Civil Liberties:
Cases and Materials

Civil Liberties:
Cases and Materials

Fourth edition

S H Bailey   MA, LLB (Cantab)
Professor of Public Law,
University of Nottingham

D J Harris   LLM, PhD (Lond)
Professor of Public International Law,
University of Nottingham

B L Jones   MA, LLB (Cantab)
Professor of Environmental Liability,
De Montfort University, Leicester

Butterworths
London, Dublin, Edinburgh
1995

United Kingdom	Butterworths, a Division of Reed Elsevier (UK) Ltd, Halsbury House, 35 Chancery Lane, LONDON WC2A 1EL and 4 Hill Street, EDINBURGH EH2 3JZ
Australia	Butterworths, SYDNEY, MELBOURNE, BRISBANE, ADELAIDE, PERTH, CANBERRA and HOBART
Canada	Butterworths Canada Ltd, TORONTO and VANCOUVER
Ireland	Butterworth (Ireland) Ltd, DUBLIN
Malaysia	Malayan Law Journal Sdn Bhd, KUALA LUMPUR
New Zealand	Butterworths of New Zealand Ltd, WELLINGTON and AUCKLAND
Puerto Rico	Butterworth of Puerto Rico, Inc, SAN JUAN
Singapore	Reed Elsevier (Singapore) Pte Ltd, SINGAPORE
South Africa	Butterworths Publishers (Pty) Ltd, DURBAN
USA	Butterworth Legal Publishers, CARLSBAD, California and SALEM, New Hampshire

A CIP Catalogue record for this book is available from the British Library.

ISBN 0 406 04590 9

Typeset in Bembo by Columns Design and Production Services Ltd, Reading
Printed by Mackays of Chatham PLC, Chatham, Kent

Preface

There have been many changes in the law of civil liberties since the third edition of this book. The main legislative development has been the enactment of the Criminal Justice and Public Order Act 1994, which has necessitated large alterations to Chapters 2 and 3 on Police Powers and Public Order respectively. Chapter 2 has also been substantially amended to reflect the revised version of the PACE Codes and new case law on police powers and the exclusion of evidence. Account is taken in Chapters 4 and 7 respectively of new review mechanisms concerning the exercise of powers under emergency legislation in Northern Ireland and new arrangements for the scrutiny of the intelligence services, DA Notices and access to official information. Chapter 8 is revised to incorporate recent case law on privacy and the latest practice of the Press Complaints Commission. The section on data protection in Chapter 8 has been omitted to save space (see next paragraph). Chapter 10 has been updated in the light of a number of developments in the law on racial discrimination, including the abolition of the limit to awards for damages effected by the Race Relations (Remedies) Act 1994. Chapter 11 on Freedom of Movement has been revised and restructured to take account of the 1994 Immigration Rules. Chapter 12 is radically revised to accommodate the mass of recent Strasbourg case law under the European Convention on Human Rights.

An important change in this edition is the omission of a chapter on prisoners' rights. The reason for this is one of space. Generally, the book has become longer with constant developments in the law concerning civil liberties and the introduction in the third edition of the book of a substantial chapter on the European Convention on Human Rights. In search for a subject that might be excluded in order to keep the new edition within bounds, we finally and reluctantly settled on prisoners' rights. Although prisoners' rights remains an important area of civil liberties, defects that were considered in previous editions—concerning disciplinary proceedings and prisoners' correspondence—have largely been remedied and the interesting body of case law that they had generated has mostly been replaced by revised Prison Rules and Standing Orders.

Finally, it may be noted that, in the short lifetime of this book, the issue of a United Kingdom Bill of Rights has become much more urgent. It is not at all impossible that a Bill of Rights will have been enacted by Parliament by the time that any fifth edition is called for.

We would wish to acknowledge the assistance given to us by a number of government departments and other bodies. These include the Home Office, the Cabinet Office, the Secretary of the Defence, Press and Broadcasting Committee, the Independent Commissioner for the Holding Centres, the Press Complaints Commission, the Commission for Racial Equality, the Broadcasting Standards Council and the Council of Europe.

We would also like to thank the following for permitting the publication of extracts from materials in respect of which they hold the copyright: the Incorporated Council of Law Reporting; Sweet and Maxwell Ltd (for extracts from the Criminal Appeal Reports); Times Newspapers Ltd; Justice of the Peace Ltd; SLS Legal Publications (NI); the New Statesman and Society; Cambridge University Press (for an extract from Wardlaw, *Political Terrorism*); Mansell Publishers Ltd (for an extract from Hepple and Szyszczak, *Discrimination: The Limits of Law*); Political Quarterly Publishing Co Ltd; the Industrial Law Society; and the Press Standards Board of Finance Ltd. Crown copyright material is reproduced with the permission of the Controller of Her Majesty's Stationery Office.

We would also like to thank the publishers for preparing the index and tables and for generally being so helpful throughout the protracted preparation of this edition.

Most of the manuscript was delivered to the publishers by early 1995. It has been possible in certain places to take into account developments that have occurred since then.

S H Bailey   July 1995
D J Harris
B L Jones

Contents

Table of statutes

References in this Table to *Statutes* are to Halsbury's Statutes of England (Fourth Edition) showing the volume and page at which the annotated text of the Act will be found.

Page references printed in **bold** type indicate where the Act is set out in part or in full.

List of cases

Page numbers in **bold** type indicate where a case is set out.

CHAPTER 1

The method of protecting civil liberties in English law

1 The present method

Report of an Interdepartmental Working Group Concerning Legislation on Human Rights, with Particular Reference to the European Convention (1976–77) HL 81.

Our arrangements for the protection of human rights are different from those of most other countries. The differences are related to differences in our constitutional traditions. Although our present constitution may be regarded as deriving in part from the revolution settlement of 1688–89, consolidated by the Union of 1707, we, unlike our European neighbours and many Commonwealth countries, do not owe our present system of government either to a revolution or to a struggle for independence. The United Kingdom—

(a) has an omnicompetent Parliament, with absolute power to enact any law and change any previous law; the courts in England and Wales have not, since the seventeenth century, recognised even in theory any higher legal order by reference to which Acts of Parliament could be held void;[1] in Scotland the courts, while reserving the right to treat an Act as void for breaching a fundamental term of the Treaty of Union [see *McCormick v Lord Advocate* 1953 SC 396], have made it clear that they foresee no likely circumstances in which they would do so;

(b) unlike other modern democracies, has no written constitution;

(c) unlike countries in the civil law tradition, makes no fundamental distinction, as regards rights or remedies, between 'public law' governing the actions of the State and its agents, and 'private law' regulating the relationships of private citizens with one another; nor have we a coherent system of administrative law applied by specialised tribunals or courts and with its own appropriate remedies;[2]

(d) has not generally codified its law, and our courts adopt a relatively narrow and literal approach to the interpretation of statutes;

(e) unlike the majority of EEC countries and the United States, does not, by ratifying a treaty or convention, make it automatically part of the domestic law (nor do we normally give effect to such an international agreement by incorporating the agreement itself into our law).

In other countries the rights of the citizen are usually (though not universally) to be found enunciated in general terms in a Bill of Rights or other constitutional document. The effectiveness of such instruments varies greatly. A Bill of Rights is not an automatic guarantee of liberty; its efficacy depends on the integrity of the institutions which apply it, and ultimately on the determination of the people that it should be maintained. The United Kingdom as such has no Bill of Rights of this kind. The Bill of Rights of 1688, though more concerned with the relationship between the English Parliament and the Crown, did contain some important safeguards for personal liberty—as did the Claim of Right of 1689, its Scottish equivalent. Among the provisions common to both the Bill of Rights and the Claim of Right are declarations that excessive bail is illegal and that it is the right of subjects to petition the Crown without incurring penalties. But the protection given by these instruments to the rights and liberties of the citizen is much narrower than the constitutional guarantees now afforded in many other democratic countries.[3]

1 *Ed.* The UK courts now recognise limitations upon parliamentary sovereignty that result from the European Union legal order: see below, p. 24.

2 *Ed.* This has ceased to be wholly true since the introduction of the present Order 53 remedy for judicial review and the distinction between public and private law used in its application: see *O'Reilly v Mackman* [1983] 2 AC 237, HL.

3 *Ed.* The Bill of Rights was relied upon (unsuccessfully) in *Williams v Home Office (No 2)* [1981] 1 All ER 1211, QBD.

The effect of the United Kingdom system of law is to provide, through the development of the common law and by express statutory enactment, a diversity of specific rights with their accompanying remedies. Thus, to secure the individual's right to freedom from unlawful or arbitrary detention, our law provides specific and detailed remedies such as habeas corpus[1] and the action for false imprisonment. The rights which have been afforded in this way are for the most part negative rights to be protected from interference from others, rather than positive rights to behave in a particular way. Those rights which have emerged in the common law can always be modified by Parliament. Parliament's role is all-pervasive—potentially, at least. It continually adapts existing rights and remedies and provides new ones, and no doubt this process would continue even if a comprehensive Bill of Rights were enacted.

The legal remedies provided for interference with the citizen's rights have in recent times been overlaid by procedures which are designed to afford not so much remedies in the strict sense of the term as facilities for obtaining independent and impartial scrutiny of action by public bodies about which an individual believes he has cause for complaint, even though the action may have been within the body's legal powers. For example, the actions of central government departments are open to scrutiny by the Parliamentary Commissioner for Administration; and complaints about the administration of the National Health Service are investigated by the Health Service Commissioners.

NOTES[2]

1. As the penultimate paragraph of the above extract from the Report[3] indicates, civil liberties are protected in the UK law by a mixture of legislation and common law. Dicey pointed out a century ago[4] that when providing such protection Parliament and the courts do not usually make general, positive statements of a right. There is, for example, no statute providing for a 'right to freedom of assembly'. Instead the technique is to legislate in detailed terms, making particular legislative provision, as in the Public Order Act 1986, from which the general right may be inferred. The courts have been similarly restrained when developing the common law.[5] While sometimes making general statements,[6] they prefer to formulate particular rules, shaped by the facts of the cases before them. Moreover, the focus of judgments is often, as it is in legislation, upon matters, such as the need to ensure public order, other than the protection of the civil liberty concerned. Another characteristic of the common law approach is that the individual's civil liberties are treated truly as liberties, not as rights. It is a negative approach by which

---

1 *Ed.* Although habeas corpus is of value in some civil liberties contexts (e.g. obtaining the release of suspects being questioned by the police, and preventing deportation (*R v Secretary of State for the Home Department, ex p Muboyayi* [1992] QB 244, CA)), it has limitations in others (e.g. achieving the release of the mentally disordered: see *X v UK*, below, p. 781). On habeas corpus, see R. J. Sharpe, *The Law of Habeas Corpus* (2nd edn, 1989) and Le Sueur, 1992 PL 13.

2 On the method of protecting civil liberties in the UK and/or the question of the introduction of a Bill of Rights, see Brennan, 9 Oxf JLS 429 (1989); R. Dworkin, *A Bill of Rights for Britain* (1990); K. Ewing, *A Bill of Rights for Britain* (1990); K. Ewing and C. Gearty, *Freedom under Thatcher* (1990); Lord Hailsham, *The Dilemma of Democracy* (1978), Chap. 26; P. Hewitt, *The Abuse of Power* (1982), Chap. 10; J. Jaconelli, *Enacting a Bill of Rights* (1980); id., (1988) 59 Pol. Quart. 343; A. Lester, *Democracy and Individual Rights* (1968); Lord Lloyd, (1976) 39 MLR 121; J. McBride, in P. Wallington, ed., *Civil Liberties* (1984), Chap. 12; A. Milne, (1977) 40 MLR 389; C. Palley, *The UK and Human Rights* (1991); Lord Scarman, *English Law—The New Dimension* (1974), pp. 10–20, 76–88; G. Robertson, *Freedom, the Individual and the Law* (7th edn, 1993), Chap. 12; P. Wallington and J. McBride, *Civil Liberties and a Bill of Rights* (1976); D. G. T. Williams, (1981) 34 CLP 25; M. Zander, *A Bill of Rights?* (3rd edn, 1985). On Northern Ireland, see Dickson, ed., *Civil Liberties in Northern Ireland* (2nd edn, 1993).

3 The Report was prepared in connection with the consideration of the question of a Bill of Rights by the House of Lords Select Committee on a Bill of Rights, as to which, see below, p. 22.

4 *An Introduction to the Study of the Law of the Constitution*, 10th edn by E. C. S. Wade, 1959, p. 197. First edition 1885.

5 See D. J. Harris, in F. Matscher, ed., *The Implementation of Economic and Social Rights* (1991) p. 201.

6 See e.g. Lord Kilbrandon in *Cassell v Broome*, below, p. 11.

a court, when faced with a civil liberties issue, seeks to discover whether there is a limitation in law upon the challenged action and, if there is not, to conclude that the action is lawful. A weakness of this approach is that it permits interferences with civil liberties as well as protection of them.[1] It is in direct contrast with the approach in the European Convention on Human Rights (ECHR), which lists in general terms the rights that it protects. The contrast was pointed out by Lord Goff in *A-G v Guardian Newspapers (No 2)* [1990] 1 AC 109 at 283:

'. . . I can see no inconsistency between English law on this subject and Article 10 of the [ECHR]. . . . The only difference is that, whereas Article 10 . . . proceeds to state a fundamental right and then to qualify it, we in this country (where everybody is free to do anything, subject only to the provisions of the law) proceed rather upon an assumption of freedom of speech, and turn to our law to discover the established exceptions to it.'

2. As the Report also states, nearly all countries protect civil liberties by means of a Bill of Rights.[2] Lord Lloyd, (1976) 39 MLR 121, 122–3 defines a Bill of Rights as a 'constitutional code of human rights' that is binding in law, is (inevitably) generally worded and has the following other key characteristics:

'(a) The code should be given some sort of overriding authority over other laws.
(b) Power should be vested in the judiciary (whether generally or by way of a Constitutional or Supreme Court) to interpret the rights set forth in the Bill of Rights and to determine judicially their proper scope, extent and limits, and their relationship inter se.
(c) The judiciary will possess the power to declare legislation invalid which it holds to be repugnant to the rights guaranteed in the Bill of Rights.'

3. The UK has no Bill of Rights in the above sense. The courts have no power to strike down statutes on the basis of such a document. Instead, in accordance with the doctrine of parliamentary sovereignty, which is the fundamental rule of the UK constitution, any statute that is enacted by the Westminster Parliament is binding upon the courts.

A power of judicial review over legislation was claimed by Coke CJ in *Dr Bonham's Case* (1610) 8 Co Rep 114a, 118: 'When an Act of Parliament is against common right and reason, or repugnant, or impossible to be performed, the common law will control it, and adjudge such Act to be void'. Had this claim been pressed and accepted, the resulting power could have been used to protect civil liberties in much the same way as a Bill of Rights does without any formal enactment. But it proved only to be rhetoric; no statute has ever been overturned on the basis of it. The current position was stated by Lord Reid in *British Railways Board v Pickin* [1974] AC 765 at 782, HL:

'The idea that a court is entitled to disregard a provision in an Act of Parliament on any ground must seem strange and startling to anyone with any knowledge of the history and law of our constitution. . . . In earlier times many learned lawyers seem to have believed that an Act of Parliament could be disregarded in so far as it was contrary to the law of God or the law of nature or natural justice, but since the supremacy of Parliament was finally demonstrated by the Revolution of 1688 any such idea has become obsolete.'

1 See E. C. S. Wade and Bradley, *Constitutional and Administrative Law*, 11th edn. by A. W. Bradley and K. D. Ewing, [1993], p. 411, who refer to the *Malone* case as an example. See also *R v Kirkless Metropolitan Borough Council, ex p C* [1993] 2 FLR 187, CA, in which counsel for a detained, mentally disordered person argued that there was no legal basis for the detention, and Stuart-Smith LJ stated that counsel had asked the wrong question: 'The real question is, on what basis can it be said that the council acted unlawfully', and there was none.
2 Australia and Israel are among the few exceptions. New Zealand adopted a Bill of Rights in 1990.

In *Oppenheimer v Cattermole* [1976] AC 249, HL, the question was whether English courts should recognise a Nazi law that deprived German Jews resident abroad of their nationality and confiscated their property. A majority of the House of Lords took the view that the law was 'so grave an infringement of human rights that the courts of this country ought to refuse to recognise it as a law at all' (Lord Cross at 278). Mann ((1978) 94 LQR 512, 513–4) refers to the case and notes that 'for more than 300 years England has been spared the necessity of facing' the question of the legality of such laws *within its own legal system*. He suggests that were it to arise 'English judges could no doubt find a legally convincing reason for reverting to the tradition of the fundamental law' and that the 'real question would be whether, in the condition which has been assumed, they would have the strength of character to search for it.'

4. Although subject to Parliament, the courts still have an important role to play in the protection of civil liberties by the interpretation of statutes, the review of administrative action and the development of the common law. As far as the interpretation of statutes is concerned, the courts have developed certain presumptions that help. The presumption against the taking of property without compensation[1] is an example. So are the presumptions against the retrospective effect of legislation;[2] against denial of access to the courts;[3] against interference with the freedom from self-incrimination;[4] and against interference with the liberty of the subject.[5] More generally, *Maxwell on Statutes* (12th edn, 1969) p. 251, reads: 'Statutes which encroach on the rights of the subject, whether as regards person or property, are subject to a strict construction in the same way as penal Acts'. The presumption that legislation complies with UK treaty obligations (see Lord Bridge in *Brind*, below, p. 7) is important in that the UK is bound by a number of international human rights treaties, including the ECHR.[6] There is also a presumption that UK legislation complies with customary international law (*Mortensen v Peters* (1906) 8 F 93, Ct of Justiciary), which contains a number of human rights guarantees (e.g. against torture): see T. Meron, *Human Rights and Humanitarian Norms of Customary Law* (1989), Chap. 2. Quite apart from such presumptions, a determined court may do a lot by way of interpretation of a statute that it considers infringes civil liberties (see the direction to the jury in *R v Bourne* [1939] 1 KB 687, CCA, interpreting the Offences against the Person Act 1861, s. 58 – an abortion, or women's rights, case). A court's attitude to the interpretation of ambiguous provisions in legislation aimed

---

1   *Central Control Board (Liquor Traffic) v Cannon Brewery Co Ltd* [1919] AC 744 at 752, HL, per Lord Atkinson. See also *R v Secretary of State, ex p de Rothschild* [1989] 1 All ER 933, CA.
2   *Waddington v Miah* [1974] 1 WLR 683, HL, below.
3   *Raymond v Honey* [1983] 1 AC 1, HL, below.
4   *Re O* [1991] 2 QB 520, CA.
5   *R v Hallstrom, ex p W* [1986] QB 1090, QBD. This presumption does not apply in wartime: *R v Halliday* [1917] AC 270, HL.
6   On the ECHR, see below, Chap. 12. Other human rights treaties in force protecting civil and political rights to which the UK is a party include the Genocide Convention 1948, UKTS 58 (1970), Cmnd 4421; the ILO Freedom of Association Convention (ILO 87), Cmnd 7638; the ILO Right to Organise Convention (ILO 98), Cmd 7852; the International Covenant on Civil and Political Rights 1966, UKTS 6 (1977), Cmnd 6702; the Convention on the Elimination of All Forms of Racial Discrimination 1966, UKTS 77 (1969), Cmnd 4108; the Convention on the Elimination of All Forms of Discrimination against Women 1979, UKTS 2 (1989), Cm 643; the UN Convention Against Torture 1984, UKTS 107 (1991), Cm 1775; the European Convention for the Prevention of Torture 1987, UKTS 5 (1991), Cm 1634; and the Convention on the Rights of the Child 1989, UKTS 44 (1992), Cm 1976. The Universal Declaration of Human Rights 1948, GAOR, 3rd Sess, Part I, Resolutions, p. 71, is not a treaty and not in itself legally binding. However, it has come, at least in part, to be recognised as stating customary international law and British courts have made reference to it: see, e.g. Lord Reid in *Waddington v Miah* [1974] 1 WLR 683, 964.

positively at protecting civil liberties can also be crucial. Consider, for example, the interpretation given to doubtful provisions in the Race Relations Acts 1965–76, below Chap. 10.

5. The courts have a well established power of judicial review of administrative action taken by national or local or other government authorities. This has long been so where the action is based upon *statutory* powers. More recently, it has been established that the exercise of *prerogative* powers may be subject to judicial review also, depending upon the subject matter of the power:[1] *Council of Civil Service Unions v Minister of the Civil Service* [1985] AC 374, HL. The courts may quash or prevent executive decisions that are not authorised by law; that are not taken in accordance with the prescribed procedures; that are erroneous in law; that infringe the rules of natural justice; or that involve an exercise of discretion that is not in accordance with guidelines (e.g. irrationality, bad faith) that the courts have developed. See, in this connection, *Ex p Brind*, below, p. 6. Cases such as *Padfield v Minister of Agriculture, Fisheries and Food* [1968] AC 997, HL, and *Secretary of State for Education and Science v Tameside Metropolitan Borough Council* [1977] AC 1014, HL, show how useful the power of judicial review can be to control ultra vires action. Action that is taken properly within the discretion given by a statute or a prerogative power is not open to challenge in court, and, as in the case of the Immigration Act 1971, s. 3, below, p. 693, the discretion that is given to the authorities may be very wide. Even if action is ultra vires, there is also the problem of finding an available remedy. On the 'application for judicial review' under Order 53, see below, p. 44.

6. The judges have a long and proud tradition of protecting civil liberties at common law against encroachment by the executive. *Entick v Carrington*, below, p. 44, is a classic example. But although cases of this sort still occur,[2] some judges are less open to persuasion than others. It is a common complaint that the courts generally are not inclined to develop the law on a grand scale, at least in the field of civil liberties. Commenting upon the failure of the courts to develop a law of privacy in the way that the American courts have, Street (*Freedom, The Individual and the Law*, (5th edn, 1982), p. 263) stated:

'But there is no spirit of adventure or progress, either in judges or counsel, in England today. Today's English judges are not the innovators that some of their distinguished predecessors were; in the hands of modern judges the common law has lost its capacity to expand. They have not been helped by counsel. Cases are argued and tried by a narrow circle of men who seldom look beyond the decided cases for guidance. The entire development of the American law of privacy can be traced to an article in a law periodical published by Harvard Law School.[3] It is inconceivable that the views of an academic journal would exercise similar influence in Britain. This inward- and backward-looking attitude of the English

---

1 In the *Council of Civil Service Unions* case, the prerogative power to determine conditions of employment in the civil service was considered 'justiciable' and hence subject to judicial review, but the powers to make treaties and to defend the realm were given (per Lord Roskill) as examples of powers that involved 'high policy' so that their exercise would not be subject to judicial review. In *R v Secretary of State for Foreign and Commonwealth Affairs, ex p Everett* [1989] QB 811, CA, the prerogative power to issue a British passport was held to be subject to judicial review. So is the prerogative of mercy: *R v Secretary of State for the Home Department, ex p Bentley* [1994] QB 349, CA. There have been over 1,000 orders made under the prerogative in the last ten years, including orders in civil liberties areas such as telephone tapping and defence matters: see 143 NLJ 656 (1993). For a debate on the scope of the prerogative, see 223 HC Debs col 487 21 April 1993.

2 See the remarkable case of *Re M* [1994] 1 AC 377, in which the Home Secretary was held in civil contempt of court for disobeying a court injunction not to deport a Zairean whose application for judicial review of the Home Office decision not to grant him asylum was under consideration by the courts. See also *R v Secretary of State for the Home Department, ex p Fire Brigades Union* [1995] 1 All ER 888, CA (Home Secretary could not introduce under the prerogative criminal injuries scheme that was radically different to statutory scheme).

3 *Ed.* See below, p. 520.

Bar serves only to increase the likelihood that the courts will fail to make the law fit the needs of the time.'

Later in the same book he wrote (pp. 318–319):

'Our judges may be relied on to defend strenuously some kinds of freedom. Their emotions will be aroused where personal freedom is menaced by some politically unimportant area of the executive: a case of unlawful arrest by a policeman, for example.[1] Their integrity is, of course, beyond criticism. Yet there are obvious limitations to what they can be expected to do in moulding the law of civil liberties. Two factors stand in their way: their reluctance to have clashes with senior members of Government, their desire not to have a repetition of the nineteenth-century strife between Parliament and the courts; and secondly, their unwillingness to immerse themselves in problems of policy, which of course loom large in many of the issues examined here.'

Does the refusal of Sir Robert Megarry VC to 'legislate in a new field' (privacy) in *Malone v Metropolitan Police Comr*, see below, p. 520, support these criticisms? Might the failure of the courts to develop a means of dealing with racial discrimination at common law be another example? (But was it ever *argued* before a court that racial discrimination might be a tort?) Are *Mandla v Dowell Lee*, below, p. 638, and *Khorasandjian v Bush*, below, p. 532, examples going the other way? And what about Ungoed-Thomas J's willingness to lead the law of breach of confidence into the unknown in *Argyll v Argyll* below, p. 552? Might the courts be better at protecting some kinds of rights (e.g. freedom from arrest) than others (e.g. freedom from inhuman or degrading treatment in prison)? Might it be relevant whether the protection needed is against the state or against a private institution or individual?[2]

R v Secretary of State for the Home Department, ex parte Brind [1991] 1 AC 696, [1991] 2 WLR 588, [1991] 1 All ER 720, House of Lords

By s. 29(3), Broadcasting Act 1981, the Home Secretary 'may at any time by notice in writing require the [Independent Broadcasting Authority (IBA)] . . . to refrain from broadcasting any matter or classes of matter specified in the notice'. (See now the 1990 Act, s. 10(3), below, p. 337.) An almost identically worded power is found in clause 13(4) of the 1981 Licence and Agreement between the Home Secretary and the BBC. Acting under these powers, in 1988, the Home Secretary issued directives to the IBA and the BBC requiring them to refrain from broadcasting on television or radio 'words spoken' by any person representing or purporting to represent certain organisations. These organisations were organisations proscribed under the Prevention of Terrorism (Temporary Provisions) Act 1984 or the Northern Ireland (Emergency Provisions) Act 1978 and also Sinn Fein, Republican Sinn Fein and the Ulster Defence Association. The prohibition applied only to the direct speech of such persons. It was permissible to report what they said or to have actors broadcasting their words. In the case of television, the latter possibility could include an actor providing a 'voice over' while the person whose direct speech was prohibited was (silently) speaking on the screen.

In this case, the applicants, who were journalists and a National Union of Journalists employee, sought judicial review for a declaration to the effect that the Home Secretary's directives were ultra vires and for certiorari to quash them. Having failed before the Divisional Court and a unanimous Court of Appeal, the applicants appealed to the House of Lords where they relied mainly on the

---

1 Eg, £40,000 exemplary damages were awarded against the police for oppressive conduct amounting to torture (suffocating with plastic bags to obtain confession): *Treadaway v Chief Constable of West Midlands* (1994) Independent, 23 September, D Ct.
2 As to the application of the ECHR to private persons, see below, p. 816.

argument that the Home Secretary's discretionary powers under the 1981 Act and the BBC Licence were exercisable subject to Article 10, ECHR. In their speeches, the House of Lords also considered other possible grounds for judicial review, including *Wednesbury* grounds and lack of 'proportionality'. The appeal was dismissed unanimously.

Lord Bridge: ... it is already well settled that, in construing any provision in domestic legislation which is ambiguous in the sense that it is capable of a meaning which either conforms to or conflicts with the Convention, the courts will presume that Parliament intended to legislate in conformity with the Convention, not in conflict with it. Hence, it is submitted, when a statute confers upon an administrative authority a discretion capable of being exercised in a way which infringes any basic human right protected by the Convention, it may similarly be presumed that the legislative intention was that the discretion should be exercised within the limitations which the Convention imposes. I confess that I found considerable persuasive force in this submission. But in the end I have been convinced that the logic of it is flawed. When confronted with a simple choice between two possible interpretations of some specific statutory provision, the presumption whereby the courts prefer that which avoids conflict between our domestic legislation and our international treaty obligations is a mere canon of construction which involves no importation of international law into the domestic field. But where Parliament has conferred on the executive an administrative discretion without indicating the precise limits within which it must be exercised, to presume that it must be exercised within Convention limits would be to go far beyond the resolution of an ambiguity. It would be to impute to Parliament an intention not only that the executive should exercise the discretion in conformity with the Convention, but also that the domestic courts should enforce that conformity by the importations into domestic administrative law of the text of the Convention and the jurisprudence of the European Court of Human Rights in the interpretation and application of it. If such a presumption is to apply to the statutory discretion exercised by the Secretary of State under section 29(3) of the Act of 1981 in the instant case, it must also apply to any other statutory discretion exercised by the executive which is capable of involving an infringement of Convention rights. When Parliament has been content for so long to leave those who complain that their Convention rights have been infringed to seek their remedy in Strasbourg, it would be surprising suddenly to find that the judiciary had, without Parliament's aid, the means to incorporate the Convention into such an important area of domestic law and I cannot escape the conclusion that this would be a judicial usurpation of the legislative function.

But I do not accept that this conclusion means that the courts are powerless to prevent the exercise by the executive of administrative discretions, even when conferred, as in the instant case, in terms which are on their face unlimited, in a way which infringes fundamental human rights. Most of the rights spelled out in terms in the Convention, including the right to freedom of expression, are less than absolute and must in some cases yield to the claims of competing public interests. Thus, Article 10(2) of the Convention spells out and categorises the competing public interests by reference to which the right to freedom of expression may have to be curtailed. In exercising the power of judicial review we have neither the advantages nor the disadvantages of any comparable code to which we may refer or by which we are bound. But again, this surely does not mean that in deciding whether the Secretary of State, in the exercise of his discretion, could reasonably impose the restriction he has imposed on the broadcasting organisations, we are not perfectly entitled to start from the premise that any restriction on the right to freedom of expression requires to be justified and that nothing less than an important competing public interest will be sufficient to justify it. The primary judgment as to whether the particular competing public interest justifies the particular restriction imposed falls to be made by the Secretary of State to whom Parliament has entrusted the discretion. But we are entitled to exercise a secondary judgment by asking whether a reasonable Secretary of State, on the material before him, could reasonably have made that primary judgment.

Applying these principles to the circumstances of the case ... I find it impossible to say that the Secretary of State exceeded the limits of his discretion. In any civilised and law-abiding society the defeat of the terrorist is a public interest of the first importance. That some restriction on the freedom of the terrorist and his supporters to propagate his cause may well be justified in support of that public interest is a proposition which I apprehend the appellants hardly dispute. ... The Secretary of State decided that it was necessary to deny to the terrorist and his supporters the opportunity to speak directly to the public through the most influential of all the media of communication and that this justified some interference with editorial freedom. I do not see how this judgment can be categorised as unreasonable. ... I should add that I do not see how reliance on the doctrine of 'proportionality' can here advance the appellants' case. But I agree with what my noble and learned friend Lord Roskill says in his speech about the possible future development of the law in that respect. ...

Lord Roskill: I agree that this appeal must be dismissed for the reasons given in the speech of my noble and learned friend Lord Bridge of Harwich. . . . I add some observations of my own only on one matter, namely, the principle of 'proportionality.' Reliance was placed on behalf of the appellants upon a passage in the speech of my noble and learned friend, Lord Diplock, in *CCSU v Minister for the Civil Service* [1985] AC 374 at 410, where, after establishing his triple categorisation of the fields in which judicial review might operate, he added:

'That is not to say that further development on a case by case basis may not in course of time add further grounds. I have in mind particularly the possible adoption in future of the principle of 'proportionality' which is recognised in the administrative law of several of our fellow members of the European Economic Community; but to dispose of the instant case the three already well-established heads that I have mentioned will suffice.'

In that passage my noble and learned friend . . . clearly had in mind the . . . adoption of this principle as a separate category and not merely as a possible reinforcement of one or more of these three stated categories such as irrationality. . . . I am clearly of the view that the present is not a case in which the first step can be taken for the reason that to apply that principle in the present case would be for the court to substitute its own judgment of what was needed to achieve a particular objective for the judgment of the Secretary of State upon whom that duty has been laid by Parliament. But so to hold in the present case is not to exclude the possible future development of the law in this respect, a possibility which has already been canvassed in some academic writings. . . .

Lord Templeman: . . . On an application for judicial review, the courts must not substitute their own views for the informed views of the Home Secretary. In terms of the Convention, as construed by the European Court, a 'margin of appreciation' must be afforded to the Home Secretary to decide whether and in what terms a restriction on freedom of expression is justified.

The English courts must, in conformity with the *Wednesbury* principles discussed by Lord Ackner, consider whether the Home Secretary has taken into account all relevant matters and has ignored irrelevant matters. These conditions are satisfied by the evidence in this case, including evidence by the Home Secretary that he took the Convention into account. If these conditions are satisfied, then it is said on *Wednesbury* principles the court can only interfere by way of judicial review if the decision of the Home Secretary is 'irrational' or 'perverse.'

The subject matter and date of the *Wednesbury* principles cannot in my opinion make it either necessary or appropriate for the courts to judge the validity of an interference with human rights by asking themselves whether the Home Secretary has acted irrationally or perversely. It seems to me that the courts cannot escape from asking themselves whether a reasonable Secretary of State, on the material before him, could reasonably conclude that the interference with freedom of expression which he determined to impose was justifiable. In terms of the Convention, as construed by the European Court, the interference with freedom of expression must be necessary and proportionate to the damage which the restriction is designed to prevent.

My Lords, applying these principles I do not consider that the court can conclude that the Home Secretary has abused or exceeded his powers. The broadcasting authorities and journalists are naturally resentful of any limitation on their right to present a programme in such manner as they think fit. But the interference with freedom of expression is minimal and the reasons given by the Home Secretary are compelling. . . .

Lord Ackner: . . . I now turn to the bases upon which it is contended that the Secretary of State exceeded his statutory powers: . . .

2. The directives were unlawful on 'Wednesbury' grounds

There remains however the potential criticism under the *Wednesday* grounds expressed by Lord Greene MR [1948] 1 KB 223, 234 that the conclusion was 'so unreasonable that no reasonable authority could ever have come to it'. This standard of unreasonableness, often referred to as 'the irrationality test', has been criticised as being too high. But it has to be expressed in terms that confine the jurisdiction exercised by the judiciary to a supervisory, as opposed to an appellate, jurisdiction. . . . To seek the court's intervention on the basis that the correct or objectively reasonable decision is other than the decision which the Minister has made, is to invite the court to adjudicate as if Parliament had provided a right of appeal against the decision—that is, to invite an abuse of power by the judiciary.

So far as the facts of this case are concerned it is only necessary to read the speeches in the Houses of Parliament . . . to reach the conclusion, that whether the Secretary of State was right or wrong to decide to issue the directives, there was clearly material which would justify a reasonable Minister making the same decision. . . .

3. *The Minister failed to have proper regard to the European Convention for the Protection of Human Rights and Fundamental Freedoms and in particular Article 10 . . .*

The Convention which is contained in an international treaty to which the United Kingdom is a party has not yet been incorporated into English domestic law. The appellants accept that it is a constitutional principle that if Parliament has legislated and the words of the statute are clear, the statute must be applied even if its application is in breach of international law. In *Salomon v Comrs of Customs and Excise* [1967] 2 QB 116 Diplock LJ at 143 stated:

'If the terms of the legislation are clear and unambiguous they must be given effect to, whether or not they carry out Her Majesty's treaty obligations.'

Much reliance was placed upon the observations of Lord Diplock in *Garland v British Rail* [1983] 2 AC 751 when he said (at 771):

'. . . it is a principle of construction of United Kingdom statutes . . . that the words of a statute passed after the Treaty has been signed and dealing with the subject matter of the international obligation of the United Kingdom, are to be construed, if they are reasonably capable of bearing such a meaning, as intended to carry out the obligation, and not to be inconsistent with it.'

I did not take the view that Lord Diplock was intending to detract from or modify what he had said in *Salomon's* case.

It is well settled that the Convention may be deployed for the purpose of the resolution of an ambiguity in English primary or subordinate legislation. The case of *R v Chief Immigration Officer, Heathrow Airport, ex p Salamat Bibi* [1976] 1 WLR 979 concerned a lady who arrived at London Airport from Pakistan with two small children saying that she was married to a man who was there and who met her. She was refused leave to enter and an application was made for an order of certiorari and also for mandamus on the ground that she ought to have been treated as the wife of the man who met her at the airport. During the course of argument a question arose about the impact of the Convention and in particular Article 8 concerning the right to private and family life and the absence of interference by a public authority with that right.

In his judgment at p. 984 Lord Denning MR said:

'The position as I understand it is that if there is any ambiguity in our statutes, or uncertainty in our law, then these courts can look to the Convention as an aid to clear up the ambiguity and uncertainty . . . but I would dispute altogether that the Convention is part of our law. Treaties and declarations do not become part of our law until they are made law by Parliament.'

In his judgment at p. 988 Geoffrey Lane LJ said:

'It is perfectly true that the Convention was ratified by this country . . . nevertheless, the Convention, not having been enacted by Parliament as a statute, does not have the effect of law in this country; whatever persuasive force it may have in resolving ambiguities it certainly cannot have the effect of overriding the plain provision of the Act of 1971 and the rules made thereunder.'. . .

Mr Lester contends that section 29(3) is ambiguous or uncertain. He submits that although it contains within its wording no fetter upon the extent of the discretion it gives to the Secretary of State, it is accepted that that discretion is not absolute. There is however no ambiguity in section 29(3). It is not open to two or more different constructions. The limit placed upon the discretion is simply that the power is to be used only for the purposes for which it was granted by the legislation (the so-called *Padfield* doctrine) and that it must be exercised reasonably in the *Wednesbury* sense. No question of the construction of the words of section 29(3) arises, as would be the case if it was alleged to be ambiguous, or its meaning uncertain.

There is yet a further answer to Mr Lester's contention. He claims that the Secretary of State before issuing his directives should have considered not only the Convention (it is accepted that he in fact did so) but that he should have properly construed it and correctly taken it into consideration. It was therefore a relevant, indeed a vital, factor to which he was obliged to have proper regard pursuant to the *Wednesbury* doctrine, with the result that his failure to do so rendered his decision unlawful. The fallacy of this submission is however plain. If the Secretary of State was obliged to have proper regard to the Convention, ie to conform with Article 10, this inevitably would result in incorporating the Convention into English domestic law by the back door. It would oblige the Courts to police the operation of the Convention and to ask itself in each case, where there was a challenge, whether the restrictions were 'necessary in a democratic society . . .' applying the principles enunciated in the decisions of the European Court of Human Rights. The treaty, not having been incorporated in English law, cannot be a source of rights and obligations and the question—did the Secretary of State act in breach of Article 10—does not therefore arise. . . .

4. The Secretary of State has acted ultra vires because he has acted in 'in a disproportionate manner'

This attack is not a repetition of the Wednesbury 'irrational' test under another guise. Clearly a decision by a Minister which suffers from a total lack of proportionality will qualify for the '*Wednesbury* unreasonable' epithet. It is, ex hypothesi, a decision which no reasonable Minister could make. This is, however, a different and severer test.

Mr Lester is asking your Lordships to adopt a different principle—the principle of 'proportionality' which is recognised in the administrative law of several members of the European Economic Community. What is urged is a further development in English administrative law, which Lord Diplock viewed as a possibility in *CCSU v Minister for the Civil Service* [1985] AC 375 at 410.

In his written submissions, Mr Lester was at pains to record 'that there is a clear distinction between an appeal on the merits and a review based on whether the principle of proportionality has been satisfied'. He was prepared to accept that to stray into the realms of appellate jurisdiction involves the Courts in a wrongful usurpation of power. Yet in order to invest the proportionality test with a higher status than the *Wednesbury* test, an inquiry into and a decision upon the merits cannot be avoided. Mr Pannick's (Mr Lester's junior) formulation—could the Minister reasonably conclude that his direction was necessary—must involve balancing the reasons, pro and con, for his decision, albeit allowing him 'a margin of appreciation' to use the European concept of the tolerance accorded to the decision-maker in whom a discretion has been vested. The European test of 'whether the interference complained of corresponds to a pressing social need' must ultimately result in the question—is the particular decision acceptable?—and this must involve a review of the merits of the decision. Unless and until Parliament incorporates the Convention into domestic law, a course which it is well-known has a strong body of support, there appears to me to be at present no basis upon which the proportionality doctrine applied by the European Court can be followed by the courts of this country.

Lord Lowry delivered a speech in which he agreed with the arguments of **Lord Ackner** and gave his own reasons for rejecting the principle of proportionality.

NOTES[1]

1. This case concerns the question whether the ECHR can be relied upon in the UK courts. As stated in the *Brind* case, it is well established that the ECHR should be referred to and followed in the interpretation of an ambiguous statute, but that it cannot prevail over a clearly worded statute that contradicts it. In this connection, it is noticeable that Lord Ackner suggested that the passage which he quoted from Lord Diplock's speech in the *Garland* case, which was made in the special context of EC law, was not intended to depart from the established position and, in particular, was not, as might be thought, intended to mean that a judge should go out of his way to find an ambiguity. What the *Brind* case is mainly authority for is that a discretionary executive power, whether under a statute or the prerogative and whether exercisable by a lowly immigration officer (who might never have heard of it) or a Secretary of State, is not to be interpreted as limited by the ECHR.[2] What reasons do Lords Bridge and Ackner give for not limiting discretionary powers by reference to the ECHR? What distinction is there between limitations that the courts do read into discretionary powers when exercising their power of judicial review (eg the rules of natural justice and the *Wednesbury* 'irrationality' rule) and a limitation that

---

1 On the *Brind* case, see J. Jowell, 1990 PL 149 and B. Thompson, 1991 PL 346. See generally on UK law and the ECHR, Bratza in Gardner, ed., *Aspects of Incorporation of the European Convention on Human Rights into Domestic Law*, Chap. 6; A. Z. Drzemczewski, *European Human Rights Convention in Domestic Law* (1983), pp. 177–87; and P. J. Duffy, (1980) 29 ICLQ 585. See also M. P. Furmston, R. Kerridge and B. E. Sufrin, eds., *The Effect on English Domestic Law of Membership of the European Communities and of Ratification of the ECHR* (1983). An application alleging a breach of the ECHR in the *Brind* case was declared inadmissible at Strasbourg: *Brind v UK* No 18714/94, 77 ADR 42 (1994). The voice ban at issue in the case no longer applies.

2 This ruling was followed in *NALGO v Secretary of State for the Environment* (1992) Times, 2 December, CA.

might stem from the European Convention? As to not introducing the ECHR by the back door (see Lord Ackner), are the courts not doing this when they take it into account in developing the common law? Is the rule whereby customary international law is a part of the common law democratic? Although the ECHR may not be relied upon, the exercise of executive discretion will be scrutinised more closely where human rights are in issue than in other cases: *R v Secretary of State for the Home Department, ex p McQuillan* (1994) Independent, 23 September, DC. In that case, the applicant was a former IRA member living in Northern Ireland who had survived two assassination attempts. An exclusion order preventing him from entering Great Britain raised human rights issues as being inhuman treatment of a person whose life was still at risk. However, although it therefore required close scrutiny, it could be justified on national security grounds.

2. Quite apart from its ruling on the question of reliance on the ECHR by the British courts, the *Brind* case is important for its consideration of other matters bearing upon the value of judicial review as a means of challenging action in breach of civil liberties. In particular, their Lordships were divided on the prospects of the principle of proportionality as a ground for judicial review in English law. As they indicated, this is a principle that applies in the law of some European countries and in EU law and that would permit a challenge to executive action contrary to civil liberties where the *Wednesbury* 'irrationality' ground for judicial review would not. Whereas Lords Ackner and Lowry rejected Lord Diplock's view in the *Civil Service Union* case that the principle might in future emerge as a separate ground for judicial review, Lords Bridge and Roskill were more sympathetic. Although it was not yet a part of English law,[1] they left the door open for its later adoption. Lord Templeman was prepared to apply the proportionality principle under Article 10 ECHR to the facts of the case. On the *Brind* case's contribution to the particular questions of the protection of freedom of speech and the permissibility of restrictions upon civil liberties to combat terrorism, see below, p. 338.

Although the UK courts have yet to accept the doctrine of proportionality, they have, as Lester notes, 1993 PL 269, 278, 'recovered their confidence' since the 1960s and are prepared to intervene to control the executive much more closely than formerly. See, for example, the *McQuillan* case, above, and their insistence that the executive give reasons for their decisions: e.g. *R v Lambeth London Borough, ex p Walters* [1994] 2 FCR 336.

3. The ECHR is increasingly being relied on by judges in the development of the common law. In *Cassell & Co Ltd v Broome* [1972] AC 1027, HL, Lord Kilbrandon said at p. 1133:

'. . . since all commercial publication is undertaken for profit, one must be watchful against holding the profit motive to be sufficient to justify punitive damages: to do so would be seriously to hamper what must be regarded, at least since the European Convention [on Human Rights] was ratified, as a constitutional right to free speech.'

In *A-G v BBC* [1981] AC 303 at 358, HL, Lord Scarman stated that if 'the issue should ultimately be . . . a question of legal policy,' regard must be had to the ECHR. In the same case, Lord Fraser (p. 352) suggested that the courts 'should have regard to the [ECHR] where our domestic law is not firmly settled'. In *A-G v*

---

1 In the *NALGO* case, above, p. 10, n. 2, the Court of Appeal noted, however, that the principle of proportionality was followed by the UK courts when applying EU law directly and by an *appellate* court when considering an exercise of *judicial* discretion. In the case of judicial review of executive discretion, in view of *Brind* it was not open to a court below the House of Lords to do more than apply the *Wednesbury* principle.

Guardian Newspapers (No 2) [1990] 1 AC 109 at 283, HL, Lord Goff, applying the equitable doctrine of breach of confidence, stated that 'I conceive it to be my duty, when I am free to do so, to interpret the law in accordance with the obligations of the Crown under this treaty [the ECHR]'.[1] Referring to the *Chowdhury* case, below, p. 591, in support, in *Derbyshire County Council v Times Newspapers* [1992] QB 770 at 812, CA, Balcombe LJ went further, stating: 'Even if the common law is certain the courts will still, when appropriate, consider whether the United Kingdom is in breach of [the ECHR]'. According to Sir Robert Megarry VC, however, the ECHR cannot be used to fill a gap where Parliament has not legislated: *Malone v Metropolitan Police Comr* [1979] 2 All ER 620, 648.

4. Despite the many references that courts have made to the ECHR, there has been no case yet in which the ECHR has been acknowledged by them as crucial to a decision. Commonly, recourse to the ECHR leads to the conclusion that the ECHR has no contribution to make; existing English law and the Convention are found to be harmonious. See, eg, *Derbyshire County Council v Times Newspapers* [1993] AC 534 at 551, HL, per Lord Keith (decision based 'upon the common law of England without finding any need to rely upon the European Convention. . . . I find it satisfactory to be able to conclude that the common law of England is consistent with the obligations assumed' under the ECHR). Generally, the impression given by the English judiciary is that they are disinclined to find that English law is in need of improvement by an alien instrument such as the ECHR – an attitude that is common in the courts of other ECHR parties also. Even so, it is clear that Strasbourg judgments have had a considerable impact upon English court decisions. Notably, they were instrumental in the English courts' abandonment of its hands off policy towards prisoners' rights, see below, p. 807, and in their adoption of ECHR reasoning and terminology ('necessary in a democratic society', 'pressing social need', etc) when considering restrictions upon rights, particularly freedom of speech. The ECHR played an important role in the freedom of speech case of *Rantzen v Mirror Group Newspapers* [1993] 3 WLR 953 at 972, CA. There the Court of Appeal had to interpret its statutory power to order a new trial in a libel action where the damages awarded by the jury were 'excessive'. When concluding for the Court that 'the common law if properly understood requires the courts to subject large awards of damages to a more searching scrutiny than was customary in the past', Neill LJ relied upon the ECHR/common law 'harmony' language in Lord Goff's speech in *Guardian Newspapers (No 2)* quoted above, p. 3. Even supposing that the Court of Appeal would in any event have suggested a 'more searching scrutiny' of libel damages, there is no doubt that the freedom of speech guarantee in Article 10, ECHR played an important part in providing it with the reasons for doing so.

5. In *R v Secretary of State for the Home Office, ex p Weeks* (1988) Times, 15 March, QBD, it was held that a prisoner who had been found by the European Court of Human Rights to have been deprived of his liberty contrary to Article 5(4), ECHR, see below, p. 783, was not entitled to compensation in the courts of this country. There is also no UK judicial remedy by which a person who wins his case at Strasbourg can require the executive to take steps to rectify the breach in other

---

1   At an earlier stage of the same case, Lords Templeman and Ackner had woven into their speeches arguments drawing upon the freedom of speech guarantees in Article 10, ECHR when applying the same doctrine: *A-G v Guardian Newspapers* [1987] 1 WLR 1248 at 1296, 1307, HL. For other cases, see Lord Scarman in the *Ahmad* case, below, p. 603, and the *Blathwayt* case, below, p. 609 (ECHR relevant to a public policy argument).

ways, e.g., by the person's release or retrial or the payment of compensation ordered by the European Court of Human Rights.

6. Potentially, European Union law could have an impact upon the protection of civil liberties in UK law.[1] In addition to certain particular provisions of EU law (e.g. Articles 48 and 119, EC Treaty, on freedom of movement within the Union for workers and sexual discrimination in employment, respectively), the European Court of Justice at Luxembourg stated in Case 4/73 *J Nold KG v EC Commission* [1974] ECR 491 at 508:

'. . . fundamental rights form an integral part of the general principles of law, the observance of which it [the court] ensures. In safeguarding these rights, the court is bound to draw inspiration from constitutional traditions common to the Member States and it cannot therefore uphold measures which are incompatible with fundamental rights recognised and protected by the Constitutions of those States.

Similarly, international treaties for the protection of human rights on which Member States have collaborated or of which they are signatories, can supply guidelines which should be followed within the framework of Community law.'

The matter has now been taken further by the Maastricht Treaty, which links the ECJ's 'fundamental rights' with the ECHR. Article F(2) of the Treaty states that the 'Union shall respect fundamental rights, as guaranteed in the European Convention . . . as general principles of law.'[2] The fundamental rights to which the Maastricht Treaty refers may be read into EU law so as to control both EU institutions[3] and member states when acting under EU law or implementing it.[4] In addition, the ECJ has held national UK law authorised by EU law to be invalid as being contrary to the 'fundamental rights' requirements of EU law.[5] However, it has been held by the Scottish Court of Session[6] that the ECHR has not been made a part of UK law 'by the back door'. It does not, that is, through being a part of the EU law incorporated into UK law by the European Communities Act 1972, s. 2, apply in the many areas of conduct (in that case deportation of a non-EU national allegedly contrary to Article 8, ECHR) that are not controlled by EU law.

7. Given the many times when UK legislation has been found to be in breach of the ECHR, it has been argued that steps should be taken by which draft primary and secondary legislation would be examined before enactment for its compliance with the ECHR and other international human rights treaties, such as the ICCPR and the ICESCR, by which the United Kingdom is bound.[7] At present, Whitehall does seek to make legislation 'Strasbourg-proof'. The argument, which makes good sense, is that, somewhat in the manner of councils of state (*conseils d'état*) found in continental Europe, Parliament should provide a Committee mechanism for the regular scrutiny of draft legislation to ensure that it complies with UK human rights obligations. The UK Government did not accept a suggestion by Lord Lester that

1 See N. Grief, 1991 PL 555.
2 As to the effect of Article F(2), see Krogsgaard, LIEI 1993/1, p. 99.
3 See, eg, *Orkem v Commission*, Case 374/87: [1989] ECR 3283 (no obligation to answer Commission questions that incriminate under EU law) and Cases 97–99/87 *Dow Chemical Iberica SA and EC Commission* [1989] ECR 3165 (Commission power of search subject to Article 8, ECHR). See also the *Prais* case, below, p. 606.
4 See, e.g., Case 222/84 *Johnston v Chief Constable of the Royal Ulster Constabulary* [1987] QB 129 (Directive to read as including the right of access to a court in Arts. 6 and 13, ECHR).
5 *R v Kirk* Case 63/83, [1984] ECR 2689 (UK delegated legislation that established a retroactive criminal offence, as the EU law that permitted the offence allowed, held to be invalid as contrary to fundamental rights in national legal systems and Article 7, ECHR).
6 *Kaur v Lord Advocate* 1980 SC 319, Ct of Sess (Outer House), per Lord Ross. On the ECHR and the law of Scotland, see J. Murdoch, 1991 PL 40.
7 See D. Kinley, *The European Convention on Human Rights: Compliance without Incorporation* (1993) Chaps. 6–8; Lord Lester, 550 HL Deb 23 November 1993; Ryle, 1993 PL 192.

Parliament should be consulted before the UK made its mandatory five-yearly report under the International Covenant on Civil and Political Rights to the UN Human Rights Committee on the protection of human rights in the UK: 553 HL Debs, 12 April 1994; col 89 WA.

2 A Bill of Rights?

Bill of Rights: a Discussion Paper. Standing Advisory Commission on Human Rights, March 1976, paras. 10 and 11 (Reprinted in the Commission's *The Protection of Human Rights by Law in Northern Ireland*, Cmnd. 7009)

On the one hand it may be argued that:
(1) It is complacent to assume that there is no need for new legal safeguards in Northern Ireland or indeed elsewhere in the United Kingdom. The existing legislative and common law safeguards against abuse of power are less comprehensive and effective than in many advanced democratic countries. . . .
(2) A Bill of Rights would remove certain fundamental values out of the reach of temporary political majorities, governments and officials and into the realm of legal principles applied by the courts. This would not be undemocratic because the exercise of political power in a democracy should not be beyond criticism or restraint.
(3) A Bill of Rights would be especially important in the context of the devolution of the present powers of Central Government in maintaining the national framework of law and order, and guaranteeing the basic rights of citizens throughout the United Kingdom.
(4) A Bill of Rights would encourage a more actively and socially responsive judicial role in protecting basic rights and freedoms; it would alter the method of judicial law-making, so as to enable the courts to recognise the fundamental importance of certain values and the relationship between them.
(5) The European Convention contains a minimum Bill of Rights for Council of Europe countries and is also being used as a source of guidance about common standards within the European Community in relation to human rights questions arising under the EEC Treaty. The enactment of a Bill of Rights in this country would enable the United Kingdom to be manifestly in conformity with its international obligations and would also enable the citizen to obtain redress from United Kingdom courts without needing, except in the last resort, to have recourse to the European Commission in Strasbourg.
(6) A Bill of Rights would not necessarily hamper strong, effective and democratic government because it could recognise that interference with certain rights would be justifiable if they were necessary in a democratic society, for example, in the interests of national security, public safety or the economic well-being of the country, for the prevention of disorder or crime, for the protection of health or morals, or for the protection of the rights and freedoms of others.
(7) The generality of a Bill of Rights makes it possible for the interpretation of such a document to evolve in accordance with changing social values and needs. This process of giving fresh meaning to basic human rights—and the obligations which flow from them—from generation to generation is valuable for its own sake, as a means of educating public opinion, and as a rallying point in the State for all who care deeply for the ideals of freedom.
(8) A Bill of Rights would not be a substitute for more specific statutory safeguards against specific abuses (e.g. anti-discrimination legislation or the Parliamentary Commissioner for Administration). It would supplement and strengthen those safeguards where they were incomplete. . . .
On the other hand it may be argued that:
(1) Because of the general nature of Bills of Rights and the increased powers of judicial law-making which they require, the scope and effect of such documents is uncertain and unpredictable.
(2) A Bill of Rights would create expectations which could not be satisfied in practice. It would be regarded as a panacea for all grievances whereas its real value (if any) would be only a limited one. It would be least effective when it was most needed: i.e. to protect fundamental rights and freedoms against powerful currents of intolerance, passion, usurpation and tyranny.
(3) A Bill of Rights might be interpreted by the courts in a manner which would hamper strong, effective or progressive government, and the role of the courts would result in important public issues being discussed and resolved in legal or constitutional terms rather than in moral or political terms. It would risk compromising the necessary independence and impartiality of the judiciary by requiring the judges to work in a more political arena.

(4) Most Bills of Rights stem from a constitutional settlement following revolution, rebellion, liberation or the peaceful attainment of independence. It would be difficult and perhaps divisive to seek to obtain a sufficient degree of political consensus about the nature and scope of a Bill of Rights in present circumstances.

(5) Human rights are at least as well protected in the United Kingdom as in countries which have Bills of Rights since they are adequately safeguarded by traditional methods, i.e., legislative measures to deal with specific problems, combined with the unwritten but effective constitutional conventions; the sense of responsibility and fair dealing in legislators and administrators; the influence of a free press and the force of public opinion; the independence of the judiciary in upholding the rule of law; and free and secret elections.

(6) The United Kingdom differs from many advanced democratic countries in lacking (a) a written constitution, (b) a system of public law, and (c) a codified legal system. A Bill of Rights involves features of all three of these distinctive characteristics of other legal systems. It would therefore represent a fundamental departure from the existing legal tradition.

(7) A Bill of Rights which did not (i) contain a modern definition of the rights and freedoms relevant to the particular circumstances obtaining whether in the United Kingdom in general or in Northern Ireland in particular, (ii) have priority over other laws, (iii) create legally enforceable rights and (iv) apply to violations of human rights by private individuals and organisations as well as by public authorities would not satisfy some prominent supporters of such a measure. On the other hand a Bill of Rights which did have these characteristics would be unlikely to obtain widespread public support.

(8) A Bill of Rights would create wasteful duplication in relation to existing statutory safeguards for human rights and would generate unnecessary litigation.

NOTES

1. The above extract weighs the arguments for and against the introduction of a Bill of Rights into UK law. The Standing Advisory Commission on Human Rights is an independent body in Northern Ireland established to advise 'the Secretary of State on the adequacy and effectiveness of the law for the time being in force in preventing discrimination on the grounds of religious belief or political opinion and in providing redress for persons aggrieved ...' (Northern Ireland Constitution Act 1973, s. 20(1)(a)). Although the Advisory Commission's paper is directed towards the question of a Bill of Rights in Northern Ireland, the arguments included in this extract apply to the UK as a whole.

2. One objection to a Bill of Rights is that it would involve the courts in political controversy. Although judges already have to rule on party political matters and other matters of social policy,[1] a power to review legislation would inevitably increase the courts' participation in such matters, and give them the last word on such questions as whether the Immigration Act 1971 results in 'degrading treatment' of black applicants for admission (Article 3, ECHR); whether legislation authorising telephone tapping is consistent with the right to privacy (Article 8, ECHR); and whether a woman has a right to abortion (see Article 8, ECHR). As to abortion, Fawcett ((1976) 73 Guardian Gaz 171) comments:

'Here it may be asked whether there should not be limits to judicial intervention in social policy; not, as is sometimes suggested, because the judiciary is too conservative or is socially insensitive – suggestions that have little contemporary justification – but because social policy rests upon consent and process and not upon unitary decision, however logical. Is it wise to allow a constitutional court to declare unconstitutional, by six votes to two, the provision of a statute enacted by a substantial majority in the national Parliament and based on a long inquiry and report of an experienced and representative Commission?

---

1 See, e.g., the *Tameside* case [1977] AC 1014, HL (comprehensive schooling), *Council of Civil Service Unions v Minister for the Civil Service* [1985] AC 374, HL (the GCHQ case), and *Hammersmith and Fulham London Borough Council v Secretary of State for the Environment* [1990] 3 All ER 589, HL (charge-capping).

This happened in the Federal Republic of Germany on the question of abortion, and is the subject of an application now before the European Commission on Human Rights.'

Does his reasoning apply equally to the powers of the European Commission and Court of Human Rights?

Although most cases arising under a Bill of Rights would not raise such large political or social issues, some would. In the US, the Supreme Court, despite its discretion not to hear cases (by refusing certiorari) and the doctrine by which it refuses to rule on 'political questions' (such as the constitutionality of the Vietnam War), is constantly a focal point and arbiter on questions of great political and social moment. Between 1934 and 1936, it held 16 social welfare laws properly passed by Congress in implementation of President Roosevelt's 'new deal' policy to be unconstitutional as infringements of 'freedom of contract' between employers and employees. A conservative majority of the Court did this on the basis of 'an economic theory [of *laissez faire*, or government non-intervention] which a large part of the country does not entertain' (Holmes J, dissenting, in *Lochner v New York* 198 US 46 (1905)). President Roosevelt sought to overcome the problem by an unsuccessful plan to increase the size of the Court (his 'court-packing' plan). It was resolved eventually by a change in the court's composition by retirement, etc. More recently, the Supreme Court has declared racial segregation to be unconstitutional (*Brown v Board of Education* 347 US 483 (1954)) and set guidelines for capital punishment statutes (*Gregg v Georgia* 428 US 153 (1976)).[1]

Should the courts, whose members are not elected by a democratic process and must necessarily be difficult to dismiss, be given a political and social role on this scale? Should issues of the sort mentioned above be resolved through the ballot box instead? (Note that Mr Allen's 1993 Human Rights Bill, below, p. 20, proposed that Parliament would be free to legislate contrary to the Bill of Rights by express provision to this effect.) Or should persons taking decisions on civil liberties (particularly those of minority groups and the unpopular) be free from the 'tyranny of the majority'? Does the experience of the judicial review of administrative action (judicial review 'writ small'), which the courts now engage in, offer a guide? Might some civil liberties be more appropriate for protection through the courts by a Bill of Rights than others? In particular, is the distinction between (1) civil and political rights and (2) economic, social and cultural rights relevant? The rights considered in this casebook are civil and political rights. As to, for example, the rights to a fair wage or to a pension, the argument runs that such economic and social rights depend upon financial resources and cannot be made the subject of legal rights enforceable in court. See Wallington and McBride, *Civil Liberties and a Bill of Rights* (1976) pp. 11–12.

On the argument that the judiciary is 'too conservative or is socially insensitive', note the following comment of Lord Milford (379 HL Deb 3 February 1977 col 996):

'Let us look at the composition of the Judges today; 89 per cent of this so-called upper class went to public school, 70 per cent went to Oxford or Cambridge, and only 22 per cent ever faced an election in their lives. . . . These men's lives are miles away from the ordinary people. Why should they be made the custodians of the liberties of the ordinary people, rather than Parliament . . .?'

His speech was interrupted to remind him that there were two female High Court judges and a number of female county court judges.[2] Wallington and McBride, *Civil*

1 On judicial review of legislation in the US, see Nowak and Rotunda, *Constitutional Law* (4th edn, 1991), Chap. 1.
2 For other information on the social background of the judiciary, see M. Berlins and C. Dyer, *The Law Machine* (3rd edn, 1989), pp. 64–66; L. Blom-Cooper and G. Drewry, *Final Appeal* (1972) Chap. VIII (of the 50 or so law lords reported on, only one had a father who 'could be described unequivocally as working class'; only one came from a redbrick university; and only one had not been to university); and J. A. G. Griffith, *The Politics of the Judiciary* (4th edn 1991) Chap. 1.

Liberties and a Bill of Rights (1976) pp. 28–29, state that 'eight of the eleven [judges] who took part in the recent case on comprehensive schools, in *Tameside* (above p. 15) had been educated at independent school, and three at grammar schools' and that 'within a week of the House of Lords' decision two commentators in the press had pronounced that the decision had killed the whole idea of a Bill of Rights as far as the Labour Party was concerned.' J. A. G. Griffith, *The Politics of the Judiciary* (4th edn, 1991), p. 325, opposing a Bill of Rights, expresses the reasons for concern on the part of some commentators on the left as follows:

'It is difficult to see how the welfare of the individual would be promoted by the enactment of [the provisions of the ECHR] . . . if they were to be interpreted by the judiciary of today.

To some, the judicial view of the public interest appears merely as reactionary conservatism. It is not the politics of the extreme right. Its insensitivity is clearly rooted more in unconscious assumptions than in a wish to oppress. But it is demonstrable that on every major social issue which has come before the courts during the last thirty years – concerning industrial relations, political protest, race relations, governmental secrecy, police powers, moral behaviour – the judges have supported the conventional, established and settled interests. And they have reacted strongly against challenges to those interests. This conservatism does not necessarily follow the day-to-day political policies currently associated with the party of that name. But it is a political philosophy nonetheless.'

K. Ewing and C. Gearty, *Freedom under Thatcher* (1990), pp. 270–1, reach a similar conclusion: 'The harsh reality is that we need to be protected by Parliament from the courts, as much as we need to be protected from the abuse of executive power.'
3. Lord Denning (369 HL Deb 25 March 1976 cols 797–8) has expressed opposition to a Bill of Rights on the different ground of the effect upon judicial independence and public confidence in the courts:

'. . . if judges were given power to overthrow sections or Acts of Parliament, they would become political, their appointments would be based on political grounds and the reputation of our Judiciary would suffer accordingly. One has only to see, in the great Constitutions of the United States of America and of India, the conflicts which arise from time to time between the judges and the Legislature. I hope we shall not have such conflicts in this country. The independence of our judges and their reputation for impartiality depend on their obeying the will of Parliament and on their being independent. The independence of the judges is the other pillar of our Constitution.'

Cf. Denning, *What Next in the Law* (1981), Chap. 12.

On the appointment of judges, an acknowledged factor in the nomination of candidates for the US Supreme Court by the President is the latter's opinion that the candidate he chooses will judge cases the right way. Note also that Supreme Court justices are by no means always appointed from the ranks of the judiciary or practising lawyers. Warren CJ was Governor of California before his appointment in 1953. 'The correlation between prior judicial experience and fitness for the functions of the Supreme Court is zero' (Justice Frankfurter, (1957) 105 U Penn LR 781, 795). If judges were to be given a power of judicial review of legislation, they would undoubtedly figure in the Sunday supplements more than they do now. Law students in the US know a lot about the judicial philosophies and quite a lot about the private lives of Supreme Court justices. How many UK law students could even name the members of the Appellate Committee at present, let alone place them on the political or philosophical spectrum? Note also the view that 'British judges are not at their best in developing social policy. Our tradition in this respect differs from the Americans where lawyers commonly discuss issues of wages, social benefits and education'.[1] Could this be overcome by more emphasis on social policy in legal education? Or would judges become more adept with greater experience anyway?

---

1 Mr Lyons, Minority Report, *Report of the Committee on Privacy*, Cmnd. 5012, p. 211.

4. If a Bill of Rights were adopted, would British judges take up the role expected of them? Many of them? Given time? One question would be the appropriate method of interpretation. As Atiyah, *Law and Modern Society* (1983), p. 111, states:

'If a Bill of Rights were ever entrenched in this country, there is no doubt that the result would be disastrous unless the judges could be persuaded to alter their traditional methods of interpretation. For traditional and crabbed methods of interpretation could often lead to the invalidation of legislation which is absolutely necessary to keep pace with changing values or conditions; huge tensions would then build up in the legal and political system, and general discredit could be thrown on the law.'

The Judicial Committee of the Privy Council, on which House of Lords judges sit, has been criticised for its jurisprudence interpreting and applying Bills of Rights in Commonwealth constitutions.[1] There could be little criticism, however, of *Pratt v A-G for Jamaica* [1993] 3 WLR 995 at 1016, in which the Privy Council stated that 'in any case in which execution is to take place more than five years after sentence there will be strong grounds for believing that the delay is such as to constitute "inhuman or degrading punishment or other treatment" '. On the response of the Canadian judiciary to a power of judicial review of legislation, see below, pp. 27–31.

5. Is the judicial forum in any event not a satisfactory one for legislation? Is an inquiry and a report marshalling all of the evidence followed by a bill drafted by parliamentary draftsmen better? Cf. Sir Robert Megarry VC in *Malone v Metropolitan Police Comr* [1979] 2 All ER 620, 642–643. And is it better for Parliament to act (at least in most cases) uninfluenced by the facts of any particular case? Hard cases make bad law. But what if Parliament doesn't have the time or the inclination? The recommendations of the Younger Report on Privacy, below, p. 524, for the reform of the law of privacy, for example, have remained largely unimplemented. Could a judge act on the basis of the Younger Report and create, say, the recommended new tort of unlawful surveillance?

6. Another important question is whether the legal profession, which, with the modest return to be gained from criminal legal aid work, has in recent years geared itself more towards commercial practice, would be ready to take up the considerable amount of work, mostly on behalf of less affluent private clients, that would result from the introduction of a Bill of Rights.

7. Documents such as the Universal Declaration of Human Rights and the ECHR have served a useful educational and promotional role by providing convenient, positive statements of civil liberties that can be used as a point of reference and as authority in argument. See, for example, the many letters in *The Times* that rely upon these sources. Might not a legally binding national Bill of Rights have the same effect in the UK, only more so?

8. How significant is the fact that the House of Lords Select Committee (Report, p. 29) 'received no evidence that human rights are in practice better protected in countries which have a code of fundamental human rights embodied in their law than they are in the United Kingdom'? Cf. Lord Hailsham's comment:[2]

'Show me a nation with a Bill of Rights and I will show you a nation which has fewer actual human rights than England or Britain because the escape clauses are used, often quite ruthlessly, by the executive of the time . . . one must not exaggerate the value of the protection given by any document of this kind.'

Note also the Select Committee's further comment (Report, p. 29):

---

1 See, e.g., Ewing, in Finnie, ed., *Edinburgh Essays in Public Law* (1991), p. 231 at n. 146.
2 369 HL Deb 25 March 1976 col 785. Note, however, that Lord Hailsham supported Lord Wade's Bill: 402 HL Deb 8 November 1979 col 1063.

'. . . in any country, whatever its constitution, the existence or absence of legislation in the nature of a Bill of Rights can in practice play only a relatively minor part in the protection of human rights. What is important, above all, is a country's political climate and traditions.'

Note also the fate of some of the Bills of Rights in the constitutions of new states.

Nonetheless, is there not some truth in the view that the negative, Diceyan approach to the protection of civil liberties (see above, p. 2) that prevails in the UK leaves an individual's liberties particularly at risk, in the absence of judicial power to control the executive, whether acting through Parliament or under the prerogative?

How would you weight the following different arguments put by Lord Scarman and Zander in favour of a Bill of Rights? Lord Scarman states (*English Law – The New Dimension* (1974) p. 15):

'When times are normal and fear is not stalking the land, English law sturdily protects the freedom of the individual and respects human personality. But when times are abnormally alive with fear and prejudice, the common law is at a disadvantage: it cannot resist the will, however frightened and prejudiced it may be, of Parliament. The classic illustration is, of course, Regulation 18(b) and *Liversidge v Anderson* [1942] AC 206.'

But would the same four judges who rejected Lord Atkin's very plausible interpretation of Regulation 18(b) in his dissenting opinion in *Liversidge v Anderson,* see below, p. 726, have decided the case differently on the basis of a 'freedom of the person' guarantee in a Bill of Rights? Zander argues (*A Bill of Rights?* (3rd edn., 1985) pp. 90–91):

'[A] Bill of Rights is desirable not because human rights are grossly abused in Britain, nor to provide against the danger of future tyranny. The former is untrue, the latter unlikely. The case for a Bill of Rights rests rather on the belief that it would make a distinct and valuable contribution to the *better* protection of human rights. Certainly it would not solve all problems. The extent of the contribution it could make must, in the end, depend on how it is regarded and interpreted by the judges. It would give them greater scope than exists in the ordinary common law and statute law. It would require of them a broader, more wide-ranging approach than has been customary.'

Note also the argument by R. Dworkin, *A Bill of Rights for Britain* (1990), pp. 1–2, 57, that 'liberty is ill in Britain'. Citing, in the 1980s, the enforcement of official secrecy laws, Spycatcher, censorship of broadcasting, telephone tapping and surveillance, public order controls on political protest and limits on the rights of suspects, he argues for the incorporation of the ECHR. On the 'decline in the culture of liberty' that a 'new constitutional charter' might help to correct, he states:

'Great Britain was once a fortress for freedom. It claimed the great philosophers of liberty – Milton and Locke and Paine and Mill. Its legal tradition is irradiated with liberal ideas: that people accused of crime are presumed to be innocent, that no one owns another's conscience, that a man's home is his castle. But now Britain offers less formal legal protection to central freedoms than most of its neighbours in Europe. I do not mean that it has become a police state, of course. Citizens are free openly to criticise the government, and the government does not kidnap or torture or kill its opponents. But liberty is nevertheless under threat by a notable decline in the culture of liberty – the community's shared sense that individual privacy and dignity and freedom of speech and conscience are crucially important and that they are worth considerable sacrifices in official convenience or public expense to protect.

The erosion of liberty is not the doing of only one party or one government. Labour governments in the 1970s compromised the rights of immigrants, tried to stop publication of embarrassing political material, and tolerated an outrageous censorship and intimidation of journalists by the newspaper unions. But most of the worst examples of the attack on liberty have occurred in the last decade, and Margaret Thatcher and her government are more open in their indifference to liberty than their predecessors were.'

Does the UK's record at Strasbourg (see below, Chap. 12) support the argument for incorporation of the ECHR? Certainly the large number of cases in which the UK has been found in breach of the ECHR suggests that, unless one rejects the standards set by the European Court of Human Rights, it is complacent and mistaken to argue that civil liberties are fully protected under UK law by our present procedures. Note also that UK experience at Strasbourg suggests that giving the last word to the courts rather than the legislature or the executive may in some cases lead to a less political resolution of an issue, to the advantage of human rights (see the *Brogan* case (arrest of terrorist suspects), below, p. 775), and may in others achieve or expedite law reforms which the Government favours but for which it has not been able to find the necessary time or support (the *Dudgeon* case (homosexual acts criminal), below, p. 812). It also suggests that it is in the area of executive discretion (see, e.g., the *Golder* case, below, p. 792), which has, at least until recently, been largely immune from control through judicial review in the British courts, that a Bill of Rights (allowing the enabling statute to be questioned) would be most valuable.

Might a domestic Bill of Rights reduce the number of cases that are taken to Strasbourg? If so, might it be better for our international reputation (as well as more convenient for the claimant) to decide the questions raised at home? The public hearing of the *Ireland v United Kingdom* case, below, p. 749, was well attended by USSR journalists. Might a statement of legal principles in a Bill of Rights assist the courts in taking an initiative to protect civil liberties? Might it avoid the thicket of case-law that sometimes results as the common law develops? Note, for example, the tangle that the law of search and seizure was in (see the first edition of this casebook, pp. 70–100) before the Police and Criminal Evidence Act 1984. From the individual's standpoint, the law of civil liberties and its remedies (which lie mostly scattered in different parts of the law of tort and crime) may seem a maze, not a mosaic. Might a Bill of Rights aimed directly at their protection and offering a tailor-made remedy encourage and facilitate a person's recourse to the courts? Might it both help develop a coherent theoretical basis for civil liberties law and facilitate the rational development of the law? For example, as Lester and Joseph[1] point out, the absence of a guarantee of equality before the law of general application in a Bill of Rights, which is made good only partially and on a piece-meal basis by particular Westminster and Brussels enactments, underlines the out-moded approach to the protection of human rights that the United Kingdom still pursues.

9. If the arguments about a Bill of Rights are evenly balanced, upon whom is the burden of proof? Those who wish to preserve the status quo? Or those who seek radical change?

3 What kind of Bill of Rights?

Human Rights (No 3) Bill

1.—(1) The fundamental rights and freedoms set out in Section 1 of the Convention and the Protocols thereto, set out in Schedule 1 to this Bill, shall, subject to the provisions of this Act and the restrictions permitted by the Convention and its Protocols and the reservations contained in Schedule 2 to this Bill, have the force of law.[2]

(2) The obligation on the part of any person to whom this Act applies to comply with the provisions of the Convention is owed to any natural person and any such person who may be adversely affected by a

1 In D. J. Harris and S. L. Joseph, eds, *The ICCPR and the UK* (1995), Chap 17.
2 *Ed.* Schedule 1 includes Arts. 2–18, ECHR and Arts. 1–3, First Protocol, ECHR. I.e. it includes all of the rights in the ECHR and in the First Protocol. The reservations referred to are those made by the UK to the right to education, below, p. 743.

breach of that obligation shall, without prejudice to any other claim, have a cause of action in like manner as in any other such claim, being a claim in tort or of delict or semi-delict under any system of law in the United Kingdom.

2.—(1) It shall be unlawful for any person or body defined in subsection (3) below to do any act which infringes any of the fundamental rights and freedoms of any natural person.

(2) It shall be the duty of any person or body defined in subsection (3) below to promote the fundamental rights and freedoms referred to in section 1 above.

(3) This section applies to—

(a) a Minister of the Crown or any person or body acting on behalf of, or for the purposes of, the Crown, and

(b) any statutory body, public body, or any person holding statutory office, any other public office or exercising any public function, or any body or person acting on behalf of, or for the purposes of, any such body or person.

3. Any natural person whose fundamental rights and freedoms are being, have been or are about to be infringed shall have an effective remedy before a tribunal or court and in the absence of, and without prejudice to, any other established remedy shall have a cause of action in the High Court or the Court of Session and in any case shall be entitled to such of the following remedies as are appropriate in all the circumstances—

(a) a declaration of the effect of those fundamental rights and freedoms in the particular circumstances;

(b) damages for such infringements including where appropriate exemplary and aggravated damages;

(c) an order restraining future infringements;

(d) an order to enforce fundamental rights and freedoms; or

(e) an order quashing the act of any person or body defined in subsection (3) of section 2 above.

4.—(1) Any provision in any enactment or in any statutory instrument made before the passing of this Act or any provision or construction of the common law taking effect before or after the passing of this Act which authorises or requires any act to be done—

(a) shall be taken to authorise or require that act to be done only in a manner and to the extent that it does not infringe any of the fundamental rights and freedoms of any natural person; and

(b) to the extent that it purports to authorise or to require any act to be done which infringes any of the fundamental rights and freedoms of any natural person, shall cease to have effect.

(2) No provision of any Act passed or statutory instrument made after the passing of this Act shall be construed or applied as if it authorised or required the doing of an act that infringes any of the fundamental rights and freedoms, or as if it conferred power to make any statutory instrument authorising or requiring the doing of any such act unless the Act contains a provision specifying that the relevant powers apply notwithstanding the fact that they are, or may be, contrary to any of the rights and freedoms referred to in subsection (1) of section 1 above. . . .

5. All courts and tribunals shall have regard to the whole of the Convention and all of its Protocols and of all judgments of the European Court of Human Rights and of all published reports and decisions of the European Commission on Human Rights established by the Convention.

NOTES

1. The Human Rights (No 3) Bill was given a first reading in the House of Commons on 11 January 1994, but made no further progress. It was introduced as a private member's bill by Mr Graham Allen, the Labour Party Frontbench Spokesperson on Democracy and the Constitution.[1] The Bill, which would be likely to be very similar to that which the Labour Party would introduce if in government, proposes, as the clauses printed above indicate, the incorporation of the ECHR as a first step. The bill provides for a United Kingdom Bill of Rights Commission that would then prepare a tailor-made bill of rights for the United Kingdom covering all civil, political, economic and social rights. The bill also provides for a Human Rights Commission whose tasks would include the making of third party interventions in

1 For Mr Allen's arguments in favour of a Bill of Rights, see 525 HC Deb, 27 May 1993, col 1023.

any court proceedings bearing upon the rights in the Bill of Rights, the initiation of proceedings in respect of any breach of the Bill of Rights and the drafting of codes of practice to promote human rights.

2. The Allen bill is the latest in a long series of private members' bills over the last 20 years or so proposing the introduction of a bill of rights. See M. Zander, *A Bill of Rights?* (3rd edn, 1985), Chap. 1. A valiant and persistent attempt at incorporation of the ECHR was made by Lord Wade with his Bill of Rights bill. Its introduction in 1977 (after a previous introduction and debate in 1976) led to the appointment of a House of Lords Select Committee to consider the question (see below, para **3**). Lord Wade's Bill was passed by the Lords in 1979 and 1981 and sent to the Commons, where it was introduced as a private member's bill but failed to obtain a second reading on either occasion in the face of Government opposition. In 1985, the immediate predecessor to the Allen bill was a bill introduced by Sir Edward Gardner, a Labour MP, to incorporate the ECHR, which received a formal second reading without a vote (115 HC Deb 8 May 1987 col 1029) and was then lost for lack of time.[1]

3. As noted above, the question of a Bill of Rights has been examined by a House of Lords Select Committee. The Committee was divided six to five in favour of a Bill of Rights; it was unanimously of the opinion that, if introduced, such a Bill should incorporate the ECHR (Report of the Select Committee on a Bill of Rights (1977–78) HL 176). Although the Convention text was not ideal, it existed and it would be politically difficult and time consuming to try and draft a new one. Moreover 'if we produced for ourselves a new and different formulation of fundamental rights, we should then have to cope with two codes which would exist side-by-side.' The Committee thought, however, that the Bill should allow for the reservation that the UK had made to Article 2, First Protocol (below, p. 743, n. **3**) and should exclude the Fourth Protocol, which the UK has not ratified.[2]

4. A key question is whether a Bill of Rights in the form of a statute could control legislation enacted after it. The House of Lords Select Committee (Report, pp. 22–6) thought not, except as a guide to interpretation:

'14. . . . there is no way in which a Bill of Rights could be made immune altogether from amendment or repeal by a subsequent Act. That follows from the principle of the sovereignty of Parliament which is the central feature of our constitution. . . . The usual way of entrenching provisions in countries with written constitutions is to require a special majority in the legislature, or in some cases a favourable vote in a referendum, for any Act amending or repealing, or otherwise overriding, the entrenched provision. The Committee think it is clear, however, that no such provision (e.g. a requirement for a two-thirds majority in the House of Commons for any Bill seeking to override a Bill of Rights) would be legally effective in the United Kingdom . . .

15. The only other possibility is a provision such as is contained in clause 3 of Lord Wade's Bill. . . .

16. If such a clause were effective, it would, in the Committee's view, in practice provide an important degree of entrenchment. In this regard, the Committee do not accept the view that has been expressed that, if such a clause were included in a Bill of Rights, Governments would have no hesitation in including in future Acts the necessary express formula to ensure that the Act would override the Bill of Rights. . . .

17. The Committee have, however, felt unable to accept the assumption . . . that a Bill of Rights could protect itself from being overridden by implication. It is contrary to the principle of Parliamentary sovereignty as it has hitherto been understood in the United Kingdom. Under that principle, Parliament cannot bind itself as to the future and a later Act must always prevail over an earlier one if it is inconsistent with it, whether the inconsistency is express or implied. The Committee are aware that some legal

---

1 There was, however, a full debate on the Bill earlier: 109 HC Deb 6 February 1987 cols 1223–1288, when the bill received a favourable vote of 94 to 16 on a closure motion.

2 For later protocols that the UK has not accepted, see below, pp. 744–5.

writers have advanced the view that the principle of Parliamentary sovereignty does not preclude Parliament from laying down a binding requirement as to the manner or form of subsequent Acts of a particular kind. . . . If this view prevailed in the courts, a provision like clause 3 of Lord Wade's Bill would be efficacious in that it does no more than lay down the form in which a subsequent Act has to be framed if it is to override a Bill of Rights. The Committee are not, however, persuaded that the view is sound.

23. It follows from the foregoing that the Committee conclude that the main scope for a Bill of Rights would be to operate on our existing law. The most that such a Bill could do would be to include an interpretation provision which ensured that the Bill of Rights was always taken into account in the construction of later Acts . . .'

When considered by the Committee in 1977, clause 3 of Lord Wade's Bill had read:

'In case of conflict between any enactment subsequent to the passing of this Act and the provisions of the said Convention and Protocols, the said Convention and Protocols shall prevail unless subsequent enactment shall explicitly state otherwise.'

Mr Allen's bill, clause 4(2), is differently worded, with the Human Rights Act prevailing over later legislation unless the later legislation expressly provides that it is to apply 'notwithstanding' the Human Rights Act. Such a provision could be adopted by an ordinary majority in Parliament. For the power to override the Canadian Charter by express provision, see s. 33, Charter, below, p. 28. Note that in the US, the constitutional Bill of Rights prevails over all later legislation, irrespective of any expressed intention or necessary implication of the legislation. Mr Allen's Bill is a more modest proposal that takes away the force of much of the argument against a Bill of Rights. The current Parliament, if it so chose, could have the last word. Mr Allen's bill would permit control of acts done under the prerogative: see clause 2(1)(3).

5. As the House of Lords Select Committee Report indicates, there are differing views as to the nature of parliamentary sovereignty that bear upon the question whether a Bill of Rights can be entrenched within the UK constitution. It is generally agreed that, under the rule of parliamentary sovereignty as it is recognised by the courts at present, Parliament can always change its mind as to the content of legislation. It could, therefore, having passed a statute containing a Bill of Rights, later enact a statute that expressly or by necessary implication contradicted a guarantee in the Bill of Rights, and the later statute in time would prevail. Even an express provision in a Bill of Rights statute to the effect that the statute could not be repealed would not prevent this. The controversy concerns the question whether Parliament can bind itself as to the 'manner and form' of subsequent legislation. Could it for example, require that a provision in a statute introducing a Bill of Rights be repealed only by express (not implied) repeal (see Mr Allen's bill), thus dictating the 'form' of legislation?[1] There are Commonwealth cases in which a special voting or referendum requirement has been held to be binding upon a legislature (e.g. *A-G for New South Wales v Thethowan* [1932] AC 526, PC (referendum)), but the Select Committee (para. 14) clearly prefers H. W. R. Wade's view (see n. 1) that these can be distinguished. An English case which supports Wade's view is *Ellen Street Estates Ltd v Minister of Health* [1934] 1 KB 590, CA.

Although H. W. R. Wade rejects the view that Parliament can limit itself as to the 'manner and form' of subsequent legislation, he does so on the basis that this is

---

1 Contrast, for example, the views of H. W. R. Wade (Lord Wade's cousin) [1955] CLJ 172 (Parliament cannot bind itself as to the manner and form of subsequent legislation) and R. F. V. Heuston, *Essays in Constitutional Law* (2nd edn., 1964) (Parliament can do so). See also Bradley, in Jowell and Oliver, eds., *The Changing Constitution*, (2nd edn., 1989), Chap. 2, and Elkind, (1987) 50 MLR 158.

the current rule of common law, which the judges can change. It is, he suggests, a special common law rule which results from an 'ultimate political fact'. It is a rule that reflects the political consensus in the country and one that should be changed by the judges if, and only if, a 'revolution' occurs by which parliamentary sovereignty in its present form (which was itself recognised by the courts only at the end of the seventeenth century as power shifted from the Crown to Parliament) no longer commands general support. So, if Parliament, speaking for the people, were to legislate, even by means of an ordinary statute, so as to introduce a Bill of Rights which was intended to limit Parliament's legislative sovereignty in the area of civil liberties, the courts should recognise it as indicating a change in the 'ultimate political fact' and modify the common law rule of parliamentary sovereignty accordingly. On this basis, Parliament could go further than Mr Allen's Bill proposes and provide that, as under the US Constitution, Parliament could not legislate contrary to the ECHR even by express enactment.

H. W. R. Wade has suggested that if the judges were called upon to recognise a change in the rule of parliamentary sovereignty, they might be assisted in doing so by a statute that required them to take an oath to uphold the constitution in which the entrenched status of the Bill of Rights was specified: *Constitutional Fundamentals* (rev edn, 1989), p. 47). Note, however, that the courts have, without any such assistance, recognised that the European Communities Act 1972 has modified the established doctrine of parliamentary sovereignty in relation to EU legislation, recognising a change in the 'ultimate political fact'.[1] It might be that they would respond similarly if a statute incorporating the ECHR were enacted. The Canadian judges have done so in respect of the Canadian Charter of Rights and Freedoms, below, p. 29, although it is true, as Hogg notes, (1984) 32 AJCL 183, 204, that the 'prolonged and highly public process by which the Charter was adopted' had 'fed the public expectation that a significant change in the Canadian Constitution occurred with the adoption of the Charter'. Note also, with regard to the EU, that British judges may have been influenced by the fact that UK entry into the EU was preceded by a referendum in which the public voted in its favour.

6. How good a Bill of Rights is the ECHR (text below, pp. 740–745) for internal UK purposes? Does it cover all the civil and political rights one would like to see protected? Would the International Covenant on Civil and Political Rights, which protects rights that the ECHR does not (e.g. equality before the law (Art. 26), be better?[2] To what extent does the ECHR protect against racial discrimination? (But a Bill of Rights can be supplemented by ordinary legislation such as the Race Relations Act 1976.) Note (1) that the ECHR represents what West European states as a whole were prepared to be legally bound by 30 years ago and (2) that it was drafted hurriedly in French as well as English and has obscurities, ambiguities and errors that reflect this. (But then statutes that come from Parliament are not always perfect.) Would the ECHR be incorporated 'bag and baggage' (i.e. with the gloss put upon it by the Strasbourg authorities) or would the British courts be free to start again in their interpretation of the ECHR for UK purposes?[3] The former approach

---

1   See *Garland v British Rail Engineering Ltd* [1983] 2 AC 751, HL and *Factortame Ltd v Secretary of State for Transport* [1990] 2 AC 85, HL.
2   On the ICCPR, see D. McGoldrick, *The Human Rights Committee: its Role in the Development of the International Covenant on Civil and Political Rights* (1991) and M. Nowak, *UN Covenant on Civil and Political Rights: CCPR Commentary* (1993, Eng. trans). On the ICCPR and the UK, see Harris and Joseph, op. cit. at p. 20, n. 2 above.
3   See clause 5, Mr Allen's Bill. See also Arnhill, 1985 PL 378.

has the disadvantage that the European Commission and Court of Human Rights (on each of which the UK has only one national) have to interpret the Convention for Europe as a whole. (Cf. the problem the Federal US Supreme Court has when interpreting the US Bill of Rights for the several states.) See the *Tyrer* case, below, p. 767 in which the British judge was outvoted on the question of judicial corporal punishment by judges from countries with different traditions. And see the different approach to contempt of court adopted by the European Court of Human Rights in the *Sunday Times* case, below, p. 823, applying Article 10, ECHR (protection of freedom of speech subject to narrowly construed exceptions, including the interest in the proper administration of justice) to that adopted by the House of Lords in the case, applying the common law (weighing the interests in freedom of speech and the administration of justice equally). The latter approach (starting again) would allow the courts to take account of UK political and social traditions (and blindspots?) but would run a greater risk of court decisions being reversed at Strasbourg.

7. The Institute for Public Policy Research (IPPR) has drafted its own tailormade Bill of Rights as a part of a written constitution for the United Kingdom.[1] This draws upon both the ECHR and the ICCPR. The commentary to the IPPR Bill points to gaps in and the out-dated nature of some of the provisions of the ECHR, as contrasted with those of the ICCPR. See also the different tailormade Bill of Rights proposed by Liberty, which makes use of the same sources.[2] Charter 88, a private pressure group, also advocates a Bill of Rights,[3] although it has not proposed its own text. Given both the undoubted limitations of the ECHR guarantee and the likelihood that time or support might well be difficult to find at Westminster for two attempts at introducing a Bill of Rights, there is a strong case for arguing that a text drawing on the ECHR and the ICCPR, but modified to meet particular United Kingdom needs, should be introduced at once.[4]

8. Of the leading political parties, the Labour and Liberal Democrat Parties are in favour of a Bill of Rights; the Conservative Party is not. The Labour Party would incorporate the ECHR.[5] The Liberal Party would adopt the IPPR's Bill of Rights (above).[6] The Conservative Party's opposition was explained by Lord Reay in the House of Lords in a Bill of Rights debate as follows:[7]

'It is the Government's firm view that imposing on the judges a duty to interpret the Convention would add a new and undesirable dimension to their current role. That new role would be to decide broad issues of policy. The more we draw judges into political matters, the more shall we impinge on the constitutional concept of the political neutrality of the judges in terms of the general public's perception of them. . . .

I do not doubt for one moment that British judges would be far better placed than those in Strasbourg to decide what does and does not comply with the Convention in the British context. But that is not the point. The point is that at present judges are charged with interpreting and applying the will of Parliament as set down in precisely drafted statute law. Interpreting the principles set down in the

---

1 For text, see IPPR, *A Written Constitution for the United Kingdom* (2nd rev. edn, 1993), pp. 34ff.
2 NCCL, *A People's Charter* (1991). On Liberty's proposals, see F Klug and J. Wadham, 1993 PL 579.
3 See *New Statesman* 2 December 1988, p 4, and N. Stanger, (1990) 8 *Index on Censorship* 14.
4 Cf. D. J. Harris, in Harris and Joseph, op. cit. at p. 20, n. 2, above, p. 67.
5 See *A New Agenda for Democracy*, a Party policy document that was adopted by the Party Conference in 1993, and Mr Allen's Human Rights (No 2) Bill, above, p. 20.
6 *Here We Stand*, Liberal Democrat Party Federal White Paper No 6, 1993.
7 524 HL Deb 5 1990 col 209. See also *Civil Liberties*, Conservative Research Department Brief, 1990, and J. Patten, *Political Culture, Conservatism and Rolling Constitutional Change*, 1991 Swinton Lecture, Conservative Political Centre publication, 1991.

Convention would be an entirely different matter, and would involve the weighing of policy issues and conclusions being reached on the basis of the judges' perceptions of the public interest. . . .

Another disadvantage of the proposal to incorporate the Convention into domestic law is that it would introduce a significant element of uncertainty into the law. Strasbourg, in finding against us, cannot strike down our law. The court and Committee of Ministers create no vacuum and time is given to reflect and make changes, if Parliament agrees.

Incorporation of the Convention would be a recipe for muddle and confusion. We might well find ourselves facing a scenario such as this: Parliament passes a law, without reserved provision, which it fully believed to conform to the Convention. Next day, or next year, this law could be struck down by a judge who, acting in good faith, took a different view according to his perceptions of the public interest. The judgment would have immediate effect which in turn could have urgent and significant administrative implications. I suggest this would impose an unpredictable burden on Parliament. If, for example, the law concerned entry to the UK, there would be enormous problems attendant thereafter on the operation of entry control procedures while a new law was being prepared.

. . . we do not have a written constitution although . . . I do not find that to be an embarrassment. Rights exist under common law in this country unless taken away by statute. Thus, an Englishman's home is his castle unless Parliament gives power to the police or others to enter it. To introduce conferred rights into our present system by way of a written constitution could have effects which are not readily apparent. The same problems do not necessarily arise in other countries which have written constitutions and the need to confer rights. Therefore, for them it is far less of a departure from tradition to incorporate the Convention. . . .

My noble friend Lord Beloff pointed out that incorporation would not be a panacea, and that as the right of individual petition would remain, litigating matters in British courts first would only add to the length of time it would take for an eventual decision to be reached in Strasbourg. . . .

The noble Lord, Lord McGregor of Durris, argued that if we accepted the Treaty of Rome provisions as part of our law, we should also accept the provisions of the European Convention on Human Rights. My answer is that the Treaty of Rome contains specific provisions. Those which have direct application are drafted in specific terms which would leave limited scope for different interpretation. On the other hand, the European Convention sets out a set of principles in general terms. That leaves much scope for interpretation, as illustrated by the differences that arise even between the Commission and the Court.'

9. There is now an impressive list of senior British judges who are on record as favouring the introduction of a Bill of Rights, in most cases by the incorporation of the ECHR into United Kingdom law. They include the Master of the Rolls (Bingham MR[1]), the Lord Chief Justice (Lord Taylor[2]) and several present or former members of the House of Lords (Lords Bridge,[3] Slynn,[4] Woolf,[5] Scarman,[6] and Simon[7]). Other judges, however, have argued constructively that much can be done by the judges to protect civil liberties further using their existing powers.[8]

---

1 (1993) 109 LQR 390.
2 The 1992 Dimbleby Lecture: see Independent, (1992) 2 December.
3 See *A-G v Guardian Newspapers* [1987] 1 WLR 1248 at 1286.
4 540 HL Deb col 1098 26 November 1992.
5 1995 PL 57. Lord Woolf argues that the UK should follow the model of the New Zealand Bill of Rights.
6 *English Law: The New Dimension* (1974), p. 77.
7 550 HL Deb col 170 23 November 1993.
8 See Lord Browne-Wilkinson, 1992 PL 397 at 409 who argues that 'membership of the EEC has incorporated the ECHR into our domestic law' in the areas to which European Union law applies and that, by developing its traditional rules of statutory construction, the common law 'could protect our freedoms from anything short of a deliberate wish by Parliament to invade them', thereby achieving all that incorporation of the ECHR subject to a 'notwithstanding' provision (see Mr Allen's bill, above) could achieve. See also Sir John Laws, 1993 PL 59.

4 The Canadian Charter of Rights and Freedoms

Canada Act 1982

Schedule B (Constitution Act 1982)

PART I: CANADIAN CHARTER OF RIGHTS AND FREEDOMS

Whereas Canada is founded upon principles that recognize the supremacy of God and the rule of law:

1. The *Canadian Charter of Rights and Freedoms* guarantees the rights and freedoms set out in it subject only to such reasonable limits prescribed by law as can be demonstrably justified in a free and democratic society.

2. Everyone has the following fundamental freedoms:
- (a) freedom of conscience and religion;
- (b) freedom of thought, belief, opinion and expression, including freedom of the press and other media of communication;
- (c) freedom of peaceful assembly; and
- (d) freedom of association.

3. Every citizen of Canada has the right to vote in an election of members of the House of Commons or of a legislative assembly and to be qualified for membership therein. . . .

6.—(1) Every citizen of Canada has the right to enter, remain in and leave Canada. . . .

7. Everyone has the right to life, liberty and security of the person and the right not to be deprived thereof except in accordance with the principles of fundamental justice.

8. Everyone has the right to be secure against unreasonable search or seizure.

9. Everyone has the right not to be arbitrarily detained or imprisoned.

10. Everone has the right on arrest or detention
- (a) to be informed promptly of the reasons therefor;
- (b) to retain and instruct counsel without delay and to be informed of that right; and
- (c) to have the validity of the detention determined by way of habeas corpus and to be released if the detention is not lawful.

11. Any person charged with an offence has the right
- (a) to be informed without unreasonable delay of the specific offence;
- (b) to be tried within a reasonable time;
- (c) not to be compelled to be a witness in proceedings against that person in respect of the offence;
- (d) to be presumed innocent until proven guilty according to law in a fair and public hearing by an independent and impartial tribunal;
- (e) not to be denied reasonable bail without just cause;
- (f) except in the case of an offence under military law tried before a military tribunal, to the benefit of trial by jury where the maximum punishment for the offence is imprisonment for five years or a more severe punishment;
- (g) not to be found guilty on account of any act or omission unless, at the time of the act or omission, it constituted an offence under Canadian or international law or was criminal according to the general principles of law recognized by the community of nations;
- (h) if finally acquitted of the offence, not to be tried for it again and, if finally found guilty and punished for the offence, not to be tried or punished for it again; and
- (i) if found guilty of the offence and if the punishment for the offence has been varied between the time of commission and the time of sentencing, to the benefit of the lesser punishment.

12. Everyone has the right not to be subjected to any cruel and unusual treatment or punishment.

13. A witness who testifies in any proceedings has the right not to have any incriminating evidence so given used to incriminate that witness in other proceedings, except in a prosecution for perjury or for the giving of contradictory evidence.

14. A party or witness in any proceedings who does not understand or speak the language in which the proceedings are conducted or who is deaf has the right to the assistance of an interpreter.

15.—(1) Every individual is equal before and under the law and has the right to the equal protection and equal benefit of the law without discrimination and, in particular, without discrimination based on race, national or ethnic origin, colour, religion, sex, age or mental or physical disability.

(2) Subsection (1) does not preclude any law, program or activity that has as its object the amelioration of conditions of disadvantaged individuals or groups including those that are disadvantaged because of race, national or ethnic origin, colour, religion, sex, age or mental or physical disability. . . .

16.—(1) English and French are the official languages of Canada and have equality of status and equal rights and privileges as to their use in all institutions of the Parliament and Government of Canada. . . .

23.—(1) Citizens of Canada
  (a) whose first language learned and still understood is that of the English or French linguistic minority population of the province in which they reside, or
  (b) who have received their primary school instruction in Canada in English or French and reside in a province where the language in which they received that instruction is the language of the English or French linguistic minority population of the province,
have the right to have their children receive primary and secondary school instruction in that language in that province.

24.—(1) Anyone whose rights or freedoms, as guaranteed by this Charter, have been infringed or denied may apply to a court of competent jurisdiction to obtain such remedy as the court considers appropriate and just in the circumstances.

(2) Where, in proceedings under subsection (1), a court concludes that evidence was obtained in a manner that infringed or denied any rights or freedoms guaranteed by this Charter, the evidence shall be excluded if it is established that, having regard to all the circumstances, the admission of it in the proceedings would bring the administration of justice into disrepute.

25. The guarantee in this Charter of certain rights and freedoms shall not be construed so as to abrogate or derogate from any aboriginal treaty or other rights or freedoms that pertain to the aboriginal peoples of Canada. . . .

26. The guarantee in this Charter of certain rights and freedoms shall not be construed as denying the existence of any other rights or freedoms that exist in Canada.

27. This Charter will be interpreted in a manner consistent with the preservation and enhancement of the multicultural heritage of Canadians.

28. Notwithstanding anything in this Charter, the rights and freedoms referred to in it are guaranteed equally to male and female persons.

29. Nothing in this Charter abrogates or derogates from any rights or privileges guaranteed by or under the Constitution of Canada in respect of denominational, separate or dissentient schools. . . .

33.—(1) Parliament or the legislature of a province may expressly declare in an Act of Parliament or of the legislature, as the case may be, that the Act or a provision thereof shall operate notwithstanding a provision included in section 2 or sections 7 to 15 of this Charter.

(2) An Act or a provision of an Act in respect of which a declaration made under this section is in effect shall have such operation as it would have but for the provision of this Charter referred to in the declaration.

(3) A declaration made under subsection (1) shall cease to have effect five years after it comes into force or on such earlier date as may be specified in the declaration.

(4) Parliament or the legislature of a province may re-enact a declaration made under subsection (1).

(5) Subsection (3) applies in respect of a re-enactment made under subsection (4).

PART VII: GENERAL

52.—(1) The Constitution of Canada is the supreme law of Canada, and any law that is inconsistent with the provisions of the Constitution is, to the extent of the inconsistency, of no force or effect.

NOTES[1]

1. The Charter is a part of the new Constitution of Canada.[2] Under s. 38, Constitution Act 1982, amendments to the new constitution, including the Charter, require acccptance by the federal Canadian Parliament and by the legislatures of two-thirds of the provinces having at least 50 per cent of the population of all of the provinces.

2. Canada had earlier adopted the Canadian Bill of Rights 1960, which remains good law. This is an ordinary federal statute, controlling only federal (not provincial) law. It provides that 'no law of Canada' should be 'so construed and applied' as to 'abrogate, abridge or infringe' the rights and freedoms that it lists. The Bill has no 'overriding' clause equivalent to s. 33, Charter. It could, nonetheless, have served as a basis for a power of judicial review of federal legislation. The Canadian judiciary, however, trained in the tradition of parliamentary sovereignty, declined to regard it as such. See W. Tarnopolsky, *The Canadian Bill of Rights* (2nd rev edn, 1975).

3. The predominant view in Canada was that the judiciary would react more positively to an entrenched, constitutional document such as the Charter. For example, Hogg, 32 AJCL 183, 204–205 (1984) stated:

The judges are unlikely to ignore the deliberate and open decision to enhance their powers vis-a-vis the eleven elected governments. In more legalistic terms, it can be said that greater respect is normally accorded constitutional rights than statutory rights. I am one of a diminishing group which holds that there are strong reasons for restraint in the exercise of a power which permits non-elected judges, acting within the confines of the litigation process, to strike down measures enacted by elected legislative bodies. But it seems likely that Canadians have now taken an irrevocable step towards the judicialization of their politics and the politicization of their judiciary. It is the beginning of a new era in Canadian constitutional law.'

These predictions are proving to be true. The Canadian Supreme Court has struck down several statutcs as contrary to the Charter. For example, in *R v Big M Drug Mart Ltd* [1985] 1 SCR 295, the Court held that the federal Lord's Day Act 1970 infringed the Charter guarantee of freedom of conscience and religion (s. 2(a)) by requiring all the inhabitants of Canada, whatever their religious belief, to observe Sunday as a religious holy day and in the *BC Motor Vehicle Reference Case* [1985] 2 SCR 486, it struck down a 1985 (post-Charter)[3] British Columbia statutory provision imposing a mandatory prison sentence for the strict liability offence of driving while suspended from doing so, on the ground that such a sentence was contrary to the Charter guarantee of 'life, liberty and security of the person' (s. 7). Then, in *R v Morgentaler (No 2)* [1988] 1 SCR 30, the Court struck down the provisions of the federal Criminal Code concerning abortion on the ground that they constituted a denial of the right of the pregnant woman to 'security of the person', other than 'in

1 See, from a large literature, C.-A. Beaudoin and E. Ratushny, eds., *The Canadian Charter of Rights and Freedoms* (2nd edn, 1989) (extensive bibliography at pp. 843–921); I. Greene, *The Charter of Rights* (1989); D. Gibson, *The Law of the Charter: General Principles* (1986); P. W. Hogg, *Constitutional Law of Canada* (3rd edn, 1992), Part III; M. Mandel, *The Charter of Rights and the Legalisation of Politics in Canada* (1989); P. J. Monahan, *Politics and the Constitution: The Charter, Federalism and the Supreme Court of Canada* (1989); R. J. Sharpe, 1987 PL 48; Symposium, [1988] PL 347.

2 The constitution is contained in the Constitution Act 1982, which is Schedule B to the Canada Act 1982. The Canada Act 1982 was enacted by the UK Parliament in accordance with the constitutional arrangements then existing under the British North America Act 1867 and the Statute of Westminster 1931. The constitutional proposals, including the Charter, that are incorporated in the Constitution Act 1982 were sent to Westminster for enactment after much public debate and with the approval of the Ottawa Parliament and all of the provinces except Quebec.

3 For the power to strike down post-Charter legislation, see s. 52, Charter, above.

accordance with the principles of fundamental justice' (s. 7). The provisions prohibited abortions unless conducted by a qualified medical practitioner with the approval of a committee of at least three doctors, which was required to certify that continuation of the pregnancy would or would be likely to endanger the life or health of the mother. In practice, the effect of the provisions was that they tended to limit and delay access to abortions even when necessary for health reasons and to cause access to vary from place to place.

Most of the cases where the Supreme Court has intervened under the Charter concern the legality of exercises of police powers, and the fairness of criminal trials, rather than direct challenges to legislation.

4. Public opinion in Canada seems generally favourable to the Charter (see P. Russell, [1988] PL 385, 398). It has, however, engendered opposition among commentators from the political left because of decisions taken in trade union cases (see, e.g., Mandel op. cit., p. 29, n. **1**). Critics have cited, for example, decisions where the courts have refused to strike down, on free association grounds, laws restricting the right to strike and, on free expression grounds, laws limiting the right to picket. According to A. C. Hutchinson and A. Petter (1988) 38 UTLJ 278, 279):

'The Charter is a potent political weapon – one that is being used to benefit vested interests in society and to weaken the relative power of the disadvantaged and the underprivileged.'

Particularly criticised (ibid) is the decision of the Supreme Court in *Retail, Wholesale and Department Store Union, Local 580 v Dolphin Delivery Ltd* (1986) 33 DLR (4th) 174, holding in a case concerning picketing that the Charter does not apply to the common law as applied in litigation concerning the relations between private persons and having no connection with the government. See also D. Beatty, (1987) 37 UTLJ 183. For the view that the Supreme Court's attitude in the field of labour relations has appropriately been one of self-restraint, see P. Weiler, (1990) 40 UTLJ 117.

The Supreme Court has adopted a 'dynamic' approach to the interpretation of the Charter, emphasising its purpose, rather than a literal approach. In *Hunter v Southam Inc*,[1] the Court stated:

'The task of expounding a constitution is crucially different from that of construing a statute. A statute defines present rights and obligations. It is easily enacted and as easily repealed. A constitution, by contrast, is drafted with an eye to the future. Its function is to provide a continuing framework for the legitimate exercise of governmental power and, when joined by a *Bill* or a *Charter of Rights*, for the unremitting protection of individual rights and liberties. Once enacted, its provisions cannot easily be repealed or amended. It must, therefore, be capable of growth and development over time to meet new social, political and historical realities often unimagined by its framers. The judiciary is the guardian of the constitution and must, in interpreting its provisions, bear these considerations in mind. Professor Paul Freund expressed this idea aptly when he admonished the American courts "not to read the provisions of the Constitution like a last will and testament lest it become one".'

5. Two provinces have made use of the override, or 'notwithstanding', power in s. 33: Quebec and Sakatchewan. Quebec, which did not assent to the Charter when it was introduced, has enacted a statute that adds a 'notwithstanding' clause to all of its pre–Charter legislation: see *Forde v Quebec* [1988] 2 SCR 712. It has also added such a clause to all of its subsequent legislation. Saskatchewan has used the power once, in a dispute settlement statute. Hogg, op. cit. at p. 29, n. 1, above, p. 898, states that, apart from the special case of Quebec, 'it seems clear that s. 33 will be

---

1 [1984] 2 SCR 145 at 156. The above approach concerns the scope of the protected rights. The Supreme Court of Canada has also placed the burden of proof upon the government when it seeks to justify a restriction upon a right under s. 1, Charter: *R v Oakes* [1986] 1 SCR 103. See generally on the interpretation of the Charter, Hogg, op. cit. at p. 29, n. 1, above, p. 809ff.

used infrequently and only when the government is persuaded that there are power-ful reasons of public policy to justify its use'. Under s. 33(3), such override clauses have effect for five years only, although they are renewable. The override power does not extend to the right to vote (s. 3) or other democratic rights (ss. 4–5), the right of citizens to enter and leave Canada (s. 6); language rights (ss. 16–23); or the right to sexual equality (s. 28). See G. A. Beaudoin and E. Ratushny, op. cit. at p. 29, n. **1**, above, p. 107.

6. The special relevance of the progress of the Canadian Charter lies in the fact that if the United Kingdom were to adopt a Bill of Rights, the British judiciary would have to assume the same alien role that has fallen to its Canadian counterpart, which had previously followed the same tradition of respect for parliamentary sovereignty.

If Canadian judges can adjust to the role of interpreting and applying a Bill of Rights, is there any reason why British judges should not do so?

CHAPTER 2

Police powers

1 Introduction

The materials in this chapter illustrate the powers and duties of the police in the enforcement of the criminal law.[1] The position has been transformed by the Police and Criminal Evidence Act 1984. In the first edition of this book we described the previous law as follows (p. 33):

The present law satisfies nobody. It is far too complex, contained in a miscellany of, often archaic, statutes and cases. Problems which are difficult enough as examination questions are trickier still for the 'police-man on the beat' who will often have to act without prolonged deliberation. If the rules are known their precise meaning may be uncertain. And when their meaning is clear their content is often unsatisfactory. Many powers of the police are of unduly wide scope and yet, at the same time, the police do not possess certain powers which many would regard as necessary to the performance of their tasks. And when the law is reasonably clear and its content reasonably satisfactory there may be difficulties in ensuring compli-ance with those rules. Police officers perform their duties subject to the possibilities of prosecution, civil claim and internal disciplinary action if they exceed their powers. Yet for most of those with whom they deal the opportunity to prosecute or sue (notwithstanding possible punitive damages – see *Cassell & Co Ltd v Broome* [1972] AC 1027, HL) may be of little practical value, and, despite new arrangements, there still exists a division of opinion as to the way in which complaints against the police are handled. Moreover, with the exception of the rules about confessions, the judges have declined to use the rules about admissibility of evidence as a method of 'policing' the police.

In the past a large amount of police work has relied on the cooperation and consent of citizens together with a certain amount of 'bluff' as to the extent of police powers. With cooperation and consent apparently diminishing and a greater awareness of people as to their 'rights' the need grows for a thorough review and reform of the law of police powers.

These matters were considered by the Royal Commission on Criminal Procedure which reported in 1981: *RCCP Report* (Cmnd 8092, 1981); *Law and Procedure* volume (Cmnd 8092–1, 1981). In a summary of the report the RCCP outlined its task:

Royal Commission on Criminal Procedure; The Balance of Criminal Justice: Summary of the Report (HMSO, 1981)

The Royal Commission on Criminal Procedure began work in February 1978. Its terms of reference were:

'To examine, having regard both to the interests of the community in bringing offenders to justice and to the rights and liberties of persons suspected or accused of crime, and taking into account also the need for the efficient and economical use of resources, whether changes are needed in England and Wales in

---

1 See generally on police powers R. Clayton and H. Tomlinson, *Civil Actions Against the Police* (2nd edn, 1992) and *Legal Action*, January 1994, p. 18; V. Bevan and K. Lidstone, *Investigation of Crime: A Guide to Police Powers* (1991); D. Feldman, *Civil Liberties and Human Rights in England and Wales* (1993), Chaps. 5, 9; M. Zander, *The Police and Criminal Evidence Act 1984* (2nd edn, 1990); Symposia, [1985] PL 388 ff; [1985] Crim LR 535 ff; [1990] Crim LR 452 ff.

i. the powers and duties of the police in respect of the investigation of criminal offences and the rights and duties of suspect and accused persons, including the means by which these are secured;

ii. the process of and responsibility for the prosecution of criminal offences; and

iii. such other features of criminal procedure and evidence as relate to the above; and to make recommendations.'

Matter of fact though these subjects may appear, they form one of the central threads in the history of liberty in Britain. Criminal justice has provided for centuries a natural arena in which the struggle to establish the rights of the individual citizen in relation to the security of society and the power of the state has been waged.

The Commission's task has been to try to achieve a balance between a host of competing rights and objectives, a task made the more difficult by the lack of consensus about the content – or even the existence – of some of the rights. On the one hand there are those who see the fight to bring criminals to justice as being of paramount necessity in today's society. They tend to see the police as struggling against increasing crime, shackled by laws and procedures which, during their investigations, their questioning of suspects, and finally at the trial, favour the criminal. On the other side are those who believe that the cards are in practice stacked against suspects and defendants, that the individual has insufficient legal protection against police power, and that the safeguards against abuse and oppression are inadequate. The majority of public and professional opinion is inevitably between the two. But where can a balance be found which will secure the confidence of the public?

In its review of investigation and prosecution, the Commission applies throughout three standards for judging both the existing system and its own recommendations. Are the arrangements, actual or proposed, fair and clear? Are they open, that is, not secret, and is there accountability? Are they workable and efficient?

The Commission recommended that police powers should be extended in a number of significant respects, but that this should be balanced by the improvement of safeguards against abuse and the extension of safeguards across the whole field of police powers. The government accepted many although not all of the recommendations concerning police powers. The Police and Criminal Evidence Act 1984 received royal assent on 31 October 1984 and generally took effect on 1 January 1986.[1]

A common theme running through many of the commentaries on the RCCP Report was that police powers were to be extended but that the proposed safeguards – requirements that a subject of the exercise of a power be informed of the reasons for it; the requirement that the reasons be recorded contemporaneously; periodic review by senior police officers or magistrates of exercises of power; improvement in complaints procedures; reliance on codes of conduct, breach of which by a police officer would constitute a disciplinary offence – were not as strong as at first sight might appear. McConville and Baldwin (op. cit., n. 1) argued (inter alia) that while the RCCP commissioned an extensive body of research, the results of that research were used selectively: for example, 'No evidence is adduced to demonstrate a need for the increased powers of stop and search, to arrest, to fingerprint, or to search property and seize goods and articles which are proposed' (p. 299).

Moreover,

'No research was conducted . . . into the efficacy of police disciplinary procedures or of civil actions either as means of inducing police compliance with the rules or as remedies to citizens in the event of breach. . . . No research was conducted to test whether the Commission's confidence that requiring police officers to record in writing their reasons, say, for arrest, for prolonged interrogation of suspects, or for refusing access to a solicitor, would provide adequate opportunity for subsequent review was well-founded or not.'

1 On the Report of the Royal Commission see the symposium in the Criminal Law Review: [1981] Crim LR 445 ff; L. H. Leigh, (1981) 44 MLR 296; B. Smythe, [1981] PL 184, 481; M. McConville and J. Baldwin, 10 *International Journal of the Sociology of Law* 287. On the Police and Criminal Evidence Bill see the *Police and Criminal Bill Briefing Guide* (Home Office, 1984); L. Bridges and T. Bunyan, (1983) 10 JLS 85; L. Christian, *Policing By Coercion* (GLC Police Committee Support Unit, 1983).

(M. McConville and J. Baldwin, 'The Research Programme' (1981) 131 NLJ 1117, 1118).

As was only to be expected, some took a more favourable view than others. L. H. Leigh, (1981) 44 MLR, 296, 307–8, noted that the RCCP Report 'engendered strong reactions, some almost Pavlovian in character': in his view, the report, with some exceptions, 'on balance ... would improve the present system and ought ... to be implemented'.

The arrangements under PACE have now been in operation for over eight years. The Home Office regularly publishes statistics on the use of certain powers under PACE. More significantly the findings of a series of research projects on particular areas have been published, and research is continuing. The research on particular areas is noted at the appropriate points in the chapter. The structure of PACE has been extended to Northern Ireland, with some modifications: see the Police and Criminal Evidence (Northern Ireland) Order 1989 (S.I. 1989 No 1341(N.I. 12)); Symposium, (1989) 40 NILQ 319 ff.

The role and powers of the police again come under a measure of scrutiny by the Royal Commission on Criminal Justice (RCCJ), chaired by Lord Runciman, which reported in 1993 (Cm 2263). Its terms of reference were:

'to examine the effectiveness of the criminal justice system in England and Wales in securing the conviction of those guilty of criminal offences and the acquittal of those who are innocent, having regard to the efficient use of resources' (p. i).

Furthermore, it was 'in particular to consider what changes are needed' in eight specific areas of the criminal justice process. The first of these was:

'the conduct of police investigations and their supervision by senior police officers, and in particular the degree of control that is exercised by those officers over the conduct of the investigation and the gathering and preparation of evidence.'

The background to the appointment of the RCCJ in 1991 was the spate of high profile cases, many involving convictions for terrorist offences, in which the Court of Appeal had found there to have been a miscarriage of justice. Police malpractice, in the form of the suppression or falsification of evidence, was a significant factor in a number of these cases. By 1993 the emphasis of the government's concerns had shifted from the problem of miscarriages of justice to a perceived lack of effectiveness of the criminal justice system in controlling crime. The RCCJ made 352 recommendations. Commentators (other than the police) have been largely hostile, noting that the recommendations seemed directed more to promoting the efficiency of the system in obtaining convictions than to the prevention or remedying of miscarriages of justice.[1]

In the area of policing, Reiner ([1993] Crim LR 808, 810) noted that the RCCJ appeared to have taken the view that the Report of the Philips Royal Commission, largely incorporated in PACE and the Prosecution of Offences Act 1985:

'laid down a framework which is broadly on the right lines. In this sense, the policing proposals of the Runciman Commission can largely be seen as a set of footnotes to Philips rather than a new departure.'

Many of the RCCJ recommendations have been accepted and incorporated in the Criminal Justice and Public Order Act 1994 or changes to regulations or

---

1 See generally M. McConville and L. Bridges, *Criminal Justice in Crisis* (1994); S. Field and P. Thomas (eds.), 'Justice and Efficiency? The Royal Commission on Criminal Justice' (1994) 21 JLS 1–164 (special issue); Symposium, [1993] Crim LR 808 ff, 926 ff; L. Bridges and M. McConville, (1994) 57 MLR 75; M. Zander, ibid. 264; reply by Bridges and McConville, ibid. 267.

practice. At the time of writing (November 1994) the government's position as to a significant number of recommendations remains unclear (see *Royal Commission on Criminal Justice Interim Government Response*, Home Office, 1994).

The main international standards relevant to the conferment and exercise of police powers include protection of the right to life (Article 2, ECHR; Article 6, ICCPR); the prohibition of torture or inhuman or degrading treatment or punishment (Article 3, ECHR; Article 7, ICCPR (which also outlaws 'cruel' treatment or punishment); the right to liberty and security of person (Article 5, ECHR; Article 9, ICCPR); and the enjoyment of the protected rights and freedoms without discrimination (Article 14, ECHR, cf Article 26, ICCPR (general entitlement without any discrimination to the equal protection of the law)).[1]

2 Developments in policing

The changes in the law relating to police powers must be seen against the background of developments in the context of policing. In particular, the accountability of the police has been the subject of much debate. The current basic structure was established by the Police Act 1964, but this was subject to significant modification by the Police and Magistrates' Courts Act 1994. The background is summarised in the following extract, which predates the 1994 Act.

S. P. Savage 'Political Control or Community Liaison' (1984) 55(1) *Political Quarterly* 48, 49–51. (footnotes omitted)

It is clear from the arguments of the various sides in the current debate that police accountability is far from a straightforward matter. It is in fact a highly complex issue, complicated by a variety of usages of the term 'accountability' itself, and by the existence of different models of police accountability already in operation. Accountability as a concept applied to any organisation can refer to relations of direction and control, to internal disciplinary procedures, to arrangements for consultation and co-operation, and so on. When applied specifically to the organisation of policing it can have a number of quite distinct meanings. First, the police are 'accountable to the law'. Legal accountability refers to the extent to which the activities of the police are subject to control through the courts; police apply the law but are not above it. Policing must or should take place within the bounds of both criminal and civil law. It is to this system which police commentators such as Robert Mark [*Policing a Perplexed Society* (1977)] refer when they claim that the British Police are 'the most accountable in the world', or David McNee when he claims that the police are 'accountable up to their eyeballs'. Secondly, accountability can refer to the guidelines, regulations and sanctions which operate under police complaints procedures.

However, even the extension of the independent element to include the actual investigation of complaints would not, in the eyes of many, constitute an effective system of accountability. Both legal accountability and complaints procedures take police accountability only so far, limiting 'control' of the police to negative sanctions and regulations. They do not allow the control of policing within those areas of activity which are completely *in accord with* the law or a disciplinary code. Even an efficient system of handling complaints, for example, would only ensure that policing policy is executed within the regulations. It would not determine that policy itself. This is precisely the province on which the third form of police accountability is pitched: political accountability.

It is no accident that the issue of political accountability of the police should have risen so sharply in importance in current political debate. Changes in the size and organisation of the average British police force, the development of specialised squads, and the expansion of technological support for policing have all played their part. Further stimulus has been given by signs of an increasing 'politicisation' of the police at both senior and rank-and-file level, and, of course, the inner-city riots of 1980 and 1981. Such

---

1 See below, pp. 740–742, 749–773, 773–785, 847–851. The application of international standards to police powers is considered by R. Reiner and L. Leigh, 'Police Power' in G. Chambers and C. McCrudden (eds.), *Individual Rights and the Law in Britain* (1993) and S. H. Bailey, 'Rights in the Administration of Justice' in D. J. Harris and S. Joseph (eds.), *The ICCPR and United Kingdom Law* (forthcoming).

developments contributed to the pressure by many on the Left and those within the civil liberties movement for a complete re-appraisal of the role of the police in Britain. New demands have been made which would place the police under the control of locally-elected representatives who would be given the power of decision in matters of policing policy. The basic thrust of such demands is an attack on the principle of the 'independence' of the police as an obstacle in the way of accountability.

To speak of 'independence' may, however, be misleading, for whatever the relationships between the police and politically representative bodies (itself an area by no means without confusion) the police are not *autonomous*. They operate within a tripartite arrangement in relation to the police authority and the Home Office (with the exception of the Metropolitan Police, whose police authority is the Home Department), each sector having distinct responsibilities. The chief constable is responsible for the '*direction and control*' of the force, the police authority for the '*maintenance*' of the force, and the Home Office for '*ensuring the efficiency*' of the force. Financial and administrative concerns do connect the operation of policing to local and central government and as such the chief police officer cannot act irrespective of *any* consideration for his political authority.

However, as far as decisions about policing policy are concerned the law does seem unequivocal: the chief constable is answerable to the law and *not* to any political authority, he is an 'independent officer of the Crown'.

'No minister of the Crown can tell him he must or must not keep observation on this place or that, he must or must not prosecute this man or that—nor can any police authority tell him so. The responsibility is on him. He is answerable to the law and the law alone.' (*R v Metropolitan Police Comr, ex p Blackburn* [[1968] 2 QB 118 at 135–136].)

This principle has been more succinctly expressed by John Alderson:

'In England, the police are associated with the law of the land rather than politics. They are neither civil servants nor local government officers.' [J. Alderson and P. Stead (eds.), *The Police We Deserve* (1973), p. 41.]

On this question chief police officers from all persuasions seem united, as if around a constitutional imperative. The police are not 'servants' of the state (whether of central or local government) but servants only to and of the law. An absolute distinction is erected, for example, between the chief constable and the chief education officer or chief planner—the latter two are public servants and exist to execute the decisions of their political authority. Not so the chief police officer, who can legitimately ignore political pressures on his duty of deciding police operations for his area. The ultimate decisions (e.g. whether to prosecute or ignore minor drug offices, deploy resources in this or that area, etc.) rest with him.

In comparison, the powers of the police authority seem limited, restricted to financial and administrative responsibilities. As laid down in the Police Act 1964 [s. 4(1)], it is the duty of a police authority to 'maintain an adequate and efficient police force', which involves the provision and maintenance of buildings, premises, vehicles, apparatus, clothing and other equipment for police purposes. Police authorities are responsible for the appointment of the chief constable, deputy and assistant chief constable, and for determining the 'establishment' of the force overall (the number of persons in each rank). Certain other duties and powers could be said to allow at least a potential for some form of control over policing. They [sic, include powers to (ed.)] require senior police officers to retire 'in the interests of efficiency' and to call for reports (in addition to the 'Annual Report') from the chief constable on any particular issue of concern [1964 Act, ss. 5(4), 6(4), 12]. But, even these powers are limited: the former by the power of veto held by the Home Office, the latter by the ability of the chief constable to simply refuse to co-operate 'in the interests of efficiency'. So although the local authority 'foot the bill' (or at least 50 per cent. of the overall cost of policing) by determining the size of the establishment, it has few if any real powers to determine in what way funds are disposed.

Another crucial fact is that police authorities are in themselves unique in that only two-thirds of their members are elected councillors, the other third being local lay magistrates. Not only is the chief constable 'independent' of the police authority, but many police authority members are not answerable to the electorate. Add to this the powers that the Home Office holds over police authorities—to 'approve' all senior appointments, and to supervise all forces through H.M. Inspectors of Constabulary—and there is every reason to appreciate the frustration and feelings of impotence which many authority members express, and which many commentators have attacked. It is against this backcloth that demands for reform in the direction of enhanced political accountability of the police have been made.

NOTES

1. The debate referred to by Savage centred on the question whether elected (or mainly elected) police authorities should be given power to determine general policing policies.[1] In 1979, a Labour MP, Jack Straw, introduced a bill designed to achieve this, and this approach has been favoured by the political left (see the discussions by M. Dean, (1982) 53 *Political Quarterly* 153; P. Hewitt, *The Abuse of Power* (1982), Chap. 3; S. Savage, (1984) 55 *Political Quarterly* 48, 51–56). Others argued that this would not be a 'happy solution' and it would be more appropriate to seek 'better explanatory accountability and a satisfactory solution to the problem of the complaints machinery procedure' (Marshall, *Constitutional Conventions* (1984), p. 145). This is the direction that reforms initially took. The Police and Criminal Evidence Act 1984, s. 106(1) provides that:

'Arrangements shall be made in each police area for obtaining the views of people in that area about matters concerning the policing of the area and for obtaining their co-operation with the police in preventing crime in the area.'

In London the arrangements are made by the Metropolitan Police Commissioner in the light of guidance issued by the Home Secretary and following consultation with local councils; elsewhere they are made by the police authority after consulting the Chief Constable. Previously, such arrangements had been informal. Lord Scarman in his report on *The Brixton Disorders* (Cmnd. 8427, 1981) stated that:

'If a rift is not to develop between the police and the public as a whole (not just the members of the ethnic minority communities) it is in my view essential that a means be derived of enabling the community to be heard not only in the development of policing policy but in the planning of many, though not all, operations against crime' (para. 5.56).

The key mechanisms were consultation and accountability. The machinery for consultation should be formalised. In response, the Home Office issued guidelines in advance of legislation: Home Office Circular 54/1982, *Local Consultation Arrangements Between the Community and the Police*. See also H.O. Circular 2/1985. Subsequent research suggests that the members of consultative committees tend to have had little to do with the police as consumers (i.e. victim or offender); they accordingly depend on the knowledge and expertise of the police officers present, who are then able to maintain control of the discussion. Police/community liaison seems to have had little effect on policing methods. The social background of members tends not to be representative of the local community: see E. Stratta, 'A Lack of Consultation?' (1990) 6 *Policing* 523.[2] Similarly, a PSI study found that local representative bodies such as consultative committees, crime prevention panels and neighbourhood watch schemes 'made no discernible input into local policing policy' (T. Johnson *et al*, *Democracy and Policing* (1994), p. 298 and Chap. 5).

---

1 For other contributions to the debate on police accountability see R. Baldwin and R. Kinsey, *Police Powers and Politics* (1982); B. Loveday, (1983) 9 *Local Government Studies* 39; P. A. J. Waddington, ibid., Vol. 10 p. 27 and Loveday, ibid., Vol. 10 p. 43; T. Jefferson and R. Grimshaw, *Controlling the Constable* (1984); S. Spencer, *Called To Account* (NCCL, 1985); L. Lustgarten, *The Governance of Police* (1986); D. Downes and T. Ward, *Democratic Policing* (Labour Campaign for Criminal Justice, 1986); I. Oliver, *Police, Government and Accountability* (1987); S. Uglow, *Policing Liberal Society* (1988), Chaps. 7, 8; R. Reiner, *Chief Constables* (1991), Chap. 11 and *The Politics of the Police* (2nd edn, 1992), Chaps. 6, 7; R. Reiner and S. Spencer (eds.), *Accountable Policing* (IPPR, 1993); T. Jones *et al.*, *Democracy and Policing* (1994); I. Loader, 'Democracy, Justice and the Limits of Policing: Rethinking Police Accountability' (1994) 3 *Social & Legal Studies* 521.
2 See further R. Morgan and C. Maggs, *Setting the PACE* (Bath Social Policy Papers 4) and (1985) 1 *Policing* 87; R. Morgan, (1986) 57 Political Quarterly 83, 'The Local Determinants of Policing Policy' in P. Wilmott (ed.), *Policing and the Community* (PSI, 1987), (1987) Brit. J. Criminol. 87, 'Policing by Consent' in R. Morgan and D. Smith (eds.), *Coming to Terms with Policing* (1989), Chap. 12, and 'Talking about Policing' in D. Downes (ed.), *Unravelling Criminal Justice* (1992), Chap. 7; G. Hughes, 'Talking Cop Shop? A Case-Study of Police Community Consultative Groups in Transition' (1994) 4 *Policing and Society* 253.

2. *Police authorities.* The major reforms effected by the Conservative government under the Police and Magistrates' Courts Act 1994 took matters in a different direction, with a change from elected (or partly elected) police authorities to smaller, appointed police authorities. The reforms were based on the White Paper, *Police Reform* (Cm. 2281, 1993), but the government's original Bill was amended significantly in a number of respects during its passage through the House of Lords following adverse criticism by influential Conservative peers.

The key points are now as follows. England and Wales is divided into 43 police areas (Police Act 1964, s. 1 and Sch. 1A, inserted by the 1994 Act, s. 1). Apart from the metropolitan police district and the City of London police area, police areas are based on one or more counties. There is a police force and police authority established for each area (Police Act 1964, ss. 2–3B, and Schs. 1B, 1C, inserted by the 1994 Act, ss. 2, 3). The police authority is now normally to comprise 17 members. Nine of these are to be members of local authorities, or the local authority, for the area (where there are two tiers of local government members are drawn from the county council(s) not the district council(s)). Five are 'independent members' appointed by the other members of the police authority from a short-list prepared by the Secretary of State, taken in turn from a list of nominations made by specially constituted local selection panels. Three are local magistrates appointed by selection panels established by regulations under s. 21(1A) of the Justices of the Peace Act 1979, or (if there is no such panel) the relevant magistrates' courts committee(s). The chairman is appointed by the authority from among its members. The government's original proposal that the independent members and chairman should be appointed by the Secretary of State was dropped following strong criticism in the House of Lords; instead there is a somewhat complex and convoluted procedure to select independent members (see Sch. 1C and the Police Authorities (Selection Panel) Regulations 1994, SI 1994/2023). The selection panels must have regard to the desirability of ensuring that the persons nominated 'represent the interests of a wide range of people within the community in the police area' and 'include persons with skills, knowledge or experience' in such fields as may be specified in regulations made by the Secretary of State (a power not as yet exercised).

It is now to be the duty of every police authority 'to secure the maintenance of an efficient and effective [rather than "adequate and efficient"] police force for its area' (Police Act 1964, s. 4(1), substituted by the 1994 Act, s. 4). In discharging its functions the authority must have regard to any:

(1) *objectives for the policing of the areas of all police authorities* determined by the Secretary of State under s. 28A of the 1974 Act (inserted by the 1994 Act, s. 15);

(2) *local policing objectives* determined annually by the authority itself after consulting the Chief Constable and considering any views obtained in accordance with arrangements under PACE, s. 106 (1964 Act, s. 4A, substituted by the 1994 Act, s. 4);

(3) *performance targets* determined by the authority; and

(4) *local policing plans* issued annually by the authority, setting out the proposed arrangements for the policing of the area during the year (1964 Act, s. 4B, inserted by the 1994 Act, s. 4).

The local policing plan must include a statement of the authority's priorities for the year, of the financial resources expected to be available and the proposed allocation of those resources. A draft is prepared initially by the Chief Constable and submitted to the authority.

Where the Secretary of State has determined an objective under s. 28A of the 1964 Act, he may direct police authorities to establish performance targets to be aimed at in seeking to achieve the objective (1964 Act, s. 28B, inserted by the 1994 Act, s. 15). He may also issue codes of practice, and give directions to police authorities after an adverse report by an Inspector of Constabulary under s. 38 of the 1964 Act (1964 Act ss. 28C, 28D, inserted by the 1994 Act, s. 15). The first objectives specified by the Secretary of State are (a) to maintain and, if possible, increase the number of detections for violent crimes; (b) to increase the number of detections for burglaries of people's homes; (c) to target and prevent crimes which are a particular local problem, including drug-related criminality, in partnership with the public and local agencies; (d) to provide high visibility policing so as to reassure the public; and (e) to respond promptly to emergency calls from the public (the Police (Secretary of State's Objectives) Order 1994 (SI 1994 No. 2678).

Police authorities must publish annual reports (1964 Act, s. 4C, inserted by the 1994 Act, s. 4); and may be required by the Secretary of State to submit a report to him on specified matters (1964 Act, s. 29A, inserted by the 1994 Act, s. 16). The Chief Constable is appointed by the police authority, but subject to the approval of the Secretary of State. The authority, also with the approval of the Secretary of State, may call upon the Chief Constable to retire 'in the interests of efficiency or effectiveness' (1964 Act, s. 5A, inserted by the 1994 Act, s. 5).

The new authorities should be in place from November 1994, initially as shadow authorities and fully operational from April 1995. See publications by the Audit Commission under the general heading *Cheques and Balances: A Framework for Improving Police Accountability* and *A Management Handbook on Police Planning and Financial Delegation* (HMSO, 1994); and B. Loveday (1994) 10 *Policing* 221.

3. *The Chief Constable*. Section 5(1) of the Police Act (as substituted by the 1994 Act, s. 5) provides that:

'a police force maintained under section 2 of this Act shall be under the direction and control of the Chief Constable. . . .'

Furthermore, in discharging his functions, every Chief Constable shall have regard to the local policing plan (1964 Act, s. 5(2), as substituted by the 1994 Act, s. 5). Civilian employees of the authority are also normally under the direction and control of the Chief Constable (1964 Act, s. 10, substituted by the 1994 Act, s. 10). The terms of s. 5(1) are virtually identical to those of the old s. 5(1).

4. *The Secretary of State*. In addition to the numerous powers already mentioned, the Secretary of State has power to alter police areas (1964 Act, ss. 21–21C, inserted by the 1994 Act, s. 14); determines the annual aggregate of grants and the amount of the grant to be made to each authority (1964 Act, s. 31, substituted by the 1994 Act, s. 17); may make regulations for police forces (1964 Act, s. 33, as amended by the 1994 Act, s. 18); appoints inspectors of constabulary (1964 Act, s. 38, as amended by the 1994 Act, s. 20); and may provide and maintain or contribute to the provision or maintenance of common organisations, facilities or services (1964 Act, s. 41, substituted by the 1994 Act, s. 23).

The Secretary of State's position in the tripartite arrangements has over the years become increasingly significant, and notwithstanding the efforts of the House of Lords (see n. **1**), has been further strengthened by the 1994 Act. Apart from formal legal powers, significant influence is maintained through Home Office circulars and arrangements for inspection by HM Inspectors of Constabulary. It is nevertheless important to note that the Secretary of State (like police authorities) has only limited powers to give directions, and these do not extend to operational matters (see below, pp. 175–176, in relation to the miners' strike).

5. *A national force?* The 1994 Act maintains the structure of locally based police forces. The case for a national force was argued by Dr. A. L. Goodhart in a memorandum of dissent to the Royal Commission on the Police (Cmnd 1728, 1962). The majority, while rejecting the argument that a national force would be a step towards a police state (pp. 45–46), recommended a more limited programme of amalgamations and greater central control, preserving the partnership between local and central government. Reiner (*The Politics of the Police* (2nd edn, 1992), pp. 236–249) identifies a whole series of factors in a 'trajectory of centralisation' including the *Northumbria* case (below, p. 175); stringent central controls over police manpower; the enhanced role of HM Inspectors 'as the linchpin of a more centralised coordination of standards and procedures'; the higher profile of the Association of Chief Police Officers; the proliferation of specialist national policing units; and the informal development of a cadre of potential chief officers, given the Home Office's power to approve the short list of candidates interviewed by police authorities and to veto the authority's selection (a power exercised in 1990 in the case of Derbyshire: see Reiner, *The Chief Constables* (1991), p. 35). Overall, while the 1962 Royal Commission rejected a *de jure* national police force,

'we have ended up with the substance of one, but without the structure of accountability for it which the explicit proposals embodied. . . . The myth of a tripartite structure of governance for essentially local policing, with constabulary independence for operational decisions, is useful for legitimating a system of de facto national control' (p. 249).

See further below, pp. 175–176.

6. *Constabulary independence.* Much has been made of the so-called doctrine of 'constabulary independence' articulated most forcefully by Lord Denning MR in *R v Metropolitan Police Comr, ex p Blackburn* [1968] 2 QB 118 at 135–136:

'I have no hestitation in holding that, like every constable in the land, he should be, and is, independent of the executive. He is not subject to the orders of the Secretary of State, save that under the Police Act 1964, the Secretary of State can call upon him to give a report, or to retire in the interests of efficiency. I hold it to be the duty of the Commissioner of Police of the Metropolis, as it is of every chief constable, to enforce the law of the land. He must take steps so to post his men that crimes may be detected; and that honest citizens may go about their affairs in peace. He must decide whether or no suspected persons are to be prosecuted; and, if need be, bring the prosecution or see that it is brought. But in all these things he is not the servant of anyone, save of the law itself. No Minister of the Crown can tell him that he must, or must not, keep observation on this place or that; or that he must, or must not, prosecute this man or that one. Nor can any police authority tell him so. The responsibility for law enforcement lies on him. He is answerable to the law and to the law alone. That appears sufficiently from *Fisher v Oldham Corporation* [1930] 2 KB 364, and *Attorney-General for New South Wales v Perpetual Trustee Co Ltd* [1955] AC 457, PC.'

Lustgarten (*The Governance of Police* (1986) pp. 64–67) comments that 'seldom have so many errors of law and logic been compressed into one paragraph'. Among these are the points that the Commissioner of Police of the Metropolis is not a constable, was not subject to the Police Act 1964 powers and has been given orders by the Secretary of State. Moreover, the cases cited merely stood for the proposition (in effect by-passed by s. 48 of the Police Act 1964) that there is no master and servant relationship between a police officer and the police authority. Nevertheless,

'the reality is that *Blackburn I* has over nearly two decades embedded itself in the lore and learning of both judges and police, and it is inconceivable that, without parliamentary intervention, the courts would resile from the position they have reached' (Lustgarten, op. cit., p. 67).

To what extent do the amendments effected by the 1994 Act impinge on 'constabulary independence'? Note that there are perfectly respectable principles of administrative law that where a discretion is conferred on a particular official or body, he or it may not act under the dictation of a third party and may not fetter the exercise of that discretion by self-created rules of police (see Sir William Wade and C. Forsyth, *Administrative Law* (8th edn, 1994), pp. 358–366). This applies as much to insulate police constables in the exercise of their powers from dictation by superiors as it does to insulate chief constables from dictation by the executive. Is this the true essence of constabulary independence? (Cf. Lustgarden, op. cit., pp. 13–15; below, pp. 137–138). In *ex p Blackburn*, Lord Denning MR indicated at p. 136 that in extreme cases, such as a directive from a chief constable 'that no person should be prosecuted for stealing any goods less than £100 in value', the courts might interfere. In the case itself, the Commissioner's decision not to enforce certain gaming laws had already been rescinded, and no order of mandamus was granted. In subsequent cases, the courts have declined to intervene: *R v Metropolitan Police Comr, ex p Blackburn (No 3)* [1973] QB 241; *R v Chief Constable of Devon and Cornwall, ex p CEGB* [1982] QB 458 (below, pp. 209–210). Decisions to prosecute may be subject to judicial review under the *Wednesbury* doctrine, but the courts are similarly reluctant to interfere: see A. Sanders and R. Young, *Criminal Justice* (1994), pp. 209–213.

7. Other related developments include (1) changes in the police complaints system (see below, pp. 47–52); (2) the introduction of schemes for lay visitors to police stations; the visitors are to be selected by the police authority and visits may be by prior arrangement or unannounced (see 97 HC Deb 26 February 1986, written answer; revised guidelines have been issued by the Home Office: see H.O. Circular 4/1992, including the strong recommendation of the Home Secretary that lay visitors are appointed directly from members of the public, rather than elected members of the police authority; S. James, [1988] PL 432; C. Kemp and R. Morgan, *Behind the Front Counter* (1989)); and (3) the establishment of the Crown Prosecution Service independent of the police, headed by the DPP under the superintendence of the Attorney-General (see the Prosecution of Offences Act 1985; S. H. Bailey and M. J. Gunn, *Smith and Bailey on The Modern English Legal System* (2nd edn, 1991), pp. 616–637, 689–692).

8. Police conduct has come under increasing scrutiny from researchers. Both the RCCP and the RCCJ commissioned a number of research projects. The Home Office Research Unit has issued a number of Research Studies in the area. The Metropolitan Police commissioned a large scale research project from the Policy Studies Institute which was published in four volumes in 1983: *Police and People in London*. The report made many detailed findings and recommendations as to selection of recruits, training, management and policing methods. The Commissioner noted that:

'In places, the Report is sharply critical of the attitudes and behaviour of a worrying number of my officers, as well as of some organisational and management aspects of the force. Although there are occasional misconceptions, the notes of criticism have, for the most part, a ring of truth'

(Report for 1983, Cmnd 9268, p. 44). The PSI Report noted, inter alia, that

'Although it has less effect on policing behaviour than might be expected, the level of racial prejudice in the force is cause for serious concern'

(Vol. IV, p. 351).
Another important finding was that:

'there is little direct supervision of the junior ranks by senior officers or of constables by sergeants and inspectors, and that there is scope for more direct supervision within the existing management structure' (ibid., p. 343).

The RCCJ was 'less satisfied' with arrangements for the supervision of routine police inquiries than with those for the most serious investigations. Indeed, research conducted for the RCCJ found little evidence here of supervision as such. Accordingly, a new approach to supervision was required throughout the police service, with improved training in the supervision of inquiries at all levels, and an overhaul of detective training and of training in investigations (Cm. 2263, pp. 18–22).[1]

For studies of policing from sociological perspectives see S. Holdaway, *Inside the British Police* (1983), D. Hobbs, *Doing the Business* (1989), M. Young, *An Inside Job* (1991) and R. Reiner, *Chief Constables* (1991). For research studies on aspects of PACE, see below, pp. 83–84, 93, 128–129, 137.

3 Review of the exercise of police powers

Issues as to the *legality* (as distinct from the propriety) of police action may arise in a number of contexts. We give here some examples of the situations which are most likely to occur. We also summarise the position as to complaints against the police.

(a) ACTIONS IN TORT

A citizen may sue a police officer for trespass to the person (assault; false imprisonment), trespass to goods or trespass to land, and the officer may seek to establish the defence that he had lawful authority for this action. Conversely, a police officer may wish to sue a citizen for assaulting him. A citizen may sue to recover property in the possession of the police or may apply to a Magistrates' Court for its return under the Police (Property) Act 1897, as amended. An application under the Act may be made by the claimant (or indeed, the police) and the court may 'make an order for the delivery of the property to the person appearing . . . to be the owner thereof, or, if the owner cannot be ascertained, make such order . . . as . . . may seem meet'. Proceedings may be brought by complaint and the court may award costs: *R v Uxbridge Justices, ex p Metropolitan Police Comr* [1981] QB 829, CA.

In recent years many actions for damages against the police have been reported. See *Allen v Metropolitan Police Comr* (1980) Times, 25 March, [1980] Crim LR 441; (£1,115 damages awarded in respect of the unreasonable use of force by police officers effecting a lawful arrest); *White v Metropolitan Police Comr* (1982) Times, 24 April, Mars-Jones J (plaintiffs awarded £20,000 exemplary damages each plus, respectively, £6,500 and £4,500 aggravated damages, for false imprisonment, assault and malicious prosecution: police officers unlawfully entered a house in Stoke Newington, on one view of their conduct 'beat up' a defenceless man in a brutal and inhuman way and thereafter prosecuted the plaintiffs for offences the officers knew they had not committed in order to escape the consequences of their own unlawful acts); *Reynolds v Metropolitan Police Comr* [1982] Crim LR 600, CA (£12,000 jury award upheld in respect of loss of a day's liberty following an arrest

1 J. Baldwin and T. Moloney, *The Supervision of Police Investigations in Serious Criminal Cases* (RCCJ Research Study No. 4, HMSO, 1992); M. Maguire and C. Norris, *The Conduct and Supervision of Criminal Investigations* (RCCJ Research Study No. 5, HMSO, 1992); B. Irving and C. Dunnighan, *Human Factors in the Quality Control of CID Investigations* (RCCJ Research Study No. 21, HMSO, 1993).

without reasonable grounds); *Hayward v Metropolitan Police Comr* (1984) Times, 24 March, Caulfield J (£1,750 awarded for an unlawful arrest and detention for 4½ hours); *George v Metropolitan Police Comr* (1984) Times, 31 March, Park J (£8,030, including £2,000 exemplary damages, awarded in respect of trespass and assault: the officers 'had deliberately lied to the court'); *Connor v Chief Constable of Cambridgeshire* (1984) Times, 11 April, French J (£2,500, including £500 exemplary damages, awarded for assault); *Treadaway v Chief Constable of West Midlands* (1994) Times, 25 October, McKinnon J (£50,000, including £40,000 exemplary damages, for a man seriously assaulted in order to obtain a confession). Note also the settlement in the Waldorf case: below, p. 44, and see T. Gifford, *LAG Bulletin*, July 1983, pp. 84–87. R. Clayton and H. Tomlinson (*Civil Actions against the Police* (2nd edn, 1992), pp. 411–431) list over 110 cases of damages awards against the police, based upon news reports as well as law reports.

In civil actions for damages, once the plaintiff has proved the trespass it is for the defendant to establish any justification in law (*R v IRC, ex p Rossminster Ltd* [1980] AC 952 at 1011, HL (per Lord Diplock)). However, if the defendant establishes the statutory conditions for the exercise of power which would justify the trespass, and the essence of the plaintiff's complaint is that there has been an ultra vires abuse of discretion, the onus lies on the plaintiff to establish the relevant facts (*Greene v Home Secretary* [1942] AC 284, HL, as explained in *R v Governor of Brixton Prison, ex p Ahsan* [1969] 2 QB 222, DC). See generally Sir William Wade and C. Forsyth, *Administrative Law* (7th edn, 1994), pp. 332–335. Most of the cases in this area have raised issues as to whether the relevant statutory conditions have been fulfilled – most commonly whether an officer is able to satisfy the court that he has had 'reasonable cause' for his actions. However, the decision of the House of Lords in *Holgate-Mohammed v Duke* [1984] AC 437, HL confirms that exercises of statutory powers by police officers are in addition subject to the principles expounded by Lord Greene MR in *Associated Provincial Picture Houses Ltd v Wednesbury Corpn* [1948] 1 KB 223, CA: public authorities or officers must not exercise statutory discretions for improper purposes; they must not take legally irrelevant matters into account or fail to have regard to legally relevant matters; and an exercise of discretion must not be so unreasonable that no reasonable authority or officer could so decide. In the *Holgate-Mohammed* case itself the House held that it was not an improper use of the power to detain after arrest where the officer did so because he believed that Mrs Holgate-Mohammed would be more likely to respond truthfully if she were questioned under arrest at the police station than if she were questioned at her home. See Commentary by D. J. Birch, [1984] Crim LR 419; G. Zellick, [1984] Crim LR 94 (on the Court of Appeal decision in the case).

In relation to tort actions against the police, two points should be noted. First, section 48 of the Police Act 1964 provides that a Chief Constable is vicariously liable in respect of torts committed by constables under his direction and control in the performance or purported performance of their functions. Secondly, under section 6 of the Constables Protection Act 1750 a police officer has a good defence to any action brought against him in respect of 'any thing done in obedience to any warrant under the hand or seal of any justice of the peace . . . notwithstanding any defect of jurisdiction in such justice'. The protection extends to 'any person or persons acting by his order and in his aid'. The defence is, however, only available if the limits of the warrant have been strictly observed. If this defence is available the only possible cause of action will be for malicious prosecution: see *Reynolds v Metropolitan Police Comr* [1984] 3 All ER 649.

(b) CRIMINAL PROSECUTIONS

A citizen who resists police action may find himself prosecuted for assault on or obstruction of the police in the execution of their duty (below, pp. 53–65) or the common law offence of escaping from lawful custody: *R v Timmis* [1976] Crim LR 129. He may wish to establish that the police action was unlawful and that the resistance or escape was as a consequence lawful. Conversely, a prosecution may be brought against the police officer for assault or false imprisonment. Between 1970 and 1979, 50 officers were convicted of assault (985 HC Deb 19 May 1980 cols 30–34, written answer). In 1983, two police officers who shot Stephen Waldorf in the mistaken belief that he was a dangerous escaped prisoner, David Martin, were tried for attempted murder and wounding with intent to cause grievous bodily harm; one of the officers who pistol-whipped him after he had been shot was charged in addition with causing grievous bodily harm with intent: the officers were acquitted (*The Times*, 13–20 October 1983). (It was reported that he subsequently received £120,000 damages plus legal expenses from the police in an out of court settlement (*The Times*, 8 March 1984).) See also below, p. 74.

(c) APPLICATIONS FOR JUDICIAL REVIEW

A citizen may challenge executive action on the ground that it is ultra vires (and on certain other grounds) by making an 'application for judicial review' to the Queen's Bench Divisional Court under RSC Order 53. A variety of remedies may be sought including, for example, certiorari (to quash a warrant: see *R v IRC, ex p Rossminster Ltd* [1980] AC 952, HL) or a declaration (that a seizure of property is unlawful: ibid.). Note, however, that the House of Lords held that if there is a substantial conflict of evidence the matter is not suitable for resolution on an application for judicial review, where evidence is normally only received in affidavit form: the matter should instead be determined by a civil action for trespass. Proceedings for habeas corpus may be brought under RSC Order 54 to challenge the legality of personal detention.

(d) THE APPROACH OF THE COURTS

The courts have been inconsistent in their approach to resolving questions concerning the scope of police powers. The following case was a landmark in requiring clear legal authority to be shown to justify invasions of the rights of others.

Entick v Carrington (1765) 19 State Tr 1029, 2 Wils 275, 95 ER 807, Court of Common Pleas Lord Camden CJ

On 6 November 1762, the Earl of Halifax, one of the principal secretaries of state, issued a warrant to four King's messengers (Nathan Carrington, James Watson, Thomas Ardran and Robert Blackmore) 'to make strict and diligent search for John Entick, the author, or one concerned in writing of several weekly very seditious papers, intitled the Monitor, or British Freeholder . . .; and him, having found you are to seize and apprehend, and to bring, together with his books and papers, in safe custody before me to be examined. . . .' The messengers entered E's house, the outer door being open, apprehended him, and searched for his books and papers in several rooms and in one bureau, one writing desk and several drawers. Where necessary these were broken open. They seized some books and papers and read others, remaining for about four hours. They then took E and the items seized to Lovel Stanhope, law-clerk to the secretaries of state. E was released on 17 November. He subsequently brought an action in trespass against the messengers. The jury gave a special verdict and assessed the damages at £300. The defendants argued that their acts were done in obedience to a lawful warrant.

Lord Camden CJ: . . . [I]f this point should be determined in favour of the jurisdiction, the secret cabinets and bureaus of every subject in this kingdom will be thrown open to the search and inspection of a messenger, whenever the secretary of state shall think fit to charge, or even to suspect, a person to be the author, printer, or publisher of a seditious libel.

This power so assumed by the secretary of state is an execution upon all the party's papers, in the first instance. His house is rifled; his most valuable secrets are taken out of his possession, before the paper for which he is charged is found to be criminal by any competent jurisdiction, and before he is convicted either of writing, publishing, or being concerned in the paper. This power, so claimed by the secretary of state, is not supported by one single citation from any law book extant. . . .

The arguments, which the defendants' counsel have thought fit to urge in support of this practice, are of this kind.

That such warrants have issued frequently since the Revolution, which practice has been found by the special verdict; . . . .

That the case of the warrants bears a resemblance to the case of search for stolen goods.

They say too, that they have been executed without resistance upon many printers, booksellers, and authors, who have quietly submitted to the authority; that no action hath hitherto been brought to try the right; and that although they have been often read upon the returns of Habeas Corpus, yet no court of justice has ever declared them illegal.

And it is further insisted, that this power is essential to government, and the only means of quieting clamours and sedition. . . .

If it is law, it will be found in our books. If it is not to be found there, it is not law.

The great end, for which men entered into society, was to secure their property. That right is preserved sacred and incommunicable in all instances, where it has not been taken away or abridged by some public law for the good of the whole. The cases where this right of property is set aside by positive law, are various. Distresses, executions, forfeitures, taxes, &c. are all of this description; wherein every man by common consent gives up that right, for the sake of justice and the general good. By the laws of England, every invasion of private property, be it ever so minute, is a trespass. No man can set his foot upon my ground without my licence, but he is liable to an action, though the damage be nothing; which is proved by every declaration in trespass, where the defendant is called upon to answer for bruising the grass and even treading upon the soil. If he admits the fact, he is bound to shew by way of justification, that some positive law has empowered or excused him. The justification is submitted to the judges, who are to look into the books; and see if such a justification can be maintained by the text of the statute law, or by the principles of common law. If no such excuse can be found or produced, the silence of the books is an authority against the defendant, and the plaintiff must have judgment.

Where is the written law that gives any magistrate such a power? I can safely answer, there is none, and therefore it is too much for us without such authority to pronounce a practice legal, which would be subversive of all the comforts of society.

But though it cannot be maintained by any direct law, yet it bears a resemblance, as was urged, to the known case of search and seizure for stolen goods.

I answer, that the difference is apparent. In the one, I am permitted to seize my own goods, which are placed in the hands of a public officer, till the felon's conviction shall intitle me to restitution. In the other, the party's own property is seized before and without conviction, and he has no power to reclaim his goods, even after his innocence is cleared by acquittal.

The case of searching for stolen goods crept into the law by imperceptible practice. It is the only case of the kind that is to be met with. No less a person than my lord Coke (4 Inst. 176,) denied its legality; and therefore if the two cases resembled each other more than they do, we have no right, without an act of parliament, to adopt a new practice in the criminal law, which was never yet allowed from all antiquity.

Observe too the caution with which the law proceeds in this singular case. . . .

I come now to the practice since the Revolution, which has been strongly urged, with this emphatical addition, that an usage tolerated from the era of liberty, and continued downwards to this time through the best ages of constitution, must necessarily have a legal commencement. . . .

With respect to the practice itself, if it goes no higher, every lawyer will tell you, it is much too modern to be evidence of the common law; and if it shoud be added, that these warrants ought to acquire some strength by the silence of those courts, which have heard them read so often upon returns without censure or animadversion. I am able to borrow my answer to that pretence from the Court of King's-bench, which lately declared with great unanimity in the Case of General Warrants, that as no objection was taken to them upon the returns, and the matter passed *sub silentio*, the precedents were of no weight. I most heartily concur in that opinion; . . .

But still it is insisted, that there has been a general submission, and no action brought to try the right.

I answer, there has been a submission of guilt and poverty to power and the terror of punishment. But it would be strange doctrine to assert that all the people of this land are bound to acknowledge that to be universal law, which a few criminal booksellers have been afraid to dispute. . . .

It is then said, that it is necessary for the ends of government to lodge such a power with a state officer; and that it is better to prevent the publication before than to punish the offender afterwards. I answer, if the legislature be of that opinion, they will revive the Licensing Act. But if they have not done that I conceive they are not of that opinion. And with respect to the argument of state necessity, or a distinction that has been aimed at between state offences and others, the common law does not understand that kind of reasoning, nor do our books take notice of any such distinction.

Serjeant Ashley was committed to the Tower in the 3d of Charles 1st, by the House of Lords only for asserting in argument, that there was a 'law of state' different from the common law; and the Ship-Money judges were impeached for holding, first that state-necessity would justify the raising money without consent of parliament; and secondly, that the king was judge of that necessity.

If the king himself has no power to declare when the law ought to be violated for reason of state, I am sure we his judges have no such prerogative. . . .

[U]pon the whole we are all of opinion, that the warrant to seize and carry away the party's papers in the case of a seditious libel, is illegal and void. . . .

NOTES

1. *Entick v Carrington* was one of four leading cases which followed the publication of No. 45 of the *North Briton* (see Sir William Holdsworth, *A History of English Law* (1938), Vol X pp. 659–672; George Rudé, *Wilkes and Liberty* (1962) Chap. II; Audrey Williamson, *Wilkes, A Friend to Liberty* (1974) Chap. IV). The *North Briton* was a weekly paper, of which John Wilkes was joint editor and a leading contributor. Its main purpose was to abuse and ridicule the recently appointed administration of the Earl of Bute. After No. 45 was published, the two secretaries of state, Lords Egremont and Halifax, issued a general warrant for the arrest of its 'authors, printers and publishers'. Over 45 people were arrested under this warrant, including Wilkes. The warrant was held to be illegal, and damages were awarded for trespass: see *Wilkes v Wood* (1763) 19 State Tr 1153; *Leach v Money* (1765) 19 State Tr 1002 and *Wilkes v Lord Halifax* (1769) 19 State Tr 1406.

2. This case is a classic illustration of the principle that any public officer must be able to point to lawful authority for actions of his which infringe the rights of others, and not merely some general conception of state necessity. It also reflects an unwillingness to 'invent' or 'discover' lawful authority, which has not been shared by some judges in more recent cases. For example, in *Chic Fashions (West Wales) Ltd v Jones* [1968] 2 QB 299 the Court of Appeal held, contrary to previous authority (see L. H. Leigh, *Police Powers in England and Wales* (1975) pp. 189–190), that

'when a constable enters a house by virtue of a search warrant for stolen goods, he may seize not only the goods which he reasonably believes to be covered by the warrant, but also any other goods which he believes on reasonable grounds to have been stolen and to be material evidence on a charge of stealing or receiving against the person in possession of them or anyone associated with him.'

(per Lord Denning MR at p. 313). Lord Denning noted, inter alia, that there was 'ever-increasing wickedness . . . about', and that if a constable who came across stolen goods not mentioned in the warrant was forced to leave in order to obtain such a warrant 'in nine cases out of ten, by the time he came back ... these other goods would have disappeared' (ibid). These appear to be the kinds of arguments disapproved of in *Entick v Carrington*. In *Ghani v Jones* [1970] 1 QB 693 Lord Denning MR, for the Court of Appeal, enunciated (1) (obiter, at p. 706) a broad principle extending the ambit of the power of a constable, executing a search or arrest warrant or effecting an arrest without warrant, to seize goods or evidence; and (2) (at pp. 708–709) a series of five principles creating a new power to seize goods or evidence where there is no warrant or arrest, and even from a person not himself criminally implicated. The first mentioned dictum was applied in *Garfinkel v Metropolitan Police Comr* [1972] Crim LR 44, Ackner J, and *Frank Truman Export Ltd v Metropolitan Police Comr* [1977] QB 952, Swanwick J, without consideration of its status as a precedent. Finally, the House of Lords in *Wills v Bowley* [1983] 1 AC 57 held by three to two that the power of a constable under s. 28 of the Town Police Clauses Act 1847 to arrest any person who 'within his view commits' one of a series of offences (here, using profane or obscene language to the annoyance of passers-by) extended to cases where the constable honestly believed on reasonable grounds derived wholly from his own observation that an offence had been committed and even though the person arrested was subsequently acquitted of the offence (see Commentary by D. J. Birch, [1982] Crim LR 580; A. Samuels (1982) 98 LQR 537; J. L. Lambert [1983] PL 234). The minority argued in vain that:

'Where the liberty of the subject is concerned, the court should not go beyond the natural construction of the statute and the strict terms of the grant of the power to arrest without warrant'

(per Lord Elwyn-Jones [1983] 1 AC 57 at 72). The majority view, expressed by Lord Bridge, was that it would be 'nonsensical' to construe such provisions 'in the sense that the legality of the arrest can only be established by an ex post facto verdict of guilty against the person arrested' and 'ridiculous' to do so in such a way as to force on the constable a choice between the risk of making an unlawful arrest and the risk of committing a criminal neglect of duty' (pp. 680, 681).

By contrast, the spirit of *Entick v Carrington* can be seen in the decisions of the House of Lords in *Morris v Beardmore* (below, p. 153) and of the Divisional Court in *McLorie v Oxford* [1982] QB 1290, DC (where *Ghani v Jones* was held not to have created a new right to *enter* premises as distinct from a right to *seize* goods). Moreover, a series of cases show that any unlawful act (subject to the de minimis principle) by a police officer will take him outside the execution of his duty (see below, pp. 53–57).

(e) COMPLAINTS AGAINST THE POLICE

Arrangements for police discipline and the handling of complaints against the police overlap but are not coterminous. The police are subject to a code of discipline. Disciplinary proceedings may be instituted as the result of a complaint from a member of the public; more commonly they are instigated internally by the force itself. Complaints may be resolved informally without recourse to disciplinary proceedings.

Section 85 of PACE requires chief officers of police to record complaints against officers other than senior officers by members of the public, and seek to resolve them informally or cause them to be investigated. Investigations have always been conducted by police officers of a designated rank (formerly superintendent; currently chief inspector), although this legal requirement is to be dropped. In some cases, the investigating officer is from a different force. An issue perenially debated is whether the investigation of complaints by the police 'themselves' can ever inspire public confidence. Major reforms since 1964 have seen the establishment of a Police Complaints Board by the Police Act 1976, with power to recommend, and in the last resort to direct, the institution of disciplinary proceedings in a particular case. The Board was replaced by the Police Complaints Authority established by Part IX of the Police and Criminal Evidence Act 1984. Its powers were further amended by the Police and Magistrates' Courts Act 1994. That Act also provided for changes to the police disciplinary arrangements.

Triennial Review of the Police Complaints Authority 1991–94 (1994–95) HC 396, Appendix A

HOW THE COMPLAINTS SYSTEM WORKS

Functions
The Authority were set up under the Police and Criminal Evidence Act of 1984[1] with three basic functions. The first is to supervise the investigation of the most serious complaints against police officers. The second is to supervise investigations into non-complaint matters voluntarily referred by police forces because of their potential gravity. The third is to review the outcome of every investigation, whether supervised or not, and to decide whether disciplinary action should be taken against any officer.

Organisation
The Authority are organised into two divisions. One, consisting of a deputy chairman and five members, carries out the supervisory function. The other, composed of a deputy chairman and six members, performs the job of review and adjudication.

Recording of complaints
The Act requires that a complaint must be recorded by the force whose officers have been complained about before an investigation can begin. Complaints must be made by, or on behalf of a member of the public; must be about the conduct of a serving officer; and may not relate to the direction or control of the force.

Every year about 1,200 people contact the Authority directly with complaints about the police. Where necessary advice and guidance is offered and the complaint is then passed to the force concerned for formal recording.

Informal resolution
The legislation provides for less serious complaints to be resolved informally. Between 30% and 40% of all recorded complaints are dealt with in this way without reaching the Authority. However, if a complainant is dissatisfied with the outcome of the informal resolution he is entitled to have his complaint considered by the formal process.

Withdrawal and dispensation
A number of complaints are withdrawn or not proceeded with. Sometimes a complainant decides not to pursue a complaint made in the heat of the moment or withdraws it once a related criminal case against him has been decided in court.

The regulations also enable the Authority to grant a force dispensation from the need to investigate a complaint if it is anonymous or repetitious; if it is vexatious, oppressive or an abuse of the procedures; if there has been more than 12 months delay between the incident and the complaint; or if it is not reasonably practical to carry out an investigation.

---

1 *Ed.* The relevant regulations are the Police (Complaints) (General) Regulations 1985 (S.I. 1985 No. 520); the Police (Complaints) (Informal Resolution) Regulations 1985 (S.I. 1985 No. 671); the Police (Complaints) (Dispensation from Requirement to Investigate Complaints) Regulations 1985 (S.I. 1985 No. 672, as amended by S.I. 1990 No. 1301); and the Police (Complaints) (Mandatory Referral etc.) Regulations 1985 (S.I. 1985 No. 673).

In granting dispensations the Authority are conscious of the fact that we are effectively removing a citizen's statutory right to have his or her complaint investigated. Applications for dispensations are, therefore, carefully scrutinised and the Authority insist that forces take every possible step to ensure that complainants are aware of the intention to seek dispensation. In considering whether to dispense with a complaint because of the complainant's failure or refusal to co-operate, the Authority's overriding concern is to decide whether or not a worthwhile investigation can still be carried out.

Supervised cases

The legislation defines the type of complaint which must be referred to the Authority for possible supervision. Forces may also refer any other complaint in which they feel that a supervised investigation is justified.

The Authority must supervise the investigation of all complaints relating to a death or serious injury.[1] In all other cases referred to them it is up to the Authority to decide whether or not to supervise. The Authority may also call in for supervision any complaint not referred to them.

Non complaint cases

Under Section 88 of the Act, forces have the power to refer for supervision any case, not based on a complaint, in which an officer may have committed an offence and which raises grave or exceptional issues. Typical examples include shooting incidents, deaths in police custody and cases of serious corruption.

What supervision means

In supervised cases the Authority must approve the appointment of the investigating officer. We also have powers to impose any requirements which we believe to be necessary for the proper conduct of the investigation. The aim is to ensure that the investigation is thorough, impartial and effective. When the investigation is complete the Authority must issue a formal statement indicating whether or not we are satisfied with it and specifying any areas about which we are concerned.

Review and adjudication

Whether the investigation has been supervised or not, the final report is submitted to the Deputy or Assistant Chief Constable of the force concerned. Under the Act, he must first consider whether the report indicates that an officer may have committed a criminal offence and, if so, whether he should be charged. If he takes that view, the case goes to the Crown Prosecution Service who must decide whether or not to prosecute. The Authority also have the power to direct that a case is submitted to the Crown Prosecution Service even though the Chief Officer has decided not to do so.

If the Crown Prosecution Service decides to prosecute, the case is heard in the criminal courts. Whatever the outcome, the officer may not be charged with a disciplinary offence based on the same facts. In all other cases the chief officer must submit a memorandum to the Authority specifying whether or not disciplinary charges are to be brought and, if not, the reasons for that decision. The Authority then review the whole case and decide whether or not to accept the force recommendations. If they disagree, the Authority have the power to recommend or, if necessary, to direct that disciplinary charges are preferred.

Less formal discipline

In a significant number of cases the completed investigation does not justify a formal disciplinary hearing but requires management action to be taken. This ranges from admonishment and warning to advice about future conduct. It is administered by a senior officer from Superintendent to Deputy Chief Constable depending on the severity of the offence. Admonishments or similar oral warnings are taken seriously and, in certain instances, are a matter of record.

Notifying the complainant

At the end of the process the Authority member responsible for making the decision writes to the complainant setting out the outcome of the case and the reasons for the Authority's decision. This letter also explains that, for a police officer to be found guilty at a disciplinary hearing, the charge must be proved 'beyond reasonable doubt' – the standard of proof required by the criminal courts. This means that a number of cases do not go to a disciplinary hearing because the available evidence does not reach this high standard.

A copy of the Authority's letter is also sent to the Deputy or Assistant Chief Constable of the force concerned so that the officer can be informed of the outcome.

---

1 *Ed.* Or assault occasioning actual bodily harm; or an offence under s. 1 of the Prevention of Corruption Act 1906; or a serious arrestable offence: added by SI 1985 No. 673, reg. 4.

NOTES

1. The Police Complaints Authority issues annual reports and has been required to report to the Secretary of State on the working of ss. 84–92 of PACE every three years. (This requirement was removed by the Police and Magistrates' Courts Act 1994, s. 37(d).) Triennial Reviews took place for 1985–88 (1987–88 HC 466), 1988–91 (1990–91 HC 352) and 1991–94 (1993–94 HC 396). A number of recommendations for change from the first two Reviews have led to amendments to legislation, regulations or the Home Office Guidance to Chief Officers; others have not been pressed in the light of developments in practice (1994 Triennial Review, pp. 5–9). The one outstanding recommendation confirmed but not yet implemented is that the current prohibition on the disclosure of information about the work of the PCA other than general statements that do not 'identify the person from whom the information was received or any person to whom it relates' (PACE, s. 98) should be amended. The PCA proposed that it should have:

'discretion to publish such information as is reasonably necessary to inform the public of the outcome of investigations without derogation from the principle of confidentiality between the Authority, complainants and those who provide information.'

This has been accepted in principle by the Home Secretary. The 1994 Review did not contain further positive recommendations, although noted continuing concerns on the ability of officers to evade disciplinary charges by obtaining medical retirement on privileged conditions and the inability of the PCA to consider complaints about the conduct of special constables or civilian staff. The latter gap is the more serious given trends in the privatisation of certain police services and plans to inrease the number of special constables from 19,000 to a target of 30,000 (1994 Review, pp. 19–20).

The Police and Magistrates' Courts Act 1994 provides for the introduction of significant changes to the disciplinary process (see n. **5**), but only limited changes to the functions and powers of the PCA. The latter changes include the following. On receipt of a report of a complaint investigation, the chief officer must determine whether it indicates that a criminal offence may have been committed by a police officer (other than a senior officer) in his force; if it does, he must send a copy of the report to the DPP (the additional requirement that the chief officer considers that the police officer concerned 'ought to be charged' has been dropped). The separate power of the PCA to direct the reference of reports to the DPP (PACE, s. 92) has been repealed (1994 Act, s. 37(b)). The awkward involvement of PCA members in disciplinary tribunals where, *inter alia*, the PCA has directed the institution of disciplinary proceedings has also been removed by the repeal of the special provision for such tribunals (PACE, s. 94, repealed by the 1994 Act, s. 37(c)). Regulations may be made for enabling the PCA to relinquish the supervision of the investigation of any complaint or other matter (PACE, s. 99(2)(ea), inserted by the 1994 Act, Sch. 5, para. 31). This will, for example, enable the PCA to cease the supervision of an investigation when a complainant's injury proves to be less serious than originally alleged (see 1994 Triennial Review, p. 6). References to disciplinary 'charges' are replaced by references to disciplinary 'proceedings'.
2. Statistics on police complaints and discipline are published annually in a Home Office Statistical Bulletin; statistics on the work of the Police Complaints Authority are set out in that body's annual report. The two sources are difficult to reconcile. In 1993, 34,894 complaints were disposed of: 14,284 (41%) were withdrawn or

granted a dispensation by the PCA; 10,126 (29%) were informally resolved; and 10,484 (30%) were investigated, of which 9,734 (28%) were unsubstantiated and 750 (2%) substantiated. The proportion of substantiated complaints has remained at the 2% level since 1990 (*Police Complaints and Discipline: England and Wales, 1993*, HOSB No. 13/94, Tables 1, 2).

In the same year, police forces referred 4,139 cases to the PCA for possible supervision, of which the PCA accepted 951 (the highest annual figure in the PCA's history). Of the 951 cases, 625 (66%) involved death or serious injury, 146 (15%) assault occasioning actual bodily harm and 64 (7%) the voluntary referral of a matter not subject to a complaint. Most forces voluntarily refer all cases involving the deaths of people who have gone to the police station as witnesses, those killed in road accidents involving vehicles driven by an on-duty police officer and anyone who dies soon after being released from police custody; the PCA's general policy is to accept all such referrals. The PCA also completed the review of the investigation of 10,916 complaints: 1,092 resulted in officers receiving advice, guidance or admonishment or being charged; 236 led to disciplinary charges (45 on the PCA's recommendation); no disciplinary charges were preferred in respect of 10,671 (9,614 for a conflict in or lack of evidence). (Annual Report of the PCA for 1993, 1993–94 HC 305, pp. 20, 22, 28.)

3. A major survey of the complaints system over 1986–88 was conducted by M. Maguire and C. Corbett (*A Study of the Police Complaints System* (HMSO, 1991)). In their concluding comments (pp. 193–201), they reported that they were generally impressed with the commitment and abilities both of police investigators and PCA members, and noted that the informal resolution procedure had made a promising start. However, apart from informally resolved cases, an overwhelming majority of complainants were dissatisfied. High proportions of both complainants and officers complained against felt excluded from the system, thought it too secretive and bureaucratic, thought that investigations took too long, that they were not kept informed of progress and that they received inadequate explanation of decisions. Only a minority of the population felt confident that, if they made a complaint, it would be investigated fairly. Maguire and Corbett concluded overall that the system had little effect in deterring police misconduct (given the extremely low proportion of substantiated complaints); did not satisfy complainants or inspire public confidence; and was only beginning to be used as a source of information by police managers in improving police performance. The greatest hope for convincing a wider public of the PCA's effectiveness appeared to lie in a greater use of 'intensive' or 'participant' supervision of investigations by PCA members, then adopted in a very small minority of cases given the PCA's resources. However, while the complaints system remained so closely interlinked with the disciplinary system (with the requirement of proof beyond reasonable doubt) there was limited scope for making responses more akin to those provided by other 'consumer-oriented' organisations where satisfaction of the consumer was accorded high priority. (Cf. n. 5, below.)

It is often suggested that public confidence would only be secured by the establishment of a fully independent system of investigation. The difficulties have been summarised by the PCA (Triennial Review, 1991–94, 1993–94 HC 396, pp. 15–16). Such a system would require substantial resources (both capital outlay and continuing commitment) in establishing its own accommodation and support services in regional centres; retired or seconded police officers would not be seen to be independent, and investigators from other bodies such as Customs and Excise or the DSS would need in-depth training and might find it more difficult to secure police co-operation. The PCA did not think such an allocation of resources was justified: 'we see no evidence to support the view that complaints against police officers are not thoroughly and impartially investigated'. Maguire and Corbett commented that with fully independent investigators:

'there might be a gain in terms of public confidence in the system, although it is by no means certain it would be more effective in other ways' (op. cit., p. 201).

Since the Maguire and Corbett study, public attitude surveys conducted for the PCA have shown an increasing awareness of the PCA (62%) and of its role (30%). 47% believed the PCA to be impartial in the handling of complaints, but 30% felt that it favoured the police; 44% would trust police officers to investigate complaints while 41% would not (Annual Report of the PCA, 1993, 1993–94 HC 305, p. 47). There are also indications that the police are making considerably greater use of the system as a provider of management information (ibid., pp. 34–35).

For further discussion of the system, see the 4th Report of the Home Affairs Committee, 1991–92 HC 179, *Police Complaints Procedures* and Government Reply, Cm. 1996, 1992 and A. Sanders and R. Young, *Criminal Justice* (1994), pp. 400–415; for comparative perspectives, see A. Goldsmith (ed.), *Complaints Against the Police: The Trend to External Review* (1991).

4. The complaints procedure may overlap with a civil action. Indeed, according to R. Clayton and H. Tomlinson, *Civil Actions against the Police* (2nd edn, 1992), p. 56, 'it seems to have become the practice of the police to treat the letter before action in a civil case as being a formal complaint'. The House of Lords has now ruled, in *R v Chief Constable of the West Midlands Police, ex p Wiley* [1995] 1 AC 274, overruling a number of Court of Appeal authorities, that a class claim to public interest immunity does not attach generally to all documents coming into existence in consequence of an investigation under Part IX of PACE. (The possibility of a class claim covering the report of the investigating officer, and of claims on a contents basis, were left open, and the first of these was subsequently recognised by the Court of Appeal in *Taylor v Anderton* [1995] 2 All ER 420, CA.) The possible use by chief constables of such material in defending civil actions, although inhibited by the earlier Court of Appeal authorities, had deterred litigants or potential litigants from instituting complaints or co-operating with complaints investigations.

5. The police discipline process is to be remodelled significantly following the enactment of the Police and Magistrates' Courts Act 1994, although at the time of writing the details are unclear (see the Home Office Consultation Paper, *Review of Police Discipline Procedures*, February 1993; J. Harrison and S. Cragg, (1993) 143 NLJ 591). It is intended that there should be a move to a more managerial approach. Where there are formal disciplinary proceedings, the civil standard of proof on the balance of probabilities is to apply rather than the criminal standard of proof beyond reasonable doubt. The 'double jeopardy' rule (PACE, s. 104(1),(2)), that where an officer was convicted or acquitted of a criminal offence, no disciplinary charges could be brought in respect of an offence that was in substance the same, has been removed (1994 Act, s. 37(f)). No officer of the rank of superintendent or below can be dismissed, required to resign or reduced in rank by a decision taken in disciplinary proceedings, unless he has been given an opportunity to elect to be legally represented at any hearing. A point of potentially great significance is that breach of the PACE codes as such is no longer required by statute to be a disciplinary offence (PACE, s. 67(8), repealed by the 1994 Act, s. 37(a)). These changes were supported by the RCCJ, which doubted 'whether the existing arrangements for police discipline do now command general public confidence' (Cm. 2263, p. 46).

4 Assaults on and obstruction of the police

Many of the cases in which the courts are called upon to determine the lawfulness of police action involve prosecutions under section 51 of the Police Act 1964.

(a) THE OFFENCES

Police Act 1964

51. (1) Any person who assaults a constable in the execution of his duty, or a person assisting a constable in the execution of his duty, shall be guilty of an offence and liable [on summary conviction to imprisonment for a term not exceeding six months or to a fine not exceeding level 5 on the standard scale or to both].
(2) (*omitted*)
(3) Any person who resists or wilfully obstructs a constable in the execution of his duty, or a person assisting a constable in the execution of his duty, shall be guilty of an offence and liable on summary conviction to imprisonment for a term not exceeding one month or to a fine not exceeding [level 3 on the standard scale], or to both.

NOTE

1. Section 51 re-enacted earlier provisions.[1] It was amended by the Criminal Law Act 1977, ss. 15, 30 and 31 and the Criminal Justice Act 1982, s. 46. The 1977 Act also removed the right to claim trial by jury under s. 51(1).

(b) 'IN THE EXECUTION OF HIS DUTY'

Coffin v Smith (1980) 71 Cr App Rep 221, Queen's Bench Divisional Court

Police officers were summoned to a boys' club by the youth leader there to ensure that various people left before a disco started. S and H assaulted the officers. The magistrates dismissed charges under the Police Act 1964, s. 51(1) on the ground that the officers were not acting in the execution of their duty as they were doing something that they were not compelled by law to do. The Divisional Court allowed the prosecutors' appeal.

Donaldson LJ: . . . The modern law on the subject is, I think, to be found in two different cases. The first is a decision of the Court of Criminal Appeal, *Waterfield and Lynn* (1963) 48 Cr App Rep 42, [1964] 1 QB 164, where Ashworth J delivering the judgment of the Court, at p. 47 and 170 respectively, said: 'In the judgment of this court it would be difficult, and in the present case it is unnecessary, to reduce within specific limits the general terms in which the duties of police constables have been expressed. In most cases it is probably more convenient to consider what the police constable was actually doing and in particular whether such conduct was prima facie an unlawful interference with a person's liberty or property. If so, it is then relevant to consider whether (a) such conduct falls within the general scope of any

---

1 See generally, G. Williams, *Textbook on Criminal Law* (2nd edn, 1983) pp. 199–205; J. C. Smith and B. Hogan, *Criminal Law* (7th edn, 1992) pp. 412–422; M. Supperstone, *Brownlie's Law Relating to Public Order* (2nd edn, 1981) pp. 105–119; K. Lidstone, 'A Policeman's Duty Not to Take Liberties' [1975] Crim LR 617; 14th Report of the Criminal Law Revision Committee on Offences against the Person (Cmnd 7844, 1980). On the obstruction offence see U. Ross, [1977] Crim LR 187; P. Murphy, [1978] Crim LR 474; R. C. Austin, [1982] CLP 187; T. Gibbons, [1983] Crim LR 21; K. Lidstone, [1983] Crim LR 29. For surveys of other offences of interfering with justice see G. Williams, [1975] Crim LR 430, 479, 608 and Smith and Hogan (6th edn, 1988), Chap. 19.

duty imposed by statute or recognised at common law and (b) whether such conduct, albeit within the general scope of such a duty, involved an unjustifiable use of powers associated with the duty.'

Applying that basis, it is quite clear that these constables were on duty, they were in uniform, and they were not doing anything which was prima facie any unlawful interference with a person's liberty or property.

Further guidance on the scope of the police officer's duty in this context is I think to be derived from the judgment of Lord Parker CJ in *Rice v Connolly* [1966] 2 QB 414, and the passage to which I would like to refer is at p. 419: 'It is also in my judgment clear that it is part of the obligations and duties of a police constable to take all steps which appear to him necessary for keeping the peace, for preventing crime or for protecting property from criminal injury. There is no exhaustive definition of the powers and obligations of the police, but they are at least those, and they would further include the duty to detect crime and to bring an offender to justice.'

In a word a police officer's duty is to be a keeper of the peace and to take all necessary steps with that in view. These officers, just like the ordinary officer on the beat, were attending a place where they thought that their presence would assist in the keeping of the peace. I know that Mr Staddon says 'Oh no, this is all part and parcel of the assistance which they gave to the youth leader in ejecting these people'. Even if that was so, they would have been doing no more than a police officer's duty in all the circumstances. In fact it is clear that there was a break. Both the respondents went away and came back. The officers were in effect simply standing there on their beat in the execution of their duty when they were assaulted. This is a very clear case indeed.

Bristow J agreed.

Appeal allowed.

NOTE

1. The term 'duty' is ambiguous. It could mean (1) a function which in a general sense can be termed part of a policeman's job but without necessarily any element of obligation; (2) the same as (1) but with the qualification that the officer be in the exercise of some specific legal power or performance of some specific legal duty; (3) a function which an officer is specifically required by his superiors or police regulations to perform; (4) a function which a police officer is obliged by law to perform in the sense that failure to do so constitutes a crime or tort. *Coffin v Smith* appears to reject meanings (3) and (4). The statement quoted from *R v Waterfield and Lynn* [1964] 1 QB 164 and other cases makes the point that if a constable is acting in the purported exercise of specific legal powers or duties he must remain within the limits set by law to those powers or duties. For example, a constable has been held to have exceeded his powers and thus acted outside the execution of his duty where he has trespassed on private land: *Davis v Lisle* (below, pp. 101–102), *McArdle v Wallace (No 2)* (below, p. 103); or assaulted someone: *Kenlin v Gardner* (below, p. 56), *Ludlow v Burgess* (below, p. 55), *Ricketts v Cox* (below, p. 60), *McBean v Parker* (below, p. 212). An exception to this principle was made in *Donnelly v Jackman* [1970] 1 WLR 562, but this was shown to be a very limited exception in *Bentley v Brudzinski* (below).

Bentley v Brudzinski (1982) 75 Cr App Rep 217, Queen's Bench Divisional Court

At about 3.30 am Constable Phillips was looking for a vehicle reported to have been taken without consent. He saw the defendant and his brother running barefoot along certain streets. They broadly fitted the description of the two men said to have taken the vehicle. The constable questioned them. They denied, truthfully, any involvement with the vehicle and after various interchanges moved off. Constable Butler, who had just arrived on the scene 'said "Just a minute" – then, not in any hostile way, but merely to attract attention – he placed his right hand on [the defendant's] left shoulder'. The defendant punched PC Butler in the face. The magistrates held there was no case to answer on a charge under s. 51(1) on the ground that PC Butler was not acting in the execution of his duty. The prosecutor's appeal to the Divisional Court was dismissed.

McCullough J: . . . *Donnelly v Jackman* (1970) 54 Cr App Rep 229, [1970] 1 WLR 562 was in some ways a similar case to the present on its facts. Mr Donnelly was charged with the same offence as here, assaulting a police constable in the execution of his duty. A Police Constable Grimmett had wanted to ask him certain questions. He had asked him to stop and tapped him on the shoulder. Mr Donnelly then tapped the officer's shoulder and said 'Now we are even, copper.' The police constable tapped Mr Donnelly on the shoulder a second time. It was found by the justices that his intention in so doing was to stop him and ask him further questions. Mr Donnelly's reaction was to strike the officer with some force. He was convicted, and appealed unsuccessfully by way of case stated to this Court.

In giving the first judgment, with which Ashworth J and Lord Parker CJ both agreed, Talbot J said at p. 232 and p. 565 of the respective reports: 'Turning to the facts of this matter, it is not very clear what precisely the justices meant or found when they said the officer touched the defendant on the shoulder, but whatever it was they really did mean, it seems clear to me that they must have felt it was a minimal matter by the way they treated this matter and the result of the case. When one considers the problem: was this officer acting in the course of his duty, one ought to bear in mind that it is not every trivial interference with a citizen's liberty that amounts to a course of conduct sufficient to take the officer out of the course of his duties. The facts that the magistrates found in this case do not justify the view that the police officer was not acting in the execution of his duty when he went up to the defendant and wanted to speak to him. Therefore the assault was rightly found to be an assault upon this officer whilst acting in the execution of his duty and I would dismiss this appeal.'

I observe that in that paragraph Talbot J simply referred to the officer going up to the defendant, wanting to speak to him and tapping him on the shoulder. He does not specifically advert in that paragraph, or anywhere in his judgment, to the justices' finding that the defendant was being stopped by the police officer.

I, for my part, think that in cases of this kind a great deal will inevitably turn on the impression that the witnesses have given to the justices. In *Donnelly's* case (supra) this Court was plainly of the view that what had happened was trivial and was not enough to take the officer out of the ordinary scope of his duties. The fact that that was the decision in *Donnelly v Jackman* (supra) does not of course necessarily mean that the decision will be the same in every case in which an officer goes up to a person in the street to ask him questions.

In the next case, *Ludlow v Burgess* (1971) 25 Cr App Rep 227, which also is in many ways rather similar to the present case, the decision went the other way. It is only reported shortly in [1971] Crim LR 238. Again it is a decision of this Court with Lord Parker CJ presiding. What had happened was this. While a constable was getting on a bus he was kicked by a youth. The constable thought it was a deliberate kick but the defendant said it was accidental. The constable, who did not have his warrant card with him, told him not to use foul language and said that he was a police officer, whereupon the defendant began to walk away. The constable put a hand on his shoulder, not with the intention of arresting him, but to detain him for further conversation and inquiries. Then the defendant struggled and kicked the constable. Others joined in. In due course the defendant was charged with the same offence as here. He was convicted. His appeal was allowed by this Court, which said that 'the detention of a man against his will without arresting him was an unlawful act and a serious interference with the citizen's liberty. Since it was an unlawful act, it was not an act done in the execution of the constable's duty.'

Although the precise circumstances of the touching are not apparent from the very short report, *Ludlow v Burgess* (supra) when compared with *Donnelly v Jackman* (supra) demonstrates that the decision in any individual case will turn on the particular circumstances in which the police officer and the citizen come into, if I may use a neutral word, engagement with one another. . . . I have no doubt, looking at the circumstances as a whole, that both constables were trying to stop the defendant and his brother from going home in order to detain them and to question them further.

We have to ask ourselves whether the justices arrived at a decision which no bench could reasonably have reached. I can well understand why they reached the decision they did. I would have reached the same decision myself.

Donaldson LJ: . . . I entirely agree with McCullough J's conclusion and the reasons which led him to that conclusion. . . .

NOTES

1. On *Donnelly v Jackman* see J. M. Evans, (1970) 33 MLR 438 and D. Lanham, [1974] Crim LR 288. For a New Zealand decision approving, obiter, the approach taken in *Donnelly*, see *Pounder v Police* [1971] NZLR 1080. S. H. Bailey and D. J. Birch commented ([1982] Crim LR at 481–482):

'The facts of [*Donnelly v Jackman* and *Bentley v Brudzinski*] are, however, difficult to reconcile. It is possible that the tap on the shoulder (*Donnelly*) was genuinely more "trivial" than the hand (*Bentley*). This would be a very fine distinction, and one arguably untenable as the intentions of the officers in the two cases seem the same, i.e. to stop for questioning. Perhaps the real explanation is that the facts of the two cases are essentially the same, that the two benches of magistrates took divergent views, and the Divisional Court was not in a position to say that either was so unreasonable or perverse as to enable it to impose a different view.'

2. In *Kerr v DPP* (1994) 158 JP 1048, K struck an officer who took hold of her arm in order to detain her, and began to caution her, in the mistaken belief that she had already been placed under arrest by another officer. The Divisional Court set aside her conviction for assaulting the officer in the execution of his duty. The officer's conduct was not so trivial as to be able to come within *Donnelly v Jackman*, he was clearly exceeding his powers and his mistaken (albeit honest and reasonable) belief was insufficient to cause him to be acting in the execution of his duty.
3. The following case confirms that the police have no common law power to detain for questioning.

Kenlin v Gardiner [1967] 2 QB 510, [1967] 2 WLR 129, [1966] 3 All ER 931, 131 JP 191, 110 Sol Jo 848, Queen's Bench Divisional Court

Two boys were visiting homes of members of their school rugby team to remind them of a forthcoming match. Two plain-clothed police officers became suspicious of the boys' behaviour. One approached the boys and asked them what they were doing. He stated that he was a policeman and showed his warrant card but this information did not register in the minds of the boys. One boys tried to run away but was restrained by the officer. The boy, not realising the restrainer was a police officer, struck the officer and escaped. Further struggle ensued. The boys were charged under section 51(1) of the Police Act 1964. They appealed against conviction.

Winn LJ: ... [W]as this officer entitled in law to take hold of the first boy by the arm ... ? ... I feel myself compelled to say that the answer to that question must be in the negative. This officer might or might not in the particular circumstances have possessed a power to arrest these boys. I leave that question open, saying no more than that I feel some doubt whether he would have had a power of arrest: but on the assumption that he had a power of arrest, it is to my mind perfectly plain that neither of these officers purported to arrest either of these boys. What was done was not done as an integral step in the process of arresting, but was done in order to secure an opportunity, by detaining the boys from escape, to put to them or to either of them the question which was regarded as the test question to satisfy the officers whether or not it would be right in the circumstances, and having regard to the answer obtained from that question, if any, to arrest them.
   I regret to say that I think there was a technical assault by the police officer. ...
Widgery J and **Lord Parker CJ** agreed.
Appeal allowed.

NOTES

1. For further judicial denials of the existence of any power at common law to detain for questioning see *R v Lemsatef* [1977] 1 WLR 812, CA per Lawton LJ at p. 816 and *R v Franciosy* (1978) 68 Cr App Rep 197, CA per Lawton LJ at pp. 205–206.
2. In *Collins v Wilcock* [1984] 3 All ER 374 the Divisional Court confirmed that a constable's act in taking hold of a woman's arm without intending to arrest her was

unlawful, notwithstanding that the constable intended to carry out the non-statutory procedure for cautioning suspected prostitutes.

3. For statutory provisions authorising detention for questioning see the Northern Ireland (Emergency Provisions) Act 1991, s. 23 (below, p. 275) and the Prevention of Terrorism (Temporary Provisions) Act 1989, s. 14 (below, pp. 303–304, 312–315).

(c) ASSAULT ON A POLICE OFFICER

A person may be guilty under s. 51(1) even if he is unaware (whether reasonably or unreasonably) that the person he is assaulting is a constable (*R v Forbes and Webb* (1865) 10 Cox CC 362). This has been strongly criticised (see e.g. Smith and Hogan, pp. 416–417; Williams, p. 200) but remains the law (*Blackburn v Bowering* [1994] 3 All ER 380, CA (CD)). However, there will normally be a good defence if D assaults a constable in the honest belief that the constable is using unlawful force against him. His mistake does not prevent him setting up the defence of self-defence (see A. Zuckerman, (1972) 88 LQR 246). In *Albert v Lavin* [1982] AC 546 the Divisional Court held that such a belief would only constitute a defence where it was based on reasonable grounds (the House of Lords affirmed the decision on different grounds: see below, p. 209). However, the limitation was disapproved by the Court of Appeal (Criminal Division) in *R v Kimber* [1983] 1 WLR 1118 and *R v Gladstone Williams* (1983) 78 Cr App Rep 276, where it was held that the reasonableness of a belief was material only to the question whether on the facts the belief was held at all. These cases concerned, respectively, the issue of consent in relation to a charge of indecent assault and a defence of using reasonable force in the prevention of crime in relation to a charge of assault occasioning actual bodily harm. Note that the 'question whether in the circumstances which the defendant believed to exist it was justifiable to use the degree of force, still depends on whether it was reasonable to do so'. Commentary on *Williams* by J. C. Smith, [1984] Crim LR at 164 (but cf *R v Scarlett* [1993] 4 All ER 629, Commentary by Sir John Smith, [1994] Crim LR 288). *Williams* was approved by the Privy Council in *Beckford v R* [1988] AC 130 and applied by the Court of Appeal (Civil Division) to the charge of assaulting a court officer in the execution of his duty (contrary to the County Courts Act 1984, s. 14(1)(b)) in *Blackburn v Bowering* [1994] 3 All ER 380. See also *R v Jackson (Kenneth)* [1984] Crim LR 674. Other limitations are (1) that a mistake of *law* as to the extent of a police officer's duty cannot be a defence (see Williams, op. cit., p. 513; see also p. 201 where it is noted that this rule operates with great rigour because the legal powers of the police are in doubt on many particulars (cf R. Austin, [1982] CLP 187)) and (2) that there is a special rule that if a person 'is in police custody and not in imminent danger of injury there is no urgency of the kind which requires an immediate decision': another person who forcibly releases him 'does so at his peril', and that is so even if he genuinely believes on reasonable grounds that the restraint is unlawful: *R v Fennell* [1971] 1 QB 428. See the analysis by Williams, op. cit., pp. 513–515.

In practice it will be much easier to establish a defence of self-defence founded on a mistake of fact where the defendant is unaware that the person assaulting or restraining him is a police officer, or honestly disbelieves the claim of, for example, a scruffy looking individual to be a constable. The defence may, however, also be established where there is a mistake of fact as to whether a constable is acting in the execution of his duty (see Roch LJ in *Blackburn v Bowering*, above, at 389).

(d) OBSTRUCTION OF A POLICE OFFICER

The offence under s. 51(3) is broader in its scope than that under s. 51(1). In Scotland it has been confined to physical obstruction (*Curlett v M'Kechnie* 1938 JC 176). In England and Wales, however, a broader view has been taken. The main cause for concern is whether it has been extended too far towards a position where simple disobedience to police instructions or even uncooperativeness may constitute the offence. There would be little need for other specific legal powers if this were the case. In the following case the court considered whether a refusal to answer questions could constitute obstruction.

Rice v Connolly [1966] 2 QB 414, [1966] 2 All ER 649, [1966] 3 WLR 17, 130 JP 322, Queen's Bench Divisional Court

Police officers patrolling late at night in an area where a number of break-in offences had just been committed observed Rice loitering about the streets. The officers asked him where he was going to, where he had come from and for his name and address. Rice gave only his surname and the name of the street on which he said he lived. The officers asked Rice to accompany them to a nearby police-box so that this information could be checked. Rice refused to move unless arrested. The officers obliged. Rice appealed against conviction under section 51(3) of the Police Act 1964.

Lord Parker CJ: What the prosecution have to prove is that there was an obstructing of a constable; that the constable was at the time acting in the execution of his duty and that the person obstructing did so wilfully. To carry the matter a little further, it is in my view clear that 'obstruct' under section 51(3) of the Police Act 1964, is the doing of any act which makes it more difficult for the police to carry out their duty. That description of obstructing I take from *Hinchliffe v Sheldon* [1955] 1 WLR 1207. It is also in my judgment clear that it is part of the obligations and duties of a police constable to take all steps which appear to him necessary for keeping the peace, for preventing crime or for protecting property from criminal injury. There is no exhaustive definition of the powers and obligations of the police, but they are at least those, and they would further include the duty to detect crime and to bring an offender to justice.

Pausing there, it seems to me quite clear that the defendant was making it more difficult for the police to carry out their duties, and that the police at the time and throughout were acting in accordance with their duties. The only remaining ingredient, and the one upon which in my judgment this case revolves, is whether the obstructing of which the defendant was guilty was a wilful obstruction. 'Wilful' in this context not only in my judgment means 'intentional' but something which is done without lawful excuse, and that indeed is conceded by Mr Skinner, who appears for the prosecution in this case. Accordingly, the sole question here is whether the defendant had a lawful excuse for refusing to answer the questions put to him. In my judgment he had. It seems to me quite clear that though every citizen has a moral duty or, if you like, a social duty to assist the police, there is no legal duty to that effect, and indeed the whole basis of common law is the right of the individual to refuse to answer questions put to him by persons in authority, and to refuse to accompany those in authority to any particular place; short, of course, of arrest.

In my judgment there is all the difference in the world between deliberately telling a false story—something which in no view a citizen has a right to do—and preserving silence or refusing to answer—something which he has every right to do. . . .

Marshall J: I agree. In order to uphold this conviction it appears to me that one has to assent to the proposition that where a citizen is acting merely within his legal rights, he is thereby committing a criminal offence. Nor can I see that the manner in which he does it can make any difference whatsoever, and for the reasons given by my Lord I agree that this appeal should be allowed.

James J: Also for the reasons given by the Lord Chief Justice, I agree that this appeal should be allowed. For my own part, I would only add this, that I would not go so far as to say that there may not be circumstances in which the manner of a person together with his silence could amount to an obstruction within the section; whether it does remains to be decided in any case that happens hereafter, not in this case, in which it has not been argued.

Appeal allowed.

NOTES

1. The decision has been criticised on the ground that a sensible result was achieved by the doubtful mechanism of holding that the word 'wilfully' incorporated the concept of 'without lawful excuse'. The former term is regarded as relating to the aspect of mens rea (the state of mind that must be proved) whereas matters of excuse relate to the actus reus of the offence (the event or state of affairs forbidden by the criminal law). See J. C. Smith and B. Hogan, *Criminal Law* (7th edn, 1992) pp. 105–106, 421–422.

2. *Rice v Connolly* requires the courts to draw a distinction between certain acts of obstruction which s. 51(3) prohibits and other acts of obstruction which remain lawful notwithstanding the apparent terms of the sub-section.

In accomplishing this task the courts have sometimes distinguished between active and passive obstruction. In *Dibble v Ingleton* [1972] 1 QB 480, DC, in order to frustrate the administration of a breathalyser test, the defendant drank from a bottle of whisky. He was convicted under s. 51(3) of the Police Act 1964 and appealed. Giving the judgment of the Divisional Court, Bridge J said, at p. 488:

'... I would draw a clear distinction between a refusal to act, on the one hand, and the doing of some positive act on the other. In a case, as in *Rice v Connolly* [1966] 2 QB 414 where the obstruction alleged consists of a refusal by the defendant to do the act which the police constable had asked him to do—to give information, it might be, or to give assistance to the police constable—one can see readily the soundness of the principle ... that such a refusal to act cannot amount to a wilful obstruction under section 51 unless the law imposes upon the person concerned some obligation in the circumstances to act in the manner requested by the police officer.

On the other hand, I can see no basis in principle or in any authority which has been cited for saying that where the obstruction consists of a positive act, it must be unlawful independently of its operation as an obstruction of a police constable under section 51. If the act relied upon as an obstruction had to be shown to be an offence independently of its effect as an obstruction it is difficult to see what use there would be in the provision of section 51 of the Police Act 1964.

In my judgment the act of the defendant in drinking whisky when he did with the object and effect of frustrating the procedure under sections 2 and 3 of the Road Safety Act 1967 was a wilful obstruction of Police Constable Tully.'

However, although obstructive inaction is more likely to be excused by the courts than obstructive action, this is not always so. For example in *Johnson v Phillips* [1975] 3 All ER 682 in order to allow the passage of an ambulance a police officer ordered the defendant to reverse the 'wrong way' down a one-way street. The defendant's refusal to do so was held to constitute an obstruction of the officer within s. 51(3). The court asserted that a constable in purported exercise of his power to control traffic on a public road has the right to disobey a traffic regulation provided that he was acting to protect life and property and such a course of action was reasonably necessary: 'if he himself has that right then it follows that he can oblige others to comply with his instructions to disobey such a regulation' (p. 685). (Note the criticisms of this case by U. Ross, [1977] Crim LR 187.) Similarly, in *Lunt v DPP* [1993] Crim LR 534, the Divisional Court held that a refusal to allow the police to exercise a right to enter his home could constitute obstruction (see further, below, p. 101). Cf. *Green v DPP* [1991] Crim LR 782, where the Divisional Court confirmed that it was not obstruction to advise a third party of his right not to answer questions. The fact that G did so in abusive terms and also told the police to 'fuck off' did not make any difference; the justices' finding that G's behaviour made it impossible for the officers to confirm or allay their suspicions of the third party meant no more than that they were unable to obtain answers.

3. The decision in *Ricketts v Cox* (1981) 74 Cr App Rep 298, DC, has been widely criticised. Here the justices found that two police officers approached Ricketts and another man named Blake, explained that a serious assault had taken place and that it was believed that coloured youths were responsible, and asked 'would you care to tell me where you have been?' R and B 'were abusive, unco-operative and positively hostile to the officers from the outset. They used obscene language calculated to provoke and antagonise the officers and ultimately made to walk away from the officers before the completion of their inquiries.' The justices held that the totality of this behaviour amounted to obstruction. R was convicted of this offence. (B was charged only with assault on the police officer in the execution of his duty, but was acquitted as the blow was in response to the unlawful act of one of the constables taking hold of his arm.) The Divisional Court merely asserted that the justices were entitled to reach this conclusion and that the case was of the kind envisaged by James J in *Rice v Connolly* (above, p. 58). On this basis the decision is highly doubtful (see Commentary by D. J. Birch, [1982] Crim LR 184; Glanville Williams, *Textbook of Criminal Law* (2nd edn, 1983) p. 204; Smith and Hogan, pp. 419–420; K. Lidstone, [1983] Crim LR 29, 33–35). If a refusal to answer questions is lawful it is difficult to see that accompanying it by abuse makes any difference. Ormrod LJ stated that the defendant had used threats (see p. 300) although no weight was attached by either the justices or the court to the threats in isolation. In fact the stated case reveals that only B had appeared to use threats: 'You only think you're fucking big because you've got that uniform on man. I'll take you white blokes on any time' (p. 299). This could not be relevant to R's liability. Would it have justified the conviction of B for obstruction? Williams (op cit, p. 204) argues not: Whatever was threatened

'the police could not reasonably have believed that they were in danger of being assaulted, because they knew that all they had to do in order to close the incident was to cease pestering him with unwelcome questions?'

However, the police are just as entitled to ask questions (provided they do not attempt to detain for questioning) as citizens are entitled to refuse to answer them (and, it appears, to tell the police to 'fuck off' or 'get stuffed' or whatever). Is it realistic to say that a threat to thump a police officer if he does not stop asking questions should not constitute an obstruction under s. 51(3)? Note that it is the threats in isolation that would constitute the obstruction, not the threats in conjunction with other lawful acts. Lidstone, (op cit, p. 34) states that R should have been acquitted as the police were not acting in the execution of their duty in 'requiring answers.' However, (1) it does not appear on the facts that the officers were 'requiring answers' up to the moment that one of the constables seized B's arm (which was rightly held to be unlawful); and (2) even if they did, their conduct (assuming no physical force was used) would not constitute a crime or tort and therefore an *unlawful* act taking the constables outside the execution of their duty. Accordingly, while the decision appears to be wrong, it is not for this reason.

4. The requirement of 'wilfulness' (which does not appear in s. 51(1)) is taken as requiring that the defendant know or at least be reckless as to whether the person he is obstructing is a police officer: *Ostler v Elliott* [1980] Crim LR 584, DC. Here, the defendant had taken a prostitute by car to a secluded place. Three 'informally dressed' young officers opened the passenger door. One said that they were police officers and asked the prostitute to get out (their intention was to arrest her for soliciting); but no identification was shown. The defendant drove off and let her out of the car. The court held that he was rightly acquitted under a charge under s. 51(3). He had reasonably supposed that the officers were accomplices of the prostitute who intended to rob him. (Note that 'reasonableness' would not be necessary: cf above, p. 57.)

5. The relevance of the purpose behind an interference with police authority has been considered in a series of cases, culminating in *Lewis v Cox*, below.

Lewis v Cox [1985] QB 509, [1984] 3 WLR 875, 148 JP 601, Queen's Bench Divisional Court

A drunk was arrested and placed in the back of a police van. C opened the rear door to ask him where he was being taken. PC Lewis, the driver, closed the door, warned C that if he opened it again he would be arrested for obstruction. C did it again, and L arrested him. The justices acquitted C on a charge under s. 51(3) of the Police Act 1964, holding that his conduct was not aimed at the police and that he did not intend to obstruct the police. The Divisional Court allowed the prosecutor's appeal.

Webster J: . . . [T]here is a line of authority . . . that the word 'wilfully' in the context of section 51(3) of the Police Act, 1964 connotes an element of mens rea. I find it necessary to consider this line of authority, although not every case in it, in some detail because it cannot, in my view, confidently be asserted that the test, whether the actions of the defendant are 'aimed at the Police', is the definitive and authoritative test.

It can, however, in my view be confidently stated, as I have already mentioned, that the word 'wilfully' imports an element of mens rea. In *Betts v Stevens* [1910] 1 KB 1, a case arising out of the warnings given at the time by AA patrol men to those who were exceeding the speed limit of the existence of a nearby Police trap, Darling J, dealing with the question of intention, said at page 8: 'The gist of the offence to my mind lies in the intention with which the things is done'.

In *Willmott v Atack* [1977] QB 498, [1976] 3 All ER 794, the defendant had intervened and obstructed a Police Officer while the Officer was attempting to restrain a man under arrest and take him to a police car. The Justices convicted him of an offence under section 51(3) of the Police Act, 1964. Although they found that the defendant had intervened in the belief that he could resolve the situation better than the Police, they concluded that his deliberate conduct had obstructed the Police, and that he was therefore guilty of wilful obstruction. This Court allowed him appeal against that conviction. Before this Court, Counsel for the defendant contended (see page 500), that: 'The proper interpretation of "wilfully obstructs" within section 51(3) of the Police Act, 1964 is that there should not merely be an intention on the part of the defendant to do something which happens to result in an obstruction of a Police Officer in the execution of his duty, but that there should also be an element of hostility and criminal intent towards the Police Officer . . .'

Croom-Johnson J, who gave the first judgment, said at pages 504–5: 'When one looks at the whole context of section 51, dealing as it does with assaults upon Constables in sub-section (1) and concluding in sub-section (3) with resistance and wilful obstruction in the execution of the duty, I am of the view that the interpretation of this sub-section for which the defendant contends is the right one. It fits the words "wilfully obstructs" in the context of the sub-section, and in my view there must be something in the nature of a criminal intent of the kind which means that it is done with the idea of some form of hostility to the Police with the intention of seeing that what is done is to obstruct, and that it is not enough merely to show that he intended to do what he did and that it did in fact have the result of the Police being obstructed'.

May J (as he then was) agreed. He observed that the word 'wilfully' had been inconsistently interpreted in various statutes which defined criminal offences, and continued: 'I agree with Croom-Johnson J that when one looks at the judgment of Darling J in *Betts v Stevens* [1910] 1 KB 1 (supra) . . . it is clear that "wilfully" in this particular statute does import a requirement of mens rea'.

Lord Widgery, in a very short judgment at page 505, agreed that the question posed should be answered in the negative, that question being (see page 502): '. . . whether upon a charge of wilfully obstructing a Police Officer in the execution of his duty it is sufficient for the prosecution to prove that the defendant wilfully did an act which obstructed the Police Officer in the execution of his duty, or must the prosecution further prove that the defendant intended to obstruct the Police Officer'.

In *Moore v Green* [1983] 1 All ER 663, DC, the facts of which are immaterial for present purposes, McCullough J, at page 665, having cited the passage from the judgment of Croom-Johnson J in *Willmott v Atack* [1977] QB 498, DC (which I have just cited) said: 'I do not understand the reference to "hostility" to indicate a separate element of the offence. I understand the word to bear the same meaning as the phrase which Croom-Johnson J used immediately afterwards, namely "the intention of seeing that what is done is to obstruct" . . .'

Griffiths LJ agreed with the judgment of McCullough J.

Finally, on this aspect of the matter, I return to *Hills v Ellis* [1983] QB 680, [1983] 1 All ER 667. In that case the appellant, while leaving a football match, saw two men fighting and formed the view that one of them was the innocent party in the fight. He then saw a Police Officer arresting the man he thought was innocent. He approached them with the intention of intervening on the part of the arrested man and, being unable to make his voice heard above the noise of the crowd, he grabbed the Police Officer's elbow to draw the Officer's attention to the fact that he was arresting the wrong man.

Another Police Officer warned the appellant that if he did not desist, he might himself be arrested for obstructing the Police. The appellant persisted in trying to stop the arrest, and was charged with wilful obstruction of a Police Officer in the execution of his duty. The Magistrates convicted him.

On his appeal he contended, inter alia, that, since his motive was to correct the Police Officer's error in arresting the wrong person, he had not acted with hostility towards the Police Officer. It was conceded that the Officer was lawfully arresting that man.

Griffiths LJ at page 670 cited the same passage from the judgment of Croom-Johnson J in *Willmott v Atack* . . . and continued: 'The appellant's Counsel argues from that passage that, as the motive here was merely to correct the policeman's error, it cannot be said that he, the appellant, was acting with hostility towards the Police. But in my view the phrase "hostility towards the Police" in that passage means no more than that the actions of the defendant are aimed at the Police. There can be no doubt here that his action in grabbing a policeman's arm was aimed at that policeman. It was an attempt to get that policeman to desist from the arrest that he was making. In my view, this is as clear a case as we can have of obstructing a Police Officer in the course of his duty, and the Justices came to the right decision'.

McCullough J agreed with the judgment of Griffiths LJ, and added, at page 671: 'I am uncertain what Croom-Johnson J had in mind when he used the word "hostility" . . . Hostility suggests emotion and motive, but motive and emotion are alike irrelevant in criminal law. What matters is intention, that is what state of affairs the defendant intended to bring about. What motive he had while so intending is irrelevant. What is meant by "an intention to obstruct"? I would construe "wilfully obstructs" as doing deliberate acts with the intention of bringing about a state of affairs which, objectively regarded, amount to an obstruction as that phrase was explained by Lord Parker in *Rice v Connolly* [1966] 2 QB 414, [1966] 2 All ER 649 at 651, ie making it more difficult for the Police to carry out their duty. The fact that the defendant might not himself have called that state of affairs an obstruction is, to my mind, immaterial. That is not to say that it is enough to do deliberate actions which, in fact, obstruct; there must be an intention that those actions should result in the further state of affairs to which I have been referring'.

Lord Parker CJ, on the same page of his judgment in *Rice v Connolly* [1966] 2 QB 414 at page 419 said that 'wilful' in the context of this section 'not only in my judgment means "intentional" but something which is done without lawful excuse'; and Lord Parker's explanation of 'wilfully obstructs' as being something which makes it more difficult for the Police to carry out their duties was taken by him from the judgment of Lord Goddard CJ in *Hinchliffe v Sheldon* [1955] 3 All ER 406, [1955] 1 WLR 1207, where Lord Goddard said: 'Obstructing, for the present purpose, means making it more difficult for the Police to carry out their duties'.

For my part I conclude that, although it may not be unhelpful in certain cases to consider whether the actions of a defendant were aimed at the Police, the simple facts which the Court has to find are whether the defendant's conduct in fact prevented the Police from carrying out their duty, or made it more difficult for them to do so, and whether the defendant intended that conduct to prevent the Police from carrying out their duty or to make it more difficult to do so.

In the present case the test which the Justices applied was whether the defendant had deliberately done some act which was aimed at the Police, they found that his actions were not aimed at the Police and they accordingly dismissed the charge. In my view, for the reasons which I have given, the justices did not ask themselves the right question for the purposes of the present case, or the whole of the right question.

[His Lordship examined the facts. He noted, inter alia, that C must have known that the police van could not be driven away with the door open, and, before he opened the door the second time, that L was about to drive the van away. It was not suggested that C had a lawful excuse for his conduct.]

In my view, therefore, if the Justices had also asked themselves whether the respondent had, by opening the door, intended to make it more difficult for the Police to perform their duties in order to carry out his intention of asking where Marsh was to be taken they must, on the evidence, have been satisfied so as to feel sure that he had such an intention.

Although the question whether a defendant's conduct is aimed at the Police may not be an unhelpful question in certain circumstances, where, as here, a defendant intended to do one thing in order to carry out his intention of doing another, that test, which might be appropriate if the Court had to find what was the defendant's predominant intention, can, in my view, mislead the Court if it is not necessary to do that.

For my part I conclude, therefore, that if the Justices had directed themselves properly in the way in which I have set out they must, on the evidence, have decided that the respondent, when he opened the door on the second occasion, intended to make it more difficult for the Police to carry out their duties, even though that was not his predominant intention, and they ought, therefore, to have convicted him of the charge against him. . . .

Kerr LJ: . . . I agree with Webster J's analysis of the authorities. The actus reus is the doing of an act which has the effect of making it impossible or more difficult for members of the Police to carry out their duty. The word 'wilfully' clearly imports an additional requirement of mens rea. The act must not only have been done deliberately, but with the knowledge and intention that it will have this obstructive effect. But in the absence of a lawful excuse, the defendant's purpose or reason for doing the act is irrelevant, whether this be directly hostile to, or 'aimed at', the Police, or whether he has some other purpose or reason. Indeed, in the majority of cases the intention to obstruct the Police will not be simply 'anti-Police', but will stem from some underlying reason or objective of the defendant which he can only achieve by an act of intentional obstruction. This may be to assist an offender, which could be termed 'hostile' to the Police. Equally, the motivation could be public-spirited, for instance, by intervening on behalf of someone whom the defendant believes to be innocent, as in *Hills v Ellis* [1983] QB 680, [1983] 1 All ER 667, DC. Or it may be for some neutral reason, for instance because the defendant considers that something else should have a higher priority than the duty on which the Police Officer is immediately engaged. In all such cases, if the defendant intentionally does an act which he realises will, in fact, have the effect of obstructing the Police in the sense defined above, he will in my view be guilty of having done so "wilfully", with the necessary mens rea. In the absence of a lawful excuse, the defendant's underlying intention, reason or purpose for intentionally obstructing the Police is irrelevant, because the intention to obstruct is present at the same time. *Willmott v Atack* [1977] QB 498, [1976] 3 All ER 794 only went the other way because the defendant's intention was in fact to assist the police. . . .

Appeal allowed. Case remitted with a direction to convict.

NOTES

1. Some of the cases discussed raise the problem of defendants with mixed purposes. A person may (1): (a) intend to obstruct a policeman in the performance of one task, (b) with the further intention of aiding him in the performance of another task (e.g. *Hills v Ellis* [1983] QB 680, [1983] 1 All ER 667); or (2): (a) intend to obstruct a policeman in the performance of a task, (b) with the further intention of pursuing some private purpose of his own (e.g. *Lewis v Cox*). The law could say either (a) that the presence of an intention to obstruct is sufficient for liability, irrespective of any other purpose, or (2) that the presence of an intention to help is sufficient for an acquittal or (3) that the answer should depend upon which motive was dominant. *Hills v Ellis* seems to adopt the first of these approaches; *Willmott v Atack* the second. It is difficult to see that the conduct in *Willmott v Atack* is distinguishable from that in *Hills v Ellis* and one of the cases is accordingly wrongly decided. Which do you prefer? *Lewis v Cox* is rightly decided on either approach as the defendant clearly is not entitled to set his own private purposes above those of the officer.

2. Some of the cases also illustrate the point that no physical obstruction is necessary. For example the offence under s. 51(3) may be committed where a warning is given in order that the commission of a crime may be suspended whilst there is a danger of detection, e.g. a warning to motorists who are speeding that a police speed trap is ahead: *Betts v Stevens* [1910] 1 KB 1; a warning to a licensee suspected of serving drinks after hours that the police are outside (so that it could not then be proved that an offence had been committed): *Hinchliffe v Sheldon* [1955] 1 WLR 1207. Similarly, warning a licensee during opening hours that the police intended to raid the premises after hours was held to be obstruction in *Moore v Green* [1983] 1 All ER 663, DC. The case had previously been before the Divisional Court: *Green v Moore* [1982] QB 1044, DC. On the earlier occasion it had been held that there was no relevant distinction between a warning given in order to *suspend* the commission of an offence whilst there was a danger of detection and a warning given in order to *postpone* the commission of an offence until after the danger of detection had passed: moreover, the offence was not limited to an obstruction where a crime was being committed or had been committed:

'Police constables maintain the Queen's peace in many different ways besides by criminal investigation. They patrol beats. They direct traffic. Is it really to be said that a police constable on point duty is not acting in the execution of his duty and that someone who wilfully obstructs his field of vision is not obstructing him in the execution of that duty? Of course not.'
(Donaldson LJ at p. 1052.)

3. Refusal to comply with police instructions given in order to prevent a breach of the peace may constitute an obstruction under s. 51(3): see *Duncan v Jones* (below, p. 248), *Piddington v Bates* (below, p. 251).

4. There is no specific power of arrest without warrant in respect of offences under s. 51 of the Police Act 1964. In respect of s. 51(1) the 'assault' will constitute a breach of the peace and so a power of contemporaneous arrest will exist (see below, pp. 207–212). In respect of offences under s. 51(3), if the obstruction does not involve an actual or apprehended breach of the peace no power of arrest exists. The police do not seem to have been much aware of this. See the arrests made in, for example, *Tynan v Balmer* [1967] 1 QB 91, DC; *Stunt v Bolton* [1972] RTR 435, DC; *Johnson v Phillips* [1975] 3 All ER 682, DC; *Wershof v Metropolitan Police Comr* [1978] 3 All ER 540, QBD; *Ledger v DPP* [1991] Crim LR 439, DC; and *Green v DPP* [1991] Crim LR 782, DC. Note also Moriarty, *Police Law* (23rd edn, 1976), p. 18 (unqualified statement that a constable may arrest without warrant a person who obstructs him in the execution of his duty).

In *Wershof v Metropolitan Police Comr*, May J stated at p. 550: 'a police constable may only arrest without a warrant anyone who wilfully obstructs him in the execution of his duty if the nature of that obstruction is such that he actually causes, or is likely to cause, a breach of the peace or is calculated to prevent the lawful arrest or detention of another'. This proposition forms part of the *ratio* of May J's judgment. The authorities cited for the proposition about arrest for conduct calculated to prevent the lawful arrest or detention of another were *Levy v Edwards* (1823) 1 C & P 40 and *White v Edmunds* (1791) Peake 123.

5. In *Riley v DPP* (1989) 91 Cr App Rep 14, police officers arrested R's brother, and then arrested R for obstruction when he attempted to push past other officers, including PC McDade, to go to his brother. R subsequently bit the thumb of PC Martin who came to PC McDade's assistance in putting R into a police van, and was subsequently convicted of assaulting PC Martin in the execution of his duty. Watkins LJ (for the Divisional Court) stated (p. 22):

'In order for there to be a lawful arrest for wilful obstruction of a constable in the execution of his duty, the Crown has to prove, in addition to the fact that he was so acting, the physical and mental element of the obstruction and further that the constable reasonably believed that if he did not make an arrest there would, or might be, a breach of the peace or an attempt to impede a lawful arrest.'

The Divisional Court quashed R's conviction on the ground (inter alia) that there was no finding of fact by the justices that any officer had a reasonable apprehension that a breach of the peace might follow. (Is 'might' sufficient in this formulation?) Moreover, as no evidence was put before the justices as to the reasons for the arrest of R's brother, the arrest for obstruction could not be justified on the basis that R intended to impede a lawful arrest. Accordingly, it was not established that the officers who arrested R's brother, and PC McDade, were acting in the execution of their duty. PC Martin, in going to PC McDade's assistance was 'unwittingly . . . acting in furtherance of an unlawful arrest of the defendant and could not consequently have been acting in the execution of his duty when he was bitten' (p. 23). The decision on this last part was criticised by Professor J. C. Smith ([1990] Crim LR 424–425): 'when M saw his colleagues struggling with a man whom they had arrested, did he not have reasonable grounds for suspecting that an arrestable offence had been committed by that man? If he did, he would have had power to make an arrest under section 24(6) of PACE, had the man not already been under arrest. . . . If it would have been lawful for him to make an arrest, it was surely also lawful for him to assist the (as he thought) lawful arrest which was taking place.' It is submitted that this goes too far: it would mean that violence used to resist an unlawful arrest by constable A would become unlawful violence as against constables B and C who came to A's assistance. The requirement that there be evidence before the court establishing that constable A in such cases was acting in the execution of his duty is appropriate and reasonable.

Riley v DPP was distinguished in *Plowden v DPP* [1991] Crim LR 850, DC. During a large demonstration against the poll tax, P was observed by PC Corby holding on to the back of another (unidentified) uniformed police officer's jacket, shouting and using abusive language, apparently attempting to prevent an arrest. The Divisional Court held that the justices were entitled to infer that the unidentified officer was acting in the execution of his duty. The line between cases where the court can draw such inferences and cases where direct evidence must be presented is, however, fine (cf. *Griffiths v DPP* (8 December 1992, unreported, DC)).

5 General aspects of police powers

(a) THE CONCEPT OF 'REASONABLE SUSPICION'

Most of the coercive powers of the police are conditioned on the presence of reasonable 'suspicion', 'cause' or 'belief' in the existence of a state of affairs – commonly that the object of the power is involved, actually or potentially, in a particular criminal offence.

Castorina v Chief Constable of Surrey (1988) NLJR 180, *Lexis*, Court of Appeal (Criminal Division).

Detectives reasonably concluded that the burglary of a company's premises was an 'inside job'. The managing director told them that she had recently dismissed someone (the plaintiff) although she did not think it would have been her, and that the documents taken would be useful to someone with a grudge. The detectives interviewed the plaintiff, having found out that she had no criminal record, and arrested her under the Criminal Law Act 1967, s. 2(4). She was detained for three and three-quarter hours at the police station and interrogated, and then released without charge. She claimed damages for wrongful arrest and detention. Judge Lermon QC held that the officers had a prima facie case for suspicion but the arrest was premature; he applied as a definition of reasonable cause 'honest belief founded on reasonable suspicion leading an ordinary cautious man to the conclusion that the person arrested was guilty of the offence', and stated that an ordinary man would have sought more information from the suspect, including an explanation for any grudge on her part. A jury awarded £4,500. The Court of Appeal (Purchas and Woolf LJJ, and Sir Frederick Lawton) allowed an appeal by the Chief Constable.

Purchas LJ: . . . The powers under which the police officers acted are contained in section 2(4) of the Criminal Law Act 1967. This section provides:

'2(4) Where a constable, with reasonable cause, suspects that an arrestable offence has been committed, he may arrest without warrant anyone whom he, with reasonable cause, suspects to be guilty of the offence.'

No question arises on the first part of this section, namely the commission of an arrestable offence. The debate centres solely around the words 'whom he, with reasonable cause, suspects to be guilty of the offence'. These powers have now been replaced by section 24(6) of the Police and Criminal Evidence Act 1984 which, however, repeats in substance the same phrase 'he may arrest without a warrant anyone whom he has reasonable grounds for suspecting to be guilty of the offence'. The exercise, therefore, is to consider the information available to the arresting officer at the time when he makes his decision to arrest in order to see whether that information is sufficient to form 'reasonable' cause for the officer's suspicion. . . .

Mr Wilson, who appeared for the appellant, submitted that the judge directed himself incorrectly on this aspect of the law. . . . He submitted that the judge's definition extended the strictness of the requirements imposed upon the arresting officer beyond those imposed in the section in the respect that the honest belief must lead an ordinary cautious man to the conclusion that the person was guilty of the offence. Mr Wilson illustrated the distinction by reference to a police officer investigating a crime which could only have been committed by one individual but where there were two or more candidates in respect of whom it was perfectly possible to hold a reasonable suspicion that one or other was guilty, whilst it would be impossible to have reason to believe in the conclusion that more than one was guilty. A similar analogy, Mr Wilson submitted, was to be found in the case of a person charged who was found in the possession of stolen goods but who might, as a result of the doctrine of recent possession, be guilty of the theft rather than handling the goods. . . .

. . . I turn first . . . to the judgment of Peter Pain J [in *Holtham v Metropolitan Police Comr* (1987) Times 8 January] which, subsequently to the judgment of Judge Lermon QC, was reversed in the Court of Appeal on 25 November 1987 [(1987) Times, 28 November]. Mr Wilson referred to an extract from the judgment of Peter Pain J which was cited by the Master of the Rolls in the *Holtham* case. This passage was part of the transcript which was before the trial judge:

'. . . the police do not have to have good evidence which would establish a prima facie case before they arrest. All they have to have is reasonable grounds for suspicion, which may be a good deal less. It may even involve matters which would not be admissible in evidence in court. But the statute requires them to have reasonable grounds for suspicion, and that, in my view, is something a good deal more than suspicion . . .'

The Master of the Rolls criticised this passage in the following terms:

'With all respect to the learned judge, I do not think that this is a correct statement of the law. As it was put by Lord Devlin in *Hussien v Chong Fook Kam* [1970] AC 942 at 948, "Suspicion in its ordinary meaning is a state of conjecture or surmise where proof is lacking: I suspect but I cannot prove". Suspicion may or may not be based upon reasonable grounds, but it still remains suspicion and nothing more. By applying a test of something which was not suspicion but was "something a good deal more than suspicion", I think that the learned judge erred and that this error was fundamental to his conclusion.'

Mr Wilson submitted that, following the approach of Peter Pain J, the judge in this case had relied upon a definition which required a state of mind higher than suspicion, namely a state of mind which concluded that the person arrested was in fact guilty of the offence.

It is clear from the notes made by the judge at the end of the evidence that the passage from the judgment of Lord Devlin in *Hussien v Chong Fook Kam* [1970] AC 942 was to the mind of the judge. It is helpful to read a little more of the context in which the passage cited by the Master of the Rolls is to be found. *Hussien*'s case concerned sections of the criminal code in Malaysia but the equivalent sections dealing with malicious prosecution, on the one hand, and false imprisonment, on the other, carried similar distinctions to those present in the law of this country. Citing from the judgment of Lord Devlin at [1970] AC page 947H:

'Mr Gratiaen has criticised the test adopted in the Federal Court. Suffian FJ, who delivered the judgment of the court, said that the information available to the police "was insufficient to prove prima facie a case against the plaintiffs under section 304A of the Penal Code or under section 34A of the Road Traffic Ordinance". Mr Gratiaen submits that this is the test appropriate in actions for malicious prosecution and not in actions for false imprisonment. . . .

Whether or not this is so – and their Lordships do not wish to add any further formulae to those already devised for the action for false imprisonment – it would appear to be a much stiffer test than the reasonable suspicion, which is the foundation of the power given in section 23(i)(a) of the Criminal Procedure Code. Suspicion in its ordinary meaning is a state of conjecture or surmise where proof is lacking: "I suspect but I cannot prove". Suspicion arises at or near the starting-point of an investigation of which the obtaining of prima facie proof is the end. When such proof has been obtained, the police case is complete; it is ready for trial and passes on to its next stage. It is indeed desirable as a general rule that an arrest should not be made until the case is complete. But if arrest before that were forbidden, it could seriously hamper the police. To give power to arrest on reasonable suspicion does not mean that it is always or even ordinarily to be exercised. It means that there is an executive discretion. In the exercise of it many factors have to be considered besides the strength of the case. The possibility of escape, the prevention of further crime and the obstruction of police inquiries are examples of those factors with which all judges who have had to grant or refuse bail are familiar. There is no serious danger in a large measure of executive discretion in the first instance because in countries where common law principles prevail the discretion is subject indirectly to judicial control.'

There are two quite distinct considerations apparent in this passage, namely what is sufficient in order to establish the right in the arresting officer to make the arrest, namely suspicion on reasonable grounds, and the second stage, namely whether in all the circumstances the officer has in making his executive decision acted within his discretion or whether he is subject to criticism under the *Wednesbury* principle (see *Associated Provincial Picture Houses v Wednesbury Corpn* [1948] 1 KB 223, [1947] 2 All ER 680) for a wrongful exercise of an executive discretion. In this appeal we are concerned solely with the first of these two aspects. . . .

I now turn to *Dumbell v Roberts* [1944] 1 All ER 326 which was the third authority listed by the judge. . . . It is to be remembered that this case concerned special powers of arrest contained in section 513 in association with section 507 of the Liverpool Corporation Act 1921. The effect of these sections was to give a power of arrest where a person was found in possession of, in that case, an excessive quantity of soap flakes for the possession of which he was unable to give a reasonable explanation. The passages upon which the judge appears to have relied in the judgment of Scott LJ are:

'The police are not called on before acting to have anything like a prima facie case for conviction; but the duty of making such inquiry as the circumstances of the case ought to indicate to a sensible man is, without difficulty, presently practicable, does rest on them; for to shut your eyes to the obvious is not to act reasonably . . .

They may have to act on the spur of the moment and have no time to reflect and be bound, therefore, to arrest, to prevent escape; but where there is no danger of the person who has ex hypothesi aroused their suspicion, that he is probably an 'offender' attempting to escape, they should make all the presently practicable enquiries from persons present or immediately accessible who are likely to be able to answer their enquiries forthwith. I am not suggesting a duty on the police to try to prove innocence; that is not their function; but they should act on the assumption that their prima facie suspicion may be ill-founded. That duty attaches particularly where slight delay does not matter because there is no probability, in the circumstances of the arrest or intended arrest, of the suspected person running away.'

Basing himself upon this passage from the judgment of Scott LJ, the learned judge formed his conclusion that the arrest was premature. . . .

In the judgment of Goddard LJ, with whom Luxmoore LJ agreed, in *Dumbell*'s case it is made clear that the majority of the court dealt with the case as one arising particularly under the provisions of the Liverpool Corporation Act in which section 513 gave a power to arrest 'when the common law grounds are absent'. The remarks of Scott LJ did not, therefore, form part of the *ratio decidendi* of the majority of the court.

Mr Wilson also attacked the reference to 'honest belief' in the legal definition of reasonable cause. The test provided by the section requires that the suspicion must arise from reasonable cause. Reasonable cause, it is not disputed, is to be determined as an objective matter from the information available to the arresting officer and cannot have anything to do with the subjective state of the officer's mind. This may well be relevant in the offence of malicious prosecution. With all respect to the learned judge it appears that he has confused belief, which plays no part in the power of arrest under the section, and suspicion, based upon reasonable grounds which does. Honest belief, therefore, cannot be relevant. To the extent that the judge has specifically found honest belief and stated it in his judgment this is an indication that he has misdirected himself. . . .

With respect to the judge I agree with Mr Wilson's submissions that, in concentration on what the officers might or might not have done by way of further inquiry before arrest, the judge's attention was deflected from the critical question, namely when they arrested her did they have reasonable cause for suspecting that the respondent was guilty of the offence? (See *Holgate-Mohammed v Duke* [1984] AC 437, [1984] 1 All ER 1054). In that case the trial judge had found that the detective constable had had reasonable cause to suspect the plaintiff of having committed an arrestable offence but, because the constable had decided not to interview her under caution but to subject her to the greater pressure of arrest and detention so as to induce a confession, there had been a wrongful exercise of the power of arrest. From the speech of Lord Diplock, who delivered the leading speech, it is clear that the failure to interrogate before arrest did not impair the lawfulness of the arrest in the first instance under the powers of section 2(4) but that the exercise of those powers before interrogation in order to enhance the chances of obtaining a confession had to be tested against the principles laid down in *Associated Provincial Picture Houses Ltd v Wednesbury Corpn* [1948] 1 KB 223, [1947] 2 All ER 680. Their Lordships decided that in the circumstances of that case there had been no such breach of the *Wednesbury* principle.

There is ample authority for the proposition that courses of inquiry which may or may not be taken by an investigating police officer before arrest are not relevant to the consideration whether, on the information available to him at the time of the arrest, he had reasonable cause for suspicion. Of course, failure to follow an obvious course in exceptional circumstances may well be grounds for attacking the executive exercise of that power under the *Wednesbury* principle. The position is very starkly pointed out in a passage . . . from the judgment of Sir John Arnold P in *Mohammed-Holgate*'s case in the Court of Appeal [1984] QB 209, [1983] 3 All ER 526 at page 216C of the former report:

'As to the proposition that there were other things which he might have done, no doubt there were other things which he might have done first. He might have obtained a statement from her otherwise than under arrest to see how far he could get. He might have obtained a specimen of her handwriting and sent that off for forensic examination against a specimen of the writing of the person who had obtained the money by selling the stolen jewellery, which happened to exist in the case. All those things he might have done. He might have carried out fingerprint investigations if he had first obtained a print from the plaintiff. But the fact that there were other things which he might have done does not, in my judgment, make that which he did do into an unreasonable exercise of the power of arrest if what he did do, namely to arrest, was within the range of reasonable choices available to him.'

At an earlier stage of the hearing in dealing with an argument as to a preliminary point, Sir John Arnold referred to the judgment of Scott LJ in *Dumbell*'s case confirming that the passage upon which the judge had relied went not to the question of suspicion on reasonable grounds but to the executive exercise of a discretionary power – see [1983] 3 All ER 526 at page 530F:

'The real reason why this line of argument fails is simply that the whole of what Scott LJ says is plainly directed in the context in which it was said not to the question of whether the police arrested with reasonable cause a person whom they suspected of having committed the crime, but whether it was reasonable to carry out the arrest even if the power were available, in other words the very point which was decided by the judge against the police and on which the main appeal is founded.'

This court has recently commented upon this part of the judgment of Scott LJ in the case of *Ward v Chief Constable of Avon and Somerset Constabulary* (unreported) Court of Appeal transcript for 25th June 1986. After pointing out that the arrest in *Dumbell*'s case was under the special powers of the Liverpool Corporation Act Croom-Johnson LJ said this:

'After saying the plaintiff's appeal would be allowed, and a new trial ordered, Lord Justice Scott made some general observations which were obiter, about what might amount to reasonable suspicion of guilt justifying an arrest. The passage relied on (p. 329G) stressed the need for the police to "make all presently practicable enquiries from persons present or immediately accessible who are likely to be able to answer their enquiries forthwith". Thus is it said here that Det Sgt Edwards' enquiries were not detailed enough.

But it is unnecessary for the police to probe every explanation. Section 2(4) of the Criminal Law Act 1967 requires the constable to have "reasonable cause" for suspicion before he arrests.'

With respect, I adopt the approach of Croom-Johnson LJ in this case. The strictures made by Judge Lermon about the failure of the arresting police officers to inquire of the respondent whether she did or did not actually have a grudge against her erstwhile employers fall within the criticism made more than once in this court of the approach based on the judgment of Scott LJ. It can be tested by asking whether the investigation would have been advanced if the police officers had pursued the point and were met with a flat denial. In my judgment, the judge was wrong to rely on the judgment of Scott LJ and this led him erroneously to conclude that the arrest was premature and, therefore, unlawful. I have, therefore, come to the conclusion that Mr Wilson's submissions on this aspect of the case are made out and that the learned judge misdirected himself in applying the provisions of section 2(4) of the Act. . . .

[Purchas LJ then rejected the plaintiff's argument that the court should order a retrial before a jury; the primary facts were not in dispute, and it was 'open to the court to draw the necessary inferences of secondary fact in order to determine whether the arresting officers had reasonable cause to suspect'. On this question, he continued:]

Mr Scrivener urged upon us that there was a duty upon the police officers to have made these inquiries, in other words that the judge was right in holding that the arrest was premature. He also submitted that there had been no lie or inconsistency in the responses given by the respondent prior to arrest, or indeed subsequent thereto. His submissions were based on an assertion that at the time of arrest, without an inquiry as to whether or not the respondent held a grudge, there was insufficient information upon which the officers could have had reasonable cause to suspect that she had committed the offence. But, with respect to Mr Scrivener, this approach discloses the fallacy of looking at what the officers might have done by way of inquiry rather than looking at the information they had gained in order to apply the test required by section 2(4). Of course, if it was relevant to consider what inquiries the officers might have made, then it would be equally relevant to consider what the result of those inquiries might have been. The evidence led before the learned judge of the inquiries made by the police officers after receiving the respondent's emphatic denial that she had a grudge, disclosed further grounds for suspicion. The note of the evidence of DC Thorne reads:

'Further enquiries. 'Phoned Mrs Wilton [sic: ed.] to learn more about ill feeling by the Plaintiff. Mrs Wilton told me that the Plaintiff had made false statements to other people about the Company. Specifically had told others within the Company that the Company was heading for financial ruin. That is the Plaintiff was running the Company down in a malicious way.'

The names of other people were obtained from Mrs Wilton but inquiries of these people did not prove fruitful. Mrs Wilton's evidence as noted by the judge was:

'Two days after the Plaintiff left I had telephone calls, one from our Manchester supervisor, Mrs Templeton. She said that the Plaintiff had told her that she had left the Company which was in financial difficulties and that it was unlikely that her interviewers would get paid for the work. Also two other telephone calls, one of a similar nature from another supervisor and one from the field director of NOP who had also been told that we were in financial difficulties. I understood then that rumours were going about the Company which concerned me. Prior to the burglary I had contacted my solicitor as a result of the 'phone calls. She suggested writing a letter threatening litigation. She drafted a letter which was sent to the Plaintiff together with her salary cheque – "unless she stopped slandering the Company we would take further proceedings".'

Had the police officers pressed their inquiries further she may well have told them all of this. This evidence demonstrates the difficult and unsatisfactory waters into which the inquiry drifts if the approach advocated by the judge had been adopted. For the reasons already given in this judgment, however, I consider that the failure to carry out this line of inquiry is not relevant to considering the objective question of reasonable cause within the meaning of section 2(4). I, therefore, find myself unable to accede to Mr Scrivener's submissions in support of the judgment based on premature arrest.

This leaves the final inquiry to be made by this court as to whether or not as an objective criterion there was sufficient information available to the arresting officers to give them 'reasonable cause to suspect that the respondent was guilty of the burglary'. I have already outlined the unusual features of the burglary which became apparent to the arresting officers on their visit to the Company's premises on the morning of 23rd June. These features need not be repeated here. They do indicate a very specific and particular character which could safely be attributed to the burglar in a number of different respects, ie experience, motive and inside knowledge of affairs within the Company's premises. In addition to this the information also given to the arresting officers by Mrs Wilton at the first stage of their inquiries identified the respondent as the only person who possessed these particular qualities. In the circumstances of this case, and I emphasise that every case has to be determined upon its particular facts, I am satisfied that the arresting officers had reasonable cause to suspect that the respondent was guilty of this unusual burglary.

For these reasons, therefore, I would allow this appeal and set aside the award of damages made by the jury enshrined in the judge's order. . . .
Woolf LJ and **Sir Frederick Lawton** delivered concurring judgments.
Appeal allowed.

NOTES

1. In his judgment, Woolf LJ stated that in a case where it is alleged that there has been an unlawful arrest, there are three questions to be answered:

' 1. Did the arresting officer suspect that the person who was arrested was guilty of the offence? The answer to this question depends entirely on the findings of fact as to the officer's state of mind.
  2. Assuming the officer had the necessary suspicion, was there reasonable cause for that suspicion? This is a purely objective requirement to be determined by the judge if necessary on facts found by a jury.
  3. If the answer to the two previous questions is in the affirmative, then the officer has a discretion which entitles him to make an arrest and in relation to that discretion the question arises as to whether the discretion has been exercised in accordance with the principles laid down by Lord Greene MR in *Associated Provincial Picture Houses Ltd v Wednesbury Corpn* [1948] 1 KB 223, [1947] 2 All ER 680.

2. R. Clayton and H. Tomlinson ('Arrest and reasonable grounds for suspicion' (1988) 85 LS Gaz. 7 September, p. 22) argue that *Castorina* was incorrect in holding that the possibility of 'further inquiries' cannot be relevant to the question whether there are reasonable grounds for an arrest:

'It is clear law that reasonable cause will only be present if a reasonable man, in the position of the officer at the time of arrest, would have thought that the plaintiff was probably guilty of the offence: see *Dallison v Caffery* [1965] 1 QB 348, 371 and *Wiltshire v Barrett* [1966] 1 QB 312, 322.
  Thus, whether or not there is "reasonable cause to suspect" depends on an overall assessment of the reliability of the evidence incriminating the suspect . . . [I]t is submitted that a reasonable man would, before thinking that a person was probably guilty of an offence, probe the evidence available to him by making any obvious and simply available inquiries' (p. 25).

They further submitted that *Castorina* was inconsistent with one of the justifications for the requirement that an officer give reasons for an arrest (see pp. 109–111), namely that the person arrested 'may be able to give more than a bare and unconvincing denial if he is in fact innocent' (per Sir John Donaldson in *Murphy v Oxford* (15 February 1988, unreported)):

'If an arresting officer is obliged to give reasons on arrest he must be under a correlative obligation to consider any answers given by the suspect and, if appropriate, to investigate them. Otherwise, the giving of reasons would simply be an empty formality (p. 26).'

Finally, the authors regard the conclusion that there was 'reasonable cause' on the facts as 'remarkable':

'If the police are justified in arresting a middle aged woman of good character on such flimsy grounds, without even questioning her as to her alibi or possible motives, then the law provides very scant protection for those suspected of crime' (p. 26).

3. The Advisory Committee on Drug Dependence (by a majority: *Powers of Arrest and Search in Relation to Drug Offences* (Home Office, 1970, paras. 111, 123–127)) and the RCCP (*Report*, Cmnd. 8092, p. 29) concluded that it would be impracticable to formulate standards for grounds of reasonable suspicion in a statute or code of practice. The RCCP concluded that the requirements of notifying reasons, making records and the monitoring of such records by superior officers would be the most effective way of reducing the risk of random action (ibid).

4. For a long time there was a dearth of cases raising the issue whether 'reasonable grounds' existed. However, a number of such cases have arisen more recently. In

King v Gardner (1979) 71 Cr App Rep 13, DC, police officers received a radio message that referred to suspects loitering: two males and one female, one with dog, and included a personal description 'blue jeans, long hair.' They stopped and detained Gardner, who was out with a woman and a dog, after he had refused to show them what was in a large canvas bag he was carrying. He was prosecuted for assaulting one of the officers. The sender of the message was not called to give evidence as to the identity of the defendant or as to acts which could be said to have given rise to reasonable suspicion. No evidence was called relating to the personal description given in the radio message, apart from PC Parker's bare assertion that Gardner fitted the description of the man in the area. The Divisional Court held that the Metropolitan Stipendiary Magistrate had been entitled to conclude that there was no satisfactory evidence that would constitute reasonable suspicion under s. 66 of the Metropolitan Police Act 1839 (below pp. 81, 82). His decision was essentially one of fact which could only be upset if it was perverse.

See also *R v Prince* [1981] Crim LR 638; *Ware v Matthews* (unreported) and *Pedro v Diss* [1981] 2 All ER 59, DC, discussed by S. H. Bailey and D. J. Birch, [1982] Crim LR at pp. 476–477.

5. In *Monaghan v Corbett* (1983) 147 JP 545, DC, a constable saw M alight from a car and noticed he smelt strongly of drink. The following day, a Saturday, he was told by neighbours that M habitually went drinking at lunchtime on Saturdays and Sundays and travelled by car. When M arrived by car he was stopped and breathalysed. M was shown to have more than the prescribed limit of alcohol. Nevertheless his conviction was quashed, the Divisional Court holding that this information did not amount to reasonable suspicion that M had consumed alcohol on this occasion as it did not arise out of the driving of the motor vehicle at the relevant time. This appears to be an artificial limit, not imposed by the statute, on the information that may be relied upon by officers: it would be contrary to common sense to hold that on all the facts there was no reasonable suspicion. (Cf. *DPP v Wilson* [1991] Crim LR 441, DC.) Conversely, in *Ward v Chief Constable of Avon and Somerset Constabulary* (1986) Times 26 June, in the course of investigations following the riots in the St Paul's area of Bristol in 1980, police officers found 13 Easter eggs in W's house. A large quantity of Easter eggs had been stolen during the riots. W stated that she had bought them from a supermarket for 37p each. DS Edwards was suspicious at the number of eggs, because they had no price labels and because 37p seemed too cheap, and arrested W. W subsequently sued for wrongful arrest and false imprisonment. The Court of Appeal held that there was sufficient evidence to show reasonable cause.

6. In *Baker v Oxford* [1980] RTR 315 the Divisional Court accepted that there was a distinction between requirements of reasonable cause to *suspect* and reasonable cause to *believe* (see S. H. Bailey and D. J. Birch, [1982] Crim LR at pp. 549–551). No opinion was expressed on what the distinction might be although it had been suggested in argument that ' "suspect" implied an imagination to exist without proof, whereas "belief" implied an acceptance of what was true'. In *Johnson v Whitehouse* [1984] RTR 38 the Divisional Court confirmed that 'the greater force of the word "believe" [than "suspect"] is an essential part of the law' (p. 47). However, an arrest was not invalid merely because the constable used the wrong word provided that the relevant grounds were present.

7. In *Siddiqui v Swain* [1979] RTR 454 the Divisional Court held that where an arrest required 'reasonable cause to suspect' it must be shown both that (1) there was 'reasonable cause' and (2) that the constable in fact 'suspected' (see Bailey and Birch, op cit, pp. 550–551). Cf. *Chapman v DPP* (1988) 89 Cr App Rep 190.

8. That 'reasonable cause to suspect' may be based on hearsay evidence was confirmed by *Erksine v Hollin* [1971] RTR 199, DC; *R v Evans* [1974] RTR 232, CA (CD) (information supplied by a fellow police officer).

9. Annex B to the original version of the Code of Practice for the Exercise by Police Officers of Statutory Powers of Stop and Search (Code A) set out guidance on the question of reasonable suspicion. In the second and third editions of Code A, Annex B was omitted and the guidance reworded:

'1.6 Whether reasonable grounds for suspicion exist will depend on the circumstances in each case, but there must be some objective basis for it. An officer will need to consider the nature of the article suspected of being carried in the context of other factors such as the time and the place, and the behaviour of the person concerned or those with him. Reasonable suspicion may exist, for example, where information has been received such as a description of an article being carried or of a suspected offender; a person is seen acting covertly or warily or attempting to hide something; or a person is carrying a certain type of article at an unusual time or in a place where a number of burglaries or thefts are known to have taken place recently. But the decision to stop and search must be based on all the facts which bear on the likelihood that an article of a certain kind will be found.

1.7 Reasonable suspicion can never be supported on the basis of personal factors alone. For example, a person's colour, age, hairstyle or manner of dress, or the fact that he is known to have a previous conviction for possession of an unlawful article, cannot be used alone or in combination with each other as the sole basis on which to search that person. Nor may it be founded on the basis of stereotyped images of certain persons or groups as more likely to be committing offences.'

For difficulties that arose from the wording of the old Annex B, see D. Dixon, *et al.*, 'Reality and Rules in the Construction and Regulation of Police Suspicion' (1989) 17 Int. Jo. of the Sociology of Law 185. They confirm that in practice, contrary to a provision of Annex B (para. 4) omitted from the revised version, the standard of suspicion applied by the police to justify a stop and search is lower (less individualised) than that applied to justify an arrest. Can this be justified on the argument that a stop and search is less intrusive than an arrest? (see pp. 194–195). They argue that some of the problems in this area might appropriately be tackled by such steps as 'clearer statements of required standards, more testing judicial scrutiny, public education and new police training' (p. 204).

(b) THE CONCEPT OF 'SERIOUS ARRESTABLE OFFENCE'

The RCCP recommended that certain of the powers of the police should be available only in respect of 'grave offences'. This was where powers were to be used against persons not themselves reasonably suspected of complicity in an offence or where the powers were particularly intrusive. The RCCP did not list 'grave offences' but suggested which broad categories would be included (*Report*, paras. 3.7–3.9). The 1984 Act used instead the concept of 'serious arrestable offence' in relation to the powers given by ss. 4 (road checks), 8 (search warrants), 42 and 43 (continued detention), 56(2) (delay in informing a friend or relative that a person has been arrested), 58(6) (delayed access to legal advice). The term 'arrestable offence' is defined by s. 24 (below, pp. 104–105). The concept of 'serious arrestable offence' is defined as follows:

Police and Criminal Evidence Act 1984

116. Meaning of 'serious arrestable offence'
(1) This section has effect for determining whether an offence is a serious arrestable offence for the purposes of this Act.

(2) The following arrestable offences are always serious—
    (*a*) an offence (whether at common law or under any enactment) specified in Part I of Schedule 5 to this Act; and
    (*b*) an offence under an enactment specified in Part II of that Schedule; [and
    (*c*) any of the offences mentioned in paragraphs (a) to (f) of section 1(3) of the Drug Trafficking Act 1994.][1]

(3) Subject to subsections (4) and (5) below, any other arrestable offence is serious only if its commission—
    (*a*) has led to any of the consequences specified in subsection (6) below; or
    (*b*) is intended or is likely to lead to any of those consequences.

(4) An arrestable offence which consists of making a threat is serious if carrying out the threat would be likely to lead to any of the consequences specified in subsection (6) below.

(5) An offence under [section 2, 8, 9, 10 or 11 of the Prevention of Terrorism (Temporary Provisions) Act 1989][2] is always a serious arrestable offence for the purposes of section 56 or 58 above, and an attempt or conspiracy to commit any such offence is also always a serious arrestable offence for those purposes.

(6) The consequences mentioned in subsections (3) and (4) above are
    (*a*) serious harm to the security of the State or to public order;
    (*b*) serious interference with the administration of justice or with the investigation of offences or of a particular offence;
    (*c*) the death of any person;
    (*d*) serious injury to any person;
    (*e*) substantial financial gain to any person; and
    (*f*) serious financial loss to any person.

(7) Loss is serious for the purposes of this section if, having regard to all the circumstances, it is serious for the person who suffers it.

(8) In this section 'injury' includes any disease or any impairment of a person's physical or mental condition.

NOTES

1. Schedule 5, Part I, mentioned in s. 116(2)(a); lists (1) treason; (2) murder; (3) manslaughter; (4) rape; (5) kidnapping; (6) incest with a girl under the age of 13; (7) buggery with a person under 16; (8) indecent assault which constitutes an act of gross indecency.

Those in Sch. 5, Part II are (1) causing an explosion likely to endanger life or property (Explosive Substances Act 1883, s. 2); (2) intercourse with a girl under 13 (Sexual Offences Act 1956, s. 5); (3) possession of firearms with intent to injure, use of firearms and imitation firearms to resist arrest and carrying firearms with criminal intent (Firearms Act 1968, ss. 16, 17(1), 18); (4) causing death by dangerous driving and causing death by careless driving when under the influence of drink or drugs (Road Traffic Act 1988, ss. 1, 3A); (5) hostage taking (Taking of Hostages Act 1982, s. 1); (6) hi-jacking (Aviation Security Act 1982, s. 1); (7) torture (Criminal Justice Act 1988, s. 134); (8) endangering safety at aerodromes, hijacking of ships and seizing or exercising control of fixed platforms (Aviation and Maritime Security Act 1990, ss. 1, 9, 10); (9) hijacking of Channel Tunnel trains (Channel Tunnel (Security) Order 1994 (S.I. 1994 No. 570)); (10) taking and distribution of indecent photographs of children (Protection of Children Act 1978, s. 1); (11) publication of obscene matter (Obscene Publications Act 1959, s. 2).[3]

2. There have been few cases offering guidance on the conditions listed in subs. (6). In *R v McIvor* [1987] Crim LR 409, Lawton LJ, sitting at first instance, held that the

---

1 Inserted by the Drug Trafficking Act 1994, Sch. 1, para. 9.
2 Inserted by the 1989 Act, Sch. 8, para. 6(7).
3 (10) and (11) were added by the Criminal Justice and Public Order Act 1994, s. 85(3).

(d) CODES OF PRACTICE

Police and Criminal Evidence Act 1984

CODES OF PRACTICE—GENERAL

66. Codes of practice
[This section requires the Secretary of State to issue Codes of Practice in connection with the matters covered by Codes A to D: see n. 1, below.]

67. Codes of practice – supplementary
(1)–(7) [This prescribes the procedure for the issue of codes of practice, with the approval of each House of Parliament.]
(9) Persons other than police officers who are charged with the duty of investigating offences or charging offenders shall in the discharge of that duty have regard to any relevant provision of such a code.
(10) A failure on the part
    (*a*) of a police officer to comply with any provision of such a code; or
    (*b*) of any person other than a police officer who is charged with the duty of investigating offences or charging offenders to have regard to any relevant provision of such a code in the discharge of that duty
shall not of itself render him liable to any criminal or civil proceedings.
(11) In all criminal and civil proceedings any such code shall be admissible in evidence; and if any provision of such a code appears to the court or tribunal conducting the proceedings to be relevant to any question arising in the proceedings it shall be taken into account in determining that question.

NOTES

1. Four Codes of Practice were issued with effect from 1 January 1986; revised versions were issued with effect from 1 April 1991. These were (1) Code A: *Code of Practice for the Exercise by Police Officers of Statutory Powers of Stop and Search*; (2) Code B: *Code of Practice for the Searching of Premises by Police Officers and the Seizure of Property found by Police Officers on Persons or Premises*; (3) Code C: *Code of Practice for the Detention, Treatment and Questioning of Persons by Police Officers*; (4) Code D: *Code of Practice for the Identification of Persons by Police Officers*. Code E, on *Tape Recording*, was issued with effect from 29 July 1988. A further revision of the five Codes was issued with effect from 10 April 1995.
2. Codes A to D have been issued, with modifications, for Northern Ireland under the Police and Criminal Evidence (Northern Ireland) Order 1989 (S.I. 1989/134).
3. By virtue of the Police and Magistrates' Courts Act 1994, s. 37(a), repealing PACE, s. 67(8), breach of one of the Codes is not automatically a disciplinary offence.
4. All of the Codes of Practice issued under the 1984 Act 'must be readily available at all police stations for consultation by police officers, detained persons and members of the public' (Codes A.1.1., B.1.1., C.1.2., D.1.1., E.1.1.).
5. It is a question of fact whether a person is 'charged with the duty of investigating offences' for the purpose of s. 67(9). Section 67(9) has been held to apply to Ladbrokes investigators (*R v Twaites and Brown* (1990) 92 Cr App Rep 106), the Federation against Copyright Theft Ltd (*Joy v FACT* [1993] Crim LR 588, DC), and a store detective (*R v Bayliss* (1993) 98 Cr App Rep 235); but not a supervising manager of the Bank of England in the course of acting to ensure that minimum criteria for authorisation by the Bank were met and maintained, under Sch. 3 to the Banking Act 1987 (*R v Smith (Wallace)* [1994] 1 WLR 1396, CA (Cr D)).

6 Powers to stop and search

Police and Criminal Evidence Act 1984

PART I

POWERS TO STOP AND SEARCH

1. Power of constable to stop and search persons, vehicles etc

(1) A constable may exercise any power conferred by this section—
   (a) in any place to which at the time when he proposes to exercise the power the public or any section of the public has access, on payment or otherwise, as of right or by virtue of express or implied permission; or
   (b) in any other place to which people have ready access at the time when he proposes to exercise the power but which is not a dwelling.
(2) Subject to subsections (3) to (5) below, a constable—
   (a) may search—
      (i) any person or vehicle;
      (ii) anything which is in or on a vehicle,
      for stolen or prohibited articles [or any article to which subsection (8A) below applies];[1] and
   (b) may detain a person or vehicle for the purpose of such a search.
(3) This section does not give a constable power to search a person or vehicle or anything in or on a vehicle unless he has reasonable grounds for suspecting that he will find stolen or prohibited articles [or any article to which subsection (8A) below applies].[1]
(4) If a person is in a garden or yard occupied with and used for the purposes of a dwelling or on other land so occupied and used, a constable may not search him in the exercise of the power conferred by this section unless the constable has reasonable grounds for believing—
   (a) that he does not reside in the dwelling; and
   (b) that he is not in the place in question with the express or implied permission of a person who resides in the dwelling.
(5) If a vehicle is in a garden or yard occupied with and used for the purposes of a dwelling or on other land so occupied and used, a constable may not search the vehicle or anything in or on it in the exercise of the power conferred by this section unless he has reasonable grounds for believing—
   (a) that the person in charge of the vehicle does not reside in the dwelling; and
   (b) that the vehicle is not in the place in question with the express or implied permission of a person who resides in the dwelling.
(6) If in the course of such a search a constable discovers an article which he has reasonable grounds for suspecting to be a stolen or prohibited article [or any article to which subsection (8A) below applies],[1] he may seize it.
(7) An article is prohibited for the purposes of this Part of this Act if it is—
   (a) an offensive weapon; or
   (b) an article—
      (i) made or adapted for use in the course of or in connection with an offence to which this subparagraph applies; or
      (ii) intended by the person having it with him for such use by him or by some other person.
(8) The offences to which subsection (7)(b)(i) above applies are—
   (a) burglary;
   (b) theft;
   (c) offences under section 12 of the Theft Act 1968 (taking motor vehicle or other conveyance without authority); and
   (d) offences under section 15 of that Act (obtaining property by deception).
[(8A) This subsection applies to any article in relation to which a person has committed, or is committing, or is going to commit an offence under section 139 of the Criminal Justice Act 1988.][1]
(9) In this Part of this Act 'offensive weapon' means any article—
   (a) made or adapted for use for causing injury to persons; or
   (b) intended by the person having it with him for such use by him or by some other person.

2. Provisions relating to search under section 1 and other powers

(1) A constable who detains a person or vehicle in the exercise—

---

1 Inserted by the Criminal Justice Act 1988, s. 140.

(*a*) of the power conferred by section 1 above; or
(*b*) of any other power—
    (i) to search a person without first arresting him; or
    (ii) to search a vehicle without making an arrest,
need not conduct a search if it appears to him subsequently—
    (i) that no search is required; or
    (ii) that a search is impracticable.
(2) If a constable contemplates a search, other than a search of an unattended vehicle, in the exercise—
    (*a*) of the power conferred by section 1 above; or
    (*b*) of any other power, except the power conferred by section 6 below and the power conferred by
        section 27(2) of the Aviation Security Act 1982—
        (i) to search a person without first arresting him; or
        (ii) to search a vehicle without making an arrest,
it shall be his duty, subject to subsection (4) below, to take reasonable steps before he commences the
search to bring to the attention of the appropriate person—
    (i) if the constable is not in uniform, documentary evidence that he is a constable; and
    (ii) whether he is in uniform or not, the matters specified in subsection (3) below;
and the constable shall not commence the search until he has performed that duty.
(3) The matters referred to in subsection (2)(ii) above are—
    (*a*) the constable's name and the name of the police station to which he is attached;
    (*b*) the object of the proposed search;
    (*c*) the constable's grounds for proposing to make it; and
    (*d*) the effect of section 3(7) or (8) below, as may be appropriate.
(4) A constable need not bring the effect of section 3(7) or (8) below to the attention of the appropriate
person if it appears to the constable that it will not be practicable to make the record in section 3(1)
below.
(5) In this section 'the appropriate person' means—
    (*a*) if the constable proposes to search a person, that person; and
    (*b*) if he proposes to search a vehicle, or anything in or on a vehicle, the person in charge of the
        vehicle.
(6) On completing a search of an unattended vehicle or anything in or on such a vehicle in the exercise
of any such power as is mentioned in subsection (2) above a constable shall leave a notice—
    (*a*) stating that he has searched it;
    (*b*) giving the name of the police station to which he is attached;
    (*c*) stating that an application for compensation for any damage caused by the search may be made to
        that police station; and
    (*d*) stating the effect of section 3(8) below.
(7) The constable shall leave the notice inside the vehicle unless it is not reasonably practicable to do so
without damaging the vehicle.
(8) The time for which a person or vehicle may be detained for the purposes of such a search is such time
as is reasonably required to permit a search to be carried out either at the place where the person or
vehicle was first detained or nearby.
(9) Neither the power conferred by section 1 above nor any other power to detain and search a person
without first arresting him or to detain and search a vehicle without making an arrest is to be construed—
    (*a*) as authorising a constable to require a person to remove any of his clothing in public other than an
        outer coat, jacket or gloves; or
    (*b*) as authorising a constable not in uniform to stop a vehicle.
(10) This section and section 1 above apply to vessels, aircraft and hovercraft as they apply to vehicles.

3. Duty to make records concerning searches

(1) Where a constable has carried out a search in the exercise of any such power as is mentioned in section 2(1) above, other than a search—
    (*a*) under section 6 below; or
    (*b*) under section 27(2) of the Aviation Security Act 1982,
he shall make a record of it in writing unless it is not practicable to do so.
(2) If—
    (*a*) a constable is required by subsection (1) above to make a record of a search; but
    (*b*) it is not practicable to make the record on the spot,
he shall make it as soon as practicable after the completion of the search.
(3) The record of a search of a person shall include a note of his name, if the constable knows it, but a
constable may not detain a person to find out his name.

(4) If a constable does not know the name of a person whom he has searched, the record of the search shall include a note otherwise describing that person.

(5) The record of a search of a vehicle shall include a note describing the vehicle.

(6) The record of a search of a person or a vehicle—

(a) shall state—
  (i) the object of the search;
  (ii) the grounds for making it;
  (iii) the date and time when it was made;
  (iv) the place where it was made;
  (v) whether anything, and if so what, was found;
  (vi) whether any, and if so what, injury to a person or damage to property appears to the constable to have resulted from the search; and

(b) shall identify the constable making it.

(7) If a constable who conducted a search of a person made a record of it, the person who was searched shall be entitled to a copy of the record if he asks for one before the end of the period specified in subsection (9) below.

(8) If—

(a) the owner of a vehicle which has been searched or the person who was in charge of the vehicle at the time when it was searched asks for a copy of the record of the search before the end of the period specified in subsection (9) below; and

(b) the constable who conducted the search made a record of it,

the person who made the request shall be entitled to a copy.

(9) The period mentioned in subsections (7) and (8) above is the period of 12 months beginning with the date on which the search was made.

(10) The requirements imposed by this section with regard to records of searches of vehicles shall apply also to records of searches of vessels, aircraft and hovercraft.

4. Road checks

(1) This section shall have effect in relation to the conduct of road checks by police officers for the purpose of ascertaining whether a vehicle is carrying—

(a) a person who has committed an offence other than a road traffic offence or a vehicles excise offence;

(b) a person who is a witness to such an offence;

(c) a person intending to commit such an offence; or

(d) a person who is unlawfully at large.

(2) For the purposes of this section a road check consists of the exercise in a locality of the power conferred by section [163] of the Road Traffic Act [1988] in such a way as to stop during the period for which its exercise in that way in that locality continues all vehicles or vehicles selected by any criterion.

(3) Subject to subsection (5) below, there may only be such a road check if a police officer of the rank of superintendent or above authorises it in writing.

(4) An officer may only authorise a road check under subsection (3) above—

(a) for the purpose specified in subsection (1)(a) above, if he has reasonable grounds—
  (i) for believing that the offence is a serious arrestable offence; and
  (ii) for suspecting that the person is, or is about to be, in the locality in which vehicles would be stopped if the road check were authorised;

(b) for the purpose specified in subsection (1)(b) above, if he has reasonable grounds for believing that the offence is a serious arrestable offence;

(c) for the purpose specified in subsection (1)(c) above, if he has reasonable grounds—
  (i) for believing that the offence would be a serious arrestable offence; and
  (ii) for suspecting that the person is, or is about to be in the locality in which vehicles would be stopped if the road check were authorised;

(d) for the purpose specified in subsection (1)(d) above, if he has reasonable grounds for suspecting that the person is, or is about to be, in that locality.

(5) An officer below the rank of superintendent may authorise such a road check if it appears to him that it is required as a matter of urgency for one of the purposes specified in subsection (1) above.

(6) If an authorisation is given under subsection (5) above, it shall be the duty of the officer who gives it—

(a) to make a written record of the time at which he gives it; and

(b) to cause an officer of the rank of superintendent or above to be informed that it has been given.

(7) The duties imposed by subsection (6) above shall be performed as soon as it is practicable to do so.

(8) An officer to whom a report is made under subsection (6) above may, in writing, authorise the road check to continue.

(9) If such an officer considers that the road check should not continue, he shall record in writing—
 (a) the fact that it took place; and
 (b) the purpose for which it took place.

(10) An officer giving an authorisation under this section shall specify the locality in which vehicles are to be stopped.

(11) An officer giving an authorisation under this section, other than an authorisation under subsection (5) above—
 (a) shall specify a period, not exceeding seven days, during which the road check may continue; and
 (b) may direct that the road check—
  (i) shall be continuous; or
  (ii) shall be conducted at specified times, during that period.

(12) If it appears to an officer of the rank of superintendent or above that a road check ought to continue beyond the period for which it has been authorised he may, from time to time, in writing specify a further period, not exceeding seven days, during which it may continue.

(13) Every written authorisation shall specify—
 (a) the name of the officer giving it;
 (b) the purpose of the road check; and
 (c) the locality in which vehicles are to be stopped.

(14) The duties to specify the purposes of a road check imposed by subsections (9) and (13) above include duties to specify any relevant serious arrestable offence.

(15) Where a vehicle is stopped in a road check, the person in charge of the vehicle at the time when it is stopped shall be entitled to obtain a written statement of the purpose of the road check if he applies for such a statement not later than the end of the period of twelve months from the day on which the vehicle was stopped.

(16) Nothing in this section affects the exercise by police officers of any power to stop vehicles for purposes other than those specified in subsection (1) above.

Criminal Justice and Public Order Act 1994

Powers of police to stop and search

60. Powers to stop and search in anticipation of violence

(1) Where a police officer of or above the rank of superintendent reasonably believes that—
 (a) incidents involving serious violence may take place in any locality in his area, and
 (b) it is expedient to do so to prevent their occurrence,
he may give an authorisation that the powers to stop and search persons and vehicles conferred by this section shall be exercisable at any place within that locality for a period not exceeding twenty four hours.

(2) The power conferred by subsection (1) above may be exercised by a chief inspector or an inspector if he reasonably believes that incidents involving serious violence are imminent and no superintendent is available.

(3) If it appears to the officer who gave the authorisation or to a superintendent that it is expedient to do so, having regard to offences which have, or are reasonably suspected to have, been committed in connection with any incident falling within the authorisation, he may direct that the authorisation shall continue in being for a further six hours.

(4) This section confers on any constable in uniform power—
 (a) to stop any pedestrian and search him or anything carried by him for offensive weapons or dangerous instruments;
 (b) to stop any vehicle and search the vehicle, its driver and any passenger for offensive weapons or dangerous instruments.

(5) A constable may, in the exercise of those powers, stop any person or vehicle and make any search he thinks fit whether or not he has any grounds for suspecting that the person or vehicle is carrying weapons or articles of that kind.

(6) If in the course of a search under this section a constable discovers a dangerous instrument or an article which he has reasonable grounds for suspecting to be an offensive weapon, he may seize it.

(7) This section applies (with the necessary modifications) to ships, aircraft and hovercraft as it applies to vehicles.

(8) A person who fails to stop or (as the case may be) to stop the vehicle when required to do so by a constable in the exercise of his powers under this section shall be liable on summary conviction to imprisonment for a term not exceeding one month or to a fine not exceeding level 3 on the standard scale or both.

(9) Any authorisation under this section shall be in writing signed by the officer giving it and shall specify the locality in which and the period during which the powers conferred by this section are

exercisable and a direction under subsection (3) above shall also be given in writing or, where that is not practicable, recorded in writing as soon as it is practicable to do so.

(10) Where a vehicle is stopped by a constable under this section, the driver shall be entitled to obtain a written statement that the vehicle was stopped under the powers conferred by this section if he applies for such a statement not later than the end of the period of twelve months from the day on which the vehicle was stopped and similarly as respects a pedestrian who is stopped and searched under this section.

(11) In this section—

    "dangerous instruments" means instruments which have a blade or are sharply pointed;

    "offensive weapon" has the meaning given by section 1(9) of the Police and Criminal Evidence Act 1984; and

    "vehicle" includes a caravan as defined in section 29(1) of the Caravan Sites and Control of Development Act 1960.

(12) The powers conferred by this section are in addition to and not in derogation of, any power otherwise conferred.

NOTES

1. Section 1(8A) of PACE, and the references to it, were added by the Criminal Justice Act 1988, s. 140. Section 139 of the 1988 Act makes it an offence for any person to have with him in a public place any article which has a blade or is sharply pointed (except a folding pocket knife whose blade does not exceed three inches). It is a defence for D to show that he had a good reason or lawful authority, or that he had the article with him for use at work, for religious reasons, or as part of any national costume.

2. Section 5 requires the annual reports of chief officers of police to include information about the number of searches and road checks carried out under ss. 3 and 4. This should facilitate independent scrutiny by police authorities and Inspectors of Constabulary to ensure that the powers are not used randomly. Section 6 enables a 'constable employed by statutory undertakers' (such as railway police) to 'stop, detain and search any vehicle before it leaves a goods area included in the premises of the statutory undertaker'.

For the definitions of 'arrestable offence' and 'serious arrestable offence' (s. 4(4)) see respectively below pp. 104–105 and above, pp. 72–74. At the last minute the House of Commons deleted a House of Lords amendment to the effect that the s. 1 powers could only be exercised by a constable *in uniform*. This issue remains relevant to s. 2(2) and 2(9)(b). Under the Road Traffic Act 1988 s. 6, only a constable 'in uniform' may require a person to provide a specimen of breath for a breath test. Whether a constable is in uniform is a question of fact. In *Wallwork v Giles* [1970] RTR 117, DC, it was held that a constable wearing his uniform except for his helmet was 'in uniform' as he was easily identifiable as a constable. Cf *Taylor v Baldwin* [1976] RTR 265, DC. A court is entitled to assume that a constable is in uniform unless the point is challenged: *Cooper v Rowlands* [1971] RTR 291, DC; *Richards v West* [1980] RTR 215, DC. This limitation also applies to powers under the Criminal Justice and Public Order Act 1994, s. 60.

3. *Stop and search.* Section 1 of PACE extended the powers of the police to stop and search without warrant in a number of important respects. First, it gave power to search for any offensive weapon: previously, there was only a power to search for firearms (Firearms Act 1968, ss. 47(3), 49(1) and (2): these powers continued to be available after the 1984 Act). Secondly, the power to search for stolen goods, previously available in the metropolitan area (Metropolitan Police Act 1839, s. 66) and in a number of other localities in the country (enshrined in local legislation) was extended throughout England and Wales, the earlier legislation being repealed (1984 Act, s. 7). Thirdly, there was a new power to stop and search for equipment used in offences such as burglary (e.g. jemmies or picklocks).

4. The new power conferred by s. 60 of the Criminal Justice and Public Order Act 1994 does not depend on any 'reasonable suspicion' held by the officer conducting the stop-search. The Minister of State at the Home Office, David Maclean MP, stated (241 HC Deb, 12 April 1994, col 69) that the government was:

'persuaded that the need to meet the tests of reasonable suspicion seriously inhibits effective preventive action by the police when they believe that violence is likely to break out.'

The power would, for example, enable the police to search a group of people after a violent incident where there are grounds to believe that some although not all are carrying a weapon (M. Shersby MP, ibid. col 76). Given that the exercise of such a power involves detention while a search is conducted, does this comply with Article 6 of the ECHR and Article 9 of the ICCPR? See also the new power to stop and search to prevent acts of terrorism: below, p. 303.

5. Another important general stop and search power is contained in the Misuse of Drugs Act 1971:

23(2). – If a constable has reasonable grounds to suspect that any person is in possession of a controlled drug in contravention of this Act or of any regulations made thereunder, the constable may—
  (a) search that person, and detain him for the purpose of searching him;
  (b) search any vehicle or vessel in which the constable suspects that the drug may be found, and for that purpose require the person in control of the vehicle or vessel to stop it;
  (c) seize and detain, for the purposes of proceedings under this Act, anything found in the course of the search which appears to the constable to be evidence of an offence under this Act.

In this subsection 'vessel' includes a hovercraft within the meaning of the Hovercraft Act 1968; and nothing in this subsection shall prejudice any power of search or any power to seize or detain property which is exercisable by a constable apart from this subsection.

This power, and certain other stop and search powers (e.g. the Wildlife and Countryside Act 1981, s. 19; the Firearms Act 1968, ss. 47(3), 49(1)(2); the Prevention of Terrorism (Temporary Provisions) Act 1984, Sch. 3, para. 6(1), now the 1989 Act, s. 15(3), below, p. 304) survived the 1984 Act, but are subject to the safeguards set out in s. 2. Note that the requirements of s. 2 operate in respect of *searches* and therefore not where a *stop* does not lead to a search.

6. Section 66 of the Metropolitan Police Act 1839 gave a power to 'stop, search and detain' any person or vehicle on which there was reason to suspect that there was stolen property: this was held to include impliedly a power to detain for questioning (*Daniel v Morrison* (1979) 70 Cr App Rep 142, DC). Section 1, by contrast, gives a power to detain for the express purpose of searching: is there room for an implied power to detain for questioning?

7. The *Code of Practice for the Exercise by Police Officers of Statutory Powers of Stop and Search* (Code A) applies to all stop and search powers except the Aviation Security Act 1982, s. 27(2) (power to search airport employees etc. for stolen goods) and the Police and Criminal Evidence Act 1984, s. 6(1) (powers of constables employed by statutory undertakers).

The Code emphasises that there is no power to stop or detain a person against his will in order to find grounds for a search (Code A.2.1); reasonable grounds cannot be retrospectively provided by questioning during detention (Code A.2.3); every reasonable effort must be made to reduce to the minimum the embarrassment that a person being searched may experience (Code A.3.1); the co-operation of the person to be searched should be sought in every case, even if he initially objects: reasonable force may be used if necessary and only in the last resort (Code A.3.2); the person or vehicle may be detained for a time that is reasonable in all the circumstances, and not beyond the time taken for the search (Code A.3.3); in the case of stop-searches based on reasonable suspicion, the thoroughness and extent of a search must depend on what is suspected of being carried and by whom (ibid.); where on reasonable grounds it is considered necessary to conduct a search more thorough than removal of an outer coat, jacket or gloves, such as removal of a T-shirt or headgear (see s. 2(9)(a)), this should be done out of public view (e.g. in a police van or a nearby police station) (Code A.3.5); any search involving the removal of more than the items specified in s. 2(9)(a) or headgear or footwear may only be made by an officer of the same sex, and may not be made in the presence of anyone of the opposite sex unless requested by the person searched (ibid.); the record should include, in addition to the matters in s. 3(3)–(6), a note of the person's ethnic origin (Code A.4.5); the record of grounds must 'briefly but informatively' explain the reason for suspecting the person concerned, whether by reference to his behaviour or other circumstances or, in the case of searches under the Criminal Justice and Public Order Act 1994, s. 60, or the Prevention of Terrorism (Temporary Provisions) Act 1989, s. 13A, state the authority provided to carry out such a search (Code A.4.7). In the case of enquiries linked to the investigation of terrorism, the officer is to give his warrant number and police station rather than his name (Code A.2.4.(i), 4(5)(x)).

For the Code's provisions as to reasonable grounds see above, p. 72.

The Notes for Guidance state that nothing in the Code affects the routine searching of persons entering sports grounds or other premises with their consent, or as a condition of entry, or the search of a person in the street on a voluntary basis (the officer should always make it clear that he is seeking the co-operation of the person concerned) (Code A.1D).

A failure to give grounds as required by s. 2(3)(c) will render the search unlawful: *R v Fennelley* [1989] Crim LR 142 (Crown Court). However, a failure to make a written record does not: *Basher v DPP* (2 March 1993, unreported, DC), where Waller J also indicated, without deciding the point, that he doubted whether a failure to give the grounds would render the search illegal.

8. Stop and search powers are particularly controversial. A study of stops carried out over a few months in four police stations, two in the provinces and two in the Metropolitan Police District (C. F. Willis, *The Use, Effectiveness and Impact of Police Stop and Search Powers, Research and Planning Unit Paper 15* (Home Office, 1983)), found that blacks, and particularly young black males, were much more likely to be stopped and searched by the police than whites. In provincial forces, stops contributed only a small proportion of arrests, although MPD figures showed that in London arrests from stop-searches made up perhaps as much as half the total arrests for relevant offences. The paper noted that:

'High rates of stopping or searching can have adverse effects on police/public relations, although the giving of clear and reasonable explanations by police officers during the stop is effective in diminishing public resentment of the police action' (p. 22).

A survey in Notting Hill confirmed that 'there was, among those stopped and searched, a generally high level of dissatisfaction with the police action': M. McConville, 'Search of Persons and Premises: New Data from London' [1983] Crim LR 605, 612.[1] Moreover,

---

1 Cf. A. Brogden, ' "Sus" is dead: but what about "Sas"?' Vol. IX No. 1, Spring-Summer 1981, *New Community*, 44–52; PSI Report, *Police and People in London* Vol 1 pp. 89–104; Vol 4 pp. 230–239, 347–350.

'[a]ll the evidence demonstrates that most stop-searches are, on any measure, unproductive. It is, therefore, very difficult to see how the requirement of reasonable suspicion can be made out in most cases.' (McConville, op. cit., p. 613).[1]

The government argued that the Act strengthened the safeguards against discriminatory or excessive searching, emphasising the need for 'reasonable grounds' to suspect that the relevant articles are being carried (see above, p. 72). The Notes for Guidance in Code A remind officers that:

'misuse of the powers is likely to be harmful to the police effort in the long term and can lead to mistrust of the police by the community.'

(Code A.*1A*). Nevertheless, the proportion of recorded stop-searches that result in no arrest has been steadily declining (17.2% to 12.6%, 1986–93) as the number of stop-searches has increased (109,800 to 442,800, 1986–93: see the *Operation of Certain Police Powers under PACE 1993* (HOSB 15/94), Table A. Moreover, there are doubts as to the reliability and helpfulness of the official statistics, given the absence of figures for stops, as distinct from stop-searches, and uncertainties in the categorisation of *voluntary* stops and searches (see the discussion by A. Sanders and R. Young, *Criminal Justice* (1994), pp. 57–62).

9. *Road checks.* Section 163(1) of the Road Traffic Act 1988 provides that:

'A person driving a motor vehicle on a road must stop the vehicle on being required to do so by a constable in uniform.'

Section 163(2) makes similar provision for a person riding a cycle and s. 163(3) makes failure to comply an offence. It has been held that it is not necessary for a constable acting under this section to be 'acting in the execution of his duty under some common law powers. It would seem on the face of it that the constable derives his duty as well as his power from the terms of section 159 [now s. 163] itself' (per Wien J in *Beard v Wood* [1980] RTR 454 at 457–458, DC). Accordingly, a constable may stop a vehicle to check whether the driver has valid documents, even though he has no reasonable grounds to suspect that he does not: (ibid.). However, a constable may not act 'in bad faith' or 'capriciously': ibid. pp. 458, 459: the section does not give a constable 'a power willy-nilly to stop a motor vehicle' (per Eveleigh LJ in *Winter v Barlow* [1980] RTR 209 at 213, DC). See also *Steel v Goacher* [1983] RTR 98, DC, Commentary by D. J. Birch, [1982] Crim LR 689 and D. P. J. Walsh, [1994] Crim LR 187. The result is that a motorist may be stopped more or less at random, provided that it is done for some purpose related to police duties. If the constable reasonably suspects the driver has been drinking the breathalyser legislation will become applicable. Although random *tests* are not permitted, (more or less) random *stops* are (D. J. Birch, op. cit.). This position was confirmed in *Chief Constable of Gwent v Dash* [1986] RTR 41, where the Divisional Court confirmed that random stops made in order to detect whether drivers could be reasonably suspected of having alcohol in their bodies did not as such constitute 'malpractice'. See also *DPP v Wilson* [1991] RTR 284, DC (below, p. 152). The reasonable suspicion may be based on such factors as the manner of driving, the smell of alcohol on the driver's breath (ibid.) or the admission by the driver that he has been drinking (*DPP v McGladrigan* [1991] RTR 297, DC). In the absence of

---

1 Similar points emerge from more recent studies: see K. Bottomley, *et al, The Impact of PACE: Policing in a Northern Force* (1991), Chap. II; C. Norris *et al*, 'Black and Blue: An Analysis of the Influence of Race on Being Stopped by the Police' (1992) 43 BJ Soc 207; W. Skogan, *The Police and Public in England and Wales* (HORS No. 117, 1990); P. Southgate and D. Crisp, *Public Satisfaction with Police Services* (HORPU Paper No. 73, 1993).

reasonable cause, evidence subsequently obtained may be excluded under s. 78 of PACE (*DPP v Godwin* [1991] RTR 303, DC; below, pp. 151–152).

Section 163 is regarded as impliedly imposing a duty on the driver (or cyclist) to remain at rest for a reasonable period after having stopped, to enable the officer to complete any lawful inquiries; however, it does not confer on the officer a power to detain the vehicle for that purpose (*Lodwick v Sanders* [1985] 1 All ER 577; *Sanders v DPP* [1988] Crim LR 605).

When the s. 163 power is used to carry out general road checks the position is governed by s. 4 of the 1984 Act. The number of road checks rose dramatically in 1993 (from 445 in 1992 to 3,560), over 3,200 being conducted in the City of London following increased terrorist activity (HOSB 15/94, Table B). These 'rolling random road blocks' involved 'stretching PACE powers to their limit' (J. Owen (then Commissioner of the City of London Police), 'The IRA Threat to the City of London' (1994) 10 *Policing* 88, 93). The Commissioner subsequently used his powers under s. 12 of the Road Traffic Regulation Act 1984 to restrict vehicle access to the City to eight streets covered by CCTV cameras. This had the incidental effect of helping reduce crime by 17% (*ibid.*, pp. 95–98). See also below, p. 303.

7 Entry, search and seizure

Police and Criminal Evidence Act 1984

PART II

POWERS OF ENTRY, SEARCH AND SEIZURE

Search warrants

8. Power of justice of the peace to authorise entry and search of premises
(1) If on an application made by a constable a justice of the peace is satisfied that there are reasonable grounds for believing—
  (*a*) that a serious arrestable offence has been committed; and
  (*b*) that there is material on premises specified in the application which is likely to be of substantial value (whether by itself or together with other material) to the investigation of the offence; and
  (*c*) that the material is likely to be relevant evidence; and
  (*d*) that it does not consist of or include items subject to legal privilege, excluded material or special procedure material; and
  (*e*) that any of the conditions specified in subsection (3) below applies,
he may issue a warrant authorising a constable to enter and search the premises.
(2) A constable may seize and retain anything for which a search has been authorised under subsection (1) above.
(3) The conditions mentioned in subsection (1)(*e*) above are—
  (*a*) that it is not practicable to communicate with any person entitled to grant entry to the premises;
  (*b*) that it is practicable to communicate with a person entitled to grant entry to the premises but it is not practicable to communicate with any person entitled to grant access to the evidence;
  (*c*) that entry to the premises will not be granted unless a warrant is produced;
  (*d*) that the purpose of a search may be frustrated or seriously prejudiced unless a constable arriving at the premises can secure immediate entry to them.
(4) In this Act 'relevant evidence' in relation to an offence, means anything that would be admissible in evidence at a trial for the offence.
(5) The power to issue a warrant conferred by this section is in addition to any such power otherwise conferred.

9. Special provisions as to access
(1) A constable may obtain access to excluded material or special procedure material for the purposes of a criminal investigation by making an application under Schedule 1 below and in accordance with the Schedule.

(2) Any Act (including a local Act) passed before this Act under which a search of premises for the purposes of a criminal investigation could be authorised by the issue of a warrant to a constable shall cease to have effect so far as it relates to authorisation of searches—

(a) for items subject to legal privilege; or

(b) for excluded material; or

(c) for special procedure material consisting of documents or records other than documents.

10. Meaning of 'items subject to legal privilege'

(1) Subject to subsection (2) below, in this Act 'items subject to legal privilege' means—

(a) communications between a professional legal adviser and his client or any person representing his client made in connection with the giving of legal advice to the client;

(b) communications between a professional legal adviser and his client or any person representing his client or between such an adviser or his client or any such representative and any other person made in connection with or in contemplation of legal proceedings and for the purposes of such proceedings; and

(c) items enclosed with or referred to in such communications and made—

(i) in connection with the giving of legal advice; or

(ii) in connection with or in contemplation of legal proceedings and for the purposes of such proceedings,

when they are in the possession of a person who is entitled to possession of them.

(2) Items held with the intention of furthering a criminal purpose are not items subject to legal privilege.

11. Meaning of 'excluded material'

(1) Subject to the following provisions of this section, in this Act 'excluded material' means—

(a) personal records which a person has acquired or created in the course of any trade, business, profession or other occupation or for the purposes of any paid or unpaid office and which he holds in confidence;

(b) human tissue or tissue fluid which has been taken for the purposes of diagnosis or medical treatment and which a person holds in confidence;

(c) journalistic material which a person holds in confidence and which consists—

(i) of documents; or

(ii) of records other than documents.

(2) A person holds material other than journalistic material in confidence for the purposes of this section if he holds it subject—

(a) to an express or implied undertaking to hold it in confidence; or

(b) to a restriction on disclosure or an obligation of secrecy contained in any enactment, including an enactment contained in an Act passed after this Act.

(3) A person holds journalistic material in confidence for the purposes of this section if—

(a) he holds it subject to such an undertaking, restriction or obligation; and

(b) it has been continuously held (by one or more persons) subject to such an undertaking, restriction or obligation since it was first acquired or created for the purposes of journalism.

12. Meaning of 'personal records'

In this Part of this Act 'personal records' means documentary and other records concerning an individual (whether living or dead) who can be identified from them and relating—

(a) to his physical or mental health;

(b) to spiritual counselling or assistance given or to be given to him; or

(c) to counselling or assistance given or to be given to him, for the purposes of his personal welfare, by any voluntary organisation or by any individual who—

(i) by reason of his office or occupation has responsibilities for his personal welfare; or

(ii) by reason of an order of a court has responsibilities for his supervision.

13. Meaning of 'journalistic material'

(1) Subject to subsection (2) below, in this Act 'journalistic material' means material acquired or created for the purposes of journalism.

(2) Material is only journalistic material for the purposes of this Act if it is in the possession of a person who acquired or created it for the purposes of journalism.

(3) A person who receives material from someone who intends that the recipient shall use it for the purposes of journalism is to be taken to have acquired it for those purposes.

14. Meaning of 'special procedure material'

(1) In this Act 'special procedure material' means—

    (*a*) material to which subsection (2) below applies; and

    (*b*) journalistic material, other than excluded material.

(2) Subject to the following provisions of this section, this subsection applies to material, other than items subject to legal privilege and excluded material, in the possession of a person who—

    (*a*) acquired or created it in the course of any trade, business, profession or other occupation or for the purpose of any paid or unpaid office; and

    (*b*) holds it subject—

        (i) to an express or implied undertaking to hold it in confidence; or

        (ii) to a restriction or obligation such as is mentioned in section 11(2)(*b*) above.

(3) Where material is acquired—

    (*a*) by an employee from his employer and in the course of his employment; or

    (*b*) by a company from an associated company,

it is only special procedure material if it was special procedure material immediately before the acquisition.

(4) Where material is created by an employee in the course of his employment, it is only special procedure material if it would have been special procedure material had his employer created it.

(5) Where material is created by a company on behalf of an associated company, it is only special procedure material if it would have been special procedure material had the associated company created it.

(6) A company is to be treated as another's associated company for the purposes of this section if it would be so treated under section 302 of the Income and Corporation Taxes Act 1970.

15. Search warrants—safeguards

(1) This section and section 16 below have effect in relation to the issue to constables under any enactment, including an enactment contained in an Act passed after this Act, of warrants to enter and search premises; and an entry on or search of premises under a warrant is unlawful unless it complies with this section and section 16 below.

(2) Where a constable applies for any such warrant, it shall be his duty—

    (*a*) to state—

        (i) the ground on which he makes the application; and

        (ii) the enactment under which the warrant would be issued;

    (*b*) to specify the premises which it is desired to enter and search; and

    (*c*) to identify, so far as is practicable, the articles or persons to be sought.

(3) An application for such a warrant shall be made ex parte and supported by an information in writing.

(4) The constable shall answer on oath any question that the justice of the peace or judge hearing the application asks him.

(5) A warrant shall authorise an entry on one occasion only.

(6) A warrant—

    (*a*) shall specify—

        (i) the name of the person who applies for it;

        (ii) the date on which it is issued;

        (iii) the enactment under which it is issued; and

        (iv) the premises to be searched; and

    (*b*) shall identify, so far as is practicable, the articles or persons to be sought.

(7) Two copies shall be made of a warrant.

(8) The copies shall be clearly certified as copies.

16. Execution of warrants

(1) A warrant to enter and search premises may be executed by any constable.

(2) Such a warrant may authorise persons to accompany any constable who is executing it.

(3) Entry and search under a warrant must be within one month from the date of its issue.

(4) Entry and search under a warrant must be at a reasonable hour unless it appears to the constable executing it that the purpose of a search may be frustrated on an entry at a reasonable hour.

(5) Where the occupier of premises which are to be entered and searched is present at the time when a constable seeks to execute a warrant to enter and search them, the constable—

    (*a*) shall identify himself to the occupier and, if not in uniform, shall produce to him documentary evidence that he is a constable;

    (*b*) shall produce the warrant to him; and

    (*c*) shall supply him with a copy of it.

(6) Where—
   (a) the occupier of such premises is not present at the time when a constable seeks to execute such a warrant; but
   (b) some other person who appears to the constable to be in charge of the premises is present,
subsection (5) above shall have effect as if any reference to the occupier were a reference to that other person.

(7) If there is no person present who appears to the constable to be in charge of the premises, he shall leave a copy of the warrant in a prominent place on the premises.

(8) A search under a warrant may only be a search to the extent required for the purpose of which the warrant was issued.

(9) A constable executing a warrant shall make an endorsement on it stating—
   (a) whether the articles or persons sought were found; and
   (b) whether any articles were seized, other than articles which were sought.

(10) A warrant which—
   (a) has been executed; or
   (b) has not been executed within the time authorised for its execution,
shall be returned—
   (i) if it was issued by a justice of the peace, to the clerk to the justices for the petty sessions area for which he acts; and
   (ii) if it was issued by a judge, to the appropriate officer of the court from which he issued it.

(11) A warrant which is returned under subsection (10) above shall be retained for 12 months from its return—
   (a) by the clerk to the justices, if it was returned under paragraph (i) of that subsection; and
   (b) by the appropriate officer, if it was returned under paragraph (ii).

(12) If during the period for which a warrant is to be retained the occupier of the premises to which it relates asks to inspect it, he shall be allowed to do so.

Entry and search without search warrant

17. Entry for purpose of arrest etc

(1) Subject to the following provisions of this section, and without prejudice to any other enactment, a constable may enter and search premises for the purpose—
   (a) of executing—
      (i) a warrant of arrest issued in connection with or arising out of criminal proceedings; or
      (ii) a warrant of commitment issued under section 76 of the Magistrates' Courts Act 1980;
   (b) of arresting a person for an arrestable offence;
   (c) of arresting a person for an offence under—
      (i) section 1 (prohibition of uniforms in connection with political objects) [. . .] of the Public Order Act 1936;
      (ii) any enactment contained in sections 6 to 8 or 10 of the Criminal Law Act 1977 (offences relating to entering and remaining on property);
      [(iii) section 4 of the Public Order Act 1986 (fear or provocation of violence);][1]
      [(iv) section 76 of the Criminal Justice and Public Order Act 1994 (failure to comply with interim possession order);][2]
   (d) of recapturing a person who is unlawfully at large and whom he is pursuing; or
   (e) of saving life or limb or preventing serious damage to property.

(2) Except for the purpose specified in paragraph (e) of subsection (1) above, the powers of entry and search conferred by this section—
   (a) are only exercisable if the constable has reasonable grounds for believing that the person whom he is seeking is on the premises; and
   (b) are limited, in relation to premises consisting of two or more separate dwellings, to powers to enter and search—
      (i) any parts of the premises which the occupiers of any dwelling comprised in the premises use in common with the occupiers of any other such dwelling; and
      (ii) any such dwelling in which the constable has reasonable grounds for believing that the person whom he is seeking may be.

(3) The powers of entry and search conferred by this section are only exercisable for the purposes specified in subsection (1)(c)(ii) [or (iv)][2] above by a constable in uniform.

---

1 Inserted by the 1986 Act, s. 40, Sch. 2, para. 7.
2 Inserted by the Criminal Justice and Public Order Act 1994, Sch. 10, para. 53.

(4) The power of search conferred by this section is only a power to search to the extent that is reasonably required for the purpose for which the power of entry is exercised.

(5) Subject to subsection (6) below, all the rules of common law under which a constable has power to enter premises without a warrant are hereby abolished.

(6) Nothing in subsection (5) above affects any power of entry to deal with or prevent a breach of the peace.

18. Entry and search after arrest

(1) Subject to the following provisions of this section, a constable may enter and search any premises occupied or controlled by a person who is under arrest for an arrestable offence, if he has reasonable grounds for suspecting that there is on the premises evidence, other than items subject to legal privilege, that relates—

    (*a*) to that offence; or

    (*b*) to some other arrestable offence which is connected with or similar to that offence.

(2) A constable may seize and retain anything for which he may search under subsection (1) above.

(3) The power to search conferred by subsection (1) above is only a power to search to the extent that is reasonably required for the purpose of discovering such evidence.

(4) Subject to subsection (5) below, the powers conferred by this section may not be exercised unless an officer of the rank of inspector or above has authorised them in writing.

(5) A constable may conduct a search under subsection (1) above—

    (*a*) before taking the person to a police station; and

    (*b*) without obtaining an authorisation under subsection (4) above,

if the presence of that person at a place other than a police station is necessary for the effective investigation of the offence.

(6) If a constable conducts a search by virtue of subsection (5) above, he shall inform an officer of the rank of inspector or above that he has made the search as soon as practicable after he has made it.

(7) An officer who—

    (*a*) authorises a search; or

    (*b*) is informed of a search under subsection (6) above,

shall make a record in writing—

    (i) of the grounds for the search; and

    (ii) of the nature of the evidence that was sought.

(8) If the person who was in occupation or control of the premises at the time of the search is in police detention at the time the record is to be made, the officer shall make the record as part of his custody report.

Seizure etc

19. General power of seizure etc

(1) The powers conferred by subsections (2), (3) and (4) below are exercisable by a constable who is lawfully on any premises.

(2) The constable may seize anything which is on the premises if he has reasonable grounds for believing—

    (*a*) that it has been obtained in consequence of the commission of an offence; and

    (*b*) that it is necessary to seize it in order to prevent it being concealed, lost, damaged, altered or destroyed.

(3) The constable may seize anything which is on the premises if he has reasonable grounds for believing—

    (*a*) that it is evidence in relation to an offence which he is investigating or any other offence; and

    (*b*) that it is necessary to seize the evidence in order to prevent it being concealed, lost, altered or destroyed.

(4) The constable may require any information which is contained in a computer and is accessible from the premises to be produced in a form in which it can be taken away and in which it is visible and legible if he has reasonable grounds for believing—

    (*a*) that—

        (i) it is evidence in relation to an offence which he is investigating or any other offence; or

        (ii) it has been obtained in consequence of the commission of an offence; and

    (*b*) that it is necessary to do so in order to prevent it being concealed, lost, tampered with or destroyed.

(5) The powers conferred by this section are in addition to any power otherwise conferred.

(6) No power of seizure conferred on a constable under any enactment (including an enactment contained in an Act passed after this Act) is to be taken to authorise the seizure of an item which the constable exercising the power has reasonable grounds for suspecting to be subject to legal privilege.

20. Extension of powers of seizure to computerised information

(1) Every power of seizure which is conferred by an enactment to which this section applies on a constable who has entered premises in the exercise of a power conferred by an enactment shall be construed as including a power to require any information contained in a computer and accessible from the premises to be produced in a form in which it can be taken away and in which it is visible and legible.

(2) This section applies—

    (a) to any enactment contained in an Act passed before this Act;

    (b) to sections 8 and 18 above;

    (c) to paragraph 13 of Schedule 1 to this Act; and

    (d) to any enactment contained in an Act passed after this Act.

21. Access and copying

(1) A constable who seizes anything in the exercise of a power conferred by any enactment, including an enactment contained in an Act passed after this Act, shall, if so requested by a person showing himself—

    (a) to be the occupier of premises on which it was seized; or

    (b) to have had custody or control of it immediately before the seizure,

provide that person with a record of what he seized.

(2) The officer shall provide the record within a reasonable time from the making of the request for it.

(3) Subject to subsection (8) below, if a request for permission to be granted access to anything which—

    (a) has been seized by a constable; and

    (b) is retained by the police for the purpose of investigating an offence,

is made to the officer in charge of the investigation by a person who had custody or control of the thing immediately before it was so seized or by someone acting on behalf of such a person, the officer shall allow the person who made the request access to it under the supervision of a constable.

(4) Subject to subsection (8) below, if a request for a photograph or copy of any such thing is made to the officer in charge of the investigation by a person who had custody or control of the thing immediately before it was so seized, or by someone acting on behalf of such a person, the officer shall—

    (a) allow the person who made the request access to it under the supervision of a constable for the purpose of photographing or copying it; or

    (b) photograph or copy it, or cause it to be photographed or copied.

(5) A constable may also photograph or copy, or have photographed or copied, anything which he has power to seize, without a request being made under subsection (4) above.

(6) Where anything is photographed or copied under subsection (4)(b) above, the photograph or copy shall be supplied to the person who made the request.

(7) The photograph or copy shall be so supplied within a reasonable time from the making of the request.

(8) There is no duty under this section to grant access to, or to supply a photograph or copy of, anything if the officer in charge of the investigation for the purposes of which it was seized has reasonable grounds for believing that to do so would prejudice—

    (a) that investigation;

    (b) the investigation of an offence other than the offence for the purposes of investigating which the thing was seized; or

    (c) any criminal proceedings which may be brought as a result of—

        (i) the investigation of which he is in charge; or

        (ii) any such investigation as is mentioned in paragraph (b) above.

22. Retention

(1) Subject to subsection (4) below, anything which has been seized by a constable or taken away by a constable following a requirement made by virtue of section 19 or 20 above may be retained so long as is necessary in all the circumstances.

(2) Without prejudice to the generality of subsection (1) above—

    (a) anything seized for the purposes of criminal investigation may be retained, except as provided by subsection (4) below,—

        (i) for use as evidence at a trial for an offence; or

        (ii) for forensic examination or for investigation in connection with an offence; and

    (b) anything may be retained in order to establish its lawful owner, where there are reasonable grounds for believing that it has been obtained in consequence of the commission of an offence.

(3) Nothing seized on the ground that it may be used—

    (a) to cause physical injury to any person;

    (b) to damage property;

    (c) to interfere with evidence; or

    (d) to assist in escape from police detention or lawful custody, may be retained when the person from whom it was seized is no longer in police detention or the custody of a court or is in the custody of a court but has been released on bail.

(4) Nothing may be retained for either of the purposes mentioned in subsection (2)(*a*) above if a photograph or copy would be sufficient for that purpose.

(5) Nothing in this section affects any power of a court to make an order under section 1 of the Police (Property) Act 1897.

Part II—Supplementary

23. Interpretation

In this Act—

'premises' includes any place and, in particular, includes—

(*a*) any vehicle, vessel, aircraft or hovercraft;

(*b*) any offshore installation; and

(*c*) any tent or movable structure; and

'offshore installation' has the meaning given to it by section 1 of the Mineral Workings (Offshore Installations) Act 1971.

SCHEDULE 1

SPECIAL PROCEDURE

Making of orders by circuit judge

1. If on an application made by a constable a circuit judge is satisfied that one or other of the sets of access conditions is fulfilled, he may make an order under paragraph 4 below.

2. The first set of access conditions is fulfilled if—

(*a*) there are reasonable grounds for believing—

(i) that a serious arrestable offence has been committed;

(ii) that there is material which consists of special procedure material or includes special procedure material and does not also include excluded material on premises specified in the application;

(iii) that the material is likely to be of substantial value (whether by itself or together with other material) to the investigation in connection with which the application is made; and

(iv) that the material is likely to be relevant evidence;

(*b*) other methods of obtaining the material—

(i) have been tried without success; or

(ii) have not been tried because it appeared that they were bound to fail; and

(*c*) it is in the public interest, having regard—

(i) to the benefit likely to accrue to the investigation if the material is obtained; and

(ii) to the circumstances under which the person in possession of the material holds it, that the material should be produced or that access to it should be given.

3. The second set of access conditions is fulfilled if—

(*a*) there are reasonable grounds for believing that there is material which consists of or includes excluded material or special procedure material on premises specified in the application;

(*b*) but for section 9(2) above a search of the premises for that material could have been authorised by the issue of a warrant to a constable under an enactment other than this Schedule; and

(*c*) the issue of such a warrant would have been appropriate.

4. An order under this paragraph is an order that the person who appears to the circuit judge to be in possession of the material to which the application relates shall—

(*a*) produce it to a constable for him to take away; or

(*b*) give a constable access to it,

not later than the end of the period of seven days from the date of the order or the end of such longer period as the order may specify.

5. Where the material consists of information contained in a computer,

(*a*) an order under paragraph 4(*a*) above shall have effect as an order to produce the material in a form in which it can be taken away and in which it is visible and legible; and

(*b*) an order under paragraph 4(*b*) above shall have effect as an order to give a constable access to the material in a form in which it is visible and legible.

6. For the purposes of sections 21 and 22 above material produced in pursuance of an order under paragraph 4(*a*) above shall be treated as if it were material seized by a constable.

Notices of applications for orders

7. An application for an order under paragraph 4 above shall be made inter partes. . . .

11. Where notice of an application for an order under paragraph 4 above has been served on a person, he shall not conceal, destroy, alter or dispose of the material to which the application relates except—
  (a) with the leave of a judge; or
  (b) with the written permission of a constable,
until—
  (i) the application is dismissed or abandoned; or
  (ii) he has complied with an order under paragraph 4 above made on the application.

Issue of warrants by circuit judge

12. If on an application made by a constable a circuit judge—
  (a) is satisfied—
    (i) that either set of access conditions is fulfilled; and
    (ii) that any of the further conditions set out in paragraph 14 below is also fulfilled; or
  (b) is satisfied—
    (i) that the second set of access conditions is fulfilled; and
    (ii) that an order under paragraph 4 above relating to the material has not been complied with,
he may issue a warrant authorising a constable to enter and search the premises.
13. A constable may seize and retain anything for which a search has been authorised under paragraph 12 above.
14. The further conditions mentioned in paragraph 12(a)(ii) above are—
  (a) that it is not practicable to communicate with any person entitled to grant entry to the premises to which the application relates;
  (b) that it is practicable to communicate with a person entitled to grant entry to the premises but it is not practicable to communicate with any person entitled to grant access to the material;
  (c) that the material contains information which—
    (i) is subject to a restriction or obligation such as is mentioned in section 11(2)(b) above; and
    (ii) is likely to be disclosed in breach of it if a warrant is not issued;
  (d) that service of notice of an application for an order under paragraph 4 above may seriously prejudice the investigation.
15.—(1) If a person fails to comply with an order under paragraph 4 above, a circuit judge may deal with him as if he had committed a contempt of the Crown Court. . . .

NOTES

1. *The common law background.* Part II of PACE extended police powers in a number of significant respects. At common law there was no general power to enter premises to search for evidence, and there was no general power to obtain warrants to authorise such searches, although there were some specific powers. Lord Denning MR noted in *Ghani v Jones* [1970] 1 QB 693, CA, that there was no power to search premises for evidence of murder. There was a power to search the premises of a person arrested there (perhaps only in his immediate vicinity) but it had to be exercised contemporaneously with the arrest (*McLorie v Oxford* [1982] QB 1290, DC). If the police were lawfully on premises, whether by consent or in the execution of a warrant or a power to enter premises without a warrant, the decision in *Ghani v Jones* [1970] 1 QB 693, CA, authorised the seizure of a wide range of material (see the first edition of this book at pp. 94–103), the ambit of the power to *seize* being wider than the powers of entry and search. The RCCP supported the extension of powers along the lines of Part II although they would have applied the special procedure involving a circuit judge to all warrants to search for evidence, and confined the power to 'grave offences' (cf. above, p. 72).
2. The main features of Part II of PACE were (1) new general powers to search for evidence (ss. 8–14 and Sch. 1); (2) provisions applying generally to search warrants (ss. 15, 16); (3) general powers of entry (s. 17); (4) a power to enter and search after arrest (s. 18); and (5) general powers of seizure (s. 19).

3. *General powers to obtain evidence.* Generally speaking, the police no longer can have direct access to items subject to legal privilege (s. 9(2)(a)). Access to excluded or special procedure material can only be authorised under s. 9(1) and Sch. 1. Of these two classes, excluded material is regarded as more sensitive, and may only be the subject of an order or warrant under Sch. 1 if, but for s. 9(2), a warrant could have been used under a pre-existing power. (See *R v Central Criminal Court, ex p Brown* (1992) Times, 7 September, DC, where it was held that no production order could be made in respect of a medical report from a hospital administration for a murder investigation as no warrant could have been issued for its seizure prior to PACE.) This restriction does not apply to special procedure material, and orders or warrants for the production of such material are much more common: see K. Lidstone, (1989) 40 NILQ 333, 344 n. 35, reporting on a survey, to which 39 of the 43 police forces of England and Wales responded, which showed that over 2,000 orders or warrants had been granted under the first set of access conditions, but only nine under the second set. Lidstone also notes that 'mortgage frauds were almost impossible to investigate before 1984, there being no legal machinery for obtaining access to material relating to such frauds held by solicitors, building societies, estate agents and the like' (ibid., p. 342 n. 29). In a survey of two forces, s. 8 had been rarely used (ibid., p. 334).

Excluded or special procedure material can be seized during the course of a search under post-arrest powers (ss. 18, 32), or under any other warranted search and whenever a constable is lawfully on premises and comes across such material (s. 19): see Lidstone, op. cit., p. 342, n. 28. In a survey of two city forces involving over 860 searches of premises, 12% were conducted under a judicial warrant and 87% under post-arrest powers (75% under s. 18, 2% under s. 32, and 6% following an entry to arrest under s. 17): Lidstone, op. cit., p. 355, n. 67. There appears to be a steady decline in the use of warrants (ibid. p. 362, n. 87). Excluded material can also be disclosed voluntarily by the maker or holder independently of s. 9(1) and Sch. 1: *R v Singleton* [1995] 1 Cr App Rep 431, CA (Cr D) (dental records).

4. The new powers to grant warrants to search for evidence under ss. 8 and 9 of PACE (and associated provisions) have given rise to a series of cases raising both procedural and substantive issues. Thus, it has been held that the material in question must be specified, either in the notice of application or otherwise: *R v Central Criminal Court, ex p Adegbesan* [1986] 1 WLR 1292; *R v Crown Court at Manchester, ex p Taylor* [1988] 1 WLR 705; but the evidence on which the application is based need not: *R v Crown Court at Inner London Sessions, ex p Baines & Baines* [1988] QB 579; cf. *R v Central Criminal Court, ex p AJD Holdings Ltd* [1992] Crim LR 669 (warrant quashed where its terms went beyond those of the sworn information on which it was based and where it would have been 'practicable' to identify the articles sought with much greater precision) and *R v Southampton Crown Court, ex p J and P* [1993] Crim LR 962 (warrants to search solicitors' premises quashed as they were wider than justified by the investigation, the judge had failed to consider the issue of legal privilege and the use of the ex parte procedure was not justified). The suspect need not be notified by the applicant if he is not the holder of the material: *R v Crown Court at Leicester, ex p DPP* [1987] 1 WLR 1371, and a bank is not impliedly under a contractual duty to notify its client or to contest the application: *Barclays Bank plc v Taylor* [1989] 3 All ER 563. This position is strongly criticised by A. A. S. Zuckerman, [1990] Crim LR 472, on the ground that the person most affected by the order is not given the opportunity to challenge it, and that if there is a risk that that person would impede or frustrate the order if he were given notice, the warrant procedure is available under Sch. 1, paras. 12–14.

As to substantive matters arising under Sch. 1, in *R v Crown Court at Bristol, ex p Bristol Press and Picture Agency Ltd* (1986) 85 Cr App Rep 190, the Divisional Court upheld the decision of Stuart-Smith J to order the applicant to produce press photographs taken during the 1986 riots in the St. Pauls area of Bristol. This was special procedure material and the first set of access conditions in Sch. 1 were applied. The court held that the judge had been entitled to conclude that there were reasonable grounds to believe that the material was 'likely to be of substantial value . . . to the investigation in connection with which the application was made' and 'likely to be relevant evidence' (para. 2(a)(iii), (iv)), notwithstanding that it could not identify any particular photograph as relating to any particular incident of violence or other criminal offence; it was likely that the press would attempt to photograph 'newsworthy' incidents, some at least relating to the actions of those engaged in violence. As to the public interest under para. 2(c), the judge was entitled to conclude that the public interest in the conviction of those guilty of serious crimes here required an access order to be made. He had taken into account the applicant's arguments that allowing access would compromise the impartiality of the press and increase the risk of injury to photographers, but had concluded (1) that the former was not undermined, given that the press would not be handing over the material voluntarily but only in response to a court order; and (2) that any risk of injury to a photographer would arise from the attackers' wish not to appear on the transmitted part of the news rather than the untransmitted part (see R. T. H. Stone, [1988] Crim LR 498, 500–501). Stone comments (ibid.):

'Once the police have established that there are reasonable grounds for believing that serious arrestable offences have occurred, and that the material they are seeking is likely to be relevant evidence, it is difficult to imagine circumstances where a court is going to be prepared to refuse access.'

See also *R v Central Criminal Court, ex p Carr* (1987) Independent, 5 March and *R v Crown Court at Maidstone, ex p Waitt* [1988] Crim LR 384, (1988) Times, 4 January, also discussed by Stone, op. cit.; *R v Crown Court at Lewes, ex p Hill* (1990) 93 Cr App Rep 60; *R v Crown Court at Leeds, ex p Switalski* [1991] Crim LR 559; *R v Crown Court at Northampton, ex p DPP* (1991) 93 Cr App Rep 376; *R v Liverpool Crown Court, ex p George Wimpey plc* [1991] Crim LR 635; *R v Acton Crown Court, ex p Layton* [1993] Crim LR 458. In *ex p Waitt*, Macpherson J stated that Sch. 1 constitutes:

'a serious inroad upon the liberty of the subject. The responsibility for ensuring that the procedure is not abused lies with circuit judges. It is of cardinal importance that circuit judges should be scrupulous in discharging that responsibility.'

On s. 8, see *R v Billericay Justices and Dobbyn, ex p Frank Harris (Coaches) Ltd* [1991] Crim LR 472, where the Divisional Court held that, unlike the position under s. 9, it was not a condition precedent to the granting of a warrant that other methods had been tried without success or would be bound to fail.

5. Hospital records of patients' admission to and discharge from a mental hospital are 'personal records' within PACE, s. 12, as they are records 'relating to' their mental health: *R v Cardiff Crown Court, ex p Kellam* (1993) 16 BMLR 76, DC.

6. By s. 10(2), 'items held with the intention of furthering a criminal purpose are not items subject to legal privilege'. In *R v Central Criminal Court, ex p Francis & Francis* [1989] AC 346, the House of Lords held by three to two (Lords Brandon, Griffiths and Goff, Lords Bridge and Oliver dissenting) that this exception (applied by the Drug Trafficking Offences Act 1986, s. 129(2)) takes effect even where the intention is that of a third party, and is not shared by either the solicitor holding the items in question or his client. Thus, production was ordered of documents held by solicitors relating to property transactions suspected to have been used by a relative of the client as a means of laundering the proceeds of drug trafficking. The majority argued that a construction that limited s. 10(2) to cases where the holder was party to the intention would lead to absurd consequences; as cases of solicitors having such an intention were 'happily rare' this 'would do little to assist' in achieving the purpose of Pt II of PACE (per Lord Brandon at p. 381). The minority argued, with some force, that the majority's interpretation could not be the grammatical meaning of the words actually used by Parliament.

An item is covered by legal professional privilege if it is a communication made in connection with the giving of advice; records of conveyancing transactions are themselves, accordingly, not privileged, although correspondence containing advice relating to such transactions would be: *R v Crown Court at Inner London Sessions, ex p Baines & Baines* [1988] QB 579. See also *R v Guildhall Magistrates' Court, ex p Primlaks Holdings Co (Panama) Inc* [1990] 1 QB 261. In *R v R* [1994] 1 WLR 758, CA (Cr D), it was held that a blood sample provided by the defendant to his doctor at the request of his solicitors for the purposes of his defence was an item subject to legal privilege.

An item not protected by legal professional privilege as a result of s. 10(2) (and so not immune from seizure) is nevertheless likely to be special procedure material, and so only obtainable via s. 9 and Sch. 1: *ex p Primlaks, supra*. However, forged material can neither be covered by legal privilege nor acquired or created in the course of the profession of a solicitor so as to be special procedure material: *R v Leeds Magistrates' Court, ex p Dumbleton* [1993] Crim LR 866.

7. Sections 55 to 57 of the Drug Trafficking Act 1994 authorise a circuit judge to make an order for the production of material which may be relevant to drug trafficking: there must be reasonable grounds for suspecting that a specified person has carried on or benefited from drug trafficking; that the material is likely to be of substantial value to the investigation and does not include items subject to legal privilege or excluded material; and that production is in the public interest. A search warrant may be granted if a production order is not complied with or such an order would be impractical or inappropriate for one or more specified reasons. See also the Prevention of Terrorism (Temporary Provisions) Act 1989, Sch. 7.

8. *Specific powers to obtain search warrants.* There are many specific powers whereby a court, judge or magistrate may issue a search warrant in respect of an offence. They have different limitations as to the geographical area for which a warrant may be granted, the persons who may execute the warrant, and the items which may be seized. The safeguards and other provisions relating to execution contained in ss. 15 and 16 are applicable to all these powers, thus removing some of these variations. See generally, D. Feldman, *The Law Relating to Entry, Search and Seizure* (1986); R. T. H. Stone, *Entry, Search and Seizure: A Guide to Civil and Criminal Powers of Entry* (2nd edn, 1989).

Examples include the following:

Theft Act 1968

26.—(1) If it is made to appear by information on oath before a justice of the peace that there is reasonable cause to believe that any person has in his custody or possession or on his premises any stolen goods, the justice may grant a warrant to search for and seize the same; but no warrant to search for stolen goods shall be addressed to a person other than a constable except under the authority of an enactment expressly so providing. . . .

(3) Where under this section a person is authorised to search premises for stolen goods, he may enter and search the premises accordingly, and may seize any goods he believes to be stolen goods.

Subsection (3) goes beyond the *ratio* of *Chic Fashions (West Wales) Ltd v Jones* (above, pp. 46–47). It is not clear whether it is an exhaustive statement of the items that may be seized under a warrant in addition to those specified in it. At common law a constable executing a warrant to search for stolen goods could seize items '- likely to furnish evidence of' the identity of the specified stolen goods (*Crozier v Cundey* (1827) 6 B & C 232) as well as goods 'reasonably believed' to be those specified in the warrant (*Chic Fashions*, above, pp. 46–47).

Misuse of Drugs Act 1971

23. Powers to search and obtain evidence
(1) A constable or other person authorised in that behalf by a general or special order of the Secretary of State . . . shall, for the purposes of the execution of this Act, have power to enter the premises of a person carrying on business as a producer or supplier of any controlled drugs and to demand the production of, and to inspect, any books or documents relating to dealings in any such drugs and to inspect any stocks of any such drugs.
(2) (*Given above at p. 82*)
(3) If a justice of the peace . . . is satisfied by information on oath that there is reasonable ground for suspecting—
  (a) that any controlled drugs are, in contravention of this Act or of any regulations made thereunder, in the possession of a person on any premises; or
  (b) that a document directly or indirectly relating to, or connected with, a transaction or dealing which was, or an intended transaction or dealing which would if carried out be, an offence under this Act, or in the case of a transaction or dealing carried out or intended to be carried out in a place outside the United Kingdom, an offence against the provisions of a corresponding law in force in that place, is in the possession of a person on any premises,
he may grant a warrant authorising any constable acting for the police area in which the premises are situated at any time or times within one month from the date of the warrant, to enter, if need be by force, the premises named in the warrant, and to search the premises and any persons found therein and, if there is reasonable ground for suspecting that an offence under this Act has been committed in relation to any controlled drugs found on the premises or in the possession of any such person, or that a document so found is such a document as is mentioned in paragraph (b) above, to seize and detain those drugs or that document, as the case may be. . . .

Note that sub-s. (3) expressly empowers a justice to issue a warrant authorising the search of *persons* found on the premises specified. In *King v R* [1969] 1 AC 304, the Privy Council held that the search of persons by virtue of a warrant granted under similar Jamaican legislation was not lawful unless the *warrant* expressly authorised such a search. Not all search warrant provisions refer expressly to authority to search persons. Is it proper to assume that these different formulations have been adopted deliberately by Parliament, so as to deny the police power to search persons under a warrant unless both the relevant statutory provisions and the warrant expressly authorise such search?

9. *The role of magistrates*. The assumption behind the requirement that warrants must in many cases be obtained from a magistrate is that this operates as a safeguard. In February 1968 four police officers went to the home of Lady Diana Cooper and executed a warrant to search for drugs. The police had acted on an anonymous telephone call. The matter was raised in Parliament (760 HC Deb 7 March 1968 cols 826–836). The Under Secretary of State for the Home Department, Mr Dick Taverne, acknowledged that a serious mistake had been made in relying on the anonymous call. There should have been an attempt to find corroborative evidence.

Following this case guidance was issued as set out in paragraph 40 of the *Home Office Evidence to the Royal Commission on Criminal Procedure, Memorandum No. III*:

'40. The decision whether or not to issue a search warrant is a matter for the magistrate concerned. The Lord Chancellor has advised those responsible for the training of Justices of the Peace that:

a. it is the duty of a magistrate before issuing a warrant to satisfy himself that it is in all the circumstances right to issue the warrant;

b. a magistrate may question the person swearing the information to this end; and

c. although a police officer who applies for a warrant should not be expected to identify his informant, the magistrate may wish to know whether the informant is known to the officer, and whether it has been possible to make further enquiries to verify the information and, if so, with what result.

Chief officers of police have been informed that this advice has been given. . . .'

A survey conducted by the Centre for Criminological and Socio-Legal Studies at the University of Sheffield indicated that 'magistrates are not at present the safeguard which constitutional theory supposes them to be' (K. Lidstone, 'Magistrates, Police and Search Warrants' [1984] Crim LR 449). Only rarely was any solid information supplied by the police, and it did not seem that questioning by magistrates was at all intensive. Most seemed unwilling to go behind assertions on oath by police officers that they had reasonable grounds for suspicion 'as a result of information from a source which is reliable.' Lidstone (p. 457) suggested that this could 'be changed by better training and the provisions of the Police and Criminal Evidence Bill could ensure that fuller information is provided.' Evidence from a later study by the same author 'suggests that this formula continues to be used, though less frequently, and that magistrates are no more questioning now than they were before the Act.' (Lidstone, (1989) 40 NILQ 333, 351 n. 55.)

10. *The execution of warrants: PACE Code requirements.* The *Code of Practice for the Searching of Premises by Police Officers and the Seizure of Property found by Police Officers on Persons or Premises* (PACE Code B; Revised Edition, 1995) applies to (a) searches of premises for the purposes of a criminal investigation, with the occupier's consent, other than routine scenes of crime searches and searches following the activation of fire or burglar alarms or calls to a fire or a burglary made on behalf of an occupier or bomb threat calls or searches under B.4.4 (below); (b) searches under ss. 17, 18 and 32 of PACE; searches of premises by virtue of a warrant issued under s. 15 or Sch. 1 of PACE or s. 15 of or Sch. 7 to the Prevention of Terrorism (Temporary Provisions) Act 1989.

Code B supplements the requirements of PACE in a number of respects. Thus, before applying for a warrant or production order, the officer must take reasonable steps to check that his information is accurate, recent and has not been provided maliciously or irresponsibly; an application may not be made on the basis of information from an anonymous source where corroboration has not been sought (Code B.2.1); he must ascertain as specifically as is possible in the circumstances the nature and location of the articles concerned (Code B.2.2); he must make reasonable inquiries about the likely occupier of the premises, and their nature, and whether they have been previously searched (Code B.2.3); no application for a search warrant may be made without the authority of an officer of at least the rank of inspector (or, in cases of urgency where no inspector is readily available, the senior officer on duty), or, in the case of a production order or warrant under Sch. 1 to PACE, or Sch. 7 to the Prevention of Terrorism (Temporary Provisions) Act 1989, an officer of at least the rank of superintendent (Code B.2.4); and, except in cases of urgency, the local police/community liaison officer must be consulted before a search if there is reason to believe that it might have an adverse effect on police/community relations (Code B.2.5). If an application is refused, no further application may be made unless supported by additional grounds (Code B.2.8).

If it is proposed to search premises with consent, that consent must be given in writing on the Notice of Powers and Rights (see below) before the search takes place; the officer must make inquiries to satisfy himself that the person is in a position to give that consent (Code B.4.1); and before seeking that consent, the officer in charge of the search must state its purpose, and inform the person concerned that he is not obliged to consent, that anything seized may be produced in evidence and, if it is so, that he is not suspected of an offence (Code B.4.2). An officer cannot enter and search, or continue to search premises by consent if the consent is given under duress or is withdrawn before the search is completed (Code B.4.3). Consent need not be sought if this would cause disproportionate inconvenience to the person concerned (e.g. a brief check of gardens along the route of a pursuit) (Code B.4.4 and 4C).

Where an entry is made without consent, the officer must first attempt to communicate with the occupier, or any other person entitled to grant access, unless (i) the premises are known to be unoccupied, (ii) the occupier etc. is known to be absent, or (iii) there are reasonable grounds for believing that to alert him would frustrate the object of the search or endanger the officers concerned or other people (Code B.5.4). Where the premises are occupied, before the search begins the officer must identify himself, if not in uniform show his warrant card, and state the purpose of the search and the grounds for undertaking it (unless (iii) above applies) (Code B.5.5).

The officer must, unless it is impracticable, provide the occupier with a Notice of Powers and Rights, (i) specifying whether the search is made under a warrant, or with consent or under ss. 17, 18 or 32 of PACE; (ii) summarising the extent of the powers of search and seizure under the Act; (iii) explaining the rights of the occupier and the owner of property seized; (iv) explaining that compensation may be payable for damage; (v) stating that a copy of the Code is available at any police station (Code B.5.7). If the occupier is present, copies of the Notice and of the warrant (if any) should if practicable be given to him before the search starts, unless the officer in charge reasonably believes that this would frustrate the object of the search or endanger the officers concerned or other people. If he is not present, copies of the Notice and the warrant (where appropriate) should be left in a prominent place on the premises and endorsed with the name of the officer in charge, his police station and the date and time of the search (Code B.5.8).

As to the conduct of searches, premises may be searched only to the extent necessary to achieve the object of the search, having regard to the size and nature of whatever is sought; a search under warrant may not continue under the authority of the warrant once all the things specified in it have been found, or the officer in charge is satisfied they are not there (Code B.5.9). Searches must be conducted with due consideration for the occupier's property and privacy, and with no more disturbance than necessary (Code B.5.10). If the occupier wishes to ask a friend, neighbour or other person to witness the search he must be allowed to do so, unless the officer in charge has reasonable grounds for believing that this would seriously hinder the investigation; a search need not be unreasonably delayed for this purpose (Code B.5.11). Premises entered by force must be left secure (Code B.5.12).

An officer of the rank of inspector or above must take charge of any search under Sch. 1 to PACE or Sch. 7 to the Prevention of Terrorism (Temporary Provisions) Act 1989; he is responsible for ensuring that the search is conducted with discretion, and so as to cause the least possible disruption (Code B.5.13).

A full record must be kept of searches (Code B.7) and a search register must be maintained at each sub-divisional police station with copies of all records required by Code B (Code B.8).

11. In *R v Longman* [1988] 1 WLR 619, the Court of Appeal held that s. 16(5) was not to be interpreted as requiring the preliminaries set out in paras. (a) to (c) to be observed before *entry* to the premises; it was sufficient that this be done before the *search* begins, as set out in Code B.5.5. (Under the revised Code B.5.5 even this is subject to the provision in Code B.5.4.(iii) (above, n. **2**)). The case concerned the execution of a warrant to enter and search L's premises for drugs. It was not the first time that the premises had been the subject of such a search and the police knew that there would almost certainly be great difficulty in effecting an entry. On this occasion, warnings were shouted as soon as the police entered. The court noted that a requirement that the preliminaries be observed before entry would stultify 'the whole object of the more important type of search operation' (p. 153); particularly in drugs cases 'because unless the officers move very quickly indeed, by the time they have reached the back of the premises the offending drugs will be flushed down the lavatory pan . . . .' (p. 153). Other points made by the court were (1) that the police were entitled to use subterfuge as an alternative to force (here, a police-woman in plain clothes pretending to be delivering flowers from Interflora); and (2) that for a warrant to be 'produced' in accordance with s. 16(5)(b), it must be made available for inspection by and not merely shown to the occupier.

In *R v Chief Constable of Lancashire, ex p Parker* [1993] QB 577, the Divisional Court held that entry, search and seizure purportedly authorised by warrants issued under s. 9 and Sch. 1 of PACE were unlawful. The occupier was shown the original warrant, but only uncertified copies of schedules that had to be read in conjunction with the warrants to comply with s. 15(6) (a breach of s. 16(5)(b)) and copies of the warrants only were left with the occupier (a breach of s. 16(5)(c)). The phrase in s. 15(1):

'an entry on or search of premises under a warrant is unlawful unless it complies with this section and section 16 below'

is ambiguous (to what is 'it' meant to refer?). However, this case makes it clear that breaches of s. 16 will render the execution of a warrant unlawful by virtue of s. 15(1).

The execution of search warrants cannot lawfully be delegated to other persons: see *R v Reading JJ, Chief Constable of Avon and Somerset and Intervention Board for Agricultural Produce, ex p South West Meat Ltd* [1992] Crim LR 672, where the Divisional Court granted declarations and awarded £25,000 damages in respect of a search under a warrant issued under PACE, s. 8, that was, *inter alia*, too general in its terms, where the search was conducted by Board officials rather than the police; and the material was then retained unlawfully by the Board, the statutory power of retention being with the police.

12. In *R v Atkinson* [1976] Crim LR 307, the Court of Appeal held that a warrant obtained under s. 23(3) for the search of 'Flat 45' in certain premises could not justify the search of Flat 30, even though the police bona fide believed that A's flat was Flat 45. However, misspellings or trivial errors in the description of premises would not necessarily invalidate a warrant.

13. *Seizure.* The RCCP recommended that the ambit of the power of seizure under a warrant should extend to items which could be the subject of a warrant: i.e. on their recommendation, goods whose possession is an offence and material relating to 'grave offences'. The Act is wider in this respect (see ss. 19, 20). Sections 8(2) and 18(2), however, authorise the seizure of only the actual material for which the search is authorised or made. In the case of warrants to search for stolen goods, the common law permitted the seizure of goods 'reasonably believed' to be the goods specified in the warrant. Should the courts permit a similar extension here, or should any seizure not justified by ss. 8(2) or 18(2) have to be justified under s. 19? Material unlawfully seized may not be retained under s. 22: *R v Chief Constable of Lancashire, ex p Parker* [1993] QB 577.

14. *Surveillance.* The obtaining by the police of information through the interception of mail or telephone calls is regulated by statute; the use of other surveillance equipment is regulated by non-statutory guidelines: see below, pp. 569–577.

15. *Entry.* For entry to premises to be justified by reference to s. 17(1)(b), the police officer entering must have reasonable grounds to suspect the person sought to be guilty of the offence in question; the provision cannot justify entry to effect an unlawful arrest: *Kynaston v DPP* (1987) 87 Cr App Rep 200, DC. Here, the justices were held to be entitled to infer that the officers had the necessary reasonable suspicion. The officers knew a robbery had taken place; they desired to arrest one Doyle for it; they had reasonable grounds for believing he was in the premises; they stated when they entered that they wished to arrest him for robbery. 'If that does not raise an inference that they had reasonable grounds for suspecting him of the robbery, I am bound to say I do not know what else it would amount to. . . . That is an inference which could have been rebutted but was not.' (per Parker LJ at 206.) Cf. *Chapman v DPP* (1988) 89 Cr App Rep 190, where the Divisional Court held that an officer's entry to arrest a person for assault on another police officer could not be justified under s. 17(1)(b). There was no evidence that the arresting officer suspected that his colleague had been injured; assault occasioning actual bodily harm is an arrestable offence but common assault is not. Furthermore, there was no evidence that the arresting officer suspected that there had been an offence of violent disorder contrary to the Public Order Act 1986, s. 2.

For entry to be justified by reference to s. 17(1)(d) ('recapturing a person who is unlawfully at large and whom [the police officer] is pursuing', there must be 'pursuit': per Lord Lowry in *D'Souza v DPP* [1992] 4 All ER 545 at 556:

'The verb in the clause "whom he is pursuing" is in the present continuous tense and therefore, give or take a few seconds or minutes – this is a question of degree – the pursuit must be almost contemporaneous with the entry into the premises. There must, I consider, be an act of pursuit, that is a chase, however short in time and distance. It is not enough for the police to form an intention to arrest, which they put into practice by resorting to the premises where they believe that the person whom they seek may be found.'

Accordingly, the House of Lords held that where a person admitted to hospital for psychiatric assessment under the Mental Health Act 1983, s. 2(4) returned home without leave granted under s. 17 of that Act, she was 'unlawfully at large'; however, the police who subsequently on the same day went to her home could not justify forcible entry under s. 17(1)(d) as there was no element of 'pursuit'. For powers to enter premises to deal with or prevent breaches of the peace see below, pp. 259–264. Note that there are many powers to enter premises granted by statute to public officials such as (to name a few) Customs and Excise officers, Inland Revenue officials, employees of gas an electricity companies and trading standards officers. For a list, see RCCP, *Law and Procedure Volume*, Appendix 4. Should police officers seeking to exercise a right of entry be required to give reasons, by analogy with *Christie v Leachinsky* (below, p. 109)? *Swales v Cox* [1981] 1 QB 849, DC suggested not, in respect of the power under the Criminal Law Act 1967, s. 2(6) to enter (if need be by force) to arrest for an arrestable offence. Section 2(6) provided a 'comprehensive code' which provided that the officer 'might enter without qualification but not that he might use force without qualification' (per Donaldson LJ at 854). Thus reasons might have to be given to justify the use of force, but this would depend on the circumstances: it might be essential for the protection of an officer following a 'very dangerous man' that he should 'give no warning of his approach by asking the leave of the criminal to enter' (ibid.). This approach was adopted in respect of the similarly worded power of entry under the Road Traffic Act 1988, s. 4(7), in *Lunt v DPP* [1993] COD 430, DC. What should the position be under s. 17 of PACE? Is the absence of an express duty to give reasons decisive?

16. The requirement that entry under s. 18 be authorised in writing is not satisfied by a note in an officer's notebook recording an oral authorisation: an independent document is required: *R v Badham* [1987] Crim LR 202 (Wood Green Crown Court). A failure to make a record in the custody record will not necessarily lead to the exclusion of evidence from the search: *R v Wright* [1994] Crim LR 55, CA (Cr D).

17. Apart from any right to enter premises conferred by law, a police officer may enter premises with the express or implied permission (or 'licence') of the owner. This point was raised in the following case.

Davis v Lisle [1936] 2 KB 434, [1936] 2 All ER 213, 105 LJKB 593, 155 LT 23, 52 TLR 475, 34 LGR 253, 30 Cox CC 412, King's Bench Divisional Court

Sidney Davis was a member of a firm which occupied a railway arch as a garage. Two police officers entered the garage to make inquiries as to the person responsible for obstructing the highway with a lorry, which lorry had subsequently been moved into the garage. D, using abusive and obscene language, told them to get out. L was in the act of producing his warrant card when D struck him in the chest and stomach with his fist, damaging his tunic. D was convicted by justices of (1) assaulting a police officer in the execution of his duty contrary to the Metropolitan Police Act 1839, s. 18; (2) obstructing an officer in the execution of his duty contrary to the Prevention of Crimes Amendment Act 1885, s. 2; and (3) maliciously damaging a serge tunic (by tearing it), to the amount of 7s 6d. D appealed unsuccessfully to quarter sessions, and then appealed to the Divisional Court by way of case stated.

Lord Hewart CJ: The point which is raised here with regard to the appellant's first two convictions is whether the officers were at the material time acting in the execution of their duty. In my opinion, they were not, and there are no grounds on which they can be held to have been so acting. The only ground which is put forward in support of the contention that they were so acting seems to me to be quite beside the point. I feel a difficulty in envisaging the legal proposition that because the police officers had witnessed an offence being committed on the highway they were acting in the execution of their duty in entering and remaining on private premises because the offenders then were on those premises. Admittedly, the officers were at liberty to enter this garage to make an inquiry, but quite a different thing to say that they were entitled to remain when, not without emphasis, the appellant had said: 'Get outside. You cannot come here without a search warrant.' From that moment on, while the officers remained where they were, it seems to me that they were trespassers and it is quite clear that the act which the respondent was doing immediately before the assault complained of was tantamount to putting forward a claim as of right to remain where he was. The respondent was in the act of producing his warrant card. That was after the emphatic order to 'get out' had been made. Mr. Raphael, with his usual candour, has admitted that, if the finding in the case that the respondent was in the act of producing his warrant card is fairly to be construed as meaning that he was asserting his right to remain on the premises, it is not possible to contend that at that moment the respondent was acting in the execution of his duty. I think it is quite clear that the act of producing his warrant card constituted the making of such a claim. I cannot think that there is any ambiguity about it. . . .

In my opinion, it is not possible to maintain the conclusion that at the material time the respondent was acting in the execution of his duty as a constable. But that conclusion by no means disposes of everything contained in this case. It does not dispose of the question whether the assault which was in fact committed was justified. We have not the materials before us which would enable us to determine that question. Nor was the appellant prosecuted for assault. He was prosecuted for assaulting and obstructing a police officer in the execution of his duty. Furthermore, the conclusion to which I have come does not affect the third conviction—that of damaging a tunic by 'wilfully and maliciously tearing' it. On that part of the case no question arises whether at that moment the officer was acting in the execution of his duty and I see no reason why we should interfere with that conviction. . . .

Du Parcq and **Goddard JJ** delivered concurring judgments.

Appeal allowed as to first two convictions.

NOTES

1. The officers in this case were not entering in order to *prevent* crime, but to *investigate*. Cf. *Thomas v Sawkins*, below, pp. 259–264.

2. In this case, the officers asserted a right to remain. Otherwise, persons requested to leave must be given reasonable time to depart. In *Robson v Hallett* [1967] 2 QB 939, a police sergeant was told to leave a private house where he was making inquiries. He at once turned and walked towards the front door but was then jumped on. Two constables went to his aid from the front path. The Divisional Court held that the sergeant had not become a trespasser the instant he was told to depart. Lord Parker CJ stated (at 952–953):

'When a licence is revoked as a result of which something has to be done by the licensee, a reasonable time must be implied in which he can do so, in this case to get off the premises; no doubt it will be a very short time, but he was doing here his best to leave the premises.'

The constables were lawfully in the front garden, as they, like any other members of the public, had implied leave and licence to walk up to the front door, and that implied licence had never been revoked (see below, p. 262). They were acting in the execution of their duty in assisting the sergeant and avoiding any further breach of the peace. Lord Parker started obiter at 953 that 'even if they had been outside the gate, it seems to me that they would have abundant right to come onto private property in those circumstances'. Diplock LJ said of the constables (at 954) that

'once a breach of the peace was taking place under their eyes, they had not only an independent right but a duty to go and stop it, and it matters not from that moment onwards whether they started off on their journey to stop it from outside the premises . . . or . . . inside . . . .'

Another example of a premature attack is *Kay v Hibbert* [1977] Crim LR 226, DC.

Robson v Hallett was distinguished by Eichelbaum J in the New Zealand High Court in *Edwards v A-G* [1986] 2 NZLR 232, where a traffic officer pursued a speeding motor cyclist, E, who returned to his friend's house, where he was staying, and drove into the garage. The officer followed E into the driveway, pushed the door up again and entered the garage. There he noticed that E had been drinking and subsequently arrested him under the drink/drive legislation. In proceedings by E for wrongful arrest, the judge held that the common law licence normally implied to permit a person to enter an unlocked gate and proceed to the door in order to make an inquiry did not extend to pursuit by a traffic officer of a suspected offender into a house or garage, or authorise forcible entry; the situation went beyond that of 'a driver, who, seeking to elude a traffic officer, dodges onto the nearest private land' where an implied licence might arise. Then in *Howden v Ministry of Transport* [1987] 2 NZLR 747, the New Zealand Court of Appeal held that it would not be reasonable to hold that an occupier gives any implied licence to police or traffic officers to enter:

'for random checking of a driver whose driving or other prior behaviour has given no cause for suspicion'

(per Cooke P at 751). Bisson J also noted (at 754) that the implied licence recognised in *Robson v Hallett*:

'may only be exercised at a time of the day or night when it is reasonable for the lawful business to be conducted. In this case it was 1.30 in the morning which would not have been a reasonable hour to knock on the door for some lawful purpose not of an urgent nature. . . .'

3. In *McArdle v Wallace* (1964) 108 Sol Jo 483, DC, a police constable entered a yard to inquire about some property in an adjoining passageway. The occupier's son told him to leave, and struck him when he did not. The magistrates found as a fact that the son had the implied authority of the father to ask the constable to leave. The Divisional Court held that the son was rightly acquitted of the charge of assaulting a police officer in the execution of his duty (see above, p. 53) 'albeit the constable did not know' of the implied authority.

4. In *Jones and Jones v Lloyd* [1981] Crim LR 340, DC, one Leach was seen by police officers attempting to open a car. He admitted he was not the owner, and said that the owner was at a party in one of the houses in the street. Inspector Lloyd asked to be taken to see her. Leach invited the officer into the house. One of the guests told them to leave, but the officers, having satisfied themselves that she was not the owner of the house, ignored her. The officers satisfied themselves about Leach's possession of the car keys, and were leaving when they were assaulted by two guests at the party. The Divisional Court held that where a guest leaves a party and then gets into difficulty, any host would be presumed to have authorised the guest to bring the police back into the house in order to clear his name. The officers were, accordingly, not trespassers. S. H. Bailey and D. J. Birch commented: ([1982] Crim LR at 478)

'This seems to be a broad view of the scope of the implied licence doctrine, but in any event it is argu-able that the fact of trespass *vis-à-vis* the owner of the house should not affect the position *vis-à-vis* guests, [Cf. below, p. 153] unless, presumably, they are acting on behalf of the owner in ejecting officers who are in fact trespassers. It should be noted here that it did not appear that the owner of the house either knew of or objected to the officers' presence.'

5. In *R v Thornley* (1980) 72 Cr App Rep 302, [1981] Crim LR 637, the Court of Appeal (Criminal Division) held that a licence to enter premises given by a wife in the course of a domestic dispute could not be revoked by the husband, who had been the subject of a complaint to the police. It was accepted that the judge had been right to direct the jury that when the officers entered the house they were not tres-passers because they had been invited to enter by the wife 'who was co-occupier'.

6. In *Riley v DPP* (1989) 91 Cr App Rep 14, the Divisional Court held that police officers were lawfully on premises when permitted to enter by the owner's son, and subsequently met by the owner, who raised no objection to their presence. Moreover, s. 17 of PACE did not set out a complete code for entry by police officers, it only applied where entry was without the occupier's consent.

7. A trespassing officer may not validly require a person to take a breath test: *Morris v Beardmore* (below, p. 153). Accordingly a number of cases have turned on whether the officer was a trespasser. It has been held that whether the words 'fuck off' used by the owner of the house constitute revocation of the implied licence to be in the driveway or mere vulgar abuse is a question of fact for the justices: *Snook v Mannion* [1982] RTR 321, DC; *Gilham v Breidenbach* [1982] RTR 328n, DC (both cases decided adversely to the defendant). (Quaere 'fuck off out of it'?). Moreover, in *Snook v Mannion, supra,* it was held to be necessary for the implied licence to be revoked expressly; it was not sufficient simply that the officer was aware that his presence on the driveway or his request for the owner to take a breath test was con-trary to the owner's wishes: such a position would be 'unworkable'. Cf. *Pamplin v Fraser* [1981] RTR 494, DC (no revocation of implied licence where D merely wound up the window of his car and locked the doors while remaining inside). In *Faulkner v Willetts* [1982] RTR 159, [1982] Crim LR 543, DC, D's wife opened the front door to a constable. He explained that he wished to interview D in connection with a road accident. She walked back into the house giving him the impression that it was an implied invitation to enter. No indication was subsequently given refusing him entry or requiring him to leave; indeed he was offered a cup of coffee. The court held that the justices were entitled to conclude that this constituted implied permission to enter.

8 Arrest

Police and Criminal Evidence Act 1984

PART III

ARREST

24. Arrest without warrant for arrestable offences
(1) The powers of summary arrest conferred by the following subsections shall apply—
  (a) to offences for which the sentence is fixed by law;
  (b) to offences for which a person of 21 years of age or over (not previously convicted) may be sentenced to imprisonment for a term of five years (or might be so sentenced but for the restrictions imposed by section 33 of the Magistrates' Court Act 1980); and
  (c) to the offences to which subsection (2) below applies,
and in this Act 'arrestable offence' means any such offence.
(2) The offences to which this subsection applies are—
  (a) offences for which a person may be arrested under the Customs and Excise Acts, as defined in section 1(1) of the Customs and Excise Management Act 1979;
  (b) offences under the Official Secrets Act [. . .] 1920 that are not arrestable offences by virtue of the term of imprisonment for which a person may be sentenced in respect of them;
  [(bb) offences under any provision of the Official Secrets Act 1989 except section 8(1), (4) or (5);][1]
  (c) offences under section [. . .][2] 22 (causing prostitution of women) or 23 (procuration of girl under 21) of the Sexual Offences Act 1956;
  (d) offences under section 12(1) (taking motor vehicle or other conveyance without authority etc.) or 25(1) (going equipped for stealing, etc.) of the Theft Act 1968; and
  [(e) any offence under the Football Offences Act 1991;][3]
  [(f) an offence under section 2 of the Obscene Publications Act 1959 (publication of obscene matter);
  (g) an offence under section 1 of the Protection of Children Act 1978 (indecent photographs and pseudo-photographs of children);][4]
  [(h) an offence under section 166 of the Criminal Justice and Public Order Act 1994 (sale of tickets by unauthorised persons);][5]
  [(i) an offence under section 19 of the Public Order Act 1986 (publishing, etc. material intended or likely to stir up racial hatred);][6]
  [(j) an offence under section 167 of the Criminal Justice and Public Order Act 1994 (touting for hire car services).][7]
(3) Without prejudice to section 2 of the Criminal Attempts Act 1981, the powers of summary arrest conferred by the following subsections shall also apply to the offences of—
  (a) conspiring to commit any of the offences mentioned in subsection (2) above;
  (b) attempting to commit any such offence [other than an offence under section 12(1) of the Theft Act 1968];[8]

1 Inserted by the 1989 Act, s. 11(1).
2 Repealed by the Sexual Offences Act 1985, s. 5(3).
3 Inserted by the Football Offences Act 1991, s. 5.
4 Inserted by the Criminal Justice and Public Order Act 1994, s. 85(2).
5 Inserted by ibid., s. 166(4).
6 Inserted by ibid., s. 155.
7 Inserted by ibid., s. 167(7).
8 Inserted by the Criminal Justice 1988 Act, Sch. 15, para. 98.

(c) inciting, aiding, abetting, counselling or procuring the commission of any such offence;

and such offences are also arrestable offences for the purposes of this Act.

(4) Any person may arrest without a warrant—

    (a) anyone who is in the act of committing an arrestable offence;

    (b) anyone whom he has reasonable grounds for suspecting to be committing such an offence.

(5) Where an arrestable offence has been committed, any person may arrest without a warrant—

    (a) anyone who is guilty of the offence;

    (b) anyone whom he has reasonable grounds for suspecting to be guilty of it.

(6) Where a constable has reasonable grounds for suspecting that an arrestable offence has been committed, he may arrest without a warrant anyone whom he has reasonable grounds for suspecting to be guilty of the offence.

(7) A constable may arrest without a warrant—

    (a) anyone who is about to commit an arrestable offence;

    (b) anyone whom he has reasonable grounds for suspecting to be about to commit an arrestable offence.

25. General arrest conditions

(1) Where a constable has reasonable grounds for suspecting that any offence which is not an arrestable offence has been committed or attempted, or is being committed or attempted, he may arrest the relevant person if it appears to him that service of a summons is impracticable or inappropriate because any of the general arrest conditions are satisfied.

(2) In this section 'the relevant person' means any person whom the constable has reasonable grounds to suspect of having committed or having attempted to commit the offence or of being in the course of committing or attempting to commit it.

(3) The general arrest conditions are—

    (a) that the name of the relevant person is unknown to, and cannot be readily ascertained by, the constable;

    (b) that the constable has reasonable grounds for doubting whether a name furnished by the relevant person as his name is his real name;

    (c) that—

        (i) the relevant person has failed to furnish a satisfactory address for service; or

        (ii) the constable has reasonable grounds for doubting whether an address furnished by the relevant person is a satisfactory address for service;

    (d) that the constable has reasonable grounds for believing that arrest is necessary to prevent the relevant person—

        (i) causing physical injury to himself or any other person;

        (ii) suffering physical injury;

        (iii) causing loss of or damage to property;

        (iv) committing an offence against public decency; or

        (v) causing an unlawful obstruction of the highway;

    (e) that the constable has reasonable grounds for believing that arrest is necessary to protect a child or other vulnerable person from the relevant person.

(4) For the purposes of subsection (3) above an address is a satisfactory address for service if it appears to the constable—

    (a) that the relevant person will be at it for a sufficiently long period for it to be possible to serve him with a summons; or

    (b) that some other person specified by the relevant person will accept service of a summons for the relevant person at it.

(5) Nothing in subsection (3)(d) above authorises the arrest of a person under sub-paragraph (iv) of that paragraph except where members of the public going about their normal business cannot reasonably be expected to avoid the person to be arrested.

(6) This section shall not prejudice any power of arrest conferred apart from this section.

26. Repeal of statutory powers of arrest without warrant or order

(1) Subject to subsection (2) below, so much of any Act (including a local Act) passed before this Act as enables a constable—

    (a) to arrest a person for an offence without a warrant; or

    (b) to arrest a person otherwise than for an offence without a warrant or an order of a court,

shall cease to have effect.

(2) Nothing in subsection (1) above affects the enactments specified in Schedule 2 to this Act.

27. Fingerprinting of certain offenders

(1) If a person—
- (a) has been convicted of a recordable offence;
- (b) has not at any time been in police detention for the offence; and
- (c) has not had his fingerprints taken—
    - (i) in the course of the investigation of the offence by the police; or
    - (ii) since the conviction,

any constable may at any time not later than one month after the date of the conviction require him to attend a police station in order that his fingerprints may be taken.

(2) A requirement under subsection (1) above—
- (a) shall give the person a period of at least 7 days within which he must so attend; and
- (b) may direct him to so attend at a specified time of day or between specified times of day.

(3) Any constable may arrest without warrant a person who has failed to comply with a requirement under subsection (1) above.

(4) The Secretary of State may by regulations make provision for recording in national police records convictions for such offences as are specified in the regulations.

(5) Regulations under this section shall be made by statutory instrument and shall be subject to annulment in pursuance of a resolution of either House of Parliament.

28. Information to be given on arrest

(1) Subject to subsection (5) below, where a person is arrested, otherwise than by being informed that he is under arrest, the arrest is not lawful unless the person arrested is informed that he is under arrest as soon as is practicable after his arrest.

(2) Where a person is arrested by a constable, subsection (1) above applies regardless of whether the fact of the arrest is obvious.

(3) Subject to subsection (5) below, no arrest is lawful unless the person arrested is informed of the ground for the arrest at the time of, or as soon as is practicable after, the arrest.

(4) Where a person is arrested by a constable, subsection (3) above applies regardless of whether the ground for the arrest is obvious.

(5) Nothing in this section is to be taken to require a person to be informed—
- (a) that he is under arrest; or
- (b) of the ground for the arrest,

if it was not reasonably practicable for him to be so informed by reason of his having escaped from arrest before the information could be given.

29. Voluntary attendance at police station etc

Where for the purpose of assisting with an investigation a person attends voluntarily at a police station or at any other place where a constable is present or accompanies a constable to a police station or any such other place without having been arrested—
- (a) he shall be entitled to leave at will unless he is placed under arrest;
- (b) he shall be informed at once that he is under arrest if a decision is taken by a constable to prevent him from leaving at will.

30. Arrest elsewhere than at police station

(1) Subject to the following provisions of this section, where a person—
- (a) is arrested by a constable for an offence; or
- (b) is taken into custody by a constable after being arrested for an offence by a person other than a constable,

at any place other than a police station, he shall be taken to a police station by a constable as soon as practicable after the arrest.

(2) Subject to subsections (3) and (4) below, the police station to which an arrested person is taken under subsection (1) above shall be a designated police station.

(3) A constable to whom this subsection applies may take an arrested person to any police station unless it appears to the constable that it may be necessary to keep the arrested person in police detention for more than six hours.

(4) Subsection (3) above applies—
- (a) to a constable who is working in a locality covered by a police station which is not a designated police station; and
- (b) to a constable belonging to a body of constables maintained by an authority other than a police authority.

(5) Any constable may take an arrested person to any police station if—

(*a*) either of the following conditions is satisfied—
  (i) the constable has arrested him without the assistance of any other constable and no other constable is available to assist him;
  (ii) the constable has taken him into custody from a person other than a constable without the assistance of any other constable and no other constable is available to assist him; and
(*b*) it appears to the constable that he will be unable to take the arrested person to a designated police station without the arrested person injuring himself, the constable or some other person.

(6) If the first police station to which an arrested person is taken after his arrest is not a designated police station he shall be taken to a designated police station not more than six hours after his arrival at the first police station unless he is released previously.

(7) A person arrested by a constable at a place other than a police station shall be released if a constable is satisfied, before the person arrested reaches a police station, that there are no grounds for keeping him under arrest.

(8) A constable who releases a person under subsection (7) above shall record the fact that he has done so.

(9) The constable shall make the record as soon as is practicable after the release.

(10) Nothing in subsection (1) above shall prevent a constable delaying taking a person who has been arrested to a police station if the presence of that person elsewhere is necessary in order to carry out such investigations as it is reasonable to carry out immediately.

(11) Where there is delay in taking a person who has been arrested to a police station after his arrest, the reasons for the delay shall be recorded when he first arrives at a police station.

(12) Nothing in subsection (1) above shall be taken to affect—
(*a*) paragraphs 16(3) or 18(1) of Schedule 2 to the Immigration Act 1971;
(*b*) section 34(1) of the Criminal Justice Act 1972; or
(*c*) [section 15(6) and (9) of the Prevention of Terrorism (Temporary Provisions) Act 1989 and paragraphs 7(4) and 8(4) and (5) of Schedule 2 and paragraphs 6(6) and 7(4) and (5) of Schedule 5 to that Act].[1]

(13) Nothing in subsection (10) above shall be taken to affect paragraph 18(3) of Schedule 2 to the Immigration Act 1971.

31. Arrest for further offence
Where—
(*a*) a person—
  (i) has been arrested for an offence; and
  (ii) is at a police station in consequence of that arrest; and
(*b*) it appears to a constable that, if he were released from that arrest, he would be liable to arrest for some other offence,
he shall be arrested for that other offence.

32. Search upon arrest
(1) A constable may search an arrested person, in any case where the person to be searched has been arrested at a place other than a police station, if the constable has reasonable grounds for believing that the arrested person may present a danger to himself or others.

(2) Subject to subsections (3) to (5) below, a constable shall also have power in any such case—
(*a*) to search the arrested person for anything—
  (i) which he might use to assist him to escape from lawful custody; or
  (ii) which might be evidence relating to an offence; and
(*b*) to enter and search any premises in which he was when arrested or immediately before he was arrested for evidence relating to the offence for which he has been arrested.

(3) The power to search conferred by subsection (2) above is only a power to search to the extent that is reasonably required for the purpose of discovering any such thing or any such evidence.

(4) The powers conferred by this section to search a person are not to be construed as authorising a constable to require a person to remove any of his clothing in public other than an outer coat, jacket or gloves [but they do authorise the search of a person's mouth].[2]

(5) A constable may not search a person in the exercise of the power conferred by subsection (2)(*a*) above unless he has reasonable grounds for believing that the person to be searched may have concealed on him anything for which a search is permitted under that paragraph.

(6) A constable may not search premises in the exercise of the power conferred by subsection (2)(*b*) above unless he has reasonable grounds for believing that there is evidence for which a search is permitted under that paragraph on the premises.

1 Inserted by the 1989 Act, s. 25(1), Sch. 8, para. 6.
2 Inserted by the Criminal Justice and Public Order Act 1994, s. 59(2).

(7) In so far as the power of search conferred by subsection (2)(*b*) above relates to premises consisting of two or more separate dwellings, it is limited to a power to search—

　(*a*) any dwelling in which the arrest took place or in which the person arrested was immediately before his arrest; and

　(*b*) any parts of the premises which the occupier of any such dwelling uses in common with the occupiers of any other dwellings comprised in the premises.

(8) A constable searching a person in the exercise of the power conferred by subsection (1) above may seize and retain anything he finds, if he has reasonable grounds for believing that the person searched might use it to cause physical injury to himself or to any other person.

(9) A constable searching a person in the exercise of the power conferred by subsection (2)(*a*) above may seize and retain anything he finds, other than an item subject to legal privilege, if he has reasonable grounds for believing—

　(*a*) that he might use it to assist him to escape from lawful custody; or

　(*b*) that it is evidence of an offence or has been obtained in consequence of the commission of an offence.

(10) Nothing in this section shall be taken to affect the power conferred by [section 15(3), (4) and (5) of the Prevention of Terrorism (Temporary Provisions) Act 1989].[1]

NOTES

1. Schedule 2 lists 42 provisions which provide for a power of arrest without warrant and which were preserved by virtue of s. 26. They include the Public Order Act 1936, s. 7(3); the Street Offences Act 1959, s. 1(3); the Immigration Act 1971, s. 24(2), Schedule 2 paras 17, 24 and 33 and Schedule 3 para 7; the Criminal Law Act 1977, ss. 6(6), 7(11), 8(4), 9(7) and 10(5); and the Mental Health Act 1983, ss. 18, 35(10), 36(8), 38(7), 136(1) and 138. Powers of arrest without warrant included in Acts passed since PACE include the Sporting Events (Control of Alcohol etc.) Act 1985, s. 7(2); Public Order Act 1986, s. 3(6) (affray), s. 4(4) (fear or provocation of violence), s. 5(4) (harassment, alarm or distress), ss. 12(7), 13(10) and 14(7) (processions and assemblies) (below, pp. 213–214, 197–198); Prevention of Terrorism (Temporary Provisions) Act 1989, s. 14 (below, p. 303).

2. *Requisites of a valid arrest.* There are a number of elements which must be present for an arrest to be valid:

　(1) There must be either an arrest warrant or a legal power to arrest without warrant (see ss. 24–26).

　(2) The factual requirements of the relevant powers must be fulfilled: commonly the requirement of 'reasonable suspicion' (see above, pp. 65–72).

　(3) At common law it was necessary for the arrestor to make it clear that the arrestee was under compulsion either (i) by physical means (such as taking him by the arm) or (ii) by notifying him of the fact of compulsion by word of mouth. There was a danger where the arrestor relied on words alone that the words might not sufficiently indicate compulsion. For example, in *Alderson v Booth* [1969] 2 QB 216, DC, following a positive breathalyser test a constable said to the defendant 'I shall have to ask you to come to the police station for further tests'. D accompanied the constable to the police station. At his trial the defendant defended charges of driving with an excess of alcohol in his blood by claiming that he had not been arrested by the constable (a lawful arrest having been made being a condition precedent to conviction under the drink and drive legislation). He was acquitted and the prosecution's appeal was dismissed. Lord Parker CJ (with whom Blain and Donaldson JJ agreed) said:

1　Inserted by the 1989 Act, s. 25(1), Sch. 8, para. 6.

'. . . the narrow point here was whether the justices were right in holding, as they did, that there never had been an arrest.

In their opinion, which is clearly partly opinion and partly finding of fact, they say:

"We were of the opinion that when the respondent accompanied the constable to the police station it was not made clear to him either physically or by word of mouth that he was under compulsion. We consider that compulsion is a necessary element of arrest, and we therefore did not regard the respondent as a person who had been arrested."

. . . I for my part have little doubt that, just looking at the words used here, "I shall have to ask you to come to the police station for further tests," they were in their context words of command which one would think would bring home to a defendant that he was under compulsion. But the justices here had the evidence not only of the police constable but of the defendant, and they were not satisfied, having heard him, that it had been brought home unequivocally to him that he was under compulsion. I confess it surprised me that he was believed but believed he was when he said or conveyed that he was not going to the police station because he thought he was under compulsion, but was going purely voluntarily. It seems to me that this is so much a question of fact for the justices that, surprising as this decision is, I feel that this court cannot interfere.

I would only say this, that if what I have said is correct in law, it is advisable that police officers should use some very clear words to bring home to a person that he is under compulsion. It certainly must not be left in the state that a defendant can go into the witness-box and merely say "I did not think I was under compulsion." If difficulties for the future are to be avoided, it seems to me that by far and away the simplest thing is for a police officer to say "I arrest you." If the defendant goes to the police station after hearing those words, it seems to me that he simply could not be believed if he thereafter said "I did not think there was any compulsion, I was only going voluntarily." '

Furthermore, where words alone were used the arrestee had to accede to the detention: if the arrestor simply said 'I arrest you' and the arrestee ran off before he was physically touched, the arrest was not complete (*Russen v Lucas* (1824) 1 C & P 153; *Sandon v Jervis* (1859) EB & E 942; Glanville Williams, [1954] Crim LR 6, 12–14).

These principles remain good law: see *Nichols v Bulman* [1985] RTR 236 (words 'I arrest you' not sufficient to constitute a lawful arrest in the absence of any prior to subsequent submission to compulsion).

(4) There is a requirement now clearly distinct from element (3) that in *all* cases the arrestee must be informed of the *fact* of arrest, except where the arrest is made by a private citizen and the fact of arrest is obvious: section 28(1), (2) and (5).

(5) The arrestee must be informed of the *ground* for arrest as soon as is practicable except where the arrest is by a private citizen and the ground of arrest is obvious. This was an important common law requirement (although the exception where the ground was 'obvious' applied to police arrests as well as citizen arrests): *Christie v Leachinsky* [1947] AC 573, HL. The reasons for the rule were stated as follows by Viscount Simon (pp. 585, 588):

'[T]his is for the obvious purpose of securing that a citizen who is prima facie entitled to personal freedom should know why for the time being his personal freedom is interfered with. Scott LJ argued that if the law circumscribed the issue of warrants for arrest in this way it would hardly be that a policeman acting without a warrant was entitled to make an arrest without stating the charge on which the arrest was made. . . . No one, I think, would approve a situation in which when the person arrested asked for the reason, the policeman replied "that has nothing to do with you: come along with me." . . .

. . . And there are practical considerations, as well as theory, to support the view I take. If the charge on suspicion of which the man is arrested is then and there made known to him, he has the opportunity of giving an explanation of any misunderstanding or of calling attention to other persons for whom he may have been mistaken, with the result that further inquiries may save him from the consequences of false accusation. . . .'

His Lordship also stated that this 'does not mean that technical or precise language need be used'. Lord Simonds put the point like this (p. 593):

'[I]t is not an essential condition of lawful arrest that the constable should at the time of arrest formulate any charge at all, much less the charge which may ultimately be found in the indictment. But this, and this only, is the qualification which I would impose upon the general proposition. It leaves untouched the principle, which lies at the heart of the matter, that the arrested man is entitled to be told what is the act for which he is arrested. The "charge" ultimately made will depend upon the view taken by the law of his act. In ninety-nine cases out of a hundred the same words may be used to define the charge or describe the act, nor is any technical precision necessary: for instance, if the act constituting the crime is the killing of another man, it will be immaterial that the arrest is for murder and at a later hour the charge of manslaughter is substituted. The arrested man is left in no doubt that the arrest is for that killing. This is I think, the fundamental principle, viz., that a man is entitled to know what . . . are "the facts which are said to constitute a crime on his part". . . .'

It was not necessary for the arrestor to indicate the grounds upon which his 'reasonable suspicion' was based: see Glanville Williams, [1954] Crim LR 161. Is that required now? In *Gelberg v Miller* [1961] 1 WLR 153, DC, the appellant parked his car outside a restaurant in London while he had a meal. Police officers asked him to move the car. He refused, preferring to finish his meal first. On being told that the police would remove the car themselves he removed the rotor arm from the distributor mechanism. He also refused to give his name and address or show his driving licence and certificate of insurance. He was arrested by one of the officers. The officer said he was arresting the appellant for 'obstructing him in the execution of his duty by refusing to move his car and refusing his name and address'. The appellant was charged under a forerunner of s. 51(3) of the Police Act 1964 (see above, p. 53). The Attorney-General conceded that there was no power to arrest for obstruction of the police as no actual or apprehended breach of the peace was involved. However, the court held that this was a valid arrest for 'obstructing the thoroughfare' (an offence under s. 54(6) of the Metropolitan Police Act 1839). Lord Parker CJ stated (at p. 161):

'To my mind it is clear that, by saying that he was arresting him for refusing to move his motor-car, he was informing the appellant of a fact which, in all the circumstances, amounted to a wilful obstruction of the thoroughfare by leaving his car in that position. It seems to me to matter not that the respondent also coupled with that the refusal to give his name and address or the allegation of obstructing him in the execution of his duty. May I test it in this way: supposing the respondent had said nothing but had just arrested him, could it really be said that the appellant did not know all the facts constituting an alleged wilful obstruction of the thoroughfare without having that particular charge made against him at the time? In my judgment, what the appellant knew and what he was told was ample to fulfil the obligation as to what should be done at the time of an arrest without warrant.'

How would this case be decided now?

In *R v Telfer* [1976] Crim LR 562 (Bristol Cr Ct) a police officer knew that the police wanted to interview the defendant in connection with a burglary. The officer encountered the defendant and when the defendant refused voluntarily to accompany the officer to the police station the officer arrested him 'on suspicion of burglary'. At the time of the arrest the officer did not know which particular burglary the defendant was suspected of having committed. The officer could have ascertained these details fairly speedily had he asked his headquarters. Instead he had merely sought confirmation that the defendant was wanted. The arrest was held unlawful. A person arrested was entitled to be told the particular burglary of which he was suspected and on the facts such information could quite easily have been given to him. Would the obligation of the officer have been less if the information had been less readily available?

In *Abbassy v Metropolitan Police Comr* [1990] 1 All ER 193, the Court of Appeal held that the trial judge in a civil action against the police, inter alia for unlawful arrest, had been wrong to hold that an arrest stated to be for 'unlawful possession' was *necessarily* insufficient as a reason for an arrest for theft of, receiving or unlawfully taking and driving away a motor vehicle. Immediately before A's arrest, he had been told by the officer that if he did not satisfy her with regard to the ownership of the vehicle he had been driving she would arrest him. (The matter was remitted for a new trial for a jury to determine as a matter of fact whether a sufficient reason had been given.)

On the application of the *Christie v Leachinsky* principles to arrests under s. 25, see *Nicholas v Parsonage*, n. **6**, below, and on arrests under the Road Traffic Act 1972 see S. H. Bailey and D. J. Birch, [1982] Crim LR at 551–554.

An arrest is unlawful if the person arrested is not told the ground of arrest in compliance with s. 28(3); however, the arrest becomes lawful once the ground is given: *Lewis v Chief Constable of the South Wales Constabulary* [1991] 1 All ER 206, applying the pre-PACE decision in *R v Kulynycz* [1971] 1 QB 367. Moreover, if it is not practicable for the ground of arrest to be given at the time of arrest the arrest is not rendered unlawful retrospectively when the ground is not supplied when this does become practicable thereafter: *DPP v Hawkins* [1988] 1 WLR 1166 (conviction for assault on a police officer under s. 51(1) of the Police Act 1964 upheld). Cf. *Edwards v DPP*, below, p. 115.

In *Dawes v DPP* [1994] RTR 209, DC, D took a car without authority; the vehicle had been prepared by the police so that when the door was opened, they were automatically informed, and after the car had been driven a few yards, the engine cut out and D was trapped inside. The police arrived on the scene within minutes and informed D that he was arrested and of the reason. The court held that D had been arrested when the doors locked on him, and that he had been given the reason as soon as practicable. Kennedy LJ did, however, say that if the police were slow to respond, a court might find that he was not informed as soon as practicable:

'It may, therefore, be prudent for police forces who wish to use this type of device to consider whether it would be practicable to put in the car something which would advise the person detained that they were under arrest and the reason why they were under arrest, but that is a matter for them' (p. 125).

(A sealed envelope marked 'For the attention of any car thief'?)

(6) The arrestor must regard his action as an arrest in the sense of a possible first step in the criminal process. For example, if he simply detains someone to question him without any thought of arrest the action will be unlawful (see *Kenlin v Gardiner* (above, p. 56) and *R v Brown* (1976) 64 Cr App Rep 231).

(7) The exercise of discretion must not be an ultra vires abuse of power (see above, p. 43); *Plange v Chief Constable of South Humberside Police* (1992) Times, 23 March, CA (arrest where officer knew that there was no possibility of a charge would be unlawful as the officer had acted on some irrelevant consideration or for an improper purpose). The use of undue force does not itself render an arrest unlawful: *Simpson v Chief Constable of South Yorkshire Police* (1991) 135 Sol Jo 383, CA.

3. Under section 1 of the Magistrates' Courts Act 1980:

'Upon an information being laid before a justice of the peace . . . that any person has, or is suspected of having, committed an offence'

the justice may either (1) issue a summons requiring that person to appear before a magistrates' court or (2) issue a warrant to arrest that person and bring him before a magistrates' court. There are geographical limitations to the justice's power (s. 1(2)) and the information must be in writing and substantiated on oath (s. 1(3)). Where the offence charged is an indictable offence, a warrant may be issued at any time notwithstanding that a summons has previously been issued (s. 1(6)). A decision to issue a warrant or summons is a 'judicial act' and cannot be delegated by a justice without express authority (*per* Lord Roskill, obiter, in *Hill v Anderton* [1982] 2 All ER 963 at 971–972, HL). The Justices' Clerks Rules 1970 (S.I. 1970/231) expressly authorise justices' clerks (but not their subordinates) to issue summonses (but not arrest warrants).

Section 125 of the Magistrates' Courts Act 1980, as amended by the 1984 Act, provides:

'(1) A warrant of arrest issued by a justice of the peace shall remain in force until it is executed or withdrawn.

(2) A warrant of arrest, warrant of commitment, warrant of distress or search warrant issued by a justice of the peace may be executed anywhere in England and Wales by any person to whom it is directed or by any constable acting within his police area. . . .

This subsection does not apply to a warrant of commitment or a warrant of distress issued under Part VI of the General Rate Act 1967.

(3) A warrant to [which this subsection applies] may be executed by a constable notwithstanding that it is not in his possession at the time; but the warrant shall, on the demand of the person arrested, be shown to him as soon as practicable. . . .'

Subsection (4) lists the warrants to which subs. (3) applies, and includes arrest warrants and various other warrants under the 1980 Act and other Acts.

There are considerable variations among police forces as to the proportions of cases initiated by (i) an arrest without warrant and charge and (ii) the issue of a summons; the arrangements whereby the police decide to prosecute also vary according to which method is adopted: see S. H. Bailey and M. J. Gunn, *Smith and Bailey on The Modern English Legal System* (2nd edn, 1991), pp. 630–632.

4. *Powers of arrest without warrant.* The general powers to arrest without warrant for 'arrestable offences' are based on those contained in s. 2 of the Criminal Law Act 1967. Section 2 had replaced common law powers of arrest in respect of felonies following the abolition of the distinction between felonies and misdemeanours (see the Seventh Report of the Criminal Law Revision Committee (Cmnd 2695, 1965) on Felonies and Misdemeanours). Sections 24(5) and 24(6) preserve a distinction that existed at common law in respect of the powers of constables and private individuals to arrest for felony. In *Walters v W H Smith & Son Ltd* [1914] 1 KB 595 the defendants reasonably suspected that Walters had stolen books from a station bookstall. At Walters' trial the jury acquitted him, believing his statements that he had intended to pay for the books. Accordingly no crime had been committed in respect of the books. Walters sued the defendants, inter alia, for false imprisonment in having arrested him for an offence that had not been committed. Sir Rufus Isaacs CJ giving judgment for the Court of Appeal held that to justify the arrest a private individual had to show not only reasonable suspicion but also that the offence for which the arrested person was given into custody had in fact been committed, albeit by somebody else. In its Seventh Report the Criminal Law Revision Committee commented:

'14. We gave serious consideration to recommending the abolition of the rule that, in order to justify an arrest, on reasonable suspicion that an offence had been committed, a private person unlike a constable, must prove that the offence was in fact committed by somebody. We recognise that there is a substantial case for abolishing the distinction. First, it seems anomalous that a private person should be liable for wrongful arrest, if he arrests a person on suspicion that an offence has been committed, merely because the suspicion (however reasonable) turns out to be wrong, whereas the reasonableness of the suspicion is a defence in the case of arrest by a constable. Secondly, it is argued that in *Walters's* case . . . the Court of Appeal, in affirming the existence of the distinction, accepted too uncritically statements to the same effect in Hale and Hawkins, without considering the question fully as one of principle; in that case however Sir Rufus Isaacs CJ said (p. 606) that he was "convinced on consideration that it [the rule] is based on sound principle" and that, in the interests of the liberty of the subject, a person who arrested another without getting a warrant should have to take the risk of its turning out, contrary to appearance, that no felony had been committed. Thirdly, it is pointed out that the existence of the distinction may be a trap to a private person who is careful instead of precipitate about deciding whether to arrest a person. If, for example, a store detective saw a person apparently shoplifting, he could arrest him under clause 2(2) on the ground that he had reasonable cause to suspect him of being in the act of committing an arrestable offence, and he would not be liable for unlawful arrest even if it turned out that he was wrong; but if he preferred out of caution to invite the other to the office to give him an opportunity of clearing himself, and then arrested him on being satisfied that he was guilty, the detective would be liable if this turned out to be wrong.

15. But the majority of the committee . . . are not in favour of recommending that the distinction should be abolished. They doubt whether it would be desirable, or acceptable to public opinion, to increase the powers of arrest enjoyed by private persons; and they think that there is a strong argument in policy that a private person should, if it is at all doubtful whether the offence was committed, put the matter in the hands of the police or, as Sir Rufus Isaacs CJ said, take the risk of liability if he acts on his own responsibility.'

The distinction between sub-s. (4) and (5) was crucial in *R v Self* [1992] 3 All ER 476, CA (Cr D). S was seen by a store detective (Mrs Stanton) to put a bar of chocolate in his pocket and leave the store without paying for it. He was followed outside and along the street by the store detective and a shop assistant (Mr Frost). They saw him throw the chocolate away and approached him, F saying 'You have been seen shoplifting'. S punched and kicked F and ran off. This was observed by a passer-by, Mr Mole, who gave chase, caught S and told him he was making a citizen's arrest. S kicked M and struggled but was subsequently restrained. At trial S gave evidence that he had forgotten about the chocolate and had no intention to steal it. He was acquitted of theft, but convicted of an assault with intent to resist or prevent his lawful apprehension contrary to s. 38 of the Offences against the Person Act 1861. The Court of Appeal quashed these convictions holding that the acquittal on the theft charge was fatal to the lawfulness of the arrest under s. 24(5) of PACE. The court dealt dismissively with an argument that the arrest might be justified by reference to s. 24(4). Per Garland J at 480:

'. . . it is said on behalf of the Crown that the court should not be assiduous to restrict the citizen's powers of arrest and that, by going back to sub-s (4) and looking at the words there, "anyone who is in the act of committing an arrestable offence", perhaps those words can be used to cover the sort of situation that arose in this case where somebody is apparently making good his escape. Having committed the offence of theft, can it be said, asks Mr Sleeman, that the thief is not in substance still committing the offence while running away?

He asks, rhetorically, should the court have to inquire into the exact moment when the ingredients of theft come together—dishonesty, appropriation, intention permanently to deprive—when to analyse the offence carefully may produce absurd results so that in one set of circumstances the offence may be complete and the situation fall within sub-s (5) and in another be still being committed and fall within sub-s (4).

The view of this court is that little profit can be had from taking examples and trying to reduce them to absurdity. The words of the statute are clear and applying those words to this case there was no arrestable offence committed.'

Is this convincing? Note that S was under the observation of the store detective throughout and so no issue of identity could arise as there might in respect of an offence that is clearly complete and in the past. Could it plausibly make a difference that the chocolate was no longer in S's possession when he was arrested? If the court's analysis is correct does it not illustrate the absurdity of the distinction between sub-ss. (4) and (5)? See Commentary by J. C. Smith, [1992] Crim LR 573–74 and J. E. Stannard, 'The Store Detective's Dilemma' (1994) 58 JCL 393.

5. The concept 'arrestable offence' includes most serious offences. For example, it includes murder, manslaughter, wounding with intend to do grievous bodily harm, unlawful wounding, criminal damage, robbery, burglary, blackmail, theft, handling

stolen goods and obtaining a pecuniary advantage by deception. The reference to offences for which the penalty is fixed by law relates to murder (Murder (Abolition of Death Penalty) Act 1965, s. 1(1)), treason (Treason Act 1814, s. 1), piracy with violence (Piracy Act 1837, s. 2) and genocide (Genocide Act 1969, s. 1(2)).

Under the 1967 Act the five-year imprisonment had to be available by virtue of an enactment. This requirement has been removed: accordingly, certain common law offences, including kidnapping, attempting to pervert the course of justice, conspiracy to defraud and false imprisonment, now fall within the concept of 'arrestable offence'. The RCCP thought that the concept should be widened to include all *imprisonable* offences: section 24 retains the 'five-year' principle.

6. Section 25 creates a power of arrest in respect of minor offences in circumstances where such a power is necessary if the suspect is to be brought to justice (as advocated, for example, by D. A. Thomas, [1966] Crim LR 639). In *Nicholas v Parsonage* [1987] RTR 199, N was seen by two police officers riding a bicycle without holding the handlebars. They told him twice to put his hands on the bars, and he then did so. When they drove off, N raised two fingers. They then stopped N, and PC Parsonage asked him for his name, telling him that it was required as he had been riding his bicycle in a dangerous manner. N refused to give his name. P informed him of his powers of arrest under PACE, and requested N's name and address. N again refused. P arrested him and told him he was being arrested for failing to give his name and address. N attempted to ride off, and a struggle ensued. N was subsequently convicted of (1) riding a pedal cycle without due care and attention, contrary to the Road Traffic Act 1972, s. 18; and (2) assaulting PC Parsonage's colleague in the execution of his duty, contrary to s. 51(1) of the Police Act 1964. The Divisional Court dismissed an appeal against the latter conviction, holding that the arrest, under s. 25 of PACE, had been lawful. Among the points made by the Divisional Court were (1) a constable exercising the power under s. 25(3)(a) and (c) is not required to say why he wants the name and address; (2) N had been adequately informed of the ground of arrest under s. 28(3), (4). 'Failure to give name and address' is not itself the ground:

'at the time of the arrest the arresting constable must indicate in some words – and there is plenty of authority for the proposition that he does not need to specify it in detail – the offence for which the defendant is being arrested. If he goes on and says: "I am arresting you because you have not given your name and address", so much the better. He has then given all the detail that could possibly be required' (per Glidewell LJ at p. 204).

The requirement was satisfied here by the reference to N's riding in a dangerous manner only a very short time before the moment of arrest. The expression 'at the time of arrest'

'comprehends a short but reasonable period of time around the moment of arrest, both before and, as the statute itself specifically says, after' (ibid.).

In *G v DPP* [1989] Crim LR 150, Gibson (G), Gill and others went to a police station to make a complaint. They refused to leave, and became abusive. Sergeant Jackson arrested Gill for violent behaviour in a police station (contrary to s. 29 of the Town Police Clauses Act 1847). G attempted to prevent this. His conviction for obstructing a police officer was subsequently quashed by the Divisional Court on the ground that Gill's arrest was unlawful. The s. 29 offence was non-arrestable. J gave evidence that, when he made the arrest, he believed the details of name and address that had been supplied by Gill when he first came to the station were false. The sole ground was that 'in the vast majority of cases . . . people who commit offences do not give their correct details'. The court found that J's suspicion was not 'reasonable' as here the details had been provided before Gill was suspected of any offence.

Aspects of both cases are criticised by A. Lawson, 'Whither the "General Arrest Conditions"?' [1993] Crim LR 567. She argues that 'for a valid arrest under section 25, satisfaction of a *general arrest* condition is just as necessary as satisfaction of the *offence* condition' (p. 571). This is undermined by Glidewell LJ's suggestion in *Nicholas v Parsonage* that it is not essential to give as a 'ground' of arrest the relevant general arrest condition as well as the offence; and by the failure of the court in *G v DPP* to state that the sergeant's belief was in any event wholly unreasonable as in effect rendering the general arrest conditions superfluous.

More reassuringly, in *Edwards v DPP* (1993) 94 Cr App Rep 301, the Divisional Court confirmed that, where it is sought to justify an arrest by reference to s. 25, there must be evidence that this was in the officer's mind at the time. Here, police officers sought to search three men suspected of possessing cannabis. One of them put the contents of his right hand in his mouth when asked by PC R to hand them over, and was arrested by R, who said 'You are nicked for obstruction'. The court held this arrest to be unlawful. There was no evidence of R's state of mind and it was not appropriate to infer what it was. Moreover, it was practicable for R to give a reason for the arrest, but he gave a reason that was not a valid one. E's conviction for obstruction of a police officer by intervening after the arrest was quashed.

7. It has been argued that a constable would have power to stop a vehicle in circumstances where he would have power to stop a person, e.g. to effect an arrest: R. Clayton and H. Tomlinson, *Civil Actions Against the Police* (2nd edn, 1992), p. 279. Similarly, once a vehicle has been stopped (e.g. under the Road Traffic Act 1988, s. 163 (above, p. 84)) and the constable reasonably suspects that it has or might have been stolen, the constable has power at common law to detain it for such reasonable time as will enable him to effect an arrest (*Lodwick v Sanders* [1985] 1 All ER 577; *Sanders v DPP* [1988] Crim LR 605).

8. *Disposition after arrest.* A person arrested by or handed over to a constable must be taken to a police station as soon as 'practicable', unless his presence elsewhere 'is necessary in order to carry out such investigations as it is reasonable to carry out immediately' (s 30(1) (10)). This appears to put into statutory form the dicta of Lord Denning MR in *Dallison v Caffery* [1965] 1 QB 348 at 366–367, CA: here, a suspect had been taken to check out an alibi instead of direct to the police station: however, as it had been done with his consent, he could not complain of it anyway. It does not appear that the suspect can require a constable to make a detour to check out an explanation of his conduct that would clear him: *McCarrick v Oxford* [1983] RTR 117, Commentary by D. J. Birch, [1982] Crim LR 751.

In *R v Keane* [1992] Crim LR 306, the Court of Appeal (Criminal Division) 'inclined to the view' that there had been breaches of s. 30(1), (10) and (11) in that it had not been necessary to interview K at the flat he was occupying, following his arrest for possessing a gun and cannabis; moreover no reasons for the delay were ever recorded. Nevertheless, the court upheld the judge's refusal to exclude the confession made during the interview under s. 78 of PACE. (See, however, the Commentary by D. J. Birch, [1992] Crim LR 307, noting that the revised Code C.11.1 was even more specific in limiting interviews other than at a police station or other authorised place of detention.) See also *R v Khan* [1993] Crim LR 54, and Commentary by D. J. Birch.

If a private person makes an arrest he 'must, as soon as he reasonably can, hand the man over to a constable or take him to the police station or take him before a magistrate' (per Lord Denning MR in *Dallison v Caffery* at pp. 366–7). However, there is no requirement that this be done immediately: *John Lewis & Co v Tims* [1952] AC 676, HL. Here, Mrs Tims and her daughter were arrested for shoplifting by store detectives employed by the appellant firm. After being arrested they were taken to the office of the chief store detective. They were detained there until the chief detective and a manager arrived to give instructions whether to bring proceedings. They were handed into police custody within an hour of arrest. Mrs Tims claimed damages for false imprisonment. She alleged that the detectives were obliged to give her into the custody of the police immediately upon arrest. The House of Lords held that the delay was reasonable in the circumstances: 'there are advantages in refusing to give private detectives a free hand and leaving the determination of whether to prosecute or not to a superior official' (per Lord Porter at p. 691).

9. *Search on arrest.* The provisions of s. 32 are similar to the powers at common law (see *Dillon v O'Brien and Davis* (1887) 16 Cox CC 245; *Bessell v Wilson* (1853) 20 LTOS 233n; *Leigh v Cole* (1853) 6 Cox CC 329, 332), but with some significant modifications. (For searches *at* police stations see ss. 54, 55, below pp. 130–132). Note there is no *automatic* right to search in every case. The search may extend to premises where the suspect had been 'immediately' before arrest; at common law it was apparently only possible to search premises where the arrestee was at the time of arrest (and possibly only in the 'immediate vicinity' of the arrestee): see *McLorie v Oxford* [1982] QB 1290; cf. *Dillon v O'Brien and Davis*, supra; *Elias v Pasmore* [1934] 2 KB 164, Horridge J. If this is not done 'immediately' entry and search must be based instead on s. 18 (above, p. 89): *R v Badham* [1987] Crim LR 202 (Wood Green Crown Court). (Is s. 32 *clearly* so limited?)

In *R v Beckford* (1991) 94 Cr App Rep 43, CA (Cr D), police officers were observing premises where they believed the ground floor flat (which had been searched under a warrant on previous occasions) was being used for drug dealing. They arrested a man, Lamptey, who emerged from the premises and who, when intercepted, dropped a package of what appeared to be (and turned out to be) heroin. On arrest, L denied that he had dropped anything. They then searched the flat in reliance on their s. 32 powers and found B and others and quantities of heroin. The Court of Appeal (Criminal Division) held that the police were entitled to assume that L had come from the ground floor flat rather than either of the other two flats in the premises in view of their previous knowledge of the use of the ground floor flat. (Note, however, that the true issue was where in fact he was immediately before the arrest not what was suspected by the police: see Commentary by D. J. Birch, [1991] Crim LR 919.) Moreover, the police were entitled to rely on s. 32 if that 'genuinely [was] the reason why police officers made their entry and search' (per Watkins LJ at 49). However, B's conviction was quashed as this issue was not left to the jury to consider. In argument, counsel for the Crown argued that the police officers entered the flat to look for evidence that would rebut L's denial that he had dropped a package of drugs, thus falling within s. 32. Counsel for B argued that the police were using L's arrest 'as a pretext for what they had really wanted to do all along, namely enter the premises without a warrant', avoiding the requirements of PACE Code B. It was difficult to imagine what further evidence was required against L; 'where a police officer knows he already has all the evidence he reasonably requires upon the arrestable offence he cannot possibly be said to believe that he needs to search for evidence relating to that offence' (p. 48).

Counsel suggested that the true state of affairs was that the police were really seeking evidence of *other* offences against *other* people, which was not within s. 32. These arguments were not considered by the court. In fact, they raise familiar public law issues as to overlapping statutory powers and exercise of powers for a plurality of purposes. If the police have two avenues lawfully open to them, one involving obtaining a warrant and the other not, why should they not choose what is to them the less burdensome (cf. in a different context *Westminster Bank Ltd v Beverley Borough Council* [1971] AC 509, HL).

If the police can properly undertake a s. 32 search, is it necessarily wrong for them to have in mind the point that, once lawfully on the premises, s. 19 of PACE confers very broad powers of seizure? If it is wrong, are the police nevertheless protected provided they 'genuinely' intend to act under s. 32; or is the exercise of power unlawful because a legally irrelevant consideration has been taken into account?

10. Section 29 makes it clear that a person at a police station 'helping police with their inquiries' is not under arrest unless he is told to the contrary. This reflects the present position although many may not realise it. Note that the Act does not require the police to inform such a person of the position (cf M. Zander, *The Police and Criminal Evidence Act 1984* (2nd edn, 1990), pp. 65–67). The Code on Detention etc. requires this to be done if he is cautioned (C.10.2). The question of 'voluntary attendance' is considered by I. McKenzie, R. Morgan and R. Reiner, [1990] Crim LR 22, 27–33. They argue that any encounter between the police and a suspect (as distinct from a witness) is inherently coercive and that all 'voluntary attenders' who are suspects should be told that they are free to leave at any time, are under no obligation to answer questions, and are entitled to have someone told of their whereabouts and to consult a solicitor in private. They also commend a formal recording procedure adopted by one force for voluntary attenders.

9 Detention

Police and Criminal Evidence Act 1984

PART IV

DETENTION

Detention—conditions and duration

34. Limitations on police detention
(1) A person arrested for an offence shall not be kept in police detention except in accordance with the provisions of this Part of this Act.
(2) Subject to subsection (3) below, if at any time a custody officer—
   (a) becomes aware, in relation to any person in police detention, that the grounds for the detention of that person have ceased to apply; and
   (b) is not aware of any other grounds on which the continued detention of that person could be justified under the provisions of this Part of this Act,
it shall be the duty of the custody officer, subject to subsection (4) below, to order his immediate release from custody.
(3) No person in police detention shall be released except on the authority of a custody officer at the police station where his detention was authorised or, if it was authorised at more than one station, a custody officer at the station where it was last authorised.
(4) A person who appears to the custody officer to have been unlawfully at large when he was arrested is not to be released under subsection (2) above.

(5) A person whose release is ordered under subsection (2) above shall be released without bail unless it appears to the custody officer—

(a) that there is need for further investigation of any matter in connection with which he was detained at any time during the period of his detention; or

(b) that proceedings may be taken against him in respect of any such matter,

and, if it so appears, he shall be released on bail.

(6) For the purposes of this Part of this Act a person arrested under [section 6(5) of the Road Traffic Act 1988] is arrested for an offence.

[(7) For the purposes of this Part of this Act a person who returns to a police station to answer to bail or is arrested under section 46A below shall be treated as arrested for an offence and the offence in connection with which he was granted bail shall be deemed to be that offence.]¹

35. Designated police stations

(1) The chief officer of police for each police area shall designate the police stations in his area which, subject to section 30(3) and (5) above, are to be the stations in that area to be used for the purpose of detaining arrested persons.

(2) A chief officer's duty under subsection (1) above is to designate police stations appearing to him to provide enough accommodation for that purpose.

(3) Without prejudice to section 12 of the Interpretation Act 1978 (continuity of duties) a chief officer—

(a) may designate a station which was not previously designated; and

(b) may direct that a designation of a station previously made shall cease to operate.

(4) In this Act 'designated police station' means a police station designated under this section.

36. Custody officers at police stations

(1) One or more custody officers shall be appointed for each designated police station.

(2) A custody officer for a designated police station shall be appointed—

(a) by the chief officer of police for the area in which the designated police station is situated; or

(b) by such other police officer as the chief officer of police for that area may direct.

(3) No officer may be appointed a custody officer unless he is of at least the rank of sergeant.

(4) An officer of any rank may perform the functions of a custody officer at a designated police station if a custody officer is not readily available to perform them.

(5) Subject to the following provisions of this section and to section 39(2) below, none of the functions of a custody officer in relation to a person shall be performed by an officer who at the time when the function falls to be performed is involved in the investigation of an offence for which that person is in police detention at that time. . . .

(7) Where an arrested person is taken to a police station which is not a designated police station, the functions in relation to him which at a designated police station would be the functions of a custody officer shall be performed—

(a) by an officer who is not involved in the investigation of an offence for which he is in police detention, if such an officer is readily available; and

(b) if no such officer is readily available, by the officer who took him to the station or any other officer.

(8) References to a custody officer in the following provisions of this Act include references to an officer other than a custody officer who is performing the functions of a custody officer by virtue of subsection (4) or (7) above.

(9) Where by virtue of subsection (7) above an officer of a force maintained by a police authority who took an arrested person to a police station is to perform the functions of a custody officer in relation to him, the officer shall inform an officer who—

(a) is attached to a designated police station; and

(b) is of at least the rank of inspector,

that he is to do so.

(10) The duty imposed by subsection (9) above shall be performed as soon as it is practicable to perform it.

37. Duties of custody officer before charge

(1) Where—

(a) a person is arrested for an offence—(i) without a warrant, or (ii) under a warrant not endorsed for bail; [. . .]

---

1 Inserted by the Criminal Justice and Public Order Act 1994, s. 29(3).

the custody officer at each police station where he is detained after his arrest shall determine whether he has before him sufficient evidence to charge that person with the offence for which he was arrested and may detain him at the police station for such period as is necessary to enable him to do so.

(2) If the custody officer determines that he does not have such evidence before him, the person arrested shall be released either on bail or without bail, unless the custody officer has reasonable grounds for believing that his detention without being charged is necessary to secure or preserve evidence relating to an offence for which he is under arrest or to obtain such evidence by questioning him.

(3) If the custody officer has reasonable grounds for so believing, he may authorise the person arrested to be kept in police detention.

(4) Where a custody officer authorises a person who has not been charged to be kept in police detention, he shall, as soon as is practicable, make a written record of the grounds for the detention.

(5) Subject to subsection (6) below, the written record shall be made in the presence of the person arrested who shall at that time be informed by the custody officer of the grounds for his detention.

(6) Subsection (5) above shall not apply where the person arrested is, at the time when the written record is made—

    (*a*) incapable of understanding what is said to him;

    (*b*) violent or likely to become violent; or

    (*c*) in urgent need of medical attention.

(7) Subject to section 41(7) below, if the custody officer determines that he has before him sufficient evidence to charge the person arrested with the offence for which he was arrested, the person arrested—

    (*a*) shall be charged; or

    (*b*) shall be released without charge, either on bail or without bail.

(8) Where—

    (*a*) a person is released under subsection (7)(*b*) above; and

    (*b*) at the time of his release a decision whether he should be prosecuted for the offence for which he was arrested has not been taken,

it shall be the duty of the custody officer so to inform him.

(9) If the person arrested is not in a fit state to be dealt with under subsection (7) above, he may be kept in police detention until he is.

(10) The duty imposed on the custody officer under subsection (1) above shall be carried out by him as soon as practicable after the person arrested arrives at the police station or, in the case of a person arrested at the police station, as soon as practicable after the arrest. . . .

(15) In this Part of this Act—

'arrested juvenile' means a person arrested with or without a warrant who appears to be under the age of 17 [. . .];

'endorsed for bail' means endorsed with a direction for bail in accordance with section 117(2) of the Magistrates' Courts Act 1980.

38. Duties of custody officer after charge

(1) Where a person arrested for an offence otherwise than under a warrant endorsed for bail is charged with an offence, the custody officer shall [, subject to section 25 of the Criminal Justice and Public Order Act 1994,]¹ order his release from police detention, either on bail or without bail, unless—

    (*a*) if the person arrested is not an arrested juvenile—

        (i) his name or address cannot be ascertained or the custody officer has reasonable grounds for doubting whether a name or address furnished by him as his name or address is his real name or address;

        [(ii) the custody officer has reasonable grounds for believing that the person arrested will fail to appear in court to answer to bail;

        (iii) in the case of a person arrested for an imprisonable offence, the custody officer has reasonable grounds for believing that the detention of the person arrested is necessary to prevent him from committing an offence;

        (iv) in the case of a person arrested for an offence which is not an imprisonable offence, the custody officer has reasonable grounds for believing that the detention of the person arrested is necessary to prevent him from causing physical injury to any other person or from causing loss of or damage to property;

        (v) the custody officer has reasonable grounds for believing that the detention of the person arrested is necessary to prevent him from interfering with the administration of justice or with the investigation of offences or of a particular offence; or

1 Inserted by the Criminal Justice and Public Order Act 1994, Sch. 10, para. 54.

(vi) the custody officer has reasonable grounds for believing that the detention of the person arrested is necessary for his own protection;][1]

(b) if he is an arrested juvenile—

(i) any of the requirements of paragraph (a) above is satisfied; or

(ii) the custody officer has reasonable grounds for believing that he ought to be detained in his own interests.

(2) If the release of a person arrested is not required by subsection (1) above, the custody officer may authorise him to be kept in police detention.

[(2A) The custody officer, in taking the decisions required by subsection (1)(a) and (b) above (except (a)(i) and (vi) and (b)(ii)), shall have regard to the same considerations as those which a court is required to have regard to in taking the corresponding decisions under paragraph 2 of Part I of Schedule 1 to the Bail Act 1976.][2]

(3) Where a custody officer authorises a person who has been charged to be kept in police detention, he shall, as soon as practicable, make a written record of the grounds for the detention.

(4) Subject to subsection (5) below the written record shall be made in the presence of the person charged who shall at that time be informed by the custody officer of the grounds for his detention.

(5) Subsection (4) above shall not apply where the person charged is, at the time when the written record is made—

(a) incapable of understanding what is said to him;

(b) violent or likely to become violent; or

(c) in urgent need of medical attention.

[(6) Where a custody officer authorises an arrested juvenile to be kept in police detention under subsection (1) above, the custody officer shall, unless he certifies—

(a) that, by reason of such circumstances as are specified in the certificate, it is impracticable for him to do so; or

(b) in the case of an arrested juvenile who has attained the [age of 12 years], that no secure accommodation is available and that keeping him in other local authority accommodation would not be adequate to protect the public from serious harm from him,

secure that the arrested juvenile is moved to local authority accommodation.

(6A) In this section—

'local authority accommodation' means accommodation provided by or on behalf of a local authority (within the meaning of the Children Act 1989);

'secure accommodation' means accommodation provided for the purpose of restricting liberty;

'sexual offence' and 'violent offence' have the same meanings as in Part I of the Criminal Justice Act 1991;

and any reference, in relation to an arrested juvenile charged with a violent or sexual offence, to protecting the public from serious harm from him shall be construed as a reference to protecting members of the public from death or serious personal injury, whether physical or psychological, occasioned by further such offences committed by him.][3]

[(6B) Where an arrested juvenile is moved to local authority accommodation under subsection (6) above, it shall be lawful for any person acting on behalf of their authority to detain him.][4]

(7) A certificate made under subsection (6) above in respect of an arrested juvenile shall be produced to the court before which he is first brought thereafter.

[(7A) In this section 'imprisonable offence' has the same meaning as in Schedule 1 to the Bail Act 1976.][5]

(8) In this Part of this Act 'local authority' has the same meaning as in the [Children Act 1989].[4]

39. Responsibilities in relation to persons detained

(1) Subject to subsections (2) and (4) below, it shall be the duty of the custody officer at a police station to ensure—

(a) that all persons in police detention at that station are treated in accordance with this Act and any code of practice issued under it and relating to the treatment of persons in police detention; and

(b) that all matters relating to such persons which are required by this Act or by such codes of practice to be recorded are recorded in the custody records relating to such persons.

(2) If the custody officer, in accordance with any code of practice issued under this Act, transfers or permits the transfer of a person in police detention—

1 Substituted by the Criminal Justice and Public Order Act 1994, s. 28(2).
2 Inserted by ibid., s. 28(3).
3 Inserted by the Criminal Justice Act 1991, s. 59, and amended by the Criminal Justice and Public Order Act 1994, s. 24.
4 Substituted by the Children Act 1989, Sch. 13, para. 53(3).
5 Inserted by the 1994 Act, s. 28(4).

(*a*) to the custody of a police officer investigating an offence for which that person is in police detention; or

(*b*) to the custody of an officer who has charge of that person outside the police station—

  (i) the custody officer shall cease in relation to that person to be subject to the duty imposed on him by subsection (1)(*a*) above; and

  (ii) it shall be the duty of the officer to whom the transfer is made to ensure that he is treated in accordance with the provisions of this Act and of any such codes of practice as are mentioned in subsection (1) above.

(3) If the person detained is subsequently returned to the custody of the custody officer, it shall be the duty of the officer investigating the offence to report to the custody officer as to the manner in which this section and the codes of practice have been complied with while that person was in his custody.

(4) If an arrested juvenile is [moved to local authority accommodation]¹ under section 38(6) above, the custody officer shall cease in relation to that person to be subject to the duty imposed on him by subsection (1) above. . . .

(6) Where—

(*a*) an officer of higher rank than the custody officer gives directions relating to a person in police detention; and

(*b*) the directions are at variance—

  (i) with any decision made or action taken by the custody officer in the performance of a duty imposed on him under this Part of this Act; or

  (ii) with any decision or action which would but for the directions have been made or taken by him in the performance of such a duty,

the custody officer shall refer the matter at once to an officer of the rank of superintendent or above who is responsible for the police station for which the custody officer is acting as custody officer.

40. Review of police detention

(1) Reviews of the detention of each person in police detention in connection with the investigation of an offence shall be carried out periodically in accordance with the following provisions of this section—

(*a*) in the case of a person who has been arrested and charged, by the custody officer; and

(*b*) in the case of a person who has been arrested but not charged, by an officer of at least the rank of inspector who has not been directly involved in the investigation.

(2) The officer to whom it falls to carry out a review is referred to in this section as a 'review officer'.

(3) Subject to subsection (4) below—

(*a*) the first review shall be not later than six hours after the detention was first authorised;

(*b*) the second review shall be not later than nine hours after the first;

(*c*) subsequent reviews shall be at intervals of not more than nine hours.

(4) A review may be postponed—

(*a*) if, having regard to all the circumstances prevailing at the latest time for it specified in subsection (3) above, it is not practicable to carry out the review at that time;

(*b*) without prejudice to the generality of paragraph (*a*) above—

  (i) if at that time the person in detention is being questioned by a police officer and the review officer is satisfied that an interruption of the questioning for the purpose of carrying out the review would prejudice the investigation in connection with which he is being questioned; or

  (ii) if at that time no review officer is readily available.

(5) If a review is postponed under subsection (4) above it shall be carried out as soon as practicable after the latest time specified for it in subsection (3) above.

(6) If a review is carried out after postponement under subsection (4) above, the fact that it was so carried out shall not affect any requirement of this section as to the time at which any subsequent review is to be carried out.

(7) The review officer shall record the reasons for any postponement of a review in the custody record.

(8) Subject to subsection (9) below, where the person whose detention is under review has not been charged before the time of the review, section 37(1) to (6) above shall effect in relation to him, but with the substitution—

(*a*) of references to the person whose detention is under review for references to the person arrested; and

(*b*) of references to the review officer for references to the custody officer.

(9) Where a person has been kept in police detention by virtue of section 37(9) above, section 37(1) to (6) shall not have effect in relation to him but it shall be the duty of the review officer to determine whether he is yet in a fit state.

---

1 Substituted by the Children Act 1989, Sch. 13, para. 53(3).

(10) Where the person whose detention is under review has been charged before the time of the review, section 38(1) to (6) above shall have effect in relation to him, but with the substitution of references to the person whose detention is under review for references to the person arrested.

(11) Where—

(a) an officer of higher rank than the review officer gives directions relating to a person in police detention; and

(b) the directions are at variance—

(i) with any decision made or action taken by the review officer in the performance of a duty imposed on him under this Part of this Act; or

(ii) with any decision or action which would but for the directions have been made or taken by him in the performance of such a duty,

the review officer shall refer the matter at once to an officer of the rank of superintendent or above who is responsible for the police station for which the review officer is acting as review officer in connection with the detention.

(12) Before determining whether to authorise a person's continued detention the review officer shall give—

(a) that person (unless he is asleep); or

(b) any solicitor representing him who is available at the time of the review,

an opportunity to make representations to him about the detention.

(13) Subject to subsection (14) below, the person whose detention is under review or his solicitor may make representations under subsection (12) above either orally or in writing.

(14) The review officer may refuse to hear oral representations from the person whose detention is under review if he considers that he is unfit to make such representations by reason of his condition or behaviour.

41. Limits on period of detention without charge

(1) Subject to the following provisions of this section and to sections 42 and 43 below, a person shall not be kept in police detention for more than 24 hours without being charged.

(2) The time from which the period of detention of a person is to be calculated (in this Act referred to as 'the relevant time')—

(a) in the case of a person to whom this paragraph applies, shall be—

(i) the time at which that person arrives at the relevant police station; or

(ii) the time 24 hours after the time of that person's arrest,

whichever is the earlier;

(b) in the case of a person arrested outside England and Wales, shall be—

(i) the time at which that person arrives at the first police station to which he is taken in the police area in England or Wales in which the offence for which he was arrested is being investigated; or

(ii) the time 24 hours after the time of that person's entry into England and Wales,

whichever is the earlier;

(c) in the case of a person who—

(i) attends voluntarily at a police station; or

(ii) accompanies a constable to a police station without having been arrested,

and is arrested at the police station, the time of his arrest;

(d) in any other case, except where subsection (5) below applies, shall be the time at which the person arrested arrives at the first police station to which he is taken after his arrest.

(3) Subsection (2)(a) above applies to a person if—

(a) his arrest is sought in one police area in England and Wales;

(b) he is arrested in another police area; and

(c) he is not questioned in the area in which he is arrested in order to obtain evidence in relation to an offence for which he is arrested;

and in sub-paragraph (i) of that paragraph 'the relevant police station' means the first police station to which he is taken in the police area in which his arrest was sought.

(4) Subsection (2) above shall have effect in relation to a person arrested under section 31 above as if every reference in it to his arrest or his being arrested were a reference to his arrest or his being arrested for the offence for which he was originally arrested.

(5) If—

(a) a person is in police detention in a police area in England and Wales ('the first area'); and

(b) his arrest for an offence is sought in some other police area in England and Wales ('the second area'); and

(c) he is taken to the second area for the purposes of investigating that offence, without being questioned in the first area in order to obtain evidence in relation to it,

the relevant time shall be—
    (i) the time 24 hours after he leaves the place where he is detained in the first area; or
    (ii) the time at which he arrives at the first police station to which he is taken in the second area,
whichever is the earlier.

(6) When a person who is in police detention is removed to hospital because he is in need of medical treatment, any time during which he is being questioned in hospital or on the way there or back by a police officer for the purpose of obtaining evidence relating to an offence shall be included in any period which falls to be calculated for the purposes of this Part of this Act, but any other time while he is in hospital or on his way there or back shall not be so included.

(7) Subject to subsection (8) below, a person who at the expiry of 24 hours after the relevant time is in police detention and has not been charged shall be released at that time either on bail or without bail.

(8) Subsection (7) above does not apply to a person whose detention for more than 24 hours after the relevant time has been authorised or is otherwise permitted in accordance with section 42 or 43 below.

(9) A person released under subsection (7) above shall not be re-arrested without a warrant for the offence for which he was previously arrested unless new evidence justifying a further arrest has come to light since his release[; but this subsection does not prevent an arrest under section 46A below.][1]

42. Authorisation of continued detention

(1) Where a police officer of the rank of superintendent or above who is responsible for the police station at which a person is detained has reasonable grounds for believing that—
    (a) the detention of that person without charge is necessary to secure or preserve evidence relating to an offence for which he is under arrest or to obtain such evidence by questioning him;
    (b) an offence for which he is under arrest is a serious arrestable offence; and
    (c) the investigation is being conducted diligently and expeditiously,
he may authorise the keeping of that person in police detention for a period expiring at or before 36 hours after the relevant time.

(2) Where an officer such as is mentioned in subsection (1) above has authorised the keeping of a person in police detention for a period expiring less than 36 hours after the relevant time, such an officer may authorise the keeping of that person in police detention for a further period expiring not more than 36 hours after that time if the conditions specified in subsection (1) above are still satisfied when he gives the authorisation.

(3) If it is proposed to transfer a person in police detention to another police area, the officer determining whether or not to authorise keeping him in detention under subsection (1) above shall have regard to the distance and the time the journey would take.

(4) No authorisation under subsection (1) above shall be given in respect of any person—
    (a) more than 24 hours after the relevant time; or
    (b) before the second review of his detention under section 40 above has been carried out.

(5) Where an officer authorises the keeping of a person in police detention under subsection (1) above, it shall be his duty—
    (a) to inform that person of the grounds for his continued detention; and
    (b) to record the grounds in that person's custody record.

(6) Before determining whether to authorise the keeping of a person in detention under subsection (1) or (2) above, an officer shall give—
    (a) that person; or
    (b) any solicitor representing him who is available at the time when it falls to the officer to determine whether to give the authorisation,
an opportunity to make representations to him about the detention.

(7) Subject to subsection (8) below, the person in detention or his solicitor may make representations under subsection (6) above either orally or in writing.

(8) The officer to whom it falls to determine whether to give the authorisation may refuse to hear oral representations from the person in detention if he considers that he is unfit to make such representations by reason of his condition or behaviour.

(9) Where—
    (a) an officer authorises the keeping of a person in detention under subsection (1) above; and
    (b) at the time of the authorisation he has not yet exercised a right conferred on him by section 56 or 58 below,
the officer—
    (i) shall inform him of that right;
    (ii) shall decide whether he should be permitted to exercise it;

---

1 Inserted by the Criminal Justice and Public Order Act 1994, s. 29(4).

(iii) shall record the decision in his custody record; and

(iv) if the decision is to refuse to permit the exercise of the right, shall also record the grounds for the decision in that record.

(10) Where an officer has authorised the keeping of a person who has not been charged in detention under subsection (1) or (2) above, he shall be released from detention, either on bail or without bail, not later than 36 hours after the relevant time, unless—

(a) he has been charged with an offence; or

(b) his continued detention is authorised or otherwise permitted in accordance with section 43 below.

(11) A person released under subsection (10) above shall not be re-arrested without a warrant for the offence for which he was previously arrested unless new evidence justifying a further arrest has come to light since his release[; but this subsection does not prevent an arrest under section 46A below.][1]

43. Warrants of further detention

(1) Where, on an application on oath made by a constable and supported by an information, a magistrates' court is satisfied that there are reasonable grounds for believing that the further detention of the person to whom the application relates is justified, it may issue a warrant of further detention authorising the keeping of that person in police detention.

(2) A court may not hear an application for a warrant of further detention unless the person to whom the application relates—

(a) has been furnished with a copy of the information; and

(b) has been brought before the court for the hearing.

(3) The person to whom the application relates shall be entitled to be legally represented at the hearing and, if he is not so represented but wishes to be so represented—

(a) the court shall adjourn the hearing to enable him to obtain representation; and

(b) he may be kept in police detention during the adjournment.

(4) A person's further detention is only justified for the purposes of this section or section 44 below if—

(a) his detention without charge is necessary to secure or preserve evidence relating to an offence for which he is under arrest or to obtain such evidence by questioning him;

(b) an offence for which he is under arrest is a serious arrestable offence; and

(c) the investigation is being conducted diligently and expeditiously.

(5) Subject to subsection (7) below, an application for a warrant of further detention may be made—

(a) at any time before the expiry of 36 hours after the relevant time; or

(b) in a case where—

(i) it is not practicable for the magistrates' court to which the application will be made to sit at the expiry of 36 hours after the relevant time; but

(ii) the court will sit during the 6 hours following the end of that period,

at any time before the expiry of the said 6 hours.

(6) In a case to which subsection (5)(b) above applies—

(a) the person to whom the application relates may be kept in police detention until the application is heard; and

(b) the custody officer shall make a note in that person's custody record—

(i) of the fact that he was kept in police detention for more than 36 hours after the relevant time; and

(ii) of the reason why he was so kept.

(7) If—

(a) an application for a warrant of further detention is made after the expiry of 36 hours after the relevant time; and

(b) it appears to the magistrates' court that it would have been reasonable for the police to make it before the expiry of that period,

the court shall dismiss the application.

(8) Where on an application such as is mentioned in subsection (1) above a magistrates' court is not satisfied that there are reasonable grounds for believing that the further detention of the person to whom the application relates is justified, it shall be its duty—

(a) to refuse the application; or

(b) to adjourn the hearing of it until a time not later than 36 hours after the relevant time.

(9) The person to whom the application relates may be kept in police detention during the adjournment.

(10) A warrant of further detention shall—

(a) state the time at which it is issued;

(b) authorise the keeping in police detention of the person to whom it relates for the period stated in it.

---

1 Inserted by the Criminal Justice and Public Order Act 1994, s. 29(4).

(11) Subject to subsection (12) below, the period stated in a warrant of further detention shall be such period as the magistrates' court thinks fit, having regard to the evidence before it.

(12) The period shall not be longer than 36 hours.

(13) If it is proposed to transfer a person in police detention to a police area other than that in which he is detained when the application for a warrant of further detention is made, the court hearing the application shall have regard to the distance and the time the journey would take.

(14) Any information submitted in support of an application under this section shall state—

(a) the nature of the offence for which the person to whom the application relates has been arrested;

(b) the general nature of the evidence on which that person was arrested;

(c) what inquiries relating to the offence have been made by the police and what further inquiries are proposed by them;

(d) the reasons for believing the continued detention of that person to be necessary for the purposes of such further inquiries.

(15) Where an application under this section is refused, the person to whom the application relates shall forthwith be charged or, subject to subsection (16) below, released, either on bail or without bail.

(16) A person need not be released under subsection (15) above—

(a) before the expiry of 24 hours after the relevant time; or

(b) before the expiry of any longer period for which his continued detention is or has been authorised under section 42 above.

(17) Where an application under this section is refused, no further application shall be made under this section in respect of the person to whom the refusal relates, unless supported by evidence which has come to light since the refusal.

(18) Where a warrant of further detention is issued, the person to whom it relates shall be released from police detention, either on bail or without bail, upon or before the expiry of the warrant unless he is charged.

(19) A person released under subsection (18) above shall not be re-arrested without a warrant for the offence for which he was previously arrested unless new evidence justifying a further arrest has come to light since his release[; but this subsection does not prevent an arrest under section 46A below.][1]

44. Extension of warrants of further detention

(1) On an application on oath made by a constable and supported by an information a magistrates' court may extend a warrant of further detention issued under section 43 above if it is satisfied that there are reasonable grounds for believing that the further detention of the person to whom the application relates is justified.

(2) Subject to subsection (3) below, the period for which a warrant of further detention may be extended shall be such period as the court thinks fit, having regard to the evidence before it.

(3) The period shall not—

(a) be longer than 36 hours; or

(b) end later than 96 hours after the relevant time.

(4) Where a warrant of further detention has been extended under subsection (1) above, or further extended under this subsection, for a period ending before 96 hours after the relevant time, on an application such as is mentioned in that subsection a magistrates' court may further extend the warrant if it is satisfied as there mentioned; and subsections (2) and (3) above apply to such further extensions as they apply to extensions under subsection (1) above.

(5) A warrant of further detention shall, if extended or further extended under this section, be endorsed with a note of the period of the extension.

(6) Subsections (2), (3) and (14) of section 43 above shall apply to an application made under this section as they apply to an application made under that section.

(7) Where an application under this section is refused, the person to whom the application relates shall forthwith be charged or, subject to subsection (8) below, released, either on bail or without bail.

(8) A person need not be released under subsection (7) above before the expiry of any period for which a warrant of further detention issued in relation to him has been extended or further extended on an earlier application made under this section.

45. Detention before charge—supplementary

(1) In sections 43 and 44 of this Act 'magistrates' court' means a court consisting of two or more justices of the peace sitting otherwise than in open court.

(2) Any reference in this Part of this Act to a period of time or a time of day is to be treated as approximate only.

1 Inserted by the Criminal Justice and Public Order Act 1994, s. 29(4).

Detention—miscellaneous

46. Detention after charge
(1) Where a person—
  (a) is charged with an offence; and
  (b) after being charged—
    (i) is kept in police detention; or
    (ii) is detained by a local authority in pursuance of arrangements made under section 38(6) above,
he shall be brought before a magistrates' court in accordance with the provisions of this section.

(2) If he is to be brought before a magistrates' court for the petty sessions area in which the police station at which he was charged is situated, he shall be brought before such a court as soon as is practicable and in any event not later than the first sitting after he is charged with the offence.

(3) If no magistrates' court for that area is due to sit either on the day on which he is charged or on the next day, the custody officer for the police station at which he was charged shall inform the clerk to the justices for the area that there is a person in the area to whom subsection (2) above applies.

(4) If the person charged is to be brought before a magistrates' court for a petty sessions area other than that in which the police station at which he was charged is situated, he shall be removed to that area as soon as is practicable and brought before such a court as soon as is practicable after his arrival in the area and in any event not later than the first sitting of a magistrates' court for that area after his arrival in the area.

(5) If no magistrates' court for that area is due to sit either on the day on which he arrives in the area or on the next day—
  (a) he shall be taken to a police station in the area; and
  (b) the custody officer at that station shall inform the clerk to the justices for the area that there is a person in the area to whom subsection (4) applies.

(6) Subject to subsection (8) below, where a clerk to the justices for a petty sessions area has been informed—
  (a) under subsection (3) above that there is a person in the area to whom subsection (2) above applies; or
  (b) under subsection (5) above that there is a person in the area to whom subsection (4) above applies,
the clerk shall arrange for a magistrates' court to sit not later than the day next following the relevant day.

(7) In this section 'the relevant day'—
  (a) in relation to a person who is to be brought before a magistrates' court for the petty sessions area in which the police station at which he was charged is situated, means the day on which he was charged; and
  (b) in relation to a person who is to be brought before a magistrates' court for any other petty sessions area, means the day on which he arrives in the area.

(8) Where the day next following the relevant day is Christmas Day, Good Friday or a Sunday, the duty of the clerk under subsection (6) above is a duty to arrange for a magistrates' court to sit not later than the first day after the relevant day which is not one of those days.

(9) Nothing in this section requires a person who is in hospital to be brought before a court if he is not well enough.

46A. [Power of arrest for failure to answer to police bail
(1) A constable may arrest without a warrant any person who, having been released on bail under this Part of this Act subject to a duty to attend at a police station, fails to attend at that police station at the time appointed for him to do so.

(2) A person who is arrested under this section shall be taken to the police station appointed as the place at which he is to surrender to custody as soon as practicable after the arrest.

(3) For the purposes of—
  (a) section 30 above (subject to the obligation in subsection (2) above), and
  (b) section 31 above,
an arrest under this section shall be treated as an arrest for an offence.][1]

NOTES

1. Part IV established a new system for police detention. It created a division of functions (wherever possible) between the officers conducting an investigation and a

---

1 Inserted by the Criminal Justice and Public Order Act 1994, s. 29(2).

'custody officer' responsible for supervising each suspect's detention, provided for written records to be kept and provided for periodic reviews of the need for the continued detention of the suspect. It does not apply to detention by immigration officers (see below, p. 723), detention under the Prevention of Terrorism (Temporary Provisions) Act 1989, s. 14 and Sch. 2 or 5 (below pp. 303–304, 318–319) or the detention of members of the armed forces as deserters, absentees or prisoners under escort: s. 51(a)–(c), and does not affect 'any right of a person in detention to apply for habeas corpus or other prerogative remedy': s. 51(d). Statistics of detention must be kept and published in the annual reports of chief officers of police: s. 50. Periods in police detention count towards custodial sentences: s. 49.

The grounds for continued detention after charge were extended by the Criminal Justice and Public Order Act 1994, s. 28(2).

2. The basic period of permitted detention without charge is limited to 24 hours from the 'relevant time': s. 41, usually the first time at which the arrestee arrives at the first police station to which he is taken after the arrest. In the case of 'serious arrestable offences' (see above, pp. 72–74) an officer of the rank of superintendent or above may authorise detention up to 36 hours from the 'relevant time': s. 42; a magistrates' court may issue a warrant of further detention for a period up to a further 36 hours: s.43; and a magistrates' court may extend the warrant for a still further period up to 36 hours, provided that the total time does not exceed 96 hours from the 'relevant time': s. 44. Times are to be treated as 'approximate only': s.45. A person must normally be brought before a magistrates' court as soon as practicable and in any event not later than the first sitting after he is charged with the offence: s. 46.

3. The provisions of the Act are supplemented by the *Code of Practice for the Detention, Treatment and Questioning of Persons by Police Officers* (PACE Code C, Revised Edition, 1995), which applies to persons who are in custody at police stations whether or not they have been arrested for an offence; and to those who have been removed to a police station as a place of safety under sections 135 and 136 of the Mental Health Act 1983 (Code C.1.10). The Notes for Guidance state that those at a police station voluntarily to assist with an investigation should be treated with no less consideration than those in custody, and enjoy an absolute right to obtain legal advice or to communicate with anyone outside the station (Code C.1*A*).

A custody record must be opened as soon as practicable for each person who is brought to a police station under arrest or is arrested at the police station having attended there voluntarily (Code C.2.1). The custody officer is responsible for the accuracy and completeness of the custody record and for ensuring that it accompanies the detained person on any transfer to another station (Code C.2.3). Where the person leaves police detention, or is taken before a court, he, his legal representative or his appropriate adult (see below, p. 136) is entitled, on request, to be given a copy of the record and, on giving reasonable notice, to inspect the original (Code C.2.4, C.2.5).

Section 15 of Code C covers reviews and extensions of detentions. Points additional to the provisions of PACE include the following. On a review of detention, persons other than a solicitor or appropriate adult who have an interest in the person's welfare may make representations (Code C.15.1); before conducting a review, the review officer must ensure that the detained person is reminded of his entitlement to free legal advice (see below) (Code C.15.3).

The Notes for Guidance state that if the detained person is likely to be asleep at the latest time when a review of detention or an authorisation of continued detention may take place, then it should be brought forward so that the detained person can make representations without being woken up (Code C.*15A*). An application for a warrant of further detention or an extension should be made between 10 am and 9 pm, and if possible during normal court hours (Code C.*15B*). A review under s. 40 of PACE or Sch. 3 to the Prevention of Terrorism (Temporary Provisions) Act 1989 may be conducted by telephone but a review to decide whether to authorise continued detention under s. 42 of PACE must be done in person (Code C.*15C*).

4. A further authorisation by a superintendent under s. 42(2) may be given even if the original 24-hour time limit has by then expired: *R v Taylor* [1991] Crim LR 541, CA (Cr D).

5. In *R v Slough Magistrates' Court, ex p Stirling* (1987) 151 JP 603, S was detained following his arrest for armed robbery for a total period of 36 hours expiring at approximately 12.53 pm on May 30, 1986. At 12.45 pm on that day an information was prepared by the police as the basis of an application to the court for a warrant of further detention. The justices were advised by their clerk that it was not practicable to hear the application at that time because of the pressure of business, and the hearing was delayed until 2.45 pm. The justices granted a warrant. This decision was quashed by the Divisional Court, which (1) rejected S's argument that s. 43(5)(b)(i) only applies where the justices are not sitting at all at the expiry of the 36-hour period, holding that the justices had a discretion to postpone a hearing to a later time (within the 6 hours permitted) where it was not practicable for them to hear the application immediately; but held that (2) s. 43(7) *required* the justices to dismiss an application if it appeared to them that it would have been reasonable for the police to apply within the 36 hour period; and (3) no reasonable bench of magistrates could have concluded that the police had acted reasonably here.

6. The role of the custody officer was designed as a key element in the protection of the rights of the detainee. However, in *Vince v Chief Constable of the Dorset Police* [1993] 2 All ER 321, the Court of Appeal held that s. 36(1) merely imposed a duty on the Chief Constable to appoint one custody officer for each designated police station and a discretion (to be reasonably exercised) to appoint more. The provision could not be read as imposing a duty to appoint a sufficient number of custody officers to ensure that the functions of such officers were ordinarily performed by duly appointed officers, and (for example) by untrained constables. Steyn LJ noted (at 335) that this conclusion showed

'that a central provision of the Act is a less effective safeguard than many may have thought'.

The custody officer is not 'statutorily debarred' from participating with other officers in a ploy involving placing suspects in a bugged cell: *R v Bailey and Smith*, below, p. 164.

The RCCJ noted that the research evidence, (including the 1993 report by Brown *et al* referred to in n. **7**) and their own observations on and discussions with custody officers:

'indicate that the police are not entirely comfortable with the role and that performance of it, though improving, still leaves something to be desired'.

(Cm 2263, p. 31.) Moreover,

'it may also be unrealistic to expect a police officer to take an independent view of a case investigated by colleagues. As far as the evidence needed to substantiate a charge is concerned, the custody officer is hardly in a position to take a different view from the investigating officer because in the nature of things he or she will not have the same direct and detailed knowledge of the case' (ibid.).

Nevertheless, they recommended that the custody officer role should remain with the police rather than be handed to the CPS or an independent body; the latter would also not have the same detailed knowledge of the case as investigating officers and it was not certain that they would be able to maintain the desired independence. The police should continue to take full responsibility for the integrity of evidence gathered, both through interviews and in other ways. Accordingly, steps should be taken to develop and strengthen the performance by the police of the custody officer role. This should include keeping the use of acting sergeants to a minimum; exploration of the possibility of delegating clerical and administrative tasks to civilians under the custody officer's control; refresher-training; the centralisation of custody functions within forces wherever practicable and their provision as a separate specialist service; the introduction of computerisation of the custody record process to a national standard; continuous video recording (including sound–track) of all the activities in the custody office, the passages and stairways leading to the cells and, if feasible, the cell passage and doors of individual cells; the testing of a simplified version of the notice to detained persons (devised by I. Clare and G. Gudjonsson, RCCJ Research Study No. 7 (HMSO, 1993)).

7. The RCCP found that about 75 per cent of suspects were dealt with within six hours and about 95 per cent within 24 hours. A survey done by the Metropolitan Police for three months in 1979 showed that only 0.4 per cent of 48,343 persons have been held for over 72 hours without charge or release: RCCP Report, para. 3.96. A study by D. Brown (*Detention at the Police Station under the Police and Criminal Evidence Act 1984*, H.O. Research Study 104, 1989) of 5,500 custody records from 3 or 4 stations in each of 10 forces, found considerable variations from station to station in the length of detention without charge, this being strongly linked with the seriousness of the crime in question, but also perhaps with differences in the custody officer's approach to PACE. The mean length of detention was just over five hours and the median three hours, 19 mins. By 24 hours, only 1% were still being held without charge. Pre-PACE comparisons suggested that detention times were now shorter in some more serious cases, but slightly longer for less serious offences. 18% of those charged were detained in custody, the mean length for detention being nearly 16 hours. Powers available to the police in respect of serious arrestable offences (e.g. detention beyond 24 hours, delayed legal advice or notification, intimate samples, non–intimate samples taken without consent) were used infrequently.[1] The RCCJ did not think any change in detention limits was necessary, although further national statistics should be maintained (Cm. 2263, 1993, p. 30). Other commentators have noted dramatic falls in the levels of complaints about treatment by the police in the charge room or cells (M. Maguire, (1988) 28 Br. J. Criminol. 19, 41) and improvements in arrangements for the welfare of suspects (ibid.; B. L. Irving and I. K. McKenzie, *Police Interrogation: the effects of the Police and Criminal Evidence Act 1984* (1989), pp. 196–198 (replicating the RCCP Research Study No. 2, 1980)). On the other hand the initial authorisation of detention by the custody officer is in practice a formality (I. McKenzie, R. Morgan and R. Reiner, [1990] Crim LR 22, 22–27).

8. Release on police bail is governed by provisions of the Bail Act 1976, as amended by Part II of the Criminal Justice and Public Order Act 1994 (ss. 25–30 and Sch. 3)

1 See also D. Dixon *et al.*, 'Safeguarding the Rights of Suspects in Police Custody' (1990) 1 *Policing and Society* 115; K. Bottomley *et al.*, *The Impact of PACE* (1991), Chap. 6; and on the last point, *Operation of Certain Police Powers under PACE: England and Wales, 1993* (HOSB 15/94), Tables C, D, E, 3, 4 and 5).

(see PACE, s. 47, as amended by the 1994 Act, s. 27). Conditions may now be attached to police bail.

9. A magistrates' court having power to remand a person in custody may, if the remand is for a period not exceeding 3 clear days, commit him to police detention for the purposes of inquiries into other offences (Magistrates' Courts Act 1980, s. 128(7)(8), as inserted by the 1984 Act, s. 48).

10 Questioning and treatment of persons in custody

Police and Criminal Evidence Act 1984

PART V

QUESTIONING AND TREATMENT OF PERSONS BY POLICE

53. Abolition of certain powers of constables to search persons
(1) Subject to subsection (2) below, there shall cease to have effect any Act (including a local Act) passed before this Act in so far as it authorises—
  (*a*) any search by a constable of a person in police detention at a police station; or
  (*b*) an intimate search of a person by a constable;
and any rule of common law which authorises a search as is mentioned in paragraph (*a*) or (*b*) above is abolished. . . .

54. Searches of detained persons
(1) The custody officer at a police station shall ascertain and record or cause to be recorded everything which a person has with him when he is—
  (*a*) brought to the station after being arrested elsewhere or after being committed to custody by an order or sentence of a court; or
  [(*b*) arrested at the station or detained there[, as a person falling within section 34(7), under section 37 above.][1]][2]
(2) In the case of an arrested person the record shall be made as part of his custody record.
(3) Subject to subsection (4) below, a custody officer may seize and retain any such thing or cause any such thing to be seized and retained.
(4) Clothes and personal effects may only be seized if the custody officer—
  (*a*) believes that the person from whom they are seized may use them—
    (i) to cause physical injury to himself or any other person;
    (ii) to damage property;
    (iii) to interfere with evidence; or
    (iv) to assist him to escape; or
  (*b*) has reasonable grounds for believing that they may be evidence relating to an offence.
(5) Where anything is seized, the person from whom it is seized shall be told the reason for the seizure unless he is—
  (*a*) violent or likely to become violent; or
  (*b*) incapable of understanding what is said to him.
(6) Subject to subsection (7) below, a person may be searched if the custody officer considers it necessary to enable him to carry out his duty under subsection (1) above and to the extent that the custody officer considers necessary for that purpose.
[(6A) A person who is in custody at a police station or is in police detention otherwise than at a police station may at any time be searched in order to ascertain whether he has with him anything which he could use for any of the purposes specified in subsection (4)(*a*) above.
(6B) Subject to subsection (6C) below, a constable may seize and retain, or cause to be seized and retained, anything found on such a search.
(6C) A constable may only seize clothes and personal effects in the circumstances specified in subsection (4) above.][3]

---

1 Substituted by the Criminal Justice and Public Order Act 1994, Sch. 10, para. 55.
2 Inserted by the Criminal Justice Act 1988, s. 147(a).
3 Inserted by the Criminal Justice Act 1988, s. 147(b).

(7) An intimate search may not be conducted under this section.

(8) A search under this section shall be carried out by a constable.

(9) The constable carrying out a search shall be of the same sex as the person searched.

55. Intimate searches

(1) Subject to the following provisions of this section, if an officer of at least the rank of superintendent has reasonable grounds for believing—

(a) that a person who has been arrested and is in police detention may have concealed on him anything which—

(i) he could use to cause physical injury to himself or others; and

(ii) he might so use while he is in police detention or in the custody of a court; or

(b) that such a person—

(i) may have a Class A drug concealed on him;

and

(ii) was in possession of it with the appropriate criminal intent before his arrest,

he may authorise [an intimate][1] search of that person.

(2) An officer may not authorise an intimate search of a person for anything unless he has reasonable grounds for believing that it cannot be found without his being intimately searched.

(3) An officer may give an authorisation under subsection (1) above orally or in writing but, if he gives it orally, he shall confirm it in writing as soon as is practicable.

(4) An intimate search which is only a drug offence search shall be by way of examination by a suitably qualified person.

(5) Except as provided by subsection (4) above, an intimate search shall be by way of examination by a suitably qualified person unless an officer of at least the rank of superintendent considers that this is not practicable.

(6) An intimate search which is not carried out as mentioned in subsection (5) above shall be carried out by a constable.

(7) A constable may not carry out an intimate search of a person of the opposite sex.

(8) No intimate search may be carried out except—

(a) at a police station;

(b) at a hospital;

(c) at a registered medical practitioner's surgery; or

(d) at some other place used for medical purposes.

(9) An intimate search which is only a drug offence search may not be carried out at a police station.

(10) If an intimate search of a person is carried out, the custody record relating to him shall state—

(a) which parts of his body were searched; and

(b) why they were searched.

(11) The information required to be recorded by subsection (10) above shall be recorded as soon as practicable after the completion of the search.

(12) The custody officer at a police station may seize and retain anything which is found on an intimate search of a person, or cause any such thing to be seized and retained—

(a) if he believes that the person from whom it is seized may use it—

(i) to cause physical injury to himself or any other person;

(ii) to damage property;

(iii) to interfere with evidence; or

(iv) to assist him to escape;

or

(b) if he has reasonable grounds for believing that it may be evidence relating to an offence.

(13) Where anything is seized under this section, the person from whom it is seized shall be told the reason for the seizure unless he is—

(a) violent or likely to become violent; or

(b) incapable of understanding what is said to him. . . .

(17) In this section—

'the appropriate criminal intent' means an intent to commit an offence under—

(a) section 5(3) of the Misuse of Drugs Act 1971 (possession of controlled drug with intent to supply to another); or

(b) section 68(2) of the Customs and Excise Management Act 1979 (exportation etc. with intent to evade a prohibition or restriction);

'Class A drug' has the meaning assigned to it by section 2(1)(b) of the Misuse of Drugs Act 1971;

1 Inserted by the Criminal Justice Act 1988, Sch. 15, para. 99.

'drug offence search' means an intimate search for a Class A drug which an officer has authorised by virtue of subsection (1)(*b*) above; and
'suitably qualified person' means—
  (*a*) registered medical practitioner; or
  (*b*) a registered nurse.

56. Right to have someone informed when arrested
(1) Where a person has been arrested and is being held in custody in a police station or other premises, he
shall be entitled, if he so requests, to have one friend or relative or other person who is known to him or
who is likely to take an interest in his welfare told, as soon as is practicable except to the extent that delay
is permitted by this section, that he has been arrested and is being detained there.
(2) Delay is only permitted—
  (*a*) in the case of a person who is in police detention for a serious arrestable offence; and
  (*b*) if an officer of at least the rank of superintendent authorises it.
(3) In any case the person in custody must be permitted to exercise the right conferred by subsection (1)
above within 36 hours from the relevant time, as defined in section 41(2) above.
(4) [Subject to subsection (5A) below, an][1] officer may give an authorisation under subsection (2) above
orally or in writing but, if he gives it orally, he shall confirm it in writing as soon as is practicable.
(5) An officer may only authorise delay where he has reasonable grounds for believing that telling the
named person of the arrest—
  (*a*) will lead to interference with or harm to evidence connected with a serious arrestable offence or
      interfere with or physical injury to other persons; or
  (*b*) will lead to the alerting of other persons suspected of having committed such an offence but not
      yet arrested for it; or
  (*c*) will hinder the recovery of any property obtained as a result of such an offence.
[(5A) An officer may also authorise delay where the serious arrestable offence is a drug trafficking offence
[or an offence to which Part VI of the Criminal Justice Act 1988 applies (offences in respect of which
confiscation orders under that Part may be made)] and the officer has reasonable grounds for believing—
  [(*a*) where the offence is a drug trafficking offence, that the detained person has benefited from drug
      trafficking and that the recovery of the value of that person's proceeds of drug trafficking will be
      hindered by telling the named person of the arrest; and
  (*b*) where the offence is one to which Part VI of the Criminal Justice Act 1988 applies that the detained
      person has benefited from the offence and that the recovery of the value of the property obtained by
      that person from or in connection with the offence or of the pecuniary advantage derived by him
      from or in connection with it will be hindered by telling the named person of the arrest].][1]
(6) If a delay is authorised—
  (*a*) the detained person shall be told the reason for it; and
  (*b*) the reason shall be noted on his custody record.
(7) The duties imposed by subsection (6) above shall be performed as soon as is practicable.
(8) The rights conferred by this section on a person detained at a police station or other premises are
exercisable whenever he is transferred from one place to another; and this section applies to each subsequent occasion on which they are exercisable as it applies to the first such occasion.
(9) There may be no further delay in permitting the exercise of the right conferred by subsection (1)
above once the reason for authorising delay ceases to subsist.
(10) In the foregoing provisions of this section references to a person who has been arrested include references to a person who has been detained under the terrorism provisions and 'arrest' includes detention
under those provisions.
(11) In its application to a person who has been arrested or detained under the terrorism provisions—
  (*a*) subsection (2)(*a*) above shall have effect as if for the words 'for a serious arrestable offence' there
      were substituted the words 'under the terrorism provisions';
  (*b*) subsection (3) above shall have effect as if for the words from 'within' onwards there were substi-
      tuted the words 'before the end of the period beyond which he may no longer be detained
      without the authority of the Secretary of State'; and
  (*c*) subsection (5) above shall have effect as if at the end there were added 'or
  (*d*) will lead to interference with the gathering of information about the commission, preparation
      or instigation of acts of terrorism; or
  (*e*) by alerting any person, will make it more difficult—
      (i) to prevent an act of terrorism; or
      (ii) to secure the apprehension, prosecution or conviction of any person in connection with
          the commission, preparation or instigation of an act of terrorism.'. . .

1 Inserted by the Drug Trafficking Offences Act 1986, s. 32.

58. Access to legal advice

(1) A person arrested and held in custody in a police station or other premises shall be entitled, if he so requests, to consult a solicitor privately at any time.

(2) Subject to subsection (3) below, a request under subsection (1) above and the time at which it was made shall be recorded in the custody record.

(3) Such a request need not be recorded in the custody record of a person who makes it at a time while he is at a court after being charged with an offence.

(4) If a person makes such a request, he must be permitted to consult a solicitor as soon as is practicable except to the extent that delay is permitted by this section.

(5) In any case he must be permitted to consult a solicitor within 36 hours from the relevant time, as defined in section 41(2) above.

[subsections (6), (7), (8), (8A), (9), (10) and (11) correspond, respectively, to s. 56(2), (4), (5), (5A), (6), (7) and (9): above p. 132]

(12) The reference in subsection (1) above to a person arrested includes a reference to a person who has been detained under the terrorism provisions.

[subsection (13) corresponds to s. 56(11): above]

(14) If an officer of appropriate rank has reasonable grounds for believing that, unless he gives a direction under subsection (15) below, the exercise by a person arrested or detained under the terrorism provisions of the right conferred by subsection (1) above will have any of the consequences specified in subsection (8) above (as it has effect by virtue of subsection (13) above), he may give a direction under that subsection.

(15) A direction under this subsection is a direction that a person desiring to exercise the right conferred by subsection (1) above may only consult a solicitor in the sight and hearing of a qualified officer of the uniformed branch of the force of which the officer giving the direction is a member.

(16) An officer is qualified for the purpose of subsection (15) above if—

    (*a*) he is of at least the rank of inspector; and

    (*b*) in the opinion of the officer giving the direction he has no connection with the case.

(17) An officer is of appropriate rank to give a direction under subsection (15) above if he is of at least the rank of Commander or Assistant Chief Constable.

(18) A direction under subsection (15) above shall cease to have effect once the reason for giving it ceases to subsist. . . .

60. Tape-recording of interviews

(1) It shall be the duty of the Secretary of State—

    (*a*) to issue a code of practice in connection with the tape-recording of interviews of persons suspected of the commission of criminal offences which are held by police officers at police stations; and

    (*b*) to make an order requiring the tape-recording of interviews of persons suspected of the commission of criminal offences, or of such descriptions of criminal offences as may be specified in the order, which are so held, in accordance with the code as it has effect for the time being.

(2) An order under subsection (1) above shall be made by statutory instrument and shall be subject to annulment in pursuance of a resolution of either House of Parliament.

65. Part V—supplementary

In this Part of this Act—

'appropriate consent' means—

    (*a*) in relation to a person who has attained the age of 17 years, the consent of that person;

    (*b*) in relation to a person who has not attained that age but has attained the age of 14 years, the consent of that person and his parent or guardian; and

    (*c*) in relation to a person who has not attained the age of 14 years, the consent of his parent or guardian;

['drug trafficking' and 'drug trafficking offence' have the same meaning as in the [Drug Trafficking Act 1994];][1] . . .

['intimate sample' means—

    (*a*) a sample of blood, semen or any other tissue fluid, urine or pubic hair;

    (*b*) a dental impression;

    (*c*) a swab taken from a person's body orifice other than the mouth;][2]

['non-intimate sample' means—

    (*a*) a sample of hair other than pubic hair;

    (*b*) a sample taken from a nail or from under a nail;

    (c) a swab taken from any part of a person's body including the mouth but not any other body orifice;

    (*d*) saliva;

1 Inserted by the Drug Trafficking Offences Act 1986, s. 32, and amended by the 1994 Act, Sch. 1, para. 8.

2 Substituted by the Criminal Justice and Public Order Act 1994, s. 58.

(e) a footprint or a similar impression of any part of a person's body other than a part of his hand.]¹

['intimate search' means a search which consists of the physical examination of a person's body orifices other than the mouth;]. . .

['speculative search', in relation to a person's fingerprints or samples, means such a check against other footprints or samples or against information derived from other samples as is referred to in section 63A(1) above; 'sufficient' and 'insufficient', in relation to a sample, means sufficient or insufficient (in point of quantity or quality) for the purpose of enabling information to be produced by the means of analysis used or to be used in relation to the sample.]¹

['the terrorism provisions' means section 14(1) of the Prevention of Terrorism (Temporary Provisions) Act 1989 and any provision of Schedule 2 or 5 to that Act conferring a power of arrest or detention; and 'terrorism' has the meaning assigned to it by section 20(1) of that Act].²

[. . . references in this Part to any person's proceeds of drug trafficking are to be construed in accordance with the [Drug Trafficking Act 1994]].³

Code of Practice for the Detention, Treatment and Questioning of Persons by Police Officers [C] Revised edition, 1995

11. Interviews: general

(a) Action

11.1A An interview is the questioning of a person regarding his involvement or suspected involvement in a criminal offence or offences which, by virtue of paragraph 10.1 of Code C, is required to be carried out under caution. Procedures undertaken under section 7 of the Road Traffic Act 1988 do not constitute interviewing for the purpose of this code.

11.1 Following a decision to arrest a suspect he must not be interviewed about the relevant offence except at a police station or other authorised place of detention unless the consequent delay would be likely:

   (a) to lead to interference with or harm to evidence connected with an offence or interference with or physical harm to other people; or
   (b) to lead to the alerting of other people suspected of having committed an offence but not yet arrested for it; or
   (c) to hinder the recovery of property obtained in consequence of the commission of an offence.

Interviewing in any of these circumstances shall cease once the relevant risk has been averted or the necessary questions have been put in order to attempt to avert that risk.

11.2 Immediately prior to the commencement or re-commencement of any interview at a police station or other authorised place of detention, the interviewing officer shall remind the suspect of his entitlement to free legal advice and that the interview can be delayed for him to obtain legal advice (unless the exceptions in paragraph 6.6 or Annex C apply). It is the responsibility of the interviewing officer to ensure that all such reminders are noted in the record of interview.

11.2A At the beginning of an interview carried out in a police station, the interviewing officer, after cautioning the suspect, shall put to him any significant statement or silence which occurred before his arrival at the police station, and shall ask him whether he confirms or denies that earlier statement or silence and whether he wishes to add anything. A 'significant' statement or silence is one which appears to be capable of being used in evidence against the suspect, in particular a direct admission of guilt, or failure or refusal to answer a question or to answer it satisfactorily, which might give rise to an inference under Part III of the Criminal Justice and Public Order Act 1994.

11.3 No police officer may try to obtain answers to questions or to elicit a statement by the use of oppression. Except as provided for in paragraph 10.5C, no police officer shall indicate, except in answer to a direct question, what action will be taken on the part of the police if the person being interviewed answers questions, makes a statement or refuses to do either. If the person asks the officer directly what action will be taken in the event of his answering questions, making a statement or refusing to do either, then the officer may inform the person what action the police propose to take in that event provided that action is itself proper and warranted.

1 Substituted by the Criminal Justice and Public Order Act 1994, ss. 58, 59(1).
2 Inserted by the 1989 Act, Sch. 8, para. 6.
3 Inserted by the Drug Trafficking Offences Act 1986, s. 32, and amended by the 1994 Act, Sch. 1, para. 8.

11.4 As soon as a police officer who is making enquiries of any person about an offence believes that a prosecution should be brought against him and that there is sufficient evidence for it to succeed, he shall ask the person if he has anything further to say. If the person indicates that he has nothing more to say the officer shall without delay cease to question him about that offence. This should not, however, be taken to prevent officers in revenue cases or acting under the confiscation provisions of the Criminal Justice Act 1988 or the Drug Trafficking Offences Act 1986 from inviting suspects to complete a formal question and answer record after the interview is concluded.

(b) Interview records

11.5 (a) An accurate record must be made of each interview with a person suspected of an offence, whether or not the interview takes place at a police station.

    (b) The record must state the place of the interview, the time it begins and ends, the time the record is made (if different), any breaks in the interview and the names of all those present; and must be made on the forms provided for this purpose or in the officer's pocket-book or in accordance with the code of practice for the tape-recording of police interviews with suspects (Code E).

    (c) The record must be made during the course of the interview, unless in the investigating officer's view this would not be practicable or would interfere with the conduct of the interview, and must constitute either a verbatim record of what has been said or, failing this, an account of the interview which adequately and accurately summarises it.

11.6 The requirement to record the names of all those present at an interview does not apply to police officers interviewing persons detained under the Prevention of Terrorism (Temporary Provisions) Act 1989. Instead the record shall state the warrant or other identification number and duty station of such officers.

11.7 If an interview record is not made during the course of the interview it must be made as soon as practicable after its completion.

11.8 Written interview records must be timed and signed by the maker.

11.9 If an interview record is not completed in the course of the interview the reason must be recorded in the officer's pocket book.

11.10 Unless it is impracticable the person interviewed shall be given the opportunity to read the interview record and to sign it as correct or to indicate the respects in which he considers it inaccurate. If the interview is tape-recorded the arrangements set out in Code E apply. If the person concerned cannot read or refuses to read the record or to sign it, the senior police officer present shall read it over to him and ask him whether he would like to sign it as correct (or make his mark) or to indicate the respects in which he considers it inaccurate. The police officer shall then certify on the interview record itself what has occurred. [See *Note 11D*]

11.11 If the appropriate adult or the person's solicitor is present during the interview, he should also be given an opportunity to read and sign the interview record (or any written statement taken down by a police officer).

11.12 Any refusal by a person to sign an interview record when asked to do so in accordance with the provisions of the code must itself be recorded.

11.13 A written record should also be made of any comments made by a suspected person, including unsolicited comments, which are outside the context of an interview but which might be relevant to the offence. Any such record must be timed and signed by the maker. Where practicable the person shall be given the opportunity to read that record and to sign it as correct or to indicate the respects in which he considers it inaccurate. Any refusal to sign should be recorded. [See *Note 11D*]

(c) Juveniles, the mentally disordered and the mentally handicapped

11.14 A juvenile or a person who is mentally disordered or mentally handicapped, whether suspected or not, must not be interviewed or asked to provide or sign a written statement in the absence of the appropriate adult unless paragraph 11.1 or Annex C applies.[1] . . .

---

1 (Ed.) Annex C applies where an officer of the rank of superintendent or above considers that delay will lead to the consequences set out in para. 11.1(a) to (c). Questioning may not continue once sufficient information to avert the immediate risk has been obtained.

11.16 Where the appropriate adult is present at an interview, he shall be informed that he is not expected to act simply as an observer; and also that the purposes of his presence are, first, to advise the person being questioned and to observe whether or not the interview is being conducted properly and fairly, and secondly, to facilitate communication with the person being interviewed.

Notes for Guidance

11A [Not used].

11B It is important to bear in mind that, although juveniles or persons who are mentally disordered or mentally handicapped are often capable of providing reliable evidence, they may, without knowing or wishing to do so, be particularly prone in certain circumstances to provide information which is unreliable, misleading or self-incriminating. Special care should therefore always be exercised in questioning such a person, and the appropriate adult should be involved, if there is any doubt about a person's age, mental state or capacity. Because of the risk of unreliable evidence it is also important to obtain corroboration of any facts admitted whenever possible.

11C It is preferable that a juvenile is not arrested at his place of education unless this is unavoidable. Where a juvenile is arrested at his place of education, the principal or his nominee must be informed.

11D When a suspect agrees to read records of interviews and of other comments and to sign them as correct, he should be asked to endorse the record with words such as 'I agree that this is a correct record of what was said' and add his signature. Where the suspect does not agree with the record, the officer should record the details of any disagreement and then ask the suspect to read these details and then sign them to the effect that they accurately reflect his disagreement. Any refusal to sign when asked to do so shall be recorded.

NOTES

1. Under Code C (see above, p. 76), where a person arrives at a police station under arrest, or is arrested there, the custody officer must tell him clearly of (1) his right to have someone informed of the arrest, (2) his right to consult privately with a solicitor, and the fact that independent legal advice is available free of charge, and (3) his right to consult the codes of practice (Code C.3.1). He must be given (1) a written notice setting out these rights, his right to a copy of the custody record, the terms of the caution (see below), and the arrangements for obtaining legal advice; and (2) an additional notice setting out his entitlements while in custody (Code C.3.2). Special arrangements apply where the person appears to be deaf, or there is doubt about his hearing, or is a juvenile, or is mentally handicapped or suffering from a mental disorder, or is blind or seriously visually handicapped or unable to read (Code C.3.6–C.3.14). These normally require the involvement of an independent third party such as an interpreter, an approved social worker or an 'approved adult' as the case may be.

A person who attends a police station voluntarily may leave at will unless arrested; if it is decided that he should not be allowed to leave, then he must at once be arrested and brought before the custody officer; if a person is not arrested, but is cautioned, the officer who cautions him must also inform him that he is not under arrest, that he is not obliged to remain at the police station, but that if he remains he may obtain free and independent legal advice (Code C.3.15). If a person at the station voluntarily asks about his entitlement to legal advice, he must be given a copy of the written notice explaining the arrangements for obtaining legal advice (Code C.3.16).

The Notes for Guidance state that the right to consult the Codes of Practice does not entitle the person concerned to delay unreasonably any necessary investigative or administrative action while he does so; procedures requiring the provision of breath, blood or urine specimens under the Road Traffic Act 1988 need not be delayed (Code C.3E, confirming *DPP v Billington* [1988] 1 All ER 435, criticised by D. Tucker, [1990] Crim LR 177).

Detailed rules govern the conditions of detention: for example, cells must be adequately heated, cleaned, ventilated and lit; bedding must be of a reasonable standard and in a clean and sanitary condition; access to toilet and washing facilities must be provided; at least two light meals and one main meal must be offered in any period of 24 hours; brief outdoor exercise must be offered daily if practicable; detainees should be visited every hour (every half hour if drunk) (Code C.8). Any complaints must be reported to an officer of the rank of inspector or above not connected with the investigation (Code C.9.1); there are detailed provisions governing the medical treatment of persons in custody (Code C.9.2–9.6).

D. Brown *et al.*, *Changing the Code: Police Detention under the Revised PACE Codes of Practice* (HORS No 129, HMSO, 1993) found that there had been improvements in the range of information provided to suspects following the introduction of revised PACE Code C in 1991; however, the required information was not always given and, in a quarter of cases, rights were not given clearly.

2. *Searches of detained persons.* Sections 54 and 55 replace any statutory or common law powers of search of arrested persons at police stations. A *search* may be carried out in any case where the custody officer considers it necessary to enable him to perform his duty of recording everything the arrestee has with him: s. 54(1) (6). This reflects standard police practice, which was previously of doubtful legality. At common law a search could only take place if there was reasonable cause to suspect that the arrestee had on his person evidence, a weapon or some other object he could use to effect an escape (see above, p. 116; *Lindley v Rutter* [1981] QB 128; *Brazil v Chief Constable of Surrey* [1983] 3 All ER 537). The power to *seize* was similarly limited. Now, anything may be seized except that limiting conditions attach to clothes and personal effects: s. 54(3)(4). Under the common law, in *R v Naylor* [1979] Crim LR 532 it was held to be unlawful for the police to seize jewellery from a woman prisoner where there was no suggestion that the rings were in any way unusual or capable of causing injury or that the earrings or necklace could cause harm to the defendant or anyone else. Similarly, in *Lindley v Rutter* [1981] QB 128 it was doubted whether it could be justifiable to remove a woman's brassière unless there was 'some evidence that female drunks in general were liable to injure themselves with their brassières or that the defendant had shown a peculiar disposition to do so' (per Donaldson LJ at p. 135). *Lindley v Rutter* also made it clear that suspects could not be searched simply because that was required by police standing orders:

'the officer having custody of the prisoner must always consider . . . whether the special circumstances of the particular case justify or demand a departure from the standard procedure either by omitting what would otherwise be done or by taking additional measures'

(per Donaldson LJ at p. 135; see also *Brazil v Chief Constable of Surrey, supra*). This principle remains applicable: the powers to search are (1) discretionary and (2) to be exercised by the officers on the spot, and must not be fettered in advance by themselves or their superiors. (This is a standard feature of all statutory discretionary powers: see above, pp. 40–41). Some doubt was, however, cast on this by the Court of Appeal in *Middleweek v Chief Constable of the Merseyside Police* [1990] 3 All ER 662 (decided in 1985 and concerning events in 1980). Here, the court rejected an argument that *Lindley v Rutter* was authority for the proposition that a search is unlawful if a standing instruction is followed without first giving consideration to the particular circumstances of the case; it was regarded as holding merely that compliance with a standing instruction is itself no conclusive answer to a complaint that a search is unlawful. If in fact there is a good reason for the search, the search will be lawful. It is submitted that this takes insufficient (or indeed any) account of the principle that statutory discretions should not be fettered and that Donaldson LJ's statement should be taken at face value.

The custody officer is responsible for ascertaining and safeguarding a detained person's property (Code C.4). Personal effects are defined as items which a person may lawfully need or use or refer to while in detention, but not cash and other items of value (Code C.4.3). The Notes for Guidance state that s. 54(1) of PACE does not require *every* detained person to be searched, but requires a search 'where it is clear that the custody officer will have continuing duties in relation to that person or where that person's behaviour or offence makes an inventory appropriate' (Code C.4A). Does it?

Intimate and strip searches must be conducted in accordance with Annex A to Code C. A strip search is a search involving the removal of more than outer clothing, and may take place only if the custody officer considers it to be necessary to remove an article which the detained person would not be allowed to keep (Code C, Annex A.10). Statistics must be kept of intimate searches under s. 55 and published in the annual reports of chief officers of police (s. 55(15)). The national figures for intimate searches have only once exceeded 100 (104 in 1986); in 1993 there were 41 (HO Statistical Bulletin 15/94, Table E). The vast majority were carried out by a 'suitably qualified person'.

3. *Right to have someone informed when arrested.* Such a right was first created by the Criminal Law Act 1977, s. 62. On the meaning of 'held in custody' in ss. 56 and 58, see *R v Kerawalla* [1991] Crim LR 451, CA (Cr D), where it was held that this meant where an appropriate authority has authorised detention in custody in a police station (criticised as too narrow an interpretation by D. J. Birch, Commentary at p. 453).

Under Code C, if the friend etc. chosen cannot be contacted, the person who made the request may choose up to two alternatives; attempts beyond these may be allowed as a matter of discretion (Code C.5.1). The person in custody may receive visits at the custody officer's discretion (Code C.5.4). If a friend etc. makes inquiries about his whereabouts, the information must be given if he agrees and unless the right not to be held incommunicado can properly be delayed (Code C.5.5). The person in custody should be supplied with writing materials on request, and allowed to speak on the telephone for a reasonable time to one person; a letter or call can be denied or delayed by an officer of the rank of inspector or above if he considers that they may result in either of the conditions in s. 56(5)(a) or (b) (in the case of a person detained for an arrestable or serious arrestable offence) or any of the grounds that justify delay of such rights (in the case of persons detained under the Prevention of Terrorism (Temporary Provisions) Act 1989) (Code C.5.6). The person must be informed that the letter, call or message (other than to a solicitor) may be read or listened to as appropriate and may be given in evidence; a telephone call may be terminated if abused; the costs can be at public expense at the discretion of the custody officer (C.5.7).

Citizens of independent Commonwealth countries and foreign nations have special rights of access to the appropriate High Commission, Embassy or Consulate (Code C.7).

4. *Right of access to legal advice.* Code C provides that all people in police detention must be informed that they may at any time consult and communicate privately, whether in person, in writing or on the telephone, with a solicitor and that independent legal advice is available free of charge from the duty solicitor (Code C.6.1). The term 'solicitor' includes any trainee solicitor, a duty solicitor representative or an accredited representative included on the register of representatives maintained by the Legal Aid Board (Code C.6.12). This right can only be delayed in accordance with s. 58(8), and provided that the suspect 'has not yet been charged with an offence' (Code C, Annex B.A.(a)1) ('an' here means 'any': *R v Samuel*, below, p. 158). A poster advertising the right to legal advice must be prominently displayed in the charging area of every police station (Code C.6.3). No police officer must at any time do or say anything with the intention of dissuading a person in detention from obtaining legal advice (Code C.6.4). A person who wants legal advice may not be interviewed or continue to be interviewed until he has received it unless

- Annex B to Code C applies (i.e. the right to legal advice can be delayed); or
- an officer of the rank of superintendent or above has reasonable grounds for believing that (i) delay will involve an immediate risk of harm to persons or serious loss of, or damage to, property; or (ii) where awaiting the arrival of a solicitor who has agreed to attend would cause unreasonable delay to the process of investigation; or
- the chosen solicitor (i) cannot be contacted; or (ii) has previously indicated that he does not wish to be contacted; or (iii) has declined to attend; and the person has been advised of the Duty Solicitor Scheme (if there is one) but has declined to ask for the duty solicitor, or the duty solicitor is unavailable. (Here, the interview may be started or continued on the authority of an inspector or above.); or
- the person who wanted legal advice changes his mind. (Here, the interview may be started or continued on the authority of an inspector or above, having inquired into the change of mind, if the person agrees on tape or in writing.) (Code C.6.6)

Where a person is permitted to consult a solicitor, who is available when the interview begins or is in progress, the solicitor must be allowed to be present at the interview (Code C.6.8). The solicitor may only be required to leave if his conduct is such that the investigating officer is unable properly to put questions, and on the authority of an officer not below the rank of superintendent (if readily available), and otherwise an officer not below the rank of inspector who is not connected with the investigation (Code C.6.9, C.6.10). A non-accredited or probationary representative is to be admitted to the police station to provide advice on behalf of a solicitor unless an officer of the rank of inspector or above considers that such a visit will hinder the investigation of crime and directs otherwise; that officer should consider whether the non-accredited or probationary representative's identity and status have been satisfactorily established, whether he is of suitable character to provide legal advice, and any other matters in any letter of authorisation sent by the solicitor; the solicitor and the detained person must be informed if access is refused (Code C.6.12–6.14).

The Notes for Guidance state that the solicitor may seek to intervene in order to seek clarification or to challenge an improper question to his client or the manner in which it is put, or advise his client not to reply to particular questions, or if he wishes to give his client further legal advice. Paragraph C.6.9 only applies if the solicitor's approach or conduct prevents or unreasonably obstructs proper questions being put to the suspect or his response being recorded (Code C.6D).

The holder of acting rank is to be treated as if he were the holder of the substantive rank (e.g. of superintendent), unless the appointment to acting rank is a colourable pretence: *R v Alladice* (1988) 98 Cr App Rep 380, CA (Cr D).

5. The Preamble to the Judges' Rules (see below, p. 150) previously provided that

'every person at any stage of an investigation should be able to communicate and to consult privately with a solicitor. This is so even if he is in custody provided that no unreasonable delay or hindrance is caused to the processes of investigation or the administration of justice by his doing so.'

This was not a legal requirement. In practice few suspects asked to see a solicitor and most such requests were refused: see M. Zander, [1972] Crim LR 342; J. Baldwin and M. McConville, [1979] Crim LR 145; P. Softley, *An Observation Study in Four Police Stations*, RCCP Research Study No. 4, 1981, p. 68.

The right of access to a solicitor is backed by a statutory 24-hour duty solicitor scheme. Research on the operation of the new arrangements indicated that there was a significant increase in the number of suspects seeking legal advice, although they still only constituted a minority; that a variety of ploys were used by the police to discourage exercise of the right; that only a small proportion of suspects had a lawyer with them during police interrogation; and that there might have been a rise in the number of suspects who refused to make admissions (see S. H. Bailey and M. J. Gunn, *Smith and Bailey on the Modern English Legal System* (2nd edn, 1991), pp. 672–675, citing D. Brown, *Detention at the Police Station under the Police and Criminal Evidence Act 1984* (HORS 104, 1989), Chap. 3 and HORPU Bulletin 26:26; A. Sanders *et al*, *Advice and Assistance at Police Stations and the 24 Hour Duty Solicitor Scheme* (LCD, 1989) and A. Sanders and L. Bridges, [1990] Crim LR 494; B. L. Irving and I. K. McKenzie, *Police Interrogation* (1989), pp. 53–59, 113–115, 157–164, 199–200). The report by Sanders *et al* was critical of the quality of service provided by duty solicitors, with a high proportion relying on telephoned advice rather than attendance in person. The Legal Aid Board has changed the rules to require, other than in exceptional circumstances, attendance in person where the suspect is to be questioned about an arrestable offence or an identity parade is to be held, or the suspect complains of serious maltreatment by the police (see E. Cape, *Legal Action*, March 1991, p. 21). The revised version of Code C expressly requires the custody officer to act without delay to secure the provision of legal advice when requested; prohibits any attempt to dissuade the suspect from obtaining advice; and requires the suspect to be reminded at various stages of the right to free legal advice. A report by Brown *et al*. following the introduction of the revised Code C in 1991 (*Changing the Code*, HORS No. 129, HMSO, 1992) revealed an increase in the proportion of suspects requesting legal advice from 24% to 32%; 25% of suspects having a legal consultation compared with 18%, two-thirds being seen in person; but legal advisers less often remaining to attend police interviews with their clinets. Other research was critical of the quality of legal advice made available (see J. Baldwin, *The Role of Legal Representatives at the Police Station* (RCCJ Research Study No. 3, HMSO, 1992); M. McConville and J. Hodgson, *Custodial Legal Advice and the Right to Silence* (RCCJ Research Study No. 16, HMSO, 1993)).

The RCCJ noted that 'there remains a substantial proportion of cases in which legal advice is neither asked for nor received'. Some of the steps they recommended (Cm. 2263, pp. 35–37) to improve arrangements for offering and securing access to legal advice have been incorporated by amendments to Code C. Accordingly, the right to waive legal advice is to be achieved by ticking alternative boxes on the custody record; the suspect should be reminded that he can speak with a duty solicitor on the telephone (see Code C.3.5, C.6.1). On the other hand, a recommended amendment to Code C to encourage the police to inform the suspect's solicitor of at least the general nature of the case and the *prima facie* evidence against the suspect (p. 36) has not been made.

The RCCJ found the evidence on the quality of legal advice to be 'disturbing' but rather weakly thought the answer lay in improved training, supervision and monitoring (pp. 37–39).

The improper denial of the right to legal advice is likely to lead to exclusion of a confession under s. 78: see *R v Samuel*, below, p. 158.

The right of access to legal advice under s. 58(1) does not extend to a person on remand in custody at a magistrates' court, but there is a right of access as soon as reasonably practicable at common law, not abrogated by the 1984 Act; accordingly, a police policy of refusing access to a solicitor on the sole ground that the request was made after 10 a.m. was unlawful: *R v Chief Constable of South Wales, ex p Merrick* [1994] 1 WLR 663, DC.

6. *Fingerprints and body samples.* PACE made separate provision for the taking of fingerprints (s. 61), intimate samples (s. 62) and non-intimate samples (s. 63). The *fingerprints* of a person detained at a police station may be taken without consent (a) on the authority of a superintendent; or (b) if he has been charged with or informed that he may be reported for a recordable offence and he has not already been fingerprinted during the investigation; any person's fingerprints may be taken without consent on his conviction for a recordable offence.

Intimate samples may be taken if there is both (a) the authority of a superintendent (or above) and (b) consent. Under PACE, the authorising officer had to have reasonable grounds to suspect involvement in a serious arrestable offence; this was enormously broadened to any recordable offence by the Criminal Justice and Public Order Act 1994, s. 54, amending s. 62. The definition of an 'intimate sample' was changed by the 1994 Act, s. 58. By comparison with the old definition, the reference to a dental impression was added, but mouth swabs switched to the non-intimate category. (The latter change was effected in Northern Ireland by the Criminal Justice Act 1988, Sch. 14; for criticism see M. Gelowitz, [1989] Crim LR 198 and C. Walker and I. Cram, [1990] Crim LR 479.) If consent is refused, a court or jury may draw such inferences as appear proper (s. 62(1)). An intimate sample other than a sample of urine may only be taken by a registered medical practitioner (or registered dentist in the case of dental impressions) (s. 62(9), as amended by the 1994 Act, s. 54(5)).

The power to take *non-intimate samples* without consent was broadened by the 1994 Act to operate on a broadly similar basis to fingerprinting, *inter alia*, extending to any recordable offence. The definition of 'non-intimate sample' in s. 65 was amended by the 1994 Act, s. 58, which added the references to the mouth and saliva.

The 1994 Act added supplementary provisions in respect of both fingerprints and samples (new s. 63A of PACE). Thus fingerprints or samples may be checked against records held by or on behalf of the police or in connection with or as a result of an investigation of an offence. Samples of hair other than pubic hair may be taken either by cutting or plucking, so long as no more are plucked than the person taking the sample reasonably considers to be necessary for a sufficient sample. Persons not in detention or custody may in certain circumstances be required to attend a police station in order to have a sample taken. Provision is made for the destruction of fingerprints or samples unless the person concerned is convicted (PACE, s. 64, as amended by the 1994 Act, s. 57, to enable samples that would otherwise have to be destroyed to be retained for statistical purposes only). An 'intimate search' has been redefined as 'the physical examination of a person's body orifices other than the mouth' (definition transferred from s. 118 to s. 65 by the 1994 Act, s. 59).

These changes are designed to facilitate the use of dental and DNA evidence, including the establishment of DNA databases, and to enable officers to remove drugs and other suspected substances from a suspect's mouth. They follow recommendations of the RCCJ (Cm. 2263, pp. 14–16), except that the latter merely recommended the extension of sampling powers to assault and burglary. The Northern Ireland provision for the reclassification of mouth swabs as non-intimate samples was said to have 'worked satisfactorily there' (p. 15), although the evidence for this was not stated. Samples taken for the purposes of one inquiry may be used as evidence in another: *R v Kelt* (1993) 99 Cr App Rep 372, CA (Cr D).

7. *The interrogation process.* Code C lays down detailed rules governing the conduct of interviews (Code C.11, above, pp. 134–136, and C.12). There are special requirements where an interpreter is needed (Code C.13). Particular difficulty has been caused by the issue of what constitutes an 'interview' for the purpose of determining whether the requirements of Code C apply (see H. Fenwick, [1993] Crim LR 174 and S. Field, (1993) 13 LS 254). The term was not defined in the first version of Code C (see *R v Maguire* (1989) 90 Cr App Rep 115, CA (Cr D)); and a Note for Guidance in the second version (para. 11A), was rightly criticised as self-contradictory by the Court of Appeal (Criminal Division) in *R v Cox* (1992) 96 Cr App Rep 464. The RCCJ recommended that the point be clarified (Cm. 2263, p. 27), and a definition is now found in Code C 11.1A. The matter is of importance because the close regulation of the conduct of interviews in the police station, including tape-recording, provide an incentive to the police to seek to obtain admissions on the way to the station, perhaps by the use of inducements or threats, or to invent confessions. The RCCJ found it 'impossible to estimate the frequency of such practices' (pp. 27–28). Research studies showed that questioning outside the police station still occurred in a significant proportion of cases (10% in one study, 8% in another). The RCCJ did not wish 'to rule out carefully researched and monitored progress towards the greater use of tape recorders outside the police station'. If this proved to be feasible, the PACE Codes should be extended. Furthermore, on the RCCJ's recommendation, PACE Code C has been amended to require at the beginning of an interview carried out at the police station 'significant statements or silence' which occurred before the interview to be put to the suspect (Code C.11.2A).

What may begin as a general inquiry may become an 'interview' (to which Code C applies) where answers to questions give rise to a suspicion that an offence has been committed. In this situation, the Court of Appeal has suggested that a record should be made of the earlier questions and answers as soon as practicable, the reason for the absence of a contemporaneous note should be recorded and the suspect given the opportunity to check the record: *R v Park* (1994) 99 Cr App Rep 270, CA (Cr D). The volunteering of information other than in response to questions is not an 'interview': *R v Menard* [1995] 1 Cr App Rep 306, CA (Cr D). See also cases where confessions outside the police station have been excluded for breach of PACE requirements: below, pp. 160–165.

Code C.12 applies to 'Interviews in Police Stations'. The custody officer is responsible for deciding whether to deliver a detained person into the custody of an interviewing officer (C.12.1). In any period of 24 hours, a detained person must normally be allowed 8 hours rest free from questioning, travel or interruption arising out of the investigation (C.12.2). No person unfit through drink or drugs to the extent that he is unable to appreciate the significance of questions put to him and his answers may be questioned except in accordance with Annex C (C.12.3). Interview rooms must as far as practicable be adequately heated, lit and ventilated (C.12.4). Interviewing officers should identify themselves and other officers present (C.12.6). Provision is made for meal and refreshment breaks (C.12.7), complaints of breaches of the Code (C.12.8) and documentation (C.12.9–C.12.13).

Where an officer considers that there is sufficient evidence to prosecute a detained person, and that there is sufficient evidence for a prosecution to succeed, and that the person has said all he wishes to say about the offence, he must without delay bring him before the custody officer, who is then responsible for considering whether he should be charged (Code C.16.1). If he is detained in respect of more than one offence, it is permissible to delay until the conditions are satisfied in respect of all the offences (subject to Code C.11.4, above, p. 135) (ibid.). When a detained person is charged with or informed that he may be prosecuted for an offence, he must be cautioned (see n. **10**, below) (Code C.16.2), and if charged, given a written notice with the particulars of the offence and other specified information (Code C.16.3). Questions relating to an offence may not be put to a person after he has been charged with, or informed that he may be prosecuted for that offence,

- unless they are necessary for the purpose of preventing or minimising harm or loss to some other person or to the public or for clearing up an ambiguity in a previous answer or statement; or
- where it is in the interests of justice that the person should have put to him and have an opportunity to comment on information concerning the offence which has come to light since that time (Code C.16.5).

The RCCJ recommended that questioning be permitted after charge provided the suspect is cautioned and has access to a solicitor (Cm. 2263, pp. 16–17). The government had not at the time of writing (May 1995) indicated its response.

Non-compliance with Code C may lead to exclusion of a confession: see below, pp. 157, 160–161, 163–164.

8. All interviews by police officers at police stations with person suspected of an indictable offence must now be tape-recorded in accordance with the provisions of the *Code of Practice on Tape Recording* (PACE Code E). The duty does not apply to interviews for terrorist offences or offences under s. 1 of the Official Secrets Act 1911 (Police and Criminal Evidence Act 1984 (Tape-recording of Interviews) (No. 1) Order 1991 (S.I. 1991 No. 2687) and (No. 2) Order 1992 (S.I. 1992 No. 2803). As a result, disputes over the contents of interviews at police stations should now be rare. The RCCJ 'unreservedly welcome[d] this advance' (Cm. 2263, p. 39). The main practical difficulties have arisen in respect of the preparation by the police of summaries (a 'written record of the interview'), originally required by PACE Code E.5.3). The exercise is very time-consuming for the police; at the same time, research by John Baldwin found that in less than a third of the cases examined could the summaries be said to provide an accurate and succinct record of the interview (*Preparing the Record of Taped Interview*, RCCJ Study No. 2, HMSO, 1992). Further guidance by the Home Office (Circular 21/1992) was, however, said by them to have led to improvements. The RCCJ (Cm. 2263, pp. 41–42) suggested that the Home Office conduct further work to establish the best practicable method for the future. The latest version of Code E merely requires that a written record be made in accordance with national guidelines approved by the Secretary of State (Note for Guidance *5A*).

Debate has now moved on to the possible introduction of video-taping of interviews (see RCCJ, Cm. 2263, pp. 39–40; J. Baldwin, *Video Taping Police Interviews with Suspects: A National Evaluation*, Police Research Series Paper No. 1, Home Office, 1992; HO Circular 6/93). The RCCJ noted Baldwin's finding that there were additional benefits to video- over audio-taping in some 20% of the cases studied, although showing such recordings to jurors and magistrates might have some prejudicial effect, for example, symptoms of nervousness might be mistaken for symptoms of guilt; a powerful visual impact might distract from what was said. The RCCJ majority recommended further research. See further A. Leonard, (1991) 141 NLJ 1512; M. McConville, [1992] Crim LR 532 and (1992) 142 NLJ 960 and 1120; J. Baldwin, (1991) 141 NLJ 1512 and (1992) 142 NLJ 1095.

9. The interrogation of persons in custody was originally discouraged by the judges, but came to be 'the principal interrogation strategy employed by the police' (M. McConville, *et al.*, *The Case for the Prosecution* (1991), p. 56). Confessions and incriminating statements have been found in some 60% of cases where there is an interrogation and around 80% of guilty pleas (A. Sanders and R. Young, *Criminal Justice* (1994), p. 184). At the same time, the importance of confessions was probably overstated (see M. McConville and J. Baldwin, *Courts, Prosecution and Conviction* (1981), Chaps. 7, 8). More recently, there has been growing recognition of the risk of false confessions (see G. Gudjonsson, *The Psychology of Interrogations, Confessions and Testimony* (1992)). Unreliable confessions, as a result of police pressure, mental instability or a combination of both, have been at the heart of many of the high-profile miscarriage of justice cases (Walker, in C. Walker and K. Starmer (eds), *Justice in Error* (1993), p. 14, citing the *Guildford Four, Birmingham Six, Judith Ward, Tottenham Three* and *Cardiff Three* cases; see also I. Dennis, [1993] PL 291). Access to taped records of interviews has demonstrated the very poor quality of much of the interviewing conducted by police officers (see J. Baldwin, 'Police Interview Techniques' (1993) 33 Brit J Criminol 325). In response

'the police service, on an official level at least, has been stressing of late that questioning a suspect is only part of the process of investigation – and a decreasingly important part.' (Baldwin, *op. cit.*, pp. 325–326).

Home Office Circular 22/1992 laid down Principles for Investigative Interviewing, emphasising, inter alia, the points that the role of interviewing should be to obtain accurate and reliable information in order to discover the truth about matters under police investigation, that interviewing should be approached with an open mind, that when questioning anyone a police officer must act fairly and that vulnerable people must be treated with particular consideration at all times. Home Office Circular 7/1993 announced the availability of a new national training package for basic interviewing skills. These developments were welcomed by the RCCJ (Cm 2263, pp. 11–14), but are at an early stage (see T. Williamson, 'Reflections on Current Police Practice' in D. Morgan and G. M. Stephenson, *Suspicion and Silence* (1994), Chap. 7, noting (at p. 111) that the principles of investigative interviewing were not yet widely understood).

Notwithstanding the many concerns, the RCCJ (by a majority) did not recommend introduction of a requirement that confessions be corroborated, but unanimously recommended that the judge should give a strong warning that great care is needed before convicting on the basis of a confession alone (Cm 2263, pp. 62–68).

10. Code C provides that a person whom there are grounds to suspect of an offence must be cautioned before questions about it are put to him regarding his involvement or suspected involvement in that offence if his answers or silence may be given in evidence to a court in a prosecution (and not, e.g. to establish his identity or his ownership of a vehicle or to search him in the exercise of a power of stop and search) (Code C.10.1). A person must be cautioned upon arrest for an offence unless it is impracticable by reason of his condition or behaviour or he has already been cautioned under para. C.10.1 (Code C.10.3).

The caution was originally in the terms:

'You do not have to say anything unless you wish to do so, but what you say may be given in evidence.'

The 1984 Act did not seek to attenuate the accused's 'right to silence'. Proposals to this effect were made by the Criminal Law Revision Committee in its Eleventh Report, *Evidence (General)* (Cmnd 4991, 1972) but received much adverse criticism and were not implemented: see e.g. M. Zander in P. Glazebrook (ed), *Reshaping the Criminal Law* (1978) pp. 349–354. The RCCP noted that the right was not a right which the generality of suspects chose to exercise and recommended, by a majority, that the present law on the right of silence should not be altered (Report, pp. 80–91). In 1988, the Home Secretary announced (after a period of public debate in which widely divergent views were expressed) that the case for change was strong; he commissioned a report by a Working Group on the precise form the change should take. The Working Group reported in 1989 that the recommendations in the 11th Report should be implemented, with modifications (*Report of the Working Group on the Right of Silence* (Home Office, 1989)). The change was, however, postponed.[1] The position was changed in Northern Ireland in 1989 (see below, p. 287). The RCCJ majority (Cm. 2263, pp. 49–56) expressed the view that adverse inferences should not be drawn from silence at the police station because of the risk that this might result in more convictions of the innocent: however, once the prosecution case was fully disclosed, defendants should be required to offer an answer to the charges made against them at the risk of adverse comment at trial on any new defence then disclosed or any departure from the defence which they previously disclosed. Apart from the latter change, the position as to silence at trial should continue.

This position was controversially rejected by the government, and the Criminal Justice and Public Order Act 1994, ss. 34–39, extends the rules applying in Northern Ireland (with some modifications) to England and Wales. 'Such inferences as appear proper' may be drawn at various stages of the trial process by a court or jury (and in some circumstances, a judge) in four situations. By s. 34(1), the first is:

'where, in any proceedings against a person for an offence, evidence is given that the accused—

(a) at any time before he was charged with the offence, on being questioned under caution by a constable trying to discover whether or by whom the offence had been committed, failed to mention any fact relied on in his defence in those proceedings; or

(b) on being charged with the offence or officially informed that he might be prosecuted for it, failed to mention any such fact,

being a fact which in the circumstances existing at the time the accused could reasonably have been expected to mention when so questioned, charged or informed, as the case may be.'

The second is where a person arrested by a constable fails or refuses to account on request for objects, substances or marks on his person, in or on his clothing or footwear, or otherwise in his possession, or in any place in which he is at the time of his arrest; the arresting or an investigating officer must reasonably believe that the object etc. may be attributable to the suspect's participation in the commission of an offence specified by the officer who must inform the suspect that he so believes (s. 36(1)). This applies to the condition of clothing or footwear as it applies to a substance or mark thereon (s. 36(3)). The constable must inform the suspect in ordinary language of the effect of the section should he fail or refuse to comply with the request (s. 36(4)). Similar provisions apply to an accused's failure or refusal to account for his presence at a place at or about the time the offence for which he was arrested is alleged to have been committed (s. 37). Finally, inferences may be drawn

---

1 For powerful adverse criticism of the proposals, see A. A. S. Zuckerman, [1989] Crim LR 855; J. Wood and A. Crawford, *The Right of Silence: The Case for Retention* (1989); S. Greer, (1990) 53 MLR 709; and B. Irving and I. McKenzie, (1990) 1 Jo. of Forensic Psychiatry 167. For arguments in favour of change, see G. Williams, 'The "Right of Silence" and the Mental Element' [1988] Crim LR 97.

from the accused's failure to give evidence at trial on his refusal, without good cause, to answer any question (s. 35).

Note that s. 34 only applies where a person is 'questioned under caution' or charged. Note also that 'interviews' outside the police station are not normally permitted (see p. 134), to that extent restricting the operation of s. 34(1)(a) to interviews at the police station. Such interviews should be properly recorded; moreover, by that time the suspect should have had the opportunity to take legal advice.

The standard caution is now: 'You do not have to say anything. But it may harm your defence if you do not mention when questioned something which you later rely on in court. Anything you do say may be given in evidence'.

In the context of serious fraud investigations, s. 2 of the Criminal Justice Act 1987 makes it an offence for a person to refuse to answer questions put by the Serious Fraud Office. Questioning may even continue after charge (*R v Director of Serious Fraud Office, ex p Smith* [1993] AC 1). However, the answers obtained cannot be subsequently used in evidence against that person unless the accused changes his story. The RCCJ rejected proposals that the latter restriction be removed (Cm. 2263, pp. 56–57). However, even the present law has been found by the Commission to be contrary to Article 6 of the European Convention on Human Rights (*Saunders v UK* (1994) Independent, 30 September). See also A. T. H. Smith, 'The Privilege Against Self-Incrimination in Cases of Serious Fraud' 18 *Archbold News*, 2 October 1994 and J. D. Jackson, (1994) 57 MLR 270. It is arguable that the 1994 Act changes on the right of silence contravene the European Convention. In *Funke v France* (A 256-A, Judgment of 25 February 1993), the European Court of Human Rights found the right of silence to be embodied in the right to a fair trial, and to have been violated by convictions for refusing to disclose bank statements and other documents to customs officials.[1]

11 Admission of evidence

Police and Criminal Evidence Act 1984

76. Confessions
(1) In any proceedings a confession made by an accused person may be given in evidence against him in so far as it is relevant to any matter in issue in the proceedings and is not excluded by the court in pursuance of this section.

(2) If, in any proceedings where the prosecution proposes to give in evidence a confession made by an accused person, it is represented to the court that the confession was or may have been obtained—

    (*a*) by oppression of the person who made it; or

    (*b*) in consequence of anything said or done which was likely, in the circumstances existing at the time, to render unreliable any confession which might be made by him in consequence thereof,

the court shall not allow the confession to be given in evidence against him except in so far as the prosecution proves to the court beyond reasonable doubt that the confession (notwithstanding that it may be true) was not obtained as aforesaid.

(3) In any proceedings where the prosecution proposes to give in evidence a confession made by an accused person, the court may of its own motion require the prosecution, as a condition of allowing it to do so, to prove that the confession was not obtained as mentioned in subsection (2) above.

---

1 For reviews of the issues surrounding the right to silence, see S. Greer and R. Morgan (eds.), *The Right of Silence Debate* (1990); S. M. Easton, *The Right to Silence* (1991); S. C. Greer, (1990) 53 MLR 709; R. Leng, *The Right to Silence in Police Interrogation: A Study of Some of the Issues Underlying the Debate* (RCCJ Research Study No. 10, HMSO, 1993); D. Morgan and G. M. Stephenson, *Suspicion and Silence* (1994); I. Dennis, [1995] Crim LR 4, 9–18.

(4) The fact that a confession is wholly or partly excluded in pursuance of this section shall not affect the admissibility in evidence—

(a) of any facts discovered as a result of the confession; or

(b) where the confession is relevant as showing that the accused speaks, writes or expresses himself in a particular way, of so much of the confession as is necessary to show that he does so.

(5) Evidence that a fact to which this subsection applies was discovered as a result of a statement made by an accused person shall not be admissible unless evidence of how it was discovered is given by him or on his behalf.

(6) Subsection (5) above applies—

(a) to any fact discovered as a result of a confession which is wholly excluded in pursuance of this section; and

(b) to any fact discovered as a result of a confession which is partly so excluded, if the fact is discovered as a result of the excluded part of the confession. . . .

(8) In this section 'oppression' includes torture, inhuman or degrading treatment, and the use or threat of violence (whether or not amounting to torture).

77. Confessions by mentally handicapped persons

(1) Without prejudice to the general duty of the court at a trial on indictment to direct the jury on any matter on which it appears to the court appropriate to do so, where at such a trial—

(a) the case against the accused depends wholly or substantially on a confession by him; and

(b) the court is satisfied—

(i) that he is mentally handicapped; and

(ii) that the confession was not made in the presence of an independent person,

the court shall warn the jury that there is special need for caution before convicting the accused in reliance on the confession, and shall explain that the need arises because of the circumstances mentioned in paragraphs (a) and (b) above.

(2) In any case where at the summary trial of a person for an offence it appears to the court that a warning under subsection (1) above would be required if the trial were on indictment, the court shall treat the case as one in which there is a special need for caution before convicting the accused on his confession.

(3) In this section—

'independent person' does not include a police officer or a person employed for, or engaged on, police purposes;

'mentally handicapped', in relation to a person, means that he is in a state of arrested or incomplete development of mind which includes significant impairment of intelligence and social functioning; and

'police purposes' has the meaning assigned to it by section 64 of the Police Act 1964.

78. Exclusion of unfair evidence

(1) In any proceedings the court may refuse to allow evidence on which the prosecution proposes to rely to be given if it appears to the court that, having regard to all the circumstances, including the circumstances in which the evidence was obtained, the admission of the evidence would have such an adverse effect on the fairness of the proceedings that the court ought not to admit it.

(2) Nothing in this section shall prejudice any rule of law requiring a court to exclude evidence.

82. Part VIII—interpretation

(1) In this Part of this Act—

'confession' includes any statement wholly or partly adverse to the person who made it, whether to a person in authority or not and whether made in words or otherwise;

'proceedings' means criminal proceedings including—[court-martial proceedings: ed.]. . .

(3) Nothing in this Part of this Act shall prejudice any power of a court to exclude evidence (whether by preventing questions from being put or otherwise) at its discretion.

NOTES

1. *Principles underlying the exclusion of admissible evidence.* Commentators have identified a number of principles that might underlie the existence of a discretion, exercisable by the judge at a criminal trial, to exclude evidence that would otherwise, according to the law of evidence, be admissible. To an extent some of these principles overlap.

Such a discretion might exist:

(i) to ensure that evidence that is unreliable, although technically admissible, is not placed before a jury: the 'reliability' principle;

(ii) to deter the police or other law enforcement agencies from obtaining evidence by illegal or improper means or to 'punish' them for so acting: the 'disciplinary' principle;

(iii) to protect the rights of citizens to be treated in accordance with the standards prescribed by law for the conduct of criminal investigations: the 'protective' principle (see A. Ashworth, [1977] Crim LR 723). This can be seen as a corollary of (ii).

(iv) to protect an accused person from being compelled to incriminate himself: the 'privilege against self-incrimination' principle (this can be regarded as an example of (iii);

(v) the right of a person to be treated fairly: the 'fairness' principle, which may simply be a general principle underlying (inter alia) principles (i), (iii) and (iv) or may operate more narrowly to ensure simply that the trial proceedings are conducted 'fairly'.

(vi) to preserve the moral authority of the verdict (see I. Dennis, (1989) CLP 21).

English common law has tended to confine the discretion so as to reflect only the reliability principle and the need to protect the right against self-incrimination, although there have been some statements that support the 'fairness' principle.

2. *Admissibility of physical evidence at common law.*[1] At common law there has been no general rule to the effect that all physical evidence obtained unlawfully or illegally is thereby inadmissible. The manner in which such evidence is obtained tends not to affect its reliability, and the exclusion of reliable evidence by a court would be done simply as a mechanism for disciplining those responsible for the illegality. It was thought sufficient to leave the disciplinary function to be fulfilled by the prosecution, actions for damages or complaints against the police. In *Kuruma v R* [1955] AC 197, the Privy Council held that relevant evidence was admissible however it was obtained except that in a criminal trial the judge had a discretion to disallow evidence if the strict rules of admissibility

'would operate unfairly against an accused. . . . If, for instance, some . . . piece of evidence, e.g. a document, had been obtained from a defendant by a trick, no doubt the judge might properly rule it out'

(per Lord Goddard CJ at p. 204). This was regarded as giving rise to a limited discretion to disallow evidence obtained oppressively, by force or by false representations: see Lord Parker CJ in *Callis v Gunn* [1964] 1 QB 495, 501, 502; cf. Lord Widgery CJ in *Jeffrey v Black* [1978] QB 490, 498. In *R v Payne* [1963] 1 WLR 637, after P was involved in a car collision, he was examined by a doctor at a police station. The Court of Criminal Appeal held that the doctor's evidence as to P's fitness to drive should be excluded as P had only agreed to be examined by him on the understanding that the purpose of the examination was to see if he was suffering from any illness or disability.

However, in *R v Sang* [1980] AC 402 the House of Lords took a restrictive view of this discretion. The House held unanimously that there was no discretion to exclude evidence merely on the basis that it was given by an *agent provocateur.* Indeed, Lord Diplock and Viscount Dilhorne indicated that apart from the well

1 See generally R Pattenden, *Judicial Discretion and Criminal Litigation* (2nd edn, 1990), pp. 264–288; J. D. Heydon, [1973] Crim LR 603, 690; A. Ashworth, [1977] Crim LR 723; R. Pattenden, (1980) 19 ICLQ 664; D. K. Allen, (1980) 43 MLR 450; M. Loewenthal, 'Evaluating the Exclusionary Rule in Search and Seizure' (1980) 9 Anglo-American LR 238; M. H. Yeo, (1981) 13 Melb ULR 31 and (1982) 6 Crim LJ 89; M. J. Allen (1982) NILQ 105.

established discretion to exclude evidence on the ground that its prejudicial effect outweighs its probative value, a discretion existed only

'with regard to admissions and confessions and generally with regard to evidence obtained from the accused after commission of the offence'

([1980] AC at 437, 442). The essential purpose underlying the discretion was to ensure that an accused was not induced to incriminate himself by deception (see Lord Diplock at p. 436). *R v Payne* was approved on this basis (see Lord Diplock at p. 435; cf. Lord Fraser at p. 449, Lord Scarman at p. 455; and see also the remarks in *R v Trump* (1979) 70 Cr App Rep 300, 302–304, CA (Cr D); and *R v Fox* [1986] AC 281, below, p. 151.

The other members of the House appeared not to assent to this narrow proposition (see J. Heydon, [1980] Crim LR 129, 132–135). Lord Salmon stated that the category of cases in which it is the duty of the trial judge to ensure that the accused receives a fair trial can not be closed ([1980] AC at 445); Lord Fraser stated that the discretion could extend to evidence obtained from 'the accused himself or from premises occupied by him' (ibid, pp. 449, 450); and Lord Scarman indicated that he would not necessarily dissent from the dicta in *Kuruma, Callis v Gunn* and *Jeffrey v Black* provided they were treated 'as relating exclusively to the obtaining of evidence from the accused' (p. 456).

R v Payne (supra) was distinguished in *R v Apicella* (1985) 82 Cr App Rep 295. A sample of body fluid was taken from A by a consultant while A was in prison; the prison doctor suspected that A was suffering from gonorrhoea and the sample was taken for therapeutic reasons. The consultant assumed that A was consenting, but in fact he only submitted because he had been told by a prison officer that he had no choice. The sample was subsequently used at A's trial for three rapes as it showed that A was suffering from the same unusual strain of gonorrhoea as had been passed to the three victims by their attackers. The Court of Appeal (Criminal Division) held (1) that there was no rule of law that an intimate sample is only admissible if taken with the suspect's consent; (2) that evidence was not inadmissible 'solely because it has been obtained as a result of a crime, such as assault, or a tort' (per Lawton LJ at pp. 299–300); and (3) that the use of this sample at the trial was not unfair: A 'was not tricked into submitting to the examination in the way which led [the court in *Payne*] . . . to exclude evidence' (per Lawson LJ at p. 300).

In Australia, the court has a broader discretion in which the significance of the invasion of civil liberties is balanced against the desirability that the guilty should be convicted: relevant factors include the nature of the offence and whether the illegality was deliberate: *R v Ireland* (1970) 44 ALJR 263; *Bunning v Cross* (1978) 19 ALR 641.

3. *Admissibility of confessions at common law.* At common law a person's confession was *admissible* provided the prosecution showed to the satisfaction of the judge that it had 'not been obtained from him either by fear of prejudice or hope of advantage exercised or held out by a person in authority' (per Lord Sumner in *Ibrahim v R* [1914] AC 599 at 609). This led to a series of cases on the definition of 'person in authority' and what was capable of amounting to an 'inducement' for these purposes, and the rule tended to be applied strictly. The courts assumed that a confession obtained in such circumstances would be unreliable, without considering whether the particular confession was unreliable. However, the decision in *DPP v Ping Lin* [1976] AC 574, HL made it clear that there had to be a causal link between the 'fear' or 'hope' and the confession for the confession to be excluded, and that the whole issue of 'voluntariness' was essentially one of fact that was not to be treated 'legalistically'. Furthermore, in *R v Rennie* [1982] 1 All ER 384, CA (Cr D), Lord Lane CJ stated that even where a confession was made with 'a hope that an admission may lead to an earlier release or a lighter sentence', and the hopes were prompted by something said or done by a person in authority, the confession would not *automatically* be regarded as involuntary. The position was the same where, as in the present case, a confession was prompted by a fear that otherwise the police would interview and perhaps arrest and charge further members of the defendant's family. The judge should 'apply his common sense' and 'remind himself that "voluntary" in ordinary parlance means "of one's own free will" ' (p. 389). The result was to narrow still further the range of confessions that were likely to be held to be involuntary.

In addition to cases applying or developing the *Ibrahim* principle, it was also held that a confession obtained as a result of 'oppression' would be treated as involuntary and thus inadmissible: *R v Prager* [1972] 1 All ER 1114, CA (Cr D).

For the guidance of the police, a set of rules governing the interrogation process was promulgated by the Queen's Bench judges, together with administrative directions from the Home Office. The first set was published in two stages in 1912 and 1918. A revised set of Judges' Rules was issued in 1964; and the Directions were amended further in 1978: see *Judges' Rules and Administrative Directions to the Police*, Home Office Circular No. 89/1978. The Rules imposed requirements as to cautioning etc. and the Directions covered such matters as the keeping of records, provision for comfort and refreshment and the interrogation of children or mentally handicapped persons. The position appeared to be that if the rules were complied with, a confession would be regarded as voluntary. However, the converse did not hold good: a confession might be held to be voluntary, and accordingly admissible, even if there had been a breach of the Judges' Rules: *R v Prager* [1972] 1 All ER 1114 at 1118, CA (Cr D); *Greaves v D and P* (1980) 71 Cr App Rep 232 at 236, DC.

At the same time, there were frequent assertions by judges of a residual *discretion* to exclude confessions. There was, however, much confusion over the permissible grounds for such exclusion, the cases referring to such matters as oppression (which in truth was not a matter of discretion at all), the use of a trick, unfairness or just breaches of the Judges' Rules.

On the admissibility of confessions at common law see R. Pattenden, op. cit., pp. 274–281; C. R. Williams, 'Judicial discretion in relation to confessions' (1983) 3 OJLS 222.

4. The interrogation process is now regulated by ss. 56–60 and 76–78 of the 1984 Act and PACE Code C (see above, p. 132 *et seq*). The admissibility of other evidence obtained improperly is governed by s. 78. A vast body of case law has considered the application of these provisions and the courts have been considerably more active than was anticipated. 'Oppression' and 'unreliability' under s. 76 were considered in *R v Fulling*, below, pp. 153–156; the question of the exclusion of confessions under s. 78 in *R v Samuel*, below, pp. 158–161, and the use of trickery by police in *R v Christou and Wright*, below, pp. 161–165. For general surveys, see D. J. Birch 'The Pace Hots Up,' [1989] Crim LR 95; D. Feldman, 'Regulating Treatment of Suspects in Police Stations' [1990] Crim LR 452.

Section 78 has been used to exclude identification evidence where there are breaches of Code D (the *Code of Practice for the Identification of Persons by Police Officers*): see e.g. *R v Gall* (1989) 90 Cr App Rep 64, CA (Cr D) (investigating officer took part in the conduct of a parade); *R v Conway* (1990) 91 Cr App Rep

143, CA (Cr D) (parade not held when requested, although no good reason); *R v Nagah* (1990) 92 Cr App Rep 344, CA (Cr D) (street identification inadmissible as identity parade was practicable) (see also *Powell v DPP* [1992] RTR 270, DC; *R v Finley* [1993] Crim LR 50, CA (Cr D); *R v Hope, Limburn and Bleasdale* [1994] Crim LR 118, CA (Cr D)); but cf. *R v Quinn* [1990] Crim LR 581, CA (Cr D) (evidence of identification of Q while on trial in a Dublin court admitted); *R v Grannell* (1989) 90 Cr App Rep 149, CA (Cr D) (breach of Code D but no unfairness); *R v Brown* [1991] Crim LR 368, CA (Cr D).

The courts have rarely used s. 78 to exclude real evidence on the ground that it has been obtained illegally or otherwise improperly. One relevant factor is whether police officers have acted in bad faith. In *Matto v Crown Court at Wolverhampton* [1987] RTR 337, the Divisional Court held that in circumstances where police officers knew they were trespassing on M's property when they required him to take a breath test it was open to the Crown Court to conclude that this adversely affected the fairness of proceedings for driving with excess alcohol based on a breath specimen obtained subsequently at the police station. The point was stressed that the officers had acted 'mala fides'. Woolf LJ stated (at p. 346):

'Whatever is the right interpretation of section 78, I am quite satisfied that it certainly does not reduce the discretion of the court to exclude unfair evidence which existed at common law. Indeed, in my view in any case where the evidence would properly be excluded in common law, it can certainly be excluded under section 78.'

This may be compared with the common law decision of the House of Lords in *R v Fox* [1986] AC 281. Here, following an accident, police officers entered F's house through the front door, which was closed but not locked, and required F to take a breath test. F refused, and was arrested and taken to the police station, where he provided specimens of breath that proved to be over the limit. His conviction for driving with excess alcohol was upheld, the House holding that the magistrates had been entitled to refuse to exclude the evidence in the exercise of their discretion. Lord Fraser stated that the Divisional Court had been right to treat the fact that he was in the police station because he had been unlawfully arrested

'merely as a historical fact, with which the court was not concerned. The duty of the court is to decide whether the appellant has committed the offence with which he is charged, and not to discipline the police for exceeding their powers. . . .
. . . of course, if the appellant had been lured to the police station by some trick or deception, or if the police officers had behaved oppressively towards the appellant, the justices' jurisdiction to exclude otherwise admissible evidence recognised in *R v Sang* might have come into play. But there is nothing of that sort suggested here. The police officers did no more than make a bona fide mistake as to their powers. . . .'
(pp. 292, 293).

It has, however, been suggested that the presence of bad faith does not automatically lead to exclusion under s. 78 (per Buckley J in *Sharpe v DPP* [1993] RTR 392, 398–399, DC). On the other hand, subsequent cases have confirmed that evidence may be excluded under s. 78 even where it is not established that the police have acted in bad faith. See *DPP v McGladrigan* [1991] RTR 297, DC (per Hodgson J at 301–302, citing *R v Samuel* (below, p. 158)); *DPP v Godwin* [1991] RTR 303 at 308. In the latter case, the Divisional Court upheld the decision of justices to exclude under s. 78 evidence of specimens obtained from G at the police station following his earlier refusal to take a breath test at the roadside; however, it was not established that the police had reasonable cause to suspect that G had alcohol in his body, specified by s. 6(1) of the Road Traffic Act 1988 as a precondition to requiring a breath test. Per Bingham LJ at 308:

'The justices were entitled to conclude that the substantial breach by the constable of the protection afforded to members of the public by section 6 was denied to the defendant, that as a result the prosecutor obtained evidence which he would not otherwise have obtained, and that as a result the defendant was prejudiced in a significant manner in resisting the charge against him.'

This may be compared with *DPP v Wilson* [1991] RTR 284, where a constable, acting on an anonymous telephone call that a particular car would be on the move any minute and he would catch a drink-driver, waited for over an hour for the car to move. He then stopped the car, spoke to the driver, noticed alcohol on his breath and administered a breath test which proved positive. The Divisional Court held that this did not constitute 'malpractice'. 'There is, in my view, no duty on a constable to warn a potential offender of a potential offence nor, in my view, is it oppressive if a constable does not do so' (per Tudor-Evans J at 291).

There is one decision at the Crown Court level where evidence obtained as the result of stop and search in the street and a strip search at the police station was excluded on the ground that the suspect was not told why he was stopped, searched and arrested: *R v Fennelley* [1989] Crim LR 142 (Acton Crown Court), criticised by D. J. Birch, ibid. pp. 143–144. By contrast, in *R v Cooke (Stephen)* [1995] 1 Cr App Rep 318, CA (Cr D), the court agreed with the trial judge that even if the plucking of a sample of C's hair from his scalp for DNA testing had been unlawful, the evidence resulting from it should not have been excluded under s. 78; that there would have been an assault did not in any way cast doubt upon the accuracy of the evidence. The court in fact held that the hair and its sheath had lawfully been taken as a non-intimate sample (see above, p. 141). Nevertheless the court would seem to contemplate the admissibility of an *intimate* sample taken without consent. Is that acceptable in view of the clear requirements of PACE? (but cf. the position at common law: *R v Apicella*, above, p. 149).

A similar reluctance to exercise the s. 78 discretion was exhibited by the Court of Appeal (Criminal Division) in *R v Khan (Sultan)* [1995] QB 27 in respect of the evidence of a tape-recorded conversation that had been overheard via a listening device covertly installed on the outside of a house where K was a visitor. The Crown conceded that there were elements of civil trespass to the outside of the building, the infliction of some degree of damage and an intrusion on privacy. The court refused to consider the question whether there was a breach of Article 8, ECHR, as the Convention was not part of English law. Furthermore, it held that the factors of trespass, damage and invasion of privacy were outweighed by the considerations that the police were proceeding in accordance with the non-statutory Home Office guidelines (apart from a breach of record-keeping requirements); the criminal conduct under investigation (large-scale drug dealing) was a type of great gravity; the issues of trespass and damage (which it inferred to be slight) were of limited importance save for their impact upon privacy and the inviolability of the home. The judge was right to conclude that the invasion of privacy was outweighed by other considerations. Should the position have been different if it had been K's home that was bugged? See further, below, pp. 569–577. An interesting feature of the decision in *Khan* is the explicit balancing of factors for and against exclusion.

'Fairness' in s. 78 comprises both fairness to the accused and fairness to the prosecution (*R v O'Loughlin and McLaughlin* (1987) 85 Cr App Rep 157, 163; *R v Hughes* [1988] Crim LR 519, CA (Cr D)). A trial within a trial must be held if an issue is raised under s. 76, and whether trial is at the Crown Court or before magistrates (*R v Liverpool Juvenile Court, ex p R* [1988] QB 1; cf. *R v Oxford City Justices, ex p Berry* [1988] QB 507). This is, however, discretionary where a challenge is made under

s. 78 (*R v Beveridge* (1987) 85 Cr App Rep 255 (at the Crown Court); *Vel v Chief Constable of North Wales* (1987) 151 JP 510 (before magistrates)).

5. In the context of the breathalyser laws, a distinction is drawn between prosecutions for refusal to provide a specimen of breath and prosecutions for driving with excess alcohol based on the evidence of a specimen that is provided. In the case of the former, a requirement to provide a specimen imposed by an officer while trespassing unlawfully in the suspect's home is itself unlawful and cannot form the basis of a conviction (*Morris v Beardmore* [1981] AC 446, HL). The issue 'relates to the ingredients of the offence itself' rather than evidence adduced in proof of the offence charged (per Lord Edmund-Davies at 459). In the case of the latter, exclusion of evidence of a specimen is regulated by the discretion to exclude evidence at common law (*R v Sang*, n. 2, above; *R v Fox* [1986] AC 281, HL) or under s. 78 of PACE (n. 4, above). Is this distinction tenable?

The practical effect of the decision in *Morris v Beardmore* was reduced by amendments to the breathalyser legislation introduced by the Transport Act 1981. See now the Road Traffic Act 1988, ss. 4–11. In particular, s. 6 gives a right of entry (if need be by force) to require the provision of a breath specimen in cases of accidents involving injury to a person other than the driver or person in charge (see sub-ss. (2) and (6)). However, if there is no accident involving injury, the *Morris v Beardmore* principle remains applicable: *Fox v Chief Constable of Gwent* [1985] 1 All ER 230 DC (this point did not arise before the House of Lords: *R v Fox*, above).

Morris v Beardmore does not, of course, apply if the officers are not trespassers (see pp. 103–104), and has been stated to be concerned only with the 'sanctity of a man's home' and not applicable where a motorist who was affected by drink was still driving his car elsewhere (per Griffiths LJ in *Steel v Goacher* [1983] RTR 98 at 104–105). It was also stated obiter in *Morris v Beardmore* that the principle only applied where the officer was a trespasser vis-à-vis the defendant: see Lord Roskill at 467–468.

R v Fulling [1987] QB 426 [1987] 2 All ER 65, [1987] 2 WLR 923 (pet dis) [1987] 1 WLR 1196, HL, Court of Appeal (Criminal Division)

F claimed over £5,000 from an insurance company in respect of a burglary at her flat. An informant subsequently told the police that the burglary was bogus, and had been instigated by one Drewery, with whom F had been living and with whom she was infatuated. F was arrested and interviewed. She initially said nothing, but eventually confessed. At her trial for obtaining property by deception, she argued that the confession was or might have been obtained by oppression. She claimed that during a break in an interview, one of the police officers told her that Drewery, her lover, had for the last three years or so been having an affair with a Christine Judge, who had also been arrested in the light of the informant's disclosures and was occupying the next cell. This so distressed her that she 'just couldn't stand being in the cells any longer', and so she agreed to make a statement. The trial judge assumed, without deciding, that her claims were true, but ruled that the confession was admissible. The Court of Appeal dismissed her appeal.

Lord Lane CJ delivered the judgment of the court (**Lord Lane CJ**, **Taylor** and **Henry JJ**):

The material part of the [trial judge's] ruling runs:

'Bearing in mind that whatever happens to a person who is arrested and questioned is by its very nature oppressive, I am quite satisfied that in section 76(2)(*a*) of the Police and Criminal Evidence Act, the word oppression means something above and beyond that which is inherently oppressive in police custody and must import some impropriety, some oppression actively applied in an improper manner by the police. I do not find that what was done in this case can be so defined and, in those circumstances, I am satisfied that oppression cannot be made out on the evidence I have heard in the context required by the statutory provision. I go on to add simply this, that I have not addressed my mind as to whether or not I believe the police or the defendant on this issue because my ruling is based exclusively upon the basis that, even if I wholly believed the defendant, I do not regard oppression as having been made out. In those circumstances, her confession—if that is the proper term for it—the interview in which she confessed, I rule to be admissible.'

Mr. Davey has drawn our attention to a number of authorities on the meaning of 'oppression'. Sachs L.J. in *R v Priestley (Note)* (1965) 51 Cr App R 1 said, at pp. 1, 2–3:

'to my mind [oppression] in the context of the principles under consideration imports something which tends to sap, and has sapped, that free will which must exist before a confession is voluntary. . . . the courts are not concerned with ascertaining the precise motive of a particular statement. The question before them is whether the prosecution have shown the statement to be voluntary, whatever the motive may be, and that is always the point to which all arguments must return. To solve it, the court has to look to the questions which I have already mentioned. First, was there in fact something which could properly be styled or might well be oppression? Secondly, did whatever happened in the way of oppression or likely oppression induce the statement in question?'

R v Prager [1972] 1 WLR 260, was another decision on note (e) to the Judges' Rules 1964, which required that a statement by the defendant before being admitted in evidence must be proved to be 'voluntary' in the sense that it has not been obtained by fear or prejudice or hope of advantage or by oppression. Edmund Davies LJ, who delivered the judgment of the court, said, at p. 266:

'As we have already indicated, the criticism directed in the present case against the police is that their interrogation constituted "oppression". This word appeared for the first time in the Judges' Rules 1964, and it closely followed the observation of Lord Parker CJ in *Callis v Gunn* [1964] 1 QB 495, 501, condemning confessions "obtained in an oppressive manner".'

Edmund Davies L.J., having cited the relevant passage from *R v Priestley (Note)*, 51 Cr App R 1 continued:

'In an address to the Bentham Club in 1968, Lord MacDermott described "oppressive questioning" as "questioning which by its nature, duration, or other attendant circumstances (including the fact of custody) excites hopes (such as the hope of release) or fears, or so affects the mind of the subject that his will crumbles and he speaks when otherwise he would have stayed silent". We adopt these definitions or descriptions . . .'

DPP v Ping Lin [1976] AC 574, was again a case in which the question was whether a statement by the defendant was shown to be voluntary. It was held that a trial judge faced by the problem should approach the task in a common sense way and should ask himself whether the prosecution had proved that the contested statement was voluntary in the sense that it was not obtained by fear of prejudice or hope of advantage excited or held out by a person in authority. Lord Wilberforce, Lord Morris of Borth-y-Gest and Lord Hailsham of St. Marylebone expressed the opinion that

'it is not necessary, before a statement is held to be inadmissible because not shown to have been voluntary, that it should be thought or held that there was impropriety in the conduct of the person to whom the statement was made' (p. 594).

What has to be considered is whether a statement is shown to have been voluntary rather than one brought about in one of the ways referred to.

Finally Mr. Davey referred us to a judgment of this court in *R v Rennie* [1982] 1 WLR 64.

Mr. Davey submits to us that on the strength of those decisions the basis of the judge's ruling was wrong; in particular when he held that the word 'oppression' means something above and beyond that which is inherently oppressive in police custody and must import some impropriety, some oppression actively applied in an improper manner by the police. It is submitted that that flies in the face of the opinions of their Lordships in *DPP v Ping Lin* [1976] AC 574.

The point is one of statutory construction. The wording of the Act of 1984 does not follow the wording of earlier rules or decisions, nor is it expressed to be a consolidating Act, nor yet to be declaratory of the common law. . . .

It is a codifying Act, and therefore the principles set out in *Bank of England v Vagliano Bros* [1891] AC 107, 144 apply. Lord Herschell, having pointed out that the Bills of Exchange Act 1882 which was under consideration was intended to be a codifying Act, said, at pp. 144–145:

'I think the proper course is in the first instance to examine the language of the statute and to ask what is its natural meaning, uninfluenced by any considerations derived from the previous state of the law, and not to start with inquiring how the law previously stood, and then, assuming that it was probably intended to leave it unaltered, to see if the words of the enactment will bear an interpretation in conformity with this view. If a statute, intended to embody in a code a particular branch of the law, is to be treated in this fashion, it appears to me that its utility will be almost entirely destroyed, and the very object with which it was enacted will be frustrated. The purpose of such a statute surely was that on any point specifically dealt with by it, the law should be ascertained by interpreting the language used instead of, as before, by roaming over a vast number of authorities in order to discover what the law was, extracting it by a minute critical examination of the prior decisions, dependent upon a knowledge of the exact effect even of an obsolete proceeding such as a demurrer to evidence.' . . .

Section 76(2) of the Act of 1984 distinguishes between two different ways in which a confession may be rendered inadmissible: (a) where it has been obtained by oppression; (b) where it has been made in consequence of anything said or done which was likely in the circumstances to render unreliable any confession which might be made by the defendant in consequence thereof. Paragraph (b) is wider than the old formulation, namely that the confession must be shown to be voluntary in the sense that it was not obtained by fear of prejudice or hope of advantage, excited or held out by a person in authority. It is wide enough to cover some of the circumstances which under the earlier rule were embraced by what seems to us to be the artifically wide definition of oppression approved in *R v Prager* [1972] 1 WLR 260.

This in turn leads us to believe that 'oppression' in section 76(2)(a) should be given its ordinary dictionary meaning. The *Oxford English Dictionary* as its third definition of the word runs as follows: 'Exercise of authority or power in a burdensome, harsh, or wrongful manner; unjust or cruel treatment of subjects, inferiors, etc.; the imposition of unreasonable or unjust burdens.' One of the quotations given under that paragraph runs as follows: 'There is not a word in our language which expresses more detestable wickedness than oppression.'

We find it hard to envisage any circumstances in which such oppression would not entail some impropriety on the part of the interrogator. We do not think that the judge was wrong in using that test. What, however, is abundantly clear is that a confession may be invalidated under section 76(2)(b) where there is no suspicion of impropriety. No reliance was placed on the words of section 76(2)(b) either before the judge at trial or before this court. Even if there had been such reliance, we do not consider that the policeman's remark was likely to make unreliable any confession of the appellant's own criminal activities, and she expressly exonerated—or tried to exonerate—her unfaithful lover.

In those circumstances, in the judgment of this court, the judge was correct to reject the submission made to him under section 76 of the Act of 1984. The appeal is accordingly dismissed.

Appeal dismissed.

NOTES

1. The partial definition in s. 76(8) was not mentioned. Might that have made a difference? To date, there are very few decisions in which a confession has been excluded on this ground. Breaches of the law or codes will not necessarily constitute oppression. In *R v Hughes* [1988] Crim LR 545, CA (Cr D), through a misunderstanding, D did not see the duty solicitor; it was held that, in the absence of police misconduct, there was no oppression. In *R v Emmerson* (1990) 92 Cr App Rep 284, CA (Cr D), it was held that the use by a police officer of a raised voice and bad language, expressing impatience and irritation, for a short time during an otherwise low-key interview, did not amount to oppression. (See also *R v Heaton* [1993] Crim LR 593, CA (Cr D); and *R v L* [1994] Crim LR 839, CA (Cr D) (pressure applied in interview did not cross the threshold of what was acceptable; *Paris* (below) distinguished.) Counsel for the defendant in *R v Samuel* [1988] QB 615, felt unable to argue that the conduct of the police there amounted to oppression. Do you agree?

An example of exclusion on this ground is *R v Beales* [1991] Crim LR 118 (Norwich Crown Court), where an officer deliberately misstated evidence in order to pressurise a person suspected of assaulting a two-year-old boy; see also *R v Ismail*

[1990] Crim LR 109, CA (Cr D). The most notorious case where oppression has been found is *R v Paris, Abdullahi and Miller* (1992) 97 Cr App Rep 99 (The 'Cardiff Three'), where the Court of Appeal (Criminal Division) quashed the convictions of the three appellants for murder. M was interviewed for some 13 hours. Having denied involvement well over 300 times, he was finally persuaded to make admissions. Lord Taylor CJ stated (at 103) that each member of the court had been 'horrified' by what they had heard in the tape recording of one interview:

'Miller was bullied and hectored. The officers ... were not questioning him so much as shouting at him what they wanted him to say. Short of physical violence, it is hard to conceive of a more hostile and intimidating approach by officers to a suspect.'

Moreover, M's solicitor

'appears to have been gravely at fault for sitting passively through this travesty of an interview'

(p. 104). The court concluded that the tenor and length of all the interviews would have been oppressive and the confessions obtained unreliable even with a suspect of normal mental capacity; in fact there was evidence that M was on the border of mental handicap. The conviction of P and A were quashed as the jury might have been prejudiced by the evidence of M's interviews.

It was stressed in *Paris* (per Lord Taylor CJ at 104) that

'it is perfectly legitimate for officers to pursue their interrogation of a suspect with a view to eliciting his account or gaining admissions. They are not required to give up after the first denial or even after a number of denials.'

The distinction between oppressive and non-oppressive conduct is a matter of degree (cf. *R v Emmerson* and *R v Heaton*, above).
2. On the interpretation of 'torture or inhuman or degrading treatment' under the ECHR, see below, pp. 749–773; on the interpretation of these words in the context of confessions under the Northern Ireland (Emergency Provisions) Act 1991, see below, pp. 271–272, 285–287.
3. The 'unreliability' hurdle has been invoked more frequently than the 'oppression' hurdle. 'The word "unreliable" ... means "cannot be relied upon as being the truth" ' (per Stuart-Smith LJ in *R v Crampton* (1990) 92 Cr App Rep 369 at 372). Moreover, the question is whether *any* confession which the accused might make in consequence of anything said or done was likely to be rendered unreliable, not whether the confession made was unreliable (ibid.). The thing 'said or done' must be by someone other than the accused himself (*R v Goldenberg* (1988) 88 Cr App Rep 285, CA (Cr D); *R v Crampton*, above (doubtful whether merely holding an interview with a suspect undergoing withdrawal symptoms is something 'done' within the meaning of s. 76(2)).

Examples include cases:
(1) where a child has been interviewed in the absence of an 'appropriate adult' (*DPP v Blake* [1989] 1 WLR 432, CA (Cr D); *R v Morse* [1991] Crim LR 195 (Wisbech Crown Court));
(2) where there have been doubts about the reliability of a confession by a person of low intelligence (*R v Harvey* [1988] Crim LR 241, Central Criminal Court (psychopathic woman of low intelligence may have confessed after hearing her lover confess, in order to protect her); *R v Everett* [1988] Crim LR 826, CA (Cr D) (man of 42 with mental age of eight: judge had taken no account of his mental condition); *R v Delaney* (1988) 88 Cr App Rep 338, CA (Cr D) (D educationally subnormal and proper records not kept); *R v Cox* [1991] Crim LR 276, CA

(Cr D); *R v Raghip* (1991) Times, 9 December, CA (Cr D) (psychological evidence of mental condition admissible and court not bound by whether D's IQ was above an arbitrary figure for the mentally defective: see P. Mirfield, (1992) 109 LQR 528); *R v Kenny* [1994] Crim LR 284, CA (Cr D) (absence of appropriate adult));

(3) where proper records of the confession have not been kept (*R v Doolan* [1988] Crim LR 747, CA (Cr D); *R v Delaney, supra; R v Walters* [1989] Crim LR 62, CA (Cr D) (W was also wrongly questioned after charge); *R v Chung* (1990) 92 Cr App Rep 314, CA (Cr D); *R v Joseph* [1993] Crim LR 205, CA (Cr D));

(4) where there has been an improper inducement (*R v Phillips* (1987) 86 Cr App Rep 18, CA (Cr D) (statement that if D confessed, offences could be taken into consideration rather than prosecuted; cf. *R v Howden-Simpson* [1991] Crim LR 49, CA (Cr D)); *R v Barry* (1991) 95 Cr App Rep 384, CA (Cr D) (prosecution unable to prove beyond reasonable doubt that statement was not made in response to offer of assistance in obtaining bail));

(5) where a drug addict was held in custody for 18 hours without being allowed the prescribed rest periods (*R v Trussler* [1988] Crim LR 446, Reading Crown Court); and

(6) where access to a lawyer has been wrongfully denied (*R v McGovern* (1990) 92 Cr App Rep 228, CA (Cr D): there were also breaches of the recording provisions; these matters more commonly lead to exclusion under s. 78: below, pp. 160–161). Under this head, a confession may be excluded where there has been no police impropriety: *R v Fulling* (above p. 153).

4. Breaches of Code C may make it more likely that a confession may be excluded under s. 76(2)(b): see, e.g. *R v Doolan* [1988] Crim LR 747, CA (Cr D).

5. Where an interview is improperly conducted this may lead to the exclusion as 'tainted' of subsequent interviews even though they are conducted according to the rules: see e.g. *R v Ismail* [1990] Crim LR 109, CA (Cr D); *R v McGovern* (1990) 92 Cr App Rep 228, CA (Cr D); *R v Glaves* [1993] Crim LR 685, CA (Cr D); *R v Neil* [1994] Crim LR 441, CA (Cr D); *R v Conway* [1994] Crim LR 838, CA (Cr D); but cf. *R v Gillard; R v Barrett* (1990) 92 Cr App Rep 61, CA (Cr D); *R v Hoyte* [1994] Crim LR 215, CA (Cr D).

6. The interests of mentally handicapped defendants are also subject to the limited protection afforded by s. 77 of PACE (above, p. 147), which requires a warning to the jury of the need for caution in the circumstances set out in the section. Failure to give the required warning may lead to the quashing of a conviction: *R v Lamont* [1989] Crim LR 813, CA (Cr D); *R v Bailey* (1995) Times, 26 January, CA (Cr D). A warning is not needed unless the case for the Crown is substantially less strong without the confession: *R v Campbell* [1995] 1 Cr App Rep 522, CA (Cr D).

Note that this section does not extend to the mentally ill. The RCCJ recommended that this point should be reconsidered, as it is inconsistent with other provisions in PACE and the PACE Codes (Cm. 2263, p. 59).

The Court of Appeal has also stated that a judge should withdraw a case from the jury where the prosecution case depends wholly on confessions, the defendant suffered from a significant degree of mental handicap, and the confessions were unconvincing to the point where a jury, properly directed, could not properly convict: *R v Mackenzie* (1992) 96 Cr App Rep 98, CA (Cr D). This principle can apply independently of any question as to the admissibility of the confessions. Cf. *R v Moss* (1990) 91 Cr App Rep 371, CA (Cr D); *R v Brine* [1992] Crim LR 122, CA (Cr D); *R v Wood* [1994] Crim LR 222, CA (Cr D). In these cases, convictions were quashed as unsafe and unsatisfactory.

R v Samuel [1988] QB 615, [1988] 2 WLR 920, [1988] 2 All ER 135, (1988) 87 Cr App Rep 232, Court of Appeal (Criminal Division)

S was arrested for armed robbery of a building society and after being questioned asked to see a solicitor. His request was refused under s. 58 by Superintendent Cresswell, who certified, inter alia, that there was a 'likelihood of other suspects to be arrested being inadvertently warned'. S had two further interviews, at the second of which he confessed to two burglaries, while denying the robbery. After he was charged with the burglaries his solicitor telephoned, but was refused access. Shortly afterwards S confessed to the robbery at a third interview, and was subsequently convicted of that offence.

The Court of Appeal quashed the conviction.

The judgment of the court (**Glidewell LJ**, **Hodgson** and **Rougier JJ**) was given by **Hodgson J** [who stated the facts and held (1) that the superintendent was entitled to conclude that the robbery had been a serious arrestable offence given the use of a shotgun and hand gun and the intention to cause serious financial loss to the society; (2) that the right to delay access to a lawyer could not be denied once S had been charged with the burglaries in view of para. 1 of Annex B(A)(a) of code C, which provided that the right could only be delayed, inter alia, if the suspect 'has not yet been charged with an offence'. His Lordship continued:]

Mr. Escott Cox's second point raises, in the judgment of this Court, more fundamental and important issues. He challenged on the voire dire and challenged before us the correctness of both Mr. Cresswell's first decision to delay access and, even more emphatically, the decision to refuse access to Mr. Warner at 4.45 p.m. on 7 August.

Perhaps the most important right given (or rather renewed) to a person detained by the police is his right to obtain legal advice. That right is given in section 58 of the Act, subsection (1) of which is precise and unambiguous.

[His Lordship read s. 58:]

The words of the section clearly imply that the officer does so believe. Therefore a court which has to decide whether denial of access to a solicitor was lawful has to ask itself two questions: 'did the officer believe?', a subjective test; 'were there reasonable grounds for that belief?,' an objective test.

What it is the officer must satisfy the court that he believed is this: (1) that delaying consultation with a solicitor (2) will (3) lead to or hinder one or more of the things set out in (8)(a) to (c). The use of the word 'will' is clearly of great importance. There were available to the draftsman many words or phrases by which he could have described differing nuances as to the officer's state of mind, for example 'might', 'could', 'there was a risk', 'there was a substantial risk', etc. The choice of 'will' must have been deliberately restrictive.

Of course, anyone who says that he believes that something will happen, unles he is speaking of one of the immutable laws of nature, accepts the possibility that it will not happen, but the use of the word 'will' in conjunction with belief implies in the believer a belief that it will very probably happen.

What is it that the officer has to satisfy the court he believed? The right denied is a right 'to consult a solicitor privately'. The person denied that right is in police detention. In practice, the only way that the person can make any of (a) to (c) happen is by some communication from him to the solicitor. For (a) to (c) to be made to happen the solicitor must do something. If he does something knowing that it will result in anything in (a) to (c) happening he will, almost inevitably, commit a serious criminal offence. Therefore, inadvertent or unwitting conduct apart, the officer must believe that a solicitor will, if allowed to consult with a detained person, thereafter commit a criminal offence. Solicitors are officers of the court. We think that the number of times that a police officer could genuinely be in that state of belief will be rare. Moreover it is our view that, to sustain such a basis for refusal, the grounds put forward would have to have reference to a specific solicitor. We do not think they could ever be successfully advanced in relation to solicitors generally.

However, the experience of some members of this court and, so he tells us, of Mr. Escott Cox, is that the practice adopted in this case is becoming more and more usual. An officer's 'reasonable belief' is more and more being based upon the 'inadvertent' or 'unwitting' conduct of a solicitor.

At first sight the wording of the subsection does not seem apt to cover inadvertent or unwitting conduct by a solicitor. But what is said is that the detained person will be able to bring about one or more of the happenings (a) to (c) by causing the solicitor to pass on unwittingly some form of coded message. Whether there is any evidence that this has or may have happened in the past we have no way of knowing. Solicitors are intelligent professional people; persons detained by the police are frequently not very clever and the expectation that one of (*a*) to (*c*) will be brought about in this way seems to contemplate a degree of intelligence and sophistication in persons detained, and perhaps a naiveté and lack of common sense in solicitors, which we doubt often occurs. When and if it does, we think it would have to have reference to the specific person detained. The archetype would, we imagine, be the sophisticated criminal who is known or suspected of being a member of a gang of criminals.

The task of satisfying a court that reasonable grounds existed at the time the decision was made, either in respect of intentional or inadvertent conduct will, we think, prove even more formidable. Any officer attempting to justify his decision to delay the exercise of this fundamental right of a citizen will, in our judgment, be unable to do so save by reference to specific circumstances including evidence as to the person detained or the actual solicitor sought to be consulted.

In this connection it is relevant to note that at many police stations a duty solicitor scheme is in operation. . . .

Duty solicitors will be well known to the police, and we think it will therefore be very difficult to justify consultation with the duty solicitor being delayed. If the duty solicitor has the reputation, deserved or not, for advising persons detained to refuse to answer questions that would, of course, be no reason for delaying consultation.

[On the facts, his Lordship concluded that whoever had decided to refuse access before the third interview could not have had reasonable grounds for the belief required by s. 58(8): by this time 'the police knew the identity of the solicitor, a highly respected and very experienced professional lawyer, unlikely to be hoodwinked by a 24-year-old'. That person was 'very probably motivated by a desire to have one last chance of interviewing the appellant in the absence of a solicitor'.]

Having ruled against the defence submissions on both the construction point and the more fundamental submissions on the exercise of the power under section 58(8), the trial judge briefly considered his discretion. He said:

'However, had I decided that "an offence" meant any offence I would, in the exercise of the discretion which I undoubtedly have, have exercised it on the basis of justice, fairness and common sense and would in any event have allowed the evidence to be given to the jury.'

It is to be noted that he there makes no reference to his decision on the second ground. Mr. Escott Cox submits that it is clear that the judge did not consider how he would have exercised his discretion if he had applied his mind to the situation at 4.45 p.m. and still held that the refusal at that time was proper. Secondly, he submits that, having found wrongly on both submissions, it was really impossible for him properly to consider how he would have exercised his discretion.

Mr. Warner gave evidence. He said it was not his policy always to advise a client not to answer questions put to him by the police. In his view, in many cases, it was of advantage to someone in detention to answer proper questions put to him. However on this occasion, knowing that his client had already been interviewed on four occasions and at each had strenuously denied complicity in the robbery and had already been charged with two serious offences, he would probably, after consultation, have advised his client, for the time being at any rate, to refuse to answer further questioning. The probable result of allowing the appellant to exercise his right would therefore, in all probability, have been that, had a further interview taken place (and we think it improbable that the police would, in those circumstances, have thought it worth their while to interview him further) no incriminating replies would have been given.

Mr. Escott Cox further submits that he was handicapped in his conduct of the appellant's defence by the judge's ruling on the construction of the Annex. That was a ruling on a point of law and therefore prevented him cross-examining the police on the propriety of the refusal of access on that ground.

It is undesirable to attempt any general guidance as to the way in which a judge's discretion under section 78 or his inherent powers should be exercised. Circumstances vary infinitely. Mr. Jones has made the extreme submission that, in the absence of impropriety, the discretion should never be exercised to exclude admissible evidence. We have no hesitation in rejecting that submission, although the propriety or otherwise of the way in which the evidence was obtained is something which a court is, in terms, enjoined by the section to take into account.

The Court of Appeal is always reluctant to interfere with the exercise of a judge's discretion but the position is different where there was no discretion to exercise on the judge's ruling and all the court has is an indication of how the judge would have exercised it. This is particularly so in this case where, on the section 58(8) point, the judge failed properly to address his mind to the point in time which was most material and did not in terms give consideration to what his decision would have been had he ruled in favour of the defence on this more fundamental issue before him.

In this case this appellant was denied improperly one of the most important and fundamental rights of a citizen. The trial judge fell into error in not so holding. If he had arrived at correct decisions on the two points argued before him he might well have concluded that the refusal of access and consequent unlawful interview compelled him to find that the admission of evidence as to the final interview would have 'such an adverse effect on the fairness of the proceedings' that he ought not to admit it. Such a decision would, of course, have very significantly weakened the prosecution case (the failure to charge earlier ineluctably shows this). In those circumstances this court feels that it has no alternative but to quash the appellant's conviction on count 1 in the indictment, the charge of robbery.

Appeal allowed.
Conviction quashed.

NOTES

1. The largest number of cases in which a confession has been excluded involve exclusion under s. 78. Examples include the following situations:

(1) Where the police have denied access to a solicitor in breach of s. 58: *R v Samuel*, above; *R v Parris* (1988) 89 Cr App Rep 68, CA (Cr D) (superintendent's order that D be kept incommunicado under s. 56 wrongly assumed to exclude access to a solicitor under s. 58); *R v Walsh* (1989) 91 Cr App Rep 161, CA (Cr D); *R v Chung* (1990) 92 Cr App Rep 314, CA (Cr D); *R v Braithwaite* (1991) Times, 9 December, CA (Cr D). Exclusion is not, however, automatic, and may not follow where D is aware of his rights: *R v Alladice* (1988) 87 Cr App Rep 380, CA (Cr D) (D admitted he was well able to cope with the interviews, that he understood the caution and was aware of his rights); *R v Dunford* (1990) 91 Cr App Rep 150, CA (Cr D) (D had a record and was aware of his right not to answer questions); *R v Oliphant* [1992] Crim LR 40, CA (Cr D) (presence of solicitor would have added nothing to what O knew of his legal rights); *R v Anderson* [1993] Crim LR 447, CA (Cr D) (even if a solicitor had been present and advised silence, A would not have acted on such advice).
A confession may also be excluded where a suspect is not told that a solicitor has come to the police station at another person's request, contrary to Code C, Annex B, para. 3: *R v Franklin* (1994) Times, 16 June, CA (Cr D) (proviso applied).

(2) Where D has not been advised of the right to legal advice: *R v Absolam* (1988) 88 Cr App Rep 332, CA (Cr D); *R v Beycan* [1990] Crim LR 185, CA (Cr D).

(3) Where a proper record of the interview was not made: *R v Abolsam*, above (no caution before questioning; no proper record); *R v Keenan* [1990] 2 QB 54, CA (Cr D) (officers unaware of Code C); *R v Walsh*, above; *R v Canale* [1990] 2 All ER 187, CA (Cr D) (where the breaches were described as 'flagrant', 'deliberate', and 'cynical'); *R v Bryce* [1992] 4 All ER 567, CA (Cr D) (interview after tape recorder switched off at B's request; no fresh caution and no contemporaneous record); *R v Cox* (1992) 96 Cr App Rep 464, CA (Cr D) (questioning before arrival at police station held to be 'interview' to which Code C.11 requirements applied); *R v Joseph* [1993] Crim LR 206, CA (Cr D) (interview after arrest away from police station not shown to be necessary; accordingly, no justification for absence of contemporaneous note); *R v Goddard* [1994] Crim LR 46, CA (Cr D) (questions to elicit admissions after arrest and caution held to be an interview; G given no opportunity to take legal advice and no contemporaneous note). In *R v Keenan*, Hodgson J emphasised the importance of these provisions as safeguards against 'verballing' by the police (i.e. 'the police inaccurately recording or inventing the words used in questioning a detained person' [1990] 2 QB 54, 63).

Cf. *R v Matthews, Dennison, Voss* (1989) 91 Cr App Rep 43, where the Court of Appeal declined to interfere with the trial judge's exercise of discretion to admit a confession notwithstanding breach of the recording requirements (the confession included correct details as to where the victim's clothes were found); and *R v Dunn* (1990) 91 Cr App Rep 237, CA (Cr D), where there were breaches of the recording requirements but a confession was held to be admissible as D's solicitor's clerk was present at the interview and so able to protect his interests.

(4) Where there was a breach of Code C.11.3 (above, p. 134): *R v Howden-Simpson* [1991] Crim LR 49, CA (Cr D) (the police indicated they would proceed on only two of a series of non-payments if D admitted theft: note the criticism by D. J. Birch, [1991] Crim LR 50–51).

(5) Where there is a breach of a requirement to caution: *R v Absolam*, above; *R v Hunt* [1992] Crim LR 582, CA (Cr D) (H seen by police officer to have a flick knife and asked what it was for; it was held that there was ample evidence to suspect commission of an offence and he should have been cautioned); *R v Bryce*, above; *R v Okafor* [1994] 3 All ER 741, CA (Cr D) (proviso applied); cf. *R v Shah* [1994] Crim LR 125, CA (Cr D) (customs officer's suspicion that S might be a drugs courier not sufficient to require a caution).

(6) Where a juvenile is interviewed in the absence of an appropriate adult: *R v Weekes* (1992) 97 Cr App Rep 222, CA (Cr D).

2. In some early cases, particularly at first instance, courts seem to have been too ready to assume that breaches of Code C render it unfair for a confession to be admitted (see D. J. Birch, [1989] Crim LR 95, 105–106). More recently the Court of Appeal has emphasised that 'not every breach or combination of breaches of the codes will justify the exclusion of interview evidence under section 76 or section 78 . . . they must be significant and substantial' (per Hodgson J in *R v Keenan* [1990] 2 QB 54, 69). Furthermore, exclusion will not follow automatically even where there is a 'significant or substantial breach':

'The task of the court is not merely to consider whether there would be an adverse effect on the fairness of the proceedings, but such an adverse effect that justice requires the evidence to be excluded'

(per Saville J, in *R v Walsh* (1989) 91 Cr App Rep 161, 163, CA (Cr D)).

On the other hand, 'if the police have acted in bad faith, the court will have little difficulty in ruling any confession inadmissible under section 78, if not under section 76' (per Lord Lane CJ in *R v Alladice* (1988) 87 Cr App Rep 380, 386, CA (Cr D)).

3. The 'burden of proof' under s. 78 is unclear, in contrast to the position under s. 76, see *R v Anderson* [1993] Crim LR 447.

R v Christou and Wright [1992] 1 QB 979, [1992] 3 WLR 228, [1992] 4 All ER 559, CA (Cr D)

In 1990, in order to combat a high rate of burglary and robbery in North London, police set up an undercover operation. A shop ('Stardust Jewellers') was established in Tottenham, run by two undercover officers ('Gary' and 'Aggi') who purported to be shady jewellers willing to buy in stolen property. Over three months, a series of transactions was recorded by cameras and sound recording equipment. The conversations included questions that would be asked by shady jewellers, such as the area of London in which it would be unwise to resell the goods. The officers also required the vendors to sign receipts recording the money paid and the specific goods. This was something which shady jewellers would be likely to do, but also had the effect of obtaining fingerprints. In the event the fingerprints were not used. C and W were vendors of stolen property charged in respect of a number of transactions. At their trial for handling stolen goods, the judge ruled that the evidence from the operation was admissible, and they accordingly pleaded guilty. Their appeal to the Court of Appeal was dismissed.

The judgment of the court (**Lord Taylor of Gosforth CJ, Boreham** and **Auld JJ**) was delivered by **Lord Taylor of Gosforth CJ**:

[His Lordship referred to dicta in *R v Sang* (above, pp. 148–149) and continued:]

In view of the terms of those dicta, the paucity of cases in which the discretion has been exercised so as to exclude legally admissible evidence is not surprising. In the present case the judge decided that, since the evidence from Stardust Jewellers had admittedly been obtained from the appellants by a trick and after the offences charged had been committed, he had a discretion to exclude the evidence if its admission would prejudice a fair trial. He also considered the alternative submission that, pursuant to section 78 of the Act of 1984, he ought to exclude the evidence. . . .

The judge held that the discretion under section 78 may be wider than the common law discretion identified in *Reg v Sang* [1980] AC 402, the latter relating solely to evidence obtained from the defendant after the offence is complete, the statutory discretion not being so restricted. However, he held that the criteria of unfairness are the same whether the trial judge is exercising his discretion at common law or under the statute. We agree. What is unfair cannot sensibly be subject to different standards depending on the source of the discretion to exclude it.

In the result the judge concluded that to admit the challenged evidence would not have an adverse effect on the fairness of the trial. He said:

'Nobody was forcing the defendants to do what they did. They were not persuaded or encouraged to do what they did. They were doing in that shop exactly what they intended to do and in all probability, what they intended to do from the moment they got up that morning. They were dishonestly disposing of dishonest goods. If the police had never set up the jewellers shop, they would, in my judgment, have been doing the same thing, though of course they would not have been doing it in that shop, at that time. They were not tricked into doing what they would not otherwise have done, they were tricked into doing what they wanted to do in that place and before witnesses and devices who can now speak of what happened. I do not think that is unfair or leads to an unfairness in the trial.'

Putting it in different words, the trick was not applied to the appellants; they voluntarily applied themselves to the trick. It is not every trick producing evidence against an accused which results in unfairness. There are, in criminal investigations, a number of situations in which the police adopt ruses or tricks in the public interest to obtain evidence. For example, to trap a blackmailer, the victim may be used as an agent of the police to arrange an appointment and false or marked money may be laid as bait to catch the offender. A trick, certainly; in a sense too, a trick which results in a form of self-incrimination; but not one which could reasonably be thought to involve unfairness. Cases such as *R v Payne* [1963] 1 WLR 637 and *R v Mason (Carl)* [1988] 1 WLR 139 are very different from the present case or the blackmail example. In *R v Mason* as in *R v Payne* [1963] 1 WLR 637, the defendant was in police custody at a police station. Officers lied to both the defendant and his solicitor. Having no evidence against the defendant, they falsely asserted that his fingerprint had been found in an incriminating place in order to elicit admissions from him. After advice from his solicitor, the defendant made admissions. This court quashed his conviction.

In the present case the argument was at one stage canvassed that requesting the receipt with the consequent obtaining of fingerprints, should be regarded separately from the main issue, that it amounted to a separate trick within a trick. However, Mr. Thornton made clear that in his submission requesting the receipt was merely an incident in the operation of the shop. The whole operation was a single trick, all the fruits of which should be excluded. We agree that the operation should be considered as a whole. In the end, the judge treated the receipts as 'part of the general deceit concerning the dishonest jewellers, the general pretence by them that it was a proper jeweller's shop'. It was not unfair. He gave, as a further reason, that had no request been made for a receipt, fingerprints could easily have been obtained in other ways, e.g., by dusting the counter. For this he relied upon *R v Apicella* (1985) 82 Cr App R 295 and *Director of Public Prosecutions v Marshall* [1988] 3 All ER 683.

The judge's exercise of his discretion could only be impugned if it was unreasonable according to *Wednesbury* principles (*Associated Provincial Picture Houses Ltd v Wednesbury Corporation* [1948] 1 KB 223): see *R v O'Leary* (1988) 87 Cr App R 387, 391. In our judgment, not only can the judge's conclusion on this issue not be so stigmatised, we think he was right.

The other ground of appeal turns on paragraph 10.1 of Code C of the PACE Codes [above, p. 144].

It is submitted that the first sentence of that paragraph applied to the conversations in the shop. Accordingly, a caution should have been given. It is obvious that if this submission is correct, setting up Stardust Jewellers would have been pointless. Mr. Thornton and Mr. Taylor grasped that nettle. They say that the operation should not have been undertaken. If a caution was required, it cannot be dispensed with simply to facilitate the operation. It is accepted that Gary and Aggi had grounds to suspect each of the appellants of an offence. The issue is whether the Code applied to this situation at all. The judge concluded it did not. . . .

In our view, although the Code extends beyond the treatment of those in detention, what is clear is that it was intended to protect suspects who are vulnerable to abuse or pressure from police officers or who may believe themselves to be so. Frequently, the suspect will be a detainee. But the Code will also apply where a suspect, not in detention, is being questioned about an offence by a police officer acting as a police officer for the purpose of obtaining evidence. In that situation, the officer and the suspect are not on equal terms. The officer is perceived to be in a position of authority; the suspect may be intimidated or undermined.

The situation at Stardust Jewellers was quite different. The appellants were not being questioned by police officers acting as such. Conversation was on equal terms. There could be no question of pressure or intimidation by Gary or Aggi as persons actually in authority or believed to be so. We agree with the judge that the Code simply was not intended to apply in such a context.

In reaching that conclusion, we should ourselves administer a caution. It would be wrong for police officers to adopt or use an undercover pose or disguise to enable themselves to ask questions about an offence uninhibited by the requirements of the Code and with the effect of circumventing it.

Were they to do so, it would be open to the judge to exclude the questions and answers under section 78 of the Act of 1984. It is therefore necessary here to see whether the questioning by Gary and Aggi was such as to require the judge in his discretion to exclude the conversation. The judge carefully reviewed the evidence on this issue. He concluded that the questions and comments from Gary and Aggi were for the most part simply those necessary to conduct the bartering and maintain their cover. They were not questions 'about the offence'. The only exception was the questioning about which area should be avoided in reselling the goods. However, even that was partly to maintain cover since it was the sort of questioning to be expected from a shady jeweller.

We are of the view that the judge's approach to the aspect of the case concerned with the Code cannot be faulted. . . .

Appeals dismissed.

NOTES

1. *Christou and Wright* deals with two distinct, but related issues: (1) the discretion to exclude evidence obtained by a trick; and (2) the question of 'entrapment'. The evidence obtained may in either event be confession or real evidence (cf. above, p. 151).

2. *Tricks.* In *R v Mason* [1988] 1 WLR 139, mentioned by Lord Taylor CJ in *R v Christou and Wright*, Watkins LJ described the conduct of the police as 'most reprehensible'. The trial judge in exercising his discretion under s. 78 had failed to take any account of the deceit practised upon M's solicitor. If he had done so, he would clearly have ruled the confession inadmissible. The court stated that 'this was not the place to discipline the police' but they hoped 'never again to hear of deceit such as this being practised upon an accused person, and more particularly possibly on a solicitor whose duty it is to advise him unfettered by false information from the police' (p. 144). The court also confirmed that s. 78 could be used to exclude evidence of confessions and admissions.

Lord Taylor in *Christou and Wright* emphasised that undercover operations must not be employed to enable police officers to ask questions about an offence uninhibited by the requirements of Code C. That line was crossed in *R v Bryce* [1992] 4 All ER 567, CA (Cr D), where an undercover police officer posed as a potential buyer and agreed by telephone to buy a stolen car (actually worth £23,000) from B for

£2,800. When they met, the officer asked B (inter alia) how long the car had been stolen, and was told two or three days. Lord Taylor noted that 'Those questions went to the heart of the vital issue of dishonesty. They were not even necessary to the undercover operation' (at 571–572). They were also hotly disputed, and there was no contemporary record (unlike the position in *Christou and Wright* where the conversations were recorded). The court held that the answers should have been excluded.

Other cases where evidence obtained by tricks or deception has been held admissible include *DPP v Marshall* [1988] 3 All ER 683, where the Divisional Court held that the justices had been wrong to exclude evidence of test purchases made by police officers, without revealing their identity, as evidence for a prosecution for selling liquor without a licence; it had not been shown that admission of the evidence would adversely affect the fairness of proceedings. (Cf. *London Borough of Ealing v Woolworths plc* [1995] Crim LR 58, DC.) Then, in *Williams and O'Hare v DPP* (1993) 98 Cr App Rep 209, the Divisional Court upheld the admissibility of evidence of interfering with a vehicle with intent to commit theft, where the police left a van unattended, with what seemed to be a valuable load of cigarettes, and W and O'H succumbed to the temptation. See also *R v Maclean and Kosten* [1993] Crim LR 775, CA (Cr D). In a number of cases, covertly recorded conversations in situations set up by the police have been held to be admissible. See *R v Jelen, R v Katz* (1989) 90 Cr App Rep 456, CA (Cr D) (tape recorded telephone conversation with a witness who had been charged and released on bail); *R v Ali (Shaukat)* (1991) Times, 19 February, CA (Cr D) (covertly recorded conversation between A and his family in the interview room at the police station after charge); *R v Bailey and Smith* [1993] 3 All ER 513, CA (Cr D) (covertly recorded conversation between the two appellants placed together in a police cell with the connivance of the custody officer, after being charged and remanded by the magistrates). Code C is held not to apply to such situations. The case that goes furthest is *Bailey and Smith* where the situation followed interviews in which B and S exercised their right to silence and involved a strategem whereby the investigating officers, in order to avoid arousing their suspicions, pretended that they had been forced to place the appellants together by an unco-operative custody officer. However, their solicitors were not given any false information or deceived, nothing had been done oppressively or so as to render unreliable any admissions made. There was no reason to doubt the essential fairness of the evidence having been held admissible (Simon Brown LJ at 523). See also *R v Cadette* [1995] Crim LR 229, CA (Cr D).

3. *Entrapment and agents provocateurs.* In *R v Smurthwaite, R v Gill* [1994] 1 All ER 898, the Court of Appeal (Criminal Division) confirmed that s. 78 had not altered the common law rule laid down in *Sang* (above, p. 148) that entrapment or the use of an agent provocateur does not per se afford a defence in law to a criminal charge. However, if the judge considered that in all the circumstances the obtaining of the evidence in that way had such an adverse affect on the fairness of the proceedings that the court ought not to admit it, it could be excluded under s. 78 (Lord Taylor CJ at 902).

His Lordship continued (at 903):

'In exercising his discretion whether to admit the evidence of an undercover officer, some, but not an exhaustive list, of the factors that the judge may take into account are as follows. Was the officer acting as an agent provocateur in the sense that he was enticing the defendant to commit an offence he would not otherwise have committed? What was the nature of any entrapment? Does the evidence consist of admissions to a completed offence, or does it consist of the actual commission of an offence? How active or passive was the officer's role in obtaining the evidence? Is there an unassailable record of what occurred, or is it strongly corroborated? In *R v Christou* [1992] 4 All ER 559, [1992] QB 979 this court held that discussions between suspects and undercover officers, not overtly acting as police officers, were not within the ambit of the codes under the 1984 Act. However, officers should not use their undercover pose to question suspects so as to circumvent the code. In *R v Bryce* [1992] 4 All ER 567 the court held that the undercover officer had done just that. Accordingly, a further consideration for the judge in deciding whether to admit an undercover officer's evidence is whether he has abused his role to ask questions which ought properly to have been asked as a police officer and in accordance with the codes.'

Here, police officers in two separate cases posed as contract killers, and were solicited by S and G to kill their respective spouses. On the facts in each case, tape recorded conversations 'showed no sign of an unwilling defendant being persuaded or cajoled into an agreement to a murder she [or he] would not otherwise have entered' (Lord Taylor CJ at 909). In S's case, all the conversations were recorded; in G's case an unrecorded conversation given in evidence by the officer was corroborated by later recorded conversations and held to be admissible.

See also *R v Latif and Shahzad* [1995] 1 Cr App Rep 270, CA (Cr D); *R v Pattemore* [1994] Crim LR 836, CA (Cr D); *R v Dixon (Paul)*, *R v Mann (Harbel)* (1994) Times, 31 December, CA (Cr D); and *R v Lawrence and Nash* (1993, unreported), cited by G. Robertson QC in 'Entrapment Evidence' [1994] Crim LR 805, 811. In the last of these cases, convictions for conspiracy to supply cannabis to an undercover police officer were quashed where the officer 'persistently and vigorously pressed the appellant to supply it' and the relevant conversations had not been recorded.

CHAPTER 3

Public order

1 Introduction[1]

The liberty of the people to assemble in public in order to express their views on political matters is generally regarded as an essential element in a free and open society. It is recognised in such international standards as Article 11 of the ECHR (below, p. 742) and Article 21, ICCPR. The extent to which that liberty may be exercised in this country depends partly on the existing state of the law, and partly on the way in which the law is enforced by police, prosecutors and courts. As this chapter shows, there are many ways in which public meetings or processions may fall foul of the law, both civil and criminal. Just as important is what is likely to happen in practice. On this latter point it is extremely difficult to generalise. Much depends on 'the policeman on the spot' (see *Williams*, Chap. 5). Moreover, the attitude of the authorities seems to vary according to current political circumstances. The more stable the political system, the greater is the toleration of political protest. As the effectiveness, or likely or even feared effectiveness, of protest increases, so toleration is reduced: the law is enforced more rigorously, and may be strengthened. In addition to being concerned with the mechanics of protest (how many protestors? where are they? are they disorderly? are they violent?), the authorities may be more inclined to focus their attention on the content of the protest (is it seditious? does it incite to disaffection?).

At present, most of the law in the context of political protest relates to its 'public order' aspect. A major theme is the control of the advocacy or use of violence as a

1 The main works cited in this chapter are: *Williams*: D. G. T. Williams, *Keeping the Peace* (1967); *Brownlie*: M. Supperstone, *Brownlie's Law of Public Order and National Security* (2nd edn, 1981); *Smith and Hogan*: J. C. Smith and B. Hogan, *The Criminal Law* (7th edn, 1992). Works published since the Public Order Act 1986 include R. Card, *Public Order: The New Law* (1987); A. T. H. Smith, *Offences against Public Order* (1987) (hereafter cited as *Smith*); A. Sherr, *Freedom of Protest, Public Order and the Law* (1989); and P. Thornton, *Public Order Law* (1987). See also: R. Benewick and T. Smith (eds), *Direct Action and Democratic Politics* (1972); V. T. Bevan, [1979] PL 163; Jo Cooper, 'Public Order Reviews' *Legal Action*, August 1992, p. 13, April 1993, p. 11, February 1994, p. 10; D. Feldman, *Civil Liberties and Human Rights in England and Wales* (1993), Chap. 17; W. Finnie, 'Public Order Law in Scotland and England 1980–1990' in Finnie, *et al.*, *Edinburgh Essays in Public Law* (1991), pp. 251–277; A. D. Grunis, (1978) 56 Can Bar Rev 393; A. Hiller, *Public Order and the Law* (1983) (Australia); E. R. H. Ivamy, (1949) CLP 183; P. E. Kilbride and P. T. Burns, (1966) 2 NZULR 1; O. Hood Phillips, (1970) 86 LQR 1; A. T. H. Smith, [1984] Crim LR 643; C. Townshend, *Making the Peace* (1993); R. Vogler, *Reading the Riot Act* (1991); D. G. T. Williams, [1970] CLJ 96; [1974] Crim LR 635–8; (1975) 1 UNSW Law Journal 94. On the *White Paper*, see P. Scraton, (1985) 12 JLS 385. On the 1986 Act, see D. Bonner and R. Stone, [1987] P.L. 449; Symposium, [1987] Crim LR 153ff; J. Driscoll, [1987] JSWL 280.

The constitutional status of public protest in Britain and the US is discussed by D. G. Barnum at [1977] PL 310 and (1981) 29 Am. Jo. of Comparative Law 59. See also L. A. Stein, [1971] PL 115; *Village of Skokie v National Socialist Party of America* 373 NE 2d 21 (1978); *Collin v Smith* 578 F 2d 1197 (1978).

means of obtaining political change (in other words the prevention of breaches of the peace (see pp. 207–212)). Another theme is the protection of other legitimate interests of citizens (e.g. the right to use the highway; the right not to have an unwanted crowd gathering in one's own front garden). This concentration on the 'public order' aspect has three consequences. Firstly, the control of political assemblies is seen as part of the general police function of keeping the peace. The problems posed by disorderly political demonstrators are regarded as analogous to those posed by vandals, quarrelling neighbours, 'mods' and 'rockers', 'football hooligans' and drunks. The laws applicable are the same for all. It is open to argument whether the law should operate in the same way in relation to all the categories mentioned, although this is a point on which a very firm view was expressed in *R v Caird* (1970) 54 Cr App Rep 499 (below, p. 219).

Secondly, by checking violent protest, it is possible that the law checks the very kind of protest which is most likely to obtain fundamental change. The justifications advanced are that any violence in society is unacceptable, and that violence in this context distorts the 'proper' democratic political process for obtaining reform.

Thirdly, laws which seek to maintain public order are easier to justify than those which impinge directly on freedom of expression. Indeed free expression is essential to the operation of those democratic processes which the maintenance of order is supposed to facilitate. However, laws preserving public order may have significant effects on freedom of expression (1) if they are enforced discriminatorily according to the nature of the political opinions held by particular individuals (as has frequently been alleged: see R. Kidd, *British Liberty in Danger* (1940) Chap. 5; B. Cox, *Civil Liberties in Britain* (1975) Chap. 1); (2) if they interfere with the *effective* communication of views (see, e.g. *Duncan v Jones* [1936] 1 KB 218, DC, below, p. 248); and (3) in so far as the use of words which incite or provoke violence is proscribed (see e.g. *Wise v Dunning* [1902] 1 KB 167, DC, below, p. 244, Public Order Act 1986, ss. 4, 4A, 5, below, pp. 213–214; the law of sedition and incitement to disaffection.)

The law relating to public order was modified and extended by the Public Order Act 1986[1] and again by the Criminal Justice and Public Order Act 1994. The latter Act significantly extends the ambit of the criminal law in seeking to control, inter alia, acts of trespass and acts that disrupt lawful activities. The 1994 Act was particularly controversial, attracting opposition from such diverse quarters as members of the House of Lords, 'clergy, lawyers, police, MPs, civil rights groups, ecology groups and the disaffected young' (*The Independent*, 4 November 1994). Mike Bennett, chairman of the Metropolitan Police Federation, described the public order provisions as unworkable, being 'legislation directed against a certain section of the population . . . people whose lifestyle, culture and attitude to life differs from other people'. On the day it was passed, 'other campaigners started a series of rolling protests across the country . . . with "mass trespass"—a new offence created under the Act—at road construction sites' (ibid.). The following day, five people climbed on the roof of Westminster Hall in protest against the Act (*The Times*, 5 November 1994). This chapter also illustrates the steady increase in the powers of the police and development of their organisation, equipment and tactics in dealing with disorder.

1 This was preceded by the *Review of the Public Order Act 1936 and related legislation* (Green Paper, Cmnd. 7891, 1980); the Fifth Report from the Home Affairs Committee, Session 1979–80, *The Law Relating to Public Order* (1979–80 HC 756: the Committee had a Conservative majority and divided on party lines on many issues); the Law Commission's Report, *Criminal Law: Offences Relating to Public Order* (Law Com No. 123, 1983) and the White Paper, *Review of Public Order Law* (Cmnd. 9510, 1985). Hereafter these are cited as *Green Paper, HAC Report, Law Com No. 123* and *White Paper*.

The Red Lion Square Disorders of 15 June 1974: Report of Inquiry by the Rt. Hon. Lord Scarman OBE (Cmnd. 5919, 1975)

FIRST PRINCIPLES

5. Amongst our fundamental human rights there are, without doubt, the rights of peaceful assembly and public protest and the right to public order and tranquillity. Civilised living collapses—it is obvious—if public protest becomes violent protest or public order degenerates into the quietism imposed by successful oppression. But the problem is more complex than a choice between two extremes—one, a right to protest whenever and wherever you will and the other, a right to continuous calm upon our streets unruffled by the noise and obstructive pressure of the protesting procession. A balance has to be struck, a compromise found that will accommodate the exercise of the right to protest within a framework of public order which enables ordinary citizens, who are not protesting, to go about their business and pleasure without obstruction or inconvenience. The fact that those who at any one time are concerned to secure the tranquillity of the streets are likely to be the majority must not lead us to deny the protesters their opportunity to march: the fact that the protesters are desperately sincere and are exercising a fundamental human right must not lead us to overlook the rights of the majority.
6. This Inquiry has been concerned to discover where the balance should be struck, and the role of the police in maintaining it. Indiscipline amongst demonstrators, heavy-handed police reaction to disorder are equally mischievous: for each can upset the balance. Violent demonstrators by creating public disorder infringe a fundamental human right which belongs to the rest of us: excessively violent police reaction to public disorder infringes the rights of the protesters. The one and the other are an affront to civilised living.

THE ROLE OF THE POLICE

7. The police are not to be required in any circumstances to exercise political judgment. Their role is the maintenance of public order—no more, and no less. When the National Front marches, the police have no concern with their political message; they will intervene only if the circumstances are such that a breach of the peace is reasonably apprehended. Even if the message be 'racist', it is not for the police to 'ban the march' or compel it to disperse unless public order is threatened. If, of course, the message appears to infringe the race relations legislation, the police have a duty to report the facts so that consideration may be given to subsequent prosecution: moreover in such circumstances a senior police officer, accompanying the march, might think it wise to warn the organisers of the march that, if it proceeds with its slogans, he will report the fact. But it is vital, if the police are to be kept out of political controversy, that in a public order situation their sole immediate concern is, and is seen to be, with public order.

2 Demonstrations and riots

The Metropolitan Police and political demonstrations by Sir Robert Mark QPM (Appendix 8 to the Report of the Commissioner of Police of the Metropolis for the year 1974)

2. . . . The total number of political demonstrations in London during 1972, 1973 and 1974 was 1,321. Only 54 of these demonstrations involved disorder, resulting in a total of 623 arrests. In these three years 297 police officers, 49 persons who were arrested and 27 other participants were reported to have been injured, none fatally until Red Lion Square. However, not every civilian participant will report minor injury and there cannot, therefore, be any true record of all casualties. The figures nevertheless suggest an avoidance of extreme violence and a tradition of containment of activities which, though usually lawful, are often controversial, sometimes provocative and occasionally open to exploitation and misrepresentation, and which are frequently the cause of inconvenience to the public. . . .
4. It is not possible to attribute to any one factor the general avoidance of extreme disorder and the comparative rarity of serious casualties in so long a history of political demonstrations. The underlying reason is perhaps our long-standing tradition of changing governments without bloodshed or tumult and a freedom of expression unsurpassed elsewhere. This has allowed a unique relationship between the people and the police, who traditionally depend on goodwill rather than force in carrying out their duties. Of the more immediate reasons for the avoidance of serious disorder and casualties, perhaps the most obvious is an adequate police presence and a lack of weaponry. The police have never had any special weapons or equipment for crowd control. We rely on manpower, supported by horses where necessary, as the most effective and least harmful means of control, and we have nothing more lethal than a wooden truncheon on which to rely in emergencies. Similarly, demonstrators in this country rarely have recourse to lethal

weapons, possession of which is, in any case, in many circumstances an offence involving liability to arrest. There is usually no intentional separation of police and demonstrators. The one escorts the other when walking in procession and even when facing each other outside an embassy or police station they are usually within touching distance; their mutual vulnerability being more evident than if seen at a distance.

5. Although the support of the public at large for police aims and methods is a major factor in keeping down the temperature at demonstrations and minimizing casualties, the lack of fatal and serious casualties had allowed unjustified complacency in the public attitude to political demonstrations. These are occasionally both violent and frightening and there has emerged a small minority of extremist causes whose adherents leave no doubt of their belief in the use of force and lack of scruple to further political aims. That these groups are contained without more serious consequences is in the main due to the fortitude, the training and the tolerance of the police and the inhibitions natural to their role. The limitation of police powers in dealing with demonstrations and demonstrators, the accountability of the police and their constant exposure to the news media and to parliamentary questions, and not least the fact that police have learnt from experience that in the long run restraint is usually the most effective way to preserve order and maintain control; all these factors have the effect of creating an unwillingness to abandon persuasion except as a last resort. This unwillingness has perhaps been reinforced over the years by growing police awareness of the tolerance of the courts in dealing with those found guilty of an offence. . . .

13. Political demonstrations seem to give satisfaction in the main to those taken part. The public as a whole are usually not interested unless affected by inconvenience or aroused by disorder and violence. Nevertheless, the right to hold them is much valued and jealously preserved. In the event of violence there is usually much comment on the extent to which the police exercised or failed to exercise control. Speculation as to whether the police should have prohibited or regulated a political demonstration usually betrays a lack of knowledge of the law or of the difficulties of applying it. No useful purpose is achieved by prohibitions or regulations incapable of enforcement, or in respect of which judicial penalties are likely to be slight. Demonstrators who can rely on massive support, such as The Committee of 100 in the sixties, are unlikely to be deterred by such restrictions and political extremists are likely to welcome them. For both, disregard or defiance is sure to achieve maximum publicity at very little cost. . . .

16. When considering what action to take in respect of the declared intention to hold extremist demonstrations in support of any political persuasion, police observe scrupulously the principle declared to the House of Commons by a former Home Secretary:—

'If this is indeed a free country and we are free people, a man is just as much entitled to profess the Fascist philosophy as any other, and he is perfectly entitled to proclaim it and expound it so long as he does not exceed the reasonable bounds which are set by law.'

18. The Metropolitan Police have always been disinclined to seek the approval of the Secretary of State for an Order prohibiting political processions for a specified period on the grounds that this encourages extremist minority groups to threaten violence with the object of achieving the suppression of opposition opinion. We believe that attempts by coercion or force to suppress free speech are not only wrong but unlawful and that behaviour of that kind must be resisted no matter what the inconvenience or cost. To give way to such threats is not just to defer to mob-rule but to encourage it. . . .

NOTES

1. In general, contrary to the popular image, in the period 1900 to 1975 there was a marked and generally downward trend in the number of violent disorders, from a high point in the first two decades of the century: see E. Dunning, *et al*, 'Violent disorders in twentieth-century Britain' in G. Gaskell and R. Benewick (eds), *The Crowds in Contemporary Britain* (1987). The same point is made in respect of industrial disputes by R. Geary, *Policing Industrial Disputes* (1985). Disorder associated with leisure and sporting events has, however, increased.

2. CS smoke was used in 1971 to dislodge a person suspected of three murders who had barricaded himself in an upstairs room. There has been a gradual extension of the kinds of equipment used by the police in Great Britain. 'CS smoke is available only for dealing with armed besieged criminals in specific circumstances' (*Report of the Commissioner of Police of the Metropolis for 1971*, Cmnd. 4986, p. 43). Protective shields were first used in disturbances arising out of a National Front march in

Lewisham in 1977, and were used again at the Notting Hill carnival in the same year. The Commissioner stated in his Report for 1977 that it 'was with extreme reluctance that the Force had to resort to the use of defensive equipment and I must stress that it does not mean that we have forsaken traditional methods of policing demonstrations and the like' (Cmnd. 7238, p. 6). At the same time riot equipment was used much more extensively in Northern Ireland. See further, below, p. 175, n. 3.

Report of Her Majesty's Chief Inspector of Constabulary for 1981 (1981–82 HC 463)

The civil disturbances

8.1 1981 saw the most serious outbreaks of public disorder in England and Wales since the end of the Second World War. The first disturbances took place at Brixton in April. No other outbreaks occurred at that time.

8.2 In July, however, disturbances occurred in many parts of the country. The first outbreak outside London began on 3 July in Toxteth, in Liverpool. A group of officers were attacked whilst attempting to arrest a youth believed to have stolen a motor cycle, and had to call for assistance. In the resulting struggle one officer sustained a broken nose. Following a warning of further trouble on the following day the police, including reinforcements from the Greater Manchester Police, were placed on standby. The disorders began in the evening, when the police were attacked with bricks and other missiles, including petrol bombs. A number of buildings were set alight. The area was then cordoned off and order restored. A reduced presence was maintained on 5 July, but was increased following warnings of further trouble. At about 5 pm, some 100 youths created disorder, which spread and soon became a concerted attack on the police. Street lighting was extinguished, oil was poured onto the road and petrol used to ignite it. Buildings were set on fire and police attempting to cordon off the area and contain the disorders were ferociously attacked: stolen vehicles, including mechanical diggers and a bulldozer, were driven at their cordons. The fire service was unable to enter the area in order to fight the fires, and the occupants of an old peoples' home had to be evacuated because of neighbouring fires. To prevent further damage and violence, the Chief Constable authorised the use of CS which resulted in the dispersal of the crowds. This was the first use on the British mainland of CS to control public disorder. Further serious outbreaks of disorder occurred on a number of nights.

8.3 At Moss Side, in Manchester the violence spread over a number of areas for the three nights of 7–9 July. A typical series of incidents occurred on 8 July, when about 100 youths set fire to a shop and stoned the fire appliance which arrived to deal with the fire. After setting fire to neighbouring shops, the gang moved to a nearby shopping precinct, looted shops and set them on fire. Similar incidents occurred elsewhere in the area but police reinforcements arrived and the area was calm by 5 am. The next day the police successfully adopted positive tactics. Sixty vans, each containing 11 officers equipped with protective equipment patrolled the area, dispersing groups before they could create serious disorder. Although some shops were damaged there were no major incidents; over 150 arrests were made and 2 police officers received minor injuries.

8.4 These disorders were the most serious which occurred outside London: their most worrying feature was the savagery of the attacks made upon the police. There were also, however, many other incidents of public disorder in other parts of the country between 3–15 July, among the most serious being those in the West Midlands, Bedfordshire, Hampshire, Kent, Leicestershire, West Yorkshire, Nottinghamshire and Derbyshire.

NOTES

1. These disturbances were foreshadowed by serious disorder in 1979 in Southall (see *Southall 23 April 1979: The Report of the Unofficial Committee of Enquiry* (NCCL, 1980); *The Death of Blair Peach: The Supplementary Report of the Unofficial Committee of Inquiry* (NCCL, 1980); C. Harlow, [1980] PL 241), and arising out of meetings held during the General Election by the National Front in Leicester, West Bromwich and Bradford (see the *Report of HM Chief Inspector of Constabulary for 1979* (1979–80

HC 725) p. 50). On 2 April 1980, there was serious disorder in the St. Paul's district of Bristol (see 983 HC Deb 28 April 1980 cols 971–981; M. Kettle and L. Hodges, *Uprising!* (1982), Chap. 1). C. Harlow ([1980] PL 241) noted the inadequacy of inquests and the police complaints system as mechanisms for investigating events of this kind.

2. The Brixton riots were the subject of an inquiry by Lord Scarman under the Police Act 1964, s. 32: *The Brixton Disorders 10–12 April 1981* (Cmnd. 8427, 1981).[1] He concluded that the riots

'[8.11] ... were not premeditated. They began as a spontaneous reaction to what was seen as police harassment: but once they had begun, an element of leadership and direction did emerge; and strangers were observed participating in the disorders. White people, as well as black people, helped to make and distribute petrol bombs on Saturday.

8.12. The disorders were communal disturbances arising from a complex political, social and economic situation, which is not special to Brixton. There was a strong racial element in the disorders; but they were not a race riot. The riots were essentially an outburst of anger and resentment by young black people against the police. . . .

8.13. A major cause of the hostility of young blacks towards the police was loss of confidence by significant sections, though not all, of the Lambeth public in the police. The reasons for this loss of confidence included the collapse of the police liaison committee in 1979; "hard" policing methods which caused offence and apprehension to many; lack of consultation about police operations; distrust of the procedure for investigating complaints against the police; and unlawful and, in particular, racially prejudiced conduct by some police officers. . . .'

An increase in crime, especially mugging, had been met by the deployment of officers of the Special Patrol Group, and this in turn provoked the hostility of young black people. Tension increased further as a result of 'Operation Swamp 81' in which over a hundred officers (not SPG) were deployed in Lambeth to detect and arrest burglars and robbers, relying on powers to stop and search for unlawfully obtained property under section 66 of the Metropolitan Police Act 1839 (above, p. 82). This was done without any warning to community leaders or local police officers.

Overall Lord Scarman found (pp. 127–134) that

'[8.20] ... the direction and policies of the Metropolitan Police are not racist. But racial prejudice does manifest itself occasionally in the behaviour of a few officers on the streets. . . .

8.22. The Metropolitan Police at District command level and above do not lack awareness of the need for good community relations. But the police in Lambeth have not succeeded in achieving the degree of

1 On the Scarman Report see (1981) 78 LS Gaz 1443–1445; G. J. Zellick, [1982] PL 1 (on Part VII, concerning the law reform proposals); S. Saeed, [1982] PL 198; (1981–82) IX (3) *New Community* 344–377 (various authors); (1982) 53 *Political Quarterly* 111–152 (various authors); M. Cain and S. Sadigh, (1982) 9 JLS 87; R. Baldwin and R. Kinsey, *Police Powers and Politics* (1982) Chap. 8; J. Benyon (ed), *Scarman and After* (1984); 13 HC Deb cols 891–900 and 425 HL Deb cols 769–778 (25 November 1981); 13 HC Deb 26 November 1981 col 1009 ff (debate on law and order); 14 HC Deb 10 December 1981 col 1001; 426 HL Deb 4 February 1982 cols 1396–1474.

On the Toxteth riots see M. Jefferson, 'The Toxteth Riots: A Select Bibliography' [1983] V (2) Liverpool LR 203; P. J. Waller, (1981–82) IX (3) *New Community* 344; and M. Brogden *The Police: Autonomy and Consent* (1982): Postscript by A. and M. Brogden (pp. 239–250). For a survey of the views and experiences of male residents in relation to the disturbances of July 1981 in Handsworth, Birmingham, see P. Southgate in *Public Disorder* (Home Office Research Study No. 72, 1982, Part II). Part I (by S. Field) is a review of research concerning Urban Disorders in Britain and America.

The 1981 riots generally are analysed by D. Cowell (*et al*) (eds), *Policing the Riots* (1982); M. Kettle and L. Hodges, *Uprising!* (1982); M. Keith, *Race, Riots and Policing* (1993); J. Lea and J. Young, 'Urban Violence and Political Marginalisation: The Riots in Britain; Summer 1981' (1982) I (3) *Critical Social Policy* 59.

public approval and respect necessary for the effective fulfilment of their functions and duties. Attitudes and methods in the senior command of "L" District had not become sufficiently adjusted to the problems of policing a multi-racial community. . . .

8.23. Although there were sometimes instances of misconduct by police officers during the disorders, in general, I reject the criticism that the police over-reacted in the handling of them.'

Broadly, 'the police response to the disorders, once they broke out, is to be commended, not criticised'. He recommended (inter alia) that there should be an urgent study of ways of improving ethnic minority recruitment into the regular police (but no quota of places reserved for ethnic minorities and no lowering of standards for recruitment); police training in community relations and in the handling of public disorder should be improved; it should be understood throughout the police that the normal penalty for racially prejudiced behaviour is dismissal; methods of policing, especially in inner city areas, should be re-examined; and arrangements for consultation between police and local community should be improved (see above p. 37). He also drew attention .ɔ failures in social policy concerning inner cities and ethnic minorities:

'there is a lack of a sufficiently well co-ordinated and directed programme for combating the problem of racial disadvantage. It is clear from the evidence of ethnic minority deprivation I have received that, if the balance of racial disadvantage is to be redressed, positive action is required' (para. 8.50).

Finally, he considered a number of proposals for law reform.
3. C. Unsworth ('The Riots of 1981: Popular Violence and the Politics of Law and Order' (1982) 9 JLS 63) regards the riots as

'not sudden explosions of violence within normally peaceful and harmonious communities, but a temporary cluster of upsurges punctuating a chronic reality of tension and aggression in the inner city. . . . The escalation . . . may be attributed to the intersection of . . . several developments . . .: provocative policing, insecurity and increasing resistance in the black communities, and traditions of resistance in white working class youth exacerbated by steeply and disproportionately rising unemployment' (p. 71).

See also J. Rex, 'The 1981 urban riots in Britain' (1982) 6 *International Journal of Urban and Regional Research* 99, who brings out differences in the background to the riots in the different parts of England. Statistics of charges arising out of the riots were given in the Home Office Statistical Bulletin No. 20/82: see (1982) 132 NLJ 977.
4. Large scale public disorder leads to enormous pressure on the courts: especially the magistrates' courts. There are dangers that as a consequence cases will not be given the individual consideration that would normally be expected in relation to applications for bail and legal aid, determining guilt and in sentencing. For example, the Nottinghamshire Law Society expressed concern at the procedure adopted by the police and Nottingham City Magistrates' Court in dealing with cases arising from street disturbances in Nottingham in July 1981.[1] For criticism of the operation of magistrates' courts dealing with cases arising out of the miners' strike, see *Legal Action*, August 1984, p. 9 and September 1984 pp. 4–5; S. McCabe and P. Wallington, *The Police, Public Order and Civil Liberties* (1988), Chap. 7.

Report of Her Majesty's Chief Inspector of Constabulary for 1984 (1984–85 HC 469)

PUBLIC ORDER

General
8.1 . . . the NUM dispute dominated public order policing in 1984, and was the greatest challenge to the police capacity to deal with disorder since the civil disturbances in 1981. In some ways its presented a

1 See (1982) 79 LS Gaz 102; Correspondence: [1982] Crim LR 255; (1982) 132 NLJ 1; (1982) 146 JPN 64. See, generally, *LAG Bulletin*, September 1981, p. 199; December 1981, p. 275; November 1982 pp. 5, 10–15.

more gruelling test of determination and stamina as the months continued and the overall levels of disorder did not significantly decrease. The largest concentration of demonstrators was at Mansfield on 14 May when 12,000 attended an NUM rally. In the disorder that followed, several hundred of those who had attended threw bricks and bottles at the police and attacked others as well, including an ITV crew who were filming the incident. More than 1,000 officers, some mounted officers among them, were deployed to deal with the disorder: 87 arrests were made and 88 officers were injured. On 29 and 30 May and 1 June thousands of pickets gathered at the Orgreave coking plant to try to prevent convoys of coke-carrying lorries from leaving the works. The attempts were unsuccessful but, over the 3 days, there was considerable violence as bricks and petrol bombs were thrown at the police. In all there were more than 100 arrests and more than 50 police injuries. On 18 June 10,000 pickets demonstrated at Orgreave and again the ensuing violence was such that mounted officers with shields and helmets had to be deployed to disperse the crowds. The incident caused 28 police injuries and led to 93 arrests.

8.2 In addition to these instances of particularly serious disorders, there were many occasions on which large numbers of pickets congregated outside collieries and elsewhere, and the tactics adopted included not just missile-throwing but the building of barricades, the spilling of oil and nails on the roads and the placing of tripwires. In the first stages of the dispute such picketing was largely in Nottinghamshire as, for example, when on 9 April 2,000 pickets demonstrated at Babbington colliery, but as the return to work spread more widely, other police force areas also faced disorder. On 2 November, for example, 3 police force areas had sites which were the targets for more than 1,000 demonstrators—Arkwright in Derbyshire, Woolley in West Yorkshire and Steetley Quarry in Durham. On other occasions pickets tried to block major routes such as the A1/M by moving slowly in convoys of large numbers. The continuing scenes of public disorder, of which the above are just a few examples, took place against a background of individual acts of criminal damage, assault and intimidation in connection with the dispute, and were on such a scale that on some days more than 8,000 officers were deployed on mutual aid. Every police force in England and Wales either provided or received mutual aid, and by 21 December the dispute had led to 1,294 police injuries and 8,945 arrests.

8.3 By comparison, the anti-nuclear demonstrations were significantly smaller in scale. . . .

8.4 Despite the different tactics and approaches adopted in the various forms of demonstration and picketing described above, the police forces continued to rely on the traditional methods of public order policing in this country, using the minimum of force to deal with violent disorder, and seeking to maintain order by co-operation and agreement whenever possible. For the most part demonstrations and pickets were policed using officers wearing ordinary uniform and in close contact with the demonstrators. Protective equipment such as overalls, shields and helmets were used where necessary, and the horses of the mounted branches again proved their worth in dispersing crowds of disorderly demonstrators. Ironically for an operation which involved such large-scale mutual aid, the policing of the NUM dispute also demonstrated chief officers' awareness of the importance of policing communities by local officers as far as possible.

Report of Her Majesty's Chief Inspector of Constabulary for 1985 (1985–86 HC 437)

NUM dispute
8.2 The decision in March by the National Union of Mineworkers to return to work ended one of the longest and most bitter industrial disputes ever seen in this country. The public order problems presented to the police were unprecedented in their scale and duration. The early and middle phases of the dispute, characterised by mass picketing and by attempts to stop supplies reaching steelworks, were covered in my report for 1984. In the final phase, as miners began to return to work at collieries which had been strikebound, bitterness between working and striking miners intensified. There were more instances of attempted intimidation involving, in some cases, personal assaults and attacks on homes. The main centres of violence were in Yorkshire, Northumberland and Durham and, to a lesser extent, in South Wales. The role of the police throughout the dispute remained constant: to maintain public order, to enforce the criminal law and to ensure that those who wished to work or otherwise to go about their lawful business could do so. Despite physical discomfort and inevitable domestic upheaval, the police sought throughout to maintain the rule of law. I was heartened by the overall level of professionalism which was displayed.

8.3 The success of the police in meeting the formidable challenges of the dispute undoubtedly owes much to the effectiveness of the mutual aid arrangements which enabled over 7,000 officers to be deployed for sustained periods on such duties. Despite misunderstanding and misrepresentation of its roles, the National Reporting Centre efficiently fulfilled its function of co-ordinating requests from Chief Officers for mutual aid. The more professional arrangements for public order training and tactics, which had followed the inner-city riots of 1981, meant that the police were much better able to handle the disorder. Protective equipment again proved its worth. It was notable that, despite the severity of the disorders, the police were able to cope without resort to the use of CS smoke, water cannon and similar equipment. It is unlikely that other police forces in Europe would have been able to cope with such disorder without the use of much more aggressive measures. I have mentioned elsewhere, however, that if the scale of violence increases in these situations the use of this type of equipment may be inevitable.

8.4 In 1985 the dispute led to a further 96 police injuries and 863 arrests. The totals for the whole dispute were 1,390 and 9,808 respectively.

8.5 The dispute also took its toll on ordinary policing throughout the country but it is not possible to say what effect, if any, the dispute had on national crime figures. The financial and resource consequences were severe, despite the scale of central assistance, and there were increased stress and welfare implications for those officers left in forces due to additional workloads and extended hours of duty.

NOTES

1. Peter Wallington's 'overview' was as follows ('Policing the Miners' Strike' (1985) 14 ILJ 145, 159):[1]

'The policing of the dispute has attracted strong comments, many almost as partisan as the positions of the protagonists to the dispute itself. The police deserve much of the praise they received for undertaking a task of such daunting magnitude and complexity. Many of the criticisms of their behaviour, unfortunately, are also deserved, and the police are not well served by the crude loyalty of some of their supporters. But the real issue for those concerned with the lessons of the policing of the dispute was whether the police role was a proper one. Effectively they filled the vacuum created by the failure of the N.C.B. and others to use the civil law; effectively they became, wittingly or otherwise, the agency by which the strike was contained and eventually broken. How far this was an inexorable product of the circumstances, and in particular the strike leaders' own tactical choices, will continue to be a matter of controversy.

The police were given whatever resources they needed to preserve law and order and access to the pits. This enabled them to make the choice to preserve order by containment or prevention of picketing. With fewer resources it might in some cases have been necessary, and would certainly have been lawful, to preserve the peace by preventing individual returning miners from attempting to pass through picket lines. Resources enabled a choice to be made as to whose activities were to be curtailed, even (certainly in the case of the operation of a blanket turn-back policy) whose lawful activities were to be curtailed. Those critics of the police who argue that they took a partisan position can at least point to legal authority that would have justified a different approach. It is scarcely conceivable in the political climate of the time that the alternative would have been adopted as a matter of policy, but that it was avoided at the cost of serious reductions in the level of policing in much of the country suggests a conscious choice.'

2. For statistics of the miners' dispute see McCabe and Wallington, op. cit., Appendix 1. In England and Wales, 9,808 people were arrested, of whom 7,917 (81%) were charged with over 10,000 offences, including conduct likely to cause a breach of the peace (4,107); obstructing a constable (1,682); criminal damage (1,019); obstructing the highway (640); unlawful assembly (509); actual bodily harm (429); assaulting police (360); theft (352); watching and besetting/intimidation (275); breach of the peace (207) and riot (137). All the riot charges failed or were dropped. The overall acquittal rate was estimated at about 25%. Conspiracy charges were 'conspicuous by their absence' (P. Wallington, (1985) 14 ILJ 145, 150).

1 For other appraisals, from varying standpoints, of the policing of the miners' strike, see B. Fine and R. Millar (eds), *Policing the Miners' Strike* (1985); P. Scraton and P. Thomas (eds), *The State v The People: Lessons from the Coal Dispute* (1985) 12 JLS, Winter issue; S. Spencer, *Police Authorities during the Miners' Strike* (Cobden Trust, 1985); P. A. J. Waddington, *The Effects of Police Manpower Depletion during the NUM Strike 1984–88* (Police Foundation, 1985); Welsh Council for Civil and Political Liberties, *Striking Back* (1985); S. McCabe and P. Wallington, *The Police, Public Order and Civil Liberties: Legacies of the Miners' Strike* (1988).

3. Since 1974 (cf. above, pp. 168–169) there have been three significant areas of development in policing disturbances. First, there have been changes in equipment. Better protective headgear and flame resistant clothing have been supplied and widely used. Water cannon, CS gas and baton rounds (plastic bullets) have been made available for use 'in the very last resort and under strict control' (*Report of HM Chief Inspector of Constabulary for 1981* (1981–82 HC 463) p. 4). In 1987, the Metropolitan Police began to acquire a fleet of armoured Land Rovers; it has also obtained quantities of 'long batons'. In *R v Secretary of State for the Home Department, ex p Northumbria Police Authority* [1989] QB 26 the Court of Appeal held that the Home Secretary had power by a circular to authorise the Home Office to supply CS gas and plastic baton rounds to a chief constable for operational use by the police, even though the local police authority declined to approve the supply of such equipment. The power was available either under s. 41 of the Police Act 1964 or under the royal prerogative to keep the peace. For criticism see H. J. Beynon, [1987] PL 146 (on the decision of the Divisional Court in this case) and A. W. Bradley, [1988] PL 298. On the use of baton rounds, see B. Robertson, (1991) 141 NLJ 340. On CS smoke, see L. Jason-Lloyd, (1991) 141 NLJ 1043, noting that it is significantly more indiscriminate in its effects to be suitable for use in public disorder situations (as distinct from sieges). Indeed it has not been used in such situations in Great Britain or Northern Ireland since the introduction of baton rounds.

The current guidelines for their use are as follows (cited by L. Jason-Lloyd, op. cit., pp. 1044–1045):

'CS or baton rounds are to be used only with the express authority of the chief officer of police (or, in his absence, his deputy), under the direction and control of a senior officer whom he has designated as officer in charge, and by police officers who have been trained in the use of the equipment and know its characteristics. CS or baton rounds are to be used only as a last resort where conventional methods of policing have been tried and failed, or must from the nature of the circumstances obtaining be unlikely to succeed if tried, and where the chief officer judges such action to be necessary because of the risk of loss of life or serious injury or widespread destruction of property. Wherever practicable, a public warning of their use is to be given.'

Second, there have been developments concerning the mutual aid arrangements under which one chief officer of police provides assistance to another whose force is under pressure. These may be co-ordinated by the Mutual Aid Co-ordination Centre (formerly known as the National Reporting Centre), located at New Scotland Yard and operated by a team under the direction of the President of the Association of Chief Police Officers, advised by a representative of HM Chief Inspector of Constabulary and a senior Home Office official. This team is 'able to set individual requests for assistance in a national context' (1981 Report, p. 5). The Centre was used during the 1981 riots and was extensively used in relation to the 1984 miners' strike (see M. Kettle in Fine and Millar, op. cit., pp. 23–33). Critics have detected the beginnings of a national police force under central government direction, but it has consistently been denied that the Centre issues operational orders. See also B. Loveday 'Central Co-ordination, Police Authorities and the Miners' Strike' (1986) 57 *Political Quarterly* 60 and R. Reiner, *Chief Constables* (1991), pp. 186–192. On the basis of interviews with chief constables, Reiner notes that many chiefs emphasized that there was no compulsion and no government pressure, and that the four Welsh chief constables opted out of NRC arrangements, declining to use English officers to police Welsh coalfields. However,

'a common claim was that the success of the voluntary mutual aid operation had prevented the establishment of a national force. A national police force would have had to be created by the Government, had the chiefs not been able to co-operate spontaneously' [p. 186].

Furthermore, there were anecdotes

'which confirmed the existence of overt central pressure when voluntarism did not produce the required goods' [p. 191].

Third, there have been developments in the training of police officers. Police Support Units have been established in all forces, each typically comprising an inspector, two sergeants and 20 constables, trained to work as a group. Some forces have established elite groups under various names (e.g. the Territorial Support Group in the Metropolitan Police). These have been associated with a more aggressive approach to disturbances

'and represent a significant move away from the traditional approach to public order policing which was based on containment and the use of minimum force'

(K. D. Ewing and C. D. Gearty, *Freedom under Thatcher* (1990), p. 105). See also T. Jefferson, *The Case Against Paramilitary Policing* (1990), Chap. 1.

New techniques, involving special formations of officers and the use of police horses, have been incorporated in the revised *Public Order Manual of Tactical Options and Related Matters* prepared by the Association of Chief Police Officers (Ewing and Gearty, op. cit., pp. 105–106; G. Northam, *Shooting in the Dark: Riot Police in Britain* (1988)). The government has formally rejected the option of establishing a 'third force' to deal specifically with public disorder, modelled on forces in European countries, such as the French CSU (Jefferson, op. cit., p. 2, referring to a Home Office Working Party between 1961 and 1971). The arguments against a 'third force' were summarised by the Chief Inspector of Constabulary in his Report for 1984 (1984–85 HC 469), pp. 4–5: mutual aid arrangements were effective in practice; we could not afford to have a large body of law enforcement officers kept in reserve for public order situations; and such a force would come under centralised control and consequently be more readily susceptible to political influence. The various developments outlined above seem to be steps towards at least the de facto establishment of the equivalent of a 'third force'. For criticism, see T. Jefferson, *The Case Against Paramilitary Policing* (1990); for the argument that paramilitary policing is the most effective way of maintaining impartial and consensual public order policing, see P. A. J. Waddington, 'Towards paramilitarism? Dilemmas in policing civil disorder' (1987) 27 Brit. J. Criminol. 37. See also, Waddington, *The Strong Arm of the Law* (1991); K. Bryett, 'Who Polices Violence' (1991) 1 *Policing & Society* 285.

4. Other instances of public disorder since 1983 have included (1) anti-nuclear demonstrations at Greenham Common and other RAF bases (1984); 'Stop the City' demonstrations (1984); serious riots at Handsworth, Brixton and Broadwater Farm, Tottenham, in which four people died (a press photographer in Brixton, two shopkeepers in a sub-post office in Handsworth and P.C. Keith Blakelock at Tottenham) (1985); the 'Peace Convoy' in the vicinity of Stonehenge (1986, 1988): see p. 205; the News International dispute at Wapping (1986): see p. 193; the poll tax riot in central London on 31 March 1990 (see D. Burns, *Poll Tax Rebellion* (1992), Chaps. 4, 5); and an increasing number of 'free festivals' attracting 'New Age travellers' (e.g. Castlemorton in May 1992: see J. Baxter, 'Castlemorton and beyond' (1992) 8 *Policing* 222 and P. Cumper and K. Stevenson, (1992) 89 LSGaz, 7 October, p. 23). Other particular matters of concern have been unlicensed acid house parties (see (1990) 154 JPN 588) and the apparent growing seriousness of disorder in rural areas (see H.O. Circular 114/1988; M. Tuck, Drinking and Disorder: A Study of Non-Metropolitan Violence (HO Research Study No. 108, 1989), suggesting that the problem was not peculiar to rural areas).

Football hooliganism has been a continuing concern. Steps taken include improved liaison between the football and public authorities; the passing of the Sporting Events (Control of Alcohol etc.) Act 1985, controlling the sale and possession of alcohol inside grounds, on entry to grounds and on football special coaches and trains; provisions of the Public Order Act 1986 (ss. 30–37) enabling exclusion orders to be made by the courts preventing persons convicted of football-related offences attending 'prescribed' football matches; the increased use of closed circuit television systems in football grounds; extensive covert operations to act against hooligan ringleaders (although a number of trials collapsed as a result of evidential difficulties); and the establishment of a National Football Intelligence Unit, operational as from March 1990, to collate police intelligence on persistent hooligans. The Football Spectators Act 1989 (ss. 2–7, unimplemented in the light of Lord Justice Taylor's Report on the Hillsborough Disaster (Cm 962, 1990)) provides the framework for a National Football Membership Scheme; Part II enables the courts to make restriction orders preventing hooligans from attending important matches abroad. The government announced its intention, following Lord Justice Taylor's recommendations (Chaps. 7, 9), to establish four new offences: (i) throwing missiles; (ii) chanting indecent and racial abuse; (iii) running on the pitch without reasonable excuse; (iv) selling tickets on the day of the match without the authority of the home club: see the Football Offences Act 1991. See generally the 2nd Report of the Home Affairs Committee for 1990–91, *Policing Football Hooliganism* (1990–91 H.C.1); *Government Reply*, Cm. 1539.

5. The investigation of offences arising out of major disorder is difficult in practice.

'Frankly, the police record for successfully prosecuting those who engage in serious public disorder is dismal. Currently, where a senior investigating officer (SIO) is appointed after the event, suspects who plead "not guilty" stand only a one in five chance of being convicted'

(Det. Supt. E. Williams, 'Investigating major disorder' (1994) 10 *Policing* 134). However, modern practice includes the use of police officers and civilian photographers as 'evidence gatherers', the use of static video cameras, the power to seek a production order for press material under PACE (above, p. 94), the organisation of hospital welfare teams to question casualties (police and public) and the establishment of charge centres (ibid.). Williams advocates the appointment of a SIO before the event rather than after.

6. For sociological studies of public disorder, including case-studies of particular occurrences, see G. Gaskell and R. Benewick (eds), *The Crowd in Contemporary Britain* (1987); D. Waddington, *et al.*, *Flashpoints: Studies in Public Disorder* (1989); D. Waddington (ed.), *Contemporary Issues in Public Disorder* (1992); E. G. Dunning, *et al.*, *The Social Roots of Football Hooliganism* (1987); P. Joyce, 'A decade of disorder' (1992) 8 *Policing* 232; M. Keith, *Race, Riots and Policing* (1993); P. A. J. Waddington, *Liberty and Order* (1994). The use of protest by the peace movement is described in J. Dewar, *et al.*, (eds), *Nuclear Weapons, the Peace Movement and the Law* (1986), Part III and J. Hinton, *Protests and Visions: Peace Politics in Twentieth-Century Britain* (1989). For comparative perspectives, see J. Roach and J. Thomaneck (eds), *Police and Public Order in Europe* (1985) and J. Brewer, *et al.*, *The Police, Public Order and the State* (1988).

3 Freedom of association

There are few legal limits on the freedom of people to associate together for political purposes. The criminal law of conspiracy only applies to agreements to commit a crime, to defraud or to do an act which tends to corrupt public morals or outrage public decency (Criminal Law Act 1977, Part I; *Smith and Hogan*, pp. 269–304). Accordingly, the fact that people associate to perform certain acts will not render them criminally liable unless those acts would be illegal if performed by an individual, subject to the three limited exceptions stated. The tort of conspiracy is committed where two or more people agree to do an unlawful act, or to do a lawful act by unlawful means, or to perform acts other than for their own legitimate benefit, with the object of inflicting damage on a third party (*Clerk and Lindsell on Torts*, 16th edn, paras 15.21–15.26; *Hubbard v Pitt* [1976] QB 142, CA, below, p. 182; *Lonrho Ltd v Shell Petroleum Co Ltd (No 2)* [1982] AC 173; *Lonrho plc v Fayed* [1992] 1 AC 448). The tort of conspiracy is thus now appreciably wider in scope than the crime, although it is necessary in tort for the plaintiff to prove that he has suffered damage.

The following section illustrates some statutory limitations on freedom of association in the public order context.

Public Order Act 1936

An Act to prohibit the wearing of uniforms in connection with political objects and the maintenance by private persons of associations of military or similar character; and to make further provision for the preservation of public order on the occasion of public processions and meetings and in public places.

1. Prohibition of uniforms in connection with political objects

(1) Subject as hereinafter provided, any person who in any public place or at any public meeting wears uniform signifying his association with any political organisation or with the promotion of any political object shall be guilty of an offence:

Provided that, if the chief officer of police is satisfied that the wearing of any such uniform as aforesaid on any ceremonial, anniversary, or other special occasion will not be likely to involve risk of public disorder, he may, with the consent of a Secretary of State, by order permit the wearing of such uniform on that occasion either absolutely or subject to such conditions as may be specified in the order. . . .

9. Interpretation, etc

(1) In this Act the following expressions have the meanings hereby respectively assigned to them, that is to say—

'Meeting' means a meeting held for the purpose of the discussion of matters of public interest or for the purpose of the expression of views on such matters;

'Private premises' means premises to which the public have access (whether on payment or otherwise) only by permission of the owner, occupier, or lessee of the premises;

'Public meeting' includes any meeting in a public place and any meeting which the public or any section thereof are permitted to attend, whether on payment or otherwise;

['Public place' includes any highway and any other premises or place to which at the material time the public have or are permitted to have access, whether on payment or otherwise;]. . . .

NOTES

1. The maximum penalty under s. 1 is currently three months' imprisonment, a fine not exceeding level 4 on the standard scale or both (1936 Act, s. 7 as amended by the Criminal Law Act 1977, s. 31, Sch. 6 and the Criminal Justice Act 1982, s. 46). The consent of the Attorney-General is required for a prosecution: s. 7(2). Section 7(3) gives a power of arrest.

2. The Public Order Acts 1936 and 1986 (for the most part: see s. 42) do not extend to Northern Ireland. The equivalent legislation there is the Public Order (Northern Ireland) Order 1987 (S.I. 1987 No. 463): see B. Hadfield, (1987) 38 NILQ 86 and [1993] Crim LR 915. See also the Prevention of Terrorism (Temporary Provisions) Act 1989, s. 3 (below, p. 310) and the Northern Ireland (Emergency Provisions) Act 1991, s. 29 (below, p. 277).

3. Section 1 was introduced in response to the increasing use of uniforms by political groups, notably the Fascists (see *Williams*, pp. 216–220). The first prosecutions were of Blackshirts: *R v Wood* (1937) 81 Sol Jo 108 (D sold Fascist newspapers while wearing a black peak cap with two emblems, black shirt, tie and leather motoring coat, dark trousers and dark footwear: fined £2); *R v Charnley* (1937) 81 Sol Jo 108 (at public meetings D wore black trousers, dark navy blue pullover, and red brassard on his left arm: convicted and bound over). See also (1937) 81 Sol Jo 509; E. R. Ivamy, [1949] CLP 184–187. Thus the wearing of a complete outfit is not necessary for a conviction. The section has also been used against members of the Ku Klux Klan (*The Times*, 8 October 1965) and supporters of the Irish republican movement (*O'Moran v DPP*; *Whelan v DPP* [1975] QB 864, DC).

In *O'Moran*, members of a funeral party accompanying the body of Michael Gaughan, a self-confessed IRA member who died on a hunger strike while in Parkhurst prison, wore black or dark blue berets, dark glasses and dark clothing. They were not identically dressed. An oration beside the coffin referred to the Irish republican movement, and an Irish tricolour flag was placed on the coffin. In *Whelan*, the defendants assembled with others at Speakers' Corner in order to march as a protest on the first anniversary of internment in Northern Ireland. The march was organised by Provisional Sinn Fein and other groups. The leaders all wore black berets and some also wore dark clothing, dark glasses and carried Irish flags and banners. The Divisional Court upheld convictions under s. 1(1). Per Lord Widgery CJ at pp. 873–874:

' "Wearing" in my judgment implies some article of wearing apparel. I agree with the submission made in argument that one would not describe a badge pinned to the lapel as being a uniform worn for present purposes. In the present instance however the various items relied on, such as the beret, dark glasses, the pullovers and the other dark clothing, were clearly worn and therefore satisfy the first requirement of the section.

The next requirement is that that which was worn was a uniform, . . . the policeman or the soldier is accepted as wearing uniform without more ado, but the isolated man wearing a black beret is not to be regarded as wearing a uniform unless it is proved that the beret in its association has been recognised and is known as the uniform of some particular organisation, proof of which would have to be provided by evidence in the usual way.

In this case [*O'Moran*] the eight men in question were together. They were not seen in isolation. Where an article such as a beret is used in order to indicate that a group of men are together and in association, it seems to me that that article can be regarded as uniform without any proof that it has been previously used as such. The simple fact that a number of men deliberately adopt an identical article of attire justifies in my judgment the view that that article is uniform if it is adopted in such a way as to show that its adoption is for the purposes of showing association between the men in question. Subject always to the de minimis rule, I see no reason why the article or articles should cover the whole of the body or a major part of the body, as was argued at one point, or indeed should go beyond the existence of the beret by itself. In this case the articles did go beyond the beret. They extended to the pullover, the dark glasses and the dark clothing, and I have no doubt at all in my own mind that those men wearing those clothes on that occasion were wearing uniform within the meaning of the Act.

Evidence has been called in this case from a police sergeant to the effect that the black beret was commonly used, or had been frequently used, by members of the IRA, and I recognise that it is possible to prove that an article constitutes uniform by that means as well.

The next point, and perhaps the most difficult problem of all, is the requirement of the section that the uniform so worn shall signify the wearer's association with any political organisation. This can be done in my judgment in two ways. The first I have already referred to. It is open to the prosecution, if they have the evidence and wish to call it, to show that the particular article relied upon as uniform has been used in the past as the uniform of a recognised association, and they can by that means, if the evidence is strong enough, and the court accepts it, prove that the black beret, or whatever it may be, is associated with a particular organisation. In my judgment it is not necessary for them to specify the particular organisation because in many instances the name of the organisation will be unknown or may have been recently changed. But if they can prove that the article in question has been associated with a political organisation capable of identification in some manner, then that would suffice for the purposes of the section.

Alternatively, in my judgment the significance of the uniform and its power to show the association of the wearer with a political organisation can be judged from the events to be seen on the occasion when the alleged uniform was worn. In other words, it can be judged and proved without necessarily referring to the past history at all, because if a group of persons assemble together and wear a piece of uniform such as a black beret to indicate their association one with the other, and furthermore by their conduct indicate that that beret associates them with other activity of a political character, that is enough for the purposes of the section.'

Public Order Act 1936

2. Prohibition of quasi-military organisations

(1)If the members or adherents of any association of persons, whether incorporated or not, are—

(a) organised or trained or equipped for the purpose of enabling them to be employed in usurping the functions of the police or of the armed forces of the Crown; or

(b) organised and trained or organised and equipped either for the purpose of enabling them to be employed for the use or display of physical force in promoting any political object, or in such manner as to arouse reasonable apprehension that they are organised and either trained or equipped for that purpose;

then any person who takes part in the control or management of the association, or in so organising or training are aforesaid any members or adherents thereof, shall be guilty of an offence under this section:

Provided that in any proceedings against a person charged with the offence of taking part in the control or management of such an association as aforesaid it shall be a defence to that charge to prove that he neither consented to nor connived at the organisation, training, or equipment of members or adherents of the association in contravention of the provisions of this section.

(2) No prosecution shall be instituted under this section without the consent of the Attorney-General.

(3) [This authorises the forfeiture of the property of an association which is unlawful under this section] . . .

(5) If a judge of the High Court is satisfied by information on oath that there is reasonable ground for suspecting that an offence under this section has been committed, and that evidence of the commission thereof is to be found at any premises or place specified in the information, he may, on an application made by an officer of police of a rank not lower than that of inspector, grant a search warrant authorising any such officer as aforesaid named in the warrant together with any other persons named in the warrant and any other officers of police to enter the premises or place at any time within one month from the date of the warrant, if necessary by force, and to search the premises or place and every person found therein, and to seize anything found on the premises or place or on any person which the officer has reasonable ground for suspecting to be evidence of the commission of such an offence as aforesaid:

Provided that no woman shall, in pursuance of a warrant issued under this subsection, be searched except by a woman.

(6) Nothing in this section shall be construed as prohibiting the employment of a reasonable number of persons as stewards to assist in the preservation of order at any public meeting held upon private premises, or the making of arrangements for that purpose or the instruction of the persons to be so employed in their lawful duties as such stewards, or their being furnished with badges or other distinguishing signs.

NOTES

1. The maximum penalties under this section are six months' imprisonment, a £5,000 fine or both on summary conviction, and two years, a fine of any amount or both on conviction on indictment (Public Order Act 1936, s. 7(1); Criminal Law Act 1977, ss. 28(2), 32(1); Magistrates' Courts Act 1980, s. 32; Criminal Justice Act 1991, s. 17(2)(c)).

2. This section was passed to meet the growth of private armies, in particular Fascist groups, between 1933 and 1936 (*Williams*, pp. 220–221; R. Benewick, 'The Threshold of Violence' in Benewick and Smith (eds), *Direct Action and Democratic Politics* (1972)).

3. Note that there is no reference to the promotion of a political object in s. 2(1)(a). Vigilante groups might accordingly offend against this provision.

4. The first prosecution under s. 2(1)(b) was *R v Jordan and Tyndall* [1963] Crim LR 124, CCA (*Williams* pp. 222–223). J and T took part in the organisation of 'Spearhead', part first of the British National Party and later of the National Socialist Movement. At various times in 1961 and 1962 uniformed members of Spearhead were seen practising foot drill, carrying out attack and defence exercises at a tower building and exchanging Nazi salutes. At a camp near Cheltenham, the Horst Wessel song was sung and cries of 'Sieg Heil' were heard. The police searched the Movement's headquarters under a warrant issued under s. 2, and found documents referring to the former German National Socialist Storm Troopers and containing phrases such as 'Task Force', 'Front Line Fighters' and 'Fighting Efficiency'. They also found tins of sodium chlorate (weed killer) which could be used in making bombs. On one tin, the words 'Jew Killer' had been written. J and T were convicted of organising Spearhead members in such a way as to arouse reasonable apprehension that they were organised to be employed for the use or display of physical force promoting a political object. The Court of Criminal Appeal approved the trial judge's direction that: 'reasonable apprehension means an apprehension or fear which is based not upon undue timidity or excessive suspicion or still less prejudice but one which is founded on grounds which to you appear to be reasonable. Moreover the apprehension or fear must be reasonably held by a person who is aware of all the facts. . . . You must try to put yourselves in the position of a sensible man who knew the whole of the facts'. J was sentenced to nine, and T to six months' imprisonment, the Court of Criminal Appeal regarding it as an appropriate occasion for the imposition of deterrent sentences (see further M. Walker, *The National Front* (1977) pp. 39–42, 44–45). The prosecution of members of the 'Free Wales Army' under s. 2 is described by D. G. T. Williams at [1970] CLJ 103. The section has also been employed in respect of the organisers of IRA units: *R v Callinan* (1973) Times, 20 January, C Cr Ct; *R v Kneafsey* (1973) Times, 23 October; *R v Fell* [1974] Crim LR 673, CA (CrD).

5. Unauthorised meetings of persons for the purpose of being trained in the use of arms or of practising military exercises, are still prohibited by the Unlawful Drilling Act 1819, s. 1. Prosecutions under the Act were not brought against those responsible for drilling the Ulster Volunteer Force in resistance to Home Rule before the First World War, or in relation to the military activities of the British Fascists in the 1930s, despite, in the latter case, assurances from the Home Secretary that appropriate action would be taken (28 HC Deb 31 January 1934 cols 360–1).

6. Certain organisations may be proscribed under the Northern Ireland (Emergency Provisions) Act 1991, s. 28 (see below, p. 277) and the Prevention of Terrorism (Temporary Provisions) Act 1989, s. 1 (see below, p. 301). In the *Review of the Public Order Act 1936 and related legislation* (Cmnd. 7891, 1980, p. 11), the government rejected an argument that since much recent disorder had resulted from confrontations between the supporters of the National Front and others, including members of the Socialist Workers Party, there were grounds for banning one or both of these organisations. Proscription had been confined to organisations openly and avowedly dedicated to violent terrorist acts and to the overthrow of the civil authorities.

4 Public meetings and processions

In this country there are no unfettered legal rights to hold public meetings or processions. The law regulates (1) the location and (2) the conduct of public assemblies.

(a) THE LOCATION OF MEETINGS AND PROCESSIONS

All land is vested in some person or institution. People may be permitted to assemble at the landowner's discretion. Assembling without permission is a trespass, although proceedings may well not be taken.[1] Meetings and processions must also conform to the common law of nuisance and to any specific statutory restrictions as to location. The residual freedom or 'liberty' to assemble must be exercised without infringement of the rights of others, and with due regard for their liberties. It is an important question whether English law gives sufficient weight to freedom of assembly. It is also open to argument whether judges have attached sufficient importance to this interest where the law only proscribes conduct that is 'unreasonable', and the conflicting interests of different people have accordingly to be balanced.

(i) The Highway

1. Tort

The use of the highway for meetings and processions is restricted by both the law of tort and the criminal law. Aspects of the law of tort which are theoretically relevant include trespass, public nuisance and private nuisance. The position in *trespass* was set out by Lopes LJ in *Harrison v Duke of Rutland* [1893] 1 QB 142 at 154, CA:

'If a person uses the soil of the highway for any purpose other than that in respect of which the dedication was made and the easement acquired, he is a trespasser. The easement acquired by the public is a right to pass and repass at their pleasure for the purpose of legitimate travel, and the use of the soil for any other purpose, whether lawful or unlawful, is an infringement of the rights of the owner of the soil, . . .'

In addition, the use of a highway for purposes incidental to passage may well be a proper use:

'Thus a tired pedestrian may sit down and rest himself. A motorist may attempt to repair a minor breakdown. Because the highway is used also as a means of access to places abutting on the highway, it is permissible to queue for tickets at a theatre or other place of entertainment, or for a bus.'

(Forbes J in *Hubbard v Pitt* [1976] QB 142, cf. *Hickman v Maisey* [1900] 1 QB 752, CA). Such user must be reasonable in extent (ibid). Technically, therefore, a stationary meeting held on the highway, or even the picketing of premises other than in furtherance of a trade dispute (according to Forbes J in *Hubbard v Pitt*) may constitute trespass against the owner of the soil of the highway. Where a highway is maintainable at the public expense, as is usually the case with made up roads, it vests in the highway authority (Highways Act 1980, ss. 1, 263, 265–267). There is in fact no reported case of such an authority suing demonstrators or the participants in a meeting for trespass. In *Hubbard v Pitt* [1976] QB 142 the defendants picketed a firm of estate agents as part of a campaign against property developers. The estate agents brought an action alleging nuisance, libel and conspiracy, and were granted an interlocutory injunction by the Court of Appeal (affirming Forbes J, although not necessarily agreeing with all aspects of his judgment). Do you think that the highway authority *could* successfully have sued for trespass in this case? Why should orderly picketing not constitute 'a reasonable and usual mode of using a highway'? Is it significantly different from resting or sketching, which A. L. Smith LJ suggested in

---

1 But see *Department of Transport and others v Williams* (1993) 138 Sol Jo LB5, where the Court of Appeal upheld the grant of interlocutory injunctions against persons demonstrating against the motorway constructions at Twyford Down to restrain trespasses and, in one case, interference with business.

Hickman v Maisey would not constitute trespass ([1900] 1 QB at 756) or queueing for theatre tickets (Forbes J in *Hubbard v Pitt*)? Note that the conduct of those held to be trespassers in *Harrison v Duke of Rutland* and *Hickman v Maisey* (below, p. 527) was detrimental to the interests of the owners of the soil of the highway in respect of their adjacent land. In what ways could picketing be detrimental to the highway authority's interests? Should a finding of some detrimental effect on the plaintiff's interests be a pre-requisite of a finding that the user of a highway is unreasonable?

To constitute *public nuisance*, the misuse of a highway must amount to 'unreasonable user' (*Lowdens v Keaveney* [1903] 2 IR 82; *R v Clark (No 2)* [1964] 2 QB 315, CCA). In *Hubbard v Pitt* Forbes J assumed that 'unreasonableness' was established if it could be shown that passage was obstructed. That assumption has been criticised (see P. Wallington, [1976] CLJ 82, 101–106). Wallington argues:

'The test is . . . not whether a demonstration is something reasonably incidental to passage, but whether it is reasonable in the context of rights of highway users generally. If passers-by must make a detour, their inconvenience must be balanced against the interest in allowing the demonstration; it will be relevant to consider the degree of obstruction and whether the demonstration could conveniently have been held at a less obstructive venue or off the highway' (ibid. p. 104).

A civil action may be brought in respect of a public nuisance only by the Attorney-General, or by a person who suffers some particular or special loss over and above the inconvenience suffered by the public at large (*Winfield and Jolowicz on Tort*, 14th edn, pp. 402–403, 433–435).

Private nuisance is described in *Winfield and Jolowicz on Tort* (14th edn, p. 404) as 'unlawful interference with a person's use or enjoyment of land, or some right over, or in connection with it'. This includes infringement of a servitude (ibid., pp. 404–405). The person who creates the nuisance may be liable whether or not he is in occupation of the land on which it originates (ibid., p. 421). The blocking of access to private premises is an example of private nuisance (ibid., pp. 435–437). Watching and besetting may constitute private nuisance (ibid., p. 587, based on *J. Lyons & Sons v Wilkins* [1899] 1 Ch 255) but Lord Denning MR took a different view in *Hubbard v Pitt*.

In his Report on the Red Lion Square disorders Lord Scarman discussed demonstrations and the public highway (Cmnd. 5919, paras. 122, 123):

'English law recognises as paramount the right of passage: a demonstration which obstructs passage along the highway is unlawful. The paramount right of passage is, however, subject to the reasonable use of the highway by others. A procession, therefore, which allows room for others to go on their way is lawful; but it is open to question whether a public meeting held on a highway could ever be lawful for it is not in any way incidental to the exercise of the right of passage. . . . I think the priority that the law gives to the right of passage is sound. Free movement between place and place and access to premises may seem workaday matters when compared with such rights as those of demonstration and protest; but society could grind to a halt if the law adopted any other priority. There is, therefore, a case, as was suggested by one party, for the specific provision of public meeting-places in our towns and cities. Public meeting-places, whether they be a speaker's corner in the centre of a great city or a village green, are as essential to civilised life as is priority for the right of passage along our highways.'

NOTES

1. In *Thomas v National Union of Mineworkers (South Wales Area)* [1985] 2 All ER 1, Scott J granted interlocutory injunctions against the branch union and its servants, agents and officers, from, inter alia, assisting, encouraging or organising members of the branch union to assemble at or near the colliery gates of each of five collieries in the area, in numbers greater than six or for any purpose outside s. 15 of the Trade Union and Labour Relations Act 1974 (below, p. 252). The judge held that the unreasonable harassment of workers who wished to use the highway to go to work was tortious: 'the tort might be described as a species of private nuisance' (p. 23). The plaintiffs (working miners) were unable to establish a cause of action for obstructing the highway, as their entry into and egress from the colliery was not physically prevented; if the pickets were obstructing the highway, the plaintiffs had not suffered any special damage (p. 21). His Lordship also held that (1) regular picketing of the home of a working miner, regardless of the number of people involved and regardless of the peaceful nature of their conduct, would constitute a common law nuisance (p. 23); and (2) mass picketing would constitute both common law nuisance and an offence under s. 7 of the Conspiracy, and Protection of Property Act 1875 (now s. 241 of the Trade Union and Labour Relations (Consolidation) Act 1992) (p. 30).

2. In *News Group Newspapers Ltd v Society of Graphical and Allied Trades '82 (No. 2)* [1987] ICR 181, Stuart-Smith J held that the daily mass picketing and demonstrations at the first plaintiff's Wapping plant constituted unreasonable use of the highway and public and private nuisance. The demonstrations arose out of the move of the printing of *The Times* and other newspapers published by the News International Group to Wapping, and the introduction of new technology. The judge held that the plaintiffs had, unlike the plaintiffs in *Thomas v NUM (South Wales Area)*, above, suffered special damage: *The Times* had lost journalists and expense had been incurred in busing in employees in vehicles with protective grilles over the windows. The judge granted interlocutory injunctions against the unions and certain individuals in a form that permitted their continuing to organise peaceful picketing and marches. It was not necessary for Stuart-Smith J to express a final view on the 'unreasonable harassment' basis of liability identified by Scott J in *Thomas v NUM (South Wales Area)*, above. However, he noted criticisms expressed by the defendants, who submitted

'that Scott J should not have invented a new tort and that it is not sufficient to found liability that there has been an unreasonable interference with the rights of others, even though when a balance is struck between conflicting rights and interests the scale comes down in favour of the plaintiffs, unless those rights are recognised by the law and fall within some accepted head of tort.'

Stuart-Smith J commented (p. 206):

'I think there is force in these criticisms, especially where it does not appear that damage is a necessary ingredient of the tort.'[1]

The Court of Appeal has since held in a case outside the context of public order that the tort of harassment does exist: *Khorasandjian v Bush* [1993] QB 727. See below, p. 532. See also *R v Coventry City Council, ex p Phoenix Aviation* [1995] 3 All ER 37, DC, where Simon Brown LJ suggested (at 41) that 'any activity which substantially inconveniences the public at large and disrupts the rights of others to go about their lawful business' was unlawful as public nuisance.

2. Crime

As we have seen, obstruction of the highway may constitute public nuisance. A public nuisance may be the subject of criminal proceedings.

1 For a discussion of the issues arising out of these cases, see H. Carty, [1985] PL 542; S. Auerbach (1987) 16 ILJ 227; K. D. Ewing and B. Napier, [1986] CLJ 285. For criticism of the policing of the dispute, in particular in relation to restrictions placed on the free movement of residents, see NCCL, *No Way in Wapping* (1986).

In *R v Clark (No 2)* [1964] 2 QB 315, C, the field secretary of the Campaign for Nuclear Disarmament, led a crowd through various streets in London in the course of a Committee of 100 demonstration during the visit of the King and Queen of Greece. Several streets were partially or completely blocked. C was convicted on a charge of inciting persons to commit a public nuisance by obstructing the highway and sentenced to 18 months' imprisonment. His conviction was quashed as the deputy chairman at the London Sessions had failed to direct the jury on the question whether, granted obstruction, there was an unreasonable user of the highway. He had merely directed that if there was a physical obstruction, that constituted nuisance, and that C, if he incited it, was guilty.

Much more commonly, criminal proceedings for obstruction of the highway are brought under the following provision.

Highways Act 1980

137. Penalty for wilful obstruction
(1) If a person, without lawful authority or excuse, in any way wilfully obstructs the free passage along a highway he shall be guilty of an offence and shall be liable in respect thereof to a fine not exceeding level 3 on the standard scale.

NOTES

1. This section was formerly section 121 of the Highways Act 1959. It is much used in respect of demonstrations – particularly where people sit down in the street. A power of arrest is available under the Police and Criminal Evidence Act 1984, s. 25(3)(d)(v) (above, p. 105), replacing a power conferred by s. 137(2).
2. It is not open to the local authority to authorise an obstruction of the highway so as to afford a defence to criminal proceedings: *Redbridge London Borough v Jacques* [1970] 1 WLR 1604, DC; *Cambridgeshire and Isle of Ely County Council v Rust* [1972] 2 QB 426, DC. See A. J. Ashworth, [1974] Crim LR 652; A. T. H. Smith, (1985) 14 Anglo-Am LR 3.
3. Cases under s. 137 and analogous statutory provisions have consistently taken the line that the obstruction of any part of the highway constitutes obstruction for these purposes, notwithstanding that there is room for persons to pass by, or that delay is minimal.

In *Homer v Cadman* (1886) 16 Cox CC 51, DC, H marched into the Bull Ring, Sedgley, an irregular triangle where six highways converge. He was accompanied by a band. He stood on a chair and addressed a crowd of between 150 and 200 people for an hour and a half. There was space between the crowd and the footpaths for vehicles or pedestrians to pass. H was convicted under the Highway Act 1835, s. 72. His appeal to the Divisional Court failed. Per Smith J at p. 54:

'The appellant was only entitled to use the highway in an authorised manner, that is, to pass over it to and fro. He certainly had used it in an unauthorised manner, and the magistrate has found that, as no person could have gone across that part of the highway where the appellant and his band were without considerable inconvenience and danger, there was an obstruction to the highway. The fact that only a part of the highway was so obstructed seems to me to make no difference.'

Cf. *Aldred v Miller* 1925 JC 117 (High Court of Justiciary).
4. Reasonable user of the highway will constitute 'lawful excuse' under s. 137. In *Nagy v Weston* [1965] 1 All ER 78, [1965] 1 WLR 280, Lajos Nagy parked his van in a lay-by where there was a bus stop, in order to sell hot-dogs from it. He was

there for five minutes before he was arrested under s. 121 of the 1959 Act. The justices found that although the road was wide, it was nevertheless busy at that time of night (10.15 p.m.), carrying heavy traffic including buses which would be pulling out of the lay-by. There was therefore unreasonable user by parking a van even for five minutes. His conviction under s. 121 was affirmed by the Divisional Court. Per Lord Parker CJ at p. 284:

'There must be proof that the use in question was an unreasonable use. Whether or not the user amounting to an obstruction is or is not an unreasonable use of the highway is a question of fact. It depends upon all the circumstances, including the length of time the obstruction continues, the place where it occurs, the purpose for which it is done, and of course whether it does in fact cause an actual obstruction as opposed to a potential obstruction. . . . [T]he justices . . . have clearly found that in the circumstances of this case there was an unreasonable use of the highway. Indeed, on the facts stated, it is difficult to see how they could conceivably arrive at any other conclusion.'

Wallington ([1976] CLJ 82, 108–9) argues that the term 'lawful' excuse could be interpreted more generously to cover all demonstrations reasonably conducted with due regard to the interests of others. The following decision acknowledges that some weight must be attached to the right of free speech.

Hirst and Agu v Chief Constable of West Yorkshire (1986) 85 Cr App Rep 143, (1986) 151 JP 304, Queen's Bench Divisional Court

H, A and four others were convicted by magistrates of obstructing the highway contrary to the Highways Act 1980, s. 137. They were members of a group of animal rights supporters who protested in Bradford City Centre outside and in the doorway of 'Lady at Lord John', a shop which sold furs. The defendants stood in varying parts of Darley Street, a spacious but busy pedestrian precinct, offering leaflets or holding a banner. A and others were arrested for conduct likely to cause a breach of the peace. H and others gathered in the shop's doorway to protest against this arrest and were in turn arrested for conduct likely to cause a breach of the peace and obstruction of the highway. In the event, only obstruction of the highway charges were brought. The defendants appealed unsuccessfully to the Crown Court, which found that their actions were not incidental to lawful user of the highway. H and A appealed to the Divisional Court by way of case stated.

Glidewell LJ: . . . [stated the facts, referred to the authorities: *Lowdens v Keaveney* [1903] 2 IR 82; *Nagy v Weston* [1965] 1 All ER 78; *Hubbard v Pitt* [1975] 3 All ER 1; *Jones v Bescoby* (8 July 1983, unreported); *Waite v Taylor* (1985) 149 JP 551; *Cooper v Metropolitan Police Comr* (1985) 82 Cr App Rep 238, and continued:]

Now it is clear in the present case that the Crown Court did not consider whether the defendants' user of the highway was reasonable or not, because that Court, considering itself bound by *Waite v Taylor* (supra), decided that handing out leaflets and holding banners was not incidental to the lawful use of the highway to pass and re-pass and, therefore, that the reasonableness of that activity was not relevant.

As I have already said, in my judgment *Nagy v Weston* (supra) is the leading modern authority and it does not apply so rigid a test as that found in the judgment of May LJ in *Waite v Taylor*, with the greatest respect to him. In *Nagy v Weston* itself, the activity being carried on, that is to say the sale of hot dogs in the street, could not in my view be said to be incidental to the right to pass and re-pass along the street. Clearly, the Divisional Court took the view that it was open to the magistrates to consider, as a question of fact, whether the activity was or was not reasonable. On the facts the magistrates had concluded that it was unreasonable (an unreasonable obstruction) but if they had concluded that it was reasonable then it is equally clear that in the view of the Divisional Court the offence would not have been made out.

That is the way Tudor Evans J approached the matter in the recent decision of *Cooper v MPC* (supra) and I respectfully agree with him.

As counsel pointed out to us in argument, if that is not right, there are a variety of activities which quite commonly go on in the street which may well be the subject of prosecution under section 137. For instance, what is now relatively commonplace, at least in London and large cities, distributing advertising material or free periodicals outside stations, when people are arriving in the morning. Clearly, that is an obstruction; clearly, it is not incidental to passage up and down the street because the distributors are virtually stationary. The question must be: is it reasonable use of the highway or not? In my judgment that is a question that arises. It may be decided that if the activity grows to an extent that it is unreasonable by reason of the space occupied or the duration of time for which it goes on that an offence would be committed, but it is a matter on the facts for the magistrates, in my view.

To take another even more mundane example, suppose two friends meet in the street, not having seen each other for some time, and stop to discuss their holidays and are more or less stationary for a quarter of an hour or 20 minutes. Obviously, they may well cause an obstruction to others passing by. What they are discussing has nothing to do with passing or re-passing in the street. They could just as well have the conversation at the home of one or other of them or in a coffee shop nearby. Is it to be said that they are guilty of an offence and the reasonableness of what they are doing is not in issue? In my judgment it cannot be said.

Some activities which commonly go on in the street are covered by statute, for instance, the holding of markets or street trading, and thus they are lawful activities because they are lawfully permitted within the meaning of the section. That is lawful authority. But many are not and the question thus is (to follow Lord Parker's dictum): have the prosecution proved in such cases that the defendant was obstructing the highway without lawful excuse? That question is to be answered by deciding whether the activity in which the defendant was engaged was or was not a reasonable user of the highway.

I emphasise that for there to be a lawful excuse for what would otherwise be an obstruction of the highway, the activity in which the person causing the obstruction is engaged must itself be inherently lawful. If it is not, the question whether it is reasonable does not arise. So an obstruction of the highway caused by unlawful picketing in pursuance of a trade dispute cannot be said to be an activity for which there is a lawful excuse. But in this case it is not suggested that the activity itself—distributing pamphlets and displaying banners in opposition to the wearing of animal furs as garments—was itself unlawful.

I suggest that the correct approach for justices who are dealing with the issues which arose and arise in the present case is as follows. First, they should consider: is there an obstruction? Unless the obstruction is so small that one can consider it comes within the rubric *de minimis*, any stopping on the highway, whether it be on the carriageway or on the footway, is prima facie an obstruction. To quote Lord Parker: 'Any occupation of part of a road thus interfering with people having the use of the whole of the road is an obstruction.'

The second question then will arise: was it wilful, that is to say, deliberate? Clearly, in many cases a pedestrian or a motorist has to stop because the traffic lights are against the motorist or there are other people in the way, not because he wishes to do so. Such stopping is not wilful. But if the stopping is deliberate, then there is wilful obstruction.

Then there arises the third question: have the prosecution proved that the obstruction was without lawful authority or excuse? Lawful authority includes permits and licences granted under statutory provision, as I have already said, such as for market and street traders and, no doubt, for those collecting for charitable causes on Saturday mornings. Lawful excuse embraces activities otherwise lawful in themselves which may or may not be reasonable in all the circumstances mentioned by Lord Parker in *Nagy v Weston* (supra). In the present case the Crown Court never considered this question. In my judgment, carefully though they dealt with the matter, they were wrong not to do so, and I would, therefore, allow the appeal.

Otton J: I agree. The courts have long recognised the right to free speech to protest on matters of public concern and to demonstrate on the one hand and the need for peace and good order on the other.

In *Hubbard v Pitt* [1975] 3 All ER 1, to which Glidewell LJ has already referred, Lord Denning MR at another passage at pp. 10D and 11B said as follows:

'Finally, the real grievance of the plaintiffs is about the placards and leaflets. To restrain these by an interlocutory injunction would be contrary to the principle laid down by the court 85 years ago in *Bonnard v Perryman* [1891] 2 Ch 269 and repeatedly applied ever since. That case spoke of the right of free speech. Here we have to consider the right to demonstrate and the right to protest on matters of public concern. These are rights which it is in the public interest that individuals should possess; and indeed, that they should exercise without impediment so long as no wrongful act is done. It is often the only means by which grievances can be brought to the knowledge of those in authority—at any rate with such impact as to gain a remedy. Our history is full of warnings against suppression of these rights. Most notable was the demonstration at St. Peter's Fields, Manchester, in 1819 in support of universal suffrage. The magistrates sought to stop it. Hundreds were killed and injured. Afterwards the Court of Common Council of London affirmed "the undoubted right of Englishmen to assemble together for the purposes of deliberating upon public grievances." Such is the right of assembly. So also is the right to meet together, to go in procession, to demonstrate and to protest on matters of public concern. As long as all is done peaceably and in good order without threats or incitement to violence or obstruction to traffic, it is not prohibited: see *Beatty v Gillbanks* (1882) 9 QBD 308. I stress the need for peace and good order. Only too often violence may break out: and then it should be firmly handled and severely punished. But, so long as good order is maintained, the right to demonstrate must be preserved. In his recent inquiry [(1975) Cmnd. 5919] on the Red Lion Square disorders, Scarman L.J. was asked to recommend "that a positive right to demonstrate should be enacted." He said at p. 28 that it was unnecessary: "The right of course exists, subject only to limits required by the need for good order and the passage of traffic." In the recent report on Contempt of Court, the committee considered the campaign of the Sunday Times about thalidomide and said that the issues were "a legitimate matter for public comment." It recognised that it was important to maintain the "freedom of protest on issues of public concern." It is time for the courts to recognise this too. They should not interfere by interlocutory injunction with the right to demonstrate and to protest any more than they interfere with the right of free speech; provided that everything is done peaceably and in good order.'

Although Lord Denning was dealing with the use of an interlocutory injunction, I consider that the passage is of importance when considering whether persons behaving like these appellants have committed a criminal offence of wilful obstruction where there is under section 137(2) of the Act a statutory right of arrest without warrant.

On the analysis of the law, given by Glidewell LJ and his suggested approach with which I totally agree, I consider that this balance would be properly struck and that the 'freedom of protest on issues of public concern' would be given the recognition it deserves.

Appeal allowed.
Convictions quashed.

NOTES

1. See G. Holgate, (1987) 151 JPN 568; P. Copling, ibid. p. 579; I. Bing, ibid. p. 628; S. Bailey, [1987] PL 495.
2. In *Waite v Taylor* (1985) 149 JP 551, DC, a busker juggling with lighted fire sticks in a pedestrian precinct was held to be guilty of the offence as he had occupied part of the highway for a purpose that could not properly be said to be ancillary to the exercise of his right to pass and repass. In *Cooper v Metropolitan Police Comr* (1985) 82 Cr App Rep 238, the Divisional Court held that the Crown Court was entitled to find that the action of a club tout in engaging people in conversation on the highway to try and persuade them to enter the club constituted an unreasonable user.

Arrowsmith v Jenkins [1963] 2 QB 561, [1963] 2 All ER 210, [1963] 2 WLR 856, 127 JP 289, 61 LGR 312, Queen's Bench Divisional Court

On 13 April 1962, a meeting was held in Nelson Street, Bootle, at which the main speaker was Pat Arrowsmith. This street linked two main roads. Meetings had been held there from time to time and police officers had on occasions attended to ensure the free passage of traffic. There was no evidence that these meetings had led to prosecutions for obstruction. At this meeting the carriageway and pavements were completely blocked from 12.35 p.m. to 12.40 p.m. A passageway for vehicles was then cleared by the police and a fire engine and other vehicles were guided through the crowd. Police officers requested the defendant to ask her audience to draw closer to her to help clear the carriageway and the defendant did so by means of a loud-hailer through which she was addressing the crowd. But the carriageway remained partly obstructed until after 12.55 p.m. when the defendant finished speaking. If it had not been for the fact that the defendant was speaking, the crowd would have dispersed and the highway would have been cleared.

A was convicted under the Highways Act 1959, s. 121. She appealed unsuccessfully to quarter sessions and to the Divisional Court.

Lord Parker CJ: I think that the defendant feels that she is under a grievance because—and one may put it this way—she says: 'Why pick on me? There have been many meetings held in this street from time to time. The police, as on this occasion, have attended those meetings and assisted to make a free passage, and there is no evidence that anybody else has ever been prosecuted. Why pick on me?' That, of course, has nothing to do with this court. The sole question here is whether the defendant has contravened section 121(1) of the Highways Act, 1959. . . .

I am quite satisfied that section 121(1) of the Act of 1959, on its true construction, is providing that if a person, without lawful authority or excuse, intentionally as opposed to accidentally, that is, by an exercise of his or her free will, does something or omits to do something which will cause an obstruction or the continuance of an obstruction, he or she is guilty of an offence. Mr. Wigoder, for the defendant, has sought to argue that if a person—and I think that this is how he puts it—acts in the genuine belief that he or she has lawful authority to do what he or she is doing then, if an obstruction results, he or she cannot be said to have wilfully obstructed the free passage along a highway.

Quite frankly, I do not fully understand that submission. It is difficult, certainly, to apply in the present case. I imagine that it can be put in this way: that there must be some mens rea in the sense that a person will only be guilty if he knowingly does a wrongful act. I am quite satisfied that that consideration cannot possibly be imported into the words 'wilfully obstructs' in section 121(1) of the Act of 1959. If anybody, by an exercise of free will, does something which causes an obstruction, then an offence is committed. There is no doubt that the defendant did that in the present case. . . .

Ashworth and **Winn JJ** agreed.

Appeal dismissed.

NOTE

A. T. H. Smith comments (*Smith*, pp. 204–205) that

'Although it could undoubtedly be said that she intended to cause an obstruction in the sense that she intended that the crowd should gather around her, it may be doubted whether in the circumstances her conduct in causing the obstruction was properly described as "wilful" . . . [W]here no contemporaneous objection is taken by those whose official function it is to preserve the way free from obstruction, it is unduly restrictive of freedom of speech for the courts to hold that the obstruction is wilful when the speaker acts in reliance on that official, and perfectly proper, connivance.'

(ii) Open Spaces

Open spaces, parks, recreation grounds and the like are usually vested in the Crown, or in a local authority. They may be subject to regulations or byelaws made under a variety of statutory powers (see *Brownlie*, pp. 35–38; Public Health Act 1875, s. 164; Open Spaces Act 1906, s. 15). The Local Government Act 1972, s. 235 empowers district and London borough councils to make byelaws for the 'good rule and government' of the whole or any part of their area, 'and for the prevention and suppression of nuisances therein'. These commonly cover such topics as the use in public of musical instruments, amplifiers or indecent language.

The general public may not acquire a private law right to hold meetings on land (*De Morgan v Metropolitan Board of Works* (1880) 5 QBD 155, DC, and *Brighton Corporation v Packham* (1908) 72 DP 318, Ch D). 'No such right . . . is known to the law' (per Lush J in *De Morgan* at 157). Moreover, challenges to byelaws which prohibit the holding of meetings at particular places or without prior consent have generally been unsuccessful: *De Morgan*, above; *Slee v Meadows* (1911) 75 JP 246, DC; *Aldred v Miller* 1925 JC 21; *Aldred v Langmuir* 1932 JC 22. Conversely, byelaws restricting access to RAF Greenham Common, made under the Military Lands Act 1892, s. 17(2), were held to be *ultra vires* in *DPP v Hutchinson; DPP v Smith* [1990] 2 AC 783, HL. The byelaws on their face prejudicially affected rights of common, and this was specifically prohibited by the enabling Acts. The appellants, who did not assert any right of common, were nevertheless entitled to argue in their defence that the byelaws were *ultra vires*. See A. W. Bradley, [1989] PL 1 and [1990] PL 193. Cf. *Bugg v DPP* [1993] 2 All ER 815, DC.

Bailey v Williamson (1873) LR 8 QB 118 concerned the validity of regulations under the Parks Regulation Act 1872 which (inter alia) prohibited public addresses in Hyde Park except at certain places. Section 1 of the Act provided that nothing in the Act authorised 'any interference with any right whatever to which any person or persons may be by law entitled'. The Court of Queen's Bench held that there was no 'right' to hold public meetings in the Park. Cockburn CJ said at 125: '. . . whatever enjoyment the public have been allowed to have of these parks and royal possessions for any purpose has been an enjoyment which the public have had by the gracious concession of the Crown'. The use of Hyde Park is now regulated by the Royal and Other Parks and Gardens Regulations 1977, S.I. 1977 No. 217.

The Trafalgar Square Regulations 1952, S.I. 1952 No. 776

The Minister of Works in exercise of the powers conferred upon him by the Trafalgar Square Act 1844, and the Parks Regulation Acts 1872 and 1926, and of all other powers enabling him in that behalf, hereby makes the following Regulations: . . .

2. Prohibited Acts.—Within the Square the following acts are prohibited:

(1) wilfully interfering with the comfort or convenience of any person in the Square;

(2) dropping or leaving litter or refuse except in a receptacle provided for the purpose;

(3) polluting any water;

(4) walking on any shrubbery or flower bed;

(5) damaging, cutting or picking any tree or plant;

(6) damaging, defacing or climbing on any structure, seat or other Government property;

(7) bathing or paddling.

3. Acts for which Written Permission is required.—Within the Square the following acts are prohibited unless the written permission of the Minister has first been obtained:

(1) selling or distributing anything or offering anything for sale or hire;

(2) carrying on any trade or business;

(3) using artificial light or a tripod or stand for photography;

(4) organising, conducting or taking part in any assembly, parade or procession;

(5) making or giving a public speech or address;

(6) placing or exhibiting any display or representation;

(7) erecting or using any apparatus for the transmission, reception, reproduction or amplification of sound or speech by electrical or mechanical means unless the sound emitted is audible to the user only;

(8) causing any obstruction to free passage;

(9) singing or playing a musical instrument.

NOTES

1. The regulations were made on 8 April 1952, and came into operation on 8 June 1952. The powers are now exercised by the Secretary of State for National Heritage. Under the present policy, the Square may be booked for meetings from 2 pm to sunset on Saturdays and from sunrise to sunset on Sundays, Bank Holidays and Good Fridays. No application is considered more than 3 months in advance of the date of a proposed meeting, and there must be at least 5 clear working days in which to consider an application (information supplied by the Department of the Environment).

2. The history of Trafalgar Square as a place of public meeting is discussed in R. Mace, *Trafalgar Square* (1976). Appendix 5 gives a list of applicants for the use of the Square for political meetings. A small minority of applications have been refused since 1952. In 1972 the Home Secretary placed a ban on all meetings concerning

Ireland following the Aldershot bombing (see 833 HC Deb 22 March 1972 cols 1497–8): this ban is still in force.

3. Two cases in 1888 confirmed that there was no right of public meeting in Trafalgar Square. In *R v Cunninghame Graham and Burns* (1888) 16 Cox CC 420 Charles J directed the jury that there was no right of public meeting 'either in Trafalgar-square' or any other public thoroughfare. . . . '[T]he use of public thoroughfares is for people to pass and repass along them' (p. 429). In *Ex p Lewis* (1888) 21 QBD 191, DC, L sought summonses against Henry Matthews, the Home Secretary, and Sir Charles Warren, the Metropolitan Police Commissioner, alleging, inter alia, conspiracy to prevent Her Majesty's subjects from exercising their constitutional and lawful rights, to endanger the public peace, and to inflict grievous bodily harm, and nuisance. The allegations were based upon the conduct of the authorities in relation to the Trafalgar Square riots of 13 November 1887 (below, p. 217). The Divisional Court declined to interfere with the magistrate's decision to refuse the summonses, and rejected the claim that there was a right of public meeting (see above, p. 189). Wills J pointed out at 198 that Trafalgar Square was vested by statute in the Crown with the powers of control and management exercised by the Commissioners of Works.

'Trafalgar Square . . . is completely regulated by Act of Parliament and whatever rights exist must be found in the statute if at all. The right of public meeting is not among them. The right of control appears to be unqualified except by what else is to be found in the Acts [53 Geo 3, c 121, 7 & 8 Vict c 60 and 14 & 15 Vict c 42] and must therefore cover the right of saying under what circumstances, and for what purposes, other than the public rights of passage given by the Acts, it shall be used . . . .'

(iii) Near Parliament

In addition to the legislative provisions mentioned below, both Houses of Parliament at the commencement of each session direct the Metropolitan Police Commissioner to keep the streets leading to Parliament open and order that the access to Parliament of Lords and members is not to be obstructed. The power to give such sessional orders derives from parliamentary privilege (see Erskine May, *Parliamentary Practice*, 21st edn, 1989, pp. 169–170). The Commissioner enforces these orders by giving directions under section 52 of the Metropolitan Police Act 1839 (below).

Sessional Order of the House of Commons 18 November 1993

METROPOLITAN POLICE

Motion made, and Question proposed.
That the Commissioner of the Police of the Metropolis do take care that during the Session of Parliament the passages through the streets leading to this House be kept free and open, and that no obstruction be permitted to hinder the passage of Members to and from this House, and that no disorder be allowed in Westminster Hall, or in the passages leading to this House, during the Sitting of Parliament, and that there be no annoyance therein or thereabouts; and that the Serjeant at Arms attending this House do communicate this Order to the Commissioner aforesaid.

Metropolitan Police Act 1839

52. Commissioners may make regulations for the route of carriages, and persons, and for preventing obstruction of the streets during public processions, etc., or in the neighbourhood of public buildings, etc.
. . . It shall be lawful for the commissioners of police from time to time, and as occasion shall require, to make regulations for the route to be observed by all carts, carriages, horses, and persons, and for preventing

obstruction of the streets and thoroughfares within the metropolitan police district, in all times of public processions, public rejoicings, or illuminations, and also to give directions to the constables for keeping order and for preventing any obstruction of the thoroughfares in the immediate neighbourhood of her Majesty's palaces and the public offices, the High Court of Parliament, the courts of law and equity, the police courts, the theatres, and other places of public resort, and in any case when the streets or thoroughfares may be thronged or may be liable to be obstructed.

NOTES

1. By s. 54(9) of this Act, 'every person' commits an offence 'who, after being made acquainted with the regulations or directions' made under s. 52, 'shall wilfully disregard or not conform himself thereunto'. The maximum penalty is a fine not exceeding level 2 on the standard scale.

2. The following direction was made by the Commissioner on 21 April 1966:

'*Processions prohibited during the sitting of Parliament.* By virtue of the powers conferred on me by section 52 of the Metropolitan Police Act 1839, I the undersigned Commissioner of Police of the metropolis do hereby give directions to all constables that during the session of Parliament the following sessional order shall be enforced: [the order was recited] And I further direct all constables in pursuance of the said order and by virtue of my powers under the said Act: (1) That all assemblies or processions of persons shall be dispersed and shall not be in or proceed along any street, square or open place within the area specified hereunder on any day on which Parliament is sitting: south side of the river Thames between Waterloo and Vauxhall Bridges, Vauxhall Bridge Road, Victoria Street (between Vauxhall Bridge Road and Buckingham Palace Road), Grosvenor Gardens, Grosvenor Place, Piccadilly, Coventry Street, New Coventry Street, Leicester Square (north side), Cranbourn Street, Long Acre, Bow Street, Wellington Street, crossing Strand and Victoria Embankment west of Waterloo Bridge. Provided that processions may be routed along the thoroughfares named except Victoria Embankment west of Waterloo Bridge. (2) That they shall prevent or remove any cause of obstruction within the area named in paragraph (1) hereof, so that every facility shall be afforded for the free passage of members to and from the Houses of Parliament on any day on which Parliament is sitting.'

This direction was at issue in *Papworth v Coventry* [1967] 2 All ER 41, [1967] 1 WLR 663, DC. P and others took part in a 'vigil' in Whitehall on both sides of Downing Street to call attention to the situation in Vietnam. They were spaced out and stationary, and were not disorderly. They refused to move when requested and were prosecuted under s. 54(9) for failure to comply with the direction. The court held (1) that the sessional order itself could have no effect outside the walls and precincts of the Houses of Parliament; and (2) that the direction was to be construed as if it referred only to such assemblies or processions of persons as are capable of causing consequential obstruction to the free passage of members to and from the Houses of Parliament or their departure therefrom, or disorder in the neighbourhood or annoyance thereabouts. Any wider sense would have been ultra vires the Commissioner. The case was remitted to the stipendiary magistrate to determine whether the conduct 'constituted an assembly which was capable of giving rise consequentially either to obstruction of streets and thoroughfares in the immediate neighbourhood of the Houses of Parliament, or to disorder, annoyance of the kind itself likely to lead to a breach of the peace.' Papworth was subsequently acquitted (*Brownlie*, p. 60).

See also *Needham v DPP* (11 March 1994, unreported) where the Divisional Court held that it was sufficient to 'acquaint' someone of a direction to summarise it (and it would be insufficient merely to state its existence). However, N's conviction under s. 54(9) in respect of her participation in a sit-down protest in the roadway in Parliament Square was quashed as the Commissioner's direction in force on that day enabled the police to stop or divert 'pedestrian traffic' but did not apply to persons sitting down on the thoroughfare.

3. The power to give directions was relied on as the basis of the use of roadblocks in the Wapping area during the News International dispute. These had a significant effect on the freedom of movement of residents: see NCCL, *No Way in Wapping* (1986). The directions were not published and copies were not given to residents. The analogous power in the City of London Police Act 1839, s. 22, was used to combat 'Stop the City' demonstrations in the City: *New Statesman*, 11 May 1984, p. 5.

4. The enforcement of sessional orders has also been secured by the prosecution of persons for wilfully obstructing the police in the execution of their duty. See *Pankhurst v Jarvis* (1910) 22 Cox CC 228, DC, and *Despard v Wilcox* (1910) 22 Cox CC 258, DC, cases concerning suffragettes.

5. Processions are stopped at the boundary of the 'Sessional Area' and marchers are allowed to proceed independently to Parliament to lobby MPs (see P. A. J. Waddington, *Liberty and Order* (1994), pp. 66–68).

6. Disorder within the precincts of Parliament is dealt with by police under the direction of the Serjeant at Arms, as in 1966, where some members of the Committee of 100 attempted to make speeches in the House of Commons, and others sat down in Old Palace Yard (*Report of the Commissioner of Police of the Metropolis for 1966*, Cmnd. 3315, p. 13).

(iv) Publicly Owned Premises

As the holding of street meetings is likely to be unlawful (see above, pp. 182–189), and therefore dependent in practice upon the goodwill of the police, it becomes even more crucial to those that wish to organise meetings that premises be available. Political meetings today seem to arouse such little public enthusiasm that finding premises is less of a problem than filling them. Extremist groups which are likely to arouse opposition naturally have most difficulty. One of the contributory factors in the decline of Mosley's British Union of Fascists after 1936 was the difficulty in hiring halls for their rallies (J. Stevenson and C. Cook, *Britain in the Depression* (1994), p. 233). Prior to the Olympia meeting in June 1934 (see below, p. 264), the police prevented a BUF rally at White City by persuading the chairman of the White City Board to demand so high a bond upon the safety of the hall that Mosley had to decline the booking.

The traditional importance of meetings during elections is recognised by sections 95 and 96 of the Representation of the People Act 1983, which entitle candidates during election campaigns to the use of a suitable school room or meeting room (maintained at public expense) for the purpose of holding public meetings. Expenses are payable and damage must be paid for but the use is otherwise free of charge. In addition the discretionary powers of management of public premises must be exercised within the constraints of the ultra vires doctrine. Accordingly, a fixed policy to refuse the use of premises to particular groups or for particular purposes may fall foul of the rule that requires individual exercises of discretion (J. M. Evans, *de Smith's Judicial Review of Administrative Action* (4th edn, 1980) pp. 311–317), and decisions based on improper considerations may also be challenged (ibid., pp. 322–343). In *R v Historic Buildings and Ancient Monuments Commission for England (English Heritage), ex p Firsoff* (19 June 1991, unreported) the Court of Appeal dismissed a renewed application for leave to apply for judicial review of English Heritage's decision to close Stonehenge over the night of the summer solstice on June 21/22 1991. EH's decision was taken on the advice of the police in view of disorder attending this occasion in previous years (see below, p. 205). Under the Ancient Monuments and

Archaeological Areas Act 1979, as amended by the National Heritage Act 1983, the public had access to Stonehenge, but EH had statutory power, if it considered it necessary or expedient to do so in the interest of safety or for the maintenance or preservation of the monument, to exclude the public from access for such period as it thought fit. The court held that there was no arguable case on any of the judicial review grounds. (See also *R v The Commissioners of English Heritage, ex p Chappell* (19 June 1986, unreported, CA), referred to in the 1991 case.)

Section 43 of the Education (No. 2) Act 1986 (below) requires the governing bodies of universities, polytechnics and colleges to take reasonable steps to ensure that freedom of speech within the law is secured for their own members, students and employees and for visiting speakers.

NOTES

1. Local councils with a general policy of refusing to allow their premises to be used for National Front meetings have been compelled to accede to requests to hold election meetings where the Front have had candidates in parliamentary elections (e.g. Manchester City Council: *The Times*, 20 April 1978). In *Webster v Southwark London Borough Council* [1983] QB 698, QBD, Forbes J granted a declaration that a National Front candidate at a parliamentary by-election was entitled to use a room in accordance with the equivalent provision in the Representation of the People Act 1949 (s. 82). In the light of continued refusal to make a room available leave was given for the issue of a writ of sequestration, although disobedience to a declaration, as a non-coercive order, did not amount to contempt of court. In *Ettridge v Morrell* (1986) 85 LGR 100, the Court of Appeal held that the right of a local election candidate to have a suitable school room made available was a private right enforceable by an action in the Queen's Bench Division and not a public law right to be protected by an application for judicial review. The court permitted the meeting to take place (Thornton, *Public Order Law* (1987), p. 162).

What is the position if the organisers of a National Front meeting, purportedly held under s. 95 of the Representation of the People Act 1983, only allow Front members or ticket holders into the meeting? What if the decision is taken by police outside in order to preserve the peace? In July 1978, Manchester City Council refused the National Front permission to hold an election meeting in a local school claiming that it would not be a public meeting, and that council employees had said they would refuse to take the steps necessary to make the room available such as opening the school. The local county court judge held that he had no jurisdiction to entertain the Front's claim for damages for breach of statutory duty (*The Times* 8 and 11 July 1978; J. F. Garner (1978) *Local Government Chronicle*, p. 778).

R. J. Clayton (*Parker's Conduct of Parliamentary Elections* (1983) pp. 101–102) argues that the expression 'public meeting', which is not defined, should be construed as 'a meeting to which the public have access' rather than 'a meeting which a section of the public is permitted to attend, whether on payment or otherwise':

'it would seem proper to construe the words narrowly so that section 95 is not construed as giving a candidate a right to use a room, on payment of bare expenses only, for the purpose of addressing the party faithful.'

See also Thornton, op. cit., pp. 162–163.

2. In October 1979, the Court of Appeal held that the Labour-controlled Great Yarmouth Council could not veto a booking for the annual conference of the

National Front which had been accepted by the council when the Conservatives had been in power. The NF had paid over £6,000 for the booking fee and insurance to cover the risk of damage to council property. Lord Denning MR stated that the conference should go ahead in the interests of freedom of speech and assembly and of the importance of upholding a contract: *Verrall v Great Yarmouth Borough Council* [1981] QB 202, CA; cf *Webster v Newham London Borough Council* (1980) Times, 22 November, CA.

3. See the *Green Paper*, pp. 24–26; *HAC Report* pp. xxv–xxvii; *White Paper*, pp. 36–37. The *HAC* proposed a procedure similar to s. 3(2) of the Public Order Act 1936 (below) to enable the Home Secretary to require a candidate to hold his meeting elsewhere in the constituency or electoral area (p. xxvi). This was rejected by the government on the ground that it would 'encroach upon the right of the candidate to convey his message to the electorate in the area of his choice; and it would involve the police and the public authorities in decisions bearing upon the political fortunes of particular candidates.'

Education (No. 2) Act 1986

43. Freedom of speech in universities, polytechnics and colleges

(1) Every individual and body of persons concerned in the government of any establishment to which this section applies shall take such steps as are reasonably practicable to ensure that freedom of speech within the law is secured for members, students and employees of the establishment and for visiting speakers.

(2) The duty imposed by subsection (1) above includes (in particular) the duty to ensure, so far as is reasonably practicable, that the use of any premises of the establishment is not denied to any individual or body of persons on any ground connected with—

    (a) the beliefs or views of that individual or of any member of that body; or

    (b) the policy or objectives of that body.

(3) The governing body of every such establishment shall, with a view to facilitating the discharge of the duty imposed by subsection (1) above in relation to that establishment, issue and keep up to date a code of practice setting out—

    (a) the procedures to be followed by members, students and employees of the establishment in connection with the organisation—

        (i) of meetings which are to be held on premises of the establishment and which fall within any class of meeting specified in the code; and

        (ii) of other activities which are to take place on those premises and which fall within any class of activity so specified; and

    (b) the conduct required of such persons in connection with any such meeting or activity;

and dealing with such other matters as the governing body consider appropriate.

(4) Every individual and body of persons concerned in the government of any such establishment shall take such steps as are reasonably practicable (including where appropriate the initiation of disciplinary measures) to secure that the requirements of the code of practice for that establishment, issued under subsection (3) above, are complied with. . . .

(6) In this section—

'governing body', in relation to any university, means the executive governing body which has responsibility for the management and administration of its revenue and property and the conduct of its affairs (that is to say the body commonly called the council of the university);

'university' includes a university college and any college, or institution in the nature of a college, in a university. . . .

(8) Where a students' union occupies premises which are not premises of the establishment in connection with which the union is constituted, any reference in this section to the premises of the establishment shall be taken to include a reference to the premises occupied by the students' union.

NOTES

1. By subs. (5), as amended, the section applies to any university, any institution other than a university within the higher education sector; any establishment of higher or further education maintained by a local education authority; and any institution within the further education sector. An LEA maintaining or assisting an institution is taken to be concerned in its government.

2. For comments on this section, see E. Barendt, 'Free Speech in the Universities' [1987] PL 344, who notes that this section

'will principally benefit controversial politicians and students disposed to listen to them. There is therefore little case in principle for imposing these unusual duties to secure free speech on university premises, when the law otherwise almost always treats freedom of speech as a mere liberty and is unwilling to recognise rights of access' (pp. 349–350).

3. In *R v University of Liverpool, ex p Caesar-Gordon* [1990] 3 All ER 821, the university authorities granted permission to the student Conservative Association to hold a meeting subject to conditions that information about the meeting be treated as confidential until 9 am on the day of the meeting; that the meeting be open only to those producing a valid staff or student card; and that the university reserved the right to charge the Association with the cost of security. Permission was subsequently withdrawn on the ground that it was likely that good order would not be maintained. The Divisional Court granted a declaration that the university was not entitled to take account of the risk of disorder other than on the university's premises, and there occasioned by members of the public over whom the university had no control. (The university had taken account of the serious concern expressed by the police at the risk of disorder in nearby Toxteth.) However, the court held that the conditions were intra vires.

4. Copies of relevant codes of practice should be available from the university or college authorities and may be set out in the institution's Calendar or Regulations.

(v) Powers to Ban or Control Processions and Assemblies

There are no general powers whereby public bodies or officials may prohibit in advance the holding of a *meeting*, although there are such powers in relation to land whose management or control is vested in the state (see, for example, pp. 189–191, 193–196). General statutory powers to ban or control *processions* were provided in section 3 of the Public Order Act 1936. The 1986 Act remodelled and extended those powers and introduced new powers to control (although not ban) meetings and static demonstrations. Moreover, any meeting or procession which constitutes an unlawful assembly may be dispersed, and it may be lawful to disperse a lawful assembly where necessary to prevent a breach of the peace (see pp. 239–256).

Public Order Act 1986

PART II

PROCESSIONS AND ASSEMBLIES

11. Advance notice of public processions
(1) Written notice shall be given in accordance with this section of any proposal to hold a public procession intended—
    (*a*) to demonstrate support for or opposition to the views or actions of any person or body of persons,
    (*b*) to publicise a cause or campaign, or
    (*c*) to mark or commemorate an event,
unless it is not reasonably practicable to give any advance notice of the procession.
(2) Subsection (1) does not apply where the procession is one commonly or customarily held in the police area (or areas) in which it is proposed to be held or is a funeral procession organised by a funeral director acting in the normal course of his business.

(3) The notice must specify the date when it is intended to hold the procession, the time when it is intended to start it, its proposed route, and the name and address of the person (or of one of the persons) proposing to organise it.

(4) Notice must be delivered to a police station—

  (a) in the police area in which it is proposed the procession will start, or

  (b) where it is proposed the procession will start in Scotland and cross into England, in the first police area in England on the proposed route.

(5) If delivered not less than 6 clear days before the date when the procession is intended to be held, the notice may be delivered by post by the recorded delivery service; but section 7 of the Interpretation Act 1978 (under which a document sent by post is deemed to have been served when posted and to have been delivered in the ordinary course of post) does not apply.

(6) If not delivered in accordance with subsection (5), the notice must be delivered by hand not less than 6 clear days before the date when the procession is intended to be held or, if that is not reasonably practicable, as soon as delivery is reasonably practicable.

(7) Where a public procession is held, each of the persons organising it is guilty of an offence if—

  (a) the requirements of this section as to notice have not been satisfied, or

  (b) the date when it is held, the time when it starts, or its route, differs from the date, time or route specified in the notice.

(8) It is a defence for the accused to prove that he did not know of, and neither suspected nor had reason to suspect, the failure to satisfy the requirements or (as the case may be) the difference of date, time or route.

(9) To the extent that an alleged offence turns on a difference of date, time or route, it is a defence for the accused to prove that the difference arose from circumstances beyond his control or from something done with the agreement of a police officer or by his direction. . . .

12. Imposing conditions on public processions

(1) If the senior police officer, having regard to the time or place at which and the circumstances in which any public procession is being held or is intended to be held and to its route or proposed route, reasonably belives that—

  (a) it may result in serious public disorder, serious damage to property or serious disruption to the life of the community, or

  (b) the purpose of the persons organising it is the intimidation of others with a view to compelling them not to do an act they have a right to do, or to do an act they have a right not to do,

he may give directions imposing on the persons organising or taking part in the procession such conditions as appear to him necessary to prevent such disorder, damage, disruption or intimidation, including conditions as to the route of the procession or prohibiting it from entering any public place specified in the directions.

(2) In subsection (1) 'the senior police officer' means—

  (a) in relation to a process being held, or to a procession intended to be held in a case where persons are assembling with a view to taking part in it, the most senior in rank of the police officers present at the scene, and

  (b) in relation to a procession intended to be held in a case where paragraph (a) does not apply, the chief officer of police.

(3) A direction given by a chief officer of police by virtue of subsection (2)(b) shall be given in writing.

(4) A person who organises a public procession and knowingly fails to comply with a condition imposed under this section is guilty of an offence, but it is a defence for him to prove that the failure arose from circumstances beyond his control.

(5) A person who takes part in a public procession and knowingly fails to comply with a condition imposed under this section is guilty of an offence, but it is a defence for him to prove that the failure arose from circumstances beyond his control.

(6) A person who incites another to commit an offence under subsection (5) is guilty of an offence. . . .

13. Prohibiting public processions

(1) If at any time the chief officer of police reasonably believes that, because of particular circumstances existing in any district or part of a district, the powers under section 12 will not be sufficient to prevent the holding of public processions in that district or part from resulting in serious public disorder, he shall apply to the council of the district for an order prohibiting for such period not exceeding 3 months as may be specified in the application the holding of all public processions (or of any class of public procession so specified) in the district or part concerned.

(2) On receiving such an application, a council may with the consent of the Secretary of State make an order either in the terms of the application or with such modifications as may be approved by the Secretary of State.

(3) Subsection (1) does not apply in the City of London or the metropolitan police district.

(4) If at any time the Commissioner of Police for the City of London or the Commissioner of Police of the Metropolis reasonably believes that, because of particular circumstances existing in his police area or part of it, the powers under section 12 will not be sufficient to prevent the holding of public processions in that area or part from resulting in serious public disorder, he may with the consent of the Secretary of State make an order prohibiting for such period not exceeding 3 months as may be specified in the order the holding of all public processions (or of any class of public procession so specified) in the area or part concerned.

(5) An order made under this section may be revoked or varied by a subsequent order made in the same way, that is, in accordance with subsections (1) and (2) or subsection (4), as the case may be.

(6) Any order under this section shall, if not made in writing, be recorded in writing as soon as practicable after being made.

(7) A person who organises a public procession the holding of which he knows is prohibited by virtue of an order under this section is guilty of an offence.

(8) A person who takes part in a public procession the holding of which he knows is prohibited by virtue of an order under this section is guilty of an offence.

(9) A person who incites another to commit an offence under subsection (8) is guilty of an offence. . . .

14. Imposing conditions on public assemblies

(1) If the senior police officer, having regard to the time or place at which and the circumstances in which any public assembly is being held or is intended to be held, reasonably believes that—

(a) it may result in serious public disorder, serious damage to property or serious disruption to the life of the community, or

(b) the purpose of the persons organising it is the intimidation of others with a view to compelling them not to do an act they have a right to do, or to do an act they have a right not to do,

he may give directions imposing on the persons organising or taking part in the assembly such conditions as to the place at which the assembly may be (or continue to be) held, its maximum duration, or the maximum number of persons who may constitute it, as appear to him necessary to prevent such disorder, damage, disruption or intimidation.

(2) In subsection (1) 'the senior police officer' means—

(a) in relation to an assembly being held, the most senior in rank of the police officers present at the scene, and

(b) in relation to an assembly intended to be held, the chief officer of police.

(3) A direction given by a chief officer of police by virtue of subsection (2)(b) shall be given in writing.

(4) A person who organises a public assembly and knowingly fails to comply with a condition imposed under this section is guilty of an offence, but it is a defence for him to prove that the failure arose from circumstances beyond his control.

(5) A person who takes part in a public assembly and knowingly fails to comply with a condition imposed under this section is guilty of an offence, but it is a defence for him to prove that the failure arose from circumstances beyond his control.

(6) A person who incites another to commit an offence under subsection (5) is guilty of an offence. . . .

[14A. Prohibiting trespassory assemblies

(1) If at any time the chief officer of police reasonably believes that an assembly is intended to be held in any district at a place on land to which the public has no right of access or only a limited right of access and that the assembly—

(a) is likely to be held without the permission of the occupier of the land or to conduct itself in such a way as to exceed the limits of any permission of his or the limits of the public's right of access, and

(b) may result—

(i) in serious disruption to the life of the community, or

(ii) where the land, or a building or monument on it, is of historical, architectural, archaeological or scientific importance, in significant damage to the land, building or monument,

he may apply to the council of the district for an order prohibiting for a specified period the holding of all trespassory assemblies in the district or a part of it, as specified.

(2) On receiving such an application, a council may—

(a) in England and Wales, with the consent of the Secretary of State make an order either in the terms of the application or with such modifications as may be approved by the Secretary of State; . . .

(3) Subsection (1) does not apply in the City of London or the metropolitan police district.

(4) If at any time the Commissioner of Police for the City of London or the Commissioner of Police of the Metropolis reasonably believes that an assembly is intended to be held at a place on land to which the public has no right of access or only a limited right of access in his police area and that the assembly—

(*a*) is likely to be held without the permission of the occupier of the land or to conduct itself in such a way as to exceed the limits of any permission of his or the limits of the public's right of access, and

(*b*) may result—

(i) in serious disruption to the life of the community, or

(ii) where the land, or a building or monument on it, is of historical, architectural, archaeological or scientific importance, in significant damage to the land, building or monument,

he may with the consent of the Secretary of State make an order prohibiting for a specified period the holding of all trespassory assemblies in the area or a part of it, as specified.

(5) An order prohibiting the holding of trespassory assemblies operates to prohibit any assembly which—

(*a*) is held on land to which the public has no right of access or only a limited right of access, and

(*b*) takes place in the prohibited circumstances, that is to say, without the permission of the occupier of the land or so as to exceed the limits of any permission of his or the limits of the public's right of access.

(6) No order under this section shall prohibit the holding of assemblies for a period exceeding 4 days or in an area exceeding an area represented by a circle with a radius of 5 miles from a specified centre.

(7) An order made under this section may be revoked or varied by a subsequent order made in the same way, that is, in accordance with subsection (1) and (2) or subsection (4), as the case may be.

(8) Any order under this section shall, if not made in writing, be recorded in writing as soon as practicable after being made.

(9) In this section and sections 14B and 14C—

'assembly' means an assembly of 20 or more persons;

'land' means land in the open air;

'limited', in relation to a right of access by the public to land, means that their use of it is restricted to use for a particular purpose (as in the case of a highway or road) or is subject to other restrictions;

'occupier' means—

(*a*) in England and Wales, the person entitled to possession of the land by virtue of an estate or interest held by him; . . .

and in subsections (1) and (4) includes the person reasonably believed by the authority applying for or making the order to be the occupier;

'public' includes a section of the public; and

'specified' means specified in an order under this section. . . .

(11) In relation to Wales, the references in subsection (1) above to a district and to the council of the district shall be construed, as respects applications on and after 1 April 1996, as references to a county or county borough and to the council for that county or county borough.

14B. Offences in connection with trespassory assemblies and arrest therefor

(1) A person who organises an assembly the holding of which he knows is prohibited by an order under section 14A is guilty of an offence.

(2) A person who takes part in an assembly which he knows is prohibited by an order under section 14A is guilty of an offence.

(3) In England and Wales, a person who incites another to commit an offence under subsection (2) is guilty of an offence. . . .]¹

[14C. Stopping persons from proceeding to trespassory assemblies

(1) If a constable in uniform reasonably believes that a person is on his way to an assembly within the area to which an order under section 14A applies which the constable reasonably believes is likely to be an assembly which is prohibited by that order, he may, subject to subsection (2) below—

(*a*) stop that person, and

(*b*) direct him not to proceed in the direction of the assembly.

(2) The power conferred by subsection (1) may only be exercised within the area to which the order applies.

(3) A person who fails to comply with a direction under subsection (1) which he knows has been given to him is guilty of an offence. . . .]²

15. Delegation

(1) The chief officer of police may delegate, to such extent and subject to such conditions as he may specify, any of his functions under sections 12 to [14A]³ to a deputy or assistant chief constable; and references in those sections to the person delegating shall be construed accordingly.

1 Inserted by the Criminal Justice and Public Order Act 1994, s. 70.
2 Inserted by ibid., s. 71.
3 Substituted by ibid., Sch. 10, para. 60.

(2) Subsection (1) shall have effect in the City of London and the metropolitan police district as if 'a deputy or assistant chief constable' read 'an assistant commissioner of police'.

16. Interpretation
In this Part—
'the City of London' means the City as defined for the purposes of the Acts relating to the City of London police;
'the metropolitan police district' means that district as defined in section 76 of the London Government Act 1963;
'public assembly' means an assembly of 20 or more persons in a public place which is wholly or partly open to the air;
'public place' means—
  (a) any highway, or in Scotland any road within the meaning of the Roads (Scotland) Act 1984, and
  (b) any place to which at the material time the public or any section of the public has access, on payment or otherwise, as of right or by virtue of express or implied permission;
'public procession' means a procession in a public place. . . .

NOTES

1. *Penalties and powers of arrest.* A person guilty of an offence under ss. 11(7), 12(5), 13(8), 14(5), 14B(2), 14C(3) is liable on summary conviction to a fine not exceeding level 3 on the standard scale; and under ss. 12(4), (6), 13(7), (9), 14(4), (6), 14B(1), (3) on summary conviction to a fine not exceeding level 4 on the standard scale, or 3 months' imprisonment, or both (1986 Act, ss. 11(10), 12(8)–(10), 13(11)–(13), 14(8)–(10), 14B(5)–(7), 14C(5)). A constable in uniform may arrest without warrant anyone he reasonably suspects is committing an offence under ss. 12(4)–(6), 13(7)–(9), 14(4)–(6), 14B and 14C (1986 Act, ss. 12(7), 13(10), 14(7), 14B(4) and 14C(4)).

Banning orders
2. Section 3 of the Public Order Act 1936 gave powers to a chief officer of police to give directions to those organising or taking part in a procession if he had reasonable grounds to apprehend that it might occasion serious public disorder. If he was 'of opinion' that this would not be sufficient, he could apply for an order to ban all or any class of public processions in the area for a specified period. These powers were introduced in response, inter alia, to disturbances arising from the activities of the British Union of Fascists in the 1930s: see J. Stevenson and C. Cook, *Britain in the Depression: Society and Politics, 1929–1939* (2nd edn, 1994), Chaps 11, 12; R. Thurlow, *The Secret State* (1994), Chap. 5.

The main changes effected by Part II of the 1986 Act were (1) the introduction of advance notice requirements for *processions* (s. 11: see n. **10** below); (2) the extension of the circumstances in which conditions may be imposed on *processions* (s. 12); and (3) a new power to impose conditions on (but not to ban) public *assemblies* (s. 14). A power to ban 'trespassory assemblies' was added by the Criminal Justice and Public Order Act 1994.

The provisions governing banning orders (s. 13) are very similar to the old s. 3. The government considered but rejected adding further grounds for banning orders (*White Paper*, Chap. 4), e.g. (1) 'that the views to be expressed would be seriously offensive: this would place an impossible task upon the police and be an unacceptable infringement of freedom of speech'; (2) a test of disruption: 'too restrictive'; (3) disproportionate cost: 'this would be haphazard in its effect and tend to concentrate major marches in the areas with larger forces'; (4) the procession 'would incite racial hatred': this 'would present insuperable problems of enforcement and could easily backfire by creating martyrs for free speech out of groups' whose policies had been decisively rejected by the electorate.

The power to impose conditions now extends to (1) 'serious damage to property'; (2) 'serious disruption to the life of the community' and (3) 'intimidation'. Ground (2) enables the police to impose conditions

'to re-route a procession in order to limit traffic congestion, or to prevent a bridge from being blocked, or to reduce the severe disruptions sometimes suffered by pedestrians, business and commerce' (*White Paper*, p. 27).

Examples include the existing policy of the Metropolitan Police to discourage demonstrators from using Oxford Street during business hours. Ground (3) enables conditions to be imposed 'to prevent the coercion of individuals', e.g. where a march is organised to 'stop' or 'smash' opponents; where the National Front organise a march through Asian districts, and the response of the local community is to board up their shops and businesses and to stay at home; where animal rights protesters march on furriers' shops or food factories with the intention of preventing the employees from working; or where a very large crowd marches on the home of an individual councillor or inquiry inspector (*White Paper*, p. 28). How these new powers are used in practice is obviously of great importance. A. T. H. Smith comments (*Public Order Offences* (1987), p. 134):

'There is a danger that, if the powers are used too freely, the symbolic significance of a demonstration may be lost. For example, if the proposed route of the march takes the participants past an embassy or a particular factory against whose occupants the organisers wish to protest, the prescription of a different route or terminus may obviate the whole point of the demonstration, and amount to in effect a disguised ban.'

The new power to impose conditions on static demonstrations and meetings was justified in the *White Paper* (p. 31) on the ground that they

'may just as frequently be the occasion of public disorder as marches. . . . Since 1980 some of the most serious public order problems have been associated with static demonstrations – at Greenham Common, the picketing at Warrington, and of the course the mass pickets during the miners' dispute'.

The government did not then propose a power to ban, noting that

'Meetings and assemblies are a more important means of exercising freedom of speech than are marches' (*White Paper*, pp. 31–32).

Nevertheless, the power to ban *trespassory assemblies* was added in 1994, prompted particularly by concern over the disruption caused by 'free festivals' (see above, p. 176, and n. **11**, below).

The 'administrative burden' of an advance notice requirement 'would far outweigh the information gain' (*White Paper*, p. 32). The scope of the new power to impose conditions would be more limited than under s. 12 'in order to prevent the imposition of conditions whose effect would be tantamount to a ban' (ibid.). The power 'might prove useful' where a rally is held after a march has been banned; in relation to picketing which results in outbreaks of serious public disorder; where disruption is caused to residents by demonstrations outside embassies; and 'where pickets deliberately try to obstruct the passage of those going to work . . . the police should be able to limit their numbers, or move them further away from the path of the workers'.

See generally on Part II of the 1986 Act, D. G. T. Williams, [1987] Crim LR 167.

3. May a specified procession be banned under s. 13(1)? If it is known that only one group is planning a march on a particular day, would it be lawful to ban 'all marches' on that day? The *White Paper* (p. 25) proposed that the law be amended to allow a single march to be banned; this change did not appear in the Act on the ground that 'it would place the police in a situation where they would be subject to allegations of political motivation and partiality whenever they exercised the power to seek a ban on a particular march' (*Smith*, pp. 136–137, citing the Minister of State at the Home Office).

4. Directions and orders under these sections are potentially reviewable in the courts under the ultra vires doctrine. A challenge might be made directly, on an application for judicial review under RSC Order 53, or collaterally, as a defence to a prosecution. There is, however, no challenge on the merits. Cf. *The Times*, 21 April 1980, p. 2. It will, however, be difficult in practice to establish that a ban or other order is ultra vires. In *Kent v Metropolitan Police Comr* (1981) Times, 15 May, a ban was made under s. 3(3) of the Public Order Act 1936 in the aftermath of the Brixton (and other) disorders, prohibiting all processions within the Metropolitan Police District (786 square miles) 'except those traditionally held on May 1 to celebrate May Day and those of a religious character customarily held.' This had the incidental effect of preventing a planned CND procession. CND sought a declaration that the ban was ultra vires on the ground that in imposing such a wide ban the Commissioner had not directed himself properly as to the matters to be considered. The Court of Appeal rejected the claim: he had considered the relevant matters, the court could not substitute its judgment for his and CND could apply under s. 9(3) (see now s. 13(5), 1986 Act) for the order to be relaxed. The Commissioner was entitled to conclude that there was a risk that either the march or the police escorting the march would be attacked by hooligans. Moreover he was entitled to ban a 'class' of marches by exclusion.

It will similarly be difficult to establish on judicial review that a refusal to ban or impose conditions is *ultra vires*. See the discussion of two cases under analogous legislation in Northern Ireland, the Public Order (N.I.) Order 1987 (S.I. 1987 No. 463) (*Re Murphy* [1991] 5 NIJB 72, QBD (NI), and 88, CA (NI); *Re Armstrong* (27 August 1992, unreported, QBD (NI)) by B. Hadfield in 'Public Order Police Powers and Judicial Review' [1993] Crim LR 915.

5. In *Application No 8440/78 Christians against Racism and Fascism v UK* (1981) 24 YBECHR 178 the Commission held inadmissible a claim that a ban under s. 3(3) of the Public Order Act 1936 in February 1978 was contrary to the ECHR Articles 5(1), 10, 11 and 14, on the ground that the claim was manifestly ill-founded. On Art. 11 the Commission noted that the right of peaceable assembly guaranteed by Art. 11(1) could not as such be taken away simply by the prospect of violent counter-demonstrations. However, the ban was justified under Art. 11(2) as it complied with the principle that:

'a general ban on demonstrations can only be justified if there is real danger of their resulting in disorder that cannot be prevented by other less stringent measures' (p. 198).

6. In *Flockhart v Robinson* [1950] 2 KB 498, DC, F was prosecuted under section 3 of the Public Order Act 1936. The Metropolitan Police Commissioner on 3 October 1949 banned all public processions of a political character within the Metropolitan Police District. On 15 October, F organised a procession of members of a political group, the Union Movement, which procession lawfully dispersed on reaching Temple Bar. Later that day he met about 150 members at Hyde Park

Corner who followed him in loose formation when he moved along Piccadilly, and then closed ranks. He gave signals to guide them through the traffic and direction signals. Members other than F sang the Horst Wessel song and shouted political slogans. F led them round Piccadilly Circus and into Coventry Street, where they were broken up by the police. F's conviction for 'organising' a procession contrary to s. 3(4) was upheld by the Divisional Court (Lord Goddard CJ and Morris J, Finnemore J dissenting). Lord Goddard CJ stated at 502: 'A procession is not a mere body of persons: it is a body of persons moving along a route. Therefore the person who organises the route is the person who organises the procession'.

7. Before 1981 bans under s. 3(2) and (3) of the 1936 Act were uncommon. However, in that year 39 banning orders were made in England and Wales, 7 inside and 32 outside the Metropolitan Police District and the City of London. 'Many of the orders were in response to tension following the civil disturbances' (*Report of HM Chief Inspector of Constabulary for 1981* (1981–82 HC 463), para 8.6). The figure fell to 13 (7 + 6) in 1982, 9 (2 + 7) in 1983 and 11 (3 + 8) in 1984. The commonest wording of a ban was 'all public processions except those of a religious, educational, festive or ceremonial character customarily held.' The Metropolitan police have on recent occasions resisted pressure to seek bans, claiming that the requirements were 'so onerous that it was a practical impossibility' and that enforcement was 'more trouble than it was worth': P. A. J. Waddington, *Liberty and Order* (1994), pp. 58–61.

Conditions on processions and assemblies

8. In practice, the power to impose conditions under the 1936 Act was rarely used, the police preferring to discuss the plans for a march with the organisers and to negotiate an informal agreement about the route and other matters (*White Paper*, pp. 26–27). Compare the power to impose conditions under ss. 12 and 14 with the common law powers of the police to preserve the peace (below, pp. 239–264).

9. An exercise of the power under s. 14 was considered in *Brickley and Kitson v Police, Legal Action*, July 1988, p. 21 (Knightsbridge Crown Court). This arose out of a picket staged by the City of London Anti-Apartheid Group outside the South African Embassy in Trafalgar Square. It was alleged that on 5 May 1987 three pickets threw red paint at the embassy causing damage. The senior officer at the scene, a chief inspector, using directions made by the Metropolitan Police Commissioner under the Metropolitan Police Act 1839, ordered the picket to move away from the front of the embassy to nearby Duncannon Street. On 6 May, the picket increased to more than 80. Four pickets crossed from Duncannon Street to the pavement outside the embassy. The chief inspector, allegedly fearing that the entire picket would cross back to the embassy and cause serious public disorder or further damage to the building, imposed a condition under s. 14 requiring the picket to remain in Duncannon Street. He addressed the four through a megaphone. Police officers then marched to them, and allegedly warned them that a s. 14 condition had been imposed and that if they did not return to Duncannon Street they would be arrested. They did not move and were arrested. The convictions by the magistrate of B and K under s. 14(5) were reversed on appeal to the Crown Court, the court not being satisfied that there had been sufficient communication to B and K to make clear to them that there was a s. 14 condition in force which applied to them as well as the Duncannon Street demonstrators, and that they were committing an offence by remaining where they were. The court was therefore not sure that they had *knowingly* been in breach of the condition.

In *Police v Reid* [1987] Crim LR 702, R was acquitted by the magistrate of a charge under s. 14(5). This case also arose out of a demonstration outside the South

African Embassy. The chief inspector in charge imposed a condition, similar to that in the previous case, when R, with about 20 others, demonstrated outside the embassy on the occasion of a reception, shouting slogans (e.g. 'Apartheid murderers, get out of Britain'), raising their arms and waving their fingers at arriving guests. The magistrates held that this conduct was intended to cause 'discomfort' and not 'intimidation': the chief inspector had equated the two, and that was the wrong test.

In *DPP v Baillie* [1995] Crim LR 446, DC, the court upheld the decision of the Crown Court to allow B's appeal against conviction for failing to comply with a s. 14 notice. B published his telephone number as a declared source of information and advice as to the time and location of free festivals. He directed callers on a Friday (in fact police officers) to Andover, and then to Crawley Down, with instructions to ring back, indicating that there was to be a festival that weekend. Police served a s. 14 notice imposing conditions requiring, inter alia, that any event be licensed under the Local Government (Miscellaneous Provisions) Act 1982, that there be advance agreement with the police as to maximum numbers in attendance and duration and that there be no damage or disruption to the life of the community resulting from inadequate sanitary arrangements. He continued to give these directions, and was arrested. The Divisional Court held that there was just sufficient evidence for a prima facie case that B was an organiser as his 'role as the purveyor of information as to the time and place of the festival was of crucial importance', but that there was insufficient evidence to show that the police were 'having regard to the time or place at which and the circumstances in which any public assembly is being held or intended to be held' in the terms of s. 14(1): 'to this day no one knows, save possibly the organisers, where or when any such public assembly was to be held. . . . [W]e do not even know that the intended assembly was going to be held in a public place as defined in s. 16 of the Act' (per McCowan LJ). The court left open the argument that, in any event at the time of B's arrest, there was still time for compliance with the conditions.

10. Section 11 introduced a general requirement of advance notice of public processions. This replaced notice requirements (in varying terms) in many local Acts. Lord Scarman, in his Report on the Red Lion Square disorders (Cmnd. 5919, 1975), had rejected suggestions for notice requirements on the ground that the need for them had not been established (paras. 128, 129). In 1981, he took a different view (The Brixton Disorders (Cmnd. 8427) p. 124) as did the Home Affairs Committee (*HAC*, pp. xii–xv) and the *White Paper*, pp. 21–22. See *Legal Action*, June 1991, p. 13, noting a case where a prosecution for breach of s. 11 in respect of a 'small and peaceful march' was dropped by the CPS; the police appeared to be aware of what was planned even though written notice had not been given. On the process of negotiation between the Metropolitan police and the organisers of demonstrations, see P. A. J. Waddington, *Liberty and Order*, Chap 4.

11. Section 39 of the Public Order Act 1986 enabled a senior police officer to direct trespassers to leave land. He had reasonably to believe that two or more persons had entered land as trespassers and were present there with the common purpose of residing there for any period; that reasonable steps had been taken by or on behalf of the occupier to ask them to leave; and that any of those persons had caused damage to property on the land or used threatening, abusive or insulting words or behaviour towards the occupier, a member of his family or an employee or agent of his, or that those persons had between them brought 12 or more vehicles on to the land. It was an offence to fail to leave the land as soon as reasonably practicable or, having left, to return as a trespasser within three months. This provision was designed as a response to large incidents of mass trespass involving such groups as Hell's Angels and hippies. In particular, in 1986, a 'Peace Convoy' of hippies attempting a pilgrimage to Stonehenge, trespassed on a farm owned by a Mr. Attwell with over 100 buses, trucks, caravans and other assorted vehicles. They stayed for seven days, and left peacefully when a High Court eviction order was granted.[1] It was doubted whether the creation of this offence was necessary (*Smith*, pp. 259–260), given the existence of recently streamlined civil remedies, the criminal damage offence and the powers of the police to deal with breaches of the peace.

Section 39 was used by the police in subsequent years to discourage mass trespass and other disorderly activity by the Peace Convoy and others in the period leading up to the summer solstice (*Reports of the Chief Inspector of Constabulary for 1987* (1987–88 HC 521), pp. 57–58; *1988* (1988–89 HC 449), p. 66). In 1989, processions and marches within a 4-mile radius of Stonehenge were banned over a short period around the summer solstice under s. 13 of the Public Order Act 1986 (*Report of the Chief Inspector of Constabulary for 1989* (1989–90 HC 524), p. 67).

The 'reasonable steps' referred to in s. 39(1) should be taken by the occupier before the direction is given by the senior police officer (*Krumpa and Anderson v DPP* [1989] Crim LR 295, DC).

An exercise of discretion to serve a notice is open to challenge on an application for judicial review, although it has been described as 'an entirely unfettered discretion to act on the information which is available': *R v Wiltshire Constabulary* (1992) (25 February, unreported, DC), per Kennedy J.

Section 39 was replaced by more extensive provisions of the Criminal Justice and Public Order Act 1994. Section 61 is similar to the old s. 39, except that the officer must reasonably believe that two or more persons 'are trespassing'; the presence of 6 vehicles rather than 12 is sufficient to trigger the power; there is express power to direct the removal of vehicles or other property; there is express provision in respect of common land; the term 'vehicle' includes any vehicle whether or not in a fit state for use on roads and any chassis or body, with or without wheels, appearing to have formed part of such a vehicle, and any load carried by, and anything attached to, such a vehicle; and there is a power for a constable to seize and remove any vehicle not removed in accordance with a direction, or taken with a person subject to a direction re-entering within three months (s. 62).

Sections 63–66 confer powers in relation to 'raves'. These are defined as gatherings on land in the open air (which includes a place partly open to the air) of 100 or more persons (whether or not trespassers) at which amplified music is played during the night and as such is, by reason of its loudness and duration and the time at which it is played, is likely to cause serious distress to the inhabitants of the locality; the term 'music' 'includes sounds wholly or predominantly characterised by the emission of a succession of repetitive beats'. If, as respects any land in the open air, a police officer of at least the rank of superintendent believes that two or more persons are making preparations for the holding of a 'rave' or ten or more persons are waiting for the rave to begin, or are attending a rave in progress, he may give a direction requiring any such persons to leave the land and remove any vehicle or property. The direction can be communicated by any constable at the scene. Persons are treated as having had a direction communicated to them if reasonable steps have been taken to bring it to

---

1 See P. Vincent-Jones, 'Private Property and Public Order: The Hippy Convoy and Criminal Trespass' (1986) 13 JLS 343; NCCL, *Stonehenge* (1986); K. D. Ewing and C. D. Gearty, *Freedom under Thatcher* (1990), pp. 125–128. For charges under s. 51(3) of the Police Act 1964 arising out of the Peace Convoy, see *Smith v Reynolds* [1986] Crim LR 559, DC.

their attention. Failure to comply with a direction, or re-entry within seven days, is an offence, subject to a defence of reasonable excuse. The section does not apply to a gathering with an entertainment licence granted by the local authority, and a direction cannot be given to an 'exempt person' (i.e. the occupier of the land, any member of his family and any employee or agent of his and any person whose home is situated on the land) (s. 63). A superintendent can authorise a constable to enter the land, and there is similar power to seize vehicles and sound equipment to that conferred by s. 62 (s. 64). Section 65 enables a constable to stop persons from proceeding to a rave in respect of which a direction is in force; this power may only be exercised within five miles of the boundary of the site of the gathering, and no direction may be given to an 'exempt person'. A person who, knowing that a constable has given him a direction, fails to comply, commits an offence. Section 66 enables the court to order forfeiture of sound equipment used at a rave following a conviction under s. 63. According to Earl Ferrers, speaking for the government in the House of Lords (554 HL Deb, 25 April 1994, col 384),

'unlicensed night time parties . . . have caused appalling misery to local residents where the peaceful lives of rural societies have suddenly been ripped apart by the all-pervasive sound of what is sometimes delicately described as "music", the noise of which travels for miles, affecting everyone in its path—both man and beast—and from which it is impossible to escape. It can be a modern-day torture for the unwilling and the unwitting.'

(b) THE CONDUCT OF PROCESSIONS AND ASSEMBLIES

(i) Introduction

There are many criminal offences which may be committed by those who take part in or disrupt meetings, processions and other activities. Some have already been mentioned, including the Police Act 1964, s. 51 (above p. 53) and the Highways Act 1980, s. 137 (above p. 185). The Criminal Damage Act 1971 makes it an offence to destroy or damage property belonging to another without lawful excuse (section 1(1); it is no defence that the defendant believes that he has the consent of God (to writing a Biblical quotation on a concrete pillar at the perimeter of the Houses of Parliament in protest at the Gulf War): *Blake v DPP* [1993] Crim LR 586). It is also an offence for a person to have with him in any public place an offensive weapon without lawful authority or reasonable excuse (Prevention of Crime Act 1953, s. 1). The Criminal Law Act 1977 made it an offence for any person other than the displaced residential occupier or a protected intending occupier to use or threaten violence to secure entry to premises (s. 6, as amended by the Criminal Justice and Public Order Act 1994, s. 72); to occupy premises as a trespasser and fail to leave on being required to do so by a displaced residential occupier or a protected intending occupier (s. 7, as substituted by the 1994 Act, s. 73); to trespass with a weapon of offence (s. 8); to trespass upon consular or diplomatic premises (s. 9); and to obstruct court officers executing process for possession against unauthorised occupiers (s. 10). A local authority may direct unauthorised campers (i.e. persons residing in a vehicle or vehicles) to leave land, and seek an order from a magistrates' court for the removal of persons and their vehicles unlawfully on land in contravention of a direction (Criminal Justice and Public Order Act 1994, ss. 77–79). We deal here with arrest for breach of the peace; the main offences under the Public Order Act 1986; and the disruption of lawful meetings and other activities.

(ii) Powers to Deal with Breaches of the Peace

R v Howell (Erroll) [1982] QB 416, [1981] 3 All ER 383, Court of Appeal (Criminal Division)

H and others had been making a disturbance at a street party. After complaints by neighbours the police arrived and told them to leave or be arrested for breach of the peace. They slowly moved off, stopping in their tracks to swear at the constables. PC Hammersley said to H 'if you swear once more you will be arrested for disturbing public order'. H said that his language was not disturbing public order, to which PC Hammersley replied 'At 4 am in the morning, and in the middle of the street, it is.' H continued to swear, whereupon the constable took hold of him in order to arrest him. In response H struck the constable in the face. H was convicted of assault occasioning actual bodily harm. He appealed to the Court of Appeal (Criminal Division) contending (inter alia) that the arrest was unlawful. Two issues were: (1) was there a power of arrest in relation to an anticipated breach of the peace?; and (2) what was the correct definition of 'breach of the peace'? On issue (1) a recorder had held in *R v Podger* [1979] Crim LR 524 that the power to arrest for breach of the peace at common law was confined to cases in which a breach was committed in the presence of the arrestor or where one had been committed and its renewal was threatened.

[The judgment of the court (**Watkins LJ, Cantley** and **Hollings JJ**) was given by **Watkins LJ**:] We entertain no doubt that a constable has a power of arrest where there is reasonable apprehension of imminent danger of a breach of the peace, so for that matter has the ordinary citizen. *R v Podger* [1979] Crim LR 524 was in our opinion wrongly decided. We hold that there is power of arrest for breach of the peace where: (1) a breach of the peace is committed in the presence of the person making the arrest or (2) the arrestor reasonably believes that such a breach will be committed in the immediate future by the person arrested although he has not yet committed any breach or (3) where a breach has been committed and it is reasonably believed that a renewal of it is threatened.

The public expects a police officer not only to apprehend the criminal but to do his best to prevent the commission of crime, to keep the peace, in other words. To deny him, therefore, the right to arrest a person who he reasonably believes is about to breach the peace would be to disable him from preventing that which might cause serious injury to someone or even to many people or to property. The common law, we believe, whilst recognising that a wrongful arrest is a serious invasion of a person's liberty, provides the police with this power in the public interest.

In those instances of the exercise of this power which depend upon a belief that a breach of the peace is imminent it must, we think we should emphasise, be established that it is not only an honest albeit mistaken belief but a belief which is founded on reasonable grounds.

A comprehensive definition of the term 'breach of the peace' has very rarely been formulated so far as, with considerable help from counsel, we have been able to discover from cases which go as far back as the 18th century. The older cases are of considerable interest but they are not a sure guide to what the term is understood to mean today, since keeping the peace in this country in the latter half of the 20th century presents formidable problems which bear upon the evolving process of the development of this branch of the common law. Nevertheless, even in these days when affrays, riotous behaviour and other disturbances happen all too frequently, we cannot accept that there can be a breach of the peace unless there has been an act done or threatened to be done which either actually harms a person, or in his presence his property, or is likely to cause such harm, or which puts someone in fear of such harm being done. There is nothing more likely to arouse resentment and anger in him, and a desire to take instant revenge, than attacks or threatened attacks upon a person's body or property.

In *Halsbury's Laws of England*, 4th edn, vol. 11 (1976), para. 108, it is stated:

'for the purpose of the common law powers of arrest without warrant, a breach of the peace arises where there is an actual assault, or where a public alarm and excitement are caused by a person's wrongful act. Mere annoyance and disturbance or insult to a person or abusive language, or great heat and fury without personal violence, are not generally sufficient.'

That is an amalgam of opinions expressed in various old cases which is principally criticised by Mr. Engels for its failure to attach the actual commission of violence to all acts which are said to be capable of causing a breach of the peace.

He makes a similar criticism of the crisp definition provided by the Attorney-General, Sir Reginald Manningham-Buller, referred to in *Gelberg v Miller* [1961] 1 WLR 153 with reference to the word 'disturbance'. Lord Parker CJ said, at p. 158:

'The Attorney-General, to whom the court is grateful for his assistance, has appeared and has told the court that he feels unable to contend that a constable is entitled to arrest somebody for obstructing him in the course of his duty which, of course, is a misdemeanour under the Prevention of Crimes Amendment Act 1885, unless the circumstances show that a breach of the peace or an apprehended breach of the peace is involved, meaning by that some affray or violence or possibly disturbance.'

The statement in *Halsbury* is in parts, we think, inaccurate because of its failure to relate all the kinds of behaviour there mentioned to violence. Furthermore, we think, the word 'disturbance' when used in isolation cannot constitute a breach of the peace.

We are emboldened to say that there is a breach of the peace whenever harm is actually done or is likely to be done to a person or in his presence to his property or a person is in fear of being so harmed through an assault, an affray, a riot, unlawful assembly or other disturbance. It is for this breach of the peace when done in his presence or the reasonable apprehension of it taking place that a constable, or anyone else, may arrest an offender without warrant. . . .

The recorder directed the jury that in order for there to have been a lawful arrest it had to be proved that P.C. Hammersley was a witness to the shouting and swearing of the defendant and had, therefore, reasonable grounds for believing, and did believe, that the defendant's conduct, either alone or as part of a general shouting and swearing, was likely to lead to the use of violence by the defendant or somebody else in the officer's presence. . . . In our view it was a clear, correct and, in the circumstances of the case, wholly appropriate direction according to law.

Appeal dismissed.

NOTES

1. See Glanville Williams, 'Dealing with Breaches of the Peace' (1982) 146 JPN 199–200, 217–219. Williams notes (inter alia) that there may have been 'faulty draftsmanship' in the omission of the requirement of 'immediacy' from head (3) by comparison with head (2): the distinction (if intended) 'seems pointless'. He suggests moreover that it 'would have been better to define a breach as an actual breach, while asserting the power to arrest and to bind over for an apprehended breach' (ibid, p. 200). The latter approach was adopted by the Court of Appeal in *Lewis v Chief Constable of Greater Manchester* (1991) The Independent, 23 October. Farquharson LJ referred to passages in *Howell* (p. 427)

'which appear to say that an act constituting a threat of violence or which puts somebody in fear of violence is itself a breach of the peace with the definition of that offence. The act which puts someone in fear of violence taking place entitles a police officer or a member of the public to detain the actor but it is not itself a breach of the peace, for the violence has not yet occurred.'

This case confirms that loud noises and disturbance (here, loud music and screaming) do not of themselves constitute a breach of the peace, the court upholding an award of £2,500 for wrongful arrest and substituting an award of £5,000 (for £17,500) for false imprisonment, in respect of L's arrest in these circumstances. The jury rejected the police claim that they honestly believed on reasonable grounds that a breach of the peace (in the narrower *Howell* sense) was imminent.

2. A further point made in *R v Howell* ([1982] QB 416 at 427–428, CA (CrD)) was that a person making an arrest when he reasonably believes a breach of the peace is about to be committed complies with the requirements of *Christie v Leachinsky* [1947] AC 573, HL (see above, p. 109) if he says merely 'I am arresting you for a breach of the peace.' Moreover, the court (at pp. 423–424), expressed the 'tentative view' that this would also suffice for an arrest under section 5 of the Public Order Act 1936 (see now section 4 of the 1986 Act).

3. *R v Howell* brings some clarification to an area of the law that previously was in doubt: see Glanville Williams, [1954] Crim LR 572; L. H. Leigh, *Police Powers in*

England and Wales (2nd edn, 1985) pp. 185–190. Nevertheless, many 'question marks' remain (Williams, (1982) 146 JPN 199).

4. In *Albert v Lavin* [1982] AC 546, A, in an attempt to board a bus, pushed past a number of people standing in a bus queue. Several objected, and L, a police constable in plain clothes, reasonably apprehended that there would be a breach of the peace. He prevented A from boarding the bus, and, after a struggle, pulled him away from the queue. He told A he was a police officer and that, if he did not stop struggling, he would arrest him. A (as the magistrates found) honestly, but unreasonably, dis-believed him and hit him five or six times. He was convicted of assaulting a police officer in the execution of his duty. The Divisional Court dealt with the case on the basis that the issue was whether an honest but unreasonable mistake was sufficient to ground a defence of self-defence: the court held that only a reasonable mistake would suffice.

The House of Lords held that this issue did not arise: per Lord Diplock at p. 565:

'every citizen in whose presence a breach of the peace is being, or reasonably appears to be about to be, committed has the right to take reasonable steps to make the person who is breaking or threatening to break the peace refrain from doing so; and those reasonable steps in appropriate cases will include detaining him against his will. At common law this is not only the right of every citizen, it is also his duty, although, except in the case of a citizen who is a constable, it is a duty of imperfect obligation.'

Accordingly L's status as a constable was irrelevant, and A's mistake on the point was consequently also irrelevant. Note that the case also makes it clear that the steps that may be taken include detention 'without arrest' (see Lord Diplock at p. 564 D–F). Glanville Williams (1982) 146 JPN 217 argues that Lord Diplock's statement is narrower than *R v Howell* in that it 'does not cover past breaches of the peace, but only those presently continuing or those feared for the future'. There is some authority to support a power of arrest *immediately* after a breach of the peace even if renewal is not apprehended, see Glanville Williams [1954] Crim LR 578 at 586–587. On the other hand there are many statements to the effect that there is no such power where a breach of the peace has occurred but it is over and there is no ground for believing that it will be renewed (see Williams, ibid). The latter view was taken in the Commentary on *R v Podger* [1979] Crim LR 524, and the Commentary was endorsed in *R v Howell* [1982] QB 416, 426, CA (Cr D), although it should be noted that this point did not arise for consideration and that the formulation 'is committed' in *Howell* (above, p. 207) might be regarded as extending to cover an immediate arrest for a concluded breach committed in the arrestor's presence.

5. There were some observations in the Court of Appeal's decision in *R v Chief Constable of the Devon and Cornwall Constabulary, ex p Central Electricity Generating Board* [1982] QB 458, CA,[1] which are difficult to reconcile with *R v Howell*. (*Howell* was cited to the court but not referred to in the judgments.) A group of protesters occupied private land in order to prevent CEGB employees from carrying out a survey to assess its suitability for a nuclear power station. The protest was intended to be peaceful and non-violent. Obstruction constituted a criminal offence but the offence did not carry a power of arrest. The CEGB sought the Chief Constable's assistance, but this was refused on the ground that there was (1) no statutory power of arrest, and (2) no common law power of arrest since there had been no breach of the peace, nor was any anticipated, nor was there any unlawful assembly to disperse. The CEGB sought mandamus requiring the Chief Constable to assist in the removal

---

1 See G. S. Morris, (1982) 45 MLR 454; A. T. H. Smith, [1982] PL 212; Glanville Williams (1982) 146 JPN 217 at 218–219.

of the protesters. The Court of Appeal refused the application on the ground that it was for the police at the site and not the court (or, as Lawton LJ emphasised at p. 835, the Chief Constable in advance) to decide whether to intervene. The court also discussed the ambit of the powers of the police. A number of possible justifications for their intervention were suggested:

(1) To assist the CEGB in exercising its right of self-help (Templeman LJ at p. 838).

(2) To deal with an actual breach of the peace. Lord Denning MR said (at p. 832):

'There is a breach of the peace whenever a person who is lawfully carrying out his work is unlawfully and physically prevented by another from doing it. . . . If anyone unlawfully and physically obstructs the worker, by lying down or chaining himself to a rig or the like, he is guilty of a breach of the peace.'

Lawton LJ took a narrower view, holding (at p. 837):

'If those obstructing do allow themselves to be removed without struggling or causing uproar (which to me seems unlikely, but I may be wrong) the police will have no reason for taking action, nor should they.'

Templeman LJ appeared to link the concept of 'breach of the peace' to that of 'violence' (p. 839, d, g). (This view was endorsed in *Percy v DPP* (below, p. 257.))

(3) To prevent a reasonably apprehended breach of the peace. Lord Denning MR (at pp. 832–833) thought that the use of force to remove even 'passive resisters' would itself constitute a breach of the peace, even where that was justified as being done in the exercise of self-help: 'in deciding whether there is a breach of the peace or the apprehension of it, the law does not go into the rights or wrongs of the matter.' Lawton LJ's view was that there would have to be a reasonable apprehension of 'struggling and uproar' (p. 834) and that 'when the manhandling starts, particularly if a man has to lay hands on a woman, struggling and uproar are likely to begin'. However, as noted above, his Lordship accepted that purely passive resistance would not constitute a breach of the peace. Templeman LJ was wholly unconvinced on the facts that resistance would stay passive (p. 839):

'An obstructor who will not leave the site unless he is forcibly removed presents a threat and danger of a breach of the peace even if he disclaims any intention of causing a breach of the peace. . . . Even Mahatma Gandhi discovered to his sorrow that in the conduct of ordinary mortals passive resistance only remains passive so long as the resistance is successful.'

(4) To prevent an unlawful assembly (i.e. the common law offence repealed by the Public Order Act 1986).

(5) (*Per* Lord Denning MR): To prevent the crime of obstruction:

'It is within the authority of the police to intervene to prevent any criminal offence being committed in their presence, even though it is only a summary offence, where the offender fails or refuses or avoids giving his name and address. Even though the statute does not give a power of arrest, the law says that a police officer can do whatever is necessary by way of restraint to prevent a criminal offence being committed or continued' (p. 833).

(This presumably rests on s. 3 of the Criminal Law Act 1967 (above, p. 74) although that makes no reference to name and address.)

Accordingly, the police had ample powers to intervene.

6. In *Kelly v Chief Constable of Hampshire* (1993) Independent, 25 March, the Court of Appeal upheld the dismissal of K's claim in damages in respect of his arrest to prevent a breach of the peace. PC Cutts came upon the scene of a heated altercation between K, a hunt saboteur, and a huntsman on horseback. K was holding the horse's reins. C arrested K 'within seconds' for conduct likely to cause a breach of the peace. Lloyd LJ stated that:

'If, on the information known to [the constable], he has reasonable cause to believe that a breach of the peace is about to occur, he is entitled to arrest one or more of the participants in order to prevent that occurrence.'

Here, C had the necessary 'reasonable cause'. The fact that, immediately prior to this incident and before C arrived, the huntsman had assaulted K with his whip (for which, indeed, K had been awarded £25 damages) was irrelevant; the answer to the question whether there was reasonable cause to believe that a breach of the peace was about to occur

'does not depend on who started the altercation or who was responsible for the apprehended violence. Where violence is imminent, the police officer does not have time to hold an inquiry or conduct an investigation. As Lord Denning said in [the *CEGB* case, above], the law does not require the constable to go into the right and wrongs of the matter at that stage. The officer has to act promptly as seems best to him in all the circumstances. The rights and wrongs as between the parties come later.'

(Lloyd LJ also stated, obiter, that if the constable *had* seen the whipping incident, that would not have been relevant. Can that be right? It would involve in effect arresting the *victim* of an assault to prevent a fight.)

The Court of Appeal also upheld the trial judge's view that K's subsequent detention was lawful. After 20 minutes, he was taken to a police station, where he was kept for a further two hours or so. The judge rejected K's argument that after 20 minutes the situation was calmer and he should have been released then. He admitted in cross-examination that if he had not been arrested he would have stayed with the hunt for the rest of the day with the possibility of a further confrontation between himself and the huntsmen. Accordingly, PC Cutts (per Lloyd LJ)

'was clearly justified in forming the view which he did, that the best way to secure the situation and to prevent a further breach of the peace was to continue the plaintiff's detention'.

7. At common law, a breach of the peace can occur on private premises. This had been assumed in statements in *Wilson v Skcock* (1949) 113 JP 294, 296; *Robson v Hallett* [1967] 2 QB 939, 953, 954–955 and *R v Chief Constable of Devon and Cornwall, ex p Central Electricity Generating Board* [1982] QB 458, 471, 479, but the point was only taken in *McConnell v Chief Constable of the Greater Manchester Police* [1990] 1 All ER 423, CA. The manager of a carpet store asked McC to leave, but he refused. PC Smith took McC outside, and, when he attempted to re-enter, arrested him on the ground that he was guilty of conduct whereby a breach of the peace might be occasioned, or, if he allowed him to re-enter, such a breach might take place. McC was taken before the magistrates to be bound over, but the magistrates declined to make a binding-over order. McC sued the police for false imprisonment claiming that the arrest was unlawful. His argument that a breach of the peace could not take place on private premises, such as a carpet store, was taken as a preliminary point, but ultimately rejected. The Court of Appeal also rejected the alternative contention that for there to be a breach of the peace on private premises, it is necessary for there to be some disturbance which would affect members of the public, or at least one other person, outside the premises themselves. Glidewell LJ pointed out (p. 429) that this would lead to an unsatisfactory distinction between the case of an abusive altercation arising between two people in an isolated house and a similar altercation between the same two people in a terraced house with thin walls and neighbours who could hear everything that was going on. The possible effect on the public would therefore only be relevant to the factual question whether the constable reasonably apprehended that a breach of the peace might occur.

8. In *McBean v Parker* (1983) 147 JP 205, DC, the Divisional Court held that 'harm' for the purpose of the definition of 'breach of the peace' in *R v Howell* 'must be unlawful harm' (p. 208) and not, as on the facts of the present case, the use of reasonable force to resist an unlawful police search. What would the position be where the force used was excessive? (Cf. Commentary [1983] Crim LR at 401.)

9. In civil proceedings arising out of an arrest for breach of the peace, it is for the judge to decide whether there was the necessary reasonable cause and for the jury to decide any disputed issues of fact relevant to the judge's decision: *Kelly v Chief Constable of Hampshire*, above, n. **6**, applying *Dallison v Caffery* [1965] 1 QB 348 at 371, per Diplock LJ (an authority on arrest for felony at common law). Diplock LJ's reasoning was of general application.

10. Note that the power to arrest for breaches of the peace was not removed by the Police and Criminal Evidence Act 1984: s. 26 (above, p. 105) repealed only statutory powers. Although mere shouting and swearing will not alone constitute a breach of the peace, it is an offence under s. 28 of the Town Police Clauses Act 1847 and may lead to an arrest under s. 25 of PACE (general arrest conditions: above, p. 105): see *Smith*, p. 182 n. 74. If it causes harassment, alarm or distress it may constitute an offence under s. 5 of the Public Order Act 1986: below, p. 213. (Cf. the facts of *G v Chief Superintendent of Police, Stroud* (1986) 86 Cr App Rep 92, DC, decided before the 1986 Act came into force.)

11. A person may be bound over by magistrates to keep the peace (see below, p. 256). On powers of entry to preserve the peace see below, pp. 259–264). Compare the power to arrest to prevent a breach of the peace with (1) the use of reasonable force in the prevention of crime (above, pp. 74–75); and (2) the power to take other (? necessary) steps to preserve the peace (below, pp. 239–256).

(iii) Part I of the Public Order Act 1986

Public Order Act 1986

PART I

NEW OFFENCES

1. Riot

(1) Where 12 or more persons who are present together use or threaten unlawful violence for a common purpose and the conduct of them (taken together) is such as would cause a person of reasonable firmness present at the scene to fear for his personal safety, each of the persons using unlawful violence for the common purpose is guilty of riot.

(2) It is immaterial whether or not the 12 or more use or threaten unlawful violence simultaneously.

(3) The common purpose may be inferred from conduct.

(4) No person of reasonable firmness need actually be, or be likely to be, present at the scene.

(5) Riot may be committed in private as well as in public places.

(6) A person guilty of riot is liable on conviction on indictment to imprisonment for a term not exceeding ten years or a fine or both.

2. Violent disorder

(1) Where 3 or more persons who are present together use or threaten unlawful violence and the conduct of them (taken together) is such as would cause a person of reasonable firmness present at the scene to fear for his personal safety, each of the persons using or threatening unlawful violence is guilty of violent disorder.

(2) It is immaterial whether or not the 3 or more use or threaten unlawful violence simultaneously.

(3) No person of reasonable firmness need actually be, or be likely to be, present at the scene.

(4) Violent disorder may be committed in private as well as in public places.

(5) A person guilty of violent disorder is liable on conviction on indictment to imprisonment for a term not exceeding 5 years or a fine or both, or on summary conviction to imprisonment for a term not exceeding 6 months or a fine not exceeding the statutory maximum or both.

3. Affray

(1) A person is guilty of affray if he uses or threatens unlawful violence towards another and his conduct is such as would cause a person of reasonable firmness present at the scene to fear for his personal safety.

(2) Where 2 or more persons use or threaten the unlawful violence, it is the conduct of them taken together that must be considered for the purposes of subsection (1).

(3) For the purposes of this section a threat cannot be made by the use of words alone.

(4) No person of reasonable firmness need actually be, or be likely to be, present at the scene.

(5) Affray may be committed in private as well as in public places.

(6) A constable may arrest without warrant anyone he reasonably suspects is committing affray.

(7) A person guilty of affray is liable on conviction on indictment to imprisonment for a term not exceeding 3 years or a fine or both, or on summary conviction to imprisonment for a term not exceeding 6 months or a fine not exceeding the statutory maximum or both.

4. Fear or provocation of violence

(1) A person is guilty of an offence if he—
  (a) uses towards another person threatening, abusive or insulting words or behaviour, or
  (b) distributes or displays to another person any writing, sign or other visible representation which is threatening, abusive or insulting,
with intent to cause that person to believe that immediate unlawful violence will be used against him or another by any person, or to provoke the immediate use of unlawful violence by that person or another, or whereby that person is likely to believe that such violence will be used or it is likely that such violence will be provoked.

(2) An offence under this section may be committed in a public or a private place, except that no offence is committed where the words or behaviour are used, or the writing, sign or other visible representation is distributed or displayed, by a person inside a dwelling and the other person is also inside that or another dwelling.

(3) A constable may arrest without warrant anyone he reasonably suspects is committing an offence under this section.

(4) A person guilty of an offence under this section is liable on summary conviction to imprisonment for a term not exceeding 6 months or a fine not exceeding level 5 on the standard scale or both.

[4A. Intentional harassment, alarm or distress

(1) A person is guilty of an offence if, with intent to cause a person harassment, alarm or distress, he—
  (a) uses threatening, abusive or insulting words or behaviour, or disorderly behaviour, or
  (b) displays any writing, sign or other visible representation which is threatening, abusive or insulting,
thereby causing that or another person harassment, alarm or distress.

(2) An offence under this section may be committed in a public or a private place, except that no offence is committed where the words or behaviour are used, or the writing, sign or other visible representation is displayed, by a person inside a dwelling and the person who is harassed, alarmed or distressed is also inside that or another dwelling.

(3) It is a defence for the accused to prove—
  (a) that he was inside a dwelling and had no reason to believe that the words or behaviour used, or the writing, sign or other visible representation displayed, would be heard or seen by a person outside that or any other dwelling, or
  (b) that his conduct was reasonable.

(4) A constable may arrest without warrant anyone he reasonably suspects is committing an offence under this section.

(5) A person guilty of an offence under this section is liable on summary conviction to imprisonment for a term not exceeding 6 months or a fine not exceeding level 5 on the standard scale or both.][1]

5. Harassment, alarm or distress

(1) A person is guilty of an offence if he—
  (a) uses threatening, abusive or insulting words or behaviour, or disorderly behaviour, or
  (b) displays any writing, sign or other visible representation which is threatening, abusive or insulting,
within the hearing or sight of a person likely to be caused harassment, alarm or distress thereby.

---

1 Inserted by the Criminal Justice and Public Order Act 1994, s. 154.

(2) An offence under this section may be committed in a public or a private place, except that no offence is committed where the words or behaviour are used, or the writing, sign or other visible representation is displayed, by a person inside a dwelling and the other person is also inside that or another dwelling.

(3) It is a defence for the accused to prove—

(a) that he had no reason to believe that there was any person within hearing or sight who was likely to be caused harassment, alarm or distress, or

(b) that he was inside a dwelling and had no reason to believe that the words or behaviour used, or the writing, sign or other visible representation displayed, would be heard or seen by a person outside that or any other dwelling, or

(c) that his conduct was reasonable.

(4) A constable may arrest a person without warrant if—

(a) he engages in offensive conduct which the constable warns him to stop, and

(b) he engages in further offensive conduct immediately or shortly after the warning.

(5) In subsection (4) 'offensive conduct' means conduct the constable reasonably suspects to constitute an offence under this section, and the conduct mentioned in paragraph (a) and the further conduct need not be of the same nature.

(6) A person guilty of an offence under this section is liable on summary conviction to a fine not exceeding level 3 on the standard scale.

6. Mental element: miscellaneous

(1) A person is guilty of riot only if he intends to use violence or is aware that his conduct may be violent.

(2) A person is guilty of violent disorder or affray only if he intends to use or threaten violence or is aware that his conduct may be violent or threaten violence.

(3) A person is guilty of an offence under section 4 only if he intends his words or behaviour, or the writing, sign or other visible representation, to be threatening, abusive or insulting, or is aware that it may be threatening, abusive or insulting.

(4) A person is guilty of an offence under section 5 only if he intends his words or behaviour, or the writing, sign or other visible representation, to be threatening, abusive or insulting, or is aware that it may be threatening, abusive or insulting or (as the case may be) he intends his behaviour to be or is aware that it may be disorderly.

(5) For the purposes of this section a person whose awareness if impaired by intoxication shall be taken to be aware of that of which he would be aware if not intoxicated, unless he shows either that his intoxication was not self-induced or that it was caused solely by the taking or administration of a substance in the course of medical treatment.

(6) In subsection (5) 'intoxication' means any intoxication, whether caused by drink, drugs or other means, or by a combination of means.

(7) Subsections (1) and (2) do not affect the determination for the purposes of riot or violent disorder of the number of persons who use or threaten violence.

7. Procedure: miscellaneous

(1) No prosecution for an offence of riot or incitement to riot may be instituted except by or with the consent of the Director of Public Prosecutions.

(2) For the purposes of the rule against charging more than one offence in the same count or information, each of sections 1 to 5 creates one offence.

(3) If on the trial on indictment of a person charged with violent disorder or affray the jury find him not guilty of the offence charged, they may (without prejudice to section 6(3) of the Criminal Law Act 1967) find him guilty of an offence under section 4.

(4) The Crown Court has the same powers and duties in relation to a person who is by virtue of subsection (3) convicted before it of an offence under section 4 as a magistrates' court would have on convicting him of the offence.

8. Interpretation

In this Part—

'dwelling' means any structure or part of a structure occupied as a person's home or as other living accommodation (whether the occupation is separate or shared with others) but does not include any part not so occupied, and for this purpose 'structure' includes a tent, caravan, vehicle, vessel or other temporary or movable structure;

'violence' means any violent conduct, so that—

(a) except in the context of affray, it includes violent conduct towards property as well as violent conduct towards persons, and

(b) it is not restricted to conduct causing or intended to cause injury or damage but includes any other violent conduct (for example, throwing at or towards a person a missile of a kind capable of causing injury which does not hit or falls short).

9. Offences abolished

(1) The common law offences of riot, rout, unlawful assembly and affray are abolished.

(2) The offences under the following enactments are abolished—

(a) section 1 of the Tumultuous Petitioning Act 1661 (presentation of petition to monarch or Parliament accompanied by excessive number of persons),

(b) section 1 of the Shipping Offences Act 1793 (interference with operation of vessel by persons riotously assembled),

(c) section 23 of the Seditious Meetings Act 1817 (prohibition of certain meetings within one mile of Westminster Hall when Parliament sitting), and

(d) section 5 of the Public Order Act 1936 (conduct conducive to breach of the peace).

10. Construction of other instruments

(1) In the Riot (Damages) Act 1886 and in section 515 of the Merchant Shipping Act 1894 (compensation for riot damage) 'riotous' and 'riotously' shall be construed in accordance with section 1 above.

(2) In Schedule 1 to the Marine Insurance Act 1906 (form and rules for the construction of certain insurance policies) 'rioters' in rule 8 and 'riot' in rule 10 shall, in the application of the rules to any policy taking effect on or after the coming into force of this section, be construed in accordance with section 1 above unless a different intention appears.

(3) 'Riot' and cognate expressions in any enactment in force before the coming into force of this section (other than the enactments mentioned in subsections (1) and (2) above) shall be construed in accordance with section 1 above if they would have been construed in accordance with the common law offence of riot apart from this Part.

(4) Subject to subsections (1) to (3) above and unless a different intention appears, nothing in this Part affects the meaning of 'riot' or any cognate expression in any enactment in force, or other instrument taking effect, before the coming into force of this section.

NOTES

1. Part I of the 1986 Act replaces the common law offences of riot, rout, unlawful assembly and affray and (inter alia) the statutory offence under section 5 of the Public Order Act 1936 (the use of threatening, abusive or insulting words or behaviour with intent to provoke a breach of the peace or whereby a breach of the peace is likely to be occasioned). It is based on the recommendations of the Law Commission (Law Com. No. 123), with some modifications. See generally on Part I, A. T. H. Smith, [1987] Crim LR 156; E. Rees, *Legal Action*, December 1989, p. 17.

Riot

2. At common law, there were five necessary elements: (1) three or more persons; (2) a common purpose; (3) execution or inception of the common purpose; (4) an intent to help one another by force if necessary against any person who might oppose them in the execution of their common purpose; and (5) force or violence displayed in such a manner as to alarm at least one person of reasonable firmness and courage (*Field v Metropolitan Police Receiver* [1907] 2 KB 853). The statutory offence is similar, but with a requirement of 12 or more persons rather than three. By contrast with the offence of violent disorder (below), the riot offence applies only to those who *use* violence. It is the most serious of the public order offences, being triable only on indictment. The consent of the DPP is required; that may be expressed by any Crown Prosecutor (Prosecution of Offences Act 1985, s. 1(6)).

The Law Commission regarded riot charges as appropriate where there is evidence of prolonged, active and direct participation in the organisation of a major public disturbance (Law Com. No. 123, paras. 6.7 to 6.10). 'In many respects, riot is simply an aggravated form of violent disorder' (*Smith*, p. 78). The distinguishing features are (1) its scale, with the involvement of 12 or more; (2) the requirement of common purpose; and (3) the requirement that the defendant be shown to have *used* unlawful violence (*White Paper*, p. 17). A defendant who does not *use* unlawful violence may, nevertheless, be convicted of riot as an aider and abettor if he encourages the use of violence by others: *R v Jefferson* [1994] 1 All ER 270, CA (Cr D), where the court confirmed that s. 8 of the Accessories and Abettors Act 1861 was potentially applicable to each of the offences in ss. 1–5 of the 1986 Act.

The principles set out in *Mahroof* (below, p. 217 n. **7**) in respect of the number of persons involved in a disturbance in relation to charges of violent disorder presumably would apply, mutatis mutandis, to riot. The requirement of 'common purpose' may be very general, for example 'celebrating the victory of England over Egypt in their World Cup match' (*Jefferson*, above), and 'demonstrating against the poll tax' (*R v Tyler* (1993) 96 Cr App Rep 332, CA (Cr D)).

3. In practice the authorities have found difficulty in securing convictions for riot following outbreaks of serious disorder. For example, in the riots in the St. Paul's district of Bristol in 1980, 134 arrests were made. The DPP decided that 16 should be charged with the common law offence of riotous assembly. (See M. Kettle and L. Hodges, *Uprising!* (1982) pp. 34–38.) The trial lasted over 7 weeks. The judge directed the acquittal of 3 defendants for lack of evidence, the jury acquitted 5 and failed to agree a verdict on the rest: 'the trial collapsed, having cost around £500,000 (the same as the cost of the riot damage). The result was seen as a resounding victory for black people and the rioters, and led the DPP . . . to comment that it may have been a mistake to bring riot charges.' It appeared that a number of the jurors were not convinced that a common purpose of 'a show of strength against the police' was sufficient to constitute a riot, even though the judge had directed that it could be (Kettle and Hodges, op. cit. p. 38). Similarly, all the charges of riotous assembly (and most of those of unlawful assembly) brought in consequence of violence during the 1984–85 miners' strike failed (see S. McCabe and P. Wallington, *The Police, Public Order and Civil Liberties* (1988), pp. 99–100; S. Kavanagh and R. Malcolm, *Legal Action*, September 1985, p. 6). The Attorney General commented that 'the law of riot creates some grave evidential problems' (63 HC Deb, 9 July 1984, col 691). These problems appear to remain under the 1986 Act. The number found guilty or cautioned each year has remained small (e.g. 3 in 1990, 31 in 1992 and 18 in 1993: *Criminal Statistics: England and Wales 1993* (Cm 2680, 1994), p. 119.

4. Most of the recent reported cases on riot have concerned claims under the Riot (Damages) Act 1886 (see A. Samuels, [1970] Crim LR 336). That Act was passed to remedy defects in the previous legislation (1827, 7 & 8 Geo IV c 31) under which compensation was paid by the hundred only in cases of the felonious destruction of certain specified kinds of property by persons riotously and tumultuously assembled. Pressure from people whose property was damaged in the Trafalgar Square riots of 8 February 1886, and who had no claim under the previous legislation, led to special provision being made for them by the Metropolitan Police (Compensation) Act 1886. The general legislation followed shortly afterwards. Claims are met by the police authority, or, in the Metropolitan Police District, by the Receiver (1886 Act ss. 3, 9 and see S.R & O. 1921 No. 1536).

Other cases under this Act include *Gunter v Metropolitan Police District Receiver* (1888) 53 JP 249, Mathews J; *Rance v Hastings Corpn* (1913) 136 LT Jo 117,

Hastings Cty Ct, (attack on a hotel where three ladies, wrongly thought by the mob to be militant suffragettes, had taken refuge: claim successful); *Ford v Metropolitan Police District Receiver* [1921] 2 KB 344, Bailhache J (a 'good humoured' crowd, some armed with crowbars and pickaxes, took woodwork and floorboards from an empty house as fuel for a 'peace night' bonfire; a neighbour gave evidence that he was afraid: claim successful); *Munday v Metropolitan Police District Receiver* [1949] 1 All ER 337, Pritchard J (crowd unable to get into Chelsea F.C.'s ground to see a match against Moscow Dynamo broke into neighbouring premises in order to watch from there, the owner's daughter was held against a wall, and gave evidence that she was afraid: claim successful). In order to establish a claim, the conduct must be 'tumultuous' as well as 'riotous' (*J W Dyer Ltd v Metropolitan Police District Receiver* [1967] 2 QB 970, Lyell J). This was endorsed by the Court of Appeal in *D H Edmonds Ltd v East Sussex Police Authority* (1988) Times, 15 July, when holding that the three or four robbers who had committed a smash and grab raid at the plaintiff's jewellery shop were assembled 'riotously' but not 'tumultuously'. To be 'tumultuous' an assembly should be of considerable size, excited and emotionally aroused and, generally although not necessarily, accompanied by noise.

'Riot' and 'riotously' in the 1886 Act are to be interpreted in accordance with s. 1: 1986 Act, s. 10(1).

Violent disorder

5. The violent disorder offence replaced the common law offence of unlawful assembly. This offence required (1) an assembly of three or more persons; (2) a common purpose (a) to commit a crime of violence or (b) to achieve some other object, whether lawful or not, in such a way as to cause reasonable men to apprehend a breach of the peace; and (3) an intention to use or abet the use of violence, or to do or abet acts which D knows to be likely to cause a breach of the peace (*Smith and Hogan*, (7th edn, 1992), p. 755). There was, however, some uncertainty as to its exact scope. It was used as a charge following serious outbreaks of disorder such as Chartist disturbances in Newport (*R v Vincent* (1839) 9 C & P 91); the Trafalgar Square riots on 'Bloody Sunday', 13 November 1887 (see *R v Cunninghame Graham and Burns* (1888) 16 Cox CC 420; V. Bailey (ed), *Policing and Punishment in Nineteenth Century Britain* (1981), Chap. 5); the disturbance at the Garden House Hotel, Cambridge (see *R v Caird*, below, p. 219); the Shrewsbury pickets case (*R v Jones* [1974] ICR 310, CA (Cr D)). *Beatty v Gillbanks* (below p. 241) was also commonly regarded as an authority on unlawful assembly.

6. The *White Paper* stated (p. 15):

'3.13. Violent disorder will be the main successor offence to unlawful assembly, and to some cases currently charged as riot. Like the Law Commission, the Government anticipates that it will be used in the future as the normal charge for serious outbreaks of public disorder. But it will be capable of being applied over a wide spectrum of situations ranging from major public disorder to minor group disturbances involving some violence.'

The offence is triable either way, but the *Practice Note* (*Offences Triable Either Way: Mode of Trial*) [1990] 3 All ER 979 states that cases of violent disorder 'should generally be committed for trial'. In practice, it has been used as a charge much more frequently than unlawful assembly: *Criminal Statistics: England and Wales: 1993* (Cm. 2680, 1994), Table 5.20: 2,652 were found guilty or cautioned in 1989 falling to 1,153 in 1993; the highest annual total for unlawful assembly in 1979–86 was 348 (in 1985).

7. The violent disorder offence requires three or more persons together using or threatening violence. In *R v Mahroof* (1988) 88 Cr App Rep 317, CA (Cr D), three defendants were charged jointly on one indictment with violent disorder, but M alone was convicted, with both his co-accused acquitted. The court held that there was a sufficient allegation made in the indictment to support M's conviction

'subject to two very important qualifications: first of all, that there is evidence before the jury that there were three people involved in the criminal behaviour, though not necessarily those named in the indictment; secondly, that the defence are apprised of what it is they have to meet' (p. 321).

On the facts there had been evidence of the involvement of others, but the defence had not been sufficiently apprised. M's conviction under s. 2 of the 1986 Act was quashed, and a conviction under s. 4 substituted (by reference to s. 7(3)). The court indicated that the best way of 'apprising' the defence was by adding the words 'and others' to the indictment, enabling the defence then to seek particulars.

Section 7(3) permits the jury to return a conviction under s. 4 where the defendant has been acquitted of a charge under s. 2: this can apply where the acquittal has been directed by the judge (*R v Carson* (1990) 92 Cr App Rep 236, CA (Cr D)) and without empanelling a jury (*R v O'Brien* (1992) 156 JP 925, CA (Cr D).

In *R v Fleming and Robinson* (1989) 153 JP 517, CA (Cr D), four persons were involved in a fight: F and R were convicted of violent disorder; one other was acquitted and the jury was unable to agree a verdict on the fourth. Applying *Mahroof*, the convictions were quashed, and convictions for affray under s. 3 substituted. Where there are three defendants under s. 2, the judge should warn the jury specifically that if any one of them should be acquitted, they must necessarily acquit the others unless satisfied that some other person not charged was taking part in the violent disorder (*R v Worton* (1989) 154 JP 201, CA (Cr D)). The defences of self defence, reasonable defence of another person and the 'taking of necessary steps to preserve the peace' may be raised: *R v Rothwell and Barton* [1993] Crim LR 662, CA (Cr D).

Affray
8. This offence is typically used in respect of fights, although cases involving very serious violence are likely to lead to charges of violent disorder or riot rather than affray. Before the 1986 Act, affray was 'by far the most important of the common law public order offences, charged against some 1,000 people per year' (*White Paper*, p. 16). It covered unlawful fighting or violence or an unlawful display of force, in such a manner that a bystander of reasonably firm character might reasonably be expected to be terrified. Statutory affray is triable either way and carries a maximum sentence (when tried on indictment) of 3 years (in comparison with life imprisonment at common law). Section 3(1) appears to contemplate both a person to whom the violence or threat is directed and a hypothetical third party of reasonable firmness. Accordingly, the offence will not cover every case of assault, as the circumstances may not be such as to cause a third party to fear for his own safety. Nevertheless, the offence may be committed in the course of domestic incidents and not just occasions of public disorder. See *R v Davison* [1992] Crim LR 31, and Commentary by Sir John Smith, and *DPP v Cotcher and Cotcher* [1993] COD 181.

On the limitation in s. 3(3) that for the purposes of affray a threat cannot be made by words alone, see *R v Dixon* [1993] Crim LR 579, CA (Cr D) (encouragement of dog to attack police officers sufficient even in the absence of evidence that the dog's subsequent attack was in response to the encouragement), and *R v Robinson* [1993] Crim LR 581, CA (Cr D) (adoption of an aggressive tone of voice insufficient), and Commentaries by Sir John Smith.

Research on the use of charges under ss. 2 and 3 of the 1986 Act (T. Newburn et al, (1990) 29 HORB 10 (see below, p. 229 n. 3) confirms that statutory affray has been 'downgraded' in comparison to common law affray. 14% of the sample studied were charged under s.3; the vast majority of incidents were generally relatively minor in character, involving little violence at most and often only the threat of violence. Section 2 (used in 6% of the cases in the sample) was employed in more serious cases, usually involving a greater number of people. Most of the incidents involved fights between groups of youths which, on occasion, resulted in quite serious injuries. A further distinction, suggested by one custody officer, was that spontaneous violence would be likely, depending on its extent, to result in s. 3 charges; anything premeditated or planned, as long as sufficient numbers were involved, would be charged under s. 2. Sections 2 or 3 would also be used as an alternative to a charge of actual or grievous bodily harm if there was doubt about the sufficiency of the evidence of these offences.

9. Section 4 of the 1986 Act was considered in *Atkin v DPP* (below, p. 221) and *R v Horseferry Road Metropolitan Stipendiary Magistrate, ex p Siadatan* (below, p. 223). Section 5 was considered in *DPP v Orum* (below, p. 226).

Section 4A, an offence of intentionally causing harassment, alarm or distress, was added by the Criminal Justice and Public Order Act 1994, s. 154. The aim was to provide higher penalties where harassment etc was deliberately inflicted, and to

'enable the courts to deal more effectively with serious racial harassment, particularly where it is persistent'.

(Earl Ferrers, 555 HL Deb, 16 June 1994, col. 1864.) The government resisted proposals for a specific offence of racial harassment, citing, inter alia, the difficulty of proving a racial motivation. See also 248 HC Deb, 20 October 1994, cols 488–503.

10. *Sentencing*
Some general considerations as regards sentencing for serious offences arising out of public protest were canvassed by Sachs LJ in *R v Caird* (1970) 54 Cr App Rep 499, CA (Cr D) (below).

R v Caird (1970) 54 Cr App Rep 499, Court of Appeal (Criminal Division)

The eight applicants were convicted of a variety of offences arising out of a disturbance at the Garden House Hotel, Cambridge. The hotel planned a dinner and dance to coincide with a 'Greek week' in Cambridge. A crowd of about 300 or 400 people assembled. The following facts were stated in the judgment. From the outset there was shouting. Soon it became clear that a large number of them had developed a common purpose of wrecking the dinner. They tried to stop people entering the hotel. One person was injured and others were frightened. A proportion of those present were determined to break through the police cordon and into the hotel. Some pounded on the windows, others climbed onto the roof. The dining room windows were broken and various missiles thrown in, including rocks, clods of earth and lighted mole fuses. Inside, tables were overturned, glass and crockery smashed, chairs brandished and thrown and curtains torn down. A constable and a proctor received serious injuries; many others received minor injuries. Many of the guests were terrified. The disturbance lasted over two and a half hours.

Fifteen defendants were tried at Hertford Assizes before Melford Stevenson J on a variety of charges. Seven were acquitted on all charges. Caird was convicted of riot, assaulting a police constable in the execution of his duty, and possessing an offensive weapon; John of riot and malicious damage; Household of unlawful assembly; Lagden of riot and malicious damage; Emley of riot and assaulting a police constable in the execution of his duty; Williams of possessing an offensive weapon; Bodea and Newton of unlawful assembly. Caird was sentenced to a total of two years' imprisonment; John and Emley to borstal training; Lagden to a total of fifteen months' imprisonment; and the others to nine months' imprisonment each. Williams and Bodea were recommended for deportation. They appealed to the Court of Appeal (Criminal Division).

Sachs LJ delivered the judgment of the court (**Sachs LJ**, **Lyell** and **Cusack JJ**): . . . That on 13 February at Cambridge there was an unlawful and riotous assembly of most serious proportions at the Garden House Hotel is something which is obvious. It has not been and could not have been disputed in this Court. . . .

Before now turning to individual sentences, it is appropriate first to mention certain general points which have been much canvassed. First, it should be observed that a plea in mitigation of 'provocation' made at one stage by Mr Myers was very properly withdrawn shortly after having been put forward. This Court could not entertain a political plea of that sort in the circumstances of this case as constituting mitigation, whatever other views it may have on it. Any suggestion that a section of the community strongly holding one set of views is justified in banding together to disrupt the lawful activities of a section that does not hold the same views so strongly or which holds different views cannot be tolerated and must unhesitatingly be rejected by the courts. When there is wanton and vicious violence of gross degree the Court is not concerned with whether it originates from gang rivalry or from political motives. It is the degree of mob violence that matters and the extent to which the public peace is being broken. It makes no difference whether the mob has attacked a first-class hotel in Cambridge or some dance hall frequented by the less well-circumstanced.

The next point to be mentioned is what might be called the 'Why pick on me?' argument. It has been suggested that there is something wrong in giving an appropriate sentence to one convicted on an offence because there are considerable numbers of others who were at the same time committing the same offence, some of whom indeed, if identified and arrested and established as having taken a more serious part, could have received heavier sentences. This is a plea which is almost invariably put forward where the offence is one of those classed as disturbances of the public peace—such as riots, unlawful assemblies and affrays. It indicates a failure to appreciate that on these confused and tumultuous occasions each individual who takes an active part by deed or encouragement is guilty of a really grave offence by being one of the number engaged in a crime against the peace. It is, moreover, impracticable for a small number of police when sought to be overpowered by a crowd to make a large number of arrests. It is indeed all the more difficult when, as in the present case, any attempt at arrest is followed by violent efforts of surrounding rioters to rescue the person being arrested. It is worse still when steps have been taken, as in the present case, to immerse the mob in darkness.

If this plea were acceded to, it would reinforce that feeling which may undoubtedly exist that if an offender is but one of a number he is unlikely to be picked on, and even if he is so picked upon, can escape proper punishment because others were not arrested at the same time. Those who choose to take part in such unlawful occasions must do so at their peril.

The present case was one of a long-lasting concerted attempt of grave proportions by aggressive force of numbers of overpower the police, to embark on wrecking, and to terrify citizens engaged in following peaceable and lawful pursuits. Any participation whatever, irrespective of its precise form, in an unlawful or riotous assembly of this type derives its gravity from becoming one of those who, by weight of numbers, pursued a common and unlawful purpose. The law of this country has always leant heavily against those who, to attain such a purpose, use the threat that lies in the power of numbers.

The general scale of the sentences adopted by the trial judge on this particular occasion was stern—but correctly so. The occasion was far more serious than that of most affrays and other disturbances of the public peace that have become all too common. In this connection it must also be emphasised that neither on the law applicable to ascertaining guilt, or on the matter of sentencing, is an adult student in any better position than any other citizen. He most certainly cannot by virtue of his education claim preferential treatment—as, for instance, to receive lighter punishment than one less well educated. . . .

It is to be emphasised that in each and every case where the jury convicted one of the seven applicants either of riotous or unlawful assembly the person convicted had been in the very forefront of the mob and had been an active participator in attempts to get past and override the police in their protective tasks. It was indeed because he was thus in the forefront that he could be identified and in certain instances seized or arrested, often after a turbulent struggle in which those alongside attempted to rescue him. Moreover, each applicant was taking his part in the course of a protracted attack, and it was of no avail to plead sudden impulse. On that footing immediately custodial sentences were clearly required. . . . [The sentences were confirmed except that Lagden was put on probation and the recommendation for deportation of Bodea was quashed.]

NOTES

1. For a critical comment on *R v Caird*, see S. Sedley, *The Listener* (1970) pp. 469–472, 783, 911; cf. A. W. Bradley, ibid. pp. 734–6; F. Bresler, ibid. pp. 736–7, 847.

2. The point that in sentencing a participant in public disorder the court must consider not only the defendant's precise individual acts, but also the fact that these were part of a wider disturbance, was confirmed by the Court of Appeal (Criminal Division) in *R v Hebron and Spencer* (1989) 11 Cr App Rep (S) 226. H and S were convicted of violent disorder following a disturbance in Hereford city centre on New Year's Eve in which up to 40 or so people among a large crowd were fighting. When the police intervened there were shouts and chants of 'Kill the Bill' and missiles were thrown at them. The police conducted three baton charges to restore order. S was shaking his fists and chanting 'Kill the Bill' with the others. Stuart-Smith LJ said (at p. 228)

'. . . in cases of violent crowd disorder, it is not only the precise individual acts that matter. It is the fact that he is taking part in violent disorder, threatening violence against other people, and is part and parcel of the whole threatening and alarming activity.'

Accordingly, a custodial sentence was justified even though S was a young offender.

On sentencing for violent disorder, see also *R v Tyler* (1992) 96 Cr App Rep 332, CA (Cr D); *R v Tomlinson, Mackie and Gladwell* (1992) Times, 2 December, CA (Cr D).

Atkin v DPP (1989) 89 Cr App Rep 199, 158 JP 383, Queen's Bench Divisional Court

Two Customs and Excise officers, accompanied by a bailiff, went to the defendant's farm to recover outstanding value added tax. The two officers conducted their business in the farmhouse while the bailiff waited outside in the car. The car was parked in the farmyard where the bailiff was unable to hear any of the conversation in the farmhouse. When the officers ascertained from the defendant that he was unable to pay the VAT due they informed him that the bailiff would have to enter the farmhouse to distrain on his goods. The defendant replied: 'If the bailiff gets out of the car he's a dead un.' No threats were made to the two officers. One of the officers noticed a gun in the corner of the room and that officer, on the instructions of her colleague, left the farmhouse and told the bailiff that the defendant had threatened him. The bailiff did not get out of the car as he felt threatened and all three then left the farm. The defendant was charged with contravening section 4 of the Public Order Act 1986. The justices were of opinion that threatening words were used in the farmhouse. The defendant did not want the bailiff to enter his house and therefore the defendant must have intended the officers to convey the threat to the bailiff in a bid to keep him out. The defendant, therefore, used threatening words towards the bailiff with intent to cause him to believe that immediate unlawful violence would be used against him. The bailiff was not in the farmhouse, so section 4(2) of the 1986 Act did not apply. The justices, therefore, convicted the defendant who appealed by way of case stated. The Divisional Court allowed the appeal.

Taylor LJ: . . . In this Court, Mr. Murray on behalf of the defendant, has highlighted the phrase in section 4(1)(*a*) 'used towards another person threatening words.' He submits that the plain and natural meaning of that phrase is that the threatening words have to be addressed directly to another person who is present and either in earshot or aimed at as being putatively in earshot. The phrase does not equate with 'used in regard to another person' or 'used concerning another person'.

He submits that approached in that way the phrase here clearly related to the use of the words within the house to those who were in earshot. The only persons in earshot were the two Customs and Excise officers. If one therefore follows through the section, the alleged offence was using 'towards those officers threatening words with intent to cause those officers to believe that immediate unlawful violence would be used against them or another person', presumably the bailiff. However, subsection (2) of section 4 provides that no offence is committed where the words are used by a person inside the dwelling and the other person is also inside that or another dwelling.

The question then arises who is meant by the phrase 'the other person'? Mr. Murray submits that the other person there must refer to the opening words of the whole section in subsection (1)(a) 'uses towards another person', the two people identified in subsection (2) being the person using the words who has to be inside the dwelling and the other person, the person towards whom they are used.

Viewed in that way the correct decision of this case would be an acquittal because the other person in section (2) would be the Customs and Excise officers and they were inside the dwelling so no offence would be committed.

We were referred to decisions of different divisions of this Court in previous cases, *Parkin v Norman* [1983] QB 92 and *Masterson v Holden* [1986] 1 WLR 1017. We have not found those citations particularly helpful as they were both concerned with an earlier Act, the Public Order Act 1936. The 1986 Act in sections 4 and 5 supersedes section 5 of the 1936 Act. The wording in the new Act is quite different. The phrase 'uses towards another person' is entirely new and the construction of section 4 is therefore not assisted, in my judgment, by considering decisions of this Court in regard to the construction of an earlier statute. This statute has, we are told, not been construed by any court and the phrase 'uses towards another person' has not been found by counsel in any other statutory provision which would give any helpful indication as to its true meaning in this context. So the exercise is one of purely looking at the wording of the section and deciding what the plain and natural meaning of the words is, bearing in mind that if there were any doubt that doubt would have to be resolved, since this is a penal provision, in favour of the appellant.

In my judgment the submissions made by Mr. Murray are correct. The phrase 'uses towards another person' means, in the context of section 4(1)(a) 'uses in the presence of and in the direction of another person directly'. I do not think, looking at the section as a whole, the words can bear the meaning 'concerning another person' or 'in regard to another person'. That conclusion is assisted by comparing sub-paragraph (a) and sub-paragraph (b) of subsection (1). If one looks at sub-paragraph (b) which concerns distributing or displaying to 'another person' any writing, it is clear that the distribution or display must be directly made to the other person. That being so, one would be surprised to find that another person had a different meaning in paragraph (a) from the meaning it holds in paragraph (b). Accordingly, I consider that when one construes in the context of this case section 4(1)(a) and the phrase 'uses towards another person' it cannot be right to regard the bailiff as being that other person because he was not in earshot and the words were not directed towards him.

Once it has been decided that the words, in the context of this case, refer to the Customs and Excise officers in 4(1)(a) one then has to look at the meaning of section 4(2). Who is the other person? Again, looking solely at the words of the section it seems to me clear that the other person refers back to section 4(1)(a), 'the other person' being the person to whom the person charged addresses or uses the words, whether they be threatening, abusive or insulting. Accordingly the conclusion I reach on this case is that 'the other person' in subsection (2), being the Customs and Excise officer, and that other person being inside the dwelling, the offence is not proved because all concerned within the ambit of the section are inside a dwelling. That being so, no offence is committed.

The other question which was raised is an academic question and suggests that it might be possible for the phrase, 'the other person' to refer back not to the person referred to in section 4(1)(a) but to 'another' later on in subsection (1) where that word is used twice; in other words the suggestion is that the other person in sub-section (2) may be the bailiff notwithstanding that the court might decide, as it has, that 'towards another person' in section 4(1)(a) referred to the Customs and Excise officers. As already indicated that would not be my construction and accordingly, although it is not specifically raised as the question in the case, I would answer the second question which the justices raised in accordance with the reasoning I have just given.

To deal with the specific question they have asked . . . in my judgment the justices were not correct in convincing the defendant on the facts outlined and accordingly I would quash this conviction.

Henry J: I agree with everything Taylor LJ has said. . . .

When one looks at the words of the exception of section 4(2) . . . it is clear that the intention of Parliament was to exclude domestic quarrels conducted within the home even in circumstances where such words or behaviour would, if repeated outside the dwelling create an offence. It also seems to me to follow from the clear words of the statute that it was the intention to exclude such domestic quarrels from criminal liability attaching to such domestic quarrels, even where the threat uttered, though spoken to the person sharing the dwelling was related to violence against someone who was not in the dwelling at the time.

For those additional reasons I agree with the conclusion of Taylor LJ as reached.

Appeal allowed.
Conviction quashed.

R v Horseferry Road Metropolitan Stipendiary Magistrate, ex p Siadatan [1991] 1 All ER 324, [1991] 1 QB 260, [1990] 3 WLR 1006, Queen's Bench Divisional Court

The applicant, Sayid Mehdie Siadatan, laid an information against Penguin Books Ltd, the publishers of *Satanic Verses* by Salman Rushdie, and sought a summons accusing them of distributing a book written by the author which contained abusive and insulting writing whereby it was likely that unlawful violence would be provoked, contrary to s. 4(1) of the Public Order Act 1986. The book was offensive to many Muslims and a bookshop owned by the publishers was subjected to a fire bomb attack while the book was on sale. The magistrate hearing the information refused to issue the summons on the ground that the information disclosed no offence because it was not alleged that 'immediate' unlawful violence would be provoked. The applicant applied for judicial review to quash the magistrate's decision, but the Divisional Court dismissed the application.

The judgment of the court (**Watkins** and **Stuart-Smith LJJ** and **Roch J**) was delivered by **Watkins LJ:** . . .

[His Lordship noted that it was not contended that distribution of the book would provoke 'immediate' unlawful violence, and continued:]

Mr Nice [counsel for the applicant] referred to the short history of the legislation as follows. Section 4(1) of the 1986 Act replaced s. 5 of the Public Order Act 1936, the offence created by which was abolished by s. 9(2)(*d*) of the 1986 Act. Section 5 provided:

'Any person who in any public place or at any public meeting—(*a*) uses threatening, abusive or insulting words or behaviour, or (*b*) distributes or displays any writing, sign or visible representation which is threatening, abusive or insulting, with intent to provoke a breach of the peace or whereby a breach of the peace is likely to be occasioned, shall be guilty of an offence . . .'

Clearly s. 5 did not require that the breach of the peace which was either intended or likely to be occasioned should follow immediately upon the actions of the defendant. . . .

[His Lordship read s. 6(3) of the 1986 Act]

In the light of those provisions Mr Nice submits that a person who intends written words to be threatening, abusive or insulting, or who is aware that written words may be threatening, abusive or insulting, should not escape criminal liability under s. 4(1) simply because the violence which the written words are likely to provoke will not be immediate. If, he said, the construction of the section for which he contended is rejected, there will be a gap in the law which did not exist under the 1936 Act, a gap which Parliament, when passing the 1986 Act, could not have intended to create.

A consequence of construing the words 'such violence' in s. 4(1) as meaning 'immediate unlawful violence' will be that leaders of an extremist movement who prepare pamphlets or banners to be distributed or carried in public places by adherents to that movement will not be committing any offence under s. 4(1) albeit that they intend the words in the pamphlets or on the banners to be threatening, abusive or insulting and it is likely that unlawful violence will be provoked by the words in the pamphlet or on the banners.

Thus, whilst recognising the right to freedom of expression which the law confers on all persons within the United Kingdom, Mr Nice argues that such rights do not include a freedom to insult or abuse other persons in such a way that it is likely that violence will be provoked. Section 4(1) provides, he said, only a partial and imperfect protection against conduct which is insulting and abusive and likely to lead to violence unless his construction of the section is correct.

He argued strongly that, whether the court seeks the 'natural and ordinary meaning' of the words of s. 4(1) or whether we construe the words of s. 4(1) 'according to the plain literal and grammatical meaning of the words', the proper construction is that 'such violence' means 'unlawful violence' unqualified in any other way.

He divided the second part of the subsection into these four parts:

'With intent: (i) to cause that person to believe that immediate unlawful violence will be used against him or another by any person, or (ii) to provoke the immediate use of unlawful violence by that person or another, or whereby: (iii) that person is likely to believe that such violence will be used, or (iv) it is likely that such violence will be provoked.'

That makes plain, he said, that the words in part (iv) 'such violence' refer back to a previous use of the word 'violence', that the normal rules of grammatical construction require a reader to look at the most recent use of the word 'violence' prior to the phrase 'such violence'. The most recent use of that word appears in part (ii), where the word 'violence' is qualified only by the word 'unlawful'.

Furthermore, he argued that the phrase 'immediate unlawful violence' could have been used expressly in each of the parts (i) to (iv). Alternatively, the phrase 'immediate unlawful violence' having been used in part (i) the words 'such violence' could have been used in parts (ii), (iii) and (iv). The change from 'immediate unlawful violence' in part (i) to 'immediate use of unlawful violence' in part (ii) can only be explained because Parliament intended the words 'such violence' where they occurred in the remainder of the subsection to refer to 'unlawful violence' and not to 'immediate unlawful violence'.

Persuasive though those somewhat intricate arguments appeared to be, as presented by Mr Nice, the contrary construction advanced for the respondents by Mr Fitzgerald and by the amicus curiae, Mr Paget, is, we think, to be preferred. In our judgment the phrase 'such violence' in s. 4(1) means 'immediately unlawful violence'. We now give our reasons for that conclusion.

We were referred to the Law Commission's report entitled *Criminal Law Offences Relating to Public Order* (Law Com no. 123 (1983)). The content and structure of s. 4(1) is foreshadowed in the very clearly expressed para 5.43 of that report thus:

Fear of violence and provoking violence:

5.43   The offence requires that each defendant use threatening etc. words or behaviour which is intended or is likely—(a) to cause another person to fear immediate unlawful violence, or (b) to provoke the immediate use of unlawful violence by another person.'

That the parliamentary draftsman, when drafting the last part of s. 4(1), did not achieve the same clarity and precision found in that paragraph is, we think, most regrettable.

The context in which s. 4(1) appears in the 1986 Act is the first matter which leads us to our conclusion. The title to the Act recounts that it is 'An Act to abolish . . . certain statutory offences relating to public order; to create new offences relating to public order . . .' Section 4 appears in the first part of the Act together with the creation of new offences, namely riot by s. 1, violent disorder by s. 2, affray by s. 3, harassment, alarm or distress by s. 5. The provisions of those sections are such that the conduct of the defendants must produce in an actual or notional person of reasonable firmness fear in relation to ss. 1, 2 and 3 which is contemporaneous with the unlawful violence being used by the defendants or harassment, alarm or distress which is contemporaneous with the threatening, abusive or insulting conduct under s. 5. We consider it most unlikely that Parliament could have intended to include, among sections which undoubtedly deal with conduct having an immediate impact on bystanders, a section creating an offence for conduct which is likely to lead to violence at some unspecified time in the future.

The second reason is that, in our view, by itself a proper reading of s. 4(1) leads to this conclusion. We accept the submission of Mr Paget that the words 'immediate unlawful violence' and the words 'the immediate use of unlawful violence' have precisely the same meaning. The change in the phraseology used by Parliament is simply a matter of style. The only violence mentioned in s. 4(1) is 'immediate unlawful violence'. The words 'such violence' refer back to the earlier use or uses of the word 'violence' in the subsection as qualified by the other words which appear in the same phrases as the word 'violence'. On the first occasion that the word 'violence' is used it is qualified by the words 'immediate unlawful' and on the second it is qualified by the words 'the immediate use of unlawful'. In our opinion, praying in aid Mr Nice's useful partition of the subsection, it is not possible in construing the words 'such violence' in part (iv), which reads 'it is likely that such violence will be provoked', to return to part (ii) and ignore the words 'the immediate use'. Parts (iii) and (iv) must have been intended by Parliament to be mirror images of parts (i) and (ii) of the subsection.

A third and very compelling reason for our conclusion on the correct construction of this subsection is that here we are construing a penal statute, of which there are, or may be, two possible readings. It is an elementary rule of statutory construction that, in a penal statute where there are two possible readings, the meaning which limits the scope of the offence thus created is that which the court should adopt. It would surely be strange indeed, if, where it could be shown that a defendant has an intent to provoke unlawful violence by another person, Parliament required the prosecution to establish an intent to provoke the immediate use of unlawful violence, but in a situation where a defendant had no such intent, but nevertheless it was likely that violence would be provoked, there was no requirement that such violence be immediate.

For these reasons we hold that the magistrate was right to refuse to issue a summons.

Finally, we consider it advisable to indicate our provisional view on the meaning of the word 'immediate'. In the Law Commission's report to which reference has already been made, at para 5.46 the Law Commission indicated that in their opinion the new offence to replace that created by s. 5 of the 1936 Act should include the element of immediacy; in the case of behaviour provoking the use of violence, it must be the immediate use of such violence. Nevertheless, the Law Commission in para 5.44 gave an example of a gang in one part of a town uttering threats directed at persons, for example, of a particular ethnic or religious group resident in another part, and stated that that would be an offence, although the threat would not be capable of being performed until the gang arrived in the other part of the town. So the Law Commission recommended there that Parliament enact a law to create an offence of the making of threats which lead to the fear of violence to the person simpliciter as opposed to an offence of the making of threats, causing fear of violence to the person hearing the threats.

It seems to us that the word 'immediate' does not mean 'instantaneous', that a relatively short time interval may elapse between the act which is threatening, abusive or insulting and the unlawful violence. 'Immediate' connotes proximity in time and proximity in causation, that it is likely that violence will result within a relatively short period of time and without any other intervening occurrence. . . .

Application dismissed.

NOTES

1. Section 4 was designed to be the direct replacement for section 5 of the Public Order Act 1936, as amended. This had provided as follows:

'Any person who in any public place or at any public meeting—
   (a) uses threatening, abusive or insulting words or behaviour, or
   (b) distributes or displays any writing, sign or visible representation which is threatening, abusive or insulting,
with intent to provoke a breach of the peace or whereby a breach of the peace is likely to be occasioned, shall be guilty of an offence.'

'Public place' was defined in s. 9 (above, p. 178). Section 5 was modelled on the Metropolitan Police Act 1839, s. 15(13) and similar offences in local legislation.

The main changes appearing in the new s. 4 were (1) that the offence can be committed in a public or *private* place (except inside a dwelling house); (2) that it is not confined to situations where a third party is likely to be *provoked* into violence, but extends also to cases where a third party *fears* violence; and (3) that the 'breach of the peace' concept is not employed. The first point was in response to the dismissal by magistrates of charges under the old s. 5 during the miners' dispute where the defendants showed that they were on National Coal Board or other private property, while the victims of the threats were on the public highway (*White Paper*, p. 14). (In fact, there was clear authority that s. 5 applied where threats etc. were directed *to* a person in a public place: *Ward v Holman* [1964] 2 QB 580; *R v Edwards*; *R v Roberts* (1978) 67 Cr App Rep 228.) The second point responded to case law such as *Marsh v Arscott* (1982) 75 Cr App Rep 211 and *Parkin v Norman* [1983] QB 92 which suggested 'that in certain circumstances intimidatory conduct may not be caught by section 5 if the victim (for example, a policeman, or an elderly lady) is someone who is not likely to be provoked into violence by the defendant's behaviour. This is clearly a loophole which needs to be closed. . . .' (*White Paper*, p. 14). The requirement of immediacy was found in the Law Commission's proposals, rejected in the *White Paper* (p. 15) but restored to the Bill (see *R v Horseferry Road Metropolitan Stipendiary Magistrates, ex p Siadatan*, above).

2. The phrase 'threatening, abusive or insulting' is common to both the old s. 5 and the new s. 4. Authorities on this aspect of the old s. 5 accordingly appear still to be relevant. See *Brutus v Cozens* (below, p. 230) and *Parkin v Norman* (below, p. 232). The phrase 'uses towards another person' did not appear in the old s. 5, and has the effect of narrowing s. 4 by comparison (see *Smith*, pp. 98–99 and *Atkin v DPP*, supra).

3. The old s. 5 was the key public order offence, and was used in preference to the more serious charges of riot, unlawful assembly and affray.

4. The exception in s. 4(2) was also applied in *R v Va Kun Hau* [1990] Crim LR 518, CA (Cr D), where the defendant became excited and aggressive when visited at home by a bailiff, accompanied by a police officer, in connection with an unpaid parking fine. He wielded and then put down, in succession, a kitchen cleaver and a kitchen knife. His conviction by the jury under s. 4 (as an alternative to the offence charged, affray, under s. 3) had to be quashed as the events took place inside a dwelling house. The communal landing outside the front door of a flat in a block of flats is not part of a 'dwelling' for the purposes of s. 4(2): *Rukwira v DPP* (1993) 158 JP 65, DC.

5. The s. 4 offence may be committed in four different ways (see the wording of s. 4(1)). In *Winn v DPP* (1992) 156 JP 881, W was convicted by justices on evidence that he threatened and abused a process server attempting to serve a county court summons, causing him to feel that W was 'going to get him'. However, the charge alleged that it was likely that unlawful violence would be provoked. W's conviction was quashed as the variation between the facts found and the particulars alleged was so substantial that the information should have been amended.

DPP v Orum [1988] 3 All ER 449, [1989] 1 WLR 88 Queen's Bench Divisional Court

O was charged with (1) an offence under s. 5(1)(a) of the Public Order Act 1986; and (2) assaulting a police officer in the execution of his duty, contrary to s. 51(1) of the Police Act 1964. The magistrates dismissed the charges, and the DPP appealed by case stated to the Divisional Court.

Glidewell LJ: . . . The magistrates heard the two charges together and found the following facts. At 1.15 am on 9 November 1987 the respondent was standing by a garden wall in a road in Victoria Park, Bristol in the company of his girlfriend. The road has terraced houses on both sides of it. The respondent and his girlfriend were eight to ten feet away from the nearest house. They were engaged in an argument and the respondent was using abusive language. He had consumed a quantity of alcohol during the course of the evening. PCs Hickman and Crossan arrived at the scene. PC Hickman approached the respondent and said: 'Quiet, you are disturbing the neighbours.' The respondent replied: 'You fuck off. This is a domestic and you can't do nothing.' PC Hickman said: 'Quiet, you are causing a breach of the peace. Quiet down, go home and sleep it off.' The respondent replied: 'You can't fucking arrest me. I know my rights. If you don't go away I am going to hit you.' PC Hickman then arrested the respondent for causing a breach of the peace and cautioned him.

The only persons present in the street were the respondent, his girlfriend and the two police constables. The respondent was placed in the rear of a police vehicle. As PC Crossan entered the vehicle, the respondent kicked him in the stomach and hit him on the head and body. The respondent was finally subdued and handcuffed. . . .

[The magistrates dismissed both charges.]

The main question which we have to answer is: can a police officer be a person who is likely to be caused harassment, alarm or distress by the threatening, abusive or insulting words or behaviour? It is apparent, as counsel who appears for the respondent sensibly concedes, that in the first part of the passage in which they set out their opinion, the magistrates firstly had taken the view that they can discount any question of harassment, alarm or distress to people living in and presumably mostly asleep in the nearby dwelling houses, because there is no evidence that any such person was likely to be caused harassment etc. Secondly, they appear to have totally discounted the effect of the respondent's conduct on his girlfriend. What they concerned themselves with, and what we are asked to concern ourselves with, is the impact of that conduct on either or both of the two police constables.

The magistrates seem to have been advised by their clerk that they could not properly, presumably as a matter of law, conclude that either of the constables was likely to be caused harassment, alarm or distress by the words or behaviour of the respondent. Counsel for the respondent argues that that is a proper conclusion provided that s. 5 of the 1986 Act is to be interpreted on the same lines as its predecessor, namely s. 5 of the Public Order Act 1936. I say 'on the same lines': what I mean is that it is conduct likely to involve a breach of the peace.

In the decision of this court in *Marsh v Arscott* (1982) 75 Cr App Rep 211 the defendant was charged under s. 5 of the Public Order Act 1936. . . .

The defendant was slumped over the bonnet of a car late on a Saturday night in the car park of a shop. The police officers who found him asked the defendant questions and received only abusive replies. The question was whether the defendant's language and behaviour was such that a breach of the peace was likely to be occasioned notwithstanding that the only witnesses to the behaviour were the police officers. McCullough J, giving the first judgment, said (at 216):

'In the circumstances here, assuming the defendant to have been acting unlawfully in using threatening words and behaviour, no breach of the peace was likely to have been occasioned. No other person was likely to have broken the peace, and all that the police were likely to do was arrest him, as they did. On that basis too an acquittal would, in my judgment, have been inevitable.'

If I may say so, respectfully, that is common sense as well as good law. However, with respect to counsel for the respondent, his argument is not. In my view, the very different wording of s. 5 of the 1986 Act, which makes no reference at all in sub-s (1) to a breach of the peace, does not allow the importation of the concept or that phrase in its interpretation.

I find nothing in the context of the 1986 Act to persuade me that a police officer may not be a person who is caused harassment, alarm or distress by the various kinds of words and conduct to which s. 5(1) applies. I would therefore answer the question in the affirmative, that a police officer can be a person who is likely to be caused harassment and so on. However, that is not to say that the opposite is necessarily the case, namely it is not to say that every police officer in this situation is to be assumed to be a person who is caused harassment. Very frequently, words and behaviour with which police officers will be wearily familiar will have little emotional impact on them save that of boredom. It may well be that, in appropriate circumstances, magistrates will decide (indeed, they might decide in the present case) as a question of fact that the words and behaviour were not likely to cause harassment, alarm or distress to either of the police officers. That is a question for the magistrates to decide having regard to all the circumstances: the time, the place, the nature of the words used, who the police officers are and so on.

It seems to me that the magistrates were advised by their clerk that they could not find that police officers could be caused harassment and so on by such words and behaviour as a matter of law. It may be that the clerk was thinking of *Marsh v Arscott* and he had in his mind the argument which counsel for the respondent advanced to us. If he did, I have already indicated that I think he was wrong so to do.

Counsel for the prosecution poses for our consideration a second question: if in fact a police officer is not likely to be caused harassment etc does he then have any power to arrest under s. 5(4)? Theoretically, the answer to that question may be Yes, but in practice, in my view, it must almost invariably be No. The reason is this. If an officer is not caused harassment alarm or distress, it is difficult to see how he can reasonably suspect, if he is the only person present, that an offence against s. 5(1) has been committed since such causation is a necessary element in the offence. If he does not reasonably suspect that such an offence has been committed, then he has no power of arrest under s. 5(4).

[His Lordship then held that the constable had lawfully arrested O for causing a breach of the peace as his conduct fell within the definition of a 'breach of the peace' set out in *R v Howell* (above, p. 207). The case was remitted to the magistrates with a direction to convict on the charge of assaulting a police officer; the acquittal on the s. 5 charge was set aside, but it was not thought necessary to send the matter back to the magistrates to determine on the facts whether the officers had been caused harassment etc.]

McCullough J: I agree both with the proposed orders and with the judgment of Glidewell LJ and would only add a few words since I was party to the decision in *Marsh v Arscott* (1982) 75 Cr App Rep 211. In enacting s. 5 of the Public Order Act 1986 in place of s. 5 of the Public Order Act 1936, Parliament advisedly deleted the requirement that a breach of the peace was either intended by the defendant or was likely to result from his conduct. In its place was put the requirement that someone within sight or sound of the defendant at the material time would be likely to be caused harassment, alarm or distress by his conduct. Thus, what matters now is not the likely physical reaction to the conduct complained of, but the likely mental reaction to it. It is improbable in the extreme that any police officer would ever be provoked by threatening, abusive or insulting words or behaviour to cause a breach of the peace, but it is by no means impossible that such an officer may not feel harassed, alarmed or distressed as a result of such words or behaviour. This distinguishes the present case from *Marsh v Arscott*.
Appeal allowed.

NOTES

1. Section 5 of the Public Order Act 1986 was a controversial extension of the law, designed to deal with 'minor acts of hooliganism' (*White Paper*, p. 18). Instances of such behaviour might include

'hooligans on housing estates causing disturbances in the common parts of blocks of flat, blockading entrances, throwing things down the stairs, banging on doors, peering in at windows, and knocking over dustbins;
groups of youths persistently shouting abuse and obscenities or pestering people waiting to catch public transport or to enter a hall or cinema;
someone turning out the lights in a crowded dance hall, in a way likely to cause panic;
rowdy behaviour in the streets, late at night which alarms local residents' (ibid.)

This control was

'particularly needed when the behaviour is directed at the elderly and others who may feel especially vulnerable, including members of ethnic minority communities' (ibid.)

Thus, the new s. 5 extends to cover 'disorderly' behaviour as well as threatening, abusive or insulting words or behaviour, provided it is within the hearing or sight of a person likely to be caused harassment, alarm or distress thereby. The *White Paper* had suggested that the behaviour must *actually* cause someone to feel harassed etc., and described this as a safeguard lest the criminal law be extended widely to cover conduct not deserving of criminal sanctions (p. 19); the Act's provisions on this point are weaker, and avoid any need to call the victim as a witness. Victims may well be reluctant to testify in the kinds of case for which s. 5 was purportedly designed. Unlike s. 4, the words or behaviour need not be shown to be 'used towards' a particular person.

'Disorderly' is presumably to be treated as an ordinary English word for the purpose of the approach in *Brutus v Cozens* (below, p. 230). Decisions on differently worded 'disorderly behaviour' offences in other jurisdictions are not likely to be appropriate authorities: see P. Sefton, (1988) 39 NILQ 292, on what he regards as doubtful references to New Zealand authorities in connection with the disorderly behaviour offence now found in the Public Order (Northern Ireland) Order 1987 (SI 1987 No. 463). For example, the Northern Ireland disorderly behaviour offence can be committed by words alone: see *Chief Inspector Clinton v Watts* (11 September 1992, unreported, CA (NI)). Can that be the case under s. 5 in view of its express wording?
2. In the House of Lords debate, Lord Denning welcomed the new offence, saying that it was 'high time that our law did something to put down disorderly behaviour'. He gave as examples of cases that would be covered: the conduct of the defendant in *Brutus v Cozens* (below, p. 230); the demonstrators in the *CEGB* case (above, p. 209); disorderly pickets; hippies invading a person's land against the owner's will; and students who do all they can to stop freedom of speech in the universities. Lord Scarman opposed the introduction of the offence:

'A very good reason for that submission I find in the entertaining and fascinating account of cases that the noble and learned Lord, Lord Denning has just given to the Committee. The Committee will have noted the extraordinary range of activities which are covered by those cases and, which it is said that this clause would cover'
(478 HL Deb, 16 July 1986, cols 935–938).

3. In practice, there were many examples of cases where magistrates had convicted defendants under the old s. 5 without sufficient regard to the requirements (1) that the defendant's conduct had been more than merely 'offensive' or 'annoying' and (2) that there had been some threat to the peace. See D. G. T. Williams, [1967] Crim LR 385 and A. Dickey, [1971] Crim LR 265. In the more recent cases, the Divisional Court has taken steps to reassert these requirements, particularly the latter (see *Marsh v Arscott* (1982) 75 Cr App Rep 211 (above, p. 236).

There are indications that the fears expressed at the time of its enactment concerning the breadth of the new s. 5 have been borne out. According to Peter Thornton, a former NCCL chair:

'In fact it had been used quite indiscriminately, for example against juveniles for throwing fake snowballs, against a man who had a birthday party for his son in his back garden (he was charged even though he agreed to turn the music down), against two 19 year old males for kissing in the street, against a nudist on a beach and against another nudist in his own house, and, most sinisterly, in the so-called Madame M case (successfully taken up by NCCL) against four students who were in the process of putting up a satirical poster during the last general election. It depicted the Prime Minister as a sadistic dominatrix'

(*Decade of Decline: Civil Liberties in the Thatcher Years* (Liberty, 1990), p. 37). It is not clear how many of these cases ended in convictions. The *Madame M* case did not, the police officers who saw the poster testified to no more than an attack of mirth (rather than harassment, alarm or distress): see C. Douzinas, *et al.*, 'The shrinking scope of public protest' (1988) 17(8) *Index on Censorship*, pp. 12, 13.

Prosecutions have been launched under s. 5 against anti-abortion protesters picketing abortion clinics, and variously displaying plastic models of human foetuses, photographs of dead foetuses and placards, and shouting slogans such as 'you are evil God will punish you' and 'do you know they are going to kill your baby?', and approaching women attending the clinics. The outcomes have been mixed. In *DPP v Clarke and others* (1991) 94 Cr App Rep 359, the Divisional Court upheld the acquittal of protesters (in a peaceful and orderly group) in respect of the display to a police officer of pictures of aborted foetuses. The justices accepted the officer's evidence that he 'found the pictures insulting to him as a father and felt abused by them and found them distressing'. Applying an objective test, they found that the defendants' conduct was not 'reasonable' within s. 5(3)(c). However, they also held, applying a subjective test, that the defendants did not intend the displays to be threatening, abusive or insulting, nor were they aware that they might be so. The Divisional Court endorsed the approach of the justices on all three points. Nolan LJ confessed 'to a feeling of some surprise' that the police officer and the justices found the pictures abusive and insulting, but stated that the question was essentially one for the justices (*Brutus v Cozens*, below, p. 230). (Presumably the more 'surprising' the view that conduct is threatening, abusive or insulting, the less likely it is that D will have the requisite intention; however, future protesters would have to take note (see Nolan LJ at 366.) See also *DPP v Fidler* (1991) 94 Cr App Rep 286 (membership of a group of anti-abortion protesters sufficient to establish a prima facie case under s. 5; offence under s. 7 of the Conspiracy and Protection of Property Act 1875 (below, p. 537) not made out where evidence shows only 'persuasion' and not 'compulsion'); *Morrow, Geach and Thomas v DPP* [1994] Crim LR 58 (anti-abortion protesters' conduct in shouting slogans, waving banners and preventing staff and patients from entering a clinic found to be disorderly and to have caused distress; no defence established under s. 5(3)(c) or s. 3 of the Criminal Law Act 1967 (above, p. 74)); *Morrow v DPP* [1993] Crim LR 58 (convictions under s. 5 upheld in respect of the invasion of a clinic by protesters).

A survey of 470 public order cases from the 1988 records at five police stations in two force areas showed that 56% of the sample led to charges under s. 5 and 24% under s. 4 (T. Newburn *et al.*, 'Policing the Streets' (1990) 29 HORB 10 and 'Increasing Public Order' (1991) 7 *Policing* 22). The authors note that during the period 1986–88 the number of prosecutions for public order offences doubled. Generally, the officers they interviewed did not feel that there had been a rise in public disorder, and suggested that the rise in the number of prosecutions was due more to the nature of the new legislation. The research supported the view 'that low-level nuisances of widely varying kinds have increasingly been brought within the ambit of the law'. Certain offences that would not formerly have led to formal action were now subject to arrest and charge; s. 5 could be used where the evidence might not support more serious charges (e.g. where a person was sexually harassed in a public place but it had been difficult for the police to secure sufficient evidence to support a charge of indecent assault); under s. 5 police officers could now be regarded as people who might be harassed, alarmed or distressed (this was seen by the police as being 'crucially important' (p. 14)); s. 5 was regarded as constituting a helpful advance in relation to 'domestic' cases given that it extended to private premises (subject to the domestic dwelling exception); it was suggested that s. 5 siphoned off cases that would formerly have been dealt with by arrest for common law breach of the peace. See also D. Brown and T. Ellis, *Policing low-level disorder* (HORS No. 135, 1994), noting variations in the use of s. 5 in different police areas and some evidence that Afro-Caribbeans were over-represented among those arrested and proceeded against.

4. In *Lodge v DPP* (1988) Times, 26 October, the Divisional Court held that the person caused 'alarm' for the purposes of s. 5 need not be concerned at physical danger to himself; it can be alarm about the safety of an unconnected third party. A policeman saw L walking into the middle of the road, shouting, kicking and gesticulating. A car approached and the police officer was seriously concerned that an accident might happen. L appeared to be at risk and a danger to traffic and he was arrested. The Divisional Court upheld L's conviction under s. 5, holding that there was ample evidence on which the justices could have concluded that alarm was likely to have been caused so far as both the policeman and the driver were concerned. Jaywalkers beware! On the power of arrest under s. 5(4), see *Groom v DPP* (1991) 155 JPN 403, DC. Note that only the officer who gives the warning may exercise the power of arrest under s. 5(4): *DPP v Hancock and Tuttle* [1995] Crim LR 139, DC. Any other officer would have to rely on s. 25 of PACE (above, p. 105).

5. The exception enshrined in s. 5(2) was considered by the Divisional Court in *Chappell v DPP* (1988) 89 Cr App Rep 82, in holding that the deposit of a letter containing threatening, abusive or insulting words through the letter box of a house, with its recipient reading it and being alarmed or distressed by it, could not constitute an offence under s. 5(1)(a) in view of the exception. (Cf. *Atkin v DPP* (above, p. 221) under s. 4). Other points made in *Chappell* were (1) that the justices had been right to hold that the deposit of the letter had been a 'display in writing' within the meaning of s. 5(1)(b); and (2) that a person writing and/or delivering a letter to another, who opens it in the absence of the sender, cannot be said to be a person who 'uses . . . words or behaviour . . . within the hearing or sight of a person . . .' who receives it. The court noted that the conduct would now fall within the provisions of the Malicious Communications Act 1988.

6. On the defence that D's conduct was reasonable, see *DPP v Clarke* and *Morrow, Geach and Thomas v DPP*, above, n. **3**. See also *Poku v DPP* [1993] Crim LR 705, where the Divisional Court held that it was open to D to argue in defence to a s. 5 charge arising out of his resistance to the seizure of his ice cream van by police ('You're not taking my fucking van' etc.) that the seizure (for unlicensed street trading) was in fact unlawful and his response therefore reasonable.

Brutus v Cozens [1973] AC 854, [1972] 2 All ER 1297, [1972] 2 WLR 521, 56 Cr App Rep 799, House of Lords

Members of the public were admitted to watch the annual open tennis tournament at Wimbledon from stands around the courts. They were not allowed access to the courts. During a tennis match involving Drysdale, a South African, B stepped on to No. 2 Court blowing a whistle. He threw around leaflets, attempted to give one to a player and sat down on the court. Upon the blowing of the whistle other persons, some bearing banners or placards on which slogans were written, came on to the court and more leaflets were distributed. Play was stopped. The appellant was charged with using insulting behaviour whereby a breach of the peace was likely to be occasioned contrary to section 5 of the Public Order Act 1936. The justices held that his behaviour had not been insulting, and dismissed the information without calling on him to give evidence.

On appeal by the respondent prosecutor, the Divisional Court held that 'insulting . . . behaviour' in section 5 of the 1936 Act was behaviour which affronted other people and evidenced a disrespect or contempt for their rights, and which reasonable persons would foresee as likely to cause resentment or protest; that on the findings of the justices, which were to be regarded as provisional, insulting behaviour by the appellant had been established and the case would be sent back to them to continue the hearing. B appealed to the House of Lords.

Lord Reid: . . . It appears that the object of this demonstration was to protest against the apartheid policy of the Government of South Africa. But it is not said that that government was insulted. The insult is said to have been offered to or directed at the spectators.

The spectators at No. 2 Court were upset: they made loud shouts, gesticulated and shook their fists and while the appellant was being removed some showed hostility and attempted to strike him. . . .

It is not clear to me what precisely is the point of law which we have to decide. The question in the case stated for the opinion of the court is, 'Whether, on the above statement of facts, we came to a correct determination and decision in point of law.' This seems to assume that the meaning of the word 'insulting' in section 5 is a matter of law. And the Divisional Court appear to have proceeded on that footing.

In my judgment that is not right. The meaning of an ordinary word of the English language is not a question of law. The proper construction of a statute is a question of law. If the context shows that a word is used in an unusual sense the court will determine in other words what that unusual sense is. But here there is in my opinion no question of the word 'insulting' being used in any unusual sense. It appears to me, for reasons which I shall give later, to be intended to have its ordinary meaning. It is for the tribunal which decides the case to consider, not as law but as fact, whether in the whole circumstances the words of the statute do or do not as a matter of ordinary usage of the English language cover or apply to the facts which have been proved. If it is alleged that the tribunal has reached a wrong decision then there can be a question of law but only of a limited character. The question would normally be whether their decision was unreasonable in the sense that no tribunal acquainted with the ordinary use of language could reasonably reach that decision.

Were it otherwise we should reach an impossible position. When considering the meaning of a word one often goes to a dictionary. There one finds other words set out. And if one wants to pursue the matter and find the meaning of those other words the dictionary will give the meaning of those other words in still further words which often include the word for whose meaning one is searching.

No doubt the court could act as a dictionary. It could direct the tribunal to take some word or phrase other than the word in the statute and consider whether that word or phrase applied to or covered the facts proved. But we have been warned time and again not to substitute other words for the words of a statute. And there is very good reason for that. Few words have exact synonyms. The overtones are almost always different.

Or the court could frame a definition. But then again the tribunal would be left with words to consider. No doubt a statute may contain a definition—which incidentally often creates more problems than it solves—but the purpose of a definition is to limit or modify the ordinary meaning of a word and the court is not entitled to do that.

So the question of law in this case must be whether it was unreasonable to hold that the appellant's behaviour was not insulting. To that question there could in my view be only one answer—No.

But as the Divisional Court [1972] 1 WLR 484, have expressed their view as to the meaning of 'insulting' I must, I think, consider it. It was said at 487:

'The language of section 5, as amended, of the Public Order Act 1936, omitting words which do not matter for our present purpose, is: "Any person who in any public place . . . uses . . . insulting . . . behaviour, . . . with intent to provoke a breach of the peace or whereby a breach of the peace is likely to be occasioned, shall be guilty of an offence." It therefore becomes necessary to consider the meaning of the word "insulting" in its context in that section. In my view it is not necessary, and is probably undesirable, to try to frame an exhaustive definition which will cover every possible set of facts that may arise for consideration under this section. It is, as I think, quite sufficient for the purpose of this case to say that behaviour which affronts other people, and evidences a disrespect or contempt for their rights, behaviour which reasonable persons would foresee is likely to cause resentment or protest such as was aroused in this case, and I rely particularly on the reaction of the crowd as set out in the case stated, is insulting for the purpose of this section.'

I cannot agree with that. Parliament had to solve the difficult question of how far freedom of speech or behaviour must be limited in the general public interest. It would have been going much too far to prohibit all speech or conduct likely to occasion a breach of the peace because determined opponents may not shrink from organising or at least threatening a breach of the peace in order to silence a speaker whose views they detest. Therefore vigorous and it may be distasteful or unmannerly speech or behaviour is permitted so long as it does not go beyond any one of three limits. It must not be threatening. It must not be abusive. It must not be insulting. I see no reason why any of these should be construed as having a specially wide or a specially narrow meaning. They are all limits easily recognisable by the ordinary man. Free speech is not impaired by ruling them out. But before a man can be convicted it must be clearly shown that one or more of them has been disregarded.

We were referred to a number of dictionary meanings of 'insult' such as treating with insolence or contempt or indignity or derision or dishonour or offensive disrespect. Many things otherwise unobjectionable may be said or done in an insulting way. There can be no definition. But an ordinary sensible man knows an insult when he sees or hears it.

Taking the passage which I have quoted, 'affront' is much too vague a word to be helpful; there can often be disrespect without insult, and I do not think that contempt for a person's rights as distinct from contempt of the person himself would generally be held to be insulting. Moreover, there are many grounds other than insult for feeling resentment or protesting. I do not agree that there can be conduct which is not insulting in the ordinary sense of the word but which is 'insulting for the purpose of this section'. If the view of the Divisional Court was that in this section the word 'insulting' has some special or unusually wide meaning, then I do not agree. Parliament has given no indication that the word is to be given any unusual meaning. Insulting means insulting and nothing else.

If I had to decide, which I do not, whether the appellant's conduct insulted the spectators in this case, I would agree with the magistrates. The spectators may have been very angry and justly so. The appellant's conduct was deplorable. Probably it ought to be punishable. But I cannot see how it insulted the spectators.

I would allow the appeal with costs.

Lords Morris of Borrth-y-Gest and **Kilbrandon** and **Viscount Dilhorne** delivered concurring speeches. **Lord Diplock** agreed.

Appeal allowed.

Parkin v Norman; Valentine v Lilley [1983] QB 92, [1982] 2 All ER 583, Divisional Court

In separate incidents, each of the defendants, P and V, was found masturbating in a public lavatory in a manner which clearly indicated that he wanted his behaviour to be seen only by the one other person present there at the time. Unknown to the defendants, the other person present in each case was a police officer in plain clothes. Both defendants were convicted of using threatening, abusive or insulting words or behaviour whereby a breach of the peace was likely to be occasioned contrary to s. 5 of the Public Order Act 1936. P's appeal to the Crown Court was dismissed. Both appealed by case stated to the Divisional Court. Counsel for P submitted (1) that there was no insulting behaviour: the officer was not insulted, P had desisted while a third person was present and there was no reason to suppose that he would not have desisted had anyone else entered; (2) that 'an insult requires an intention to insult'; and (3) that no breach of the peace was likely to be occasioned.

McCullough J read the judgment of the court (**Donaldson LJ** and **McCullough J**): . . .

In our judgment, threats, abuse and insults are within the section whether or not they were intended to be threats, abuse or insults. 'Threatening, abusive or insulting words or behaviour' are simply words or behaviour that are threatening, abusive or insulting in character. . . . If the conduct in question is of this character it does not, in our judgment, matter whether anyone feels himself to have been threatened, abused or insulted. Insulting behaviour does not lose its insulting character simply because no one who witnessed it was insulted, any more than it would lose its liability to provoke a breach of the peace merely because no one who witnessed it broke the peace. In *Ballard v Blythe* (3 November 1980, unreported) the appellant insulted, abused, threatened and spat at a man who, unknown to him, was a headmaster, and who reacted with an unusual degree of self-restraint. In dismissing his appeal, Donaldson LJ said:

> 'the court has to find the circumstances in which the conduct takes place and to consider the question posed by the statute: is this conduct such as is inherently likely to occasion a breach of the peace? . . . the general test is "What is the natural and probable result of the conduct?" '

Where the defendant is addressing an audience which he knows has special susceptibilities, a breach of the peace may be the natural and probable result of behaviour which would not provoke an audience not having this susceptibility in such a way. . . .

The Act does not make it criminal to use offensive or disgusting behaviour whereby a breach of the peace is likely to be occasioned. It requires in the circumstances material to this case, 'insulting behaviour'. What then is an insult? We do not propose to attempt any sort of definition, particularly after the speeches in *Brutus v Cozens* [1973] AC 854, but some consideration of its characteristics are necessary in the light of counsel's submissions that behaviour of the type here is not insulting.

One cannot insult nothing. The word presupposes a subject and an object and, in this day and age, a human object. An insult is perceived by someone who feels insulted. It is given by someone who is directing his words or his behaviour to another person or persons. When A is insulting B, and is clearly directing his words and behaviour to B alone, if C hears and sees is he insulted? He may be disgusted, offended, annoyed, angered and no doubt a number of other things as well; and he may be provoked by what he sees and hears into breaking the peace. But will he be insulted?

One must take care not to become too analytical or too refined about these things, and we are not beginning to attempt either to define or to lay down any sort of principle, but these considerations may help to clear the mind before one asks oneself whether homosexual behaviour of the type in question here is really properly described as 'insulting.'

At one stage, a third person did come in, but he, so far as we know, saw nothing. So he was not insulted, nor was he likely to have been. Had further people come in the position would no doubt have been the same. If, by chance, anyone had surprised the defendant and seen what was happening, we think it would be difficult to say that he would have been insulted.

The defendant's conduct was aimed at one person and only one person. He obviously hoped, and after a little while would presumably have believed, that the person to whom it was directed was another homosexual. Whatever he was trying to do, he was not trying to insult him. Whatever another homosexual would have felt, he would not, presumably, have felt insulted. In fact, the second person was a police officer. Was he insulted? He had gone there in plain clothes to catch anyone whom he saw doing this sort of thing, and he caught one. It seems to us quite unrealistic to say that he would have felt insulted. Suppose, as was possible, that the person to whom the behaviour was directed had been a heterosexual using the lavatory for its proper purpose. He would almost certainly have felt disgusted and perhaps angry, but would he have felt insulted? The argument that he would, is that the behaviour was tantamount to a statement: 'I believe you are another homosexual,' which the average heterosexual would surely regard as insulting. We regard this as the only basis upon which the behaviour could fairly be characterised as 'insulting'. However, that did not happen in this case. The only person importuned, for that is what it comes to, was the police officer, but the person importuned might very well have been an ordinary heterosexual using the lavatory for its proper purpose. On this basis we think that the behaviour can fairly be regarded as potentially insulting, and we would regard this as sufficient to give it the description 'insulting behaviour'.

For this reason, and this reason alone, we are not prepared to say that the court was in error in making a finding that there had been 'insulting behaviour'. And as has already been indicated, we do not think the court was prevented from making this finding by the fact that the defendant did not intend to insult, nor by the fact that no one was insulted, nor by his having taken steps to ensure that no third person saw what he was doing. This is not to hold that such a finding was inevitable. It was for the court to decide on the whole of the evidence. We could only interfere if it had been demonstrated that the finding must have been wrong.

But was a breach of the peace likely to result? Neither the defendant nor the police officer was likely to break the peace. No third party was likely to have seen. One came in and the defendant desisted. Had others come in, he would no doubt have done the same. It is true that someone might have caught him unawares and there must have been a possibility that such a person might have gone so far as to cause a breach of the peace, i.e., to use or threaten violence, but we think counsel for the defendant is right in saying that on the evidence, as we assume it to have been, no court could have been sure that this was likely. It our judgment the court can only have reached the conclusion that it did by treating 'likely' as if it had read 'liable', which it does not.

We therefore quash this conviction.

Appeal allowed.

NOTES

1. The appeal in *Valentine v Lilley* [1983] QB 92, DC, was allowed on the ground that the justices had not applied the test for a 'breach of the peace' laid down in *R v Howell* [1982] QB 416, CA (above, p. 207), in determining whether such a breach was 'likely' for the purpose of the old s. 5. Note that ss. 4 and 5 require D to intend his words etc. to be threatening, abusive or insulting etc. or to be aware that they may be (1986 Act, s. 6(3), (4)).

2. The decision of magistrates on a question of fact will only be reversed on appeal to the High Court if it is one which no reasonable bench of magistrates could reach or if it is totally unsupported by evidence (*Bracegirdle v Oxley* [1947] KB 349, DC). In most cases it is accepted that different magistrates may reasonably come to different conclusions, and the court will not interfere solely because the judges would personally have taken a different view.

An example of a case where a conviction was upset is *Hudson v Chief Constable, Avon and Somerset Constabulary* [1976] Crim LR 451. H was on the terraces at a football match. He became excited, jumping up and down and clapping his hands above his head. He fell forward and knocked the persons in front, causing a surge in the crowd. He was convicted of using threatening behaviour whereby a breach of the peace was likely to be occasioned, but the Divisional Court held that the facts found contained nothing which constituted a threat. Conversely, in *Simcock v Rhodes* (1977) 66 Cr App Rep 192, [1977] Crim LR 751, the Divisional Court upheld a conviction under the old s. 5. A police sergeant instructed a disorderly group of about 15 young people who had emerged from a dance hall to be quiet and go home. The defendant shouted to him to 'fuck off'. The words were insulting and could have resulted in a breach of the peace. In *Maile v McDowell* [1980] Crim LR 586, the Divisional Court held that an acquittal had been perverse. The defendant had been one of a crowd of 'away' supporters at a football match who had been jumping up and down, waving their fists and shouting aggressive slogans. The justices held that D's behaviour had 'not been threatening since the crowd habitually behaved in that manner, and in any event it had not been likely to occasion a breach of the peace because of a fence separating the rival groups of supporters.' The court allowed the prosecutor's appeal, holding that everybody had been guilty of threatening behaviour and that the 'presence of a Berlin-type wall to separate rival groups should not be necessary and the fact that such fencing stopped different groups from reaching each other could not of itself prevent a breach of the peace.' More doubtful cases where the High Court has declined to interfere with the justices' decision are *DPP v Clarke* (above, p. 229: display of photograph of aborted foetus found to be 'insulting'); and *Herrington v DPP* (23 June 1992, unreported, DC). In the latter case, H stood naked in his back garden, staring for some time in the direction of his neighbour's kitchen window, where he was observed by her while at her kitchen sink. This was found to be 'threatening' behaviour; although H could not have seen her at that distance as he was without his glasses, he must have been aware that his behaviour might be threatening.

3. In *Bryan v Robinson* [1960] 1 WLR 508, DC, a hostess at a non-alcoholic refreshment house in Dean Street London stood at the doorway, leaned out, smiled, beckoned and spoke to three men in the street. The men were annoyed and walked across the street. The Divisional Court allowed the hostess's appeal against conviction under the Metropolitan Police Act 1839, s. 54(13) (above, p. 225). *Per* Lord Parker CJ at 509:

'I find it very difficult to see how a mere leaning out, smiling and beckoning without more could amount to such insulting behaviour of a character whereby a breach of the peace may be occasioned. It is true that three men were annoyed, but clearly somebody can be annoyed by behaviour which is not insulting behaviour. The mere fact that they were annoyed really carries the matter no further. Even if it can be said that a reasonable person would be likely to treat the gestures as insulting, they were certainly not, in my judgment, of such a character whereby a breach of the peace may be occasioned.'

This approach is difficult to reconcile with a later decision under s. 54(13), *Masterson v Holden* [1986] 3 All ER 39, DC. The two defendants, both men, were standing by a bus stop in Oxford Street at about 2 a.m., kissing and cuddling and one fondling the other. They appeared to be unaware of others in the vicinity. They were seen by two young women, who stopped. One of them raised a hand to her mouth and both then ran to tell two young men whom they were with. The men then walked towards the defendants and one shouted 'You filthy sods. How dare you in front of our girls?' The defendants were then arrested by police officers. The justices convicted them of using 'insulting behaviour whereby a breach of the peace may be occasioned', ordered absolute discharges, and bound them over to keep the peace and be of good behaviour. The Divisional Court dismissed the defendants' appeal. Glidewell LJ rejected an argument that McCullough J's judgment in *Parkin v Norman* was

'authority for the proposition that in the case of some sort of overt behaviour between two male persons that behaviour could only be said to be insulting if it amounts to a statement that they believe that the person who sees it is a homosexual.'

That was a correct appreciation of the situation where only two persons are present in a public lavatory and one displays some homosexual activity; it was not applicable to the conduct here: 'it was in the open street, one of the busiest streets in the United Kingdom, although it was 1.55 a.m.' (p. 43).

The other argument was that in order to be insulting, conduct must be directed at another person or persons; the defendants could not be said to be directing the insult at anybody given the findings that they appeared wholly unaware of other persons in the vicinity. The response of Glidewell LJ was as follows (p. 44):

'the magistrates were perfectly entitled to infer that the two appellants must have known that other people would be likely to be present and if they had glanced up for a moment they would have seen that four people were present. Their conduct, therefore, if in the ordinary sense it was capable of being insulting, would be likely to make some impact upon anybody who was nearby in the vicinity. In that sense, while not disagreeing with the way McCullough J. put it, in circumstances such as this it can properly be said that the conduct could be insulting, albeit it was not deliberately aimed at a particular person or persons if in fact it could be insulting to any member of the public who might be passing by. So one comes back to this. Was it conduct which within the ordinary meaning of the word could be said to be insulting? The magistrates have found as a question of fact that it was. In my judgment, they were entitled so to find. Overt homosexual conduct in a public street, indeed overt heterosexual conduct in a public street, may well be considered by many persons to be objectionable, to be conduct which ought to be confined to a private place. The fact it is objectionable does not constitute an offence. But the display of such objectionable conduct in a public street may well be regarded by another person, particularly by a young woman, as conduct which insults her by suggesting that she is somebody who would find such conduct in public acceptable herself. The magistrates do not say that that was the reason for their finding. We cannot say for certain that that was their reasoning. Certainly it may have been. I content myself with saying that in my view in the ordinary use of the word "insulting" on the material in this case they were perfectly entitled to conclude that the conduct was insulting.'

Could this argument not be used to turn any objectionable conduct into 'insulting' conduct? Could it have been applied in *Bryan v Robinson*? Consider whether the defendants here would have been guilty under (1) s. 4 or (2) s. 5 of the 1986 Act.

4. In *Jordan v Burgoyne* [1963] 2 QB 744, DC, J, a leader of the National Socialist movement, was addressing a rally in Trafalgar Square. A group of young people near the speakers' platform contained many Jews, supporters of CND and communists who intended to prevent the meeting. When J used the words

'... more and more people every day ... are opening their eyes and coming to say that Hitler was right. They are coming to say that our real enemies ... were not Hitler and the National Socialists of Germany but world Jewry and its associates in this country' there was complete disorder, an outcry and a general surge forward by the crowd towards the speakers' platform. The police stopped the meeting. J was convicted of using insulting words whereby a breach of the peace was likely to be occasioned, contrary to s. 5 of the Public Order Act 1936. Quarter Sessions allowed his appeal holding that while his words were highly insulting they were not likely to lead ordinary reasonable persons to commit breaches of the peace. This decision was reversed by the Divisional Court.

Lord Parker LJ said (pp. 748, 749):

'I cannot myself, having read the speech, imagine any reasonable citizen, certainly one who was a Jew, not being provoked beyond endurance, and not only a Jew but a coloured man, and quite a number of people of this country who were told that they were merely tools of the Jews, and that they had fought in the war on the wrong side, and matters of that sort.

But, be that as it may, in my judgment, there is no room here for any test as to whether any member of the audience is a reasonable man or an ordinary citizen. . . .

This is . . . a Public Order Act, and if in fact it is apparent that a body of persons are present – and let me assume in the defendant's favour that they are a body of hooligans – yet if words are used which threaten, abuse or insult – all very strong words – then that person must take his audience as he finds them, and if those words to that audience or that part of the audience are likely to provoke a breach of the peace, then the speaker is guilty of an offence.'

Accordingly, on the assumption that the body of young persons near the platform was a body of hooligans ('I am not saying that they were') and assuming that they had come with the preconceived idea of preventing him from speaking, J committed the s. 5 offence when he addressed to them these words:

'As for the red rabble here present with us in Trafalgar Square it is not a very good afternoon at all. Some of them are looking far from wholesome, more than usual I mean. We shall of course excuse them if they have to resort to smelling salts or first aid. Meanwhile, let them howl these multi-racial warriors of the Left. It is a sound that comes natural to them, it saves them from the strain of thinking for themselves.'

These words were

'intended to be and were deliberately insulting to that body of persons being restrained by the police . . .'

His Lordship denied that there was any inroad into the doctrine of free speech:

'A man is entitled to express his own views as strongly as he likes, to criticise his opponents, to say disagreeable things about his opponents and about their policies, and to do anything of that sort. But what he must not do is – and these are the words of the section – he must not threaten, he must not be abusive and he must not insult them, "insult" in the sense of "hit by words".'

(See D. G. T. Williams, (1963) 26 MLR 425; A. Dickey, [1971] Crim LR 265, 272–275).

How would this case be decided under the new s. 4 (or s. 5)?

A. T. H. Smith argues (*Offences against Public Order* (1987), p. 14) that, notwithstanding Lord Parker's statement, there is room for a 'reasonable man' test in determining whether words are 'insulting' in the first place. This question 'must be assessed objectively, by the standards of ordinary people'. He also suggests (ibid., pp. 110–111) that the change in language from 'occasioned' in the old s. 5 to 'provoked' in the new s. 4

'might be an occasion for the rethinking of the doctrine enunciated by Lord Parker . . . that the speaker must take his audience as he finds it.'

There was no doubt that Jordan intended to provoke part of his audience; however,

'a person may be the occasion of violence without necessarily provoking it.'

Lord Parker's dictum

'has dire consequences for those who would seek to exercise freedom of speech in public. Effectively it confers on those who seek to disrupt a "heckler's veto" ' (ibid., p. 13).

5. On the facts of *Beatty v Gillbanks* (below, p. 241), would the Salvationists have committed any offence under Part I of the Public Order Act 1986?

(iv) Disruption of Lawful Activities

The statutory provisions given below afford a measure of protection to lawful meetings. Those who disrupt lawful meetings may commit other criminal offences not related in particular to meetings (see pp. 206–237). They may be ejected, and those who organise a meeting on private premises may employ stewards to preserve order (Public Order Act 1936, s. 2(6), above, p. 180). It is arguable that the police should act first against persons who disrupt or threaten to disrupt a lawful meeting, and disperse the meeting itself only if necessary in the last resort (see pp. 239–256). As to police powers of entry to prevent disorder, see *Thomas v Sawkins*, below, pp. 259–264. The Criminal Justice and Public Order Act 1994 (below) introduced new provisions in respect of disruptive trespasses.

Public Meetings Act 1908

1. Penalty on endeavour to break up public meeting.
(1) Any person who at a lawful public meeting acts in a disorderly manner for the purpose of preventing the transaction of the business for which the meeting was called together shall be guilty of an offence . . . .
(2) Any person who incites others to commit an offence under this section shall be guilty of a like offence.
(3) If any constable reasonably suspects any person of committing an offence under the foregoing provisions of this section, he may if requested so to do by the chairman of the meeting require that person to declare to him immediately his name and address and, if that person refuses or fails so to declare his name and address or gives a false name and address he shall be guilty of an offence under this subsection and liable on summary conviction thereof to a fine not exceeding [level 1 on the standard scale.]
(4) This section does not apply as respects meetings to which section 97 of the Representation of the People Act 1983 applies.

NOTES

1. Sub-s. (3) was added by the Public Order Act 1936, s. 6. The maximum penalty under s. 1(1) is now six months' imprisonment, a fine not exceeding level 5 on the standard scale. The Act does not apply to election meetings, but they are protected by analogous provisions in the Representation of the People Act 1983, s. 97, as amended by the Representation of the People Act 1985, Sch. 4, para. 39. Breach of s. 97 is an 'illegal practice' under election law (see the 1983 Act, ss. 169, 173, 174). A power to arrest a suspect for failure to give a satisfactory name and address was repealed by the Police and Criminal Evidence Act 1984, Sch. 7, and replaced, in effect, by the 1984 Act, s. 25 (above, p. 105).
2. In *Burden v Rigler* [1911] 1 KB 337, DC, justices hearing a prosecution brought under the Act held that any meeting on the highway was ipso facto unlawful. The Divisional Court held that the justices had 'no right to assume that, simply because the meeting was held on a highway it could be interrupted notwithstanding the provisions of the Public Meeting Act 1908' (Lord Alverstone CJ at 340). The case was remitted for the justices to consider inter alia whether there was an obstruction.

Criminal Justice and Public Order Act 1994

Disruptive trespassers

68. Offence of aggravated trespass

(1) A person commits the offence of aggravated trespass if he trespasses on land in the open air and, in relation to any lawful activity which persons are engaging in or are about to engage in on that or adjoining land in the open air, does there anything which is intended by him to have the effect—

    (a) of intimidating those persons or any of them so as to deter them or any of them from engaging in that activity,

    (b) of obstructing that activity, or

    (c) of disrupting that activity.

(2) Activity on any occasion on the part of a person or persons on land is 'lawful' for the purposes of this section if he or they may engage in the activity on the land on that occasion without committing an offence or trespassing on the land. . . .

(5) In this section 'land' does not include—

    (a) the highways and roads excluded from the application of section 61 by paragraph (b) of the definition of 'land' in subsection (9) of that section;[1] . . . .

69. Powers to remove persons committing or participating in aggravated trespass

(1) If the senior police officer present at the scene reasonably believes—

    (a) that a person is committing, has committed or intends to commit the offence of aggravated trespass on land in the open air; or

    (b) that two or more persons are trespassing on land in the open air and are present there with the common purpose of intimidating persons so as to deter them from engaging in a lawful activity or of obstructing or disrupting a lawful activity,

he may direct that person or (as the case may be) those persons (or any of them) to leave the land.

(2) A direction under subsection (1) above, if not communicated to the persons referred to in subsection (1) by the police officer giving the direction, may be communicated to them by any constable at the scene.

(3) If a person knowing that a direction under subsection (1) above has been given which applies to him—

    (a) fails to leave the land as soon as practicable, or

    (b) having left again enters the land as a trespasser within the period of three months beginning with the day on which the direction was given,

he commits an offence. . . .

(4) In proceedings for an offence under subsection (3) it is a defence for the accused to show—

    (a) that he was not trespassing on the land, or

    (b) that he had a reasonable excuse for failing to leave the land as soon as practicable or, as the case may be, for again entering the land as a trespasser. . . .

(6) In this section 'lawful activity' and 'land' have the same meaning as in section 68.

NOTES

1. The penalties for offences under ss. 68 and 69 are three months' imprisonment or a fine not exceeding level 4 on the standard scale or both (ss. 68(3), 69(3)). A constable in uniform who reasonably suspects that a person is committing an offence may arrest him without a warrant (ss. 68(4), 69(5)).

2. In the House of Commons, the Home Secretary, Michael Howard, noted (235 HC Deb, 11 January 1994, col 29):

'In recent months we have seen many examples of disruptive and threatening behaviour—at the Grand National, during country sports and even fishing. Those who dislike such activities have a perfect right to campaign to change the law, but they do not have the right to trespass, threaten and intimidate.'

1 ie highways other than a footpath, bridleway, by-way open to all traffic, road used as a public place or cycle track.

The main target, however, appears to be the hunt saboteurs, and the new powers were so employed immediately when they came into force on the passing of the Act on 3 November 1994. (See *Civil Liberty Agenda* 13, March 1995, p. 7.) Note that a *trespassing* hunt is not a lawful activity.

3. If the senior police officer's 'reasonable belief' is in fact incorrect, could that be raised as a matter of 'reasonable excuse' under sub-s. (4)?

(c) PREVENTIVE POWERS

(i) Powers of dispersal

According to the cases in this section, police or magistrates may take direct action against persons not acting unlawfully where necessary to preserve the peace. This action may include committing what would otherwise be assaults (*Humphries v Connor*, below; *O'Kelly v Harvey*, below, p. 245). *Duncan v Jones* (below p. 248) goes one step further: it supports the proposition that resistance to a police order to disperse may constitute the offence of obstruction of the police in the execution of their duty. These cases have been adversely criticised by commentators, although not in the courts.

Humphries v Connor (1864) 17 ICLR 1, Court of Queen's Bench in Ireland

Anne Humphries sued Daniel Connor for assault. C pleaded that he was a sub-inspector of Constabulary in Cavan; and at the time of the committing of the alleged assault, H was walking through Swanlinbar at about noon wearing a party emblem (an orange lily) the wearing of which 'was calculated and tended to provoke animosity between different classes of Her Majesty's subjects'. A number of people were provoked by the emblem, followed her, caused great noise and disturbance and threatened her with personal violence. She refused C's request to remove the emblem. C's pleadings continued:

'Whereupon the defendant . . . in order to preserve the public peace, which was likely to be broken by and in consequence of the said conduct of the plaintiff, and to protect the plaintiff from the said threatened violence, and which violence the said several persons who were provoked by the conduct of the plaintiff, as aforesaid, in consequence of her said conduct, were likely to inflict on the plaintiff, and in order to restore order and tranquillity in said town, then gently and quietly, and *necessarily and unavoidably*, removed said emblem from the plaintiff, doing her no injury whatever; and in so doing, and for the purpose of so doing, *necessarily* committed the said alleged trespass . . . and thereby protected the plaintiff from said threatened personal violence, which would otherwise have been inflicted on her, and preserved the public peace, which was likely to be, and would otherwise have been broken.'

The plaintiff demurred to this defence on the grounds that the wearing of the lily was a perfectly legal act, and afforded no excuse for any turbulence on the part of others, and that it was the duty of the defendant to protect the plaintiff and not to assault or restrain her in the exercise of a legal right. The court held that, on the assumption that the facts alleged were true, the defence was good in law.

O'Brien J: . . . With respect to the first ground . . . that it was defendant's duty as a constable to preserve the public peace, and to prevent the breach of it by disturbance or otherwise; and it appears to me that some of the authorities cited in the argument show that, under the circumstances stated in the defence, he was justified in acting as therein mentioned. The observations of Baron Alderson in *Cook v Nethercote* (1835) 6 C & P 741), and in *R v Brown* ((1841) Car & M 314), and those of Baron Parke, in *Ingle v Bell* ((1836) 1 M & W 516), show the power which policemen have, even to arrest a party, in order to prevent a breach of the peace being committed or renewed. In another case—*R v Hagan* ((1837) 8 C & P 167)—where it appeared that a man playing the bagpipes at night had attracted a crowd of dissolute persons about him, Coltman J, held that a constable who had directed the man to move on did not exceed his duty by merely laying his hand on the man's shoulder, with that view only.

According to the statements in this defence now before us, the act complained of . . . though an assault in point of law, was not a greater one than those complained of in some of the cases referred to; and it was done by defendant for the purpose of preventing a breach of the public peace, &c., and was necessary for that purpose. It has, however, been urged by plaintiff's Counsel that injurious consequences would result from our decision in defendant's favour—giving to constables a power so capable of being abused. I think it sufficient, in answer to this argument, to say that our decision would not be applicable to a state of facts where the power was abused; and that it would not protect a constable from any unnecessary, excessive, or improper exercise of such power in other cases.

Hayes J: . . . A constable, by his very appointment, is by law charged with the solemn duty of seeing that the peace is preserved. The law has not ventured to lay down what precise measures shall be adopted by him in every state of facts which calls for his interference. But it has done far better; it has announced to him, and to the public over whom he is placed, that he is not only at liberty, but is bound, to see the peace be preserved, and that he is to do everything that is necessary for that purpose, neither more nor less. What he does, he does upon the peril of answering to a jury of his country, when his conduct shall be brought into question, and he shall be charged either with exceeding or falling short of his duty. In the present case it is said that it would be a lamentable thing if an individual were to be obstructed and assaulted when doing a perfectly legal act; and that there is no law against wearing an emblem or decoration of one kind or another. I agree with that in the abstract; but I think it is not straining much the legal maxim, *sic utere tuo ut alienum non lædas*—to hold that people shall not be permitted to use even legal rights for illegal purposes. When a constable is called upon to preserve the peace, I know no better mode of doing so than that of removing what he sees to be the provocation to the breach of the peace; and, when a person deliberately refuses to acquiesce in such removal, after warning so to do, I think the constable is authorised to do everything necessary and proper to enforce it. It would seem absurd to hold that a constable may arrest a person whom he finds committing a breach of the peace, but that he must not interfere with the individual who has wantonly provoked him to do. But whether the act which he did was or was not, under all the circumstances, *necessary* to preserve the peace, is for the jury to decide. The defendant in his defence asserts that it was; and, for the purposes of this demurrer, we must take that assertion to be true. In my opinion the plea is good.

Fitzgerald J: . . . I entertain a doubt—and I may add a very serious doubt—as to the correctness of the judgment of the Court, though I defer to the greater experience and sounder opinions of my Brothers. . . . With respect to a constable, I agree that his primary duty is to preserve the peace; and he may for that purpose interfere, and, in the case of an affray, arrest the wrong-doers; or, if a breach of the peace is imminent, may, if necessary, arrest those who are about to commit it, if it cannot otherwise be prevented. But the doubt which I have is, whether a constable is entitled to interfere with one who is not about to commit a breach of the peace, or to do, or join in any illegal act, but who is likely to be made an object of insult or injury by other persons who are about to break the Queen's peace. . . .

I do not see where we are to draw the line. If a constable is at liberty to take a lily from one person, because the wearing of it is displeasing the others, who may make it an excuse for a breach of the peace, where as we to stop? It seems to me that we are making, not the law of the land but the law of the mob supreme, and recognising in constables a power of interference with the rights of the Queen's subjects, which, if carried into effect to the full extent of the principle, might be accompanied by constitutional danger. If it had been alleged that the lady wore the emblem with an intent to provoke a breach of the peace, it would render her a wrongdoer; and she might be chargeable as a person creating a breach of the peace.

NOTES

1. According to the pleadings the plaintiff's conduct was 'calculated and tended' to provoke animosity. The term 'calculated' normally means 'likely' rather than 'intended'. See Glanville Williams, *Textbook on Criminal Law* (2nd edn, 1983) p. 141. Note the difference of view as to the relevance of the plaintiff's intentions. What would be the position where a person totally unwittingly provokes a breach of the peace, as where a person wears an emblem unaware of any political connotations? Should the availability of this defence depend upon the state of mind of the person against whom the action is taken? If so, what should the relevant state of mind be?

2. In *Hughes v Casares* (1967) 111 Sol Jo 637, the defendant, a police officer, was struggling with a person under arrest in the course of transferring him to a police car. The plaintiff stood in front of the door and did not move when requested. The defendant pushed the plaintiff aside and the latter fell injuring his ankle. His claim for damages failed. Blain J held that there was no evidence of deliberate or unnecessary violence, and that the defendant's reaction was reasonable and 'no more than the occasion demanded'.

Beatty v Gillbanks (1882) 15 Cox CC 138, 9 QBD 308, 51 LJMC 117, 47 LT 194, 46 JP 789, Queen's Bench Divisional Court

Case stated by the Axbridge justices.

The three appellants, Beatty, Mullins and Bowden, were charged on the complaint of Superintendent Gillbanks that they had unlawfully and tumultuously assembled with more than 100 others in public thoroughfares and other places in Weston-super-Mare to the disturbance of the public peace. The justices found the allegations proved and bound the appellants over to keep the peace for twelve months. They stated a case for the opinion of the Divisional Court. The following facts were found to be proved. The Salvation Army had for some time organised processions in the streets of Weston-super-Mare. The Salvationists formed at the Army's Hall, were headed by a band and flags and banners, and collected a mob as they marched. There was much shouting and singing and noise. Beatty was a captain, and the other appellants leaders, of the Salvation Army, and they organised its meetings and processions. There was another organised body of persons called the Skeleton Army which also paraded the streets, and was antagonistic to the Salvationists. Other people collected in support of one or other faction. On several occasions 'a free fight, great uproar, blows, tumults, stone-throwing and disorder' ensued between the two groups. On 23 March 1882 the Salvation Army's procession was accompanied by a disorderly and riotous mob of over 2,000. The police were for a long time unable to cope with the fighting and disturbance in this mob. The Salvation Army forced their way through the streets to the Railway-parade where a general fight took place. B led the Salvationists on this occasion but neither he nor the other appellants were seen to commit any overt act of violence. In consequence, two justices issued a notice, copies of which were posted in the town and served on B, which stated that there were 'reasonable grounds for apprehending a repetition of such riotous and tumultuous assembly' and that 'we do hereby require, order, and direct all persons to abstain from assembling to the disturbance of the publice peace' in the parish.

On Sunday 26 March, the Salvation Army, under the appellants' direction, formed a procession of 100 or more and marched off. They were surrounded by a tumultuous and shouting mob of some 100 persons, which rapidly increased as they passed on. They were met and stopped by the police. The sergeant in charge told B that he must obey the notice, and disperse at once, or he would be arrested. B refused to comply, marched on at the head of the procession some 20 yards, told the sergeant that he should still proceed, and was arrested. Mullins and Bowden were also arrested when they persisted in leading the procession on. None of the appellants were guilty of any overt act of violence, and all submitted quietly to their arrest. The final two paragraphs of the case stated that this assembling of the Salvation Army was a terror to the peaceable inhabitants of Weston-super-Mare,

'and was calculated to endanger and did endanger, and was calculated to cause a breach of the public peace; and there was good and sufficient cause for the inhabitants to suppose, and any rational person knowing the aforesaid circumstances would suppose that, unless the procession and mob were dispersed, there would be a repetition of the aforesaid violent and tumultuous acts, and that there would be a breach of the peace. The appellants intended to parade their procession through the principal streets and public places of the town, and to collect on their march a large mob of persons to accompany them; and they had good reason to expect that they would come into collision with the said Skeleton Army and other persons antagonistic to the procession, and they had good reason to expect that there would be the same fighting, stone-throwing, and disturbance, as there had been on previous occasions, and intended on meeting such opposition to force their way through the said streets and places as they had done on previous occasions.'

The questions of law stated for the opinion of the court were, whether these facts so found to be proved as aforesaid constituted the offence charged in the complaint, and whether the order made – that the defendants should find sureties to keep the peace – was valid.

Field J: I am of opinion that this order cannot be supported, and must therefore be discharged. The appellants, it appears, together with a large number of other people, belong to a body of persons called the Salvation Army, who are associated together for a purpose which cannot be said to be otherwise than lawful and laudable, or at all events cannot be called unlawful, their object and intention being to induce a class of persons who have little or no knowledge of religion and no taste or disposition for religious exercises or for going to places of worship, to join them in their processions, and so to get them together to attend and take part in their religious exercises, in the hope that they may be reclaimed and drawn away from vicious and irreligious habits and courses of life, and that a kind of revival in the matter of religion may be brought about amongst those who were previously dead to any such influences. That undoubtedly is the object of the Salvation Army, and of the appellants, and no other object or intention has been or can be imputed to them; and, as has been said by their learned counsel, and doubtless with perfect truth, so far are they from desiring to carry out that object by means of any force or violence, their principles are directly and entirely opposed to any conduct of that kind, or to the exercise or employment of anything like physical force; and, indeed, it appears that on the occasion in question they used no personal force or violence, but, on the contrary, when arrested by the police, they submitted quietly without the exhibition of any resistance either on their own parts or on that of any other member of their body. Such being their lawful object and intention, and having no desire or intention of using force or violence of any kind, it appeared that on this 26th day of March they assembled, as they had previously done on other occasions, in considerable numbers at their hall, and proceeded to march thence in procession through the streets of the town of Weston-super-Mare. Now that, in itself, was certainly not an unlawful thing to do, nor can such an assembly be said to be an unlawful one. Numerous instances might be mentioned of large bodies of persons assembling in much larger numbers, and marching, accompanied by banners and bands of music, through the public streets, and no one has ever doubted that such processions were perfectly lawful. Now the appellants complain that, for having so assembled as I have before stated, they have been adjudged guilty of the offence of holding an unlawful assembly, and have in consequence been ordered to find sureties to keep the peace, in the absence of any evidence of their having broken it. It was of course necessary that the justices should find that some unlawful act had been committed by the appellants in order to justify the magistrates in binding them over. The offence charged against them was 'unlawfully and tumultuously assembling with others to the disturbance of the public peace, and against the peace of the Queen', and of course before they can be convicted upon the charge clear proof must be adduced that the specific offence charged has been committed. Now was that charge sustained? There is no doubt that the appellants did assemble together with other persons in great numbers, but that alone is insufficient. The assembly must be a 'tumultuous assembly,' and 'against the peace,' in order to render it an unlawful one. But there was nothing so far as the appellants were concerned to show that their conduct was in the least degree 'tumultuous' or 'against the peace'. All that they did was to assemble together to walk through the town, and it is admitted by the learned counsel for the respondent, that as regards the appellants themselves, there was no disturbance of the peace, and that their conduct was quiet and peaceable. But then it is argued that, as in fact their line of conduct was the same as had on previous similar occasions led to tumultuous and riotous proceedings with stone-throwing and fighting, causing a disturbance of the public peace and terror to the inhabitants of the town, and as on the present occasion like results would in all probability be produced, therefore the appellants, being well aware of the likelihood of such results again occurring, were guilty of the offence charged against them. Now, without doubt, as a general rule it must be taken that every person intends what are the natural and necessary consequences of his own acts, and if in the present case it had been their intention, or if it had been the natural and necessary consequence of their acts, to produce the disturbance of the peace which occurred, then the appellants would have been responsible for it, and the magistrates would have been right in binding them over to keep the peace. But the evidence as set forth in the case shows that, so far from that being the case, the acts and conduct of the appellants caused nothing of the kind, but, on the contrary, that the disturbance that did take place was caused entirely by the unlawful and unjustifiable interference of the Skeleton Army, a body of persons opposed to the religious views of the appellants and the Salvation Army, and that but for the opposition and molestation offered to the Salvationists by these other persons, no disturbance of any kind would have taken place. The appellants were guilty of no offence in their passing through the streets, and why should other persons interfere with or molest them? What right had they to do so? If they were doing anything unlawful it was for the magistrates and the police, the appointed guardians of law and order, to interpose. The law relating to unlawful assemblies, as laid down in the books and the cases, affords no support to the view of the matter for which the learned counsel for the respondent was obliged to contend, viz., that persons acting lawfully are to be held responsible and punished merely because other persons are thereby induced to act unlawfully and create a disturbance. In 1 Russell on Crimes (4th edn. p. 387), an unlawful assembly is defined as follows: 'An unlawful assembly, according to the common opinion, is a disturbance of the peace by persons barely assembling together with the intention to do a thing which, if it were executed, would make them rioters, but neither actually executing it nor making a motion towards the execution of it.' It is clear that, according to this definition of the offence, the appellants were not guilty, for it is not pretended that they had, but, on the contrary, it is admitted that they had not, any intention to create a riot, or to commit any riotous or other unlawful act. Many examples of what are unlawful assembles are given in Hawkins' Pleas of the Crown, book 1, cap. 28, sects. 9 and 10, in all of which the necessary circumstances of terror are present in the assembly itself, either as regards the object for which it is gathered together, or in the manner of its assembling and proceeding to carry out that object. The present case, however, differs from the cases there stated; for here the only terror that existed was caused by the unlawful resistance wilfully and designedly offered to the proceedings of the Salvation Army by an unlawful organisation outside and distinct from them, called the Skeleton Army. It was suggested by the respondent's counsel that, if these Salvation processions were allowed, similar opposition would be offered to them in future, and that similar disturbances would ensue. But I cannot believe that that will be so. I hope, and I cannot but think, that when the Skeleton Army, and all other persons who are opposed to the proceedings of the Salvation Army, come to learn, as they surely will learn, that they have no possible right to interfere with or in any way obstruct the Salvation Army in their lawful and peaceable processions, they will abstain from opposing or disturbing them. It is usual happily in this country for people to respect and obey the law when once declared and understood, and I have hope and have no doubt that it will be so in the present case. But, if it should not be so, there is no doubt that the magistrates and police, both at Weston-super-Mare and everywhere else, will understand their duty and not fail to do it efficiently, or hesitate, should the necessity arise, to deal with the Skeleton Army and other disturbers of the public peace as they did in the present instance with the appellants, for no one can doubt that the authorities are only anxious to do their duty and to prevent a disturbance of the public peace. The present decision of the justices, however, amounts to this, that a man may be punished for acting lawfully if he knows that his so doing may induce another man to act unlawfully—a proposition without any authority whatever to support it. Under these circumstances, the questions put to us by the justices must be negatively answered, and the order appealed against be discharged.

Cave J: I am entirely of the same opinion . . .

[His Lordship referred to Hawkins' Pleas of the Crown and Dalton's Country Justice]

Now, putting these several passages from these old authorities together, it seems to me to be impossible to hold that the appellants here have been brought within them as being guilty of unlawfully and tumultuously assembling. The meeting or assembly of the Salvation Army was for a purpose not unlawful. Was there an intention on their part to use violence? If, though their meeting was in itself lawful, they intended, if opposed, to meet force by force, that would render their meeting an unlawful assembly; but it does not appear that they entertained any such intention. On the contrary, when met and resisted by the Skeleton Army, they used no violence of any kind, and manifested no intention of meeting their opponents with like violence to that which the latter offered to them. . . .

Appeal allowed.

NOTES

1. This was not a *prosecution* for unlawful assembly. The justices had no jurisdiction to try that offence. It was nevertheless regarded as an authority on the scope of the offence: see *Brownlie*, pp. 125–126. Its primary importance lies in its recognition of the point that a group of persons acting lawfully are not to be regarded as acting unlawfully when others threaten to cause a breach of the peace. See generally *Smith*, pp. 12–15.

2. Between 1878 and 1891 there were 'Salvation Army riots' in at least 60 towns and cities: see V. Bailey, 'Salvation Army Riots, the "Skeleton Army" and Legal Authority in the Provincial Town' in A. P. Donajgrodzki (ed), *Social Control in Nineteenth Century Britain* (1977), Chap. 9. The organised opposition to the Salvationists owed much to the brewery trade, but was also encouraged by persons in a 'higher social position' who objected to the disruption of 'the customary quiet of the town' and indeed by both police and magistracy (Bailey, op. cit., pp. 241, 243–44). Many borough authorities sought to rely on a common law power to prohibit processions where they would lead to breaches of the peace. In this they relied on the advice of the Home Secretary (*The Times*, 11 October 1881, p. 6). *Beatty v Gillbanks* showed, however, that such prohibitions lacked legal force. In consequence, the authorities turned to provisions in byelaws and local Acts prohibiting, for example, singing and the playing of music in public or Sunday processions (see e.g. *Kruse v Johnson* [1898] 2 QB 91, DC) and in some areas, police protection of street parades was withdrawn, the aim being to restrict the work of Salvationists to indoor meetings (Bailey, op. cit., pp. 245–247).

3. How convincing is the argument that the disturbances were not *caused* by the Salvationists? Had the Salvationists not marched there would have been no disturbances. Moreover, the disturbances were both foreseeable and foreseen. To what extent would you regard the court's interpretation of the facts found as unduly favourable to the Salvationists? Note the criticisms expressed in *O'Kelly v Harvey* below, pp. 245–247.

4. The question whether those who 'innocently' provoke a breach of the peace can be guilty of unlawful assembly is separate from the question whether direct action may be taken against them in order to preserve the peace (see above, pp. 239–241 and below, pp. 245–248).

5. In *R v Londonderry Justices* (1891) 28 LR Ir 440, QBD, the court granted certiorari to quash orders binding over certain Salvationists to keep the peace. Their parades attracted a hostile crowd, but there was no act of hostility and no act of misconduct on the part of the Salvationists. The court held there was no evidence to support the orders.

6. *Beatty v Gillbanks* was distinguished in *Wise v Dunning* [1902] 1 KB 167, DC. 'Pastor' George Wise conducted a Protestant 'crusade' in Liverpool. He addressed a series of street meetings, using insulting and provocative language and gestures. At one meeting he put beads round his neck and waved a crucifix above his head. At another he referred to Roman Catholics as 'rednecks'. He did not himself commit any breach of the peace, nor did he incite his supporters to do so, but his conduct provoked his opponents to do so. He was bound over to keep the peace and be of good behaviour for 12 months. He appealed by case stated arguing that the magistrate had no jurisdiction (1) to bind him over to keep the peace because there was no evidence that he had committed a breach of the peace, or (2) to bind him over to be of good behaviour because it was not 'justly suspected' that he intended to break the peace. 'The appellant's conduct was lawful, and he cannot be bound over because the conduct of others was, or was likely to be, unlawful: *Beatty v Gillbanks*' (F. E. Smith, in argument). The Divisional Court upheld the order. Darling and Channell JJ held that breaches of the peace were the 'natural consequence' of W's provocative conduct. Channell J stated at 179 and 180 that while 'the law does not as a rule regard an illegal act as being the natural consequence of a temptation which may be held out to commit it . . . the cases with respect to apprehended breaches of the peace show that the law does regard the infirmity of human temper to the extent of considering that a breach of the peace, although an illegal act, may be the natural consequence of insulting or abusive language or conduct.'

Darling J pointed out (at p. 179) in relation to *Beatty v Gillbanks* and *R v Londonderry Justices* 'the whole question is one of fact and evidence'.

Lord Alverstone CJ referred to the Liverpool Improvement Act 1842 s. 149, which was identical in terms to the Metropolitan Police Act 1839 s. 54(13), (above p. 225), and said that it has a 'very important bearing on this case' (p. 176), (although no charge was actually brought under the Act).

'[W's] language and conduct went very far indeed towards inciting people to commit, or was, at any rate, language and behaviour likely to occasion, a breach of the peace' (p. 177).

7. *Beatty v Gillbanks* was the subject of comment by Hutton J in *R v Secretary of State for Northern Ireland, ex p Atkinson* [1987] 8 NIJB 6, 26–33 (for a summary see below, p. 255). No express argument was based by the plaintiff on *Beatty v Gillbanks*, but it was regarded as implicit in some of counsel's submissions. Hutton J stated that

'there is clear authority that there is a limitation to the *Beatty v Gillbanks* principle. This limitation was laid down by the Irish Court of Appeal in *O'Kelly v Harvey* [below]' (p. 27).

Accordingly, the Magherafelt band could be stopped from going to Keady even though it was not unlawful for the band to do so.

O'Kelly v Harvey (1883) 15 Cox CC 435, 10 LR Ir 285, 14 LR Ir 105, Exchequer Division and Court of Appeal in Ireland

The plaintiff claimed damages for assault and battery. H, a magistrate, had laid his hand on him in the course of dispersing a meeting held on 7 December 1880 to encourage tenant farmers not to pay their rents. The 13th paragraph of the defence stated that the meeting had been advertised in advance as a 'Great Land Demonstration' which would probably be addressed by C. S. Parnell and other MPs. In response the following notice was circulated:

Orangemen of Fermanagh, will you allow your country to be disgraced by letting a Land League meeting be held (as advertised) at Brookeborough, on 7th Dec. inst., where addresses are to be delivered not only dishonest but treasonable, and opposed to your principles?

When the Government won't protect Protestant life and property, it is time we should do so ourselves, and put a stop to all treasonable proceedings in our loyal county Fermanagh.

Remember the treatment of your brethren at Lough Mask!!! Assemble in your thousands at Brookeborough on Tuesday, and give Parnell and his associates a warm reception.

God save the Queen.

Brookeborough, Dec. 4th, 1880.

The defendant claimed that he believed, and had reasonable and probable grounds for believing that if the meeting were held many Orangemen would meet in pursuance of the second notice and the public peace would be broken. Para. 13 continued:

'The defendant . . . believed, *and had reasonable and probable grounds for believing*, that a breach of the peace would occur if said meeting were allowed to be held and continued; and that the public peace and tranquillity could not otherwise be preserved than by separating and dispersing the plaintiff and said other persons so assembled as aforesaid; and the defendant, being present at said meeting, requested the plaintiff and said other persons so assembled to disperse, which they neglected to do; and thereupon the defendant laid his hand on the plaintiff, in order to separate and disperse the plaintiff and said other persons so assembled as aforesaid, using no more violence than was necessary for the purpose aforesaid, which is the assault and battery complained of.'

The plaintiff demurred on the ground that this did not disclose a defence. The Exchequer Division (Palles CB, Fitzgerald and Dowse BB) and the Court of Appeal (Law LC, Morris CJ, Deasy and Fitzgibbon LJJ) held that the defence was good.

The judgment of the Court of Appeal was delivered by **Law LC**: . . . The question then seems to be reduced to this: assuming the plaintiff and others assembled with him to be doing nothing unlawful, but yet that there were reasonable grounds for the defendant believing as he did that there would be a breach of the peace if they continued so assembled, and that there was no other way in which the breach of the peace could be avoided but by stopping and dispersing the plaintiff's meeting—was the defendant justified in taking the necessary steps to stop and disperse it? In my opinion he was so justified under the peculiar circumstances stated in the defence, and which for the present must be taken as admitted to be there truly stated. Under such circumstances the defendant was not to defer action until a breach of the peace had actually been committed. His paramount duty was to preserve the peace unbroken, and that by whatever means were available for the purpose. Furthermore, the duty of a justice of the peace being to preserve the peace unbroken, he is, of course, entitled, and in fact bound to intervene the moment he has reasonable apprehensions of a breach of the peace being imminent; and, therefore, he must in such cases necessarily act on his own reasonable and *bonâ fide* belief as to what is likely to occur. Accordingly, in the present case, even assuming that the danger to the public peace arose altogether from the threatened attack of another body on the plaintiff and his friends, still; if the defendant believed and had just grounds for believing that the peace could only be preserved by withdrawing the plaintiff and his friends from the attack with which they were threatened, it was I think the duty of the defendant to take that course. This indeed was, as it appears to me, substantially decided here some years ago by the Court of Queen's Bench in the case of *Humphries v Connor* (1864) 17 ICLR 1. . . .

So also here the vital averment that the defendant had reasonable grounds for his belief that the peace could not be preserved by any other means than those which he adopted must, I think, be regarded as a sufficient statement of a matter or fact on which the plaintiff could safely take issue, as no doubt he has done, and which, if not proved at the trial to the satisfaction of the jury, the defence must necessarily fail. If it be suggested that the defence should have been more communicative and distinct as to the defendant's grounds of belief, the answer is that any embarrassment so caused—if, indeed, there was any, which I do not myself belief there was—should have been dealt with by motion. On the record, however, as it stands, no such point as this is open for consideration. During the argument the recent case of *Beatty v Gillbanks* ((1882) 9 QBD 308) was much relied on by the plaintiff's counsel. I frankly own that I cannot understand that decision, having regard to the facts stated in the special case there submitted to the court, and which, with all deference to the learned judges who decided it, appear to me to have presented all the elements necessary to constitute the offence known as 'unlawful assembly.' Field J quotes a passage from Serjeant Hawkins to the effect that any meeting of great numbers of people, with such circumstances of terror as cannot but endanger the public peace and raise fears and jealousies among the King's subjects, is an unlawful assembly, and suggests that, for this purpose, the 'circumstances of terror' must exist in the assembly itself. Well, even supposing this to be so, what is to be said as to the paragraph of the case which stated (sect. m) that the particular assemblage in question was a terror to the peaceable inhabitants of the town, and especially to those then going to their respective places of worship, and was calculated to endanger, and did endanger, the public peace, I should have thought that an assemblage of that character had in itself sufficient 'circumstances of terror' to make it unlawful. But, again, we find it stated that Beatty and his friends constituting this Salvation Army procession knew they were likely to be attacked on this occasion, as before, by the body which had been organised in antagonism to them, and that there would be fighting, stone-throwing, and disturbance as there had been on previous occasions; and further, that they intended, on meeting such opposition, to fight and force their way through the streets and public places as they had done before. I confess I should have thought that this, too, was no bad description of an unlawful assembly. Indeed, I have always understood the law to be that any needless assemblage of persons in such numbers and manner and under such circumstances as are likely to provoke a breach of the peace, was itself unlawful; and this, I may add, appears to be the view taken by the very learned persons who revised the Criminal Code Bill in 1878. But, after all, that decision of Field and Cave JJ is no authority against the view I take of the case now before us. I assume here that the plaintiff's meeting was not unlawful. But the question still remains. Was not the defendant justified in separating and dispersing it if he had reasonable grounds for his belief that by no other possible means could he perform his duty of preserving the peace? For the reasons already given I think he was so justified, and therefore that the defence in question is good; . . .
Appeal dismissed.

NOTES

1. The reference to Lough Mask relates to the social ostracism of Captain Charles Boycott, land agent for Lord Erne, who lived in Lough Mask House, Co. Mayo (see J. Marlow, *Captain Boycott and the Irish* (1973)). The Land League was founded in 1879 under the presidency of C. S. Parnell, and proceeded to hold meetings, particularly in Connaught. Its aims were the reduction of rent and evictions, and the ultimate achievement of tenant ownership. The first meeting organised in Ulster was at Belleek on 9 November 1880:

'Some disturbance was anticipated and an opposition meeting was talked of, but it did not take place, and the proceedings passed off quietly. A large force of police and military was sent down from Eniskellen and kept under arms during the day, but there was no need for their services'
(*The Times*, 10 November 1880).

For the meeting on 7 December 1880, over 100 extra police were brought into Brookeborough, and over 100 men of the 2nd Dragoons were billeted nearby. J. J. O'Kelly MP and others arrived by train from Dublin. They drove to the field

'and found it occupied by a crowd of people and a strong force of police under the direction of Mr Harvey RM. When Mr O'Kelly entered the field, Mr Harvey, advancing to him, asked what he had come for, and on his replying that he had come to attend the meeting, Mr Harvey took him by the shoulders and gave him into the custody of a constable. He demanded by what authority the magistrate did so, and Mr Harvey directed the constable to remove him from the field .... Mr O'Kelly and his friends ... drove away to the distance of about half a mile, in the direction of the railway, where a crowd collected and a meeting was hastily formed. Apprehending the interference of the police, the promoters of it cut short the proceedings ....'
(*The Times*, 8 December 1880).

Interestingly, the authorities took a different approach in respect of a meeting at Scotstown, Co. Monaghan on 9 December, which O'Kelly and John Dillon MP attended. A counter demonstration by Orangemen had been announced. The 2nd Dragoons were moved in from Brookeborough and there was a strong force of police. The time, the Land League meeting was not prohibited. Instead, Major Blair RM and others persuaded Lord Rossmore, County Grand Master of the Orange Order, to adjourn the Orange meeting (*The Times*, 10 December 1880). On the origins and development of the land war in Ulster see R. W. Kirkpatrick in F. S. L. Lyons and A. J. Hawkins (eds), *Ireland under the Union* (1980) pp. 201–235.

O'Kelly had formerly been a soldier in the French Foreign Legion, a captain in the French army and a war correspondent in Cuba and the USA. In this last capacity he had been with US troops in the war against the Sioux chief, Sitting Bull (H. Boyland, *A Dictionary of Irish Biography* (1978) p. 272).

2. Compare the principle of *Humphries v Connor* and *O'Kelly v Harvey* with (1) the law on arrest for breach of the peace, above, p. 207 and (2) s. 3 of the Criminal Law Act 1967, above p. 74. If the circumstances are such as to justify detention, then the use of force short of arrest is similarly justified.

3. It is clear that ample legal powers are available to deal with the persons who are threatening disorder in situations such as these. The principle of these cases is designed to assist the policeman on the spot who may be faced with practical problems. Nevertheless, the principle is dangerous, if acceptable at all. It should be confined to cases of genuine last resort. If not it might become too easy to suppress the expression of unpopular views by threatening violence against those who express them. Where the police had advance warning of a problem of the *O'Kelly v Harvey* kind, should they be allowed to rely on the principle endorsed by that case, or should they be required to mobilise sufficient support to deal with the 'hostile' group?

4. Cf. *R v Coventry City Council ex p Phoenix Aviation* [1995] All ER 37, DC, where it was held that port and airport authorities were not entitled to bar live animal exports in response to unlawful threats.

Duncan v Jones [1936] 1 KB 218, 105 LJKB 71, 154 LT 110, 99 JP 399, 52 TLR 26, 79 Sol Jo 903, 33 LGR 491, 30 Cox CC 279, King's Bench Divisional Court
Case stated by the County of London Quarter Sessions.

At 1 p.m. on 30 July 1934, about thirty people, including the appellant, Mrs Katherine Duncan, collected with a view to holding a meeting in Nynehead Street, New Cross, Deptford, a cul-de-sac, near to the entrance to an unemployed training centre. The meeting was to protest against the Incitement to Disaffection Bill. At the entrance to Nynehead Street a notice was written across the roadway as follows:—

'SEDITION'

Meeting at the Test Centre to-day (now) 1 p m
Speakers: R. Kidd (Council for Civil Liberties),
A. Bing (Barrister-at-Law),
E. Hanley (Amalgamated Engineers' Union),
K. Duncan (National Unemployed Workers' Movement),
Defend the right of free speech and public meeting.

A box was placed in the roadway opposite the entrance to the training centre, on which the appellant was about to mount, when the chief constable of the district, with whom was Inspector Jones, told her that a meeting could not be held in Nynehead Street, but that it could be held in Desmond Street, some 175 yards distant. The appellant then said: 'I'm going to hold it,' stepped on to the box, and started to address the people who were present, when the respondent immediately took her into custody, to which she submitted without resistance.

D was convicted by a magistrate of obstructing J in the execution of his duty contrary to the Prevention of Crimes Act 1871, s. 12, as amended by the Prevention of Crimes Amendment Act 1885, s. 2. She was fined 40s, and appealed to London Quarter Sessions.

At the hearing of the appeal it was not alleged . . . that there was any obstruction of the highway or of the access to the training centre, save in the sense of the obstruction necessarily caused by the box which was placed in the roadway and by the presence of the people surrounding it. Neither was it alleged that the appellant nor any of the persons present at the meeting had either committed, incited or provoked any breach of the peace.

It was proved or admitted that on 25 May 1933, a meeting had been held opposite the entrance to the training centre, and the appellant had addressed that meeting. Following the meeting and on the same day a disturbance took place inside the training centre. The superintendent of the training centre, who attributed the disturbance to the meeting, sent for the police to prevent a breach of the peace. Subsequently, and in spite of the disturbance and of warnings by the police, the appellant, for some reason unexplained by her, made one or more attempts to hold a meeting at the same spot, which were frustrated by the police. Before 30 July 1934, the superintendent of the training centre, who feared a repetition of the previous disturbance, communicated with the police, and by reason of such communication and of reports by the police in the course of their duty, the chief constable of the district and the respondent apprehended that a breach of the peace would result if the meeting now in question were held.

The deputy-chairman of quarter sessions was of opinion: (1.) that in fact (if it be material) the appellant must have known of the probable consequences of her holding the meeting—namely, a disturbance and possibly a breach of the peace—and was not unwilling that such consequences should ensue; (2.) that in fact the respondent reasonably apprehended a breach of the peace; (3.) that in law it thereupon became his duty to prevent the holding of the meeting; and (4.) that in fact, by attempting to hold the meeting, the appellant obstructed the respondent when in the execution of his duty. The appeal was, therefore, dismissed. A case was stated for the opinion of the Court whether there was evidence on which the deputy-chairman could so decide in point of law.

Lord Hewart CJ: There have been moments during the argument in this case when it appeared to be suggested that the Court had to do with a grave case involving what is called the right of public meeting. I say 'called,' because English law does not recognize any special right of public meeting for political or other purposes. The right of assembly, as Professor Dicey puts it (Dicey's Law of the Constitution, 8th edn., p. 499), is nothing more than a view taken by the Court of the individual liberty of the subject. If I thought that the present case raised a question which has been held in suspense by more than one writer on constitutional law—namely, whether an assembly can properly be held to be unlawful merely because the holding of it is expected to give rise to a breach of the peace on the part of persons opposed to those who are holding the meeting—I should wish to hear much more argument before I expressed an opinion. This case, however, does not even touch that important question.

Our attention has been directed to the somewhat unsatisfactory case of *Beatty v Gillbanks* ((1882) 9 QBD 308). The circumstances of that case and the charge must be remembered, as also must the important passage in the judgment of Field J, in which Cave J concurred. Field J said (Ibid. 314): 'I entirely concede that everyone must be taken to intend the natural consequences of his own acts, and it is clear to me that if this disturbance of the peace was the natural consequence of acts of the appellants they would be liable, and the justices would have been right in binding them over. But the evidence set forth in the case does not support this contention; on the contrary, it shows that the disturbances were caused by other people antagonistic to the appellants, and that no acts of violence were committed by them.' Our attention has also been directed to other authorities where the judgments in *Beatty v Gillbanks* have been referred to, but they do not carry the matter any further, although they more than once express a doubt about the exact meaning of the decision. In my view, *Beatty v Gillbanks* is apart from the present case. No such question as that which arose there is even mooted here.

The present case reminds one rather of the observations of Bramwell B in *R v Prebble* ((1858) 1 F&F 325 at 326), where, in holding that a constable, in clearing certain licensed premises of the persons thereon, was not acting in the execution of his duty, he said: 'It would have been otherwise had there been a nuisance or disturbance of the public peace, or any danger of a breach of the peace.'

The case stated which we have before us indicates a causal connection between the meeting of May 1933, and the disturbance which occurred after it—that the disturbance was not only *post* the meeting but was also *propter* the meeting. In my view, the deputy-chairman was entitled to come to the conclusion to which he came on the facts which he found and to hold that the conviction of the appellant for wilfully obstructing the respondent when in the execution of his duty was right. This appeal should, therefore, be dismissed.

Humphrey J: I agree. I regard this as a plain case. It has nothing to do with the law of unlawful assembly. No charge of that sort was even suggested against the appellant. The sole question raised by the case is whether the respondent, who was admittedly obstructed, was so obstructed when in the execution of his duty.

It does not require authority to emphasize the statement that it is the duty of a police officer to prevent apprehended breaches of the peace. Here it is found as a fact that the respondent reasonably apprehended a breach of the peace. It then, as is rightly expressed in the case, became his duty to prevent anything which in his view would cause that breach of the peace. While he was taking steps so to do he was wilfully obstructed by the appellant. I can conceive no clearer case within the statutes than that.

Singleton J: On the facts stated in the case I am satisfied that the respondent at the material time was doing that which it was his duty to do, and that, therefore, the obstruction of him by the appellant constituted obstruction of him when in the execution of his duty. Authorities in other branches of the law do not carry the matter any further. I agree that the appeal should be dismissed.

Appeal dismissed.

NOTES

1. This case has received widespread condemnation from academic commentators. See E. C. S. Wade, (1937) 6 CLJ 175; *Williams*, pp. 119–123; *Brownlie*, pp. 111–115; T. C. Daintith, [1966] PL 248. It has been followed in New Zealand: *Burton v Power* [1940] NZLR 305, but not the Australian Capital Territory (see n. **10** below).

2. An alternative version of events is given in A. Barrister, *Justice in England* (1938) pp. 247–260. See also *Williams*, pp. 127–128 on the ban on meetings.

3. 'The police are set up by this judgment as the arbiters of what political parties or religious sects shall and shall not be accorded the rights of freedom of speech and freedom of assembly' (R. Kidd, *British Liberty in Danger* (1940) p. 24). Do you agree?

4. How convincing is the finding of fact that a breach of the peace was reasonably apprehended? Consider the width of the discretion which may be exercised by the police. Is there any suggestion that the police action was *necessary* in the *last resort*? Should this be a precondition to dispersal of a lawful meeting? (cf. *Humphries v*

Connor, O'Kelly v Harvey, above). Note that the meeting in *Duncan v Jones* was not alleged to be unlawful. On the facts given, however, what offences might have been committed?

5. Is it possible to reconcile *Duncan v Jones* with *Beatty v Gillbanks* (above, p. 241) (1) in law; (2) in spirit? (See T. C. Daintith, [1966] PL 248; S. A. de Smith, *Constitutional and Administrative Law*, (5th edn, 1985) pp. 513–518) (a passage omitted from subsequent editions). Does it matter, given that both are merely decisions of the Divisional Court? An important point made by Daintith is that obstructing the police in the execution of their duty was a summary offence under a variety of statutory provisions at the time of *Beatty v Gillbanks* and could have been used by the prosecutor in that case (op. cit. p. 251). He suggests that the reason why it was not used was that 'not until 1936 was it revealed that facts insufficient to establish the offence of unlawful assembly might yet amount to obstruction of the police in the execution of their duty. . . . [U]nless an assembly was unlawful, the police had no duty to disperse it . . .' (op. cit. pp. 251–2).

6. Compare the reasoning in *Duncan v Jones* with that of *Thomas v Sawkins* (below, p. 259), and that of *R v Waterfield* [1964] 1 QB 164. Note that other cases have taken a more restrictive view of what conduct, and in particular, disobedience to what commands, may amount to obstruction of the police in the execution of their duty (above pp. 58–65).

7. D. N. Pritt, who defended Mrs Duncan in the court, sponsored by the NCCL, told the House of Commons: 'You can always lend an air of plausibility to the enterprise of stopping the meeting by offering . . . an alternative site 175 yards away. . . . [I]f you cannot get an audience 175 yards away you might as well be 175 miles away' (314 HC Deb 10 July 1936 col 1551).

8. The basic issue is one of policy. Where X 'innocently' provokes Y to commit breaches of the peace, and the police wish to take direct action against X, the alternatives are (1) the police pay compensation (damages) to X (who is after all 'innocent'), with the money coming out of public (police) funds; or (2) the police needn't pay damages (*Humphries v Connor*); or (3) the police needn't pay damages, and any resistance is an offence (*Duncan v Jones*).

9. The police in practice rely on *Duncan v Jones* to control the numbers of pickets outside places of work, and the judges do not show much inclination to challenge assertions by police officers that they had reasonable grounds to apprehend breaches of the peace. See *Piddington v Bates* (below p. 251). It has been extended to persons stopped at some distance from the place they appear to be intending to picket. See *Moss v McLachlan*, below p. 253.

10. In *Forbutt v Blake*, *Reid v Eggins*, *Vickers v Pearson* (1980) 51 FLR 465 Connor ACJ in the Supreme Court of the Australian Capital Territory declined to follow *Duncan v Jones*. The appellants had been part of a group of about 15 young women who wished to protest about women raped in war. They proposed to march in or alongside the Anzac Day parade (which is equivalent to a Remembrance Day parade). They were dressed in black and some carried placards with inscriptions such as 'Patriots kill' and 'Heroes rape'. On the day in question they disobeyed an instruction from a police officer not to march and they were subsequently convicted of obstructing a police officer in the execution of his duty. Connor ACJ allowed their appeal. He held that there was prima facie evidence:

(1) that the police officer had reasonable grounds to believe that some members of the public might be provoked into committing acts against the group which would constitute a breach or breaches of the peace;

(2) that this was 'imminent':

'Imminence must be a relative concept and in these circumstances I would not hesitate to describe a breach of the peace which might well have occurred during the ensuing five to ten minutes as "imminent" (p. 471)';

(3) that the arrests were 'necessary to preserve the peace': it could not be said

'that the peace could have been preserved equally well by less drastic means such as perhaps removing the placards and the wreath and ordering the members of the group to disperse' (ibid);

(4) that the women were not committing an offence at the time the order was given and were not suspected to be about to commit any offence.

However, disobedience to the police order could not in these circumstances constitute the offence charged: the most the police

'could legally have done was to arrest the appellants in order to bring them before a court to seek to have them bound over to keep the peace' (p. 476).

'If this were not so it seems to me that quite extraordinary results would follow. A policeman might bona fide form the view that the attendance of a person, holding an exalted public office, at an official function might provoke some errant members of the public to commit breaches of the peace. He could presumably order that person to stay away from the function and, if he disobeyed, could charge him with obstructing the police in the execution of their duty. Members of Parliament could thus be forbidden to address hostile audiences during election campaigns. It is to be observed that the penalty for the offence of obstructing the police, if tried on indictment, is imprisonment for two years. I am quite unable to attribute an intention to the legislature to expose a person to such a penalty for disobeying a police order to cease a lawful activity in circumstances where the only relevant police duty is to prevent a breach of the peace by other citizens against him. What was said by O'Brien J in *R v Londonderry Justices* (1891) 28 LR Ir 440 seems much in point: "If danger arises from the exercise of lawful rights resulting in a breach of the peace, the remedy is the presence of sufficient force to prevent the result, not the legal condemnation of those who exercise those rights"' (ibid, at p. 450).

His Lordship regarded *Wise v Dunning* [1902] 1 KB 167, DC (above, p. 244) as authority for the proposition that

'a binding over order may be available against a person who has not committed any offence in circumstances where the consequences of his lawful conduct is likely to produce a breach of the peace by other persons' (p. 476).

Piddington v Bates [1961] 1 WLR 162, [1960] 3 All ER 660, Queen's Bench Divisional Court

Eighteen men arrived to picket a printer's works where about eight of the normal complement of twenty-four were working. Chief Inspector Bates told the appellant that two pickets at each of the two entrances were sufficient. He replied 'I'm going there and you can't stop me', 'I know my rights', and 'I can stand by the gate if I want to' and finally, 'I'm going to join them. If you don't want me to, you'd better arrest me'. He then pushed gently past the prosecutor and was gently arrested. He was convicted of obstructing the prosecutor in the execution of this duty, and appealed.

Lord Parker CJ: . . . First, the mere statement by a constable that he did anticipate that there might be a breach of the peace is clearly not enough. There must exist proved facts from which a constable could reasonably anticipate such a breach. Secondly, it is not enough that his contemplation is that there is a remote possibility; there must be a real possibility of a breach of the peace. Accordingly, in every case, it becomes a question of whether, on the particular facts, it can be said that where there were reasonable grounds on which a constable charged with this duty reasonably anticipated that a breach of the peace might occur . . . . The magistrate found, so far as it is material: 'Having regard to the whole of the evidence the [prosecutor] was in my opinion justified in anticipating the possibility of a breach of the peace unless steps were taken to prevent it, and in my opinion it was his duty to decide what those steps should be.' That is challenged by the defendant on two grounds. The first and lesser ground is a criticism of the word 'possibility' of a breach of the peace. It is said that there must be something more than a mere possibility. I agree with that, but I do not read the finding of the magistrate as saying that it was just a mere remote possibility. I think he was referring to it as a real possibility.

The other point goes to an analysis of the evidence, from which it is said that no reasonable man could possibly anticipate a breach of the peace. It is pointed out that there was no obstruction in the street; that there was no actual intimidation; and that there were no threats or intimations of violence. It is said that there was really nothing save the fact that picketing was going on to suggest that a breach of the peace was a real possibility.

As I have said, every case must depend upon its exact facts, and the matter which influences me in this case is the matter of numbers. It is, I think, perfectly clear from the wording of the case, although it is not expressly so found, that the police knew that in these small works there were only eight people working. They found two vehicles arriving, with 18 people milling about the street, trying to form pickets at the doors. On that ground alone, coupled with the telephone call which, I should have thought, intimated some sense of urgency and apprehension, the police were fully entitled to think as reasonable men that there was a real danger of something more than mere picketing to collect or impart information or peaceably to persuade. I think that in those circumstances the prosecutor had reasonable grounds for anticipating that a breach of the peace was a real possibility. It may be, and I think this is the real criticism, that it can be said: Well, to say that only two pickets should be allowed is purely arbitrary; why two? Why not three? Where do you draw the line? I think that a police officer charged with the duty of preserving the Queen's peace must be left to take such steps as on the evidence before him he thinks are proper. I am far from saying that there should be any rule that only two pickets should be allowed at any particular door. There, one gets into an arbitrary area, but so far as this case is concerned I cannot see that there was anything wrong in the action of the prosecutor.

Finally, I would like to say that all these matters are so much matters of degree that I would hesitate, except on the clearest evidence, to interfere with the findings of magistrates who have had the advantage of hearing the whole case and observing the witnesses. . . .

Ashworth and **Elwes JJ** agreed.

Appeal dismissed.

NOTES

1. See also *Tynan v Balmer* [1967] 1 QB 91, DC and *Kavanagh v Hiscock* [1974] QB 600, DC. Wallington ([1972] 1 ILJ 219, 222) observes that 'any form of mass picketing almost inevitably involves the commission of offences, unless the pickets remain quiet and orderly, do not obstruct the street or the footway, and do as they are told by the police.'

2. *Duncan v Jones* appears to have been relied upon by the police during operations in respect of the miners' strike. For example, on 18 March 1984 the police attempted to stop anyone who appeared to be a miner or who was travelling north to aid the strike from crossing the Thames via the Dartford Tunnel. (See S. Miller and M. Walker, *A State of Siege* (A Report to the Yorkshire Area NUM) (1984) pp. 19–23.) Miners claimed that they had been told they would be arrested if they crossed the county boundary; the police claimed that they were warned that they could later be arrested for causing a breach of the peace. On the assumption that the miners' version is correct, would that fall within the principle of *Duncan v Jones*? Would the police be entitled to prevent a 'working miner' entering a pit on the ground that this would provoke pickets to commit breaches of the peace? (Cf. (1984) 134 NLJ 325–326.) Why do you think the police did not take such action? See also *Moss v McLachlan* below, p. 253. On the use of bail conditions to restrict picketing, see *R v Mansfield Justices, ex p Sharkey* [1985] 1 All ER 193, DC.

3. The current statutory protection for peaceful picketing is section 220 of the Trade Union and Labour Relations (Consolidation) Act 1992:

'(1) It shall be lawful for a person in contemplation or furtherance of a trade dispute to attend
   (*a*) at or near his own place of work; or

(b) if he is an official of a trade union, at or near the place of work of a member of that union whom he is accompanying and whom he represents,

for the purpose only of peacefully obtaining or communicating information, or peacefully persuading any person to work or abstain from working.'

This protects pickets from civil actions in trespass or for inducing breaches of contract, but not in respect of unreasonable obstruction of access to premises, unreasonable obstruction of the highway or simply attendance in large numbers (whose purposes will not be regarded as 'peacefully obtaining or communicating information' etc.: *Thomas v National Union of Mineworkers (South Wales Area)* [1985] 2 All ER 1, 20) (*Sweet & Maxwell's Encyclopaedia of Employment Law*, para. 1.8427). It also absolves a picket from criminal liability 'where an act which is reasonably necessary for the communication of information involves a criminal act, such as technical obstruction' (R. Kidner, *Trade Union Law* (2nd edn, 1983) p. 187). Again this will not extend to unreasonable obstructions of the highway (*Tynan v Balmer* [1967] 1 QB 91) or offences such as breaches of the Public Order Act 1986 (above, pp. 212–237), and breaches of section 241 of the Trade Union and Labour Relations (Consolidation) Act 1992 (see below, p. 537, and Kidner, pp. 194–198; *Galt v Philp* [1984] IRLR 156; K. Miller, (1984) 13 ILJ 111). In 1980, the government (with Parliament's approval) issued a Code of Practice on picketing and a revised version was issued in 1992 (*Encyclopaedia of Employment Law*, paras. 6.0056 et seq.), which, inter alia, states that 'pickets and their organisers should ensure that in general the number of pickets does not exceed six at any entrance to or exit from a workplace; frequently a smaller number will be appropriate' (para. 51). A person's failure to observe the code 'shall not of itself render him liable to any proceedings' but in proceedings before a court or tribunal the code is admissible in evidence and, if relevant, is to be 'taken into account' (1992 Act, s. 207). The code has been used as the basis of the grant of injunctions limiting the number of pickets in attendance at a particular place to six (*Thomas v NUM (South Wales Area)*, above; *News Group Newspapers Ltd v Society of Graphical and Allied Trades 1982* [1986] ICR 716). No one can be obliged to stop and listen (*Broome v DPP* [1974] AC 587, HL, *Kavanagh v Hiscock* [1974] QB 600, DC) and s. 220 does not confer a right to attend on land against the wish of the owner of that land (*British Airports Authority v Ashton* [1983] 3 All ER 6, DC).[1]

Moss v McLachlan (1984) 149 JP 167, [1985] IRLR 76, Queen's Bench Divisional Court

During the miners' strike a number of police officers were stationed at Junction 27 on the M1, which was 1½–2 miles from two collieries, which were ½ mile away from each other, and 4–5 miles from two others, also ½ mile apart. Their object was to stop cars carrying persons who appeared to be striking miners. Those who satisfied them that they were not were allowed to proceed; the rest would be turned back. Moss and three others were travelling in a convoy of 25 cars carrying 60–80 striking miners (clearly identifiable as such from their badges and stickers on their cars). The police told them of their fear that a breach of the peace would occur if they continued, and that if they did so they would be liable to arrest for obstructing the police in the execution of their duty. After 40 minutes or so, 40 miners who attempted to force their way through the police cordon were arrested on the ground that the police feared a breach of the peace at one of the four collieries. Moss and

1 See further on picketing: I. T. Smith and Sir John Wood, *Industrial Law* (5th edn, 1993), pp. 565–577; P. Davies and M. Freedland, *Labour Law: Text and Materials*, (1984) pp. 842–861; R. Kidner, *Trade Union Law* (2nd edn, 1983) Chap. 11.

three others were among those subsequently convicted of obstruction offences and appealed to the Divisional Court by case stated. They conceded that they had wilfully obstructed the officers but argued that the latter had not been acting in the execution of their duty. The Divisional Court dismissed the appeal.

The judgment of the court (**Skinner** and **Otton JJ**) was delivered by **Skinner J**: . . . .

Subject to one submission by Mr. Mansfield, to which I shall return later, the law on this subject is clear. If a constable apprehends, on reasonable grounds, that a breach of the peace may be committed, he is not only entitled but is under a duty to take reasonable steps to prevent that breach occurring.

The magistrates concluded that 'The police honestly and on reasonable grounds feared that there would be a breach of the peace if there were a mass demonstration at whichever Nottinghamshire colliery the appellants and their colleagues chose to congregate.'

The appellants submit that there was no finding of fact by the magistrates to support that conclusion: there was no conduct from which any constable could reasonably have apprehended a breach of the peace. Mr. Mansfield submits that the conduct in question must be conduct by the appellants themselves in the presence of the arresting officer, though he concedes that the latter is entitled to take into account the conduct of a group of which the appellants were members. He also contends that the fears must be specific. It is not enough, he says, to fear a breach of the peace at one or more of the collieries involved by some or all of the miners involved. The officer must be able to say which pit, which miners and when.

Mr. Milmo replies that a police officer has to look at all the facts within his knowledge. He has the power to act if they raise in his mind a fear that the person or persons he is dealing with may cause a breach of the peace, even if he cannot precisely pinpoint when and where.

On this basis he relies on the magistrates' findings that: (a) there were four pits within five miles of the cordon; (b) over 25 cars carrying over 60 striking miners were involved in the attempt to break through the police cordon; (c) while waiting at the junction, angry shouts from the National Union of Mineworkers members at passing National Coal Board lorries and other comments by them made it plain that the police's suspicions that the men were intent on a mass demonstration or picket were justified; (d) the police suspicions that the gathering of a large picket would lead to a breach of the peace were based on their own experiences in the current and other trade disputes, on the knowledge gleaned from those experiences, from their colleagues and from the widespread public dissemination of the news that there had been severe disruptions of the peace, including many incidents of violence, at collieries within the Nottinghamshire coalfield area in the days and weeks of the dispute before April 20, 1984. The officers however had no way of knowing which colliery it was the intention of the miners to picket.

The appellants say this is not enough. The police were not entitled to take into account the experience of others or what they had heard or read on television or in the press. They could only prevent the men from proceeding if it was clear from the words and deeds of the men at the junction that a breach of the peace was intended.

In our judgment there was ample evidence before the magistrates to support their conclusion. That is enough to dispose of Mr. Mansfield's argument that the magistrates here were dealing with action by the police to prevent the appellants from exercising their undoubted right to demonstrate peacefully in order to show support for and solidarity with fellow trade unionists.

On the magistrates' findings of fact anyone with knowledge of the current strike would realize that there was a substantial risk of an outbreak of violence. The mere presence of such a body of men at the junction in question in the context of the current situation in the Nottinghamshire coalfields would have been enough to justify the police in taking preventive action. In reaching their conclusion the police themselves are bound to take into account all they have heard and read and to exercise their judgment and common sense on that material as well as on the events which are taking place before their eyes.

The situation has to be assessed by the senior police officers present. Provided they honestly and reasonably form the opinion that there is a real risk of a breach of the peace in the sense that it is in close proximity both in place and time, then the conditions exist for reasonable preventive action including, if necessary, the measures taken in this case.

The findings of fact by the magistrates therefore dispel any suggestion that (1) the belief of the officers present was other than honest or reasonable, or (2) that the steps taken were other than reasonable.

But, says Mr. Mansfield, the police can only take preventive action if a breach of the peace is imminent and there was no such imminence here. In support of this proposition he relied on a passage in the judgment of Watkins LJ in *R v Howell* (1982) 146 JP 13, [1981] 3 All ER 383 at p 388: '. . . there is a power of arrest for breach of the peace where . . . (2) the arrestor reasonably believes that such a breach will be committed in the immediate future by the person arrested although he has not yet committed any breach . . . .'

This passage must be read in the light of the judgment of Parker LCJ in *Piddington v Bates* [1960] 3 All ER 660 at 663, in which he says the police must anticipate 'a real, not a remote, possibility' of a breach of the peace before they are justified in taking preventive action.

We do not think that there is any conflict between the two approaches. The possibility of a breach must be real to justify any preventive action. The imminence or immediacy of the threat to the peace determines what action is reasonable. If the police feared that a convoy of cars travelling towards a working coal field bearing banners and broadcasting, by sight or sound, hostility or threats towards working miners might cause a violent episode, they would be justified in halting the convoy to inquire into its destination and purpose. If, on stopping the vehicles, the police were satisfied that there was a real possibility of the occupants causing a breach of the peace one and a half miles away, a journey of less than five minutes by car, then in our judgment it would be their duty to prevent the convoy from proceeding further and they have the power to do so.

If and in so far as there may be any differences between the two approaches (and we do not believe there is), we respectfully prefer that of Lord Parker LCJ in *Piddington v Bates*.

We also repeat the words of Parker LCJ, at p. 663 of that case: 'For my part, I think that a police officer charged with the duty of preserving the Queen's peace must be left to take such steps as, on the evidence before him, he thinks proper.'

For the reasons we have given, on the facts found by the magistrates, a breach of the peace was not only a real possibility but also, because of the proximity of the pits and the availability of cars, imminent, immediate and not remote. In our judgment the magistrates were correct in their reasoning and conclusions and we would dismiss these appeals.

NOTES

1. See the generally critical comments of R. East and P. A. Thomas, (1985) 135 NLJ 63, (1985) 12 JLS 77; G. S. Morris (1985) 14 ILJ 109; F. P. Davidson, (1985) 19 LT 142; A. L. Newbold, [1985] PL 30.

2. Do you agree that there is no real difference between the approaches in *Howell* and *Piddington v Bates*?

3. *Duncan v Jones* and *Moss v McLachlan* were relied upon in *R v Secretary of State for Northern Ireland, ex p Atkinson* [1987] 8 NIJB 6, Queen's Bench Division (Crown Side), High Court in Northern Ireland. Hutton J rejected A's application for judicial review seeking a declaration that the police had acted unlawfully in preventing the Magherafelt Ulster Democratic Unionist Party Flute Band joining a band parade at Keady, County Armagh. The great majority of the citizens of Keady were Nationalist, but the Keady No Surrender Branch Club of the Apprentice Boys of Derry decided to hold a very large parade at Keady on 8 August 1986, to which over 100 Apprentice Boys of Derry Clubs and over 100 bands and Orange Lodges were invited. Conditions were attached to the route of the parade under Article 4(1) of the Public Order (Northern Ireland) Order 1981 (see now art. 4 of the 1987 Order) on the ground that the parade might occasion a breach of the peace or serious public disorder (the test under art. 4(1)). Concerned that there was still a risk of very serious public disorder, and unwilling to seek a ban on the parade, the police decided that in an attempt to prevent or minimise the risk, bands which had a reputation for, and record of, disorderly behaviour should be prevented from travelling to Keady to take part in the parade. (In the event, serious disorder did indeed occur.) The Magherafelt band was stopped by the police between Moneymore and Cookstown, but allowed to proceed to take part in the parade having left their instruments at Magherafelt.

Hutton J held (1) that there were ample facts from which police officers could reasonably have anticipated a grave breach of the peace in Keady that evening; (2) that this risk was a strong probability and not merely a remote possibility; (3) that the police had reasonable grounds for believing their actions in stopping the band were necessary to preserve the peace (a test derived from *O'Kelly v Harvey* (above, p. 245) to be applied in preference to that of Lord Parker in *Piddington v Bates* (above, p. 251: 'such steps as, on the evidence before him, he thinks are proper') in so far as the tests were different); (4) that this was so notwithstanding that the distance at which the band was stopped was much further than that in *Moss v McLachlan*: 'the police had reasonable grounds for fearing that their task of seeking to preserve the peace in Keady and limiting the spread of disorder, if a breach of the peace occurred, would be much more difficult if they stopped the bus in close proximity to Keady . . .' (p. 23); (5) that the band had a record of disorderly behaviour and the police had reasonable grounds for fearing that it would have an inflammatory effect if it took part in the parade.

4. *Holmes v Bournemouth Crown Court* (6 October 1993, unreported, DC) is a particularly disturbing decision. H, a 'scruffy' anti-smoking campaigner, took up a position within five or six feet of delegates attending the Conservative Party conference rather than in a designated lobbying area further away. He held up a placard and shouted messages about the danger of smoking but at no time used, offered or threatened violence or did anything amounting to a breach of the peace. He refused to comply with the request of police officer, PC Caddy, that he move into the designated area, and was arrested, and subsequently convicted of obstructing PC Caddy in the execution of his duty. The judges of the Crown Court accepted PC Caddy's evidence that if H stayed in his original position he feared 'there might be a breach of the peace', and stated that they considered it reasonable for PC Caddy to entertain that fear, and found that he was acting in the execution of his duty. The Divisional Court (Kennedy LJ and Pill J) upheld the decision. Pill J stated:

'The police have a duty to take all reasonable steps which appear to be necessary to keep the peace. It needs no underlining in this Court that there are security risks at the annual conferences of the major political parties. The police must take reasonable steps to keep the peace and prevent crimes being committed against those lawfully attending conferences, whether they do so as delegates or in any other capacity. The proper discharge of that duty may involve placing restrictions upon the positions which may be taken up by those wishing to lobby delegates and others attending the conference centres. The police clearly must plan a security operation in advance if security at such a conference is to be effective. It does not necessarily take action outside the proper discharge of police duties that the effect of the measures they take may be to exclude law-abiding members of the public from certain areas.'

Here the attention of the court seems focused on the facilitation of the security operation rather than (as it should have been) on the question whether H's conduct gave rise to a risk of a breach of the peace. Is the conclusion of the judges of the Crown Court remotely plausible? What breach of the peace was to be anticipated— that smokers among the delegates might stub out their cigarettes on H in annoyance at his slogans?

(ii) Binding Over[1]

The common law power of justices (and any court of record having a criminal jurisdiction: Justices of the Peace Act 1968, section 1(7); Administration of Justice Act 1973, Schedule 5) to bind persons over to keep the peace, and their wider power

---

1 On binding-over generally see G. Williams, 'Preventive Justice and the Rule of Law' (1953) 16 MLR 417; *Williams*, Chap. 4; *Brownlie*, pp. 312–315; (1961) 25 Journal of Criminal Law 220; A. D. Grunis, [1976] PL 16; D. G. T. Williams, [1970] CLJ 96, 104–106; M. Dodds, (1985) 149 JPN 259, 278; Law Commission Report No. 222, *Binding Over* (Cm. 2439, 1994). On the historical origins, see D. Feldman, 'The King's Peace, the Royal Prerogative and Public Order: the Roots and Early Development of Binding Over Powers' [1988] CLJ 101.

under the Justices of the Peace Act 1361 (34 Edw III c 1) to bind persons over to be of good behaviour, have frequently been employed in the context of public order.

The power to require a person to enter into a recognisance to keep the peace, either generally, or towards a particular person, may be exercised where there is reasonable apprehension of a future breach of the peace (see above pp. 207–212). The recognisance may be forfeited by any unlawful action that 'either is or tends to a breach of the peace' (Blackstone, Book IV, Chap. XVIII).

The statutory power 'to take of all of them that be [not] of good fame, where they shall be found, sufficient surety and mainprise of their good behaviour towards the King and his people, . . .', according to Blackstone (ibid.), may be exercised:

'for causes of scandal, *contra bonos mores*, as well as *contra pacem*: as, for haunting bawdy-houses with women of bad fame; or for keeping such women in his own house; or for words tending to scandalize the government, or in abuse of the officers of justice, especially in the execution of their office. Thus also a justice may bind over all night-walkers; eavesdroppers; such as keep suspicious company, or are reported to be pilferers or robbers; such as sleep in the day, and wake in the night; common drunkards; whore-masters; the putative fathers of bastards; cheats; idle vagabonds; and other persons whose misbehaviour may reasonably bring them within the general words of the statute, as persons not of good fame . . . .'

NOTES

1. An order may be made on a complaint to a magistrates' court under s. 115 of the Magistrates' Courts Act 1980; however, the binding-over powers may be exercised by justices of the peace at any stage of other proceedings. An appeal lies against a binding-over order made by a magistrates' court to the Crown Court (Magistrates' Courts (Appeals from Binding Over Orders) Act 1956; the appeal should be conducted by way of rehearing: *Shaw v Hamilton* [1982] 2 All ER 718, DC), or, by case stated on a point of law, to the Divisional Court (e.g. *Beatty v Gillbanks*, above p. 241; *Wise v Dunning*, above p. 244). An order may be challenged on an application for judicial review (see *R v Londonderry Justices* (1891) 28 LR Ir 440; *R v Central Criminal Court, ex p Boulding* [1984] 1 All ER 766, DC; *R v Ilminster Justices, ex p Hamilton* (1983) Times, 23 June, DC (binding-over orders quashed on the ground of breach of natural justice); *R v Morpeth Ward Justices, ex p Ward* (1992) 95 Cr App Rep 215, DC (the court noting, however, that the appeal by case stated was normally the appropriate method of challenge)).

In *R v South Molton Justices, ex p Ankerson* (1989) 90 Cr App Rep 158, Taylor LJ stated (at p. 162) that when justices are minded to order a binding-over (sc. to keep the peace)

'(1) there should be material before them justifying the conclusion that there is a risk of a breach of the peace unless action is taken to prevent it. (2) They must indicate to the defendant their intention to bind him over and the reasons for it so that he or his lawyer can make representations. (3) They must obtain consent to the bind-over from the defendant himself. (4) Before fixing the amount of the recognisance they should inquire as to the defendant's means. (5) The binding-over should be for a finite period.'

Point (4) has been emphasised on a number of occasions: see *R v Central Criminal Court, ex p Boulding*, above; *R v Atkinson* (1988) 10 Cr App Rep(S) 470, CA (Cr D); *R v Crown Court at Nottingham, ex p Brace* (1989) 154 JP 161, CA. The concept of a breach of the peace is limited to violence or threats of violence as set out in *R v Howell* (above, p. 207): *Percy v DPP* [1995] 3 All ER 124, DC. The court also inclined to the view, without deciding, that the criminal standard of proof applies to the hearing of a complaint. However, the civil standard is applicable to proceedings for forfeiture of a recognisance: *R v Marlow Justices, ex p O'Sullivan* [1983] 3 All ER

578, DC. There is no power to attach conditions to a binding-over order to keep the peace or be of good behaviour (*R v Randall* (1986) 8 Cr App Rep (S) 433, CA (Cr D)).

2. Binding-over orders have been made in many cases following conviction for a criminal offence against public order (see *Williams*, pp. 94–95). In addition, they have been made against persons who incite disorder. The most celebrated instance is *Lansbury v Riley* [1914] 3 KB 229, DC, where George Lansbury spoke in support of militant suffragettes at a time when there were many attacks on property. He said that women 'ought to break the law on every possible occasion, short of taking human life' (*Williams*, p. 97). He was bound over in the sum of £1,000 with two sureties of £500. In the 1930s, several officers of the National Unemployed Workers' Movement were imprisoned for refusing to be bound over (Wal Hannington in 1922 and 1931; Sid Elias in 1931; Tom Mann and Emrhys Llewellyn in 1932: see *Williams*, pp. 99–100; J. Stevenson and C. Cook, *Society and Politics, 1929–1939, Britain in the Depression* (1994), p. 251). See also *Wise v Dunning*, above p. 244, and *Beatty v Gillbanks*, above p. 241. Compare *Beatty v Gillbanks* with *R v Morpeth Ward Justices, ex p Ward* (1992) 95 Cr App Rep 215, where the Divisional Court upheld binding-over orders to keep the peace imposed on demonstrators who disrupted a pheasant shoot by invading the field where the shoot was taking place, and shouting and swearing. There was no evidence of any acts by them which physically harmed persons or property or put anyone in fear of such harm being done. There was, however, a threat by a member of the shooting party to one of the demonstrators, 'If you don't move, I'll kill you.' Brooke J stated (at 221) that

'because provocative disorderly behaviour which is likely to have the natural consequence of causing violence, even if only to the persons of the provokers, is capable of being treated as conduct likely to cause a breach of the peace, then it would be quite impossible to say that the justices were perverse in finding that there was a risk that the applicants were likely, unless bound over, to cause a breach of the peace.'

Should it have made a difference if the demonstrators had marched across the field singing hymns?

Ex p Ward may in turn be compared with *Percy v DPP* (1994) Times, 13 December, where the Divisional Court allowed an appeal against an order for the committal of P for 14 days for refusing to be bound over to keep the peace. On five occasions, P had entered the air base at RAF Alconbury to protest against abuse of byelaws and the continuing expansion of the war machine; the court held that it was highly improbable that her non-violent acts of trespass would provoke trained US servicemen to violent reaction.

3. In *Hughes v Holley* (1986) 151 JP 233, the Divisional Court upheld an order binding Hughes over to be of good behaviour. He was found to have accosted a young woman in the 'red light' district of Leicester and solicited her to have sexual intercourse with him. It was a common occurrence in the area for respectable women to be thus accosted, and this caused anger and frustration among respectable residents. In order to deal with the problem, the young woman, a police officer, had been sent on duty in civilian clothes to walk in the area in question. Glidewell LJ stated that it was clear that the magistrates 'do have a very wide discretion in deciding whether to bind over' (p. 238). They could bind someone over whose conduct was '*contra bonos mores*' and that simply meant

'contrary to a good way of life. What is a good way of life is for the magistrates to decide.... [I]t means conduct which has the property of being right rather than wrong, and "*contra bonos mores*" is conduct which has the property of being wrong rather than right in the judgment of the majority of contemporary fellow citizens (p. 240).'

There was material here on which the magistrates could properly exercise their power to bind over.

This case highlights the breadth of the binding-over power, and that it may be employed where there is no threat to the peace. See Bazell, (1987) 151 JPN 456. A survey conducted for the Law Commission (see below) showed that a large majority (79%) of orders were made both to keep the peace and be of good behaviour; 12% were to keep the peace and 9% to be of good behaviour (Law Commission Working Paper No. 103, 1987, pp. 31–35 (Statistical Survey)). For a list of examples of public order and other cases where orders have been used see ibid., pp. 39–43.

4. The Law Commission (Law Com. No. 222) has firmly recommended that these binding-over powers should be repealed without replacement, notwithstanding the view of the majority of those responding to their consultation document that they should be retained. Relevant considerations included (op. cit., pp. 5–6) (1) the criminal sanctions now applicable to many of the forms of anti-social practice for which a binding-over was formerly used (e.g. the Public Order Act ss. 4, 5; the Sexual Offences Act 1985 (kerb crawling); the Malicious Communications Act 1988 (poison pen letters); the Telecommunications Act 1984, s. 43 (covering, inter alia, persistent telephoning to cause annoyance, inconvenience or distress)); (2) modern developments in cautioning and diverting anti-social offenders from the court system; (3) the many defects in practice in procedure which could not satisfactorily be cured without 'depriving the procedure of the informality which is regarded as one of its main attractions'. The conclusion in favour of abolition was buttressed by the view that binding-over fell short of the requirements of the European Convention on Human Rights (in fact here reflecting fundamental principles of English law) as to the certainty and ascertainability of a citizen's obligations, the limitations on arrest and detention (article 5), the requirements of a fair trial (article 6) and the guarantees of free expression and assembly (articles 10 and 11) (op. cit., pp. 59–67).

(iii) Powers of Entry to Preserve the Peace

Thomas v Sawkins [1935] 2 KB 249, 104 LJ KB 572, 153 LT 419, 99 JP 295, 51 TLR 514, 33 LGR 330, 30 Cox CC, King's Bench Divisional Court

Case stated by Glamorgan (Newcastle and Ogmore) justices.

On 17 August 1934 a public meeting was held at the Large Hall of the Caerau Library to protest against the Incitement to Disaffection Bill then before Parliament and to demand the dismissal of the chief constable of the county of Glamorgan, at which meeting between 500 and 700 people were present. The principal speaker was to be Alun Thomas (the appellant). He had previously addressed meetings at Nantymoel (9 August), Caerau (14 August) and Maesteg (15 August). He had lodged a written complaint against the refusal of police officers to leave the Nantymoel meeting, had threatened physically to eject the police if they attended the meeting on 17 August, and had stated at the Maesteg meeting: 'If it were not for the presence of these people' – pointing to police officers – 'I could tell you a hell of a lot more.'

The Library Hall was hired by one Fred Thomas, and the public were invited to attend, free of charge. The meeting was convened by (among others) Fred Thomas and Alun Thomas. Sergeant Sawkins (the respondent), together with Inspector Parry and Sergeant Lawrence, was refused admission by Fred Thomas. Nevertheless, the three officers entered the hall and sat on the front row. They also refused to leave on two occasions when requested to do so by Alun Thomas. Alun Thomas then stated that the police officers would be ejected, and he laid his hand on Inspector Parry to eject him. Sergeant Sawkins thereupon pushed Alun Thomas's arm and hand from Parry, saying: 'I won't allow you to interfere with my superior officer.' About 30 other police officers entered with batons drawn, and no further attempt was made to eject the police. In attempting to remove Parry, Alun Thomas used no more force than was reasonably necessary for that purpose, and Sawkins used no more force than was reasonably necessary (assuming that he and Parry had a right to be there) to protect Parry and to prevent him from being ejected.

The respondent did not allege that any criminal offence was committed. There was no breach of the peace or disorder at any time.

Alun Thomas preferred an information against Sergeant Sawkins alleging that Sawkins had committed assault and battery contrary to section 42 of the Offences against the Person Act 1861. He claimed that the police officers were trespassers. If that was correct, he would be entitled to use reasonable force to eject them, and forcible resistance by the police officers would be illegal. The justices concluded (33 LGR at 333):

'Upon the above facts and evidence given before us we were and are of the opinion that the respondent and other police officers had reasonable grounds for believing that if they were not present at the meeting seditious speeches would be made and/or incitements to violence and/or breaches of the peace would take place and that they were entitled to enter and remain in the said hall and meeting.'

They dismissed the information. Alun Thomas appealed. It was argued, inter alia, on behalf of Sawkins that:

'The respondent was entitled to be present at the meeting. A constable by his oath swears to cause the peace to be preserved and to prevent the commission of all offences. Where, therefore, the police have reasonable grounds for believing that an offence may be committed or a breach of the peace occur, they have a right to enter private premises to prevent the commission of the offence or the ocurrence of the breach of the peace. If that were not so, it would be extremely difficult for the police to exercise their powers of watch and ward and their duty of preventive justice' ([1935] 2 KB at 253).

Lord Hewart CJ: It is apparent that the conclusion of the justices in this case consisted of two parts. One part was a conclusion of fact that the respondent and the police officers who accompanied him believed that certain things might happen at the meeting which was then about to be held. There were ample materials on which the justices could come to that conclusion. The second part of the justices' finding is no less manifestly an expression of opinion. Finding the facts as they do, and drawing from those facts the inference which they draw, they go on to say that the officers were entitled to enter and to remain on the premises on which the meeting was being held.

Against that determination, it is said that it is an unheard-of proposition of law, and that in the books no case is to be found which goes the length of deciding, that, where an offence is expected to be committed, as distinct from the case of an offence being or having been committed, there is any right in the police to enter on private premises and to remain there against the will of those who, as hirers or otherwise, are for the time being in possession of the premises. When, however, I look at the passages which have been cited from Blackstone's Commentaries, vol. i., p. 356, and from the judgments in *Humphries v Connor* (1864) 17 ICLR 1 [above p. 239] and *O'Kelly v Harvey* (1883) 14 LR Ir 105 [above p. 245] and certain observations of Avory J in *Lansbury v Riley* [1914] 3 KB 229 at 236, 237, I think that there is quite sufficient ground for the proposition that it is part of the preventive power, and, therefore, part of the preventive duty, of the police, in cases where there are such reasonable grounds of apprehension as the justices have found here, to enter and remain on private premises. It goes without saying that the powers and duties of the police are directed, not to the interests of the police, but to the protection and welfare of the public.

It was urged in one part of the argument of Sir Stafford Cripps that what the police did here amounted to a trespass. It seems somewhat remarkable to speak of trespass when members of the public who happen to be police officers attend, after a public invitation, a public meeting which is to discuss as one part of its business the dismissal of the chief constable of the county. It is elementary that a good defence to an action for trespass is to show that the act complained of was done by authority of law, or by leave and licence.

I am not at all prepared to accept the doctrine that it is only where an offence has been, or is being, committed, that the police are entitled to enter and remain on private premises. On the contrary, it seems to me that a police officer has ex virtute officii full right so to act when he has reasonable ground for believing that an offence is imminent or is likely to be committed.

I think, therefore, that the justices were right and that this appeal should be dismissed.

Avory J: I am of the same opinion. I think that it is very material in this particular case to observe that the meeting was described as a public meeting, that it was extensively advertised, and that the public were invited to attend. There can be no doubt that the police officers who attended the meeting were members of the public and were included in that sense in the invitation to attend. It is true that those who had hired the hall for their meeting might withdraw their invitation from any particular individual who was likely to commit a breach of the peace or some other offence, but it is quite a different proposition to say that they might withdraw the invitation from police officers who might be there for the express purpose of preventing a breach of the peace or the commission of an offence.

With regard to the general question regarding the right of the police to attend the meeting notwithstanding the opposition of the promoters, I cannot help thinking that that right follows from the description of the powers of a constable which Sir Stafford Cripps relies on in Stone's Justices' Manual, 1935, p. 208, where it is said that when a constable hears an affray in a house he may break in to suppress it and may, in pursuit of an affrayer, break in to arrest him. If he can do that, I cannot doubt that he has a right to break in to prevent an affray which he has reasonable cause to suspect may take place on private premises. In other words, it comes within his duty, as laid down by Blackstone (Commentaries, vol. i., p. 356), to keep the King's peace and to keep watch and ward. In my view, the right was correctly expressed in *R (Feehan) v Queen's County JJ* (1882) 10 LR Ir 294 at 301 where Fitzgerald J said: 'The foundation of the jurisdiction [to bind persons to be of good behaviour] is very remote, and probably existed prior to the statute of 1360–61; but whatever its foundation may be, or by whatever language conveyed, we are bound to regard and expound it by the light of immemorial practice and of decision, and especially of direct modern decisions. It may be described as a branch of preventive justice, in the exercise of which magistrates are invested with large judicial discretionary powers, for the maintenance of order and the preservation of the public peace.' That passage was expressly approved in *Lansbury v Riley* [1914] 3 KB 229 at 236 and the statement of the law which it contains was adopted by Lord Alverstone CJ in *Wise v Dunning* [1902] 1 KB 167 at 175; *R v Queen's County JJ* is there referred to sub nom *R v Cork JJ* (1882) 15 Cox CC 149. In principle I think that there is no distinction between the duty of a police constable to prevent a breach of the peace and the power of a magistrate to bind persons over to be of good behaviour to prevent a breach of the peace.

I am not impressed by the fact that many statutes have expressly given to police constables in certain circumstances the right to break open or to force an entrance into private premises. Those have all been cases in which a breach of the peace was not necessarily involved and it, therefore, required express statutory authority to empower the police to enter. In my opinion, no express statutory authority is necessary where the police have reasonable grounds to apprehend a breach of the peace, and in the present case I am satisfied that the justices had before them material on which they could properly hold that the police officers in question had reasonable grounds for believing that, if they were not present, seditious speeches would be made and/or that a breach of the peace would take place. To prevent any such offence or a breach of the peace the police were entitled to enter and to remain on the premises, and I agree that this appeal should be dismissed.

Lawrence J: As my Lord has pointed out, our judgment proceeds on the particular facts of this case, and on those facts I agree with the conclusion. I will only add that I am unable to follow the distinction which Sir Stafford Cripps has drawn between the present matter and the cases which have been cited. If a constable in the execution of his duty to preserve the peace is entitled to commit an assault, it appears to me that he is equally entitled to commit a trespass.

Appeal dismissed.

NOTES

1. Background information not available from the law reports is given in D. G. T. Williams, *Keeping the Peace* (1967), pp. 142–149, and (1985) Cambrian LR 116. The case was adversely criticised by A. L. Goodhart in (1936–8) CLJ 22.

2. What is the *ratio decidendi* of the judgment of Lord Hewart CJ? Is it the *ratio decidendi* of the case?

3. Where Lord Hewart states that a police officer may enter and remain on private premises 'when he has reasonable ground for believing that an offence is imminent or is likely to be committed', do you think that the point he was considering was (a) the *point of time* at which the police may intervene, or (b) the nature of the *offence* which has to be anticipated, or (c) both? Does Lord Hewart's judgment amount to an endorsement of the argument of counsel for Sawkins that there is a power to enter premises to prevent *any* offence? Note that the Police and Criminal Evidence Act 1984, s. 17(5)(6) abolishes all common law powers of entry except to deal with or prevent a breach of the peace (see above, p. 89). Does s. 17(6) constitute an endorsement of *Thomas v Sawkins*?

4. Could Alun Thomas have been convicted of the offences of assaulting or obstructing a police officer in the execution of his duty? (cf. *Duncan v Jones* [1936] 1 KB 218, above, p. 248).

5. In principle, the occupier of land may grant or refuse permission (a 'licence') to someone seeking to go on to the land according to his own wishes, unless that other has a right to enter conferred by law. A gratuitous licence may be revoked at any time provided that reasonable notice is given (Megarry and Wade, *The Law of Real Property* (5th edn, 1984), p. 799.) A licensee must be given reasonable time to depart before his continued presence on the land constitutes trespass (*Robson v Hallett* [1967] 2 QB 939, above, p. 102; unless he makes it clear that he will not leave voluntarily (*Davis v Lisle* [1936] 2 KB 434, above, p. 101).

Apart from the situation where there is a right to remain conferred by law, a licence will only be irrevocable where (a) it is protected by estoppel or equity; (b) the licence is coupled with a proprietary interest in other property; or (c) (in some circumstances) where the licence is granted by contract (see *Megarry v Wade*, pp. 801–805). In view of this, would it be correct to say that the persons who hired the hall could *only* 'withdraw their invitation from any particular individual who was likely to commit a breach of the peace or some other offence'? (cf. Avory J). How is the position of the organiser of a *public* meeting different from that of a *private* meeting? Is it not simply the difference between a meeting to which there is a general invitation to the public, and one to which specific invitations are given? Can the fact that a meeting is 'public' limit the power of the *occupier* to refuse entry or to eject, as distinct (possibly) from marking the limit of the right of the *police* to enter private premises in anticipation of the commission of offences? Is a Premier League football match with an attendance of 40,000 a public or private meeting? What about a match attended by a few hundred spectators? Or by an old man and a dog? Is a private dinner party a 'private meeting'?

6. Consider the situation where a police officer purchases a ticket to attend a public meeting. What is the position if he attends in plain clothes, knowing that the organisers would not have sold him a ticket had they known his true identity? (Cf. *Said v Butt* [1920] 3 KB 497; *Cheshire, Fifoot and Furmston's Law of Contract* (11th edn, 1986) pp. 238–245, 247–248).

7. Consider the statement of Lawrence J that if a constable is 'entitled to commit an assault, . . . he is equally entitled to commit a trespass' in the light of section 3 of the Criminal Law Act 1967 (above, p. 74).

8. What is the position where a police officer has no legal right of entry but obtains permission to enter premises:

(1) by concealing the fact that he is a police officer in circumstances where he knows that a policeman would not be admitted; or
(2) by a false representation of fact (e.g. 'I thought I saw a burglar'); or
(3) by a false representation of law (e.g. 'I have a legal power to enter'); or
(4) by acquiescing in the self deception of the occupier (e.g. 'You've a right to come in so I suppose I'd better let you').

9. The judges rely on analogies (a) with the power of police and magistrates to commit acts which would otherwise constitute assaults where this is necessary in the last resort to preserve the peace (above, pp. 239–256) and (b) with the preventive power of magistrates to bind people over to keep the peace or be of good behaviour (above, pp. 256–259). How apt are these analogies? (See Goodhart, (1936–8) 6 CLJ 22, 25–29).

10. In *Handcock v Baker* (1800) 2 Bos & P 260, the defendants were held entitled to break into a house where they had reasonable cause to believe that the occupier was about to kill his wife. Moreover, a constable may enter premises in fresh pursuit of a person who has committed a breach of the peace within his view (see *R v Walker* (1854) Dears CC 358; *R v Marsden* (1868) LR 1 CCR 131).

11. In *McGowan v Chief Constable of Kingston upon Hull* [1967] Crim LR 34, the Divisional Court held that police officers were entitled to enter and remain in a private house where they feared there would be a breach of the peace arising out of a domestic quarrel. *Thomas v Sawkins* was not mentioned in the report, but was presumably the relevant authority. In *McLeod v Metropolitan Police Comr* [1994] 4 All ER 553, the Court of Appeal upheld the dismissal of Mrs McLeod's claim against the police for trespass to land arising out of the removal of her ex-husband's furniture from her house by him, his brother and sister, in the presence of a solicitor's clerk and two police officers. The door was opened by Mrs McLeod's elderly mother, but there was no consent to the entry. It was common ground that the officers had entered the property and that an 'excuse in law' was required. The court held that the *Thomas v Sawkins* principle was not confined to public meetings. *Per* Neill LJ at 560:

'I am satisfied that Parliament in s. 17(6) [of PACE] has now recognised that there is a power to enter premises to prevent a breach of the peace as a form of preventive justice. I can see no satisfactory basis for restricting that power to particular classes of premises such as those where public meetings are held. If the police reasonably believe that a breach of the peace is likely to take place on private premises, they have power to enter those premises to prevent it. The apprehension must of course be genuine and it must relate to the near future.'

On the facts, the court upheld the trial judge's decision that the police officers here had the necessary reasonable grounds: they had been told to go to the house on the information of a solicitor that there might be trouble and the solicitor's fears were well founded in the light of the previous history of the parties. Neill LJ (at 560) added a word of caution:

'It seems to me it is important that when exercising his power to prevent a breach of the peace a police officer should act with great care and discretion; this will be particularly important where the exercise of his power involves entering on private premises contrary to the wishes of the owners or occupiers. The officer must satisfy himself that there is a real and imminent risk of a breach of the peace, because, if the matter has to be tested in court thereafter there may be scrutiny not only of his belief at the time but also of the grounds for his belief.

It may be necessary in some future case to consider how far in advance of a possible breach of the peace the right to enter arises. It will depend on the facts of the case, and on the nature and scale of the apprehended breach.'

Does s. 17(6) necessarily support the court's conclusion? Given that the concept of a 'public meeting' is used in other areas of public order law, why should that not form a 'satisfactory basis' for restricting *Thomas v Sawkins*?

12. See above, pp. 207–212 on the concept of a 'breach of the peace'.

13. Before *Thomas v Sawkins*, it was generally accepted that the police had no power to enter meetings on private premises unless they had reason to believe that a breach of the peace was actually taking place. This was stated to be the position by the

Departmental Committee on the Duties of the Police with respect to the Preservation of Order at Public Meetings (Cd. 4673, 1909, p. 6), and by the Home Secretary, Sir John Gilmour, in a debate arising out of the Fascist meeting at Olympia on 7 June 1934 where there was considerable violence (290 HC Deb 14 June 1934 col 1968). Cf. *Robson v Hallett*, above, p. 102.

14. Contrary to expectations which might be engendered by *Thomas v Sawkins* D. G. T. Williams has noted 'the apparent determination of the police to avoid wherever possible any entanglement in the protests and demonstrations taking place on private property' ([1970] CLJ 96, 116). This was particularly marked in relation to sit ins at universities in the late 1960s. Cf. *R v Dytham* [1979] QB 722, CA (Cr D), where a constable was convicted of the common law misdemeanour of misconduct of a public officer in that he failed to fulfil his duty to preserve the peace. He had witnessed a man being beaten and kicked to death outside a club, but had taken no steps to intervene.

CHAPTER 4

Emergency powers; the problem of political terrorism

1 Introduction

The most extreme form of emergency which the country may face is war. In earlier times, the Crown relied on prerogative powers to take steps necessary for the conduct of war (see Wade and Bradley, *Constitutional and Administrative Law*, 11th edn, 1993, pp. 588–590). Each of the two world wars saw the creation of a complex edifice of statutory powers, mostly contained in delegated legislation made under the Defence of the Realm Acts 1914–15 and the Emergency Powers (Defence) Acts 1939–40. Every aspect of national life was closely regulated. Commentators were able to poke fun at the inevitable fatuity of some of the controls (see, e.g. C. K. Allen, *Law and Disorder* (1954)). The interest of civil liberties was equally inevitably and equally swiftly relegated to a lesser rank in the order of national priorities. These measures have attracted both support, inasmuch as Britain had 'created the means of preserving itself from disaster without sacrificing the essential processes of democracy' (C. P. Cotter, (1953) 5 Stanford LR 382, 416), and stringent criticism (see C. K. Allen, *Law and Orders* (1st edn, 1945); R. Kidd, *British Liberty in Danger* (1940), Part Two; N. Stammers, *Civil Liberties in Britain during the Second World War* (1983)). Economic difficulties caused certain aspects of wartime regulation to be prolonged after the cessation of hostilities.

In addition, the Emergency Powers Act 1920[1] enables the state to obtain wide ranging powers by regulation to meet peacetime emergencies. Section 1(1) of the Act (as amended by the Emergency Powers Act 1964) provides that

'If at any time it appears to His Majesty that [there have occurred, or are about to occur, events of such a nature] as to be calculated, by interfering with the supply and distribution of food, water, fuel, or light, or with the means of locomotion, to deprive the community, or any substantial portion of the community, of the essentials of life, His Majesty may, by proclamation (hereinafter referred to as a proclamation of emergency) declare that a state of emergency exists. . . .'

A proclamation may not be in force longer than a month, without prejudice to the issue of further proclamations (ibid.). During the currency of a proclamation, regulations may be made by Order in Council 'for securing the essentials of life to the community'. The Act has been used solely in relation to major strikes. The most recent proclamation was in the winter of 1973/1974. The regulations were contained in S.I. 1974 No. 350.

That the royal prerogative is also a source of legal powers in relation to the maintenance 'of what is popularly called the Queen's peace within the realm' was

---

1 See generally, G. Morris, [1979] PL 317 and *Strikes in Essential Services* (1986), Chap. 3; K. Jeffery and P. Hennessy, *States of Emergency* (1983); S. Peak, *Troops in Strikes* (Cobden Trust, 1984); D. Bonner, *Emergency Powers in Peacetime* (1985), Chap. 5.

affirmed by the Court of Appeal in *R v Secretary of State for the Home Department, ex p Northumbria Police Authority* [1989] QB 26. The court held that

'the Crown does have a prerogative power to keep the peace, which is bound up with its undoubted right to see that crime is prevented and justice administered;'

that the power could be used by the Home Secretary to make plastic baton rounds and CS gas available to chief constables, without the approval of the police authority, the prerogative not having been curtailed by s. 4(4) of the Police Act 1964 (which gave the police authority power to provide equipment); and that the power was not confined to use *in* an emergency, but could be used

'in times when there is reason to apprehend outbreaks of riot and serious civil disturbance'

(per Croom-Johnson LJ at pp. 563–565). The court could have dealt with the matter simply by reference to the Secretary of State's statutory powers under the Police Act 1964 but chose to deal with the prerogative issue as well. For criticism that 'in several respects the judges' approach to the subject failed to conform with important constitutional traditions' see A. W. Bradley, [1988] PL 298.

This chapter concentrates in particular on how the pressures for additional legal powers to combat terrorism can be reconciled with legitimate demands for the protection of civil liberties. The international standards applicable to the exercise of police powers (above, p. 35) apply here, subject to the point that some may be (and have been) the subject of derogation by the UK (see below, p. 850).

2 Political terrorism[1]

Political terrorism has been defined as

'the use, or threat of use, of violence by an individual or a group, whether acting for or in opposition to established authority, when such action is designed to create extreme anxiety and/or fear-inducing effects in a target larger than the immediate victims with the purpose of coercing that group into acceding to the political demands of the perpetrators'

(G. Wardlaw, *Political Terrorism* (2nd edn, 1989), p. 16). While the systematic employment of terrorist tactics can be traced back to the French Revolution and various political movements in late nineteenth century Europe, there have over the last 25 years been both a dramatic increase in the incidence of terrorism in the world, and significant changes in its nature. These changes are related to various factors, including technological developments in weaponry, the increasing sophistication of the news media (media coverage often being a major objective of terrorists), the dependence of heavily industrialised societies on a decreasing number of critical locations or processes (e.g. commercial aircraft, gas pipelines, electric power grids, government computers) and the development of links between terrorist groups in different countries (see Wardlaw, op. cit., Chap. 3). For liberal democracies, the choice of appropriate measures poses problems:

'The primary objective of counter-terrorist strategy must be the protection and maintenance of liberal democracy and the rule of law. It cannot be sufficiently stressed that this aim overrides in importance even the objective of eliminating terrorism and political violence as such. Any bloody tyrant can "solve"

---

1 For general surveys, see R. Clutterbuck (ed), *The Future of Political Violence* (1986) and *Terrorism and Guerilla Warfare* (1990); C. Gearty, *Terror* (1991); J. Lodge (ed), *The Threat of Terrorism* (1988); G. Wardlaw, *Political Terrorism* (2nd edn, 1989); P. Wilkinson, *Political Terrorism* (1974), *Terrorism and the Liberal State* (2nd edn, 1986) and (ed), *British Perspectives on Terrorism* (1981); P. Wilkinson and A. M. Stewart (eds), *Contemporary Research on Terrorism* (1987).

the problem of political violence if he is prepared to sacrifice all considerations of humanity, and to trample down all constitutional and judicial rights.'
(P. Wilkinson, *Terrorism and the Liberal State* (1977) p. 121)

This point is developed in the following extract (Wardlaw, op. cit., pp. 69–70):

'However serious the threat of terrorism, we must not be tempted to use repressive methods to combat it. To believe that we can "protect" liberal democracy by suspending our normal rights and methods of government is to ignore the numerous examples in contemporary history of countries where "temporary", "emergency" rule has subsided quickly and irrevocably into permanent dictatorial forms of government. While we must avoid the easy move to repression as a counter to terrorism, it is equally vital that we do not allow ourselves to be so overcome by our democratic sensibilities that our response is weak and vacillating, and characterised by inaction. It is as much a betrayal of our beliefs and responsibilities to do not enough as to do too much. We must uphold constitutional authority and law and order, and we must do so with firmness and determination. To do so requires political will; but most importantly it requires citizen support. To gain such support the political will must be translated into effective action. First, the government must be open and honest about its policies and objectives. As will be stressed when we come to examine the role of the army in counter-terrorism, it is particularly important in a society such as ours to spell out clearly the circumstances under which military aid to the civil power would be invoked, the rights and responsibilities of military personnel operating in an internal security role, and the lines of control and command.

Second, the government must accord full and proper support to its civil and security force personnel who are involved in counter-terrorist operations. In particular, it is necessary to avoid sudden changes in security policy which could undermine both official and public confidence in the government's ability to handle difficult situations. Policy vacillations also expose weaknesses and differences within the government ranks which can be exploited by terrorists.

Third, any anti-terrorist measures must be, and be seen to be, directed only at terrorists. The response must be limited, well-defined, and controlled. It must also, wherever at all possible, be publicly explained. . . .

It is most important that executive control of anti-terrorist and security policy rests with the civil authorities (the elected government) who are accountable to the people for their actions. Further, it should be both policy and practice for the government and its security forces to act within the law. Not only does failure to do so place the government in a morally difficult position (if it does not obey the law, why should anyone?) but also such action is likely to undermine their support and provide valuable ammunition for a terrorist cause. Propaganda capital can very easily be made out of violations of the law by government servants, and such propaganda can be used as additional justification for a terrorist campaign. While the law can be a refuge for the law-breaker and a hindrance to the law enforcement official, the law is the basis of our system of government and must be upheld. Otherwise are we any better than the terrorist who also argues on the grounds of expediency?'

In the United Kingdom the major problem of terrorism has been created by the Northern Ireland conflict, although there have, in addition, been a number of terrorist incidents reflecting struggles between groups of foreign nationals rather than campaigns directed at the UK government (e.g. the Iranian Embassy siege in 1980 (see G. Brock *et al, Siege* (1980)) and the Libyan Embassy siege in 1984). The position in Northern Ireland is considered in the following section, and the response to the activities of terrorists in mainland Britain in section 4.

3 Northern Ireland

The situation in Ireland has long generated a requirement for additional legal powers to aid the preservation of peace. 'Emergency powers' or 'special powers' have existed in Ireland without a break from the nineteenth century. Current provisions for Northern Ireland are contained in the Northern Ireland (Emergency Provisions) Act 1991 (below, p. 271 ff).

The materials which follow concentrate upon Northern Ireland's security problems. This is not the whole picture. Between the inception of the state of Northern Ireland in 1921 and 1972 its government was in the hands of the Protestant Ulster Unionist party. The decision that Northern Ireland should comprise six of the nine counties in the Province of Ulster was indeed based on the desire to ensure a Unionist majority in the Parliament of Northern Ireland. The voting strength of Unionists and Nationalists in Ulster as a whole was roughly equal (see N. Mansergh, *The Irish Question 1840–1921* (3rd edn, 1975) Chap. VI). The Catholic minority during this period was the object of serious discrimination in a number of important areas. Official recognition of this came in 1969 with the report of the Cameron Commission on *Disturbances in Northern Ireland*, whose conclusions in this regard are summarised below. Both before and after the imposition of direct rule in 1972 a number of legislative measures sought to end the regime of discrimination. Fourteen reforms are listed in the Report of the Standing Advisory Commission on Human Rights on *The protection of human rights by law in Northern Ireland* (Cmnd. 7009, 1977) pp. 11–14, covering such matters as universal adult suffrage in local elections, and the establishment of a Parliamentary Commissioner for Administration (government departments), a Commissioner for Complaints (local councils and public bodies), a Police Complaints Board, a central housing authority, an independent police authority, a Director of Public Prosecutions and a Fair Employment Agency. All legislative and execution actions of central and local government and statutory bodies which are discriminatory on religious or political grounds are unlawful under Part III of the Northern Ireland Constitution Act 1973. Nevertheless, as the Advisory Commission pointed out (at p. 14):

'What might have succeeded at another time or in different circumstances has not been sufficient to change a situation where violence has become a way of life for some and perpetual terror for others. . . . The continuing state of emergency has not only seriously impaired the effectiveness of the substantial legislative and administrative reforms which have been made since 1969 for the better protection of human rights but has also inevitably resulted in the restriction of certain basic rights and freedoms in Northern Ireland.'

One matter for concern for those who believe that legal processes may be of value in the protection of civil liberties has been why the minority did not seek legal redress for such of their grievances as lay against public authorities. The discriminatory abuse of statutory powers is potentially reviewable under the ultra vires doctrine. Judicial review of administrative action may in theory at least be used as a vehicle for civil rights litigation. The Government of Ireland Act 1920 contained specific guarantees against discriminatory legislation. However, commentators have pointed to the absence of 'the necessary confidence in the judicial system as a means of securing justice' (K. Boyle, T. Hadden and P. Hillyard, *Law and State* (1975) p. 1).[1]

The possibilities of judicial review have, however, been illustrated in a series of cases in which the courts have upheld and enforced the legal rights of Sinn Fein councillors (the government having decided not to ban the political activities of members of Sinn Fein), and in cases vindicating prisoners' rights. See C. Hill QC and S. Lee, 'Without Fear or Favour? Judges and Human Rights in Northern Ireland' (Annex B to the SACHR 18th Report, 1992–93 HC 739, p. 81 at 83–90). However, Hill and Lee argue that the judges 'might be accused of being less successful in policing the criminal justice system itself, in policing (or judging) themselves' (ibid., at 90–92).[2]

1 On the avenues of legal redress, see also Boyle, Hadden and Hillyard, Chap. 2; W. D. Carroll, (1973) 6 NY Univ Journal of International Law and Politics p. 28, 47–53; T. Hadden and P. Hillyard, *Justice in Northern Ireland* (1973) Chap. II; Northern Ireland Constitution Act 1973 Part III; *Purvis v Magherafelt District Council* [1978] NI 26.

2 See also B. Dickson, 'Northern Ireland's Troubles and the Judges' in B. Hadfield (ed.), *Northern Ireland, Politics and the Constitution* (1992), Chap. 9. For criticism of the general reluctance of the House of Lords to scrutinise closely the exercise of emergency powers, to ensure the individual rights are only derogated from the extent clearly mandated by Parliament, see S. Livingstone, 'The House of Lords and the Northern Ireland Conflict' (1994) 57 MLR 333.

At the time of writing (November 1994), cease-fires have been announced by both Republican and loyalist paramilitary groups and steps are being taken in pursuit of a political solution. The prospects remain very uncertain, and there have not this far been any moves to dismantle the body of 'emergency' legislation. Indeed, royal assent was given to the Criminal Justice and Public Order Act 1994 after the cease-fire announcements, the Act adding further powers to the existing edifice.[1]

Disturbances in Northern Ireland: Report of a Commission appointed by the Governor of Northern Ireland, Chairman: Lord Cameron [Cmd. 532, 1969]

SUMMARY OF CONCLUSIONS ON CAUSES OF DISORDERS

(a) General

(1) A rising sense of continuing injustice and grievance among large sections of the Catholic population in Northern Ireland, in particular Londonderry and Dungannon, in respect of (i) inadequacy of housing provision by certain local authorities (ii) unfair methods of allocation of houses built and let by such authorities, in particular, refusals and omissions to adopt a 'points' system in determining priorities and making allocations (iii) misuse in certain cases of discretionary powers of allocation of houses in order to perpetuate Unionist control of the local authority.

(2) Complaints, now well documented in fact, of discrimination in the making of local government appointments, at all levels but especially in senior posts, to the prejudice of non-Unionists and especially Catholic members of the community, in some Unionist controlled authorities.

(3) Complaints, again well documented, in some cases of deliberate manipulation of local government electoral boundaries and in others a refusal to apply for their necessary extension, in order to achieve and maintain Unionist control of local authorities and so to deny to Catholics influence in local government proportionate to their numbers.

(4) A growing and powerful sense of resentment and frustration among the Catholic population at failure to achieve either acceptance on the part of the Government of any need to investigate these complaints or to provide and enforce a remedy for them.

(5) Resentment, particularly among Catholics, as to the existence of the Ulster Special Constabulary (the 'B' Specials) as a partisan and para-military force recruited exclusively from Protestants.

(6) Widespread resentment among Catholics in particular at the continuance in force of regulations made under the Special Powers Act, and of the continued presence in the statute book of the Act itself.

(7) Fears and apprehensions among Protestants of a threat to Unionist domination and control of Government by increase of Catholic population and powers, inflamed in particular by the activities of the Ulster Constitution Defence Committee and the Ulster Protestant Volunteers, provoked strong hostile reaction to civil rights claims as asserted by the Civil Rights Association and later by the People's Democracy which was readily translated into physical violence against Civil Rights demonstrators. . . .

---

1 For general surveys of the operation of the Northern Ireland system in relation to terrorism see Boyle, Hadden and Hillyard, op. cit.; K. Boyle, T. Hadden and P. Hillyard, *Ten Years On in Northern Ireland* (1980); K. Boyle 'Human Rights and the Northern Ireland Emergency' in J. A. Andrews (ed), *Human Rights in Criminal Procedure* (1982), pp. 144–164; D. P. J. Walsh, *The Use and Abuse of Emergency Legislation in Northern Ireland* (1983); C. Palley in International Commission of Jurists, *States of Emergency: Their Impact on Human Rights* (1983) pp. 217–246; D. Bonner, *Emergency Powers in Peacetime* (1985), Chap. 3; G. Hogan and C. Walker, *Political Violence and the Law in Ireland* (1989) (hereafter, *Hogan and Walker*); A. Jennings (ed), *Justice Under Fire: The Abuse of Civil Liberties in Northern Ireland* (rev. edn, 1990) (hereafter, *Jennings*); Amnesty International, *United Kingdom: Human Rights Concerns* (1991); *Human Rights in Northern Ireland: A Helsinki Watch Report* (1991); Liberty, *Broken Covenants: Violations of International Law in Northern Ireland* (1993). The constitutional background to 1972 is considered by C. Palley, (1972) 1 Anglo-Am LR 368–476. For contributions to the debate on ways out of the current political situation, see A. Pollak (ed.), *A Citizens' Inquiry: The Opsahl Report on Northern Ireland* (1993) (considered by B. Thompson, [1993] PL 588); B. O'Leary et al., *Northern Ireland: Sharing Authority* (IPPR, 1993); K. Boyle and T. Hadden, *Northern Ireland: The Choice* (1994); *Frameworks for the Future* (1995).

The problems of the control of emergency powers are considered by M. P. O'Boyle, (1977) 28 NILQ 160; C. Warbrick in F. E. Dowrick (ed), *Human Rights* (1979), Chap. 7; and for a comparative survey see G. J. Alexander, 'The Illusory Protection of Human Rights by National Courts during Periods of Emergency' (1984) 5 HRLJ 1.

Report of a Committee to consider, in the context of civil liberties and human rights, measures to deal with terrorism in Northern Ireland, Chairman: Lord Gardiner (Cmnd. 5847, 1975)

CIVIL LIBERTIES AND HUMAN RIGHTS

15. Our terms of reference require us to consider the problem of terrorism and subversion . . . with due consideration for the preservation of civil liberties and human rights. We have been set the difficult task of maintaining a double perspective; for, while there are policies which contribute to the maintenance of order at the expense of individual freedom, the maintenance without restriction of that freedom may involve a heavy toll in death and destruction. Some of those who have given evidence to us have argued that such features of the present emergency provisions as the use of the Army in aid of civil power, detention without trial, arrest on suspicion and trial without jury are so inherently objectionable that they must be abolished on the grounds that they constitute a basic violation of human rights. We are unable to accept this argument. While the liberty of the subject is a human right to be preserved under all possible conditions, it is not, and cannot be, an absolute right, because one man may use his liberty to take away the liberty of another, and must be restricted from doing so. Where freedoms conflict, the state has a duty to protect those in need of protection. . . .

17. The suspension of normal legal safeguards for the liberty of the subject may sometimes be essential, in a society faced by terrorism, to counter greater evils. But if continued for any period of time it exacts a social cost from the community; and the price may have to be paid over several generations. It is one of the aims of terrorists to evoke from the authorities an over-reaction to the violence, for which the terrorists are responsible, with the consequence that the authorities lose the support of those who would otherwise be on the side of government.

18. In the present situation there are neighbourhoods in Northern Ireland where natural social motivation is being deployed against lawful authority rather than in support of it. Any good society is compounded of a network of natural affection and loyalties; yet we have seen and heard of situations in which normal human responses such as family affection, love of home, neighbourliness, loyalty to friends and patriotism are daily invoked to strengthen terrorist activity.

19. The imposition of order may be successful in the short term; but in the long term, peace and stability can only come from that consensus which is the basis of law. The tragedy of Northern Ireland is that crime has become confused with politically motivated acts. The common criminal can flourish in a situation where there is a convenient political motive to cover anti-social acts; and the development of a 'prisoner-of-war' mentality among prisoners with social approval and the hope of an amnesty, lends tacit support to violence and dishonesty.

20. We acknowledge the need for firm and decisive action on the part of the security forces; but violence has in the past provoked a violent response. The adoption of methods of interrogation 'in depth', which involved forms of ill-treatment that are described in the Compton Report (Cmnd. 4823), did not last for long. Following the Report of the Parker Committee in 1972 (Cmnd. 4901) these methods were declared unlawful and were stopped by the British Government; but the resentment caused was intense, widespread and persistent.

21. **The continued existence of emergency powers should be limited both in scope and duration**. Though there are times when they are necessary for the preservation of human life, they can, if prolonged, damage the fabric of the community, and they do not provide lasting solutions. **A solution to the problems of Northern Ireland should be worked out in political terms, and must include further measures to promote social justice between classes and communities. Much has been done to improve social conditions in recent years, but much remains to be done.**[1]

The following sections of this chapter concentrate on political terrorism in the context of Northern Irish affairs. The main statutes are now the Northern Ireland (Emergency Provisions) Act 1991 and the Prevention of Terrorism (Temporary Provisions) Act 1989. Despite their titles, these Acts are but the latest in a line going back (under these titles), respectively to 1973 and 1974. The point is well made that it is misleading simply to characterise these as 'emergency' laws:

T. Hadden (1990) 41 NILQ 391 (Review of G. Hogan and C. Walker, Political Violence and the Law in Ireland)

States of legal emergency are increasingly the norm rather than the exception in many countries throughout the world. This is not just a phenomenon of the Third World, to be shrugged off by liberal

1 Paragraph 21 was endorsed as 'no less relevant today than at the time when they were made' by the Standing Advisory Commission on Human Rights (17th Report, 1991–92 HC 54, p. 12).

democracies. Both parts of Ireland have been under a more or less permanent state of emergency since partition in the 1920s and arguably for many years before that. For long periods these states of emergency were formal rather than actual in the sense that the wide powers granted to the executive to deal with politically motivated violence and other forms of subversion were used only sporadically. But they have now been in active operation for more than twenty years both in Northern Ireland and in the Irish Republic. And many of the most draconian powers are now in active operation throughout the United Kingdom, on a similarly 'temporary' basis.

The persistence of quasi-permanent states of emergency of this kind has not until recently attracted the attention it deserves from constitutional lawyers. There has always been a temptation for them to relegate emergency powers to a footnote, on the ground that because they are exceptional and temporary they are of little practical or theoretical importance. The sheer bulk of the legislation is now forcing them to write more extensively on the issue. But there is still a tendency to deal with emergency powers as exceptions to the prevailing rule of law rather than as an integral part of modern constitutional law. The analysis of the rule of law in national systems and of human rights under international law is incomplete without a detailed consideration of the nature and extent of emergency powers and of the related derogations from human rights commitments. For it is precisely in these circumstances that the rule of law and the protection of individual human rights are most at risk.

Northern Ireland (Emergency Provisions) Act 1991

PART I

Scheduled offences

[Part I contains various provisions as to proceedings for 'scheduled offences' i.e. those listed in Schedule 1. These are the crimes commonly committed by terrorists, including, for example, murder, manslaughter, riot, kidnapping, false imprisonment, assault occasioning actual bodily harm, robbery involving weapons, theft, burglary or obtaining by deception (in relation to nuclear material), various firearms and explosives offences and various offences under the 1991 Act and the Prevention of Terrorism (Temporary Provisions) Act 1989. In relation to some of these the Attorney-General for Northern Ireland may certify that a particular case is not to be treated as a scheduled offence. Trials on indictment of scheduled offences are normally held at the Belfast Crown Court (section 9) and are conducted by a judge sitting without a jury (section 10). Reasons for conviction must be given (section 10(5)). A person convicted may appeal to the Court of Criminal Appeal on any ground without leave.]

11. Admissions by persons charged with scheduled offences

(1) In any criminal proceedings for a scheduled offence, or for two or more offences at least one of which is a scheduled offence, a statement made by the accused may be given in evidence by the prosecution in so far as—

(a) it is relevant to any matter in issue in the proceedings, and

(b) it is not excluded by the court in pursuance of subsection (2) below or in the exercise of its discretion referred to in subsection (3) below (and has not been rendered inadmissible by virtue of such a direction as is mentioned in subsection (2)(iii) below).

(2) Where in any such proceedings—

(a) the prosecution proposes to give, or (as the case may be) has given, in evidence a statement made by the accused, and

(b) prima facie evidence is adduced that the accused was subjected to torture, to inhuman or degrading treatment, or to any violence or threat of violence (whether or not amounting to torture), in order to induce him to make the statement,

then, unless the prosecution satisfies the court that the statement was not obtained by so subjecting the accused in the manner indicated by that evidence, the court shall do one of the following things, namely—

(i) in the case of a statement proposed to be given in evidence, exclude the statement;

(ii) in the case of a statement already received in evidence, continue the trial disregarding the statement; or

(iii) in either case, direct that the trial shall be restarted before a differently constituted court (before which the statement in question shall be inadmissible).

(3) It is hereby declared that, in the case of any statement made by the accused and not obtained by so subjecting him as mentioned in subsection (2)(b) above, the court in any such proceedings as are mentioned in subsection (1) above has a discretion to do one of the things mentioned in subsection (2)(i) to (iii) above if it appears to the court that it is appropriate to do so in order to avoid unfairness to the accused or otherwise in the interests of justice.

(4) This section does not apply to a summary trial.

12. [This section reverses the onus of proof in relation to certain offences of possessing firearms, explosives etc.]. . . .

PART II

Powers of arrest, search and seizure, etc

16. Entry and search of premises for purpose of arresting terrorists
For the purpose of arresting a person under section 14(1)(b) of the Prevention of Terrorism (Temporary Provisions) Act 1989 (arrest of persons suspected of being connected in acts of terrorism) a constable may enter and search any premises or other place where that person is or where the constable has reasonable grounds for suspecting him to be.

17. Constables' general power of arrest and seizure
(1) Any constable may arrest without warrant any person who he has reasonable grounds to suspect is committing, has committed or is about to commit a scheduled offence or an offence under this Act which is not a scheduled offence.

(2) For the purpose of arresting a person under this section a constable may enter and search any premises or other place where that person is or where the constable has reasonable grounds for suspecting him to be.

(3) A constable may seize anything which he has reasonable grounds to suspect is being, has been or is intended to be used in the commission of a scheduled offence or an offence under this Act which is not a scheduled offence.

18. Powers of arrest and seizure of members of Her Majesty's forces
(1) Any member of Her Majesty's forces on duty may arrest without warrant, and detain for not more than four hours, a person who he has reasonable grounds to suspect is committing, has committed or is about to commit any offence.

(2) A person effecting an arrest under this section complies with any rule of law requiring him to state the ground of arrest if he states that he is effecting the arrest as a member of Her Majesty's forces.

(3) For the purpose of arresting a person under this section a member of Her Majesty's forces may enter and search any premises or other place—
  (a) where that person is, or
  (b) if there are reasonable grounds for suspecting that that person is a terrorist or has committed an offence involving the use or possession of an explosive substance or firearm, where there are reasonable grounds for suspecting him to be.

(4) Any member of Her Majesty's forces may seize, and detain for not more than four hours, anything which he has reasonable grounds to suspect is being, has been or is intended to be used in the commission of an offence under section 24 or 25 below.

19. Power to search for munitions, radio transmitters and scanning receivers
(1) Any member of Her Majesty's forces on duty or any constable may enter any premises or other place other than a dwelling-house for the purpose of ascertaining—
  (a) whether there are any munitions unlawfully at that place; or
  (b) whether there is a transmitter at that place;
and may search the place for any munitions or transmitter with a view to exercising the powers conferred by subsection (7) below.

(2) Any member of Her Majesty's forces on duty authorised by a commissioned officer of those forces or any constable authorised by an officer of the Royal Ulster Constabulary not below the rank of chief inspector may enter any dwelling-house in which there are reasonable grounds for suspecting that there are unlawfully any munitions or that there is a transmitter and may search it for any munitions or transmitter with a view to exercising the said powers.

(3) If it is necessary for the purpose of effectively carrying out a search—
  (a) a member of Her Majesty's forces or constable exercising the powers conferred by subsection (1) above may be accompanied by other persons; and

(b) any authority given under subsection (2) above may authorise other persons to accompany the member of Her Majesty's forces or constable to whom the authority is given.

(4) If the member of Her Majesty's forces or constable carrying out a search under subsection (1) or (2) above reasonably believes that it is necessary to do so for the purpose of effectively carrying out the search or of preventing the frustration of its object he may—

(a) require any person who when the search begins is on, or during the search enters, the premises or other place where the search is carried out ('the place of search') to remain in, or in a specified part of, that place, to refrain from entering a specified part of it or to go from one specified part of it to another specified part;

(b) require any person who is not resident in the place of search to refrain from entering it; and

(c) use reasonable force to secure compliance with any such requirement.

(5) No requirement imposed under subsection (4) above shall have effect after the conclusion of the search in relation to which it was imposed; and no such requirement shall be imposed or have effect after the end of the period of four hours beginning with the time when that or any other requirement was first imposed under that subsection in relation to the search in question but an officer of the Royal Ulster Constabulary not below the rank of superintendent may extend that period by a further period of four hours if he reasonably believes that it is necessary to do so for the purpose mentioned in that subsection.

(6) Any member of Her Majesty's forces on duty or any constable may—

(a) stop any person in any public place and, with a view to exercising the powers conferred by subsection (7) below, search him for the purpose of ascertaining whether he has any munitions unlawfully with him or any transmitter with him; and

(b) with a view to exercising the said powers—

(i) search any person not in a public place who he has reasonable grounds to suspect has any munitions unlawfully with him or any transmitter with him; and

(ii) search any person entering or found in a dwelling-house entered under subsection (2) above.

(7) Where a member of Her Majesty's forces or a constable is empowered by virtue of any provision of this Act to search any premises or other place or any person—

(a) he may seize any munitions found in the course of the search (unless it appears to him that the munitions are being, have been and will be used only lawfully) and may retain and, if necessary, destroy them; and

(b) he may seize any transmitter found in the course of the search (unless it appears to him that the transmitter has been, is being and is likely to be used only lawfully) and may retain it.

(8) Where a member of Her Majesty's forces or a constable carries out a search under subsection (1) or (2) above he shall, unless it is not practicable to do so, make a written record of the search which shall specify—

(a) the address of the premises, or a description of the place, which is searched;

(b) the date and time of the search;

(c) any damage caused in the course of the search; and

(d) anything seized in the course of the search.

(9) Such a record shall also include the name (if known) of any person appearing to the person making the record to be the occupier of the premises or other place searched; but—

(a) a person may not be detained to find out his name; and

(b) if the person making the record does not know the name of a person appearing to him to be the occupier of the premises or other place searched, he shall include in the record a note otherwise describing him.

(10) Such a record shall identify the person by whom the search is carried out—

(a) in the case of a constable, by reference to his police number; and

(b) in the case of a member of Her Majesty's forces, by reference to his service number, rank and regiment.

(11) Where a record of a search is made under this section a copy of the record shall be supplied at once or, where that is not practicable, as soon as is practicable to any person appearing to the person making the record to be the occupier of the premises or other place searched.

(12) Any person who wilfully fails to comply with a requirement imposed under subsection (4) above or wilfully obstructs, or seeks to frustrate the object of, a search in relation to which such a requirement has been or could be imposed is guilty of an offence and liable—

(a) on conviction on indictment, to imprisonment for a term not exceeding two years or a fine or both;

(b) on summary conviction, to imprisonment for a term not exceeding six months or a fine not exceeding the statutory maximum or both.

(13) The preceding provisions of this section shall have effect in relation to scanning receivers as they have effect in relation to transmitters.

(14) In this section—
'munitions' means—
(a) explosives, explosive substances, firearms and ammunition; and
(b) anything used or capable of being used in the manufacture of any explosive, explosive substance, firearm or ammunition;
'scanning receiver' means—
(a) any apparatus for wireless telegraphy designed or adapted for the purpose of automatically monitoring selected frequencies, or automatically scanning a selected range of frequencies, so as to enable transmissions on any of those frequencies to be detected or intercepted; or
(b) part of any such apparatus;
'transmitter' means any apparatus for wireless telegraphy designed or adapted for emission, as opposed to reception, or part of any such apparatus;
'wireless telegraphy' has the same meaning as in section 19(1) of the Wireless Telegraphy Act 1949.

20. Powers of explosives inspectors
[This section gives powers of entry, search and seizure in respect of explosives to inspectors appointed under section 53 of the Explosives Act 1875.]

21. Entry to search for persons unlawfully detained
(1) Where any person is believed to be unlawfully detained in such circumstances that his life is in danger, any member of Her Majesty's forces on duty or any constable may, subject to subsection (2) below, enter any premises or other place for the purpose of ascertaining whether that person is so detained there.
(2) A dwelling-house may be entered in pursuance of subsection (1) above—
(a) by a member of Her Majesty's forces, only when authorised to do so by a commissioned officer of those forces; and
(b) by a constable, only when authorised to do so by an officer of the Royal Ulster Constabulary not below the rank of chief inspector.

22. Examination of documents
(1) Where a member of Her Majesty's forces or a constable is empowered by virtue of any provision of this Act to search any premises or other place or any person he may examine any document or record found in the course of the search so far as reasonably required for ascertaining whether it contains any such information as is mentioned in section 31(1)(a) or (b) below.
(2) A document or record which cannot be conveniently or thoroughly examined at the place where it is found may be removed for examination to another place and retained there until the examination has been completed.
(3) This section shall not be taken to authorise the examination, removal or retention of a document or record by a person at a time when he has reasonable cause for believing it to be an item subject to legal privilege (within the meaning of the Police and Criminal Evidence (Northern Ireland) Order 1989).
(4) Where a document or record is examined under this section it shall not be photographed or copied.
(5) Where a document or record is examined under this section the person who examines it shall make a written record of the examination at once or, where it is not practicable to make one at once, as soon as is practicable.
(6) A record of an examination of a document or record which is made under this section shall specify—
(a) a description of the document or record;
(b) the object of the examination;
(c) the address of the premises, or a description of the place, where the document or record was found;
(d) where the document or record was found in the course of a search of a person, the name of that person;
(e) where the document or record was found in the course of a search of any premises or other place, the name of any person appearing to the person making the record to be the occupier of the premises or other place or to have had custody of the document or record when it was found;
(f) where the document or record was removed for examination from the place where it was found, the date and time when it was removed from that place; and
(g) where the document or record was examined at the place where it was found, the date and time when it was examined.
(7) Such a record shall identify the person by whom the examination was carried out—
(a) in the case of a constable, by reference to his police number; and
(b) in the case of a member of Her Majesty's forces, by reference to his service number, rank and regiment.

(8) Where a record of an examination of a document or record is made under this section a copy of the record shall be supplied at once or, if that is not practicable, as soon as is practicable—

(a) in the case where the document or record was found in the course of a search of a person, to that person; and

(b) in a case where the document or record was found in the course of a search of any premises or other place, to any person appearing to the person making the record to be the occupier of the premises or other place or to have had custody or control of the document or record when it was found.

(9) Subject to subsection (10) below, a document or record may not be retained by virtue of subsection (2) above for more than forty-eight hours.

(10) An officer of the Royal Ulster Constabulary not below the rank of chief inspector may authorise the retention of a document or record by a constable for a further period or periods; but no such authorisation shall permit the retention of a document or record beyond the end of the period of ninety-six hours from the time when it was removed for examination from the place where it was found.

(11) Any person who wilfully obstructs a member of Her Majesty's forces or a constable in the exercise of the powers conferred by this section is guilty of an offence. . . .

23. Power to stop and question

(1) Any member of Her Majesty's forces on duty or any constable may stop any person for so long as is necessary in order to question him for the purpose of ascertaining—

(a) that person's identity and movements;

(b) what he knows concerning any recent explosion or any other recent incident endangering life or concerning any person killed or injured in any such explosion or incident; or

(c) any one or more of the matters referred to in paragraphs (a) and (b) above.

(2) Any person who—

(a) fails to stop when required to do so under this section, or

(b) refuses to answer, or fails to answer to the best of his knowledge and ability, any question addressed to him under this section,

is guilty of an offence and liable on summary conviction to a fine not exceeding level 5 on the standard scale.

24. General powers of entry and interference with rights of property and with highways

(1) Any member of Her Majesty's forces on duty or any constable may enter any premises or other place—

(a) if he considers it necessary to do so in the course of operations for the preservation of the peace or the maintenance of order; or

(b) if authorised to do so by or on behalf of the Secretary of State.

(2) Any member of Her Majesty's forces on duty, any constable or any person specifically authorised to do so by or on behalf of the Secretary of State may, if authorised to do so by or on behalf of the Secretary of State—

(a) take possession of any land or other property;

(b) take steps to place buildings or other structures in a state of defence;

(c) detain any property or cause it to be destroyed or moved;

(d) do any other act interfering with any public right or with any private rights of property, including carrying out any works on any land of which possession has been taken under this subsection.

(3) Any member of Her Majesty's forces on duty, any constable or any person specifically authorised to do so by or on behalf of the Secretary of State may, so far as he considers it immediately necessary for the preservation of the peace or the maintenance of order—

(a) wholly or partly close a highway or divert or otherwise interfere with a highway or the use of a highway; or

(b) prohibit or restrict the exercise of any right of way or the use of any waterway.

(4) Any person who, without lawful authority or reasonable excuse (the proof of which lies on him), interferes with works executed, or any apparatus, equipment or any other thing used, in or in connection with the exercise of powers conferred by this section, is guilty of an offence and liable on summary conviction to imprisonment for a term not exceeding six months or a fine not exceeding level 5 on the standard scale or both.

(5) Any authorisation to exercise any powers under any provision of this section may authorise the exercise of all those powers, or powers of any class or a particular power specified, either by all persons by whom they are capable of being exercised or by persons of any class or a particular person specified.

25. [This section gives the Secretary of State power to direct the closure or diversion of roads, and makes it an offence to interfere with works in connection with the closure or diversion or to execute by-pass works.]

26. Supplementary provisions

(1) Any power conferred by this Part of this Act—

    (a) to enter any premises or other place includes power to enter any vessel, aircraft or vehicle;

    (b) to search any premises or other place includes power to stop and search any vehicle or vessel or any aircraft which is not airborne and search any container;

and in this Part of this Act references to any premises or place shall be construed accordingly.

(2) Where a document or record examined under section 22 above was found in the course of a search of a vehicle, vessel or aircraft—

    (a) the reference in subsection (6) of that section to the address of the premises, or a description of the place, where the document or record was found shall be construed as a reference to the location of the vehicle, vessel or aircraft when it was found together (in the case of a vehicle) with its registration number; and

    (b) the references in that section to the occupier of the premises or place where it was found shall be construed as references to the person in charge of the vehicle, vessel or aircraft.

(3) In this Part of this Act references to a dwelling-house include references to a vessel or vehicle which is habitually stationary and used as a dwelling.

(4) Any power conferred by this Part of this Act to enter any place, vessel, aircraft or vehicle shall be exercisable, if need be, by force.

(5) Any power conferred by virtue of this section to search a vehicle or vessel shall, in the case of a vehicle or vessel which cannot be conveniently or thoroughly searched at the place where it is, include power to take it or cause it to be taken to any place for the purpose of carrying out the search.

(6) Where by virtue of this section under section 19(1) or (2) above is carried out in relation to a vessel, aircraft or vehicle, the person carrying out the search may, if he reasonably believes that it is necessary to do so for the purpose mentioned in subsection (4) of that section—

    (a) require any person in or on the vessel, aircraft or vehicle to remain with it or, in the case of a vessel or vehicle which by virtue of subsection (5) above is removed for the purpose of the search, to go to and remain at the place to which it is removed; and

    (b) use reasonable force to secure compliance with any such requirement;

and subsections (5) and (12) of section 19 above shall apply to a requirement imposed under this subsection as they apply to a requirement imposed under subsection (4) of that section.

(7) The requirement to make a record of a search under subsection (1) or (2) of section 19 above shall apply in the case of a vehicle, vessel or aircraft (other than one which is habitually stationary) searched by virtue of this section only where the search takes place after the vehicle, vessel or aircraft is removed for the purpose of the search by virtue of subsection (5) above; and in the case of such a search—

    (a) the reference in subsection (8) of that section to the address of the premises, or a description of the place, which is searched shall be construed as a reference to the location where the vehicle, vessel or aircraft is searched together (in the case of a vehicle) with its registration number; and

    (b) the references in that section to the occupier of the premises or place searched shall be construed as references to the person in charge of the vehicle, vessel or aircraft.

(8) Any power conferred by virtue of this section to search any vessel, aircraft, vehicle or container includes power to examine it.

(9) Any power conferred by this Part of this Act to stop any person includes power to stop a vessel or vehicle or an aircraft which is not airborne.

(10) Any person who, when required by virtue of this section to stop a vessel or vehicle or any aircraft which is not airborne, fails to do so is guilty of an offence and liable on summary conviction to imprisonment for a term not exceeding six months or a fine not exceeding level 5 on the standard scale or both.

(11) A member of Her Majesty's forces exercising any power conferred by this Part of this Act when he is not in uniform shall, if so requested by any person at or about the time of exercising that power, produce to that person documentary evidence that he is such a member.

(12) The Documentary Evidence Act 1868 shall apply to any authorisation given in writing under this Part of this Act by or on behalf of the Secretary of State as it applies to any order made by him.

PART III

Offences against public security and public order

27. Directing terrorist organisation

Any person who directs, at any level, the activities of an organisation which is concerned with the commission of acts of terrorism is guilty of an offence and liable on conviction on indictment to imprisonment for life.

28. Proscribed organisations

(1) Subject to subsection (6) below, any person who—

(a) belongs or professes to belong to a proscribed organisation; or

(b) solicits or invites support for a proscribed organisation other than support with money or other property; or

(c) solicits or invites any person to become a member of a proscribed organisation or to carry out on behalf of a proscribed organisation orders or directions given, or requests made, by a member of that organisation; or

(d) arranges or assists in the arrangement or management of, or addresses, any meeting of three or more persons (whether or not it is a meeting to which the public are admitted) knowing that the meeting—

(i) is to support a proscribed organisation; or

(ii) is to further the activities of such an organisation; or

(iii) is to be addressed by a person belonging or professing to belong to such an organisation,

is guilty of an offence. . . .

(2) The organisations specified in Schedule 2 to this Act are proscribed organisations for the purposes of this Act: and any organisation which passes under a name mentioned in that Schedule shall be treated as proscribed, whatever relationship (if any) it has to any other organisation of the same name.

(3) The Secretary of State may by order add to Schedule 2 to this Act any organisation that appears to him to be concerned in terrorism or in promoting or encouraging it.

(4) The Secretary of State may also by order remove an organisation from Schedule 2 to this Act.

(5) The possession by a person of a document—

(a) addressed to him as a member of a proscribed organisation; or

(b) relating or purporting to relate to the affairs of a proscribed organisation; or

(c) emanating or purporting to emanate from a proscribed organisation or officer of a proscribed organisation,

shall be evidence of that person belonging to the organisation at the time when he had the document in his possession.

(6) A person belonging to a proscribed organisation shall—

(a) if the organisation is a proscribed organisation by virtue of an order under subsection (3) above; or

(b) if this section has ceased to be in force but has been subsequently brought into force by an order under section 68(3) below,

not be guilty of an offence under this section by reason of belonging to the organisation if he has not after the coming into force of the order under subsection (3) above or the coming into force again of this section, as the case may be, taken part in any activities of the organisation.

(7) Subsection (6) above shall apply in relation to a person belonging to the Red Hand Commando, the Ulster Freedom Fighters, the Ulster Volunteer Force, the Irish National Liberation Army or the Irish People's Liberation Organisation as if the organisation were proscribed by virtue of an order under subsection (3) above with the substitution in subsection (6) for the reference to the coming into force of such an order of a reference—

(a) as respects a person belonging to the Red Hand Commando or the Ulster Freedom Fighters, to 12th November 1973;

(b) as respects a person belonging to the Ulster Volunteer Force, to 4th October 1975;

(c) as respects a person belonging to the Irish National Liberation Army, to 3rd July 1979;

(d) as respects a person belonging to the Irish People's Liberation Organisation, to 29th March 1990.

29. Display of support in public for a proscribed organisation

Any person who in a public place—

(a) wears any item of dress; or

(b) wears, carries or displays any article,

in such a way or in such circumstances as to arouse reasonable apprehension that he is a member or supporter of a proscribed organisation is guilty of an offence . . . .

30. Possession of items intended for terrorist purposes

(1) A person is guilty of an offence if he has any article in his possession in circumstances giving rise to a reasonable suspicion that the item is in his possession for a purpose connected with the commission, preparation or instigation of acts of terrorism connected with the affairs of Northern Ireland.

(2) It is a defence for a person charged with an offence under this section to prove that at the time of the alleged offence the article in question was not in his possession for such a purpose as is mentioned in subsection (1) above . . . .

(4) Subsections (1), (2) and (5) of section 12 above shall apply where a person is charged with possessing an article in such circumstances as to constitute an offence under this section as they apply where a person is charged with possessing a proscribed article in such circumstances as are there mentioned.

31. Unlawful collection, etc. of information
(1) No person shall, without lawful authority or reasonable excuse (the proof of which lies on him)—
  (a) collect, record, publish, communicate or attempt to elicit any information with respect to any person to whom this paragraph applies which is of such a nature as is likely to be useful to terrorists;
  (b) collect or record any information which is of such a nature as is likely to be useful to terrorists in planning or carrying out any act of violence; or
  (c) have in his possession any record or document containing any such information as is mentioned in paragraph (a) or (b) above.
(2) Subsection (1)(a) above applies to any of the following persons, that is to say—
  (a) any constable or member of Her Majesty's forces;
  (b) any person holding judicial office;
  (c) any officer of any court;
  (d) any person employed for the whole of his time in the prison service in Northern Ireland; and
  (e) any person who has at any time been a person falling within any of the preceding paragraphs.
(3) In subsection (1) above any reference to recording information includes a reference to recording it by means of photography or by any other means. . . .
(5) The court by or before which a person is convicted of an offence under this section may order the forfeiture of any record or document mentioned in subsection (1) above which is found in his possession.
(6) Without prejudice to section 18 of the Interpretation Act 1978 (offences under two or more laws), nothing in this section shall derogate from the operation of the Official Secrets Acts 1911 to 1989.

32. Training in making or use of firearms, explosives or explosive substances
(1) Subject to subsection (2) below, any person who instructs or trains another or receives instruction or training in the making or use of firearms, explosives or explosive substances is guilty of an offence. . . .
(2) In any prosecution for an offence under this section it shall be a defence for the person charged to prove that the instruction or training was given or received with lawful authority or for industrial, agricultural or sporting purposes only or otherwise with good reason.
(3) The court by or before which a person is convicted of an offence under this section may order the forfeiture of any thing which appears to the court to have been in his possession for purposes connected with the offence.
(4) Without prejudice to section 18 of the Interpretation Act 1978 (offences under two or more laws), nothing in this section shall derogate from the operation of the Unlawful Drilling Act 1819.

33. Wearing of hoods, etc. in public places
Any person who, without lawful authority or reasonable excuse (the proof of which lies on him), wears in a public place or in the curtilage of a dwelling-house (other than one in which he is residing) any hood, mask or other article whatsoever made, adapted to be used for concealing the identity or features is guilty of an offence. . . .

PART IV

Detention orders

34. Detention orders
Schedule 3 to this Act shall have effect with respect to the detention of terrorists and persons suspected of being terrorists.

PART V

Regulation of the provision of private security services

[Sections 35 to 42 provide that it is an offence for a person to offer security services for reward without a certificate from the Secretary of State and establish a procedure for obtaining a certificate; a certificate may only be refused if the Secretary of State is satisfied that a proscribed organisation (or associated organisation) would be likely to benefit from its issue, or that the applicant has persistently failed to comply with the requirements of Part V.]

PART VI

Persons in police custody under terrorism provisions

43. The terrorism provisions and police custody

(1) In this Part of this Act 'the terrorism provisions' means section 14 of the Prevention of Terrorism (Temporary Provisions) Act 1989 and any provision of Schedule 2 or 5 to that Act conferring a power of arrest or detention.

(2) A person is held in police custody for the purposes of this Part of this Act if he is detained at a police station or is detained elsewhere in the charge of a constable except that a person who is at a court after being charged with an offence is not held in police custody for the purposes of section 44 below.

44. Right to have someone informed of detention under terrorism provisions

(1) A person who is detained under the terrorism provisions and is being held in police custody shall be entitled, if he so requests, to have one friend or relative or other person who is known to him or is likely to take an interest in his welfare told that he is being detailed under those provisions and where he is being held in police custody.

(2) A person shall be informed of the right conferred on him by subsection (1) above as soon as practicable after he has become a person to whom that subsection applies.

(3) A request made by a person under subsection (1) above, and the time at which it is made, shall be recorded in writing.

(4) If a person makes such a request, it must be complied with as soon as is practicable except to the extent that any delay is permitted by this section.

(5) Any delay in complying with such a request is only permitted if—

    (a) it is authorised by an officer of at least the rank of superintendent; and

    (b) it does not extend beyond the end of the period referred to in subsection (6) below.

(6) That period is—

    (a) except where paragraph (b) below applies, the period of forty-eight hours beginning with the time when the detained person was first detained under the terrorism provisions;

    (b) where the detained person was, prior to the time when he was first so detained, being examined in accordance with paragraph 2 of Schedule 5 to the Prevention of Terrorism (Temporary Provisions) Act 1989, the period of forty-eight hours beginning with the time when he was first so examined.

(7) An officer may give an authorisation under subsection (5) above orally or in writing but, if he gives it orally, he shall confirm it in writing as soon as is practicable.

(8) An officer may only authorise a delay in complying with a request under subsection (1) above where he has reasonable grounds for believing that telling the person named in the request of the detention of the detained person—

    (a) will lead to interference with or harm to evidence connected with a scheduled offence or interference with or physical injury to any person; or

    (b) will lead to the alerting of any person suspected of having committed such an offence but not yet arrested for it; or

    (c) will hinder the recovery of any property obtained as a result of such an offence; or

    (d) will lead to interference with the gathering of information about the commission, preparation or instigation of acts of terrorism; or

    (e) by alerting any person, will make it more difficult—

        (i) to prevent an act of terrorism; or

        (ii) to secure the apprehension, prosecution or conviction of any person in connection with the commission, preparation or instigation of an act of terrorism.

(9) If any delay is authorised, then, as soon as is practicable—

    (a) the detained person shall be told the reason for authorising it; and

    (b) the reason shall be recorded in writing.

(10) Any authorisation under subsection (5) above shall cease to have effect once the reason for giving it ceases to subsist.

(11) The right conferred by subsection (1) above may be exercised by a person to whom that subsection applies on each occasion when he is transferred from one place to another; and this section applies to each subsequent occasion on which that right is so exercised as it applies to the first such occasion.

(12) Subsection (11) above shall not be construed as prejudicing the operation of a request by a person to whom subsection (1) above applies which was made, but not complied with, before he was transferred.

45. Right of access to legal advice

(1) A person who is detained under the terrorism provisions and is being held in police custody shall be entitled, if he so requests, to consult a solicitor privately.

(2) A person shall be informed of the right conferred on him by subsection (1) above as soon as practicable after he has become a person to whom that subsection applies.

(3) A request made by a person under subsection (1) above, and the time at which it is made, shall be recorded in writing unless it is made by him while at a court after being charged with an offence.

(4) If a person makes such a request, he must be permitted to consult a solicitor as soon as is practicable except to the extent that any delay is permitted by this section.

(5) Any delay in complying with a request under subsection (1) above is only permitted if—

(a) it is authorised by an officer of at least the rank of superintendent; and

(b) it does not extend beyond the relevant time.

(6) In subsection (5) above 'the relevant time' means—

(a) where the request is the first request made by the detained person under subsection (1) above, the end of the period referred to in section 44(6) above; or

(b) where the request follows an earlier request made by the detained person under that subsection in pursuance of which he has consulted a solicitor, the end of the period of forty-eight hours beginning with the time when that consultation began.

(7) An officer may give an authorisation under subsection (5) above orally or in writing but, if he gives it orally, he shall confirm it in writing as soon as is practicable.

(8) An officer may only authorise a delay in complying with a request under subsection (1) above where he has reasonable grounds for believing that the exercise of the right conferred by that subsection at the time when the detained person desires to exercise it—

(a) will lead to interference with or harm to evidence connected with a scheduled offence or interference with or physical injury to any person; or

(b) will lead to the alerting of any person suspected of having committed such an offence but not yet arrested for it; or

(c) will hinder the recovery of any propery obtained as a result of such an offence; or

(d) will lead to interference with the gathering of information about the commission, preparation or instigation of acts of terrorism; or

(e) by alerting any person, will make it more difficult—

(i) to prevent an act of terrorism; or

(ii) to secure the apprehension, prosecution or conviction of any person in connection with the commission, preparation or instigation of an act of terrorism.

(9) If any delay is authorised, then, as soon as is practicable—

(a) the detained person shall be told the reason for authorising it; and

(b) the reason shall be recorded in writing.

(10) If an officer of at least the rank of Assistant Chief Constable has reasonable grounds for believing that, unless he gives a direction under subsection (11) below, the exercise by a person of the right conferred by subsection (1) above will have any of the consequences specified in subsection (8) above, he may give a direction under subsection (11) below.

(11) A direction under this subsection is a direction that a person desiring to exercise the right conferred by subsection (1) above may only consult a solicitor in the sight and hearing of a qualified officer of the uniformed branch of the Royal Ulster Constabulary.

(12) An officer is qualified for the purposes of subsection (11) above if—

(a) he is of at least the rank of inspector; and

(b) in the opinion of the officer giving the direction, he has no connection with the case.

(13) Any authorisation under subsection (5) above or direction under subsection (11) above shall cease to have effect once the reason for giving it ceases to subsist. . . .

PART VII

Confiscation of proceeds of terrorist-related activities

[Sections 47 to 56, as amended by the Criminal Justice Act 1993, enable a court which convicts a person of specified scheduled offences to make a confiscation order in respect of the amount by which he has benefited from terrorist-related activities, and make it an offence to assist another to retain proceeds of terrorist-related activities or to conceal or transfer the proceeds of terrorist-related activities.]

PART VIII

Miscellaneous

57. Additional investigation powers

(1) If, on an application made in writing by an officer of the Royal Ulster Constabulary not below the rank of superintendent, it appears to the Secretary of State—

(*a*) that an investigation to which this section applies is taking place; and

(*b*) that the investigation could be more effectively carried out with the participation of a person who is not a constable and who is named in the application,

the Secretary of State may authorise that person to exercise for the purposes of the investigation the powers conferred by Schedule 5 to this Act.

(2) Those powers shall be exercisable in Great Britain as well as in Northern Ireland and accordingly this section and that Schedule shall extend to the whole of the United Kingdom.

(3) Where a person who has been authorised under subsection (1) above to exercise the powers there mentioned considers that any material may be relevant to the investigation in relation to which the authority was given, Schedule 7 to the Prevention of Terrorism (Temporary Provisions) Act 1989 (terrorist investigations) shall have effect in relation to the material as if—

(*a*) the references to a constable in paragraphs 2(1), 3(1) and (2)(*b*), 5(1) and (3), 6(1), 12(2)(*b*), 14(3) and 15(1);

(*b*) the first of the references to a constable in paragraph 3(6); and

(*c*) the references to a procurator fiscal in paragraphs 12(1) and (6), 13(2), 14(1) and 15(1),

included references to that person, and where (by virtue of this subsection) such a person has made an application for an order under paragraph 3 of that Schedule, the reference in paragraph 4(2)(*b*) to the constable on whose application the order was made or any constable serving in the same police station shall be construed as referring to that person.

(4) This section applies to any investigation by the Royal Ulster Constabulary into the existence of—

(*a*) the resources of a proscribed organisation;

(*b*) funds which may be applied or used for the commission of, or in furtherance of or in connection with, acts of terrorism connected with the affairs of Northern Ireland; or

(*c*) the proceeds of the commission of such acts of terrorism or of activities engaged in furtherance of or in connection with such acts.

(5) Paragraph (*a*) of subsection (4) above includes any money or property which is or is to be applied or made available for the benefit of a proscribed organisation; and paragraph (*c*) of that subsection includes any property which in whole or in part directly or indirectly represents such proceeds as are there mentioned. . . .

PART IX

Supplementary

65. Restriction of prosecutions

A prosecution in respect of an offence under this Act shall not be instituted in Northern Ireland except by or with the consent of the Director of Public Prosecutions for Northern Ireland or in England and Wales except by or with the consent of the Director of Public Prosecutions.

66. General interpretation

In this Act, except so far as the context otherwise requires—

'dwelling-house' means any building or part of a building used as a dwelling;

'explosive' means any article or substance manufactured for the purpose of producing a practical effect by explosion;

'explosive substance' means any substance for the time being specified in regulations made under section 3 of the Explosives Act (Northern Ireland) 1970;

'firearm' includes an air gun or air pistol;

'proscribed organisation' means an organisation for the time being specified in Schedule 2 to this Act, including an organisation which is to be treated as a proscribed organisation by virtue of section 28(2) above;

'public place' means a place to which for the time being members of the public have or are permitted to have access, whether on payment or otherwise; . . .

'terrorism' means the use of violence for political ends and includes any use of violence for the purpose of putting the public or any section of the public in fear;

'terrorist' means a person who is or has been concerned in the commission or attempted commission of any act of terrorism or in directing, organising or training persons for the purpose of terrorism;

'vehicle' includes a hovercraft. . . .

Schedule 2

PROSCRIBED ORGANISATIONS

The Irish Republican Army.

Cumann na mBan.

Fianna na hEireann.

The Red Hand Commando.

Saor Eire.

The Ulster Freedom Fighters.

The Ulster Volunteer Force.

The Irish National Liberation Army.

The Irish People's Liberation Organisation.

[The Ulster Defence Association.]

NOTES

1. Section 58 enables the Secretary of State to make supplementary regulations for promoting the preservation of peace and the maintenance of order (see S.I. 1991 No. 1759). Section 61 requires him to make Codes of Practice in connection with the detention, treatment, questioning and identification of persons detained under the 1989 Act, and enables him to make Codes in respect of (a) the exercise by police officers of powers conferred by Part II of this Act or the Prevention of Terrorism (Temporary Provisions) Act 1989; and (b) the seizure and retention of property found by police officers conducting a search under the 1989 or 1991 Acts. Section 62 enables him to make a Code of Practice in connection with the exercise of powers under Part II of this Act by members of the armed forces. Drafts of each Code must be laid before Parliament, but the approval of Parliament is not required. Contravention of a provision of the Code does not of itself give rise to civil or criminal liability, but may lead to disciplinary proceedings. The Secretary of State has made the mandatory code under s. 61 (*Northern Ireland Office: Northern Ireland (Emergency Provisions) Act 1991: Section 61: Codes of Practice* (HMSO, Belfast, 1994)). He has not made a code for the armed forces (although the SACHR has recommended that this be done: 17th Report, 1991–92 HC 54, p. 14). Instead, he has published a non-statutory *Guide to the Emergency Powers* (Northern Ireland Office, HMSO, Belfast, 1994). Lord Colville (1992 Report on the EPA, pp. 59–60) recommended the introduction of a code of practice for the exercise of stop-search powers by the security forces, in particular the armed forces. There is also a Code of Practice concerning the exercise by authorised investigators of the powers conferred by Sch. 5. Section 63 gives a right to compensation for interference with property under this Act. Parts I to VIII (with certain exceptions) were to expire on 15 June 1992 unless continued in force by order (s. 69). Continuance orders have been made every 12 months.

Except where indicated, the offences in the provisions set out above are triable either way, with maximum penalties on conviction on indictment of 10 years' (ss. 28(1), 30(3), 31(4), 32), 2 years' (ss. 19(8), 22(11)) or 1 years' (ss. 29, 33) imprisonment or a fine or both, and on summary conviction, six months' imprisonment or a fine not exceeding the statutory maximum or both.

2. There have been many occasions in Irish history when the government of the day has secured the enactment of wider statutory powers to deal with the problem of security than those normally available in Great Britain. See generally C. Townshend, *Political Violence in Ireland* (1983). In the nineteenth century, for example, the Protection of Person and Property Act (Ireland) 1881, 44 Vict c4, the

Peace Preservation (Ireland) Act 1881, 44 Vict c5, the Prevention of Crime (Ireland) Act 1882, 45 & 46 Vict c25, and the Criminal Law and Procedure (Ireland) Act 1887, 50 & 51 Vict c20, included many provisions similar to those contained in the 1991 Act, including powers of detention, arrest and search, and trial without a jury for certain kinds of offence. In addition there were at various times powers to prohibit meetings, provisions as to special juries and the change of venue of trials, and provisions making intimidation an offence.

In the twentieth century, the main piece of 'emergency' legislation in Northern Ireland was the Civil Authorities (Special Powers) Act (NI) 1922 and the regulations made thereunder. This was originally intended as a temporary measure, but was renewed annually until 1928 and then for five years to 1933. It was then provided that the Act 'shall continue in force until Parliament otherwise determines' by the Civil Authorities (Special Powers) Act (NI) 1933, s. 2. The content of the regulations was altered from time to time, and certain features were strongly criticised.[1] One of the most objectionable provisions was section 2(4) of the 1922 Act which provided that:

'If any person does any act of such a nature as to be calculated to be prejudicial to the preservation of the peace or maintenance of order in Northern Ireland and not specifically provided for in the regulations, he shall be deemed to be guilty of an offence against the regulations.'

This has had no counterpart in the successive Northern Ireland (Emergency Provisions) Acts.

The legal procedures to deal with terrorist activities were reviewed by the Diplock Commission (Report, Cmnd. 5185, 1972; see W. L. Twining, [1973] Crim LR 407). The Northern Ireland (Emergency Provisions) Act 1973 (which repealed the Special Powers Acts) was based upon their recommendations. The legislation was amended in 1975, consolidated in 1978, amended again in 1987 and consolidated with yet further amendments in 1991. It has been the subject of major reviews.[2] One of its features has been a steady increase in size and scope.[3]

The 1991 Act is analysed by B. Dickson, 'Northern Ireland's Emergency Legislation' [1992] PL 592. Dickson argues (p. 597) that:

'Whatever the position in the early 1970s, the objective behind anti-terrorist legislation today, whether in Northern Ireland or in Great Britain, is no longer the prevention of atrocities or the detection and punishment of those who perpetrate them. Its real pupose is to placate the electorate, as well as some of the elected, who demand that some steps must be taken by the law to counteract terrorism, regardless of how effective these might prove in practice. Emergency law, in other words, is being exploited for its symbolic significance.'

3. *Monitoring arrangements*

The 1978 Act was unlimited in its duration, but subject to renewal by order every six months. The 1987 Act provided, however, that the 1978 and 1987 Acts would expire five years after the passing of the 1987 Act (i.e. on 16 June 1992), and was subject to annual renewal by order. The 1991 Act accordingly replaced the 1978

---

1 See the *Report of a Commission of Inquiry appointed to examine the purpose and effect of the Civil Authorities (Special Powers) Acts (NI) 1922 and 1933* (NCCL, 1936); *A Review of the 1936 NCCL Commission of Inquiry in the light of subsequent events* (NCCL, 1972); J. Ll. J. Edwards, [1956] Crim LR 7; H. Calvert, *Constitutional Law in Northern Ireland* (1968) pp. 380–386; *Emergency Powers: A Fresh Start*, Fabian Tract 416 (1972).

2 The Gardiner Committee (Cmnd. 5847, 1975: above, p. 270); the Bennett Committee Inquiry into *Police Interrogation Procedures in Northern Ireland* (Cmnd. 7497, 1989); Sir George Baker, *Review of the Operation of the Northern Ireland (Emergency Provisions) Act 1978* (Cmnd. 9222, 1984); Viscount Colville, *Review of the Northern Ireland (Emergency Provisions) Act 1978 and 1987* (Cm. 1115, 1990); J. J. Rowe QC, *Review of the Northern Ireland (Emergency Provisions) Act 1991* (Cm. 2706, 1995) (hereafter, *Rowe Review (EPPr)*).

3 On the 1987 Act, see J. D. Jackson, (1988) 39 NILQ 235.

and 1987 Acts in anticipation of their expiry. It is not expressly limited in overall duration, but is subject to annual renewal. The operation of the Emergency Provisions
legislation was from 1987 to 1992 the subject of an annual report by Viscount Colville
of Culross QC (who made similar reports on the Prevention of Terrorism (Temporary
Provisions) legislation). From 1993, the reporter has been John Rowe QC. These are
published by the Northern Ireland Office, and form the background to the annual
renewal debates. Lord Colville conducted a more substantial review in 1990 and John
Rowe in 1994 (see p. 283, n. **2**). John Rowe recommended that, notwithstanding the
cease-fires, the bulk of the 1991 Act should be re-enacted.

Issues arising out of the exercise of emergency powers may arise in prosecutions or
civil actions by or against the authorities. In addition, there are separate procedures
for dealing with non-criminal complaints against the police and the army. The
former involve the Independent Commission for Police Complaints, established by
the Police (Northern Ireland) Order 1987 (S.I. 1987 No. 938 (NI 10)). The latter are
subject to review by the Independent Assessor of Military Complaints Procedures in
Northern Ireland, appointed under the 1991 Act, s. 60 and Sch. 6. The Assessor,
unlike the ICPC, has no powers of oversight over the actual investigation of specific
complaints and no powers of direction. His reports (unlike the annual review of the
operation of the EPA and PTA) are published by HMSO (1993 Report: 1993–94
HC 369; 1994 Report: 1994–95 HC 471). The government resisted Labour Party
proposals for an Army Ombudsman: B. Dickson, [1992] PL 592, 603.

4. *Trial by judge alone*

This was introduced following recommendations of the Diplock Commission
(Cmnd. 5185, pp. 17–19). The Commission took the view that there was a serious
threat of intimidation to jurors, and a danger of perverse acquittals of 'loyalist
extremists' by the predominantly Protestant juries. The Gardiner Committee concluded (Cmnd. 5847, p. 11) that the new system 'has worked fairly and well', that
'the right to a fair trial has been respected and maintained and that the administration of justice has not suffered'. Accordingly they supported the continuation
of these provisions. Boyle (*Current Law Statutes Annotated 1978*, note to s. 7) gave
figures which showed a pattern of declining acquittal rates for trials by judge alone
over the period 1973–1977, and noted that 'concern has been voiced over the
spectre of judges becoming case-hardened. . .'. Cf. D. Greer, (1980) 31 NILQ 205,
233, who argued that comparisons of acquittal rates were 'not entirely valid and the
allegation of case-hardening cannot be regarded as having been established'. Sir
George Baker (Report, p. 37) stated that each Northern Ireland judge 'is continually thinking of the possibility and warning himself against leaning or even
appearing to lean to the prosecution or against the defence', that the fall in acquittal
rates might be explained by greater care taken by the prosecuting authorities in the
preparation or selection of cases, and that the rates had in fact risen in 1981 and
1982. He concluded that the time was not ripe for a return to jury trials: 'the overwhelming weight of opinion from those best qualified to judge is that members of
juries in serious cases would be in more danger today than ever before' (ibid.,
p. 30). He also rejected the alternative possibilities of courts comprising two or
three judges or a judge with assessors or resident magistrates (ibid., pp. 31–39). The
same position was taken in the *Colville Review (EPA)*, (Cm. 1115, 1990) Chap. 9.
There was insufficient judge-power to support two- or three-judge panels. A proposal for anonymous juries, hidden from public view was also rejected:

'It is far from certain . . . that a person who suddenly deserts his normal way of life and disappears for five
days a week . . . is safe from the deduction that he is on jury service' (ibid. para. 9.1).

The acquittal rate in contested 'Diplock' cases has fluctuated, increasing in the early 1980s, most markedly in 1984 and 1985 (mainly as a result of the rejection of 'supergrass' evidence (see p. 288)), but then falling (although not to the low levels of the late 1970s): see *Hogan and Walker*, Table 4.2 (p. 104) and *Jennings*, p. *xxvii*. There have been limited additions to the lists of offences that may be 'certified-out', but also additions to the list of scheduled offences. See A. Jennings and D. Wolchover, (1984) 134 NLJ 659, 687 and S. Greer and A. White, *Abolishing the Diplock Courts* (Cobden Trust, 1986) and *Jennings*, Chap. 3, for arguments in support of the restoration of trial by jury. For a general discussion see *Hogan and Walker*, pp. 100–109. They argue that special trials are overused, and that the problem should be tackled by providing further protection for juries, the descheduling of certain offences, the extension of certification powers to any scheduled offence and, possibly, moving to a requirement of certifying-in (cf. the *Colville Review (EPA)*, Chap. 8). For a critical analysis of the scheduling system in the light of research on the operation of juries in ordinary cases, see J. Jackson and S. Doran, 'Diplock and the Presumption Against Jury Trial' [1992] Crim LR 755.

5. *Admissions*[1]

Section 11 re-enacts s. 8 of the 1978 Act, as substituted by the 1987 Act, s. 5. The reference to 'torture or inhuman or degrading treatment' is taken from Art. 3 of the ECHR (below, p. 740). In *R v McCormick* [1977] NI 105, 111, Belfast City Commission, McGonigal LJ stated that s. 6 of the 1973 Act (the forerunner of s. 8) left 'it open to an interviewer to use a moderate degree of physical maltreatment for the purpose of inducing a person to make a statement'. This observation was based on the view of the European Commission that assaults did not necessarily amount to 'inhuman treatment' under Art. 3/ECHR (see e.g. *Application No. 4220/69X v United Kingdom* 14 YBECHR p. 250; L. Doswald-Beck, (1978) 25 Ned. International L. Rev. 24). However, McGonigal LJ's view was doubted by Lord Lowry CJ in *R v O'Halloran* [1979] NI 45, 47, (NI CA):

'This court finds it difficult in practice to envisage any form of physical violence which is relevant to the interrogation of a suspect in custody and which, if it had occurred could at the same time leave a court satisfied beyond reasonable doubt in relation to the issue for decision under section 6.'

(See also the cases cited by Greer, (1980) 31 NILQ 205, 213, n. 37). It was unclear how far s. 8 permitted psychological pressure to be applied to a suspect (see Greer, op. cit., pp. 213–215).

In *R v McGrath* [1980] NI 91 the Northern Ireland Court of Appeal endorsed the view of the trial judge that

'the ill-treatment which would fall within the section must be done with the intention of causing either physical or mental suffering and that physical or mental suffering must be of a very high degree and it must have been done also as the section indicates with the purpose of inducing a statement (p. 92).'

Accordingly, suffering inflicted through negligence or lack of judgment or sensitivity did not come within s. 8: there had to be an intention to cause suffering. The object of Art. 3, and accordingly s. 8(2), 'was to outlaw certain forms of conduct and not simply to obviate the admission of unreliable evidence.' Moreover, there had to be an intention, by causing that suffering, to induce the suspect to confess (see also on this point *R v Milne* [1978] NI 110 at 117, Belfast City Commission) and a causal link between the ill-treatment and the statement (Greer, (1980) 31 NILQ 205, 215–217). However, once a prima facie case had been raised that the

1 See generally D. S. Greer, (1973) 24 NILQ 199 and (1980) 31 NILQ 205; *Hogan and Walker*, pp. 109–119.

defendant had been subjected to improper treatment under the section, the onus shifted to the Crown to establish *beyond reasonable doubt* that admissions were not so obtained (*R v Hetherington* [1975] NI 164 at 166, Belfast City Commission; *R v Brophy* [1982] AC 476, Belfast City Commission).

There was an important qualification to these principles: it was held that while section 8 had replaced the common law test of voluntariness, the judges retained their discretion to disallow relevant evidence 'on the ground that . . . its prejudicial effect outweighs its probative value and that to admit the evidence would not be in the interests of justice' (*R v Corey* (1973) reported at [1979] NI 49 (Note), Belfast City Commission; *R v Hetherington* [1975] NI 164 at 169–180). Indeed, the discretion seemed a little broader than this wording would suggest. In *R v Culbert* [1982] NI 90, 93, (NI CA) Lord Lowry CJ referred without disapproval to the formulation of O'Donnell J in *R v McCracken* (Unreported: 1975) where he stated that there was

'an overall discretion to exclude statements which have been unfairly obtained which might prejudice the fair trial of the defendant even if not induced by torture, inhuman or degrading treatment.'

In *R v McCormick* [1977] NI 105 at 114 McGonigal LJ stated that this discretion should not be used so as to negative the effects of s. 6 of the 1973 Act 'and under the guise of the discretionary power have the effect of reinstating the old common law test in so far as it depended on the proof of physical or mental maltreatment'. It should only be exercised where maltreatment has rendered a statement 'in itself' suspect by reason of the method as a result of which it was obtained. See also *R v Milne* [1978] NI 110, Belfast City Commission, and *R v O'Halloran* [1979] NI 45, (NI CA) and Greer, (1980) 31 NILQ 205, 217–244. The existence of the discretion was affirmed by the Northern Ireland Court of Appeal in *R v Dillon* [1984] NI 292 and *R v McBrien and Harman* [1984] NI 280.

The Bennett Committee concluded that reports of cases decided by the judges as to the discretion to exclude evidence 'necessarily leave areas of uncertainty from the point of view of police practice' (Bennett Report (1979) p. 136). This led the Committee 'to consider whether the control exercised by the court over the means by which statements are induced and obtained should be supplemented by more direct regulation operating immediately on the interviewing officers' (ibid. p. 31: see below, pp. 315–317).

Sir George Baker (Report (1984) pp. 54–58 and Appendix J) recommended that s. 8 should be redrafted to prohibit violence and include the judges' discretion expressly. This change was effected by the Northern Ireland (Emergency Provisions) Act 1987, s. 5, re-enacted in s. 11 of the 1991 Act. Note that s. 11(2)(b) is not confined to actual or threatened *physical* violence, but is limited to *deliberate* violence (see *Hogan and Walker*, p. 114). The question of the admissibility of confessions in cases where s. 11 does not apply is now determined by Articles 74–76 of the PACE (Northern Ireland) Order 1989 (S.I. 1989 No. 1341) (cf. above, pp. 146–165). The *Colville Review (EPA)* recommended that 'an enabling power to transfer to the PACE standard, if it becomes appropriate to do so, should . . . be made' (Cm. 1115, para. 10.5.7.6). Boyle (*Current Law Statutes Annotated 1987*, note to s. 5) argues that there 'can be little doubt that the PACE standards are more demanding'. Is there any justification for maintaining different standards? See the *Rowe Review (EPA)*, pp. 17–19.

The Northern Ireland Court of Appeal has held that the use of foul and obscene language by interrogating officers was on the facts of the case not 'degrading treatment' for the purposes of s. 11 (then s. 8) and not sufficient to justify exclusion in the exercise of discretion (*R v Mullan* [1988] 10 NIJB 36). Moreover, searching and persistent questioning over a period which causes an accused to speak when otherwise he would have remained silent should not of itself be regarded as 'oppression' so as to justify discretionary exclusion (although it might have constituted 'oppression' at common law: see *R v Priestley* (1967) 51 Cr App Rep 1n, above, p. 154) (*R v McBrien and Harman* [1984] NI 280; *R v Dillon* [1984] NI 292). Similarly, the offering of an inducement does not necessarily require exclusion (*R v Cowan* [1987] NI 338). Reliance 'on the threat of unlawful vengeance from a third party as a lever with which to apply pressure on a suspect' has, however, been held to be improper and to justify exclusion (*R v Howell* [1987] 5 NIJB 10).

Dermot P. J. Walsh (in *Jennings*, Chap. 2) is critical of what is now s. 11 and its interpretation by the judges:

'The cumulative effect of these judicial interpretations is that the RUC can subject a prisoner to lengthy, repetitive and debilitating interrogations, threats, bribes, trickery, verbal abuse and possibly even a moderate degree of physical ill-treatment to obtain a confession without that confession being ruled inadmissible.' (p. 38)

6. *The 'right to silence'*

Apart from the question of the admissibility of confessions, the Criminal Evidence (Northern Ireland) Order 1988 (S.I. 1988 No. 1987 (NI 20)) enables a court in any criminal trial to draw adverse inferences from an accused's failure to mention a relevant fact during police questioning or when charged (Art. 3); his refusal to give evidence at trial (Art. 4); his failure to account for the presence of an object, substance or mark on his person, in or on his clothing or footwear, otherwise in his possession or in any place in which he is at the time of his arrest (Art. 5); or his failure to account for his presence when found by a constable at a place at or about the time the offence for which he was arrested is alleged to have been committed (Art. 6). See J. D. Jackson, (1989) 40 NILQ 105, 105–118; *Colville Review (EPA)*, para. 10.6. After initial caution (J. D. Jackson, [1991] Crim LR 404), the judges have drawn inferences under Article 4 in a series of cases (Jackson, *Legal Action*, December 1992, p. 8). In *Murray v DPP* [1994] 1 WLR, 97 Cr App Rep 151, the House of Lords upheld M's convictions for the attempted murder of a soldier and possession of a firearm with intent to endanger life where the trial judge had drawn an inference under Article 4. Lord Slynn (for a unanimous House of Lords) noted that the prosecutor must first establish a prima facie case (otherwise there could be a successful submission of no case to answer by the defence). The judge (as trier of fact) could then draw 'such inferences from the refusal [to testify] as appear proper' (Art. 4(4)(b)). This would

'depend on the circumstances of the particular case and is a question to be decided by applying ordinary commonsense'

(*per* Lord Slynn at 160, citing Lord Diplock in *Haw Tua Tau v Public Prosecutor* [1982] AC 136, 153). Here, there was forensic evidence linking M with the attempted murder (especially a thumb print on the mirror of the car used by the attackers, cartridge residue and mud on his jeans) and the trial judge was entitled 'to infer that there was no innocent explanation to the prima facie case and that the accused was guilty'. The judge had clearly not proceeded on the erroneous basis that 'simply because the accused did not give evidence he was therefore guilty' (Lord Slynn at 161). Moreover, it was not necessary for the judge to spell out what precise inference he drew from each aspect of the circumstantial evidence relied on; he was

'entitled to have regard to the circumstantial evidence as a whole and to conclude that a refusal to deal with it or any of it justified an inference of guilt' (ibid.).

For criticism of *Murray*, see J. D Jackson, 'Inferences from Silence: from Common Law to Common Sense' (1993) 44 NILQ 103, who argues that the House could have adopted a narrower approach, limiting the operation of Article 4 to cases where the prosecution case is otherwise 'on the brink of proof beyond reasonable doubt' (pp. 107–108) or to inferences which undermine the defence case as distinct from inferences drawn directly to bolster the prosecution case (p. 108). He also criticises the lack of any guidelines on the application of 'common sense'.

Note that a prima facie case here means:

'a case consisting of direct evidence which, if believed and combined with legitimate inferences based upon it, could lead a properly directed jury to be satisfied beyond reasonable doubt . . . that each of the essential elements of the offence is proved'

(per Lord Mustill at 154).

The *Murray* case has been taken to Strasbourg: see *John Murray v UK* (Application No. 18731/91), where the Commission on 27 June 1994 found that the drawing of adverse inferences from silence did not infringe Article 6(1) (below, p. 741) but denial of access to a solicitor did. The Northern Ireland provisions have been adopted for England and Wales (with modifications that are also to be made in Northern Ireland) (above, p. 145).

7. 'Supergrasses'

From 1981 onwards, a number of trials, commonly involving large numbers of defendants, were conducted on the basis of the evidence of informers variously termed 'converted terrorists', 'accomplices' or 'supergrasses'. The Attorney-General (47 HC Deb, 24 October 1983 cols 3–5, written answer) explained that the principles governing accomplice evidence were the same in England and Northern Ireland, in that the judge was required to warn the jury (or himself, if the trier of fact) that, although it (or he) may convict on such evidence, it is dangerous to do so unless it is corroborated. It was for the DPP

'to consider each case on its own facts and in the light of the interest of the public that criminals, and particularly dangerous criminals, should be brought to justice. Where the evidence of an accomplice appears to be credible and cogent and relates to serious terrorist crime, there is an overriding public interest in having charges brought before the court.'

Any immunity from prosecution would only be given in respect of offences which the witness discloses and of which he has given a truthful account. The prospect of saving lives would weigh heavily in making such a decision.

Critics stressed the dangers of relying on the evidence of accomplices (see Walsh, op. cit., pp. 90–92; T. Gifford, *Supergrasses: The Use of Accomplice Evidence in Northern Ireland* (1984)). It was suggested that the judges were not always sufficiently discriminating in accepting some parts of an accomplice's testimony while rejecting others, and in convicting on some counts without corroboration (see the comments by Gifford on the cases concerning the informers Bennett (*R v Graham* [1983] 7 NIJB, Belfast Cr. Ct), Black, and McGrady (*R v Gibney* [1983] 13 NIJB, Belfast Cr. Ct)). (Cf. the Baker Report, pp. 47–50). Indeed, the Northern Ireland Court of Appeal subsequently quashed convictions where they were based on the uncorroborated testimony of a 'supergrass' or other informer (see *R v McCormick* [1984] NI 50; *R v Graham* [1984] 18 NIJB 23; *R v Donnelly* [1986] 4 NIJB 32; *R v Gibney* [1986] 4 NIJB 1; *R v Crumley* (1987) 3 BNIL n. 83), and the use of 'supergrasses' ceased. Whether this was simply to be explained by an absence of informers willing to testify, or a change in prosecution policy in the light of the critical response of the judiciary was unclear. The Attorney-General stated in 1986 that it was unlikely that there would be any further prosecutions in Northern Ireland based solely on accomplice evidence (94 H. C. Deb, 19 March 1986, col. 186, written answer).[1]

8. *Internment*

The detention of persons without trial has been employed by the authorities in both Northern Ireland and the Republic of Ireland (see J. McGuffin, *Internment* (1973)). The changes in legislation authorising the 'extrajudicial deprivation of liberty' are traced in the Judgment of the European Court of Human Rights in *Ireland v The United Kingdom* (1978) pp. 31–39. These were in turn (1) Regulation 12(1) of the Special Powers Regulations; (2) the Detention of Terrorists (Northern Ireland) Order 1972 (made under the Northern Ireland (Temporary Provisions) Act 1972 and in operation between 7 November 1972 and 8 August 1973); (3) the Northern Ireland (Emergency Provisions) Act 1973 s. 10(5) and Sch. 1 (7 August 1973–21 August 1975); and (4) the Northern Ireland (Emergency Provisions) (Amendment) Act 1975 s. 9 and Sch. 1 (21 August 1975—now consolidated in s. 34 and Sch. 3 of the 1991 Act).

The internment powers were invoked on 9 August 1971 (see The Sunday Times Insight Team, *Ulster* (1972) Ch. 15; *Ireland v UK,* pp. 16–18).

In 1975, the Gardiner Committee concluded:

148. After long and anxious consideration, we are of the opinion that detention cannot remain as a long-term policy. In the short term, it may be an effective means of containing violence, but the prolonged effects of the use of detention are ultimately inimical to community life, fan a widespread sense of grievance and injustice, and obstruct those elements in Northern Ireland society which could lead to reconciliation. Detention can only be tolerated in a democratic society in the most extreme circumstances; it must be used with the utmost restraint and retained only as long as it is strictly necessary. We would like to be able to recommend that the time has come to abolish detention; but the present level of violence, the risks of increased violence, and the difficulty of predicting events even a few months ahead make it impossible for us to put forward a precise recommendation on the timing.'

Should such measures still be regarded as necessary, the Committee recommended a return to the system where the sole and ultimate responsibility for detention should be that of the Secretary of State, advised by a Detention Advisory Board, but with no attempt to emulate, even approximately, quasi-judicial procedures of the kind operative between 1972 and 1975 (Cmnd. 5847, pp. 45–49). Revised arrangements were incorporated in the 1975 and 1978 statutes but were not used. The last detainees were released on 5 December 1975, and the policy of 'internment' abandoned.[2] Sir George Baker (Report, Chap. 6) recommended 'without qualification' that the provisions of s. 12 and Schedule 1 should now be repealed. The *Colville Review (EPA)* (Cm 1115, Chap. 11) endorsed this recom-mendation 'with vigour' as has the SACHR (17th Report, 1991–92 HC 54, pp. 222–223) but it has not been accepted by the government. For arguments in favour of retention of the power to detain without trial for use in a genuine emergency, while noting the dangers of overuse, see *Hogan and Walker,* pp. 86–96. John Rowe QC now favours the removal of these powers (*Rowe Review (EPA),* pp. 32–33). Section 34 and Sch. 3 are on the statute book but have not been brought into force. A commencement order would be made if and when necessary.

1 See further on 'supergrasses', P. Hillyard and J. Percy-Smith, (1984) 11 JLS 335; S. C. Greer, *Supergrasses: Anti-terrorist Law Enforcement in Northern Ireland* (1994) and *Jennings,* Chap. 4; D. Bonner, (1988) 51 MLR 23; A. Boyd, *The Informers* (1984); *Hogan and Walker,* pp. 123–126.
2 See E. Rauch, (1973) 6 NY Univ Journal of International Law and Politics 1; R. J. Spjut, (1975) 10 *Irish Jurist* (ns) 272 and (1986) 49 MLR 712; K. Boyle, T. Hadden and P. Hillyard, *Law and State* (1975), Chap. 5.

The compatibility of internment with the European Convention on Human Rights was considered in *Ireland v UK* (below, pp. 749–756).

9. *Arrest*

(i) *EPA arrests.* A wide power of arrest was conferred by section 11 of the Northern Ireland (Emergency Provisions) Act 1978: 'Any constable may arrest without warrant any person whom he suspects of being a terrorist'. It was designed to be used as the start of the procedure leading to internment, although it was also widely used to lead to questioning and, possibly, proceedings for a specific criminal offence. Over time, the RUC made increasing use of the power to arrest under section 12 of the Prevention of Terrorism (Temporary Provisions) Act 1984. It was indeed RUC policy to arrest every terrorist suspect, even if caught in the act of committing a specific offence, under one of these powers, as they gave more time in which to conduct investigations. Arrest powers under s. 13 of the 1978 Act (now s. 17 of the 1991 Act) or s. 2 of the Criminal Law Act (Northern Ireland) 1967 were rarely used (see Walsh (1982) 9 JLS, 37, 41). The Northern Ireland (Emergency Provisions) Act 1987 abolished the arrest power under s. 11, leaving arrests to be made either under s. 14 of the Prevention of Terrorism (Temporary Provisions) Act 1989 (below, p. 303), which replaced s. 12 of the 1984 Act, or under specific arrest powers (e.g. those conferred now by the PACE (Northern Ireland) Order 1989 (S.I. 1989 No. 1341 (NI 12))). For a detailed comparison of s. 11 of the EPA and what is now s. 14 of the 1991 Act, see *Hogan and Walker*, pp. 47–50.

In *Fox, Campbell and Hartley v United Kingdom* (1990) 13 EHRR 157, below, p. 773 the European Court of Human Rights held that the arrest of the complainants under s. 11 of the 1978 Act on suspicion of being terrorists was unlawful as contrary to Article 5(1)(c) of the ECHR (below, p. 740), which required 'reasonable suspicion' to justify detention, the matter being judged by reference to the facts of the case rather than the form of the legislation. See W. Finnie, (1991) 54 MLR 288.

(ii) *Army arrests and searches.* Section 18(2) dispenses with the normal *Christie v Leachinsky* requirements (as to which see above pp. 109–111). This was justified by the Diplock Commission (Cmnd. 5185) on the ground that it was not practicable for the initial arrest of a suspected terrorist in 'extremist strongholds' to be effected by a police officer:

'45. It is, we think, preposterous to expect a young soldier making an arrest under these conditions to be able to identify a person whom he has arrested as being a man whom he knows to be wanted for a particular offence so as to be able to inform him accurately of the grounds on which he is arresting him. It is impossible to question arrested persons on the spot to establish their identity. In practice this cannot usually be ascertained until they have been taken to the safety of battalion headquarters. Even here it may be a lengthy process, as suspects often give false names or addresses or, giving their true names, which are often very common ones, assert that some relation or other person of the same name is the real person who is "wanted" for a particular offence. It is only when his identity has been satisfactorily established that it is possible to be reasonably certain of the particular ground on which he was liable to arrest and inform him of it.'

The House of Lords has held, moreover, that observance of even the limited requirement of s. 18(2) can be delayed (*Murray v Ministry of Defence* [1988] 2 All ER 521). The House approved what appeared to be the army's standard practice when effecting an arrest at the home of a person suspected of an offence in connection with the IRA: the suspect was identified on entry to the house, but the house was searched, with its occupants detained in the living room, before the ground of arrest was given. This procedure was justified by the House of Lords on the ground that there would be a real risk that the alarm might be raised and an attempt made to resist arrest. (For criticism of this 'new exception to *Christie v Leachinsky*', see C. Walker, (1989) 40 NILQ 1, 6–10, pointing out that the House 'applied a plausible reason for delay which did not in fact pertain' (p. 10), and G. Williams, (1991) 54 MLR 408).

A further deviation from normal standards was formerly found in ss. 13, 14 and 15(2) of the 1978 Act (now ss. 17, 18 and 19(2) of the 1991 Act) in that the powers of arrest and search there were exercisable on the basis of 'suspicion'. This was changed to a requirement of 'reasonable suspicion' by the Northern Ireland (Emergency Provisions) Act 1987, Sched. 1.

(iii) *Arrest-search procedure.* The House of Lords in *Murray v Ministry of Defence* [1988] 2 All ER 521 held that the search procedure summarised above was lawful by reference to the power of search in s. 14(3) of the 1978 Act (now s. 18(3) of the 1991 Act), notwithstanding that the search was conducted *after* the person whom the army had come to arrest had been identified. The House accepted that there was no power to search for incriminating evidence, but held that

'It is . . . a proper exercise of the power of search for the purpose of effecting the arrest to search every room for other occupants of the house in case there may be those there who are disposed to resist the arrest. The search cannot be limited solely to looking for the person to be arrested and must also embrace a search whose object is to secure that the arrest should be peaceable' (*per* Lord Griffiths at p. 527).

C. Walker ((1989) 40 NILQ 1, 18) argues that this

'improperly widens the notion of the "purpose" to include the rounding up of possible malcontents removed from the arrest scene. . . . Furthermore, the search was unnecessary in *Murray v Ministry of Defence* since the arrest had already been executed without demur.'

The House also indicated, obiter, that the detention of the occupants of the house in one room while the rest of the house was searched was lawful. These dicta were applied by the High Court in Northern Ireland in the context of an alleged detention, ancillary to a munitions search: *Kirkpatrick v Chief Constable of the Royal Ulster Constabulary* [1988] NI 421. Kelly LJ stated that

'there must necessarily be some degree of control over the activities of the members of the household, especially at the outset of the search, when certain preliminaries and formalities are gone through. Such degree of control will be slight and minimal and must substantially depend on the consent, tacit or passive though it may be, of the household. The interference with the habits and convenience of the household will also be minimal and must at all times be justifiable on the ground that it is reasonably necessary for the execution of a speedy and efficient search' (pp. 429–430).

On the facts, however, the court found that the level of restraint imposed on the occupants did not amount to a detention or imprisonment; the occupants had consented in acceding to a request to assemble in one room at the start of the search (p. 86). Express authority was subsequently given for some of these matters in connection with munitions searches (but not searches on arrest) (Prevention of Terrorism (Temporary Provisions) Act 1989, s. 21; see now the 1991 Act, ss. 19(4)(5), 26(6)).

See C. Walker (1989) 40 NILQ 1, 11–18, who argues that 'the reasoning supporting both these judicially created powers is profoundly wrong' and that the issues would have been more appropriately dealt with 'as an aspect of the use of reasonable force in making an arrest, as governed by section 3(1) of the Criminal Law Act (Northern Ireland) 1967' (p. 18). In *Murray v UK* (1994) 19 EHRR 193, Series A No. 300-A, the European Court of Human Rights rejected claims that the arrest and the arrest procedure violated Articles 5 and 8, ECHR.

(iv) *Former army arrest powers.* Many regulations made under the Civil Authorities (Special Powers) Act (NI) 1922 purported to give powers to members of the armed forces on duty. It was held in *R (Hume) v Londonderry Justices* [1972] NI 91, QBD (NI), that such regulations were *ultra vires* in view of the Government of Ireland Act 1920, s. 4(1), which provided that the Northern Ireland Parliament was not to have power to make laws in respect of 'the navy, the army, the air force, . . . or the defence of the realm, or any other naval, military, or air force matter. . . .'

Parliament immediately passed legislation to regularise the position retrospectively in the Northern Ireland Act 1972, s. 1. An application in which the Republic of Ireland argued that the 1972 Act conflicted with Article 7 of the Convention was withdrawn when the UK Attorney-General gave an undertaking in proceedings before the Commission that no one had or would be held guilty as a result of the 1972 Act for an act or omission which did not constitute a criminal offence at the time it was committed (A 5451/72, 41 CDE Comm HR, pp. 82–83 (1972)).

In *Re McElduff* [1972] NI 1, QBD (NI), McGonigal J held that the usual common law requirements as to arrests were applicable to arrests under the Civil Authorities (Special Powers) Act Regulations. Accordingly, a person could not be validly arrested unless (1) the arrestor took reasonable steps to bring the fact of the arrest to the notice of the person arrested; (2) the person arrested was informed at the time of the arrest or at the earliest opportunity thereafter, (i) under what powers he had been arrested, and (ii) of the general nature of the suspicion leading to the arrest. McElduff was arrested on 9 August 1971 under Regulation 10 (power to arrest and detain for up to 48 hours for the purposes of interrogation) as part of 'Operation Demetrius' (see *Ireland v UK*, below, p. 749). Later the same day, he was pur- portedly rearrested under Regulation 11(1) (power to arrest persons suspected of acting in a manner prejudicial to peace or order). The arresting officer did not suffi- ciently distinguish this from the earlier arrest, merely stating that McElduff was 'being arrested' under the Special Powers Act. As a valid and subsisting arrest under Regulation 11(1) was a necessary prerequisite for a valid detention order under Regulation 11(2), habeas corpus was granted. McGonigal J stated obiter that the power to arrest a person whom the arrestor 'suspects' of acting in the prescribed manner did not import a standard of reasonableness:

'The test is therefore whether the arrestor suspected. That does not appear to me to be open to an object- ive test. It may be based on purely arbitrary grounds, on grounds on which the court, if this were an objective test of reasonableness, might consider unreasonable. . . . What is required by the regulation is a suspicion existing in the mind of the constable. That is a subjective test. If that is correct, the courts enquiring into the exercise of the power, can only enquire as to the bona fides of the existence of the sus- picion. Did the constable in his own mind suspect? And in my view the only other question for the courts is, "Was this an honest suspicion" ' (p. 19).[1]

(v) *Reasonable suspicion for EPA arrests.* In *McKee v Chief Constable* [1983] 11 NIJB the majority of the Northern Ireland Court of Appeal (Kelly J and O'Donnell LJ, Jones LJ dissenting) held that suspicion that a person was a member of a proscribed organisation was insufficient to constitute suspicion that he was a 'terrorist' (as defined in s. 31 of the 1978 Act, now s. 66 of the 1991 Act); for that, he had to be suspected of the commission or attempted commission of an *act* of terrorism or of the directing, organising or training of persons for the purpose of terrorism. A further point that the court unanimously accepted was that 'when a Constable receives instructions from a superior officer or an equal it is sufficient if he bona fide accepts the suspicion that those instructions contain or imply. The suspicion of

---

1 An earlier attempt by McElduff to obtain habeas corpus from the High Court in London failed on jurisdictional grounds: *In Re Keenan* [1972] 1 QB 533. See K. Boyle (1972) 23 NILQ 334 and *Kelly v Faulkner* [1973] NI 31, QBD (NI).

the other becomes the arrestor's suspicion when accepted' (per Kelly J at p. 3 of his judgment). An appeal to the House of Lords was allowed ([1984] 1 WLR 1358). The decision on the second point was affirmed. However, the House held that the arresting officer at the time of arrest did in fact suspect that McKee was an *active* terrorist; the correctness of the Court of Appeal's interpretation of 'terrorism' was left open. For criticisms of this interpretation see C. Walker, (1985) 36 NILQ 145. It is not clear whether it is applicable to an arrest under s. 14 of the 1989 Act (below, p. 303) as that power expressly applies in respect of the preparation or instigation of terrorism (see *Hogan and Walker*, p. 48).

Where the arresting officer relies on the suspicions of another officer in accordance with the decision in *McKee*, it is not necessary in defending an action for false imprisonment that that other officer be called as a witness to establish that *he* had reasonable grounds for suspicion: *Stratford v Chief Constable of the Royal Ulster Constabulary* [1988] NI 361. If that officer were to supply false information to the arresting officer, an action might lie against the former for maliciously and without reasonable cause procuring his arrest (ibid. at p. 364). See further, below, p. 314.

(vi) *Purpose of arrest.* The Army have found it necessary to obtain information about the population in Republican areas. Indeed, a population census has been described as 'the fundamental tool for defeating terrorism and insurrection' (R. Evelegh, *Peace-Keeping in a Democratic Society* (1978), p. 119). One aspect of this has been the use of the arrest powers under the Emergency Provisions Acts to detain people in Republican areas for questioning (see K. Boyle, T. Hadden and P. Hillyard, *Law and State* (1975), pp. 41–48; Evelegh, op. cit., pp. 63–67, 119–122). The use of powers of arrest for purposes other than that of commencing criminal proceedings is of dubious legality. Moreover, according to Evelegh (who commanded an army battalion in Belfast in 1972 and 1973) 'the vast majority of those arrested by the Army in Northern Ireland were arrested without being suspected of anything except in the most general sense' (op. cit., p. 120). Is the proper response to criticise the illegality, or to argue the case for the extension of powers to detain for questioning, or both?

The use of arrest powers *solely* for the purpose of general intelligence gathering would seem to be a use of power for an improper purpose, and thus *ultra vires* (cf. *Holgate-Mohammed v Duke*, above, p. 43). It will, however, be difficult in practice for the arrestee to establish that this was the sole purpose. In *Murray v Ministry of Defence* [1988] 2 All ER 521, the trial judge was satisfied that the soldier who arrested M under s. 14 of the 1978 Act did genuinely suspect M of having committed offences involving the collection of money for the IRA, and that the subsequent interrogation of M was at least in part directed to these offences, although much of it ranged over her private life. The House of Lords upheld the conclusion that the interrogation was lawful, declining to hold that the permitted scope of questioning was confined to matters *directly* related to the suspected offence (p. 530). For further discussion of this question see C. Walker, (1989) 40 NILQ 1, 18–24; *Hogan and Walker*, pp. 53–54.

(vii) Where it is established that a prisoner is seriously assaulted during interrogation, the detention becomes unlawful and the detainee is entitled to the issue of a writ of habeas corpus (*Re Gillen's Application* [1988] NI 40). Here, G made out a strong prima facie case of a serious assault on him, based on medical reports, and an interlocutory injunction was granted restraining the police from interrogating him, while his allegations were investigated by the Chief Constable, and pending a final ruling by the court on whether they were made out. In the event, the Chief

Constable did not subsequently file affidavits contesting the allegations, and G was released. In 1990, G received an out of court settlement of £7,500 (*Just News*, Vol. 5 No. 11/Vol. 6 No. 1, p. 4). See further below, p. 315, on conditions in detention.

10. *Search and the examination of documents*

Powers of entry and search in relation to arrests are conferred by ss. 16–18. Section 19 gives powers to search for munitions, radio transmitters and scanning receivers. The power to enter and search any place other than a dwelling-house (s. 19(1)) and the power to stop-search in any 'public place' (s. 19(6)) do not require reasonable grounds to suspect that munitions etc. are to be found. 'Public place' is not defined, but includes a public house (*McShane v Chief Constable of the RUC* (15 December 1993, unreported, QBD (NI)).

The power to examine documents (s. 22) was introduced by the 1991 Act. The SACHR have recommended that exercise be made conditional on reasonable suspicion (16th Report, 1990–91 HC 488), p. 91 (see B. Dickson [1992] PL 592 at 618–619). Lord Colville heard of no complaints on the operation of s. 22 (1991 Report on the EPA, p. 8, 1992 Report on the EPA, p. 80).

11. *Unlawful collection of information*

In *R v Lorenc* [1988] NI 96, the Northern Ireland Court of Appeal held that the offence in s. 31 (then s. 22 of the 1978 Act) was committed when L was found in possession of three Army Manuals pertaining to the use of rifles, booby traps and incendiaries. The court rejected an argument that the offence only applied to information likely or intended to be *used* in planning or carrying out an act of violence. Conversely, in *R v McLoughlin* (8 October 1993, unreported, CA (Cr D) (NI)) the court quashed McLoughlin's conviction under this provision in respect of his collection of a list of radio frequencies used by the RUC. The court was satisfied that he had established on the balance of probabilities the 'reasonable excuse' of being a 'radio buff' and not a terrorist.

12. *Proscription*

Some of the proscribed organisations were proscribed under previous legislation (see *McEldowney v Forde* [1971] AC 632, HL; D. N. MacCormick (1970) 86 LQR 171; (1969) 20 NILQ 1; (1970) 21 NILQ 191: proscription of ' "Republican Clubs" or any like organization howsoever described'). The UDA were added to the list by the Northern Ireland (Emergency Provisions) Act 1991 (Amendment) Order 1992 (S.I. 1992 No. 1958). Sinn Fein was proscribed between 8 August 1973 and 23 May 1974.

In *R v Adams* [1978] 5 NIJB, Belfast City Commission, Lowry LCJ declined to infer IRA membership from the defendant's conduct in parading in a compound of the Maze Prison run by the inmates on quasi-military lines.

A proscription power is also available under the Prevention of Terrorism (Temporary Provisions) Act 1989 (below, p. 301), which applies to Great Britain. Only the IRA and INLA are proscribed under the 1989 Act. Is the difference in the lists justifiable? Lord Colville took the view that it was 'since it reflects as it should the activities of terrorist organisations in different parts of the UK' (*Colville Review (EPA)*, p. 5); cf. Lord Jellicoe, below, p. 308). For further discussion, see *Hogan and Walker*, pp. 138–143.

13. *Directing terrorist organisations*

The offence of directing terrorist organisations, introduced in the 1991 Act (s. 27) is criticised by C. Walker and K. Reid, [1993] Crim LR 669 on the grounds that it is too wide (it is not limited to proscribed organisations and all directions are penalised, even if lawful) and unnecessary, and that 'it is politically unwise to apply such vague and broad offence as part of the police of criminalisation' (p. 676). There has been one conviction (*Rowe Review (EPA)*, p. 30. B. Dickson commented ([1992] PL at 617):

'Perhaps no more than any other offence contained in the emergency legislation section 27 illustrates the "symbolic law-making" described earlier [above, p. 283].'

Attorney-General for Northern Ireland's Reference (No 1 of 1975) [1977] AC 105, [1976] 2 All ER 937, [1976] 3 WLR 235, House of Lords (NI)

A British soldier on patrol in Northern Ireland in the exercise of his power to prevent crime under section 3(1) of the Criminal Law Act (NI) 1967 (which is in the same terms as the Criminal Law Act 1967, s. 3(1), above p. 74) shot and killed an unarmed man, who had run away when challenged. The soldier had the honest and reasonable, though mistaken, belief that he was a terrorist. A judge sitting without a jury acquitted him of murder holding that he had no conscious intention to kill or seriously injure and that the killing was justifiable. The Attorney-General referred two matters to the Court of Criminal Appeal in Northern Ireland, and an appeal was taken to the House of Lords. The House held that the first matter raised no point of law, since it was in essence whether or not the soldier had used reasonable force, and that was a question of fact for the judge. The second matter accordingly did not arise. Lord Diplock made some observations as to the legal position.

Lord Diplock: . . . There is little authority in English law concerning the rights and duties of a member of the armed forces of the Crown when acting in aid of the civil power; and what little authority there is relates almost entirely to the duties of soldiers when troops are called upon to assist in controlling a riotous assembly. Where used for such temporary purposes it may not be inaccurate to describe the legal rights and duties of a soldier as being no more than those of an ordinary citizen in uniform. But such a description is in my view misleading in the circumstances in which the army is currently employed in aid of the civil power in Northern Ireland. . . . In theory it may be the duty of every citizen when an arrestable offence is about to be committed in his presence to take whatever reasonable measures are available to him to prevent the commission of the crime; but the duty is one of imperfect obligation and does not place him under any obligation to do anything by which he would expose himself to risk of personal injury, nor is he under any duty to search for criminals or seek out crime. In contrast to this a soldier who is employed in aid of the civil power in Northern Ireland is under a duty, enforceable under military law, to search for criminals if so ordered by his superior officer and to risk his own life should this be necessary in preventing terrorist acts. For the performance of this duty he is armed with a firearm, a self-loading rifle, from which a bullet, if it hits the human body, is almost certain to cause serious injury if not death. . . .

What amount of force is 'reasonable in the circumstances' for the purpose of preventing crime, is in my view, always a question for the jury in a jury trial, never a 'point of law' for the judge.

The form in which the jury would have to ask themselves the question in a trial for an offence against the person in which this defence was raised by the accused, would be: Are we satisfied that no reasonable man (a) with knowledge of such facts as were known to the accused or reasonably believed by him to exist (b) in the circumstances and time available to him for reflection (c) could be of opinion that the prevention of the risk of harm to which others might be exposed if the suspect were allowed to escape justified exposing the suspect to the risk of harm to him that might result from the kind of force that the accused contemplated using?

The jury would have also to consider how the circumstances in which the accused had to make his decision whether or not to use force and the shortness of the time available to him for reflection, might affect the judgment of a reasonable man. In the facts that are to be assumed for the purposes of the reference there is material upon which a jury might take the view that the accused had reasonable grounds for apprehension of imminent danger to himself and other members of the patrol if the deceased were allowed to get away and join armed fellow-members of the Provisional IRA who might be lurking in the neighbourhood, and that the time available to the accused to make up his mind what to do was so short that even a reasonable man could only act intuitively. This being so, the jury in approaching the final part of the question should remind themselves that the postulated balancing of risk against risk, harm against harm, by the reasonable man is not undertaken in the calm analytical atmosphere of the court-room after counsel with the benefit of hindsight have expounded at length the reasons for and against the kind and degree of force that was used by the accused; but in the brief second or two which the accused had to decide whether to shoot or not and under all the stresses to which he was exposed.

In many cases where force is used in the prevention of crime or in effecting an arrest there is a choice as to the degree of force to use. On the facts that are to be assumed for the purposes of the reference the only options open to the accused were either to let the deceased escape or to shoot at him with a service rifle. A reasonable man would know that a bullet from a self-loading rifle if it hit a human being, at any rate at the range at which the accused fired, would be likely to kill him or to injure him seriously. So in one scale of balance the harm to which the deceased would be exposed if the accused aimed to hit him was predictable and grave and the risk of its occurrence high. In the other scale of the balance it would be open to the jury to take the view that it would not be unreasonable to assess the kind of harm to be averted by preventing the accused's escape as even graver—the killing or wounding of members of the patrol by terrorists in ambush, and the effect of this success by members of the Provisional IRA in encouraging the continuance of the armed insurrection and all the misery and destruction of life and property that terrorist activity in Northern Ireland has entailed. The jury would have to consider too what was the highest degree at which a reasonable man could have assessed the likelihood that such consequences might follow the escape of the deceased if the facts had been as the accused knew or believed them reasonably to be.

Lords Simon of Glaisdale, **Edmund-Davies** and **Russell of Killowen** expressed their agreement with **Lord Diplock's** opinion.

NOTES

1. In *R v MacNaughton* [1975] NI 203,[1] a sergeant was tried by Lowry LCJ (sitting without a jury) on charges of attempted murder and causing grievous bodily harm. He was in command of a foot patrol in South Armagh. They met a man, W, coming from the direction of an explosion and, suspecting him of being implicated in it, arrested him. The defendant claimed that W then tried to escape over a fence, and that he had shot at W after calling on him to stop. Lowry LCJ held that there had been a lawful arrest, that the defendant's evidence raised a triable issue that the force used was reasonable, and that the prosecution had been unable to prove beyond reasonable doubt that the degree of force was not reasonable on this occasion.

His Lordship took into account the factors that the patrol was working in active service conditions in a hostile area; that judging by the explosion, it was operating in the possible presence of an ambush; that there was a danger of booby-traps; that there was a possibility of masking a line of fire; the gravity of the suspected offence; and the likelihood that if W escaped he would undertake terrorist acts.

2. In *Farrell v Secretary of State for Defence* [1980] 1 All ER 1667, the commanding officer of an army unit (X) received information that a bomb attack would be made by three men on a bank in Newry. He instructed an NCO, soldier A, and three other soldiers to take up a position on the roof of a building opposite the bank. During the night, soldier B saw two men attempt to open the bank's night safe; they were then attacked by three other men. B called soldier A, who saw only the second group. He called on them to halt. They stopped and looked up and down the street. One of them shouted 'run' and they made off. Soldier A shouted 'Halt, I am ready

---

1 See also *Report of the Tribunal appointed to inquire into the events on Sunday, 30 January, 1972, which led to loss of life in connection with the procession in Londonderry on that day* by The Rt Hon Lord Widgery (1972 HC 220), S. Dash, *Justice Denied* (NCCL, 1972), E. McCann, *Bloody Sunday in Derry* (1992), B. M. E. McMahon, (1974) 6 *The Human Context* 681; *Ireland v UK*, Application 5310/71 41 CDE Comm HR p. 3 (1972) (application under Article 2 ECHR in respect of the deaths of certain persons in Northern Ireland declared inadmissible); *R v Bohan* [1979] 5 NIJB, Belfast Crown Court; *McLaughlin v Ministry of Defence* [1978] 7 NIJB, (NI CA): on appeal, *Farrell v Secretary of State for Defence* [1980] 1 All ER 1667, HL; *McGuigan v Ministry of Defence* [1982] 19 NIJB, QBD (NI); *Lynch v Ministry of Defence* [1983] NI 216; *R v Hegarty* [1986] NI 343; *Magill v Ministry of Defence* [1987] NI 194; *Hegarty, Doyle and Kelly v Ministry of Defence* [1989] 9 NIJB 88.

to fire.' They did not stop. A opened fire, as did his colleagues, and all three were killed. The widow of one of them sued the Secretary of State. The jury held that the soldiers had reasonable cause to suspect that the three men were attempting to place at the bank an explosive device that would endanger life, and that it was reasonable in the circumstances for the soldiers to shoot to kill, in the prevention of crime or in effecting a lawful arrest (s. 3(1) of the Criminal Law Act (Northern Ireland) 1967: in the same terms as s. 3(1) of the Criminal Law Act 1967, above p. 74). The Northern Ireland Court of Appeal ordered a new trial on the ground that the jury should have been invited to consider whether there had been negligence in the planning of the operation: it had emerged that X had only given instructions to one soldier, A; that he had given no instructions about summoning help; that there was no agreed procedure for the four soldiers reporting back to base; only four soldiers out of 80 in X's command were selected for the operation; all four were ordered to go on the roof; they did not have a loud hailer; they were left in a situation where the only way to stop a suspected terrorist if he refused to stop was by firing at him. The House of Lords allowed an appeal, holding (1) that the term 'circumstances' in s. 3(1) did not extend to include the planning of the operation; and (2) that negligence had not been pleaded against any person other than the four soldiers at the scene. On the first point, Viscount Dilhorne stated (at p. 172):

'I am unable to agree that the phrase "in the circumstances" in s. 3(1) should be given the wide interpretation given to it in the Court of Appeal. That section is contained in a statute dealing with the criminal law. It may provide a defence for a person sued. In each case when such a defence is put forward the question to be determined is whether the person who is accused or sued used such force as was reasonable in the circumstances in which he was placed in the prevention of crime or in bringing about a lawful arrest of an offender or suspected offender.

Section 3(1) would provide no defence to soldier X in respect of a claim for negligence in the planning of the operation. It can only provide a defence for those who have used force and if the force the four soldiers used was reasonable in the circumstances in which they used it, the defects, if there were any, in the planning of the operation would not deprive them of that defence and render the force used unreasonable.'

This narrow approach has been criticised: D. S. Greer, (1980) 31 NILQ 151, 154–155. See also on the *Farrell* case C. P. Walker, (1980) 43 MLR 591 and G. Bennett and P. Rowe, (1981) 131 NLJ 991. Many commentators, including Greer, Walker, Bennett and Rowe and the Standing Advisory Commission on Human Rights (9th Annual Report for 1982–83 (1983–84 HC 262) p. 21–23 and Appendix B) have argued that s. 3(1) provides insufficient guidance on the general nature of the circumstances in which potentially lethal force may be used.[1]

3. The *Farrell* case was taken to Strasbourg and a claim under Article 2 ECHR admitted for consideration on the merits: *Farrell v United Kingdom* (1983) 5 EHRR 466. The case was then the subject of a friendly settlement, the British government agreeing to pay substantial damages to Mrs Farrell. In *Stewart v United Kingdom* (decn admiss of 10 July 1984), the applicant's son died after being struck on the head by a plastic bullet fired by a British soldier in Northern Ireland. It was held that the use of plastic bullets was not per se contrary to Articles 2 or 3, ECHR. Then, in *Kelly v United Kingdom* (App. No. 17579/90), the Commission found that the shooting dead of a joyrider attempting to evade an army checkpoint did not contravene Article 2, ECHR (below, p. 740), as the soldiers had a genuine and reasonable belief that the youth was a terrorist and had fired 'in order to effect a

---

1 See also Glanville Williams, *Textbook of Criminal Law* (2nd edn, 1983) pp. 493–500; J. C. Smith and B. Hogan, *Criminal Law* (7th edn, 1992) pp. 253–261; P. J. Rowe and C. J. Whelan (eds), *Military Intervention in Democratic Societies* (1985), Chap. 9; *Hogan and Walker*, pp. 64–69; R. J. Spjut, [1986] PL 38; J. C. Smith, (1994) 47(2) CLP 101.

lawful arrest' within Article 2(2). This has been cogently criticised (Sir John Smith, (1994) 144 NLJ 354; D. J. Harris, (1994) 1 *Maastricht Journal of European and Comparative Law* 123, 134–137) on the ground that the national court had rejected a claim for damages on the basis of the force being reasonable force in the prevention of crime (a basis not found in Article 2), and that the soldiers were neither seeking nor had power to arrest in the circumstances. See also the decision of the Commission in *McCann, Farrell and Savage v UK* (App. No. 18984/91) that the shooting in Gibraltar of three members of the IRA was not disproportionate to the aim of defending other persons from unlawful violence.

It is argued that s. 3 is broader than the test prescribed by Article 2, ECHR: see e.g. SACHR, 18th Report, 1992–93 HC 739, p. 12, and n. **7**, below.

4. According to A. Jennings ('Shoot to Kill: The Final Courts of Justice' in Jennings (ed) *Justice under Fire* (Rev. edn. 1990), chap. 5), writing in 1988, over 270 individuals, at least 155 of them 'civilians', had been killed by the security forces in Northern Ireland since 1969. Between 1982 and 1985, 35 individuals were so killed, 23 in covert operations. Twenty-one members of the security forces had been prosecuted for killings using firearms on duty, of whom one was convicted of manslaughter (*R v Davidson* (1981, unreported)) and one of murder (*R v Thain* [1985] NI 457). There were suspicions of the existence of a 'shoot-to-kill' policy in the 1982–1985 period, associated particularly with undercover surveillance units. John Stalker, then Deputy Chief Constable of Greater Manchester, conducted an inquiry into a series of killings, including those at two incidents where prosecutions of members of the security forces ended in acquittals (*R v Robinson* [1984] 4 NIJB; *R v Montgomery* (1984, unreported). The terms of reference did not, however, include an investigation of the existence of a shoot-to-kill policy. The inquiry was completed by Colin Sampson, Chief Constable of West Yorkshire, following Stalker's suspension for alleged disciplinary offences. The outcome of the inquiry was not made public. However, the Attorney-General announced in 1988 that eight RUC officers involved in a conspiracy to pervert the course of justice and responsible for obstructing the Stalker inquiry would not be prosecuted for reasons of national security. There was no evidence of a shoot-to-kill policy (126 HC Deb, 25 January 1988, cols 21–35).

John Stalker has subsequently suggested that there was

'no written instruction, nothing pinned upon a noticeboard. But there was a clear understanding on the part of the men whose job it was to pull the trigger that that was what was expected of them' (*The Times*, 9 February 1988, cited by Jennings, op. cit., p. 120).

Jennings concludes that

'The sheer number of incidents and the circumstances in which they occurred during 1977–78 and 1982–5 points towards the deliberate planning of operations in which opportunities for the use of lethal force would arise' (op. cit., p. 123).[1]

Similar controversy was caused by the killing by the army of three members of the Provisional IRA in Gibraltar in 1988, and the programme about the shootings, 'Death on the Rock', subsequently made by Thames Television. An inquest jury returned majority verdicts of lawful killing.[2]

1 See also *Shoot to Kill? International Lawyers' Inquiry into the Lethal Use of Firearms by the Security Forces in Northern Ireland* (Chairman, Kader Asmal, 1985) and M. Urban, *Big Boys' Rules* (1992). On the Stalker affair, see J. Stalker, *Stalker* (1988); P. Taylor, *Stalker: The Search for the Truth* (1987); K. Taylor, *The Poisoned Tree* (1990); D. Murphy, *The Stalker Affair and the Press* (1991).
2 See A. Jennings (ed), *Justice under Fire* (Rev. edn, 1990), pp. xx–xxii; Amnesty International, *Investigating Lethal Shootings: the Gibraltar Inquest* (1989); The *Windelsham/Rampton Report on 'Death on the Rock'* (1989); NCCL, *The Gibraltar Report*; R. Bolton, *Death on the Rock and other stories* (1990) and below, p. 340. The European Commission of Human Rights has referred a complaint alleging breach

More recently, one member of the Parachute Regiment was convicted of murder and another of attempted murder (*R v Clegg and Aindow* (4 June 1993, unreported, Cr Ct)). In this case 'the crucial evidence ... came from a policeman, on patrol with the army unit on the night the incident occurred, who was unable to sustain the army's version of events' (*Just News* (1993) Vol. 8 No. 6, p. 3). The victims were teenage joyriders in a stolen car. Campbell J held that the defendants were justified in firing shots at the car when speeding towards them, but not in shooting after the car had passed their patrol. On appeal, the Northern Ireland Court of Appeal dismissed C's appeal but substituted a conviction for malicious wounding for A's conviction for attempted murder (Unreported, 30 March 1994). The House of Lords dismissed on appeal: [1995] 1 All ER 334. Following a campaign on his behalf, C was released on licence in July 1995.

By early 1994, the number of deaths caused by the security forces had risen to 351 (*Just News* (1994) Vol. 9 No. 2, p. 1). Compare the acquittals in *R v Elkington and Callaghan* (23 December 1993, unreported, Cr Ct; *Just News* (1994) Vol. 9 No. 1, p. 1) and *R v Hanley* (25 January 1994, unreported, Cr Ct; *Just News* (1994) Vol. 9 No. 2, p. 4). For a critical overview, see Amnesty International, *Political Killings in Northern Ireland* (1994).

5. On the possible liability of members of the armed forces in negligence see the Court of Appeal in *McLaughlin v Ministry of Defence*, (1978) 7 NIJB; Greer (1980) 31 NILQ 151, 156–159; *Doherty v Ministry of Defence* (1980, unreported, HL), noted by P. J. Rowe, (1981) 44 MLR 466; *McGuigan v Ministry of Defence*, [1982] 19 NIJB. In *McGuigan*, Hutton J noted that while in a criminal case, once the accused has raised by evidence the defence of reasonable force under s. 3(1) the onus rests on the *prosecution* to prove beyond a reasonable doubt that the force used was not reasonable in the circumstances, in a civil case the onus lies on the *defence* to establish a defence of reasonable force on the balance of probabilities.

6. Where a plaintiff establishes a case in trespass against the police, the damages may be reduced on account of the plaintiff's contributory negligence. Thus in *Wasson v Chief Constable of the Royal Ulster Constabulary* [1987] NI 420, the plaintiff was taking part in a 'very serious' riot, when he was struck on the head by a baton round and badly injured. The police were held liable in trespass, having failed to show on a balance of probabilities that the baton round was not fired above leg level, and, as a result, being unable to establish a defence under s. 3(1) of the 1967 Act. However, the plaintiff's damages were halved in view of his participation in the riot. (Cf. *Tumelty v Ministry of Defence* [1988] 3 NIJB 51, where in a somewhat similar case, an 80% reduction in damages was made.)

7. The absence of clear guidelines has been criticised by a number of commentators. See n. **2**, above. The SACHR has recommended that a specific code of conduct to govern the use of legal force should be introduced, and has prepared a draft code for consideration (16th Report, 1990–91 HC 488, Annex C, Appendix 2). This code is based in part on the *Yellow Card* for 1972 and for 1980 (internal guidance for the armed forces) and on the terms of the *United Nations Instrument on Basic Principles on the Use of Force and Firearms by Law Enforcement Officials* (adopted in the 8th UN Congress on the Prevention of Crime and the Treatment of Offenders, Havana, 7 September 1990). Further recommendations by the Commission are that:

of Article 2, ECHR, arising out of the Gibraltar incident to the Court, although it ruled by 11 to 6 that the force used did not violate the Convention: see p. 298.

' (i) The Government should review the law on the use of lethal force and publish the outcome of its deliberations.

(ii) Section 3 of the Criminal Law Acts should be amended to meet the United Kingdom's obligations under the European Convention on Human Rights.

(iii) A specific detailed statutory code on the use of force by soldiers, police officers and other law enforcement officials should be enacted. The sanction for breach of this code in cases where a charge of murder or manslaughter is not appropriate should be limited to internal army or police disciplinary proceedings.

(iv) Consideration should be given to the general law relating to murder and manslaughter in the whole of the United Kingdom.

(v) Following on from (iv) above, charges of murder should be reserved for cases in which there is a preplanned intention to kill regardless of the legality of such action or at least of a deliberate disregard of the law in circumstances in which there was ample time for those responsible to decide whether to use lethal force.

(vi) A charge of manslaughter should be made available in cases in which the soldier or police officer in using lethal force acted honestly though in excess of what the circumstances would have warranted. This would require the introduction of a specific statutory provision of general application.

(vii) The Government should issue a detailed response on the Commission's earlier recommendations on reform of the law on inquests'

(18th Report, 1992–93 HC 739, pp. 11–15.) On the other hand, the Commission is against the creation of a new offence of the reckless or dangerous use of firearms, or any offence which relates only to the actions of soldiers or police officers.[1]

In *R v Clegg and Aindow* (above, p. 299), the Northern Ireland Court of Appeal endorsed the view that Parliament should consider a change in the existing law to permit a conviction for manslaughter where a soldier or police officer causes death with the intention to kill or cause grievous bodily harm, reacting wrongly but without malice or evil motive to a situation arising in the course of his duty. The House of Lords stated that any change should be made by Parliament and not by the House in its judicial capacity: [1995] 1 All ER 334, 345–347.

The government's subsequent response on inquests was that 'the present arrangements generally work well in practice' (229 HC Deb, 27 July 1993, col 753, written answer), a view disputed by the SACHR (19th Report, 1993–94 HC 495, p. 17).

8. The gap between theory and practice as regards military aid to the civil power is discussed by Evelegh (op. cit.). 'By contrast with 19th century practice, the "civil power" that may call in the armed forces appears no longer to be the local magistracy, but the Home Secretary, acting on a request from the chief officer of police' (A. W. Bradley and K. Ewing, *Wade and Bradley: Constitutional and Administrative Law* (11th edn., 1993), p. 580).[2]

---

1 See S. Doran, 'The doctrine of excessive defence: developments past, present and potential' (1985) 36 NILQ 314 and 'The use of force by the security forces in Northern Ireland: a legal perspective' (1987) 7 LS 291; Lord Colville's Annual Reports on the Northern Ireland (Emergency Provisions) Acts for 1987, pp. 28–30, 1988, pp. 34–38; paper by T. Hadden, SACHR 18th Report, Annex E.

2 See also the *Manual of Military Law*, Part II, Section V, (1968); *Queen's Regulations for the Army*, Reg. J. 11.002; *Report of the Committee appointed to inquire into the Circumstances connected with the Disturbances at Featherstone on 7th of September, 1893* (C 7234); R. Neville, 'The Yorkshire Miners and the 1893 Lockout: The Featherstone "Massacre" ' (1976) XXI *International Review of Social History*, 337; *Report of the Departmental Committee on Riot* (1895, C 7650); *Report of the Commissioner of Police of the Metropolis for 1975*, Cmnd. 6496, Appendix 9; *Report of the Tribunal of Inquiry into Violence and Civil Disturbances in Northern Ireland* (Chairman, Scarman J) (Cmd. 566, 1972) especially Part VI, and pp. 193–195, 201–206, 220–221; K. Jeffery in P. J. Rowe and C. J. Whelan, *Military Intervention in Democratic Societies* (1985), Chap. 2; A. Babington, *Military Intervention in Britain* (1990); C. J. Whelan, (1979) 8 ILJ 222; C. Townshend, (1982) 25 *The Historical Journal* 167; S. Greer, 'Military Intervention in Civil Disturbances: the Legal Basis Reconsidered' [1983] PL 573, criticised by B. Robertson, (1990) xxix *The Military Law and Law of War Review* 309; C. Walker, 'The Role and Powers of the Army in Northern Ireland' in B. Hadfield (ed.), *Northern Ireland: Politics and the Constitution* (1992), Chap. 8, pp. 113–116.

4 The Prevention of Terrorism (Temporary Provisions) Act 1989

PART I

PROSCRIBED ORGANISATIONS

1. Proscribed organisations

(1) Any organisation for the time being specified in Schedule 1 to this Act is a proscribed organisation for the purposes of this Act; and any organisation which passes under a name mentioned in that Schedule shall be treated as proscribed whatever relationship (if any) it has to any other organisation of the same name.

(2) The Secretary of State may by order made by statutory instrument—

    (*a*) add to Schedule 1 to this Act any organisation that appears to him to be concerned in, or in promoting or encouraging, terrorism occurring in the United Kingdom and connected with the affairs of Northern Ireland;

    (*b*) remove an organisation from that Schedule.

[Subss. (3)–(5) provide that an order shall not be made unless a draft is approved by each House of Parliament, except in urgent cases, where an order can be made, but must be approved by each House within 40 days.]

(6) In this section 'organisation' includes any association or combination of persons.

2. Membership, support and meetings

(1) Subject to subsection (3) below, a person is guilty of an offence if he—

    (*a*) belongs or professes to belong to a proscribed organisation;

    (*b*) solicits or invites support for a proscribed organisation other than support with money or other property; or

    (*c*) arranges or assists in the arrangement or management of, or addresses, any meeting of three or more persons (whether or not it is a meeting to which the public are admitted) knowing that the meeting is—

        (i) to support a proscribed organisation;

        (ii) to further the activities of such an organisation; or

        (iii) to be addressed by a person belonging or professing to belong to such an organisation. . .

(3) A person belonging to a proscribed organisation is not guilty of an offence under this section by reason of belonging to the organisation if he shows—

    (*a*) that he became a member when it was not a proscribed organisation under the current legislation; and

    (*b*) that he has not since he became a member taken part in any of its activities at any time while it was a proscribed organisation under that legislation.

(4) In subsection (3) above 'the current legislation', in relation to any time, means whichever of the following was in force at that time—

    (*a*) the Prevention of Terrorism (Temporary Provisions) Act 1974;

    (*b*) the Prevention of Terrorism (Temporary Provisions) Act 1976;

    (*c*) the Prevention of Terrorism (Temporary Provisions) Act 1984; or

    (*d*) this Act.

(5) The reference in subsection (3) above to a person becoming a member of an organisation is a reference to the only or last occasion on which he became a member.

3. Display of support in public

(1) Any person who in a public place—

    (*a*) wears any item of dress; or

    (*b*) wears, carries or displays any article,

in such a way or in such circumstances as to arouse reasonable apprehension that he is a member or supporter of a proscribed organisation, is guilty of an offence. . . .

(3) In this section 'public place' includes any highway . . . and any premises to which at the material time the public have, or are permitted to have, access, whether on payment or otherwise.

PART II

EXCLUSION ORDERS

4. Exclusion orders: general

(1) The Secretary of State may exercise the powers conferred on him by this Part of this Act in such a way as appears to him expedient to prevent acts of terrorism to which this Part of this Act applies.

(2) The acts of terrorism to which this Part of this Act applies are acts of terrorism connected with the affairs of Northern Ireland.

(3) An order under section 5, 6 or 7 below is referred to in this Act as an 'exclusion order'.

(4) Schedule 2 to this Act shall have effect with respect to the duration of exclusion orders, the giving of notices, the right to make representations, powers of removal and detention and other supplementary matters of this Part of this Act.

(5) The exercise of the detention powers conferred by that Schedule shall be subject to supervision in accordance with Schedule 3 to this Act.

5. Orders excluding persons from Great Britain

(1) If the Secretary of State is satisfied that any person—

    (*a*) is or has been concerned in the commission, preparation or instigation of acts of terrorism to which this Part of this Act applies; or

    (*b*) is attempting or may attempt to enter Great Britain with a view to being concerned in the commission, preparation or instigation of such acts of terrorism,

the Secretary of State may make an exclusion order against him.

(2) An exclusion order under this section is an order prohibiting a person from being in, or entering, Great Britain.

(3) In deciding whether to make an exclusion order under this section against a person who is ordinarily resident in Great Britain, the Secretary of State shall have regard to the question whether that person's connection with any country or territory outside Great Britain is such as to make it appropriate that such an order should be made.

(4) An exclusion order shall not be made under this section against a person who is a British citizen and who—

    (*a*) is at the time ordinarily resident in Great Britain and has then been ordinarily resident in Great Britain throughout the last three years; or

    (*b*) is at the time subject to an order under section 6 below.

6. Orders excluding persons from Northern Ireland [This section is identical in terms to s. 5, with the substitution of 'Northern Ireland', for 'Great Britain']

7. Orders excluding persons from United Kingdom [Subss. (1)–(3) are identical in terms to s. 5(1)–(3), with the substitution of 'Great Britain or Northern Ireland' for 'Great Britain' in subs. (1), and 'United Kingdom' for 'Northern Ireland' in subss. (2) and (3)]

(4) An exclusion order shall not be made under this section against a person who is a British citizen.

8. Offences in respect of exclusion orders

(1) A person who is subject to an exclusion order is guilty of an offence if he fails to comply with the order at a time after he has been, or has become liable to be, removed under Schedule 2 to this Act.

(2) A person is guilty of an offence—

    (*a*) if he is knowingly concerned in arrangements for securing or facilitating the entry into Great Britain, Northern Ireland or the United Kingdom of a person whom he knows, or has reasonable grounds for believing, to be an excluded person; or

    (*b*) if he knowingly harbours such a person in Great Britain, Northern Ireland or the United Kingdom.

(3) In subsection (2) above 'excluded person' means—

    (*a*) in relation to Great Britain, a person subject to an exclusion order made under section 5 above who has been, or has become liable to be, removed from Great Britain under Schedule 2 to this Act;

    (*b*) in relation to Northern Ireland, a person subject to an exclusion order made under section 6 above who has been, or has become liable to be, removed from Northern Ireland under that Schedule; and

    (*c*) in relation to the United Kingdom, a person subject to an exclusion order made under section 7 above who has been, or has become liable to be, removed from the United Kingdom under that Schedule. . . .

PART III

FINANCIAL ASSISTANCE FOR TERRORISM

[This Part (ss. 9–13), as amended, creates offences in respect of contributions to acts of terrorism (s. 9), contribution to the resources of proscribed organisations (s. 10), and assisting in the retention or control of terrorist funds (s. 11), and provides that a person may, notwithstanding any restriction on the disclosure of information imposed by statute or otherwise, disclose to a constable a suspicion or belief that any money or other property is or is derived from terrorist funds or any matter on which such a suspicion or belief is based; such disclosure may also provide a defence to a charge under ss. 9, 10 or 11 (s. 12).]

PART IV

[POWERS OF ARREST, STOP AND SEARCH, DETENTION AND CONTROL OF ENTRY][1]

[13A. Powers to stop and search vehicles etc. and persons
(1) Where it appears to—
  (a) any officer of police of or above the rank of commander of the metropolitan police, as respects the metropolitan police area;
  (b) any officer of police of or above the rank of commander of the City of London police, as respects the City of London; or
  (c) any officer of police of or above the rank of assistant chief constable for any other police area,
that it is expedient to do so in order to prevent acts of terrorism to which this section applies he may give an authorisation that the powers to stop and search vehicles and persons conferred by this section shall be exercisable at any place within his area or a specified locality in his area for a specified period not exceeding twenty eight days.
(2) The acts of terrorism to which this section applies are—
  (a) acts of terrorism connected with the affairs of Northern Ireland; and
  (b) acts of terrorism of any other description except acts connected solely with the affairs of the United Kingdom or any part of the United Kingdom other than Northern Ireland.
(3) This section confers on any constable in uniform power—
  (a) to stop any vehicle;
  (b) to search any vehicle, its driver or any passenger for articles of a kind which could be used for a purpose connected with the commission, preparation or instigation of acts of terrorism to which this section applies;
  (c) to stop any pedestrian and search any thing carried by him for articles of a kind which could be used for a purpose connected with the commission, preparation or instigation of acts of terrorism to which this section applies.
(4) A constable may, in the exercise of those powers, stop any vehicle or person and make any search he thinks fit whether or not he has any grounds for suspecting that the vehicle or person is carrying articles of that kind.
(5) This section applies (with the necessary modifications) to ships and aircraft as it applies to vehicles.
(6) A person is guilty of an offence if he—
  (a) fails to stop or (as the case may be) to stop the vehicle when required to do so by a constable in the exercise of his powers under this section; or
  (b) wilfully obstructs a constable in the exercise of those powers. . . .
(8) If it appears to a police officer of the rank specified in subsection (1)(a), (b) or (c) (as the case may be) that the exercise of the powers conferred by this section ought to continue beyond the period for which their exercise has been authorised under this section he may, from time to time, authorise the exercise of those powers for a further period, not exceeding twenty eight days.
(9) Where a vehicle is stopped by a constable under this section, the driver shall be entitled to obtain a written statement that the vehicle was stopped under the powers conferred by this section if he applies for such a statement not later than the end of the period of twelve months from the day on which the vehicle was stopped; and similarly as respects a pedestrian who is stopped under this section for a search of anything carried by him.
(10) In this section—
  'authorise' and 'authorisation' mean authorise or an authorisation in writing signed by the officer giving it; and
  'specified' means specified in an authorisation under this section.
(11) Nothing in this section affects the exercise by constables of any power to stop vehicles for purposes other than those specified in subsection (1) above.][1]

14. Arrest and detention of suspected persons
(1) Subject to subsection (2) below, a constable may arrest without warrant a person whom he has reasonable grounds for suspecting to be—
  (a) a person guilty of an offence under section 2, 8, 9, 10 or 11 above;

1 Inserted by the Criminal Justice and Public Order Act 1994, s. 81.

(b) a person who is or has been concerned in the commission, preparation or instigation of acts of terrorism to which this section applies; or

(c) a person subject to an exclusion order.

(2) The acts of terrorism to which this section applies are—

(a) acts of terrorism connected with the affairs of Northern Ireland; and

(b) acts of terrorism of any other description except acts connected solely with the affairs of the United Kingdom or any part of the United Kingdom other than Northern Ireland.

(3) The power of arrest conferred by subsection (1)(c) above is exercisable only—

(a) in Great Britain if the exclusion order was made under section 5 above; and

(b) in Northern Ireland if it was made under section 6 above.

(4) Subject to subsection (5) below, a person arrested under this section shall not be detained in right of the arrest for more than forty-eight hours after his arrest.

(5) The Secretary of State may, in any particular case, extend the period of forty-eight hours mentioned in subsection (4) above by a period or periods specified by him, but any such further period or periods shall not exceed five days in all and if an application for such an extension is made the person detained shall as soon as practicable be given written notice of that fact and of the time when the application was made.

(6) The exercise of the detention powers conferred by this section shall be subject to supervision in accordance with Schedule 3 to this Act.

(7) The provisions of this section are without prejudice to any power of arrest exercisable apart from this section.

15. Provisions supplementary to s. 14

(1) If a justice of the peace is satisfied that there are reasonable grounds for suspecting that a person whom a constable believes to be liable to arrest under section 14(1)(b) above is to be found on any premises he may grant a search warrant authorising any constable to enter those premises for the purpose of searching for and arresting that person. . . .

(3) In any circumstances in which a constable has power under section 14 above to arrest a person, he may also, for the purpose of ascertaining whether he has in his possession any document or other article which may constitute evidence that he is a person liable to arrest, stop that person and search him.

(4) Where a constable has arrested a person under that section for any reason other than the commission of a criminal offence, he, or any other constable, may search him for the purpose of ascertaining whether he has in his possession any document or other article which may constitute evidence that he is a person liable to arrest.

(5) A search of a person under subsection (3) or (4) above may only be carried out by a person of the same sex.

(6) A person detained under section 14 above shall be deemed to be in legal custody at any time when he is so detained and may be detained in such a place as the Secretary of State may from time to time direct. . . .

(9) Where a person is detained under section 14 above, any constable or prison officer, or any other person authorised by the Secretary of State, may take all such steps as may be reasonably necessary for photographing, measuring or otherwise identifying him. . . .

[Subsection (10) and sub-ss. (11)–(14) (inserted by the Criminal Justice and Public Order Act 1994, Sch. 10, para. 61(2)) apply with modifications the provisions of the Police and Criminal Evidence Act 1984 concerning the taking of fingerprints (s. 61(1)–(8)), intimate samples (s. 62(1)–(11)) and non-intimate samples (s. 63(1)–(9)) (see above, p. 141).]

16. Port and border controls

(1) Schedule 5 to this Act shall have effect for conferring powers to examine persons arriving in or leaving Great Britain or Northern Ireland and for connected purposes. . . .

[PART IVA

OFFENCES AGAINST PUBLIC SECURITY

16A. Possession of articles for suspected terrorist purposes

(1) A person is guilty of an offence if he has any article in his possession in circumstances giving rise to a reasonable suspicion that the article is in his possession for a purpose connected with the commission, preparation or instigation of acts of terrorism to which this section applies.

(2) The acts of terrorism to which this section applies are—

(a) acts of terrorism connected with the affairs of Northern Ireland; and

(b) acts of terrorism of any other description except acts connected solely with the affairs of the United Kingdom or any part of the United Kingdom other than Northern Ireland.

(3) It is a defence for a person charged with an offence under this section to prove that at the time of the alleged offence the article in question was not in his possession for such a purpose as is mentioned in subsection (1) above.

(4) Where a person is charged with an offence under this section and it is proved that at the time of the alleged offence—

(a) he and that article were both present in any premises; or

(b) the article was in premises of which he was the occupier or which he habitually used otherwise than as a member of the public,

the court may accept the fact proved as sufficient evidence of his possessing that article at that time unless it is further proved that he did not at that time know of its presence in the premises in question, or, if he did know, that he had no control over it. . . .

(6) This section applies to vessels, aircraft and vehicles as it applies to premises.

16B. Unlawful collection, etc. of information

(1) No person shall, without lawful authority or reasonable excuse (the proof of which lies on him)—

(a) collect or record any information which is of such a nature as is likely to be useful to terrorists in planning or carrying out any act of terrorism to which this section applies; or

(b) have in his possession any record or document containing any such information as is mentioned in paragraph (a) above.

(2) The acts of terrorism to which this section applies are—

(a) acts of terrorism connected with the affairs of Northern Ireland; and

(b) acts of terrorism of any other description except acts connected solely with the affairs of the United Kingdom or any part of the United Kingdom other than Northern Ireland.

(3) In subsection (1) above the reference to recording information includes a reference to recording it by means of photography or by any other means. . . .

(5) The court by or before which a person is convicted of an offence under this section may order the forfeiture of any record or document mentioned in subsection (1) above which is found in his possession.][1]

PART V

INFORMATION, PROCEEDINGS AND INTERPRETATION

17. Investigation of terrorist activities

(1) Schedule 7 to this Act shall have effect for conferring powers to obtain information for the purposes of terrorist investigations. . . .

18. Information about acts of terrorism

(1) A person is guilty of an offence if he has information which he knows or believes might be of material assistance—

(a) in preventing the commission by any other person of an act of terrorism connected with the affairs of Northern Ireland; or

(b) in securing the apprehension, prosecution or conviction of any other person for an offence involving the commission, preparation or instigation of such an act,

and fails without reasonable excuse to disclose that information as soon as reasonably practicable—

(i) in England and Wales, to a constable;

(ii) in Scotland, to a constable or the procurator fiscal; or

(iii) in Northern Ireland, to a constable or a member of Her Majesty's Forces. . . .

(3) Proceedings for an offence under this section may be taken, and the offence may for the purposes of those proceedings be treated as having been committed, in any place where the person to be charged is or has at any time been since he first knew or believed that the information might be of material assistance as mentioned in subsection (1) above.

[18A. Failure to disclose knowledge or suspicion of offences under section 9 to 11]

[This section makes it an offence to fail without reasonable excuse to disclose knowledge or suspicion that another person is providing financial assistance to terrorism, where the information or matter on which this is based is acquired in the course of his trade, profession, business or employment. It does not apply to a professional legal adviser who fails to disclose information or other matter which came to him in privileged circumstances, although that does not apply where it is communicated or given with a view to furthering any criminal purpose.][2]

1 Inserted by the Criminal Justice and Public Order Act 1994, s. 82.
2 Inserted by the Criminal Justice Act 1993, s. 51.

19. Prosecutions and evidence

(1) Proceedings shall not be instituted—

    (a) in England and Wales for an offence under section 2, 3, 8, 9, 10, 11, 17[, 18 or 18A]¹ above or Schedule 7 to this Act except by or with the consent of the Attorney General; or

    [(aa) in England and Wales for an offence under sections 13A, 16A or 16B except by or with the consent of the Director of Public Prosecutions;]²

    (b) in Northern Ireland for an offence under section 8, 9, 10, 11, 17[, 18 or 18A]¹ above or Schedule 7 to this Act except by or with the consent of the Attorney General for Northern Ireland. . . .

[19A. Extension of certain offences to Crown servants]³

[This section enables the Secretary of State to make regulations applying ss. 9–11, 17 and 18A to prescribed Crown servants, and providing that s. 18A shall not apply to specified regulators. See the Prevention of Terrorism (Temporary Provisions) Act 1989 (Crown Servants and Regulators etc.) Regulations 1994 (S.I. 1994 No. 1758).]

20. Interpretation

(1) In this Act—

    'aircraft' includes hovercraft;

    'captain' means master of a ship or commander of an aircraft;

    'examining officer' has the meaning given in paragraph 1 of Schedule 5 to this Act;

    'exclusion order' has the meaning given by section 4(3) above but subject to section 25(3) below;

    'the Islands' means the Channel Islands or the Isle of Man;

    'port' includes airport and hoverport;

    'premises' includes any place and in particular includes—

    (a) any vehicle, vessel or aircraft;

    (b) any offshore installation as defined in section 1 of the Mineral Workings (Offshore Installations) Act 1971; and

    (c) any tent or moveable structure;

    'property' includes property wherever situated and whether real or personal, heritable or moveable and things in action and other intangible or incorporeal property;

    'ship' includes every description of vessel used in navigation;

    'terrorism' means the use of violence for political ends, and includes any use of violence for the purpose of putting the public or any section of the public in fear;

    'vehicle' includes a train and carriages forming part of a train.

(2) A constable or examining officer may, if necessary, use reasonable force for the purpose of exercising any powers conferred on him under or by virtue of any provision of this Act other than paragraph 2 of Schedule 5; but this subsection is without prejudice to any provision of this Act, or of any instrument made under it, which implies that a person may use reasonable force in connection with that provision.

(3) The powers conferred by Part II and section 16 of, and Schedules 2 and 5 to, this Act shall be exercisable notwithstanding the rights conferred by section 1 of the Immigration Act 1971 (general principles regulating entry into and stay in the United Kingdom).

(4) Any reference in a provision of this Act to a person having been concerned in the commission, preparing or instigation of acts of terrorism shall be taken to be a reference to his having been so concerned at any time, whether before or after the passing of this Act.

Schedule 1

PROSCRIBED ORGANISATIONS

Irish Republican Army

Irish National Liberation Army

NOTES

1. Part I and ss. 13A and 15(1) and Part IVA do not extend to Northern Ireland; s. 15(10) extends only to England and Wales; Sch. 7 Part I extends only to England, Wales and Northern Ireland.

1 Inserted by the Criminal Justice Act 1993, Sch. 5, para. 15.
2 Inserted by the Criminal Justice and Public Order Act 1994, Sch. 10, para. 63(3).
3 Inserted by the 1993 Act, Sch. 4, para. 4.

The maximum penalties on conviction on indictment are 14 years' (ss. 9, 10, 11), 10 years' (ss. 2(1), 16A, 16B) or 5 years' (ss. 8, 17(2), 18) imprisonment, or a fine or both. The maximum penalties on summary conviction under these sections are 6 months' imprisonment or a fine not exceeding the statutory maximum. The maximum penalty under ss. 3(1) and 13A(6) is, on summary conviction, 6 months' imprisonment or a fine not exceeding level 5 on the standard scale or both. Section 13(2)–(8) and Sch. 4 provide powers for the court to order forfeiture of money and other property by persons convicted under ss. 9 and 10.

Schedule 2 contains further provisions on exclusion orders; Sch. 3 introduces arrangements for reviews of persons in detention; Sch. 4 concerns forfeiture orders; Sch. 5, port and border control; Sch. 6, designated ports; and Sch. 7, powers in the investigation of terrorism.

2. This Act has its origins in the Prevention of Violence (Temporary Provisions) Act 1939 (see O. G. Lomas, [1980] PL 16) which was also designed to deal with terrorism relating to Irish affairs, and was in force between 1939 and 1954. The Prevention of Terrorism (Temporary Provisions) Act 1974 (see H. Street, [1975] Crim LR 192) was passed in the aftermath of the Birmingham public house bombings of 21 November 1974 when 21 people were killed and over 180 injured. The Bill was introduced on 27 November and received the Royal Assent on 29 November. It was re-enacted, with some amendments, as the Prevention of Terrorism (Temporary Provisions) Act 1976.[1] The 1976 Act was replaced by the Prevention of Terrorism (Temporary Provisions) Act 1984 following Lord Jellicoe's *Review of the Operation of the Prevention of Terrorism (Temporary Provisions) Act 1976* (Cmnd. 8803, 1983).[2] The 1984 Act was in turn replaced by the present provisions,[3] following Lord Colville's *Review of the Operation of the Prevention of Terrorism (Temporary Provisions) Act 1984* (Cm. 264, 1987) (hereafter, *Colville Review (PTA)*). The Labour Party is committed to the repeal of the 1989 Act (see H. Arnott, 'Breaking the Silence', *Legal Action*, May 1990, p. 25.

3. Statistics as to the operation of the Act are now given regularly in Home Office Statistical Bulletins, and in annual reviews conducted by John Rowe QC (who performs the same function in respect of the Northern Ireland (Emergency Provisions) legislation. John Rowe has conducted reviews since 1993, reviews in 1984 and 1985 having been conducted by Sir Cyril Philips, and between 1986 and 1992 by Lord Colville.

4. *Proscribed organisations.* The power to proscribe terrorist organisations in Northern Ireland is contained in the Northern Ireland (Emergency Provisions) Act 1991, s. 28 above, pp. 277 and 294.

---

1 The operation of the 1976 Act was monitored by the National Council for Civil Liberties (see C. Scorer, *The Prevention of Terrorism Acts 1974 and 1976* (NCCL, 1976) and was reviewed by Lord Shackleton in a report for the Home Office (*Review of the Operation of the Prevention of Terrorism (Temporary Provisions) Acts 1974 and 1976* (Cmnd. 7324, 1978)). The provisions concerning exclusion orders were discussed by D. Bonner, [1982] PL 262.

2 See D. Bonner, 'Combating Terrorism: The Jellicoe Approach' [1983] PL 224; C. P. Walker, (1983) 46 MLR 484; J. Sim and P. Thomas, (1983) 10 JLS 71; *Current Law Statutes 1984* (annotations by D. S. Greer); C. Walker, (1984) 47 MLR 704; A. Samuels, [1984] PL 365; D. Bonner, *Emergency Powers in Peacetime* (1985), Chap. 4.

3 On the 1989 Act, see D. Bonner, [1989] PL 440; W. Finnie, 1990 JR 1; B. Dickson, (1989) 40 NILQ 250; C. Walker, *The Prevention of Terrorism in British Law* (2nd edn., 1992). The case for repeal without replacement is argued by C. Scorer and P. Hewitt, *The New Prevention of Terrorism Act: The Case for Repeal* (3rd edn., 1985). The impact on individuals' lives of the operation of the legislation is documented by P. Hillyard, *Suspect Community* (1993). On the position in the Channel Islands and the Isle of Man, see C. Walker, (1992) 12 LS 178.

The 'Irish Republican Army' (which term covers both the 'Official' and 'Provisional' wings) was proscribed under the 1974 Act. The Irish National Liberation Army was proscribed in July 1979 (S.I. 1979 No. 745). The group had claimed responsibility for the killing of Mr Airey Neave, Opposition spokesman on Northern Ireland. Both groups are still proscribed (Sch. 1). To the end of 1989, seven persons had been charged with offences under what is now s. 2(1)(b) and three under s. 3(1)(b): these were the only charges under Part I, and all were brought under the 1973 or 1976 Acts. Section 10 was, by contrast, used in 43 cases (to the end of 1982), and the penalties on conviction were consistently higher than for other offences. Lord Jellicoe commented (1983 Report, pp. 80 ff):

[207] . . . [P]roscribing an organisation is unlikely either to impair substantially its capacity for carrying out terrorist attacks or to deter those most deeply involved in its activities. But the terms of legislation suggest a wider range of purposes than the merely symbolic. At the least practical level, it enshrines in legislation public aversion to organisations which use, and espouse, violence as a means to a political end. But the legislation also prohibits public displays by or in support of proscribed organisations. The effect of this, if successful, will be not only the avoidance of public outrage, but also the averting of any danger of this outrage being expressed in disorder. More practically still, proscription is designed to stem the flow of funds to the organisations concerned.

208. It is at the more presentational level that proscription under this Act (ie in Great Britain) seems to have been most successful, in that there have apparently been few demonstrations or open displays of support by or on behalf of either the IRA or the INLA. The financial aspects of proscription, on the other hand, appear to have had less effect. . . . On the other hand, the police have told me that the flow of funds to proscribed organisations from sources on the mainland is relatively limited, which may be due in part to proscription. At the least, open collections for proscribed organisations are banned. . . . **I conclude, therefore, that proscription has had some—albeit relatively limited—beneficial effects.** . . .

210. The basic argument of principle against proscription is that banning an organisation is an unacceptable infringement of freedom of speech; instead, its members should be prosecuted for the criminal offences which they commit. I have much sympathy with this view. If one were starting absolutely with a clean slate, proscription would I believe be low on the list of priorities for inclusion in counter-terrorist legislation. But this is not the case. There is presently proscription in Great Britain, and the arguments againt proscription are not necessarily the same as those in favour of deproscription. It cannot reasonably be argued that by not proscribing a particular organisation, the Government is indicating approval of it or condoning its activities. Deproscription, on the other hand, would be understood as implying a change either in the Government's attitude towards an organisation, or in the attitude and conduct of the organisation itself. The proscription provisions of the 1974 Act were introduced on an understandable wave of public resentment, and were, indeed, considered by many to be among the Act's most important provisions. I believe that time has proved this judgment to be mistaken; but there would be a further, equally understandable, wave of public resentment were the IRA or INLA to be deproscribed in Great Britain in the absence of a change in the conduct and attitude towards violence of these organisations.

211. I believe that this also answers those who argued to me that there should be "symmetry" in proscription between Great Britain and Northern Ireland. (Under the Northern Ireland (Emergency Provisions) Act 1978, several organisations engaged in terrorism on behalf of the Loyalist cause are proscribed, as well as the IRA and INLA.) It is a reasonable argument that an organisation posing a threat in one part of the United Kingdom should be regarded in law as posing a threat to the United Kingdom as a whole. It has also been suggested that by proscribing in Great Britain only the IRA and INLA, the Government is discriminating against Irish Republicanism, or against the Irish Catholic community in Great Britain. I believe this argument to be fallacious. The proscription of these organisations is based not on their political views or aims, but on their open and avowed use of violence to achieve those aims. Were their use of violence to cease, there would no longer be any ground for their continued proscription. **I should be loath to see any addition to the list of proscribed organisations in the absence of a clear and demonstrable need for this, and I do not believe that a search for "symmetry", whether between Northern Ireland and Great Britain or between Republican and Loyalist terrorist groups, is a sufficient reason for adding to the list.**

212. This brings me to the argument, advanced by a number of witnesses, that the effect of proscription has been to inhibit free discussion about the future of Northern Ireland. I fully accept that frank and untrammelled political discussion is essential to political progress in Northern Ireland. I was very concerned to read in the evidence of a number of organisations representing the Irish community in Great Britain that the proscription provisions of this legislation have been widely seen within that community as creating an atmosphere in which the discussion had been curtailed for fear of police action. If this were a necessary and inevitable result of proscription, then I should recommend without hesitation that the power to proscribe should lapse forthwith. But I cannot believe that this is the case, despite the obvious sincerity of those who argued it to me. The power to proscribe may be exercised only against organisations involved in violence for political ends, and it cannot be emphasised too strongly or too often that it is not the ends themselves which are the target of these provisions. I do, however, agree with these witnesses that there is a potential problem here. It is asking a lot of the police service to apply these provisions fully in relation to the proscribed organisations themselves, while not affecting the free expression of views about Northern Ireland. **Accordingly, I recommend that the police service throughout Great Britain should be given guidance by circular on the proper use, and limits on the use, of sections 1 and 2 of the Act.**

(b) Contributions towards acts of terrorism

213. By contrast, section 10 of the Act is far less controversial. Prosecutions and convictions for offences under the section, particularly in Great Britain, suggest that it fills a genuine need.

The recommendation in para. 212 was accepted, and a Home Office circular issued on 9 August, 1983 (*Current Law Statutes 1984*, notes to s. 1(1)).

Lord Colville expressed similar views to those of Lord Jellicoe in the *Colville Review (PTA)* (Cm. 264, 1987, Chap. 13). He rejected the argument that the power to proscribe should be extended to international terrorist organisations:

'This would place the Secretary of State in the most unenviable position of having to monitor all manner of foreign quarrels and their manifestations in the United Kingdom and to determine which of them posed a sufficiently serious and lasting threat in this country to justify proscription. The international terrorism scene is in a constant state of flux. Proscription seems to me to be too blunt and inflexible a weapon to use against international terrorism.' (ibid. p. 46)

Compare the s. 3 offences of displaying support for a proscribed organisation with s. 1 of the Public Order Act 1936, banning political uniforms (above, pp. 178, 179). Is the s. 3 offence necessary or desirable? See the debate by W. Finnie, 1990 JR 1, 6; B. Robertson, 1991 JR 250; C. Walker, 1993 JR 90; and Finnie, 1994 JR 118.

5. *Exclusion orders.* These are perhaps the most controversial provisions of the Act. Between 1984 and the end of 1994, 107 orders were made in Great Britain (out of 122 applications), 58 orders remained in force at the end of 1994 (John Rowe's 1994 Report on the PTA, Table 11). Comparative figures for orders made in Northern Ireland between 1980 and 1992 were, respectively, 26, 27, and 10 (*Colville Review (PTA)* (1987), p. 38; Annual Reports by Lord Colville, 1987–92 and John Rowe, 1993–94). Orders under the 1976 Act were of indefinite duration, but from 1979, following a recommendation by Lord Shackleton (Review, para. 127), a system of three-year reviews was introduced. Orders now expire after three years (Sch. 2, para. 1). A person on whom notice of an exclusion order is served has the rights, within 7 (or in some cases 14) days, to make written representations to the Secretary of State, and to request a personal interview with an Adviser nominated by the Secretary of State. In most cases there is a right to a personal interview (Sch. 2, para. 3). The Divisional Court has, however, held that the Secretary of State is not required to give reasons for making an exclusion order: 'to do so would be fraught with difficulty and danger' (per Watkins LJ in *R v Secretary of State for the Home Department, ex p Stitt* (1987) Times, 3 February). That point was confirmed by the Court of Appeal in *R v Secretary of State for the Home Department, ex p*

Gallagher (1994) Times, 16 February, the court emphasising the security context.
The court also held that the applicant was not obliged to disclose the name of the
persons nominated to hear objections to the renewal of an order; naming the panel
of advisers would in all likelihood expose them to danger and the applicant was not
prejudiced by not being informed of the adviser's name. However, questions
whether the Home Secretary breached Article 9 of Council Directive 64/221/EEC
by making an order before obtaining the opinion of a competent authority, and
whether the adviser was a competent authority were referred under Article
177/EEC to the European Court of Justice. See also *R v Secretary of State for the
Home Department, ex p Adams* [1995] All ER (EC) 177, where the Divisional Court
confirmed that judicial review would in practice be available in the most exceptional circumstances, but also referred certain questions to the European Court.
The order, in respect of Gerry Adams, the President of Sinn Fein, was subsequently
revoked following the IRA cease-fire. See S. Douglas-Scott and J. A. Kimbell,
'The Adams Exclusion Order Case: New Enforceable Civil Rights in the Post-
Maastricht European Union' [1994] PL 516.

Lord Jellicoe (1983 Report, Chap. 9) found that 'the exclusion of some people
under these powers has materially contributed to public safety in the United
Kingdom and that this could not have been achieved through the normal criminal
process' (p. 68). The power

'has been used, for instance, against individuals who there was good reason to believe had come to Great
Britain in order to set up a Provisional IRA "active service unit", or who were being used by the
Provisional IRA as couriers of information or materials; their exclusion will undoubtedly have disrupted
the IRA's lines of communication. Other exclusion orders have been made against people who had
travelled from Northern Ireland to Scotland for the purpose of obtaining arms or explosives for use by
extreme loyalist organisations' (p. 69).

Accordingly, the powers should remain. However, he saw the force of the critics'
argument that exclusion 'turns Northern Ireland into a dumping-ground for terrorists' (pp. 70–71):

'They are obliged to receive someone with substantial terrorist connections, who, though probably born
in Northern Ireland, has left it some years earlier to set up home in the mainland. He is already, presumably, deeply alienated from government policy in relation to Northern Ireland or he would not have
turned to terrorism in the first place. His exclusion, which will mean uprooting him and his family from
the mainland, is almost certain to alienate him still further, and it is Northern Ireland which will have to
bear the brunt of this. This seems to me wrong.'

Moreover, he accepted that exclusion could cause considerable financial hardship
and emotional suffering to the family of the excluded person:

'Much of the evidence presented to me critical of exclusion has focused on cases of people excluded from
Great Britain following substantial periods of residence there—as much as nineteen years in a few cases—
who had married English wives and had had children who had never lived anywhere but England. It has
been pointed out that the effect of exclusion in such a case is either to break up the family or to require
the wife and children to uproot themselves to live in an alien and possibly hostile environment, where
also unemployment is substantially worse than on the mainland.'

Accordingly the period of ordinary residence for the purposes of ss. 5(4) and 6(4)
was reduced from 20 years to 3 years. (Note, however, that 'only 27 out of 263
persons excluded from Great Britain up to the end of 1982 had been resident in
Great Britain for more than three years and less than 20 years' and 'no person with
more than three years' residence was excluded from Northern Ireland' (*Current Law
Statutes 1984*, notes to the 1984 Act, ss. 4(4) and 5(4)).)

On the other hand, he was 'convinced that all those who had administered the
system . . . have done so with fairness and integrity' and in all the exclusion cases he

examined there were 'grounds on which the Secretary of State could be satisfied of the subject's involvement in terrorism. But many of these cases are finely balanced' (pp. 72, 73). He rejected arguments in favour of a right of appeal to a judicial tribunal (pp. 74, 75). The needs of security would require the use of screens and voice scramblers to protect witnesses, the use of hearsay evidence and in camera sessions (as had been the case in relation to internment between 1972 and 1975) (see above, p. 289). This 'would in practice constitute no more than a parody of due legal process and would thus contribute to a loss of public confidence in the legal system' (p. 75). (For the case in favour of a judicial tribunal, see D. Bonner, [1980] PL 262.) On the application of exclusion orders to MPs see C. P. Walker, [1983] PL 537.

Lord Colville, unlike Lord Jellicoe, recommended that the powers to make exclusion orders should be repealed (*Colville Review (PTA)* (1987), p. 40). He agreed that

'it is probably an effective way of getting rid of people from an area where otherwise they might cause great trouble; and that it disrupts terrorist lines of communication and supply of arms, ammunition and explosives. However, I am not convinced that the ends justify these means.'

To repeal the power would be the correct decision

'both in terms of civil rights in the United Kingdom and this country's reputation in that respect among the International Community.'

The Government rejected this recommendation. Lord Colville's view on this matter does not seem to be shared by his successor, John Rowe QC (1993 Report on the PTA, Chap. 2). The SACHR has consistently recommended that the power to make exclusion orders should be repealed, arguing that it contravenes a number of provisions of the ECHR (Articles 6, 8 and 11, and Article 2 of the 4th protocol: below, pp. 741–742, 744). If there is enough evidence to satisfy police that someone has been involved in terrorist activity, that person should be charged; if the evidence is sufficient to create a suspicion, the person should be kept under surveillance (19th Report, 1993–94, pp. 14–15). In the absence of any repeal, the SACHR has also recommended that there should be express power to suspend orders for exceptional reasons, e.g. compassionate grounds (ibid).

See further on exclusion orders, *Walker*, Chap. 6; *Bonner*, pp. 191–209; D. Bonner, [1989] PL 440, 452–456; P. Hillyard, *Suspect Community* (1993), Chaps. 9, 10.

6. *Withholding information.* Section 18, formerly s. 11 of the 1984 Act, began life as a controversial amendment to the 1976 Bill. Lord Shackleton (1978 Report, para. 133) recommended that it should be allowed to lapse except (perhaps) in Northern Ireland, but this was not accepted (980 HC Deb 4 March 1980 col. 409). Lord Jellicoe concluded that 'the section is of significant value to the police service, but that the service could operate without it if required to do so' (1983 Report, p. 85). However, he accepted that there was 'substantial potential for abuse of a provision of this kind in the counter-terrorist sphere', especially at the interrogation stage:

'Three possible dangers have been instanced to me. First, . . . is the danger of unfair pressure being placed by the police on, for instance, the relative of a terrorist who, without any involvement in terrorism himself, happens to pick up information of the type covered by the section. Such a person would have the choice between providing the information and perhaps seeing the individual concerned convicted, with the risk of reprisals to add to the inevitable conflict of loyalty; and not providing the information and risking prosecution. Such a choice will probably put a relative under considerable strain, and it is a strain which can be occasioned simply by the police bringing to his notice the provisions of section 11. As I argued above, in extreme cases—where the withholding of information might lead to death, serious injury or the escape of a terrorist offender—I believe that this can be justified; but it is vital that it is not used in a routine manner. **I recommend that the police throughout the United Kingdom be advised by circular that section 11 should be used only where they suspect that information is being withheld which could if revealed prevent acts of terrorism or lead to the apprehension of terrorist offenders.'**

The circular issued in consequence (9 August, 1983) went further:

'A relative of a terrorist who is not involved in terrorism himself should not be put under strain by being reminded in a routine manner of the provisions of section 11. The use of section 11 can only be justified in extreme cases—where the withholding of information might lead to death, serious injury, or the escape of a terrorist offender' (Baker Report (see above, p. 283 n. 2.) p. 73).

Secondly, reasonable suspicion of an offence under s. 11 should no longer be a sufficient ground for an arrest under s. 12 of the 1984 Act (see now ss. 14(1)(a) of the 1989 Act). Thirdly, it should be made clear that s. 11 could not be used to put pressure on people to make self-incriminating statements (following *HM Advocate v Von* 1979 SLT (Notes) 62) (see now s. 18(1)(a), which includes the words 'any other person').

Lord Colville (*Colville Review (PTA)* (1987), Chap. 15) recommended that the offence should be repealed, arguing that there is nothing special about withholding information about terrorism, and noting (inter alia) that the offence is hardly used, is in practice not used in Scotland in view of doubts about the admissibility of evidence so obtained and enables pressure to be brought by the police. This recommendation was rejected by the government. See further, *Walker*, pp. 98–112.

It is necessary for the prosecution to establish, for a conviction under s. 18(1)(b), that an actual terrorist offence was committed (*Re Reference under Section 15 of the Criminal Appeal (Northern Ireland) Act 1980* (Unreported, 2 September 1993, CA (Cr D) (NI)).

7. *Arrest and detention.*

(i) To the end of 1982, 5,555 people were detained in Great Britain: exclusion orders were made against 261 (nearly 5 per cent) and 394 (about 7 per cent) were charged with a criminal offence; the equivalent figures for Northern Ireland (to 30 September) were 1,975, 24 (all exclusions whether or not following arrest under s. 12) and 847 (about 40 per cent) (Jellicoe Report, Annex D, Tables 1, 10 and 11). Lord Jellicoe came 'to the firm conclusion that if the power of extended detention were abolished, the police both in Northern Ireland and on the mainland would be seriously handicapped in dealing with terrorists' (p. 22). He continued:

'66. In evidence to this review, witnesses critical of the power of extended detention have deployed a number of arguments, amounting to a claim that the power is abused or is open to abuse. Some have suggested, on the basis of statistical or anecdotal evidence, that the power is used in many if not most cases with no prospect of a criminal charge resulting. Witnesses have given as evidence for this the alleged fact that questioning has focussed more on the arrested person's political beliefs and activities than on possible terrorist involvement. There have been claims that many arrested people have simply been held in custody for seven days without any attempt to question them at all, suggesting the use of the power as a form of preventive detention; and that it has been used for low-level intelligence gathering, with detention for up to seven days (rather than any physical maltreatment) employed as a means of putting pressure on arrested persons to provide information about their associates. Finally, critics of the power as applied on the mainland have claimed that it has been used largely as a means of harassing the Irish population resident in Great Britain.

67. It would be wrong to suggest that abuses of the power have never occurred. But I am satisfied on the basis of wide consultation, examination of individual cases, and the statistical evidence set out in the previous chapter that in the great majority of cases arrests are made and extensions of detention sought under section 12 because the police believe this to be necessary to prevent terrorist acts or to bring to justice those responsible for their commission. . . . Clearly, extended detention should not be used for the purpose of gleaning minor information. But good intelligence can save lives, and if sensitive use of this power, under careful supervision, can aid the collection of such information from individuals who are themselves involved in terrorism, I see no objection to this.'

Nevertheless, the police should be reminded that the power of arrest under s. 12 'should be exercised only where the use of no other power is appropriate to the end sought' (p. 23); 'wherever possible, applications for extended detention should specify the period required (which in many cases ought to be less than five days) and justify this by reference to the results anticipated' (p. 25); 'where circumstances permit, all applications should be seen and approved by the appropriate secretary of state personally, and not by a junior minister alone' (ibid.); and a full five day extension should only be granted 'when he is satisfied that this, rather than a lesser period, is necessary' (ibid.). It would not, however, be appropriate for extensions to be granted by a court rather than a Minister (pp. 24–25) (cf. PACE, s. 43, above, p. 124).

Between 1984 and the end of 1994, 1,651 people were detained in Great Britain in connection with Northern Irish terrorism, leading to 84 exclusion orders, 252 persons charged with an offence, and 1,315 (80 per cent) persons not excluded or charged. Comparative figures for those detained in Great Britain in connection with international terrorism between 1984 and 1994 were 331 detained, 56 deported, excluded or removed, 49 charged and 226 (68 per cent) persons not deported etc. or charged. By contrast, in Northern Ireland, 1,509 persons were detained, with 336 charged, in 1994 alone. (Home Office Statistical Bulletin 2/95, *Statistics on the Operation of the Prevention of Terrorism Legislation—1994*; John Rowe's Annual Report for 1994, Table 1.) In Northern Ireland, s. 14 is now the major terrorist arrest power following the repeal of s. 11 of the Northern Ireland (Emergency Provisions) Act 1978 (above, p. 290).

Lord Colville reported that the arrest power under s. 12 of the 1984 Act (now s. 14 of the 1989 Act) was justified as it enabled the police to arrest on reasonable suspicion 'at the preparatory stage of the commission of offences of violence'; reliance on ordinary powers to arrest for an attempt would be 'leaving things rather late' and proving conspiracy 'will often be more difficult than proving an attempt' and was surrounded by jurisdictional and other difficulties (*Colville Review (PTA)* (1987), Chap. 4). There were still good reasons for permitting a period of detention of up to seven days (ibid, Chap. 5).

The powers providing for extended detention without the authority of a judicial officer have been held by the European Court of Human Rights to be contrary to the ECHR (*Brogan v United Kingdom* (1988) 11 EHRR 117, below, p. 775). The government's response has been for the UK to derogate from the relevant provisions of the ECHR and the International Convenant on Civil and Political Rights: see pp. 777, 852. This move has been criticised by the SACHR, who argue that the initial period of detention should be limited to 48 hours, with extensions for further periods up to 120 hours in all permitted on application to a magistrates' court (17th Report, 1991–92 HC 54, p. 217). Alternatively, the establishment of a special tribunal could be considered (18th Report, 1992–93, HC 739, p. 17). Extended detention can be authorised by a junior minister: *R v Harper* [1990] 4 NIJB 75.

A recent change has been the introduction of periodic reviews of detention under Sch. 3 to the 1989 Act, modelled on the provisions of PACE (ss. 40–44, above, p. 121). A detention must be reviewed as soon as practicable after the beginning of the detention and subsequently at interviews of not more than 12 hours (Sch. 3, para. 1). However, in contrast with the PACE provisions, all reviews are conducted by police officers, albeit senior officers not directly involved with the case; there is no requirement for authorisation by magistrates or another judicial officer at the later stages of detention. Moreover, even if the review officer refuses to authorise an

extension of detention, an extension may still be granted by the Secretary of State
(Sch. 3, para. 3(1)(b)). 'On close examination . . . the new review system appears
inadequate' (B. Dickson, (1989) 40 NILQ 250, 257).

(ii) The s. 14 arrest power (then s. 12 of the 1976 Act) was considered by the
Northern Ireland Court of Appeal in *Ex p Lynch* [1980] NI 126 (see W. Finnie,
(1982) 45 MLR 215). The court held first, that the arresting officer complied with
the requirements of *Christie v Leachinsky* (above, p. 109) by telling L that he was
arresting him under s. 12 as he suspected him of being involved in terrorism:

'an arrest [under s. 12] is not necessarily . . . the first step in a criminal proceedings against a suspected
person on a charge which was intended to be judicially investigated. Rather it is usually the first step in
the investigation of the suspected person's involvement in terrorism' (per Lord Lowry LCJ at p. 131).

Secondly, the court held that

'we can find nothing in section 11 of the [Northern Ireland (Emergency Provisions) Act 1978: see above,
p. 290] or section 12 of the 1976 Act to place a fetter on the right of arrest first under one Act and then under
the other, or indeed twice in quick succession under the same provision. . . .' (per Lord Lowry LCJ at p. 133)

This holding is cogently criticised by C. P. Walker, 'Arrest and Rearrest' (1984) 35
NILQ 1. Sir George Baker (Report, p. 87) commented:

'I am assured that it is not RUC practice initially to arrest under section 11 and then at the end of 72
hours to re-arrest under section 12, so I cannot recommend a specific prohibition against so doing. Fresh
evidence would in any event justify a further arrest. I suggest however that the arrest provisions in the
new Act should be so drawn as to avoid this suggested danger.'

As to the first point, in *Fox, Campbell and Hartley v United Kingdom* (1990) 13
EHRR 157, the European Court held that the use of this formula (in respect of an
arrest under s. 11 of the Northern Ireland (Emergency Provisions) Act 1978, since
repealed (see p. 290)) was not sufficient to comply with Article 5(2) of the ECHR
(below, p. 740). However, it was not necessary for compliance that the required
information be supplied on arrest; here, the information had been provided during
interrogation, and in the present context 'intervals of a few hours [between arrest
and interrogation] cannot be regarded as falling outside the constraints of time
imposed by the notion of promptness in Article 5(2)' (p. 171). Then in *Oscar v Chief
Constable of the Royal Ulster Constabulary* [1992] 9 NIJB 27 the Northern Ireland
Court of Appeal held it sufficient for an arrest under what is now s. 14(1) for the
arresting officer to say:

'I arrest you under section 12(1)(*b*) of the Prevention of Terrorism (Temporary Provisions) Act 1984 as I
have reasonable grounds for suspecting you have been concerned in the commission, preparation or
investigation of acts of terrorism.'

The arrest

'was not unlawful because the constable failed to tell him of the nature of the terrorist acts which he was
suspected to have committed'

(per Hutton LCJ at 54).

(iii) The principle of *McKee v Chief Constable of the RUC* (above, p. 292) that bona
fide acceptance of instructions from a superior officer may amount to reasonable suspicion, has been applied in subsequent cases involving arrests under the Prevention of
Terrorism legislation. See *Clinton v Chief Constable of the Royal Ulster Constabulary*
[1991] 2 NIJB 53, QBD (NI); *Brady v Chief Constable of the Royal Ulster Constabulary*
[1991] 2 NIJB 22, QBD (NI) (see 'A Barrister', (1992) 43 NILQ 66); *Oscar v Chief
Constable of the RUC* [1992] 9 NIJB 27, CA (NI); *O'Hara v Chief Constable of the
RUC* (6 May 1994, unreported, CA (NI)). The outcome in *O'Hara* was that:

'the information given at the briefing to the arresting officer was admissible and although [in the words of the trial judge] "scanty", it was sufficient to constitute the required state of mind of an arresting officer under s. 12(1)(b) of the [1984 Act]'

(per Kelly LJ). The arresting officer was simply briefed that O'Hara had been 'involved in' a particular murder.

(iv) The restriction on the scope of the powers that is now found in s. 14(2) was introduced by the 1984 Act, s. 12(2). The power under s. 12 of the 1976 Act had been used in respect of Scottish nationalist extremists (see *Colville Review (PTA)*, Chap. 7). Lord Colville recommended against removing the restriction: were this done

'it could be perceived that Parliament had deliberately judged there to be an indigenous terrorism problem in Great Britain with no international nor Irish flavour. . . . There might then be apprehension that the police were being given extra and controversial powers over a range of domestic political activities which warrant no such thing' (ibid., p. 21).

8. *Conditions in detention*
(i) *Treatment in detention in Northern Ireland.* In *Ireland v UK* (below, p. 749), the European Court of Human Rights found that the adoption of the 'five techniques' in the operation of the policy of internment and detention in 1971 constituted inhuman treatment. The use of these techniques was officially abandoned following the Parker Report (Cmnd. 4901). Allegations of ill-treatment in the period following that considered by the European Court were substantiated: see the *Report of an Amnesty International Mission to Northern Ireland* (1978), the Bennett Report, (Cmnd. 7497, 1979) and P. Taylor, *Beating the Terrorists?* (1980). The Bennett Committee's examination of medical evidence revealed 'cases in which injuries, whatever their precise cause, were not self-inflicted and were sustained in police custody' (Bennett Report, p. 136). The Committee made a number of suggestions for improving the supervision of interrogations and the police complaints procedures. For example, interviews should not last longer than the interval between normal meal times or extend over meal breaks or continue after midnight except for urgent operational reasons; not more than two officers at a time or six in all should interview a prisoner; prisoners should be seen by a medical officer at least every 24 hours; interrogation rooms should be covered by closed circuit television and monitored by uniformed, supervisory officers; a training programme should be introduced for interrogators, and a code of conduct incorporated into the RUC Code. In addition, prisoners should be given an unconditional right of access to a solicitor after 48 hours and every 48 hours thereafter, although the solicitor should not be permitted to be present at interviews.

These recommendations were mostly accepted, and implemented by changes to the RUC Code (see Lord Jellicoe's *Review of the Operation of the Prevention of Terrorism (Temporary Provisions) Act 1976* (Cmnd. 8803) pp. 29–35, 39–44).

Following the implementation of the Bennett recommendations, the number of allegations of physical abuse declined significantly. Lord Jellicoe reported that the Bennett recommendations had 'on the whole . . . been implemented fully and fairly. . . . Even witnesses in other respects strongly critical both of the continued existence of the emergency legislation and of its application assured me that well-founded allegations of mistreatment during interview were now rare and justified complaints of physical assault virtually non-existent' (Report, pp. 30, 31). Nevertheless, there have been persistent allegations of verbal abuse and the application of pressure on suspects to act as informers (see Walsh, *The Use and Abuse of Emergency Legislation in Northern Ireland* (1983), pp. 54–78; *Hogan and Walker*, p. 118), and, indeed, continuing allegations of assaults against persons in detention at the 'holding centres' (Castlereagh and Gough Barracks, Londonderry) where most terrorist suspects are taken when arrested. In the period 1990–93 there were over 1,000 allegations of assault by persons detained in the holding centres, although none were substantiated, the proof required being 'beyond reasonable doubt' (B. Dickson, (1994) 45 NILQ 210, 216). Moreover, in the 1989–92 period, the Police Authority settled 18 civil claims in which one factor in the calculation of damages was an allegation of assault in a holding centre (ibid.). In *R v Nash* (Unreported, December 1992, Cr Ct) the trial judge, Hutton LCJ, excluded N's confession under s. 11 of the Northern Ireland (Emergency Provisions) Act 1991 on the ground that it was not proved beyond reasonable doubt that an assault had not been committed on him. Evidence was given that the officers with responsibility for watching CCTV monitors spent up to 20 minutes patrolling the corridors rather than watching the screens. In July 1993, the European Committee for the Prevention of Torture and Inhuman or Degrading Treatment or Punishment visited Northern Ireland and was told by both medical staff and senior paramilitaries 'that instances of physical ill-treatment had sharply decreased in recent times'. However, many allegations were made of various forms of psychological ill-treatment and this gave rise to 'legitimate concern' (Report to the UK Government, CPT/Inf(94)17). The government responded that there had been no specific complaints of psychological ill-treatment since 1 January 1993 and that all complaints were fully investigated (Response, CPT/Inf (94) 18, pp. 8–9).

Steps taken to improve the regulation of detention at the holding centres include the introduction of the Code of Practice under s. 61 of the Northern Ireland (Emergency Provisions) Act 1991 (above, p. 282), and the appointment under the royal prerogative of an Independent Commissioner for the Holding Centres. His terms of reference state that his principal purpose is

'to provide further assurance to the Secretary of State that persons detained in Holding Centres are fairly treated and that both statutory and administrative safeguards are being properly applied'

(Second Annual (1994) Report, Annex). He (and his deputy) make irregular visits to the centres, normally without prior notice, inspect records and interview detainees (with their consent). The first appointee is Sir Louis Blom-Cooper QC. His deputy is a consultant psychiatrist. His first annual report to the Secretary of State for Northern Ireland covered 1993 and was published in March 1994. He reported:

'I have found absolutely nothing that might give anyone the slightest cause for concern about the care and treatment of detainees held in the custody of uniformed officers of the RUC' (p. 118).

The few complaints that were received related either to incidents on arrest, on the journey to the holding centre or during interviews by detectives. As regards the last of these,

'in 1994 public confidence can only be secured only if there is in place a form of surveillance over and a method of accountability for the conduct of non-uniformed police officers conducting interrogations in the interview rooms of the Holding Centres' (p. 120).

Steps that have been recommended but (to date) rejected include the video-recording of the silent CCTV signal from interrogation rooms (supported by Lord Colville (e.g. *Colville Review (EPA)*, pp. 15–16); the SACHR (e.g. 18th Report, 1992–93 HC 739, pp. 20–21); and John Rowe QC (1993 Report on the EPA, pp. 35–36). These advisers also expressed the view that audio-taping of interrogations should be introduced; Sir Louis Blom-Cooper (1993 Report, pp. 109–117; 1994 Report, pp. 36–38) and the SACHR (op. cit.) also favour trials for full video-recording. The RUC argument against recording has been that good quality information would become scarce because of the risk that a terrorist organisation would obtain access to the transcript or tape. John Rowe's answer was that:

'it may be possible, even under the present system of interviewing, for the organisation to ascertain what has been said in interview'

(1993 Report on the EPA, p. 35; cf. the *Rowe Review (EPA)*, p. 37).

Once it has been decided to charge a person he is normally taken to a designated police station; at the moment of charge they apparently become PACE prisoners even though the PACE Code of Practice explicitly states in its opening sub-paragraph that the Code does not apply to persons arrested or detained under the PTA (B. Dickson and N. O'Loan, (1994) 45 NILQ 210, 217). Designated police stations (but not the holding centres) are subject to periodic unannounced visits by lay visitors (see Dickson and O'Loan, op. cit.).

(ii) *Access to legal advice in Northern Ireland.* A legal right of access is now conferred by s. 45 of the Northern Ireland (Emergency Provisions) Act 1991 (above, p. 279). Statements given some 24 hours beyond the legal 48 hour deferral period permitted by s. 45(6) were excluded by Judge Russell in *R v Gilgunn* (10 October 1991, unreported, Cr Ct) and by Pringle J in *R v Lynch* (19 October 1993, unreported, Cr Ct, discussed in the SACHR 19th Report, 1993–94 HC 495, p. 11).

Breach of the right of access to a solicitor does not give rise to an action for damages for breach of statutory duty (*Cullen v Chief Constable of the Royal Ulster Constabulary* (6 May 1994, unreported, Crown Court, McDermott LJ). However, the decision to delay access to a lawyer is subject to judicial review: see *Re McKenna's Application* [1992] NIJB (QBD (NI)); *Re Duffy's Application* (20 September 1991, unreported, QBD (NI)) (authorisation quashed); *Re Application by Maher and others* (25 March 1992, unreported, QBD (NI)) (authorisation upheld the *bona fides* of the solicitor were not challenged, but the police were found to have had reasonable grounds for believing that INLA would force him to reveal information).

Restrictions that do not apply in ordinary cases are that consultations with a lawyer take place in the hearing of an officer and that lawyers are not present during interrogations. The SACHR regard the former limitation as contrary to international standards (17th Report, 1991–92 HC 54, pp. 218–219) and has expressed concern on the latter (18th Report, 1992–93 HC 739, p. 24), noting that these restrictions do not apply to interrogations of terrorist suspects in Great Britain (the power to require consultations to be in the sight and hearing of an officer is very seldom used: in 2% of 384 consultations in the study by D. Brown, *Detention under the Prevention of Terrorism (Temporary Provisions) Act 1989: Access to Legal Advice and Outside Contact*, HORPU Paper 75, 1992).

Sir Louis Blom-Cooper found that the legal advice service currently available to detainees was 'less than adequate' and proposed that the Law Society of Northern Ireland should establish a full-time legal advice unit at the holding centres, funded by the Northern Ireland Office, negating the need to defer access (1993 Report, Chap. IX). This was supported by the SACHR (19th Report, p. 11), but rejected by the Law Society. Sir Louis subsequently submitted a modified proposal (*Delayed Choice or Instant Access? Legal Advice for Detainees in Holding Centres: Report to the Secretary of State for Northern Ireland, November 1994*).

(iii) *PTA detention in England and Wales.* Detention under the PTA in England and Wales is regulated by the PACE regime, albeit with modifications (see PACE, Part V and Code C; above, pp. 130–146). A two-year experiment with audio-taping of interviews began on 1 December 1992 (see Home Office Circular 108/1992). Research on PTA detentions in England and Wales (D. Brown, *Detention under the Prevention of Terrorism (Temporary Provisions) Act 1989: Access to Legal Advice and Outside Contact* (HORPU Paper 75, 1993) showed that the exercise of rights to legal advice and to have someone notified of their detention were delayed in a far higher proportion of PTA than ordinary PACE detentions (26%, 44% of the sample), and a far higher percentage (40%) are held for more than 24 hours. The report also noted shortcomings in record-keeping. However, nearly 40% of detainees successfully obtained legal advice (a far higher proportion than for PACE prisoners) and

'scrupulous attention to the detainee's physical well-being through regular medical examination and reviews by senior officers was also common, particularly where detention was lengthy' (p. 56).

For frequently critical views and experiences of conditions in PTA detention, see P. Hillyard, *Suspect Community* (1993), Chap. 7.

9. *Financial assistance for terrorism.* Sections 9 to 13A of the 1989 Act extend the law dealing with terrorist funds. Section 9 (contributions towards acts of terrorism) re-enacted s. 10 of the 1984 Act, extended to acts of international terrorism; s. 10 (contributions to resources of proscribed organisations) extends to organisations proscribed under the Northern Ireland (Emergency Provisions) Act 1991 (above p. 277) as well as those proscribed under the 1989 Act, as do provisions of ss. 11 and 13. Section 11 (assisting in retention or control of terrorist funds) was a new offence. Section 12 enables, for example, a bank to disclose a suspicion to the police that money is derived from terrorist funds, notwithstanding any statutory or other[1] restriction on disclosure. Section 13 provides for the forfeiture on conviction of money or property related to offences under ss. 9, 10 and 11. The provisions were modelled on the Drug Trafficking Offences Act 1986, but relaxed in favour of the prosecution in a number of respects, for example in placing the onus of proof of certain defences on the accused. (For criticism, see D. Bonner [1989] PL 440, 457–464 and D. Wheatley, (1989) 139 NLJ 499.) Bonner notes that

'Sensitive use of the Attorney-General's role in sanctioning prosecutions will be necessary if these offences are not to prove oppressive in penalising those merely indulging in the normal social and economic intercourse of certain areas or by doubly penalising the unfortunate victim of intimidation' (p. 460).

Sections 9 to 13 were amended by the Criminal Justice Act 1993, s. 49. The 1993 Act modified the distinct confiscation régimes under the Drug Trafficking Offences Act 1986 (now the Drug Trafficking Act 1994), the Criminal Justice Act 1988 (confiscation of the proceeds of crime) and the Northern Ireland (Emergency Powers) Act 1991 (confiscation of the proceeds of terrorist related activities).

10. *Travel controls.* Section 16 and Sch. 5 set out the system of travel controls previously found in subordinate legislation (see D. Bonner, [1989] PL 440, 443–447). Examining officers have power to examine any person on arrival or departure from Great Britain or Northern Ireland by ship or aircraft, or travelling by land between Northern Ireland and the Republic, to determine whether he appears to be a person who is or has been concerned in the commission, preparation or instigation of acts of terrorism, or subject to an exclusion order, or whether there are grounds to suspect that he has committed an offence under s. 8 of the Act. There need be no prior suspicion. Examination may last for up to 24 hours, although only beyond 12

1 Extended from contractual restrictions by the Criminal Justice Act 1993, s. 49.

hours if there are reasonable grounds to suspect involvement in terrorism. The person may, however, be formally detained for up to 48 hours pending conclusion of the examination, or consideration by the Secretary of State whether to make an exclusion order, or by the DPP, Attorney-General, Lord Advocate, or Attorney-General or DPP for Northern Ireland whether to institute criminal proceedings. The period may be extended by the Secretary of State up to a total of 5 days on the pattern of detention under s. 14. Examination without detention beyond 12 hours, and detention itself, under Sch. 5 is subject to the review arrangements under Sch. 3. Examining officers also have powers to require the production of information, to search, and to require the completion of landing embarkation cards.

In *McVeigh v UK* (1983) 5 EHRR 71, the applicants had been arrested under s. 13 of the 1976 Act (now s. 16 and Sch. 5 of the 1989 Act) upon their arrival at Liverpool from Ireland. They were detained for 45 hours, during which time they were questioned, searched, fingerprinted and photographed, the fingerprints and photographs being retained. The Committee of Ministers, agreeing with the opinion of the European Commission on Human Rights, held that Articles 5(1)(*b*) and 8, ECHR had not been infringed on these facts in the emergency situation that existed. It held, however, that the right to respect for family life in Article 8, ECHR had been infringed insofar as two of the applicants had been refused permission to contact their wives (one a common law wife) during the 45 hours to alert them of their detention. See C. Warbrick, (1983) 32 ICLQ 757.

11. *Terrorist investigations.* Section 17 and Sch. 7 introduced new powers in connection with the investigation of terrorism, modelled on the Drug Trafficking Offences Act 1986, ss. 27–33. Investigations may be into the commission, preparation or investigation of acts of terrorism to which s. 14 of the 1989 Act applies; any other act which appears to have been done in furtherance of or in connection with such acts of terrorism; the resources of a proscribed organisation; and investigations into whether there are grounds for proscribing an organisation (s. 17(1)). The disclosure of information likely to prejudice an investigation or proposed investigation and the falsification, concealment or destruction of relevant material are offences (s. 17(2)–(4A), as amended by the Criminal Justice Act 1993, s. 50). Sch. 7, para. 2, enables a justice of the peace to issue warrants authorising the police to search for evidence (other than excluded or special procedure material or material subject to legal privilege) in the course of a 'terrorist investigation'. Sch. 7, para. 3 (as amended by the Criminal Justice and Public Order Act 1994, s. 83(1)) enables a circuit judge (or county court judge in Northern Ireland) to order the production of, or grant a warrant authorising the police to search for excluded or special procedure material, analogous to s. 9 of and Sch. 1 to PACE (above, pp. 85, 91). Applications are made ex parte but there may be an inter partes hearing of an application to discharge or vary an order (see *R v Crown Court at Middlesex Guildhall, ex p Salinger* [1993] 2 All ER 310, where the Divisional Court gave guidance as to the procedure to be adopted, stating that the nature of the information on which the application is based, but not the nature and identity of its source, should normally be disclosed). Disobedience to a production order is a contempt: see *DPP v Channel 4 Television Co Ltd.*, below, p. 440. In urgent cases, a police officer of at least the rank of superintendent may by a written order give to any constable the authority which may be given by a search warrant (the superintendent must 'have reasonable grounds for believing that the case is one of great emergency and that in the interests of the State immediate action is necessary': Sch. 7, para. 7(1)). A 'Secretary of State's production order' may be made in relation to a terrorist investigation concerning any act which appears to the Secretary of State to constitute an offence under Part III of the Act (Sch. 7, para. 8). Unlike the PACE and Drug Trafficking Offences Act powers, there need not be a suspicion of specific criminal offences; indeed, the powers are 'designed to apply much earlier than an arrest' (D. Bonner, [1989] PL 440, 465, citing Standing Committee B, cols. 472–473). See generally, Bonner, op. cit., pp. 464–473.

12. Part IV of the 1984 Act (arrest, detention and port powers) extended to international terrorism (see s. 12(3)). Further provisions in the 1989 Act have similarly been extended. The Home Office has advised the police that:

'In the case of acts of international terrorism committed outside the United Kingdom, the powers should be used only when it appears that there is some prospect of a charge before United Kingdom courts or of the person concerned being deported. That is to say that the powers should not be used unless either deportation is in prospect or it is thought that the involvement of the person concerned in such acts constitutes an offence under United Kingdom law. This restriction is likely to mean that although the powers may be freely used in connection with acts of international terrorism committed in the United Kingdom, their use will rarely be justified in connection with acts of international terrorism committed ouside the United Kingdom'

(449 HL Deb 15 March 1984 col 867).

Note that hijacking and other acts of damaging or endangering the safety of aircraft are made offences by the Aviation Security Act 1982, Part I, and that hostage-taking is made an offence by the Taking of Hostages Act 1982, s. 1. The Aviation and Maritime Security Act 1990 extended powers in relation to aviation security (Part I), and introduced provisions in respect of terrorism against ships and fixed platforms (Part II) and ship and harbour security (Part III). See the extensive annotations on the 1990 Act by N. Gaskell, *Current Law Statutes Annotated 1990* and, more generally, *Walker*, pp. 273–278.

13. The 1984 Act was subject to annual renewal, and expired after five years (s. 17). The present Act is not expressly limited in overall duration, but is subject to annual renewal (s. 27). The government has undertaken that unless in any particular circumstances there are overriding reasons against doing so, each renewal order will be laid in ample time for Parliament to debate it: the government will accordingly have time to substitute a revised order if so persuaded by Parliament. Moreover there will be a report on the general operation of the Act by an independent person (currently John Rowe QC: see above, p. 307) in good time before the debate (448 HL Deb 23 February 1984 cols 945–946 and 449 HL Deb 8 March 1984 cols 405–406 (Lord Elton)).

CHAPTER 5

Freedom of expression: censorship and obscenity

This chapter, and the ones which immediately follow, have as a unifying theme the issue of 'freedom of expression'. This freedom is commonly considered to be of fundamental importance in Western-style democracies.[1] The First Amendment to the US Constitution includes the slogan 'Congress shall make no law . . . abridging the freedom of speech, or of the press'; Art. 19(2) of the International Convenant on Civil and Political Rights provides that 'everyone shall have the right to freedom of expression: this right shall include freedom to seek, receive and impart information and ideas of all kinds, regardless of frontiers, either orally, in writing or in print, in the form of art, or through any other media of his choice'; and Art. 10 of the European Convention on Human Rights proclaims 'Everyone has the right to freedom of expression. This right shall include freedom to hold opinions and to receive and impart information and ideas without interference by public authority.'[2]

The philosophical underpinnings of this freedom have been much discussed.[3] Desire to protect freedom of speech is to an extent simply an aspect of the more general ideal that individual freedom of behaviour be protected: that incursions on an individual's liberty should be permitted only in situations where this is necessary to prevent harm to another, or where one person's liberty must be curtailed in order to preserve the liberty of others.

However, in addition to this general reason for seeking to protect liberty of expression, other more specific justifications may be offered. Some have pointed to the importance of freedom of expression in terms of the 'fulfilment' and 'development' of the individual in society, by means of the exposure of individuals to a free and wide-ranging flow of information, experience, ideas and opinions. Such exposure should at one and the same time both provide a stimulus to individual personality development, and also act as a safeguard against an unduly restricted diet of 'information' and 'opinion' fed from official sources. It follows that there is a need, in a society which places a high value on the individual, for there to be freedom of

1 In August 1994 the French Constitutional Council held that certain recently enacted laws, designed to purge English words and phrases from the French language, were invalid as contrary to the freedom of expression guarantees of the Declaration of the Rights of Man of 1789, protected under the French Constitution. The law had purported to outlaw the use of 'unapproved' foreign words on television, on radio, and in the press. The law was upheld, however, to the extent that it applied to the language which the state required to be used by its own officials in the performance of their duties.
2 Note also two recent decisions of the High Court of Australia in which some of the judgments countenance the notion of 'implied' rights to freedom of expression within the Australian Constitution: such rights being implicit in the Constitution's fundamental principles of governmental accountability and representative government. See *Australian Capital Television Pty Ltd v The Commonwealth* (1992) 66 AJLR 695, and *Nationwide News Pty Ltd v Wills* (1992) 66 AJLR 658: and comment by Justice M. D. Kirby (1992) ALJ 775.
3 See, for excellent surveys, E. Barendt, *Freedom of Speech* (Oxford, 1985) Chap. 1; G. Marshall, [1992] Pub. Law 40.

artistic, literary and political expression. An adjunct to this is that the operation of democracy requires that there should be both open and informed discussion of issues of contemporary significance. Well known are the words of Mr Justice Brandeis of the US Supreme Court in *Whitney v California* (274 US 357 (1927)), speaking of those whose ideals had shaped the terms of the US Constitution. They

'believed that freedom to think as you will and to speak as you think are means indispensable to the discovery and spread of political truth: that without free speech and assembly, discussion would be futile: that with them, discussion affords ordinarily adequate protection against the dissemination of noxious doctrine: that the greatest menace to freedom is an inert people: that public discussion is a political duty; and that this should be a fundamental principle of the American government. . . .'

And in the still stronger words of Alexander Meiklejohn:

'when a question of policy is "before the house", free men choose it not with their eyes shut, but with their eyes open. To be afraid of ideas, any idea, is to be unfit for self-government' (Free Speech and its Relation to Self-Government (New York, 1948, p. 19)).

This is not, of course, to suggest that there should be no limits to this liberty: only that in assessing the limits which should be drawn it is well to remember what may be the reasons underlying this ideal. In the sections which follow in this chapter we shall look at liberty of expression in the theatre, the cinema, on video and in the broadcasting media, in the published media and in the world of art. There then follows a chapter which looks at the extent to which free expression may be restricted in the interests of the due administration of justice; and this in turn is followed by a chapter which addresses these issues in the context of the 'openness' or otherwise of governmental information and activity.

1 Theatre censorship

Theatres Act 1968

1. Abolition of censorship of the theatre
(1) The Theatres Act 1843 is hereby repealed; and none of the powers which were exercisable thereunder by the Lord Chamberlain of Her Majesty's Household shall be exercisable by or on behalf of Her Majesty by virtue of Her royal prerogative.
(2) In granting, renewing or transferring any licence under this Act for the use of any premises for the public performance of plays or in varying of the terms, conditions or restrictions on or subject to which any such licence is held, the licensing authority shall not have power to impose any term, condition or restriction as to the nature of the plays which may be performed under the licence or as to the manner of performing plays thereunder:
   Providing that nothing in this subsection shall prevent a licensing authority from imposing any term, condition or restriction which they consider necessary in the interests of physical safety or health or any condition regulating or prohibiting the giving of an exhibition, demonstration or performance of hypnotism within the meaning of the Hypnotism Act 1952.

NOTES

1. The Theatres Act 1968 ended official censorship of plays. Originating in legislation of 1737 (provoked by Sir Robert Walpole's sensitivity to his caricaturisation in plays), and extended in 1843 for the preservation of 'good manners' and 'decorum', the power of the Lord Chamberlain as regards the licensing of plays was, even in the years immediately preceding the 1968 Act, certainly no dead letter. Political characterisation, let alone satire, was closely controlled by the Lord Chamberlain, thus imposing significant restrictions on dramatic treatment of political issues of the day. Equally, the Lord Chamberlain firmly acted as guardian of the theatre-going public's 'decency'. A particularly strict line was taken as regards any allusions to homosexuality, with little or no regard taken to considerations of dramatic or other merit.

Although unpopular with dramatists and directors, commercial theatre managers quite favoured the Lord Chamberlain's activities. It was unlikely that any prosecution (e.g. for obscenity) would be brought in respect of the performance of any play in respect of which he had granted his approval. Managers could therefore feel confident that they would only be involved in the presentation of 'safe' plays unlikely to cause much controversy amongst audiences or the public at large. (Compare the establishment, by the film industry itself, of the British Board of Film Censors.) Writers and directors took a less sanguine view of the restrictions imposed by this licensing control, and, following a campaign mounted by the state-subsidised Royal Shakespeare Company, the matter was considered by a Parliamentary Joint Committee which reported in 1967. The Committee's recommendation that theatre censorship be abolished was implemented by the 1968 Act. It remains, however, the case that a theatrical performance may involve the commission of a criminal offence, although the opportunity was taken in the Theatres Act 1968 to modify legislation on obscenity and incitement to racial hatred as it applies to the theatre. See below, pp. 364–366.

The absence of 'official' censorship of the theatre does not, of course, mean that writers and directors may not encounter difficulties staging plays with controversial content. Commercial theatre managers may prefer to present pieces with more assured audience attraction, and even the subsidised theatre has from time to time been said to act with one eye on the attitude of its funding bodies.

2. For accounts of the Lord Chamberlain's exercise of his powers of censorship, see R. Findlater, *Banned! A Review of Theatrical Censorship in Britain* (1967); P. O'Higgins, *Censorship* (1972) pp. 95–99; G. Robertson, *Freedom, the Individual and the Law* (7th edn, 1993) pp. 238–241.

2 Film censorship

Cinemas Act 1985

Control of exhibitions

1. Licence required for exhibitions

(1) . . . no premises shall be used for a film exhibition unless they are licensed for the purpose under this section.

(2) A licensing authority may grant a licence under this section to such a person as they think fit to use any premises specified in the licence for the purpose of film exhibitions on such terms and conditions and subject to such restrictions as . . . they may determine.

(3) Without prejudice to the generality of subsection (2) above, it shall be the duty of a licensing authority, in granting a licence under this section as respects any premises,—

    (*a*) to impose conditions or restrictions prohibiting the admission of children to film exhibitions involving the showing of works designated, by the authority or by such other body as may be specified in the licence, as works unsuitable for children; and

    (*b*) to consider what (if any) conditions or restrictions should be imposed as to the admission of children to other film exhibitions involving the showing of works designated, by the authority or by such other body as may be specified in the licence, as works of such other description as may be so specified.

2. Consent required for exhibitions for children

(1) . . . no premises shall be used, except with the consent of the licensing authority, for a film exhibition organised wholly or mainly as an exhibition for children.

(2) . . . a licensing authority may, without prejudice to any conditions or restrictions imposed by them on the granting of a licence, impose special conditions or restrictions on the granting of a consent under this section.

NOTES

1. The Cinemas Act 1985 consolidates earlier legislation dating from 1909. By 'film exhibition' is meant any exhibition of moving pictures, but not the simultaneous reception and transmission of television programmes included in a programme service within the meaning of the Broadcasting Act 1990 (1985 Act, s. 21(1); 1990 Act, s. 201). The licensing authorities are, now, the London boroughs and the district councils elsewhere. A right of appeal against refusal, or against conditions imposed, lies to the Crown Court (s. 16). An appeal lies on behalf of 'any person aggrieved'. For modern judicial discussion of this phrase, see *Cook v Southend Borough Council* [1990] 2 WLR 61. Would (should) the following have standing to appeal against a restrictive local authority licensing decision: the distributors of a film; a local resident annoyed at being denied a local opportunity to view a film? For the scope of appellate review in the Crown Court, see *Sagnata Investments Ltd v Norwich Corporation* [1971] 2 QB 614.

2. In addition to the express obligation imposed on licensing authorities to exercise their functions so as to protect children (under 16), the Act authorises the Secretary of State to make regulations in respect of the 'safety', 'health' and 'welfare' of children attending film exhibitions.

3. Sections 5 and 6 exclude from licensing control certain film exhibitions to which the public are not admitted and which are not presented for private gain. This applies, in particular, to domestic presentations and to members-only, non-commercial, cinema clubs (e.g. non-profit-making film societies). However, since 1982, 'commercial' cinema clubs have been subject to these local authority licensing controls: see s. 20 – restrictive definition of 'private gain'.

4. In *R v Greater London Council, ex p Blackburn* [1976] 1 WLR 550, CA, Lord Denning MR said, at p. 553:

'. . . [The Cinematograph Act 1909] was passed in the early days and was concerned with safety in cinemas, not with censorship. . . . Although the Act was concerned with safety, nevertheless the courts two years later held that a county council could impose conditions which related to other matters so long as they were not unreasonable. So, in 1911, the courts held that a condition saying that premises should not be opened on Sundays was valid: see *LCC v Bermondsey Bioscope Co Ltd* [1911] 1 KB 445. Soon afterwards the county councils began to insert a condition that no film shown should be of a licentious or indecent character. Such a condition was accepted as valid, but it did not permit any censorship beforehand. Next the county councils tried to insert a power of censorship by delegating it to three justices. This was held to be invalid: see *R v Burnley JJ, ex p Longmore* [1916–17] All ER Rep 346. Once again they tried. They sought to hand over all power of censorship to the British Board of Film Censors, but this was held invalid because the county councils were not allowed to delegate their powers: see *Ellis v Dubowski* [1921] 3 KB 621. But in 1924 there was a breakthrough. The courts gave a decision which allowed censorship by the British Board of Film Censors provided that that body did not have the final say, but was subject to review by the county council itself: see *Mills v LCC* [1925] 1 KB 213. That decision has held the field since that time and must, I think, be accepted as good law. It was recognised as such by Parliament itself[1] when it made it compulsory for conditions to be imposed for the protection of children. Under that section the county council are under a duty to impose conditions so as to ensure

1 *Ed.* In the Cinematograph Act 1952.

that, if a film is designated as unsuitable for children, then children are not to be admitted to see it. Such designation is to be done 'by the licensing authority or such other body as may be specified in the licence'. In speaking of such other body Parliament no doubt had in mind the British Board of Film Censors. To that extent, therefore, the Board has Parliamentary approval. . . . The British Board of Film Censors . . . goes back for 60 years. There is a president, . . . who is responsible for broad policy. There is a secretary, . . . who makes executive decisions. There are . . . film examiners. . . . They put films into . . . categories, according to their suitability for various age groups. . . . They sometimes require cuts before giving a certificate. The examiners are recruited from outside the film industry. . . .

I do not think the county councils can delegate the whole of their responsibilities to the board . . . but they can treat the board as an advisory body whose views they can accept or reject, provided that the final decision – aye or nay – rests with the county council. If the exhibitor – or any member of the public – brings the film up before the county council, they ought themselves to review the decision of the British Board of Film Censors and exercise their own judgment on it. That is, I think, the right way to interpret *Mills v LCC*. When the Board issues a certificate permitting the exhibition of a film – and the county council take no objection – that is equivalent to a permission by the county council themselves. When the board refuses a certificate, the exhibitor can appeal to the county council. . . .

The upshot of it all is this. The county council are in law the body which has the power to censor films for exhibitions in cinemas, but in practice it is the board which carries out the censorship, subject to review by the county council.'

Most local authorities have adopted the model licensing conditions suggested by the Home Office, which include the following:

(1) no film, other than a current newsreel, shall be exhibited unless it has received a certificate of the British Board of Film Classification or is the subject of the licensing authority's permission;
(2) no young people shall be admitted to any exhibition of a film classified by the Board as unsuitable for them, unless with the local authority's permission;
(3) no film shall be exhibited if the licensing authority gives notice in writing prohibiting its exhibition on the ground that it 'would offend against good taste or decency or would be likely to encourage or incite to crime or to lead to disorder or to be offensive to public feeling';
(4) the nature of the certificate given to any film shall be indicated in any advertising for the film, at the cinema entrance (together with an explanation of its effect), and on the screen immediately before the film is shown;
(5) displays outside the cinema shall not depict any scene or incident not in the film as approved;
(6) no advertisement shall be displayed at the premises if the licensing authority gives notice in writing objecting to it on the same grounds as apply to the prohibition of films.

Cinema licences in London carry the following additional conditions:

'No film shall be exhibited at the premises—
(1) which is likely—
    (a) to encourage or to incite to crime; or
    (b) to lead to disorder; or
    (c) to stir up hatred against any section of the public in Great Britain on grounds of colour, race or ethnic or national origins, or sexual orientation or sex; or
    (d) to promote sexual humiliation or degradation of or violence towards women; or
(2) the effect of which is, if taken as a whole, such as to tend to deprave and corrupt persons who are likely to see it; or
(3) which contains a grossly indecent performance thereby outraging the standards of public indecency.'

5. The film industry established the British Board of Film Censors in 1912 as a response to the assertion, under the 1909 Act, of censorship powers by local authorities. The aim was to establish a body which would be independent of both central and local government and which might help to secure achievement of reasonably informed, and reasonably uniform, decision-making on this matter by councils across the country. Being a non-statutory body its powers (in relation to film) are only those of advice, but in the main, its objectives seem to have been achieved. Councils have been willing to accept the classification decisions of the BBFC in most cases, and film makers have gained familiarity with the criteria adopted by the BBFC in deciding whether or not to grant a certificate, and if so, what viewing classification to impose. Inevitably, not all film makers (as compared with film distributors) have been happy with this system of 'control'. As the present President of the BBFC, the Earl of Harewood, has explained, 'one man's safeguards are another's shackles'. Controversy has arisen, over the years, in connection with numerous films. In some cases councils have chosen to ban a film from being shown in their areas even though it was passed by the BBFC – e.g. *Straw Dogs*, *Clockwork Orange*, *Life of Brian*. In other cases councils have chosen to allow films to be shown despite the fact that the BBFC felt unable to grant a certificate – e.g. *More about the Language of Love*, *Texas Chain Saw Massacre* (both passed by the former Greater London Council). In truth, however, it appears that most councils have no wish to devote resources to the regular scrutiny of films and have been pleased to rely on the judgment of the BBFC – see D. Holbrook (1973) 123 NLJ 701 and correspondence at pp. 754, 775, 794, 833, and 915; and Report of the Williams Committee on Obscenity and Film Censorship (1979) Cmnd. 7772 p. 27.

A virtue of the BBFC system is that decisions are taken by persons who have actually seen the film in question; and where a film is controversial it is seen by two pairs of film examiners, as well as by a senior member of the BBFC staff before any decision is taken. Film examiners are drawn from outside the film industry, and comprise an equal number of men and woman. They comprise persons with a broad range of ages and backgrounds (including from the ethnic minority communities: note that many films and videos are in foreign languages, designed for Hindi and Cantonese audiences). The BBFC views around 400 films and 4,000 videos annually.

By contrast to these arrangements, there have been occasions where a local council has banned the showing of a feature film, basing its decision upon press reports of the film's nature and content alone. See, for example, G. Phelps, *Sight and Sound*, Vol. 42 No. 3 p. 138, discussing press reports about, and local authority decisions in respect of, *Last Tango in Paris*. In 1988 concern was expressed in the press about the allegedly blasphemous content of a film, *The Last Temptation of Christ* (directed by Martin Scorsese). The Board received some 1,870 letters and petitions about the film even prior to its arrival in the UK. On viewing the film the BBFC came to the conclusion that it was a 'reinterpretation' of Christ's life and passion rather than a scurrilous attack on the Christian religion! An '18' certificate was granted. The BBFC took the view that the film did not contravene the offence of blasphemy. This was, however, not sufficient to prevent the film being banned by a number of local authorities.

The functions of the BBFC (renamed the British Board of Film Classification) were significantly extended in 1985 by the Video Recordings Act 1984. See further, below, p. 332. In this connection the BBFC takes decisions which themselves have legal effect under the Act. As regards films it continues to have no more than the power of recommendation to local authorities as to the exercise of their functions.

The BBFC currently classifies films (and videos) in accordance with the following published guidelines:

U—Universal: suitable for all: contains no theme, action or dialogue that could be construed as disturbing, harmful or offensive.

Uc—Universal: particularly suitable for very young and pre-school children. Used for videos only – introduced in 1985 at the request of the video industry.

PG—Parental Guidance: general viewing but some scenes unsuitable for young children. May contain mild violence, occasional non-sexual nudity, bed scenes (without 'serious suggestion' of sexual activity, limited scatological language (but no sexual expletives), no drug use or condonation of immoral behaviour unless clearly mitigated by context (e.g. comedy), and no undue emphasis on weapons (e.g. flick knives).

12—Passed only for persons of 12 years and over. Implications of sex (within a relationship) permitted; stronger language, but only rarely a sexual expletive; more realistic violence but limits as regards length and intensity; no drug use. This category was introduced for films in 1989 to deal with the film *Batman*. It was extended to videos in 1994.

15—Passed only for persons of 15 years and over. May involve themes requiring a more mature understanding; full-frontal nudity in a non-sexual context; brief or 'impressionistic' sex; more extensive use of expletives; mildly graphic violence and/or horror (but 'limited gore'); soft drugs may be seen in use, but not so as to condone or normalise. In 1989 the 'Bond' film, *Licence to Kill*, was passed as '15' only after a number of cuts had been ordered. Earlier Bond films had all been classified PG and the distributors evidently had hoped to market the film at an audience including young teenagers. However, the BBFC regarded the film as much too violent for a '12' classification: the character of Bond had been altered from 'urbane intelligence man' to 'embittered vigilante seeking revenge'.

18—Passed only for persons of 18 years and over. Themes requiring an adult understanding (e.g. complex sexual relationships, controversial religious subjects); simulated sex (or, in some educational contexts, real sex); full nudity in a sexual context; unglamourised use of hard drugs; no censorship of sexual expletives (although 'pornographic descriptions' may be cut); graphic violence provided that it does not encourage sadistic pleasure nor glamourise weapons.

R18—Restricted 18. Passed only for restricted distribution through specially licensed cinemas or sex shops to which no one under 18 is admitted. For such licensing see n. **6**, below. Consenting, non-violent, sex may be depicted with a degree of explicitness limited only by the law (as to which, see below, pp. 349–372). No censorship of pornographic language, provided it does not encourage or incite to sexual crime.

If a film or video work is obscene within the meaning of the Obscene Publications Act or offends against other provisions of the criminal law in such manner that in the view of the BBFC no amount of cutting can make the work acceptable for national distribution, the work will be refused a certificate altogether. Since cinema licences permit the option of a local certificate, film companies are free to submit their product to any local authority if it is felt that a different view might be taken. There is a right of appeal against *video* classification decisions to the statutory Video Appeals Committee.

The majority of cuts ordered by the BBFC fall into the following categories:

(1) Sexual violence: the Board maintains a strict policy on material that attempts to glamourise rape or sexual assault. The Board considers that there is research evidence that sexual violence towards women does influence a significant minority of men: such images are therefore not permitted for purely entertainment purposes.

(2) Emphasis on the process of violence: scenes of torture or where violence is presented as prolonged enjoyment. The Board acknowledges that the relationship between media violence and society is a complex one: the media both mirror and feed into reality. According to the Board, 'few now believe that people simply copy what they see on screen or are influenced in a direct way. On the other hand there is certainly some effect, particularly over the long term and in specific areas.'

(3) Sexual explicitness: such as falls foul of the obscenity legislation.

(4) Glamourisation of weapons: a strong line is taken as regards weapons which are dangerous and are not already well known in Britain.

(5) Ill-treatment of animals or child actors: details of imitable, dangerous or criminal techniques; blasphemous images or dialogue.

Note, however, that although the BBFC has made known the 'guidelines' described above, it also asserts that it 'does not rely on a written set of guidelines but operates a system of precedent, so that every decision is taken in the light of previous ones. The Board's view is that context, treatment and the intention of the film-maker are as important as the actual images shown, so that a list of prohibitions is unhelpful. Virtually any theme can be accepted if the treatment is responsible, and the same images may be acceptable in one context but not in another.

In considering films (and videos) the BBFC is, as the above system of categories shows, primarily concerned to protect children. It by no means follows that a film which has received a particular classification for cinema release will receive the same video classification. Thus, for example, *Rambo III* was cut more extensively for video than for the cinema: principally limiting its glamourisation of weaponry – the Rambo knife and cross-bow. Note, however, a more recent tendency for distributors to agree cuts so as to achieve a teenage cinema audience, but to reinstate cuts, and accept an '18' video classification. In this way it may be that films known to be popular with young audiences at the cinema are viewed in rather different form (wittingly or unwittingly) by video audiences in the home. The Board has expressed concern over the very considerable differences between the cinema (12) version of the surfing thriller *Point Blank* and its video version (15). Likewise, *Kindergarten Cop.* *Lethal Weapon 2* received cuts to allow it a '15' classification for the cinema. When it came to consideration for video classification the Board took into account the desire of under 18 year olds to view the video – following recommendations from such young cinema-goers. This, together with the Board's general concern that under 18s may view videos rented by adults, led the Board to refuse to reinstate the two most violent scenes for the '18' video release. If the making of cuts to a film or video would permit it to be granted a certificate, or be granted a wider category classification, the BBFC indicates in some detail what is required. It will often offer a choice of classification depending on whether the maker wishes to make specified cuts: in this way any decision to cut merely in order to make a work available to a wider and younger audience is one taken, ultimately, by the distributor and not by the Board. The Board will consider alternative suggestions as to cuts. This may be felt desirable by makers for artistic reasons. In practice relatively few British films require cuts to be ordered. The makers are reasonably familiar with the attitudes of the BBFC. If requested the BBFC is willing to give a non-binding preliminary view as to certificate and classification on being submitted the script of a film prior to shooting.

If a film or video is considered to be obscene within the meaning of the Obscene Publications Acts (see further, below, pp. 349–363), or is considered to offend against some other aspect of the criminal law, a certificate will be refused altogether. In 1989 the BBFC refused a certificate to an 18 minute erotic video, *Visions of Ecstasy*, on grounds of blasphemy. Its nudity and sexual imagery were well within the normal bounds of an '18' classification. However, the sexual imagery focused on the crucified figure of Christ, and featured overt expressions of sexuality on the part of a nun. Having taken legal advice on the issue of blasphemy the BBFC denied a certificate, and the decision was upheld by the Video Appeals Committee (see below).

Where a film company is unable to obtain the decision it wishes from the BBFC it is at liberty to lobby individual local authorities with a view to them permitting the film to be shown, or for it to be shown to a wider audience than that which the BBFC has thought appropriate. In the case of video decisions there is a Video Appeals Committee to which decisions of the BBFC may be taken.

The BBFC has been willing in its Annual Reports, and elsewhere, to explain its approach to certain issues which it has to tackle. The Reports address matters of concern in an order which seems to reflect the Board's view of their seriousness: 'violence', 'sexual violence', 'weapons and imitable criminal or dangerous techniques', and 'horror' proving more problematic than depiction of 'sex and sexuality'.

As regards violence a distinction is drawn between acceptable 'stylised' violence – the thrill associated with the traditional kind of horror or adventure/thriller film – and depictions of realistic and brutal violence (especially towards women) in works of an exploitative nature. The Board seeks to take into consideration the frequency and intensity of violence, as well as the moral context in which it occurs.

In its 1990 Report the Board referred to violence as having become a major ingredient in Hollywood films of the 1980s and to Hollywood's continuing tendency to take violence to ever further extremes. Martial arts films from Hong Kong and the Far East also gave rise to concern. Certain violence cuts were required of *Robocop 2* in order to achieve an '18' classification (both film and video). Particularly sensitive decisions are necessary in respect of films and videos of a 'horror' variety intended for children. Small cuts were accepted by co-operative distributors of a film of Roald Dahl's, *The Witches* (PG). The Board conducted trial screenings before young audiences in order to assess whether any, and which, scenes might need to be cut.

Note that the Board has sought to acknowledge and recognise the legitimacy of violent films which also promote a proper moral message. For example, *Reservoir Dogs* and *Romper Stomper* were both described by the Board as 'moral tales about the break-down of morality'. Contrast the Board's view of the 'moral blankness' of *Henry – Portrait of a Serial Killer*. Notwithstanding excellent reviews, the Board felt it necessary to order cuts to the '18' video version: a judgment it reached following advice from a forensic psychiatrist about the effect of repeated video viewing on certain categories of viewer.

In recent years the problem of sexual violence, or sexualised violence, to women in films and videos appears to the Board to have declined. Nevertheless a careful watch is maintained, particularly for 'films that revel in cruelty and pain inflicted on helpless women to provide a sense of vicarious retribution for male anger at failed relationships, or no relationships at all'. 'That such scenes may prove cathartic to those who seek them out is insufficient justification, since the gratification they provide can easily validate and reinforce this hatred and taste for retribution' (Annual Report for 1989, p. 11). The Board's general policy is to order cuts of material which link 'pain, degradation or loss of volition to sexual pleasure' (1990 Report, p. 12).

The mere fact that material is sexually explicit is less likely to lead to denial of a certificate (though perhaps only in the R18 category), than is the nature of the sexual activity. Although changing attitudes in society have encouraged the Board to take a less strict view than formerly as regards less conventional forms of consensual sexual conduct, the Board has not relaxed its approach to the depiction of forcible sex. The Board seeks to take a firm line against the 'pornographic treatment of rape, bondage, flagellation, child sex, and other harmful or coercive forms of sexual exploitation' (Annual Report, 1985 para. 36). But context and treatment is important. The BBFC aims to act against material designed to reveal the 'pleasures of sadism' or which is objectionable in the way in which it may seek to eroticise rape. At the same time a number of the listed matters are important subjects which film-makers should not be required to ignore. Critical questions will include whether the depiction is such as to encourage imitation of the activity in question, whether it suggests toleration of the activity, whether the sexual violence is indulged in for its own sake, where seems to lie the sympathy of the film-maker, and whether the camerawork or editing belie an ostensibly moral stance taken by the film (Annual Report, 1985 para. 32 and p. xxxii).

The importance of context, both in the Board's own assessment of material and also its assessments of the ambit of the general law on obscenity, has resulted in a number of sex education videos being granted '18' classification. These date from the first *Lovers' Guide*, released in 1991. The 'educational context' has permitted leading stockists (e.g. W. H. Smith) to sell videos containing fleeting visual representations of sexual activity of a nature more explicit than generally permitted in '18R' classifications. In such educational videos the Board stresses the need for 'safer sex' practices to be emphasised.

Recent Annual Reports have noted the apparent failure of the R18 classification system. With substantially less than 100 retail outlets (see below, p. 331) the legitimate market for such films and videos is too small to be financially viable. Very few videos and practically no films are put forward for this category classification. Instead, products which would most naturally have fitted the R18 category are offered in substantially cut form to gain an '18' certificate: producing what may be regarded as the worst of all worlds. Rows of enticingly (albeit not indecently – see below, p. 371) labelled videos lie open to general public view, containing emasculated films, providing satisfaction to no one. In addition, the Board has noted the availability of hard-core pornography, going well beyond its own 18R limits, following the recent liberalisation of customs restrictions and checks at EC internal frontiers. Note also the ready availability of material via mail order from abroad, and the broadcasting into Britain of foreign television channels devoted to graphic depiction of sexual activity. See further, below, p. 345.

The effect of a work as regards imitation of the conduct depicted is a matter of concern for the Board. It has ordered cuts where techniques for the commission of crime are too closely depicted, where the taking of 'soft' drugs (e.g. cannabis and glue-sniffing) is depicted as a part of normal behaviour, and where martial arts films show actions such as neck chops and double ear-claps which may result in severe harm if imitated. Cuts were ordered to the children's film *Teenage Mutant Ninja Turtles* to remove all depiction of flails: this at a time when it appeared that such flails were re-emerging as a street weapon in some parts of London. The Board's policy on techniques such as double ear-claps was, it seems, vindicated when several children were taken to hospital with punctured ear drums following the depiction of such action during a television advertisement for Tango orange drink (Annual Report for 1992).

In 1989 the BBFC refused a certificate to *International Guerrillas*, a video which appeared to depict the author, Salman Rushdie, as a drunken murderer of muslims. The BBFC feared that the video might be blasphemous. The Appeals Committee rejected this view (see further on blasphemy, below, pp. 591–598). A second refusal by the Board was based upon the view that the video involved a *criminal* libel of Rushdie. This decision was also overturned by the Appeals Committee, following a plea against such censorship from Rushdie himself.

See further on film censorship, N. March Hunnings, *Film Censors and the Law* (1967) pp. 29–148; Williams Committee on Obscenity and Film Censorship (1979) Cmnd 7772 Appendix 2; J. Trevelyan, *What the Censor Saw* (1973) and 'Film Censorship and the Law' in R. Dhavan and C. Davies (eds.) *Censorship and Obscenity* (1978) pp. 98–108; G. Phelps, *Film Censorship* (1975); B. Brown, *Screen*, Vol. 23 No. 5 p. 2; E. Wistrich, *I Don't Mind the Sex it's the Violence* (1972); G. Robertson, *Freedom, the Individual and the Law* (7th edn, 1993, pp. 258–272); James C. Robertson, *The British Board of Film Censors: Film Censorship in Britain 1896–1950*, and *The Hidden Cinema: British Film Censorship in Action 1913–1972*; S. Brody, *Screen Violence and Film Censorship* (HMSO).

6. The Local Government (Miscellaneous Provisions) Act 1982, s. 2 provides that district councils, the London Boroughs, and the Common Council of the City of London may by resolution, followed by public notice, adopt the provisions of Schedule 3 to the Act relating to the 'Control of Sex Establishments'. This Schedule provides, on pain of criminal penalty, that 'no person shall knowingly . . . use any premises, vehicle, vessel or stall as a sex establishment except under and in accordance with the terms of a licence granted' by the local authority (para. 6(1)). For the requirement of *mens rea* see *Westminster City Council v Croyalgrange Ltd* [1986] 2 All ER 353, HL. Paras. 8–11 lay down in some detail the procedure for applying for the grant, renewal or transfer of such a licence, and for the handling of such applications by the local authority (e.g. public notice of the application, account to be taken of objectors' views, rights of appearance for the applicant prior to an adverse decision). Para. 12 lists persons and bodies to whom licences 'shall not be granted' (e.g. persons under 18, bodies incorporated outside the United Kingdom), and states, in respect of eligible applicants, the grounds on which applications may be refused (e.g. the unsuitability of the applicant; the number of sex establishments in the locality already being such as the local authority thinks appropriate – which number may be nil; the character of the locality; the use to which premises in the vicinity are put). Para. 13 empowers local authorities to make regulations prescribing standard conditions applicable to licences granted (e.g. relating to displays, or the visibility of the interior to passers-by). Paras. 17 and 18 provide for the variation and revocation of licences, and para. 19 authorises authorities to charge for licences 'a reasonable fee' – a power interpreted by some authorities as authorising annual fees of several thousand pounds. Para. 27 provides that unsuccessful applicants, applicants aggrieved by conditions, and holders whose licences have been revoked may appeal on the 'merits' to the magistrates' court, with a further right of appeal to the Crown Court.

Note that the possession of a licence under the Schedule provides no legal immunity in respect of charges of any offence at common law or under any enactment (except, of course, the offence under the Schedule itself). Nor does it protect against forfeiture proceedings under, e.g., the Obscene Publications Act 1959 (below, p. 359).

The expression 'sex establishment' means a 'sex cinema' or a 'sex shop', and these terms are themselves further defined. 'Sex cinema' means premises etc. used to a 'significant degree' (a much criticised expression) for the exhibition of 'moving pictures, by whatever means produced' which:

(1) are concerned primarily with the portrayal of, or primarily deal with or relate to, or are intended to stimulate or encourage—
   (i) sexual activity; or
   (ii) acts of force or restraint which are associated with sexual activity; or
(2) are concerned primarily with the portrayal of, or primarily deal with or relate to, genital organs or urinary or excretory functions.

Likewise, 'sex shop' means premises etc. used for a 'business which consists to a significant degree of selling, hiring, exchanging, lending, displaying or demonstrating 'sex articles' (itself further defined) or 'other things intended for use in connection with, or for the purpose of stimulating or encouraging (i) sexual activity; or (ii) acts of force or restraint which are associated with sexual activity'.

By virtue of the Greater London Council (General Powers) Act 1986, London borough councils may, by adopting the amendment to Sch. 3 of the 1982 Act embodied in s. 12(4) of the 1986 Act, exercise still further controls. The amended Sch. 3 extends, for the benefit of such adopting councils, the notion of 'sex establishment' to embrace also what are called 'sex encounter establishments'. Such premises comprise, inter alia, those at which

'performances . . . are given by one or more persons present and performing, which wholly or mainly comprise the sexual stimulation of persons admitted to the premises (whether by verbal or any other means); or, . . . [where] any services . . . which do not include sexual activity are provided by one or more persons who are without clothes or who expose their breasts or genital, urinary or excretory organs at any time while they are providing the service; or . . . [where] entertainments . . . are provided by one or more persons who are without clothes. . . .'

For prosecution of the proprietor of an unlicensed Soho 'peep-show', see *McMonagle v Westminster City Council* [1990] 1 All ER 991, HL.

7. The Video Recordings Act 1984 established 'censorship' controls over the distribution of video recordings. The need felt for some such control stemmed from concern over 'video-nasties'; and, in particular, newspaper assertions as to the large numbers of children who were viewing such videos (see further, J. Petley, *Screen*, Vol. 25 No. 2 p. 68). The provisions of the 1984 Act, superseding an earlier 'voluntary' BBFC classification system, extend beyond those necessary simply to deal with the 'video-nasties' problem, and have introduced for video a thorough-going statutory system of video classification and censorship modelled on that which has long applied to the cinema.

The basic offences under the Act are those of (i) supplying, or offering to supply, a video recording of an unclassified work, (ii) possessing such a recording for the purposes of supply, and (iii) supplying a video recording in breach of its classification (ss. 9–11). The Act provides quite complex definitions of terms used. 'Video recording' refers to the disc or tape containing the 'video work': any 'series of images' that is 'produced electronically by the use of information contained on any disc (lazer or compact), magnetic tape or any other device capable of storing data electronically'. 'Supply' need not be for reward, and includes sales, lettings on hire, exchanges and loans. 'Classified' means that a 'classification certificate' has been issued by the BBFC. Where such a certificate is issued it must state (i) that the work is suitable for general viewing and unrestricted supply, or (ii) that the work is suitable for viewing only by persons above an age specified in the certificate (not being more than 18) and that no recording containing the work is to be supplied to any person below that age, or (iii) that in addition to the statement in (ii) above, no recording containing the work is to be supplied other than in a licensed sex shop (see above, p. 331). Some video works will be refused classification certificates altogether. In reaching its decisions the designated authority is required to have 'special regard to the likelihood of video works . . . being viewed in the home' (s. 4(1)(a)).

The certification requirements do not, however, apply to 'exempted works' or to 'exempted supplies'. The former are works which, taken as a whole, are designed to 'inform, educate or instruct', are concerned with 'sport, religion or music' or are 'video games'. However, such works are not exempt if to any significant extent they depict 'human sexual activity or acts of force or restraint associated with such activity; mutilation or torture of, or other acts of gross violence towards, humans or animals; human genital organs or human urinary or excretory functions; or techniques likely to be useful in the commission of offences. Exemption is also forfeit if a work is likely to any significant extent to stimulate or encourage sexual activity, is likely to any extent to encourage gross violence to humans or animals, or depicts criminal activity which is likely to stimulate or encourage commission of offences (s. 2). 'Exempted supplies' include supplies other than for reward and not in the course or furtherance of business, and supplies to participants of recordings of events or occasions so long as not significantly depicting anything referred to in section 2 (above) i.e. the video-recording of a wedding ceremony but not the honeymoon. If dissatisfied with a decision of the BBFC in relation to a video recording an appeal may be taken to the Video Appeals Committee. Enforcement of the provisions of the 1984 Act became in 1988 a matter for local 'weights and measures' authorities (Criminal Justice Act 1988 s. 162).

Note the general defence added by the Video Recordings Act 1993: it is a defence to a charge of committing any offence under the 1983 Act 'to prove (a) that the commission of the offence was due to the act or default of a person other than the accused, and (b) that the accused took all reasonable precautions and exercised all due diligence to avoid the commission of the offence by any person under his control'.

In the autumn of 1993 two young boys were convicted of the murder of two year old James Bulger. In passing sentence the trial judge, Morland J, commented that there might have been some connection between the behaviour of the two boys and the fact that the father of one of them had over the previous year rented several hundred 'adult' videos, including one of particular notoriety (*Child's Play 3*).

Subsequently, there was much press coverage of a report authored by Professor Elizabeth Newson, a professor of developmental psychology, in which, purporting to speak also for others in her profession, she wrote:

'Many of us hold our liberal freedom of expression dear, but begin to feel we were naive in our failure to predict the extent of damaging material and its all too free availability to children. It now seems that professionals in child health and psychology underestimated the degree of brutality and sustained sadism that film makers were capable of inventing and willing to portray . . . and we certainly underestimated how easy would be children's access to them' (Sunday Times, 3 April 1994).

This apparent change of stance amongst child development professionals at one and the same time spurred on those who sought tighter controls over video content and availability, and also produced a critical response on the part of those who had studied the evidence as regards the particular effect of film on children and others. For example, Dr Guy Cumberpatch (an academic applied psychologist) was quoted as commenting that although research showed that violent children liked violent films there was no firm evidence to show that such films cause violent or criminal behaviour. Studies suggesting the contrary, mostly American, have been difficult to replicate this side of the Atlantic. Further concern was expressed by film-makers themselves. In a letter to *The Times* (28 May 1994) nine leading film directors commented,

'This is the most heavily censored country in Europe and also the one with the largest prison population. We only have to point to the lower crime rates in countries such as Japan and Holland, where there is minimal censorship, to question the validity of any further restrictive measures. Although there is no conclusive research that the viewing of violent images results in violent activity, there is research that shows that deprivation within society and the family can lead to criminality. . . . The Victorian era is often referred to with nostalgia but juvenile crime and child prostitution were rife—and there were no videos, TV or films to blame then. Freedom of expression is essential for any democracy and trying to cover the wounds in our society by curtailing that freedom is dangerous and short-sighted.'

The response of Government was to incorporate the following provisions into the Criminal Justice and Public Order Bill, then before the House of Commons. Section 90 of the 1994 Act now provides criteria to which the BBFC is required to have 'special regard' in the exercise of its functions under the 1984 Act. Such special regard shall be had to

'any harm that may be caused to potential viewers or, through their behaviour, to society by the manner in which the work deals with – (a) criminal behaviour, (b) illegal drugs, (c) violent behaviour or incidents, (d) horrific behaviour or incidents, or (e) human sexual activity'.

The 1994 Act also stiffens the penalties which may be imposed following conviction for offences under the 1984 Act. Thus, for example, in relation to the principal offence under s. 9 (supplying video recording of an unclassified work) trial may now be on indictment (formerly summary only); and in either case a prison term may be imposed (maximum two years and six months respectively).

3 Broadcasting

In this section we shall be principally concerned with the following issues – (i) the independence of broadcasting authorities from governmental influence and control; (ii) the political impartiality of the broadcasting media – issues of political 'neutrality' and political 'balance'; and (iii) the regulation and enforcement of standards to be observed by broadcasters as regards matters of sex, violence, taste and decency.

The importance of these issues is easily demonstrated. In the modern world most people obtain the bulk of their information on matters of contemporary interest from the broadcasting media. A state which controls the broadcasters thereby possesses considerable power to manipulate opinion. There should, therefore, be a presumption in any Western-style democracy against governmental influence over broadcasters. Any influence or control should be restricted to wholly exceptional or emergency situations; and even then the fact of influence should, wherever possible, be declared to viewers and listeners.

As worrying as governmental influence over broadcasting is the possibility of limits being imposed, on what is broadcast, by those in control of the broadcasting stations. How independent, and how influential, are the, government appointed, Governors of the BBC? Who owns the 'independent' television and radio channels? Might the identity of the corporate owner make certain issues taboo? Might ownership of a broadcasting station be regarded as a way of wielding corporate political influence? These questions have commonly been raised in Britain in relation to ownership of the press. They are coming to be asked in relation to television and radio. During the 1980s, and also now in the 1990s, the BBC has, on several occasions, encountered the hostility of members of the Government and of the Conservative Party; and it was not clear to all observers that the Governors were as resistant to governmental influence and as supportive of broadcasters as might have been the case.

The 1990s have seen new arrangements for the franchising of independent television and radio. Provided a 'quality control' threshold is satisfied, the franchise under the terms of the Broadcasting Act 1990, goes to the highest bidder. Some safeguards are, however, provided. Provisions exist to prevent any individual or corporation achieving an excessive degree of media dominance. Also, the tradition in British broadcasting that no overt editorial stance shall be taken continues in force. Moreover, the new legislation preserves, and elaborates upon, the traditional obligation, as a part of the requirement of station neutrality, to achieve 'political balance' in programmes.

As well as being of prime significance in the way in which it informs us, and moulds our ideas, the broadcasting medium is unique in the way in which it 'intrudes' into our homes. Individuals can quite easily choose to avoid reading books, or looking through magazines, or watching films or videos, if these will offend them. By contrast, there appears to be a public expectation that television and radio should, although 'invited' into the home, behave there as reasonable guests, not offending or outraging those who might be expected to be watching at the time in question. Controversy here, inevitably, concerns the point at which the mark is overstepped. What one person may regard as an appropriately forceful presentation, in dramatic form or as a news or current affairs item, of an important issue of the day, will likely shock or affront another. Difficulty in drawing this line should not mean that such issues be avoided, nor that they should be treated in a wholly anodyne way.

Broadcasting Act 1990

[Section 1 established, as from 1 January 1991, the Independent Television Commission. This public body has replaced the former Independent Broadcasting Authority and the Cable Authority. It licenses and regulates non-BBC television services – these include Channels 3 and 4 (and the proposed Channel 5), and cable and satellite services. Section 2 requires that the ITC discharge its functions in the manner it considers best to ensure that a wide range of television programme services is available throughout the UK, and that the programmes (taken as a whole) are of high quality and cater for a variety of tastes and interests. During 1991 the ITC was engaged in allocating 16 new Channel 3 licences, operative from 1 January 1993. The ITC was required to allocate these by competitive tender (i.e. to the highest bidder), subject to the tenderer satisfying certain threshold qualifying criteria. Thus, the ITC may not grant a licence to any person unless 'satisfied that he is a fit and proper person to hold it'; moreover, the ITC must do all it can to ensure that a franchise owner is not a person falling within Sch. 2 of the Act, imposing restrictions on the holding of licences (non-EEC nationals, political bodies, religious bodies, advertising agencies, prevention of accumulations of interests in licensed services, and restrictions on controlling interests in both the press and broadcasting services). Licences are not transferable except with the consent of the ITC.]

6. General requirements as to licensed services
(1) The Commission shall do all that they can to secure that every licensed service complies with the following requirements, namely—
   (a) that nothing is included in its programmes which offends against good taste or decency or is likely to encourage or incite to crime or to lead to disorder or to be offensive to public feeling;
   (b) that any news given (in whatever form) in its programmes is presented with due accuracy and impartiality;

    (c) that due impartiality is preserved on the part of the person providing the service as respects matters of political or industrial controversy or relating to current public policy;

    (d) that due responsibility is exercised with respect to the content of any of its programmes which are religious programmes, and that in particular any such programmes do not involve—

        (i) any improper exploitation of any susceptibilities of those watching the programmes, or

        (ii) any abusive treatment of the religious views and beliefs of those belonging to a particular religion or religious denomination; and

    (e) that its programmes do not include any technical device which, by using images of very brief duration or by any other means, exploits the possibility of conveying a message to, or otherwise influencing the minds of, persons watching the programmes without their being aware, or fully aware, of what has occurred.

(2) In applying subsection (1)(c) a series of programmes may be considered as a whole.

(3) The Commission shall—

    (a) draw up, and from time to time review, a code giving guidance as to the rules to be observed in connection with the application of subsection (1)(c) in relation to licensed services; and

    (b) do all that they can to secure that the provisions of the code are observed in the provision of licensed services;

and the Commission may make different provision in the code for different cases or circumstances.

(4) Without prejudice to the generality of subsection (1), the Commission shall do all that they can to secure that there are excluded from the programmes included in a licensed service all expressions of the views and opinions of the person providing the service on matters (other than the provision of programme services) which are of political or industrial controversy or relate to current public policy.

(5) The rules specified in the code referred to in subsection (3) shall, in particular, take account of the following matters—

    (a) that due impartiality should be preserved on the part of the person providing a licensed service as respects major matters falling within subsection (1)(c) as well as matters falling within that provision taken as a whole; and

    (b) the need to determine what constitutes a series of programmes for the purposes of subsection (2).

(6) The rules so specified shall, in addition, indicate to such extent as the Commission consider appropriate—

    (a) what due impartiality does and does not require, either generally or in relation to particular circumstances;

    (b) the ways in which due impartiality may be achieved in connection with programmes of particular descriptions;

    (c) the period within which a programme should be included in a licensed service if its inclusion is intended to secure that due impartiality is achieved for the purposes of subsection (1)(c) in connection with that programme and any programme previously included in that service taken together; and

    (d) in relation to any inclusion in a licensed service of a series of programmes which is of a description specified in the rules—

        (i) that the dates and times of the other programmes comprised in the series should be announced at the time when the first programme so comprised is included in that service, or

        (ii) if that is not practicable, that advance notice should be given by other means of subsequent programmes so comprised which include material intended to secure, or assist in securing, that due impartiality is achieved in connection with the series as a whole;

and those rules shall, in particular, indicate that due impartiality does not require absolute neutrality on every issue or detachment from fundamental democratic principles.

(7) The Commission shall publish the code drawn up under subsection (3). . . .

7. General code for programmes

(1) The Commission shall draw up, and from time to time review, a code giving guidance—

    (a) as to the rules to be observed with respect to the showing of violence, or the inclusion of sounds suggestive of violence, in programmes included in licensed services, particularly when large numbers of children and young persons may be expected to be watching the programmes;

    (b) as to the rules to be observed with respect to the inclusion in such programmes of appeals for donations; and

    (c) as to such other matters concerning standards and practice for such programmes as the Commission may consider suitable for inclusion in the code;

and the Commission shall do all that they can to secure that the provisions of the code are observed in the provision of licensed services.

(2) In considering what other matters ought to be included in the code in pursuance of subsection (1)(c), the Commission shall have special regard to programmes included in licensed services in circumstances such that large numbers of children and young persons may be expected to be watching the programmes.

(3) . . .

(4) The Commission shall publish the code . . .

8. General provisions as to advertisements

(1) The Commission shall do all that they can to secure that the rules specified in subsection (2) are complied with in relation to licensed services.

(2) Those rules are as follows—

(a) a licensed service must not include—

(i) any advertisement which is inserted by or on behalf of any body whose objects are wholly or mainly of a political nature,

(ii) any advertisement which is directed towards any political end, or

(iii) any advertisement which has any relation to any industrial dispute (other than an advertisement of a public service nature inserted by, or on behalf of, a government department);

(b) in the acceptance of advertisements for inclusion in a licensed service there must be no unreasonable discrimination either against or in favour of any particular advertiser; and

(c) a licensed service must not, without the previous approval of the Commission, include a programme which is sponsored by any person whose business consists, wholly or mainly, in the manufacture or supply of a product, or in the provision of a service, which the licence holder is prohibited from advertising by virtue of any provision of section 9.

(3) Nothing in subsection (2) shall be construed as prohibiting the inclusion in a licensed service of any party political broadcast which complies with the rules (so far as applicable) made by the Commission. . . .

(4) . . .

(5) . . .

9. Control of advertisements

(1) It shall be the duty of the Commission—

(a) after the appropriate consultation, to draw up, and from time to time review, a code—

(i) governing standards and practice in advertising and in the sponsoring of programmes, and

(ii) prescribing the advertisements and methods of advertising or sponsorship to be prohibited, or to be prohibited in particular circumstances; and

(b) to do all that they can to secure that the provisions of the code are observed in the provision of licensed services;

and the Commission may make different provision in the code for different kinds of licensed services.

(7) The Commission may give directions to persons holding any class of licences with respect to the times when advertisements are to be allowed.

(8) Directions under this section may be, to any degree, either general or specific and qualified or unqualified; and directions under subsection (7) may, in particular, relate to—

(a) the maximum amount of time to be given to advertisements in any hour or other period,

(b) the minimum interval which must elapse between any two periods given over to advertisements and the number of such periods to be allowed in any programme in any hour or day,

(c) the exclusion of advertisements from a specified part of a licensed service,

and may make different provision for different parts of the day, different days of the week, different types of programmes or for other differing circumstances.

10. Government control over licensed services

(1) If it appears to him to be necessary or expedient to do so in connection with his functions as such, the Secretary of State or any other Minister of the Crown may at any time by notice require the Commission to direct the holders of any licences specified in the notice to publish in their licensed services, at such times as may be specified in the notice, such announcement as is so specified, with or without visual images of any picture, scene or object mentioned in the announcement; and it shall be the duty of the Commission to comply with the notice.

(2) Where the holder of a licence publishes any announcement in pursuance of a direction under subsection (1), he may announce that he is doing so in pursuance of such a direction.

(3) The Secretary of State may at any time by notice require the Commission to direct the holders of any licences specified in the notice to refrain from including in the programmes included in their licensed services any matter or classes of matter specified in the notice; and it shall be the duty of the Commission to comply with the notice.

(4) Where the Commission—

(a) have given the holder of any licence a direction in accordance with a notice under subsection (3), or

(b) in consequence of the revocation by the Secretary of State of such a notice, have revoked such a direction, or where such a notice has expired, the holder of the licence in question may publish in the licensed service an announcement of the giving or revocation of the direction or of the expiration of the notice, as the case may be.

11. Monitoring by Commission of programmes included in licensed services
(1) For the purpose of maintaining supervision over the programmes included in licensed services the Commission may make and use recordings of those programmes or any part of them.
(2) A licence shall include conditions requiring the licence holder—
  (a) to retain, for a period not exceeding 90 days, a recording of every programme included in the licensed service;
  (b) at the request of the Commission, to produce to them any such recording for examination or reproduction;
  (c) at the request of the Commission, to produce to them any script or transcript of a programme included in the licensed service which he is able to produce to them.
(3) Nothing in this Part shall be construed as requiring the Commission, in the discharge of their duties under this Part as respects licensed services and the programmes included in them, to view such programmes in advance of their being included in such services.

NOTES

1. The provisions set out above are closely paralleled in Part III of the 1990 Act by provisions establishing the Independent Radio Authority, and conferring upon it licensing and regulatory functions. See ss. 83–97.
2. These provisions of the 1990 Act relate to non–BBC broadcasting. The BBC, by contrast, is a body established under Royal Charter, which operates under the terms of that Charter and also its Licence and Agreement from the Home Secretary. See, Cmnd 8313 and 8233 respectively. These instruments impose on the BBC obligations similar to those outlined above (e.g. in relation to programme quality, variety of content, good taste and decency, encouragement to crime, offence to public feeling, due impartiality, avoidance of editorial opinion, scheduling of programmes to protect children, and obligations to broadcast Ministerial announcements and to comply with any 'veto' imposed by the Home Secretary on the broadcasting of any matter or class of matter).
3. The formal power of 'veto', described above, has rarely been used by government. In the early days of broadcasting, in 1927, the BBC was directed not to broadcast matters of political, industrial or religious controversy. This directive only lasted until 1928. Later, in 1955, the BBC and the independent broadcasting authorities were ordered not to derogate from the primacy of Parliament as the proper forum for debating the affairs of the nation by broadcasts of their own programmes or discussions on the matter without 14 days of the Parliamentary debate. This embargo on discussion of issues of current concern also lasted for only a short period.
  More recently this formal power has been used by government to seek to deprive terrorists of the 'oxygen of publicity'. In October, 1988, the Home Secretary ordered that the BBC and the independent companies refrain from broadcasting words spoken by representatives, or purported representatives, of certain specified organisations, or words spoken in support of, or which solicited or invited support for such an organisation. Words spoken by representatives were only proscribed when the representative was speaking in that capacity rather than in a personal capacity – a distinction requiring of broadcasters a careful exercise of judgment. When speaking as a representative of such an organisation the ban applied however innocent the actual content of the words. The organisations covered were those

proscribed under the terms of the Northern Ireland (Emergency Provisions) legislation (see, above, pp. 277 and 294) as well as Sinn Fein, Republican Sinn Fein and the Ulster Defence Association. The directions did not extend to words spoken in the UK Parliament, nor words spoken by or in support of a candidate pending a Parliamentary, European Parliamentary or a local election. The directions applied only to direct statements, not to reported speech. In other words, it was permitted to show a film of a proscribed speaker, together with a 'voice-over' reading verbatim the speaker's words. The directions applied equally to current matters and to programmes about events of the past. In September 1990 Ulster Television discovered it could not broadcast directly the words of Eamonn de Valera or Sean McBride in its proposed six-part school history of Ulster.

For an early list of programmes which could not be broadcast in their original form, see *Index on Censorship* (1988) Vol. 17 No. 8. The ban was unsuccessfully challenged by the National Union of Journalists and others, but not the broadcasting organisations themselves) in judicial review proceedings in *R v Secretary of State for the Home Department, ex p Brind* [1991] 2 WLR 588. See extract, above, pp. 6–10. Following the IRA declaration of a total cessation of violence, in September 1994, the ban was lifted.

4. The 1988 ban followed a considerable period of tension between broadcasters and government about the broadcasting of Irish affairs. As far back in the present troubles as 1972 controversy arose over a proposed BBC programme, *The Question of Ulster*: a programme in which both loyalist and republican proponents were to be given full opportunity to argue their cases. Following representations from the Home Secretary about the proposed programme, the Chairman and Director-General met the minister and told him that if the government felt that the programme should not be shown the proper course was for the minister to ban the programme and for the BBC to broadcast the fact of the ban. The Home Secretary apparently made further representations about the programme but declined to exercise his powers to prevent it from occurring.

In 1978 the BBC was criticised by government for having broadcast an interview with a member of the outlawed Irish National Liberation Army. In 1979, controversy surrounded the filming by a Panorama film crew (reporter, Jeremy Paxman) of an IRA road block at Carrickmore. It was alleged that the BBC had liaised with the IRA in staging the event. The Governors set up an inquiry and, in due course, denied the main charges. The filmed footage was not broadcast. However, the terms of the denial were seen as a message to documentary film-makers to avoid issues likely to engender governmental criticism. In 1985, the Home Secretary, Leon Brittan, wrote an open letter to the Chairman of the BBC contending that a proposed programme (*At the Edge of the Union*) in a series called *Real Lives* should not be broadcast. The programme was to feature interviews with both Martin McGuinness (IRA) and Gregory Campbell, a hardline loyalist. The Governors immediately took the highly unusual step of previewing the programme themselves, rather than referring the matter for the judgment of the Director-General. In this case the D-G was, in fact, temporarily unavailable and the preview took place in his absence. Following their viewing of the film the Governors withdrew the programme from the schedules. The Home Secretary denied having brought improper pressure on the BBC, claiming that it was appropriate for a minister to let the government's opinion on broadcasting by terrorists be known. He denied that the decision to ban the programme was anything other than the exercise of independent judgment by the Governors. Nevertheless, journalists at both the BBC and independent television staged a one-day strike a week after this action of the Governors, protesting at the failure of the Board to take a clear stance to protect news and current affairs journalism from government pressures. In due course the programme was shown, minor cuts having been made. See further, C. Horrie and S. Clarke, *Fuzzy Monsters: Fear and Loathing at the BBC* (1994) pp. 47–49. In 1988, Thames Television broadcast a *This Week* documentary, *Death on the Rock*, investigating the circumstances of the shooting of three, as it transpired unarmed, members of the IRA in Gibraltar earlier in the year. Government explanations were that the killings were of members of an active service unit of the IRA intent on planting a bomb on the island; and that they were shot by members of the SAS acting in self defence. The documentary, however, included evidence from a 'new' witness to the events who asserted that those killed had been shot without warning and with their hands in the air. The documentary rekindled debate about the existence of a 'shoot-to-kill' policy on the part of the security forces in dealing with terrorists. The documentary was strongly denounced by the Prime Minister, Mrs Thatcher; and similar material in a BBC programme shown in Northern Ireland met with expressions of disapproval from the Foreign Secretary, Sir Geoffrey Howe. The IBA (the forerunner of the ITC) supported the showing of the Thames documentary. Thames later set up an independent inquiry under Lord Windlesham. His report largely exonerated the documentary makers: Windlesham Report, *Death on the Rock* (1989). See also, R. Bolton, *Death on the Rock and Other Stories* (1990).

In addition to these events in connection with *Irish* affairs a number of other recent examples of government seeking to interfere with broadcasting freedom (or of governmental annoyance at broadcasting bias!) may be noted. In 1986 a critical analysis of television news coverage was published by the Conservative Party. This followed strong criticism by Mr Tebbitt of the BBC's coverage of the US air raid, launched from UK bases, on Tripoli earlier in the year. In 1987, the BBC responded to government concerns and banned the showing of a documentary, on the secret *Zircon* spy-satellite project, made by Duncan Campbell in his *Secret Society* series. See further, below, pp. 454–455. The film was eventually shown, in slightly altered form, in 1988. Also not shown in this series was a documentary on the working of Cabinet government. The film was re-made by Channel 4 and eventually broadcast in 1991. See further, P. Fiddich, 'Broadcasting: A Catalogue of Confrontation', in N. Buchan and T. Sumner (eds) *Glasnost in Britain: Against Censorship and in Defence of the Word* (1989). Note also the decision of the IBA (the predecessor of the ITC) not to permit the broadcast of a programme in the *20/20 Vision* series in which a former employee of MI5, Cathy Massiter, had spoken of the very wide scope of that body's surveillance activities. The ban was eventually lifted following wide knowledge of the contents of the programme. Was this an example of undue deference to governmental desire for secrecy as regards the activities of the security services, or simply proper action on the part of a regulatory body in response to evidence of clear breach of the Official Secrets legislation? Over the years a number of Panorama programmes have been substantially revised following an elaborate 'referral up' process within the BBC: e.g. in 1990 'Who Pays for the Party' – an investigation of Conservative Party finances; and an episode on the Iraqi Super-gun. Note also the controversy following the Panorama film, 'Maggie's Militant Tendency' (1984). See C. Horrie and S. Clarke, *Fuzzy Monsters: Fear and Loathing at the BBC* (1994), passim.

5. The ITC published its Programme Code in February 1991: the current version dates from January 1993. The section which deals with impartiality on matters of political or industrial controversy explains that broadcasters do not have to be absolutely neutral on every controversial issue, in particular, broadcasters do not have to remain detached from fundamental democratic principles. However, 'opinion' should be clearly distinguished from 'fact', and opposing points of view should be dealt with even-handedly. 'Due impartiality' does not mean that balance is required in any simple mathematical sense, nor that equal time must be given to each opposing view. Although there are times when it will be appropriate to include opposing viewpoints within a single programme (e.g. where the issues are of current or active controversy), it is also permissible to invite individuals to make programmes which express their personal views. This is, however, limited by the obligation on the licence-holder not to use programmes to put forward its own views, to make clear that the programme expresses the views of the contributor (whilst also taking care to ensure that those views are not based on any falsification of facts), and the obligation that the broadcasting service be impartial over a period of time. In other words, balance may be achieved through the presentation of a series of programmes. Where this is the intention the fact that a programme is a part of a balanced series should be drawn to the attention of the viewer. Moreover, it is not permissible to argue, as might a newspaper or magazine, that a 'biased' service is compensated for by other channels with different biases. Each broadcasting service is separately required to achieve impartiality in its programming.

6. The ITC Programme Guide deals also with matters of good taste, decency and the portrayal of violence. It requires that early evening broadcasts conform to the requirements of the Family Viewing Policy. This policy states that prior to 9.00 pm nothing should be broadcast which is unsuitable to be viewed by children (15 and under); after this time, and until 5.30 am progressively less suitable material may be shown, reflecting the diminishing proportion of young persons likely to be watching. Between these hours it is expected that parents should share with the broadcasters the responsibility of determining what young persons may and may not view. Unsuitability may result from depiction of violence, from bad language, profanity, crude innuendo, explicit sexual behaviour and scenes of extreme distress. Even after the Family Viewing watershed of 9.00 pm the Code warns against bad language which is not defensible in terms of context and authenticity, and states that profanity is of concern in relation to *any* religious faith. As regards sex and nudity the Code stresses that context is important, and that it should be presented with tact and discretion so as not to offend. Representations of sexual intercourse must normally await the 9.00 p.m. watershed. The Code stresses, however, that entertainment and comedy have traditionally made use of sexual innuendo and suggestive behaviour. This is permissible so long as 'mere crudity' is avoided. Equally, much great drama has involved love and passion and these matters may be treated forcefully (even with intention to 'shock' and 'disturb') in television drama so long as not so as to give offence. The Code requires broadcasters to take care to avoid bad taste and offence in humour. Whilst acknowledging that much humour has its basis in deviations from the normal and the familiar, special care is needed if physical and mental disability is to be treated humorously. Humour based on differences in racial characteristics may give offence, and may give a false impression as to acceptable attitudes, and so should be closely monitored; as also humour based upon other, vulnerable minorities – old people, homosexuals, religious minorities.

As regards material which has been considered by the BBFC (see above p. 325) the Code states that no 'R18' material should ever be shown, that '18' rated material should not start before 10.00 pm, and that '15' and '12' rated material should not start before 9.00 pm and 8.00 pm respectively. These should, however, be regarded as minimum requirements. Thus, for example, the film *The Life of Brian* was screened, albeit controversially, with the equivalent of an '18' certificate in cinemas but was not shown on television until 1991.

The Code's provisions on violence note that violence should not be regarded as something which can be excluded from broadcast material. Television should, at times at least, seek to reflect the world, and this includes its violent aspects. News and current affairs items may properly depict scenes of suffering and distress, or deal with the fact and consequences of violent behaviour. Drama commonly is based upon conflict, and conflict may erupt into violence. However, the depiction of violence may cause offence, may be psychologically disturbing to young or emotionally insecure viewers, may lead to imitative behaviour, may lead to a feeling that such behaviour is acceptable, and may result in indifference to suffering. Furthermore, the Code stresses that the depiction of violence towards the achievement of good ends is likely to be as harmful as violence for the achievement of evil; and the Code takes the view that it is not possible to regard 'sanitised' violence – violence the results of which are concealed or minimised – as innocuous. Although it may be less likely to give offence, there may be danger in so disguising the true consequences of violent behaviour. With these considerations in mind the Code makes the usual references to the Family Viewing watershed and to the vital importance of context in dramatic presentation. More specifically, it contains specific guidelines in relation to dangerous behaviour which may easily be imitated by children (e.g. 'hanging' scenes, or violent use of readily accessible articles); and as regards the portrayal of suicide (in particular showing method) and the handling of exorcism and occult practices in adult presentations. The Code also states that it may be appropriate to warn viewers about the content of programmes, although programmes broadcast during Family Viewing Time should not be such as to require such announcement.

7. Other matters dealt with in the Code include Privacy and Methods of Gathering Information; Party Political and Parliamentary broadcasting; and Terrorism, Crime and Anti-Social Behaviour. Broadly similar guidelines operate in relation to broadcasts by the BBC.

8. Unlike its predecessor, the Independent Broadcasting Authority, the ITC will not act as censor in the sense of itself becoming involved in the previewing of scheduled programmes and determining whether or not to allow transmission. For cases challenging, unsuccessfully, the exercise by the IBA of these powers, see *A-G (ex rel McWhirter) v Independent Broadcasting Authority* [1973] QB 629, CA (proposed showing of documentary film about Andy Warhol), and *R v Independent Broadcasting Authority, ex p Whitehouse* (1985) Times, 4 April, CA (showing on Channel 4 of controversial, X certificate, feature film *'Scum'* – film based on television play which the BBC had in 1978 decided not to transmit – depiction of violence within penal institution). In both cases the court decided that the IBA had not broken, or failed to perform, its statutory duties in allowing transmission. The latter decision made clear that the IBA was not required by the legislation then in force to involve itself in 'day to day' editorial decisions on programmes. Such involvement by the IBA, both in relation to drama and current affairs programmes, had brought upon it much criticism from programme makers for meddling too closely in their freedom of communication. By contrast, the recently established ITC has from 1993 no longer involved itself in the vetting of programmes. It has, however, sanctions which it is able to impose in relation to any programme which breaches the provisions of the legislation or the Code. These sanctions include the imposition of fines on the company in default, and the revocation or non-renewal of its broadcasting licence.

9. Examples of drama programmes commissioned but not broadcast by the BBC or independent television include – *The War Game* (1965), a film depicting the horrific nature of nuclear war – made but not shown for some 20 years; *Brimstone and Treacle* (1976), a play by Dennis Potter which the BBC considered would outrage viewers in a way which was unjustifiable – play subsequently made into feature film – play eventually broadcast in 1987; *Scum* (1978), a play by Roy Minton and Alan Clarke – see above, n. **8;** *Solid Geometry* (1978), a play by Ian McEwan banned by BBC at rehearsal stage, objection being taken to certain lines about menstruation and the proposed appearance on screen of a preserved penis in a specimen jar; *Headcrash* (1987), a play by Michael Wall – cancelled after Wall refused to agree to cuts in violence in the script. In other instances programmes have been shown, albeit after cuts have been ordered against the wishes of the programme's writers and makers. Thus, for example, in 1978 a play, *The Legion Hall Bombing,* was broadcast in a shorter version than had been made by author Caryl Churchill and director Roland Joffe. The cuts removed criticisms of the fairness of the court system in Northern Ireland (non-jury 'Diplock' courts). Churchill and Joffe took proceedings to have their names removed from the play's credits and released the full script to the press. In 1983, the BBC cut some two and a half minutes from a play, *The Falklands Factor.* Its author, Don Shaw, considered this to be 'political censorship': the BBC explained the decision as a desire not to cause distress to families of soldiers.

Broadcasting Act 1990

THE BROADCASTING STANDARDS COUNCIL

152. Preparation by Council of code relating to broadcasting standards
(1) It shall be the duty of the Council to draw up, and from time to time review, a code giving guidance as to—
  (a) practices to be followed in connection with the portrayal of violence in programmes to which this Part applies,
  (b) practices to be followed in connection with the portrayal of sexual conduct in such programmes, and
  (c) standards of taste and decency for such programmes generally. . . .
(3) It shall be the duty of each broadcasting or regulatory body, when drawing up or revising any code relating to standards and practice for programmes, to reflect the general effect of so much of the code referred to in subsection (1) (as for the time being in force) as is relevant to the programmes in question.
(4) The Council shall from time to time publish the code referred to in subsection (1) (as for the time being in force).
(5) Before drawing up or revising the code the Council shall consult—
  (a) each broadcasting or regulatory body; and
  (b) such other persons as appear to the Council to be appropriate.

153. Monitoring by Council of broadcasting standards
(1) It shall be the duty of the Council to monitor programmes to which this Part applies with a view to enabling the Council—
  (a) to make reports on the portrayal of violence and sexual conduct in, and the standards of taste and decency attained by, such programmes generally, and
  (b) to determine whether to issue complaints in respect of such programmes under section 154(7).
(2) Subject to section 160(2), the Council may make reports on the matters specified in subsection (1)(a) on such occasions as they think fit; and any such report may include an assessment of either or both of the following, namely—
  (a) the attitudes of the public at large towards the portrayal of violence or sexual conduct in, or towards the standards of taste and decency attained by, programmes to which this Part applies, and

(b) any effects or potential effects on the attitudes or behaviour of particular categories of persons of the portrayal of violence or sexual conduct in such programmes or of any failure on the part of such programmes to attain such standards.

(3) The Council may publish any report made by them in pursuance of subsection (1)(a). . . .

154. Consideration by Council of complaints relating to broadcasting standards

(1) Subject to the provisions of this section, it shall be the duty of the Council to consider complaints which are made to them under this section and relate—

(a) to the portrayal of violence or sexual conduct in programmes to which this Part applies, or

(b) to alleged failures on the part of such programmes to attain standards of taste and decency,

and to make findings on such complaints, taking into account any relevant provisions of the code.

(2) Any such complaint must be in writing and give particulars of the matters complained of.

(5) The Council shall not entertain, or proceed with the consideration of, a complaint if it appears to them—

(a) that the matter complained of is the subject of proceedings in a court of law in the United Kingdom, or

(b) that the matter complained of is a matter in respect of which the complainant has a remedy by way of proceedings in a court of law in the United Kingdom, and that in the particular circumstances it is not appropriate for the Council to consider a complaint about it, or

(c) that the complaint is frivolous, or

(d) that for any other reason it is inappropriate for them to entertain, or proceed with the consideration of, the complaint.

(7) If it appears to the Council to be appropriate to do so, they may of their own motion issue complaints relating to matters falling within subsection (1)(a) or (b).

(8) Any such complaint shall give particulars of the matters complained of.

155. Consideration of complaints

(1) Subject to the provisions of section 154, every complaint made to or issued by the Council under that section shall be considered by them either without a hearing or, if they think fit, at a hearing (and any such hearing shall be held in private unless the Council decide otherwise).

156. Publication of Council's findings

(1) Where the Council have considered and made their findings on any complaint, they may give the following directions, namely—

(a) where the relevant programme was broadcast by a broadcasting body, directions requiring that body to publish the matters mentioned in subsection (2) in such manner, and within such period, as may be specified in the directions; and

(b) where the relevant programme was included in a licensed service, directions requiring the appropriate regulatory body to direct the licence holder to publish those matters in such manner, and within such period, as may be so specified.

(2) Those matters are—

(a) a summary of the complaint; and

(b) the Council's findings, and any observation by them, on the complaint, or a summary of those findings and any such observations.

(3) The form and content of any such summary as is mentioned in subsection (2)(a) or (b) shall be such as may be approved by the Council.

(4) A broadcasting or regulatory body shall comply with any directions given to them under this section.

(5) Any licence to provide a licensed service which is granted by a regulatory body under this Act shall include conditions requiring the licence holder to comply with such directions as may be given to him by that body for the purpose of enabling them to comply with any directions give to them under this section.

NOTES

1. The Broadcasting Standards Council was established by government in 1988 as a consumer 'watchdog' over the activities of the broadcasters as regards matters of sex, violence, taste and decency: or, in the words of its first Chairman (Lord Rees-Mogg), as 'an institution which . . . can provide a bridge between audiences and broadcasters . . ., sustaining . . . dialogue . . .'. It achieved statutory status in the Broadcasting Act 1990. Its Chairman is Lord Rees-Mogg. It published a Code of

Practice on the matters within its remit in November 1989, and the terms of this Code are reflected in the relevant parts of the ITC Programme Code described above. In addition to adjudicating upon complaints (and finding against most complainants), it has a general monitoring function over programmes broadcast. It has sought to engage in dialogue with the public about the public's principal concerns, and has sought to inform itself as to the latest research on relevant matters, such as the effects of the mass media. See, further, F. Coleman [1993] Pub. Law 488.

2. An example of the exercise by the BSC of its power under s. 153 (above) to make reports to the Secretary of State on issues identified during its monitoring which appear to raise questions of general broadcasting policy came in 1992. The Council became aware from press reports of a satellite broadcast channel, Red Hot Dutch (later Red Hot Television, and transmitted from Denmark). The service was available via the Eutelsat satellite on the payment of a quarterly decoder rental of some £47.50p. For this price viewers would receive broadcasts of what was billed as totally explicit sex each Saturday and Sunday night from midnight until 4.00 a.m. (subsequently Wednesday night also). The Council obtained such a decoder and, using the steerable dish on the roof of its offices, tuned in from the very first broadcast (25 July 1992). The content of the programmes did, indeed, show explicit heterosexual sex, including close-up shots of penetration and ejaculation and oral sex. Buggery of females by males, and the penetration of anal passages of males and females by means of sexual aids, was also featured. Explicit lesbian scenes also were shown. The Council took the view that there was, in the films shown, commonly an association between aggression and sexual action. Women were frequently shown in what it regarded as degrading and humiliating positions and circumstances.

The Council reported to the Secretary of State in late November 1992. The Council noted the times at which the broadcasts were transmitted. The times, in its view, made the situation all the worse in so far as the unsociable hours would only increase the extent to which the films were recorded on video rather than watched 'live', and this produced a substantial risk that the films would in due course be viewed by young persons. Much of the material was of a nature not legally available on video in the UK.

The Secretary of State responded in March 1993 by making Orders (SI 1993/1024) under the 1990 Act proscribing the satellite service for the purpose of s. 178. It thereby became an offence in various ways to lend succour to the satellite broadcaster of this channel – e.g. by publication of programme details, or by supplying decoder equipment. The broadcasters challenged the Orders by way of judicial review. The Divisional Court denied an injunction to prevent the Orders having effect, but referred to the ECJ certain points of interpretation of the EC Broadcasting Directive 89/552. See [1993] 2 CMLR 333.

3. Part V of the Broadcasting Act 1990 provides for the continued existence of the Broadcasting Complaints Commission, first established under the Broadcasting Act 1981. The function of the BCC is to consider and adjudicate on complaints of unjust or unfair treatment in television and radio programmes, or of unwarranted infringement of privacy in (or in connection with the obtaining of material included in) such programmes. The provisions of the Act relating to complaints, hearings and the duty to publicise findings closely parallel those set out above in relation to the BSC. See 1990 Act ss. 142–150. For forceful criticism of the procedures and the decisions reached by the BCC see G. Robertson, *Freedom, the Individual and the Law* (7th edn, 1993) pp. 295–300.

4 Obscenity and indecency

(a) INTRODUCTION

The extent to which it is appropriate for the law to impose criminal penalties in relation to the publication or display of material which is obscene or indecent has been, and remains, a matter of acute theoretical and practical debate.

In terms of theory, a helpful discussion may be found in Joel Bakan (1984) 17 Ottawa Law Review 1. Bakan identifies three principal factions in this 'law and morality' debate: 'liberals', 'legal moralists' and 'feminists'. He writes, perhaps a little over-simply,

'all appear to agree that, in certain circumstances, restrictions on pornography are justified, but they vehemently disagree as to why and in what circumstances such restrictions are justified. Liberals argue that restricting pornography means curtailing freedom of expression and the right to individual liberty, and that such restrictions are only justified where the exercise of these rights and freedoms can be shown to cause harm. . . . Legal moralists, on the other hand, argue that restrictions on pornography are necessary even where no harm to individuals can be shown. Pornography, they claim, is immoral, and the law must protect society from breaches of its moral standards. Feminists are not concerned with the moral or the immoral nature of pornography, but with the harm that pornography causes to . . . women. In this sense the feminist position is consistent with liberal theory. . . .'

Note that for 'liberals' any restraints imposed (whether pre-publication censorship or post-publication sanctions) may infringe both their cherished 'freedom of expression' and also the more general notion of 'liberty of the individual'. This will be the case at any rate in circumstances where the obscene material can be regarded as an 'expressive' act. See further, below.

As regards the liberal thesis much may depend on what is meant by 'harm to others': their accepted justification for constraints. Two particular arguments are commonly deployed in attempts to justify aspects of obscenity/indecency laws in terms of liberal principles. First, it is argued by some that pornographic material does indeed have an adverse and harmful effect on those who are its consumers. The truth or falsity of this assertion has long been controversial, and will probably remain so. At the time of the Williams Committee Report (1979) the prevailing view appeared to be that no causal link had been clearly demonstrated between pornography and such 'harm', either in terms of intrinsic 'corruption' of the mind of the individual consumer – arguably not harm in the liberal sense – or in terms of harm being caused by such persons to others. The difficult matter is the demonstration of causality. To some it is highly plausible that one who has exposed himself to, for example, violent and sadistic pornography may go on to commit sex offences (and, of course, from time to time it is discovered that such offenders have indeed collected such material). To others, in contrast, it may seem inconceivable that any person without a propensity to such criminal behaviour might be driven to commit such acts as a result of exposure to such material. A middle view, albeit in a context where middle views tend not to be voiced, might be to believe that for some people at least such exposure might just 'tip the scales'. A further complication, however, to note in this discussion of pornography and harm is the contrary view that for some persons who may have a propensity towards anti-social/criminal sexual behaviour the availability of pornography may constitute a 'safety-valve', offering catharsis to help them to refrain from such harmful behaviour.

Over the past decade those who assert a causal connection between pornography, violence and anti-social/criminal behaviour have become inclined to assert that studies are tending to support their contentions. Compare in this connection the approach to this issue of the (US) Federal Commission on Obscenity and Pornography (1970) and the (UK) Williams Committee (1979), with that of the (US) Mees Commission in 1986. However, sceptics remain sceptical, arguing that research findings from US studies have been difficult to replicate, and may be flawed in terms of methodology.

It will be apparent that the range of possible connections between pornography and behaviour, and the difficulties of proof of causality, are considerable. This leads discussion on to the question: assuming that clear proof of a connection is not possible, what stance should the law take? Should it strive to offer protection to those who may be the victims of pornography on the basis that even in the absence of a proven connection a 'precautionary' approach is appropriate. Or should freedom of liberty/expression be regarded as inviolable in the absence of clear proof of harm?

Another 'harm' argument, and this time one commonly accepted by the liberal camp, involves the harm of causing offence by foisting obscene or indecent displays onto unwitting and undesiring individuals. It is one thing for images to be presented on the inside pages of a magazine which would only be opened by a person well aware of the likely contents; it is another, as one writer has put it, to utilise a 'billboard on Times Square to promulgate to the general populace the techniques and the pleasures of sodomy'. This notion of harm justifies controls on the basis of the nuisance caused by unsolicited experience of obscene and indecent material. As will be seen in the materials which follow it forms the basis of several pieces of legislation over the past two decades. It is not, however, a justification which is without some theoretical difficulty: at any rate in so far as we may be considering material which may be said to intend to communicate ideas or seek to promote some set of values. To proscribe involuntary exposure of others to such material is to accept that one person's liberty to express those ideals/values may be restrained because another person may thereby hear and see things which he or she does not wish to hear and see. The right to be an ostrich takes precedence over the liberty to bring before others one's ideas of right and wrong, of moral and immoral, or whatever. Perhaps most people would defend an individual's right of choice not to be unwittingly exposed to ideas which may be shocking and disturbing: and some have, in any event, argued that pornography does not express ideas and values, and so does not warrant protection on the grounds of freedom of expression – a protection to be afforded, in principle, to even the most offensive views and opinions. But this may be too easy an escape from the problem. Civil rights organisations have long wrestled with the tricky question of their attitude towards the pornographer. Some have taken up controversial stances, acknowledging that the issues are difficult ones which cannot be simply resolved. A spokesperson for the American Civil Liberties Union not so long ago made clear that whatever, ultimately, should be the law relating to pornography it was not right to seek to deny that pornography (and other lewd and indecent entertainment) presents and promotes to the world certain ideas, implicit within its explicitness, of the legitimacy of particular kinds of sexual behaviour.

A further notion of harm is that which has attracted the attention of feminist writers. This literature, which is itself quite diverse, has enhanced the debate by focusing on additional and rather different and subtle notions of harm which may be a consequence of pornography. In particular, feminists have argued that pornography has potential, by its demeaning and degrading images of women and in some instances in the hatred of women it seems to display, to provoke misogynist attitudes in men. In other words, over and above the fear of particular incidents of anti-social/criminal sexual conduct, exposure to pornography may also harm women by its influence on the way in which men perceive women. Additionally, feminists have argued strongly that it must be considered to be harmful to the female portion of the population that they have to live in a community which appears (because men make and enforce the laws) to tolerate a substantial and profitable industry sector which is involved in the production for men of material which, at best, does little to foster respect and mature relations between the sexes.

It is at this point that considerations of the 'equality' between the sexes under the law come into the picture. Feminists have argued that to debate the pornography issue in terms of protecting individual liberty and protecting freedom of expression is to debate in terms of constitutional libertarian principles devised essentially for men and by men. Once the debate is turned towards equal treatment under the law, and the promotion of fairness and equity within the state, different considerations may apply and different conclusions be drawn.

For a recent decision of the Canadian Supreme Court considering the relationship between the Constitutional Guarantees of the Charter of Rights and the obscenity offences of the Canadian Criminal Code, see *R v Butler* (1992) 89 DLR 449: offences were prima facie in violation of freedom of expression guarantee, but 'saved' because the provisions constituted a reasonable limit prescribed by law. The Court reviewed carefully the scope and definition of the matter which might fall within the obscenity offences, and concluded that the offence was reasonably restricted to kinds of material in respect of which it was fair to presume that harm of various kinds might result, and therefore that criminal sanction was legitimate. Note that the court referred expressly to the idea that the kinds of material covered by the offences under the Code were such as to undermine the ideas of equality and dignity of all human beings, and referred to the 'equality' guarantees of the Charter: 'There is a substantial body of opinion that holds that the portrayal of persons being subjected to degrading and dehumanising sexual treatment results in harm, particularly to women, and therefore to society as a whole'.

Note also the New Zealand decision in *Comptroller of Customs v Gordon and Gotch (NZ) Ltd* [1987] 2 NZLR 80 in which the High Court held that under New Zealand legislation defining indecency for purposes of customs control – in this case, importation of issues of *Knave* and *Fiesta* – in terms of injury to the public good, it was not necessary that any actual injury be proven by evidence: it was for the decision-making body to use its experience and judgment to determine whether such harm was likely. However, the Court considered that the approach of the minority of the Tribunal below had been misconceived. The minority had erred in adopting a feminist approach (and without alerting counsel to their thinking on this issue) of supposing that material 'depicting a representational view of women that degraded all women' (i.e. as the sexual playthings of men) could thereby be indecent under the Act. The minority had stated that some of the portfolios of photographs of women in the magazines were

'injurious to the public good because of: the contrived positions the women are placed in . . .; the surrounding context of the photographs, and the symbolic representation of women depicted. Such portfolios promote social values which degrade, not just the single model posing, but all women as a social class. Women are portrayed as subordinates who are always sexually available and have limited choice. . . . The total effect of such representation suggests that women have an inferior social status and lack autonomy. . . . Publications which promote social values degrading a class or group would be considered harmful to the public good (and discriminatory) if that group were a racial or religious group. Similarly when the group is determined by sex. . . . We do not consider that, for the requirement of injury to be satisfied, the harm must be manifest by action. Injury may occur in the province of attitudes or perceptions, particularly if these are widely shared, and consistently suggest that one class is inferior to another.'

(b) OBSCENE PUBLICATIONS ACTS 1959 AND 1964

(i) The Offences

Obscene Publications Act 1959

An Act to amend the law relating to the publication of obscene matter; to provide for the protection of literature; and to strengthen the law concerning pornography.

2. Prohibition of Publication of Obscene Matter

(1) Subject as hereinafter provided, any person who, whether for gain or not, publishes an obscene article [or who has an obscene article for publication for gain (whether gain to himself or gain to another)][1] shall be liable—

    (a) on summary conviction to a fine not exceeding [£5,000] or to imprisonment for a term not exceeding six months;

    (b) on conviction on indictment to a fine or to imprisonment for a term not exceeding three years or both.

(3) A prosecution for an offence against this section shall not be commenced more than two years after the commission of the offence.

(3A)[2] Proceedings for an offence under this section shall not be instituted except by or with the consent of the Director of Public Prosecutions in any case where the article in question is a moving picture film of a width of not less than sixteen millimetres and the relevant publication or the only publication which followed or could reasonably have been expected to follow from the relevant publication took place or (as the case may be) was to take place in the course of a film exhibition; and in this subsection 'the relevant publication' means—

    (a) in the case of any proceedings under this section for publishing an obscene article, the publication in respect of which the defendant would be charged if the proceedings were brought; and

    (b) in the case of any proceedings under this section for having an obscene article for publication for gain, the publication which, if the proceedings were brought, the defendant would be alleged to have had in contemplation.

(4) A person publishing an obscene article shall not be proceeded against for an offence at common law consisting of the publication of any matter contained or embodied in the article where it is of the essence of the offence that the matter is obscene.

(4A)[2] Without prejudice to subsection (4) above, a person shall not be proceeded against for an offence at common law—

    (a) in respect of a film exhibition or anything said or done in the course of a film exhibition, where it is of the essence of the common law offence that the exhibition or, as the case may be, what was said or done was obscene, indecent, offensive, disgusting or injurious to morality; or

    (b) in respect of an agreement to give a film exhibition or to cause anything to be said or done in the course of such an exhibition where the common law offence consists of conspiring to corrupt public morals or to do any act contrary to public morals or decency.

(5) [See below, p. 363]

(6) [See below, p. 353]

(7) [In this section 'film exhibition' has the same meaning as in the Cinemas Act 1985][3]

NOTES

1. The Obscene Publications Act 1964, s. 1(2) provides that for the purpose of any proceedings for an offence under s. 2 of the 1959 Act 'a person shall be deemed to have an article for publication for gain if with a view to such publication he has the article in his ownership, possession or control'.

2. The Obscene Publications Act 1964, s. 1(5) provides that the term 'publication for gain' shall mean 'any publication with a view to gain, whether the gain is to accrue by way of consideration for the publication or in any other way'.

1 Words in square brackets added by the Obscene Publications Act 1964, s. 1(1).
2 S. 2(3A) and s. 2(4A) added by the Criminal Law Act 1977, s. 53.
3 See above, p. 323.

3. The Obscene Publications Acts 1959 and 1964 have superseded, though without actually abolishing, the common law offence of obscene libel. The 1959 Act followed recommendations of a committee set up by the Society of Authors (Chairman, Sir Alan Herbert) in response to a 'spate' of prosecutions of 'serious literature' during 1954, and the deliberations of a Parliamentary Select Committee (1956–57 HC 245; 1957–58 HC 122 and 123). For the 1954 prosecutions and the unsatisfactory features of the common law offence they revealed see C. H. Rolph, *Books in the Dock* (1969) pp. 93–109; N. St. John-Stevas, [1954] Crim LR 817 and *Obscenity and the Law* (1956); series of unattributed articles in (1954) 118 JPN at 664, 680, 694, 709, 725, 812; G. Robertson, *Obscenity* (1979), Chap. 2. Note however the much praised summing-up of Stable J in *R v Martin Secker Warburg* [1954] 2 All ER 683, [1954] 1 WLR 1178. The 1964 Act was passed to remedy certain flaws that had become apparent in the provisions of the 1959 Act (see e.g. *R v Clayton and Halsey* [1963] 1 QB 163, CCA and *Mella v Monahan* [1961] Crim LR 175, DC).

The 1959 Act was intended to provide greater safeguards for those who create or deal in works of 'art' or 'literature' whilst, at the same time, making better provision for the effective prosecution of those who create or deal in 'pornography' and for the seizure and forfeiture of such material. Neither aim appears to have been achieved. The protection afforded to literature depends more on levels of tolerance of jurors and magistrates than on the law itself, and pornography is such profitable business that the possibility of conviction, or forfeiture of material, provides no real deterrent. Moreover, the publicity which such proceedings bring may well provide a more than compensatory boost to future sales. The difficulties of enforcing the obscenity laws prompted Sir Robert Mark, then Metropolitan Police Commissioner, to describe the task as 'a self-defeating attempt to eradicate the ineradicable' (Sir R. Mark, *Policing a Perplexed Society* (1977) p. 60). See also *R v Metropolitan Police Comr, ex p Blackburn (No 3)* [1973] QB 241, CA. A further difficulty for the police has been the vigilance necessary to ensure that their own officers do not succumb to offers of bribes held out by the pornographers. For accounts of such corruption and its 'rooting out' see B. Cox, J. Shirley and M. Short, *The Fall of Scotland Yard* (1977); Sir R. Mark, *In the Office of Constable* (1978) pp. 173–4, 263–269; Report of the Williams Committee on Obscenity and Film Censorship (Cmnd 7772, 1979) pp. 39–41.

Inevitably there have been many proposals for reform of the law. Some have sought to provide a more workable legal formula for distinguishing what is permissible from what is not. See e.g. *Pornography: The Longford Report* (1972); *The Pollution of the Mind: New Proposals to Control Public Indecency and Obscenity* – Society of Conservative Lawyers (1972); Obscene Publications Bill 1986. Others have favoured relaxation of the obscenity laws, though usually recognising the need to afford children some protection. A distinction has commonly been drawn between those who *foist* offensive displays on others and those who simply supply material to those who *actively seek* it. See e.g. *The Obscenity Laws: Report of Arts Council Working Party* (1969); proposals of the Defence of Literature and the Arts Society (DLAS), reported at (1978) 128 NLJ 423. For appraisals of a variety of possible reforms see C. H. Rolph, *Books in the Dock* (1969), Chap. 6; G. Robertson, *Obscenity* (1979), Chap. 11. A committee, chaired by Professor Bernard Williams, was appointed in 1977 to review, inter alia, 'the laws concerning obscenity, indecency and violence in publications, displays and entertainments in England and Wales, except in the field of broadcasting'. It reported in 1979 – Cmnd 7772. It recommended that the existing variety of laws be scrapped and a fresh start made, avoiding the uncertainties resulting from couching criminal laws in terms like 'obscene', 'indecent', 'deprave' and 'corrupt'. In determining the scope of laws on these matters the committee considered that the following basic principles should govern. It was necessary to draw a clear distinction between material which should be 'prohibited', and thereby denied even to those who wish access to it; and material which should not be prohibited but merely 'restricted' – which should not be thrust, so as to cause offence, on to the ordinary public. Material should only be 'prohibited', and denied to those who wish to see it, where harm is likely to be caused by the material. The committee regarded the current state of scientific evidence as justifying only very limited prohibitions on adult access to material. The committee acknowledged, however, that the law should provide for broader categories of material to be kept from, more vulnerable, young persons. The committee also felt that a distinction should also be drawn between the printed word and other material. It recommended that the former should never be prohibited nor restricted. By its very nature it is not 'immediately offensive' in the way in which other material foisted on an unsuspecting public might be; and a specially protected status is justified for the written word because of its importance in conveying ideas. The many detailed recommendations of the Williams Committee, fleshing out these principles into more concrete proposals, have not, in terms, been implemented. Note, however, that certain of these ideas, but not the whole 'balanced package', have been implemented in the sex cinema/sex shop licensing legislation, in the R18 film and video classification system and the Video Recordings Act 1984, and in the Indecent Displays (Control) Act 1981. See further, pp. 331, 332 and 371. For discussion of the Williams Report see C. Manchester, (1980) 31 NILQ 103 and (1980) 14 UWAL Rev 172; S. Coldham, (1980) 43 MLR 306; A. W. B. Simpson, *Pornography and Politics – the Williams Report in Retrospect* (1983) – discussion by member of the committee; R. Dworkin, (1981) 1 OJLS 177.

4. The provisions in s. 2(4) of the 1959 Act were intended to prevent defendants being denied the various safeguards contained in the 1959 Act by being charged at common law with obscene libel. It has, however, been held that the subsection does not prevent charges of conspiracy to corrupt public morals or conspiracy to outrage public decency since in such cases the essence of the offence is not the *publication* of obscene matter but the *agreement* to act in a corrupting or outrageous manner. See *Shaw v DPP* [1962] AC 220, HL, at 268, 290, 291; and *Knuller v DPP* [1973] AC 435, HL, at 456 per Lord Reid: 'Technically the distinction . . . is correct but it appears to me to offend against the policy of the Act. . . .' Fears lest the bringing of such charges might circumvent the Obscene Publications Acts led to assurances to Parliament from the Law Officers that such charges would not be brought where to do so would deprive defendants of those Acts' safeguards. See 695 HC Deb 3 June 1964 col 1212; 698 HC Deb 7 July 1964 cols 315–6. Note, however, the prosecution brought, and the decision of the Court of Appeal in *R v Gibson* [1990] 2 QB 619. Two defendants were convicted of having outraged public decency contrary to common law. The charges followed the display at an art gallery run by one of the defendants of an item made by the other defendant. The offending item was a pair of earrings, each of which was made out of a freeze-dried foetus of three or four months gestation. The gallery was in a parade of shops and was open to the public to enter to browse. On appeal it was argued that the charges brought were precluded by the terms of s. 2(4) above. The Court of Appeal began by confirming that there was an offence at common law of outraging public decency, adopting the words of Lord Reid in *Shaw's* case: 'it is an indictable offence to say or do or exhibit anything in public which outrages public decency, whether or not it also tends to corrupt and deprave those who see or hear it'. The next issue was whether, as was required for s. 2(4) to apply, the obscenity of the earrings was the essence of the offence charged. This depended, the Court held, on whether the word 'obscenity' was used in the subsection in its colloquial sense (which would cover an item's tendency to outrage public decency), or in its narrower sense, as defined in s. 1(1) of the Act, as depending solely on an item's tendency to deprave or corrupt. There being no suggestion that the display was likely to corrupt or deprave any member of the public, the court held that the essence of the offence was the likely outrage to decency caused by the display. Interpreting s. 2(4) the court held that there was no reason to depart from the Act's usual meaning of the term 'obscene'. Accordingly, the appellants' arguments failed. The court was unwilling to accept that this interpretation denied a defendant the 'artistic' merit safeguard intended by the enactment of the 1959 Act. It took the view that in the kind of case where a prosecution for outraging public decency might succeed it was 'unlikely that a defence of public good could possibly arise'.

Would the court have been able to have come to the same decision had the charge at common law been that of '*corruption*' of public morals? Note that the 'public good' defence proceeds on the basis that an admittedly obscene publication should not constitute the commission of a criminal offence because of its aesthetic value. In other words the defence does not negative obscenity – it justifies obscenity. Does this not suggest that the view of the court in *Gibson*, that this defence would be inapplicable in the case of an item which outrages decency, is misguided? See also, on *Gibson*, M. Childs [1991] Pub. Law 20.

For full discussion of these conspiracy offences see Smith and Hogan, *Criminal Law* (7th edn, 1992) pp. 291–293, 748; *Law Commission Report No. 76 Conspiracy and Criminal Law Reform* (1976) pp. 74–80; G. Robertson, *Obscenity* (1979) pp. 210–236.

Note the more comprehensive words in the 1959 Act s. 2(4A) (the parallel provisions relating to prosecutions in respect of films added by Criminal Law Act 1977, s. 53), and also in the Theatres Act 1968, s. 2(4) (below, p. 364) in respect of obscene plays.

5. An undertaking was given by the then Solicitor-General, during the passage of the 1964 Act through Parliament, that a publisher who indicated that he would continue 'publication' of an article notwithstanding successful *forfeiture* proceedings would instead be *prosecuted* by the Crown, thus giving the publisher the opportunity to defend the article in question before a jury.

6. The time limit on prosecutions contained in the 1959 Act, s. 2(3) protects those who 'publish' or 'have for publication' rather than secondary parties who aid and abet such 'publication', e.g. authors, cameramen, actors. Time runs from the 'publication' or 'having for publication' rather than from the, perhaps much earlier, date of the secondary party's contribution to that eventual 'having' or 'publication'. See G. Robertson, *Obscenity* (1979) at pp. 74–6 quoting from transcript of the Court of Appeal judgment in *R v Barton* [1976] Crim LR 514. The Court of Appeal suggested that a person will not be regarded as having aided or abetted publication if he 'disassociated' himself from such publication, but did not give guidance as to what conduct would amount to such a 'disassociation'.

7. On the appropriate sentences to be imposed in respect of offences under the Obscene Publications Acts note the guidance of Lawton LJ in *R v Holloway* (1982) 4 Cr App Rep (S) 128, CA at 131:

'Experience has shown, ... that fining these pornographers does not discourage them. Fines merely become an expense of the trade and are passed on to purchasers of the pornographic matter, so that prices go up and sales go on.

... the only way of stamping out this filthy trade is by imposing sentences of imprisonment on first offenders and all connected with the commercial exploitation of pornography: otherwise front men will be put up and the real villains will hide behind them. It follows ... that the salesmen, projectionists, owners and suppliers behind the owners should on conviction lose their liberty. For first offenders sentences need only be comparatively short, but persistent offenders should get the full rigour of the law. In addition courts should take the profit out of this illegal filthy trade by imposing very substantial fines.

... We wish to make it clear that the guidelines we have indicated apply to those who commercially exploit pornography. We do not suggest that sentences of imprisonment would be appropriate for a newsagent who is carrying on a legitimate trade in selling newspapers and magazines and who has the odd pornographic magazine in his possession ... [H]e can be discouraged ... by a substantial fine from repeating his carelessness. Nor do we suggest that a young man who comes into possession of a porno-graphic video tape and who takes it along to his rugby or cricket club to amuse his friends by showing it should be sentenced to imprisonment. On conviction he too can be dealt with by the imposition of a fine. The matter might be very different if owners or managers of clubs were to make a weekly practice of showing 'blue' films to attract custom.... When news of this judgment reaches Soho it is to be hoped, and we think it is likely, that there will be a considerable amount of stocktaking within the next 72 hours; because if there is not there is likely to be a depletion in the population of that area in the next few months.'

Note the custodial sentences imposed, albeit reduced in severity on appeal, in *R v Wallace* (1992) 13 Cr App R (S) 628, CA, and *R v Xenofhontos and Mace* (1992) 13 Cr App R (S) 580, CA. A sentence of five months' imprisonment was upheld on appeal in *R v Jack (Colin Mason)* [1994] 9CL 144 (Norwich Crown Ct). The case involved computer pornography. The defendant had pleaded guilty to having nine computer discs (imported from the USA) for gain. Each disc contained several thousand files containing 'hard-core' pornographic material. Adult home computer users had gained access via an 0898 premium rate telephone line, enabling them to view explicit images on their computer screens. D was of good character and had made some £14,000 from the service over a ten-month period.

(ii) The Definition of 'Obscene'

Obscene Publications Act 1959

1. Test of obscenity
(1) For the purposes of this Act an article shall be deemed to be obscene if its effect or (where the article comprises two or more distinct items) the effect of any one of its items is, if taken as a whole, such as to tend to deprave and corrupt persons who are likely, having regard to all relevant circumstances, to read, see or hear the matter contained or embodied in it.
(2) In this Act 'article' means any description of article containing or embodying matter to be read or looked at or both, any sound record, and any film or other record of a picture or pictures.

2. Prohibition of publication of obscene matter
(6) In any proceedings against a person under this section the question whether an article is obscene shall be determined without regard to any publication by another person unless it could reasonably have been expected that the publication by the other person would follow from publication by the person charged.

Obscene Publications Act 1964

1. Obscene articles intended for publication for gain
(3) In proceedings brought against a person under the said section 2[1] for having an obscene article for publication for gain the following provisions shall apply in place of subsections (5) and (6) of that section, that is to say,—

1 I.e. Obscene Publications Act 1959, s. 2.

(a) [See below, p. 363]
(b) the question whether the article is obscene shall be determined by reference to such publication for gain of the article as in the circumstances it may reasonably be inferred he had in contemplation and to any further publication that could reasonably be expected to follow from it, but not to any other publication.

NOTES

1. The Obscene Publications Act 1964, s. 2(1) extends the meaning of 'article' as defined in s. 1(2) of the 1959 Act. It provides:

'The Obscene Publications Act 1959 (as amended by this Act), shall apply in relation to anything which is intended to be used, either alone or as one of a set, for the reproduction or manufacture therefrom of articles containing or embodying matter to be read, looked at or listened to, as if it were an article containing or embodying that matter so far as that matter is to be derived from it or from the set.'

Whether or not such an article is obscene is to be determined in accordance with the Obscene Publications Act 1964, s. 2(2) which provides:

'For the purposes of the Obscene Publications Act 1959 (as so amended), an article shall be deemed to be had or kept for publication if it is had or kept for the reproduction or manufacture therefrom of articles for publication; and the question whether an article so had or kept is obscene shall—
(a) for the purposes of section 2 of the Act be determined in accordance with section 1(3)(b) above as if any reference to publication of them were a reference to publication of articles reproduced or manufactured from it; and
(b) for purposes of section 3 of the Act by determined on the assumption that articles reproduced or manufactured from it would be punished in any manner likely having regard to the circumstances in which it was found, but in no other manner.'

(For the Obscene Publications Act 1959, s. 3, see below, p. 359).
2. In *A-G's Reference (No 5 of 1980)* [1980] 3 All ER 816, CA (CD) it was held that a video-cassette was an 'article' within section 2(1) above in that it was a 'record of . . . pictures'; and that a cinema showing video films was 'publishing' such article because the cassettes were being 'played or projected' (as required by section 1(3), below, p. 359).
3. In *DPP v Whyte* [1972] AC 849, HL at 860, Lord Wilberforce, commenting on the statutory test of obscenity, said:

'. . . the Act has adopted a relative conception of obscenity. An article cannot be considered obscene in itself: it can only be so in relation to its likely readers . . . in every case, the magistrates, or the jury are called upon to ascertain who are likely readers and then to consider whether the article is likely to deprave and corrupt them.'

An example of the application of the test was given by Lord Pearson at 864:

'The question whether an article is obscene depends not only on its inherent character but also on what is being or is to be done with it. Suppose that there is a serious book on *Psychopathia Sexualis* designed to be read only by medical men or scientists concerned with such matters, and that it is kept in the library of a hospital or university and so far as possible reserved for use by such medical men or scientists. Such a book should not be regarded as obscene for the purpose of the Act, because it is not likely to come (though possibly it might come) into the hands of anyone who might be corrupted by it.'

Lord Simon commented at 867:

'The intention of the Act was . . . to enable serious literary, artistic, scientific or scholarly work to draw on the amplitude of human experience without fear of allegation that it could conceivably have a harmful effect on persons other than those to whom it was in truth directed . . .'

The defence raised in *Whyte*, which the magistrates had accepted, was that by virtue of a policy of excluding young persons from the defendant's bookshop, the likely purchasers of the pornographic books were males of middle age and upwards described by the magistrates as 'inadequate, pathetic, dirty-minded men . . . addicts to this type of material, whose morals were already in a state of depravity and corruption'. Since this likely audience was no longer open to immoral influence (being already corrupt and depraved) the articles could not be considered obscene within the meaning of the 1959 Act. The prosecutor appealed to the House of Lords. The majority held that the facts as found by the magistrates were sufficient to constitute the offence charged. The minority (Lords Simon and Salmon) held that the magistrates' conclusions on the facts could not be interfered with, as it had not been shown that they lacked any evidential basis. Their Lordships were generally agreed that the Act covered more than cases of once and for all corruption. Lord Wilberforce explained, at 863:

'. . . the Act's purpose is to prevent the depraving and corrupting of men's minds by certain types of writing: it could never have been intended to except from the legislative protection a large body of citizens merely because, in different degrees, they had previously been exposed, or exposed themselves, to the "obscene" material. The Act is not merely concerned with the once and for all corruption of the wholly innocent; it equally protects the less innocent from further corruption, the addict from feeding or increasing his addiction.'

Lord Simon said, at 867:

'. . . a defence is available not merely that the likely exposé is too aesthetic, too scientific or too scholarly to be likely of corruption by the particular matter in question, but also that he is too corrupt to be further corrupted by it. I would, however, express my concurrence with the view . . . that the language of the statute is apt to extend to the maintenance of a state of corruption which might otherwise be escaped, and . . . that a person can be recorrupted . . .'

Lord Salmon, at 876, commented:

'. . . there was no finding that these dirty minded old men were other than depraved and corrupted long before they became customers of the respondents, nor that what they found there made them any worse than they already were or kept them in a state of depravity or corruption from which they might otherwise have escaped.'

4. The courts have deprecated judicial attempts to explain to juries the meaning of the terms 'corrupt and deprave'. See, for example, Salmon LJ in *R v Calder and Boyars Ltd* [1969] 1 QB 151 at 168 referring to 'attempts to improve upon or re-define' the statutory formula. In general the matter should be left at large for the jury; and see *R v O'Sullivan* (1994) Times, 3 May: judge's summing-up should inform juries of the words of 1959 Act, s. 1(1) and 1(3), and 1964 Act, s. 1(3)(b), adding only a comment about the proportion of the audience which need be shown to have been corrupted – see below, n. **6.** However judges have, from time to time, stressed the seriousness of the terms. For example, in *Knuller v DPP* [1973] AC 435, HL at 456 Lord Reid commented that one may 'lead persons morally astray without depraving and corrupting them.' On the other hand, in *DPP v Whyte* [1972] AC 849 the House of Lords stressed that the formula covered moral or spiritual corruption and depravity not manifesting itself in corrupt and depraved conduct. If an article produces in the minds of its audience thoughts which a magistrate or jury, as the case may be, regards as having corrupted and depraved the audience's minds, the article is obscene.

How far, and in what ways, might it be possible to define more precisely the content of an obscenity law? Consider the principle that justice requires that the criminal law should be clear in its terms. An American judge once despaired of the search for a judicial yardstick to delimit the extent to which obscenity laws might make inroads on freedom of expression: 'I know it when I see it', per Stewart J, *Jacobelli v Ohio* (1964) 378 US 184.

5. A consequence of defining obscenity in terms of tendency to deprave and corrupt is that the concept is not confined to sexual matters. In *Calder (John) (Publications) Ltd v Powell* [1965] 1 QB 509, DC, Lord Parker CJ said at 515:

'In my judgment it is perfectly plain that depravity, and, indeed, obscenity (because obscenity is treated as a tendency to deprave) is quite apt to cover what was suggested by the prosecution in this case. This book – the less said about it the better – concerned the life, or imaginary life, of a junkie in New York, and the suggestion of the prosecution was that the book high-lighted the favourable effects of drug-taking and, so far from condemning it, advocated it, and that there was a real danger that those into whose hands the book came might be tempted at any rate to experiment with drugs and get the favourable sensations high-lighted by the book.

In my judgment there is no reason whatever to confine obscenity and depravity to sex, and there was ample evidence upon which the justices could hold that this book was obscene.'

During 1984 a number of comics and pamphlets dealing with the taking of drugs were the subject of prosecutions at the Old Bailey. Note criticisms of the trials in the *New Statesman*, June 8 and August 3, 1984. See *R v Skirving* [1985] QB 819, CA, below p. 358. What other matter might be regarded as having a tendency to deprave and corrupt? Violence? See *DPP v A and BC Chewing Gum Ltd* [1968] 1 QB 159, DC.

6. Some guidance has been given by the courts as to what proportion of an article's audience a magistrate or jury need regard as being susceptible to an article's corrupting and depraving effect for the article to be obscene. In *R v Calder and Boyars Ltd* [1969] 1 QB 151 Salmon LJ said at 168: 'the jury should have been directed to consider whether the effect of the book was to tend to deprave and corrupt a significant proportion of those persons likely to read it. What is a significant proportion is a matter entirely for the jury to decide.' Earlier he had said that the term 'persons' in s. 1 of the 1959 Act 'clearly . . . cannot mean all persons, nor can it mean any person, for there are individuals who may be corrupted by almost anything. On the other hand, it is difficult to construe "persons" as meaning the majority of persons or the average reader. . . .' Salmon LJ's formulae were approved by the House of Lords in *DPP v Whyte* [1972] AC 849, Lord Cross explaining that 'a significant proportion of a class means a part which is not numerically negligible but which may be much less than half' and Lord Pearson stating that 'if a seller of pornographic books has a large number of customers who are not likely to be corrupted by such books, he does not thereby acquire a licence to expose for sale or sell such books to a small number of customers who are likely to be corrupted by them.' The concept of 'more than a negligible number' was approved in the Court of Appeal in *R v O'Sullivan* (1994) Times, 3 May.

7. A defence sometimes raised is that an article does not deprave and corrupt its audience if it so revolts them that it averts them from the sort of conduct it depicts. In *R v Calder and Boyars Ltd* [1969] 1 QB 151, CA (Cr D), Salmon LJ said at 168:

'The defence . . . was that the book . . . gave a graphic description of the depths of depravity and degradation in which life was lived in Brooklyn. This description was compassionate and condemnatory. The only effect that it would produce in any but a minute lunatic fringe of readers would be horror, revulsion and pity; it was admittedly and intentionally disgusting, shocking and outrageous; it made the reader share in the horror it described and thereby so disgusted, shocked and outraged him that, being aware of the truth, he would do what he could to eradicate those evils and the conditions of modern society which so callously allowed them to exist. In short, according to the defence, instead of tending to encourage anyone to homosexuality, drug-taking or senseless, brutal violence, it would have precisely the reverse effect. Unfortunately, whilst the judge told the jury in general terms that it was not enough for the Crown to prove merely that the book tended to horrify, shock, disgust or nauseate, he never put a word of the specific defence to the jury when he summed up on the issue of obscenity.

This is a serious defect in the summing-up. . . . With a book such as this, in which words appear on almost every page and many incidents are described in graphic detail which, in the ordinary, colloquial sense of the word, anyone would rightly describe as obscene, it is perhaps of particular importance to explain to the jury what the defendant alleges to be the true effect of those words and descriptions within their context in the book.'

In *R v Anderson* [1972] 1 QB 304 at 314, CA (Cr D), Lord Widgery CJ said:

'. . . the defence . . . said this material in the magazine [Oz No. 28 School Kids Issue] was not likely to deprave or corrupt; that it may shock is accepted, but it is not likely to cause people to act in a depraved or corrupted fashion. One of the arguments advanced in support of that line of defence was that many of the illustrations in the magazine were so grossly lewd and unpleasant that they would shock in the first instance and then would tend to repel. In other words, it was said that they had an aversive effect and that far from tempting those who had not experienced the acts to take part in them, they would put off those who might be tempted so to conduct themselves. The argument which Mr Mortimer [counsel for the defendant] put forward on this point is that the trial judge never really got over to the jury this argument of aversion, . . . Strangely enough the same situation arose in [an] earlier decision in this court . . . *R v Calder and Boyars Ltd* . . . was in fact a then well-publicised criminal trial dealing with the book *Last Exit to Brooklyn* and Mr Mortimer appeared for the defence, and in this court Mr Mortimer argued, and this court held rightly argued, that the failure of the judge to put what one might call the aversion argument was fatal to the retention of the conviction.'

The appellants' convictions under s. 2 were accordingly quashed. (Cf. below, p. 367.)

8. Section 1(1) of the 1959 Act requires that an article be considered as a whole in estimating its effect on its likely audience. This contrasts with the position prior to 1959 in trials for obscene libel when prosecutors might read 'purple passages' in isolation from their context to juries. Note the effect, however, of s. 1(1) of the 1959 Act on articles comprising more than one item. In *R v Anderson* [1972] 1 QB 304 at 312 CA (Cr D), Lord Widgery CJ said:

'. . . At the trial the prosecution accepted the proposition that in deciding whether the offences under the Act of 1959 had been made out, it was right for the jury to consider the magazine as a whole and not to look at individual items in isolation. That was a proposition accepted by the prosecution . . . largely in fairness to the defence, and, being accepted by both parties, it was a proposition which was accepted by the judge as well. It certainly did the defence no harm; it was much to their interests; but in the judgment of this court it was entirely wrong. It is in our view quite clear from section 1 that where you have an article such as this comprising a number of distinct items, the proper view of obscenity under section 1 is to apply the test to the individual items in question. It is equally clear that if, when so applied, the test shows one item to be obscene that is enough to make the whole article obscene.

Now that may seem unfair at first reading, but it is the law in our judgment without any question. A novelist who writes a complete novel and who cannot cut out particular passages without destroying the theme of the novel is entitled to have his work judged as a whole, but a magazine publisher who has a far wider discretion as to what he will, and will not, insert by way of items is to be judged under the Act on what we call the "item by item" basis. This was not done in this case. Our main concern in mentioning the point now is to ensure that it will be done in future. . . .'

9. The courts have usually refused to permit expert evidence as to the effect that an article may have on its likely audience. The matter is one for the jury to assess without expert guidance (cf. the use of expert testimony under s. 4 of the 1959 Act, see below, p. 361). In *R v Anderson* [1972] 1 QB 304, CA (Cr D), Lord Widgery CJ said at 313:

'. . . a majority of the expert evidence called by the defence in this case . . . was . . . directed to showing that the article was not obscene. In other words, it was directed to showing that in the opinion of the witness it would not tend to deprave or corrupt. Now whether the article is obscene or not is a question exclusively in the hands of the jury, and it was decided in this court in *R v Calder and Boyars Ltd* [1969] 1 QB 151 that expert evidence should not be admitted on the issue of obscene or no. It is perfectly true that there was an earlier Divisional Court case in which a somewhat different view had been taken. It was *DPP v A and BC Chewing Gum Ltd* [1968] 1 QB 159. That case in our judgment should be regarded as highly exceptional and confined to its own circumstances, namely, a case where the alleged obscene matter was directed at very young children, and was of itself of a somewhat unusual kind. In the ordinary run of the mill cases in the future the issue "obscene or no" must be tried by the jury without the assistance of expert evidence on that issue, and we draw attention to the failure to observe that rule in this case in order that that failure may not occur again.

We are not oblivious of the fact that some people, perhaps many people, will think a jury, unassisted by experts, a very unsatisfactory tribunal to decide such a matter. Those who feel like that must campaign elsewhere for a change of the law. We can only deal with the law as it stands, and that is how it stands on this point.'

In *DPP v Jordan* [1977] AC 699, HL, Viscount Dilhorne expressed some doubt about the correctness of the *Chewing Gum* case and felt the exception certainly should not be extended. Lord Wilberforce stated the alleged exception to the general rule and commented, at 718:

'we are not obliged to validate, or otherwise this exception or to define its scope, because the evidence was not directed to showing that the class of likely readers consisted of, or as to a significant number included, sexual abnormals or deviants. The case was one of normal readers, and was to be judged by the jury in relation to them, and, since normal readers were in question here, [expert] evidence ... was inadmissible at the stage when section 1 was being considered.'

Note, however, the decision in *R v Skirving* [1985] QB 819, CA (Cr D). The appellants, partners in a book distribution business, had been convicted of having an obscene article for publication for gain, contrary to s. 1(1) of the 1959 Act. The article in question was a pamphlet entitled '*Attention Coke Lovers – Freebasing, the Greatest Thing Since Sex*', copies of which had been discovered by police following a search of their office premises. The pamphlet contained instructions ('recipes') as to how to take cocaine to maximum effect – in particular, how to smoke or 'freebase' the drug. The prosecution had, at the trial, obtained leave to adduce expert evidence from a professor of addiction behaviour as to the effects of taking cocaine. This had been permitted by the trial judge on the ground that the jury would need to consider the effects of 'freebasing', and that this was not within the knowledge or experience of the ordinary person. On appeal, the appellants argued that such evidence should not have been admitted. The Court of Appeal upheld the decision of the trial judge, holding that unlike the sexual obscenity cases (such as *Anderson* and *Jordan*) where the jury were in a reasonable position to assess from their own experience the likely effect of material, in this case the jury would have been 'in the dark' 'guessing and no more' at its likely effect. The Court of Appeal did emphasise, however, that the proper question for the jury was not whether the act of taking cocaine 'corrupted or depraved', but, rather, the linked but separate question whether the pamphlet itself could be said to have that effect. The court was content, however, that the trial judge had properly distinguished these questions in his summing-up.

10. For summaries of research into the effect of the portrayal of sex and violence in the various media see M. Yaffé, Appendix 5 to *Pornography: the Longford Report* (1972), and Appendix V to the *Williams Committee Report*; S. Brody, *Screen Violence and Film Censorship* – Home Office Research Study No. 40 (1977); E. Wistrich, *I Don't Mind the Sex it's the Violence – Film Censorship Explored* (1978) pp. 45–47, 83–89, 96–101; R. Dhavan and C. Davies (eds) *Censorship and Obscenity* (1978), pp. 111–182; Belson, *Television Violence and the Adolescent Boy* (1978); G. Cumberpatch and D. Howitt, *A Measure of Uncertainty – The Effects of the Mass Media* (1989); Report of the Williams *Committee on Obscenity and Film Censorship* (1979) Cmnd. 7772 Chapter 6 and para. 10.8 (burden of proving harm caused by pornography fairly clearly not discharged). Contrast, however, *R v Holloway* (1982) 4 Cr App Rep (S) 128, per Lawton LJ:

'In the course of our judicial experience we have dealt with cases of sexual offenders who have undoubtedly been incited to engage in criminal conduct by pornographic material ... Pornography, and particularly the type known as "hard porn," in our experience has a corrupting influence. Those of us who have had to deal with matrimonial cases in the Family Division . . . know that sometimes matrimonial troubles are started by husbands who have been reading or seeing this kind of material and try to introduce in the matrimonial bed what they have read or seen. There is an evil in this kind of pornography. It is an evil which in our opinion has to be stopped.'

Note also feminist writing since the mid 1970s. Compare the opposing approaches (evident from their titles) of Andrea Dworkin, *Pornography: Men Possessing Women* (1981) and Carole Vance (ed), *Pleasure and Danger: Exploring Female Sexuality* (1984).

(iii) The Definition of 'Publication'

Obscene Publications Act 1959

1. (3) For the purposes of this Act a person publishes an article who—
    (a) distributes, circulates, sells, lets on hire, gives, or lends it, or who offers it for sale or for letting on hire; or
    (b) in the case of an article containing or embodying matter to be looked at or a record, shows, plays or projects it, or, where the matter is data stored electronically, transmits that data:
Provided that[1]. . . .

NOTE

1. In *R v Taylor (Alan)* (1994) Times, 4 February 1994, CA, T had developed and printed photographic films depicting obscene acts. The Court of Appeal held that the sale of the prints to the owners of the developed film constituted a 'publication'. 'High Street' photographic developing-processing outlets have long exercised some caution in the material they are willing to return to customers. Periodically, press reports appear of difficulties experienced by would-be serious artists in securing the return, for self-portrait purposes, of 'snaps' they have taken of themselves. Camcorders have, no doubt, eased the difficulties of others with less legitimate purposes.

(iv) Forfeiture of Obscene Articles

Obscene Publications Act 1959[2]

3. Powers of search and seizure
(1) If a justice of the peace is satisfied by information on oath that there is reasonable ground for suspecting that, in any premises in the petty sessions area for which he acts, or on any stall or vehicle in that area, being premises or a stall or vehicle specified in the information, obscene articles are, or are from time to time, kept for publication for gain, the justice may issue a warrant under his hand empowering any constable to enter (if need be by force) and search the premises, or to search the stall or vehicle, and to seize and remove any articles found therein or thereon which the constable has reason to believe to be obscene articles and to be kept for publication for gain.
(2) A warrant issued under the foregoing subsection shall, if any obscene articles are seized under the warrant, also empower the seizure and removal of any documents found in the premises or, as the case may be, on the stall or vehicle which relate to a trade or business carried on at the premises or from the stall or vehicle.
(3) [Subject to subsection (3A) of this section] any articles seized under subsection (1) of this section shall be brought before a justice of the peace acting for the same petty sessions area as the justice who issued the warrant, and the justice before whom the articles are brought may thereupon issue a summons to the occupier of the premises or, as the case may be, the user of the stall or vehicle to appear on a day specified in the summons before a magistrates' court for that petty sessions area to show cause why the articles

1 Proviso excluded television and radio from scope of Act: proviso ceased to have effect as from 1 January 1991: s. 162, Broadcasting Act 1990.
2 Words in square brackets and second proviso added by Criminal Law Act 1977.

or any of them should not be forfeited; and if the court is satisfied, as respects any of the articles, that at the time when they were seized they were obscene articles kept for publication for gain, the court shall order those articles to be forfeited:

Provided that if the person summoned does not appear, the court shall not make an order unless service of the summons is proved.

Provided also that this subsection does not apply in relation to any article seized under subsection (1) of this section which is returned to the occupier of the premises or, as the case may be, the user of the stall or vehicle in or on which it was found.

Obscene Publications Act 1964

1. Obscene articles intended for publication for gain
(4) Where articles are seized under section 3 of the Obscene Publications Act 1959 . . . and a person is convicted under section 2 of that Act of having them for publication for gain, the court on his conviction shall order the forfeiture of those articles:. . . .

Obscene Publications Act 1959

3. Powers of search and seizure
(3A)[1] Without prejudice to the duty of a court to make an order for the forfeiture of an article where section 1(4) of the Obscene Publications Act 1964 applies (orders made on conviction), in a case where by virtue of subsection (3A) of section 2 of this Act proceedings under the said section 2 for having an article for publication for gain could not be instituted except by or with the consent of the Director of Public Prosecutions, no order for the forfeiture of the article shall be made under this section unless the warrant under which the article was seized was issued on an information laid by or on behalf of the Director of Public Prosecutions.
(4) In addition to the person summoned, any other person being the owner, author or maker of any of the articles brought before the court, or any other person through whose hands they had passed before being seized, shall be entitled to appear before the court on the day specified in the summons to show cause why they should not be forfeited.
(5) Where an order is made under this section for the forfeiture of any articles, any person who appeared, or was entitled to appear, to show cause against the making of the order may appeal to the Crown Court;. . . .
(6) If as respects any articles brought before it the court does not order forfeiture, the court may if it thinks fit order the person on whose information the warrant for the seizure of the articles was issued to pay such costs as the court thinks reasonable to any person who has appeared before the court to show cause why those articles should not be forfeited; and costs ordered to be paid under this subsection shall be enforceable as a civil debt.
(7) For the purposes of this section the question whether an article is obscene shall be determined on the assumption that copies of it would be published in any manner likely having regard to the circumstances in which it was found, but in no other manner.
(8) The Obscene Publications Act 1857 is hereby repealed, ...

NOTES

1. The Criminal Justice Act 1967, s. 25 provides that a warrant under s. 3 may not be issued except on an information laid by or on behalf of the DPP or by a constable. This restriction followed the successful private forfeiture proceedings, in 1966, against *Last Exit to Brooklyn*. These proceedings forced the hand of the DPP to reverse his original decision not to prosecute the publishers under s. 2. See further *R v Calder and Boyars Ltd* [1969] 1 QB 151, CA (Cr D). The use made of the seizure and forfeiture procedure has increased considerably in recent years. In 1969 only 31 forfeiture orders were made throughout England and Wales compared with 550 in 1978. The number of items seized by the Metropolitan Police increased from 35,390 in 1969 to 1,229,111 in 1978 (Williams Report, Appendix 7), and rose further to 2,071,190 in 1983. More recently, in 1989, the volume of figures fell to

---

1 S. 3(3A) added by the Criminal Law Act 1977, s. 53.

some 185,000 articles, as the police concentrated resources on investigating child pornography. In view of the volume of material seized, the Divisional Court has upheld the practice of magistrates and judges not examining each and every item, but reaching decisions having examined representative samples selected by the police and the defendant – see *R v Crown Court at Snaresbrook, ex p Metropolitan Police Comr* (1984) 148 JP 449.

2. For criticism of the way in which magistrates operate the burden of proof under s. 3 see G. Robertson, *Obscenity* (1979) pp. 93–100.

3. The provision in s. 3(4) of the 1959 Act granting rights to appear to interested parties other than the occupier of the premises searched was regarded as an important new provision in the 1959 Act. The opportunity it provides to authors etc. to defend their work is somewhat diminished by the absence of any procedure for making such interested persons aware of the existence of the forfeiture proceedings. Much depends on press publicity of the seizure or the actions of the person from whom the articles were seized in contacting such other interested parties.

4. Prior to the 1959 Act a practice had developed whereby the police, having discovered articles which they and the DPP considered obscene, would persuade the occupier of the premises to sign a form disclaiming any interest in the articles. The police would then destroy the articles and no court proceedings would take place. This practice was disapproved by the 1957 *Parliamentary Select Committee on Obscene Publications* (1957–58 HC 123–1). Section 3(3) of the 1959 Act (as amended) requires articles seized to be returned to the occupier or brought before the magistrates. See also the adverse comments of the Court of Appeal concerning the 'disclaimer' practice in *R v Metropolitan Police Comr, ex p Blackburn (No 3)* [1973] QB 241 at 252–254.

5. It not uncommonly appears that there are differences between the attitudes of magistrates and juries in their application of the test of obscenity. For example, comment was aroused when magistrates at Watford ordered forfeiture of an edition of the magazine *Men Only* at about the time that an Old Bailey jury acquitted the editors of *Nasty Tales* of the offence under s. 2 (see (1973) 127 JPN 82). Note also the jury acquittal of the publishers of *Inside Linda Lovelace* in 1976 and comment at (1976) 126 NLJ 126 and in the Williams Committee Report at p. 35:

'. . . the view was expressed to us by representatives of the Metropolitan Police that the failure of that prosecution meant that the law was unlikely to be invoked again against the written word. Their view (which appeared from his summing up to have been shared by the trial judge) was that it was difficult to imagine what written material would be regarded as obscene if that was not'.

6. In *Darbo v DPP* (1994) Times, 11 July, D was convicted under Police Act 1964, s. 51(3) for having obstructed a police officer in the execution of his duty. The officer had been seeking to execute a warrant which purported to authorise the search for 'any other material of a sexually explicit nature . . .'. D's appeal succeeded. Under the 1959/1964 Acts it was not possible to equate the notions of 'obscene' and 'sexually explicit': and only searches for, and seizure of, material of the former kind could be authorised by a s. 3 warrant. See further on s. 51(3) Police Act 1964, above, p. 53.

(v) Defence of 'Public Good'

Obscene Publications Act 1959

4. Defence of Public Good[1]

(1) [Subject to subsection (1A) of this section] a person shall not be convicted of an offence against section two of this Act, and an order for forfeiture shall not be made under the foregoing section, if it is

1 Words in square brackets, s. 4(1A) and s. 4(3) added by the Criminal Law Act 1977, s. 53.

(c) THEATRES ACT 1968

Theatres Act 1968

2. Prohibition of presentation of obscene performances of plays

(1) For the purpose of this section a performance of a play shall be deemed to be obscene if, taken as a whole, its effect was such as to tend to deprave and corrupt persons who were likely, having regard to all the circumstances, to attend it.

(2) Subject to sections 3 and 7 of this Act, if an obscene performance of a play is given, whether in public or private, any person who (whether for gain or not) presented or directed that performance shall be liable—

    (a) on summary conviction, to a fine not exceeding [£5,000] or to imprisonment for a term not exceeding six months;

    (b) on conviction on indictment, to a fine or to imprisonment for a term not exceeding three years, or both.

(3) A prosecution on indictment for an offence under this section shall not be commenced more than two years after the commission of the offence.

(4) No person shall be proceeded against in respect of a performance of a play or anything said or done in the course of such a performance—

    (a) for an offence at common law where it is of the essence of the offence that the performance or, as the case may be, what was said or done was obscene, indecent, offensive, disgusting or injurious to morality;

and no person shall be proceeded against for an offence at common law of conspiring to corrupt public morals, or to do any act contrary to public morals or decency, in respect of an agreement to present or give a performance of a play, or to cause anything to be said or done in the course of such a performance.

3. Defence of public good

(1) A person shall not be convicted of an offence under section 2 of this Act if it is proved that the giving of the performance in question was justified as being for the public good on the ground that it was in the interests of drama, opera, ballet or any other art, or of literature or learning.

(2) It is hereby declared that the opinion of experts as to the artistic, literary or other merits of a performance of a play may be admitted in any proceedings for an offence under section 2 of this Act either to establish or negative the said ground.

6. Provocation of breach of peace by means of public performance of a play

(1) Subject to section 7 of this Act, if there is given a public performance of a play involving the use of threatening, abusive or insulting words or behaviour, any person who (whether for gain or not) presented or directed that performance shall be guilty of an offence under this section if—

    (a) he did so with intent to provoke a breach of the peace; or

    (b) the performance, taken as a whole, was likely to occasion a breach of the peace.

(2) A person guilty of an offence under this section shall be liable—

[on summary conviction to a fine not exceeding level 5 on the standard scale [currently £5,000] or to imprisonment for a term not exceeding 6 months or to both].

7. Exceptions for performances given in certain circumstances

(1) Nothing in sections 2 to 4 of this Act shall apply in relation to a performance of a play given on a domestic occasion in a private dwelling.

(2) Nothing in sections 2 to 6 of this Act shall apply in relation to a performance of a play given solely or primarily for one or more of the following purposes, that is to say—

    (a) rehearsal; or

    (b) to enable—

        (i) a record or cinematograph film to be made from or by means of the performance; or

        (ii) the performance to be broadcast; or

        (iii) the performance to be included in a programme service (within the meaning of the Broadcasting Act 1990) other than a sound or television broadcasting service,

but in any proceedings for an offence under section 2 or 6 of this Act alleged to have been committed in respect of a performance of a play or an offence at common law alleged to have been committed in England and Wales by the publication of defamatory matter in the course of a performance of a play, if it is proved that the performance was attended by persons other than persons directly connected with the giving of the performance or the doing in relation thereto of any of the things mentioned in paragraph (b) above, the performance shall be taken not to have been given solely or primarily for one or more of the said purposes unless the contrary is shown.

(3) In this section—
'broadcast' means broadcast by wireless telegraphy (within the meaning of the Wireless Telegraphy Act 1949), whether by way of sound broadcasting or television;
'cinematograph film' means any print, negative, tape or other article on which a performance of a play or any part of such a performance is recorded for the purposes of visual reproduction;
'record' means any record or similar contrivance for reproducing sound, including the sound-track of a cinematograph film;

8. Restriction on institution of proceedings
Proceedings for an offence under section 2 or 6 of this Act or an offence at common law committed by the publication of defamatory matter in the course of a performance of a play shall not be instituted in England and Wales except by or with the consent of the Attorney-General.

18. Interpretation
(1) In this Act . . .
'play' means—
  (a) any dramatic piece, whether involving improvisation or not, which is given wholly or in part by one or more persons actually present and performing and in which the whole or a major proportion of what is done by the persons performing, whether by way of speech, singing or acting, involves the playing of a role; and
  (b) any ballet given wholly or in part by one or more persons actually present and performing, whether or not it falls within paragraph (a) of this definition;
'premises' includes any place;
'public performance' includes any performance in a public place within the meaning of the Public Order Act 1936 and any performance which the public or any section thereof are permitted to attend, whether on payment or otherwise;
(2) For the purposes of this Act—
  (a) a person shall not be treated as presenting a performance of a play by reason only of his taking part therein as a performer;
  (b) a person taking part as a performer in a performance of a play directed by another person shall be treated as a person who directed the peformance if without reasonable excuse he performs otherwise than in accordance with that person's direction; and
  (c) a person shall be taken to have directed a performance of a play given under his direction notwithstanding that he was not present during the performance;
and a person shall be not treated as aiding or abetting the commission of an offence under section 2 or 6 of this Act in respect of a performance of a play by reason only of his taking part in that performance as a performer.

NOTES

1. For the prosecution of indecent performances not coming within the terms of the 1968 Act see R. T. H. Stone, (1977) 127 NLJ 452.
2. In 1981 a play, *The Romans in Britain*, containing a scene depicting the homosexual rape of a young druid priest by three Roman soldiers, was presented at the National Theatre. Mrs Mary Whitehouse called upon the Attorney-General to bring, or consent to, a prosecution under the Theatres Act 1968 (e.g. for the offence under s. 2). Such consent was refused on the ground that a prosecution was not likely to succeed. Mrs Whitehouse thereupon commenced a private prosecution under s. 13 of the Sexual Offences Act 1956 – alleging the procurement by the (male) director, Michael Bogdanov, of the commission by one male actor of an act of gross indecency with another male actor. Since this was not a charge under the Theatres Act 1968 the consent of the Attorney-General was not necessary; and since it was not a charge of an offence of indecency at *common law* the provisions of s. 2(4) were not applicable. At the conclusion of the prosecution case Staughton J held that there was no case to answer: at which point the prosecution

was dropped. Accordingly, no decision was reached as to whether or not the performance had involved commission of the offence charged. In particular, the defence was denied the opportunity to argue that there was no 'procurement' by the director because the scene had taken place with the actors' fullest agreement; and further, that the scene was not grossly indecent because of the serious manner of its performance, involving nothing by way of eroticism or titillation. See further, G. Zellick, [1982] PL 165–167; G. Robertson and A. Nicol, *Media Law* (3rd edn, 1992, pp. 144–147). Note also that it was reported that the leader of the Greater London Council, Sir Horace Cutler, who had walked out of a performance in disgust, had subsequently threatened termination of the Council's substantial grant to the National Theatre. See P. R MacMillan, *Censorship and Public Morality* (1983) p. 308.

Public Order Act 1986

20. Public performance of play

(1) If a public performance of a play is given which involves the use of threatening, abusive or insulting words or behaviour, any person who presents or directs the performance is guilty of an offence if—

    (a) he intends thereby to stir up racial hatred, or

    (b) having regard to all the circumstances (and, in particular, taking the performance as a whole) racial hatred is likely to be stirred up thereby.

(2) If a person presenting or directing the performance is not shown to have intended to stir up racial hatred, it is a defence for him to prove—

    (a) that he did not know and had no reason to suspect that the performance would involve the use of the offending words or behaviour, or

    (b) that he did not know and had no reason to suspect that the offending words or behaviour were threatening, abusive or insulting, or

    (c) that he did not know and had no reason to suspect that the circumstances in which the performance would be given would be such that racial hatred would be likely to be stirred up.

(3) This section does not apply to a performance given solely or primarily for one or more of the following purposes—

    (a) rehearsal,

    (b) making a recording of the performance, or

    (c) enabling the performance to be broadcast or included in a cable programme service;

but if it is proved that the performance was attended by persons other than those directly connected with the giving of the performance or the doing in relation to it of the things mentioned in paragraph (b) or (c), the performance shall, unless the contrary is shown, be taken not to have been given solely or primarily for the purposes mentioned above.

(4) For the purposes of this section—

    (a) a person shall not be treated as presenting a performance of a play by reason only of his taking part in it as a performer,

    (b) a person taking part as a performer in a performance directed by another shall be treated as a person who directed the performance if without reasonable excuse he performs otherwise than in accordance with that person's direction, and

    (c) a person shall be taken to have directed a performance of a play given under his direction notwithstanding that he was not present during the performance;

and a person shall not be treated as aiding or abetting the commission of an offence under this section by reason only of his taking part in a performance as a performer.

(5) In this section 'play' and 'public performance' have the same meaning as in the Theatres Act 1968.

(d) OFFENCES INVOLVING INDECENCY

Post Office Act 1953

11. Prohibition on sending by post of certain articles

(1) A person shall not send or attempt to send or procure to be sent a postal packet which—

    (a) . . .; or

(b) encloses any indecent or obscene print, painting, photograph, lithography, engraving, cinematograph film, book, card or written communication, or any indecent or obscene article whether similar to the above or not; or

(c) has on the packet, or on the cover thereof, any words, marks or designs which are grossly offensive or of an indecent or obscene character.

(2) If any person acts in contravention of the foregoing subsection, he shall be liable on summary conviction to a fine not exceeding [£5,000] or on conviction on indictment to imprisonment for a term not exceeding twelve months.

NOTES

1. See, generally, C. Manchester, [1983] Crim LR 64.

2. The meaning of the words 'indecent or obscene' was considered in *R v Stanley* [1965] 2 QB 327, CCA. Lord Parker CJ explained, at 333:

'... The words "indecent or obscene" convey one idea, namely, offending against the recognised standards of propriety, indecent being at the lower end of the scale and obscene at the upper end of the scale ... As it seems to this court, an indecent article is not necessarily obscene, whereas an obscene article almost certainly must be indecent. ...'

Lord Parker also quoted with approval the following passage from Lord Sands' judgment in *McGowan v Langmuir* 1931 JC 10:

'I do not think that the two words "indecent" and "obscene" are synonymous. The one may shade into the other, but there is a difference of meaning. It is easier to illustrate than define, and I illustrate thus. For a male bather to enter the water nude in the presence of ladies would be indecent, but it would not necessarily be obscene. But if he directed the attention of a lady to a certain member of his body his conduct would certainly be obscene. ...'

In *R v Anderson* [1972] 1 QB 304, CA (Cr D), it was held to have been no misdirection on the charge under the Post Office Act 1953 for the trial judge to have directed the jury to consider whether the material was 'repulsive', 'filthy' 'loathsome' or 'lewd'.

In assessing 'indecency' under this section the courts have refused to look beyond the intrinsic qualities of the material itself to consider the circumstances of its distribution – e.g. to consider its effect on its recipient. See *Kosmos Publications v DPP* [1975] Crim LR 345, DC. Such effect would be crucial to a charge under the Obscene Publications Act 1959, s. 2.

In *Customs and Excise Comrs v Sun and Health Ltd* (1973), cited in G. Robertson and A. Nicol, *Media Law* (3rd edn, 1992) p. 131, a book comprising 122 photographs of naked boys, with their genitals as the focal point of interest, was held indecent under the customs legislation (see below). Bridge J accepted that the book could not be regarded as 'obscene'.

Note also the words of Lord Bridge in *McMonagle v Westminster City Council* [1990] 1 All ER 993:

'Newspapers and magazines which in varying degrees overtly exploit nudity for the purposes of titillating the sexual appetite, and many of which, in the first half of this century, would certainly have led to prosecution of the publisher, are now on sale in any newsagent's shop. So also, in films, on television and on the stage varying degrees of nudity have come to be accepted as commonplace. In saying this I do not overlook, of course, that there are strongly held opinions in some sections of society which deplore this state of affairs and actively campaign for the restoration of what they regard as minimal standards of decency. It is nevertheless inevitable that in the current climate of opinion prosecutions for public indecency offences have become rare and since any such prosecution will, if the defendant so elects, be tried by jury the standard likely to be applied in determining what amounts to a public indecency offence is in a high degree unpredictable.'

Customs Consolidation Act 1876

42. Prohibitions and restrictions
The goods enumerated and described in the following table of prohibitions and restrictions inwards are hereby prohibited to be imported or brought into the United Kingdom, save as thereby excepted . . .

Goods prohibited to be imported

Indecent or obscene prints, paintings, photographs, books, cards, lithographic and other engravings, or any other indecent or obscene articles.

Customs and Excise Management Act 1979

49. Forfeiture of goods improperly imported
(1) Where—
  (*a*) . . .
  (*b*) any goods are imported, landed or unloaded contrary to any prohibition or restriction for the time being in force with respect thereto under or by virtue of any enactment; or
  (*c*) . . .
those goods shall . . . be liable to forfeiture.

NOTES

1. The forfeiture of indecent material under the customs legislation set out above has been challenged as being in breach of EC obligations. In Case 121/85, *Conegate Ltd v Customs and Excise Comrs* [1987] QB 254, the appellants had sought to import into the UK from West Germany a quantity of life-size rubber dolls of a sexual nature and other erotic articles. The items were forfeited by customs officers at Heathrow airport. The appellants contended that the prohibition imposed by s. 42 of the 1876 Act constituted a quantitative restriction on imports between EC states contrary to Art. 30 of the EC Treaty. Although there is a provision in Art. 36 which permits restriction where this is justified on grounds, inter alia, of public morality, the appellants argued that this could not protect the seizure because at least in so far as the materials were indecent rather than obscene such materials could be manufactured and sold perfectly legally within the UK (though certain restrictions might apply to the public display of the items, or to sending them through the post). In other words the restriction on importation was in reality an act of discrimination in favour of domestic producers of such items and against foreign competitors. The matter was referred to the Court of Justice of the European Communities. The ECJ upheld the contentions of the appellants, and when the case returned to the English courts the forfeiture order was quashed and the goods returned. Following this decision the customs authorities could have operated a differential policy depending on whether the import is from an EC or non-EC country. In fact it appears that a general policy not to forfeit merely indecent articles is being followed. It remains the case that where an item is obscene within the meaning of the 1959 legislation its forfeiture may be justified under Art. 36. See also *R v Henn and Darby* [1981] AC 850, [1980] 2 All ER 166, ECJ and HL: affirming that for the purpose of Art. 36 each Member State may determine the requirements of public morality in accordance with its own scale of values. Customs forfeitures of 'obscene' material were upheld in *R v Bow St Metropolitan Stipendiary Magistrate, ex p Noncyp Ltd* [1990] 1 QB 123, and in *R v Uxbridge Justices, ex p David Webb* [1994] CMLR 288, DC. Both these cases involved proceedings in respect of explicit homosexual material. In the former the court refused to admit evidence on the issue of 'public good', holding that there could be no lawful trade in obscene articles within the UK even in circumstances where a public good defence might succeed.

2. Note that a directive issued by the Customs Department in 1978 instructs officers to ignore the importation by individuals of small quantities of single copies of prohibited material if imported purely for personal use. See G. Robertson, *Obscenity* (1979) p. 194. And see, generally, C. Manchester, [1981] Crim LR 531. Note the marked fall in the number of items seized in the decade prior to the *Williams Report*: 2,252,173 in 1969 compared with 125,394 in 1978.

3. For offences relating to breach of s. 42 see the Customs and Excise Management Act 1979, ss. 50 and 170. Note also the provisions of the 1979 Act, s. 154(2) as to the burden of proof in proceedings relating to customs and excise. For severity of sentence in relation to commercial importation of pornography, see *R v Nooy and Schyff* (1982) 4 Cr App Rep (S) 308 per Lawton LJ at p. 311:

'The word should go round the Continent of Europe and the Americas that importing on a commercial basis indecent and obscene matter into the United Kindgom is nearly as hazardous an operation as importing dangerous drugs – ie sentences of imprisonment and heavy fines to be imposed in order to stamp out the "flood of filth".'

Protection of Children Act 1978

1. Indecent photographs of children

(1) It is an offence for a person—

    (a) to take, or permit to be taken or to make, any indecent photograph or pseudo-photograph of a child; or

    (b) to distribute or show such indecent photographs or pseudo-photographs; or

    (c) to have in his possession such indecent photographs or pseudo-photographs, with a view to their being distributed or shown by himself or others; or

    (d) to publish or cause to be published any advertisement likely to be understood as conveying that the advertiser distributes or shows such indecent photographs or pseudo-photographs, or intends to do so.

(2) For purposes of this Act, a person is to be regarded as distributing an indecent photograph or pseudo-photograph if he parts with possession of it to, or exposes or offers it for acquisition by, another person.

(3) Proceedings for an offence under this Act shall not be instituted except by or with the consent of the Director of Public Prosecutions.

(4) Where a person is charged with an offence under subsection (1)(b) or (c), it shall be a defence for him to prove—

    (a) that he had a legitimate reason for distributing or showing the photographs or pseudo-photographs or (as the case may be) having them in his possession; or

    (b) that he had not himself seen the photographs or pseudo-photographs and did not know, nor had any cause to suspect, them to be indecent . . .

2. Evidence . . .

(3) In proceedings under this Act relating to indecent photographs of children a person is to be taken as having been a child at any material time if it appears from the evidence as a whole that he was then under the age of 16.

6. Punishments

(1) Offences under this Act shall be punishable either on conviction on indictment or on summary conviction.

(2) A person convicted on indictment of any offence under this Act shall be liable to imprisonment for a term of not more than three years, or to a fine or to both.

(3) A person convicted summarily of any offence under this Act shall be liable—

    (a) to imprisonment for a term not exceeding 6 months; or

    (b) to a fine not exceeding the prescribed sum [currently £5,000] . . ., or to both.

7. Interpretation

(1) The following subsections apply for the interpretation of this Act.

(2) References to an indecent photograph include an indecent film, a copy of an indecent photograph or film, and an indecent photograph comprised in a film.

(3) Photographs (including those comprised in a film) shall, if they show children and are indecent, be treated for all purposes of this Act as indecent photographs of children and so as respects pseudo-photographs.

(4) References to a photograph include—

    (a) the negative as well as the positive version; and

    (b) data stored on a computer disc or by other electronic means which is capable of conversion into a photograph.

(5) 'Film' includes any form of video-recording.

(6) 'Child', subject to subsection (8), means a person under the age of 16.

(7) 'Pseudo-photograph' means an image, whether made by computer graphics or otherwise howsoever, which appears to be a photograph.

(8) If the impression conveyed by a pseudo-photograph is that the person shown is a child, the pseudo-photograph shall be treated for all the purposes of this Act as showing a child and so shall a pseudo-photograph where the predominant impression conveyed is that the person shown is a child notwithstanding that some of the physical characteristics are those of an adult.

(9) References to an indecent pseudo-photograph include—

    (a) a copy of an indecent pseudo-photograph; and

    (b) data stored on a computer disc or by other electronic means which is capable of conveying information as a pseudo-photograph.

Criminal Justice Act 1988

160. Summary offence of possession of indecent photograph of child

(1) It is an offence for a person to have any indecent photograph or pseudo-photograph of a child in his possession.

(2) Where a person is charged with an offence under subsection (1) above, it shall be a defence for him to prove—

    (a) that he had a legitimate reason for having the photograph or pseudo-photograph in his possession; or

    (b) that he had not himself seen the photograph or pseudo-photograph and did not know, nor had any cause to suspect, it to be indecent; or

    (c) that the photograph or pseudo-photograph was sent to him without any prior request made by him or on his behalf and that he did not keep it for an unreasonable time.

(3) A person shall be liable on summary conviction of an offence under this section to imprisonment for a term not exceeding six months or a fine not exceeding level 5 on the standard scale or both [currently, £5,000].

(4) Sections 1(3), 2(3), 3 and 7 of the Protection of Children Act 1978 shall have effect as if any reference in them to that Act included a reference to this section.

NOTES

1. Sections 4 and 5 of the 1978 Act provide powers to entry, search, seizure and forfeiture in terms substantially similar to the provisions of the Obscene Publications Act 1959, s. 3, above, p. 359.

2. See further the annotation of this Act by M. D. A. Freeman in *Current Law Statutes Annotated 1978*. For events leading to the passage of the Act, see M. A. McCarthy and R. A. Moodie (1981) xxxiv *Parliamentary Affairs* 47.

3. In *R v Graham-Kerr* [1988] 1 WLR 1098, a naturist was convicted under s. 1(1) of the above Act of having taken photographs of a naked seven year old boy at a naturists-only session at a swimming pool. The prosecution at the trial adduced evidence of the purpose and motive for having taken the photos (i.e. sexual gratification) in order to seek to show that the pictures were indecent. The Court of Appeal, allowing the appeal against conviction, held that the photos should be considered objectively, as to whether they infringed recognised standards of propriety, without consideration being given to the motivation of the person who had taken them. That person's state of mind would only be relevant where an issue arose as to whether pictures were taken intentionally or by accident.

Indecent Displays (Control) Act 1981

Indecent Displays

1.—(1) If any indecent matter is publicly displayed the person making the display and any person causing or permitting the display to be made shall be guilty of an offence.

(2) Any matter which is displayed in or so as to be visible from any public place shall, for the purposes of this section, be deemed to be publicly displayed.

(3) In subsection (2) above, 'public place', in relation to the display of any matter, means any place to which the public have or are permitted to have access (whether on payment or otherwise) while that matter is displayed except—

(*a*) a place to which the public are permitted to have access only on payment which is or includes payment for that display; or

(*b*) a shop or any part of a shop to which the public can only gain access by passing beyond an adequate warning notice;

but the exclusions contained in paragraphs (*a*) and (*b*) above shall only apply where persons under the age of 18 years are not permitted to enter while the display in question is continuing.

(4) Nothing in this section applies in relation to any matter—

(*a*)[1] included by any person in a television broadcasting service or other television programme service (within the meaning of Part I of the Broadcasting Act 1990); or

(*b*) included in the display of an art gallery or museum and visible only from within the gallery or museum; or

(*c*) displayed by or with the authority of, and visible only from within a building occupied by, the Crown or any local authority; or

(*d*) included in a performance of a play (within the meaning of the Theatres Act 1968); or

(*e*)[2] included in a film exhibition as defined in the Cinemas Act 1985—

(i) given in a place which as regards that exhibition is required to be licensed under section 1 of that Act or by virtue only of sections 5, 7, or 8 of that Act, is not required to be so licensed; or

(ii) which is an exempted exhibition to which section 6 of that Act applies given by an exempted organisation as defined in subsection (6) of that section.

(5) In this section 'matter' includes anything capable of being displayed, except that it does not include an actual human body or any part thereof; and in determining for the purpose of this section whether any displayed matter is indecent—

(*a*) there shall be disregarded any part of that matter which is not exposed to view; and

(*b*) account may be taken of the effect of juxtaposing one thing with another.

(6) A warning notice shall not be adequate for the purposes of this section unless it complies with the following requirements—

(*a*) The warning notice must contain the following words, and no others—

'WARNING

Persons passing beyond this notice will find material on display which they may consider indecent. No admittance to persons under 18 years of age.'

(*b*) The word 'WARNING' must appear as a heading.

(*c*) No pictures or other matter shall appear on the notice.

(*d*) The notice must be so situated that no one could reasonably gain access to the shop or part of the shop in question without being aware of the notice and it must be easily legible by any person gaining such access.

NOTES

1. See C. Manchester, [1982] Stat LR 31; R. Stone, (1981) 45 MLR 62, and annotations to the Act in *Current Law Statutes Annotated 1981*; C. Munro, (1981) 132 NLJ 629.

2. Section 2(2) authorises constables to seize articles reasonably believed to be, or to contain, indecent matter and to have been used in the commission of an offence under the Act. Section 2(3) authorises justices of the peace to issue warrants authorising any constable to enter specified premises (if need be by force) and to seize any

1 As substituted by Broadcasting Act 1990.
2 As substituted by Cinemas Act 1985.

article reasonably believed to be, or to contain, indecent matter and to have been used in the commission of an offence under the Act. The justice of the peace must be satisfied that there are reasonable grounds for suspecting commission of an offence under the Act.

3. Section 3 provides for the criminal liability of directors, managers, secretaries and other officers of corporate bodies which commit offences under the Act. The consent, connivance or neglect of the individual in question must be proven.

CHAPTER 6

Freedom of expression: contempt of court

1 Introduction[1]

It is obvious that the administration of justice must be preserved free from improper interference and obstruction, and more or less inevitable that the courts will play a significant part in securing that end. There are a number of substantive criminal offences relating to the administration of justice, for example, perjury, subornation (i.e. inducing a witness to commit perjury), embracery (i.e. attempting to corrupt or improperly to influence a jury), perversion or obstruction of the course of public justice, and impeding the prosecution of a person who has committed an arrestable offence, contrary to section 4(1) of the Criminal Law Act 1967. These offences have been considered by the Law Commission, who proposed the creation or retention of over 20 specific offences in order to bring more certainty into this area of the law (see *Law Commission Report No. 96 on Offences relating to Interference with the Course of Justice* (1979); R. Leng, [1981] Crim LR 151).

Superimposed upon these criminal offences is the power of the superior courts to punish contempts. The contempt power is of wide and uncertain scope, and in the United Kingdom is exercised according to a summary procedure unknown to any other branch of the law. Trial on indictment is a theoretical possibility, but proceedings are today almost invariably conducted summarily (see below pp. 441–442). The summary procedure is of doubtful historical origin (see *R v Almon* (1765) Wilm 243; Sir John Fox, *Contempt of Court* (1927); Frankfurter and Landis, 37 Harv LR 1010, 1046 ff.). However, it is now too late to argue that the courts may not punish contempts summarily, given that many judges of high authority have acted on the then unchallenged assumption that they could (see *James v Robinson* (1963) 109 CLR 593; Frankfurter J in *Green v United States* 356 US 165 at 189 (1958)).

---

1 The main works cited in this chapter are: *Abraham*: H. J. Abraham and B. A. Perry, *Freedom and the Court*, (6th edn, 1994); *Borrie and Lowe*: N. Lowe, *Borrie and Lowe's Law of Contempt* (2nd edn, 1983); *Dobbs*: D. B. Dobbs, 'Contempt of Court: A Survey' (1971) 56 Cornell LR 183; *Goldfarb*: R. L. Goldfarb, *The Contempt Power* (1963); *Miller*: C. J. Miller, *Contempt of Court* (2nd edn, 1989); *Phillimore*: *Report of the Committee on Contempt of Court* (Cmnd. 5794, 1974); *Smith and Hogan*: J. C. Smith and B. Hogan, *Criminal Law* (6th edn, 1988): the 7th edn., 1992, omits coverage of contempt of court. In addition, see: A. Arlidge and D. Eady, *The Law of Contempt* (1982); Zelman Cowen, *Individual Liberty and the Law*, Chapters 6 and 7 (1977); Zelman Cowen, *Sir John Latham and other papers*, Chapter 2 (1965); *Contempt of Court: A Discussion Paper* (Cmnd. 7145, 1978); D. Feldman, *Civil Liberties and Human Rights in England and Wales* (1993), Chap. 16; A. L. Goodhart, (1935) 48 Harv LR 885; A. E. Hughes, (1900) 16 LQR 292; T. Ingman, 'Interference with the Proper Administration of Justice: Some Recent Developments' (1992) 11 CJQ 175; JUSTICE Report on Contempt of Court (1959); JUSTICE Report on Law and the Press (1965) pp. 5–17; H. J. Laski, (1928) 41 Harv LR 1031; J. Laws, (1990) 43 CLP 99; M. Lippman and T. Weber, [1978] 2 Crim LJ 198; Oswald, *Contempt of Court* (3rd edn, 1910); C. J. Miller, [1992] Crim LR 107; G. Robertson, *Freedom, the Individual and the Law* (7th edn, 1993) pp. 326–338; G. Robertson and A. G. L. Nicol, *Media Law* (3rd edn, 1992), Chaps. 6–8; S. Walker, 'Freedom of Speech and Contempt of Court: The English and Australian Approaches Compared' (1991) 40 ICLQ 583.

Classification of contempt is not easy. A basic distinction is drawn in England (although not in Scotland) between 'civil' and 'criminal' contempts. The former are cases of disobedience to an order of a court made in civil proceedings such as an injunction, the object of such contempt proceedings being essentially coercive (although occasionally punitive: see *Enfield London Borough Council v Mahoney* [1983] 2 All ER 901, CA). Other illustrations of civil contempts include breaches of under-takings given by litigants or their lawyers, illustrated graphically by the decision of the House of Lords in *M, Re* [1994] 1 AC 377 that Ministers of the Crown are amenable to this aspect of the contempt jurisdiction (see also *Harman v Secretary of State for the Home Department* [1983] 1 AC 280, HL; RSC Ord. 24, r. 14A; *Miller*, pp. 338–342). Criminal contempts are cases of interference with the administration of justice, and the aims of the proceedings are punitive and deterrent. There are some minor differences between the two forms. The most significant used to be that in civil contempt, committals could be *sine die*, until the contempt is purged: in criminal contempts, committals could only be for a fixed term.

Criminal contempts may be grouped under five headings (see *Borrie and Lowe*): (1) publications prejudicial to a fair criminal trial; (2) publications prejudicial to fair civil proceedings; (3) publications interfering with the course of justice as a continuing process; (4) contempt in the face of the court; and (5) acts which interfere with the course of justice. The materials given here concentrate on the first three aspects, as these tend to impinge most on freedom of expression, and the fourth, as this gener-ates problems of natural justice. The general principles underlying the law of contempt are discussed in *A-G v Times Newspapers Ltd* [1974] AC 273, the first con-tempt case to reach the House of Lords (see below, p. 405, in the section on publications prejudicial to civil proceedings).

The contempt power gives rise to concern on a number of points. Firstly, there is uncertainty as to its scope, which is undesirable given the heavy punishments that may be imposed. Secondly, it may inhibit unduly freedom of expression. Thirdly, the summary process may lack the qualities of procedural fairness thought essential for orthodox criminal proceedings. These considerations led the Phillimore Committee on Contempt of Court (Cmnd. 5794, 1974) to recommend that con-duct *intended* to pervert the course of justice should be dealt with as a criminal offence unless there are compelling reasons requiring it to be dealt with as a matter of urgency by means of summary contempt procedures. Where there is no such intention, then the law of contempt should apply, but on a narrower basis than pre-viously. Accordingly, strict liability should only attach to publications (and no other kinds of conduct) which create a risk of serious prejudice to the course of justice and which are addressed to the public at large during the currency of proceedings. The relevant time limits should be more narrowly drawn than the existing sub judice period. 'Scandalising the court' should no longer be punished as contempt, but as a criminal offence. Contempt in the face of the court should where appropriate be dealt with as a criminal offence, and where dealt with summarily there should be additional procedural safeguards for the defendant. The distinctions between 'civil' and 'criminal' contempt should be abolished. Many of these proposals were imple-mented in the Contempt of Court Act 1981 (see below pp. 376–380) although the government took the view that on a number of points the Phillimore proposals for reducing the scope of contempt were too radical (Cmnd. 7145). The 1981 Act has had some effect in narrowing and clarifying the law of contempt. However, recent decisions have shown that the common law of contempt, outside the 1981 Act, is by no means defunct. There have been important decisions dealing with publications *intended* to interfere with the administration of justice (pp. 402–405) and conduct which involves failure to respect the terms of an injunction directed to third parties (pp. 411–416). The latter in particular has opened up what is in effect a new field of criminal contempt.

Ultimately, in this context the law must draw an appropriate balance between the protection of free expression and ensuring fairness in the administration of justice. Both interests are reflected in explicit guarantees in the European Convention on Human Rights (Articles 10 and 6: see below, pp. 741, 742). The first case before the European Court of Human Rights from the UK dealing with these issues, *Sunday Times v UK* (below, p. 823), led to the Contempt of Court Act 1981 (below, p. 376), but whether English law has yet got the balance right remains controversial.

In the United States of America, the contempt power has been much more narrowly defined by comparison with the British position. The Supreme Court has applied the Constitution's First Amendment guarantees of freedom of speech and of the press strictly against exercises of the contempt power. In *Bridges v California; Times-Mirror v California* 314 US 252 (1941), the Court held by 5–4 that utterances can only be punished as contempt where there is a clear and present danger to the orderly and fair administration of justice in relation to pending litigation: 'The substantive evil must be extremely serious and the degree of imminence extremely high before utterances can be punished' (per Black J at p. 263). A 'reasonable tendency' is not sufficient. Subsequent cases have shown that the law of contempt is virtually a dead letter in protecting the trial process from prejudicial comment (see below, p. 399). In addition, the constitutional right to jury trial in serious criminal cases (Fifth, Sixth and Fourteenth Amendments) has been held applicable to contempt cases (*Bloom v Illinois* 391 US 194 (1968); *Miller* pp. 192–194). In federal courts, the summary contempt power is limited by statute (18 US Code, Section 401, as derived originally from an Act of 1831) to: '(1) Misbehaviour of any person in its presence or so near thereto as to obstruct the administration of justice; (2) Misbehaviour of any of its officers in their official transactions; (3) Disobedience or resistance to its lawful writ, process, order, rule, decree, or command.' The words 'so near thereto' have been held by the Supreme Court to bear a geographical rather than a causative meaning (*Nye v United States* 313 US 33 (1941)). Some states have similar legislation narrowing the scope of the contempt power.

2 The Contempt of Court Act 1981

In this section we set out the provisions of the Contempt of Court Act 1981. This Act does not codify the whole of the law of contempt of court. It simply modifies certain aspects of the previously existing law. One significant feature that should be noted is that the first seven sections deal with what the Act terms the 'strict liability rule', as defined in s. 1. Accordingly, conduct *intended* to interfere with the course of justice will be regulated by (1) the common law of contempt except insofar as it is modified by the remaining provisions of the 1981 Act or (2) the substantive offences relating to the administration of justice (see above, p. 373).

In the remaining sections (3–8) of the chapter we consider in turn the main varieties of criminal contempt, and within each section the position at common law is set out first, followed by a summary of the position following the enactment of the Contempt of Court Act 1981.

Contempt of Court Act 1981

Strict liability

1. The strict liability rule
In this Act 'the strict liability rule' means the rule of law whereby conduct may be treated as a contempt of court as tending to interfere with the course of justice in particular legal proceedings regardless of intent to do so.

2. Limitation of scope of strict liability
(1) The strict liability rule applies only in relation to publications, and for this purpose 'publication' includes any speech, writing, [programme included in a programme service][1] or other communication in whatever form, which is addressed to the public at large or any section of the public.
(2) The strict liability rule applies only to a publication which creates a substantial risk that the course of justice in the proceedings in question will be seriously impeded or prejudiced.
(3) The strict liability rule applies to a publication only if the proceedings in question are active within the meaning of this section at the time of the publication.
(4) Schedule 1 applies for determining the times at which proceedings are to be treated as active within the meaning of this section.
[(5) In this section 'programme service' has the same meaning as in the Broadcasting Act 1990.][2]

3. Defence of innocent publication or distribution
(1) A person is not guilty of contempt of court under the strict liability rule as the publisher of any matter to which that rule applies if at the time of publication (having taken all reasonable care) he does not know and has no reason to suspect that relevant proceedings are active.
(2) A person is not guilty of contempt of court under the strict liability rule as the distributor of a publication containing any such matter if at the time of distribution (having taken all reasonable care) he does not know that it contains such matter and has no reason to suspect that it is likely to do so.
(3) The burden of proof of any fact tending to establish a defence afforded by this section to any person lies upon that person. . . .

4. Contemporary reports of proceedings
(1) Subject to this section a person is not guilty of contempt of court under the strict liability rule in respect of a fair and accurate report of legal proceedings held in public, published contemporaneously and in good faith.
(2) In any such proceedings the court may, where it appears to be necessary for avoiding a substantial risk of prejudice to the administration of justice in those proceedings, or in any other proceedings pending or imminent, order that the publication of any report of the proceedings, or any part of the proceedings, be postponed for such period as the court thinks necessary for that purpose.
(3) For the purposes of subsection (1) of this section and of section 3 of the Law of Libel Amendment Act 1888 (privilege) a report of proceedings shall be treated as published contemporaneously—
   (a) in the case of a report of which publication is postponed pursuant to an order under subsection (2) of this section, if published as soon as practicable after that order expires;
   (b) in the case of a report of [an application for dismissal under section 6 of the Magistrates' Courts Act 1980][3] of which publication is permitted by virtue only of [subsection (5) or (7) of section 8A of that Act],[3] if published as soon as practicable after publication is so permitted. . . .

5. Discussion of public affairs
A publication made as or as part of a discussion in good faith of public affairs or other matters of general public interest is not to be treated as a contempt of court under the strict liability rule if the risk of impediment or prejudice to particular legal proceedings is merely incidental to the discussion.

6. Savings
Nothing in the foregoing provisions of this Act—
   (a) prejudices any defence available at common law to a charge of contempt of court under the strict liability rule;

1 Substituted by the Broadcasting Act 1990, Sch. 20, para. 31.
2 Added by the Broadcasting Act 1990, Sch. 20.
3 Substituted by the Criminal Justice and Public Order Act 1994, Sch. 4, para. 50, from a day to be appointed.

(b) implies that any publication is punishable as contempt of court under that rule which would not be so punishable apart from those provisions;

(c) restricts liability for contempt of court in respect of conduct intended to impede or prejudice the administration of justice.

7. Consent required for institution of proceedings

Proceedings for a contempt of court under the strict liability rule (other than Scottish proceedings) shall not be instituted except by or with the consent of the Attorney-General or on the motion of a court having jurisdiction to deal with it.

Other aspects of law and procedure

8. Confidentiality of jury's deliberations

(1) Subject to subsection (2) below, it is a contempt of court to obtain, disclose or solicit any particulars of statements made, opinions expressed, arguments advanced or votes cast by members of a jury in the course of their deliberations in any legal proceedings.

(2) This section does not apply to any disclosure of any particulars—

(a) in the proceedings in question for the purpose of enabling the jury to arrive at their verdict, or in connection with the delivery of that verdict, or

(b) in evidence in any subsequent proceedings for an offence alleged to have been committed in relation to the jury in the first mentioned proceedings,

or to the publication of any particulars so disclosed.

(3) Proceedings for a contempt of court under this section (other than Scottish proceedings) shall not be instituted except by or with the consent of the Attorney-General or on the motion of a court having jurisdiction to deal with it.

9. Use of tape recorders

(1) Subject to subsection (4) below, it is a contempt of court—

(a) to use in court, or bring into court for use, any tape recorder or other instrument for recording sound, except with the leave of the court;

(b) to publish a recording of legal proceedings made by means of any such instrument, or any recording derived directly or indirectly from it, by playing it in the hearing of the public or any section of the public, or to dispose of it or any recording so derived, with a view to such publication;

(c) to use any such recording in contravention of any conditions of leave granted under paragraph (a).

(2) Leave under paragraph (a) of subsection (1) may be granted or refused at the discretion of the court, and if granted may be granted subject to such conditions as the court thinks proper with respect to the use of any recording made pursuant to the leave; and where leave has been granted the court may at the like discretion withdraw or amend it either generally or in relation to any particular part of the proceedings.

(3) Without prejudice to any other power to deal with an act of contempt under paragraph (a) of subsection (1), the court may order the instrument, or any recording made with it, or both, to be forfeited; and any object so forfeited shall (unless the court otherwise determines on application by a person appearing to be the owner) be sold or otherwise disposed of in such manner as the court may direct.

(4) This section does not apply to the making or use of sound recordings for purposes of official transcripts of proceedings.

10. Sources of information

No court may require a person to disclose, nor is any person guilty of contempt of court for refusing to disclose, the source of information contained in a publication for which he is responsible, unless it be established to the satisfaction of the court that disclosure is necessary in the interests of justice or national security or for the prevention of disorder or crime.

11. Publication of matters exempted from disclosure in court

In any case where a court (having power to do so) allows a name or other matter to be withheld from the public in proceedings before the court, the court may give such directions prohibiting the publication of that name or matter in connection with the proceedings as appear to the court to be necessary for the purpose for which it was so withheld.

12. Offences of contempt of magistrates' courts

(1) A magistrates' court has jurisdiction under this section to deal with any person who—

(a) wilfully insults the justice or justices, any witness before or officer of the court[1] or any solicitor or counsel having business in the court, during his or their sitting or attendance in court or in going to or returning from the court; or

(b) wilfully interrupts the proceedings of the court or otherwise misbehaves in court.

(2) In any such case the court may order any officer of the court, or any constable, to take the offender into custody and detain him until the rising of the court; and the court may, if it thinks fit, commit the offender to custody for a specified perod not exceeding one month or impose on him a fine not exceeding [£2,500] or both. . . .

[(2A) A fine imposed under subsection (2) above shall be deemed, for the purposes of any enactment, to be a sum adjudged to be paid by a conviction.][2]

(4) A magistrates' court may at any time revoke an order of committal made under subsection (2) and, if the offender is in custody, order his discharge.

(5) The following provisions of the Magistrates' Courts Act 1980 apply in relation to an order under this section as they apply in relation to a sentence on conviction or finding of guilty of an offence, namely: section 36 (restriction on fines in respect of young persons); sections 75 to 91 (enforcement); section 108 (appeal to Crown Court); section 136 (overnight detention in default of payment); and section 142(1) (power to rectify mistakes). . . .

Penalties for contempt and kindred offences

14. Proceedings in England and Wales

(1) In any case where a court has power to commit a person to prison for contempt of court and (apart from this provision) no limitation applies to the period of committal, the committal shall (without prejudice to the power of the court to order his earlier discharge) be for a fixed term, and that term shall not on any occasion exceed two years in the case of committal by a superior court, or one month in the case of committal by an inferior court.

(2) In any case where an inferior court has power to fine a person for contempt of court and (apart from this provision) no limit applies to the amount of the fine, the fine shall not on any occasion exceed [£2,500]. . . .

[(2A) A fine imposed under subsection (2) above shall be deemed, for the purposes of any enactment, to be a sum adjudged to be paid by a conviction.][3]

(4) and (4A) [*Persons suffering from mental illness or severe mental impairment*]

[(4A) For the purposes of the preceding provisions of this section a county court shall be treated as a superior court and not as an inferior court.] . . .

19. Interpretation

In this Act

'court' includes any tribunal or body exercising the judicial power of the State, and 'legal proceedings' shall be construed accordingly;

'publication' has the meaning assigned by subsection (1) of section 2, and 'publish' (except in section 9) shall be construed accordingly; . . .

'the strict liability rule' has the meaning assigned by section 1;

'superior court' means the Court of Appeal, the High Court, the Crown Court, the Courts-Martial Appeal Court, the Restrictive Practices Court, the Employment Appeal Tribunal and any other court exercising in relation to its proceedings powers equivalent to those of the High Court, and includes the House of Lords in the exercise of its appellate jurisdiction.

SCHEDULES

SCHEDULE 1

TIMES WHEN PROCEEDINGS ARE ACTIVE FOR PURPOSES OF SECTION 2

Preliminary

1. In this Schedule 'criminal proceedings' means proceedings against a person in respect of an offence, not being appellate proceedings or proceedings commenced by motion for committal or attachment in

---

1 The reference to any officer of the court includes a reference to any court security officer assigned to the court-house in which the court is sitting: Criminal Justice Act 1991, Sch. 11, para. 29. On court security officers, see the 1991 Act, ss. 76–79.

2 Substituted by the Criminal Justice Act 1993, Sch. 3, para. 6(4).

3 Substituted by the Criminal Justice Act 1993, Sch. 3, para. 6(5).

England and Wales or Northern Ireland; and 'appellate proceedings' means proceedings on appeal from or for the review of the decision of a court in any proceedings.

2. Criminal, appellate and other proceedings are active within the meaning of section 2 at the times respectively prescribed by the following paragraphs of this Schedule; and in relation to proceedings in which more than one of the steps described in any of those paragraphs is taken, the reference in that paragraph is a reference to the first of those steps.

Criminal proceedings

3. Subject to the following provisions of this Schedule, criminal proceedings are active from the relevant initial step specified in paragraph 4 until concluded as described in paragraph 5.

4. The initial steps of criminal proceedings are:—
   (a) arrest without warrant;
   (b) the issue, or in Scotland the grant, of a warrant for arrest;
   (c) the issue of a summons to appear, or in Scotland the grant of a warrant to cite;
   (d) the service of an indictment or other document specifying the charge;
   (e) except in Scotland, oral charge.

5. Criminal proceedings are concluded
   (a) by acquittal or, as the case may be, by sentence;
   (b) by any other verdict, finding, order or decision which puts an end to the proceedings;
   (c) by discontinuance or by operation of law.

6. The reference in paragraph 5(a) to sentence includes any order or decision consequent on conviction or finding of guilt which disposes of the case, either absolutely or subject to future events, and a deferment of sentence under section 1 of the Powers of Criminal Courts Act 1973, section 219 or 432 of the Criminal Procedure (Scotland) Act 1975 or Article 14 of the Treatment of Offenders (Northern Ireland) Order 1976.

7. Proceedings are discontinued within the meaning of paragraph 5(c)—
   (a) in England and Wales or Northern Ireland, if the charge or summons is withdrawn or a *nolle prosequi* entered;
   [(aa) in England and Wales, if they are discontinued by virtue of section 23 of the Prosecution of Offences Act 1985;][1]
   (b) in Scotland, if the proceedings are expressly abandoned by the prosecutor or are deserted *simpliciter*;
   (c) in the case of proceedings in England and Wales or Northern Ireland commenced by arrest without warrant, if the person arrested is released, otherwise than on bail, without having been charged.

8. Criminal proceedings before a court-martial or standing civilian court are not concluded until the completion of any review of finding or sentence.

9. Criminal proceedings in England and Wales or Northern Ireland cease to be active if an order is made for the charge to lie on the file, but become active again if leave is later given for the proceedings to continue.

[9A. Where proceedings in England and Wales have been discontinued by virtue of section 23 of the Prosecution of Offences Act 1985, but notice is given by the accused under subsection (7) of that section to the effect that he wants the proceedings to continue, they become active again with the giving of that notice.][2]

10. Without prejudice to paragraph 5(b) above, criminal proceedings against a person cease to be active—
   (a) if the accused is found to be under a disability such as to render him unfit to be tried or unfit to plead or, in Scotland, is found to be insane in bar of trial; or
   (b) if a hospital order is made in his case under [section 51(5) of the Mental Health Act 1983] . . .
but become active again if they are later resumed.

11. Criminal proceedings against a person which become active on the issue or the grant of a warrant for his arrest cease to be active at the end of the period of twelve months beginning with the date of the warrant unless he has been arrested within that period, but become active again if he is subsequently arrested.

Other proceedings at first instance

12. Proceedings other than criminal proceedings and appellate proceedings are active from the time when arrangements for the hearing are made or, if no such arrangements are previously made, from the time the hearing begins, until the proceedings are disposed of or discontinued or withdrawn; and for the purposes of this paragraph any motion or application made in or for the purposes of any proceedings, and any pre-trial review in the county court, is to be treated as a distinct proceeding.

---

1 Added by the Prosecution of Offences Act 1985, Sch. 1, para. 4.
2 Added by the Prosecution of Offences Act 1985, Sch. 1, para. 5.

13. In England and Wales or Northern Ireland arrangements for the hearing of proceedings to which paragraph 12 applies are made within the meaning of that paragraph—

    (a) in the case of proceedings in the High Court for which provision is made by rules of court for setting down for trial, when the case is set down;

    (b) in the case of any proceedings, when a date for the trial or hearing is fixed.

14. In Scotland arrangements for the hearing or proceedings to which paragraph 12 applies are made within the meaning of that paragraph—

    (a) in the case of an ordinary action in the Court of Session or in the sheriff court, when the Record is closed;

    (b) in the case of a motion or application, when it is enrolled or made;

    (c) in any other case, when the date for a hearing is fixed or a hearing is allowed.

Appellate proceedings

15. Appellate proceedings are active from the time when they are commenced—

    (a) by application for leave to appeal or apply for review, or by notice of such an application;

    (b) by notice of appeal or of application for review;

    (c) by other originating process,

until disposed of or abandoned, discontinued or withdrawn.

16. Where, in appellate proceedings relating to criminal proceedings, the court—

    (a) remits the case to the court below; or

    (b) orders a new trial or a venire de novo, or in Scotland grants authority to bring a new prosecution,

any further or new proceedings which result shall be treated as active from the conclusion of the appellate proceedings.

NOTES

1. By mistake, two subsections (4A) have been inserted in section 14. The second (the one printed here) was introduced by the County Court (Penalties for Contempt) Act 1983 and was enacted to deal with the restriction on the powers of county courts to deal with civil contempts highlighted by the decision of the House of Lords in *Peart v Stewart* [1983] 2 AC 109, HL. The fines in ss. 12(2) and 14(2) were increased by the Criminal Justice Act 1991, Sch. 4. The limits to the penalties for contempt apply to civil as well as criminal contempts: *Linnett v Coles* [1987] QB 555, CA. A judge may not impose on one occasion consecutive sentences which cumulatively exceed two years: *Re R (a minor) (contempt: sentence)* [1994] 2 All ER 144; *Villiers v Villiers* [1994] 2 All ER 149, CA. A person found guilty of criminal contempt is not 'convicted of an offence' and so may not be put on probation: *R v Palmer* [1992] 3 All ER 289, CA (Cr D).[1]

2. The real impetus to reform seems to have been the decision of the European Court of Human Rights in the *Sunday Times* case (below, p. 823) that the restrictions placed upon freedom of speech by the injunction against the newspaper, upheld by the House of Lords in *A-G v Times Newspapers Ltd* (below, p. 405), was contrary to Article 10 of the European Convention on Human Rights. The Bill was introduced in the House of Lords by Lord Hailsham of St. Marylebone L.C. (415 HL Deb December 9 1980 cols 657–665). He said that his 'poor little ewe lamb' of a Bill was intended to be a liberalising measure. The three main purposes of the first group of sections, dealing with the so-called rule of strict liability in criminal contempt, were (1) implementation of the main recommendations of the Phillimore report, with 'minor deviations'; (2) harmonisation of the law of England and Wales with the

---

1 The Act is considered in the following works: *Borrie and Lowe*; *Miller*; A. Arlidge and D. Eady, *The Law of Contempt* (1982); *Current Law Statutes Annotated 1981* (annotations by A. G. L. Nicol and (for Scotland) C. H. W. Gane); N. Lowe, [1982] PL 20; C. J. Miller, [1982] Crim LR 71; S. H. Bailey, (1982) 45 MLR 301; P. J. Cooke [1983] V (1) Liverpool LR 35.

European Court's judgment in the *Sunday Times* case; and (3) harmonisation of the laws of England, Scotland and Northern Ireland into a coherent set of rules. The other sections either sought to implement other recommendations of the Phillimore Committee or to deal with problems that had arisen since the Committee reported. The Act came into force on 27 August, 1981. It has been a matter of debate whether the Act does enough to bring English law into conformity with the European Convention on Human Rights (see the articles cited below, p. 410 n. **5**).

3 Publications prejudicial to a fair criminal trial

The main area where uncertainties in the law of contempt cast a shadow over free expression is that of publications which tend to prejudice the fair trial of either criminal or civil proceedings, or otherwise interfere with the course of justice. The important criticisms made to the Phillimore Committee were (1) 'the lack of clear definition of the kind of statement, criticism or comment which will be held to amount to contempt' (para. 83) and (2) 'the uncertainty as to the time when the law of contempt applies' (para. 84). Where it is sought to hold persons liable under the 'strict liability rule' (Contempt of Court Act 1981, s. 1; above p. 376) the law on these points has been modified by sections 2 and 3 and Schedule 1 of the 1981 Act (above, pp. 376 and 378–380 and below pp. 384–391, and 416–421). Prior to the 1981 Act it was more or less settled that the common law imposed strict liability for this form of contempt, subject to certain statutory defences (see below, pp. 401–402). Strict liability can now only be imposed by virtue of sections 1 to 7 of the 1981 Act. Recent cases have made it clear that publications (and indeed other conduct) *intended* to interfere with justice can still be dealt with under the common law of contempt. Here, the issues of what constitutes contempt, when the sub judice rule applies and the scope of liability are regulated by the common law and not the 1981 Act (see below, pp. 381–384, 400–405, 411–416).

The balance between freedom of expression and the right to a fair trial is different in the UK and the United States, and there are important sectors of opinion in each country which express dissatisfaction with their country's own position.

(a) WHAT CONSTITUTES CONTEMPT?

(i) At Common Law

R v Evening Standard Co Ltd [1954] 1 QB 578, [1954] 1 All ER 1026, [1954] 2 WLR 861, Queen's Bench Divisional Court

On 23 February 1954, a Mr Kemp was indicted at Chelmsford Assizes for the murder of his wife, who had been dead for a considerable time before his arrest and whose body was discovered in a trunk which the prisoner had caused to be moved with his effects. Part of the case for the Crown was that the defendant had told many lies with regard to the disappearance of his wife. A Miss Briggs gave evidence that the defendant had told her that he was unmarried, and a Mrs Darmody said that he had told her that he had been married but that his wife had died. That evening, the *Evening Standard* carried a report of the trial under the headline 'Trunk Trial Story of Marriage Offer – Husband is Accused', which stated that Mrs Darmody 'said at the assizes that a man accused of murdering his wife asked her to marry him.'

In fact, Mrs Darmody had not given that evidence. Miss Briggs had given evidence before the examining justices that the prisoner had, after the death of his wife, asked her to marry him; but at the trial, when Miss Briggs had just begun to give evidence, the judge ruled, after a discussion in the absence of the jury, that that part of her evidence should not be given as it was highly prejudicial to the defendant; and no such evidence was given at the trial.

The reporter at the trial was responsible for the error – he had attended the committal proceedings, and had left the trial during the discussion as to the admissibility of part of Miss Briggs' evidence, returning just after she had completed her evidence. In fact the jury found the defendant not guilty.

The Attorney-General applied for leave to issue a writ of attachment against the Evening Standard Co Ltd, the editor of the *Evening Standard* and the reporter.

According to an affidavit filed by the editor the reporter had for 10 years been a trusted reporter on the staff of the newspaper and had previously reported many trials without any complaint as to the accuracy of his reports, and had proved himself a thoroughly competent and reliable reporter. He had thought the report perfectly accurate and genuine and he and the proprietors had published it in good faith.

Lord Goddard CJ delivered the judgment of the court (**Lord Goddard CJ**, **Hilbery** and **Hallett JJ**): . . .
This is surely a proper matter to bring before this court. It is just as well that the nature of the jurisdiction which this court exercises on these occasions with regard to reports of trials in newspapers should be understood. It is called contempt of court, and that is a convenient expression because it is akin to a contempt. But the essence of the jurisdiction is that reports, if they contain comments on cases before they are tried, or alleged histories of the prisoner who is on trial—such as in the case of the *Daily Mirror* (*R v Bolam, ex p Haigh* (1949) 93 Sol Jo 220), in which this court had to intervene about five years ago—and all misreports are matters which tend to interfere with the due course of justice. The foundation of the jurisdiction is that such reports are an interference with the due course of justice, and one of the earliest cases, if not the earliest, in which this jurisdiction was invoked was in 1742, in a case known as *The St. James Evening Post* ((1742) 2 Atk 469) before that great judge, Lord Hardwicke LC. In that case there was a motion to commit an editor for publishing a libel upon a litigant and it was objected that it was not a matter for the summary jurisdiction of the court because there was a remedy at law for libel. Lord Hardwicke pointed out that he was dealing with the matter of the publication of a libel upon a litigant in a case which had not then come to a conclusion or been heard. He started his judgment by saying (ibid.): 'Nothing is more incumbent upon courts of justice, than to preserve their proceedings from being misrepresented;—that is, of course, what has happened here—'nor is there any thing of more pernicious consequence, than to prejudice the minds of the public against persons concerned as parties in causes, before the cause is finally heard.' After rejecting the argument that he could not deal summarily with the case because there was a remedy at law, he considered the different sorts of contempt. The last one was (ibid. p. 471): 'There may be also a contempt of this court, in prejudicing mankind against persons before the cause i· heard. There cannot be any thing of greater consequence, than to keep the streams of justice clear and pure, that parties may proceed with safety both to themselves and their characters.' . . .
We have said, perhaps more frequently in recent years, that the summary jurisdiction of this court should only be invoked and will only be exercised in cases of real and serious moment; and have deprecated in certain cases a motion to attach where there has not really been a serious interference with justice. This case might have been a disastrous interference with justice; but, as Lord Hewart CJ said in *R v Editor of the New Statesman, ex p DPP* (1928) 44 TLR 301 at 303 the gravity of the penalty or sanction which the court will impose must depend upon the circumstances of each particular case. If a comment is gratuitously published either in a newspaper or in any other form of public dissemination, this court would not hesitate to impose a severe penalty, and even, as in the recent case of the *Daily Mirror* (*R v Bolam, ex p Haigh* (1949) 93 Sol Jo 220) to inflict the penalty of imprisonment. In this case, however, I am glad to be able to come to the conclusion that there was here no intentional interference with the course of justice. I cannot believe that the reporter for a moment deliberately or intentionally sent out false information. He, as a responsible journalist, would know that doing so would land him in the gravest possible difficulty. Nor can one attach moral blame, if I may use that expression, to the editor, who had no reason to suppose that a reporter of the 'Standard' had sent him information in an inaccurate form. There are, therefore, mitigating circumstances, and one can only be thankful that the matter did

not react unfavourably on the prisoner, though, as I have said whether it reacts favourably or unfavourably upon the prisoner is not the test.

Sir Hartley Shawcross said that, while his clients desired to abide by the well understood rule of journalism that the editor and proprietors of papers must in a case such as this take responsibility, he would suggest to the court that vicarious liability, as it is called, ought not in law to be visited upon them and that they ought not to be made vicariously liable for the mistake or misconduct of the reporter. I do not think that we can possibly agree with that submission, which seems contrary to what Lord Russell and Wright J said in *R v Payne* [1896] 1 QB 577 where they pointed out that the court would interfere where the publication was intended or calculated or likely to interfere with the course of justice. Wright J (ibid. p. 582) used the word 'likely,' Lord Russell (ibid. p. 580) used the word 'calculated'.

[The court held that all the defendants were guilty of contempt, but that no penalty should be imposed on the editor and reporter. The publishers were fined £1,000.]

NOTES

1. Note that the Divisional Court was not concerned with the actual effect upon proceedings, but the potential effect, particularly on a jury (cf. *A-G for New South Wales v John Fairfax & Sons Ltd* [1980] 1 NSWLR 362, 368 (NSWCA)).

The cases show that the test at common law was whether a publication was 'calculated' or 'likely' to interfere with the course of justice or, in other words, whether it created a real risk that the fair and proper trial of pending proceedings might be prejudiced. This remains the test where contempt proceedings are taken in respect of conduct *intended* to interfere with the course of justice, with the possible qualification that the proceedings need not be pending or imminent (see below, pp. 402–405). The common law is also of relevance in as much as s. 6(b) of the Contempt of Court Act 1981 provides that nothing in ss. 1–5 implies that any publication is punishable as contempt of court under the strict liability rule which would not have been so punishable apart from those provisions: i.e. at common law.

2. The following are some examples of contempt in cases decided before the 1981 Act came into operation:

(i) Prejudging the merits of a case

R v Bolam, ex p Haigh (1949) 93 Sol Jo 220. B, the editor of the *Daily Mirror*, was imprisoned for three months, and the proprietors were fined £10,000 for describing Haigh as a 'vampire' and, after saying that he was charged with one murder, stating that he had committed others, giving the names of the victims (cf. *R v Odham's Press Ltd, ex p A-G* [1957] 1 QB 73).

In the 1920s, various newspapers conducted systematic 'criminal investigations' whose results were then published. This led to fines of £1,000 imposed on the *Evening Standard*, and of £300 on two other newspapers, with a warning that repetition of the offence would lead to imprisonment (*R v Evening Standard, ex p DPP* (1924) 40 TLR 833).

In the *Sunday Times* case, below p. 405, the House of Lords held that prejudgment of the merits amounted to a contempt of court. The facts concerned civil proceedings, but a distinction between civil and criminal proceedings was not drawn for this purpose. However, in subsequent cases the Divisional Court held that prejudgment only amounted to contempt where it created a real risk that the fair and proper trial of pending proceedings might be prejudiced. So, in *Blackburn v BBC* (1976) Times, 15 December, James Ferman, secretary designate of the British Board of Film Censors, referred in a television interview to pending criminal proceedings instituted by B in relation to the showing of the film 'The Language of Love', and said 'The context of the film was seriously educational and could do nothing but good in the board's opinion and my opinion.' The court held that there was no risk of prejudice given that the words were spoken in the middle of a general discussion about film censorship and were immediately followed by an expression of F's opinion that the courts should be the final arbiter. Moreover, the programme was only shown in the south-west, and it was unlikely that a prospective Old Bailey juror would see or recollect the words. The same test was applied in *R v Bulgin, ex p BBC* (1977) Times, 14 July.

(ii) Comments on a defendant's character

R v Thomson Newspapers Ltd, ex p A-G [1968] 1 All ER 268. The *Sunday Times* published an article about Michael Abdul Malik who was awaiting trial on a charge under the Race Relations Act 1965. Beneath a photograph of M was the comment that he 'took to politics after an unedifying career as brothel keeper, procurer and property racketeer.' The proprietors were fined £5,000 for contempt. However, M's appeal against conviction on the ground (inter alia) that there was a danger that he had not had a fair trial was dismissed. The Court of Appeal (Criminal Division) felt that in the light of all the evidence at the trial, M had not been prejudiced (*R v Malik* [1968] 1 All ER 582n). In *R v Border Television Ltd, ex p A-G; R v Newcastle Chronicle and Journal Ltd, ex p A-G* (1978) 68 Cr App Rep 375, DC, the defendants had stated that a person being tried by jury on six charges of obtaining by deception and six charges of theft had pleaded guilty to four deception charges. That information had been kept from the jury, which had to be discharged. The publication was held to be a contempt. Lord Widgery CJ pointed out at 380 that 'every fledgling reporter' should be aware of two simple forms of contempt: 'publishing material relating to other offences or publishing material which has been deliberately kept from the jury's ears'. In 1981, similar proceedings were taken against the *North Western Evening Mail* (*UK Press Gazette*, 16 February 1981, p. 4) and the *Northampton Chronicle and Echo* (*The Times*, 31 March 1981). See further, p. 396.

(iii) The publication of photographs

R v Evening Standard Co Ltd, ex p A-G (1976) Times, 3 November, DC. The company was fined £1,000 for publishing a photograph of Peter Hain, together with an article, on the front page of the *Evening Standard*, on the day that he was due to take part in an identification parade after he had been charged with the theft of £490 from a bank in Putney. H was ultimately acquitted. In assessing the penalty, the court took into account the nature of the contempt, how the contempt happened, the degree of distribution of the newspaper, and the effect on the administration of justice. The court seemed to think that it had had no effect on the identification parade, but Peter Hain has stated that several bank officials who attended the parade as witnesses had seen a copy of the paper that morning at the bank (P. Hain, *Mistaken Identity* (1976), pp. 21–2, 39–40, 42, 85). Another factor the court took into account was that 'it would be a great pity if the courts allowed newspapers to think that the cost of their legal department was unjustified'.

(ii) Under the 'Strict Liability Rule'

Section 2 of the Contempt of Court Act 1981 (above, p. 376) provides that there can only be liability for contempt under the strict liability rule where a 'publication' (see s. 2(1)) 'creates a substantial risk that the course of justice in the proceedings in question will be seriously impeded or prejudiced' (s. 2(2)). This is more stringent than the test at common law.

NOTES

1. This test was based on that recommended by the Phillimore Committee (Cmnd. 5794, 1974), pp. 44–49, but with the addition of the word 'substantial'. Note that strict liability is now confined to 'publications', as recommended by the Phillimore Committee (pp. 33–35), whose view was that strict liability should be confined to public conduct.

2. To what extent does the new test constitute a real and not merely a 'semantic' or 'cosmetic' relaxation in the application of the law of contempt? See *Borrie and Lowe*, pp. 90–91. Do you think that any of the cases where D was convicted at common law would have been decided differently had the new test been in operation? Section 2(2) has been applied in *A-G v English* [1983] 1 AC 116, HL, and *A-G v Times Newspapers* (1983) Times, 12 February, DC (below). As to its application in respect of civil cases, see pp. 416–421.

A-G v English [1983] 1 AC 116, [1982] 2 All ER 903, [1982] 3 WLR 278, House of Lords

In October 1981 the *Daily Mail* published an article under the heading 'The vision of life that wins my vote' written by the journalist and broadcaster Malcolm Muggeridge in support of a parliamentary candidate, Mrs Marilyn Carr, who was seeking election as a pro-life candidate. The article was concerned with preserving the sanctity of human life. It also noted that Mrs Carr had been born without arms and continued: 'Today the chances of such a baby surviving would be very small indeed. Someone would surely recommend letting her die of starvation, or otherwise disposing of her.' The article was published on the third day of the trial of a consultant paediatrician, Dr Leonard Arthur, for the murder of John Pearson, a baby suffering from Down's syndrome. The trial judge, Farquharson J, referred the article to the Attorney-General, who applied to the Divisional Court for an order of committal against the editor of the *Daily Mail*, David English, and the newspaper's owners. He relied on the 'strict liability rule' contained in section 1 of the Contempt of Court Act 1981. The defendant relied on section 5 of the 1981 Act (above, p. 376). The Divisional Court held that the publication amounted to contempt. No penalty was imposed on the editor; he had been absent from the office at the relevant times and was not personally responsible for the publication. A 'nominal' fine of £500 was imposed on the owners. The defendants appealed to the House of Lords.

Lord Diplock: . . . There is, of course, no question that the article in the *Daily Mail* of which complaint is made by the Attorney-General was a 'publication' within the meaning of section 2(1). That being so, it appears to have been accepted in the Divisional Court by both parties that the onus of proving that the article satisfied the conditions stated in section 2(2) lay upon the Attorney-General and that, if he satisfied that onus, the onus lay upon the appellants to prove that it satisfied the conditions stated in section 5. For my part, I am unable to accept that this represents the effect of the relationship of section 5 to section 2(2). Section 5 does not take the form of a proviso or an exception to section 2(2). It stands on an equal footing with it. It does not set out exculpatory matter. Like section 2(2) it states what publications shall *not* amount to contempt of court despite their tendency to interfere with the course of justice in particular legal proceedings.

[L]ogically the first question always is: has the publication satisfied the criterion laid down by section 2(2) i.e. that it 'creates a substantial risk that the course of justice in the proceedings in question will be seriously impeded or prejudiced.'

My Lords, the first thing to be observed about this criterion is that the risk that has to be assessed is that which was created by the publication of the allegedly offending matter at the time when it was published. The public policy that underlies the strict liability rule in contempt of court is deterrence. Trial by newspaper or, as it should be more compendiously expressed today, trial by the media, is not to be permitted in this country. That the risk that was created by the publication when it was actually published does not ultimately affect the outcome of the proceedings is, as Lord Goddard CJ said in *R v Evening Standard Co Ltd* [1954] 1 QB 578, 582 'neither here nor there.' If there was a reasonable possibility that it might have done so if in the period subsequent to the publication the proceedings had not taken the course that in fact they did and Dr Arthur was acquitted, the offence was complete. The true course of justice must not at any stage be put at risk.

Next for consideration is the concatenation in the subsection of the adjective 'substantial' and the adverb 'seriously', the former to describe the degree of risk, the latter to describe the degree of impediment or prejudice to the course of justice. 'Substantial' is hardly the most apt word to apply to 'risk' which is a noumenon. In combination I take the two words to be intended to exclude a risk that is only remote. With regard to the adverb 'seriously' a perusal of the cases cited in *A-G v Times Newspapers Ltd* [1974] AC 273 discloses that the adjective 'serious' has from time to time been used as an alternative to 'real' to describe the degree of risk of interfering with the course of justice, but not the degree of interference itself. It is, however, an ordinary English word that is not intrinsically inapt when used to describe the extent of an impediment or prejudice to the cause of justice in particular legal proceedings, and I do not think that for the purposes of the instant appeal any attempt to paraphrase it is necessary or would be helpful. The subsection applies to all kinds of legal proceedings, not only criminal prosecutions before a jury. If, as in the instant case and probably in most other criminal trials upon indictment, it is the outcome of the trial or the need to discharge the jury without proceeding to a verdict that is put at risk, there can be no question that that which in the course of justice is put at risk is as serious as anything could be.

My Lords, that Mr Malcolm Muggeridge's article was capable of prejudicing the jury against Dr Arthur at the early stage of his trial when it was published, seems to me to be clear. It suggested that it was a common practice among paediatricians to do that which Dr Arthur was charged with having done, because they thought that it was justifiable in the interest of humanity even though it was against the law. At this stage of the trial the jury did not know what Dr Arthur's defence was going to be; and whether at that time the risk of the jury's being influenced by their recollection of the article when they came eventually to consider their verdict appeared to be more than a remote one, was a matter which the judge before whom the trial was being conducted was in the best position to evaluate, even though this evaluation, although it should carry weight, would not be binding on the Divisional Court or on your Lordships. The judge thought at that stage of the trial that the risk was substantial, not remote. So, too, looking at the matter in retrospect, did the Divisional Court despite the fact that the risk had not turned into an actuality since Dr Arthur had by then been acquitted. For my part I am not prepared to dissent from this evaluation. I consider that the publication of the article on the third day of what was to prove a lengthy trial satisfied the criterion for which section 2(2) of the Act provides.

The article, however, fell also within the category dealt with in section 5. It was made, in undisputed good faith, as a discussion in itself of public affairs, viz, Mrs Carr's candidature as an independent pro-life candidate in the North West Croydon by-election for which the polling day was in one week's time. It was also part of a wider discussion on a matter of general public interest that had been proceeding intermittently over the last three months, upon the moral justification of mercy killing and in particular of allowing newly born hopeless handicapped babies to die. So it was for the Attorney-General to show that the risk of prejudice to the fair trial of Dr Arthur, which I agree was created by the publication of the article at the stage the trial had reached when it was published, was not 'merely incidental' to the discussion of the matter with which the article dealt.

My Lords, any article published at the time when Dr Arthur was being tried which asserted that it was a common practice among paediatricians to let severely physically or mentally handicapped new born babies die of starvation or otherwise dispose of them would (as, in common with the trial judge and the Divisional Court, I have already accepted) involve a substantial risk of prejudicing his fair trial. But an article supporting Mrs Carr's candidature in the by-election as a pro-life candidate that contained no such assertion would depict her as tilting at imaginary windmills. One of the main planks of the policy for which she sought the suffrage of the electors was that these things did happen and ought to be stopped.

I have drawn attention to the passages principally relied upon by the Divisional Court as causing a risk of prejudice that was not 'merely incidental to the discussion'. The court described them as 'unnecessary' to the discussion and as 'accusations'. The test, however, is not whether an article could have been written as effectively without these passages or whether some other phraseology might have been substituted for them that could have reduced the risk of prejudicing Dr Arthur's fair trial; it is whether the risk created by the words actually chosen by the author was 'merely incidental to the discussion', which I take to mean: no more than an incidental consequence of expounding its main theme. The Divisional Court also apparently regarded the passages complained of as disqualified from the immunity conferred by section 5 because they consisted of 'accusations' whereas the court considered, [1983] 1 AC p. 128E–F, that 'discussion' was confined to 'the airing of views and the propounding and debating of principles and arguments'. I cannot accept this limited meaning of 'discussion' in the section. As already pointed out, in the absence of any accusation, believed to be true by Mrs Carr and Mr Muggeridge, that it was a common practice among some doctors to do what they are accused of doing in the passages complained of, the article would lose all its point whether as support for Mrs Carr's parliamentary candidature or as a contribution to the wider controversy as to the justifiability of mercy killing. The article would be emasculated into a mere contribution to a purely hypothetical problem appropriate, it may be, for debate between academic successors of the mediaeval schoolmen, but remote from all public affairs and devoid of any general public interest to readers of the *Daily Mail*.

My Lords, the article that is the subject of the instant case appears to me to be in nearly all respects the antithesis of the article which this House (pace a majority of the judges of the European Court of Human Rights) held to be a contempt of court in *A-G v Times Newspapers Ltd.* [1974] AC 273. There the whole subject of the article was the pending civil actions against Distillers Co. (Biochemicals) Ltd, arising out of their having placed upon the market the new drug thalidomide, and the whole purpose of it was to put pressure upon that company in the lawful conduct of their defence in those actions. In the instant case, in contrast, there is in the article no mention at all of Dr Arthur's trial. It may well be that many readers of the *Daily Mail* who saw the article and had read also the previous day's report of Dr Arthur's trial, and certainly if they were members of the jury at that trial, would think, 'that is the sort of thing that Dr Arthur is being tried for; it appears to be something that quite a lot of doctors do.' But the risk of their thinking that and allowing it to prejudice their minds in favour of finding him guilty on evidence that did not justify such a finding seems to me to be properly described in ordinary English language as 'merely incidental' to any meaningful discussion of Mrs Carr's election policy as a pro-life candidate in the by-election due to be held before Dr Arthur's trial was likely to be concluded, or to any meaningful discussion of the wider matters of general public interest involved in the current controversy as to the justification of mercy killing. To hold otherwise would have prevented Mrs Carr from putting forward and obtaining publicity for what was a main plank in her election programme and would have stifled all discussion in the press upon the wider controversy about mercy killing from the time that Dr Arthur was charged in the magistrates' court in February 1981 until the date of his acquittal at the beginning of November of that year; for those are the dates between which, under section 2(3) and Schedule 1, the legal proceedings against Dr Arthur would be 'active' and so attract the strict liability rule.

Such gagging of bona fide public discussion in the press of controversial matters of general public interest, merely because there are in existence contemporaneous legal proceedings in which some particular instance of those controversial matters may be in issue, is what section 5 of the Contempt of Court Act 1981 was in my view intended to prevent. I would allow this appeal.

Lords Elwyn-Jones, **Keith**, **Scarman** and **Brandon** agreed with **Lord Diplock's** speech.
Appeal allowed.

NOTES

1. See G. J. Zellick, [1982] PL 343; A. Ward, (1983) 46 MLR 85; M. Redmond, [1983] CLJ 9.
2. The word 'noumenon' means an 'object of intellectual intuition devoid of all phenomenal attributes' (OED).
3. Are the interpretation and application of s. 2(2) satisfactory? In the Divisional Court, Watkins LJ noted ([1983] 1 AC at pp. 123–125) that while the article made no express reference to the Arthur trial, the circumstances of the trial were 'unusual' and 'had received very great publicity'. It seemed to their Lordships 'inevitable that all sensible people, including the jurors at the Crown Court at Leicester, would conclude' that assertions in the article such as 'someone would surely recommend letting her die of starvation' referred to the Arthur trial. The article 'contains undisguised assertions or insinuations that babies who are born with certain kinds of handicaps are caused or allowed by those in charge of them to die within days of birth of starvation among other means'. Such statements 'may wrongly prejudice

jurors'. The 'poison of prejudice' must be kept away from the 'well of justice.' 'If it is not, then the possibility of a miscarriage of justice inevitably accompanies prejudice.' Accordingly, the Divisional Court was satisfied 'beyond reasonable doubt' that the publication 'created a substantial risk of serious prejudice in the trial of Dr Arthur.' Consider (1) whether the word 'substantial' in s. 2(2) should have been accorded such a narrow interpretation by the House of Lords and (2) whether, even on that narrow approach, you would be satisfied the publication created the necessary risk. (See Zellick, op. cit., p. 344, who argues that the decision on this point 'seriously misinterpreted the subsection and confirms the traditional breadth of the contempt law which Parliament had been at pains to curb', and Redmond, op. cit., pp. 12–13).

4. *A-G v English* may be contrasted with the decisions of the Divisional Court in *A-G v Times Newspapers Ltd* (heard with four other cases) (1983) Times, 12 February, DC. The Attorney-General brought contempt proceedings under the strict liability rule against the publishers of five newspapers in respect of news stories and articles about Michael Fagan, an intruder into the Queen's bedroom. He had already been charged with offences arising out of three previous incidents: (1) a charge of burglary in respect of a previous entry into Buckingham Palace, during which he had drunk some wine; (2) a charge of taking a motor vehicle without the owner's consent; and (3) a charge of assaulting his stepson. Lord Lane CJ noted that under s. 2(2) a slight or trivial risk of serious prejudice was not enough nor was a substantial risk of slight prejudice. Five cases were heard together.

(1) *The Sun* was prosecuted in respect of assertions that Fagan had a long standing drug problem, was a glib liar and had stolen cigars from the Palace. Lord Lane 'accepted the view that jurors were to be credited with more independence of mind than was sometimes suggested'. The risk that the fair trial on the burglary charge would be prejudiced was 'too remote to qualify for the description of substantial.'

(2) The *Daily Star* had published allegations similar to *The Sun* and was accordingly acquitted in respect of those. In addition, it had asserted (i) that Fagan admitted to stealing the wine and (ii) that he intended to commit suicide, the inferential suggestion being that he was unbalanced. Assertion (i) amounted to contempt, but assertion (ii) did not: 'However independent minded a jury might be and however cynical about the accuracy of newspaper reporting nevertheless there would inevitably be a real risk, whether the judge gave a warning about disregarding extraneous facts or not, that the memory of [assertion (i)] would remain in the jurors' minds and would affect the outcome of their deliberations.' It was conceded that s. 5 provided no defence. Nevertheless, no penalty was imposed.

(3) Neither of the matters complained of against the *Sunday People* amounted to contempt: (i) allegations that Fagan had been addicted to drugs were similar to those made by *The Sun* and the *Daily Star*; (ii) reported comments, said to have emanated from a Palace spokesman, that some of Fagan's reported statements were 'quite absurd and fanciful suggestions' (thus implying that he was untruthful) were not likely to influence a juror.

(4) *The Mail on Sunday* had published an article by Lady Falkender which contained the clear suggestion of a possible homosexual liaison between Fagan and Commander Trestrail, who had recently resigned as Queen's Police Officer because of a homosexual relationship with a male prostitute. It also referred to Fagan as a 'rootless neurotic with no visible means of support'. The court held that this could not fail to have an effect on anyone considering Fagan's honesty. Although the burglary charge was not mentioned, everybody reading any newspaper would be

well aware of it. 'Accordingly the article had the necessary ingredient under s. 2.' However, it fell within s. 5: 'the appalling state of the safeguards designed to protect Her Majesty together with the proclivities of her bodyguard were matters which were of the greatest public concern' and 'the article was part of the discussion about the Queen's safety'.

(5) *The Sunday Times* had alleged that Fagan was charged with stabbing his step-son in the neck with a screwdriver: it was now conceded that there was never any such allegation and that the only allegation was one of assault. This inaccuracy 'on its own did not cause the publication to amount to contempt. Where however the inaccuracy was of that extent and was given front-page prominence then the publisher put himself at risk.' A second article repeated the false suggestion that Fagan was charged with wounding and also stated that the whole affair arose out of a genuine misunderstanding that the boy had received his injuries not at Fagan's hands but in some earlier incident before Fagan arrived on the scene. These statements were held to be prejudicial to the trial of the assault charge. The second article also stated, falsely, that the charge of taking a motor vehicle had been dropped. This was held to be prejudicial to the prosecution in respect of this charge. Section 5 was not applicable. The alleged assault was no more than a domestic fracas that was irrelevant to the public discussion of the matter of the Queen's security. The articles nevertheless went into great detail about it and could not be described as 'merely incidental' to the expounding of the main theme. Ackner LJ agreed with Lord Lane CJ. Oliver LJ generally agreed, but doubted whether *The Mail on Sunday* article fell foul of s. 2, and held that the first *Sunday Times* article did so not because of any possible influence on jurors but because it caused Fagan, on legal advice, to elect for jury trial rather than summary trial: any extraneous factor which impeded or restricted the defendant's right of election was a serious prejudice.

Borrie and Lowe (p. 122) note that these decisions 'have done much to dispel earlier fears, widely voiced in the English press after the *English* decision, that the courts were interpreting the Act particularly restrictively. Indeed, some would argue that the Divisional Court went too far in favour of the media.' Do you agree?

More recent cases where the courts have dismissed contempt proceedings on the basis that no breach of s. 2(2) was established include the following. In *A-G v Guardian Newspapers* [1992] 3 All ER 38, the publication of the fact that one unidentified defendant out of six on trial in Manchester was awaiting trial in the Isle of Man on other charges was held not to give rise to any practical risk of engendering bias in a juror of ordinary good sense. In *A-G v Independent Television News Ltd and others* [1995] 2 All ER 370, DC, TV news and newspapers (the *Daily Mail, Today, Daily Express* and *Northern Echo*) published the fact that Patrick Magee, who had been arrested for the murder of a special constable and the attempted murder of a police constable, was a convicted IRA terrorist who had escaped from jail in Belfast where he was serving a life sentence for the murder of an SAS officer. The court held that there was no contempt given the likely (and actual) lapse of time of over nine months before any trial, the ephemeral nature of a single news item on TV news, and the limited circulation of the first (and only offending) editions of the newspapers in question. In particular in the case of the *Northern Echo*, where only 146 copies were distributed in London, at King's Cross Station, there was no risk.

These cases tend to reinforce the view expressed in *Borrie and Lowe* quoted above.

5. In *A-G v TVS Television Ltd* (1989) Times, 7 July, DC, TVS broadcast a programme, 'The New Rachman', on 29 January 1988, exposing certain landlords in Reading who were alleged to be obtaining money by deception from the DHSS, as part of a general discussion of the causes of a new wave of Rachmanism in Southern England. The trial of one of the landlords, which had commenced on 4 January, had to be aborted (at a cost of £215,000). TVS accepted that the broadcast was a publication which had created a substantial risk of serious prejudice, and the Attorney-General accepted that TVS had acted in good faith. The court held that the s. 5 defence was not available: the reference to the landlords was not 'merely incidental' to the matter of general public interest discussed in the programme: the thrust of the discussion was directed to the Reading landlords. TVS were fined £25,000. In *A-G v Henry* [1990] COD 307, the *News of the World* was fined £15,000 for publishing particulars of previous offences by John Cannon, after his arrest for attempted robbery and for the abduction of Shirley Banks (he was subsequently convicted of her murder). The court accepted, with some reluctance, that there had been an 'honest, if wholly unprofessional, mistake rather than a deliberately contumacious or risky course of conduct'. In *A-G v BBC* [1992] COD 264, the BBC was fined £5,000 for broadcasting on *Midlands Today* a misleading and inaccurate report of a trial at Shrewsbury Crown Court while the trial was continuing; the report contained matters not put before the jury, and was seen by four jurors. The matter was dealt with by a warning to the jury. However, there was a breach of s. 2(2) as it was on the cards that the jury would have to be discharged.

6. To what extent is the defendant's intention relevant to the s. 5 limitation? See Redmond, op. cit., pp. 11–12. Is the test for 'good faith' objective or subjective? See N. Lowe, (1981) 131 NLJ 1167, 1169. Note that s. 5 was held to be applicable in *The Mail on Sunday* case (above) notwithstanding that the article mentioned the accused (cf. *A-G v English*, above, p. 385). In *A-G v TVS Television Ltd* (1989) Times, 7 July, Lloyd LJ stated that in determining whether a risk was merely incidental

'... a better and surer test is simply to look at the subject matter of the discussion and see how closely it relates to the particular legal proceedings. The more closely it relates the easier it will be for the Attorney-General to show that the risk of prejudice is not merely incidental to the discussion. The application of the test is largely a matter of first impression.'

In *A-G v Guardian Newspapers* [1992] 3 All ER 38 (see above, p. 389), Mann LJ (at 45) agreed that the application of the test was largely one of impression. The Divisional Court held that the s. 5 defence was made out where in the course of an article criticising the alleged propensity of judges in major fraud trials to impose reporting restrictions, reference was made to a particular case where restrictions were imposed because a defendant was awaiting trial elsewhere. Brooke J stated (at 49) that the inclusion of examples was 'no more than an incidental consequence of expounding the main theme of the article'. On the burden of proof, Prof J. C. Smith, [1982] Crim LR 744 points out that while s. 3(3) (above, p. 376) states explicitly that the onus of proving the defence of innocent publication or distribution is on the defendant there is no such provision in ss. 4 or 5. Nevertheless, in *A-G v TVS Television Ltd* (1989) Times, 7 July, DC, the Attorney-General accepted that the burden of proving liability rested on him for the purposes of both ss. 2(2) and 5 of the 1981 Act. Professor Smith also considers whether an article written with reference to the issue of principle raised by the trial itself would amount to contempt:

'Arguably, proceedings are not "impeded" or "prejudiced" by a discussion in good faith of issues of principle, even if it is intended to influence the court to reach a "correct" decision. Many commentaries on decisions of the Court of Appeal published in this *Review* have been written in the hope they might influence the House of Lords, either directly or through their adoption by counsel, to reach a particular decision and have not (so far) been treated as contemptuous. If, in the course of the published debate following the acquittal of Dr. Arthur, a similar charge had been brought against another doctor, would it have been necessary to suspend the debate? It is submitted that it would not.'

Does section 5 apply only in respect of incidental risks created by the continuation of an *existing* public debate or does it extend in addition to articles which *initiate* such a debate (see C. J. Miller, [1982] Crim LR 71, 78–79).

(iii) Other Aspects of Contempt

NOTES

1. *Protection of inferior courts and tribunals.* Inferior courts generally only have power to punish contempts in the face of the court (see below, p. 428 ff.). However, the Divisional Court fulfils a protective role over the proceedings of inferior courts and tribunals. Accordingly, it has been held that that court can punish publications likely to prejudice proceedings before quarter sessions (see *R v Davies* [1906] 1 KB 32), consistory courts (*R v Daily Herald, ex p Bishop of Norwich* [1932] 2 KB 402), coroners courts (see *R v Clarke, ex p Crippen* (1910) 103 LT 636, 641, per Lord Coleridge CJ; *Peacock v London Weekend Television* (1985) 150 JP 71, CA), courts martial (see *R v Daily Mail, ex p Farnsworth* [1921] 2 KB 733) and county courts (see *R v Edwards, ex p Welsh Church Temporalities Comrs* (1933) 49 TLR 383 and *R v Bloomsbury County Court, ex p Brady* (1987) Times, 16 December, CA (where it was emphasised that a county court has no jurisdiction over criminal contempts of court other than contempt in the face of the court).) However, in *A-G v BBC* [1981] AC 303 the House of Lords held that the contempt jurisdiction was not co-extensive with the High Court's general supervisory jurisdiction, but was only exercisable in relation to 'inferior courts' (see RSC Ord 52, r 1(2)(a)(iii)). The House was unanimous in holding that this contempt power did not apply to local valuation courts.

In *Pickering v Liverpool Daily Post and Echo Newspapers plc* [1991] 2 AC 370, [1990] 1 All ER 335, the Court of Appeal held the definition in s. 19 of the Contempt of Court Act 1981 (above, p. 378) 'must be intended to reflect the common law concept of what is a "court" for the purposes of the common law jurisdiction of the courts in relation to contempt of court' (per Lord Donaldson MR at p. 341). Applying that definition, a Mental Health Review Tribunal was to be regarded as a 'court' for these purposes. Since the passing of the Mental Health (Amendment) Act 1982 (consolidated in the Mental Health Act 1983), these tribunals had been given power to determine whether a restricted patient should be released from detention; previously they had only had the power to make recommendations. Indeed this change had been necessitated by the ruling of the European Court of Human Rights in *X v United Kingdom* (1981) 4 EHRR 188, which had applied Art. 5(4) of the Convention to decisions of Mental Health Review Tribunals: this entitled persons deprived of their liberty by arrest or detention to have the lawfulness of the detention 'decided speedily by a court'. Lord Donaldson pointed out that if a Tribunal were not a 'court' for all purposes, the Convention would not be complied with. The decision of the Court of Appeal on this point was approved on appeal by the House of Lords: [1991] 2 AC 370. An industrial tribunal is an 'inferior court' for these purposes: *Peach Grey & Co. (a firm) v Sommers* [1995] 2 All ER 513.

2. *Powers to sit in camera.* In general court proceedings must take place in public. However, courts have inherent power to sit in private where that is necessary to serve

the ends of justice, and there are also statutory exceptions. The principles were stated as follows by Lord Diplock in *A-G v Leveller Magazine Ltd* [1979] AC 440 at 450:[1]

'The application of this principle of open justice has two aspects: as respects proceedings in the court itself it requires that they should be held in open court to which the press and public are admitted and that, in criminal cases at any rate, all evidence communicated to the court is communicated publicly. As respects the publication to a wider public of fair and accurate reports of proceedings that have taken place in court the principle requires that nothing should be done to discourage this.

However, since the purpose of the general rule is to serve the ends of justice it may be necessary to depart from it where the nature or circumstances of the particular proceedings are such that the application of the general rule in its entirety would frustrate or render impracticable the administration of justice or would damage some other public interest for whose protection Parliament has made some statutory derogation from the rule. Apart from statutory exceptions, however, where a court in the exercise of its inherent power to control the conduct of proceedings before it departs in any way from the general rule, the departure is justified to the extent and to no more than the extent that the court reasonably believes it to be necessary in order to serve the ends of justice.'

This last stated point may in appropriate circumstances justify a decision to sit *in camera* or the imposition of restrictions on the reporting of certain matters (see n. **3**).

A decision to sit *in camera* may be challenged (in the case of an inferior court or tribunal) on an application for judicial review or (in the case of a trial on indictment) an appeal to the Court of Appeal under the Criminal Justice Act 1988, s. 159. See, e.g. *Re Crook* (1989) 93 Cr App Rep 17, where the Court of Appeal gave guidance as to the circumstances in which applications in connection with trials on indictment could properly be heard in chambers. If the public are exclued from a hearing, the Press should be excluded as well (ibid.). The policy of a particular bench to withhold the names of justices during the hearing of cases and from both public and press afterwards was held to be unlawful (as contrary to the principles of open justice) in *R v Felixstowe Justices, ex p Leigh* [1987] QB 582. See also *R v Malvern Justices, ex p Evans* below, p. 395.

3. *Powers to prohibit reporting; Contempt of Court Act 1981, s. 11.* It has been established that a judge has jurisdiction to order that the name of a witness should not be disclosed in the proceedings if there is a danger that a lack of anonymity would deter such witnesses from coming forward. Disclosure may then amount to contempt. In *R v Socialist Worker Printers and Publishers Ltd, ex p A-G* [1975] QB 637, DC, prosecution witnesses at the trial of Janie Jones on charges (inter alia) of blackmail were referred to in court as 'Y' and 'Z' by direction of the judge. Their names were published in the *Socialist Worker*. There was no specific direction to the press not to publish the names. Nevertheless, the publishers and editor (Paul Foot) were each fined £250 for contempt. This was both 'an affront to the authority of the court' and 'an act calculated to interfere with the due course of justice' (per Lord Widgery CJ at 151).

The New Zealand Court of Appeal has similarly held that it is contempt to disobey directions not to reveal the identities of members of the NZ Security Intelligence Service who were prosecution witnesses in a well publicised trial (*A-G v Taylor* [1975] 2 NZLR 675; *A-G v Hancox* [1976] 1 NZLR 171; W. C. Hodge, (1976) 7 NZ Universities LR 171).

In *A-G v Leveller Magazine Ltd* [1979] 1 All ER 745, HL, three newspapers (*Leveller, Peace News* and *Journalists*) published the name of a witness in the committal

---

1 See also *Scott v Scott* [1913] AC 417, HL; *B (otherwise P) v A_G* [1965] 3 All ER 253; *R v Ealing Justices, ex p Weafer* (1982) 74 Cr App Rep 204, [1983] Crim LR 182, DC; *R v Reigate Justices, ex p Argus Newspapers and Larcombe* (1983) 147 JP 385, DC; *R v Chief Registrar of Friendly Societies, ex p New Cross Building Society* [1984] QB 227; *Polly Peck International plc v Nadir* (1991) Times, 11 November; Law Commission *Report on the Powers of Appeal Courts to Sit in Private and the Restrictions upon Publicity in Domestic Proceedings* (Cmnd 3149, 1966); *Robertson and Nicol*, pp. 309–323.

proceedings which led to the 'ABC trial' (below p. 462). He had been allowed to give evidence as 'Colonel B' for security reasons. They were convicted of contempt and fined, on the ground that 'a flouting (or deliberate disregard) outside the court will be a contempt if it frustrates the court's ruling' (per Lord Widgery CJ, [1978] 3 All ER 731 at 736). The House of Lords allowed the defendants' appeals on a variety of grounds.

(1) (Lord Diplock, Viscount Dilhorne and Lord Russell). In evidence at the committal proceedings 'Colonel B' gave the name and number of his unit and referred to the fact that his posting was recorded in a particular issue of 'Wire', the Royal Signals magazine, which was available to the general public. His identity could thus be deduced from evidence given in open court without objection from the prosecution. Accordingly, the disclosure could not interfere with the due administration of justice and could not amount to contempt. In the words of Lord Russell, 'the gaff was already blown' (p. 764). Viscount Dilhorne (at 754) and Lord Russell (at 764) gave this as the only reason for their decision.

(2) (Lord Edmund-Davies). The Attorney-General had sought the orders of committal on the basis that the defendants had ignored an explicit *direction* of the magistrates. It subsequently appeared from the affidavit of the court clerk that no such direction had been given. Lord Edmund-Davies held at 759 that

'it was not open to the Divisional Court (and particularly after refusing to allow him to amend his grounds of application) to entertain an entirely different case on which to commit the appellants for criminal contempt. . . . Persons charged with criminal misconduct are entitled to know with reasonable precision the basis of the charge.'

The speeches of their Lordships do not, however, give clear guidance as to when a publication of information will amount to contempt. Would it be sufficient for the court simply to rule that a witness's name should not be revealed in the court? Publication of the name, following such a ruling, might well amount ipso facto to contempt in the opinions of Viscount Dilhorne at 755, 756 and Lord Russell of Killowen at 764. The speeches of the other members of the House seemed to require further conditions to be fulfilled before a conviction for contempt. Lord Edmund-Davies' view was nearest to that of Viscount Dilhorne and Lord Russell, although he did express doubts as to the *ratio decidendi* of *R v Socialist Worker*. Viscount Dilhorne at 756 (as did Lord Scarman) expressly approved the decision in that case and Lord Russell can be taken as having done so by implication.

Lord Diplock:

'. . . [W]here (1) the reason for a ruling which involves departing in some measure from the general principle of open justice within the courtroom is that the departure is necessary in the interests of the due administration of justice and (2) it would be apparent to anyone who was aware of the ruling that the result which the ruling is designed to achieve would be frustrated by a particular kind of act done outside the courtroom, the doing of such an act with knowledge of the ruling and of its purpose may constitute a contempt of court, not because it is a breach of the ruling but because it interferes with the due administration of justice.

What was incumbent on [the magistrates] was to make it clear to anyone present at, or reading an accurate report of, the proceedings, what in the interests of the due administration of justice, was the result that was intended by them to be achieved by the limited derogation from the principle of open justice within the courtroom which they had authorised, and what kind of information derived from what happened in the courtroom would if it were published frustrate that result.

There may be many cases in which the result intended to be achieved by a ruling by the court as to what is to be done in court is so obvious as to speak for itself; it calls for no explicit statement. Sending the jury out of court during a trial within a trial is an example of this; so may be the common ruling in prosecutions for blackmail that a victim called as a witness be referred to in court by a pseudonym.'

Lord Edmund-Davies: . . .

'For [contempt] to arise something more than disobedience of the court's direction needs to be established. That something more is that the publication must be of such a nature as to threaten the administration of justice either in the particular case in relation to which the prohibition was pronounced or in relation to cases which may be brought in the future. . . .

[N]othing I have said should be regarded as implying that there can be no committal for contempt unless there has been some sort of warning against publication. While, it would be wise to warn, the court is under no obligation to do so. And there will remain cases where a court could not reasonably have considered a warning even desirable, such as where the later conduct complained of should not have been contemplated as likely to occur. *R v Newcastle Chronicle and Journal Ltd* [above, p. 384] is an example of such a case.'

Lord Scarman: . . .

'If a court is satisfied that for the protection of the administration of justice from interference it is necessary to order that evidence either be heard in private or be written down and not given in open court, it may so order. Such an order or ruling may be the foundation of contempt proceedings against any person who, with knowledge of the order, frustrates its purpose by publishing the evidence kept private or information leading to its exposure. The order or ruling must be clear and can be made only if it appears to the court reasonably necessary. There must be material (not necessarily evidence) made known to the court on which it could reasonably reach its conclusion, and those who are alleged to be in contempt must be shown to have known, or to have had a proper opportunity of knowing of the existence of the order. . . .'

Note that there are three distinct statements by justices which are possible: (a) a 'ruling' that a witness should be allowed to remain anonymous in court; (b) a 'direction' that the witness's identity should not be published in or out of court; (c) a 'warning' that publication may amount to or be dealt with as contempt. Which of these statements do you think each of their Lordships has in mind as a precondition of liability in contempt? There seemed to be general agreement that disobedience to statements of any of these kinds would not *automatically* constitute contempt. See Viscount Dilhorne at 734, Lord Edmund-Davies at 761 and Lord Scarman at 768. Lord Diplock at 751 left the point open. See R. T. H. Stone, (1980) 96 LQR 22. (Contrast the New Zealand decision in *A-G v Taylor* [1975] 2 NZLR 675 where it was held that the court had power to make an order binding on outsiders disobedience to which would automatically constitute contempt.)

It would seem that in order for contempt proceedings to succeed (1) there must be a valid anonymity order (not a mere request) (see Lord Scarman); (2) D must know or (per Lord Scarman) must have had the opportunity of knowing of the order; (3) either there must be a warning from the court that the order is made to protect the administration of justice and that publication will constitute contempt or the object of the order must be apparent to anyone; and (4) (per Lord Edmund-Davies) the publication must constitute a real risk of interfering with the administration of justice (see *Borrie and Lowe*, pp. 193–196).

The difficulties of the *Leveller* case are not solved by s. 11 of the Contempt of Court Act 1981 (see above, p. 377). Note that s. 11 does not *confer* any power to withhold information in court, does not indicate what consequences are to flow from a breach of a direction made under the section, and does not make it clear whether the deliberate publication of matter withheld in court may constitute contempt where there has not also been an express direction to the press to refrain from publication. It has, however, been held that an order cannot be made under s. 11 prohibiting the publication of a name in connection with proceedings unless the name has been withheld during the proceedings: *R v Arundel Justices, ex p Westminster Press Ltd* [1985] 2 All ER 390, DC, following dicta in *R v Central Criminal Court, ex p Crook* (1984) Times, 8 November, DC. Anonymity orders have been made, for example, to protect witnesses in blackmail trials (*R v Socialist Worker*, above), in connection with security matters (*R v Leveller*, above), in pornography trials (*R v Hove Justices, ex p Gibbons* (1981) Times, 19 June) and to prohibit the publication of the name and address of a person with a notifiable disease against whom an *ex parte* order was made under the Public Health (Control of Disease) Act 1984, s. 37, requiring his removal to hospital (*Birmingham Post and Mail Ltd v Birmingham City Council* (1993) Times, 25 November: the s. 11 order was, however, not to be continued once all reasonable opportunity to challenge the hospital order had passed). Anonymity orders may also be justified where a witness is in fear for himself or his family (*R v Watford Magistrates' Court, ex p Lenman* [1993] Crim LR 388 [1992] COD 474, DC; *R v Taylor (Gary)* (1994) Times, 17 August, CA (Cr D)). The growing use of powers to sit *in camera* (see nn. **1** above and **5** below) and to make orders under s. 11 was viewed with concern by the National Union of Journalists, the Association of British Editors and the Press Council. However, the tide was to an extent stemmed by two decisions of the Divisional Court.

In *R v Malvern Justices, ex p Evans* [1988] QB 540, the Divisional Court affirmed the jurisdiction of a magistrates' court to sit *in camera* if the administration of justice so required, but doubted that the court's discretion to do so had been properly exercised in the circumstances of the case. A woman pleaded guilty to driving with excess alcohol but sought to advance special reasons why she should not be disqualified which concerned embarrassing and intimate details of her personal life with her husband and her pending divorce proceedings. The justices acceded to her request that this be heard *in camera*. The case was only argued on the question of jurisdiction, but Watkins LJ also indicated that he regarded the justices' reason for sitting *in camera* as 'wholly unsustainable and out of accord with principle' (p. 550). Moreover, it was held in *R v Evesham Justices, ex p McDonagh* [1988] QB 553, DC, that a magistrates' court has no power to make a s. 11 order prohibiting publication of the defendant's address merely on the ground that he feared he would be subjected to severe harassment by his ex-wife if his address were made public; it could not be said that the application of the general rule requiring openness would in this case 'frustrate or render impracticable the administration of justice' (the test suggested by Lord Diplock in *A-G v Leveller Magazines Ltd* (above, p. 392) for departing from the principle of open justice). Similarly, in *R v Dover Justices, ex p Dover District Council and Wells* (1991) 156 JP 433, the Divisional Court held that the justices could not prevent or restrict publicity of proceedings against a restaurant business alleging offences against food hygiene regulations on account of the very severe economic damage to the business that publicity would cause. (See H. Scheer, [1993] CLJ 37.)

An application for a hearing to be held *in camera*, or for suppression of (for example) a name or address, should itself be heard *in camera*: the court can then determine whether there is any substance in the application without prejudicing the applicant: *R v Tower Bridge Magistrates' Court, ex p Osborne* (1987) 88 Cr App Rep 28, DC. Here a woman defendant sought to conceal her current address from her husband. The stipendiary magistrate refused to hear her application for a s. 11 order *in camera*, and her solicitor was obliged to reveal what were, in the words of Watkins LJ, 'very sensitive matters indeed, the publication of which could, in my view, have had serious consequences for the applicant' (p. 30). The magistrates in the event refused to make a s. 11 order. The court granted an injunction preventing (with certain exceptions) publication of any matter revealed in the making of the application before the magistrate. The decision to refuse the s. 11 order was not, apparently, challenged.

4. *Statutory reporting restrictions.* There are various statutory provisions which impose reporting restrictions disobedience to which constitutes a statutory offence.[1] See e.g. the Magistrates' Court Act 1980, s. 8A (substituted by the Criminal Justice and Public Order Act 1994, Sch. 4, Part I) (applications for dismissal); ibid, s. 71 (family proceedings); the Criminal Justice Act 1987, s. 11 (applications to the Crown Court for dismissal of charges and preparatory hearings in serious fraud cases); Children and Young Persons Act 1933, ss. 39 (children or young persons involved in court proceedings), 49 (substituted by the Criminal Justice and Public Order Act 1994, s. 49: youth court and other proceedings); Judicial Proceedings (Regulation of Reports) Act 1926 (indecent matter); Sexual Offences (Amendment) Act 1976, as amended by the Criminal Justice Act 1988, s. 158 (complainants and accused in rape trials). The position as to reporting proceedings properly held in private is governed by section 12 of the Administration of Justice Act 1960. See *Re F (a minor) (Publication of Information)* [1977] Fam 58; *Re L (a minor) (wardship: freedom of publication)* [1988] 1 All ER 418; *Pickering v Liverpool Daily Post and Echo Newspapers plc* [1991] 2 AC 370, HL; and below, p. 544.

5. *Powers to delay reporting; Contempt of Court Act 1981, s. 4.* Distinct from the powers set out in the previous note are the powers of a court to *postpone* publication of certain matters. The position at common law was uncertain. See *R v Clement* (1821) 4 B & Ald 218; *R v Poulson* [1974] Crim LR 141; cf. *R v Kray* (1969) 53 Cr App Rep 412, CA (Cr D).

Apart from those authorities, it was accepted that a criminal court had power to hold a 'trial within a trial' in the absence of the jury (e.g. to determine whether evidence is legally admissible) and to withhold information from a jury (e.g. that the accused has pleaded guilty to some but not all the charges). The premature publication of these matters was regarded as an obvious contempt (see above, p. 384).

The position is now regulated by section 4 of the Contempt of Court Act 1981 (above, p. 376). Section 4 was considered by the Court of Appeal in *R v Horsham Justices, ex p Farquharson* [1982] QB 762, CA, where a journalist and others sought judicial review to quash an order made by magistrates under s. 4(2). The court held that an order could validly be made under s. 4(2) restricting the reporting of 'old style' committal proceedings notwithstanding that the restrictions imposed by s. 3 of the Criminal Justice Act 1967 (now the Magistrates' Courts Act 1980, s. 8) had been lifted under s. 3(2). The two sections were regarded as applying in different situations and for different purposes. However, the magistrates' order was quashed on the ground that it was too wide. Another point concerned the relationship between s. 4(2) and s. 6(b). Counsel for the applicants argued that breach of a s. 4(2) order could only amount to contempt if it (a) constituted a breach of the 'strict liability rule' (s. 2(2)) and (b) that the conduct would have amounted to contempt at common law (s. 6(b)). Lord Denning MR (at pp. 790–795) accepted this argument, but it was rejected by his brethren. Ackner LJ held that 'a new head of contempt of court has been created, separate and distinct from the strict liability rule. . . . If a journalist reports proceedings that are the subject matter of a postponement order under s. 4(2) then he is guilty of a contempt of court' (p. 805). Shaw LJ stated that 'a premature publication in contravention of an order of which the publisher is aware could not be said to be in good faith' (p. 798) and would accordingly fall outside the protection of s. 4(1). Both the Divisional Court and the Court of Appeal were,

---

1 See generally M. Jones, *Justice and Journalism* (1974); B. Harris, *The Courts, the Press and the Public* (1976); *Borrie and Lowe*, pp. 212–221; G. Robertson and A. Nicol, *Media Law* (3rd edn, 1992) Chap. 7; D. Brogarth and C. Walker, (1988) 138 NLJ 909.

however, agreed that the press are entitled under s. 4(1) to publish anything occurring in open court unless an order has been made under s. 4(2); accordingly an order is now necessary to prohibit reporting of a 'trial within a trial' or guilty pleas (cf. above, p. 384: the *Border TV* case would now be decided differently). An order can only be made under s. 4(2) to postpone publication of reports of 'legal proceedings held in public'; this term means proceedings held in court at a hearing, and does not enable a court to ban the showing of a film of the defendant's arrest: *R v Rhuddlan Justices, ex p HTV Ltd* [1986] Crim LR 329.

In 1982 a Practice Direction was made by Lord Lane CJ in respect of orders under ss. 4(2) and 11 (*Practice Direction (Contempt: Reporting Restrictions)* [1982] 1 WLR 1475):

'It is necessary to keep a permanent record of such orders for later reference. For this purpose all orders made under section 4(2) must be formulated in precise terms, having regard to the decision of *R v Horsham Justices, ex p Farquharson* [1982] QB 762, and orders under both sections must be committed to writing either by the judge personally or by the clerk of the court under the judge's directions. An order must state (a) its precise scope, (b) the time at which it shall cease to have effect, if appropriate, and (c) the specific purpose of making the order.

Courts will normally give notice to the press in some form that an order has been made under either section of the Act and court staff should be prepared to answer any inquiry about a specific case, but it is, and will remain, the responsibility of those reporting cases, and their editors, to ensure that no breach of any order occurs and the onus rests with them to make inquiry in any case of doubt.'

On a number of occasions newspapers and journalists have applied successfully to the trial judge for the order to be revoked (*Robertson and Nicol*, 3rd edn, pp. 345–350). It was subsequently stated that representations to a trial judge should only be made by counsel for the prosecution or counsel for a defendant; counsel acting on behalf of the media or a witness did not have standing: *R v Central Criminal Court, ex p Crook* (1984) Times, 8 November. A different view was, however, taken by the Divisional Court in *R v Clerkenwell Metropolitan Stipendiary Magistrate, ex p The Telegraph plc* [1993] QB 462, which held that the court had a discretion to hear representations from the media, which should ordinarily be exercised when the media asked to be heard either on the making of an order or in regard to its continuance. (For subsequent proceedings, see *R v Clerkenwell Justice, ex p Trachtenberg* [1993] COD 93, where the Divisional Court upheld the magistrate's decision to revoke a s. 4(2) order.) Orders under ss. 4 or 11 imposed by inferior courts or the Crown Court (other than in respect of a trial on indictment) may be challenged on an application for judicial review under the ultra vires doctrine. Orders in relation to a trial on indictment can now be challenged by a 'person aggrieved' by way of an appeal to the Court of Appeal: Criminal Justice Act 1988, s. 159, under which the role of the court is to form its own view and not merely review the decision of the trial judge: *Ex p Telegraph plc* [1993] 2 All ER 971, 977, CA (Cr D). Applications for leave to appeal and appeals under s. 159 are determined on written submissions without a hearing (Criminal Appeal Rules 1968 (S.I. 1968 No. 1262), r. 16B(6),(7): upheld as *intra vires* by the Divisional Court in *Ex parte Guardian Newspapers* (1993) Times, 26 October).

In *Re Central Independent Television plc* [1991] 1 All ER 347, the Court of Appeal allowed an appeal against an order under s. 4(2) which prohibited the reporting of a trial by radio or television on the evening that the jury had to spend at a hotel after having retired to consider their verdict. The judge had taken the view that they should be able to relax and watch television or listen to the radio; the Court of Appeal held there was no substantial risk of prejudice to the administration of justice to justify an order.

The Court of Appeal (Criminal Division) also took a robust approach in setting aside or restricting s. 4(2) orders in *R v Beck, ex p Daily Telegraph plc* [1993] 2 All ER 177 and *Ex parte Telegraph plc* [1993] 2 All ER 971. In *Beck*, the court set aside an order restricting reporting of the trial of three social workers on the first of three indictments alleging serious offences of sexual and physical abuse of children in the care of Leicestershire Social Services, until end of the trial, when the matter would be reconsidered. The court had to consider separately (1) whether there was a substantial risk of prejudice and (2) whether, if so, it was necessary to make an order. The latter step involving balancing the considerations that supported a fair trial against the requirement of open justice and a legitimate public interest and concern in the matters in question. Here, there was a substantial risk of prejudice if the first trial were reported, but in view of the widespread public concern over the circumstances that gave rise to the trial, no order should be made. A similar approach was adopted in *Ex p Telegraph plc*, confirming that the question of the court's discretion was in practice merged with the requirement of necessity (Lord Taylor CJ at 975). The court removed restrictions on the identification of the principal prosecution witness (an alleged accomplice) at the first of what was to be a series of major trials in respect of the importation, manufacture and supply of the drug 'Ecstasy'. There was no substantial risk of prejudice and, even if there had been, the case was important and one in which there was a considerable and legitimate public interest because of the nature and quantity of the drug involved; the restrictions in question would make the case almost impossible to report.

See also *MGN Pension Trustees Ltd v Bank of America National Trust and Savings Association* [1995] 2 All ER 355, where Lindsay J refused to make a s. 4(2) order prohibiting reporting civil proceedings alleging breach of trust and fraud in the management of pension funds of companies associated with the late Robert Maxwell. There was no substantial risk of prejudice to criminal proceedings due to start in April 1995. The allegations were not detailed and the press so far had been either uninterested or thoroughly responsible. The possible postponement of reporting of the judgment was stood over to an appropriate time.

On s. 4(2) orders and committal proceedings, see *R v Beaconsfield Justices ex p Westminster Press Ltd* (1994) 158 JP 1055, QBD.

For a proposal that there should be a unified statutory code governing the reporting of criminal cases, see C. Walker, I. Cram and D. Brogarth, 'The Reporting of Crown Court Proceedings and the Contempt of Court Act 1981' (1992) 55 MLR 647. See also M. J. Beloff, Fair Trial – Free Press? Reporting Restrictions in Law and Practice' [1992] PL 92.

A decision to refuse an order under s. 4(2), made at a preparatory hearing under Part I of the Criminal Justice Act 1987, may be challenged on an appeal to the Court of Appeal, but only if erroneous in law: *Re Saunders* (1990) Times, 8 February (where the Court of Appeal upheld the decision of Henry J to refuse an order restricting reporting of the first of the two 'Guinness' trials).

6. Media coverage *during* a trial that creates a real risk of prejudice against the defendant may cause the conviction to be quashed as unsafe and unsatisfactory. In *R v McCann and others* (1990) 92 Cr App R 239, CA (Cr D), convictions of the 'Winchester three' for conspiracy to murder Tom King, the Secretary of State for Northern Ireland, were quashed following extensive media coverage during the trial of the government's proposals to change the law on the right to silence. This included interviews with Tom King and Lord Denning, expressing in strong terms the view that in terrorist cases a failure to answer questions or to give evidence was tantamount to guilt; two defendants had refused to answer questions and all had elected not to give evidence at trial. The Court of Appeal held that the jury should have been discharged. The risk of prejudice could not be eliminated by the judge's direction.

In *R v Taylor and Taylor* (1993) 98 Cr App R 361, CA (Cr D) coverage had been sensational and inaccurate, with headlines such as 'Love Crazy Mistress Butchered Rival Wife Court Told' (the court 'had been told no such thing': per McCowan LJ at 369). Apart from the effect on the fairness of the trial, the court also declined to order a retrial on the ground that a fair trial would not now be possible. The papers were sent to the Attorney-General, but he decided that no further action should be taken. Leave to apply for judicial review of this decision has been granted.

See B. Naylor, 'Fair Trial or Free Press: Legal Responses to Media Reports of Criminal Trials' [1994] CLJ 492.

7. In an appropriate case the High Court may grant an injunction to restrain a publication that would be a contempt of court by prejudicing criminal proceedings: see *Coe v Cental Television* (1993) Independent, 11 August, where the Court of Appeal discharged an injunction restraining the broadcasting of material in the 'Cook Report' relating to allegations against Coe of computer pornography. Proceedings had not yet been instigated, and the court was not satisfied on the evidence that the publication risked prejudice to the administration of justice and was motivated by an intention to create that risk of prejudice so as to amount to contempt at common law. On injunctions in the context of publications in respect of civil proceedings, see below, pp. 405–416.

8. The strong line taken by the Supreme Court of the United States against inhibitions on freedom of expression and freedom of the press (see above, p. 375) has meant that broadcasting and press publication of prejudicial material have been a considerable problem. There has been an extensive debate on whether the balance between the right of free expression and the right to a fair trial is correctly drawn (see e.g. *Abraham*, pp. 174–186; Donnelly and Goldfarb, (1961) 24 MLR 239). The Supreme Court has had to quash convictions in some extreme *causes célèbres*: *Irwin v Dowd* 366 US 717 (1961); *Estes v Texas* 381 US 532 (1965) (where the courtroom, according to the *New York Times*, 'was turned into a snake-pit by the multiplicity of cameras, wires, microphones and technicians milling about the chamber' (*Abraham*, p. 177)); and *Sheppard v Maxwell* 384 US 333 (1966). In the last case, Sheppard's conviction was quashed after he had been in prison for ten years convicted of murder after a sensationalised 'circus-like' trial. He was acquitted following a re-trial. The disquiet engendered by such cases has led to the employment of a number of safety devices: use of the voir dire examination of jurors to determine whether they are capable of ignoring pre-trial publicity; sequestration of the jury during the trial; transferring a case to another county; and the exercise of control by judges and public authorities over police officers, lawyers and court officials to prevent the release of prejudicial information. In addition, there is the encouragement of self-regulation by the press – the voluntary observation of proper standards of press coverage. These devices are constitutional, but doubts are expressed as to their efficacy. Following *Sheppard v Maxwell*, with its emphasis on the defendant's right to a fair trial under the Sixth and Fourteenth Amendments, trial courts have imposed specific reporting restrictions ('gag orders') on the press in individual cases where prejudicial publicity is apprehended. In *Nebraska Press Association v Stuart* 427 US 539 (1976), the Supreme Court held that a 'gag order' will normally be an unconstitutional restriction on press freedom (see A. M. Schatz, (1975) 10 Harvard Civil Rights–Civil Liberties Law Review 608; Note (1977) 87 Yale LJ 342). The debate in the United States continues.

(b) WHEN DOES THE SUB JUDICE RULE APPLY?

(i) At Common Law

1. Commencement

There were uncertainties both as to the commencement and the conclusion of the period within which matters were sub judice so as to render comments or acts that were prejudicial, contempts. If proceedings were 'pending' they were clearly sub judice. Proceedings were held to be 'pending' where a defendant had been arrested by virtue of a warrant (*R v Clarke, ex p Crippen* (1910) 103 LT 636, DC), and it was suggested obiter in the same case that they were 'pending' from the time the warrant was issued. The authorities conflicted on the question whether matters were sub judice when proceedings were merely 'imminent'. In *James v Robinson* (1963) 109 CLR 593, the High Court of Australia held that, as a matter of law, contempt of court could not be committed before the proceedings in question began. The view that the law of contempt applied when proceedings were merely imminent was expressed in *R v Savundranayagan* [1968] 3 All ER 439n, but those were not contempt proceedings. In *R v Beaverbrook Newspapers Ltd* [1962] NI 15, QBD (NI), Sheil and McVeigh JJ held that the word 'imminent' in section 11 of the Administration of Justice Act 1960 (see below p. 402) 'cannot be ignored if effect is to be given to the section as a whole. Whatever may be said to be the distinction between "proceedings pending" and "proceedings imminent", it is clear from the use of the words "as the case may be" that a distinction was intended' (Shiel J at 21). The *Daily Express* published photographs and other details (including the past criminal record) of a man who was arrested and charged with murder within two days of the publication. At the time of the publication, the reporter who supplied the material knew that the man was under close police surveillance, and indeed the *Daily Express* referred to him as the 'No. 1 Suspect'. Fines were imposed on the editors and proprietors of the *Daily Express*.

The Phillimore Committee concluded (pp. 49–52) that the application of the concept of 'imminence' presented too many problems, and that the right starting point in England and Wales was the moment when the suspected man was charged or a summons served.

2. Conclusion

Technically, the proceedings were not over until the trial had been completed and either the time for appealing had expired, or any appeals had finally been determined (see *Delbert-Evans v Davies and Watson* [1945] 2 All ER 167, DC; *R v Duffy, ex p Nash* [1960] 2 QB 188, DC). However, it was unlikely that any comment would be regarded as giving rise to any risk of prejudice to the fair conduct of proceedings. 'A judge is in a very different position to a juryman. Though in no sense superhuman, he has by his training no difficulty in putting out of his mind matters which are not evidence in the case' (*per* Lord Parker CJ in *R v Duffy, ex p Nash* [1960] 2 QB 188 at 198). The Phillimore Committee recommended that the law of contempt should cease to apply at the conclusion of the trial or hearing at first instance unless (1) sentence is postponed, in which case restrictions should continue until sentence is passed; or (2) no verdict is reached, in which case restrictions should continue unless and until it is clear that there will be no further trial; or (3) a new trial is ordered on appeal, in which case restrictions should again apply; or (4) there is an appeal from a magistrate's court to the Crown Court, in which case restrictions should apply from the moment the appeal is set down (para. 132).

(ii) Publications Intended to Interfere with Justice

In *A-G v News Group Newspapers plc* [1989] QB 110, the Divisional Court indicated (below p. 402) that where a publication was intended to interfere with justice and created a real risk of prejudice to proceedings, contempt proceedings could be taken notwithstanding that proceedings were neither pending nor imminent. On the facts, however, the proceedings were properly to be regarded as 'imminent'. However, in *A-G v Sport Newspapers Ltd* [1992] 1 All ER 503, the Divisional Court was divided on the point, Bingham LJ following the *News Group* case (with some reluctance), but Hodgson J holding that proceedings had to be pending. The court was agreed that the requisite intention had not been proved (see below, p. 404).

(iii) Under the 'Strict Liability Rule'

The time limits for the sub judice period in relation to the 'strict liability rule' are now to be found in s. 2(3)(4) and Schedule 1 of the Contempt of Court Act 1981 (see above, pp. 376, 378–380).

NOTES

1. The government took the view that the Phillimore proposal in relation to commencement went 'too far in allowing prejudicial publication before a formal charge is made, so endangering the trial of accused persons' (Cmnd 7145, 1978, para. 14). Accordingly the provisions in Schedule 1, para. 4 were enacted. It should be noted that proceedings are not technically 'active' while a person is voluntarily 'helping police with their inquiries.' It may be difficult for outsiders to discover whether an arrest warrant has been issued or an arrest without warrant effected. Note the defence in s. 3 of the 1981 Act (above, p. 376).

2. The rules for the conclusion of the sub judice period are found in Schedule 1, paras. 5–11. The provision in para. 11 was intended to cover the 'Lucan situation' i.e. where a suspect remains undiscovered or goes abroad and cannot be extradited.

3. Appellate proceedings will be 'active' according to the provisions of Schedule 1, para. 15 (above, p. 380). These are wider than those recommended by the Phillimore Committee (see above, p. 399). Do you think that the possible effect of comments on appellate judges is sufficient to justify this? (Cf. below, pp. 418–421.)

(c) THE SCOPE OF LIABILITY

(i) At Common Law Generally

A defendant was liable for contempt if he published matter in circumstances where such publication, objectively judged, created a real risk that the fair trial of proceedings might be prejudiced. An intention to prejudice proceedings was not apparently enough if there was in fact no risk of prejudice: *R v Ingrams, ex p Goldsmith* (1976) 120 Sol Jo 835, [1977] Crim LR 40, DC. However authorities to the contrary collected in *Borrie and Lowe* at pp. 64–66 were not mentioned by the members of the Divisional Court in *R v Ingrams*, and Eveleigh J was reported as saying that he did not think the article in question 'would – or had been intended to – prejudice the fair trial of the litigation' against *Private Eye*.

There appeared to be no requirement of mens rea beyond an intention to publish the matter in question and no defence of 'innocent dissemination' at common law (*R v Odhams Press Ltd* [1957] 1 QB 73, DC; *R v Griffiths, ex p A-G* [1957] 2 QB 192, DC). However, section 11 of the Administration of Justice Act 1960 provided defences in two situations where publication could be said to be 'innocent': (1) where the defendant 'did not know and had no reason to suspect that the proceedings were pending, or that such proceedings were imminent, as the case may be' (s. 11(1)); and (2) where the distributor of a publication 'did not know that it contained any [matter calculated to interfere with the course of justice in connection with any proceedings pending or imminent at the time of publication] and had no reason to suspect that it was likely to do so' (s. 11(2)).

It was also argued that the person who supplied information to a newspaper should not be held liable unless he had mens rea (see *Smith and Hogan* (6th edn, 1988) p. 776, criticising *R v Evening Standard Co Ltd* [1954] 1 QB 578; but cf. *Borrie and Lowe*, pp. 260–262).

The Phillimore Committee recommended that the unintentional creation of a risk of prejudice should continue to be regarded as contempt:

'The risk of damage resulting from potentially prejudicial publications is such that we are sure that, broadly speaking, no change of principle is required. A liability which rested only on proof of intent or actual foresight would favour the reckless at the expense of the careful. Most publishing is a commercial enterprise undertaken for profit, and the power of the printed or broadcast word is such that the administration of justice would not be adequately protected without a rule which requires great care to be taken to ensure that offending material is not published.' (para. 74).

This recommendation was taken up: see section (iii) below (p. 405) on the strict liability rule.

(ii) Common Law Liability for Intended Contempt

This category is of significance where the circumstances fall outside the scope of the 'strict liability rule' (below). The leading cases are *A-G v Times Newspapers Ltd* [1992] 1 AC 191, [1991] 2 All ER 398 (below p. 411) in the section on publications prejudicial to civil proceedings) and *A-G v News Group Newspapers plc* [1989] QB 110, DC (below).

A-G v News Group Newspapers plc [1989] QB 110, [1988] 2 All ER 906, [1988] 3 WLR 163, 132 Sol Jo 934, 87 Cr App Rep 323, Queen's Bench Divisional Court

The respondents, proprietors of the *Sun*, published articles entitled 'Rape Case Doc: Sun Acts', 'He's a real swine' and 'Beast must be named says MP,' accusing a Dr B of raping an 8-year old girl. The second article, 'Rape Case Doc' and 'Doc groped me, says girl', named the girl and accused him of the indecencies. NGN wrote to the girl's mother's solicitor offering to fund a private prosecution, as the police and the DPP had decided, in the absence of corroboration, not to prosecute Dr B. Nine months later, a private prosecution of the doctor resulted in his acquittal. The Attorney-General applied to the court for NGN to be fined for contempt of court at common law, proceedings not having been active for the purposes of the strict liability rule. NGN argued that at the time of publication proceedings were neither pending nor imminent.

Watkins LJ: . . . The Contempt of Court Act 1981 made fairly extensive provision for what might be called statutory contempts but by section 6 it made the following material saving, namely:

'Nothing in the foregoing provisions of this Act—. . . . (c) restricts liability for contempt of court in respect of conduct intended to impede or prejudice the administration of justice.'

In order to tell whether it has been established that a contempt has been committed by reason of a newspaper publication, it is a first and necessary finding that the contents of the publication present a risk of prejudice to a fair trial assuming that at the time of publication, proceedings have commenced or there has been an arrest and the commencement of proceedings is thereafter inevitable. The risk predicated must be real as opposed to a remote possibility: see *R v Duffy, ex p Nash* [1960] 2 QB 188, 200.

No one could possibly resist the conclusion that in the circumstances I have assumed for the present purpose that the contents of the articles complained of here posed a real risk of prejudice to a fair trial of Dr B. Publication of them during pending proceedings could not, in my view, have failed to have had that effect, so grave are the allegations made against the doctor and so prominent, widespread and so savage, in headline at least, is the publicity given to them. . . .

. . . I feel bound to say that I should be surprised if the law were authoritatively declared to be that something less than a specific intent will do. After all, what is in contemplation here, as has been in some previous cases of criminal contempt, is serious criminal conduct accompanied by the possibility of the infliction of drastic penalty.

The ascertainment of the existence of intention is, of course, quite a different matter. . . .

Mr Alexander [counsel for NGN] submits that it would be wrong to infer the required intent from the contents of the articles, for which proposition he relies on *R v Moloney* [1985] AC 905.

If, in so submitting, he intended us to conclude that the contents are all we have to consider, I cannot agree with him, nor do I accept that the contents of these articles are not alone capable of giving rise to the inference that the respondent intended to prejudice the fair trial of Dr. B, if and when that proceeding took place. I agree with Mr. Pannick, who appeared with Mr. Laws [counsel for the A-G], that we are not bound to accept the editor's assertion that he did not intend to interfere with the course of administration of justice. But the articles do not stand alone. The respondent's affidavits and financial support to the mother stand with them in forming the whole of the circumstances to be considered for the purpose of ascertaining by inference whether the intent required was present.

Mr. Laws submits that we should draw the inference that the respondent intended to prejudice the fair trial because (1) the contents of the articles strikingly showed that it took the view that Dr B. was guilty; in paragraph 11 of his affidavit, Mr Mackenzie states: 'I believe that what we were publishing was true;' (2) although the risk of being in contempt was never mentioned, so they say, in discussions between him and Mr Crone [NGN's deputy legal manager], Mr Crone thought there would be an answer to an allegation of being in contempt in regard to which he states in paragraph 10 of his affidavit that he dismissed this as a likely danger since the proceedings were not in an active period under Schedule 1 to the Act of 1981 and that any proceedings likely to ensue were a long way off; (3) Mr Mackenzie and Mr Crone thought proceedings were likely to ensue otherwise why go to the lengths they did to put the mother in funds and, further, they could only have printed articles of such a kind if they were campaigning for a conviction, as they clearly were.

I regard that as a powerful and persuasive submission. I simply cannot accept that an experienced editor such as Mr. Mackenzie could have failed to have foreseen that the material which he published in the articles complained of and the steps he announced he was taking to assist the mother to prosecute would incur a real risk of prejudicing the fairness of a trial of Dr B. The inescapable inference is, in my judgment, that Mr Mackenzie became so convinced of Dr. B's guilt and incensed by that and the failure to prosecute him that he endeavoured to persuade readers of 'The Sun' to take a similar view. Some of those obviously could possibly have formed part of a jury to try the doctor. That is trial by newspaper, a form of activity which strikes directly at a jury's impartiality.

Furthermore, what conceivable reason could there be for publishing the article headed 'Doc groped me, says girl' unless it was intended to prejudice a fair trial by bringing to the notice of readers of 'The Sun,' including possibly potential jurors, extremely damaging matter affecting Dr. B. which would be inadmissible as evidence in his trial. . . .

[His Lordship then held that recklessness was insufficient for mens rea for this form of contempt, expressing agreement with Lloyd LJ in *A-G v Newspaper Publishing plc* [1988] Ch 333, 381–383. He then proceeded to consider whether this head of contempt only applies where proceedings are pending or imminent and if so whether the proceedings here satisfied that test.]

Mr Pannick, who, as I have said, appeared with Mr. Laws, most impressively submitted that 'imminent proceedings' is a vague and uncertain phrase which cannot be confined to any particular length of time as a matter of principle. Its application depends on all the circumstances of the case. The concept is necessarily imprecise because it is intended to be applied by reference to its purpose. There are cases, he said, where although proceedings are not yet active, they are likely to be commenced in the near future. Some proceedings are imminent when there is a likelihood or a real risk that they will be instituted in the near future and when there is a real risk that the kind of publication as here would interfere with the course of justice.

In the present case, he submitted, proceedings were imminent, the respondent intended they should be commenced at their expense as soon as possible and actively pursued that goal because they were determined to see Dr B. charged, tried and convicted. The possibility of counsel advising against proceedings did not remove the likelihood or real risk that proceedings would be instituted in the near future.

Alternatively, he argued, that if the proceedings here could not be said to be imminent, common law contempt applied nonetheless in the whole of the circumstances of this case. This is because the purpose of the contempt jurisdiction is to prevent interference with the course of justice. The more distant the commencement of proceedings, the less likely such interference. But here, he said, the contents of the articles created a real risk that a fair trial would be impeded.

There is, he contended, no authority which states that common law contempt cannot be committed where proceedings cannot be said to be imminent, but where there is a specific intent to interfere with the course of justice accompanied by a real risk that the published matter will impede a fair trial, the occurrence of which is in contemplation. The authorities are not concerned with the scope of common law contempt where such an intent exists in relation to proceedings in the contemplation of a respondent who deliberately assists a private prosecutor to prosecute as soon as possible.

I have found that a formidable contention. The circumstances in which a criminal contempt at common law can be committed are not necessarily, in my judgment, confined to those in which proceedings are either pending or imminent, 'an imprecise word by which to mark out a period of time,' *per* Windeyer J in *James v Robinson* (1963) 109 CLR 593, 618. The common law surely does not tolerate conduct which involves the giving of encouragement and practical assistance to a person to bring about a private prosecution accompanied by an intention to interfere with the course of justice by publishing material about the person to be prosecuted which could only serve to and was so intended to prejudice the fair trial of that person. This is especially so where the publisher of them makes it plain that he believes the person referred to in the articles is guilty of serious crime, is deserving of punishment for that and that he has committed some other similar crime.

The common law is not a worn out jurisprudence rendered incapable of further development by the ever increasing incursion of Parliamentary legislation. It is a lively body of law capable of adaptation and expansion to meet fresh needs calling for the exertion of the discipline of law. . . .

The need for a free press is axiomatic, but the press cannot be allowed to charge about like a wild unbridled horse. It has, to a necessary degree, in the public interest, to be curbed. The curb is in no circumstance more necessary than when the principle that every man accused of crime shall have a fair trial is at stake. It is a principle which, in my experience, newspaper proprietors and editors are usually as alert as anyone to avoid violating.

There may not have been in fact, as was suggested, another case quite like this, but the kind of threat which the articles complained of posed to the proper administration of justice is by no means novel, as reports of previous cases of criminal contempt committed by publishers of newspaper articles show.

The respondent here had very much in mind particular proceedings which it was determined, as far as it lay within its power and influence, to ensure took place. If it is necessary for the Attorney-General to establish that proceedings were imminent, he has, I think, done so. In my judgment, where a prosecution is virtually certain to be commenced and particularly where it is to be commenced in the near future, it is proper to describe such proceedings as imminent. Such was the case here.

Thus, for the reasons I have explained, I find that the Attorney-General justifiably complains of the conduct of the respondent whom I would hold is in contempt of court at common law and liable to be punished therefor.

Mann LJ agreed.

NOTES

1. The respondent was fined £75,000, with costs. The House of Lords refused leave to appeal ([1989] QB 135). In *A-G v Sport Newspapers* [1992] 1 All ER 503, the Divisional Court dismissed the Attorney-General's application against the publishers and editors of the *Sport*, a tabloid newspaper that carried 'some general news stories, many of them with a sexual slant and generally written in a sensational style' (Bingham LJ at 506). The Attorney-General alleged that the deliberate publication of a wanted man's previous convictions, contrary to the wishes of the police expressed at a press conference, amounted to common law contempt. The court, however, held that it had not been proved beyond reasonable doubt that at the date of publication the editor had the specific intention to prejudice the fair conduct of proceedings, whose existence he regarded at that time as being speculative and remote. (An arrest warrant was issued two days after publication of the article; the wanted man, David Evans, was arrested three days later in France, extradited, and subsequently convicted of murder.) See A. T. H. Smith, [1992] CLJ 203.

2. On the difficulties surrounding use of the term 'specific intent', see *Smith and Hogan*, pp. 70–71. Smith and Hogan state (6th edn., 1988, p. 779) that

'Where D has an "intent" to interfere with the course of justice, he may be liable whatever form his conduct takes, whether or not there is a substantial risk that the course of justice will be impeded, or the impediment serious. . . .'

(Cf. above, p. 416).

(iii) The 'Strict Liability Rule'

By virtue of s. 1 of the Contempt of Court Act 1981 (above, p. 376) conduct may be treated as a contempt of court as tending to interfere with the course of justice 'regardless of intent to do so'. However, it will still be necessary to prove that the defendant intended to publish the material in question (see *Borrie and Lowe*, pp. 70–76, 91). Moreover, the 1981 Act enacts a number of defences and limitations to liability under the 'strict liability rule' (but not other aspects of the law of contempt e.g. scandalising the court (below pp. 421–427)). These provisions follow the recommendations of the Phillimore Committee (pp. 52–62). Section 3 (above, p. 376) corresponds to s. 11 of the Administration of Justice Act 1960 (which is now repealed). Section 4(1) (above, p. 376) enacts what was probably a defence at common law (see *Borrie and Lowe*, pp. 185–192); s. 5 (above, p. 376) enacts a limitation to the scope of liability which is recognised in the Commonwealth (*Re Truth and Sportsman Ltd, ex p Bread Manufacturers Ltd* (1937) 37 SRNSW 242) and might have been recognised in this country (cf. Lord Simon in *A-G v Times Newspapers Ltd* [1974] AC 273 at 321). The leading case on s. 5 is *A-G v English* (above, pp. 385–388).

4 Publications prejudicial to civil proceedings

(a) AT COMMON LAW

As the jury is today rarely used in civil proceedings, so the risk of prejudice to the fairness of trials from the publication of information and comments concerning pending litigation is accordingly reduced. However, where there is trial by jury the law of contempt obviously applies in the same way as in criminal proceedings, see above, pp. 384 ff., and the *Sunday Times* case (below) illustrated that the law protected litigants and witnesses from improper pressure, and indeed protected the administration of justice from being devalued by the development of 'trial by newspaper'.

A-G v Times Newspapers Ltd [1974] AC 273, [1973] 3 All ER 54, [1973] 3 WLR 298, House of Lords

In 1958, Distillers, a drug company, began to make and sell in the United Kingdom a sedative which contained the drug thalidomide. The product was prescribed for many pregnant women for whom it was said to be quite safe. Many of the mothers who had taken the drug gave birth to babies suffering from grave deformities. It was subsequently established that the deformities were caused by the action of thalid-omide on the unborn child at certain stages of the pregnancy. As soon as that was realised Distillers withdrew the product in 1961. Between 1962 and 1968 some 70 actions for negligence were brought against Distillers on behalf of the deformed children. Early in 1968 a settlement was reached in those pro-ceedings. Subsequently further writs were issued; by February 1969, 248 writs had been issued in proceedings which were not covered by the 1968 settlement. Negotiations took place with a view to a settlement and no further steps were taken in the proceedings in which writs had been issued to bring the actions to trial. Distillers made it a condition of any settlement that all claimants should accept it. The parties were, however, unable to come to agreement. In June 1972 Distillers made new proposals but they were not accepted; there were then some 389 claims outstanding. The editor of the *Sunday Times* took a keen interest in the matter. On 24 September 1972 the newspaper published a long and powerful article which criticised the law relating to the liability of drug companies and the methods of assessing damages. The sting of the article was however contained in a paragraph which stated that 'the thalid-omide children shame Distillers' and urged Distillers to offer much more than they had done so far. The paragraph continued: '. . . the law is not always the same as justice. There are times when to insist on the letter of the law is as exposed to criticism as infringement of another's legal rights. The figure in the pro-posed settlement is £3.25m., spread over 10 years. This does not shine as a beacon against pre-tax profits last year of £64.9 million and company assets worth £421 million. Without in any way surrendering on negligence, Distillers could and should think again.' Distillers brought the article to the attention of the Attorney-General maintaining that it was a contempt of court. The Attorney-General decided to take no action and Distillers let the matter drop. The editor of the *Sunday Times* was, however, minded to publish a further article of a different character. That article consisted in the main of detailed evidence and argu-ment intended to show that Distillers had not exercised due care to see that thalidomide was safe for pregnant mothers before they put it on the market. The editor sent the article to the Attorney-General who commenced proceedings for an injunction against the respondents, the proprietors of the *Sunday Times*, restraining them from publishing that article. The Divisional Court ([1972] 3 All ER 1136) granted an injunction but the Court of Appeal ([1973] 1 All ER 815) allowed the respondents' appeal and discharged the injunction on the grounds, inter alia, that the article contained comments which the authors honestly believed to be true on matters of outstanding public interest and did not prejudice pend-ing litigation since the litigation had been dormant for several years and no active steps had been taken or were likely to be taken to bring it before the courts. The Attorney-General appealed.

The House held unanimously (1) that the Attorney-General was a proper person to commence contempt proceedings, and (2) that an injunction should be granted to restrain publication of the second article. Lords Reid and Cross of Chelsea stated obiter that the first article did not amount to contempt. Lords Diplock and Simon of Glaisdale disagreed. They held that the first article improperly held Distillers up to public obloquy. Lord Simon would in addition have held that 'private pressure' to forgo legal rights was in general impermissible, and could only be justified within narrow limits as where there existed such a common interest that fair, reasonable and moderate personal representations could be appropriate. Lord Diplock took the view that 'private pressure' could not constitute contempt.

Lord Reid: . . . The law on this subject is and must be founded entirely on public policy. It is not there to protect the private rights of parties to a litigation or prosecution. It is there to prevent interference with the administration of justice and it should, in my judgment, be limited to what is reasonably neces-sary for that purpose. Public policy generally requires a balancing of interests which may conflict. Freedom of speech should not be limited to any greater extent than is necessary but it cannot be allowed where there would be real prejudice to the administration of justice. . . .

We are particularly concerned here with 'abusing parties' and 'prejudicing mankind' against them. Of course parties must be protected from scurrilous abuse: otherwise many litigants would fear to bring their cases to court. But the argument of the Attorney-General goes far beyond that. His argument was based on a passage in the judgment of Buckley J in *Vine Products Ltd v Green* [1966] Ch 484 at 495–496:

'It is a contempt of this court for any newspaper to comment on pending legal proceedings in any way which is likely to prejudice the fair trial of the action. That may arise in various ways. It may be that the comment is one which is likely in some way or other to bring pressure to bear upon one or other of the parties to the action, so as to prevent that party from prosecuting or from defending the action, or encourage that party to submit to terms of compromise which he otherwise might not have been prepared to entertain, or influence him in some other way in his conduct in the action, which he ought to be free to prosecute or to defend, as he is advised, without being subject to such pressure.'

I think that this is much too widely stated. It is true that there is some authority for it but . . . it does not seem to me to be in accord with sound public policy. Why would it be contrary to public policy to seek by fair comment to dissuade Shylock from proceeding with his action? Surely it could not be wrong for the officious bystander to draw his attention to the risk that, if he goes on, decent people will cease to trade with him. Or suppose that his best customer ceased to trade with him when he heard of his lawsuit. That could not be contempt of court. Would it become contempt if, when asked by Shylock why he was sending no more business his way, he told him the reason? Nothing would be more likely to influence Shylock to discontinue his action. It might become widely known that such pressure was being brought to bear. Would that make any difference? And though widely known must the local press keep silent about it? There must be some limitation of this general statement of the law.

And then suppose that there is in the press and elsewhere active discussion of some question of wide public interest, such as the propriety of local authorities or other landlords ejecting squatters from empty premises due for demolition. Then legal proceedings are begun against some squatters, it may be by some authority which had already been criticised in the press. The controversy could hardly be continued without likelihood that it might influence the authority in its conduct of the action. Must there then be silence until that case is decided? And there may be a series of actions by the same or different landlords. Surely public policy does not require that a system of stop and go shall apply to public discussion.

I think that there is a difference between direct interference with the fair trial of an action and words or conduct which may affect the mind of a litigant. Comment likely to affect the minds of witnesses and of the tribunal must be stopped for otherwise the trial may well be unfair. But the fact that a party refrains from seeking to enforce his full legal rights in no way prejudices a fair trial, whether the decision is or is not influenced by some third party. There are other weighty reasons for preventing improper influence being brought to bear on litigants, but they have little to do with interference with the fairness of a trial. There must be absolute prohibition of interference with a fair trial but beyond that there must be a balancing of relevant considerations. . . .

So I would hold that as a general rule where the only matter to be considered is pressure put on a litigant, fair and temperate criticism is legitimate, but anything which goes beyond that may well involve contempt of court. But in a case involving witnesses, jury or magistrates, other considerations are involved: there even fair and temperate criticism might be likely to affect the minds of some of them so as to involve contempt. But it can be assumed that it would not affect the mind of a professional judge. . . .

The crucial question on this point of the case is whether it can ever be permissible to urge a party to a litigation to forgo his legal rights in whole or in part. The Attorney-General argues that it cannot and I think that the Divisional Court has accepted that view. In my view it is permissible so long as it is done in a fair and temperate way and without any oblique motive. The *Sunday Times* article of 24 September 1972, affords a good illustration of the difference between the two views. It is plainly intended to bring pressure to bear on Distillers. It was likely to attract support from others and it did so. It was outspoken. It said: 'There are times when to insist on the letter of the law is as exposed to criticism as infringement of another's legal rights' and clearly implied that that was such a time. If the view maintained by the Attorney-General were right I could hardly imagine a clearer case of contempt of court. It could be no excuse that the passage which I quoted earlier was combined with a great deal of other totally unobjectionable material. And it could not be said that it created no serious risk of causing Distillers to do what they did not want to do. On the facts submitted to your Lordships in argument it seems to me to have played a large part in causing Distillers to offer far more money than they had in mind at that time. But I am quite unable to subscribe to the view that it ought never to have been published because it was in contempt of court. I see no offence against public policy and no pollution of the stream of justice by its publication.

Now I must turn to the material to which the injunction applied. . . . [I]t consists in the main of detailed evidence and argument intended to show that Distillers did not exercise due care to see that thalidomide was safe before they put it on the market.

If we regard this material solely from the point of view of its likely effect on Distillers I do not think that its publication in 1972 would have added much to the pressure on them created, or at least begun, by the earlier article of September 24. . . .

But, to my mind, there is another consideration even more important than the effect of publication on the mind of the litigant. The controversy about the tragedy of the thalidomide children has ranged widely but as yet there seems to have been little, if any, detailed discussion of the issues which the court may have to determine if the outstanding claims are not settled. The question whether Distillers were negligent has been frequently referred to but, so far as I am aware, there has been no attempt to assess the evidence. If this material were released now, it appears to me to be almost inevitable that detailed answers would be published and there would be expressed various public prejudgments of this issue. That I would regard as very much against the public interest.

There has long been and there still is in this country a strong and generally held feeling that trial by newspaper is wrong and should be prevented. I find, for example, in the report in 1969 of Lord Salmon's committee dealing with the Law of Contempt in relation to Tribunals of Inquiry (Cmnd. 4078) a reference to the 'horror' in such a thing (p. 12, para. 29). What I think is regarded as most objectionable is that a newspaper or television programme should seek to persuade the public by discussing the issues and evidence in a case before the court, whether civil or criminal, that one side is right and the other wrong. If we were to ask the ordinary man or even a lawyer in his leisure moments why he has that feeling, I suspect that the first reply would be—'well, look at what happens in some other countries where that is permitted.' As in so many other matters, strong feelings are based on one's general experience rather than on specific reasons, and it often requires an effort to marshal one's reasons. But the public policy is generally the result of strong feelings, commonly held, rather than of cold argument. . . .

There is ample authority for the proposition that issues must not be prejudged in a manner likely to affect the mind of those who may later be witnesses or jurors. But very little has been said about the wider proposition that trial by newspaper is intrinsically objectionable. That may be because if one can find more limited and familiar grounds adequate for the decision of a case it is rash to venture on uncharted seas.

I think that anything in the nature of prejudgment of a case or of specific issues in it is objectionable, not only because of its possible effect on that particular case but also because of its side effects which may be far reaching. Responsible 'mass media' will do their best to be fair, but there will also be ill-informed, slapdash or prejudiced attempts to influence the public. If people are led to think that it is easy to find the truth, disrespect for the processes of the law could follow, and, if mass media are allowed to judge, unpopular people and unpopular causes will fare very badly. Most cases of prejudging of issues fall within the existing authorities on contempt. I do not think that the freedom of the press would suffer, and I think that the law would be clearer and easier to apply in practice if it is made a general rule that it is not permissible to prejudge issues in pending cases. . . .

There is no magic in the issue of a writ or in a charge being made against an accused person. Comment on a case which is imminent may be as objectionable as comment after it has begun. And a 'gagging' writ ought to have no effect.

But I must add to prevent misunderstanding that comment where a case is under appeal is a very different matter. For one thing it is scarcely possible to imagine a case where comment could influence judges in the Court of Appeal or noble and learned Lords in this House. And it would be wrong and contrary to existing practice to limit proper criticism of judgments already given but under appeal.

Now I must deal with the reasons which induced the Court of Appeal to discharge the injunction. It was said that the actions had been dormant or asleep for several years. Nothing appears to have been done in court, but active negotiations for a settlement were going on all the time. No one denies that it would be contempt of court to use improper pressure to induce a litigant to settle a case on terms to which he did not wish to agree. So if there is no undue procrastination in the negotiations for a settlement I do not see how in this context an action can be said to be dormant.

Then it was said that there is here a public interest which counter-balances the private interests of the litigants. But contempt of court has nothing to do with the private interests of the litigants. I have already indicated the way in which I think that a balance must be struck between the public interest in freedom of speech and the public interest in protecting the administration of justice from interference. I do not see why there should be any difference in principle between a case which is thought to have news value and one which is not. Protection of the administration of justice is equally important whether or not the case involves important general issues. . . .

Lord Diplock: . . .

The due administration of justice requires *first* that all citizens should have unhindered access to the constitutionally established courts of criminal or civil jurisdiction for the determination of disputes as to their legal rights and liabilities; *secondly*, that they should be able to rely upon obtaining in the courts the arbitrament of a tribunal which is free from bias against any party and whose decision will be based upon those facts only that have been proved in evidence adduced before it in accordance with the procedure adopted in courts of law; and *thirdly* that, once the dispute has been submitted to a court of law, they should be able to rely upon there being no usurpation by any other person of the function of that court to decide it according to law. Conduct which is calculated to prejudice any of these three requirements or to undermine the public confidence that they will be observed is contempt of court. . . .

My Lords, to hold a party up to public obloquy for exercising his constitutional right to have recourse to a court of law for the ascertainment and enforcement of his legal rights and obligations is calculated to prejudice the *first* requirement for the due administration of justice: the unhindered access of all citizens to the established courts of law. Similarly, 'trial by newspaper,' i.e., public discussion or comment on the merits of a dispute which has been submitted to a court of law or on the alleged facts of the dispute before they have been found by the court upon the evidence adduced before it, is calculated to prejudice the *third* requirement: that parties to litigation should be able to rely upon there being no usurpation by any other person of the function of that court to decide their dispute according to law. If to have recourse to civil litigation were to expose a litigant to the risk of public obloquy or to public and prejudicial discussion of the facts or merits of the case before they have been determined by the court, potential suitors would be inhibited from availing themselves of courts of law for the purpose for which they are established.

It is only where a case is to be heard by a tribunal which may be regarded as incapable of being influenced by public criticism of the parties or discussion of the merits or the facts and any witnesses likely to be called are similarly immune, that conduct of this kind does not also offend against the *second* requirement for the due administration of justice; . . .

[His Lordship went on to hold that the second article was in contempt as it 'discussed prejudicially the facts and merits of Distillers' defence to the charge of negligence brought against them in the actions before these have been determined by the court or the actions disposed of by settlement'. The first article was also in contempt as a passage in it 'does hold Distillers up to public obloquy for . . . relying upon the defence, available to them under the law as it stands, that they were not guilty of any negligence. . . .' That did not mean that action should have been taken as it was a 'short passage in a long and trenchant article which was otherwise unobjectionable'.]

Lord Cross of Chelsea: . . . I agree with my noble and learned friend [Lord Reid] that we should maintain the rule that any 'prejudging' of issues, whether of fact or of law, in pending proceedings—whether civil or criminal—is in principle an interference with the administration of justice although in any particular case the offence may be so trifling that to bring it to the notice of the court would be unjustifiable . . . .

Appeal allowed.

NOTES

1. The injunction was discharged in 1976 (*The Times*, 24 June), and the article subsequently appeared in the *Sunday Times*.[1]

2. The Phillimore Committee did not like the 'prejudgment' test propounded by the House of Lords, while recognising the force of the policy arguments against 'trial by newspaper' or 'trial by television':

'111. The test of prejudgment might well make for greater certainty in one direction – provided a satisfactory definition of prejudgment could be found – but it is by no means clear that it is satisfactory in others, for instance, in the case of the "gagging" writs. . . . It can be arbitrary in its application. For example, an opinion expressed on a legal issue in a learned journal would fall within the description of prejudgment given by Lord Cross of Chelsea. Again, there has been much discussion and expression of opinion in scientific journals as to the manner in which thalidomide operates to produce deformities. These, too, would fall within the test of prejudgment and would therefore be contempts. Furthermore, the scope and precise meaning of the words "prejudge" or "prejudgment" as used in the House of Lords are no easier to determine in practice than the phrase "risk of prejudice". At what point does legitimate discussion or expression of opinion cease to be legitimate and qualify as prejudgment? This may depend as much upon the quality and the authority of the party expressing the opinion as upon the nature of the opinion and the form of its expression. . . . Further, the expression of opinion and even its repetition can be so framed as to disclaim clearly any intention to offer a concluded judgment and yet be of highly persuasive and influential character. The simple test of prejudgment therefore seems to go too far in some respects and not far enough in others. We conclude that no satisfactory definition can be found which does not have direct reference to the mischief which the law of contempt is and always has been designed to suppress. That mischief is the risk of prejudice to the due administration of justice.'

1 See casenotes by C. J. Miller, (1974) 37 MLR 96; M. O'Boyle, (1974) 25 NILQ 57; D. G. T. Williams, [1973] CLJ 177; and see C. J. Miller, [1975] Crim LR 132 and M. Rosen, *The Sunday Times Thalidomide Case* (1979).

The Committee's preferred test for contempt under the strict liability rule formed the basis of what is now s. 2(2) of the Contempt of Court Act 1981 (see p. 376).
3. It was formerly thought that once a writ for libel was issued, subsequent repetition of the libel would amount to contempt of court. So, persons with little or no intention of pursuing proceedings issued so-called 'gagging' writs in order to stifle further comment. The best view, prior to the 1981 Act, was that the issue of a writ did not *automatically* render repetition of the alleged libel contempt, but that repetition might be contempt if there was a risk of prejudice to the pending proceedings. If a court was not convinced that the plaintiff genuinely intended to proceed, or if the repetition was well before the trial, then there was likely to be no risk of prejudice and so no contempt. Salmon LJ seemed to go further when he offered the following encouragement to the press (obiter) in *Thomson v Times Newspapers Ltd* [1969] 3 All ER 648 at 651, CA:

'It is a widely held fallacy that the issue of a writ automatically stifles further comment. There is no authority that I know of to support the view that further comment would amount to contempt of court. Once a newspaper has justified, and there is some prima facie support for the justification, the plaintiff cannot obtain an interlocutory injunction to restrain the defendants from repeating the matters complained of [under the rule in *Bonnard v Perryman*, below, p. 538]. In these circumstances it is obviously wrong to suppose that they could be committing a contempt by doing so. It seems to me to be equally obvious that no other newspaper that repeats the same sort of criticism is committing a contempt of court. They may be publishing a libel, and if they do so, and they have no defence to it, they will have to pay whatever may be the appropriate damages; but the writ does not, in my view, preclude the publication of any further criticism: it merely puts the person who makes the further criticism on risk of being sued for libel; and he takes the same risk whether or not there has been any previous publication. I appreciate that very often newspapers are chary about repeating criticism when a writ for libel has been issued because they feel they are running some risk of being proceeded against for contempt. Without expressing any final view, because the point is not before this court for decision, I think that in this they are mistaken. No doubt the law relating to contempt could and should be clarified in this respect.'

This was approved by Lord Denning MR in *Wallersteiner v Moir* [1974] 3 All ER 217 at 230, CA. Note also Lord Reid's remark in the *Sunday Times* case (above, p. 408) that 'a gagging writ ought to have no effect.' There is now less scope for 'gagging writs' in view of the provisions of the Contempt of Court Act 1981 that (1) delay commencement of the sub judice period in civil cases (Sch. 1); (2) strengthen the test for contempt (s. 2(2): see *A-G v News Group Newspapers Ltd* below p. 417 n. 3); and (3) establish a public interest defence (s. 5: above, p. 376). However, it has been held that the rule in *Bonnard v Perryman* does not apply if there is an infringement of the strict liability rule (*A-G v News Group Newspapers Ltd*, below, p. 417 n. 3). See further on 'gagging writs': Borrie and Lowe, pp. 135–138; Miller, pp. 247–252.
4. The *Sunday Times* case was distinguished in *Schering Chemicals Ltd v Falkman Ltd* [1982] QB 1, CA. Here, the Court of Appeal declined to grant an injunction to prevent the showing of a television film about a drug ('Primodos') that had been alleged to be harmful to unborn children, sought on the ground that it would be in contempt of court in relation to pending civil litigation. There was no risk of prejudice as the issues were not prejudged, there was no improper pressure and it would be arranged that the judge who tried the action would not have seen the broadcast. (An injunction was, however, granted (Lord Denning MR dissenting) on the ground of breach of confidence: see below p. 554. See (1982) 98 LQR 5–8.)
5. The decision of the European Court of Human Rights in the *Sunday Times* case is considered below at p. 823. The Contempt of Court Act 1981 was intended to fulfil the requirements of that decision. It has been a matter of debate whether this has been achieved: see N. V. Lowe in M. P. Furmston (*et al*) (eds), *The Effect on*

English Domestic Law of Membership of the European Communities and of Ratification of the European Convention on Human Rights (1983), Chap. 10; A. Arlidge and D. Eady, *The Law of Contempt* (1982) pp. 144–150.

6. *Borrie and Lowe* (pp. 145–149) argue that in *A-G v Times Newspapers* (above) Lords Reid, Cross and Morris took the view that fair and temperate criticism of a litigant, whether public or private, designed, for example, to encourage him to settle or not to insist on his strict legal rights, is not contempt (cf. Hunt J in *Commercial Bank of Australia Ltd v Preston* [1981] 2 NSWLR 554, Sup Ct NSW). For an example of illegitimate pressure, see *Dove Group plc and Jaguar Cars Ltd v Hynes* [1993] COD 174, where H conducted a campaign of harassment against Dove Jaguars in respect of a Jaguar Sovereign car which was the subject of pending litigation between the parties in the county court. H's actions included driving the car around with a large cardboard box on the roof simulating a battery and making it clear that it was insufficiently powered, arranging for the car to be towed around the streets by shire horses having alerted the media beforehand, interfering with car salesmen and visiting Mr Dove's country home in his absence to Mrs Dove's alarm. H was fined. The Phillimore Committee (pp. 25–30) recommended that only conduct directed against a litigant which amounts to intimidation or unlawful threats should be capable of being treated as a contempt. The Green Paper (Cmnd. 7145, pp. 15–17) expressed the view that this would tip the balance too far against the interests of justice. The Law Commission (Law Com No. 96, pp. 59–62) proposed an offence of making an unwarranted demand with menaces that a person should either not institute judicial proceedings, or should withdraw or should settle those proceedings. No action has been taken on these recommendations.

7. The following case considers liability for intentional contempt at common law.

A-G v Times Newspapers Ltd [1991] 2 All ER 398, [1992] 1 AC 191, [1991] 2 WLR 994, House of Lords

In 1985, the Attorney-General obtained an interim injunction in Australia restraining Peter Wright from publishing *Spycatcher: The Candid Memoirs of an Intelligence Officer*. In June 1986, before the trial of the Australian proceedings, the *Guardian* and the *Observer* published articles outlining allegations contained in the Wright memoirs. The Attorney-General obtained interlocutory injunctions against the newspapers restraining them, with certain exceptions, from disclosing any information obtained by Wright in his capacity as a member of the security service (*A-G v Observer Newspapers Ltd and the Guardian* [1986] NLJ Rep 799, CA). He intended to seek final injunctions, based on Mr Wright's breach of confidence. In April 1987, the *Independent*, the *London Evening Standard* and the *London Daily News*, who were not parties to the 1986 injunctions, published further material derived from Wright's memoirs. The Attorney-General brought proceedings for contempt of court. A preliminary issue of law was tried, namely whether a publication made in knowledge of an outstanding injunction against another party and which if made by that party would be in breach of the injunction, could constitute a criminal contempt of court on the ground that it interfered with the process of justice in relation to that injunction. Sir Nicolas Browne-Wilkinson V-C held that the law of contempt did not apply where the only act complained of was not a breach of the express terms of the order and the alleged contemnor was neither party nor privy to any breach of the order by others. The Attorney-General appealed. He conceded that the strict liability rule did not apply as proceedings were not active, but argued that the defendants could be liable for contempt at common law as their conduct was intended to impede or prejudice the administration of justice. On 15 July 1987, the Court of Appeal ([1988] Ch 333) held that the respondents' publications could amount to contempt of court, and remitted the case for trial. Meanwhile, on 12 July, the *Sunday Times*, having been advised by leading counsel that it would not constitute contempt, published extracts from *Spycatcher*. On 13 July, the Attorney-General commenced contempt proceedings against the publishers of the *Sunday Times* (Times Newspapers Ltd) and its editor, Andrew Neil.

Both sets of proceedings were heard by Morritt J. At this stage the Attorney-General pressed for substantive relief only against the *Independent* and the *Sunday Times*. Morritt J held ([1989] 1 FSR 457) that the publishers and editors of these papers had been guilty of contempt by publishing extracts from or summaries of *Spycatcher*. The respective publishers were each fined £50,000. On appeal, the Court of Appeal (*A-G v Newspaper Publishing Ltd plc* (1990) Times, 28 February) upheld the finding of contempt, but discharged the fines. Times Newspapers appealed to the House of Lords. The only matter at issue was whether the appellants had committed the actus reus of contempt. The House of Lords unanimously dismissed the appeal.

Lord Oliver: . . . The appellants' primary submission is that it not only was not, but was not capable of being, a contempt of court because, although they were fully aware of the orders which had been made against 'The Guardian' and the 'Observer,' they were not themselves bound by those orders nor were they assisting in or procuring or inciting a breach of those orders by the two newspapers which were bound.

The submission involves some analysis of the particular type of contempt with which the appeal is concerned. A distinction (which has been variously described as 'unhelpful' or 'largely meaningless') is sometimes drawn by what is described as 'civil contempt,' that is to say, contempt by a party to proceedings in matters of procedure, and 'criminal contempt.' One particular form of contempt by a party to proceedings is that constituted by an intentional act which is in breach of the order of a competent court. Where this occurs as a result of the act of a party who is bound by the order or of others acting at his direction or on his instigation, it constitutes a civil contempt by him which is punishable by the court at the instance of the party for whose benefit the order was made and can be waived by him. The intention with which the act was done will, of course, be of the highest relevance in the determination of the penalty (if any) to be imposed by the court, but the liability here is a strict one in the sense that all that requires to be proved is service of the order and the subsequent doing by the party bound of that which is prohibited. When, however, the prohibited act is done not by the party bound himself but by a third party, a stranger to the litigation, that person may also be liable for contempt. There is, however, this essential distinction that his liability is for criminal contempt and arises not because the contemnor is himself affected by the prohibition contained in the order but because his act constitutes a wilful interference with the administration of justice by the court in the proceedings in which the order was made. Here the liability is not strict in the sense referred to, for there has to be shown not only knowledge of the order but an intention to interfere with or impede the administration of justice – an intention which can of course be inferred from the circumstances.

The distinction is very well brought out in the judgment of Eveleigh LJ in *Z Ltd v A-Z and AA-LL* [1982] QB 558, where the question arose whether a third party could be liable for contempt in doing, at a time before the party enjoined had himself received notice of the order, that which was prohibited by the order. Eveleigh LJ observed, at p. 578:

'It was argued that the liability of a third party arose because he was treated as aiding and abetting the defendants (i.e. he was an accessory) and as the defendant could himself not be in breach unless he had notice it followed that there was no offence to which the third party could be accessory. In my opinion this argument misunderstands the true nature of the liability of the third party. He is liable for contempt of court committed by himself. It is true that his conduct may very often be seen as possessing a dual character of contempt of court by himself and aiding and abetting the contempt by another, but the conduct will always amount to contempt of court by himself. It will be conduct which knowingly interferes with the administration of justice by causing the order of the court to be thwarted.'

Mr Lester, on behalf of the appellants, accepts this as an accurate statement of the principle but nevertheless contends that it is restricted to cases in which it can be demonstrated that the third party was privy in some way to a breach by the party enjoined and that therefore the decision of the Court of Appeal in the instant case constituted an unwarranted extension of the law of contempt in a way which is both contrary to principle and unwarranted by authority. That submission is encapsulated in paragraph 19 of the appellants' printed case where it is asserted:

'The authorities decide that a third party is not liable for contempt by performing an act prohibited by the court except where he has aided and abetted (or incited or otherwise assisted) the performance of the act by the party enjoined.'

I will consider in a moment the authorities upon which Mr Lester relies for this proposition, but a moment's reflection will, I think, demonstrate that it cannot possibly be valid as a general proposition. Of course, aiding and abetting or inciting a breach is an obvious example of the sort of situation in which a third party will subject himself to liability, but if the underlying basis of his liability is, as Mr Lester accepts that it is, that stated by Eveleigh LJ, there can be no logical reason for restricting the liability in the way that he suggests. Take a simple example. A has a right of way over a roadway on C's land which constitutes the only access to his premises. A, having built a wall on his premises which obstructs the light of his next-door neighbour B, B commences proceedings for an injunction. On motion in that action A proffers and the court accepts an undertaking by A to use his best endeavours to remove the wall by a given date. A accordingly instructs contractors to carry out the work of demolition. C, who knows of the undertaking but wishes to pursue a private spite against B, in order to prevent the demolition of the wall, obstructs the access to the premises by blocking the right of way and employs security guards to prevent A's contractors from removing the obstruction. C is not bound by the terms of the undertaking nor can he conceivably be under any obligation to assist A in fulfilling it. Nor, obviously, does he aid and abet a breach by A of his undertaking, which the latter has in fact fulfilled by instructing contractors. But equally obviously C has impeded the administration of justice by deliberately thwarting an undertaking given to the court and designed to secure the removal of the wall. In circumstances such as these, it would seem to me unarguable that C is not in contempt of court in exactly the same way as if he had obstructed an officer of the court and I cannot imagine any court accepting as a defence to a motion for committal the proposition that no contempt is committed because C was not a party to the action or the undertaking.

Nor, in my judgment, do the authorities cited by Mr. Lester support the broad proposition for which he contends. *Lord Wellesley v Earl of Mornington* (1848) 11 Beav 181 was a case in which the earl's agent had cut wood with notice of an injunction against the earl. It was certainly said that the agent was liable to be committed for contempt as a third party who had aided and abetted a breach by the earl, but there is in fact nothing in the report of the proceedings to suggest that the earl was even aware of the agent's acts much less that he had authorised them. *Seaward v Paterson* [1897] 1 Ch 545, was a case where the contemnors had actively aided and abetted the defendant in the action in a breach of the injunction and it is not surprising therefore that the judgments treat of contempt in that context. But the principle enunciated by the Court of Appeal, and which is expressed in the judgments of both Lindley LJ and Rigby LJ, was the quite general one that any member of the public is under a duty not to obstruct the course of justice. . . .

[His Lordship referred to *A-G v Leveller Magazine Ltd* [1979] AC 440: above p. 392].

My Lords, there can be no logical distinction between a case where the court seeks to protect or preserve the interests of justice by a procedural ruling in the course of a hearing and one where it seeks to achieve the same end by a formal prohibition directed to one of the parties. Once one gets away, as these authorities compel, from the notion that the binding effect of an order is an essential ingredient in the offence of contempt, Mr Lester's proposition that the actus reus of contempt is narrowly confined solely to those who aid, abet or incite breaches by the party bound is seen to be untenable. It could not have made the slightest difference to the liability of Murray and Shepherd in *Seaward v Paterson* [1897] 1 Ch 545, if they had arranged and conducted the offending boxing match without Paterson's knowledge or authority. Both had been served with copies of the order made for the protection of the plaintiffs from disturbance and restraining Paterson from using or suffering the premises to be used otherwise than as a private club and their use of the premises for the holding of a boxing match was an intentional act having the inevitable consequence of frustrating the very purpose for which the court had made its order.

Once the conclusion is reached that the fact that the alleged contemnor is not party to or personally bound by the court's order then, given the intention on his part to interfere with or obstruct the course of justice, the sole remaining question is whether what he has done has that effect in the particular circumstances of the case. In the Court of Appeal it was said that the administration of justice was interfered with because the publication, as it was variously put, 'rendered nugatory the trial of the action' [[1988] Ch 358, 373 per Sir John Donaldson MR], 'destroyed in whole or in part the subject matter of the action' [Lloyd LJ, at pp. 378–380] or 'rendered the trial . . . pointless' [Balcombe LJ, at p. 387]. I respectfully question, however, whether the mere fact that an act of a third party foreseeably has the result that the issue in the action becomes academic or that it is no longer worth pursuing, so that the court's order ceases to fulfil any useful purpose, necessarily involves the conclusion that it constitutes the actus reus of contempt. It is not difficult to imagine circumstances in which a stranger to litigation acting in the pursuit of his own interests can quite permissibly take steps which he knows perfectly well will render pending litigation pointless or destroy, for practical purposes, the subject matter of a pending action. For example, in the course of the argument, I instanced the case of an action in which a company obtains an ex parte injunction until the next motion day to prevent a creditor whose debt is disputed from presenting and advertising a winding-up petition. A petition presented the next day with knowledge of the injunction by an unpaid creditor whose debt is not capable of being disputed would clearly have the effect of rendering any further proceeding in the action entirely pointless. But it would be absurd to suggest that a perfectly proper use of the court's own machinery, even if for the express purpose of affecting the course of other pending litigation, could constitute the actus reus of contempt. Other examples are not difficult to come by and they illustrate the difficulty and, sometimes, the danger of attempting to formulate a universal test of what constitutes interfering with or impeding the administration of justice.

For my part, I doubt the value of cataloguing a series of hypothetical circumstances which can do no more than serve as illustrations of conduct which can or may fall on one side of the line or the other. I think that a more dependable guide is to be found in the way in which the gravamen of the offence is expressed in the respondent's case and which, I think, must be based upon the speeches in this House in the *Leveller Magazine* case, [1979] AC 440: 'The publication . . . frustrates, thwarts, or *subverts the purpose* of the court's order and thereby interferes with the due administration of justice in the particular action.' 'Purpose,' in this context, refers, of course, not to the litigant's purpose in obtaining the order or in fighting the action but to the purpose which, in seeking to administer justice between the parties in the particular litigation of which it had become seized, the court was intending to fulfil.

The appellants raise two principal objections to addressing the purpose of the order in this context. In the first place, it is said that the purpose of an order is something which can be gathered only from its terms and thus becomes synonymous with the text of the order. By that test, of course, the act of a third party, not an aider or abettor, has no effect upon the order at all. If the order forbids the doing of an act by A, A has done nothing and remains bound by the order which thus cannot be said to be frustrated. It was, on its face, designed to inhibit A. It achieves that purpose. Any other approach, it is said, leads to uncertainty, but how otherwise is the court's purpose to be ascertained? And can it be right in the context of a criminal offence that members of the public should be obliged to enquire beyond the terms of the order itself?

I can see the force of this in a case where the court's purpose is not manifest from the mere making of the order and this was, indeed, one of the matters which troubled Lord Edmund-Davies in the *Leveller Magazine* case [1979] AC 440. But the difficulty is more imaginary than real. None of their lordships who decided the *Leveller Magazine* case experienced any difficulty where the purpose of the order or ruling is obvious and manifest. Where there is room for genuine doubt about what the court's purpose is, then the party charged with contempt is likely to escape liability, not because of failure to prove the actus reus but for want of the necessary mens rea, for an intention to frustrate the purpose of the court would be difficult to establish if the purpose itself was not either known or obvious. In the instant case, there could never have been any doubt in anybody's mind what the court's purpose was in making the order. It was to preserve, until the trial of the action, the plaintiff's right to keep confidential and unpublished the information obtained by Mr Wright in the course of his employment – a right which the plaintiff enjoyed against all the world but which had been specifically threatened by the defendants in the action. . . .

The appellants fairly take the point that the third party who learns of the order and is thus put in the position of considering whether he is at liberty to do that which the party to the order is forbidden to do, has not been heard by the court and has, thus, not had the opportunity of putting before the court any arguments which he may have for contending that he is free to do what he desires in his own interest to do. That is perfectly true, but the answer is surely that that is by his own choice. 'The Sunday Times' in the instant case was perfectly at liberty, before publishing, either to inform the respondent and so give him the opportunity to object or to approach the court and to argue that it should be free to publish where the defendants were not, just as a person affected by notice of, for example, a *Mareva* injunction is able to, and frequently does, apply to the court for directions as to the disposition of assets in his hands which may or may not be subject to the terms of the order. In the end, therefore, I find myself unpersuaded by this argument. . . .

[His Lordship then rejected the argument that the effect of the present decision was to criminalise an act retroactively: there was nothing retroactive about 'the application of perfectly well known principles to a novel set of circumstances – novel only in the sense that no precise analogue can be found in any previously reported proceedings.' The argument that maintenance of the injunctions was in conflict with Article 10 of the ECHR was precluded by the statement to the contrary by Lord Templeman in *A-G v Guardian Newspapers Ltd* [1987] 3 All ER 316, 356 (below, p. 486).]

Finally, it is said that, because of the impending publication of Mr Wright's book in the United States, 'The Sunday Times' publication did not in fact interfere with the administration of justice since such confidentiality as remained was about to be destroyed in any event. The short answer to this is that the act has to be looked at the date when it was performed. It cannot be open to one who has frustrated the court's order to excuse himself by saying that someone else was about to do the same thing.

It seems, at first sight, a startling proposition that the doing by a person not a party to an action of an act which he is at liberty, in his own interests, to do and which he is not prohibited by order from doing, should subject him to proceedings for contempt merely because he is affected by knowledge that an order has been made against somebody else. But the circumstances are unusual and I cannot readily envisage circumstances likely in practice to occur, apart from claims for breach of confidence, where such an act would have the effect of impeding the administration of justice. As the Master of the Rolls observed in the instant case, breach of confidence is a uniquely fragile cause of action and the publication, once made, can have the effect of destroying for good and all the right which the law seeks to protect. Whilst newspapers have a legitimate interest and an important and necessary function in disseminating information, their rights are no higher than the right of a private individual to preserve the inviolability of that which he has imparted to another under an obligation of confidence and ought not to be permitted to override that right save where the public interest compulsively demands. A fortiori is that the case where a competent court has intervened to protect such right. The respondent to this appeal is the Attorney-General, but it has to be stressed as was emphasised in both the courts below, that in this case he was in no different position from any other private citizen entitled to preserve the sanctity of confidential information. In the end, I have found the logic of the respondent's arguments inescapable and I accordingly agree that the Court of Appeal reached the right conclusion and that the appeal must be dismissed. I confess, however, that I do so with a measure of disquiet, not because I doubt the validity of the conclusion, but because of the possibilities that open up. As I have said, I think that this sort of question is unlikely to arise except in cases of threatened publication of confidential material. But in those cases the important stage of the proceedings is almost always and inevitably the interlocutory one and it is, I think, important that a vigilant eye should be kept on the possibility that the law of contempt may be invoked in support of claims which are in truth insupportable. The guidelines laid down by this House in *American Cyanamid Co v Ethicon Ltd* [1975] AC 396, have come to be treated as carved on tablets of stone, so that a plaintiff seeking interlocutory relief has never to do more than show that he has a fairly arguable case. Thus the effect in a contest between a would-be publisher and one seeking to restrain the publication of allegedly confidential information is that the latter, by presenting an arguable case, can effectively through the invocation of the law of contempt, restrain until the trial of the action, which may be two or more years ahead, publication not only by the defendant but by anyone else within the jurisdiction and thus stifle what may, in the end, turn out to be perfectly legitimate comment until it no longer has any importance or commands any public interest. In cases where there is a contest as to whether the information is confidential at all or whether the public interest in any event requires its publication despite its confidentiality, this could be very important and experience shows that orders for speedy trial do not always achieve the hoped for result. I speak only for myself, but I cannot help feeling that in cases where it is clearly of importance that publication, if it takes place at all, should take place expeditiously, it may be necessary for courts to balance the rights of the parties and to decide the issue, as they sometimes did before the *Cyanamid* case, at the interlocutory stage on the prima facie merits and on the evidence then available.

Lords Brandon, Ackner and **Jauncey** delivered concurring speeches. **Lord Keith** concurred. *Appeal dismissed*

NOTES

1. The other members of the House of Lords did not express any misgiving of the kind mentioned by Lord Oliver, although Lord Jauncey did say (p. 427) that it 'can only be in a limited type of case that independent action by a third party will have the effect of interfering with the operation of an order to which he is not a party. Cases involving confidential information are obvious examples.' Others might include destruction of a valuable object or demolition of a listed building, but it would 'only be in exceptional circumstances that a third party would be free to achieve this result without also incurring liabilities other than for contempt of court.'

2. The question of mens rea was considered by the Court of Appeal (1990) Times (28 February). It was common ground by this stage that recklessness was insufficient for mens rea and that what was necessary was a 'specific intent' to impede or prejudice the administration of justice (in accordance with observations in *A-G v Newspaper Publishing plc* [1988] Ch 333, 374 (Sir John Donaldson MR), 382 (Lloyd LJ), 387 (Balcombe LJ)). What was in issue was how that intention was to be established. In the present case, the Court of Appeal held that the following passage from the judgment of Lord Lane CJ in *R v Nedrick* [1986] 3 All ER 1, 3–4, was applicable to criminal contempt of court.

'When determining whether the defendant had the necessary intent, it may therefore be helpful for a jury to ask themselves two questions. (1) How probable was the consequence which resulted from the defendant's voluntary act? (2) Did he foresee that consequence?

If he did not appreciate that death or serious harm was likely to result from his act, he cannot have intended to bring it about. If he did, but thought that the risk to which he was exposing the person killed was only slight, then it may be easy for the jury to conclude that he did not intend to bring about that result. On the other hand, if the jury are satisfied that at the material time the defendant recognised that death or serious harm would be virtually certain (barring some unforeseen intervention) to result from his voluntary act, then that is a fact from which they may find it easy to infer that he intended to kill or do serious bodily harm, even though he may not have had any desire to achieve that result.

As Lord Bridge said in *R v Moloney* [1985] 1 All ER 1025 at 1036, [1985] AC 905 at 925:
'. . . the probability of the consequence taken to have been foreseen must be little short of overwhelming before it will suffice to establish the necessary intent.'
Later he uses the expression 'moral certainty' (see [1985] 1 All ER 1025 at 1037, [1985] AC 905 at 926) and says, 'will lead to a certain consequence unless something unexpected supervenes to prevent it' (see [1985] 1 All ER 1025 at 1039, [1985] AC 905 at 929).

Where the charge is murder and in the rare cases where the simple direction is not enough, the jury should be directed that they are not entitled to infer the necessary intention unless they feel sure that death or serious bodily harm was a virtual certainty (barring some unforeseen intervention) as a result of the defendant's actions and that the defendant appreciated that such was the case.

Where a man realises that it is for all practical purposes inevitable that his actions will result in death or serious harm, the inference may be irresistible that he intended that result, however little he may have desired or wished it to happen. The decision is one for the jury to be reached on a consideration of all the evidence.'

See further, J. Laws, (1990) 43 CLP 99, 105–110.

3. Is there any room in the law on intentional contempt for any public interest defence analogous to s. 5 of the Contempt of Court Act 1981 (above p. 376). J. Laws ((1990) 43 CLP 99, 110–111) argues that public interest considerations cannot affect the actus reus of intended contempt (if D intends to impede justice he can hardly argue that he was discussing *in good faith* matters of general public interest). They might, however, tend to negative the necessary intent. In *Times Newspapers Ltd v A-G*, Lord Jauncey did consider the public interest, and concluded 'that in these cases the public interest in having justice done unimpeded between parties must prevail over that interest in the freedom of the press.'

(b) UNDER THE STRICT LIABILITY RULE

The test for contempt under the 'strict liability rule' is to be found in s. 2(2) of the Contempt of Court Act 1981 (above, p. 376) and is the same as for criminal cases (above, pp. 384–391). The time limits are enacted in Schedule 1, paras. 12–14 and (for appellate proceedings) paras. 15 and 16 (above, pp. 379–380). These largely follow the recommendations of the Phillimore Committee, which took the view that in the light of the length of civil proceedings as compared with criminal, the decrease in jury trials and the unlikelihood that judges will be improperly influenced, strict liability need not be imposed from the commencement of proceedings in civil cases. The defences under ss. 3, 4(1) and 5 of the 1981 Act are available (see above, pp. 376, 385–391, 405).

NOTES

1. How would the *Sunday Times* case be decided under the 1981 Act? Consider (1) the test for contempt; (2) the time limits; (3) the defences. Note Lord Diplock's remarks in *A-G v English* (above, p. 387) and *Re Lonrho plc* (below, p. 420).

2. Coroners' inquests are active once they have opened, and until they have been closed by a finding as to the cause of death; they remain active even though adjourned *sine die* while police investigations take place: *Peacock v London Weekend Television* (1985) 150 JP 71, CA. In this case, an injunction was granted to prevent a televised reconstruction of events that led to the death of a black Hell's Angel in police custody; this was held to constitute a substantial risk that the coroner's proceedings would be seriously impeded or prejudiced. Watkins LJ regarded the proposed programme as 'very emotive': 'newspapers and broadcasters must beware of wittingly or unwittingly usurping the functions of courts. In our land we do not allow trial by television or newspaper' (p. 80). Croom-Johnson LJ did not regard the programme as 'balanced'. As to the suggestion that the passage of time would cause the memories of watchers to fade, 'nowadays one has to remember the existence of the video' (pp. 82–83).

3. The relationship between the rule in *Bonnard v Perryman* (below p. 538) and the law of contempt of court was considered by the Court of Appeal in *A-G v News Group Newspapers Ltd* [1987] QB 1. In 1984, Ian Botham, the England Test cricketer, began libel proceedings in respect of an article in the *Mail on Sunday* alleging, inter alia, the misuse of drugs while on tour in New Zealand. The defendants intended to plead justification and the case was set down for trial no earlier than March 1987. Under the rule in *Bonnard v Perryman*, applicable under the law of defamation, the plaintiff would not be able to seek an interlocutory injunction restraining the defendants from repeating the allegations subsequently. On 6 April 1986, the *News of the World* repeated the allegations, and a further story, with further details, was intended for publication on 13 April. The Attorney-General sought an injunction restraining the defendants from publishing allegations covering substantially the same ground as the *Mail on Sunday* allegations of 1984. The Court of Appeal held that the rule in *Bonnard v Perryman* was decisive only in so far as the strict liability rule was not invoked. However, on the facts here, the proposed publication by the *News of the World* at this time would not involve a breach of the strict liability rule. Per Sir John Donaldson at pp. 15, 16:

'There has to be a *substantial* risk that the course of justice in the proceedings in question will be *seriously* impeded or prejudiced. This is a double test. First, there has to be some risk that the proceedings in question will be affected at all. Second, there has to be a prospect that, if affected, the effect will be serious. The two limbs of the test can overlap, but they can be quite separate. I accept Mr Laws' submission that "substantial" as a qualification of "risk" does not have the meaning of "weighty," but rather means "not insubstantial" or "not minimal". The "risk" part of the test will usually be of importance in the context of the width of the publication. To declare in a speech at a public meeting in Cornwall that a man about to be tried in Durham is guilty of the offence charged and has many previous convictions for the same offence may well carry no substantial risk of affecting his trial, but, if it occurred, the prejudice would be most serious. By contrast, a nationwide television broadcast at peak viewing time of some far more innocuous statement would certainly involve a substantial risk of having some effect on a trial anywhere in the country and the sole effective question would arise under the "seriousness" limb of the test. Proximity in time between the publication and the proceedings would probably have a greater bearing on the risk limb than on the seriousness limb, but could go to both. . . .

. . . Whatever else may be said about the "News of the World," it is a newspaper with a nationwide circulation and there is a reasonable chance that it will have been read by at least one member of the jury which eventually hears Mr Botham's claims against the "Mail on Sunday." Whilst it is true that these actions are not yet in the jury list, I wholly reject Mr Gray's suggestion that there is any significance in the time at which the case comes into that list or in a period of about three months before trial. To accept such a submission would be to substitute a new test for "activity" for the purposes of the Act of 1981.

However, proximity to the trial is clearly a factor of great importance and this trial will not take place for at least 10 months, by which time many wickets will have fallen, not to mention much water having flowed under many bridges, all of which would blunt any impact of the publication. Furthermore, whilst I have never been a great believer in the efficacy of a conscious effort to put something out of one's mind—an acceptance of the fact that it is likely to remain there, but a determination not to take it into account, is more effective—and whilst I fully accept that judges may have an exaggerated belief in the extent to which juries are prepared to be guided by them in such mental gymnastics, the fact is that for one reason or another a trial, by its very nature, seems to cause all concerned to become progressively more inward looking, studying the evidence given and submissions made to the exclusion of other sources of enlightenment. This is a well-known phenomenon. As Lawton J put it on the basis of vast experience of jury trials, both at the Bar and on the Bench: "the drama, if I may use that term, of a trial almost always has the effect of excluding from recollection that which went before": *R v Kray* (1969) 53 Cr App Rep 412, 415.

The time may well come when a national newspaper would be in breach of the strict liability rule if it referred to the disputed incidents which are the subject matter of the "Mail on Sunday" actions. But in my judgment that day has not yet arrived, because it is not at present possible to say that there is a substantial risk of the "Mail on Sunday" trials being seriously prejudiced.'

See also *Pickering v Liverpool Daily Post and Echo Newspapers plc* [1990] 1 All ER 335 where the plaintiff, a restricted mental patient detained under the Mental Health Act 1983 following his brutal killing of a 14-year old girl, sought an injunction restraining the defendants from publishing the fact that he had applied to a Mental Health Review Tribunal for his discharge, the date of the hearing or the tribunal's decision. Previous applications by him had given rise to considerable media controversy. The Court of Appeal held that such an injunction could not be granted here on the basis of a threatened breach of the strict liability rule: the publication of the information 'would not *necessarily* impede or prejudice the course of justice, although, according to when, and where and how it is published, considerable discretion and restraint may have to be exercised if it is not to do so' (per Lord Donaldson MR at p. 342). A modified injunction was, however, granted under the specific procedural rules applicable to Mental Health Appeal Tribunals, and the court indicated, obiter, that a deliberate breach of restrictions imposed by those rules might constitute contempt of court by virtue of s. 12 of the Administration of Justice Act 1960 (see above, p. 396). The injunction was in turn set aside by the House of Lords ([1991] 2 AC 370) on the grounds (1) that breach of the rules did not itself give rise to a cause of action; and (2) that in any event the rules would not be breached by the publication of the information in question. (Cf. *A-G v Associated Newspapers Group plc* [1989] 1 All ER 604, DC, where proceedings for criminal contempt arising out of publicity surrounding a previous application by the plaintiff to a Mental Health Review Tribunal were dismissed, inter alia, on the ground that any risk of prejudice by any effect on the tribunal or expert witnesses was remote.)

4. The application of the strict liability rule to appellate proceedings was considered by the Appellate Committee of the House of Lords in *Re Lonrho plc* [1990] 2 AC 154. This case arose out of the long campaign by Lonrho to acquire House of

Fraser, the owners of a series of stores including Harrods. In 1985, House of Fraser was acquired by the Al Fayed brothers. In 1987 the Secretary of State appointed inspectors under the Companies Act 1985, s. 432(2), to investigate and report on this acquisition. In 1988, the Secretary of State received this report, and sent a copy to the Serious Fraud Office. He decided that it should not be published while this might hinder the S.F.O.'s investigation and the fair trial of anyone prosecuted in consequence. He also decided not to refer the acquisition to the Monopolies and Mergers Commission. Lonrho sought judicial review of these decisions. They succeeded in the Divisional Court but the Secretary of State's appeal to the Court of Appeal was allowed. Lonrho's appeal to the House of Lords was fixed for hearing on 10 April 1989. On 23 March, Lonrho's chief executive, 'Tiny' Rowland, came into possession of two unauthorised copies of the report. On 30 March, a special edition of *The Observer* (a Lonrho subsidiary) was published containing extracts from and comments on the report. An injunction was obtained against *The Observer* but too late to prevent widespread distribution. 3,000 copies were sent by Lonhro to various recipients including four of the five Law Lords who were due to hear the appeal. Further campaign literature against the Al Fayeds was subsequently sent to some of the Law Lords. The Appellate Committee that was due to hear the judicial review appeal commenced contempt proceedings against Lonrho, Rowland, three Lonrho directors, The Observer Ltd, the editor of *The Observer*, Donald Trelford, and two lawyers. An amicus curiae was instructed to present the case. The Committee subsequently held (1) that the proceedings should be heard by the House, no other court having jurisdiction; and (2) that although there was nothing to prevent the Committee itself from determining impartially whether there had been a contempt, the alleged contemnors should not be left with a sense of grievance, and so proceedings should be heard before a differently constituted Committee.

A fresh Committee, comprising Lords Bridge, Goff and Jauncey, held that the respondents' conduct had not constituted contempt of court. Charges relating to the material sent to Law Lords were not proceeded with: the copies of the special edition had been sent to the Law Lords by mistake, steps having been taken to remove them from the mailing list; the subsequent sending of propaganda material did not fall within the original order of the House authorising contempt proceedings.

The Committee considered whether the publication of the special edition constituted contempt under the strict liability rule (1) by prejudging these issues; or (2) by pre-empting the outcome of the judicial review proceedings. On prejudgment, the Committee noted that the test for contempt under the strict liability rule (s. 2(2)) had to be applied without any preconception derived from *A-G v Times Newspapers Ltd* (above, p. 405) as to what kind of publication is likely to impede or prejudice the course of justice:

'7.3 . . . Whether the course of justice in particular proceedings will be impeded or prejudiced by a publication must depend primarily on whether the publication will bring influence to bear which is likely to divert the proceedings in some way from the course which they would otherwise have followed. The influence may affect the conduct of witnesses, the parties or the court. Before proceedings have come to trial and before the facts have been found, it is easy to see how critical public discussion of the issues and criticism of the conduct of the parties, particularly if a party is held up to public obloquy, may impede or prejudice the course of the proceedings by influencing the conduct of witnesses or parties in relation to the proceedings. If the trial is to be by jury, the possibility of prejudice by advance publicity directed to an issue which the jury will have to decide is obvious. The possibility that a professional judge will be influenced by anything he has read about the issues in a case which he has to try is very much more remote. He will not consciously allow himself to take account of anything other than the evidence and argument presented to him in court.

7.4 After an action has been tried or an application for judicial review determined and when proceedings are pending on appeal from the decision of first instance or, as here, from the Court of Appeal to the House of Lords, the possibility that a publication which discusses the issues arising on the appeal or the merits of the decision appealed against or of the conduct of the parties in relation thereto will impede or prejudice the course of justice in those proceedings is very much narrower. In the ordinary case, as here, there will be no question of influencing witnesses. In general terms the possibility that the parties will be influenced is remote. When a case has proceeded so far it is unlikely, save in exceptional circumstances, that criticism would deter an appellant from pursuing his appeal or induce a respondent to forgo the judgment in his favour or to reach a compromise of the appeal. So far as the appellate tribunal is concerned, it is difficult to visualise circumstances in which any court in the United Kingdom exercising appellate jurisdiction would be in the least likely to be influenced by public discussion of the merits of a decision appealed against or of the parties' conduct in the proceedings. Discussion and criticism of decisions of first instance or of the Court of Appeal which are subject to pending appeals are a commonplace in legal journals, but on matters of more general public interest examples also readily spring to mind of criticism in the general press directed against, for example, criminal convictions, sentences imposed, damages awarded in libel actions and other court decisions which arouse public controversy. No case was drawn to our attention in which public discussion of the issues arising in, or criticism of the parties to, litigation already decided at first instance has been held to be a contempt on the ground that it was likely to impede or prejudice the course of justice in proceedings on appeal from that decision.

7.5 The publication in "The Observer" special edition of extracts from the inspectors' report falls for consideration as possible contempt under the heading of "pre-emption". The vice at which the strictures in the speeches in *A-G v Times Newspapers Ltd* against "trial by newspaper" and "prejudgment" were directed is exhibited, if at all, in the editorial comment, in particular the accusation that the Secretary of State acted in bad faith in deciding to defer publication of the inspectors' report. . . . Having heard full argument, we do not consider that the editorial comment in "The Observer" special edition, however intemperate the language in which it was expressed may have been, created any risk that the Secretary of State, having succeeded in the Court of Appeal in both appeals, would be deterred from seeking to uphold those decisions in opposition to the appeals or deflected from the course he would otherwise have followed in relation to the appellate proceedings. Nor was the publication in this regard capable of exerting any influence on the decision of the Appellate Committee on either appeal.'

As to the argument that the publication of the special edition 'pre-empted' the ruling of the House on the legality of the Secretary of State's decision to defer publication, the Committee commented:

'8.4 In the light of these apparent anomalies we must ask whether there is any support in principle or authority for the proposition that a litigant who seeks a judicial remedy compelling a certain course of action creates a risk that the course of justice in the proceedings in which the remedy is sought would be impeded or prejudiced if he takes direct action to secure for himself the substance of the remedy sought without the assistance of the court. The example was put in the course of argument of the plaintiff who complains that his neighbour has built a wall obstructing his right of way and seeks an injunction to have it removed. He succeeds at first instance, loses in the Court of Appeal and appeals to the House of Lords. While the appeal is still pending he loses patience and knocks the wall down. In this example, if the plaintiff succeeds in the appeal, he will no longer need a mandatory injunction. If he loses, he will have rendered himself liable in damages and possibly criminally. In either event, however deplorable his conduct, it is difficult to see how the course of justice, in determining the legal rights of the parties is likely to have been impeded or prejudiced in any way. It is easy to think of many other examples of litigants resorting to this kind of self-help. In all or nearly all of them their conduct may involve a breach of civil or criminal law or both. But so far as we are aware, no case has ever been before the court in which conduct of this character has been held to amount to contempt of court. We think that it would be a novel extension of the law of contempt to hold that direct action taken by a litigant to secure the substance of a remedy which he was seeking in judicial proceedings amounted to a contempt in relation to those proceedings and that the publication of extracts from the inspectors' report in "The Observer" special edition did not create any risk that the course of justice in the appellate proceedings challenging the lawfulness of the Secretary of State's decision to deter publication would be impeded or prejudiced.'

(In this case an injunction was obtained *after* publication; had one been obtained *before* publication, would the principle of *A-G v Times Newspapers Ltd* (above, pp. 414–416) have been applicable?) See D. G. T. Williams, [1990] CLJ 1.

In *R v Bow Street Magistrates' Court, ex p Mirror Group Newspapers Ltd* [1992] COD 15, the Divisional Court quashed an order under s. 4(2) of the 1981 Act (see above,

p. 376 and pp. 396–398) insofar as it prevented the applicants from publishing the magistrates' reasons for ordering that committal proceedings of four police officers charged with conspiracy to pervert the course of justice be stayed as an abuse of process. The purpose of the s. 4 order was to prevent prejudice to the administration of justice in the Divisional Court, to which the DPP was expected to apply for judicial review of the stay. However, it was doubtful whether such publicity could properly be considered by the Divisional Court when reviewing the validity of the stay; in any event, it could not be said that the s. 4 order was 'necessary' or the risk of prejudice 'substantial'.

5. In *A-G v Hislop* [1991] 1 QB 514, Ian Hislop and Pressdram Ltd, respectively editor and publisher of *Private Eye*, were fined £10,000 each in respect of two articles relating to Sonia Sutcliffe, the wife of Peter Sutcliffe, the so-called 'Yorkshire Ripper'. They were published in 1989, when the trial of a libel action by Mrs Sutcliffe against *Private Eye*, arising out of allegations that she had sold her story to the *Daily Mail* for £250,000, was about three months away. The articles alleged that Mrs Sutcliffe had provided a false alibi for her husband, knew about his activities before his arrest and was defrauding the DSS. Mrs Sutcliffe was successful in the first action, although the damages were reduced by consent following an appeal to the Court of Appeal, and a second libel action arising out of 1989 articles was settled in her favour. In the present proceedings, the Court of Appeal, reversing Popplewell J, held that the articles constituted both common law contempt and contempt under the strict liability rule in that they constituted improper pressure on Mrs Sutcliffe to discontinue the first libel action; and contempt under the strict liability rule in that they created a substantial risk that a juror or jurors might be prejudiced against her. On the first point Parker LJ noted that the articles 'went far further than fair and temperate criticism. They were plain abuse' (p. 527). There was no defence under s. 5 of the 1981 Act: 'Mr Hislop's intention negatived the existence of good faith' (per Nicholls LJ at p. 532). On the second point, Parker LJ commented (p. 528):

'That anyone reading the articles might be prejudiced is, as it seems to me, beyond doubt. The impact of the charges was great. They were admittedly very damaging to Mrs. Sutcliffe and blackened her character. The trial was only three months away and Mr. Sutcliffe was notorious. I am fully satisfied that anyone who happened to read the articles and found himself on a jury three months later would be likely to remember them and in that case to mention the content of them to other jurors. I am also satisfied that there was a substantial risk of one or more jurors having read one or both of the articles. With the trial in London and the readership of the magazine as large as it was, I cannot accept that the risk was only a remote possibility.'

5 Publications interfering with the course of justice as a continuing process

(a) SCANDALISING THE COURT

R v Gray [1900] 2 QB 36, 69 LJQB 502, 82 LT 534, 64 JP 484 Queen's Bench Divisional Court

On 15 March 1900, one Wells was tried before Darling J at Birmingham Assizes for publishing certain obscene and filthy words, and for publishing an obscene libel. Before the trial commenced Darling J made some observations in court, pointing out that, whatever might be the rights of the case, it was inexpedient that the press should give anything like a full or detailed account of what passed at the trial, and that, although a newspaper had the right to publish accounts of proceedings in a law court, and for many purposes was protected for doing so, there was absolutely no protection to a newspaper for the publication of objectionable, obscene, and indecent matter, and any newspaper which did so might as easily be prosecuted as anybody else. He further said that, although he hoped and believed that his advice would be taken, if it was disregarded he should make it his business to see that the law was in that respect enforced.

The following day, after the Wells trial was over, Gray wrote and published in the *Birmingham Daily Argus* an article which included the following passage (printed in 82 LT 534):

'No newspaper can exist except upon its merits, a condition from which the Bench, happily for Mr Justice Darling, is exempt. There is not a journalist in Birmingham who has anything to learn from the impudent little man in horsehair, a microcosm of conceit and empty-headedness, who admonished the Press yesterday. It is not the credit of journalism, but of the English Bench, that is imperilled in a speech like Mr Justice Darling's. One is almost sorry that the Lord Chancellor had not another relative to provide for on that day that he selected a new judge from among the larrikins of the law. One of Mr Justice Darling's biographers states that "an eccentric relative left him much money". That misguided testator spoiled a successful bus conductor. Mr Justice Darling would do well to master the duties of his own profession before undertaking the regulation of another.'

The Attorney-General brought the matter to the attention of the Queen's Bench Divisional Court on 27 March.

Lord Russell of Killowen CJ delivered the judgment of the court (**Lord Russell CJ**, **Grantham** and **Phillimore JJ**): . . .
Any act done or writing published calculated to bring a Court or a judge of the Court into contempt, or to lower his authority, is a contempt of Court. That is one class of contempt. Further, any act done or writing published calculated to obstruct or interfere with the due course of justice or the lawful process of the Courts is a contempt of Court. The former class belongs to the category which Lord Hardwicke LJ characterised as 'scandalising a Court or a judge' (*Re Read and Huggonson* (1742) 2 Atk 291, 469). That description of that class of contempt is to be taken subject to one and an important qualification. Judges and Courts are alike open to criticism, and if reasonable argument or expostulation is offered against any judicial act as contrary to law or the public good, no Court could or would treat that as contempt of Court. The law ought not to be astute in such cases to criticise adversely what under such circumstances and with such an object is published; but it is to be remembered that in this matter the liberty of the press is no greater and no less than the liberty of every subject of the Queen. Now, as I have said, no one has suggested that this is not a contempt of Court, and nobody has suggested, or could suggest, that it falls within the right of public criticism in the sense I have described. It is not criticism: I repeat that it is personal scurrilous abuse of a judge as a judge. We have, therefore, to deal with it as a case of contempt, and we have to deal with it brevi manu. This is not a new-fangled jurisdiction; it is a jurisdiction as old as the common law itself, of which it forms part. . . . It is a jurisdiction, however, to be exercised with scrupulous care, to be exercised only when the case is clear and beyond reasonable doubt; because, if it is not a case beyond reasonable doubt, the Courts will and ought to leave the Attorney-General to proceed by criminal information.
[The court fined Gray £100, with £25 costs]

R v Metropolitan Police Commissioner, ex p Blackburn (No 2) [1968] 2 QB 150, [1968] 2 All ER 319, [1968] 2 WLR 1204, Court of Appeal

In January 1968 the Court of Appeal delivered judgment in an application by a private citizen, [Raymond Blackburn], for an order of mandamus against the Metropolitan Police Commissioner in connection with the non-enforcement of the Gaming Acts. In their judgments the court expressed opinions on the conduct of the police and on earlier decisions on the Acts in the Queen's Bench Divisional Court [see [1968] 2 QB 118]. After reports of the judgments had appeared in the Press, [Quintin Hogg], a Privy Councillor who was also a Member of Parliament and Queen's Counsel, wrote an article in the weekly newspaper *Punch* in a section entitled 'Political Parley' in which he vigorously criticised the Court of Appeal and its dicta, wrongly attributing to that court decisions of the Divisional Court.

The applicant applied to the same Court of Appeal for an order that the writer had been guilty of contempt of court in (a) that the article falsely stated that the Act was 'rendered virtually unworkable by the unrealistic, contradictory and, in the leading case, erroneous decisions of the courts, including the Court of Appeal' and ridiculed that court by suggesting that it should apologise for the expense and trouble to which it had put the police; (b) that without proper knowledge of the facts the writer sought to ridicule the court for its alleged 'blindness'; and (c) that the writer had stated that 'a prudent policeman may well turn a some-what blind eye towards a law which does not make sense and which Parliament may be about to repeal,' thereby encouraging police officers to flout the court's decision and commit breaches of their duty to enforce the law. For the writer it was stated that no disrespect of the court was intended but that he was exercising his right to criticise on a matter which he believed to be of public importance.

Lord Denning MR: . . .
That article is certainly critical of this court. In so far as it referred to the Court of Appeal, it is admittedly erroneous. This court did not in the gaming cases give any decision which was erroneous, nor one which was overruled by the House of Lords. But is the article a contempt of court?

This is the first case, so far as I know, where this court has been called on to consider an allegation of contempt against itself. It is a jurisdiction which undoubtedly belongs to us but which we will most sparingly exercise: more particularly as we ourselves have an interest in the matter.

Let me say at once that we will never use this jurisdiction as a means to uphold our own dignity. That must rest on surer foundations. Nor will we use it to suppress those who speak against us. We do not fear criticism, nor do we resent it. For there is something far more important at stake. It is no less than freedom of speech itself.

It is the right of every man, in Parliament or out of it, in the Press or over the broadcast, to make fair comment, even outspoken comment, on matters of public interest. Those who comment can deal faithfully with all that is done in a court of justice. They can say that we are mistaken, and our decisions erroneous, whether they are subject to appeal or not. All we would ask is that those who criticise us will remember that, from the nature of our office, we cannot reply to their criticisms. We cannot enter into public controversy. Still less into political controversy. We must rely on our conduct itself to be its own vindication.

Exposed as we are to the winds of criticism, nothing which is said by this person or that, nothing which is written by this pen or that, will deter us from doing what we believe is right; nor, I would add, from saying what the occasion requires, provided that it is pertinent to the matter in hand. Silence is not an option when things are ill done.

So it comes to this: Mr Quintin Hogg has criticised the court, but in so doing he is exercising his undoubted right. The article contains an error, no doubt, but errors do not make it a contempt of court. We must uphold this right to the uttermost.

I hold this not to be a contempt of court, and would dismiss the application.

Salmon LJ: The authority and reputation of our courts are not so frail that their judgments need to be shielded from criticism, even from the criticism of Mr Quintin Hogg. Their judgments, which can, I think, safely be left to take care of themselves, are often of considerable public importance. It is the inalienable right of everyone to comment fairly upon any matter of public importance. This right is one of the pillars of individual liberty—freedom of speech, which our courts have always unfailingly upheld.

It follows that no criticism of a judgment, however vigorous, can amount to contempt of court, providing it keeps within the limits of reasonable courtesy and good faith. The criticism here complained of, however rumbustious, however wide of the mark, whether expressed in good taste or in bad taste, seems to me to be well within those limits. . . .

No one could doubt Mr Hogg's good faith. I, of course, entirely accept that he had no intention of holding this court up to contempt; nor did he do so. Mr Blackburn complains that Mr Hogg has not apologised. There was no reason why he should apologise, for he owes no apology, save, perhaps, to the readers of *Punch* for some of the inaccuracies and inconsistencies which his article contains. I agree that this application should be dismissed.

Edmund Davies LJ delivered a concurring judgment.
Application dismissed.

NOTES

1. On the historical background to this head of contempt, see D. Hay, 'Contempt by Scandalizing the Court: A Political History of the First Hundred Years' (1987) 25(3) OHLJ 431 and, for Australia, H. Burmester, (1985) 15 Melb ULR 313. On the position more recently, see C. Walker, 'Scandalising in the Eighties' (1985) 101 LQR 359.

2. In *McLeod v St Aubyn* [1899] AC 549, PC, attacks upon the competence and partiality of St. Aubyn, the Acting Chief Justice of St. Vincent, appeared in the

Federalist newspaper. McLeod gave a copy of the newspaper to a librarian. It was not alleged that he was the author of either the article or the letter in question, although he was the paper's agent and correspondent in St. Vincent. Neither was he aware of the contents of the offending issue. The Privy Council held that McLeod was not guilty of contempt. 'A printer and publisher intends to publish, and so intending cannot plead as a justification that he did not know the contents. The appellant in this case never intended to publish' (per Lord Morris at 562). Lord Morris also stated (at 561):

'The power summarily to commit for contempt of Court is considered necessary for the proper administration of justice. It is not to be used for the vindication of the judge as a person. He must resort to action for libel or criminal information. Committal for contempt of Court is a weapon to be used sparingly, and always with reference to the interests of the administration of justice. Hence, when a trial has taken place and the case is over, the judge or the jury are given over to criticism.

It is a summary process, and should be used only from a sense of duty and under the pressure of public necessity, for there can be no landmarks pointing out the boundaries in all cases. Committals for contempt of Court by scandalising the Court itself have become obsolete in this country. Courts are satisfied to leave to public opinion attacks or comments derogatory or scandalous to them. But it must be considered that in small colonies, consisting principally of coloured populations, the enforcement in proper cases of committal for contempt of Court for attacks on the Court may be absolutely necessary to preserve in such a community the dignity of and respect for the Court.'

The case of *R v Gray*, decided the following year, showed that this aspect of contempt was not obsolete. A. E. Hughes ((1900) 16 LQR 292) argued strongly that Lord Morris's view was to be preferred. According to Abel-Smith and Stevens (*Lawyers and the Courts* (1967) pp. 126–7): 'within a decade [of *R v Gray*] the criticism of judicial behaviour which had been so outspoken was replaced in the press by almost unbroken sycophantic praise for the judges'.

3. In *Ambard v A-G for Trinidad and Tobago* [1936] AC 322, PC, a reasoned criticism of the sentences passed in two cases in a Port of Spain court was held by the Privy Council not to constitute contempt. There was no evidence to support the finding of the Supreme Court of Trinidad that the article was written 'with the direct object of bringing the administration of the criminal law in this Colony by the judges into disrepute and disregard'. Lord Atkin stated (at 335):

'But whether the authority and position of an individual judge, or the due administration of justice, is concerned, no wrong is committed by any member of the public who exercises the ordinary right of criticising, in good faith, in private or public, the public act done in the seat of justice. The path of criticism is a public way: the wrong headed are permitted to err therein: provided that members of the public abstain from imputing improper motives to those taking part in the administration of justice, and are genuinely exercising a right of criticism, and not acting in malice or attempting to impair the administration of justice, they are immune. Justice is not a cloistered virtue: she must be allowed to suffer the scrutiny and respectful, even though outspoken, comments of ordinary men.'

4. In *R v New Statesman Editor, ex p DPP* (1928) 44 TLR 301, DC, the defendant wrote that the verdict in a libel action against Marie Stopes was a miscarriage of justice – prejudice against her work 'ought not to be allowed to influence a court of justice in the manner in which they appeared to influence Mr Justice Avory in his summing-up. . . . [A]n individual owning to such views as those of Dr Stopes cannot apparently hope for a fair hearing in a Court presided over by Mr Justice Avory – and there are so many Avorys'. The Divisional Court held this to be a contempt, although they imposed no penalty in view of the editor's unqualified expressions of regret, and the absence of any intention to interfere with the performance of Avory J's judicial duties.

5. The last successful contempt proceedings of this nature in England were in the 1930s (*R v Wilkinson* (1930) Times, 16 July; *R v Colsey* (1931) Times, 9 May). It is

noteworthy that contempt proceedings were not instituted in respect of attacks on the National Industrial Relations Court which were at times virulent (see *Phillimore*, para. 160 and Chap. 11). There have, however, been more recent examples in the Commonwealth. See *R v Glanzer* (1963) 38 DLR (2d) 402; *Re Wiseman* [1969] NZLR 55; *Re Borowski* (1971) 19 DLR (3d) 537; *Re Ouellet* (1976) 67 DLR (3d) 73; and *Gallagher v Durack* (1983) 57 ALJR 191, HCA (see T. Caillard, (1983) 14 Melb ULR 311). However, in *R v Kopyto* (1987) DLR 213, following the dismissal of a civil action against the police, the plaintiff's lawyer, K, criticised the decision in a newspaper interview as a 'mockery of justice. It stinks to high hell . . . [the plaintiff and I are] wondering what is the point of appealing and continuing this charade of the Courts in this country which are warped in favour of protecting the police.' A majority of the Ontario Court of Appeal held that K's conviction for scandalising the court in respect of his expression of opinion was contrary to the guarantee of freedom of expression in s. 2(b) of the Canadian Charter of Rights and Freedoms. While the objective of protecting the administration of justice was of sufficient importance to warrant overriding a constitutionally protected right or freedom, the means chosen were not reasonable and demonstrably justified. In particular, the scandalizing offence did not require the Crown to prove that the statements actually constituted a serious danger to the administration of justice, merely that they were 'calculated' to have that effect. Of the three judges in the majority on this point two (Cory and Goodman JJA) thought that the offence could be redefined so as to meet constitutional standards (e.g. where statements cause a clear, significant and imminent or present danger to the fair and effective administration of justice); the third (Houlden JA) thought that it could not, stating that the Canadian judiciary and courts were strong enough to withstand criticism after a case has been decided no matter how outrageous or scurrilous.

6. The Privy Council in *Badry v DPP of Mauritius* [1983] 2 AC 297 held that this head of contempt is only applicable to 'courts of justice properly so called' and the judges of such courts: statements made against a judge in his capacity as sole commissioner under the Commissions of Inquiry Ordinance (Mauritius), to conduct an inquiry into allegations of fraud and corruption made against the appellant in his capacity as a government minister, could not, accordingly, form the basis of contempt proceedings (cf. *A-G v BBC*, above, p. 391). Lord Hailsham (at p. 979) also made it clear that this head of contempt was not obsolete:

'[w]hilst nothing really encourages courts or Attorneys General to prosecute cases of this kind in all but the most serious examples, or courts to take notice of any but the most intolerable instances, nothing has happened in the intervening eighty years to invalidate the analysis by the first Lord Russell of Killowen CJ in *R v Gray*.'

7. *Mens Rea.* It is not clear whether mens rea is required for liability for this form of contempt (see *Miller*, pp. 378–379; *Borrie and Lowe*, pp. 243–244). *R v New Statesman Editor, ex p DPP* (1928) 44 TLR 301, above p. 424, seems to indicate that it does not. This was followed in New Zealand in *Solicitor General v Radio Avon Ltd* [1978] 1 NZLR 225, NZCA. Authorities to the contrary are *S v Van Niekerk* [1970] 3 SA 655 (T) and *Re Ouellet* (1976) 67 DLR (3d) 73, 91–92 (Qu Sup Ct).

In *S v Van Niekerk* [1970] 3 SA 655 (T), the defendant, a senior lecturer in law, wrote in an article in the South African Law Journal ((1969) 86 SALJ 457 and (1970) 87 SALJ 60) that a significant proportion of judges and advocates who responded to a questionnaire believed that justice as regards capital punishment was meted out to the different races on a deliberately differential basis. Claassen J held (at 657) that 'before a conviction can result the act complained of must not only be wilful and calculated to bring into contempt but must also be made with the intention of bringing the judges in their judicial capacity into contempt or of casting suspicion on the administration of justice'. As Van N did not have that intention he was not convicted. See H. R. Hahlo, (1971) 21 U of Toronto LJ 378 and J. R. L. Milton, (1970) 87 SALJ 424.

8. There is some Commonwealth authority in support of a defence of fair comment: per Griffith CJ in *R v Nicholls* (1911) 12 CLR 280 at 286; *A-G for New South Wales v Mundey* [1972] 2 NSWLR 887 at 910; *Solicitor-General v Radio Avon Ltd* [1978] 1 NZLR 225 at 231; but against a defence of justification: *A-G v Blomfield* (1914) 33 NZLR 545.

9. This variety of the law of contempt is virtually a dead letter in the United States. In *Bridges v California; Times-Mirror Co v California* 314 US 252 (1941), in applying the 'clear and present danger' test (see above, p. 375), Black J discounted 'disrespect for the judiciary' as a 'substantive evil' which could properly be averted by restricting freedom of expression: 'The assumption that respect for the judiciary can be won by shielding judges from published criticism wrongly appraises the character of American public opinion. For it is a prized American privilege to speak one's mind, although not always with perfect good taste, on all public institutions. And an enforced silence, however limited solely in the name of preserving the dignity of the bench, would probably engender resentment, suspicion, and contempt much more than it would enhance respect' (pp. 270–271).

Press allegations of judicial bias, directed to pending proceedings, have been held not to constitute a clear and present danger to the administration of justice (*Pennekamp v Florida* 328 US 331 (1946); *Re Turner* 174 NW (2d) 895 (1969)).

10. Does the law on scandalising the court comply with Art. 10 of the ECHR? Cf. *Barfod v Denmark* (1989) 13 EHRR 493, ECtHR (Series A No. 149), where the court held that a conviction in the Greenland High Court for defaming two lay judges (imputing biased voting in a tax case in favour of their employer, the Greenland Local Government) did not violate Art. 10. The interference with freedom of expression was prescribed by law, and justifiable as necessary in a democratic society for the protection of the reputation of others and, indirectly, the maintenance of the authority of the judiciary. B was perfectly entitled to question the composition of the court, but not to allege actual bias without any supporting evidence.

11. *Reform.* The Phillimore Committee recommended that attacks on courts or judges should not be dealt with under the law of contempt, unless there is a risk of serious prejudice to particular proceedings in progress. However, there should be a substantive criminal offence consisting of the publication of matter imputing improper or corrupt judicial conduct with the intention of impairing confidence in the administration of justice. It should be triable only on indictment, and only with the leave of the Attorney-General or the Lord Advocate. The Law Commission in their Report (No. 96) on *Offences Relating to Interference with the Course of Justice* (pp. 67–68) took the view that there would be difficulties in interpreting the 'intent' provision, and that it would be too wide to include imputations of 'improper' conduct. Accordingly they recommended that it should be an offence to publish or distribute false matter, with intent that it be taken as true and knowing it to be false or being reckless whether it is false, when it imputes corrupt judicial conduct to any judge, tribunal or member of a tribunal. A prosecution could only be brought with the consent of the Attorney-General but the offence would be triable either way.

12. (i) Is the law of defamation sufficient to protect the judges from scurrilous abuse, or do you agree with either proposal for a criminal offence to replace contempt proceedings in this context?

(ii) Does the present law of contempt give sufficiently clear guidance to those who wish to criticise the judiciary?

(iii) Do you agree with Harold Laski's view that 'To argue that the expression, even the strong expression, of . . . doubts [as to judicial impartiality] is an "interference with the course of justice" because the result is to undermine public confidence in the judiciary is to forget that public confidence is undermined not so much by the comment, as by the habit which led to the comment. . . .' ((1928) 41 Harv LR 1031 at 1036)?

(iv) Should reports of research into the administration of justice ever be regarded as contempt (cf. *S v Van Niekerk*)?

(b) PUBLICATION OF JURY SECRETS[1]

This is now regulated by s. 8 of the Contempt of Court Act 1981 (above, p. 377). The section as originally drafted incorporated the limitation that it was not to apply to publications which did not identify the proceedings, or the names of particular jurors, and which did not enable such matters to be identified. Moreover, the disclosure or the solicitation of the disclosure of particulars was only to be an offence when done in the contemplation that they would be published. Neither the Criminal Law Revision Committee (Tenth Report: Secrecy of the Jury Room, Cmnd 3750, 1968), the Phillimore Committee nor the Law Commission had recommended legislation. Interesting accounts by jurors of their jury service had indeed been published (see e.g. E. Devons, (1965) 28 MLR 561). However, the publication in the *New Statesman* of an interview with a juror after the trial of Jeremy Thorpe and others led to contempt proceedings against the newspaper (*A-G v New Statesman* [1981] QB 1; M. J. Richardson, [1980] II Liverpool LR 126). The juror was interviewed after the trial was over and no money was paid. It was conceded that the publication could not in any respect interfere with the administration of justice in the *Thorpe* case and that the juror's comments showed that the jury had approached its task in a sensible and reasonable manner, but it was contended that any disclosure of jury-room secrets would tend to imperil the finality of jury verdicts and affect adversely the attitude of future jurymen. The Divisional Court held that if a publication had that tendency it was capable of being a contempt, but did not accept that the disclosure of jury-room secrets would necessarily have that effect, and did not accept that the article in question constituted contempt. The court did not explain why it thought the article in question was not objectionable; it indicated that no exception could be taken to disclosures which did not indentify the persons concerned, but the *New Statesman* article could not of course be exonerated on that ground.

It was argued by some that the exceptions built into the original clause were too narrow. However, Lord Hutchinson and Lord Wigoder persuaded the House of Lords at the last minute to remove the exceptions altogether on the ground that any approaches to jurors were undesirable, whether by 'respectable professors from Birmingham', 'Marxist professors from the English Faculty at Cambridge', by 'any scribbler or any journalist,' or by that 'most dangerous animal, the sociologist' (416

---

1 See generally J. Baldwin and M. McConville, *Jury Trials* (1979) Chap. 1, pp. 130–134 and (1981) 145 JPN 575; E. Campbell, (1985) 11(4) Monash ULR 169; Mr. Justice McHugh in M. Findlay and P. Duff (eds), *The Jury Under Attack* (1988), Chap. 4; P. Robertshaw, (1993) 14 Jo Media Law and Practice 114.

HL Deb 20 January 1981 col 371, 422 HL Deb July 1981 cols 239–254). Accordingly, it is now a contempt for any juror to disclose particulars of a case to anyone, even a spouse or a friend. The only safeguard is the requirement of the Attorney-General's consent to prosecution, and even this is not necessary where proceedings are instituted on the motion of a court. It is appropriate to rely upon that safeguard where the ambit of a law is uncertain and the considerations to be borne in mind when exercising the discretion to prosecute are particularly sensitive. It is clearly undesirable to have to rely upon that safeguard in relation to an offence that is drawn so widely that it catches many situations about which there is general agreement that they should not be regarded as criminal at all.

In *A-G v Associated Newspapers Ltd* [1994] 1 All ER 556, the House of Lords held that the prohibition against 'disclosure' in s. 8 extended to the publication by a newspaper of the deliberations of jurors in the jury room, obtained from a source other than the jurors. The *Mail on Sunday* had published material from transcripts of interviews apparently conducted by independent 'researchers' with jurors at the 'Blue Arrow' fraud trial. The House rejected the argument that s. 8 should be construed narrowly to apply only to a revelation by a juror to another person; the section was not ambiguous and what the appellants had done amounted to 'disclosure' within the ordinary meaning of that word. The House upheld fines of £30,000 on the publishers, £20,000 on the editor, Stewart Steven, and £10,000 on the responsible journalist, Clive Wolman.

Inquiries of jurors concerning matters other than juror deliberations (here, the use of a mobile telephone by a juror in the jury room) do not infringe s. 8, but should only be undertaken with the leave of the trial court or (after verdict and sentence) the Court of Appeal: *R v McCluskey* (1993) 94 Cr App R 216, CA (Cr D). See also *R v Mickleburgh* [1995] 1 Cr App Rep 297, CA (Cr D); *R v Young (Stephen)* (1994) Times, 30 December (use of ouija board by jurors in hotel overnight; conviction quashed).

The Royal Commission on Criminal Justice (Cm 2263, 1993) has recommended (p. 2) that s. 8 should be amended to enable research to be conducted into juries' reasons for their verdicts.

6 Contempt in the face of the court

It is obvious that the public interest in the due administration of justice requires that legal proceedings be free from disruption or direct interference. Some kinds of disruption are ordinary criminal offences, for example violent attacks on judges or jurors. All kinds of disruption will also amount to contempt in the face of the court, and may be dealt with summarily (e.g. *Balogh v Crown Court at St Albans* [1975] QB 73, below, p. 429). The law of contempt in this context does to an extent inhibit freedom of expression, such as the expression of the views of a disappointed litigant as to the defects of the English legal system in general, and the defects of the judge who has just tried his case in particular. Moreover, the disruption of legal proceedings in order to gain publicity for a particular cause has been roundly condemned in the Court of Appeal (*Morris v Crown Office* [1970] 2 QB 114, below p. 431). However, the law here cannot convincingly be criticised on the basis of interference with free speech. Most of the criticism has centred on the summary nature of the procedure. The two main criticisms made to the Phillimore Committee were, 'first, that the judge appears to assume the role of prosecutor and judge in his own cause, especially where the missile or insult is directed against him personally; and secondly, that the contemnor usually has little or no opportunity to defend himself or make a plea in mitigation' (*Phillimore*, para. 29). The refusal of a witness to answer a question or produce a document may also constitute contempt in the face. This can pose particular problems for journalists, who may be required to divulge their sources of information. This is now regulated by section 10 of the Contempt of Court Act 1981 (above, p. 377), which was considered by the House of Lords in *X Ltd v Morgan-Grampian (Publishers) Ltd* [1991] 1 AC 1 (below, p. 435).

Balogh v St Albans Crown Court [1975] QB 73, [1974] 3 All ER 283, [1974] 3 WLR 314, Court of Appeal

Balogh, a temporary clerk in a solicitor's office, while attending a criminal trial at a Crown Court, devised a plan to enliven the proceedings by releasing nitrous oxide ('laughing gas') down a ventilation duct on the roof into the trial court. He stole a cylinder of the gas from a hospital lorry and climbed up on to the roof at night to locate the particular inlet duct. The next morning he left the cylinder in his briefcase in the public gallery of the court next door (Court 1) from which there was access to the roof, intending to carry out his plan later in the day. Police, who had seen him on the roof, found his brief case, opened it, and later cautioned Balogh who at once admitted what he had done and planned to do. He was charged with theft of the cylinder. The police reported the matter to Melford Stevenson J, the senior judge, who was presiding in Court 1. Balogh was brought before the judge who said that his admitted conduct was a serious contempt of court and that he would consider the penalty overnight. Balogh was to be kept in custody.

The next morning Balogh told the judge that he did not feel competent to conduct his own case on contempt and that he understood that the only charge against him was theft. The judge said that he would not deal with that charge, but committed him to six months' imprisonment for contempt of court. Balogh then said: 'You are a humourless automaton. Why don't you self-destruct.' Subsequently, he wrote from prison to the Official Solicitor asking to be allowed to apologise in the hope that his contempt would be purged. Accordingly, he appealed to the Court of Appeal.

Lord Denning MR: . . .

The jurisdiction of the Crown Court

The Crown Court is a superior court of record: section 4(1) of the Courts Act 1971. In regard to any contempt of court, it has the like powers and authority as the High Court: section 4(8) [see now the Supreme Court Act 1981, s. 45(1)(4)]. . . .
[RSC Order 52 r. 5] . . . preserves the power of the High Court 'to make an order of committal of its own motion against a person guilty of contempt of court' . . . .
   In what circumstances can the High Court make an order 'of its own motion?' In the ordinary way the High Court does not act of its own motion. An application to commit for contempt is usually made by motion either by the Attorney-General or by the party aggrieved: . . . and such a motion can, in an urgent case be made ex parte: see *Warwick Corpn v Russell* [1964] 2 All ER 337, [1964] 1 WLR 613. . . .
All I find in the books is that the court can act upon its own motion when the contempt is committed 'in the face of the court'. Wilmot CJ in his celebrated opinion in *R v Almon* (1765) Wilm 243 at 254 said: 'It is a necessary incident to every court of justice to fine and imprison for a contempt to the court, acted in the face of it.' *Blackstone* in his *Commentaries*, 16th edn. (1825), Book IV, p. 286, said: 'If the contempt be committed in the face of the court, the offender may be instantly apprehended and imprisoned, at the discretion of the judges'. In *Oswald on Contempt*, 3rd edn. (1910), p. 23 it is said: 'Upon contempt in the face of the court an order for committal was made instanter' and not on motion. But I find nothing to tell us what is meant by 'committed in the face of the court'. It has never been defined. Its meaning is, I

think, to be ascertained from the practice of the judges over the centuries. It was never confined to conduct which a judge saw with his own eyes. It covered all contempts for which a judge of his own motion could punish a man on the spot. So 'contempt in the face of the court' is the same thing as 'contempt which the court can punish of its own motion'. It really means 'contempt in the cognisance of the court'.

Gathering together the experience of the past, then, whatever expression is used, a judge of one of the superior courts or a judge of Assize could always punish summarily of his own motion for contempt of court whenever there was a gross interference with the course of justice in a case that was being tried, or about to be tried or just over—no matter whether the judge saw it with his own eyes or it was reported to him by the officers of the court, or by others—whenever it was urgent and imperative to act at once. This power has been inherited by the judges of the High Court and in turn by the judges of the Crown Court. To show the extent of it, I will give some instances:

(i) *In the sight of the court.* There are many cases where a man has been committed to prison at once for throwing a missile at the judge, be it a brickbat, an egg, or a tomato. Recently, too, when a group of students broke up the trial of a libel action Lawton J very properly sent them at once to prison: see *Morris v Crown Office* [1970] 2 QB 114. There is an older case, too, of great authority, where a witness refused to answer a proper question. The judge of Assize at York Castle at once sentenced him to prison for six months and imposed a fine of £500: see *Ex p Fernandez* (1861) 10 CBNS 3.

(ii) *Within the court room but not seen by the judge.* At the Old Bailey a man distributed leaflets in the public gallery inciting people to picket the place. A member of the public reported it to a police officer, who reported it to the judge. The offender denied it. Melford Stevenson J immediately heard the evidence on both sides. He convicted the offender and sentenced him to seven days' imprisonment. The man appealed to this court. His appeal was dismissed: *Lecointre v Court's Administrator of the Central Criminal Court* (1973) 8 February Bar Library Transcript No 57A (unreported).

(iii) *At some distance from the court.* At Bristol 22 men were being tried for an affray. The first witness for the prosecution was a school girl. After she had given her evidence, she went to a café for a meal. A man clenched his fist at her and threatened her. She told the police, who told the judge. Park J had the man arrested. He asked counsel to represent him. He broke off the trial. He heard evidence of the threat. He committed the man. He sentenced him to three months' imprisonment. The man appealed to this court. His appeal was dismissed: *Moore v Clerk of Assize, Bristol* [1972] 1 All ER 58. Another case was where a man was summoned to serve on a jury. His employer threatened to dismiss him if he obeyed the summons. Melford Stevenson J said it was a contempt of court which made him liable to immediate imprisonment: see 'The Rule of Law and Jury Service' (1966) 130 JP 622.

Those are modern instances. I have no doubt that there were many like instances in the past which were never reported, because there was until recently no right of appeal. They bear out the power which I have already stated—a power which has been inherited by the judges of the Crown Court.

This power of summary punishment is a great power, but it is a necessary power. It is given so as to maintain the dignity and authority of the court and to ensure a fair trial. It is to be exercised by the judge of his own motion only when it is urgent and imperative to act immediately—so as to maintain the authority of the court—to prevent disorder—to enable witnesses to be free from fear—and jurors from being improperly influenced—and the like. It is, of course, to be exercised with scrupulous care, and only when the case is clear and beyond reasonable doubt: see *R v Gray* [1900] 2 QB 36 at 41 by Lord Russell of Killowen CJ. But properly exercised it is a power of the utmost value and importance which should not be curtailed.

Over 100 years ago Erle CJ said that '. . . these powers, . . . as far as my experience goes, have always been exercised for the advancement of justice and the good of the public': see *Ex p Fernandez* (1861) 10 CBNS 3 at 38. I would say the same today. From time to time anxieties have been expressed lest these powers might be abused. But these have been set at rest by section 13 of the Administration of Justice Act 1960, which gives a right to appeal to a higher court.

As I have said, a judge should act of his own motion only when it is urgent and imperative to act immediately. In all other cases he should not take it upon himself to move. He should leave it to the Attorney-General or to the party aggrieved to make a motion in accordance with the rules in RSC Ord 52. The reason is that he should not appear to be both prosecutor and judge: for that is a role which does not become him well.

Returning to the present case, it seems to me that up to a point the judge was absolutely right to act of his own motion. The intention of Mr Balogh was to disrupt the proceedings in a trial then taking place. His conduct was reported to the senior judge then in the court building. It was very proper for him to take immediate action, and to have Mr Balogh brought before him. But once he was there, it was not a case for summary punishment. There was not sufficient urgency to warrant it. Nor was it imperative. He was already in custody on a charge of stealing. The judge would have done well to have remanded him in custody and invited counsel to represent him. If he had done so counsel would, I expect, have taken the point to which I now turn.

The conduct of Mr Balogh

Contempt of court is a criminal offence which is governed by the principles applicable to criminal offences generally. In particular, by the difference between an attempt to commit an offence and an act preparatory to it.

[His Lordship held that B's conduct amounted at most to 'acts preparatory'] . . .

So here Mr Balogh had the criminal intent to disrupt the court, but that is not enough. He was guilty of stealing the cylinder, but no more.

On this short ground we think the judge was in error. We have already allowed the appeal on this ground. But, even if there had not been this ground, I should have thought that the sentence of six months was excessive. Balogh spent 14 days in prison: and he has now apologised. That is enough to purge his contempt, if contempt it was.

Conclusion

There is a lesson to be learned from the recent cases on this subject. It is particularly appropriate at the present time. The new Crown Courts are in being. The judges of them have not yet acquired the prestige of the Red Judge when he went on Assize. His robes and bearing made eveyone alike stand in awe of him. Rarely did he need to exercise his great power of summary punishment. Yet there is just as much need for the Crown Court to maintain its dignity and authority. The judges of it should not hesitate to exercise the authority they inherit from the past. Insults are best treated with disdain—save when they are gross and scandalous. Refusal to answer with admonishment—save where it is vital to know the answer. But disruption of the court or threats to witnesses or to jurors should be visited with immediate arrest. Then a remand in custody and, if it can be arranged, representation by counsel. If it comes to a sentence, let it be such as the offence deserves—with the comforting reflection that, if it is in error, there is an appeal to this court. We always hear these appeals within a day or two. The present case is a good instance. The judge acted with a firmness which became him. As it happened, he went too far. That is no reproach to him. It only shows the wisdom of having an appeal.

Stephenson and **Lawton LJJ** delivered concurring judgments.

Appeal allowed.

NOTES

1. Lord Denning MR equates 'contempt in the face of the court' and the power to the High Court to 'make an order of committal on its own motion'. *Borrie and Lowe* (pp. 9–11) argue that the concept of 'contempt in the face' should be construed more narrowly, particularly in the context of the inherent powers of *inferior* courts to punish contempts, to cover misconduct in the court room and (perhaps) other misbehaviour that actually interrupts proceedings or where there is an admission by the defendant or all the witnesses are before the court. In *McKeown v R* (1971) 16 DLR (3d) 390, 408 Laskin J (in a dissenting judgment) held that the concept of contempt in the face was confined to cases where 'all the circumstances are in the personal knowledge of the court' (contra, *Registrar, Court of Appeal v Collins* [1982] 1 NSWLR 682, NSWCA).

2. In *Morris v Crown Office* [1970] 2 QB 114, CA, a group of young Welsh students interrupted the proceedings in a libel action (*Broome v Cassell & Co*) being heard by Lawton J. They shouted slogans, scattered pamphlets and sang songs. The judge adjourned the hearing. When order was restored, the judge returned to court and sentenced three students to three months' imprisonment each for contempt. At the rising of the court, he dealt with 19 others. Eight apologised, and were fined £50 each and bound over to keep the peace. Eleven did not apologise, saying that they acted as a matter of principle on behalf of the Welsh language. They each received three month sentences. The eleven students appealed to the Court of Appeal, arguing (inter alia) (1) that s. 39(1) and (3) of the Criminal Justice Act 1967 required the sentences to be suspended, and (2) that the sentences were too severe. The Court of Appeal held that the 1967 Act was not applicable as there was no machinery for following up a suspended sentence passed in such circumstances, and that the sentences when passed were appropriate. However, as the students had spent a week in prison, and shown respect to the court, the prison sentences were remitted and the defendants bound over to be of good behaviour, to keep the peace, and to come up to judgment if called on to do so. On the problem of disruptive defendants see G. Zellick, (1980) 43 MLR 121 and 284; *R v Logan* [1974] Crim LR 609; *R v Aquarius* (1974) 59 Cr App Rep 165.

3. In *R v Powell* (1993) 98 Cr App R 224, the Court of Appeal (Criminal Division) upheld P's conviction for contempt in the face of the court in respect of a loud wolf-whistle at a female juror as the jury came into court to deliver its verdict. The court stated that while the general principles applicable were to be found in the *Balogh* and *Morris* cases (above), 'when it comes to the detail [section 12 of the Contempt of Court Act] gives a good indication of the sort of behaviour which should be considered contempt of that nature' (*per* Staughton LJ at 227). Here, the wolf-whistle was

'potentially an insult and potentially offensive, and a serious interference with the administration of justice and the process of the court. . . . [J]urors do not come to these courts, as they are under a duty to do when summoned, in order to have comments, even flattering comments, publicly made on their personal appearance. The administration of justice is not to be interrupted at the tense moment when the jury return with their verdict' (ibid. at 228).

However, the judge's sentence of 14 days' imprisonment was quashed as excessive. As P had served one day in custody before his release on bail by Russell LJ of the Court of Appeal, no further penalty was imposed.

4. In England, inferior courts have statutory power to punish certain kinds of conduct amounting to contempt in the face. For county courts see the County Courts Act 1984, ss. 14(1) (assault on officer of the court), 55(1) (refusals to produce documents, to be sworn or to give evidence), 118(1) (insults towards judge, juror, witness or officer of the court, and misbehaviour in court). For magistrates' courts see the Magistrates' Courts Act 1980, s. 97(4) (refusals to produce documents, to be sworn or to give evidence) and s. 12 of the Contempt of Court Act 1981 (above p. 377). Binding-over powers may be used, and offenders can be removed from the court. The Phillimore Committee recommended that magistrates courts be given statutory power to punish contempt in the face of the court with a maximum penalty the same as that prescribed by s. 77(4) of the 1952 Act (now s. 97(4) of the 1980 Act), namely 7 days' imprisonment, with an alternative of a £20 fine. In the event, the penalties prescribed by section 12 of the 1981 Act were much higher than those recommended, and this was a cause of criticism (G. J. Zellick, [1981] PL 148). The penalty under s. 97(4) was increased in line with s. 12 by the Criminal Justice Act 1991, Sch. 4, Pt. I. In Parliament, the main point of controversy was whether the power to deal with insults was necessary or even desirable. Where the object of the insult is the magistrate he will be 'the victim, the witness, the prosecution, the judge and the jury' (Lord Gifford, 416 HL Deb 20 January 1981 col 385). This is already accepted to be the main cause of concern with the law of contempt in the face of the court, but one may perhaps have greater confidence in the objectivity of High Court judges than of magistrates. In 1981 a man was reported to have been imprisoned for one month for refusing to stand while certain charges against him were read out in court ((1981) Times, 19 December). In *Re Hooker (Patricia) and the Contempt of Court Act 1981* [1993] COD 190, the Divisional Court set aside a conviction under s. 12(1)(b) of the 1981 Act and a £500 fine in respect of the use of a tape recorder by H, a court reporter, without leave, contrary to s. 9(1)(a) (see above, p. 377). In construing the words 'otherwise misbehaves' in s. 12(1)(b), regard had to be had to the fact that this was a criminal statute and that the other prohibitions in s. 12 were qualified by the word 'wilfully'. Accordingly, there had to be some other element of defiance, or at least conduct such that the court could not reasonably be expected to tolerate. Neither element was present here.

In *R v Tamworth Justices, ex p Walsh* (1994) Times, 3 March, the Divisional Court quashed the justices' order that a solicitor be detained in custody under s. 12(2) until the rising of the court following an insult to the clerk of the court (a reference to 'ridiculous listing' by the clerk). The court noted that the justices could have ordered the solicitor's removal from the court (should he have refused to withdraw the remark), reported him to the Law Society or adjourned the matter to another day. Instead, they 'had taken a sledgehammer to crack a nut'.

Threats to a witness outside the court do not constitute 'insults' which can be dealt with under s. 12(1)(a): *R v Havant Justices, ex p Palmer* [1985] Crim LR 658. Proceedings can be 'interrupted' under s. 12(1)(b) by acts done outside, as well as inside the court: *Bodden v Metropolitan Police Comr* [1990] 2 QB 397, CA (use of loudhailer in the street outside court preventing witness being heard). The interruption is 'wilful' if the defendant commits the acts causing the interruption deliberately with the intention that they should interrupt proceedings or if, knowing that there was a risk of interruption, he nevertheless goes on deliberately to do those acts (ibid). The power under s. 12(1) includes all incidental powers necessary to enable the court to exercise its jurisdiction in a judicial manner, such as power to direct an officer of the court to bring a person reasonably believed to be responsible for a wilful interruption before the court (ibid.).

5. Section 41 of the Criminal Justice Act 1925 prohibits (in general) photography and sketching in court. Tape-recording in court is now regulated by s. 9 of the Contempt of Court Act 1981 (above, p. 377). See *Practice Direction* [1981] 3 All ER 848 (applicable to the Supreme Court and county courts), Home Office Circular No. 79/1981 (26 August 1981) (magistrates' courts) and *Re Hooker*, above.

6. The fact that many examples of contempt in the face of the court have their humorous side should not conceal the very real difficulties faced by judges in 'political' trials. These seem to be more endemic in the United States than in Britain. See, for example, the *Transcript of the Contempt Citations, Sentences, and Responses of the Chicago Conspiracy 10* (1970). For entertainment, see R. E. Megarry, *A Second Miscellany-at-Law* (1973) pp. 70–83.

7. An excellent illustration of the dangers inherent in use of the summary procedures in this context is *McKeown v R* (1971) 16 DLR (3d) 390, where the Supreme Court of Canada managed to uphold a contempt conviction based on slender evidence, over strong dissents by Spence and Laskin JJ. See also *Maharaj v A-G for Trinidad and Tobago (No 2)* [1979] AC 385, where the Privy Council held that the failure of a judge to make plain the specific nature of the contempt with which M was being charged vitiated the judge's order committing M to the 'Royal Goal' [sic] for contempt in the face of the court. Subsequently the Privy Council held that M was entitled to claim damages for the imprisonment, under the Constitution of Trinidad and Tobago, on the ground that he had been deprived of his liberty otherwise than by due process of law (*Maharaj v A-G for Trinidad and Tobago (No 2)* [1979] AC 385, PC). For a discussion of the problems arising out of alleged misconduct by lawyers in the face of the court, see P. Butt, [1978] Crim LR 463.

8. The Phillimore Committee recommended (in Chap. 3) that the practice whereby the judge deals with contempts in the face of the court himself should continue, and that:

'(a) the judge should always ensure that the contemnor is in no doubt about the nature of the conduct complained of, and give him an opportunity of explaining or denying his conduct, and of calling witnesses;

(b) before any substantial penalty is imposed there should be a short adjournment, with power to remand the contemnor in custody. The judge should have power to obtain a background report on the contemnor, and the contemnor should be entitled to speak in mitigation of sentence;

(c) for the purposes of defending himself and of making a plea in mitigation the contemnor should be entitled to legal representation, and the court should have power to grant legal aid immediately for this purpose where appropriate;

(d) if the contempt also amounts to a criminal offence, the judge should consider referring it to the prosecuting authorities to be dealt with under the ordinary criminal law, and should so refer it in serious cases unless reasons of urgency or convenience require that it be dealt with summarily' (p. 95).

For provisions on legal aid see section 29 of the Legal Aid Act 1988. Recent cases have emphasised the need for natural justice to be observed in summary contempt proceedings. The defendant must be given the chance to defend himself and in appropriate cases, should be given the opportunity of being legally represented. In *R v K* (1983) 78 Cr App Rep 82, K refused to testify against a fellow inmate of Camp Hill prison at the latter's trial on a charge of wounding K: the judge did not offer him legal representation, brusquely prevented him from giving any explanation for his refusal and sentenced him to a further three months' imprisonment. The Court of Appeal (Criminal Division) quashed the conviction. In fact, K could have presented evidence of duress which might have constituted a valid defence. Per Watkins LJ at p. 87: 'calm reflection and consideration of how best to deal with such a situation is called for. The rules of natural justice obviously apply in these circumstances and have as much force as they do in any other proceedings in our courts and tribunals.' (See also *Re Dr A S Rayan* (1983) 148 JP 569 and *R v Chowdhury; R v Crone* (1984) Times, 29 March.) In *R v Phillips* (1983) 78 Cr App Rep 88 the Court of Appeal (Criminal Division) stated that it was advisable in cases of refusals to testify to deal with the matter at the conclusion of the trial or, at the very soonest, the end of the prosecution case: to do so earlier, at the end of the second day of a five day trial, was 'precipitous'. Moreover, the effect on the course of the trial was a relevant consideration when considering sentence: here, it transpired that P's evidence would have added little or nothing by way of weight, support or confirmation of other witnesses. Accordingly, the sentence of four months' imprisonment was replaced by one of 14 days' detention. See also *R v Moran* (1985) 81 Cr App Rep 51, CA (Cr D) (order of committal quashed where the judge had acted precipitately, failed to give an opportunity to apologise and did not ask anyone in court to offer advice to the defendant); *R v Hill* [1986] Crim LR 457, CA (CrD) (insults from public gallery, committal to prison for seven days upheld); *R v Griffin* (1988) 88 Cr App Rep 63, CA (CrD) (committal for nine months for threatening witness outside court quashed: summary process not well suited in the circumstances, and should in any event have been postponed to the end of the trial); *R v Selby JJ, ex p Frame* [1992] QB 72 (no opportunity for F to deny or admit his disturbance of the court; no representation; committals under s. 12 of the 1981 Act quashed); *Re Hooker* [1993] COD 190 (see n. 4) (legal representation not permitted). In *R v Renshaw* [1989] Crim LR 811, a case widely publicised at the time, Judge Pickles found R to be in contempt, and sentenced her to seven days' imprisonment, when she refused to testify for the prosecution in respect of an assault on her by W., with whom she had cohabited. The Court of Appeal held that she had not had a fair trial: the judge had interrupted excessively; R had been threatened, apparently by W's friends; W had agreed to be bound over. In *R v Montgomery* [1995] 2 All ER 28, the Court of

Appeal (Criminal Division) set out sentencing guidelines in respect of witnesses refusing to testify, stating, inter alia, that an immediate custodial sentence was the only appropriate sentence unless the circumstances were wholly exceptional.

In cases of sudden outbursts in court that interrupt proceedings it has been said that it may be necessary for the court to take swift punitive action without affording an opportunity of legal representation: *per* Stephenson LJ (obiter) in *Balogh v St Albans Crown Court* [1975] QB 73, (citing *Morris v Crown Office* as an example); per Watkins LJ (obiter) in *R v K* (1983) 78 Cr App Rep 82, 87; *R v Newbury Justices, ex p Du Pont* (1983) 148 JP 248; *R v Moran* (1985) 81 Cr App Rep 51, 53. In the *Newbury* case 11 women created a disturbance in court which seriously disrupted the court's business and were removed to the cells. Three subsequently apologised and were released; eight refused and were committed for 14 days for contempt. They were not afforded access to legal advice. The Divisional Court, however, held that in the circumstances this was not a requirement of natural justice. Given that order had been restored (as in the *Morris* case) is this decision justifiable?

9. Is it contempt of court for a member of the public to raise two fingers in the direction of a limousine carrying two High Court judges on their way to court? Should it make any difference that the member of the public believes the car to be that of the local mayor, whom he regards as responsible for the latest increase in rates? Cf. the case of Mr Bangs (*Miller*, pp. 109–110, *The Times*, 24 May 1973, *The Daily Telegraph*, 23 May 1973). Mr Bangs spent two hours in a cell before being admonished by Lawson J.

10. *Mens Rea.* It is clear that it must be shown that the accused intended to do the act in question. At common law it was uncertain whether it was necessary to prove in addition an intention to interfere with the course of justice (*A-G v Butterworth* [1963] 1 QB 696; *Borrie and Lowe*, pp. 53–54, 274–275). It does seem that such an intention must be shown where it is sought to hold an advocate or witness in contempt for failure to attend court: *Weston v Central Criminal Court Courts' Administrator* [1976] QB 32, 43 (*per* Lord Denning MR); *Re Dr A S Rayan* (1983) 148 JP 569, DC; or interference with jurors is alleged: *R v Giscombe* (1985) 79 Cr App Rep 79, CA (CrD). It has also been argued that the Contempt of Court Act 1981, by limiting the scope of strict liability in relation to conduct alleged to interfere with the course of justice in particular proceedings (see ss. 1, 2: above p. 376), now imports a full *mens rea* requirement for contempt in the face of the court (*Borrie and Lowe*, ibid; cf. *Miller*, p. 134, suggesting that the 1981 Act affords at best a weak inference to this effect.) In principle, however, there should be a full *mens rea* requirement, although this might properly extend to include recklessness (see *Miller*, p. 135).

X Ltd v Morgan-Grampian (Publishers) Ltd [1991] 1 AC 1, [1990] 2 WLR 421, [1990] 1 All ER 616, House of Lords

A highly confidential draft business plan was stolen from the plaintiffs, two associated private companies. The following day, the third defendant, William Robin Goodwin, a trainee journalist employed by the first and second defendants, publishers of *The Engineer*, was telephoned by an unidentified source and given information which could be inferred to have been obtained from the stolen plan. He decided to write an article based on the information and contacted the plaintiffs to check certain facts. The plaintiffs immediately sought and obtained an ex parte injunction against the publishers restraining them from publishing information derived from the draft plan, on the ground that the information had been imparted to them in breach of confidence.

It being their intention to bring proceedings against the source for recovery of the plan, they applied for an order requiring the journalist and publishers to disclose the source, and sought discovery of Mr Goodwin's notes of the telephone conversation as a means of discovering the source's identity. The publishers did not know the source's identity and had no means of coercing Mr Goodwin. Accordingly, the plaintiffs directed their attention on Mr Goodwin. Hoffmann J granted the orders sought ([1990] 1 All ER 608); on appeal, the Court of Appeal varied the order by giving him the option of disclosing the notes, or delivering them to court in a sealed envelope which would remain sealed until final determination of his appeal against the order. Mr Goodwin declined to comply. The Court of Appeal dismissed the defendants' appeal against the orders ([1991] 1 AC 1). The defendants appealed to the House of Lords. The House of Lords held unanimously that the court had jurisdiction to make an order against the defendants requiring disclosure of the source's identity: the defendants were parties to the injunction proceedings for breach of confidence, and were in any event 'mixed up in the tortious acts' of the source (cf. Lord Reid in *Norwich Pharmacal Co v Customs and Excise Comrs* [1974] AC 133, 175). The House also considered the scope of section 10 of the Contempt of Court Act 1981.

Lord Bridge: . . . *Privilege from disclosure*
The courts have always recognised an important public interest in the free flow of information. How far and in what circumstances the maintenance of this public interest operated to confer on journalists any privilege from disclosure of their sources which the common law would recognise admitted of no short and simple answer on the authorities. But the matter is no longer governed by the common law and I do not think any assistance is to be gained from the authorities preceding the coming into force of section 10 of the Contempt of Court Act 1981 which is in these terms: [see above, p. 377].

It has been accepted in this case at all levels that the section applies to the circumstances of the instant case notwithstanding that the information obtained by Mr Goodwin from the source has not been 'contained in a publication'. The information having been communicated and received for the purposes of publication, it is clearly right to treat it as subject to the rule which the section lays down, since the purpose underlying the statutory protection of sources of information is as much applicable before as after publication. It is also now clearly established that the section is to be given a wide, rather than a narrow, construction in the sense that the restriction on disclosure applies not only to direct orders to disclose the identity of a source but also to any order for disclosure of material which will indirectly identify the source and applies notwithstanding that the enforcement of the restriction may operate to defeat rights of property vested in the party who seeks to obtain that material: *Secretary of State for Defence v Guardian Newspapers Ltd* [1984] Ch 156, 166–167, per Griffiths LJ; [1985] AC 339, 349–350, per Lord Diplock. As a statement of the rationale underlying this wide construction I cannot do better than quote from the passage in the judgment of Griffiths LJ to which I have referred, where he said:
'The press have always attached the greatest importance to their ability to protect their sources of information. If they are not able to do so, they believe that many of their sources would dry up and this would seriously interfere with their effectiveness. It is in the interests of us all that we should have a truly effective press, and it seems to me that Parliament by enacting section 10 has clearly recognised the importance that attaches to the ability of the press to protect their sources. . . . I can see no harm in giving a wide construction to the opening words of the section because by the latter part of the section the court is given ample powers to order the source to be revealed where in the circumstances of a particular case the wider public interest makes it necessary to do so.'
It follows then that, whenever disclosure is sought, as here, of a document which will disclose the identity of a source within the ambit of section 10, the statutory restriction operates unless the party seeking disclosure can satisfy the court that 'disclosure is necessary' in the interests of one of the four matters of public concern that are listed in the section. I think it is indisputable that where a judge asks himself the question: 'Can I be satisfied that disclosure of the source of *this* information is necessary to serve *this* interest?' he has to engage in a balancing exercise. He starts with the assumptions, first, that the protection of sources is itself a matter of high public importance, secondly, that nothing less than necessity will suffice to override it, thirdly, that the necessity can only arise out of concern for another matter of high public importance, being one of the four interests listed in the section.

What assistance is to be derived from the authorities as to the proper tests to be applied in carrying out this balancing exercise?

[His Lordship referred to Lord Diplock and himself in *Secretary of State for Defence v Guardian Newspapers Ltd* [1985] AC 339, 345, 372; Lord Griffiths and Lord Oliver in *Re an Inquiry under the Company Securities (Insider Dealing) Act 1985* [1988] AC 660, 704, 708–709, and continued:]

. . . I cannot help wondering whether these dicta do not concentrate attention too much on only one side of the picture. They suggest that in determining whether the criterion of necessity is established one need only look at, in the one case, the interests of national security and, in the other case, the prevention of crime. In the context of cases dealing with those two grounds of exception to the protection of sources, it is perfectly understandable that they should do so. For if non-disclosure of a source of information will imperil national security or enable a crime to be committed which might otherwise be prevented, it is difficult to imagine that any judge would hesitate to order disclosure. These two public interests are of such overriding importance that once it is shown that disclosure will serve one of those interests, the necessity of disclosure follows almost automatically; though even here if a judge were asked to order disclosure of a source of information in the interests of the prevention of crime, he 'might properly refuse to do so if, for instance, the crime was of a trivial nature': [1988] AC 660, 703, per Lord Griffiths.

But the question whether disclosure is necessary in the interests of justice gives rise to a more difficult problem of weighing one public interest against another. A question arising under this part of section 10 has not previously come before your Lordships' House for decision. In discussing the section generally Lord Diplock said in *Secretary of State for Defence v Guardian Newspapers Ltd* [1985] AC 339, 350:

'The exceptions include no reference to "the public interest" generally and I would add that in my view the expression "justice", the interests of which are entitled to protection, is not used in a general sense as the antonym of "injustice" but in the technical sense of the administration of justice in the course of legal proceedings in a court of law, or, by reason of the extended definition of "court" in section 19 of the Act of 1981 before a tribunal or body exercising the judicial power of the state.'

I agree entirely with the first half of this dictum. To construe 'justice' as the antonym of 'injustice' in section 10 would be far too wide. But to confine it to 'the technical sense of the administration of justice in the course of legal proceedings in a court of law' seems to me, with all respect due to any dictum of the late Lord Diplock, to be too narrow. It is, in my opinion, 'in the interests of justice', in the sense in which this phrase is used in section 10, that persons should be enabled to exercise important legal rights and to protect themselves from serious legal wrongs whether or not resort to legal proceedings in a court of law will be necessary to attain these objectives. Thus, to take a very obvious example, if an employer of a large staff is suffering grave damage from the activities of an unidentified disloyal servant, it is undoubtedly in the interests of justice that he should be able to identify him in order to terminate his contract of employment, notwithstanding that no legal proceedings may be necessary to achieve that end.

Construing the phrase 'in the interests of justice' in this sense immediately emphasises the importance of the balancing exercise. It will not be sufficient, per se, for a party seeking disclosure of a source protected by section 10 to show merely that he will be unable without disclosure to exercise the legal right or avert the threatened legal wrong on which he bases his claim in order to establish the necessity of disclosure. The judge's task will always be to weigh in the scales the importance of enabling the ends of justice to be attained in the circumstances of the particular case on the one hand against the importance of protecting the source on the other hand. In this balancing exercise it is only if the judge is satisfied that disclosure in the interests of justice is of such preponderating importance as to override the statutory privilege against disclosure that the threshold of necessity will be reached.

Whether the necessity of disclosure in this sense is established is certainly a question of fact rather than an issue calling for the exercise of the judge's discretion, but, like many other questions of fact, such as the question whether somebody has acted reasonably in given circumstances, it will call for the exercise of a discriminating and sometimes difficult value judgment. In estimating the weight to be attached to the importance of disclosure in the interests of justice on the one hand and that of protection from disclosure in pursuance of the policy which underlies section 10 on the other hand, many factors will be relevant on both sides of the scale.

It would be foolish to attempt to give comprehensive guidance as to how the balancing exercise should be carried out. But it may not be out of place to indicate the kind of factors which will require consideration. In estimating the importance to be given to the case in favour of disclosure there will be a wide spectrum within which the particular case must be located. If the party seeking disclosure shows, for example, that his very livelihood depends upon it, this will put the case near one end of the spectrum. If he shows no more than that what he seeks to protect is a minor interest in property, this will put the case at or near the other end. On the other side the importance of protecting a source from disclosure in pursuance of the policy underlying the statute will also vary within a wide spectrum. One important factor will be the nature of the information obtained from the source. The greater the legitimate public interest in the information which the source has given to the publisher or intended publisher, the greater will be the importance of protecting the source. But another and perhaps more significant factor which will very much affect the importance of protecting the source will be the manner in which the information was itself obtained by the source. If it appears to the court that the information was obtained legitimately this will enhance the importance of protecting the source. Conversely, if it appears that the information was obtained illegally, this will diminish the importance of protecting the source unless, of course, this factor is counterbalanced by a clear public interest in publication of the information, as in the classic case where the source has acted for the purpose of exposing iniquity. I draw attention to these considerations by way of illustration only and I emphasise once again that they are in no way intended to be read as a code.

In the circumstances of the instant case, I have no doubt that Hoffmann J and the Court of Appeal were right in finding that the necessity for disclosure of Mr Goodwin's notes in the interests of justice was established. The importance to the plaintiffs of obtaining disclosure lies in the threat of severe damage to their business, and consequentially to the livelihood of their employees, which would arise from disclosure of the information contained in their corporate plan while their refinancing negotiations are still continuing. This threat, accurately described by Lord Donaldson of Lymington MR, ante p. 28E, as 'ticking away beneath them like a time bomb' can only be defused if they can identify the source either as himself the thief of the stolen copy of the plan or as a means to lead to the identification of the thief and thus put themselves in a position to institute proceedings for the recovery of the missing document. The importance of protecting the source on the other hand is much diminished by the source's complicity, at the very least, in a gross breach of confidentiality which is not counterbalanced by any legitimate interest which publication of the information was calculated to serve. Disclosure in the interests of justice is, on this view of the balance, clearly of preponderating importance so as to override the policy underlying the statutory protection of sources and the test of necessity for disclosure is satisfied. . . .

The position of Mr. Goodwin . . .

The maintenance of the rule of law is in every way as important in a free society as the democratic franchise. In our society the rule of law rests upon twin foundations: the sovereignty of the Queen in Parliament in making the law and the sovereignty of the Queen's courts in interpreting and applying the law. While no one doubts the importance of protecting journalists' sources, no one, I think seriously advocates an absolute privilege against disclosure admitting of no exceptions. Since the enactment of section 10 of the Act of 1981 both the protection of journalists' sources and the limited grounds on which it may exceptionally be necessary to override that protection have been laid down by Parliament. I have not heard of any campaign in the media suggesting that the law itself is unjust or that the exceptions to the protection are too widely drawn. But if there were such a campaign, it should be fought in a democratic society by persuasion, not by disobedience to the law. Given the law as laid down by section 10, who, if not the courts, is to interpret it and to decide in the circumstances of any given case whether the protection is to prevail or whether the case is brought within one of the exceptions? The journalist cannot be left to be judge in his own cause and decide whether or not to make disclosure. This would be an abdication of the role of Parliament and the courts in the matter and in practice would be tantamount to conferring an absolute privilege. Of course the courts, like other human institutions, are fallible and a journalist ordered to disclose his source may, like other disappointed litigants, feel that the court's decision was wrong. But to contend that the individual litigant, be he a journalist or anyone else, has a right of 'conscientious objection' which entitles him to set himself above the law if he does not agree with the court's decision, is a doctrine which directly undermines the rule of law and is wholly unacceptable in a democratic society. Any rule of professional conduct enjoining a journalist to protect his confidential sources must, impliedly if not expressly, be subject to whatever exception is necessary to enable the journalist to obey the orders of a court of competent jurisdiction. Freedom of speech is itself a right which is dependent on the rule of law for its protection and it is paradoxical that a serious challenge to the rule of law should be mounted by responsible journalists.

Lords Templeman, Oliver and **Lowry** delivered concurring speeches. **Lord Griffiths** agreed.
Appeal dismissed.

NOTES

1. For full discussions of this and related cases, see T. R. S. Allan, 'Disclosure of Journalists' Sources, Civil Disobedience and the Rule of Law' [1991] CLJ 131; S. Palmer, 'Protecting Journalists' Sources: Section 10, Contempt of Court Act 1981' [1992] PL 61; see also I. Cram (1992) 55 MLR 400 (casenote on *X v Morgan-*

Grampian) and S. Walker, (1991) 14(2) UNSWLJ 302. In *Goodwin v UK*, the
European Commission on Human Rights ruled that the order violated Goodwin's
right to freedom of expression under Article 10, ECHR (see *The Guardian*, 26 May
1994).

2. For cases at common law in this area, which have now been superseded by s. 10,
see pp. 307–308 of the 2nd edition of this book.

3. As Lord Bridge points out, where disclosure is necessary in the interests of national
security or the prevention of crime, the courts are unlikely to allow sources to be protected. Where one of the other interests specified in s. 10 is invoked, the picture is
more mixed. Thus, in *Maxwell v Pressdram Ltd* [1987] 1 All ER 656, the Court of
Appeal declined to order disclosure of the source of a libellous article in *Private Eye*,
which alleged that Robert Maxwell had financed Neil Kinnock's trips abroad in order
to be recommended for a peerage. At the trial of the libel action arising out of the
article, *Private Eye* withdrew their plea of justification. The plaintiff claimed that disclosure could be ordered under s. 10 because it was necessary in the interests of justice
to determine whether *Private Eye* had published the articles recklessly or knowing
them to be false, and were accordingly liable for aggravated and exemplary damages.
The Court of Appeal held that while disclosure might be relevant and important for
this purpose it was not *necessary*. The trial judge had not been wrong to take the view
that the matter could be dealt with adequately by a strong direction to the jury.
Similarly, in *X v Y* [1988] 2 All ER 648, Rose J refused to order the disclosure of the
source of stories in a national newspaper identifying two doctors who were carrying
on general practice despite having contracted AIDS. The stories were based on
information obtained from hospital records by one or more employees of the plaintiff
health authority, and passed to the newspaper for payment. The health authority
argued that disclosure was necessary 'for the prevention of crime'; there was prima
facie evidence of offences of corruption under the Public Bodies Corrupt Practices Act
1889 and the Prevention of Corruption Act 1906, and they wished to ensure that such
disclosures in breach of confidence did not happen again. Rose J held that the evidence adduced fell short of establishing necessity; prevention of crime was not one of
the health authority's tasks and it was not clear that criminal investigation was the
intended or likely consequence of disclosure. Then, in *Broadmoor Hospital v Hyde*
(1994) Times, 18 March, Sir Peter Pain held that a disclosure order against a journalist
and his news agency in respect of the leaking of a confidential report by the general
manager of Broadmoor concerning two convicted murderers who had escaped was
not 'necessary' within s. 10; the applicant had failed to make personal enquiries in
order to discover the source of the leak and there was insufficient evidence to show
that the sources would have been revealed if enquiries had been made.

By contrast, in *Re an Inquiry under the Company Securities (Insider Dealing) Act 1985*
[1988] AC 660, Jeremy Warner, a financial journalist, was required by inspectors
appointed under the 1985 Act to investigate suspected leaks from government
departments of price-sensitive information about take-over bids, to reveal the sources
of information on which he had based articles in *The Times* and *The Independent*. The
inspectors certified his refusal to answer questions to the High Court under s. 178 of
the Financial Services Act 1986, the High Court having power to punish a person
who refuses to answer questions, without reasonable excuse, as if he had been guilty
of contempt. The House of Lords held that the test set out in s. 10 should be applied
to determine whether Mr Warner had a 'reasonable excuse', but that disclosure
would here be 'necessary . . . for the prevention of . . . crime.' The House rejected a
narrow construction of this test that would have limited it to a situation where

disclosure would lead to the prevention of a particular identifiable future crime or crimes; it was sufficient that it would lead to the prevention of leaks of information and criminal insider dealing generally. Mr Warner persisted in his refusal, and was fined £20,000 (*Re an Inquiry under the Company Securities (Insider Dealing) Act 1985* (1988) Times, 27 January).

4. Disobedience to an order made by a circuit judge under the Prevention of Terrorism (Temporary Provisions) Act 1989, Sch. 7, para. 3, requiring the production of information is punishable as a contempt. Such proceedings should invariably be heard in the Divisional Court; that court has no jurisdiction in contempt proceedings to review the exercise of the circuit judge's discretion – the order must be obeyed until set aside. These propositions were established in *DPP v Channel 4 Television Co Ltd and another* [1993] 2 All ER 517, where the Divisional Court fined Channel 4 and Box Productions £75,000 for refusing to divulge material collected in the preparation of a programme in the 'Dispatches' series which made allegations of widespread and systematic collusion between members of the RUC and loyalist terrorists. The companies feared that the disclosure of their source would imperil both his life and that of their researcher, and had promised the source anonymity. Woolf LJ stated (at 529) that the companies should not have given unqualified assurances in view of the terms of the 1989 Act and the fact than an inquiry into the allegations was inevitable. Accordingly, they were responsible for their own dilemma of being compelled for genuinely held moral considerations to disobey what they knew to be their legal duty, and had to accept the consequences. However, the court refused the Attorney-General's application for sequestration orders against the companies, accepting the reality that they would not now change their stance. Section 10 of the 1981 Act was not relied on by the companies 'since, presumably, it was accepted it provided no protection' (Woolf LJ at 530). This case has been described as dealing 'a severe blow to investigative journalism' (R. Costigan, (1992) 142 NLJ 1417, 1418).

7 Interference with the course of justice

This head of contempt covers a variety of matters including interference with witnesses (e.g. *A-G v Butterworth* [1962] 3 All ER 326; *Moore v Clerk of Assize, Bristol* [1972] 1 All ER 58 (above, p. 431); *R v Mulvaney* [1982] Crim LR 462, DC; *A-G v Jackson* [1994] COD 171, DC), jurors (*R v Martin* (1848) 5 Cox CC 356; *R v Owen* [1976] 3 All ER 239; *R v Goult* (1982) 76 Cr App Rep 140; *A-G v Judd* (1994) Times, 15 August), and judges and court officers, whether the interference takes place before, during or after the relevant proceedings. In *R v Runting* (1988) 89 Cr App Rep 243, the Court of Appeal quashed a conviction for contempt of court of a *Sun* photographer who pursued a defendant outside court in an attempt to take a close-up picture. The photographer had not struck or physically jostled his quarry; there were no intentional acts of sufficient gravity to amount to the actus reus of contempt of court by way of an interference with the course of justice.

Intentional interferences are clearly contempts: it is unclear, however, how far mens rea is a requirement, both at common law and after the enactment of the 1981 Act (see *Borrie and Lowe*, pp. 274–275, 277–279; *A-G v Butterworth* (above)). The issue of mens rea was left open in *R v Runting,* above.

Other illustrations include bringing improper pressure to bear on parties (cf. *A-G v Times Newspapers* [1974] AC 273, HL (above, p. 405) and interfering with a prisoner's right of access to the courts (*Raymond v Honey* [1983] 1 AC 1, HL); and inspecting documents on a court file if it was known that leave was required or to gain access to a court file by deception or subterfuge (*Dobson v Hastings* [1992] Ch 394 (on the facts there was no contempt as a journalist had obtained access to a court file without deception or trickery, and the editor responsible for the subsequent publication of information acquired from the file had no intention to interfere with the course of justice)).

For consideration of whether the victimisation of anti-discrimination complainants may amount to contempt, see E. Ellis and C. J. Miller, [1993] PL 80.

Intimidation of persons assisting in the investigation of offences, jurors and potential witnesses or jurors is now a substantive offence. Similarly, it is an offence to harm or threaten to harm a person because they have been so involved. This is in addition to any offence at common law. See the Criminal Justice and Public Order Act 1994, s. 51.

8 Jurisdiction

The position as to the jurisdiction to deal with criminal contempts is complex (see *Borrie and Lowe*, Chap. 11). In brief, the superior courts of record (e.g. House of Lords, Court of Appeal, High Court) have inherent power, acting on their own motion, to punish contempts committed both in the face and outside the court. Formal applications for committal, as by the Attorney-General (cf. s. 7 of the Contempt of Court Act 1981 (above, p. 377)) must be made to the Queen's Bench Divisional Court: (1) if the alleged contempt is committed in connection with criminal proceedings (except where the contempt is committed in the face of the court or consists of disobedience to a court order or breach of an undertaking (RSC Ord. 52 r. 1(2)(a)(ii)); (2) if the alleged contempt concerns an inferior court (ibid r. 1(2)(a)(iii); above p. 391); or (3) if the contempt is committed otherwise than in connection with any proceedings (ibid, r. 1(2)(b)). However, the Court of Appeal may also exercise jurisdiction in relation to contempt of itself (ibid). Criminal contempts committed in relation to civil proceedings may be dealt with by a High Court judge of the appropriate Division (ibid, r. 1(3)). Inferior courts have inherent or statutory powers to deal with contempt in the face (see above, p. 432). Applications for injunctions (e.g. by the Attorney-General: *A-G v Times Newspapers* (above, p. 405)) should be made to the High Court (on the role of the Attorney-General in contempt proceedings see J. Ll J. Edwards, *The Attorney-General, Politics and the Public Interest* (1984) pp. 161–176). Proceedings under the strict liability rule can only be brought by or with the consent of the Attorney-General or on the motion of a court with jurisdiction to deal with such a contempt (1981 Act, s. 7, above p. 377; *Taylor v Topping* (1990) Times, 15 February). This restriction does not, however, apply to proceedings for an injunction to restrain the likely commission of an offence under the Act: *Peacock v London Weekend Television* (1985) 150 JP 71, CA (above p. 417).

Appeals are governed by section 13 of the Administration of Justice Act 1960. In most cases they lie to the Court of Appeal (Civil Division) but appeals against decisions of the Crown Court lie to the Court of Appeal (Criminal Division) (Supreme Court Act 1981, s. 53(2)(b); Criminal Justice Act 1988, s. 159) and against the decisions of some inferior courts to the Queen's Bench Divisional Court. Appeals lie from the Divisional Court or Court of Appeal to the House of Lords.

The possibility of trial on indictment for contempt was thought to be obsolete, the last such prosecution being *R v Tibbits and Windust* [1902] 1 KB 77. In *R v D* [1984] 1 All ER 574 a contempt of court count was included in an indictment charging a variety of offences arising out of D's conduct in taking his child, a ward of court, out of her mother's care and control and outside England and Wales without the consent of the court. The Court of Appeal (Criminal Division) quashed (inter alia) the conviction for contempt, holding that it was 'highly undesirable that that form of proceeding should be resorted to' (p. 583). (The House of Lords restored a conviction for kidnapping but the decision on the contempt point was not certified for consideration by the House: [1984] 2 All ER 449.)

CHAPTER 7

Government secrecy and national security

1 Introduction[1]

The materials in this chapter illustrate a variety of legal and extra-legal inhibitions on freedom of expression and access to information which protect the interest of the state in keeping certain matters secret. At the heart of the legal restrictions are the Official Secrets Acts (below pp. 444–470) which cover matters ranging from serious breaches of national security to the unauthorised disclosure of certain classes of official information. These have reinforced the tendency towards excessive secrecy which has been one of the hallmarks of the public service. There have been moves towards more open government (below, pp. 512–515). Government departments are prepared (and obliged) to release more information than formerly. The Official Secrets Act 1989, which repealed the 'catch all' provisions of section 2 of the Official Secrets Act 1911, narrowed the scope of criminal sanctions. There are rather more tentative suggestions for the creation of legal rights of access to information. The courts have restricted the circumstances in which a public authority may decline to divulge information in the course of legal proceedings on the ground that it would be contrary to the public interest (below, p. 515). At the same time, the state has taken advantage of the developing law relating to the restraint by injunction of breaches of confidence (below, pp. 474–492).

Extra-legal factors are equally significant in the maintenance of secrecy and security. The press have to an extent acceded to a system of self-censorship in defence and security matters ('D' (now 'DA') Notices: below pp. 470–474). There are extensive measures for maintaining the physical security of classified information. There are procedures for vetting applicants for positions in the Civil Service aimed in particular at excluding persons with Communist associations or character defects from sensitive positions. Civil Servants responsible for unauthorised disclosures may be disciplined or dismissed.

---

1 See generally, D. G. T. Williams, *Not in the Public Interest* (1965), (1968) 3 Federal LR 20 and 'Official Secrecy and the Courts' in P. Glazebrook (ed), *Reshaping the Criminal Law* (1978) (hereafter cited as D. G. T. *Williams* (1978)); G. Robertson, *Freedom, the Individual and the Law*, (7th edn, 1993) Chap. 4; D. Leigh, *The Frontiers of Secrecy* (1980); J. Michael, *The Politics of Secrecy* (1982); A. Nicol and G. Robertson, *Media Law* (3rd edn, 1992), Chap. 10; D. Hooper, *Official Secrets* (1987); P. Birkinshaw, *Freedom of Information: The Law, the Practice and the Ideal* (1988), *Government and Information* (1990) and *Reforming the Secret State* (1990); J. D. Baxter, *State Security, Privacy and Information* (1990); S. Shetreet (ed.), *Free Speech and National Security* (1991); P. Gill, *Policing Politics: Security Intelligence and the Liberal Democratic State* (1994); L. Lustgarten and I. Leigh, *In from the Cold: National Security and Parliamentary Democracy* (1994).

2 The Official Secrets Acts

(a) THE OFFICIAL SECRETS ACTS 1911–1989

Official Secrets Act 1911

1. Penalties for spying

(1) If any person for any purpose prejudicial to the safety or interests of the State—

    (*a*) approaches, [inspects, passes over] or is in the neighbourhood of, or enters any prohibited place within the meaning of this Act; or

    (*b*) makes any sketch, plan, model, or note which is calculated to be or might be or is intended to be directly or indirectly useful to an enemy; or

    (*c*) obtains, [collects, records, or publishes,] or communicates to any other person [any secret official code word, or pass word, or] any sketch, plan, model, article, or note, or other document or information which is calculated to be or might be or is intended to be directly or indirectly useful to an enemy;

he shall be guilty of felony . . . .

(2) On a prosecution under this section, it shall not be necessary to show that the accused person was guilty of any particular act tending to show a purpose prejudicial to the safety or interests of the State, and, notwithstanding that no such act is proved against him, he may be convicted if, from the circumstances of the case, or his conduct, or his known character as proved, it appears that his purpose was a purpose prejudicial to the safety or interests of the State; and if any sketch, plan, model, article, note, document, or information relating to or used in any prohibited place within the meaning of this Act, or anything in such a place [or any secret official code word or pass word], is made, obtained, [collected, recorded, published], or communicated by any person acting under lawful authority, it shall be deemed to have been made, obtained, [collected, recorded, published] or communicated for a purpose prejudicial to the safety or interests of the State unless the contrary is proved. . . .

3. Definition of prohibited place

For the purposes of this Act, the expression 'prohibited place' means—

    [(*a*) Any work of defence, arsenal, naval or air force establishment or station, factory, dockyard, mine, minefield, camp, ship, or aircraft belonging to or occupied by or on behalf of His Majesty, or any telegraph, telephone, wireless or signal station, or office so belonging or occupied, and any place belonging to or occupied by or on behalf of His Majesty and used for the purpose of building, repairing, making, or storing any munitions of war, or any sketches, plans, models, or documents relating thereto, or for the purpose of getting any metals, oil, or minerals of use in time of war]; and

    (*b*) any place not belonging to His Majesty where any [munitions of war], or any [sketches, models, plans] or documents relating thereto, are being made, repaired, [gotten] or stored under contract with, or with any person on behalf of, His Majesty, or otherwise on behalf of His Majesty; and

    (*c*) any place belonging to [or used for the purposes of] His Majesty which is for the time being declared [by order of a Secretary of State] to be a prohibited place for the purposes of this section on the ground that information with respect thereto, or damage thereto, would be useful to an enemy; and

    (*d*) any railway, road, way, or channel, or other means of communication by land or water (including any works or structures being part thereof or connected therewith), or any place used for gas, water, or electricity works or other works for purposes of a public character, or any place where any [munitions of war], or any [sketches, models, plans] or documents relating thereto, are being made, repaired, or stored otherwise than on behalf of His Majesty, which is for the time being declared [by order of a Secretary of State] to be a prohibited place for the purposes of this section, on the ground that information with respect thereto, or the destruction or obstruction thereof, or interference therewith, would be useful to an enemy. . . .

6. Power to arrest

Any person who is found committing an offence under this Act . . . or who is reasonably suspected of having committed, or having attempted to commit, or being about to commit, such an offence, may be apprehended and detained. . . .

7. Penalty for harbouring spies

If any person knowingly harbours any person whom he knows, or has reasonable grounds for supposing, to be a person who is about to commit or who has committed an offence under this Act, or knowingly permits to meet or assemble in any premises in his occupation or under his control any such persons, or if any person having harboured any such person, or permitted to meet or assemble in any premises in his occupation or under his control any such persons, [wilfully omits or refuses] to disclose to a superintendent of police any information which it is in his power to give in relation to any such person he shall be guilty of a misdemeanour. . . .

8. Restriction on prosecution
A prosecution for an offence under this Act shall not be instituted except by or with the consent of the Attorney-General.

9. Search warrants
(1) If a justice of the peace is satisfied by information on oath that there is reasonable ground for suspecting that an offence under this Act has been or is about to be committed, he may grant a search warrant authorising any constable . . . to enter at any time any premises or place named in the warrant, if necessary, by force, and to search the premises or place and every person found therein, and to seize any sketch, plan, model, article, note, or document, or anything of a like nature or anything which is evidence of an offence under this Act having been or being about to be committed, which he may find on the premises or place or on any such person, and with regard to or in connexion with which he has reasonable ground for suspecting that an offence under this Act has been or is about to be committed.
(2) Where it appears to a superintendent of police that the case is one of great emergency and that in the interests of the State immediate action is necessary, he may by a written order under his hand give to any constable the like authority as may be given by the warrant of a justice under this section. . . .

12. Interpretation
In this Act, unless the context otherwise requires,—

Any reference to a place belonging to His Majesty includes a place belonging to any department of the Government of the United Kingdom or of any British possessions, whether the place is or is not actually vested in His Majesty; . . .

Expressions referring to communicating . . . include any communicating . . . whether in whole or in part, and whether the sketch, plan, model, article, note, document, or information itself or the substance, effect, or description thereof only be communicated . . . expressions referring to obtaining or retaining any sketch, plan, model, article, note, or document, include the copying or causing to be copied the whole or any part of any sketch, plan, model, article, note, or document; and expressions referring to the communication of any sketch, plan, model, article, note or document include the transfer or transmission of the sketch, plan, model, article, note or document;

The expression 'document' includes part of a document;

The expression 'model' includes design, pattern, and specimen;

The expression 'sketch' includes any photograph or other mode of representing any place or thing;

[The expression 'munitions of war' includes the whole or any part of any ship, submarine, aircraft, tank or similar engine, arms and ammunition, torpedo, or mine, intended or adapted for use in war, and any other article, material or device, whether actual or proposed, intended for such use;]

The expression 'superintendent of police' includes any police officer of a like or superior rank [and any person upon whom the powers of a superintendent of police are for the purposes of this Act conferred by a Secretary of State];

The expression 'office under His Majesty' includes any office or employment in or under any department of the Government of the United Kingdom, or of any British possession;

The expression 'offence under this Act' includes any act, omission, or other thing which is punishable under this Act.

Official Secrets Act 1920

1. (2) If any person—
   (a) retains for any purpose prejudicial to the safety or interests of the State any official document, whether or not completed or issued for use, when he has no right to retain it, or when it is contrary to his duty to retain it, or fails to comply with any directions issued by any Government Department or any person authorised by such department with regard to the return or disposal thereof; or
   (b) allows any other person to have possession of any official document issued for his use alone, or communicates any secret official code word or pass word so issued, or, without lawful authority or excuse, has in his possession any official document or secret official code word or pass word issued for the use of some person other than himself, or on obtaining possession of any official document by finding or otherwise, neglects or fails to restore it to the person or authority by whom or for whose use it was issued, or to a police constable; or

(c) without lawful authority or excuse, manufactures or sells, or has in his possession for sale any such die, seal or stamp as aforesaid;

he shall be guilty of a misdemeanour.

(3) In the case of any prosecution under this section involving the proof of a purpose prejudicial to the safety or interests of the State, subsection (2) of section one of the principal Act shall apply in like manner as it applies to prosecutions under that section.

6. Duty of giving information as to commission of offence

[(1) Where a chief officer of police is satisfied that there is reasonable ground for suspecting that an offence under section one of the principal Act has been committed and for believing that any person is able to furnish information as to the offence or suspected offence, he may apply to a Secretary of State for permission to exercise the powers conferred by this subsection and, if such permission is granted, he may authorise a superintendent of police, or any police officer not below the rank of inspector, to require the person believed to be able to furnish information to give any information in his power relating to the offence or suspected offence, and, if so required and on tender of his reasonable expenses, to attend at such reasonable time and place as may be specified by the superintendent or other officer; and if a person required in pursuance of such an authorisation to give information, or to attend as aforesaid, fails to comply with any such requirement or knowingly gives false information, he shall be guilty of a misdemeanour.

(2) Where a chief officer of police has reasonable grounds to believe that the case is one of great emergency and that in the interest of the State immediate action is necessary, he may exercise the powers conferred by the last foregoing subsection without applying for or being granted the permission of the Secretary of State, but if he does so shall forthwith report the circumstances to the Secretary of State.

(3) References in this section to a chief officer of police shall be construed as including references to any other officer of police expressly authorised by a chief officer of police to act on his behalf for the purposes of this section when by reason of illness, absence, or other cause he is unable to do so.]

7. Attempts, incitements, etc.

Any person who attempts to commit any offence under the principal Act or this Act, or solicits or incites or endeavours to persuade another person to commit an offence, or aids or abets and does any act preparatory to the commission of an offence under the principal Act or this Act, shall be guilty of a felony or a misdemeanour or a summary offence according as the offence in question is a felony, a misdemeanour or a summary offence, and on conviction shall be liable to the same punishment, and to be proceeded against in the same manner, as if he had committed the offence.

Official Secrets Act 1989

1. Security and intelligence

(1) A person who is or has been—
  (a) a member of the security and intelligence services; or
  (b) a person notified that he is subject to the provisions of this subsection,
is guilty of an offence if without lawful authority he discloses any information, document or other article relating to security or intelligence which is or has been in his possession by virtue of his position as a member of any of those services or in the course of his work while the notification is or was in force.

(2) The reference in subsection (1) above to disclosing information relating to security or intelligence includes a reference to making any statement which purports to be a disclosure of such information or is intended to be taken by those to whom it is addressed as being such a disclosure.

(3) A person who is or has been a Crown servant or government contractor is guilty of an offence if without lawful authority he makes a damaging disclosure of any information, document or other article relating to security or intelligence which is or has been in his possession by virtue of his position as such but otherwise than as mentioned in subsection (1) above.

(4) For the purposes of subsection (3) above a disclosure is damaging if—
  (a) it causes damage to the work of, or of any part of, the security and intelligence services; or
  (b) it is of information or a document or other article which is such that its unauthorised disclosure would be likely to cause such damage or which falls within a class or description of information, documents or articles the unauthorised disclosure of which would be likely to have that effect.

(5) It is a defence for a person charged with an offence under this section to prove that at the time of the alleged offence he did not know, and had no reasonable cause to believe, that the information, document or article in question related to security or intelligence or, in the case of an offence under subsection (3), that the disclosure would be damaging within the meaning of that subsection.

(6) Notification that a person is subject to subsection (1) above shall be effected by a notice in writing served on him by a Minister of the Crown; and such a notice may be served if, in the Minister's opinion,

the work undertaken by the person in question is or includes work connected with the security and intelligence services and its nature is such that the interests of national security require that he should be subject to the provisions of that subsection.

(7) Subject to subsection (8) below, a notification for the purposes of subsection (1) above shall be in force for the period of five years beginning with the day on which it is served but may be renewed by further notices under subsection (6) above for periods of five years at a time.

(8) A notification for the purposes of subsection (1) above may at any time be revoked by a further notice in writing served by the Minister on the person concerned; and the Minister shall serve such a further notice as soon as, in his opinion, the work undertaken by that person ceases to be such as is mentioned in subsection (6) above.

(9) In this section 'security or intelligence' means the work of, or in support of, the security and intelligence services or any part of them, and references to information relating to security or intelligence include references to information held or transmitted by those services or by persons in support of, or of any part of, them.

2. Defence

(1) A person who is or has been a Crown servant or government contractor is guilty of an offence if without lawful authority he makes a damaging disclosure of any information, document or other article relating to defence which is or has been in his possession by virtue of his position as such.

(2) For the purposes of subsection (1) above a disclosure is damaging if—

  (a) it damages the capability of, or of any part of, the armed forces of the Crown to carry out their tasks or leads to loss of life or injury to members of those forces or serious damage to the equipment or installations of those forces; or

  (b) otherwise than as mentioned in paragraph (a) above, it endangers the interests of the United Kingdom abroad, seriously obstructs the promotion or protection by the United Kingdom of those interests or endangers the safety of British citizens abroad; or

  (c) it is of information or of a document or article which is such that its unauthorised disclosure would be likely to have any of those effects.

(3) It is a defence for a person charged with an offence under this section to prove that at the time of the alleged offence he did not know, and had no reasonable cause to believe, that the information, document or article in question related to defence or that its disclosure would be damaging within the meaning of subsection (1) above.

(4) In this section 'defence' means—

  (a) the size, shape, organisation, logistics, order of battle, deployment, operations, state of readiness and training of the armed forces of the Crown;

  (b) the weapons, stores or other equipment of those forces and the invention, development, production and operation of such equipment and research relating to it;

  (c) defence policy and strategy and military planning and intelligence;

  (d) plans and measures for the maintenance of essential supplies and services that are or would be needed in time of war.

3. International relations

(1) A person who is or has been a Crown servant or government contractor is guilty of an offence if without lawful authority he makes a damaging disclosure of—

  (a) any information, document or other article relating to international relations; or

  (b) any confidential information, document or other article which was obtained from a State other than the United Kingdom or an international organisation,

being information or a document or article which is or has been in his possession by virtue of his position as a Crown servant or government contractor.

(2) For the purposes of subsection (1) above a disclosure is damaging if—

  (a) it endangers the interests of the United Kingdom abroad, seriously obstructs the promotion or protection by the United Kingdom of those interests or endangers the safety of British citizens abroad; or

  (b) it is of information or of a document or article which is such that its unauthorised disclosure would be likely to have any of those effects.

(3) In the case of information or a document or article within subsection (1)(b) above—

  (a) the fact that it is confidential, or

  (b) its nature or contents,

may be sufficient to establish for the purposes of subsection (2)(b) above that the information, document or article is such that its unauthorised disclosure would be likely to have any of the effects there mentioned.

(4) It is a defence for a person charged with an offence under this section to prove that at the time of the alleged offence he did not know, and had no reasonable cause to believe, that the information, document or article in question was such as is mentioned in subsection (1) above or that its disclosure would be damaging within the meaning of that subsection.

(5) In this section 'international relations' means the relations between States, between international organisations or between one or more States and one or more such organisations and includes any matter relating to a State other than the United Kingdom or to an international organisation which is capable of affecting the relations of the United Kingdom with another State or with an international organisation.

(6) For the purposes of this section any information, document or article obtained from a State or organisation is confidential at any time while the terms on which it was obtained require it to be held in confidence or while the circumstances in which it was obtained make it reasonable for the State or organisation to expect that it would be so held.

4. Crime and special investigation powers

(1) A person who is or has been a Crown servant or government contractor is guilty of an offence if without lawful authority he discloses any information, document or other article to which this section applies and which is or has been in his possession by virtue of his position as such.

(2) This section applies to any information, document or other article—

   (a) the disclosure of which—

      (i) results in the commission of an offence; or

      (ii) facilitates an escape from legal custody or the doing of any other act prejudicial to the safekeeping of persons in legal custody; or

      (iii) impedes the prevention or detection of offences or the apprehension or prosecution of suspected offenders; or

   (b) which is such that its unauthorised disclosure would be likely to have any of those effects.

(3) This section also applies to—

   (a) any information obtained by reason of the interception of any communication in obedience to a warrant issued under section 2 of the Interception of Communications Act 1985, any information relating to the obtaining of information by reason of any such interception and any document or other article which is or has been used or held for use in, or has been obtained by reason of, any such interception; and

   (b) any information obtained by reason of action authorised by a warrant issued under section 3 of the Security Services Act 1989 [or under section 5 of the Intelligence Services Act 1994 or by an authorisation given under section 7 of that Act],[1] any information relating to the obtaining of information by reason of any such action and any document or other article which is or has been used or held for use in, or has been obtained by reason of, any such action.

(4) It is a defence for a person charged with an offence under this section in respect of a disclosure falling within subsection (2)(a) above to prove that at the time of the alleged offence he did not know, and had no reasonable cause to believe, that the disclosure would have any of the effects there mentioned.

(5) It is a defence for a person charged with an offence under this section in respect of any other disclosure to prove that at the time of the alleged offence he did not know, and had no reasonable cause to believe, that the information, document or article in question was information or a document or article to which this section applies.

(6) In this section 'legal custody' includes detention in pursuance of any enactment or any instrument made under an enactment.

5. Information resulting from unauthorised disclosures or entrusted in confidence

(1) Subsection (2) below applies where—

   (a) any information, document or other article protected against disclosure by the foregoing provisions of this Act has come into a person's possession as a result of having been—

      (i) disclosed (whether to him or another) by a Crown servant or government contractor without lawful authority; or

      (ii) entrusted to him by a Crown servant or government contractor on terms requiring it to be held in confidence or in circumstances in which the Crown servant or government contractor could reasonably expect that it would be so held; or

      (iii) disclosed (whether to him or another) without lawful authority by a person to whom it was entrusted as mentioned in sub-paragraph (ii) above; and

   (b) the disclosure without lawful authority of the information, document or article by the person into whose possession it has come is not an offence under any of those provisions.

---

1 Inserted by the Intelligence Services Act 1994, Sch. 4, para. 4.

(2) Subject to subsections (3) and (4) below, the person into whose possession the information, document or article has come is guilty of an offence if he discloses it without lawful authority knowing, or having reasonable cause to believe, that it is protected against disclosure by the foregoing provisions of this Act and that it has come into his possession as mentioned in subsection (1) above.

(3) In the case of information or a document or article protected against disclosure by sections 1 to 3 above, a person does not commit an offence under subsection (2) above unless—

    (a) the disclosure by him is damaging; and

    (b) he makes it knowing, or having reasonable cause to believe, that it would be damaging;

and the question whether a disclosure is damaging shall be determined for the purposes of this subsection as it would be in relation to a disclosure of that information, document or article by a Crown servant in contravention of section 1(3), 2(1) or 3(1) above.

(4) A person does not commit an offence under subsection (2) above in respect of information or a document or other article which has come into his possession as a result of having been disclosed—

    (a) as mentioned in subsection (1)(a)(i) above by a government contractor; or

    (b) as mentioned in subsection (1)(a)(iii) above,

unless that disclosure was by a British citizen or took place in the United Kingdom, in any of the Channel Islands or in the Isle of Man or a colony.

(5) For the purposes of this section information or a document or article is protected against disclosure by the foregoing provisions of this Act if—

    (a) it relates to security or intelligence, defence or international relations within the meaning of section 1, 2 or 3 above or is such as is mentioned in section 3(1)(b) above; or

    (b) it is information or a document or article to which section 4 above applies;

and information or a document or article is protected against disclosure by sections 1 to 3 above if it falls within paragraph (a) above.

(6) A person is guilty of an offence if without lawful authority he discloses any information, document or other article which he knows, or has reasonable cause to believe, to have come into his possession as a result of a contravention of section 1 of the Official Secrets Act 1911.

6. Information entrusted in confidence to other States or international organisations

(1) This section applies where—

    (a) any information, document or other article which—

        (i) relates to security or intelligence, defence or international relations; and

        (ii) has been communicated in confidence by or on behalf of the United Kingdom to another State or to an international organisation,

    has come into a person's possession as a result of having been disclosed (whether to him or another) without the authority of that State or organisation or, in the case of an organisation, of a member of it; and

    (b) the disclosure without lawful authority of the information, document or article by the person into whose possession it has come is not an offence under any of the foregoing provisions of this Act.

(2) Subject to subsection (3) below, the person into whose possession the information, document or article has come is guilty of an offence if he makes a damaging disclosure of it knowing, or having reasonable cause to believe, that it is such as is mentioned in subsection (1) above, that it has come into his possession as there mentioned and that its disclosure would be damaging.

(3) A person does not commit an offence under subsection (2) above if the information, document or article is disclosed by him with lawful authority or has previously been made available to the public with the authority of the State or organisation concerned or, in the case of an organisation, of a member of it.

(4) For the purposes of this section 'security or intelligence', 'defence' and 'international relations' have the same meaning as in sections 1, 2 and 3 above and the question whether a disclosure is damaging shall be determined as it would be in relation to a disclosure of the information, document or article in question by a Crown servant in contravention of sections 1(3), 2(1) and 3(1) above.

(5) For the purposes of this section information or a document or article is communicated in confidence if it is communicated on terms requiring it to be held in confidence or in circumstances in which the person communicating it could reasonably expect that it would be so held.

7. Authorised disclosures

(1) For the purposes of this Act a disclosure by—

    (a) a Crown servant; or

    (b) a person, not being a Crown servant or government contractor, in whose case a notification for the purposes of section 1(1) above is in force,

is made with lawful authority if, and only if, it is made in accordance with his official duty.

(2) For the purposes of this Act a disclosure by a government contractor is made with lawful authority if, and only if, it is made—

(a) in accordance with an official authorisation; or

(b) for the purposes of the functions by virtue of which he is a government contractor and without contravening an official restriction.

(3) For the purposes of this Act a disclosure made by any other person is made with lawful authority if, and only if, it is made—

(a) to a Crown servant for the purposes of his functions as such; or

(b) in accordance with an official authorisation.

(4) It is a defence for a person charged with an offence under any of the foregoing provisions of this Act to prove that at the time of the alleged offence he believed that he had lawful authority to make the disclosure in question and had no reasonable cause to believe otherwise.

(5) In this section 'official authorisation' and 'official restriction' mean, subject to subsection (6) below, an authorisation or restriction duly given or imposed by a Crown servant or government contractor or by or on behalf of a prescribed body or a body of a prescribed class.

(6) In relation to section 6 above 'official authorisation' includes an authorisation duly given by or on behalf of the State or organisation concerned or, in the case of an organisation, a member of it.

8. Safeguarding of information

(1) Where a Crown servant or government contractor, by virtue of his position as such, has in his possession or under his control any document or other article which it would be an offence under any of the foregoing provisions of this Act for him to disclose without lawful authority he is guilty of an offence if—

(a) being a Crown servant, he retains the document or article contrary to his official duty; or

(b) being a government contractor, he fails to comply with an official direction for the return or disposal of the document or article,

or if he fails to take such care to prevent the unauthorised disclosure of the document or article as a person in his position may reasonably be expected to take.

(2) It is a defence for a Crown servant charged with an offence under subsection (1)(a) above to prove that at the time of the alleged offence he believed that he was acting in accordance with his official duty and had no reasonable cause to believe otherwise.

(3) In subsections (1) and (2) above references to a Crown servant include any person, not being a Crown servant or government contractor, in whose case a notification for the purposes of section 1(1) above is in force.

(4) Where a person has in his possession or under his control any document or other article which it would be an offence under section 5 above for him to disclose without lawful authority, he is guilty of an offence if—

(a) he fails to comply with an official direction for its return or disposal; or

(b) where he obtained it from a Crown servant or government contractor on terms requiring it to be held in confidence or in circumstances in which that servant or contractor could reasonably expect that it would be so held, he fails to take such care to prevent its unauthorised disclosure as a person in his position may reasonably be expected to take.

(5) Where a person has in his possession or under his control any document or other article which it would be an offence under section 6 above for him to disclose without lawful authority, he is guilty of an offence if he fails to comply with an official direction for its return or disposal.

(6) A person is guilty of an offence if he discloses any official information, document or other article which can be used for the purpose of obtaining access to any information, document or other article protected against disclosure by the foregoing provisions of this Act and the circumstances in which it is disclosed are such that it would be reasonable to expect that it might be used for that purpose without authority.

(7) For the purposes of subsection (6) above a person discloses information or a document or article which is official if—

(a) he has or has had it in his possession by virtue of his position as a Crown servant or government contractor; or

(b) he knows or has reasonable cause to believe that a Crown servant or government contractor has or has had it in his possession by virtue of his position as such.

(8) Subsection (5) of section 5 above applies for the purposes of subsection (6) above as it applies for the purposes of that section.

(9) In this section 'official direction' means a direction duly given by a Crown servant or government contractor or by or on behalf of a prescribed body or a body of a prescribed class.

9. Prosecutions

(1) Subject to subsection (2) below, no prosecutions for an offence under this Act shall be instituted in England and Wales or in Northern Ireland except by or with the consent of the Attorney General or, as the case may be, the Attorney General for Northern Ireland.

(2) Subsection (1) above does not apply to an offence in respect of any such information, document or article as is mentioned in section 4(2) above but no prosecution for such an offence shall be instituted in England and Wales or in Northern Ireland except by or with the consent of the Director of Public Prosecutions or, as the case may be, the Director of Public Prosecutions for Northern Ireland.

10. Penalties

(1) A person guilty of an offence under any provision of this Act other than section 8(1), (4) or (5) shall be liable—

  (a) on conviction on indictment, to imprisonment for a term not exceeding two years or a fine or both;

  (b) on summary conviction, to imprisonment for a term not exceeding six months or a fine not exceeding the statutory maximum or both.

(2) A person guilty of an offence under section 8(1), (4) or (5) above shall be liable on summary conviction to imprisonment for a term not exceeding three months or a fine not exceeding level 5 on the standard scale or both.

11. Arrest, search and trial

(3) Section 9(1) of the Official Secrets Act 1911 (search warrants) shall have effect as if references to offences under that Act included references to offences under any provision of this Act other than section 8(1), (4) or (5); and the following provisions of the Police and Criminal Evidence Act 1984, that is to say—

  (a) section 9(2) (which excludes items subject to legal privilege and certain other material from powers of search conferred by previous enactments); and

  (b) paragraph 3(b) of Schedule 1 (which prescribes access conditions for the special procedure laid down in that Schedule),

shall apply to section 9(1) of the said Act of 1911 as extended by this subsection as they apply to that section as originally enacted. . . .

(4) Section 8(4) of the Official Secrets Act 1920 (exclusion of public from hearing on the grounds of national safety) shall have effect as if references to offences under that Act included references to offences under any provision of this Act other than section 8(1), (4) or (5).

(5) Proceedings for an offence under this Act may be taken in any place in the United Kingdom.

12. 'Crown servant' and 'government contractor'

(1) In this Act 'Crown servant' means—

  (a) a Minister of the Crown;

  (b) a person appointed under section 8 of the Northern Ireland Constitution Act 1973 (the Northern Ireland Executive etc.);

  (c) any person employed in the civil service of the Crown, including Her Majesty's Diplomatic Service, Her Majesty's Overseas Civil Service, the civil service of Northern Ireland and the Northern Ireland Court Service;

  (d) any member of the naval, military or air forces of the Crown including any person employed by an association established for the purposes of the Reserve Forces Act 1980;

  (e) any constable and any other person employed or appointed in or for the purposes of any police force (including a police force within the meaning of the Police Act (Northern Ireland) 1970);

  (f) any person who is a member or employee of a prescribed body or a body of a prescribed class and either is prescribed for the purposes of this paragraph or belongs to a prescribed class of members or employees of any such body;

  (g) any person who is the holder of a prescribed office or who is an employee of such a holder and either is prescribed for the purposes of this paragraph or belongs to a prescribed class of such employees.

(2) In this Act 'government contractor' means, subject to subsection (3) below, any person who is not a Crown servant but who provides, or is employed in the provision of, goods or services—

  (a) for the purposes of any Minister or person mentioned in paragraph (a) or (b) of subsection (1) above, of any of the services, forces or bodies mentioned in that subsection or of the holder of any office prescribed under that subsection; or

  (b) under an agreement or arrangement certified by the Secretary of State as being one to which the government of a State other than the United Kingdom or an international organisation is a party or which is subordinate to, or made for the purposes of implementing, any such agreement or arrangement.

(3) Where an employee or class of employees of any body, or of any holder of an office, is prescribed by an order made for the purposes of subsection (1) above—

(a) any employee of that body, or of the holder of that office, who is not prescribed or is not within the prescribed class; and

(b) any person who does not provide, or is not employed in the provision of, goods or services for the purposes of the performance of those functions of the body or the holder of the office in connection with which the employee or prescribed class of employees is engaged,

shall not be a government contractor for the purposes of this Act.

13. Other interpretation provisions

(1) In this Act—

'disclose' and 'disclosure', in relation to a document or other article, include parting with possession of it;

'international organisation' means, subject to subsections (2) and (3) below, an organisation of which only States are members and includes a reference to any organ of such an organisation;

'prescribed' means prescribed by an order made by the Secretary of State;

'State' includes the government of a State and any organ of its government and references to a State other than the United Kingdom include references to any territory outside the United Kingdom.

(2) In section 12(2)(b) above the reference to an international organisation includes a reference to any such organisation whether or not one of which only States are members and includes a commercial organisation.

(3) In determining for the purposes of subsection (1) above whether only States are members of an organisation, any member which is itself an organisation of which only States are members, or which is an organ of such an organisation, shall be treated as a State. . . .

15. Acts done abroad and extent

(1) Any act—

(a) done by a British citizen or Crown servant; or

(b) done by any person in any of the Channel Islands or the Isle of Man or any colony,

shall, if it would be an offence by that person under any provision of this Act other than section 8(1), (4) or (5) when done by him in the United Kingdom, be an offence under that provision.

(2) This Act extends to Northern Ireland. . . .

16. Short title, citation, consequential amendments, repeals, revocation and commencement

(1) This Act may be cited as the Official Secrets Act 1989.

(2) This Act and the Official Secrets Acts 1911 to 1939 may be cited together as the Official Secrets Acts 1911 to 1989. . . .

NOTES

1. The words in square brackets in the 1911 Act were added by the Official Secrets Act 1920. Section 6 of the 1920 Act was substituted by the Official Secrets Act 1939, s. 1. The maximum penalty under s. 1 of the 1911 Act is 14 years' imprisonment, and for the other offences under the two Acts (other than sections 4 and 5 of the 1920 Act) is two years' imprisonment.

There are special provisions concerning atomic energy. Section 11 of the Atomic Energy Act 1946 makes it an offence to communicate to an unauthorised person information relating to atomic energy plant (see S. R. & O. 1947 No. 100). Section 13 makes it an offence for any person to disclose, without authority, any information obtained in the exercise of powers under the Act. Any place belonging to or used for the purposes of the Authority may be declared to be a prohibited place under the Official Secrets Act 1911, s. 3(c) (Atomic Energy Authority Act 1954, s. 6(3)). Similar provisions apply to the Civil Aviation Authority (Civil Aviation Act 1982, s. 18), the holders of a nuclear site licence (Nuclear Installations Act 1965, Sch. 1) and public telecommunications operators (Telecommunications Act 1984, Sch. 4, para. 12(2)). It is also an offence for a member of any Euratom institution or committee, an officer or servant of Euratom or a person who has dealings with

Euratom to disclose classified information acquired from that source (European Communities Act 1972, s. 11(2)). The current orders under s. 3(c) are The Official Secrets (Prohibited Places) Orders 1955 and 1975, S.I.s 1955 No. 1497 and 1994 No. 968. They cover the Capenhurst and Sellafield works of British Nuclear Fuels Ltd., and various establishments of the Atomic Energy Authority, including Dounreay, Windscale and Harwell. On the implications for civil liberties generally of nuclear power see J. C. Woodliffe, [1983] PL 440; Justice Report on *Plutonium and Liberty* (1978); M. Flood and R. Grove-White, *Nuclear Prospects* (1976).

2. It is an offence under section 1(1) of the 1920 Act to use specified false pretences for the purpose of gaining admission to a prohibited place or for any other purpose prejudicial to the safety or interests of the State. These include the use without lawful authority of official uniform (e.g. military or police) or any uniform so nearly resembling it as to be calculated to deceive; making false statements; tampering with a pass (or similar document); possessing a pass (or similar document) that has been forged, altered or is otherwise 'irregular'; personating a person holding office under the Crown or a person entitled to use an official pass (or similar document), code word, or pass word; unauthorised use or possession of any die, seal or stamp of a government department or any diplomatic, naval, military or air force authority under the Crown, or die, seal or stamp so closely resembling one as to be calculated to deceive.

It is also an offence to obstruct, knowingly mislead or otherwise interfere with or impede any police officer, or any member of the forces on guard, patrol or similar duty, 'in the vicinity of a prohibited place' (1920 Act, s. 3).

3. The fact that a person has been in communication with a foreign agent constitutes evidence in proceedings against him under s. 1 of the 1911 Act that he has for a purpose prejudicial to the safety or the interests of the State, obtained or attempted to obtain information which may be useful to an enemy (1920 Act, s. 2). There is also a power whereby a Secretary of State may require the production of telegrams (1920 Act, s. 4). Persons who carry on the business of receiving postal packets for delivery or forwarding must be registered with the police (1920 Act, s. 5).

4. If, in the course of any court proceedings under the Acts:

'. . . application is made by the prosecution, on the ground that the publication of any evidence to be given or of any statement to be made in the course of the proceedings would be prejudicial to the national safety, that all or any portion of the public shall be excluded during any part of the hearing, the court may make an order to that effect, but the passing of sentence shall in any case take place in public.' (1920 Act, s. 8(4)).

5. The 1911 Official Secrets Bill[1] was presented by the government as a measure which was aimed at spying and was essential on grounds of national security (Franks Report, p. 24). Section 2 (see below, p. 460) was not mentioned. It passed all its Commons stages in less than an hour. The files show that the legislation had been desired for some time by governments, the Official Secrets Act 1889 having proved inadequate to prevent the leakage of official information by civil servants, and that it had been carefully prepared over a period of years (Franks Report, p. 25). The background to the 1989 Act is discussed below, pp. 460–465.

6. *Aspects of interpretation.* The term 'enemy' includes a potential enemy, and so all the provisions of section 1 are applicable in peace time (*R v Parrott* (1913) 8 Cr App

---

1 The origins of the Officials Secrets Acts are discussed in D. G. T. Williams, *Not in the Public Interest* (1965) Chap. 1; Report of the Franks Committee on Section 2 of the Official Secrets Act 1911, Cmnd. 5104, Ch. 4 and Appendix III; D. French, 'Spy Fever in Britain, 1900–1915', *The Historical Journal*, 21, 2 (1978) p. 355; K. G. Robertson, *Public Secrets* (1982), Chaps. 4 and 5.

Rep 186, CCA). The leading case on section 1, *Chandler v DPP*, is given below, p. 455. Section 3 of the 1920 Act was used in a prosecution of four members of the Committee of 100, including Pat Arrowsmith, in 1964. They were fined £25 for inciting people to obstruct police officers at the USAF base at Ruislip in connection with a demonstration there (D. G. T. Williams, *Not in the Public Interest* (1965) p. 109). Williams points out (at p. 111) that it was not necessary for the Official Secrets Acts to be invoked against the nuclear disarmers in the 1960s, in preference to prosecutions for the general public order offences.

In *Adler v George* [1964] 2 QB 7, A obstructed a member of the armed forces engaged in security duty while within the boundaries of Marham RAF station. His conviction under s. 3 of the 1920 Act was upheld by the Divisional Court, which held that the words 'in the vicinity of' had to be read as meaning 'in or in the vicinity of'.

Another alteration in the statutory language to the detriment of a defendant was made by the Court of Criminal Appeal in *R v Oakes* [1959] 2 QB 350. The court treated section 7 of the 1911 Act as if it read 'aids or abets *or* does any act preparatory' so as to render liable a person who had done an 'act preparatory' without 'aiding or abetting'.

'It seems to the court that it is quite clear in the present case what the intention was, and that there has been merely a faultiness of expression'
(per Lord Parker CJ at p. 357).

O had also been convicted under s. 2 of the 1911 Act. In *R v Bingham* [1973] QB 870 the Court of Appeal (Criminal Division) held that an 'act preparatory' was 'an act done by the accused with the commission of an offence under the principal Act in mind', and that it was sufficient to show that the transmission of prejudicial information was 'possible' and not 'probable' (*per* Lord Widgery CJ at p. 875). Is it necessary for something to be an offence which is even more remote from the substantive offence than an attempt to commit it?

7. *Powers of search.* The powers of search granted by s. 9 of the 1911 Act were relied upon by the police in the 'Zircon affair'.[1] In 1986 the BBC commissioned Duncan Campbell to make a series of programmes entitled *Secret Society*. One of these revealed the existence of a secret Ministry of Defence project, Project Zircon, to put a spy satellite in space. The programme also revealed its cost (c. £500m) and the fact that the existence and cost of the project had been concealed from Parliament, but not its technical details. On 15 January 1987, the programme was banned on national security grounds by Alasdair Milne, the BBC's Director General (having previously been cleared by Assistant Director General Alan Protheroe). An injunction was obtained against Duncan Campbell on 21 January, but not served in time to prevent the Zircon story being told in the *New Statesman* of 23 January 1987 ('Spy in the Sky'), published on 22 January. On the same day, the Attorney-General failed to obtain an injunction to prevent the programme being shown in the Palace of Westminster, Ian Kennedy J stating that it was for the House to regulate its own proceedings; but persuaded the Speaker, after a briefing 'on Privy Counsellor terms', to impose a ban on its being shown while the injunction against Campbell was in force (it was lifted on 25 February in the light of a detailed undertaking given by Campbell).

1 See generally the *New Statesman* for 23 and 30 January and 6 February 1987; P. Thornton, *The Civil Liberties of the Zircon Affair* (NCCL, 1987); P. Gill, (1987) 9 Liverpool LR 189; debates on the Special Branch Raids 109 HC Deb 2 and 3 February 1987, cols 691–700, 815–858; K. D. Ewing and C. A. Gearty, *Freedom Under Thatcher* (1990), pp. 147–152.

Over the weekend of 24–25 January, Special Branch police officers searched the offices of the *New Statesman*; on 25 January, officers searched Duncan Campbell's home, and on 31 January, the Glasgow offices of BBC Scotland. Substantial quantities of documents were removed, especially from the BBC. The London warrants were granted under the Police and Criminal Evidence Act 1984, s. 9 and Sch. 1 under the warrant procedure exceptionally available as an alternative to obtaining an order inter partes. The basis of the warrant in Glasgow was s. 9 of the 1911 Act, the PACE provisions not extending to Scotland (see G. J. Zellick, (1987) 137 NLJ 160). It was claimed that the legal proceedings involved were instigated by the Attorney-General in England and the Lord Advocate in Scotland rather than ministers (see e.g. 110 HC Deb 19 February 1977 cols 796–798, written answer by Malcolm Rifkind MP, Secretary of State for Scotland).

The government's actions were widely criticised as an attempt to intimidate the press, particularly in view of the broad terms in which the search warrants were granted. The question why the authorities, who had known about the proposed programme since the middle of 1986, waited until early 1987 to take any action was never satisfactorily answered.

A majority of the Committee of Privileges subsequently concluded that the Speaker had acted 'wholly correctly in this matter', and stated that the private showing of the programme could not constitute a 'proceeding in Parliament' protected by Parliamentary privilege. See *First Report from the Committee of Privileges 1986–87, Speaker's Order of 22 January 1987 on a Matter of National Security* (1986–87 H.C. 365); A. W. Bradley [1987] PL 1 and 488.

Section 9(2) and Sch. 1, para. 3(b) of PACE (above, pp. 86, 91) now apply to warrants under s. 9(1) of the 1911 Act (Official Secrets Act 1989, s. 11(3)).

(b) SECTION 1 OF THE OFFICIAL SECRETS ACT: ESPIONAGE, SABOTAGE AND WHAT ELSE?

Chandler v Director of Public Prosecutions [1964] AC 763, [1962] 3 All ER 142, [1962] 3 WLR 702, House of Lords

The appellants, five men and a woman, were members of the Committee of 100 who sought to further the aims of the Campaign for Nuclear Disarmament by non-violent demonstrations of civil disobedience. They took part in organising a demonstration held on 9 December 1961, at Wethersfield Airfield, which was a 'prohibited place' within section 3 of the Official Secrets Act 1911, and which was occupied at the material time by United States Air Force squadrons assigned to the Supreme Commander Allied Forces, Europe. The plan was that on 9 December 1961, some demonstrators would take up a position outside the entrances to the airfield and would remain there sitting for five hours, while others would enter the airfield and, by sitting in front of the aircraft, would prevent them from taking off. On that date, many demonstrators did travel to Wethersfield, but were prevented from entering the airfield. The admitted objects were to ground all aircraft, to immobilise the airfield and to reclaim the base for civilian purposes. The appellants were charged with conspiring together to incite diverse persons to commit, and with conspiring together and with others to commit, 'a breach of section 1 of the Official Secrets Act 1911, namely, for a purpose prejudicial to the safety or interests of the State to enter a Royal Air Force Station . . . at Wethersfield'. A prosecution witness, Air Commodore Magill, gave evidence that interference with the ability of aircraft to take off was prejudicial to the safety or interests of the State. The judge refused to allow counsel for the defence to cross-examine or call evidence as to the appellants' beliefs that their acts would benefit the State or to show that the appellants' purpose was not in fact prejudicial to the safety or interests of the State. The appellants were convicted and sentenced to terms of imprisonment (18 months each for the men and 12 for the woman).

They appealed on the grounds that the facts did not disclose a conspiracy to commit a breach of section 1 of the Act of 1911, and that the judge was wrong in excluding cross-examination and evidence as to the facts on which the appellants' beliefs were based, and as to whether the appellants' purpose was in fact prejudicial to the State. Their appeals were dismissed by the Court of Criminal Appeal [1964] AC 771 and the House of Lords.

Lord Reid: . . . In cross-examination [of Air Commodore Magill] objection was taken to his being asked as to the armament of these squadrons. Counsel for the accused said that they sought to adduce evidence that their purpose was not prejudicial to the interests of the State, and that the basis of the defence was that these aircraft used nuclear bombs and that it was not in fact in the interests of the State to have aircraft so armed at that time there. So, he said, it would be beneficial to the State to immobilise these aircraft. Then counsel further submitted that he was entitled to adduce evidence to show that the accused believed, and reasonably believed, that it was not prejudicial but beneficial to the interests of the State to immobilise these aircraft: the jury were entitled to hold that no offence had been committed because the accused did not have a purpose prejudicial to the State, and it was for the jury to determine their purpose. . . . [C]ounsel said that his evidence would deal with the effect of exploding a nuclear bomb and . . . reference was made to the possibility of accident or mistake, and other reasons against having nuclear bombs. He said that he wished to cross-examine as to the basic wrongness of the conception of a deterrent force and the likelihood of it attracting hostile attack. In reply the Attorney-General submitted that an objective test must determine whether the purpose of grounding aircraft was a prejudicial purpose, that the accuseds' beliefs were irrelevant and so was the reasonableness of their beliefs. Havers J then ruled that the defence were not entitled to call evidence to establish that it would be beneficial for this country to give up nuclear armament or that the accused honestly believed that it would be. . . . [Section 1 of the Official Secrets Act 1911] has a side note 'Penalties for spying', and it was argued that this limits its scope. In my view side notes cannot be used as an aid to construction. They are mere catchwords and I have never heard of it being supposed in recent times that an amendment to alter a side note could be proposed in either House of Parliament. Side notes in the original Bill are inserted by the draftsman. During the passage of the Bill through its various stages amendments to it or other reasons may make it desirable to alter a side note. In that event I have reason to believe that alteration is made by the appropriate officer of the House—no doubt in consultation with the draftsman. So side notes cannot be said to be enacted in the same sense as the long title or any part of the body of the Act. Moreover, it is impossible to suppose that the section does not apply to sabotage and what was intended to be done in this case was a kind of temporary sabotage.

The first word in the section that requires consideration is 'purpose'. . . . The accused both intended and desired that the base should be immobilised for a time, and I cannot construe purpose in any sense that does not include that state of mind. A person can have two different purposes in doing a particular thing and even if their reason or motive for doing what they did is called the purpose of influencing public opinion that cannot alter the fact that they had a purpose to immobilise the base. And the statute says 'for any purpose'. There is no question here of the interference with the aircraft being an unintended or undesired consequence of carrying out a legitimate purpose.

Next comes the question of what is meant by the safety or interests of the State. 'State' is not an easy word. It does not mean the Government or the Executive. And I do not think that it means, as counsel argued, the individuals who inhabit these islands. The statute cannot be referring to the interests of all those individuals because they may differ and the interests of the majority are not necessarily the same as the interests of the State. . . . Perhaps the country or the realm are as good synonyms as one can find and I would be prepared to accept the organised community as coming as near to a definition as one can get.

Who, then, is to determine what is and what is not prejudicial to the safety and interests of the State? The question more frequently arises as to what is or is not in the public interest. I do not subscribe to the view that the Government or a Minister must always or even as a general rule have the last word about that.

But here we are dealing with a very special matter—interfering with a prohibited place which Wethersfield was. The definition in section 3 shows that it must either be closely connected with the armed forces or be a place such that information regarding it or damage to it or interference with it would be useful to an enemy. It is in my opinion clear that the disposition and armament of the armed forces are and for centuries have been within the exclusive discretion of the Crown and that no one can seek a legal remedy on the ground that such discretion has been wrongly exercised. I need only refer to the numerous authorities gathered together in *China Navigation Co Ltd v A-G* [1932] 2 KB 197. Anyone is entitled, in or out of Parliament, to urge that policy regarding the armed forces should be changed; but until it is changed, on a change of Government or otherwise, no one is entitled to challenge it in court.

Even in recent times there have been occasions when quite large numbers of people have been bitterly opposed to the use made of the armed forces in peace or in war. The 1911 Act was passed at a time of grave misgiving about the German menace, and it would be surprising and hardly credible that the Parliament of that date intended that a person who deliberately interfered with vital dispositions of the armed forces should be entitled to submit to a jury that Government policy was wrong and that what he did was really in the best interests of the country, and then perhaps to escape conviction because a unanimous verdict on that question could not be obtained. Of course we are bound by the words which Parliament has used in the Act. If those words necessarily lead to that conclusion then it is no answer that it is inconceivable that Parliament can have so intended. The remedy is to amend the Act. But we must be clear that the words of the Act are not reasonably capable of any other interpretation.

I am prepared to start from the position that, when an Act requires certain things to be established against an accused person to constitute an offence, all of those things must be proved by evidence which the jury accepts, unless Parliament has otherwise provided. But normally such things are facts and where questions of opinion arise they are on limited technical matters on which expert evidence can be called. Here the question whether it is beneficial to use the armed forces in a particular way or prejudicial to interfere with that use would be a political question—a question of opinion on which anyone actively interested in politics, including jurymen, might consider his own opinion as good as that of anyone else. Our criminal system is not devised to deal with issues of that kind. The question therefore is whether this Act can reasonably be read in such a way as to avoid the raising of such issues.

The Act must be read as a whole and paragraphs (*c*) and (*d*) of section 3 appear to me to require such a construction. Places to which they refer become prohibited places if a Secretary of State declares that damage, obstruction or interference there 'would be useful to an enemy'. Plainly it is not open to an accused who has interfered with or damaged such a place to a material extent to dispute the declaration of the Secretary of State and it would be absurd if he were entitled to say or lead evidence to show that, although he had deliberately done something which would be useful to an enemy, yet his purpose was not prejudicial to the safety or interests of the State. So here at least the trial judge must be entitled to prevent the leading of evidence and to direct the jury that if they find that his purpose was to interfere to a material extent they must hold that his purpose was prejudicial. If that be so, then, in view of the matters which I have already dealt with, it appears to me that the same must necessarily apply to the present case.

I am therefore of opinion that the ruling of Havers J excluding evidence was right and that his direction to the jury was substantially correct. . . . I think it was proper to give to the jury a direction to the effect that if they were satisfied that the intention and desire of the accused was to procure the immobilisation of these aircraft in a way which they knew would or might substantially impair their operational effectiveness then the offence was proved and they should convict.

Viscount Radcliffe: . . . When a man has avowed that his purpose in approaching an airfield forming part of a country's defence system was to obstruct its operational activity, what, if any, evidence is admissible on the issue as to the prejudicial nature of his purpose? In my opinion the correct answer is, virtually none. This answer is not surprising if certain considerations that lie behind the protection of official secrets are borne in mind. The defence of the State from external enemies is a matter of real concern, in time of peace as in days of war. The disposition, armament and direction of the defence forces of the State are matters decided upon by the Crown and are within its jurisdiction as the executive power of the State. So are treaties and alliances with other States for mutual defence. An airfield maintained for the service of the Royal Air Force or of the air force of one of Her Majesty's allies is an instrument of defence, as are the airplanes operating from the airfield and their armament.

It follows, I think, that if a man is shown to the satisfaction of the jury to have approached an airfield with the direct purpose of obstructing its operational use, a verdict of guilty must result, provided that they are also satisfied that the airfield belongs to Her Majesty and was at the relevant date part of the defence system maintained by the Crown for the protection of the realm. . . .

[E]ven if all these matters [on which the accused wished to adduce evidence] were to be investigated in court, they would still constitute only various points of consideration on the ultimate general issue, is it prejudicial to the interests of the State to include nuclear armament in its apparatus of defence? I do not think that a court of law can try that issue or, accordingly, can admit evidence upon it. It is not debarred from doing so merely because the issue is what is ordinarily known as 'political'. Such issues may present themselves in courts of law if they take a triable form. Nor, certainly, is it because Ministers of State have any inherent general authority to prescribe to the courts what is or is not prejudicial to the interests of the State. But here we are dealing with a matter of defence of the realm and with an Act designed to protect State secrets and the instruments of the State's defence. If the methods of arming the defence forces and the disposition of those forces are at the decision of Her Majesty's Ministers for the time being, as we know that they are, it is not within the competence of a court of law to try the issue whether it would be better for the country that that armament or those dispositions should be different.

Lords Hodson, Devlin and **Pearce** delivered concurring speeches.

Appeal dismissed.

NOTES

1. Lord Devlin's reasoning differed in some respects from the other members of the House, although he concurred in the result. The question whether an act was for a prejudicial purpose was for the jury to consider, and they should take account of all the consequences of the act which were reasonably to be apprehended. There was no justification for restricting the relevant consequences, as the Crown had argued, to those which occurred in the prohibited place or which could otherwise be regarded as 'immediate'. Whether the general immobilisation of nuclear weapons would be a good thing for the country would have had to be considered by the jury had it not been for the words 'to the safety and interests of the State'. In this context, the term 'state' denoted 'the organs of government' (p. 807), which in relation to the armed forces meant the Crown:

'So long as the Crown maintains armed forces for the defence of the realm, it cannot be in its interests that any part of them should be immobilised' (p. 807).

It was for the Crown to indicate, and not for the jury to determine, what its 'interests' were:

'Suppose that the statute made it an offence to be in a factory for a purpose prejudicial to the interests of the owner, I should not allow the accused to cross-examine the owner to suggest that the factory was unprofitable and that the sooner it closed down the better for the owner, nor to call expert evidence to show that his views were economically sound. A man is entitled to decide for himself how he should govern his life, his business and his other activities, and when the decision is taken, it dictates what his interests are. It is not to the point to say that if the decision had been a better one, his interests would have been different.' (p. 807) . . .

'In a case like the present, it may be presumed that it is contrary to the interests of the Crown to have one of its airfields immobilised just as it may be presumed that it is contrary to the interests of an industrialist to have his factory immobilised . . . But the presumption is not irrebuttable. Men can exaggerate the extent of their interests and so can the Crown. It is the duty of the Courts to be as alert now as they have always been to prevent abuse of the prerogative. But in the present case there is nothing at all to suggest that the Crown's interest in the proper operation of its airfields is not what it may naturally be presumed to be or that it was exaggerating the perils of interference with their effectiveness' (p. 809).

2. The decision in this case has been severely criticised by D. Thompson ([1963] PL 201). He points out that Parliament had been assured by two Attorneys-General (Sir Gordon Hewart and Sir Hartley Shawcross) and Lord Maugham LC that s. 1 applied only to espionage, and that the expression 'for a purpose prejudicial to the safety or interests of the state' would be for the courts to construe and determine. Indeed the current form of section 6 of the 1920 Act was adopted in order to limit its operation to cases of espionage, and linking it with s. 1 of the 1911 Act was thought to have that effect. While reference to proceedings in Parliament was not permissible as an aid to construction, 'it was indefensible on the part of the Attorney-General to press arguments upon the courts to give the section a wider meaning' (pp. 210–211).

Thompson also challenges the legal reasoning (cf. J. C. Smith and B. Hogan, *Criminal Law* (6th edn, 1988), pp. 839–841; G. Marshall in R. F. Bunn and W. G. Andrews (eds), *Politics and Civil Liberties in Europe* (1967), pp. 5–35).

3. Apart from *Chandler v DPP*, prosecutions under s. 1 have generally been confined to cases of espionage. It is certainly open to the Attorney-General to have regard to assurances given to Parliament in exercising the discretion whether to authorise a prosecution. However, the then Attorney-General, Sir Reginald Manningham-Buller said:

'In considering whether or not to prosecute, I must direct my mind to the language and spirit of the Acts and not to what my predecessors said about them many years ago in an entirely different context' (657 HC Deb 5 April 1962 col 611).

Persons convicted for contravening or conspiring to contravene section 1 since the war include Dr Fuchs, the members of the Portland 'spy ring', George Blake (sentenced to fourteen years' imprisonment on each of five separate counts the first three to run consecutively: (1961) 45 Cr App Rep 292), and W. J. C. Vassall (see the Report of the Radcliffe Tribunal of Inquiry, (Cmnd 2009, 1963). In 1978 proceedings were instituted under ss. 1 and 2 against John Berry, a former corporal in the Intelligence Corps, and two journalists, Duncan Campbell and Crispin Aubrey. B communicated information to the journalists concerning Britain's Signals Intelligence Organization. Mars-Jones J hinted that the use of charges under s. 1 was oppressive in a non-spying case. None of the defendants intended to use the information to assist an enemy. Counsel for the prosecution offered to prove that the defendants' conduct was prejudicial, notwithstanding that the burden of proof as to this matter technically lay on the defendants under s. 1(2). Mars-Jones J was unable to accept this arrangement in view of the clear words of s. 1(2). The Attorney-General decided to drop the s. 1 charges (*The Times*, 31 October 1978). See further, below p. 462. Other matters of significance were (1) the proceedings for contempt of court brought in relation to the disclosure of the identity of one of the witnesses (see above, pp. 392–394; and (2) the revelation that the potential jurors had been vetted for their potential loyalty or disloyalty (see H. Harman and J. Griffith, *Justice Deserted* (NCCL, 1979)).

More recent prosecutions under s. 1 have related to espionage. In 1982, Geoffrey Arthur Prime pleaded guilty to seven counts on an indictment charging offences under s. 1. He had been engaged in signals intelligence work at Government Communications Headquarters (GCHQ) in Cheltenham and had passed a vast quantity of information concerning this work to the Russian Intelligence Service. He was sentenced to a total of 35 years' imprisonment (consecutive terms of 14, 14 and 7 years' imprisonment with other terms concurrent), with an additional 3 years for indecently assaulting three young girls. The Lord Chief Justice commented that he had done 'incalculable harm to the interests of security of this country . . . and of our friends and allies'. An application for leave to appeal against the sentence was dismissed ('*The Times*, 11, 12 November 1982; *The Sunday Times*, 14 November 1982; *R v Prime* (1983) 5 Cr App Rep (S) 127; Report of the Security Commission, May 1983 (Cmnd 8876); Statement by the Prime Minister, 42 HC Deb 12 May 1983 cols 431–434, written answer). Shortly afterwards, a Canadian economist, Professor Hugh Hambleton, admitted passing secret NATO documents to KGB agents and was sentenced to 10 years' imprisonment (*The Times*, 30 November and 1, 2, 3, 7, 8 December 1982). Lance-Corporal Philip Aldridge pleaded guilty to doing an act preparatory to the commission of an offence under s. 1 in abstracting a highly classified document with the intention of communicating it to the Russian Intelligence Service; he was sentenced to four years' imprisonment (*The Times*, 19 January 1983; Report of the Security Commission, March 1984 (Cmnd 9212, 1984)). Michael Bettaney, an MI5 counter-espionage officer, was convicted of six charges under s. 1(1) of the 1911 Act and four under s. 7 of the 1920 Act, and was sentenced to a total of 23 years' imprisonment. He had communicated some secret information to the Russians and had collected much more for the purposes of becoming an agent for them. Lord Lane CJ ruled that most of the trial should be held *in camera*, apart from a brief opening statement by the Attorney–General and the delivery of the verdict (*The Sunday Times*, 25 March 1984; *The Times*, 9, 11, 17 April 1984). Sentences of 10 years' imprisonment on two East Germans who settled in England with a view to espionage were upheld in *R v Schulze and Schulze* (1986) 8 Cr App Rep (S) 463.

In 1984 and 1985, prosecutions under s. 1 of eight young servicemen from the Cyprus Signals Intelligence base, for passing official secrets in return for 'favours', failed after lengthy trials estimated to have cost £5m, doubts having been cast on the reliability of confessions they had made. In one case the judge had ruled the defendant's statements inadmissible, the rest were acquitted by the jury. An inquiry by David Calcutt QC (Cmnd. 9781, 1986) found that they had all or most of the time been held in custody unlawfully, and interrogated oppressively (albeit without the use of sensory deprivation techniques or physical violence). Ex gratia payments were made. See A. W. Bradley, [1986] PL 363 and the Report of the Security Commission, October 1986, Cmnd. 9923. The Report criticised the lack of knowledge of officers and senior NCOs about the behaviour of the young servicemen under their command and recommended, inter alia, that so far as possible postings of very young servicemen and women to sensitive locations should be avoided.

In 1993, Michael Smith, who worked for two top defence research companies, was sentenced to 25 years' imprisonment for spying for the Russians (*The Times*, 19 November 1993).

(c) UNAUTHORISED DISCLOSURES: THE OFFICIAL SECRETS ACT 1989

The Official Secrets Act 1989 replaced, at long last, s. 2 of the Official Secrets Act 1911. Section 2, as amended by the Official Secrets Act 1920, was the product of a highly convoluted piece of draftsmanship. However, its essence was simple and breathtakingly wide in its scope. Section 2(1) penalised the disclosure of official information by D to anyone 'other than a person to whom he is authorised to communicate it, or a person to whom it is in the interest of the State his duty to communicate it'. The categories of protected information in question included any information which was obtained in contravention of the Act or owing to D's position or former position as an office holder under the Crown or as a government contractor. Section 2(2) penalised the receipt of any information by D, knowing or having reasonable ground to believe that the information was communicated to him in contravention of the Act, unless he proved that the communication was contrary to his desire.

The breadth of these provisions was widely regarded as unsatisfactory. The Franks Committee on s. 2 of the Official Secrets Act 1911 (Cmnd. 5104, 1972) recommended the repeal of s. 2 and its replacement by narrower and more specific provisions. Various bills, both government and private member's, designed to secure reform, failed. Ultimately, the government, following the White Paper, *Reform of Section 2 of the Official Secrets Act 1911* (Cm. 408, 1988), secured the passage of the Official Secrets Act 1989. The extent to which this would prove in practice to be a liberalising measure was, however, hotly debated.

NOTES

1. The breadth of s. 2 of the 1911 Act was often emphasised. Sir Lionel Heald, a former Attorney-General, commented that s. 2 'makes it a crime, without any possibility of defence, to report the number of cups of tea consumed per week in a government department, or the details of a new carpet in the minister's room. . . . The Act contains no limitation as to materiality, substance or public interest' (*The Times*, 20 March 1970, cited in *D. G. T. Williams* (1978) pp. 160–1). 'The Act has been variously described as a "blunderbuss", a "mangy old sheep", a "punt gun", and a "fishing net"; and that only includes the more recent and polite terms' (J. Michael, *The Politics of Secrecy* (1982) p. 36). The Franks Committee noted that over 2,000 differently worded charges could be brought under s. 2 and described it as a 'catch-all' (Cmnd. 5104, p. 14) and a 'mess' (ibid, p. 37). The only significant safeguard was that a prosecution under the Acts might only be brought by or with the consent of the Attorney-General (1911 Act, s. 8). Summaries of prosecutions under the Acts (including all since 1945) are given in the Franks Report, Appendix II (1911–1971); 955 HC Deb 1 August 1978 cols 230–231, written answer (1972–1978); and 36 HC Deb 9 February 1983 cols 367–368, written answer (1978–1983). See also D. Hooper, *Official Secrets* (1987), Appendix I, which summarises many of the cases brought under s. 2 between 1915 and 1987.

About a third of the prosecutions between 1945 and 1983 concerned the improper disclosure of police information for the purposes of crime or to journalists or private detectives. Among the others, in 1981 a DHSS employee and a private detective were convicted summarily of communicating and retaining personal information about members of the public stored on the DHSS computer and a former detective sergeant, Edward Dodsworth, was fined £750 for disclosing information concerning the 'Yorkshire Ripper' inquiry to a journalist (*The Times*, 28 May 1981). In 1982, Rhona Ritchie, formerly a second secretary at the British embassy in Tel Aviv, was convicted under s. 2 for wrongfully communicating confidential information to her lover, an official in the Egyptian embassy in Tel Aviv. She was given a nine month suspended prison sentence; he was promoted (see *The Times*, 30 November 1982; Report of the Security Commission, 46 HC Deb 28 July 1983 cols 517–523, written answer). In 1983, Robin Gordon-Walker, a government information officer, was fined £500 for failing to take reasonable care of classified Foreign Office papers, which he lost on the way to Heathrow: a report on the papers and extracts from them were published in the magazine *City Limits* and on the same day the Crown obtained an injunction banning further publication. This was a rare example of a prosecution under s. 2(1)(c), which made it an offence to fail to take reasonable care of official documents or information (*The Times*, 7 January 1983; cf. *R v Treu* (1979) 49 CCC (2d) 222, Qu CA).

In *Loat v Andrews* [1986] ICR 679, the Divisional Court held that a civilian who operated police computers under the supervision of police officers was thereby employed 'under' a person who held office under Her Majesty. Accordingly, he was properly convicted under s. 2 of the 1911 Act and s. 7 of the 1920 Act for passing information from the computer about the location of recent burglaries to the representative of a burglar alarm company.

2. In some cases prosecutions under s. 2 either failed spectacularly or attracted criticism even though successful. In *R v Aitken* (1971) a confidential assessment of the situation in Nigeria during the Biafran conflict, written by the Defence Adviser at the British High Commission in Lagos, was passed through various hands to Jonathan Aitken, a journalist (subsequently an MP and cabinet minister). Aitken passed copies to the *Sunday Telegraph*, which gave the report wide coverage. The report contained information at variance with statements made by the government to Parliament and included various criticisms of the Nigerian government. Aitken, Brian Roberts (the editor of the *Sunday Telegraph*) and others were prosecuted for various offences under s. 2, but acquitted by the jury. The trial judge, Caulfield J, ruled that mens rea was a necessary requirement and left to the jury Aitken's defence that it was his duty in the interest of the State to communicate the report to the *Sunday Telegraph*. His Lordship's suggestion that the government consider whether s. 2 'should be pensioned off' and replaced by a provision of greater clarity was followed by the appointment of the Franks Committee.

The defendants in *R v Berry* (the *ABC* case: A. Nicol, [1979] Crim LR 284 and C. Aubrey, *Who's Watching You?* (1981)) were John Berry, a former corporal in the Intelligence Corps, Duncan Campbell, a journalist with the *New Statesman*, and Crispin Aubrey, a journalist with *Time Out*. B communicated information to the journalists concerning Britain's signals intelligence (SIGINT) organisation. They were convicted under s. 2. The journalists were given conditional discharges, and B a six month suspended prison sentence. The outcome, given that charges were originally brought under s. 1 (see above, p. 459) was less than a triumph for the prosecution. As to mens rea, Mars-Jones J rejected B's argument that he was entitled to be acquitted if he honestly believed that in the interests of the State it was his duty to communicate the information to C. What was in the interests of the State was a wholly inappropriate question for a jury. He followed *R v Fell* [1963] Crim LR 207 where the Court of Criminal Appeal stated that the offence under s. 2(1) 'is absolute and is committed whatever the document contains, whatever the nature of the disclosure and whether or not the disclosure is prejudicial to the state'. Contra, *R v Aitken*, above.

Also controversial was the prosecution of Sarah Tisdall, a clerk in the Foreign Secretary's private office, who leaked copies of two documents to *The Guardian*. One related to the delivery of cruise missiles to the RAF base at Greenham Common, naming the date when the first would arrive, and the other concerned the security arrangements at the base connected with the deliveries. Both were classified SECRET. The text of the first was printed in *The Guardian*; the other was destroyed. The Court of Appeal, on the application of the Secretary of State for Defence, ordered *The Guardian* to return the photocopy of the first document: *Secretary of State for Defence v Guardian Newspapers Ltd* [1984] Ch 156 (see above, p. 436). From markings on the photocopy the police were able to narrow down the source to one small group of civil servants, including Miss Tisdall, and she confessed. She subsequently explained that she had learned from the memorandum that the Secretary of State proposed to delay the announcement of the arrival of the cruise missiles until after they had arrived, to make the announcement at the end of question time when there would be no time for him to answer questions, and to leave the House immediately. She regarded this as objectionable 'political subterfuge'. She pleaded guilty to a charge under s. 2 and was sentenced to six months' imprisonment. The judge stated that she had known that she was committing a criminal offence and a breach of trust. It was not possible to decide that such an action would do no harm. If secret documents were leaked for publication, that would weaken the confidence of this country's allies in the trustworthiness of the government. Unless other arrangements could be made in time, people fundamentally opposed to the missiles would have obstructed the arrival, and this had involved the danger of violent confrontation.

'[U]nfortunately in these days it is necessary to make perfectly clear by example that any person in contact with material classified as secret, who presumes to give himself permission to decide to publish, will not escape from a custodial sentence, however honestly he thought it would do no harm' (*The Guardian*, 24 March 1984; *The Times*, 26 and 27 March 1984).

When questioned in the House of Commons the Prime Minister said that no government could carry on its business unless it could trust civil servants to keep classified documents to themselves (57 HC Deb 27 March 1984 col 138). The Attorney-General defended his decision to prosecute and indicated that it was based on the same general guidelines on the criteria for prosecution which he had issued in March 1983 and which were applicable to all criminal cases (see (1983) 127 Sol Jo 134). He used s. 2 'sparingly and only when absolutely necessary' (58 HC Deb 9 April 1984, cols 13–15).

Some critics argued that the prosecution should not have been brought, claiming that the disclosure had caused much political embarrassment rather than constituting a serious threat to national security; a larger number thought that the sentence was excessive. Some expressed surprise that *The Guardian* had not been prosecuted.

Among comments about the sentence, *The Times* (26 March 1984) stated that 'a month's imprisonment, with strict warning that heavier sentences could be expected by anyone else who acted as she had done, . . . would almost certainly have been sufficient to meet . . . [the judge's] own purpose of setting an example.' Lord Hunt, a former member of the Parole Board, argued that, in his experience, exemplary sentences were 'unlikely to have any generally deterrent effect' (*The Times*, 29 March 1984). Sir Douglas Wass, former Joint Head of the Home Civil Service, commented: 'I would have sacked her summarily. But sending her to jug for six months is absurd' (*The Times*, 11 May 1984). The Court of Appeal (Criminal Division) refused Miss Tisdall's application for leave to appeal against the sentence (*The Times*, 10 April 1984). See *Hooper*, Chap. 11 and R. Pyper, (1985) 57 *Political Quarterly* 72.

3. The last straw for the government was the acquittal of Clive Ponting: *R v Ponting* [1985] Crim LR 318.[1] Ponting was an Assistant Secretary at the Ministry of Defence. In the belief that the government was deliberately misleading Parliament, the Select Committee on Foreign Affairs and the public on the circumstances of the sinking of the Argentinian warship, the *General Belgrano*, during the Falklands campaign, he sent two documents to Tam Dalyell MP, a known critic of the government on the *Belgrano* sinking. Ponting was prosecuted under s. 2(1) of the

1 See generally, C. Ponting, *The Right to Know* (1985) and (1987) 14 JLS 366; R. Norton-Taylor, *The Ponting Affair* (1985); *Hooper*, Chap. 12; R. Thomas, 'The British Official Secrets Act 1911–1939 and the Ponting Case', [1986] Crim LR 491 and pp. 95–122, of R. Chapman and M. Hunt (eds), *Open Government* (1987); G. Drewry, [1985] PL 203; N. MacCormick in P. Wallington and R. Merkin (eds), *Essays in Memory of F. H. Lawson* (1986); and, on parliamentary privilege in the context of 'leaks' to Parliament, A. I. L. Campbell, [1985] PL 212.

1911 Act. His defence was that Dalyell was a person to whom it was his duty in the interest of the state to pass the information. It was accepted that the leak itself had not damaged national security. McCowan J directed the jury that mens rea was not required under s. 2(1) and that the interests of the state were synonymous with the interests of the government of the day (following the approach of Lord Reid in *Chandler v DPP*, above, p. 456, on the interpretation of 'interests of the state' under s. 1). The jury acquitted, notwithstanding the fact that the judge's ruling on the law had favoured the prosecution. It has been suggested that the acquittal 'no doubt related to a jury refusing to be browbeaten by a judge, prosecution handling the case less adroitly than it should, a feeling that the Government was actively involved in manipulating an outcome, and the Attorney-General appearing to prejudge guilt in a radio broadcast. And Ponting's lawyers mounted a very successful campaign outside the courtroom' (P. Birkinshaw, *Freedom of Information* (1988), p. 81).

Following Ponting's acquittal, it was noteworthy that no prosecution under the Official Secrets Acts was brought in respect of revelations by Cathy Massiter, formerly an officer in the Security Service, and an anonymous retired MI5 clerk, in a Channel 4 programme, *MI5's Official Secrets*, prepared by the 20/20 Vision production company. Massiter claimed that MI5 tapped telephones of trade unionists involved in strike action, and, in one case had burgled the house of Ken Gill, general secretary of TASS, in order to plant a bugging device; persistently disregarded the rules as to telephone tapping (see below, p. 572); had placed leading CND members under surveillance; and had maintained files on NCCL officers such as Patricia Hewitt, its general secretary, and Harriet Harman, its legal officer. The terms of reference of MI5 provided that its task was the defence of the realm from espionage, sabotage and subversion; the peaceful activities of CND and the NCCL did not fall within this definition. The IBA initially banned the programme, pending a decision as to whether Massiter and the producers would be prosecuted. It was, however, screened in the House of Commons and elsewhere. On 5 March 1985, Sir Michael Havers announced his decision that there would be no prosecution, and the programme was shown on 8 March. Lord Bridge, following an inquiry begun on 28 February and concluded on 6 March, reported that all authorised taps had in fact been properly authorised. Given the large number of taps (6,129) that apparently had to have been checked, and the point that the allegations were that there had been *un*authorised taps, Lord Bridge's report was widely criticised. (In fact all that Lord Bridge had done was to look at the files of the individuals (about a dozen) named by Massiter: see Lustgarten and Leigh, op. cit., p. 489.)

The prosecutions of Sarah Tisdall and Clive Ponting can also be contrasted with the lack of any prosecution of two cabinet ministers, Cecil Parkinson and Leon Brittan. Parkinson was alleged to have revealed information to his lover, Sarah Keays, concerning the Falklands campaign (Parkinson being then a member of the War Cabinet) (see *Hooper*, Chap. 15). Brittan, as Secretary of State for Trade and Industry, authorised the selective leaking of a confidential letter written by the Solicitor-General to Michael Heseltine, the Secretary of State for Defence, in connection with the proposed sale of Westland Helicopters, in order to discredit Heseltine. Heseltine was in favour of a bid by a European consortium, and Brittan a bid by Sikorski/Fiat. The Prime Minister maintained subsequently that she was not aware of the proposed leak (her Press Secretary, Bernard Ingham, was); Brittan was, however, under the impression that the leak had her approval. On one view, the disclosure was not in breach of s. 2 as it was authorised by a cabinet minister; the better view is, however, that such authorisation could only properly have been given by the Prime Minister. The Westland affair led to the resignation of both ministers. See M. Linklater and D. Leigh, *Not with Honour: The Inside Story of the Westland Scandal* (1986); *Hooper*, Chap. 15; R. Austin, (1986) 39 CLP 269.

4. The Official Secrets Act 1989[1] (above, p. 446) was based on the government's White Paper, *Reform of Section 2 of the Official Secrets Act 1911* (Cm 408, 1988).

The Act narrows the scope of protection of official information by the criminal law to categories: (1) security and intelligence; (2) defence; (3) international relations; (4) information obtained in confidence from other states or international organisations; (5) information disclosure of which is likely to result in the commission of an offence or to impede the prevention or detection of offences; and (6) information obtained by special investigations authorised by warrant (1989 Act ss. 1–4). The categories reflect the post-Franks consensus that Cabinet documents and economic information should not automatically be protected. The unauthorised disclosure of information in these categories by a Crown servant or government contractor is an offence. In categories (2) to (5), the disclosure must be 'damaging' in the ways specified in the sections. The tests for 'damage' are more precise but less strict than those envisaged by Franks, and there is no system of ministerial certification (except, in effect, under s. 1(4)(b): see P. Birkinshaw, *Reforming the Secret State* (1990), pp. 11, 20). In category (1), the unauthorised disclosure or purported disclosure by a member of the security and intelligence services, and others notified that they are subject to this provision, of information obtained by virtue of their work, is an offence without any proof of damage; damage must, however, be proved where a disclosure of information relating to security and intelligence is otherwise made by a Crown servant or government contractor. Similarly, there is no requirement to prove damage in respect of category (6). It is also an offence in certain circumstances for any person to make, without authority, (1) a damaging disclosure of protected information that has come into his possession following an unauthorised disclosure by a current (not former) Crown servant or government contractor, or the breach of a requirement of confidence imposed by a Crown servant or government contractor, or (2) a disclosure of information acquired as a result of a breach of s. 1 of the 1911 Act (1989 Act s. 5). It is an offence for a person to make, without authority, a damaging disclosure of information in categories (1) to (3) communicated in confidence by the UK to another state or an international organisation and disclosed without the authority of that state or organisation (1989 Act, s. 6). There are also offences relating to the retaining or failure to take care of protected documents and articles and disclosing information which facilitates unauthorised access to protected material (1989 Act, s. 8). Mere receipt of information is no longer an offence.

It is generally a defence for the accused to prove that he did not know that the information fell into the protected category in question, or that disclosure would be damaging in the relevant sense (1989 Act, ss. 1(5), 2(3), 3(4), 4(4), (5)). Under s. 5, it is for the prosecution to prove that the accused knew or had reasonable cause to believe that the information was protected against disclosure and that disclosure would be damaging (s. 5(2), (3); cf. similar provisions in s. 6(2)). There is no defence that disclosure was in the public interest or (except in the limited situation covered in s. 6(3)) that the information had previously been published. As to the first, the

---

1 See generally on the 1989 Act, J. A. G. Griffith, (1989) 16 JLS 273; S. Palmer, [1990] PL 243; Annotations by J. Mayhew and P. O'Higgins in *Current Law Statutes Annotated 1989*; I. N. Stevens, (1989) Denning LJ 169; P. Birkinshaw, *Reforming the Secret State* (1990) pp. 15–29. On the White Paper, see S. Palmer, [1988] PL 523.

government argued that such a defence would make the law less clear and was in any event inappropriate given that the criminal law would be confined to 'information which demonstrably requires its protection in the public interest'; as to the second, prior publication should at most be regarded as a factor in determining whether a disclosure would be damaging in a relevant way (White Paper, paras. 58–64).

The narrowing of the scope of the criminal law in the area can only be welcomed. There are, however, a number of criticisms that were forcefully articulated during the passage of the Bill but which left the government unmoved. These include:

(1) the blanket prohibition of disclosure of information by members of the security and intelligence services irrespective of damage;
(2) the blanket prohibition of disclosure of information derived from e.g. authorised telephone tapping, also irrespective of damage;
(3) the absence of any public interest defence and any general defence of prior publication;
(4) the imposition of the burden of proof to establish certain defences on the accused, contrary to normal principle.

As to (1), the absolute prohibition would extend to prevent, for example, the exposure of unlawful behaviour and thus is to be contrasted with the law of confidence (below, pp. 474–492). Amendments proposed to prevent the Secretary of State from unreasonably withholding consent to the disclosure of information (e.g. in memoirs) by a former member of the security and intelligence services, or to establish a Publications Review Board with power to authorise disclosure, were rejected . A mechanism for considering complaints has, however, been established by the Security Service Act 1989 (below, p. 501), although this falls short of providing independent scrutiny. The absence of a public interest defence is designed to discourage 'whistleblowers'. Again, a mechanism has been created whereby members and former members of the security and intelligence services may approach a 'staff counsellor' with any grievance about their work. The counsellor has unrestricted access to the Prime Minister, and access to all documents, to all levels of management and the Cabinet Secretary (see 121 HC Deb cols 508 (2 November 1987) and 796 (3 November 1987)). Public disclosure is not, however, to be available in the last resort where other avenues have been exhausted.

5. In 1991, Arthur Henry Price and Joseph Terrence Wilson pleaded guilty to making a damaging disclosure to a foreign power. W, a security guard at the VSEL shipyard in Barrow-in-Furness, stole an acoustic tile used on submarines from the yard. W and F (a mini-cab driver) subsequently offered to sell it to a man (Nick) believed to be a Russian for £3m. The man turned out to be a British security agent. W's counsel said that the exercise had been conceived and executed as a joke. 'My indications are that Nick's Russian accent was wholly unconvincing. He kept saying "Ja" as in German, and he couldn't pronounce "Moscow".' The security services had got in touch with W and P via an advert in the local press. W had subsequently seen police officers enter the phone booths they had just left and start dusting for fingerprints. Nevertheless, the matter was not treated as a joke by Brooke J, who sentenced each of them to 15 months' imprisonment. Charges of conspiracy to contravene the 1911 Act were changed to charges under the 1989 Act, with the authority of the Attorney-General. (See the *North-Western Evening Mail*, 8–11 July 1991.)

6. A number of persons and bodies are prescribed under s. 12(1)(f) and (g) of the 1989 Act by the Official Secrets Act 1989 (Prescription) Order 1990 (S.I. 1990 No.

200, as amended by the Intelligence Services Act 1994, Sch. 4, para. 5). These include (under s. 12(1)(f)) employees and Board members of British Nuclear Fuels plc and Urenco Ltd., and members, officers and employees of the UK Atomic Energy Authority and (under s. 12(1)(g)), the Comptroller and Auditor General and the staff of the National Audit office, their Northern Ireland equivalents, officers of the Parliamentary Commissioner for Administration, the Health Service Commissioner and the Northern Ireland P.C.A. not otherwise Crown servants, and a private Secretary to the sovereign.

7. *Civil servants and ministers.* Following the Ponting affair (above, p. 463), the Head of the Home Civil Service, Sir Robert Armstrong, issued Notes for Guidance on *The Duties and Responsibilities of Civil Servants in Relation to Ministers* (reproduced at 74 HC Deb, cols 128–130, written answer, 26 February 1985). The Armstrong Memorandum stated, inter alia, that:

'Civil servants are servants of the Crown. For all practical purposes the Crown in this context means and is represented by the Government of the day. . . . The duty of the individual civil servant is first and foremost to the Minister of the Crown who is in charge of the Department in which he or she is serving. It is the Minister who is responsible, and answerable in Parliament, for the conduct of the Department's affairs. . . .

Civil servants are under an obligation to keep the confidences to which they become privy in the course of their official duties. . . . There is and must be a general duty upon every civil servant, serving or retired, not to disclose, in breach of that obligation, any document or information or detail about the course of business, which has come his or her way in the course of duty as a civil servant.'

However, a civil servant should not be required to do anything unlawful; if he was, the matter should be reported to the permanent head of the Department. A 'fundamental issue of conscience' should be raised with a superior officer or, in the last resort, the permanent head of the Department. The possibility of an appeal to the Head of the Home Civil Service was introduced into a revised version of the memorandum issued in 1987 (123 HC Deb, cols 572–575, written answer, 2 December 1987) following a recommendation of the Treasury and Civil Service Committee (7th Report, *Civil Servants and Ministers: Duties and Responsibilities*, 1985–86 HC 92 I, II: see G. Drewry, [1986] PL 514). This revision also enabled a civil servant to use the procedures where he considers an instruction to be 'improper, unethical or in breach of constitutional conventions, or . . . otherwise inconsistent with the standards of conduct prescribed' in the Armstrong Memorandum (para. 12). Appeals to the Head of the Home Civil Service must be submitted through the Permanent Head of Department or, if that is impracticable or inappropriate, through the Principal Establishment Officer or equivalent. All appeals must be forwarded unless the HoD or PEO considers it vexatious or frivolous; the HoD or PEO may add comments but not amend the appeal itself. If there is insufficient time to complete these steps where, for example, events develop quickly, the individuals concerned, having satisfied themselves that there is no alternative action available to them under the procedure, 'should carry out the request or instruction in question and immediately afterwards formally record in writing their dissent and the reasons for it'. The minute should then be sent to the HoD, who must advise the Departmental Minister, if appropriate, and inform the Head of the Home Civil Service (*Civil Service Management Code*, paras. 7.7.5 to 7.7.7). The appeal procedures apply where a civil servant has a 'crisis of confidence, for example in respect of an instruction to do something which appears to be illegal or improper or which may raise questions of maladministration' (para. 7.7.5). Thus the Code appears to contemplate in urgent cases requiring a civil servant to obey what may turn out to be an illegal requirement first and ask questions afterwards. Is that acceptable?

The appeal procedures have been used once, in connection with conscientious reservations about a government department's approach to theoretical research (5th Report of the Treasury and Civil Service Committee, *The Role of the Civil Service*, 1994–95 HC 27-I, p. xxvi). The Armstrong Memorandum is reproduced in the *Civil Service Management Code*, 4.1 Annex A. This code replaced the *Civil Service Pay and Conditions of Service Code* in 1993. The Code also states, inter alia, that civil servants:

— 'are expected to be prepared to make available official information which is not held in confidence within Government, in accordance with Government policy and departmental or agency instructions. They must not, without relevant authorisation, disclose official information which has been communicated in confidence within Government or received in confidence from others' (para. 4.2.2);
— 'must continue to observe this duty of confidentiality after they have left Crown employment' (para. 4.2.3);
— 'must not seek to frustrate the policies or decisions of Ministers by the use or disclosure outside the Government of any information to which they have had access as civil servants' (para. 4.2.6).

The Treasury and Civil Service Committee has concluded that the Armstrong Memorandum appears increasingly dated and cannot be viewed as an authoritative summary of the constitutional position and role of the civil service; the appeal procedures do not command the confidence of all civil servants. They recommended the introduction of a Civil Service Code and a final appeal to an independent and strengthened body of Civil Service Commissioners (5th Report, 1994–95 HC 27-I, pp. xxi–xxxiv) and this has been accepted by the government: *The Civil Service: Taking Forward Continuity and Change* (Cm. 2748, 1995).[1]

These arrangements, as with the Official Secrets Act 1989 and unlike the law of breach of confidence (below, pp. 474–492), provide no protection to the 'whistleblower' who reveals information in the public interest. In other jurisdictions, legislation specifically protects those who reveal such matters as violations of the law, gross wastage of funds, and threats to public health and safety.[2]

8. *Other means of maintaining security.* The Franks Committee proposals were shaped by their view that s. 2 was properly described as 'a long stop or a safety net. . . . Section 2 is not the main protection: its function is to provide an extra margin of protection, in case other measures should fail' (Franks Committee, p. 30). The 'other measures' are discussed in Chap. 5 of the Committee's report. They point out that a civil servant who is regarded as unreliable, or who tends to overstep the mark and talk too freely, may fail to obtain promotion or may be given less important and attractive jobs. Breach of the formal discipline code (see n. **7**, above) may lead to penalties ranging from reprimand to dismissal. (Action taken for the purpose of safeguarding national security may not form the basis of a complaint for unfair dismissal under the Employment Protection (Consolidation) Act 1978: ibid., Sch. 9, para. 2(1), and a certificate purporting to be signed by or on behalf of a Minister is conclusive evidence that the action was taken for that purpose: ibid., Sch. 9, para. 2(2).) See

---

1 For further discussion, see O. McDonald, *The Future of Whitehall* (1992), Chap. 5 (on 'Civil Service Ethics'); R. A. Chapman (ed.), *Ethics in Public Service* (1993); N. Lewis and D. Longley, 'Ethics and the Public Service' [1994] PL 596.
2 See R. A. Parker, 'Whistleblowing legislation in the United States: a preliminary appraisal' (1988) 41 *Parliamentary Affairs* 149; G. Zellick, [1987] PL 311; (1989) 63 ALJ 592; J. G. Starke, 'Public Service Whistleblowers' (1991) 65 ALJ 205, 252; R. Fox, 'Protecting the Whistleblower' (1993) 15(2) Adelaide LR 137; J. McMillan, 'The Whistleblower versus the Organisation—Who Should be Protected?' in T. Campbell and W. Sadurski (eds), *Freedom and Communication* (1994) and see 'Canadian law reform report on "Whistleblowing" by public servants' (1987) 61 ALJ 319.

generally Y. Cripps, [1983] PL 600 and below, p. 499. The government's recruitment procedures are designed to ensure fitness for appointment. There are vetting procedures to check the suitability of those with access to particularly sensitive information (see below, pp. 492–499). Precautions are also taken to ensure the physical security of documents according to their classification. Following the report of the Security Commission on the Prime case (Cmnd. 8876, 1983: see above p. 459) random searches have been made of staff leaving GCHQ premises.

In 1994, the government revised its approach to the classification of documents, as explained by John Major in a written answer (240 HC Deb, 23 March 1994, cols 259–260):

'**The Prime Minister**: In recent years, the nature of the threats of Government security has changed. While some of the traditional threats to national security may have somewhat reduced, others have not. The security of Government is also increasingly threatened by, for example, theft, copying and electronic surveillence, as well as by terrorism.

To ensure that one approach to security reflects current threats, the Government have recently completed a review of arrangements for the management of protective security in Departments and agencies. This has recommended a new protective marking system for documents which will help identify more precisely those which need protecting, enabling them to be protected more effectively according to their value. The new system will also be more closely related to the code of practice on Government information announced in the Government's White Paper on openness [below, p. 512].

In addition, the review has concluded that existing security measures should be examined closely to ensure they are necessary in relation to today's threats; that commercially available security equipment should be more widely used; and that personnel vetting enquiries should be streamlined particularly in routine cases. Overall, the aim is to give departments and agencies, and management units within them, greater responsibility for assessing the nature of the risks they face and for making decisions, within the framework of common standards of protection, about the security measures they need to put in place. Substantial cost savings will result.

The first stage of the implementation of the proposals of this review will be the introduction of a new protective marking system with effect from 4 April 1994 alongside the code of practice on access to Government information. The new definitions, which will allow fewer Government documents to be classified, particularly at the higher levels, are set out. The other elements of the new approach to protective security will be put in place in due course.

The four categories of protective marking: Definitions

The markings to be allocated to any asset, including information, will be determined primarily by reference to the practical consequences that are likely to result from the compromise of that asset or information. The levels in the new protective marking system are defined as follows:

TOP SECRET: the compromise of this information or material would be likely: to threaten directly the internal stability of the United Kingdom or friendly countries; to lead directly to widespread loss of life; to cause exceptionally grave damage to the effectiveness or security of United Kingdom or allied forces or to the continuing effectiveness of extremely valuable security or intelligence operations; to cause exceptionally grave damage to relations with friendly governments; to cause severe long-term damage to the United Kingdom economy.

SECRET: the compromise of this information or material would be likely: to raise international tension; to damage seriously relations with friendly governments; to threaten life directly, or seriously prejudice public order, or individual security or liberty; to cause serious damage to the operational effectiveness or security of United Kingdom or allied forces or the continuing effectiveness of highly valuable security or intelligence operations; to cause substantial material damage to national finances or economic or commercial interests.

CONFIDENTIAL: the compromise of this information or material would be likely: materially to damage diplomatic relations (ie cause formal protest or other sanction); to prejudice individual security or liberty; to cause damage to the operational effectiveness or security of United Kingdom or allied forces or the effectiveness of valuable security or intelligence operations; to work substantially against national finances or economic and commercial interests; substantially to undermine the financial viability of major organisations; to impede the investigation or facilitate the commission of serious crime; to impede seriously the development or operation of major government policies; to shut down or otherwise substantially disrupt significant national operations.

RESTRICTED: the compromise of this information or material would be likely: to affect diplomatic relations adversely; to cause substantial distress to individuals; to make it more difficult to maintain the operational effectiveness or security of United Kingdom or allied forces; to cause financial loss or loss of earning potential to or facilitate improper gain or advantage for individuals or companies; to prejudice the investigation or facilitate the commission of crime; to breach proper undertakings to maintain the confidence of information provided by third parties; to impede the effective development or operation of government policies; to breach statutory restrictions on disclosure of information; to disadvantage government in commercial or policy negotiations with others; to undermine the proper management of the public sector and its operations.'

3 DA Notices

Defence Press and Broadcasting Advisory Committee

GENERAL INTRODUCTION TO THE DEFENCE ADVISORY NOTICES

1. Public discussion of the United Kingdom's defence and counter-terrorist policy and overall strategy does not impose a threat to national security and is welcomed by Government. It is important however that such discussion should not disclose details which could damage national security. The DA Notice System is a means of providing advice and guidance to the media about defence and counter-terrorist information the publication of which would be damaging to national security. The system is voluntary, it has no legal authority and the final responsibility for deciding whether or not to publish rests solely with the editor or publisher concerned.
2. DA Notices are issued by the Defence, Press and Broadcasting Advisory Committee (DPBAC), an advisory body composed of senior civil servants and editors from national and regional newspapers, periodicals, news agencies, television and radio. It operates on the shared belief that there is a continuing need for a system of guidance and advice such as the DA Notice System, and that a voluntary, advisory basis is best for such a system.
3. The 1993 edition of the DA Notices recognises the changed circumstances following the break-up of the Soviet Union and Warsaw Pact and the UK's involvement in smaller-scale conflicts, the undiminished and currently high threat from terrorist attacks and the risk of proliferation of weapons of mass destruction. It also takes account of the continued targeting of the UK by foreign intelligence services.
4. Compliance with the DA Notice system does not relieve the editor of responsibilities under the Official Secrets Acts.
5. The Secretary DPBAC (the DA Notice Secretary) is the servant of the Government and the Press and Broadcasting sides of the Committee. He is available at all times to Government departments and the media to give advice on the system and, after consultation with Government departments as appropriate, to help in assessing the relevance of a DA Notice to particular circumstances.

HOW THE SYSTEM WORKS

Purpose

1. The Defence, Press and Broadcasting Advisory Committee oversees a voluntary code which operates between those Government departments which have responsibilities for national security and the media; using as its vehicle the DA Notice system.

Composition

2. The Committee is chaired by the Permanent Under-Secretary of State for Defence.
3. Membership may be varied from time to time by agreement. At present there are three members representing Government departments, one each from the Home Office, the Ministry of Defence and the Foreign and Commonwealth Office.
4. At present there are eleven members nominated by the media; three by the Newspaper Publishers Association, two by the Newspaper Society, two by the Periodical Publishers Association and one each by the Scottish Daily Newspaper Society, the Press Association, the British Broadcasting Corporation and Independent Television News. The Publishers Association was invited in 1982 to nominate a representative but declined.
5. The press and broadcasting members select one of their number as Chairman of their side and Vice Chairman of the Committee. He leads for their side at Committee meetings and provides a point of day-to-day contact for them and for the Secretary.

6. The Committee is served by a full-time Secretary and part-time Deputy Secretary who substitutes in the Secretary's absence on leave etc.

Responsibility of membership

7. The Press and Broadcasting members respond to proposals from the government departments concerned and advise the Committee on those areas of information in which it may be reasonable to invite guidance reflecting the interests of national security. Official proposals may not be issued in DA Notice form without the consent of the Press and Broadcasting members.

Meetings

8. The Committee normally have a Spring and Autumn meeting each year. It reviews the Secretary's report of guidance sought and advice offered over the previous six months. It also reviews the content of the DA Notices as necessary to ensure that amendments are made to meet the changing needs of national security.

DA Notices

9. The DA Notices are intended to provide to national and provincial newspaper editors, to periodicals editors, to radio and television organisations and to relevant book publishers general guidance on those areas of national security which the Government considers it has a duty to protect. The Notices, together with a General Introduction, details of the Committee and how to contact the Secretary, are widely distributed to editors, producers and publishers and also to officials in Government departments, military commanders, chief constables and some institutions. The Notices have no legal standing and advice offered within their framework may be accepted or rejected partly or wholly.

10. Although the system is normally applied through the standing DA Notices, should it be found necessary to issue a DA Notice on a specific matter, the Government department concerned will agree a draft of the proposed Notice with the Secretary who, from his experience, can advise upon the form and content which are likely to make it acceptable to the press and broadcasting members. The Secretary will then seek the agreement of both sides of the DPBAC to the draft and, if it is obtained, issue the text as a DA Notice.

Secretary DPBAC

11. The Secretary is normally a retired two-star officer from the Armed Forces, employed as a Civil Servant on the budget of the Ministry of Defence. He is the servant of the Government and Press and Broadcasting sides of the Committee, a fact which is recognised by the Vice Chairman being involved in the process of his selection. Similar arrangements apply for the Deputy Secretary who is also normally a retired service officer.

12. The Secretary (or Deputy Secretary) is available at all times to Government departments and the media to give advice on the system, taking into account the general guidance given to him by the Committee. DA Notices are necessarily drafted in somewhat general terms and it is the application of a DA Notice to a particular set of circumstances on which the Secretary is expected to give guidance, consulting as necessary with appropriate departmental officials. He is not invested with the authority to give rulings nor to advise on considerations other than national security.

NOTES

1. The pre-1965 position as to D Notices is discussed in D. G. T. Williams, *Not in the Public Interest* (1965) pp. 80–87. The Report of the (Radcliffe) Committee of Privy Counsellors (Cmnd. 3309, 1967) concerned the revelation by Chapman Pincher in the *Daily Express* that private cables and telegrams were vetted by the security authorities. The government claimed, and persisted in claiming notwithstanding the contrary view expressed by the Radcliffe Committee, that this contravened two D Notices (see the White Paper, Cmnd. 3312 (1967), P. Hedley and C. Aynsley, *The D Notice Affair* (1967) and Chapman Pincher, *Inside Story* (1978)).

Chapman Pincher suggested that the minority of government representatives on the Committee almost always got their way and that prior to 1967, journalists tended to rely heavily on the view of the Secretary as to whether a story was covered by a D Notice, confident that clearance by the Secretary would cover them in practice as regards possible prosecution under the Official Secrets Act (although it could not affect the legal position). According to Pincher, the affair, 'effectively destroyed the D-notice system', which he thereafter 'virtually ignored' (op. cit., p. 244). This seems to stem from his loss of confidence in the changed role of the Secretary and the emphasis in the revised arrangements that clearance by the Secretary would not affect the position under the Official Secrets Act. In the Oral Evidence to the Franks Committee the Chairman of the Defence, Press and Broadcasting Committee, Sir James Dunnett, stated that it would be an 'extreme case' in which the DPP would want to prosecute an editor where clearance had been given, and that the Attorney-General in deciding to give his fiat under the Act would wish to know whether the editor had been in touch with the Secretary to the Committee (p. 57).

2. The system was reviewed by the House of Commons Defence Committee in its Third Report, 1979–80 HC 773, 640 i–v, *The D Notice System*. The Committee concluded that the system as at present constituted was failing to fulfil the role for which it was created, but concluded that it was necessary that advice should continue to be given to the press and broadcasting on what could be disseminated without damage to national security, and (by the Conservative majority) that the Committee should be retained at least until there was a fundamental review of the Official Secrets Acts. An internal review led to the publication of a Revised Introduction to the D Notices and a reduction in their number from 12 to 8, phrased in more general terms. See J. Jaconelli, [1982] PL 37.

3. The D Notice system was again put under strain in 1987 over a proposed BBC radio series, *My Country Right or Wrong*, which was to examine issues raised by the *Spycatcher* litigation. On the eve of the first programme, Henry J granted an interlocutory injunction sought by the Attorney-General to prevent the broadcasting of any interviews with or information derived from members or past members of the security and intelligence services relating to any aspect of the work of the services, including their identity as members. The terms of the injunction were subsequently modified by agreement to permit fair and accurate reports of proceedings in Parliament and the courts (see D. Oliver in D. Kingsford-Smith and D. Oliver (eds), *Economical with the Truth* (1990), p. 43). The injunction was subsequently continued by Owen J: *A-G v BBC* (1987) Times 18 December, applying the *American Cyanamid* principles (below, p. 485) and *A-G v Guardian Newspapers* [1987] 1 WLR 1248 (below, pp. 485–487). (The injunction was lifted in respect of one of the programmes in March 1988, and the others in May 1988, after the scripts had been vetted: see P. Thornton, *Decade of Decline* (1989), pp. 9–11.) The programme's producer had previously obtained an indication from the Secretary to the D Notice Committee that he did not advise that the broadcast would be potentially prejudicial to national security (the nearest the Secretary gets to giving a 'clearance': see D. Fairley, (1990) 10 OJLS 430, 431, 435). The apparent contradiction was subsequently explained by the Secretary on the basis that his advice concerned the lack of a threat to national security whereas the government's claim to an injunction was based on breach of confidence. It was, he said, 'a pity that the two issues have become entwined' (*The Guardian* 10 December 1987). Nevertheless, as Fairley comments,

'Given that the policy argument upon which the existence and scope of the alleged duty of confidentiality depended in *Spycatcher* was that of potential damage to national security, it is hard to see how there can be two separate issues. . . .' ((1990) 10 OJLS 430, 435).

He argues (ibid.) that the real difference lay in the approach to the assessment of the implications for national security; the Secretary was concerned solely with prejudice arising from the *contents* of the particular document or broadcast, whereas the government was asserting the broader basis for the duty of confidence also put forward in *A-G v Guardian Newspapers Ltd (No 2)* (below, p. 477) and *Lord Advocate v Scotsman Publications Ltd* (below, p. 487), namely that there would be long term damage to the security service as a result of media pressure on MI5 members for similar disclosures, and loss of confidence in MI5 on the part of other countries and potential informants. This broader basis was ultimately rejected by the House of Lords in the *Scotsman* case (below, p. 487) (where, again, the editor had obtained a 'no advice' response from the D Notice Secretary before publication). This does not, however, remove the difficulty: Fairley argues that a claim to confidentiality based on the *contents* of a document would be likely to succeed before the courts even if the Secretary had offered 'no advice' ((1990) 10 OJLS 430, 437).

Fairley's survey of newspaper and periodical editors showed that formal participation in the system was fairly widespread, but actual use infrequent: most of the respondents

'felt that, in the light of recent Government behaviour, they would be more influenced by the advice of their lawyers than by that of the Secretary of the D Notice Committee' ((1990) 10 OJLS 430, 438).

The effect of the government's increasing use of the civil courts has been to 'marginalize the significance of the D Notice system and to destroy the atmosphere of mutual trust' between press and government on which voluntary prior restraint can be based. Nevertheless, evidence of a 'no advice' response by the Secretary still may be of relevance to a civil action, or to a prosecution under the Official Secrets Act 1989 (e.g. in respect of an argument that there was no reasonable cause to believe that damage would result from disclosure of information), or in respect of sentence (Fairley, op. cit., pp. 439, 440).

4. The system was again reviewed by the Committee in 1992, leading to a number of changes (see *The Defence Advisory Notices: A Review of the D Notice System* (Ministry of Defence Open Government Document No. 93/06)). The aim of the review 'was to make the system more transparent and relevant in the light of international changes and the increased emphasis on openness in Government' (op. cit.). The Notices were revised, reduced in number from 8 to 6 and renamed Defence Advisory Notices 'better to reflect the voluntary and advisory nature of the system'. The introduction and procedure are set out above (p. 470). The content of the six DA Notices is now freely published. They cover: No. 1, Operations, Plans and Capabilities; No. 2, Non-nuclear weapons and operational equipment; No. 3, Nuclear weapons and equipment; No. 4, Ciphers and Secure Communications; No. 5, Identification of Specific Installations; and No. 6, United Kingdom Security and Intelligence Services. Each notice is accompanied by a stated 'rationale'. For example, DA Notice No. 6 states:

'**United Kingdom Security and Intelligence Services**

1. It is requested that information falling within the following categories should not be published without first seeking advice:
   a. specific operations, sources and methods of the Security Service, SIS and GCHQ and those involved with them, the application of those methods, including the interception of communications, and their targets; the same applies to those engaged on sensitive counter-terrorist operations;
   b. the identities, whereabouts and tasks of staff employed by these services or engaged on such work, including details of their families and home addresses, and any other information, including photographs, which could assist terrorist or other hostile organisations to identify a target (with the exception of details which have been officially announced);

c. the addresses and telephone numbers used by these services, other than those which have been the subject of an official announcement.

2. It is also requested that where other individuals are likely targets for attacks by terrorists, care should be taken not to publish details of their home addresses without first seeking advice.

Rationale

3. Identified staff from the intelligence and security services, others engaged on sensitive counter-terrorist operations and those who are likely targets for attack are at real risk from terrorists. Security and intelligence operations, contacts and techniques are easily compromised, and therefore need to be pursued in conditions of secrecy. Publicity about an operation which is in train finishes it. Publicity given even to an operation which has been completed, whether successfully or not, may well deny the opportunity for further exploitation of a capability, which may be unique against other hostile and illegal activity. The disclosure of identities can prejudice past, present and future operations. Even inaccurate speculation about the source of information on a given issue can put intelligence operations (and, in the worst cases, lives) at risk and/or lead to the loss of information which is important is the interests of national security.'

5. Some journalists and writers have expressly disassociated themselves from the D Notice system. J. Bloch and P. Fitzgerald, authors of *British Intelligence and Covert Action* (1983), which named British officials it claimed were, or had been, involved in British Intelligence, 'freely admit ignoring D Notice No. 6 (and several others besides). Neither ourselves nor our publishers are represented on the D Notice Committee, nor are we party to any other cosy agreement between Whitehall and the media' (letter to *The Times*, 25 April 1984). In response to this book preparatory work was apparently undertaken on a draft law to prohibit the naming in public of MI5 and MI6 officers and agents (P. Hennessy, *The Times*, 9 April 1984). The Whitehall consensus on this book was that 'its publication was "indefensible" as unlike most other studies of British intelligence, it covered events and personalities "so near to the present day", as one insider put it' (ibid.). The DA Notice 'request' that nothing shall be published without reference to the DPBAC Secretary which identifies officers can be contrasted with the US Intelligence Identities Protection Act 1982, which makes it an offence for persons with access to classified information intentionally to reveal the identities of covert agents working outside the USA for agencies such as the CIA, and for other persons to do so 'in the course of a pattern of activities intended to identify and expose covert agents . . . with reason to believe that such activities would impair or impede the foreign intelligence activities of the United States' (50 USC § 421–426). The maximum penalties are (1) $50,000/ten years' imprisonment/both for 'insiders' who have had access to classified information which identifies the agent(s); (2) $25,000/five years' imprisonment/both for 'insiders' who learn the identity as a result of their access to classified information in general; and (3) $15,000/three years' imprisonment/both for 'outsiders'. The legislation is directed at those such as the former CIA agent, Philip Agee, who wished to expose and nullify covert political intervention in the affairs of other countries. The Act's constitutionality is considered by S. D. Charkes, (1983) 83 Colum L Rev 727.

4 Breach of confidence

The use of the law of breach of confidence to protect official secrets was thrown into prominence in the *Spycatcher* litigation, in which the Attorney-General, in a number of jurisdictions throughout the world, sought to restrain the publication of the memoirs of Peter Wright, a former member of MI5. As the chronology set out below shows, the litigation was lengthy and complex, and saw the invocation of the law of contempt as well as the law of confidence against a variety of parties. So far as the UK and the law of breach of confidence was concerned, the matter culminated in the decision of the House of Lords in *A-G v Guardian Newspapers Ltd (No 2)*, below, p. 477.

Chronology of the Spycatcher litigation

1985	A-G commences proceedings in NSW against Peter Wright and Heinemann Publishers Australia Pty Ltd seeking an injunction restraining publication of *Spycatcher* or, alternatively, an account of profits. Pending trial, undertakings restraining publication of the book or disclosure of information obtained by W as a MI5 officer were given by W, H, and Malcolm Turnbull, the solicitor acting for them.
22, 23 June 1986	*The Observer* and *The Guardian* publish articles reporting on the forthcoming hearing.
27 June 1986	Ex parte injunctions against the newspapers granted by Macpherson J.
11 July 1986	Inter partes injunctions against the newspapers granted by Millett J, restraining them from disclosing any information obtained by W as an MI5 officer or from attributing any information about MI5 to him, with certain exceptions: [1989] 2 FSR 3.
25 July 1986	The Court of Appeal upholds the injunctions, with slight modifications: *A-G v Observer Newspapers Ltd* (1986) Times, 26 July, [1986] NLJ Rep 799, [1989] 2 FSR 15.
17 November 1986	NSW trial begins before Powell J.
13 March 1987	A-G's action dismissed: (1987) 8 NSWLR 341. Undertakings continued pending appeal.
27 April 1987	Articles published by *The Independent*, the *Evening Standard* and the *London Daily News* based on the contents of the book.
3 May 1987	The *Washington Post* publishes extracts from the manuscript of *Spycatcher*.
7 May 1987	Proceedings for contempt commence against the newspapers in respect of the articles of 27 April.
14 May 1987	Viking Penguin Inc announces its intention to publish *Spycatcher* in the U.S.A.
2 June 1987	Sir Nicolas Browne-Wilkinson V-C holds on a preliminary point of law that contempt proceedings against *The Independent*, the *Evening Standard* and the *London Daily News* cannot succeed as they were not party to the Millett injunctions: *A-G v Newspaper Publishing plc* [1988] Ch 333 (above, p. 411).
12 July 1987	*The Sunday Times*, having obtained a copy of the manuscript from Viking Penguin in the US, publishes extracts from *Spycatcher* in its second edition.

13 July 1987	A-G commences contempt proceedings against *The Sunday Times*. *Spycatcher* on sale in the US.
15 July 1987	(reasons given 17 July) Court of Appeal allows an appeal against the decision of the Vice-Chancellor, holding that the publication of the 27 April articles could constitute contempt: *A-G v Newspaper Publishing plc* [1988] Ch 333 (above, pp. 411–412).
16 July 1987	A-G granted interlocutory injunction restraining *The Sunday Times* from publishing further extracts from *Spycatcher*.
22 July 1987	Sir Nicolas Browne-Wilkinson V-C discharges the Millett injunctions on the ground that the book was now 'freely available to all': *A-G v Guardian Newspapers Ltd* [1987] 3 All ER 316.
24 July 1987	Millett injunctions restored by the Court of Appeal: [1987] 3 All ER 316, in modified form, permitting the publication of a 'summary in very general terms' of W's allegations.
30 July 1987	(reasons given 13 August) Appeal to the House of Lords dismissed by 3–2. Millett injunctions endorsed, and without the exceptions, inter alia, permitting the reporting of what had taken place in open court in the Australian proceedings: [1987] 3 All ER 316.
2 August 1987	*News on Sunday* publishes an article with quotations from the *Sunday Times* article of 12 July.
24 September 1987	New South Wales Court of Appeal dismisses A-G's appeal: *A-G for the United Kingdom v Heinemann Publishers Australia Pty Ltd* (1987) 75 ALR 353.
29 September 1987	Deane J in the High Court of Australia declines to grant temporary injunctions pending the hearing of an application by the A-G for leave to appeal to the HCA.
12, 13 October 1987	*Spycatcher* goes on sale in Ireland and Australia.
27 October 1987	A-G commences proceedings against *The Sunday Times* for breach of confidence.
21 December 1987	Scott J discharges the interlocutory injunctions against *The Observer* and *The Guardian*, holds that *The Sunday Times* is accountable for profits resulting from the first extract of the serialisation on 12 July, and refuses the A-G an injunction restraining future publication of information derived from W: *A-G v Guardian Newspapers Ltd (No 2)* [1990] 1 AC 109, [1988] 3 All ER 545.
10 February 1988	Decision of Scott J upheld by Court of Appeal: *A-G v Guardian Newspapers Ltd (No 2)* [1990] 1 AC 109, [1988] 3 All ER 545, 594.

2 June 1988   High Court of Australia dismisses A-G's appeal: *A-G (UK) v Heinemann Publishers Australia Pty Ltd (No 2)* (1988) 165 CLR 30, 78 ALR 449.

13 October 1988   Decision of Scott J and the Court of Appeal upheld by the House of Lords (4–1): [1990] 1 AC 109, [1988] 3 All ER 545, 638 (below).

8 May 1989   *The Independent, The Sunday Times* and the *News on Sunday* each fined £50,000 for contempt by Morritt J; contempt proceedings against the *Evening Standard*, the *London Daily News* and *The Daily Telegraph* dismissed: *A-G v Newspaper Publishing plc*: [1989] FSR 457.

27 February 1990   Decision of Morritt J upheld by the Court of Appeal: *A-G*
11 April 1991   *v Newspaper Publishing plc* (1990) Times, 28 February; and the House of Lords: *A-G v Times Newspapers Ltd* (above, p. 410).

26 November 1991   European Court of Human Rights gives judgment in *Observer and Guardian v UK* (Series A No. 216) and *Sunday Times v UK (No 2)* (Series A No. 217) (below, p. 487).

A-G v Guardian Newspapers Ltd (No 2) [1990] 1 AC 109, [1988] 3 All ER 545, House of Lords

The facts are set out in Lord Keith's speech. The House of Lords held:

(1) (Lord Griffiths dissenting) that the publications by *The Observer* and *The Guardian* on 22 and 23 June 1986 did not constitute an actionable breach of confidence, as they were not damaging to the public interest;

(2) that *The Sunday Times'* publications on 12 July 1987 did constitute a breach of confidence, for which the Crown was entitled to an account of profits;

(3) that no injunction should lie against (a) *The Observer* and *The Guardian* or (b) (Lord Griffiths dissenting) *The Sunday Times* to prevent any future serialisation of the book; neither would the newspaper be liable for any account of profits: the information was now in the public domain;

(4) that the A-G was not entitled to any general injunction restraining future publication of information derived from Mr Wright or other members or ex-members of the security service.

Lord Keith of Kinkel: My Lords, from 1955 to 1976 Peter Wright was employed in a senior capacity by the counter-espionage branch of the British Security Service known as MI5. In that capacity he acquired knowledge of a great many matters of prime importance to the security of the country. Following his retirement from the service he went to live in Australia and later formed the intention of writing and publishing a book of memoirs describing his experiences in the service. He wrote the book in association with a man named Paul Greengrass, and it was accepted for publication by Heinemann Publishers Pty. Ltd., the Australian subsidiary of a well known English publishing company. The Attorney-General in right of the Crown, learning of the intended publication of the book, instituted in 1985 proceedings in New South Wales against Mr. Wright and Heinemann Publishers claiming an injunction to restrain the publication in Australia or alternatively an account of profits. Pending trial, Mr. Wright, the publishers and their solicitors gave undertakings not to reveal the contents of the book. The Attorney-General's action failed before Powell J and again before the Court of Appeal of New South Wales. Special leave to appeal was granted by the High Court of Australia, but the respondents were released from their undertakings. So the book was published in Australia on 13 October 1987, under the title of *Spycatcher*. On 2 June 1988 the High Court dismissed the Attorney-General's appeal upon the sole ground that an Australian court should not accept jurisdiction to enforce an obligation of confidence owed to a foreign government so as to protect that government's intelligence secrets and confidential political information. In the meantime *Spycatcher* had on 14 July 1987 been published in the United States of America by Viking Penguin Inc., a subsidiary of an English publishing company. Her Majesty's Government had been advised that, in view of the terms of the First Amendment to the United States Constitution, any attempt to restrain publication there would be certain to fail. Publication also took place in Canada, the Republic of Ireland, and a number of other countries. Her Majesty's Government decided that it was impracticable and undesirable to take any steps to prevent the importation into the United Kingdom of copies of the book, and a very substantial number of copies have in fact been imported. So the contents of the book have been disseminated world-wide and anyone in this country who is interested can obtain a copy without undue difficulty.

. . . The issues raised in the litigation are thus summarised in the judgment of Sir John Donaldson M.R. in the Court of Appeal, ante, pp. 180H–181C:

'(1) Were the "Observer" and "The Guardian" in breach of their duty of confidentiality when, on 22 and 23 June 1986, they respectively published articles on the forthcoming hearing in Australia? If so, would they have been restrained from publishing if the Attorney-General had been able to seek the assistance of the court? . . . (2) Was "The Sunday Times" in breach of its duty of confidentiality when, on 12 July 1987 it published the first extract of an intended serialisation of *Spycatcher*? . . . (3) Is the Attorney-General now entitled to an injunction (a) in relation to the "Observer" and "The Guardian" and (b) in relation to "The Sunday Times" with special consideration to further serialisation? . . . (4) Is the Attorney-General entitled to an account of the profits accruing to "The Sunday Times" as a result of the serialisation of *Spycatcher*? . . . (5) Is the Attorney-General entitled to some general injunction restraining future publication of information derived from Mr. Wright or other members or ex-members of the Security Service?'

As regards issue (1) Scott J. and the majority of the Court of Appeal (Dillon and Bingham L.JJ.; Sir John Donaldson M.R. dissenting) held that the publication of the articles in question was not in breach of an obligation of confidence.

On issue (2) Scott J. and the majority of the Court of Appeal (Bingham L.J. dissenting) held that the publication of the first extract from *Spycatcher* was in breach of an obligation of confidence.

Upon issue (3) Scott J. and the Court of Appeal held that the Attorney-General was not entitled to an injunction against the 'Observer' and 'The Guardian' nor (Sir John Donaldson M.R. dissenting) against further serialisation of *Spycatcher* by 'The Sunday Times'.

As to issue (4) Scott J. and the majority of the Court of Appeal (Bingham L.J. dissenting) decided this in favour of the Attorney-General.

Issue (5) was decided against the Attorney-General both by Scott J. and by the Court of Appeal.

The Attorney-General now appeals to your Lordships' House upon all the issues on which he failed below. 'The Sunday Times' cross-appeals against the decision on account of profits.

The Crown's case upon all the issues which arise invokes the law about confidentiality. So it is convenient to start by considering the nature and scope of that law. The law has long recognised that an obligation of confidence can arise out of particular relationships. Examples are the relationships of doctor and patient, priest and penitent, solicitor and client, banker and customer. The obligation may be imposed by an express or implied term in a contract but it may also exist independently of any contract on the basis of an independent equitable principle of confidence: *Saltman Engineering Co Ltd v Campbell Engineering Co Ltd* (1963) 65 RPC 203. It is worthy of some examination whether or not detriment to the confider of confidential information is an essential ingredient of his cause of action in seeking to restrain by injunction a breach of confidence. Presumably that may be so as regards an action for damages in respect of a past breach of confidence. If the confider has suffered no detriment thereby he can hardly be in a position to recover compensatory damages. However, the true view may be that he would be entitled to nominal damages. Most of the cases have arisen in circumstances where there has been a threatened or actual breach of confidence by an employee or ex-employee of the plaintiff, or where information about the plaintiff's business affairs has been given in confidence to someone who has proceeded to exploit it for his own benefit: an example of the latter type of case is *Seager v Copydex Ltd* [1967] 1 WLR 923. In such cases the detriment to the confider is clear. In other cases there may be no financial detriment to the confider, since the breach of confidence involves no more than an invasion of personal privacy. Thus in *Duchess of Argyll v Duke of Argyll* [1967] Ch 302 an injunction was granted against the revelation of marital confidences. The right to personal privacy is clearly one which the law should in this field seek to protect. If a profit has been made through the revelation in breach of confidence of details of a person's private life it is appropriate that the profit should be accounted for to that person. Further, as a general rule, it is in the public interest that confidences should be respected, and the encouragement of such respect may in itself constitute a sufficient ground for recognising and enforcing the obligation of confidence even where the confider can point to no specific detriment to himself. Information about a person's private and personal affairs may be of a nature which shows him up in a favourable light and would by no means expose him to criticism. The anonymous donor of a very large sum to a very worthy cause has his own reasons for wishing to remain anonymous, which are unlikely to be discreditable. He should surely be in a position to restrain disclosure in breach of confidence of his identity in connection with the donation. So I would think it a sufficient detriment to the confider that information given in confidence is to be disclosed to persons whom he would prefer not to know of it, even though the disclosure would not be harmful to him in any positive way.

The position of the Crown, as representing the continuing government of the country may, however, be regarded as being special. In some instances disclosure of confidential information entrusted to a servant of the Crown may result in a financial loss to the public. In other instances such disclosure may tend to harm the public interest by impeding the efficient attainment of proper governmental ends, and the revelation of defence or intelligence secrets certainly falls into that category. The Crown, however, as representing the nation as a whole, has no private life or personal feelings capable of being hurt by the disclosure of confidential information. In so far as the Crown acts to prevent such disclosure or to seek redress for it on confidentiality grounds, it must necessarily, in my opinion, be in a position to show that the disclosure is likely to damage or has damaged the public interest. How far the Crown has to go in order to show this must depend on the circumstances of each case. In a question with a Crown servant himself, or others acting as his agents, the general public interest in the preservation of confidentiality, and in encouraging other Crown servants to preserve it, may suffice. But where the publication is proposed to be made by third parties unconnected with the particular confidant, the position may be different. The Crown's argument in the present case would go to the length that in all circumstances where the original disclosure has been made by a Crown servant in breach of his obligation of confidence any person to whose knowledge the information comes and who is aware of the breach comes under an equitable duty binding his conscience not to communicate the information to anyone else irrespective of the circumstances under which he acquired the knowledge. In my opinion that general proposition is untenable and impracticable, in addition to being unsupported by any authority. The general rule is that anyone is entitled to communicate anything he pleases to anyone else, by speech or in writing or in any other way. That rule is limited by the law of defamation and other restrictions similar to these mentioned in article 10 of the Convention for the Protection of Human Rights and Fundamental Freedoms (1953) (Cmd. 8969). All those restrictions are imposed in the light of considerations of public interest such as to countervail the public interest in freedom of expression. A communication about some aspect of government activity which does no harm to the interests of the nation cannot, even where the original disclosure has been made in breach of confidence, be restrained on the ground of a nebulous equitable duty of conscience serving no useful practical purpose.

There are two important cases in which the special position of a government in relation to the preservation of confidence has been considered. The first of them is *A-G v Jonathan Cape Ltd* [1976] QB 752. That was an action for injunctions to restrain publication of the political diaries of the late Richard Crossman, which contained details of Cabinet discussions held some ten years previously, and also of advice given to Ministers by civil servants. Lord Widgery C.J. said, at pp. 770–771:

'In these actions we are concerned with the publication of diaries at a time when 11 years have expired since the first recorded events. The Attorney-General must show (a) that such publication would be a breach of confidence; (b) that the public interest requires that the publication be restrained, and (c) that there are no other facets of the public interest contradictory of and more compelling than that relied upon. Moreover, the court, when asked to restrain such a publication, must closely examine the extent to which relief is necessary to ensure that restrictions are not imposed beyond the strict requirement of public need.'

Lord Widgery went on to say that while the expression of individual opinions by Cabinet Ministers in the course of Cabinet discussions were matters of confidence, the publication of which could be restrained by the court when clearly necessary in the public interest, there must be a limit in time after which the confidential character of the information would lapse. Having read the whole of volume one of the diaries he did not consider that publication of anything in them, ten years after the event, would inhibit full discussion in the Cabinet at the present time or thereafter, or damage the doctrine of joint Cabinet responsibility. He also dismissed the argument that publication of advice given by senior civil servants would be likely to inhibit the frankness of advice given by such civil servants in the future. So in the result Lord Widgery's decision turned on his view that it had not been shown that publication of the diaries would do any harm to the public interest.

The second case is *Commonwealth of Australia v John Fairfax & Sons Ltd* (1980) 147 CLR 39. That was a decision of Mason J. in the High Court of Australia, dealing with an application by the Commonwealth for an interlocutory injunction to restrain publication of a book containing the texts of government documents concerned with its relations with other countries, in particular the government of Indonesia in connection with the 'East Timor Crisis'. The documents appeared to have been leaked by a civil servant. Restraint of publication was claimed on the ground of breach of confidence and also on that of infringement of copyright. Mason J. granted an injunction on the latter ground but not on the former. Having mentioned, at p. 51, an argument for the Commonwealth that the government was entitled to protect information which was not public property, even if no public interest is served by maintaining confidentiality, he continued, at pp. 51–52:

'However, the plaintiff must show, not only that the information is confidential in quality and that it was imparted so as to import an obligation of confidence, but also that there will be "an unauthorised use of that information to the detriment of the party communicating it" (*Coco v A N Clark (Engineers) Ltd* [1969] RPC 41, 47). The question then, when the executive government seeks the protection given by equity, is: What detriment does it need to show?

'The equitable principle has been fashioned to protect the personal, private and proprietary interests of the citizen, not to protect the very different interests of the executive government. It acts, or is supposed to act, not according to standards of private interest, but in the public interest. This is not to say that equity will not protect information in the hands of the government, but it is to say that when equity protects government information it will look at the matter through different spectacles.

'It may be a sufficient detriment to the citizen that disclosure of information relating to his affairs will expose his actions to public discussion and criticism. But it can scarcely be a relevant detriment to the government that publication of material concerning its actions will merely expose it to public discussion and criticism. It is unacceptable in our democratic society that there should be a restraint on the publication of information relating to government when the only vice of that information is that it enables the public to discuss, review and criticise government action.

'Accordingly, the court will determine the government's claim to confidentiality by reference to the public interest. Unless disclosure is likely to injure the public interest, it will not be protected.

'The court will not prevent the publication of information which merely throws light on the past workings of government, even if it be not public property, so long as it does not prejudice the community in other respects. Then disclosure will itself serve the public interest in keeping the community informed and in promoting discussion of public affairs. If, however, it appears that disclosure will be inimical to the public interest because national security, relations with foreign countries or the ordinary business of government will be prejudiced, disclosure will be restrained. There will be cases in which the conflicting considerations will be finely balanced, where it is difficult to decide whether the public's interest in knowing and in expressing its opinion, outweighs the need to protect confidentiality.'

I find myself in broad agreement with this statement by Mason J. In particular I agree that a government is not in a position to win the assistance of the court in restraining the publication of information imparted in confidence by it or its predecessors unless it can show that publication would be harmful to the public interest.

In relation to Mr. Wright, there can be no doubt whatever that had he sought to bring about the first publication of his book in this country, the Crown would have been entitled to an injunction restraining him. The work of a member of MI5 and the information which he acquires in the course of that work must necessarily be secret and confidential and be kept secret and confidential by him. There is no room for discrimination between secrets of greater or lesser importance, nor any room for close examination of the precise manner in which revelation of any particular matter may prejudice the national interest. Any attempt to do so would lead to further damage. All this has been accepted from beginning to end by each of the judges in this country who has had occasion to consider the case and also by counsel for the respondents. It is common ground that neither the defence of prior publication nor the so called 'iniquity' defence would have availed Mr. Wright had he sought to publish his book in England. The sporadic and low key prior publication of certain specific allegations of wrongdoing could not conceivably weigh in favour of allowing publication of this whole book of detailed memoirs describing the operations of the Security Service over a lengthy period and naming and describing many members of it not previously known to be such. The damage to the public interest involved in a publication of that character, in which the allegations in question occupy a fairly small space, vastly outweighs all other considerations. The question whether Mr. Wright or those acting for him would be at liberty to publish *Spycatcher* in England under existing circumstances does not arise for immediate consideration. These circumstances include the world-wide dissemination of the contents of the book which has been brought about by Mr. Wright's wrongdoing. In my opinion general publication in this country would not bring about any significant damage to the public interest beyond what has already been done. All such secrets as the book may contain have been revealed to any intelligence services whose interests are opposed to those of the United Kingdom. Any damage to the confidence reposed in the British Security and Intelligence Services by those of friendly countries brought about by Mr. Wright's actions would not be materially increased by publication here. It is, however, urged on behalf of the Crown that such publication might prompt Mr. Wright into making further disclosures, would expose existing and past members of the British Security and Intelligence Services to harassment by the media and might result in their disclosing other secret material with a view, perhaps, to refuting Mr. Wright's account and would damage the morale of such members by the spectacle of Mr. Wright having got away with his treachery. While giving due weight to the evidence of Sir Robert Armstrong on these matters, I have not been persuaded that the effect of publication in England would be to bring about greater damage in the respects founded upon than has already been caused by the widespread publication elsewhere in the world. In the result, the case for an injunction now against publication by or on behalf of Mr. Wright would in my opinion rest upon the principle that he should not be permitted to take advantage of his own wrongdoing.

The newspapers which are the respondents in this appeal were not responsible for the world-wide dissemination of the contents of *Spycatcher* which has taken place. It is a general rule of law that a third party who comes into possession of confidential information which he knows to be such, may come under a duty not to pass it on to anyone else. Thus in *Duchess of Argyll v Duke of Argyll* [1967] Ch 302 the newspaper to which the Duke had communicated the information about the Duchess was restrained by injunction from publishing it. However, in that case there was no doubt but that the publication would cause detriment to the Duchess in the sense I have considered above. In the present case the third parties are 'The Guardian' and the 'Observer' on the one hand and 'The Sunday Times' on the other hand. The first two of these newspapers wish to report and comment upon the substance of the allegations made in *Spycatcher*. They say that they have no intention of serialising it. By virtue of section 6 of the Copyright Act 1956 they might, without infringing copyright, quote passages from the book for purposes of 'criticism or review'. 'The Sunday Times' for their part, wish to complete their serialisation of *Spycatcher*. The question is whether the Crown is entitled to an injunction restraining the three newspapers from doing what they wish to do. This is the third of the issues identified by Sir John Donaldson MR in the court below. For the reasons which I have indicated in dealing with the position of Mr. Wright, I am of the opinion that the reports and comments proposed by 'The Guardian' and the 'Observer' would not be harmful to the public interest, nor would the continued serialisation by 'The Sunday Times'. I would therefore refuse an injunction against any of the newspapers. I would stress that I do not base this upon any balancing of public interests nor upon any considerations of freedom of the press, nor upon any possible defences of prior publication or just cause or excuse, but simply upon the view that all possible damage to the interest of the Crown has already been done by the publication of *Spycatcher* abroad and the ready availability of copies in this country.

It is possible, I think, to envisage cases where, even in the light of widespread publication abroad of certain information, a person whom that information concerned might be entitled to restrain publication by a third party in this country. For example, if in the *Argyll* case the Duke had secured the revelation of the marital secrets in an American newspaper, the Duchess could reasonably claim that publication of the same material in England would bring it to the attention of people who would otherwise be unlikely to learn of it and who were more closely interested in her activities than American readers. The publication in England would be more harmful to her than publication in America. Similar considerations would apply to, say, a publication in America by the medical adviser to an English pop group about diseases for which he had treated them. But it cannot reasonably be held in the present case that publication in England now of the contents of *Spycatcher* would do any more harm to the public interest than has already been done.

In relation to future serialisation by 'The Sunday Times' the Master of the Rolls took the view that this newspaper stood in the shoes of Mr. Wright by virtue of the licence which it has been granted by the publishers. The cost of this licence was £150,000 of which £25,000 was to be paid at once and the balance after the serialisation. So Mr. Wright and his publishers will benefit from future instalments of it. The Master of the Rolls considered that there was a strong public interest in preventing Mr. Wright and his publishers from profiting from their wrongdoing. There can be no doubt that the prospect of Mr. Wright receiving further sums of money from 'The Sunday Times' as a reward for his treachery is a revolting one. But a natural desire to deprive Mr. Wright of profit does not appear to me to constitute a legally valid ground for enjoining the newspaper from a publication which would not in itself damage the interests of the Crown. Indeed, it appears that Mr. Wright would have no legally enforceable claim against 'The Sunday Times' for payment, upon the principle of ex turpi causa non oritur actio. Whether 'The Sunday Times' is bound to account for the profits of serialisation I shall consider later.

The next issue for examination is conveniently the one as to whether 'The Sunday Times' was in breach of an obligation of confidentiality when it published the first serialised extract from *Spycatcher* on 12 July 1987. I have no hesitation in holding that it was. Those responsible for the publication well knew that the material was confidential in character and had not as a whole been previously published anywhere. Justification for the publication is sought to be found in the circumstance that publication in the United States of America was known to be imminent. That will not hold water for a moment. It was Mr. Wright and those acting for him who were about to bring about the American publication in breach of confidence. The fact that a primary confidant, having communicated the confidential information to a third party in breach of obligation, is about to reveal it similarly to someone else, does not entitle that third party to do the same. The third party to whom the information has been wrongfully revealed himself comes under a duty of confidence to the original confider. The fact that his informant is about to commit further breaches of his obligation cannot conceivably relieve the third party of his own. If it were otherwise an agreement between two confidants each to publish the confidential information would relieve each of them of his obligation, which would be absurd and deprive the law about confidentiality of all content. The purpose of 'The Sunday Times' was of course to steal a march on the American publication so as to be the first to reveal, for its own profit, the confidential material. The evidence of Mr. Neil, editor of 'The Sunday Times', makes it clear that his intention was to publish his instalment of *Spycatcher* at least a full week before the American publication and this was in the event reduced to two days only because circumstances caused that publication to be brought forward a week. There can be no question but that the Crown, had it learned of the intended publication in 'The Sunday Times', would have been entitled to an injunction to restrain it. Mr. Neil employed peculiarly sneaky methods to avoid this. Neither the defence of prior publication nor that of just cause or excuse would in my opinion have been available to 'The Sunday Times'. As regards the former, the circumstance that certain allegations had been previously made and published was not capable of justifying publication in the newspaper of lengthy extracts from *Spycatcher* which went into details about the working of the Security Service. As to just cause or excuse it is not sufficient to set up the defence merely to show that allegations of wrongdoing have been made. There must be at least a prima facie case that the allegations have substance. The mere fact that it was Mr. Wright, a former member of MI5 who, with the assistance of a collaborator, had made the allegations, was not in itself enough to establish such a prima facie case. In any event the publication went far beyond the mere reporting of allegations, in so far as it set out substantial parts of the text of *Spycatcher*. For example, the alleged plot to assassinate Colonel Nasser occupies but one page of a book, in paperback of 387 pages, and the alleged plot to destabilise Mr Wilson's government about five pages. In this connection it is to be noted that counsel for 'The Sunday Times' accepted that neither of the two defences would have availed Mr. Wright had he sought to publish the text of *Spycatcher* in England. There is no reason of logic or principle why 'The Sunday Times' should have been in any better position acting as it was under his licence.

This leads on to consideration of the question whether 'The Sunday Times' should be held liable to account to the Crown for profits made from past and future serialisation of *Spycatcher*. An account of profits made through breach of confidence is a recognised form of remedy available to a claimant: *Peter Pan Manufacturing Corpn v Corsets Silhouette Ltd* [1963] 3 All ER 402, [1964] 1 WLR 96; cf. *Reading v A-G* [1951] AC 507. In cases where the information disclosed is of a commercial character an account of profits may provide some compensation to the claimant for loss which he has suffered through the disclosure, but damages are the main remedy for such loss. The remedy is, in my opinion, more satisfactorily to be attributed to the principle that no one should be permitted to gain from his own wrongdoing. Its availability may also, in general, serve a useful purpose in lessening the temptation for recipients of confidential information to misuse it for financial gain. In the present case 'The Sunday Times' did misuse confidential information and it would be naive to suppose that the prospect of financial gain was not one of the reasons why it did so. I can perceive no good ground why the remedy should not be made available to the Crown in the circumstances of this case, and I would therefore hold the Crown entitled to an account of profits in respect of the publication on 12 July 1987. I would add that in my opinion 'The Sunday Times', in the taking of the account, is not entitled to deduct in computing any gain the sums paid to Mr. Wright's publishers as consideration for the licence granted by the latter, since neither Mr. Wright nor his publishers were or would in the future be in a position to maintain an action in England for recovery of such payments. Nor would the courts of this country enforce a claim by them to the copyright in a work the publication of which they had brought about contrary to the public interest: cf. *Glyn v Weston Feature Film Co* [1916] 1 Ch 261, 269. Mr. Wright is powerless to prevent anyone who chooses to do so from publishing *Spycatcher* in whole or in part in this country, or to obtain any other remedy against them. There remains of course, the question whether the Crown might successfully maintain a claim that it is in equity the owner of the copyright in the book. Such a claim has not yet been advanced, but might well succeed if it were to be.

In relation to future serialisation of further parts of the book, however, it must be kept in mind that the proposed subject matter of it has now become generally available and that 'The Sunday Times' is not responsible for this having happened. In the circumstances 'The Sunday Times' will not be committing any wrong against the Crown by publishing that subject matter and should not therefore be liable to account for any resultant profits. It is in no different position from anyone else who now might choose to publish the book by serialisation or otherwise.

The next matter for consideration, though the point is not now of any practical importance is whether the 'Observer' and 'The Guardian' were in breach of an obligation of confidence by the publication of their articles on 22 and 23 June 1986. The circumstances were that Mr. Wright and Heinemann and their solicitors had given to the New South Wales court, pending trial of the action there, undertakings not to disclose any information gained by Mr. Wright in the course of his service with MI5. Scott J. found, and it has never been disputed by counsel for the two newspapers, that information about the allegations described in the two articles must have been obtained from someone in the office of the publishers or in that of their solicitors. Scott J. also inferred that the newspapers must have known of the undertakings that had been given. There can be no question of the articles having been a fair and accurate report of proceedings in the New South Wales court. Such a report could only cover matters which had actually been divulged in open court. The newspapers knew that the information in question was of a confidential nature, deriving as it did from Mr. Wright and relating to his experiences in MI5. Some of the allegations, albeit of minor significance, had never previously been published at all. The allegations about Sir Roger Hollis had received quite widespread publicity in various books and newspapers and had been made by Mr. Wright himself on a Granada television programme in July 1984. Allegations about the Nasser plot and the Wilson plot and the bugging of embassies and other places had been made in a number of published books, but had been attributed to Mr. Wright only in an 'Observer' article of 15 March 1985 and another of 9 February 1986, and then only in a somewhat oblique fashion. I do not consider that an injunction would have been granted against publication of the fact that Mr. Wright was repeating in his memoirs the allegations about Sir Roger Hollis, because it was quite well known that he had been making that allegation for a considerable time. The specific attribution to Mr. Wright of the other allegations is perhaps a different matter. But I would regard it as highly doubtful that the publication of that attribution could reasonably be regarded as damaging to the public interest of the United Kingdom in the direct sense that the information might be of value to unfriendly foreign intelligence services, or as calculated to damage that interest indirectly in any of the ways spoken of in evidence by Sir Robert Armstrong. I consider that on balance the prospects are that the Crown would not have been held entitled to a permanent injunction. Scott J. and the majority of the Court of Appeal took that view, and I would not be disposed to differ from them.

The final issue is whether the Crown is entitled to a general injunction against all three newspapers restraining them from publishing any information concerned with the *Spycatcher* allegations obtained by any member or former member of the Security Service which they know or have reasonable grounds for believing to have come from any such member or former member, including Mr. Wright, and also from attributing any such information in any publication to any member or former member of the Security Service. The object of an injunction on these lines is to set up a second line of defence, so to speak, for the confidentiality of the operations of the Security Service. The first and most important line of defence is obviously to take steps to secure that members and ex-members of the service do not speak about their experiences to the press or anyone else to whom they are not authorised to speak. Obviously the Director-General of the Service is in a position to impose a degree of discipline upon the existing members of the service so as to prevent unauthorised disclosures, and it is reasonable to suppose that in any event the vast majority of these members are conscientious and would never consider making such disclosures. In so far as unconscientious ex-members are concerned, in particular Mr. Wright, the position under existing circumstances is more difficult, although measures may now be introduced which are apt to discourage breaches of confidence by such people. There are a number of problems involved in the general width of the injunction sought. Injunctions are normally aimed at the prevention of some specific wrong, not at the prevention of wrongdoing in general. It would hardly be appropriate to subject a person to an injunction on the ground that he is the sort of person who is likely to commit some kind of wrong, or that he has an interest in doing so. Then the injunction sought would not leave room for the possibility that a defence might be available in a particular case. If Mr. Wright were to publish a second book in America or Australia or both and it were to become readily available in this country, as has happened in regard to his first book, newspapers which published its contents would have as good a defence as the respondents in the present case. It would not be satisfactory to have the availability of any defence tested on contempt proceedings. In my opinion an injunction on the lines sought should not be granted.

A few concluding reflections may be appropriate. In the first place I regard this case as having established that members and former members of the Security Service do have a lifelong obligation of confidence owed to the Crown. Those who breach it, such as Mr. Wright, are guilty of treachery just as heinous as that of some of the spies he excoriates in his book. The case has also served a useful purpose in bringing to light the problems which arise when the obligation of confidence is breached by publication abroad. The judgment of the High Court of Australia reveals that even the most sensitive defence secrets of this country may not expect protection in the courts even of friendly foreign countries, although a less extreme view was taken by Sir Robin Cooke P. in the New Zealand Court of Appeal (*A-G v Wellington Newspapers Ltd (No 2)* [1988] 1 NZLR 180). The secrets revealed by Mr. Wright refer to matters of some antiquity, but there is no reason to expect that secrets concerned with matters of great current importance would receive any different treatment. Consideration should be given to the possibility of some international agreement aimed at reducing the risks to collective security involved in the present state of affairs. The First Amendment clearly poses problems in relation to publication in the United States of America, but even there there is the prospect of defence and intelligence secrets receiving some protection in the civil courts, as is shown by the decision of the Supreme Court in *Snepp v United States* (1980) 444 US

507. Some degree of comity and reciprocity in this respect would seem desirable in order to promote the common interests of allied nations. . . .

Lords Brightman, **Goff** and **Jauncey of Tullichettle** delivered generally concurring speeches. **Lord Griffiths** dissented in part.

Appeal and cross-appeal dismissed

NOTES

1. The important question of the circumstances in which the duty of confidence owed by an officer of the security and intelligence services might be overridden was addressed more explicitly by Scott J at first instance, who stated that this

'would not extend to information of which it could be said that, notwithstanding the needs of national security, the public interest required disclosure. Nor, in my opinion, would the duty extend to information which was trivial or useless or which had already been disclosed under the authority of the government' ([1988] 3 All ER 545, 585).

For example, the duty of confidence could not be used to prevent the press from informing the public of the allegation of a plot to assassinate President Nasser, and the press were entitled to report the fact that allegations of an MI5 plot to destabilise the Wilson government had been repeated by an insider:

'The press has a legitimate role in disclosing scandals by government. An open democratic society requires that that be so. If an allegation be made by an insider that, if true, would be a scandalous abuse by officers of the Crown of their powers and functions, and the allegation comes to the attention of the press, the duty of confidence cannot, in my opinion, be used to prevent the press from repeating the allegation. . . . Nor is it, in my opinion, necessarily an answer to say that the allegation should not have been made public but should have been reported to some proper investigating authority. In relation to some, perhaps many, allegations made by insiders, that may be the only proper course open to the press. But the importance to the public of this country of the allegation that members of MI5 endeavoured to undermine and destroy public confidence in a democratically elected government makes the public the proper recipient of the information' ([1988] 3 All ER 545, 588–589).

In the House of Lords, Lord Griffiths denied the existence of an exception for trivia. He was, however, prepared to countenance a public interest defence, while finding it very difficult to envisage the circumstances where the facts would justify it:

'But, theoretically, if a member of the service discovered that some iniquitous course of action was being pursued that was clearly detrimental to our national interest, and he was unable to persuade any senior member of his service or any member of the establishment, or the police, to do anything about it, then he should be relieved of his duty of confidence so that he could alert his fellow citizens to the impending danger' ([1988] 3 All ER 545, 650).

However, no such considerations arose in *Spycatcher*. Lord Goff's position was similar ([1988] 3 All ER 545, 660–661). Lord Keith was more concerned with the point that the public interest defence would not in any event have been open to Mr Wright on the facts.

2. Opinions were expressed on a number of other points that did not directly arise for consideration.

(1) Would Peter Wright or his publishers be restrained now from publishing *Spycatcher* in the UK? Lord Griffiths and Lord Jauncey of Tullichettle were clear that he would, on the ground that his duty of confidence persisted ([1990] 1 AC 109, 271, 293); Lord Goff was very doubtful ([1990] 1 AC 109, 284–289); Lord Keith and Lord Brightman left the point open, but indicated that such an injunction would be based on the principle that he should not be permitted to take advantage of his own wrongdoing, and not on the basis of breach of confidence ([1990] 1 AC 109, 259, 265–266).

(2) The position as to copyright. The House was clear that neither Wright nor his publishers had any copyright in *Spycatcher* that was enforceable in the UK (see Lord Keith at pp. 262–263, Lord Brightman at p. 267, Lord Griffiths at pp. 275–276 and Lord Jauncey at p. 294) and, indeed, it was suggested that copyright might well be vested in the Crown (see Lord Keith at p. 263, Lord Brightman at p. 266, Lord Griffiths at p. 276 and Lord Goff at p. 288). See Y. Cripps, [1989] PL 13, noting that the government had based its claim for an account of profits on breach of confidence and not on a constructive trust imposed on any copyright which Wright or his publishers might hold. In a future case, the law of copyright might prove more fruitful, especially as there is no 'public domain' defence (ibid., pp. 14–15, 19–20).[1]

3. The question for the House of Lords at the 'interlocutory stage' was whether the Millett interlocutory injunctions should be continued or discharged. The general approach to be adopted when considering whether an interlocutory injunction should be granted was laid down by the House of Lords in *American Cyanamid Co v Ethicon Ltd* [1975] AC 396, and requires the judge to consider (1) whether the plaintiff applicant for the injunction has an arguable case in law; (2) if so, whether damages would be an adequate or appropriate remedy should an interlocutory injunction be refused and the plaintiff ultimately succeed at trial; and (3) if not, where the balance of convenience lay. Sir Nicolas Browne-Wilkinson V-C held that since the Millett injunctions had been granted in 1986 there had been a material change in the circumstances, given the publicity given to the Australian trial, the widespread publication of *Spycatcher* material in the foreign press and the publication of *Spycatcher* itself in the US. The government had taken the view that proceedings in the US to restrain publication would be doomed to failure, in the light of the 1st Amendment guarantees of freedom of speech. It also decided not to seek to prevent importation of *Spycatcher*, which could accordingly be obtained in the UK by mail order or simply brought back by travellers (it was apparently a best seller on the bookstall at JF Kennedy Airport). The Vice-Chancellor (*A-G v Guardian Newspapers Ltd* [1987] 3 All ER 316) concluded, with reluctance, that the A-G had an arguable case for permanent injunctions; it was clear that damages would not be an appropriate remedy. However, the balance of convenience was against continuing the injunctions: the public interest in terms of deterring the publication of memoirs by members of the security service was small compared with the public interest in freedom of the press: 'One of the safeguards of our country and our system is to have a press that can search matters out, disclose them, and give rise to informed public discussion. . . . [O]ne should not restrain publication in the press unless it is unavoidable' ([1987] 3 All ER at 331). Moreover, 'If the courts were to make orders manifestly incapable of achieving their avowed purpose, such as to prevent the dissemination of information which is already disseminated, the law would to my mind indeed be an ass' (ibid., p. 332).

The Court of Appeal allowed an appeal by the A-G, and a further appeal by the newspapers was dismissed by the House of Lords (*A-G v Guardian Newspapers Ltd*

---

1 The various stages of the *Spycatcher* litigation are considered by D. G. T. Williams, [1988] CLJ 2, 329, [1989] CLJ 1 and (1989) 12 Dalhousie LJ 209; Y. Cripps, [1989] PL 13 (on breaches of copyright and confidence) and E. Barendt, [1989] PL 204 (on freedom of speech); S. Lee, (1987) 103 LQR 506 (on the interlocutory stage); F. A. Mann, (1988) 104 LQR 497; M. Turnbull and M. Howard (1989) 19 UWALR 117, (1989) 105 LQR 382 (on the Australian decisions); P. Birks, (1989) 105 LQR 501; J. Michael, (1989) 52 MLR 389; B. J. Narain, (1988) 39 NILQ 73; D. Burnet and R. Thomas, (1989) 16 JLS 210; Lord Oliver of Aylmerton, (1989) 23 Israel LR 409; G. Jones (1989) 42 CLP 49; D. Kingsford-Smith and D. Oliver (eds), *Economical with the Truth* (1990), chapters by D. Pannick and R. Austin; K. D. Ewing and C. D. Gearty, *Freedom under Thatcher* (1990), pp. 152–169. See also M. Turnbull, *The Spycatcher Trial* (1988).

[1987] 3 All ER 316) by 3–2 (Lords Brandon, Templeman and Ackner, Lords Bridge and Oliver dissenting). The decision was announced on 30 July with reasons given later. Their Lordships were agreed that the injunctions had originally properly been granted and that the compromise solution adopted by the Court of Appeal, permitting publication of 'a summary in very general terms' of the *Spycatcher* allegations, was unworkable. The majority were agreed that the A-G still had an arguable case for permanent injunctions. Lord Brandon argued that discharge of the injunctions now would cause permanent and irrevocable damage to the A-G's case for permanent injunctions; their continuance would merely postpone reporting by the newspapers, should *they* ultimately prevail at trial. The potential injustice to the A-G of the first course of action outweighed the potential injustice to the newspapers of the second. The approaches of Lord Templeman and Lord Ackner were more robust. Lord Templeman condemned Peter Wright's 'treachery' and held that there were good reasons for continuing the injunctions: the mass circulation of extracts from *Spycatcher* in the UK would expose members of the security service to the harassment of accusations to which they could not respond; discharge of the injunctions would create an 'immutable precedent' for 'any disgruntled public servant or holder of secret or confidential information relating to the security service' to 'achieve mass circulation in this country of damaging truths and falsehoods by the device of prior publication anywhere else abroad' (p. 357); the newspaper reports were contrary to the object and purpose of the Millett injunctions, had originated with Wright and his publishers abroad, and were intended to bring pressure on the English courts to allow *Spycatcher* to be published here. Moreover, these reasons would make the interference with freedom of expression 'necessary in a democratic society in the interests of national security' and thus justified in terms of Art. 10 of the European Convention on Human Rights. Finally, the injunctions should be modified so as to prevent reporting of extracts from *Spycatcher* read in open court in Australia. Lord Ackner's speech was on similar lines, although he was even more critical of the conduct of the press, in particular in their response to the decision to continue the injunction that was announced on 30 July:

'It has required no imagination to anticipate the resentment which the newspaper, and, indeed, the entire media, would feel and vociferously express if we ultimately imposed a restraint on publication, albeit a temporary restraint. Moreover, it is a fact of life, however regrettable, that there are elements in the press as a whole which lack not only responsibility but integrity. . . . It would have been absurd and naive of your Lordships not to have appreciated that every attempt would inevitably have been made to frustrate your Lordship's orders. The "antic disposition" of the press and the media following the announcement of the orders establishes this fully' (p. 365).

The modification to the injunctions was necessary to close a 'loophole' that might have been used by such elements to nullify the temporary damage limitation operation determined essential by the majority.

The speeches of the minority provided a stark contrast. Given the publication of *Spycatcher* in the US, an injunction would, in the view of Lord Bridge, now be 'futile'. Any remaining national security interest which the Millett injunctions were capable of protecting was of insufficient weight 'to justify the massive encroachment on freedom of speech' which their continuance would necessarily involve. He continued (pp. 346–347):

'Having no written constitution, we have no equivalent in our law to the First Amendment to the Constitution of the United States of America. Some think that puts freedom of speech on too lofty a pedestal. Perhaps they are right. We have not adopted as part of our law the European Convention on Human Rights (Convention for the Protection of Human Rights and Fundamental Freedoms (Rome, 4 November 1950; TS 71 (1953); Cmd 8969)) to which this country is a signatory. Many think that we should. I have hitherto not been of that persuasion, in large part because I have had confidence in the capacity of the common law to safeguard the fundamental freedoms essential to a free society including the right to freedom of speech which is specifically safeguarded by art. 10 of the convention. My confidence is seriously undermined by your Lordships' decision. All the judges in the courts below in this case have been concerned not to impose any unnecessary fetter on freedom of speech. I suspect that what the Court of Appeal would have liked to achieve, and perhaps set out to achieve by its compromise solution, was to inhibit the Sunday Times from continuing the serialisation of *Spycatcher*, but to leave the press at large at liberty to discuss and comment on the *Spycatcher* allegations. If there were a method of achieving these results which could be sustained in law, I can see much to be said for it on the merits. But I can see nothing whatever, either in law or on the merits, to be said for the maintenance of a total ban on discussion in the press of this country of matters of undoubted public interest and concern which the rest of the world now knows all about and can discuss freely. Still less can I approve your Lordships' decision to throw in for good measure a restriction on reporting court procedings in Australia which the Attorney General had never even asked for.

Freedom of speech is always the first casualty under a totalitarian regime. Such a regime cannot afford to allow the free circulation of information and ideas among its citizens. Censorship is the indispensable tool to regulate what the public may and what they may not know. The present attempt to insulate the public in this country from information which is freely available elsewhere is a significant step down that very dangerous road. The maintenance of the ban, as more and more copies of the book *Spycatcher* enter this country and circulate here, will seem more and more ridiculous. If the government are determined to fight to maintain the ban to the end, they will face inevitable condemnation and humiliation by the European Court of Human Rights in Strasbourg. Long before that they will have been condemned at the bar of public opinion in the free world.'

Lord Oliver endorsed the approach that had been taken by the Vice-Chancellor. Continuance of the injunctions 'on which I may call the Admiral Byng principle, "pour encourager les autres" ' would involve misuse of the injunctive remedy, as would be its use to punish Mr Wright. (Lord Goff expressly agreed with this view in *A-G v Guardian Newspapers Ltd (No 2)* [1990] 1 AC 109, 288.) The newspapers were not responsible for the publication of *Spycatcher* in the US. He did not think the A-G would have an arguable case for a permanent injunction at trial. In the event, of course, permanent injunctions were refused.

4. In *The Observer and The Guardian v United Kingdom*, Judgment of 26 November 1991, Series A No. 216 and *The Sunday Times v United Kingdom*, Judgment of 26 November 1991, Series A No. 217, the grant of the interlocutory injunctions was considered by the European Court of Human Rights. The court concluded by 14 to 10 that the injunctions up until the publication of *Spycatcher* in the United States in July 1987 did not violate Article 10, ECHR, but concluded unanimously that the continuation of the injunctions thereafter was such a violation. See below, p. 829, and J. McDermott (1992) Jo of Media Law & Practice 137 and S. Colyer, ibid, p. 142.

5. It was clear in the outcome of the *Spycatcher* litigation that the law of confidence, like the criminal law, will be ineffective in reaching persons outside the jurisdiction. Lord Oliver, for one, argued that 'in the end, the preservation of security secrets has to depend on the imposition on members of the security services of extremely tight *contractual* obligations which can be enforced interlocutorially without the assumption of any burden beyond the proof of the contract' ((1989) 23 Israel LR at 424) (cf. the position in the US, below, pp. 491–492). Section 1 of the Official Secrets Act 1989 (above, p. 446) now imposes a 'lifelong duty of confidence' on members of the security services.

6. *A-G v Guardian Newspapers Ltd (No 2)* was applied by the House of Lords in *Lord Advocate v Scotsman Publications Ltd* [1990] 1 AC 812. Anthony Cavendish was an officer of MI6 from 1948 to 1953. In 1987 he sought authorisation for the publication of his memoirs, *Inside Intelligence*, which included some information about his

time in MI6. Authorisation was refused. He distributed 279 of 500 copies he had printed at his own expense to private individuals. One of them gave a copy to the *Scotsman*, which published an article including some material from the book on 5 January 1988. The Lord Advocate sought an interim interdict restraining the *Scotsman* and any person having notice of the interdict from publishing (with certain exceptions) any information obtained by C in the course of his employment in MI6. The Lord Ordinary and the Second Division of the Court of Session refused the application (1988 SLT 490). The Lord Advocate appealed without success to the House of Lords. During argument before the Second Division, the Crown conceded that the book contained no information the disclosure of which was capable of damaging national security. In the light of this, the House held that the public interest did not require publication by the *Scotsman* to be restrained. Lord Keith (pp. 858–859) pointed out that the decision did not mean that any newspaper which received such an unsolicited book of memoirs by an intelligence officer would be free to publish: if there had been no previous publication, and no concession that the contents were innocuous, 'the newspaper would undoubtedly itself come under an obligation of confidence and be subject to restraint. If there had been a minor degree of prior publication, and no such concession, it would be a matter for investigation whether further publication would be prejudicial to the public interest, and interim interdict would normally be appropriate'.

Lords Griffiths and Goff agreed with Lord Keith. Lords Templeman and Jauncey noted that the decision mirrored the provision of sections 1 and 5 of the Official Secrets Act 1989 (not then in force): under that provision, members and former members of the security services can be liable notwithstanding that no damage is proved; a third party could only be liable if a disclosure is damaging. See N. Walker, 'Spycatcher's Scottish Sequel' [1990] PL 354, noting the confusion between contents-based and non-contents-based arguments put foward by the Crown, and criticising the reliance on the terms of legislation in determining the scope of private law.

7. *Cabinet documents.* The foundation for the use of the law of confidence by the Crown was provided by the decision of Lord Widgery CJ in *A-G v Jonathan Cape Ltd* [1976] QB 752 (the Crossman Diaries case), discussed by Lord Keith (above, p. 479).[1]

8. In June 1976 extracts from Cabinet minutes were used in an article in *New Society* by Frank Field (17 June 1976) criticising the government for deciding to postpone the introduction of a child benefit scheme (see 914 HC Deb 28 June 1976 cols 39–106). An investigation did not reveal the identity of the person responsible for the leak. A Committee of Privy Counsellors on Cabinet Document Security, chaired by Lord Houghton, subsequently made various recommendations for tightening the physical security of documents, applying the 'need to know' principle to the circulation of documents and improving the relevant administrative machinery (Cmnd. 6677). In general, they found that 'our public servants . . . maintain a very high standard for the protection of the written word' (p. 10).

9. Cabinet documents may also be protected from disclosure in litigation by a claim that disclosure would be contrary to the public interest (see below, p. 515). Note that in relation to both claims of public interest immunity and government applications to restrain threatened breaches of confidence the courts must balance

---

1 On this case see Hugo Young, *The Crossman Affair* (1976); R. K. Middlemass, (1976) 47 *Political Quarterly* 39; M. W. Bryan, (1976) 92 LQR 180; D. G. T. Williams, [1976] CLJ 1; D. L. Ellis, 'Collective Ministerial Responsibility and Collective Solidarity' [1980] PL 367.

competing interests. In the former, the public interest in the proper administration of justice is balanced against the public interest in keeping certain matters confidential. In the latter the public interest in confidentiality is balanced against other public interests, such as the freedom of speech.

10. The conventions as to the publication of ministerial memoirs were considered by the *Committee of Privy Counsellors on Ministerial Memoirs* (Chairman, Lord Radcliffe (Cmnd. 6386, 1976)). The committee endorsed the view taken by the Cabinet in 1946 that it was necessary

'to keep secret information of two kinds, disclosure of which would be detrimental to the public interest:
(*a*) In the international sphere, information whose disclosure would be injurious to us in our relations with other nations, including information which would be of value to a potential enemy.
(*b*) In the domestic sphere, information the publication of which would be destructive of the confidential relationships on which our system of government is based and which may subsist between Minister and Minister, Ministers and their advisers, and between either and outside bodies or private persons' (p. 7).

The committee suggested further 'working rules' as to the reticence due from an ex-Minister:

'(*a*) In dealing with the experience that he has acquired by virtue of his official position, he should not reveal the opinions or attitudes of colleagues as to the Government business with which they have been concerned. That belongs to their stewardship, not to his. He may, on the other hand, describe and account for his own.
(*b*) He should not reveal the advice given to him by individuals whose duty it has been to tender him their advice or opinions in confidence. If he wishes to mention the burden or weight of such advice, it must be done without attributing individual attitudes to identifiable persons. Again, he will need to exercise a continuing discretion in any references that he makes to communications received by him in confidence from outside members of the public.
(*c*) He should not make public assessments or criticisms, favourable or unfavourable, of those who have served under him or those whose competence or suitability for particular posts he has had to measure as part of his official duties' (pp. 20–21).

As to enforcement, the committee did not regard the legal principles expounded by Lord Widgery CJ in the Crossman Diaries case as providing 'a system which can protect and enforce those rules of reticence that we regard as called for when ex-Ministers compose their memoirs. . . .' According to his Lordship, each case would have to be decided on its own facts – there were 'no fixed principles of legal enforceability' (p. 24). The committee did not regard a judge as 'so equipped as to make him the best arbitrator of the issues involved. The relevant considerations are political and administrative. . . .' Moreover, the legal principles did not protect confidences of or about civil servants. Neither did legislation offer the right solution. The 'burden of compliance' should be 'left to rest on the free acceptance of an obligation of honour' (p. 26). Whenever a former minister intends to publish information derived from his ministerial experience he should submit the full text in advance to the Secretary of the Cabinet. If clearance is refused in relation to information concerning national security or international affairs, the minister may appeal to the Prime Minister, whose decision is final. If clearance is refused in relation to other information it is for the minister to decide whether to publish; moreover, the information may be published after 15 years in any event, except that beyond that point he should not reveal the advice tendered by individuals who are still members of the public service nor make public assessment or criticisms of them. The government accepted these recommendations (903 HC Deb 22 January 1976 cols 521–523) but not all ministers have observed them (see B. Castle, *The Castle Diaries* (1980), H. Jenkins, *The Culture Gap* (1979)). 'Everything which the Government failed to have decided in its favour in the *Crossman Diaries* case was duly enshrined in [these] constitutional conventions' (G. Robertson, *Freedom, the Individual and the Law* (7th edn, 1993), p. 194). See further R. Brazier, *Constitutional Practice* (2nd edn., 1994), pp. 123–124.

Civil servants whether serving or retired are required to submit manuscripts relating to service matters for prior approval before entering a contract for publication (Robertson, op. cit., p. 195). For example, Prof. A. V. Jones' book, *Most Secret War*, which concerned Britain's secret scientific intelligence operations during the Second World War, was cleared by the Cabinet Office, MI6 and the D Notice Committee (*The Times*, 10 May 1977; *Brownlie*, pp. 266–267). The power has been used 'to delete or dilute criticisms of still-serving ministers' (Robertson, op. cit., in relation to the autobiography of Bernard Ingham, Mrs Thatcher's press secretary). The criteria for authorising publications by former members of the security and intelligence services were set out by the Foreign Secretary, Douglas Hurd, in 241 HC Deb, 20 April 1994, cols 539–540, written answer. The statement noted the duty of confidence and obligations under s. 1(1) of the Official Secrets Act 1989 applicable to former employees of the security and intelligence agencies. It continued:

'The need to protect sensitive information is fully recognised in the Intelligence Services Bill, as it is in the Security Service Act 1989. The Bill defines strictly the circumstances under which information may properly be disclosed by the intelligence services including disclosure of records in accordance with the Public Records Act 1958 and 1967, which of course applies only to matters over 30 years old.

Authorisation for publication or other disclosure will accordingly be especially rare and exceptional with regard to events which happened less than 30 years ago. In any case where a former member of the security and intelligence agencies or a person notified under section 1(1)(b) [of the 1989 Act] . . . wishes to publish or otherwise disclose material relating to his official duties, whether older than 30 years or not, he will need to apply to his former employer for authority to disclose. But there may, in the case of older material, be more likelihood that there will be no objection to disclosure. Any applications made in good faith would be looked at on their individual merits, and would still be judged on whether disclosure of any particular piece of information would jeopardise national security, whether directly or indirectly. If not, the service would be able so to inform the prospective author and give him authority to make the disclosure, so that it would not be contrary to section 1(1) of the Official Secrets Act 1989 nor in breach of his civil duty of confidence. Authorisation would imply only that there were no concerns about national security. It would not imply that the Crown had endorsed the publication or confirmed the accuracy of its contents. The Crown would reserve the right not to give authorisation in cases where an officer had committed breaches of the criminal law or his civil obligations.'

11. An injunction will only rarely be granted by a civil court to restrain a threatened breach of the criminal law, such as a breach of the Official Secrets Acts. See *Gouriet v Union of Post Office Workers* [1978] AC 435; D. G. T. Williams, [1977] Crim LR 703; D. Feldman, (1979) 42 MLR 369; J. M. Evans, *de Smith's Judicial Review of Administrative Action* (4th edn., 1980) pp. 455–457. In the *Gouriet* case Lord Wilberforce stated at p. 481 that it is 'an exceptional power confined, in practice, to cases where an offence is frequently repeated in disregard of a, usually, inadequate penalty – see *A-G v Harris* [1961] 1 QB 74; or to cases of emergency – see *A-G v Chaudry* [1971] 1 WLR 1614.' Threatened breaches of the Official Secrets Acts might well count as an 'emergency' for these purposes, at least where 'grave and irreparable' harm (see *de Smith*, p. 456) would be caused. Cf. *Commonwealth of Australia v John Fairfax & Sons Ltd* (1980) 55 ALJR 45, 147 CLR 39; HCA. Here, the federal government discovered that long extracts from unpublished government documents were to be printed in two newspapers and a book. The documents related to various defence and foreign affairs issues, but did not contain technical information of military significance. Many of them were classified. The government sought an interim injunction on three grounds: (1) the threatened breach of section 79 of the Crimes Act 1914 (Cth), which is similar in terms to the Official Secrets

Act 1911, s. 2(1)(a) and (b); (2) breach of confidence; and (3) breach of copyright. Mason J acceded to the application on ground (3) alone. On ground (1) his Lordship stated (at 147 CLR at p. 50):

'It may be that in some circumstances a statutory provision which prohibits and penalizes the disclosure of confidential government information or official secrets will be enforceable by injunction. This is more likely to be the case when it appears that the statute, in addition to creating a criminal offence, is designed to provide a civil remedy to protect the government's right to confidential information. I do not think that s. 79 is such a provision. It appears in the *Crimes Act* and its provisions are appropriate to the creation of a criminal offence and to that alone. The penalties which it imposes are substantial. There is nothing to indicate that it was intended in any way to supplement the rights of the Commonwealth to relief by way of injunction to restrain disclosure of confidential information or infringement of copyright. There is no suggested inadequacy in these two remedies which would lead me to conclude that it is inappropriate to regard s. 79 as a foundation for injunctive relief.'

Do you think these observations would be applicable to a threatened breach of the Official Secrets Acts? Are they unduly restrictive? This case was referred to by Lord Keith on the breach of confidence point (above, p. 479). On the copyright point, note that actual Crown documents were involved, and not merely a work written by a former Crown servant.

12. In the United States there is a heavy presumption against any prior restraint on the freedom of the press guaranteed by the First Amendment. In *New York Times v United States* 403 US 713 (1971) the Supreme Court rejected by 6:3 the government's application for an injunction to prevent publication of the 'Pentagon Papers', a series of secret government documents dealing with the origins of the United States' involvement in Vietnam. Black and Douglas JJ held that the First Amendment prevented any judicial restraint on speech and press. Brennan, Stewart and White JJ held, in varying degrees, that the government had failed to show that publication *would* (not could) cause direct, immediate and irreparable harm to the nation. Marshall J held that an injunction could not be issued in the absence of the specific statutory authority of Congressional legislation. Burger CJ and Harlan and Blackmun JJ held that the courts should not refuse to enforce the executive branch's claim, provided that a Cabinet-level officer personally so decided (see N. Sheehan *et al*, *The Pentagon Papers* (1971); L. Henkin, 120 U Pa L Rev 271 (1971); Nimmer, 26 Stan L Rev 311 (1974); M. Supperstone, *Brownlie's Law of Public Order and National Security* (2nd edn., 1981) pp. 271–274; C. R. Sunstein, 74 Calif LR 889). It was left unclear whether the strict tests propounded by Brennan, Stewart and White would be applicable where there was a specific statutory provision.

In 1979 a US district judge granted an injunction to restrain publication of materials on the hydrogen bomb: these had been specifically defined as 'restricted data' in the Atomic Energy Authority Act 1954, and the Act had also empowered the courts to issue injunctions against the publication of such material (42 USC §, 2014 (y) – 2162, 2274, 2280): *United States v Progressive Inc* 467 F Supp 990 (1979) (the litigation was dropped after similar materials were published elsewhere).

Then in 1980 the Supreme Court held that an agreement requiring CIA employees not to publish any information about the agency without specific prior approval was a judicially enforceable contract applicable to both classified and non-classified information. Moreover, CIA employees were in a fiduciary position. An ex-employee of the CIA published without permission a highly critical account (*Decent Interval*) of the CIA's evacuation of South Vietnam after the fall of Saigon. The Supreme Court imposed a constructive trust on all profits from the sales in favour of the CIA and permanently enjoined the author from publishing future writings concerning the CIA or intelligence activities without submitting them to the CIA for prepublication review. This was notwithstanding the concession that the book contained no information that the CIA could have suppressed under the secrecy agreement: *Snepp v United States* 444 US 507 (1980) (see Comment, 14 Harv Civ Rights – Civ Lib L Rev 665 (1979); Comment, 32 Stan L Rev 409 (1980); D. F. Orentlicher, 81 Colum LR 662 (1981); C. R. Sunstein, 74 Calif LR 889, 912–921).

5 Security vetting

(a) THE 'PURGE' PROCEDURE

In 1945, the defection of Igor Gouzenko stimulated a chain of events which led to the unravelling of major spy rings in Canada, the United States and Britain. This included the arrest and conviction in 1946 of Dr Alan Nunn May, a nuclear scientist who had spied for Russia while working in Canada. A number of civil servants, suspected of communist or fascist sympathies, were transferred to non-sensitive posts. (See P. Hennessy and G. Brownfeld, 'Britain's Cold War Security Purge: The Origins of Positive Vetting', *The Historical Journal*, 25, 4 (1982) pp. 965–973.) 'MI5 feared its covert purge might be "blown" as the number of transferees grew.' Accordingly, in 1948 the prime minister, Mr Attlee, made a public statement to the effect that

'the only prudent course to adopt is to ensure that no one who is known to be a member of the Communist Party, or to be associated with it in such a way as to raise legitimate doubts about his or her reliability, is employed in connection with work, the nature of which is vital to the security of the state'.

(448 HC Deb 15 March 1948, cols 1703–1704). The same rule was to govern persons known to be actively associated with Fascist organisations. These were included to give the appearance of impartiality: Communists were considered the real threat. 'The security authorities were overjoyed when they eventually found a fascist in one of the service departments': Hennessey and Brownfeld, op. cit., p. 968). The procedure was revised in 1957, 1962 and 1985 and is set out in the following extract.

Statement of the procedure to be followed when the reliability of a public servant is thought to be in doubt on security grounds (Cabinet Office)

2. The Minister (that is, the Minister responsible for the department or organisation to which the public servant belongs) will have before him information on which to decide whether the reliability of the public servant is prima facie to be regarded as in doubt on the security grounds. His reliability will be so regarded if
   (a) he is, or is to be, employed in connection with work the nature of which is vital to the security of the State; and simultaneously;
   (b) (i) he is, or has recently been, a member of a communist or fascist organisation, or of a subversive group, acknowledged as such by the Minister, whose aims are to undermine or overthrow parliamentary democracy in the United Kingdom of Great Britain and Northern Ireland by political, industrial or violent means; or
   (ii) he is, or recently has been, sympathetic to or associated with members or sympathisers of such organisations or groups, in such a way as to raise reasonable doubts about his reliability; or
   (iii) he is susceptible to pressure from such organisations or groups.
   No statement of general application can be made as to what constitutes sympathy or association under (b)(ii) or what can be regarded as susceptibility to pressure under (b)(iii) above. Each case will be assessed in the light of the particular facts.

3. If the Minister rules that there is a prima facie case, the public servant is at once to be so informed and will where necessary be sent on special leave with pay, care being taken as far as possible not to disclose the reasons for his absence to his colleagues.

4. The public servant will at the same time be given any particulars, such as the date of his alleged membership, or the nature of the alleged sympathies, associations or connections that might enable him to clear himself. There will however have to be limits to the information given for he cannot be given such particulars as might involve the disclosure of the sources of the evidence.

5. At the same time the public servant will be asked to say whether he accepts or denies the allegation. If he accepts the allegation he will be dealt with as described in paragraphs 10 and 11 below. If he does not admit the allegation he shall have fourteen days in which to make written representations to the Minister if he so wishes.

6. The Minister will reconsider his prima facie ruling in the light of any representations the public servant may make. If the Minister decides that there is no reason for varying it, the public servant shall be so informed and shall then have seven days in which to decide whether to ask for a reference to the Three Advisers. If he does not ask for such a reference he will be dealt with as in paragraph 9 below. If he does ask for a reference to the Three Advisers the latter will be asked to consider the case as soon as possible.

7. The function of the Three Advisers is set out in their terms of reference. Where there is no suggestion of communist, fascist or other subversive associations, sympathies or connections, cases involving aspects of character or conduct will not be referred to the tribunal, and appeals will be dealt with under the normal grievance or similar procedures of departments.

8. In discharging their functions the Advisers will take into account the representations made by the public servant. They will hear him in person if he so wishes and he may be accompanied by a 'friend', who may be a trade union official, to help him in presenting his opening statement in reply to the charge. At the discretion of the Three Advisers, the 'friend' may remain to assist the appellant for as much of the proceedings as the Three Advisers consider appropriate. The 'friend' must withdraw when asked to do so. The public servant may also ask third parties to appear before the Advisers separately to testify to them as to his record, reliability and character. In the special circumstances of these cases the proceedings must be governed by the requirement that neither sources of evidence nor evidence which might involve the disclosure of sources can be given to the person against whom the charge is brought. The Advisers will therefore count it as an important part of their functions to see that anyone appearing before them can make his points effectively and will adapt their procedure in such a way as to give him the best possible opportunity of bringing out the points which he wishes to bring to their notice.

9. On receiving the report of the Three Advisers, the Minister will reconsider his prima facie ruling and if he decides to uphold it, he will give the public servant an opportunity of making representations to himself or his representative before action is finally taken. Similar opportunity will be given when the public servant does not wish his case to go to the Advisers.

10. If the prima facie ruling is finally upheld, a public servant will be posted to or retained in a non-secret branch within his own department, or, if this is not practicable, will be posted to a non-secret branch in another department. If he belongs to a category which it is impossible to employ in any other than a secret branch, or if his qualifications or experience are such that no alternative employment elsewhere in the government service can found, he will have to be dismissed unless he accepts the option, which should always be afforded in such cases, of resigning.

11. Before a decision to re-post, or in the last resort, to dismiss (with resignation as the alternative) is made effective, the public servant's trade union should be afforded an opportunity of suggesting any alternative re-posting that it may think more suitable, or of suggesting a possible re-posting as an alternative to dismissal or resignation.

12. A public servant will be given a similar opportunity to make representations to the responsible Minister and to have his case referred to the Three Advisers as described above if:

    (a) he is an official of a union with members in the civil and public services who may acquire access to classified information in the course of negotiations or while visiting secret establishments, and the responsible Minister issues a notice of refusal to negotiate with him or of denial of access to a secret establishment on any of the grounds described in paragraph 2(b);

    (b) he is removed from classified work or is refused a positive vetting clearance and in consequence his career is likely to be prejudiced because he, his spouse (or any person who is regarded or lives as his spouse) or other close relative has overseas connections which are judged to constitute a security risk because they may impose a strain on his loyalties or make him vulnerable to pressure from a foreign intelligence service;

    (c) he is a British citizen employed by an international defence organisation, whether on secondment or directly recruited, and:

      (i) the responsible Minister rules that there is a prima facie case for withdrawing his security clearance on any of the grounds described in paragraph 2(b) or sub-paragraph 12(b) above, and

      (ii) he would be liable to dismissal or to suffer financial loss as a result of such withdrawal.

NOTES

1. The procedure applies to the public service (excluding the armed forces); the UK Atomic Energy Authority (including British Nuclear Fuels Ltd and UK employees of URENCO Ltd); the Civil Aviation Authority; British Telecom; the Post Office; police forces (including civilian employees); civilian employees of the Territorial Army and Auxiliary Forces Association; 'employees of firms engaged on classified government contracts, departmental consultants and employees of NAAFI who are liable to dismissal or to suffer financial loss as a result of the responsible minister issuing a directive that secret matters should not be disclosed to them' (para. 1).

2. The 'Terms of Reference of the Three Advisers' require them to advise the minister whether there are reasonable grounds for supposing that the individual has or has recently had the relevant sympathies or associations. If they are in doubt, they are to give their assessment of the evidence. In any event they should give their grounds. Character defects are only to be taken into account where they bear on these sympathies and associations. It is for the minister to determine whether employment is 'in connection with work vital to the security of the state'. See D. G. T. Williams, *Not in the Public Interest* (1965) pp. 170–185; D. C. Jackson, (1957) 20 MLR 364; M. R. Joelson, [1963] PL 51. Revisions in the procedure followed the *Statement on the Findings of the Conference of Privy Counsellors on Security* (Cmd 9715, 1956) which had been set up following the defections of Burgess and Maclean to the USSR (see 563 HC Deb cols 152–156, written answer, 29 January 1957). They were further revised in 1985, when a widened definition of 'subversive' activities was incorporated, and express provision was made for the public servant to be accompanied by a friend (see I. Linn, *Application Refused* (1990) pp. 15–16). The Three Advisers also have jurisdiction in respect of persons refused clearance under 'positive vetting' procedures (see below pp. 495–499) and in some deportation cases (see below pp. 734–736).

3. According to Williams (op cit, p. 171) by November 1954, 124 civil servants had been removed from their posts for security reasons. Between 20 and 30 were dismissed; almost as many resigned; the remainder were transferred. There have been no cases under the purge procedure since 1969; this case was not, in the end, referred to the Three Advisers (information supplied by the Cabinet Office).

4. The position of government contractors dealing with classified information is the subject of a memorandum by the Ministry of Defence to the *Franks Committee on Section 2 of the Official Secrets Act 1911* Vol. 2 Written Evidence pp. 39–52 (see also Chap. 7 of the Radcliffe Report on *Security Procedures in the Public Service* (Cmnd 1681, 1962)). Standard conditions of government contracts may, inter alia, (1) require contractors to take all reasonable steps to ensure that all persons employed on work in connection with the contract have notice that the Official Secrets Acts apply; (2) enable the government to require that secret matters shall not be disclosed to a named employee of the contractor; (3) enable the government to require that specified employees sign a statement that they understand that the Official Secrets Acts are applicable. The sanctions for failure to comply include the determination of the contract and the withdrawal of future contracts. The main cause célèbre in this context was the decision of the government to require ICI to move their Assistant Solicitor from a position where he could have access to secret information as his wife had formerly been a member of the Communist Party (see 197 HL Deb cols 122ff 21 June 1956; H. Street, *Freedom, the Individual and the Law* (5th edn, 1982 pp. 240–241). At that time there was no right of appeal to the Three Advisers, but such a right was created on the recommendation of the Conference of Privy Counsellors on Security (Cmd 9715, 1956).

5. The Three Advisers have not sat since 1967 (information supplied by the Cabinet Office).

6. The main issue here is whether the security considerations justify a procedure that obviously fails to conform to basic standards of natural justice. In particular, the appellant is not made fully aware of the case against him. In 1956 the Conference of Privy Counsellors concluded that it was 'right to continue the practice of tilting the balance in favour of offering greater protection to the security of the State rather than in the direction of safeguarding the rights of the individual' (Cmd 9715, para. 15). On the other hand the procedure has been adversely criticised by the Council of Civil Service Unions in evidence to the House of Commons Defence Committee (First Special Report, Session 1982–83 HC 242, pp. 93–94). Professor Street noted that 'the political accountability of a Minister is a completely inadequate substitute for the right to take one's case before the courts' and that these procedures 'are a travesty of justice as Englishmen are accustomed to it' (*Freedom, the Individual and the Law* (5th edn, 1982), pp. 242, 244). A further issue concerns the broader definition of subversion incorporated in the 1985 revisions, and which has now been adopted in the Security Service Act 1989 (see below, p. 501). See the criticisms expressed by the NCCL Trade Union Liaison Committee, *The Purging of the Civil Service* (1985).

7. The purge procedure was originally established to consider cases of suspected Communist associations. It was soon recognised that security risks could equally arise where there was some character defect, such as drunkenness, drug addiction or homosexuality, which might make a man unreliable or expose him to blackmail or influence by foreign agents. However, it was not until the Statement of the Findings of the Conference of Privy Counsellors on Security in 1956 (Cmd 9715) that the government publicly declared that character defects might affect a civil servant's postings or promotion. These cases are outside the jurisdiction of the Three Advisers, but there is a right of appeal to the permanent head of the department.

(b) POSITIVE VETTING

'By today's standards, the purge procedure was rudimentary, almost naive' (Hennessy and Brownfeld, op. cit., p. 967). The United States authorities regarded it as 'feeble' (ibid, p. 969). The arrest and conviction of Klaus Fuchs in 1950, a nuclear scientist who had leaked atomic secrets to the Russians, led to the introduction of 'positive vetting'. Instead of simply ensuring that the security service had no adverse record of a candidate, a conscious effort should be made to confirm his reliability. The introduction of positive vetting was announced in a press statement released on 8 January 1952. The arrangements have been revised on a number of occasions, the latest being in 1994, as explained in the following extract from *Hansard*.

Vol. 251 HC Deb, cols 764–766, written answer, 15 December 1994

The Prime Minister: [. . . To] ensure that security measures and procedures reflect current threats, the Government have recently completed a fundamental review of their arrangements for the management of protective security in Departments and agencies. In the area of personnel security, the review concluded that the vetting process served a worthwhile purpose, not only in disclosing circumstances which might lead to breaches of security but as a deterrent to those who might otherwise seek to undermine that security. The review recommended, however, that there should be a streamlining of the procedures that made up the vetting process. That work has now been completed.

The new framework should ensure that personnel security objectives are properly defined and that responsibility for achieving them is clearly established. There will be a greater emphasis on ensuring that personnel security resources are targeted on, and proportionate to, the threat and add necessarily and cost-effectively to the protection of government assets. Between 1 January and 31 March 1995, the existing arrangements will be replaced by a new personnel security regime which will consist of two levels of vetting, a security check and developed vetting. A security check will be similar to the current PV(S) – positive vetting (secret) – clearance, but will in addition include a check on the financial status of the individual. Developed vetting will replace the present PV(TS) – positive vetting (top secret) – and EPV – extended positive vetting – levels of vetting. The current system of counter terrorist checks will remain unchanged, but will be subject to review.

As at present, all candidates for security vetting will be asked to complete a security questionnaire which will explain the purpose of the procedure and invite them to provide the personal details required for the necessary checks to be carried out. Vetting will then be carried out on the basis of the statement of policy set out below.

Statement of HM Government's vetting policy

In the interests of national security, safeguarding the Parliamentary democracy and maintaining the proper security of the Government's essential activities, it is the policy of HMG that no one should be employed in connection with work the nature of which is vital to the interests of the state who:

is, or has been involved in, or associated with any of the following activities:
— espionage,
— terrorism,
— sabotage,
— actions intended to overthrow or undermine Parliamentary democracy by political, industrial or violent means; or
is, or has recently been:
— a member of any organisation which has advocated such activities; or
— associated with any organisation, or any of its members in such a way as to raise reasonable doubts about his or [sc. her] reliability; or
is susceptible to pressure or improper influence, for example because of current or past conduct; or
has shown dishonesty or lack of integrity which throws doubt upon their reliability; or
has demonstrated behaviour, or is subject to circumstances which may otherwise indicate unreliability.

In accordance with the above policy, Government departments and agencies will carry out a Security Check (SC) on all individuals who require long term, frequent and uncontrolled access to SECRET information or assets. A Security Check may also be applied to staff who are in a position directly or indirectly to bring about the same degree of damage as such individuals or who need access to protectively marked material originating from other countries or international organisations. In some circumstances, where it would not be possible for an individual to make reasonable progress in their career without clearance to SECRET level, it may be applied to candidates for employment whose duties do not, initially, involve such regular access.

An SC clearance will normally consist of:

a check against the National Collection of Criminal Records and relevant departmental and police records;
in accordance with the Security Service Act 1989, where it is necessary to protect national security, or to safeguard the economic well-being of the United Kingdom from threats posed by persons outside the British Islands, a check against Security Service records; and
credit reference checks and where appropriate, a review of personal finances.

In some circumstances further enquiries, including an interview with the subject, may be carried out.

Individuals employed on government work who have long term, frequent and uncontrolled access to TOP SECRET information or assets, will be submitted to the level of vetting clearance known as Developed Vetting (DV). This level of clearance may also be applied to people who are in a position directly or indirectly to cause the same degree of damage as such individuals and in order to satisfy the requirements for access to protectively marked material originating from other countries and international organisations. In addition to a Security Check, a DV will involve:

an interview with the person being vetted; and
references from people who are familiar with the person's character in both the home and work environment. These may be followed up by interviews. Enquiries will not necessarily be confined to past and present employers and nominated character referees.

It is also the Government's policy that departments and agencies will carry out Counter Terrorist Checks (CTC) in the interest of national security before anyone can be:

authorised to take up posts which involve proximity to public figures at particular risk of attack by terrorist organisations, or which give access to information or material assessed to be of value to terrorists; granted unescorted access to certain military, civil and industrial establishments assessed to be at particular risk of attack by a terrorist organisation.

The purpose of such checks is to prevent those who may have connections with terrorist organisations, or who may be vulnerable to pressure from such organisations, from gaining access to certain posts, and in some circumstances, premises, where there is a risk that they could exploit that position to further the aims of a terrorist organisation. A CTC will include a check against Security Service records. Criminal record information may also be taken into account.

Departments and agencies generally assure themselves, through the verification of identity, and written references from previous employers, that potential recruits are reliable and trustworthy. Such Basic Checks (BC) are already standard procedure for many departments and agencies. Where access needs to be granted to Government information or assets at CONFIDENTIAL level, departments, agencies and contractors engaged on government work are required to complete such checks. In some cases, at the CONFIDENTIAL level, where relevant, the Basic Check may be augmented with some of the checks normally carried out for security clearances.

NOTES

1. PV procedures were considered in the report of the *Committee on Security Procedures in the Public Service* chaired by Lord Radcliffe (Cmnd 1681, 1961) and the *Statement on the Recommendations of the Security Commission* (Cmnd 8540, 1982). Furthermore, the Security Commission reported on the operation of procedures in the case of two persons convicted under the Official Secrets Acts who had received PV clearance: Geoffrey Arthur Prime (Report of May 1983, Cmnd 8876) and Philip Leslie Aldridge (Report of March 1984, Cmnd 9212) and Lord Bridge reported on the PV clearance of Commander Trestrail, who resigned as Queen's Police Officer following the revelation of his homosexuality. Information is also contained in memoranda to the Defence Committee (1982–83 HC 242) although the Committee did not have time to complete its work. See generally M. Hollingsworth and R. Norton-Taylor, *Blacklist: The Inside Story of Political Vetting* (1988); S. Fredman and G. S. Morris, *The State as Employer* (1989), pp. 232–236; I. Linn, *Application Refused: Employment Vetting by the State* (1990). The 1994 guidelines replaced guidelines published in 1990 (177 HC Deb, 24 July 1990, cols 159–161, written answer). While the procedures have been streamlined, the policy is generally similar, except that it applies to people whose work is vital to the 'interests' rather than the 'security' of the state; there is a general reference to susceptibility to pressure or improper influence (not just pressure from a subversive organisation, a foreign intelligence service or a hostile power); character defects that expose the person to blackmail or other influence by a subversive organisation or foreign intelligence service are no longer expressly mentioned as indications of unreliability (but presumably still are). There seems to be an intention to apply a higher degree of scrutiny (including financial checks) to a narrower range of personnel (see *The Independent*, 16 December 1994).

2. In 1950 it was contemplated that PV would be applied to about 1,000 posts (Hennessy and Brownfeld, op. cit., p. 969). By 1982 the number of posts covered had risen to 68,000 (Cmnd 8540, p. 5). The Commission noted that the procedure was expensive and time-consuming, and recommended that the number of PV posts should be reviewed. In particular PV should no longer be an automatic requirement for officials of Under-Secretary rank and above and officials in the private offices of ministers. It remains a requirement for all members of the Diplomatic Service and the police special branches. It is also used in the UK Atomic Energy Authority and in firms which have contracts involving access to classified material. Following the review, some 2,000 posts were removed from the PV category (Linn, op. cit., p. 21). Records of the number of posts subject to security vetting are, however, not kept centrally (information from the Cabinet Office).

PV clearance does not apply to political ministers, although on appointment they are given specific instructions upon security problems and procedures. It does, however, apply to special advisers to ministers where they have regular access to highly classified information.

3. *Criteria for clearance.* These are summarised in the 1994 statement. The policy on homosexuality was reviewed in 1991 (195 HC Deb, 23 July 1991, col 474, written answer):

'Because homosexual acts, even between consenting adults, remain criminal offences in a number of overseas countries, evidence of homosexuality, even if acknowledged, has been treated under this policy as a bar to clearance at PV (TS) – positive vetting (top secret) – or enhanced positive vetting (EPV) level in overseas posts and therefore as a bar to recruitment to certain areas of employment, including the diplomatic service. In the light of changing social attitudes towards homosexuality in this country and abroad, and the correspondingly greater willingness on the part of homosexuals to be open about their sexuality, their lifestyle and their relationships, the Government have reviewed this policy and concluded that in future there should be no posts involving access to highly classified information for which homosexuality represents an automatic bar to security clearance, except in the special case of the armed forces where homosexual acts remain offences under the service disciplinary Acts.

The susceptibility of the subject to blackmail or pressure by a foreign intelligence service will continue to be a factor in the vetting of all candidates for posts involving access to highly classified information. An individual assessment is made in each case, taking account of the evidence which emerges in the course of the vetting process and the level of security clearance required.'

4. *Appeals.* If an officer is refused PV clearance on the ground of character defect, and his career will be adversely affected thereby, he is normally informed and allowed to appeal to the permanent head of department. In the MOD, where possible the individual is given a written statement of the facts on which the decision is based, and if he wishes he may be accompanied at any appeal interview by a friend or trade union representative (1982–83 HC 242, p. 4). The Security Commission recommended that a statement should normally be given: the government undertook to consider this (Cmnd 8540, p. 14). Where the refusal is based on other security reasons, an appeal lies to the Three Advisers (see above). In the case of members of the services an appeal lies to the appropriate Service Board. The Council of Civil Service Unions has argued that in *all* cases PV procedures should include (1) as full as possible a statement of the allegation against the civil servant; (2) the right of appeal to a body, such as the Three Advisers, *outside* the department; and (3) the right to be represented *throughout* the PV process by a 'friend', who may be a trade union representative (1982–83 HC 242, pp. 92–95). PV procedures may be applied to the employees of firms involved in classified work (cf, above, p. 494). An employee refused PV clearance may appeal to the Three Advisers. This was formerly possible in the case of (1) suspected Communist sympathies and (2) character defect, but following the *Statement on the Recommendations of the Security Commission* (Cmnd 8540, 1982, p. 9) the right has been restricted to ground (1), in line with the position for civil servants. An applicant for employment has no such entitlement (Linn, op cit, p. 32).

5. The limitations of judicial review as a mechanism for protecting the interests of those refused PV clearance were shown in *R v Director of Government Communications Headquarters, ex p Hodges* (1988) Times, 26 July. H, who had been employed at

GCHQ since he was 16, informed his employers, when he was 21, that he had concluded that he was homosexual. Although he was entirely open about this, and had a current steady relationship, his PV clearance was removed as it was thought he might be subject to blackmail because of his lifestyle. The Divisional Court rejected his application for judicial review holding (1) that, in the light of the decision of the House of Lords in *Council of Civil Service Unions v Minister for the Civil Service* [1985] AC 374, the court was not entitled even to consider whether the decision was *Wednesbury* unreasonable; and (2) that the procedure adopted was procedurally fair, notwithstanding that notes of an interview with his employers were not revealed. (H had been given a résumé of the facts, and had indeed been interviewed on a number of occasions.) In case he was wrong on point (1), Glidewell LJ also indicated that on the facts the Director's decision was not *Wednesbury* unreasonable.

The Employment Protection (Consolidation) Act 1978, Sch. 9, para. 2 (above, p. 468) was considered in *R v Secretary of State for the Foreign and Commonwealth Office, ex p Vidler* [1993] COD 305, where Popplewell J rejected an application for judicial review of a ministerial certificate that V had failed to obtain the level of security clearance necessary to hold a post in the FCO, and his dismissal was directly linked to that failure. His Lordship rejected the respondent's argument that the certificate was sufficient to prevent any further discussion on any aspect of the case, including the question of possible alternative employment elsewhere in the public service; however, that issue had not arisen for consideration by the industrial tribunal.

A similar procedure is found in the Race Relations Act 1976, ss. 41, 69(2), (3): see *R v Secretary of State for Transport, ex p Evans* [1992] COD 196.

6. In his report on the *Trestrail* case (1982–83 HC 59) Lord Bridge concluded that the PV procedures were not and could not be infallible: here, they were carried out efficiently and thoroughly. Where the subject was determined to conceal disqualifying factors this would present the PV investigator with an almost impossible task. They might be discovered by a 'system of random and covert surveillance of the subject's private activities'. However, this would '(a) add enormously to the cost of PV; (b) not necessarily be successful – this would depend on the length of the surveillance and the frequency of the subject's irregular behaviour; and (c) be strongly resented by most public servants as an unjustifiable invasion of their privacy' (ibid, pp. 21–22).

7. The 1990 reforms at least ensure that all candidates for vetting are aware that the procedures are to be carried out. They also expressly set out the procedure for individuals requiring access to less than Top Secret material (also in the past termed 'negative vetting': see Linn, op cit, pp. 17–21).

8. Following a major controversy in 1985, security vetting of staff in the BBC's domestic services has ended, except for those who may be invited to participate in the planning and operation of the wartime broadcasting service. See M. Hollingworth and R. Norton-Taylor, *Blacklist* (1988), Chap. 5 and Linn, op cit, pp. 49–50 and Appendix VII.

6 The security and intelligence services

There is now a vast literature on the activities of the security and intelligence services, ranging from works of historical scholarship,[1] through books by

---

1 E.g. C. Andrew, *Secret Service* (1985); F. H. Hinsley and C. A. G. Simkins, *British Intelligence in the Second World War* (1990); I. Leigh and L. Lustgarten, *In from the Cold* (1994).

knowledgeable observers apparently based on inside information[1] to journalistic pot-boilers. It has only been where the authors have themselves been members or former members of the relevant services that the government has taken serious steps to prevent publication, ultimately with comparatively little success (see above, pp. 474–491). With the growth in the amount of information about the services that has been made public has come increased concern at the constitutional position of the services, and at the illegality or impropriety of some of their activities. Examples of the latter include Peter Wright's claims that he and others 'bugged and burgled our way across London at the State's behest, while pompous, bowler-hatted civil servants in Whitehall pretended to look the other way' (*Spycatcher* (1987), p. 54); his claims of an MI5 plot to destabilise the Wilson government (ibid, pp. 362–372; D. Leigh, *The Wilson Plot* (1988)); and the revelations of Cathy Massiter (above p. 464). The last of these led to an application for judicial review by three prominent CND members (Joan Ruddock, Bruce Kent and John Cox) challenging inter alia the legality of the tapping of Cox's telephone: *R v Secretary of State for the Home Department, ex p Ruddock* [1987] 2 All ER 518 (see I. Leigh, [1987] PL 12). The challenge ultimately failed, but was nevertheless embarrassing for the government. Moreover, in autumn 1988, the European Commission on Human Rights declared admissible a case brought by two former NCCL officers, Patricia Hewitt and Harriet Harman, com-plaining of their classification as 'subversive' by MI5, which had placed them under surveillance (*H and H v UK* App No 12175/86). One of their grounds of challenge was the absence of any effective remedy for complainants. In May 1989, the Commission found that there had been breaches of Articles 8 and 13, ECHR (1989) 14 EHRR 657, below, p. 808. In response the government secured the passage of the Security Service Act 1989. This places the Security Service (MI5) on a statutory footing, but does little to answer the many concerns that have been expressed.

The Security Service operates at home and in the colonies, and has traditionally been concerned with counter-espionage. The Secret Intelligence Service (MI6), which mainly operates abroad, in co-operation with the Foreign Office, collects intelligence by covert means. Government Communications Headquarters (GCHQ) intercepts and analyses signals intelligence, including the communications of foreign countries, friendly and otherwise, companies and private individuals. SIS and GCHQ have now also been placed on a statutory basis by the Intelligence Services Act 1994. The work of the Security Service has been summarised in a glossy book-let issued by HMSO: *MI5, The Security Service* (1993). The 'current approximate allocation of the Service's resources' were counter-terrorism: Irish and other domestic 44%, and international 26%; counter espionage and counter proliferation (of weapons of mass destruction) 25%; and subversion, 5%' (p. 12). The threat from subversive organisations 'has diminished over a number of years and is now very low' (p. 17). Nevertheless, the Service is 'alert to any new threats . . . from left-wing or right-wing subversive organisations. It also monitors the possibility of extreme right-wing, nationalist and racist groups on the Continent establishing contact with sympathisers in the country' (p. 17). In October 1992, it took over from Special Branch lead responsibility for the intelligence effort against Irish Republican terror-ism on the British mainland (p. 28). In the aftermath of the IRA cease-fire on 31 August 1994, there have been suggestions that the Service is seeking a greater role in

---

1 E.g. books by Nigel West (the pseudonym of Rupert Allason MP), including *MI5: British Security Service Operations 1909–45* (1981); *A Matter of Trust: MI5 1945–72* (1982); *MI6: British Secret Intelligence Service Operations 1909–45*; *Molehunt* (1986); *GCHQ: The Secret Wireless War 1909–86*; *The Friends: Britain's Post-War Secret Intelligence Operations* (1988).

acting on the intelligence and surveillance arm of the police on serious crimes, drug trafficking and organised crime, although it has also been denied that the Service is seeking to be involved in crime that does not threaten national security (see *Statewatch* November–December 1994, pp. 17–19; *The Times*, 4 November 1994, reporting a lecture by the Director of MI5, Stella Rimington). The 1994 Act amended the 1989 Act to enable the Service to disclose information 'for the purpose of any criminal proceeding' (s. 2(2)).

Security Service Act 1989

1. The Security Service

(1) There shall continue to be a Security Service (in this Act referred to as 'the Service') under the authority of the Secretary of State.

(2) The function of the Service shall be the protection of national security and, in particular, its protection against threats from espionage, terrorism and sabotage, from the activities of agents of foreign powers and from actions intended to overthrow or undermine parliamentary democracy by political, industrial or violent means.

(3) It shall also be the function of the Service to safeguard the economic well-being of the United Kingdom against threats posed by the actions or intentions of persons outside the British Islands.

2. The Director-General

(1) The operations of the Service shall continue to be under the control of a Director-General appointed by the Secretary of State.

(2) The Director-General shall be responsible for the efficiency of the Service and it shall be his duty to ensure—

    (*a*) that there are arrangements for securing that no information is obtained by the Service except so far as necessary for the proper discharge of its functions or disclosed by it except so far as necessary for that purpose or for the purpose of preventing or detecting serious crime [or for the purpose of any criminal proceeding][1]; and

    (*b*) that the Service does not take any action to further the interests of any political party.

(3) The arrangements mentioned in subsection (2)(*a*) above shall be such as to ensure that information in the possession of the Service is not disclosed for use in determining whether a person should be employed, or continue to be employed, by any person, or in any office or capacity, except in accordance with provisions in that behalf approved by the Secretary of State.

[(3A) Without prejudice to the generality of subsection (2)(*a*) above, the disclosure of information shall be regarded as necessary for the proper discharge of the functions of the Security Service if it consists of—

    (*a*) the disclosure of records subject to and in accordance with the Public Records Act 1958; or

    (*b*) the disclosure, subject to and in accordance with arrangements approved by the Secretary of State, of information to the Comptroller and Auditor General for the purposes of his functions.][2]

(4) The Director-General shall make an annual report on the work of the Service to the Prime Minister and the Secretary of State and may at any time report to either of them on any matter relating to its work. . . .

4. The Security Service Commissioner

(1) The Prime Minister shall appoint as a Commissioner for the purposes of this Act a person who holds or has held high judicial office within the meaning of the Appellate Jurisdiction Act 1876.

(2) The Commissioner shall hold office in accordance with the terms of his appointment and there shall be paid to him by the Secretary of State such allowances as the Treasury may determine.

(3) In addition to his functions under the subsequent provisions of this Act the Commissioner shall keep under review the exercise by the Secretary of State of his [powers, so far as they relate to applications made by the Service, under sections 5 and 6 of the Intelligence Services Act 1994.][3]

(4) It shall be the duty of every member of the Service and of every official of the department of the Secretary of State to disclose or give to the Commissioner such documents or information as he may require for the purpose of enabling him to discharge his functions.

1 Inserted by the Intelligence Services Act 1994, Sch. 4, para. 1(1).
2 Inserted by ibid., para. 1(2).
3 Substituted by the Intelligence Services Act 1994, Sch. 4, para. 3.

(5) The Commissioner shall make an annual report on the discharge of his functions to the Prime Minister and may at any time report to him on any matter relating to his discharge of those functions.

(6) The Prime Minister shall lay before each House of Parliament a copy of each annual report made by the Commissioner under subsection (5) above together with a statement as to whether any matter has been excluded from that copy in pursuance of subsection (7) below.

(7) If it appears to the Prime Minister, after consultation with the Commissioner, that the publication of any matter in a report would be prejudicial to the continued discharge of the functions of the Service, the Prime Minister may exclude that matter from the copy of the report as laid before each House of Parliament.

(8) The Secretary of State may, after consultation with the Commissioner and with the approval of the Treasury as to numbers, provide the Commissioner with such staff as the Secretary of State thinks necessary for the discharge of his functions.

5. Investigation of complaints

(1) There shall be a Tribunal for the purpose of investigating complaints about the Service in the manner specified in Schedule 1 to this Act.

(2) Schedule 2 to this Act shall have effect with respect to the constitution, procedure and other matters relating to the Tribunal.

(3) The Commissioner shall have the functions conferred on him by Schedule 1 to this Act and give the Tribunal all such assistance in discharging their functions under that Schedule as they may require.

(4) The decisions of the Tribunal and the Commissioner under that Schedule (including decisions as to their jurisdictions) shall not be subject to appeal or liable to be questioned in any court. . . .

7. Short title, commencement and extent

. . . .

(3) This Act extends to Northern Ireland.

(4) Her Majesty may by Order in Council direct that any of the provisions of this Act specified in the Order shall extend, with such exceptions, adaptations and modifications as may be so specified, to the Isle of Man, any of the Channel Islands or any colony.

SCHEDULE 1

INVESTIGATION OF COMPLAINTS

Preliminary

1. Any person may complain to the Tribunal if he is aggrieved by anything which he believes the Service has done in relation to him or to any property of his; and, unless the Tribunal consider that the complaint is frivolous or vexatious, they shall investigate it in accordance with this Schedule.

Investigations and determinations

2. (1) The Tribunal shall investigate whether the complainant has been the subject of inquiries by the Service.

(2) If the Tribunal find that the Service has made inquiries about the complainant but that those inquiries had ceased at the time when the complaint was made, they shall determine whether, at the time when the inquiries were instituted, the Service had reasonable grounds for deciding to institute inquiries about the complainant in the discharge of its functions.

(3) If the Tribunal find that inquiries by the Service about the complainant were continuing at the time when the complaint was made, they shall determine whether, at that time, the Service had reasonable grounds for deciding to continue inquiries about the complainant in the discharge of its functions.

(4) Where it appears to the Tribunal that the inquiries had been or were being made about the complainant on the ground of his membership of a category of persons regarded by the Service as requiring investigation in the discharge of its functions, the Tribunal shall regard the Service as having reasonable grounds for deciding to institute or continue inquiries about the complainant if the Tribunal consider that the Service had reasonable grounds for believing him to be a member of that category.

3. If and so far as the complainant alleges that the Service has disclosed information for use in determining whether he should be employed, or continue to be employed, by any person or in any office or capacity specified by him, the Tribunal shall investigate whether the Service has disclosed information for that purpose and, if the Tribunal find that it has done so, they shall determine whether the Service had reasonable grounds for believing the information to be true.

4. (1) If and so far as the complainant alleges that anything has been done by the Service in relation to any property of his, the Tribunal shall refer the complaint to the Commissioner who shall investigate whether a warrant has been issued under section 3 of this Act in respect of that property and if he finds that such a warrant has been issued he shall, applying the principles applied by a court on an application for judicial review, determine whether the Secretary of State was acting properly in issuing or renewing the warrant.

(2) The Commissioner shall inform the Tribunal of his conclusion on any complaint so far as referred to him under this paragraph.

Report of conclusions

5. (1) Where the Tribunal determine under paragraph 2 or 3 above that the Service did not have reasonable grounds for the decision or belief in question, they shall—

(*a*) give notice to the complainant that they have made a determination in his favour under that paragraph; and

(*b*) make a report of their findings to the Secretary of State and to the Commissioner.

(2) The Tribunal shall also give notice to the complainant of any determination in his favour by the Commissioner under paragraph 4 above.

(3) Where in the case of any complaint no such determination as is mentioned in sub-paragraph (1) or (2) above is made by the Tribunal or the Commissioner the Tribunal shall give notice to the complainant that no determination in his favour has been made on his complaint.

Remedies

6. (1) Where the Tribunal give a complainant notice of such a determination as is mentioned in paragraph 5(1) above, the Tribunal may—

(*a*) if the determination is under paragraph 2 above, order inquiries by the Service about the complainant to be ended and any records relating to such inquiries to be destroyed;

(*b*) if the determination is under that paragraph or paragraph 3 above, direct the Secretary of State to pay to the complainant such sum by way of compensation as may be specified by the Tribunal.

(2) Where the Tribunal give a complainant notice of such a determination as is mentioned in paragraph 5(2) above the Tribunal may—

(*a*) quash any warrant in respect of any property of the complainant which the Commissioner has found to have been improperly issued or renewed and which he considers should be quashed;

(*b*) if the Commissioner considers that a sum should be paid to the complainant by way of compensation, direct the Secretary of State to pay to the complainant such sum as the Commissioner may specify.

References to the Commissioner

7. (1) If in a case investigated by the Tribunal under paragraph 2 above they consider that the Service may not be justified in regarding all members of a particular category as requiring investigation they shall refer that matter to the Commissioner.

(2) If in any case investigated by the Tribunal—

(*a*) the Tribunal's conclusions on the matters which they are required to investigate are such that no determination is made by them in favour of the complainant; but

(*b*) it appears to the Tribunal from the allegations made by the complainant that it is appropriate for there to be an investigation into whether the Service has in any other respect acted unreasonably in relation to the complainant or his property,

they shall refer that matter to the Commissioner.

(3) The Commissioner may report any matter referred to him under this paragraph to the Secretary of State who may take such action in the light of the report as he thinks fit, including any action which the Tribunal have power to take or direct under paragraph 6 above.

Supplementary

8. (1) The persons who may complain to the Tribunal under this Schedule include any organisation and any association or combination of persons.

(2) References in this Schedule to a complainant's property include references to any place where the complainant resides or works.

9. (1) No complaint shall be entertained under this Schedule if and so far as it relates to anything done before the date on which this Schedule comes into force.

(2) Where any inquiries about a person were instituted before that date and no decision had been taken before that date to discontinue them, paragraph 2 above shall have effect as if they had been instituted on that date.

Intelligence Services Act 1994

The Secret Intelligence Service

1. The Secret Intelligence Service

(1) There shall continue to be a Secret Intelligence Service (in this Act referred to as 'the Intelligence Service') under the authority of the Secretary of State; and, subject to subsection (2) below, its functions shall be—

    (*a*) to obtain and provide information relating to the actions or intentions of persons outside the British Islands; and

    (*b*) to perform other tasks relating to the actions or intentions of such persons.

(2) The functions of the Intelligence Service shall be exercisable only—

    (*a*) in the interests of national security, with particular reference to the defence and foreign policies of Her Majesty's Government in the United Kingdom; or

    (*b*) in the interests of the economic well-being of the United Kingdom; or

    (*c*) in support of the prevention or detection of serious crime.

2. The Chief of the Intelligence Service

(1) The operations of the Intelligence Service shall continue to be under the control of a Chief of that Service appointed by the Secretary of State.

(2) The Chief of the Intelligence Service shall be responsible for the efficiency of that Service and it shall be his duty to ensure—

    (*a*) that there are arangements for securing that no information is obtained by the Intelligence Service except so far as necessary for the proper discharge of its functions and that no information is disclosed by it except so far as necessary—

        (i) for that purpose;

        (ii) in the interests of national security;

        (iii) for the purpose of the prevention or detection of serious crime; or

        (iv) for the purpose of any criminal proceedings; and

    (*b*) that the Intelligence Service does not take any action to further the interests of any United Kingdom political party.

[Subsections (3) and (4) follow the terms of s. 2(3A) and (4) of the Security Service Act 1989 (above, p. 501).]

GCHQ

3. The Government Communications Headquarters

(1) There shall continue to be a Government Communications Headquarters under the authority of the Secretary of State; and, subject to subsection (2) below, its functions shall be—

    (*a*) to monitor or interfere with electromagnetic, acoustic and other emissions and any equipment producing such emissions and to obtain and provide information derived from or related to such emissions or equipment and from encrypted material; and

    (*b*) to provide advice and assistance about—

        (i) languages, including terminology used for technical matters, and

        (ii) cryptography and other matters relating to the protection of information and other material,

    to the armed forces of the Crown, to Her Majesty's Government in the United Kingdom or to a Northern Ireland Department or to any other organisation which is determined for the purposes of this section in such manner as may be specified by the Prime Minister.

(2) The functions referred to in subsection (1)(*a*) above shall be exercisable only—

    (*a*) in the interests of national security, with particular reference to the defence and foreign policies of Her Majesty's Government in the United Kingdom; or

    (*b*) in the interests of the economic well-being of the United Kingdom in relation to the actions or intentions of persons outside the British Islands; or

    (*c*) in support of the prevention or detection of serious crime.

(3) In this Act the expression 'GCHQ' refers to the Government Communications Headquarters and to any unit or part of a unit of the armed forces of the Crown which is for the time being required by the Secretary of State to assist the Government Communications Headquarters in carrying out its functions.

4. The Director of GCHQ

(1) The operations of GCHQ shall continue to be under the control of a Director appointed by the Secretary of State.

(2) The Director shall be responsible for the efficiency of GCHQ and it shall be his duty to ensure—

    (a) that there are arrangements for securing that no information is obtained by GCHQ except so far as necessary for the proper discharge of its functions and that no information is disclosed by it except so far as necessary for that purpose or for the purpose of any criminal proceedings; and

    (b) that GCHQ does not take any action to further the interests of any United Kingdom political party.

[Subsections (3) and (4) follow the terms of s. 2(3A) and (4) of the Security Service Act 1989 (above, p. 501).]

Authorisation of certain actions

5. Warrants: general

(1) No entry on or interference with property or with wireless telegraphy shall be unlawful if it is authorised by a warrant issued by the Secretary of State under this section.

(2) The Secretary of State may, on an application made by the Security Service, the Intelligence Service or GCHQ, issue a warrant under this section authorising the taking, subject to subsection (3) below, of such action as is specified in the warrant in respect of any property so specified or in respect of wireless telegraphy so specified if the Secretary of State—

    (a) thinks it necessary for the action to be taken on the ground that it is likely to be of substantial value in assisting, as the case may be,—

        (i) the Security Service in carrying out any of its functions under the 1989 Act; or

        (ii) the Intelligence Service in carrying out any of its functions under section 1 above; or

        (iii) GCHQ in carrying out any function which falls within section 3(1)(a) above; and

    (b) is satisfied that what the action seeks to achieve cannot reasonably be achieved by other means; and

    (c) is satisfied that satisfactory arrangements are in force under section 2(2)(a) of the 1989 Act (duties of the Director-General of the Security Service), section 2(2)(a) above or section 4(2)(a) above with respect to the disclosure of information obtained by virtue of this section and that any information obtained under the warrant will be subject to those arrangements.

(3) A warrant authorising the taking of action in support of the prevention or detection of serious crime may not relate to property in the British Islands.

(4) Subject to subsection (5) below, the Security Service may make an application under section (2) above for a warrant to be issued authorising that Service (or a person acting on its behalf) to take such action as is specified in the warrant on behalf of the Intelligence Service or GCHQ and, where such a warrant is issued, the functions of the Security Service shall include the carrying out of the action so specified, whether or not it would otherwise be within its functions.

(5) The Security Service may not make an application for a warrant by virtue of subsection (4) above except where the action proposed to be authorised by the warrant—

    (a) is action in respect of which the Intelligence Service or, as the case may be, GCHQ could make such an application; and

    (b) is to be taken otherwise than in support of the prevention or detection of serious crime.

6. Warrants: procedure and duration, etc.

(1) A warrant shall not be issued except—

    (a) under the hand of the Secretary of State; or

    (b) in an urgent case where the Secretary of State has expressly authorised its issue and a statement of that fact is endorsed on it, under the hand of a senior official of his department.

(2) A warrant shall, unless renewed under subsection (3) below, cease to have effect—

    (a) if the warrant was under the hand of the Secretary of State, at the end of the period of six months beginning with the day on which it was issued; and

    (b) in any other case, at the end of the period ending with the second working day following that day.

(3) If at any time before the day on which a warrant would cease to have effect the Secretary of State considers it necessary for the warrant to continue to have effect for the purpose for which it was issued, he may by an instrument under his hand renew it for a period of six months beginning with that day.

(4) The Secretary of State shall cancel a warrant if he is satisfied that the action authorised by it is no longer necessary.

(5) In the preceding provisions of this section 'warrant' means a warrant under section 5 above.

(6) As regards the Security Service, this section and section 5 above have effect in place of section 3 (property warrants) of the 1989 Act, and accordingly—

    (a) a warrant issued under that section of the 1989 Act and current when this section and section 5 above come into force shall be treated as a warrant under section 5 above, but without any change in the date on which the warrant was in fact issued or last renewed; and

    (b) section 3 of the 1989 Act shall cease to have effect.

7. Authorisation of acts outside the British Islands

(1) If, apart from this section, a person would be liable in the United Kingdom for any act done outside the British Islands, he shall not be so liable if the act is one which is authorised to be done by virtue of an authorisation given by the Secretary of State under this section.

(2) In subsection (1) above 'liable in the United Kingdom' means liable under the criminal or civil law of any part of the United Kingdom.

(3) The Secretary of State shall not give an authorisation under this section unless he is satisfied—

(a) that any acts which may be done in reliance on the authorisation or, as the case may be, the operation in the course of which the acts may be done will be necessary for the proper discharge of a function of the Intelligence Service; and

(b) that there are satisfactory arrangements in force to secure—

(i) that nothing will be done in reliance on the authorisation beyond what is necessary for the proper discharge of a function of the Intelligence Service; and

(ii) that, in so far as any acts may be done in reliance on the authorisation, their nature and likely consequences will be reasonable, having regard to the purposes for which they are carried out; and

(c) that there are satisfactory arrangements in force under section 2(2)(a) above with respect to the disclosure of information obtained by virtue of this section and that any information obtained by virtue of anything done in reliance on the authorisation will be subject to those arrangements.

(4) Without prejudice to the generality of the power of the Secretary of State to give an authorisation under this section, such an authorisation—

(a) may relate to a particular act or acts, to acts of a description specified in the authorisation or to acts undertaken in the course of an operation so specified;

(b) may be limited to a particular person or persons of a description so specified; and

(c) may be subject to conditions so specified.

(5) An authorisation shall not be given under this section except—

(a) under the hand of the Secretary of State; or

(b) in an urgent case where the Secretary of State has expressly authorised it to be given and a statement of that fact is endorsed on it, under the hand of a senior official of his department.

(6) An authorisation shall, unless renewed under subsection (7) below, cease to have effect—

(a) if the authorisation was given under the hand of the Secretary of State, at the end of the period of six months beginning with the day on which it was given;

(b) in any other case, at the end of the period ending with the second working day following the day on which it was given.

(7) If at any time before the day on which an authorisation would cease to have effect the Secretary of State considers it necessary for the authorisation to continue to have effect for the purpose for which it was given, he may by an instrument under his hand renew it for a period of six months beginning with that day.

(8) The Secretary of State shall cancel an authorisation if he is satisfied that any act authorised by it is no longer necessary.

The Commissioner, the Tribunal and the investigation of complaints

[Sections 8 and 9 provide for the appointment of a Commissioner and a Tribunal for the purposes of this Act following the terms of ss. 4 and 5 of the Security Services Act 1989 (above, pp. 501–502).]

The Intelligence and Security Committee

10. The Intelligence and Security Committee

(1) There shall be a Committee, to be known as the Intelligence and Security Committee and in this section referred to as 'the Committee', to examine the expenditure, administration and policy of—

(a) the Security Service;

(b) the Intelligence Service; and

(c) GCHQ.

(2) The Committee shall consist of nine members—

(a) who shall be drawn both from the members of the House of Commons and from the members of the House of Lords; and

(b) none of whom shall be a Minister of the Crown.

(3) The members of the Committee shall be appointed by the Prime Minister after consultation with the Leader of the Opposition, within the meaning of the Ministerial and other Salaries Act 1975; and one of those members shall be so appointed as Chairman of the Committee.

(4) Schedule 3 to this Act shall have effect with respect to the tenure of office of members of, the procedure of and other matters relating to, the Committee; and in that Schedule 'the Committee' has the same meaning as in this section.

(5) The Committee shall make an annual report on the discharge of their functions to the Prime Minister and may at any time report to him on any matter relating to the discharge of those functions.

(6) The Prime Minister shall lay before each House of Parliament a copy of each annual report made by the Committee under subsection (5) above together with a statement as to whether any matter has been excluded from that copy in pursuance of subsection (7) below.

(7) If it appears to the Prime Minister, after consultation with the Committee, that the publication of any matter in a report would be prejudicial to the continued discharge of the functions of either of the Services or, as the case may be, GCHQ, the Prime Minister may exclude that matter from the copy of the report as laid before each House of Parliament. . . .

12. Short title, commencement and extent

. . . .

(3) This Act extends to Northern Ireland.

(4) Her Majesty may by Order in Council direct that any of the provisions of this Act specified in the Order shall extend, with such exceptions, adaptations and modifications as appear to Her to be necessary or expedient, to the Isle of Man, any of the Channel Islands or any colony.

NOTES

1. Schedule 1 of the 1994 Act makes provision for the investigation of complaints by the Tribunal established by that Act. It is similar in terms to Sch. 1 of the 1989 Act, but there are modifications. Complaints relating to property or authorisations under s. 7 of the 1994 Act must be referred to the Commissioner. Otherwise, the Tribunal must investigate (para. 3):

'(a) whether the Intelligence Service or, as the case may be, GCHQ has obtained or provided information or performed any other tasks in relation to the actions or intentions of the complainant; and
(b) if so, whether, applying the principles applied by a court on an application for judicial review, the Intelligence Service or GCHQ had reasonable grounds for doing what it did.'

Likewise, the Commissioner must determine whether the Secretary of State was acting properly in issuing or renewing a warrant or authorisation by applying judicial review principles (para. 4). The provisions as to the report of conclusions and special references to the Commissioner are broadly similar. If a complaint is upheld, the Tribunal may, as the case may be, quash a warrant or authorisation directing the payment of compensation by the Secretary of State, or (para. 8):

'direct that the obtaining and provision of information in relation to the complainant or, as the case may be, the conduct of other activities in relation to him or to any property of his shall cease and that any records relating to such information so obtained or provided or such other activities shall be destroyed'.

2. The composition of the Tribunals under the two Acts is set out, respectively, in Sch. 2 of the 1989 Act and Sch. 2 of the 1994 Act. In each case it comprises between three and five lawyers of at least ten years' standing, appointed by the Queen for renewable five year periods. A President and Vice-President may be designated (the first President of the Security Service Tribunal was Simon Brown J). Each Tribunal's functions may be performed by any two or more members at any place in the UK. Every member of the three services must disclose such documents or information as the relevant Tribunal may require for the purpose of enabling it to carry out its functions. Each Tribunal may determine its own procedure. However, it must not disclose without consent any document or information given to it by any person, to any complainant, Crown servant (other than the Commissioner) or other person, and accordingly must not, except in reports under Sch. 1, para. 5(1)(b) of the 1989 Act or Sch. 1, para. 6(1)(b) of the 1994 Act, give any reason for a determination notified by it to a complainant.

3. In his first Commissioner's Report under the 1989 Act, for 1990 (Cm 1480, 1991) Stuart-Smith LJ concluded that the Secretaries of State had properly exercised their powers, and noted that all complaints had been rejected. He applied judicial review principles to the review of warrants under s. 4(3) of the 1989 Act and has concluded that it would not be in the public interest to publish statistics of warrants (1990 Report, paras. 12 and 14). In interpreting s. 1(2) of the Act he noted that the term 'national security' was not defined in the Act, and was not limited to the matters listed 'in particular' in that subsection (ibid., para. 10):

'The concept of national security . . . is wider than this and is not easily defined; indeed it is probably undesirable that I attempt an all embracing definition. In my opinion it includes the defence of the realm and the government's defence and foreign policies involving the protection of vital national interests in this country and abroad. In this regard I would draw a distinction between national interests and the interests, which are not necessarily the same, of the government of the day. What is a vital national interest is a question of fact and degree, more easily recognised when being considered than defined in advance.'

To date, the Commissioner has remained satisfied that powers are exercised properly and no complaint has been upheld (Annual Reports for 1991, 1992, 1993 and 1994 (Cm. 1946, 2174, 2523 and 2827)). In his 1992 Report, Stuart-Smith LJ noted in the three years 1990–92, 40 complaints had been referred to him concerning property, and in no case did he find that a warrant had been issued. While being unable to be categorical, it was his opinion that unauthorised operations were not undertaken. His reasons were (Cm. 2174, para. 8):

'First, I believe that very tight control over such operations as are conducted is exercised by those in managerial positions in the Service. Secondly, technical operations of this kind are complex and expensive in money and human resources; it is unlikely that such resources would be squandered on unauthorised as opposed to authorised operations. Thirdly, such is the complexity of most technical operations that it would not be feasible to conceal from the management and colleagues the number of people, use of equipment and time which would need to be deployed on such unauthorised activity. Fourthly, if the target is a legitimate one within the functions of the Service, there should be no difficulty in obtaining a warrant; the Service can have no interest or reason to conduct unauthorised operations which, if discovered, would give rise to possible legal action and certain scandal.'

4. The reception of the Security Service Act 1989 and the Intelligence Services Act 1994 has generally been critical.[1] Among the criticisms of the 1989 Act made by Leigh and Lustgarten, (1989) 52 MLR 801 were:

(1) The broad definition of 'subversion' reflected in s. 1(2): 'Actions intended to overthrow or undermine parliamentary democracy by political, industrial or violent means'. This was based on, but even broader than a definition given by Lord Harris when a Home Office Minister in a House of Lords debate:

'activities which threaten the safety or wellbeing of the state, and are intended to undermine or overthrow parliamentary democracy by political, industrial or violent means'

(357 HL Deb, col 947, 26 February 1975; endorsed by the Home Secretary, Merlin Rees, 947 HC Deb, col 618, 6 April 1978: see R. J. Spjut, (1979) 6 BJLS 254). Leigh and Lustgarten argue that this is unacceptably broad given the inherent right-wing bias of security agencies (see (1989) 52 MLR 801, 805–809). While

1 On the 1989 Act, see I. Leigh and L. Lustgarten, (1989) 52 MLR 801; P. Birkinshaw, *Reforming the Secret State* (1990), pp. 34–43. On the 1994 Act, see J. Wadham, (1994) 57 MLR 916; M. Supperstone, [1994] PL 329.

'subversion' at present accounts for a very small proportion of the Service's work (above, p. 500), the involvement of the Service and Special Branch in the past in the surveillance of such bodies as the NCCL (above, p. 464) and in covert operations against the NUM in the miners' strike (see S. Milne, *The Enemy Within: MI5, Maxwell and the Scargill Affair* (1994)) is not reassuring.[1]

(2) Lack of clarity in the arrangements for ministerial responsibility and control (ibid, pp. 810–814). The Act failed to acknowledge the central place of the Prime Minister in the security and intelligence scheme, and left unclear the extent to which the Director-General may be given direct orders and the extent to which, conversely, ministers should be consulted by the Director-General. See now n. **8**, below.

(3) Absence of any form of parliamentary oversight, or even a non-parliamentary oversight committee comprising privy councillors (ibid, pp. 814–822). See now n. **9**, below.

(4) The broad legal powers conferred by section 3 (see now ss. 5, 6 of the 1994 Act) (ibid, pp. 822–828). Warrants are issued by the Secretary of State rather than a judicial officer; unlike under PACE there are no privileged or exempted categories of information (see above, pp. 85–87); and there are no requirements as to the degree of detail required in warrant applications.

'The section amounts to statutory authorisation of ministerial general warrants for reasons of state necessity of the kind which the common law disapproved in the celebrated case of *Entick v Carrington* (above, p. 44).'

It is also uncertain whether the royal prerogative may continue as a source of legal power for the service (cf. *R v Secretary of State for the Home Department, ex p Northumbria Police Authority* [1988] 1 All ER 556).

(5) The inadequacy of the complaints mechanism ((1989) 52 MLR 801, 828–835). Particular difficulties include how a person will know whether he has been 'bugged, burgled or investigated' (service personnel who feel they have been asked to behave improperly in this way are *not* permitted to complain to the Tribunal or Commissioner); the complainant will not be given reasons for the Tribunal's decision; judicial review is excluded.

5. In *R v Security Service Tribunal, ex p Hewitt* (Unreported, 14 February 1992), Kennedy J refused to hold that the retention of records by the Service necessarily meant that there was no 'discontinuance' of 'inquiries,' giving the tribunal jurisdiction under Sch. 1, para. 9, to deal with the question whether files on the applicants were still open and in the possession of the service. His Lordship refused leave to apply for judicial review, having accepted 'for today's purposes' that it is arguable that in certain circumstances the court could entertain such an application notwithstanding s. 5(4) of the 1989 Act.

6. In three cases, the European Commission of Human Rights has rejected as inadmissible complaints that the structure of the 1989 Act was insufficiently certain for interference with private life to be 'in accordance with the law' and thus justifiable under Article 8, ECHR. See *Eskester v UK* (App. No. 18601/91, 2 April 1993), *Redgrave v UK* (App. No. 20271/92, 1 September 1993) and *Hewitt and Harman v UK* (App. No. 20317/92, 1 September 1993) (a further application), discussed by Stuart-Smith LJ in his 1993 Report (Cm. 2523).

---

1 See also the accounts, from an earlier era, of the surveillance of the Communist Party of Great Britain, the National Unemployed Workers Movement and the NCCL: R. Thurlow, *The Secret State* (1994), Chap. 5 ('Reds in the Bed'); J. Morgan, *Conflict and Order* (1987), Chap. 8 ('The Police and the Unemployed Marchers, 1918–1939'); Liberty, *Agenda*, Summer 1993, pp. 10–11.

7. Given the absence, prior to the 1989 Act, of any specific legal powers, the Security Service has in practice operated in conjunction with the Special Branches attached to each police force. According to the *Guidelines on Special Branch Work in Great Britain* (Home Office, Scottish Office, July 1994):

'Special Branches exist primarily to acquire intelligence, to assess its potential operational value, and to contribute more generally to its interpretation. They do so both to meet local policing needs and also to assist the Security Service.'

Its single most important function is counter-terrorism. On the historical background R. Allason, *The Branch: A History of the Metropolitan Police Special Branch 1883–1983* (1983); and B. Porter, *The Origins of the Vigilant State* (1987). An investigation into Special Branch by the House of Commons Home Affairs Committee was hampered by limitations on the information made available to it: *Fourth Report from the Home Affairs Committee*, 1984–85 HC 71.

8. The Intelligence Services Act put the Secret Intelligence Service (sometimes known as MI6) and GCHQ on the same statutory footing as the Security Service. Points (4) and (5) made by Leigh and Lustgarten in relation to the 1989 Act (see n. **4**) remain relevant here. However, there has been clarification of the arrangements for ministerial responsibility (see the booklet on the *Central Intelligence Machinery* published by HMSO in 1993), and some provision for external oversight (see n. **9**). The Prime Minister is responsible for intelligence and security matters overall, supported by the Secretary of the Cabinet. The Home Secretary is responsible for the Security Service, the Foreign Secretary for SIS and GCHQ and the Secretary of State for Defence for the Defence Intelligence Staff. There is a Ministerial Committee on the Intelligence Services, assisted by the Permanent Secretaries' Committee on the Intelligence Service (PSIS). The Joint Intelligence Committee, based in the Cabinet Office, sets the UK's national intelligence requirements and produces a weekly survey on intelligence. It includes senior officials, the heads of the three services and the Intelligence Co-Ordinator. Its chairman has direct access to the Prime Minister.

The existence of GCHQ was formally acknowledged by the Prime Minister after the Prime affair (see above, p. 459). The decision to ban trade unionism at GCHQ led to litigation that was ultimately unsuccessful (*Council of Civil Service Unions v Minister for the Civil Service* [1985] AC 374) and the dismissal of some employees. See S. Fredman and G. S. Morris, *The State as Employer* (1989), pp. 98–102; K. D. Ewing and C. Gearty, *Freedom under Thatcher* (1990), pp. 130–136; H. Canning and R. Norton-Taylor, *A Conflict of Loyalties: GCHQ 1984–1991* (1991).

Section 7 of the 1994 Act is the 'statutory equivalent of James Bond's "licence to kill" ' (J. Wadham, (1994) 57 MLR 916, 922, noting that 'the Minister has stated that: "It is inconceivable that, *in ordinary circumstances*, . . . the Secretary of State . . . would authorise the use of lethal force" ' (emphasis supplied), HC Standing Committee E, col 34, 3 March 1994).

9. The Intelligence Services Act 1994 also introduced an element of independent oversight (the Intelligence and Security Committee). The government did not accept a proposal by the Home Affairs Select Committee that it should provide oversight, and declined to respond in detail to the Committee's view that the Service in any event fell within its jurisdiction as an associated body of the Home Office (see the 1st Report of the HAC, 1992–93 HC 265, *Accountability of the Security Service*, and Government Reply, Cm 2197, 1993). Detailed provision for the Committee is made by Sch. 3. A member of the Committee holds office for the duration of the Parliament in which he is appointed, but must vacate office if he ceases to be an MP or member of the House of Lords or becomes a minister, may be replaced by the Prime Minister or may resign. If the Committee seeks information from any of the heads of the intelligence services, he must either disclose it in accordance with arrangements approved by the Secretary of State, or inform the Committee that it cannot be disclosed (i) because it is sensitive information which in his opinion should not be made available, or (ii) because the Secretary of State has determined that it should not be disclosed. The Secretary of State may override the head of service's view under (i) if he 'considers it desirable in the public interest' (para. 3(3)). He may not make a determination under (ii) 'on the grounds of national security alone', and, subject to that, 'he shall not make such a determination unless the information appears to him to be of such a nature that, if he were requested to produce it before a Departmental Select Committee of the House of Commons, he would think it proper not to do so' (para. 3(4)). Disclosures under para. 3 are to be regarded as disclosures necessary for the proper discharge of the functions of the respective services, for the purposes of the 1989 and 1994 Acts (para. 3(5)). 'Sensitive information' is defined as (para. 4):

'(a) information which might lead to the identification of, or provide details of, sources of information, other assistance or operational methods available to the Security Service, the Intelligence Service or GCHQ;

(b) information about particular operations which have been, are being or are proposed to be undertaken in pursuance of any of the functions of those bodies; and

(c) information provided by, or by an agency of, the Government of a territory outside the United Kingdom where that Government does not consent to the disclosure of the information.'

It will be noted that while the Committee is comprised of Members of Parliament, it is appointed by and responsible to the Prime Minister, although its reports are to be laid before Parliament in the same way as those of the Tribunals and Commissioners under the 1989 and 1994 Acts. The members are to be notified under s. 1(1)(b) of the Official Secrets Act 1989 (above, p. 446: see J. Wadham, (1994) 57 MLR at 926–927). Why should the Committee's access to information be more restricted than the Commissioners (see Wadham, op. cit., at p. 926)? The first chairman is Tom King MP, the former Defence Secretary, and comprises five Conservatives (including Lord Howe), three Labour and one Liberal Democrat MPs (*The Times*, 15 December, 1994; *Interim Report* (Cm. 2873, 1995)).

These arrangements may be compared with those in other jurisdictions. In Canada, the domestic security service was put on a statutory basis by the Canadian Security Intelligence Service Act 1984, with oversight provided by an Inspector-General and a Security Intelligence Review Committee comprising Privy Councillors who are not members of the Senate or the House of Commons. The Australian Security Intelligence Organisation Act 1956 (Cth) put ASIO on a statutory basis. In 1986, two oversight mechanisms were established. The Inspector-General of Intelligence and Security's remit includes inquiry into ASIO's compliance with the law, ministerial directions and human rights, and the propriety of their activities. The Parliamentary Joint Committee on ASIO comprises seven members, with a majority of government members, and a majority from the House of Representatives, appointed after consultation with the leaders of each political party represented in Parliament. The latter development was controversial, but the Committee's powers are circumscribed (see H. P. Lee, (1989) 38 ICLQ 890; Lustgarten and Leigh, op. cit., pp. 455–458). On Canada's arrangements, see Lustgarten and Leigh, op. cit., pp. 458–466; A. Goldsmith, [1985] PL 39; J. Ll. J.

Edwards, (1985) 5 UJLS 143; and M. Rankin, (1986) 36 UTLJ 249; S. Garson, [1992] PL 377.

For an overview of the issues of accountability, see P. Gill, *Policing Politics: Security Intelligence and the Liberal Democratic State* (1994). Gill concludes that 'there has been inadequate political or ministerial control of the agencies so that they have been able to operate autonomously' and that 'the complete lack of effective external review of security intelligence operations has led to serious abuses of civil rights' (p. 311). He calls for a wide-ranging inquiry, emphasising the 'paramount need' for information (p. 313).

10. The new Intelligence and Security Committee must be distinguished from the Security Commission, a body that advises the Prime Minister, normally on breaches of security: see I. Leigh and L. Lustgarten, 'The Security Commission: Constitutional Achievement or Curiosity?' [1991] PL 215 and Lustgarten and Leigh, op. cit., pp. 476–491.

7 Access to information

1. There is no general public legal right of access to official information. There has, however, been a series of moves to make government more open, the most recent and significant development being a review in 1992–93 to identify areas of excessive secrecy and to propose ways of increasing openness. The results of the review were presented in a White Paper, *Open Government* (Cm 2290, 1993), and involved, apart from the continued provision of information on targets and performance under the Citizen's Charter (p. 5):

'(i)   a new Code of Practice on access to information held by central government and public bodies, and consultation on the introduction of similar Codes for the National Health Service and local authorities;
(ii)   a role for the Parliamentary Ombudsman in investigating complaints that departments have not complied with the Code;
(iii) a statutory right for people to see government information relating to them;
(iv)   a statutory right of access to health and safety information;
(v)   selective introduction of 'harm tests' into the criminal provisions covering unauthorised disclosure of information entrusted to government;
(vi)   a reduction in the number of public records withheld from release beyond thirty years.'

2. Public records in the Public Records Office are not available for public inspection

'[until the expiration of the period of thirty years beginning with the first day of January in the year next after that in which they were created, or such other period] . . . as the Lord Chancellor may, with the approval or at the request, of the Minister or other person, if any, who appears to him to be primarily concerned, for the time being prescribe as respects any particular class of public records.' (Public Records Act 1958 s. 5(1), as amended by the Public Records Act 1967).

Longer periods have been prescribed for the following categories (White Paper on *Open Government*, Chap. 9):

(i)   'Exceptionally sensitive records containing information, the disclosure of which would not be in the public interest *in that* it would harm defence, international relations, national security (including the maintenance of law and order) or the economic interests of the UK and its dependent territories.'
(ii)   'Documents containing information supplied in confidence the disclosure of which would or might constitute a breach of good faith.'
(iii) 'Documents containing information about individuals the disclosure of which would cause either: substantial distress, or endangerment from a third party, to persons affected by disclosure or their descendants.'

Further details and guidance are given in Annex C to the White Paper. Criteria (i) and (iii) are narrower than those previously applicable (based on the Report of the Wilson Committee on *Modern Public Records* (Cmnd 8204)) and follow the recommendations of a review group established by the Lord Chancellor in 1992. Records in category (i) are to be reviewed every 10 years; recommended closure periods between 40 and 100 years are specified for other cases by Annex C to the White Paper.

Under s. 3(4) of the 1958 Act departments may, with the approval of the Lord Chancellor, retain records after 30 years if they are 'required for administrative purposes or ought to be retained for any other special reason'. The latter covers, inter alia, security and intelligence and atomic energy material, and is subject to review at least every ten years (White Paper, p. 68). The security and intelligence 'blanket' as regards the records of the security and intelligence agencies is to continue, but intelligence-related documents held by other departments are reviewed as part of the normal procedures (White Paper, p. 69).

As resources permit, departments are to review all material currently withheld for longer than 30 years, to use a blanking-out procedure to delete sensitive information from otherwise releasable documents, to consider blocks of records which, although not 30 years old, may be releasable, and to consider ad hoc requests from historians in respect of blocks of records closed for longer than 30 years (White Paper, pp. 69–70).

The programme of release has been extended to security and intelligence records of historical interest (see White Paper, Annex D).

3. There are many specific statutory provisions preventing the disclosure without lawful authority of information acquired from citizens. See Y. Cripps, [1983] PL 600, 628–631, and the lists of statutes set out in Birkinshaw, *Government and Information* (1990), pp. 345–348. Annex B to the White Paper on *Open Government* lists over 200 provisions concerning disclosure of official information, most protecting third-party information. The government proposes that in future it will assess the cause for harm tests in legislation on disclosure, and to review existing provisions as and when legislative opportunities arise (White Paper, Chap. 8).

4. The main feature of the 1993 White Paper was the proposal for a *Code of Practice on Access to Government Information*. After consultation, the Code was published by the Cabinet Office with effect from 4 April 1994. Under Part I of the Code, the information which the government will release is as follows:

'3. Subject to the exemptions in Part II, the Code commits departments and public bodies under the jurisdiction of the Parliamentary Commissioner for Administration (the Ombudsman):[1]
  (i) to publish the facts and analysis of the facts which the Government considers relevant and important in framing major policy proposals and decisions; such information will normally be made available when policies and decisions are announced;
  (ii) to publish or otherwise make available, as soon as practicable after the Code becomes operational, explanatory material on departments' dealings with the public (including such rules, procedures, internal guidance to officials and similar administrative manuals as will assist better understanding of departmental action in dealing with the public) except where publication could prejudice any matter which should properly be kept confidential under Part II of the Code;
  (iii) to give reasons for administrative decisions to those affected;[2]

1 In Northern Ireland, the Parliamentary Commissioner for Administration and the Commissioner for Complaints.
2 There will be a few areas where well-established convention or legal authority limits the commitment to give reasons, for example decisions on citizenship applications (see s. 44(2) of the British Nationality Act 1981) or certain decisions on merger and monopoly cases or on whether to take enforcement action.

(iv) to publish in accordance with the Citizen's Charter:
  • full information about how public services are run, how much they cost, who is in charge, and what complaints and redress procedures are available;
  • full and, where possible, comparable information about what services are being provided, what targets are set, what standards of service are expected and the results achieved;
(v) to release, in response to specific requests, information relating to their policies, actions and decisions and other matters related to their areas of responsibility.
4. There is no commitment that pre-existing documents, as distinct from information, will be made available in response to requests. The Code does not require departments to acquire information they do not possess, to provide information which is already published, to provide material which the Government did not consider to be reliable information, or to provide information which is provided as part of an existing charged service other than through that service.'

Information is to be provided as soon as practicable, with a target for simple requests of 20 working days. The Code applies to the Government departments and other bodies within the jurisdiction of the Parliamentary Commissioner for Administration, including agencies, and contractors acting on behalf of a department or public body. Charges may be made. The Code does not override the Public Records Act arrangements, and does not extend to information held by courts or in court documents. A complaint that information which should have been provided was not, or that unreasonable charges have been demanded, should be made first to the department or body concerned; if the applicant remains dissatisfied, a complaint can be made via an MP to the PCA.

There is, however, an extensive list of exemptions. Part II sets out 15 categories. In many cases, the exemption only applies if there is actual harm or prejudice, or a reasonable expectation of harm or prejudice, and it is to be considered here whether any harm or prejudice arising out of disclosure is outweighed by the public interest in making information available. The 15 category headings are: (1) Defence, security and international relations; (2) Internal discussion and advice; (3) Communications with the Royal Household; (4) Law enforcement and legal proceedings; (5) Immigration and nationality; (6) Effective management of the economy and collection of tax; (7) Effective management and operations of the public service; (8) Public employment, public appointments and honours; (9) Voluminous or vexatious requests; (10) Publication and prematurity in relation to publication; (11) Research statistics and analysis; (12) Privacy of an individual; (13) Third party's commercial confidences; (14) Information given in confidence; (15) Statutory and other restrictions. Some categories are very broad. For example, category (2) covers 'information whose disclosure would harm the frankness and candour of internal discussion', including proceedings of Cabinet and Cabinet committees; internal opinion, advice, recommendation, consultation and deliberation; analysis of alternative policy options; and confidential communications between departments, public bodies and regulatory bodies.

The proposed Code was welcomed by almost all the 103 respondents to the White Paper as 'an important step to greater openness'. However, 14 respondents still favoured freedom of information legislation, and some criticised the point that access is to *information* not *documents* and the width of the exemptions (see *Open Government: Summary of Consultation Comments and Government Response* (Cabinet Office (OPSS) 29 March 1994). The government's preference for a Code rather than legislation is justified as follows:

'The Government believes that a code of practice will be more effective than freedom of information legislation in changing administrative culture so that in future the presumption will be in favour of permitting access. The Code of Practice also recognises that the policy process of Government is something in which Parliament, rather than the courts, has the ultimate interest, and ensures that the principle of ministerial accountability to Parliament remains intact. The Code will be less legalistic and confrontational than a statutory approach where private rights are not at issue. Review and interpretation will be more flexible, with less scope for legal costs and delays.'

The PCA has been given additional resources to support this extension of his activities. Supporters of a statutory right of access include the Campaign for Freedom of Information and Liberty. A Right to Know Bill, proposed by Mark Fisher MP, was talked out in July 1993 (see CFI, *Questions and Answers about the Right to Know Bill; Secrets* (Newspaper of the CFI, August 1993).

5. The Campaign for Freedom of Information has been prominent in support of a series of private member's bills that have reached the statute book and which improve access to information in specific areas away from central government. See the Local Government (Access to Information) Act 1985 (introduced by Robin Squire MP, widening access to information held by local authorities); the Access to Personal Files Act 1987 (Archy Kirkwood MP, enabling regulations to be made covering local authority housing and social work records): see Access to Personal Files (Social Services) Regulations 1989 (S.I. 1989 No. 206) and Access to Personal Files (Housing) Regulations 1989 (S.I. 1989 No. 503); the Access to Medical Reports Act 1988 (Archy Kirkwood MP, covering reports supplied by a doctor to an insurance company or employer); and the Environment and Safety Information Act 1988 (Chris Smith MP, establishing public registers of notices issued by authorities enforcing the Fire Precautions Act 1971, the Health and Safety at Work etc. Act 1974, the Safety at Sports Grounds Act 1975 and the Food and Environmental Protection Act 1985); and the Access to Health Records Act 1990. This is not to say that the legislation has always emerged as the Campaign would have wished: the Access to Personal Files Act 1987 in particular emerged in an 'eviscerated' form (see the notes by P. Birkinshaw in *Current Law Statutes Annotated 1987*). Other Bills have been blocked.

6. Many overseas countries have enacted freedom of information laws creating a general public right of access, subject to exceptions, including the United States of America, Sweden, Norway, Denmark, New Zealand, Australia and Canada.[1]

7. Government information may be protected from disclosure by a claim of public interest immunity. See P. P. Craig, *Administrative Law* (3rd edn., 1994), pp. 712–722 and Simon Brown LJ, [1994] PL 579. In *Balfour v Foreign and Commonwealth Office* [1994] 1 WLR 681, the Court of Appeal held that while the court must always be vigilant to ensure that a claim of public interest immunity is raised only in appropriate circumstances and with appropriate particularity, once a minister certifies that disclosure of documents poses a risk to national security, the court should not exercise its right to inspect those documents. On the controversial PII claims in the course of the prosecution of Matrix Churchill executives for deception in obtaining licences to export machine tool to Iraq, for use in armaments manufacture, see G. Ganz, (1993) 56 MLR 564, (1995) 58 MLR 417; T. R. S. Allan, [1993] Crim LR 660; I. Leigh, [1993] PL 630 and A. Tomkins, ibid., p. 650.

8. It is argued that the 'right to know' cannot be an integral part of freedom of expression, on the ground that the freedom would then be claimed 'where there is no willing speaker' (E. Barendt, *Freedom of Speech* (1987), pp. 82–83, 107–113). For a different view, see P. Bayne, 'Freedom of Information and Political Free Speech' in T. Campbell and W. Sadurski, *Freedom of Communication*, Chap. 10.

---

1 See generally J. Michael, *The Politics of Secrecy* (1982); K. G. Robertson, *Public Secrets* (1982); N. S. Marsh (ed.), *Public Access to Government: Held Information: A Comparative Symposium* (1987); R. Chapman and M. Hunt (eds), *Open Government* (1987); P. Birkinshaw, *Freedom of Information* (1988).

CHAPTER 8

The right to privacy

1 Introduction[1]

The right to privacy was described by Cooley as 'the right to be let alone' (*Torts* (2nd edn, 1888) p. 29). Both the Justice Report (*Privacy and the Law* (1970) p. 5) and the Younger Committee Report (*Report of the Committee on Privacy*, 1972, Cmnd. 5012, p. 17) pointed out the difficulty of finding 'a precise or logical formula which could either circumscribe the meaning of the word "privacy" or define it exhaustively' (Justice Report, p. 5). Each, however, suggested a working definition. The Justice Report (ibid) understood privacy as meaning

'that area of a man's life which, in any given circumstances, a reasonable man with an understanding of the legitimate needs of the community would think it wrong to invade.'

Cf. the definition adopted by A. F. Westin, *Privacy and Freedom* (1970) p. 7:

'Privacy is the claim of individuals, groups, or institutions to determine for themselves when, how, and to what extent information about them is communicated to others. Viewed in terms of the relation of the individual to social participation, privacy is the voluntary and temporary withdrawal of a person from the general society through physical or psychological means, either in a state of solitude or small-group intimacy or, when among larger groups, in a condition of anonymity or reserve.'

The Younger Committee (Report, p. 10) 'conceived of the right of privacy as having two main aspects':

'The first of these is freedom from intrusion upon oneself, one's home, family and relationships. The second is privacy of information, that is the right to determine for oneself how and to what extent information about oneself is communicated to others.'

More recently, the Calcutt Committee[2] adopted the following, similar, working definition of the right to privacy:

---

1 On the right to privacy, see J. D. Baxter, (1977) 8 Cambrian LR 7; S. I. Benn, (1978) 52 Aust LJ 601, 686; L. Brittan, (1963) 37 Tul LR 235; P. Burns, (1976) 54 Can BR 1; Z. Cowen, *Individual Liberty and the Law* (1977) Chaps. 4 & 5; G. Dworkin, (1967) 2 U Tas LR 418; J. Fleming, *Law of Torts* (7th edn, 1987) Chap. 26; P. Goode, (1973-6) 5 Adelaide LR 13; P. Hewitt, *Privacy: The Information Gatherers* (1977); M. Jones (ed.) *Privacy* (1974); D. Madgwick, *Privacy under Attack* (1968); D. Madgwick and T. Smythe, *The Invasion of Privacy* (1974); B. S. Markensis, (1990) 53 MLR 802; G. Marshall, (1975) 21 McGill LJ 242; A. R. Miller, *The Assault on Privacy* (1971); B. Neill, (1962) 25 MLR 393; W. F. Pratt, *Privacy in Britain* (1979); J. B. Rule, *Private Lives and Public Surveillance* (1973); D. J. Siepp, (1983) 3 OJLS 325; S. Stoljar, (1984) 4 Legal Studies 67; J. Swanton, (1974) 48 Aust LJ 91; S. Stromholm, *Right of Privacy and Rights of the Personality* (1967); G. D. S. Taylor, (1971) 34 MLR 288; R. Wacks, (1980) 96 LQR 73; id, *The Protection of Privacy* (1980); id, *Personal Information* (1989); S. Warren and L. Brandeis, (1890) 4 Harv LR 193; A. F. Westin, *Privacy and Freedom* (1970); P. Winfield, (1931) 47 LQR 23; T. L. Yang, (1966) 15 ICLQ 175.
2 *Report of the Committee on Privacy and Related Matters*, Cm 1102 (1990), p. 7.

516

'The right of the individual to be protected against intrusion into his personal life or affairs, or those of his family, by direct physical means or by publication of information.'[1]

The 'principal areas of complaint with regard to intrusions into privacy' *in the private sector* were identified by the Younger Committee (Report, p. 7) as follows: (i) unwanted publicity (by the press and broadcasting); (ii) misuse of personal information (by credit rating agencies, banks, employers, educational institutions (student records) and the medical profession (particularly in industry)); (iii) intrusions on home life (by prying neighbours, landlords, the press, doorstep and postal and telephone sales and promotional methods and private detectives); and (iv) intrusion in business life (industrial espionage).[2] To these may be added *in the public sector* (i) intrusion in the course of the administration of the criminal law, for example, by personal and property searches (the law as to which is considered in Chapter 2), telephone tapping, fingerprinting, and the use of breathalysers and (ii) the misuse of personal information held by public authorities such as income tax, census, social security, council housing and family welfare authorities and the police.[3]

The protection afforded to privacy by English law is piecemeal, incomplete and indirect. There is no general right to privacy. Concern about the adequacy of the protection given has long been voiced (see, e.g., Winfield, (1931) 47 LQR 23) and has in recent years reached the point where it has been the subject of three reports and several private members' bills. The reasons for this activity were identified by the Younger Committee Report, p. 6, as follows:

'18 To some extent the new public concern on this subject is the direct result of new technological developments. Numerous sophisticated electronic devices have been invented and marketed, which greatly increase the possibilities of surreptitious supervision of people's private activities and of spying upon business rivals. Computers have been designed which facilitate the centralisation of information about people's private affairs and its dissemination for purposes other than those for which it was supplied. And, accompanying these technical developments, there has been a spectacular growth in the collection and distribution of information as a commercial activity, which has given rise to anxiety in connection with the granting of credit, mail-order business and other forms of promotion.
19 Furthermore, but by no means least important, there has been a fairly steady flow of complaints about intrusions into privacy by the mass information media. This is a subject as old as the popular press, but its importance has been enhanced in the context of radio and television and by the growing tendency of all media to engage increasingly in "investigative journalism". Press and broadcasting organisations see themselves as the watchdogs of the public in investigating and exposing conduct of many kinds which, though not necessarily involving breaches of the law, may arguably be considered of concern to society and therefore fair game for revelation and public comment in the press or on the air. This may involve the reporting of intimate details of the lives of individuals which would not normally be thought of as being in the public domain.
20 From a wider point of view concern for the protection of privacy has been stimulated by the growing pressures exerted by modern industrial society upon the home and daily life, including such factors as the density of urban housing, the consequent difficulty of escaping from the observation of neighbours, the annoyance of commercial advertising and the increasing inquisitiveness of social surveys, polls and market research about the lives of private citizens.'

1 See also the definitions in the US *Restatement*, below, p. 521, and in the conclusions of the 1967 Nordic Conference on the Right of Privacy (Justice Committee Report, Appendix B, and S. Stromholm, *Right of Privacy and Rights of the Personality* (1967) p. 237). And see W. A. Parent, (1983) 2 Law and Philosophy 305.
2 The problems posed by press conduct, which have been the most persistent and serious cause for concern, were identified in detail by the Calcutt Committee (Report, p. 10).
3 For the result of a survey of complaints to solicitors on privacy invasions which suggested that the privacy problem was a large one, see R. Wacks, [1983] PL 260. On the problem of the 1971 census, see *Security of the Census of Population* (Cmnd. 5365). On prying in the enforcement of the cohabitation rule by the Supplementary Benefits Commission (now abolished), see the extracts in M. Jones (ed), *Privacy* (1974) p. 107.

Although each of these reasons remains valid, it is probably correct to say that concern about the threat posed by computers has declined,[1] while exasperation with unethical or irresponsible press conduct has increased, as indicated by the appointment of the Calcutt Committee.

2 A general right of privacy?

Kaye v Robertson [1991] FSR 62, Court of Appeal

The plaintiff, the star of 'Allo! Allo!', a popular television comedy series, underwent extensive surgery to his head and brain after injuries resulting from storm debris falling on his car. In the interests of Mr Kaye's health, which remained a matter of serious concern, the hospital authorities placed a notice on the door of Mr Kaye's private room asking visitors to contact a member of the hospital staff before visiting. Acting on the instructions of their editor, a journalist and a photographer from *Sunday Sport*, a national newspaper, went to the hospital and, ignoring the notice on the door, entered Mr Kaye's room. They interviewed him and took photographs showing the injuries to his head. This, the editor claimed, was a 'great old-fashioned scoop.' The plaintiff obtained an injunction, based mainly upon *Tolley v Fry*, requiring the first and second defendants, the newspaper editor and publisher respectively, to refrain from publishing the interview and photographs. The defendants appealed to the Court of Appeal.

Glidewell LJ: It is well-known that in English law there is no right to privacy, and accordingly there is no right of action for breach of a person's privacy. The facts of the present case are a graphic illustration of the desirability of Parliament considering whether and in what circumstances statutory provision can be made to protect the privacy of individuals.

In the absence of such a right, the plaintiff's advisers have sought to base their claim to injunctions upon other well-established rights of action. . . .

1. Libel

The basis of the plaintiff's case under this head is that the article as originally written clearly implied that Mr. Kaye consented to give the first 'exclusive' interview to *Sunday Sport*, and to be photographed by their photographer. This was untrue: [according to medical evidence] Mr. Kaye was in no fit condition to give any informed consent, and such consent as he may appear to have given was, and should have been known by *Sunday Sport*'s representative to be, of no effect. The implication in the article would have the effect of lowering Mr. Kaye in the esteem of right-thinking people, and was thus defamatory.

The plaintiff's case is based on the well-known decision in *Tolley v J S Fry & Sons Ltd* [below, p. 488] . . .

Mr. Milmo for the defendants submits that, assuming that the article was capable of having the meaning alleged, this would not be a sufficient basis for interlocutory relief. In *William Coulson & Sons v James Coulson & Co* (1887) 3 TLR 846, this court held that, though the High Court has jurisdiction to grant an interim injunction before the trial of a libel action, it is a jurisdiction to be exercised only sparingly.[2] . . .

This is still the rule in actions for defamation, despite the decision of the House of Lords in *American Cyanamid Co v Ethicon Ltd* [1975] AC 396 in relation to interim injunctions generally. This court so decided in *Herbage v Times Newspapers Ltd*, unreported but decided on 1 May 1981.[3] . . .

It is in my view certainly arguable that the intended article would be libellous, on the authority of *Tolley v Fry*. I think that a jury would probably find that Mr. Kaye had been libelled, but I cannot say that such a conclusion is inevitable. It follows that I agree with Mr. Milmo's submission and in this respect I disagree with the learned judge; I therefore would not base an injunction on a right of action for libel.

1 The problem is tackled by the Data Protection Act 1984. See the annual reports of the Data Protection Registrar, which are published as House of Commons papers.
2 *Ed*. Cf. *Bonnard v Perryman*, below, p. 538.
3 *Ed*. See also *Herbage v Pressdram* [1984] 2 All ER 769, CA.

2. Malicious falsehood

The essentials of this tort are that the defendant has published about the plaintiff words which are false, that they were published maliciously, and that special damage has followed as the direct and natural result of their publication. As to special damage, the effect of section 3(1) of the Defamation Act 1952 is that it is sufficient if the words published in writing are calculated to cause pecuniary damage to the plaintiff. Malice will be inferred if it be proved that the words were calculated to produce damage and that the defendant knew when he published the words that they were false or was reckless as to whether they were false or not.

The test in *Coulson v Coulson (supra)* applies to interlocutory injunctions in actions for malicious falsehood as it does in actions for defamation. However, in relation to this action, the test applies only to the requirement that the plaintiff must show that the words were false. In the present case I have no doubt that any jury which did not find that the clear implication from the words contained in the defendants' draft article were false would be making a totally unreasonable finding. Thus the test is satisfied in relation to this cause of action.

As to malice I equally have no doubt from the evidence, including the transcript of the tape-recording of the 'interview' with Mr. Kaye in his hospital room which we have read, that it was quite apparent to the reporter and photographer from *Sunday Sport* that Mr. Kaye was in no condition to give any informed consent to their interviewing or photographing him. Moreover, even if the journalists had been in any doubt about Mr. Kaye's fitness to give his consent, Mr. Robertson [the first defendant] could not have entertained any such doubt after he read the affidavit sworn on behalf of Mr. Kaye in these proceedings. Any subsequent publication of the falsehood would therefore inevitably be malicious.

As to damage, I have already recorded that Mr. Robertson appreciated that Mr. Kaye's story was one for which other newspapers would be willing to pay 'large sums of money'. It needs little imagination to appreciate that whichever journal secured the first interview with Mr. Kaye would be willing to pay the most. Mr. Kaye thus has a potentially valuable right to sell the story of his accident and his recovery when he is fit enough to tell it. If the defendants are able to publish the article they proposed, or one anything like it, the value of this right would in my view be seriously lessened, and Mr. Kaye's story thereafter be worth much less to him.

I have considered whether damages would be an adequate remedy in these circumstances. They would inevitably be difficult to calculate, would also follow some time after the event, and in my view would in no way be adequate. It thus follows that in my opinion all the preconditions to the grant of an interlocutory injunction in respect of this cause of action are made out. . . .

3. Trespass to the person

. . . The plaintiff's case in relation to this cause of action is that the taking of the flashlight photographs may well have caused distress to Mr. Kaye and set back his recovery, and thus caused him injury. In this sense it can be said to be a battery. . . . I am prepared to accept that it may well be the case that if a bright light is deliberately shone into another person's eyes and injures his sight, or damages him in some other way, this may be in law a battery. But in my view the necessary effects are not established by the evidence in this case. Though there must have been an obvious risk that any disturbance to Mr. Kaye would set back his recovery, there is no evidence that the taking of the photographs did in fact cause him any damage.

Moreover, the injunction sought in relation to this head of action would not be intended to prevent another anticipated battery, since none was anticipated. The intention here is to prevent the defendants from profiting from the taking of the photographs, i.e. from their own trespass. Attractive though this argument may appear to be, I cannot find as a matter of law that an injunction should be granted in these circumstances. . . .

4. Passing off

Mr. Caldecott submits . . . that the essentials of the tort of passing off, as laid down by the speeches in the House of Lords in *E Warnink BV v J Townend & Sons (Hull) Ltd* [1979] AC 731, are satisfied here. . . . I think that the plaintiff is not in the position of a trader in relation to his interest in his story about his accident and his recovery, and thus fails from the start to have a right of action under this head. . . .

Bingham LJ: The defendants' conduct towards the plaintiff here was 'a monstrous invasion of his privacy' (to adopt the language of Griffiths J in *Bernstein v Skyviews Ltd* [1978] QB 479 at 489G). If ever a person has a right to be let alone by strangers with no public interest to pursue, it must surely be when he lies in hospital recovering from brain surgery and in no more than partial command of his faculties. It is this invasion of his privacy which underlies the plaintiff's complaint. Yet it alone, however gross, does not entitle him to relief in English law.

Leggatt LJ: . . . In view of the importance of the topic I add a note about the way in which the common law has developed in the United States to meet the need which in the present case we are unable to fulfil satisfactorily. . . .

It [the right to privacy] is manifested in several forms. . . . One example is such intrusion upon physical solitude as would be objectionable to a reasonable man. So when in *Barber v Time Inc* 159 SW 2d 291 (1942) the plaintiff was confined to a hospital bed, the publication of her photograph taken without consent was held to be an invasion of a private right of which she was entitled to complain. Similarly, a so-called 'right of publicity' has developed to protect the commercial interest of celebrities in their identities. . . . *Carson v Here's Johnny Portable Toilets Inc* 698 F 2d 831 (1983) at page 835.

We do not need a First Amendment to preserve the freedom of the press, but the abuse of that freedom can be ensured only by the enforcement of a right to privacy. This right has so long been disregarded here that it can be recognised now only by the legislature. Especially since there is available in the United States a wealth of experience of the enforcement of this right both at common law and also under statute, it is to be hoped that the making good of this signal shortcoming in our law will not be long delayed.

NOTES

1. Although the Court of Appeal was unanimously of the opinion that an interlocutory injunction should be granted on the basis of malicious falsehood, the appeal was allowed in part, the original injunction being discharged as having been wrongly granted on the basis of the claim of libel.[1] In accordance with the law of malicious falsehood, the new injunction was more limited than the original one. It allowed the publication of the story and certain less objectionable photographs (one of Mr Kaye lying in bed asleep was published) provided that it was not claimed that the plaintiff had given his consent.

2. Exemplary and aggravated damages are available in malicious falsehood: per Sir Michael Kerr in *Joyce v Sengupta* [1993] 1 All ER 897, CA.[2] A case may be brought in malicious falsehood rather than defamation at the discretion of the plaintiff in order to obtain legal aid, which is not available in defamation proceedings: ibid.

3. The Court of Appeal's acknowledgment that there is no right of privacy in English law follows similar pronouncements in *Malone v Metropolitan Police Comr* [1979] Ch 344 Ch D, per Sir Robert Megarry, VC, and *Re X (A Minor)* [1975] Fam 47 CA, per Lord Denning MR. Note that judges have nevertheless on a number of occasions referred to 'the right to privacy' in the course of considering other remedies. See e.g. *Morris v Beardmore* [1981] AC 446, 462 at 464–5, 465, HL. In addition to malicious falsehood, which will only occasionally provide a remedy, torts (mainly trespass, nuisance and defamation) provide indirect remedies in some cases, as does the law of copyright and breach of confidence. Criminal law occasionally helps: see below, p. 564. The Press Complaints Commission, see below, p. 565, and other complaints or standard-setting bodies play a role.[3]

4. As noted by Leggatt LJ, the position contrasts sharply with that in the United States where the courts in most jurisdictions have developed a tort of invasion of privacy or one has been provided by legislation. The inspiration to do so came from an article by Warren and Brandeis ((1890) 4 Harv LR 193) prompted by the press coverage of the wedding of the daughter of one of the authors. Somewhat ironically, the article argued for the existence of a right of privacy in tort largely on the basis of English precedents such as *Prince Albert v Strange*, below, p. 550. The

1 On *Kaye v Robertson*, see D. Bedingfield, (1992) 55 MLR 111; B. S. Markensis, (1992) 55 MLR 118; and P. Prescott, (1991) 54 MLR 451.
2 See, however, the ruling on exemplary damages in the *AB* case, below, p. 529.
3 E.g. the Broadcasting Complaints Commission, below, p. 569, and the Data Protection Registrar.

tort—or more accurately the four interrelated torts—that has developed in the US is defined in the *Restatement, 2d, Torts* as follows:[1]

'(1) One who invades the right of privacy of another is subject to liability for the resulting harm to the interests of the other.
(2) The right of privacy is invaded by
   (a) unreasonable intrusion upon the seclusion of another . . .; or
   (b) appropriation of the other's name or likeness . . .; or
   (c) unreasonable publicity given to the other's private life . . .; or
   (d) publicity that unreasonably places the other in a false light before the public.'

5. When rejecting the claim in passing off, the Court of Appeal accepted that it applied only to unfair trading competition. The Court did not, however, refer to *Sim v Heinz* [1959] 1 WLR 313, CA, in which the question whether an action for passing off lies for the unauthorised use by impersonation of an actor's voice (in that case the impersonation of Alaister Sim's voice in an advertisement) was left open. B. S. Markesinis, (1990) 53 MLR 802, 803, asks 'if that could be done for the voice of an actor, why not for his image, especially when the appropriation of the likeness is used to enrich another person?'
6. Why, as all three judges in *Kaye v Robertson* asserted, is it impossible for the courts to develop a tort of invasion of privacy in the absence of legislative action? Might it not be easier for the courts to act to control the press than for the Government?
7. Would the new criminal offences proposed by the Calcutt Committee, see below, p. 526, have been of value in the circumstances of *Kaye v Robertson*?

Report of the Committee on Privacy and Related Matters, Chairman: David Calcutt QC (Cm 1102, 1990)

12.5 We have concluded that an overwhelming case for introducing a statutory tort of infringement of privacy has not so far been made out and that the better solution lies with the measures set out elsewhere in this report. We therefore *recommend* that such a tort should not presently be introduced. . . . We make our recommendation on the assumption that the improved scheme for self-regulation recommended . . . will be made to work. Should this fail, the case for a statutory tort of infringement of privacy might have to be reconsidered.

12.6 . . . if unwarranted intrusion is taking place and sufficient remedy is lacking, there must be a case in principle for seeking to fill this gap. We are satisfied that the absence of sufficient protection for the individual against intrusion by the press satisfies the criterion of 'pressing social need'. . . . This need is especially pressing in the case of individuals who are vulnerable to exploitation because, for example, of age, immaturity, infirmity, grief or the need to undergo medical treatment. There is a clear precedent in the law of defamation for providing compensation for distress, hurt feelings and anxiety without it having to be established that a plaintiff has suffered actual damage. We see no difficulty in principle in the adoption of such an approach for intrusions into privacy.

12.7 We have considered, however, whether the pressing social need requires the creation of a new tort or whether it would be better met by the proposals elsewhere in this report. . . .

12.9 Any consideration of a possible tort of infringement of privacy must begin with the definition of the proposed tort and of the defences to it. This is the issue on which all other proposed legislation has foundered. . . .

12.10 The problem was clearly expressed by the Vice-Chancellor, Sir Nicolas Browne-Wilkinson, in his address to the International Press Institute assembly in Istanbul in 1988, as follows:

1 1977, para. 652A. The *Restatement* represents the preponderance of opinion in American jurisdictions. See further on privacy in American law, Prosser, *Law of Torts* (4th edn, 1971), Chap. 20. On privacy in other European states, see Raab, 72 Pub Admin 95.

'I think it is extremely difficult for a legal system to apply a general concept of privacy, because it is hard to distinguish what is meant by it. On the other hand, it seems to me impossible to draw a comprehensive list of those things which, in any one society, are to be treated as private. As a legal technician, I would be unhappy dealing with the law of privacy. . . .'

12.12   We accept that it would be impracticable to create a general wrong of infringement of privacy, since this would give rise to an unacceptable degree of uncertainty. However, this would not necessarily rule out the formulation of a tort directed towards the publication of personal information to the world at large. The absence of a precise or exhaustive definition has not presented insuperable problems in the areas of negligence and defamation. . . . Concepts such as 'the reasonable man' and 'right-thinking members of society' are to be found there in daily use. . . . Our grounds for recommending against a new tort do not, therefore, include difficulties of definition. . . .

12.17   We are satisfied that it would be possible to define a statutory tort of infringement of privacy. This could specifically relate to the publication of personal information (including photographs). It could follow Mr Browne's approach rather than Mr Cash's in excluding physical intrusion (for which we make specific recommendations . . .).[1] Personal information could be defined in terms of an individual's personal life, that is to say, those aspects of life which reasonable members of society would respect as being such that an individual is ordinarily entitled to keep them to himself, whether or not they relate to his mind or body, to his home, to his family, to other personal relationships, or to his correspondence or documents.

12.18   We would not see any advantage in laying down a more detailed definition of personal information on the face of any statute. The courts could develop their interpretation on a case by case basis. . . .

12.19   All proposals for a tort of infringement of privacy have included a number of defences. These have been of two kinds: the specific and the general. Specific defences have included consent, legal privilege, lawful authority and absence of intent. Defences of this kind would clearly be necessary if a tort were ever to be introduced. . . .

12.22   . . . we have serious reservations about a general defence merely labelled 'public interest'. We would not consider it appropriate for any tort of infringement of privacy. A defence to cover the justified disclosure of personal information would, however, clearly be necessary, but it would need to be tightly drawn and specific. The possible definition of personal information which we have set out (see *paragraphs 12.17–12.18*) would already provide for flexible interpretation by the courts. We would see difficulty in introducing a further variable which would be likely to mean different things to different people. . . .

12.24   . . . We do not accept that such a tort would be the thin end of a wedge leading towards censorship. A law designed solely for the protection of individual citizens and their personal lives should offer no scope for Government interference. Furthermore, there is no necessary inter-relationship between protection of individual privacy (in the terms in which we discuss it in this report) and censorship by Government. We cannot, therefore, accept the argument that no tort of infringement of privacy should be introduced unless balanced by some provision for the entrenchment of freedom of speech or a Freedom of Information Act.

12.25   Nor do we agree that a narrowly-drawn tort would inhibit serious investigative journalism or that responsible newspapers would suffer for the misdeeds of others. Serious investigative journalism would be outside the scope of such a law, especially when exposing serious wrong-doing. There is a clear distinction between infringements of privacy deriving from prurient curiosity and those associated with legitimate journalism. . . . Most people have little difficulty in recognising where the boundary lies.

12.26   Many of those opposed to the creation of a statutory tort argued that it would be disproportionate and an undue restriction upon freedom of speech in the light of our treaty obligations. We cannot accept the argument that Article 10 of the European Convention on Human Rights must be regarded as conclusive against a law of privacy. Due weight must be given to Article 8 in which privacy is described as a 'right'. Furthermore, Article 10(2) provides for legitimate exceptions to freedom of expression, including the protection of the rights of others. We note that a number of our European partners have had laws for the protection of privacy for many years and reconcile this with adherence to Article 10. . . .

1   The references are to the Right of Privacy and Protection of Privacy bills introduced in the sessions 1987/88 and 1988/89 by Messrs Cash and Browne MPs respectively. For the texts of these bills, see *Infringement of Privacy*, Lord Chancellor's Dept. Consultation Paper, 1992, Annex D.

12.27   Although Article 10 does not form part of our domestic law, it is clear that it is having an impact upon our jurisprudence (see . . . *A-G v Guardian Newspapers Ltd* [above, p. 12]) . . .

In any case, freedom of speech has long been recognised as of fundamental importance in the English common law. The clearest example is the so-called rule in *Bonnard v Perryman* [see below, p. 538] . . .

12.28   On the other hand, we are conscious that a tort of infringement of privacy would mark a new departure in the law. It might extend restrictions on the press even to situations where the information was not only true but also where it:

(a) would not necessarily cause any significant or lasting harm;
(b) had been obtained by reputable means; and
(c) was already known within the complainant's own circle of acquaintances.

12.29   In addition a tort might have the effect of stifling reports about the failings of people in the public eye who use the media to promote themselves. We have the impression that many people would agree with the sentiments expressed by Lord Denning, the Master of the Rolls, in *Woodward v Hutchins* [see below, p. 561]. . . .

12.30   One of the main arguments in favour of a new tort of infringement of privacy is that the courts would be able to grant an injunction to restrain publication. Such an injunction would be of far greater value to a plaintiff than an apology or compensation after an intrusion into his privacy. . . .

12.31   It has been argued that, when applied to true personal information, such a restraint upon the press would be excessive. Some mechanism would be necessary to guard against those with guilty secrets obtaining such an injunction. The availability of injunctions could, therefore, be restricted in England and Wales by imposing a limitation comparable to that which already exists in defamation cases. . . . Prior restraint of publication, in particular on the basis of an *ex parte* interlocutory injunction, is, however, undoubtedly still a major restraint upon press freedom. . . .

12.32   As well as the arguments of principle in *paragraphs 12.24–12.31*, we have considered whether a new statutory tort would be the most effective way to tackle the problems [of physical intrusion and the publication of intrusive material by the press that have led to complaints]. . . . We have concluded that the need could be met by a combination of the more sharply-focused remedies recommended elsewhere in this report. . . .

12.33   . . . we do not consider that physical intrusion as such is best tackled by means of a civil remedy. That is why we propose the creation of new criminal offences and why we would exclude such intrusion from the definition of infringement of privacy in any tort (see *paragraph 12.17*). A civil remedy would, however, be valuable against the imminent or actual publication of material obtained by means of physical intrusion. Accordingly, . . . we recommend that anyone having a sufficient interest should be able to seek an injunction and damages in respect of the publication of private material or photographs obtained by committing any of the proposed offences. . . . We consider that such a tightly-drawn civil remedy, closely linked to acts that most people would regard as clearly wrong, would tackle many of the worst forms of infringement of individual privacy. . . .

12.34   Any form of legal action in tort suffers from a number of limitations. The individual who has been wronged has the daunting task of mounting and pursuing an action in the courts. Many find the financial risks a deterrent. One of the main shortcomings of a tort of infringement of privacy would be that it would not provide a readily accessible remedy. Even if legal aid were made available, which we would consider essential, many would still fall outside its scope. . . . we set ourselves the test of asking whether any proposed remedy would satisfy the criteria of speed, cheapness and readiness of access. We are not persuaded that a tort of infringement of privacy would perform very well against such criteria. We consider this a major weakness.

12.35   On the other hand, the provision of a legal remedy in tort would provide a more certain redress, particularly for those seeking prior restraint (see *paragraphs 12.30–12.31*). It would also enable the courts to award compensation. Furthermore, it can be argued that the introduction of a new form of legal protection should not be rejected on what are essentially administrative grounds.

12.36   Nevertheless, an improved form of self-regulation, under which, once the initial complaint had been made, action was taken forward by the proposed non-statutory Press Complaints Commission . . ., would undoubtedly be less daunting to many people than having to use a new tort. The people whose privacy we consider most needs protecting should they, for example, become the victims of a crime or a disaster, or suffer from a disfiguring illness, are precisely those who hold no office, play no prominent role in society, have no publicity agent and also probably lack the means to sue. Thus, while we have not based our rejection of a general tort of infringement of privacy on accessibility alone, it is, nevertheless, an important factor in deciding whether the case for a tort has been made out. . . .

NOTES

1. The Calcutt Committee Report is the third report on privacy in the past 20 years. It follows the Justice Report (1970) and the Younger Committee Report (1972).[1] The Justice Report, which was privately sponsored, considered the threat to privacy posed by both state and private action and prepared a draft bill recommending a general statutory right of action for invasion of privacy. The Younger Committee, which was government appointed, was called upon to consider privacy in the private sector only (the press, private detectives, etc.). It came out against a general right of privacy, *inter alia*, because of the difficulty that the courts would face in handling 'so ill-defined and unstable a concept';[2] the effect upon freedom of speech; and the unrealised potential of the existing law (particularly breach of confidence) to respond to invasions of privacy.

The Younger Committee did, however, favour strengthening and adding to existing legal and extra-legal rules and remedies. Its main recommendations for changes in the law were for:

(i) a criminal offence of surreptitious unlawful surveillance by means of a technical device;
(ii) a tort of unlawful surveillance by such means;
(iii) a tort of disclosure or other use of information unlawfully acquired;
(iv) a legally enforceable right of access to information held by a credit agency about oneself (implemented by the Consumer Credit Act 1974, s. 158).

The Committee also recommended changes in the working of the former Press Council (which were implemented); the taking of steps by the institutions and persons concerned to improve the confidentiality of personal information held by banks, universities and employers; the licensing of private detectives; and the adoption of a voluntary code by computer users (see now the Data Protection Act 1984). Only where indicated above have the Committee's proposals been implemented.

The Younger Committee was not unanimous. Mr Lyon and Mr Ross appended dissenting opinions. Mr Lyon presented the advantages of a general tort as follows:

17.   *First*, . . . Parliamentary time is restricted and every new advance demands a long and sometimes exhausting campaign. It is much better to set out the principles on which the courts can act and leave them to develop the law as need requires . . . .

1 For references to these reports, see above, p. 516.
2 Report, p. 206. The Committee stated:

> We have found privacy to be a concept which means widely different things to different people and changes significantly over relatively short periods. In considering how the courts could handle so ill-defined and unstable a concept, we conclude that privacy is ill-suited to be the subject of a long process of definition through the building up of precedents over the years, since the judgments of the past would be an unreliable guide to any current evaluation of privacy. . . .
>
> On the 'unstable' nature of privacy, contrast the reaction now and 40 years ago to the information that an unmarried couple are living together. Note also that the revelation of a person's income was placed only below the revelation of facts about his sex life as an invasion of privacy in the public opinion survey done for the Younger Committee (Report, p. 239). In contrast, in Sweden one's income is a matter of public record in the sense that it is possible to buy a book which lists the income tax that everyone pays. The land ownership list kept by the Land Registry identifies the owner and mortgagee of land subject to registration in England and Wales. Access to the list became open to the public on written application in 1990 after having always been confidential.

19.   *Second*, it gives a remedy to all those seriously prejudiced by intrusions into privacy . . . .

20.   *Third*, it gives teeth to many of our other recommendations. If a computer operator knew that his activities might lead to a suit for damages, he would be more likely to respond to the code of principles we enunciate.

21.   *Fourth*, it allows juries to set the standards in a constantly changing area of human values. If private enquiry agents are to lose their certificates of registration for unreasonable intrusion into privacy, who is to decide what is reasonable? The Home Office? The police? I would prefer a jury as more representative of public opinion.

22.   *Fifth*, it would provide an effective remedy for any unreasonable behaviour. Not only would damages reimburse financial loss or mollify injured feelings, but an injunction would be a useful deterrent to prevent anticipated intrusions into privacy . . . .

23.   *Sixth*, no general remedy is likely to gain Parliamentary approval if it did not include government activities. The result of my colleagues' recommendations is that the government has succeeded in keeping its activities to itself although many would agree that government intrusion is potentially more dangerous and annoying. A general tort would easily have been amended to cover all those government activities which were not authorised by law . . . .

24.   *Seventh*, we would have fulfilled our obligations under the United Nations Declaration of Human Rights and the European Convention. One of the ironies of the majority report is that the European Court may choose in time to give a remedy for English litigants which my colleagues would deny to them. [See the *Malone* case, below, p. 804] . . .

26.   Early in my researches on this subject I came across the case of a Mrs X whose policeman husband took a mistress. The wife prevailed upon him to give up the mistress and they were reconciled. The jealous lover told a national newspaper. When their reporter was rebuffed by Mrs X, they printed the story under the headlines 'The love life of a detective'. The family had to move; the husband had to give up his job; the child was teased at school. What do I now tell Mrs X? 'Truth must prevail'. 'We cannot protect privacy except where there has been a breach of confidence or the intruder used offensive new methods like bugging devices.' 'A reformed Press Council will censure the newspaper!'

2. The Calcutt Committee, which was appointed by the government following mounting concern about the conduct of the press, was required:

'to consider what measures (whether legislative or otherwise) are needed to give further protection to individual privacy from the activities of the press and improve recourse against the press for the individual citizen' (Report, p. 1).

Like the Younger Committee, the Calcutt Committee recommended against a general right of privacy, for reasons both of principle and practicality. Although, in accordance with its terms of reference, the Committee had particularly in mind ill-conduct *by the press*, its discussion of the question of a general right has wider application. The Committee would appear to have found the arguments fairly evenly balanced and its recommendation was, in a sense, a provisional one – dependent upon the success of the new system of self-regulation that it proposed. Following the Calcutt Committe Report, a Press Complaints Commission was established by the industry in place of the Press Council, although the Commission is not composed or functioning in the way that the Calcutt Committee Report proposed: see below, p. 569. Other changes proposed by the Committee have been postponed by the government pending the outcome of the new arrangements for self-regulation. The particular changes in the criminal law recommended by the Calcutt Committee to combat physical intrusion were that the following acts be criminal offences (Report, p. ix):

(a) entering private property, without the consent of the lawful occupant, with intent to obtain personal information with a view to its publication;

(b) placing a surveillance device on private property, without the consent of the lawful occupant, with intent to obtain personal information with a view to its publication; and

(c) taking a photograph, or recording the voice, of an individual who is on private property, without his consent, with a view to its publication and with intent that the individual shall be identifiable.

The Committee also made certain recommendations for legal restrictions to protect the privacy of individuals from the press reporting of court proceedings (Report, p. ix):

5.   Consideration should be given to amending the legislation on the non-identification of minors in England and Wales to eliminate any inconsistencies or uncertainties. . . .

6.   The statutory prohibition on identifying rape victims in England and Wales should be extended to cover the victims of the sexual assaults listed at *appendix H*.[1] . . .

7.   In any criminal proceedings in England and Wales, the court should have the power to make an order prohibiting the publication of the name and address of any person against whom the offence is alleged to have been committed, or of any other matters likely to lead to his or her identification. This should only be exercised if the court believes that it is necessary to protect the mental or physical health, personal security or security of the home of the victim. . . .

8.   After consulting the press and the broadcasting authorities, the Press Complaints Commission . . . should issue early guidance on jigsaw identification.

The Committee, however, recommended against the establishment of a statutory right to reply (Report, pp. x, 44).

3. How do you reconcile the fact that the Court of Appeal in *Kaye v Robertson* was clearly of the opinion that Parliament should act to introduce a statutory remedy for invasion of privacy when the Calcutt Committee, and the Younger Committee before it, recommended otherwise?

4. The Calcutt Committe regarded the Press Complaints Commission that it proposed as providing the 'final chance' for the press 'to prove that voluntary self-regulation can be made to work' (Report, p. x). Should the Commission fail, it proposed a statutory Press Complaints Tribunal applying a statutory code of practice with powers to award compensation (ibid, p. xi). Elsewhere in its Report (p. 46), the Committee stated that if the Press Complaints Commission system of voluntary self-regulation fails, 'the case for a statutory tort of infringement of privacy might have to be reconsidered'.

5. As proposed when the Calcutt Committee Report was published, Sir David Calcutt was asked some 18 months after the new regime of voluntary self-regulation had become operational by the then Home Secretary, Mr David Mellor, to conduct a review of the effectiveness of the new regime and to consider whether the arrangements 'should be modified or placed on a statutory basis'. In his *Review of Press Self-Regulation*, 1993, Cm 2135, Sir David Calcutt was highly critical of the Press Complaints Commission. He found its composition, methods of work and bias in favour of the press unsatisfactory. He considered that it had been ineffective in protecting privacy in a number of cases concerning both private individuals and persons in public life and that in some high profile cases the individuals whose privacy

---

1 *Ed.* These include intercourse with under age girls, incest and indecent assaults. Anonymity for victims of male rape is provided by amendments made by the Criminal Justice and Public Order Act 1994, Sch. 10, para. 36. There is no anonymity for persons accused of rape.

had arguably been invaded had not sought to invoke its jurisdiction.[1] Sir David Calcutt's conclusion was the new regime had not proved an effective regulator and that the Government should introduce a statutory regime. In particular, he proposed a remedy for individuals against the press for infringements of privacy before a statutory Press Complaints Tribunal along the lines suggested in the Calcutt Committee Report. The Tribunal would be fully independent of the press, with a judge or senior lawyer appointed by the Lord Chancellor as chairman. It would draw up a statutory code of practice and have powers to restrain publication in breach of the code and receive complaints alleging breaches of it. The Commission would be able to award compensation and costs, impose fines and require the printing of apologies, corrections and replies. Sir David Calcutt also recommended that the Government give further consideration to the introduction of a statutory tort of infringement of privacy that would apply not only to the press. His view was that the proposed Tribunal dealing only with the press should be established at once; it would be open to the Government if it thought fit to allow this tailor-made remedy to continue in parallel with any general tort that it introduced.

6. Sir David Calcutt's proposals have not yet been implemented by the Government. The Lord Chancellor's Department has published a Consultation Paper, *Infringement of Privacy*, 1993, which invited comments on the 'proposal that the right to privacy should now be recognised, as a matter of principle, in English law and in Scots law'. The consultation period is over and the many comments made remain under consideration. The House of Commons National Heritage Select Committee has published a report (Privacy and Media Intrusion, Fourth Report, HC 291–1, 1993), which proposes the enactment of a Protection of Privacy Act, which would contain civil and criminal remedies for invasion of privacy and would apply not only to the press.

3 Existing remedies in law

The remedies that exist in English law are found in various parts of the criminal and, particularly, the civil law. In terms of the two main kinds of invasion of privacy, protection from physical intrusion is offered mainly by the torts of trespass and nuisance. Informational privacy is to some extent safeguarded by the law of defamation, the court's jurisdiction to protect juveniles, breach of copyright and breach of confidence.

(a) TRESPASS

Hickman v Maisey [1900] 1 QB 752, 69 LJQB 511, 82 LT 321, Court of Appeal

The plaintiff owned and occupied land on which for a fee he allowed a racehorse trainer to train horses. The defendant, a racing tout, observed the horses from a

---

1 One case in which no complaint had been brought concerned Mr David Mellor and the actress Ms Antonia de Sancha in which *The People* published a story of an affair that came to light after a telephone conversation had been recorded by electronic bugging. Another case concerned the publication in the *Daily Mirror* of compromising long-lens pictures of the Duchess of York and a Texan friend at a villa in France. The Duchess obtained damages in a French court for invasion of privacy; there would have been no legal liability in English law. A third case, to which the Chairman of the Press Complaints Commission responded by a statement reminding the press of the threat of government intervention, concerned press publicity about Mr Paddy Ashdown's affair with his secretary. Mr Ashdown had obtained an injunction to prevent the publication of the story in England, which had been obtained following the theft of documents in a break-in. He admitted the affair when *The Scotsman*, which was not bound by the injunction, published details.

highway that crossed the plaintiff's land. The plaintiff brought an action in trespass for damages and an injunction. The jury found for the plaintiff, awarding damages of one shilling, and the judge granted an injunction. The defendant appealed to the Court of Appeal.

A. L. Smith LJ: . . . Many authorities shew that prima facie the right of the public is merely to pass and repass along the highway; but I quite agree with what Lord Esher MR said in *Harrison v Duke of Rutland* [1893] 1 QB 142. . . . namely, that, though highways are dedicated prima facie for the purpose of passage, 'things are done upon them by everybody which are recognised as being rightly done and as constituting a reasonable and usual mode of using a highway as such'; and, 'if a person on a highway does not transgress such reasonable and usual mode of using it', he will not be a trespasser; but, if he does 'acts other than the reasonable and ordinary user of a highway as such' he will be a trespasser. For instance . . . if a man took a sketch from the highway, I should say that no reasonable person would treat that as an act of trespass. But I cannot agree with the contention of the defendant's counsel that the acts which this defendant did, not really for the purpose of using the highway as such, but for the purpose of carrying on his business as a racing tout to the detriment of the plaintiff by watching the trials of race-horses on the plaintiff's land, were within such an ordinary and reasonable user of the highway as I have mentioned. . . . In the case of *Harrison v Duke of Rutland* [1893] 1 QB 142 the point which arises in this case was not precisely similar to that in the present case. In that case the plaintiff went upon a highway, the soil of which was vested in the defendant, while a grouse drive was taking place on adjoining land of the defendant, for the purpose of interfering with the drive, which the defendant's keepers prevented him from doing by force. The plaintiff thereupon brought an action for assault against the defendant, and the defendant counter-claimed in trespass. . . . It was clear upon the facts that he was not using the highway for the purpose of passing or repassing along it, but solely for the purpose of interfering with the defendant's enjoyment of his right of shooting over his land, and it was held therefore that the plaintiff's user of the highway was a trespass. I cannot see any real distinction between that case and the present. . . . I do not agree with the argument of the defendant's counsel to the effect that the intention and object of the defendant in going upon the highway cannot be taken into account in determining whether he was using it in a lawful manner. I think that his intention and object were all-important in determining that question.

Collins and **Romer LJJ** delivered concurring judgments.
Appeal dismissed.

NOTES

1. It was crucial in this case that the defendant was using the highway for commercial purposes to the detriment of the plaintiff. The case concerned a highway the soil of which was the property of the plaintiff. In most cases (a private road would be an exception), the soil will be vested in a highway authority: a local authority or the Transport Secretary. Although the same rule (ordinary and reasonable user) applies, it will be unlikely in such cases that a person who wishes to rely upon it will be as fortunate as the racehorse trainer in *Hickman v Maisey* was in persuading the owner of the soil to bring proceedings.

2. The trainer could not have brought an action in trespass to land because he was not in possession of the land. Similarly, in cases which reached the Press Council in which the press had entered hospitals surreptitiously to interview or photograph a patient (see, e.g. the Aneurin Bevan case, 8th Report 1961, p. 39), the hospital authorities could have brought proceedings in trespass, but not the patient or his family. So also, 'the ordinary overnight visitor at an hotel may sleep in but does not "occupy" the bedroom allotted to him and hence has no remedy against an intruder who plants a microphone in the room; the hotel proprietor will have an action in trespass but he may be unwilling to bring it; indeed he may have put the microphone in the room himself or be in collusion with someone who did so' (Younger Report, p. 290). But 'where there is a contract between a hotel guest and the hotel proprietor it might be argued that it is an implied term of such a contract that the former's room should be free from devices intruding on his privacy' (ibid). This, of course, would only give a claim against the hotel.

3. The plaintiff would not have had a remedy in trespass to land if the defendant had watched the horses from land that was not the plaintiff's. There has to be a physical presence on the plaintiff's land.[1] The Younger Committee (p. 289) suggested that a 'method of spying which involved the projection into airspace above the plaintiff's land of beams (as for radar) could presumably be treated as trespass to land or perhaps nuisance'. The Committee added:

'An entry is unauthorised . . . if permission to enter is obtained by fraud, as when an enquiry agent posing as a post office engineer obtains entry to a building and puts a bugging device in a telephone receiver; and an entry lawfully made may become trespassing when the entrant takes advantage of the occasion to do things (e.g. to carry out a search of the premises) not covered by his permission to enter.'

See the Press Council cases (e.g. 18th Report 1971, p. 49) in which reporters have been invited into a house and then taken a photograph without consent.

4. In addition to the limitations upon trespass to land as a remedy for invasion of privacy noted above, trespass has two other limitations. Firstly, although an injunction may be granted to prevent a future trespass, one may not be available to prevent the publication of information or a photograph obtained as a result of a trespass: *Kaye v Robertson and Sport Newspapers Ltd*, above, p. 518. Secondly, there is also the question of the measure of damages. As the Younger Report states (p. 290):

'In any case where invasion of privacy is the real issue, there is not likely to be any substantial claim for damage to the land, at least by comparison with what the plaintiff is likely to feel he ought to receive for the invasion of privacy. Damages for the latter can only be covered by a claim for aggravated or for punitive (or exemplary) damages i.e. for a sum which will offer the plaintiff some recompense for the attack made on his feelings and dignity or which will punish the defendant for the outrageous form which the trespass has taken. . . . It would seem that . . . a journalist, for example, who forced his way into a house to get a story for his newspaper might find himself liable to pay substantial damages, even though he had done little or no damage to the house. However, the cases in which punitive damages may be awarded appear to have been severely limited by the House of Lords in *Rookes v Barnard* [1964] AC 1129 and *Cassell & Co v Broome* [1972] AC 1027.'

Aggravated and exemplary (or punitive) damages are distinct and different concepts. *Aggravated* damages were awarded in *Jolliffe v Willmett & Co* [1971] 1 All ER 478, QBD, in which a private detective acting for the husband in a matrimonial dispute gained entry to the matrimonial home where the wife only was still living by deceit and force. The defendant pretended to be the postman and, when the door was opened, pushed past the wife to discover evidence of the sleeping arrangements. £250 damages were awarded for an 'insolent and high-handed trespass'. In *Rookes v Barnard*, Lord Devlin stated that *exemplary* damages were available only in (i) cases of 'oppressive, arbitrary or unconstitutional action by the servants of the government' (the government includes local government and the police: *Cassell v Broome*); (ii) cases 'in which the defendant's conduct has been calculated by him to make a profit for himself which may well exceed the compensation payable to the plaintiff'; and (iii) where 'exemplary damages are expressly authorised by statute'. Exemplary damages are not available in respect of causes of action for which they had not been awarded before 1964: *AB v South West Water Services Ltd* [1993] 2 WLR 507, CA. Some privacy cases involving, for example, police or press action will come within

---

1 *Sheen v Clegg, Daily Telegraph* (1961), 22 June, cited in the Younger Committee Report, p. 289 (microphone placed by trespass over plaintiff's marital bed) and *Greig v Greig* [1966] VR 376, S Ct Vict (microphone placed in plaintiff's flat by trespass). See also *Francome v Mirror Group Newspapers Ltd*, below, p. 562.

the first or second of Lord Devlin's categories. For a privacy case of breach of copyright in which punitive damages were awarded, see *Williams v Settle*, below, p. 549.

5. In 1965 the *Sunday Express* and *The People* published pictures of the Queen and Princess Margaret showing them water-skiing at the Great Pond, Sunninghill Park. The Park is Crown land but has a public footpath running through it some distance from the lake and from which part of the lake can be seen. The pictures had been bought from a professional photographer who claimed to have taken them from the footpath with a telephoto lens. The case was investigated by the Press Council (12th Report 1965, p. 3) which found 'that the photographs . . . were taken surreptitiously by Mr R. Bellisario when the Queen and the Princess obviously were unaware that the pictures were being taken and that Mr Bellisario was trespassing on the private ground of Her Majesty [i.e. off the footpath] at the time.' After concluding that the newspapers had acted in good faith, having been deceived by the photographer, the Council 'unreservedly' condemned the photographer. It also censured a *Daily Express* photographer who was one of two photographers discovered 'hidden in the undergrowth lying on the ground, with their cameras trained on the hut where Her Royal Highness was changing her clothes'. Clearly actions in trespass could have been brought to protect privacy on these facts. Could one have been brought against Mr Bellisario if his claim to have taken the pictures from the footpath had been correct?

6. Another Press Council case (4th Report 1957, p. 22) in which there would have been a remedy in trespass was that in which the *Daily Sketch* published a reporter's story of how she had gatecrashed the Duke of Kent's 21st birthday party in the boot of a car. The editor was found 'guilty of a flagrant violation of good manners'. In one case, the Council (23rd Report 1976, p. 113) condoned trespass by deception when a *News of the World* reporter claimed to be homeless to gain admission to the Centrepoint hostel in London to check a story that homeless youngsters were sleeping in a mixed sex dormitory. The Press Council ruled that 'the use of subterfuge can be justified in cases involving public interest or the exposure of crime'. However, the Council found against the *Sunday People* in a case in which reporters had posed as hospital volunteers to investigate allegations of sexual promiscuity among mental patients. The public interest defence was defeated by the need to maintain confidence in the system of voluntary helpers (26th Report 1979, p. 68).[1] Journalists should generally disclose that they are such when seeking information (*Daily Mail* condemned because journalists failed to do so when seeking an interview with hospital patient: 27th/28th Reports 1980/81, p. 177).

7. In *Baron Bernstein of Leigh v Skyviews and General Ltd* [1978] QB 479, the plaintiff's land was flown over and an aerial photograph of his house taken without his knowledge or consent. He refused the offer to sell him the photograph and sued the defendant in trespass and invasion of privacy instead. Rejecting the claim, Griffiths J stated:

'I can find no support in authority for the view that a landowner's rights in the air space above his property extend to an unlimited height. In *Wandsworth Board of Works v United Telephone Co Ltd* [1884] 13 QBD 904 Bowen LJ described the maxim, usque ad coelum, as a fanciful phrase, to which I would add that if applied literally it is a fanciful notion leading to the absurdity of a trespass at common law being committed by a satellite every time it passes over a suburban garden. . . . The problem is to balance the rights of an owner to enjoy the use of his land against the rights of the general public to take advantage of all that science now offers in the use of air space. This balance is in my judgment best struck in our present society by restricting the rights of an owner in the air space above his land to such height as is

---

1 See also the case in which a complaint by Ms Germaine Greer that a *Mail on Sunday* journalist had gained admission to her house by pretending to be homeless was upheld: Press Complaints Commission Report No 23, Jan–Feb 1994, p. 18.

necessary for the ordinary use and enjoyment of his land and the structures upon it, and declaring that above that height he has no greater rights in the air space than any other member of the public.

Applying this test to the facts of this case, I find that the defendants' aircraft did not infringe any rights in the plaintiff's air space, and thus no trespass was committed. It was on any view of the evidence flying many hundreds of feet above the ground and it is not suggested that by its mere presence in the air space it caused any interference with any use to which the plaintiff put or might wish to put his land. The plaintiff's complaint is not that the aircraft interfered with the use of his land but that a photograph was taken from it. There is, however, no law against taking a photograph, and the mere taking of a photograph cannot turn an act which is not a trespass into the plaintiff's air space into one that is a trespass.

The present action is not founded in nuisance for no court would regard the taking of a single photograph as an actionable nuisance. But if the circumstances were such that a plaintiff was subjected to the harassment of constant surveillance of his house from the air, accompanied by the photographing of his every activity, I am far from saying that the court would not regard such a monstrous invasion of his privacy as an actionable nuisance for which they would give relief.'

See R. Wacks (1977) 93 LQR 491.

8. There is no right in law to prevent a person taking and publishing one's picture. In *Sports and General Press Agency v Our Dogs Publishing Co Ltd* [1916] 2 KB 880, the Ladies' Kennel Association purported to sell the 'sole photographic rights' to their dog show (held at a place of which they were in exclusive occupation for the day). An injunction was sought to prevent a magazine publishing photographs taken at the show by another photographer whose ticket of admission said nothing about taking photographs. In the absence of any trespass, Horridge J held for the defendant:

'In my judgment no one possesses a right of preventing another person photographing him any more than he has a right of preventing another person giving a description of him, provided the description is not libellous or otherwise wrongful.'

The Younger Committee reported (Report, p. 35) that it was suggested to it that if a person is photographed by the press without permission 'the negative and all the prints should be considered his property'. Would you agree?

9. A lot of Press Council or Press Complaints Commission cases raising questions of privacy have concerned the publication of photographs. These may raise questions of physical intrusion as well as of informational privacy. In 1982, the Press Council condemned the publication by the *Daily Star* and *The Sun* of pictures taken by long-lens photography of the Princess of Wales sun-bathing in a bikini on a beach on holiday in the Bahamas when five months pregnant as 'a gross intrusion into her personal privacy' (*The Times*, 4 March 1982). The Council stated: 'Whether the beach was public or private is immaterial to this offence. There was no legitimate public interest to excuse that intrusion. Personal consent would have been required for the publication of pictures in these circumstances of any woman who was pregnant.' *The Sun* apologised, reprinting the offending pictures to demonstrate its offence. In the most recent royal family case, the Press Complaints Commission ruled that five national daily newspapers were in breach of the Press Code of Practice when they printed a picture of Prince Edward and his girl friend kissing outside a house on the private Balmoral estate.[1]

---

1 Press Complaints Commission Report No 25, May–July 1994, p. 6. The case was the first under the current, 1993 version of the Code, below, p. 565, which now expressly makes the 'use of long-lens photography to take pictures of people on private property without their consent ... generally unacceptable'. For other, pre-1993 royal family cases in which breaches of the Code involving long-lens photographs were found, see the *Bellassario* case, above, p. 530, and the case in which *The People* published a picture of the Duke of York's baby daughter running naked in a high-walled garden: Press Complaints Commission Report No 2, July–Sept 1991, p. 18. In other, non-royal family cases, the *Sun* was condemned by the Press Council for publishing long-lens pictures of Brigitte Bardot sunbathing topless by her private swimming pool (*The Times* 12 April 1984) and of David Niven showing him in a distressed state shortly before his death (*The Times* 12 January 1984).

10. The public opinion survey done for the Younger Committee (Report, Appendix E) showed that 'callers at the door' were regarded as invading privacy, with Jehovah's Witnesses being mentioned in particular. In *Robson v Hallett* [1967] 2 QB 939, DC, Diplock LJ stated at 953–4 that

'when a householder lives in a dwelling house to which there is a garden in front and does not lock the gate of the garden, it gives an implied licence to any member of the public who has lawful reason for doing so to proceed from the gate to the front door or back door, and to inquire whether he may be admitted and to conduct his lawful business.'

Diplock LJ stated that such an implied licence may be rebutted, as by a notice on the gate (e.g. 'No hawkers').

11. The above materials concern trespass to land. With statutory exceptions,[1] trespass to land is not a criminal offence. When Michael Fagan climbed into Buckingham Palace and surprised the Queen by sitting on her bed, he thereby committed no offence. He was charged and acquitted of burglary in respect of an entry into the Palace a month earlier when he had stolen wine (*The Times* 24 September 1982). Following the second incident, the enactment of an offence of trespassing on residential property in a 'manner likely to cause the occupier alarm or distress', was considered but no government bill has resulted: Calcutt Report, p. 10. Trespass to goods may also occasionally provide a remedy for invasion of privacy, as where a document is taken.

12. See also the additional criminal offences suggested by the Calcutt Committee, above, p. 526, which respond to certain of the above limitations on the law of trespass.

(b) NUISANCE

Khorasandjian v Bush [1993] QB 727, Court of Appeal

The plaintiff, aged 18, and the defendant, aged 23, had been friends. When the plaintiff indicated that she no longer wished to see the defendant, he reacted badly. Over a period of time, he assaulted her, threatened further violence and pestered her with telephone calls at her parents' home, where she lived. The plaintiff brought a civil action and obtained an interlocutory injunction against the defendant restraining him from 'using violence to, harassing, pestering or communicating with' her. The defendant appealed against the injunction on the ground that the court lacked jurisdiction to restrain him from 'harassing, pestering or communicating with' the plaintiff because these terms did not relate to a tort which the plaintiff could later claim was infringed in the substantive proceedings. The Court of Appeal dismissed the appeal.

Dillon LJ: Miss Harry Thomas, for the defendant, concedes . . . that an injunction could be granted to restrain the defendant from assaulting or threatening to assault the plaintiff. She concedes also that an injunction could be granted to restrain the defendant from interfering with the plaintiff's property. . . . In relation to the telephone calls, she concedes that if the plaintiff's mother has a freehold or leasehold interest in the parental home, the plaintiff's mother could complain of persistent unwanted telephone calls made by the defendant to the plaintiff's mother in the parental home, as that would fall within the tort of private nuisance. But she submits, in reliance on the decision of this court in *Malone v Laskey* [1907] 2 KB 141, that the basis of the tort of private nuisance is interference with the enjoyment of a person's

---

1 E.g. trespass using violence to secure entry (Criminal Law Act 1977, s. 6) and aggravated trespass (Criminal Justice and Public Order Act 1994, ss. 68–9, above, p. 238).

property, and therefore the plaintiff, as in law a mere licensee in her mother's property with no propriet-ary interest, cannot invoke the tort of private nuisance or complain of unwanted and harassing telephone calls made to her in her mother's home.

To my mind, it is ridiculous if in this present age the law is that the making of deliberately harassing and pestering telephone calls to a person is only actionable in the civil courts if the recipient of the calls happens to have the freehold or a leasehold proprietary interest in the premises in which he or she has received the calls. Miss Harry Thomas submits, however, that English law does not recognise any tort of harassment or invasion of privacy or, save in the different context of such a case as *Rookes v Barnard* [1964] AC 1129 [concerning industrial disputes], intimidation. Therefore, she says that, save as expressly conceded as set out above, the defendant's conduct to the plaintiff is, even on the plaintiff's version of it, under the English civil law, legitimate conduct of which the plaintiff has no power or right to complain. I apprehend that it is correct, historically, that the tort of private nuisance, which originated as an action on the case, was developed in the beginning to protect private property or rights of property, in relation to the use or enjoyment of land. . . .

That a legal owner of property can obtain an injunction, on the ground of private nuisance, to restrain persistent harassment by unwanted telephone calls to his home was decided by the Appellate Division of the Alberta Supreme Court in *Motherwell v Motherwell* (1976) 73 DLR (3d) 62. . . . notwithstanding *Malone v Laskey*,[1] the court held that the wife of the owner had also the right to restrain harassing telephone calls to the matrimonial home. Clement JA, who delivered the judgment of the court, said, at p. 78:

> 'Here we have a wife harassed in the matrimonial home. She has a status, a right to live there with her husband and children. I find it absurd to say that her occupancy of the matrimonial home is insufficient to found an action in nuisance. In my opinion she is entitled to the same relief as is her husband, the brother.'

I respectfully agree, and in my judgment this court is entitled to adopt the same approach. The court has at times to reconsider earlier decisions in the light of changed social conditions. . . . If the wife of the owner is entitled to sue in respect of harassing telephone calls, then I do not see why that should not also apply to a child living at home with her parents.

Damage is . . . a necessary ingredient in the tort of private nuisance. . . . So far as the harassing tele-phone calls are concerned, however, the inconvenience and annoyance to the occupier caused by such calls, and the interference thereby with the ordinary and reasonable use of the property are sufficient damage. The harassment is the persistent making of the unwanted telephone calls, even apart from their content; if the content is itself as here threatening and objectionable, the harassment is the greater.

In relation to harassment by telephone calls, there is also the decision of this court (Sir John Arnold P. and Sir Roualeyn Cumming-Bruce) in *Burnett v George* [1992] 1 FLR 525 decided on 6 March 1986 but only recently reported. There, in a context in which, as in the present case, section 1 of the Domestic Violence and Matrimonial Proceedings Act 1976 was not applicable, it was held that an injunction to restrain harassment by telephone calls should only be granted if there was evidence that the health of the plaintiff was being impaired by molestation or interference calculated to cause such impairment, in which case the relief should be granted to the extent necessary to avoid the impairment of health.

It is to be observed that in that case the attention of the court was not directed to the cases concerned with interference with the ordinary and reasonable enjoyment of property as being a nuisance. It was directed instead to a different line of authority (*Wilkinson v Downton* . . . and *Janvier v Sweeney* . . .) which establishes that false words or verbal threats calculated to cause, uttered with the knowledge that they are likely to cause, and actually causing, physical injury to the person to whom they are uttered are action-able: see the judgment of Wright J in *Wilkinson v Downton* [1897] 2 QB 57, 59, cited by Bankes LJ in *Janvier v Sweeney* [1919] 2 KB 316, 321–322 [see below, p. 563]. There was a wilful false statement, or unfounded threat, which was in law malicious, and which was likely to cause and did in fact cause physical injury, viz., illness of the nature of nervous shock.

From this two points follow. First, in my judgment, *Burnett v George* [1992] 1 FLR 525 does not pre-clude this court from taking a wider view of the telephone harassment under the heading of private nuisance in the light of the interference with the ordinary and reasonable enjoyment of property since that was not considered at all in *Burnett v George*. Secondly, *Janvier v Sweeney* [1919] 2 KB 316 is authority that verbal threats made orally to a person are actionable if they cause illness. This is of somewhat less importance in the present case, since the actual threats (as opposed to other acts of pestering in addition to the telephone calls) were threats to assault and it is not in doubt that, even without consequent illness, such threats can be restrained by injunction, because they are threats to commit a tort.

The injury for which damages were claimed in *Wilkinson v Downton* and *Janvier v Sweeney* was in both those cases described as 'nervous shock'. On modern authorities in the law of negligence, that term is

---

1 *Ed*. In the *Malone* case, the wife of the occupier was held to have no action in nuisance.

understood as referring to recognisable psychiatric illness with or without psychosomatic symptoms (see per Lord Bridge in *McLoughlin v O'Brian* [1983] 1 AC 410, 431H) or, as put by Lord Wilberforce in the same case, at p. 418B, recognisable and severe physical damage to the human body and system caused by the impact, through the senses, of external events on the mind. It is distinguished from mere emotional distress. From the judgment of Bankes LJ in *Janvier v Sweeney*, it seems that he had much the same concept in mind, in that he refers in various citations to physical damage inflicted through the medium of the mind.

In the present case, the plaintiff in her evidence referred to the defendant's conduct as putting her under an enormous weight of stress. This is amply borne out by much else that she says. On the facts in evidence that is the predictable and, so far as the defendant is concerned, intended effect of the defendant's conduct. There is no medical evidence, and it could not as yet be said, that the plaintiff is suffering from any physical or psychiatric illness. But there is, in my judgment, an obvious risk that the cumulative effect of continued and unrestrained further harassment such as she has undergone would cause such an illness. The law expects the ordinary person to bear the mishaps of life with fortitude and, as was put in a case cited by Lord Bridge in *McLoughlin v O'Brian*, customary phlegm; but it does not expect ordinary young women to bear indefinitely such a campaign of persecution as that to which the defendant has subjected the plaintiff. Therefore, in my judgment, on the facts of this case and in line with the law as laid down in *Janvier v Sweeney*, the court is entitled to look at the defendant's conduct as a whole and restrain those aspects on a quia timet basis also of his campaign of harassment which cannot strictly be classified as threats. . . .

I come now to *Patel v Patel* [1988] 2 FLR 179, decided by a division of this court consisting of May LJ and Waterhouse J. This was a dispute between a father-in-law, the plaintiff, and his son-in-law, the defendant. There had been an injunction against the defendant restraining him from assaulting, molesting, or otherwise interfering with the plaintiff or communicating with the plaintiff otherwise than through solicitors and from trespassing upon the plaintiff's property or from approaching within 50 yards of it. A judge had discharged that injunction and substituted an injunction to the effect that the defendant should not assault or molest the plaintiff or trespass on his property. The plaintiff appealed; . . . he sought (1) to reinstate the order restraining the defendant from approaching within 50 yards of the plaintiff's property and (2) to have a fine of £25 which the judge had imposed on the defendant for minor acts of molestation increased.

May LJ rejected both grounds of appeal. As to (1) he said that unless an actual trespass was committed or was more than likely to be committed, it did not seem to him that merely to approach to within 50 yards of a person's house gave a cause of action which might be restrained by an injunction in those terms. As to (2) he drew attention to the very minor acts of molestation which the judge had found proved, and to the fact that many more serious allegations had not been accepted by the judge. That judgment of May LJ, while good warrant for Judge Stockdale's curtailment of the earlier injunction granted by the Barnet County Court in the present case, does not, in my judgment, affect the present appeal in the circumstances of the present case.

Waterhouse J agreed with May LJ and endorsed the approach adopted by the judge in reformulating the injunctions. He added, however, at p. 182:

'The essence of the appellant's complaint is that he has been the victim of repeated harassment since May 1985, but in the present state of the law there is no tort of harassment. The judge was right, in my judgment, in limiting the scope of the injunctions in the way that he did.'

I find it difficult to give much weight to that general dictum that there is no tort of harassment, when the reformulated injunctions which Waterhouse J approved included an injunction restraining the defendant from molesting the plaintiff. . . .

For the reasons I have endeavoured to indicate, I regard the injunction granted by Judge Stockdale as in principle justified in law as an interlocutory injunction on the facts of this case as they were before him. . . . I would dismiss this appeal.

I have had the advantage of reading in draft the judgment of Peter Gibson J. I note that he would qualify the injunction by adding words such as 'by doing acts calculated to cause the [plaintiff] harm.' I regard such a qualification as undesirable, because it would complicate enforcement of the injunction pending trial of the action; the defendant would assert that any act of pestering or harassment of which complaint was made was not by itself calculated to cause the plaintiff harm. I also regard the qualification as unnecessary because (i) the campaign of harassment has to be regarded as a whole without consideration of each ingredient in isolation, and viewed as a whole it is plainly calculated to cause the plaintiff harm, and can be restrained quia timet because of the danger to her health from a continuation of the stress to which she has been subjected; (ii) threats of violence can be restrained per se, whether or not the threat, without the subsequent violence, is calculated to cause the plaintiff harm; and (iii) telephone harassment is, in my judgment, as indicated above, an actionable interference with her ordinary and reasonable use and enjoyment of property where she is lawfully present, and thus, on the past history, can be restrained quia timet without further proof of damage.

Rose LJ agreed with the judgment of **Dillon LJ**. **Peter Gibson LJ** dissented.

NOTES

1. Before the *Khorasandjian* case, the limited potential of the tort of nuisance as a remedy for invasion of privacy by way of physical intrusion was explained in the Younger Committee Report (Appendix I, para 18) as follows:

'Private nuisance, giving rise to a civil action at the suit of an aggrieved individual, has on occasions been very widely defined to cover virtually any unreasonable interference with that individual's enjoyment of land which he occupies. But an action for private nuisance is normally brought for *some physical invasion of the plaintiff's land by some deleterious subject-matter*—such as noise, smell, water or electricity—in circumstances which would not amount to trespass to land. It is much more doubtful if it would cover an activity which had no physical effects on the plaintiff's land, although it detracts from the plaintiff's enjoyment of that land. Thus spying on one's neighbour is probably not in itself a private nuisance although watching and besetting a man's house with a view to compelling him to pursue (or not to pursue) a particular course of conduct has been said to be a nuisance at common law. With regard to the latter type of conduct, however, it must be admitted that it is concerned with a situation very different from the typical case in which complaint is made of an invasion of privacy. The eavesdropper or spy does not seek to change the behaviour of his victim; on the contrary he hopes that it will continue unchanged, so that he may have the opportunity of noting it unobserved. . . .

As a remedy for invasions of privacy private nuisance has the same basic disadvantages as the action for trespass to land, namely that it can only be brought by the person who is from a legal point of view the 'occupier' of the land, enjoyment of which is affected by the nuisance.'

2. The *Khorasandjian* case takes a more innovative approach to the particular question of nuisance as a remedy for persistent[1] telephone tapping than the Younger Committee might have anticipated. The Court followed the Canadian case of *Motherwell v Motherwell*.[2] There an injunction was granted on a basis of nuisance to restrain a mentally disturbed woman from, inter alia, telephoning her father and brother in the houses of which they were the lawful occupiers; her brother at his office; and her sister-in-law in the matrimonial home that she shared with the brother. It was the last of these rulings that was relied upon in the *Khorasandjian* case. The law of nuisance would now seem to extend to protect all close family members of the occupier living on the premises from persistent telephone calls. What is not clear is whether it extends to persistent telephone calls to all persons in their places of residence or to all or some persons other than the occupier in respect of other kinds of nuisance.

3. In *Robbins v Canadian Broadcasting Corpn* (1958) 12 DLR (2d) 35, Quebec Sup Ct, the plaintiff wrote to the producer of a television programme criticising it. The letter was read on the programme and viewers were invited to telephone (the number was given) or write to the plaintiff to cheer him up. For three days afterwards, the plaintiff's telephone rang nonstop until he was obliged to change his number. He also received 102 letters and had pranks played upon him. He was awarded damages by the Quebec Superior Court under the Quebec Civil Code for damage caused by the fault of another. This case differs on its facts from the

1 A single telephone call, even in the middle of the night (see 11th Press Council Report 1964, pp. 32, 35), is not a nuisance.
2 Cf *Stokes v Brydges* 1958 5, S Ct Queensland, in which the defendant, annoyed by the noise made by milkmen, retaliated by making telephone calls to the homes of the directors of the milk company to disturb their sleep. The directors were granted an injunction.

Khorasandjian case, inter alia, because the telephone calls, etc, were from different people. Cf. a Press Council case (12th Report 1965, p. 97) in which the *Daily Sketch* was censured for publishing the home telephone number of Christine Keeler at the height of the Profumo affair causing 'a constant stream of abusive calls'.

4. The criminal law also controls persistent telephone calls. A person commits a summary offence contrary to the Telecommunications Act 1984, s. 43, if he 'for the purpose of causing annoyance, inconvenience or needless anxiety to another . . . persistently makes use for that purpose of a public telecommunications system'. It is also a summary offence to send to another person with intent to 'cause distress or anxiety' a letter or other article which conveys, inter alia, an indecent or grossly offensive message, a threat or information which is known or believed to be false: Malicious Communications Act 1988, s. 1.

5. In *Victoria Park Racing and Recreation Grounds Co Ltd v Taylor* (1938) 58 CLR 479 (Aust HC), the first defendant owned land adjacent to the plaintiff's racecourse. The second defendant erected a platform on the land and broadcast descriptions of the races from it. The plaintiff was refused an injunction to prevent the broadcasts. Latham CJ stated at 494–6:

> 'Any person is entitled to look over the plaintiff's fences and to see what goes on in the plaintiff's land. . . . The court has not been referred to any principle of law which prevents any man from describing anything which he sees anywhere if he does not make defamatory statements, infringe the law as to offensive language, &c, break a contract, or wrongfully reveal confidential information. . . .
>
> The claim under the head of nuisance has also been supported by an argument that the law recognizes a right of privacy which has been infringed by the defendant. However desirable some limitation upon invasions of privacy might be, no authority was cited which shows that any general right of privacy exists.'

Winfield, (1931) 47 LQR 23, 27) suggests that 'peeping toms', however persistent, do not commit a nuisance. But they may be bound over to be of good behaviour, see below, p. 564. The Younger Committee's recommendation on unlawful surveillance by technical devices (below, p. 577) would not apply. 'Peeping toms' would be liable for invasion of privacy in the form of 'intrusion upon seclusion' in the sense of the *Restatement, 2d, Torts*, above, p. 521.

6. Would the conduct of newspaper reporters who gather at the door of a person's house and will not go away unless they are given an interview or a picture be actionable in nuisance? On constant surveillance as nuisance, see the *Bernstein* case, above, p. 530. Might the reasoning in *Khorasandjian* apply? In the Yorkshire Ripper case, the Press Council concluded:[1]

18.29 . . . in this case the relatives of those at the centre of the story—victim and accused—were subjected to wholly unacceptable and unjustifiable pressures by journalists and other media representatives anxious either to interview or photograph them or to bid for the right to publish their stories. The conduct of journalists who laid siege to their homes in the circumstances described above can best be characterised in the old phrase—watching and besetting. The targets of this attention were people in deep personal grief or grave anxiety and they were harassed by the media ferociously and callously.

18.30. The descriptions of the attempts by reporters and photographers to make contact with Mr and Mrs Hill and Mrs Szurma-Sutcliffe cannot be read without a feeling of revulsion.

See also the *Christine Keeler* case, below, p. 542. Would the conduct of the press in the *Yorkshire Ripper* or *Christine Keeler* cases constitute a criminal offence contrary to s. 241, Trade Union and Labour Relations Act 1992?[1] The Calcutt Committee considered that, although aimed at harassment during industrial disputes, the offence in

1 *Press Conduct in the Sutcliffe Case* (1983), Press Council Booklet No 7, pp. 162–3.

s. 7[1] 'could be committed by journalists following someone or surrounding his house', although in practice 'it is unlikely to be invoked against the press', the police normally limiting themselves 'to moving the press aside so that someone can pass' (Report, p. 18). Note, however, Glanville Williams' comment that 'Parliament has not yet found itself able to make harassment by journalists an offence' (*Textbook of Criminal Law* (2nd edn, 1983), p. 210.) As between spouses, an injunction may be granted restraining one spouse 'from molesting' the other or a child living with the other: Domestic Violence and Matrimonial Proceedings Act 1976, s. 1. 'Molesting' does not necessarily imply violence; it 'applies to any conduct which can properly be regarded as such a degree of harassment as to call for the intervention of the court'.[2] The Calcutt Committee suggested that the offences in the Public Order Act 1986, ss. 4 and 5, above, p. 213, might apply in some press harassment cases (Report, p. 18).

7. It is unclear whether there is a tort of harassment at common law. In *Patel v Patel*, Waterhouse J was quite clear that there was not: see the quotation in the judgment of Dillon LJ in the *Khorasandjian* case, above, p. 534. In the later case, however, Dillon LJ questioned this, without actually stating that such a tort did exist.

8. The Broadcasting Complaints Commission upheld a complaint concerning Channel 4's 'The Big Breakfast' programme. The presenter Mr Keith Chegwin and a camera crew arrived unannounced in the early morning on the doorstep of Mr Mike Smith and Ms Sarah Greene. They sought to attract attention by shouting through the letter box, etc. When the occupants failed to respond, the broadcasting team continued with their live broadcast and did not leave the property. The Commission held that the manner of obtaining material for the broadcast and its showing was an invasion of the complainant's privacy in breach of broadcasting standards. See the Broadcasting Complaints Commission adjudication of 20 April 1994.

(c) DEFAMATION

Corelli v Wall (1906) 22 TLR 532, Chancery Division, Swinfen Eady J

The plaintiff, a well known authoress and a resident of Stratford-on-Avon, sought an interlocutory injunction to restrain the defendants, publishers in the same town, from publishing a series of postcards depicting imaginary scenes in the private life of the plaintiff. The injunction was sought pending the hearing of a libel action based upon the cards. The scenes included the plaintiff feeding ponies, on the river Avon in a gondola, and in an imaginary garden. The plaintiff's annoyance reached its height when the defendants hired sandwichmen to parade through Stratford, particularly near the plaintiff's home, to advertise the postcards.

---

1 S. 241 reads:

> Every person who, with a view to compel any other person to abstain from doing or to do any act which such other person has a legal right to do or abstain from doing, wrongfully and without legal authority . . .
>
> 2. Persistently follows such other person about from place to place; or . . .
>
> 4. Watches or besets the house or other place where such other person resides, or works, or carries on business, or happens to be, or the approach to such house or place; or,
>
> 5. Follows such other person with two or more other persons in a disorderly manner in or through any street or road . . .
>
> [commits an offence].

2 *Homer v Homer* [1982] 4 FLR 50, per Ormrod LJ. For a molestation case concerning unmarried partners not within the 1976 Act, see *Johnson v Walton* [1990] 1 FLR 350, CA.

Swinfen Eady J:
The real ground of the plaintiff's motion is that the cards constitute a libel upon her and that their sale ought to be restrained on that ground. Although it is well settled that a person may be defamed as well by a picture or effigy as by written or spoken words, I am not satisfied that the cards are libellous; and in any event the case is not so clear as to justify the Court in intervening before the fact of libel has been established. The case of *Bonnard v Perryman* [1891] 2 Ch 269 shows how careful the Court should be in granting interlocutory injunctions in cases of alleged libel. It is also urged that the plaintiff as a private person was entitled to restrain the publication of a portrait of herself which had been made without her authority and which, although professing to be her portrait, was totally unlike her. No authority in support of this proposition was cited. The plaintiff has not established, for the purpose of this motion, that she has any such right. Under these circumstances I do not see my way to grant any interlocutory injunction. When it is known that the sale of the postcards is in direct opposition to the plaintiff's wishes, and is the subject of grave annoyance to her, most respectable persons will probably do as Messrs. W. H. Smith and Son have done, and refuse to have anything to do with them.
Motion dismissed.

NOTES

1. The case illustrates that even if an action in defamation is available, the remedy may be limited to damages. Although an interlocutory injunction will often be much the more effective remedy from the privacy point of view, one will only be granted under the rule in *Bonnard v Perryman* [1891] 2 Ch 269 at 284, CA 'in the clearest cases, where any jury would say that the matter complained of was libellous . . .'. An interlocutory injunction will not be granted if the defendant's defence is justification (see, e.g. Fox LJ in *Francome v Mirror Newspapers* [1984] 2 All ER 408 at 414, CA).

2. Did *Corelli v Wall* decide that there was no remedy in English law for invasion of privacy in the form of the 'appropriation' of a person's 'name or likeness' (*Restatement, 2d, Torts*, above, p. 521)? Or only that an injunction could not be granted on the facts of the case?

3. In *Monson v Tussauds* [1894] 1 QB 671, CA the plaintiff had been tried and acquitted of murder. He sued the defendants for libel for including in their exhibition a wax model of him with the gun that was thought to be the murder weapon close-by. Under the rule in *Bonnard v Perryman*, the Court of Appeal refused an injunction pending trial of the libel action. In the Divisional Court, Collins J expressly left open 'the question whether a private person can restrain the publication of a portrait or effigy of himself which has been obtained without his authority' (p. 679). In the Court of Appeal, Lord Halsbury touched upon the question of invasion of privacy in more general terms (p. 687):

'If I understand the argument correctly, it comes to this—that the exhibition in question is dedicated to the gratification of public curiosity in regard to every person or event which may for the moment be interesting. I confess I regard such a claim with something like dismay. Is it possible to say that everything which has once been known may be reproduced with impunity in print or picture; every incident of a criminal or other trial be produced, and its publication justified; not only trials, but every incident which has actually happened in private life, furnish material for the adventurous exhibitor, dramatized peradventure, and justified because, in truth, such an incident did really happen? That it is done for gain does not in itself make it unlawful if it be in other respects legitimate; but it is not altogether immaterial as excluding such a publication from the category of those which are made in the fulfilment of some moral or legal duty.'

4. In *Tolley v J S Fry & Sons Ltd* [1931] AC 333, HL, the defendants published an advertisement for their chocolate showing, without his knowledge or consent, a caricature of the plaintiff, a well known amateur golfer, playing golf with a packet of their chocolate in his pocket. The plaintiff recovered damages in defamation on the basis that the advertisement carried an innuendo that he had prostituted his amateur status by advertising the defendant's goods for reward. On the question whether a remedy would have existed if the advertisement had not been defamatory, Greer LJ stated in the Court of Appeal ([1930] 1 KB at 477–8):

'Some men and women voluntarily enter professions which by their nature invite publicity, and public approval or disapproval. It is not unreasonable in their case that they should submit without complaint to their names and occupations and reputations being treated as matters of public interest, and almost as public property. On the other hand a great many people outside the professions I have referred to resent any attempt to utilize their names or their doings as public property. And I can very well imagine that an amateur sportsman, though success necessarily brings about a certain amount of publicity, strongly objecting to the use of his name in connection with an advertising campaign aimed at increasing the sales of a commodity which he may either dislike, or at any rate in which he is not the least interested. I have no hesitation in saying that in my judgment the defendants in publishing the advertisement in question, without first obtaining Mr Tolley's consent, acted in a manner inconsistent with the decencies of life, and in doing so they were guilty of an act for which there ought to be a legal remedy. But unless a man's photograph, caricature, or name be published in such a context that the publication can be said to be defamatory within the law of libel, it cannot be made the subject-matter of complaint by action at law: *Dockrell v Dougall* and *Corelli v Wall* [above].'

In *Dockrell v Dougall*[1] the defendant had used the plaintiff's name without his knowledge or consent in an advertisement for a quack medicine ('Dr Dockrell says "Nothing had done his gout so much good" '). After a jury had held that the advertisement was not libellous, the plaintiff unsuccessfully sought an injunction. Smith LJ stated:

'If it could be made out that a man has a property in his own name *per se* and there has been an unauthorised use of his name, then the plaintiff might be entitled to an injunction. In order, however, to be entitled to an injunction, it seems to me that the plaintiff must show injury to him in his property, business, or profession. Upon that ground I think that the appeal fails.'

5. A man who opened a copy of a medical textbook in a public library was surprised to find a full frontal nude photograph of himself giving his initials, hospital record number and details of his case, all without his consent. The Health Service Commissioner, or Ombudsman, found that there had been a breach of confidentiality by the Health Authority.[2]

The Goolagong Case (20th Press Council Report 1973, p. 44)

Publication by the *Sun* of drawings purporting to show Miss Evonne Goolagong, the Australian tennis player, in the nude, was an infringement of privacy said the Council after the All England Lawn Tennis and Croquet Club had complained that the *Sun* published the drawings without Miss Goolagong's knowledge and consent and that the drawings caused her great distress. . . . The drawings . . . were published under the heading 'On Wimbledon's opening day Goolagong in the Altogether'.

Miss Goolagong wrote to the Secretary of the All England Club (Major A. D. Mills) saying (inter alia) that when she went on court on the first Tuesday she felt all eyes were turned on her and that she was being undressed publicly. . . . Major Mills protested to the Editor [Mr Lamb] about the drawings and the Editor's Personal Assistant . . . replied that they were published because they believed they had artistic merit and were in no way offensive. They had had no complaint from Miss Goolagong. They would be distressed to think they had upset her. The newspaper was the first to note her charm, professional potential and appeal in 1971. . . .

1 (1899) 80 LT 556 at 557, CA. See also *Blennerhassett v Novelty Sales Services Ltd* (1933) 175 LT Jo 393. On appropriation of personality, see T. Frazer, (1983) 99 LQR 281.
2 *Report of the Health Service Commissioner, Selected Investigations Oct 1984–Mar 1985*, p. 35. Liability for invasion of privacy was established in a somewhat similar US case: *Banks v King Features Syndicate* 30 F Supp 352 (1939) (surgical clamp left accidentally in a patient's abdomen; press photograph of the clamp in situ without the patient's knowledge or consent).

Mr Lamb replied that his information was that Miss Goolagong was distressed not so much by the drawings as the behaviour of a fellow competitor who publicly accused her of having posed for them. He was unable to accept that the drawings, which were wholly sympathetic, were below 'acceptable standards' or that they constituted an infringement of privacy. . . .

The adjudication was: In the view of the Press Council the publication of drawings purporting to portray Miss Goolagong in the nude without her knowledge and consent was an infringement of her privacy. The complaints against the *Sun* are upheld.

NOTE

1. Would there have been a remedy at law on these facts?

Melvin v Reid 112 Cal App 285 (1931) 297 Pac 91, District Court of Appeal, 4th District, California

The plaintiff, a prostitute, was acquitted of murder in 1918. Thereafter, she abandoned her former way of life and became a respectable married housewife. She made many friends who did not know of her past. In 1925, the defendants made a film without the plaintiff's knowledge or consent based upon her earlier life and trial and identifying the plaintiff by using her maiden name. The plaintiff sued in the California state courts inter alia for invasion of privacy. The plaintiff appealed against the judgment of the trial court rejecting her claim.

Marks J:
. . . the use of the incidents from the life of appellant in the moving picture is in itself not actionable. These incidents appeared in the records of her trial for murder, which is a public record, open to perusal of all. . . . Had respondents, in the story of 'The Red Kimono,' stopped with the use of those incidents from the life of appellant which were spread upon the record of her trial, no right of action would have accrued. They went further, and in the formation of the plot used the true maiden name of appellant. If any right of action exists, it arises from the use of this true name in connection with the true incidents from her life together with their advertisements in which they stated that the story of the picture was taken from true incidents in the life of Gabrielle Darley, who was Gabrielle Darley Melvin.

In the absence of any provision of law, we would be loath to conclude that the right of privacy as the foundation of an action in tort, in the form known and recognized in other jurisdictions, exists in California. We find, however, that the . . . right to pursue and obtain happiness is guaranteed to all by the fundamental law of our state [Article 1(1) Calif. Const.]. This right by its very nature includes the right to live free from the unwarranted attack of others upon one's liberty, property and reputation. . . .

. . . [E]ight years before the production of 'The Red Kimono' appellant had abandoned her life of shame, had rehabilitated herself, and had taken her place as a respected and honored member of society. This change having occurred in her life, she should have been permitted to continue its course without having her reputation and social standing destroyed by the publication of the story of her former depravity with no other excuse than the expectation of private gain by the publishers. . . .

We believe that the publication by respondents of the unsavoury incidents in the past life of appellant after she had reformed, coupled with her true name, was not justified by any standard of morals or ethics known to us, and was a direct invasion of her inalienable right guaranteed to her by our Constitution, to pursue and obtain happiness. Whether we call this a right of privacy or give it any other name is immaterial, because it is a right guaranteed by our Constitution that must not be ruthlessly and needlessly invaded by others. . . .

Barnard PJ and **Jennings J** concurred.
Judgment reversed.

NOTES

1. This would have been a case of invasion of privacy in the form of 'unreasonable publicity' for a person's 'private life' according to the classification of invasion of privacy in the *US Restatement, 2d, Torts*, above, p. 521. The *Restatement* states that publicity is not actionable if it is on a 'matter of legitimate public concern'. It also states that the private lives of both voluntary (e.g. politicians, actors, criminals) *and* involuntary (e.g. relatives of criminals, victims of crime, witnesses of catastrophes) public figures are such matters 'to some reasonable extent'. Some American courts are less protective of privacy than others. Contrast *Melvin v Reid* with *Sidis v F-R Pub Corpn* 113 F 2d 806 (2d Circ, 1940) (a cruel 'where are they now' article on a failed childhood prodigy; no liability). In the US it has been held that there can be no liability for invasion of privacy for publishing a matter of public record: *Cox Broadcasting Corpn v Cohn* 420 US 469 (1975) (name of a rape victim discovered in court records and broadcast on TV). This case may protect freedom of the press unduly. A distinction may be drawn between cases in which information is available for those who go and seek it out in public records and cases in which it is conveniently made available for the public at large in a newspaper or on television. Even though a matter is generally a matter of public knowledge, much distress may also be caused by repeated invasions of privacy: see *R v Broadcasting Complaints Commission*, below, p. 569.

2. There would have been no liability in defamation in English law in *Melvin v Reid* because justification, or truth, is always a defence (but see the Rehabilitation of Offenders Act 1974, below). 'Newspapers are free in this country to rake up a man's forgotten past, and ruin him deliberately in the process, without incurring tortious liability' (Street, *Torts* (8th edn, 1988) p. 405). In 1981, the Press Council severely censured the *Lancashire Evening Post* for a 'sordid piece of journalism' when it recalled details about a woman murdered several years earlier and published her parents' name and address, noting that the parents had refused to answer the newspaper's questions.[1] In most Australian jurisdictions truth is only a defence to defamation if the publication is for the 'public benefit' or in the 'public interest': see Fleming, *The Law of Torts* (8th edn, 1992, p. 557). Dworkin (2 U Tas LR 418 at 425 (1967)) suggests that if such a limitation were introduced into English law, cases of invasion of privacy of the 'unjustified publicity' kind which were not controlled by law would be 'reduced to negligible proportions'.

3. Under the Rehabilitation of Offenders Act 1974, a conviction leading to a sentence of no more than 30 months' imprisonment becomes 'spent' after a period of time ranging from 5 to 10 years. The effect of a conviction becoming 'spent' is, inter alia, that the convicted person (i) need not reveal it in judicial proceedings or for employment or insurance purposes and (ii) may recover in defamation against a person who reveals the conviction provided that he proves that the publication is made 'with malice' (s. 8). There are some exceptions. For a case in which malice was not shown, see *Herbage v Pressdram Ltd* [1984] 2 All ER 769, CA. A case that does not fall within the 1974 Act may nonetheless infringe the Press Code of Practice. The *North-West Daily Mail* was condemned for the prominent way in which it reported that a man had lost his job when it became known he had been convicted of a murder some 14 years earlier.[2]

4. In *Re X (A Minor) (Wardship: Jurisdiction)*,[3] Lord Denning noted that a dead person could not be defamed:

'Suppose the mother of the child were to bring an action for defamation on the ground that the passages were untrue and a gross libel on her dead husband. Many might think she should be able to prevent the publication, especially as it would bring such grief and distress to his relatives, and, in addition, emotional

---

1 (27th/28th Reports, 1980/81, p. 184). For other 'raking up the past' cases, see ibid, pp. 108, 173.
2 Press Council Press Release, 17 May 1988. The report caused the family distress and made re-employment unlikely. The case was decided under the Press Council's Declaration of Principle on Privacy.
3 [1975] Fam 47. For the facts, see Neill LJ in the *Central Independent Television plc* case, below, p. 545.

damage to his child. But the law of defamation does not permit any such proceedings. It says simply that no action lies for a libel on a dead man: on the ground that on balance it is in the public interest that no such action should lie: see *R v Topham* (1791) 4 Term Rep 126; *R v Ensor* (1887) 3 TLR 366.

The Calcutt Committee rejected a suggestion that a right of action be allowed to close relatives for defamation of the dead (Report, p. 30):

'However, distress and hurt feelings are central to defamation claims; a dead person can have no hurt feelings. In practice, the most immediate impact is upon the grieving relatives. The truth would be even more difficult than usual to establish in such cases. Problems would also arise over the discovery of documents. Furthermore, any change in the law would need to include clear guidance on the length of time after death during which a person could be libelled and whether any time limit should start from the events referred to or from the death of the individual. Some of the problems are illustrated by the play which falsely alleged, some years after his death, that Sir Winston Churchill had been responsible for the death of the Polish exiled leader, General Sikorski, during the Second World War. A time limit would have to be set, if only to permit research by historians. We do not consider that extending the law of defamation to cover the dead would provide a practical solution to intrusions into privacy.
     . . . We consider, however, that the immediate family of a person who is recently dead should be entitled to have recourse for intrusive press coverage, but only insofar as the intrusion infringes their own privacy. Stories about the private lives of the recently dead and their immediate families, and the reporting methods used to obtain those stories, should fall within the scope of the proposed expanded code of practice [for journalists].

5. Christine Keeler had been a prominent figure in the Profumo Affair in the early 1960s. In spite of a request by her, several newspapers published her new name and address when she married several years later. The Press Council (13th Report 1966, p. 95) considered that her request had been 'a reasonable one' and regretted 'that this was either overlooked or disregarded by a number of newspaper editors'. The complainant 'told the Council that from the Saturday afternoon on which her whereabouts were discovered by the Press, until the following Monday afternoon, reporters and photographers were almost continually outside her house. Repeated requests that she and her husband should pose for photographs were refused'. Eventually the photographers went away after Miss Keeler and her husband agreed to walk from the house to their car while photographs were taken. The Council did not comment specifically upon this harassment but noted that it 'was inevitable that Miss Keeler's marriage should be reported as a matter of public interest'. Would these facts give a remedy in English law? Should they?

6. The Press Council has ruled upon a lot of complaints about the revelation of current information about a person's life. In one case (6th Report 1959, p. 30) the *Sunday Mercury* was censured for revealing, contrary to a coroner's request, the name of a married mother who had had an affair with a man who had committed suicide. The woman then committed suicide herself, apparently because of the revelation. In another, the *Sunday Pictorial* had, much to the embarrassment of the family, stopped a wedding in church because the bride was under age. The Council found that the family could have been given the opportunity to tell the clergyman beforehand but the press, quite improperly, were looking for a sensational story (4th Report 1957, p. 24). In two other cases, the Council censured the *Daily Mail* for revealing 'the name, age and school of a six year old girl from whom her parents had kept the opinion of doctors that she would die from a rare blood disease before she reached teen-age' (9th Report 1962, p. 36) and a story about a girl who had plagiarised a poem in a poetry competition and who, following the report (which gave her name and address) had received 'threats of violence, filthy letters and other kinds of abuse' (11th Report 1964, p. 53). In the early days of heart transplants, the Press Council

(16th Report 1969, p. 70 and 17th Report 1970, p. 47) rejected complaints that newspapers had ignored hospital and, in one case, family requests that the name of the recipient should not be published. The Council considered that the matter was one for editorial discretion.

In 1977, the Council (24th Report 1977, p. 72) rejected a complaint that the *Daily Mail* had invaded the privacy of Ms Maureen Colquhoun (then an MP, later defeated in the 1979 election) by revealing in its Diary that Ms Colquhoun had left her matrimonial home to share a house with a close woman friend. Applying its Declaration of Principle on Privacy,[1] the Council considered that whereas her status as an MP would not by itself have justified the story, the fact that Ms Colquhoun was an MP 'who has taken a very strong stand on feminist issues and has not been loath to publicise her views upon them' did. It brought the story into 'the area of those matters which the public is entitled to know as being capable of affecting the performance of her public duties or affecting public confidence in her views as a Member of Parliament'. A public interest defence was also upheld in a claim against *The Sun* after it had published allegations about the personal life of Helen Smith, the British nurse who fell to her death from a balcony in Saudi Arabia. The allegations were relevant to the manner of her death, which had become a matter of legitimate public concern (27th/28th Council Reports, 1980/81, p. 135).

7. For an unsuccessful attempt in Parliament to restrict by law the publication in the media of the details of wills, see the suggestion by Sir Anthony Meyer in 1975: 895 HC Deb 14 July 1975 col 1059. In the public opinion survey conducted for the Younger Committee (Report, p. 238), publication of the details of a large legacy left to a person was regarded by most people as an invasion of privacy that ought to be prohibited by law. For a Press Council case on unwanted publicity for football pool winners, see 13th Report 1966, p. 80. The Press Complaints Commission has issued guidance to the press on the treatment and identification of National Lottery winners: PCC Press Release, 4 April 1995.

8. In a case of false attribution, the Press Council (23rd Report 1976, p. 111) upheld a complaint against the *Daily Express* in respect of the publication of 'an article on abortion purporting to have been written by Labour MP Mrs Helene Hayman, when in fact she was not the author and was not consulted about the presentation of her views in that way'. The *Express* had telephoned Mrs Hayman and asked for comments on the then current controversy in Parliament on abortion. Mrs Hayman's comments were used as the basis for an article under her name without her knowledge or consent that they would be used in this way. Had Mrs Hayman written the article, she would have presented her views in a very different way. 'The Council strongly criticised the practice of presenting interviews as if they were the personal contribution of the interviewee'. Would there have been a remedy for defamation in this case? Or for the tort of passing off? See above, p. 521. In the US this would have been a case of invasion of privacy by placing a person in a 'false light' in the sense of the *Restatement, 2d, Torts*, above, p. 521.[2]

1 The Declaration preceded the present Press Code of Practice. A public interest defence was rejected in another case concerning the MP Ms Clare Short: Press Complaints Commission Report No 1, Jan–June 1991, p. 9. In that case, the *News of the World* had interviewed Ms Short's former boy-friend and published a story headed "MP Clare's Ex-Boyfriend was Gun Murder Victim", in which his convictions for serious criminal offences were revealed. The Press Complaints Commission could find no public interest reason for this story.
2 For a 'false light' case in which defamation provided a remedy in English law, see *Fry v Daily Sketch* (1968) Times, 29 June. See also the Press Council ruling in the same case: 15th Report 1968, p. 100.

(d) COURT JURISDICTION TO PROTECT MINORS

R v Central Independent Television plc [1994] Fam 192, Court of Appeal

The defendant company was responsible for a series of television programmes called 'Scotland Yard' that depicted the work of the police. One programme in the series concerned the investigation by the Obscene Publications Squad of a man who was eventually convicted of offences involving indecency with young boys and sentenced to six years' imprisonment. When the plaintiff saw a trailer of the programme, she recognised the man as her former husband and the father of her daughter, then five years old. In order to avoid potential harm to the daughter, who knew nothing of her father's offences, the plaintiff sought to have the programme altered so as to prevent it being possible to identify the man as her father. Following negotiations, the defendant agreed to remove from the broadcast any picture showing the exterior or interior of the plaintiff's house where the man had been arrested and to exclude pictures of the plaintiff and her daughter. When the defendant refused to agree to obscure pictures of the man so that he could not be recognised, the plaintiff obtained an injunction from Kirkwood J to the effect that the programme could only be broadcast if 'moving pictures of the father are obscured'. The Court of Appeal unanimously allowed an appeal by the defendant.

Neill LJ: . . . The jurisdiction of the court to protect minors has been recognised for many centuries. The basis of the jurisdiction was explained . . . by Lord Halsbury LC in *Barnado v McHugh* [1891] AC 388, 395:

> '[A court of equity] interferes for the protection of infants, qua infants, by virtue of the prerogative which belongs to the Crown as parens patriae, and the exercise of which is delegated to the Great Seal. . . .

The law which restricts the publication of information relating to proceedings in private is now statutory. Section 12(1) of the Administration of Justice Act 1960 . . . provides . . .:

> 'The publication of information relating to proceedings before any court sitting in private shall not of itself be contempt of court except in the following cases, that is to say—(a) where the proceedings—(i) relate to the exercise of the inherent jurisdiction of the High Court with respect to minors; (ii) are brought under the Children Act 1989; or (iii) otherwise relate wholly or mainly to the maintenance or upbringing of a minor; . . .'

Other statutory restrictions on newspaper reports of proceedings affecting children are contained in section 39(1) of the Children and Young Persons Act 1933 . . . and in section 49(1) of the Act of 1933, amended by section 10(1) of the Children and Young Persons Act 1969 and Schedule 11 to the Criminal Justice Act 1991.

In *In re F (A Minor)* [1977] Fam 58 . . . in the context of contempt proceedings to which section 12 of the Act of 1960 applied the Court of Appeal was careful to confine the protection of the ward to 'information relating to the wardship proceedings.'

In several cases decided in the last 10 years, however, the jurisdiction to protect the ward has been exercised on a somewhat wider basis. In *In re X (A Minor) (Wardship: Injunction)* [1984] 1 WLR 1422 the ward's mother had achieved notoriety in 1968 when, as a child, she had been found guilty of the manslaughter of two small boys. On her release from prison she changed her name. In May 1984 the mother gave birth to a child and almost immediately the local authority for the area in which the mother was living applied for the child to be made a ward of court. . . . In July 1984 the birth came to the attention of a newspaper which wished to publish an article about the mother, though they offered undertakings that the new name of the mother and the names of the ward and other relatives would not be published. In the light of these undertakings the judge refused to make an order to prevent the publication of the fact that 'as Mary Bell' she had had a daughter. . . .

A few days later, however, the newspaper made a further application to the court contending that there was no jurisdiction to prevent publication of material which might identify Mary Bell by her new name and thus the ward. In the course of his judgment Balcombe J. referred to the decision of the Court of Appeal in *In re F* [1977] Fam 58 and concluded that without an order of the court there could be no objection to the publication of the present identity of Mary Bell or the child, or of the child's father. He then turned to consider whether he was entitled to prevent publication in the exercise of the wardship injunction. He continued, at pp. 1425–1426:

'it seems to me that I have jurisdiction in this case to make an order which has the effect of prohibiting publication by anybody of details which would enable the present identity of Mary Bell and her child to become known. . . .

I come next to the decision in *In re C (A Minor) (Wardship: Medical Treatment) (No 2)* [1990] Fam 39. In that case the child concerned was terminally ill. A national newspaper wished to publish an article relating to her care and treatment, though it was accepted on behalf of the newspaper that nothing should be published which might identify the child or her parents. The newspaper did wish, however, to refer in the article to the hospital and to the medical practitioners and staff who were looking after the child, and to be free to carry out interviews with the staff. It was said that in view of her condition the child herself would never be capable of understanding anything written about her, and that if an injunction in wide terms were granted it would have the effect of protecting from criticism or comment public authorities which should be accountable to the public for the decisions they take. Nevertheless, the Court of Appeal imposed an injunction which prevented the newspaper from identifying those who had looked after the child in the past, as well as those who were currently caring for her and from soliciting information from them. Nicholls L.J. said, at p. 55, that the terms imposed represented:

'a sensible balance, in a case of considerable public importance, between on the one hand the right of the public to be kept informed of what is going on in court and, on the other hand, the need for the welfare of baby C not to be put at risk by public identification of her, her parents and those who are or have been involved in her care. . . .'

[After referring to *In re M and N (Minors)* (see below), **Neill LJ** continued:]

In re W [1992] 1 WLR 100 was a similar case. A boy of 15 with a disturbed background, and who had been involved in the past in homosexual activities with older men, had been made a ward of court and placed in the care of a local authority. The local authority decided to foster the boy with two men who had had a stable homosexual relationship with each other for many years. A national newspaper learnt of the placement and wished to publish an article about it. In this case also the Court of Appeal approved the grant of an injunction, though to a more limited extent than had the judge. It was held that the newspaper should be allowed to include in the article all the ingredients of the story which were of public concern, but that the article should not identify the boy or his foster parents nor give any other particulars which might directly lead to the identification either of him or of the foster parents. It was in this context that in *In re W* I set out the guidelines which should be taken into account when in a case involving a ward the court is asked to restrain the publication of material relating to him.

The crucial point about these cases, however, was that the publications restrained related to the care and upbringing of children over whose welfare the court was exercising a supervisory role. It is true that the restraints imposed went further than to prevent only publication of accounts of the wardship proceedings which had already taken place, but the activities restrained were not only likely to affect the welfare of the ward himself but also the ability of the carers to carry out their obligations to the court for the care of the ward. The court itself therefore had an interest in the integrity of its own wardship jurisdiction.

The present case, however, is quite different. The programme was in no way concerned with the care or upbringing of S. Indeed, the present case is much nearer to *In re X (A Minor) (Wardship: Jurisdiction)* [1975] Fam 47. In that case the stepfather of a girl aged 14 made her a ward of court for the purpose of applying for an injunction to restrain the publishers and author of a book which was on the point of publication from publishing it, so long as it contained an account describing the aberrant private activities and practices of the ward's deceased father.

Latey J. granted an injunction on the basis that the book might come to the attention of the ward and that grave injury would be caused to her emotional psychological health. The Court of Appeal discharged the injunction. . . .

In the Court of Appeal Lord Denning M.R. rejected the idea that there was any balancing exercise to be carried out in such a case. He referred to the importance of the freedom of the press and continued, at pp. 58–59:

'. . . I do not think the wardship jurisdiction should be extended so as to enable the court to stop publication of this book. The relatives of the child must do their best to protect her by doing all they can to see the book does not come into her hands. . . . In my opinion it would be extending the wardship jurisdiction too far and infringing too much upon the freedom of the press for us to grant an injunction in this case.'

Counsel for Mrs R, however, drew our attention to passages in the judgments of Roskill LJ and Sir John Pennycuick in *In re X* [1975] Fam 47, which suggested that even in that case a balancing exercise had to be carried out and that the court had to weigh the interests of the child against the rights of free speech. Thus . . . Sir John Pennycuick . . . said . . .

'The court must hold a proper balance between the protection of the ward and the rights of outside parties. Specifically, it seems to me, the court must hold a proper balance between the protection of the ward and the right of free publication enjoyed by outside parties and should hesitate long before interfering with that right of free publication. It would be impossible and not, I think, desirable to draw any rigid line beyond which the protection of a ward should not be extended. . . .'

For my part, . . . I am unable to accept the proposition that a balancing act has to be carried out in every case where a threatened publication may be likely to affect a ward. In my view the judgments of Roskill LJ and Sir John Pennycuick in *In re X (A Minor) (Wardship: Jurisdiction)* [1975] Fam 47, when read as a whole, do not support so wide a proposition.

A balancing exercise only becomes necessary where the threatened publication touches matters which are of direct concern to the court in its supervisory role over the care and upbringing of the ward. Whether in any particular case the relevant publication is in this category will depend on the facts and on the nature of the publication. In the earlier cases to which I have referred the court was closely concerned with the impact of the threatened publicity on the future care of baby X, of the dying baby C, of the two boys M and N in their new foster homes and of the boy W with his two male foster parents.

In the present case, as I have already observed, the programme had nothing whatever to do with the care or upbringing of S. There was nothing to put in the balance against the freedom to publish. I am reminded of the words of Lord Donaldson of Lymington MR in *In re M and N* [1990] Fam 211, where he said, at p. 231:

'. . . I regard injunctive protection of children from publicity which, though inimical to their welfare, is not directed at them or at those who care for them, but is an incidental part of life, as being in a special category . . .'

For these reasons I thought it right to uphold the television company's submission that they were entitled to publish the programme in full, and that there was no legal bar to prevent them from including pictures of the place of arrest.

On the other hand, I would wish to applaud, and to say nothing to discourage, the responsible attitude taken by the television company in this case. They did what they could to reduce the risk of identification and the risk of harm to the welfare of S. One would hope that in similar circumstances others would act in a similar way. The press and broadcasters are entitled to publish the results of criminal proceedings and questions as to what should be left out are in the main a matter for editorial decision. It is always to be remembered, however, that the families of those convicted have a heavy burden to bear and the effect of publicity on small children may be very serious. . . .

The motives which impel judges to assume a power to balance freedom of speech against other interests are almost always understandable and humane on the facts of the particular case before them. Newspapers are sometimes irresponsible and their motives in a market economy cannot be expected to be unalloyed by considerations of commercial advantage. Publication may cause needless pain, distress and damage to individuals or harm to other aspects of the public interest. But a freedom which is restricted to what judges think to be responsible or in the public interest is no freedom. Freedom means the right to publish things which government and judges, however well motivated, think should not be published. It means the right to say things which 'right-thinking people' regard as dangerous or irresponsible. This freedom is subject only to clearly defined exceptions laid down by common law or statute.

Furthermore, in order to enable us to meet our international obligations under the Convention for the Protection of Human Rights and Fundamental Freedoms (1953) (Cmd 8969), it is necessary that any exceptions should satisfy the tests laid down in article 10(2). . . . It cannot be too strongly emphasised that outside the established exceptions, or any new ones which Parliament may enact in accordance with its obligations under the Convention, there is no question of balancing freedom of speech against other interests. It is a trump card which always wins.

This is why I respectfully think that Lord Denning MR was right in *In re X (A Minor) (Wardship: Jurisdiction)* [1975] Fam 47 when he said that the wardship jurisdiction did not permit the courts to balance the competing interests of the child and the freedom of the press. The exceptions to freedom of speech were, he said, at p. 58F 'already staked out by the rules of law.' Section 12(1)(*a*) of the Administration of Justice Act 1960 prohibits the publication of information relating to a private court hearing in proceedings which concern children. It does not however apply to information which relates to the child but not to the proceedings: see *In re F (orse A) (A Minor) (Publication of Information)* [1977] Fam 58. It would be wrong, said Lord Denning MR in *In re X (A Minor) (Wardship: Jurisdiction)* [1975] Fam 47, 58 to extend the law:

'so as to give the judges a power to stop publication of true matter whenever the judges—or any particular judge—thought that it was in the interests of a child to do so. . . .'

It is true that in a series of decisions commencing with *In re C (A Minor) (Wardship: Medical Treatment) (No 2)* [1990] Fam 39 the courts have, without any statutory or, so far as I can see, other previous authority, assumed a power to create by injunction what is in effect a right of privacy for children. The power is said to be based on the powers of the Crown as parens patriae and the 'machinery for its exercise' is the wardship jurisdiction: see Butler-Sloss LJ in *In re M and N (Minors) (Wardship: Publication of Information)* [1990] Fam 211, 223. The novelty of this jurisdiction is shown by the fact that as recently as 1977, Scarman LJ in *In re F* [1977] Fam 58, 99 was able to say that apart from section 12(1)(*a*) of the Administration of Justice 1960, 'the ward enjoys no greater protection against unwelcome publicity than other children.' In *In re M and N* Butler-Sloss LJ said, at p. 224, that the power to restrain publication was needed because:

'There has, since *In re X* [1975] Fam 47, been an upsurge in investigative journalism with an interest in situations affecting children which has led the media to publish or attempt to publish more widely and more frequently than ever contemplated in the early 1970s.'

I would not for a moment dispute either this perception or the fact that a right of privacy may be a legitimate exception to freedom of speech. After all, other countries also party to the Convention have a right of privacy for grown-ups as well. But we do not and there may be room for constitutional argument as to whether in a matter so fundamentally trenching upon the freedom of the press as the creation of a right of privacy, it would not be more appropriate for the remedy to be provided by the legislature rather than the judiciary. In recent years Parliament has not been slow to act in the interests of children. However that may be, the existence of a jurisdiction to restrain publication of information concerning a child and its upbringing is no longer open to dispute in this court.

But this new jurisdiction is concerned only with the privacy of children and their upbringing. It does not extend, as Lord Donaldson of Lymington MR made clear in *In re M and N*, at p. 231B to 'injunctive protection of children from publicity which, though inimical to their welfare, is not directed at them or those who care for them.' It therefore cannot apply to publication of the fact that the child's father has been convicted of a serious offence, however distressing it may be for the child to be identified as the daughter of such a man. If such a jurisdiction existed, it could be exercised to restrain the identification of any convicted criminal who has young children. It may be that the decision of Balcombe J in *X County Council v A* [1985] 1 All ER 53 can be brought within Lord Donaldson of Lymington MR's language because the child's mother, at whose past the intended publication was directed, was actually caring for the child at the time of the application. But the events in question had happened long before the child was born. The publication was not directly concerned with the child or its upbringing, and for my part I think that the judge, for wholly commendable reasons, was asserting a jurisdiction which did not exist. . . .
Waite LJ delivered a concurring judgment.

NOTES

1. The *Central Independent Television plc* case concerned the prerogative power of the Crown parens patriae, exercisable through the courts, to protect children. This power is normally used in respect of a child whom a court has decided to make a ward of court. As the present case illustrates, it may also be invoked to request a court order to protect other children. Although the power was invoked unsuccessfully in the present case, the courts have in several cases in recent years used their wardship jurisdiction to make orders protecting children in cases raising privacy or related issues, as several of the cases considered by Neill LJ indicate. In the *Central Independent Television plc* case, the Court of Appeal drew a distinction between cases where the publication that is challenged contains information (e.g. concerning the child's medical treatment) that has a direct bearing upon a child and his welfare, for which the courts are responsible, and cases where the publication has a less direct connection (e.g. where personal details are given about a close relative). In the former kind of case, the prerogative jurisdiction parens patriae is available to censor a publication provided that on balance this should be done. In other kinds of cases, such as the *Central Independent Television plc* case, no balancing act is called for: freedom of expression simply prevails. The guidelines applicable when considering the former kind of case were set out by Neill LJ in the earlier case of *In re W*[1] as follows:

'(1) The court will attach great importance to safeguarding the freedom of the press. . . .

(2) The court will also take account of art 10 of the Convention for the Protection of Human Rights and Fundamental Freedoms. . . .

(3) These freedoms, however, are subject to exceptions, which include restrictions upon publication which are imposed for the protection of children.

(4) In considering whether to impose a restriction upon publication to protect a ward of court the court has to carry out a balancing exercise. It is to be noted, as Butler-Sloss LJ pointed out in *Re M and anor (minors) (wardship: freedom of publication)* [1990] 1 All ER 205 at 210, [1990] Fam 211 at 223, that: "In this situation the welfare of the child is not the paramount consideration."

(5) In carrying out the balancing exercise the court will weigh the need to protect the ward from harm against the right of the press (or other outside parties) to publish or to comment. An important factor will be the nature and extent of the public interest in the matter which it is sought to publish. A distinction can be drawn between cases of mere curiosity and cases where the press are giving information or commenting about a subject of genuine public interest.

(6) It is to be anticipated that in almost every case the public interest in favour of publication can be satisfied without any identification of the ward to persons other than those who already know the facts. It seems to me, however, that the risk of *some* wider identification may have to be accepted on occasions if the story is to be told in a manner which will engage the interest of the general public.

(7) Any restraint on publication which is imposed is intended to protect the ward and those who care for the ward from the risk of harassment. The restraint must therefore be in clear terms and be no wider than is necessary to achieve the purpose for which it is imposed. It also follows that, save perhaps in an exceptional case, the ward cannot be protected from any distress which he may be caused by reading the publication himself.'

2. A feature of the *Central Independent Television plc* case is that the Court of Appeal accepted the defendant's submission that it was 'entitled to publish the programme in full and that there was no legal bar to prevent them from including pictures of the place of arrest' (Neill LJ). In fact, the programme was broadcast without any of the deletions as to the place of arrest, etc, to which the defendant had agreed during negotiations. What is remarkable about this statement by the Court of Appeal is that, as the Court was aware, the pictures inside the house that were included in the film had been obtained without consent by means of a concealed camera and sound recording equipment. An action in trespass in respect of this entry by deceit was dropped when the defendant agreed in negotiations to exclude the material thus illegally obtained. Commenting on the case, J. Gardiner, 145 NLJ 225, 226 (1995) states:

'The pictures of the place of arrest were obtained by a trespass and included pictures and words of people not concerned in the arrest at all.

These pictures were then included in a documentary film about the work of the police. The fact of the suspect's conviction and sentence was the culmination of a thirty-minute film broadcast some eighteen months after the arrest. The local newspaper had not found the integrity of its contemporaneous report of the proceedings compromised in any way by omitting reference to the man's identity. As far as Mrs R is aware, no other media person had found her ex-husband's case of any interest to the general public.

Neill LJ's comment concerning the television company's entitlement to publish the programme in full suggests that the Court of Appeal will never be prepared to intervene to prevent publication of "fly-on-the-wall" film material. If the publication of such material really has anything to do with the freedom of the press, then one wonders whether it is now time for press freedoms to be defined and limited: not for the protection only of politicians and other public entertainers, but also of real people doing their best to bring up children and live their lives out of range of the apparently insatiable information industry.'

1 [1992] 1 All ER 794, CA. See also *Re H-S (Minors: Protection of Identity)* [1994] 3 All ER 390, CA (parent could write in press about his sex change operation, subject to restrictions to safeguard the identity of the children).

The Broadcasting Complaints Commission dismissed a complaint of invasion of privacy brought by the plaintiff in the *Central Independent Television plc* case, ruling that the broadcast of the full programme was justified in the public interest.

(e) BREACH OF COPYRIGHT

Williams v Settle [1960] 1 WLR 1072, [1960] 2 All ER 806, Court of Appeal

The defendant, a professional photographer, took the photographs at the plaintiff's wedding. Two years later, when the plaintiff's wife was pregnant, her father was murdered. The case attracted publicity and, when the national press came looking for photographs, the defendant sold them copies of the wedding photographs. He did so without the knowledge or consent of the plaintiff, who held the copyright. One of the photographs—a family group with the father in it—was published five days after the wife gave birth with captions identifying the persons in it. One newspaper gave a particular description of the plaintiff's wife. The plaintiff successfully sued the defendant for breach of copyright in the county court. He was awarded £1,000 damages. The defendant's appeal to the Court of Appeal on the ground that the county court had lacked jurisdiction to award such a high amount of damages was rejected. The following extract concerns the appeal on the amount of damages.

Sellers LJ: In the present action the judge was clearly justified, in the circumstances in which the defendant, in breach of the plaintiff's copyright, handed these photographs to the press knowing the use to which they were going to be put, in awarding substantial and heavy damages of a punitive nature. The power so to do, quite apart from the ordinary law of the land, is expressly given by statute. By section 17(3) of the Copyright Act 1956, it is provided: 'Where in an action under this section an infringement of copyright is proved or admitted, and the court, having regard (in addition to all other material considerations) to—(a) the flagrancy of the infringement, and (b) any benefit shown to have accrued to the defendant by reason of the infringement, is satisfied that effective relief would not otherwise be available to the plaintiff, the court, in assessing damages for the infringement, shall have power to award such additional damages by virtue of this subsection as the court may consider appropriate in the circumstances.' It seems that this is not a case where there is any effective relief which could be given. The benefit which can be shown to have accrued to the defendant is meagre . . . It is the flagrancy of the infringement which calls for heavy damages, because this was a scandalous matter in the circumstances, which I do not propose to elaborate and about which I do not propose to express a view. It is sufficient to say that it was a flagrant infringement of the right of the plaintiff, and it was scandalous conduct and in total disregard not only of the legal rights of the plaintiff regarding copyright but of his feelings and his sense of family dignity and pride. It was an intrusion into his life, deeper and graver than an intrusion into a man's property.
Willmer and **Harman LJJ** delivered concurring judgments.
Appeal dismissed.

NOTES

1. The plaintiff also obtained £52 10s damages and costs from the *Daily Express*, an apology and undertakings from the *Daily Mail* and a ruling in his favour from the Press Council.[1] The power to award 'additional damages' in s. 17(3) of the 1956 Act has been re-enacted in similar terms in s. 97(2), Copyright, Designs and Patents Act 1988.

---

1 See [1960] 1 WLR 1074–5. On the case, see (1961) 77 LQR 12 and G. Dworkin, (1961) 24 MLR 185. On the public interest defence available in breach of copyright cases, see the *Lion Laboratories* case, below, p. 559.

2. The first owner of the copyright in a 'work', including a photograph or letter, is its author (other than in the case of an employee acting in the course of his employment): Copyright, Designs and Patents Act 1988, s. 11. A person 'who for private and domestic purposes commissions the taking of a photograph or the making of a film has, where copyright subsists in the resulting work, the right not to have', inter alia, 'copies of the work issued to the public' or 'the work exhibited or shown in public': 1988 Act, s. 85. This right may, however, be waived, by contract or otherwise: 1988 Act, s. 87.

3. The *Daily Mail* was sued for breach of copyright by Princess Margaret's lady in waiting for publishing photographs taken by her at a private house party which showed Princess Margaret dressed as Mae West and a Valkyrie and her friend Mr Llewellyn as a wizard: *Lady Anne Tennant v Associated Newspapers Group Ltd* [1979] FSR 298. The photographs had been taken from the plaintiff's home by her son and sold to the *Daily Mail* without her knowledge or consent. A court order was made against the defendant requiring the return of the photographs. Damages were agreed out of court.

(f) BREACH OF CONFIDENCE

Prince Albert v Strange (1849) 1 Mac and G 25, 1 H & TW 1, Court of Chancery

Queen Victoria and the plaintiff had for their private amusement made etchings of their children and other subjects of personal interest. The defendant obtained copies and planned to exhibit them and to publish a catalogue listing and describing the etchings for profit. The etchings had been kept privately by the Royal Family, although a few copies had been given to friends. The plates for the etchings had been entrusted to a printer in Windsor for him to make further impressions. It appeared that, without the printer's knowledge or consent, one of his employees had made unauthorised copies of the etchings and the defendant had purchased these. The plaintiff obtained an injunction preventing the exhibition and the publication of the catalogue. In these proceedings, the defendant, who accepted that the exhibition should not proceed, applied to have the injunction amended to allow him to publish the catalogue. He appealed to the Lord Chancellor against the refusal of his application by Knight Bruce V-C ((1848) 2 De G and Sm 652), who had referred in his judgment to 'sordid spying into the privacy of domestic life' (p. 698).

Lord Cottenham LC: . . . the Defendant insists that he is entitled to publish a catalogue of the etchings, that is to say, to publish a description or list of works or compositions of another, made and kept for the private use of that other, the publication of which was never authorised, and the possession of copies of which could only have been obtained by surreptitious and improper means. It was said by one of the learned counsel for the Defendant, that the injunction must rest upon the ground of property or breach of trust; both appear to me to exist. The property of an author or composer of any work, whether of literature, art, or science, in such work unpublished and kept for his private use or pleasure, cannot be disputed . . . the Plaintiff is entitled to the injunction of this Court to protect him against the invasion of such right and interest by the Defendant, which the publication of any catalogue would undoubtedly be; but this case by no means depends solely upon the question of property, for a breach of trust, confidence, or contract, would of itself entitle the Plaintiff to an injunction . . . and upon the evidence on behalf of the Plaintiff, and in the absence of any explanation on the part of the Defendant, I am bound to assume that the possession of the etchings by the Defendant . . . has its foundation in a breach of trust, confidence, or contract . . . upon this ground also I think the Plaintiff's title to the injunction sought to be discharged, fully established. The observations of Vice-Chancellor Wigram in *Tipping v Clarke* ((1843) 2 Hare 383) are applicable to this part of the case. He says: 'Every clerk employed in a merchant's counting-house is under an implied contract that he will not make public that which he learns in the execution of his duty as clerk. If the Defendant has obtained copies of books, it would very probably be by means of

some clerk or agent of the Plaintiff; and if he availed himself surreptitiously of the information which he could not have had except from a person guilty of a breach of contract in communicating it, I think he could not be permitted to avail himself of that breach of contract. . . . This was the opinion of Lord Eldon, expressed in the case of *Wyatt v Wilson* in 1820, respecting an engraving of George the Third during his illness, in which, according to a note with which I have been favoured by Mr Cooper, he said, 'If one of the late king's physicians had kept a diary of what he heard and saw, this court would not, in the king's lifetime, have permitted him to print and publish it.'
Motion refused.

NOTES[1]

1. The Younger Committee (Report, p. 26) considered that the 'law on breach of confidence offers the most effective protection of privacy in the whole of our existing law, civil or criminal'. In its opinion 'the extent of its potential effectiveness is not widely recognised'. Although this may well be true, the value of breach of confidence as a remedy is inevitably limited in that it only concerns informational privacy; it does not extend to physical intrusion. Moreover, even in the context of informational privacy, serious breaches by the press and others often involve no obligation of confidence. Nonetheless, as the Younger Committee states, breach of confidence 'affords a measure of protection for all specific and reasonably implied confidences'. On its recommendation, breach of confidence was referred to the Law Commission, which produced its Report in 1981. It recommended that the present law of breach of confidence be replaced by a statutory tort of breach of a duty of confidence, binding on the Crown as well as others: Report No 110, p. 102. However, the 'Government do not propose, particularly in the light of recent judgments which restate that law, to give its implementation high priority at present': 148 HC Deb 2 March 1989 WA col 257. The Calcutt Committee recommended against the introduction of a statutory tort on breach of confidence, preferring to allow the judge-made law to develop (Report, p. 32). Although the Law Commission accepted the close relationship between breach of confidence and privacy, it stressed that the two are not identical. For example, the obligation of confidence will not always be owed to the person whose privacy is at risk: see the Law Commission obituary example, below, p. 559.

2. *Prince Albert v Strange* is the seminal case in the development of the equitable doctrine of breach of confidence. Insofar as judgment was given for the plaintiff on a basis other than that of his property right in the etchings, was it given purely because of breach of confidence or because of an implied term in the rogue employee's contract of employment? As the cases Lord Cottenham refers to at the end of the above extract indicate, the common law has, in the absence of an express term, implied a term in a contract of employment by which an employee may not divulge confidential information obtained during employment to any third party without consent while he is still employed and thereafter. In practice this has mainly been relevant (as has the law of breach of confidence) in the context of trade secrets, but

1 See on breach of confidence, G. Dworkin, *Confidence in the Law* (1971); G. Forrai, (1971) 6 Sydney LR 382; F. Gurry, *Breach of Confidence* (1984, reissued in 1991); J. Jacob and R. Jacob, (1969) 119 NLJ 133; G. Jones, (1970) 86 LQR 463; Meagher, Gummow and Lehane, *Equity Doctrines and Remedies* (3rd edn, 1992), Chap. 41; P. M. North, (1972) 12 JSPTL 149; S. Ricketson, (1977) 11 Mel ULR 223, 289; A. M. Tettenborn, (1982) 11 Anglo-Am LR 273; R. Wacks (1977) 127 NLJ 328. And see Law Commission Report on Breach of Confidence (1981), Report No 110, Cmnd. 8388, and the Australian Law Commission Report on Unfair Publication, Defamation and Privacy (1970). On the Law Commission Report, see M. W. Bryan, [1982] PL 188; G. Jones, [1982] CLJ 40; J. Michael, (1981) 131 NLJ 1201; A. M. Tettenborn, (1983) 34 NILQ 248.

it can apply to more personal matters, as the unreported case of *Wyatt v Wilson*, above, p. 551, indicates. The conditions of service of members of the Royal Household contain a confidentiality clause. See the Press Council's 2nd Report 1955, p. 35, in connection with a case in which the *Sunday Pictorial* had published the memoirs of the Duke of Edinburgh's valet.

Duchess of Argyll v Duke of Argyll [1967] Ch 302, [1965] 1 All ER 611, [1965] 2 WLR 790, Ungoed-Thomas J

The first defendant, the Duke of Argyll and former husband of the plaintiff, Margaret, Duchess of Argyll, had published in *The People* the first two of a series of articles in which he wrote of their married life. The plaintiff sought injunctions against the first defendant and against the editor and publisher of *The People* to prevent the publication in the remaining articles of 'secrets of the plaintiff relating to her private life, personal affairs or private conduct, communicated to the first defendant in confidence during the subsistence of his marriage to the plaintiff and not hitherto made public property'.

Ungoed-Thomas J: . . . it is clear that the court may restrain breach of confidence arising out of contract or any right to property. The question whether the court's protection is limited to such cases was considered in two authorities to which I shall refer.

[His Lordship discussed *Prince Albert v Strange*, above, and *Pollard v Photographic Co* (1888) 40 Ch D 345, Ch D. Referring to the latter, he said:]

. . . In that case a photographer, who had taken a negative likeness of a lady to supply her with copies for money, was restrained from selling or exhibiting copies, both on the ground that there was an implied contract not to use the negative for such purposes, and also on the ground that such sale or exhibition was a breach of confidence. . . .

These cases, in my view, indicate (1) that a contract or obligation of confidence need not be expressed but can be implied; (2) that a breach of confidence or trust or faith can arise independently of any right of property or contract other, of course, than any contract which the imparting of the confidence in the relevant circumstances may itself create; (3) that the court in the exercise of its equitable jurisdiction will restrain a breach of confidence independently of any right at law.

. . . Marriage is, of course, far more than a mere legal contract and legal relationship, and even legal status; but it includes legal contract and relationship. If, for the court's protection of confidence and, contrary to my view, the confidence must arise out of a contractual or property relationship, marriage does not lack its contract. It is basically a contract to be and, according to our Christian conception of marriage, to live as man and wife. It has been said that the legal consideration of marriage—that is the promise to become and to remain man and wife—is the highest legal consideration which there is. And there could hardly be anything more intimate or confidential than is involved in that relationship, or than in the mutual trust and confidences which are shared between husband and wife. The confidential nature of the relationship is of its very essence and so obviously and necessarily implicit in it that there is no need for it to be expressed. To express it is superfluous; it is clear to the least intelligent. So it seems to me that confidences between husband and wife during marriage are not excluded from the court's protection by the criteria appearing in the cases to which I have referred. . . .

[His Lordship then considered and distinguished *Rumping v DPP* [1964] AC 814, HL, in which the House of Lords ruled that an intercepted communication between a husband and wife was admissible in evidence in criminal proceedings against the husband.]

It thus seems to me that the policy of the law, so far from indicating that communication between husband and wife should be excluded from protection against breaches of confidence given by the court in accordance with *Prince Albert v Strange* strongly favours its inclusion, and in view of that policy it can hardly be an objection that such communications are not limited to business matters. . . . if there are communications which should be protected and which the policy of the law recognises should be protected, even to the extent of being a foundation of the old rule making husband and wife incompetent as witnesses against each other, then the court is not to be deterred merely because it is not already provided with fully developed principles, guides, tests, definitions and the full armament for judicial decision. It is sufficient that the court recognises that the communications are confidential, and their publication within the mischief which the law as its policy seeks to avoid, without further defining the scope and limits of the jurisdiction; and I have no hesitation in this case in concluding that publication of some of the passages complained of is in breach of marital confidence. . . .

Should the plaintiff be denied the injunction which she would otherwise get because she has herself to an extent broken confidence and because she, after the confidences of whose breach she complains, adopted an immoral attitude towards her marriage? A person coming to Equity for relief—and this is equitable relief which the plaintiff seeks—must come with clean hands: but the cleanliness required is to be judged in relation to the relief that is sought.

First, I do not consider that the plaintiff's own articles [written in another Sunday newspaper before the defendant's articles and revealing information about him] justify the objectionable passages in the Duke's articles or, of themselves, should disentitle the plaintiff to the court's protection.

Secondly, with regard to the plaintiff's immorality. . . . [it] is not in my view just that adultery should have retrospective operation on a marriage and not only break the marriage for the future but nullify it for the past. The plaintiff's adultery, repugnant though it be, should not in my view license the husband to broadcast unchecked the most intimate confidences of earlier and happier days.

It is in my view established by *Lord Ashburton v Pape* [1913] 2 Ch 469, in accordance with the references already made to *Prince Albert v Strange*, that an injunction may be granted to restrain the publication of confidential information not only by the person who was a party to the confidence but by other persons into whose possession that information has improperly come.

Injunction granted.

NOTES

1. Breach of confidence may thus be a basis for a claim in equity in the absence of any express or implied term in a contract in order to protect confidential communications which the policy of the law recognises should be protected, including marital secrets.
2. In *Saltman Engineering Co Ltd v Campbell Engineering Co Ltd* [1963] 3 All ER 413, CA (a trade secrets case), Lord Greene MR stated (p. 415) that the information must have 'the necessary quality of confidence about it, namely, it must not be something which is public property and public knowledge'. The 'public domain' doctrine was applied in *Woodward v Hutchins*, below, p. 561. See also *Lennon v News Group Newspapers Ltd*,[1] in which John Lennon was refused an injunction to prevent the publication in the *News of the World* of an article by his former wife about their married life. Distinguishing *Argyll v Argyll*, Lord Denning MR stated:

The reasoning of that case, it was said, was put on the fact that marriage has been said to be the highest legal consideration and the court will protect the confidences arising out of it.

That may well be in normal marriages, but I cannot say, looking at this case, that either of these two parties have had much regard for the sanctity of marriage. . . . we have been shown a whole series of articles from various newspapers—some by the former wife, Cynthia Lennon, talking to newspapers about their relationships; some by Mr Lennon himself talking about their relationships—going into the most intimate affairs, accusing one another, obviously just for the satisfaction of the public and, no doubt, for their own reward.

It seems to me as plain as can be that the relationship of these parties has ceased to be their own private affair. They themselves have put it into the public domain.

What if medical information about an individual published by a local newspaper in breach of confidence by a doctor is then republished in a national newspaper? See

1 [1978] FSR 573, CA. See also *Khashoggi v Smith* (1980) 130 NLJ 168, CA (application by Mrs K for an injunction to prevent publication in the *Daily Mirror* of an article by her former housekeeper refused partly because Mrs K had courted publicity).

tattle outside the protection of the law. He says that the law does not protect information relating to grossly immoral behaviour, and relies by analogy on the refusal of the courts to enforce copyright in literary works of a grossly immoral nature. Further, he submits that any sexual conduct whether hetero-sexual or homosexual—and he draws no distinction between the two—necessarily lacks the quality of confidentiality because, by taking part in the sexual activity itself, both sexual partners know what has happened, and accordingly neither of them can claim that the information is confidential to either of them. . . .

In my judgment those arguments are not well-founded. As to the submission that the law will not enforce a duty of confidentiality relating to grossly immoral conduct, the submission is founded on *Glyn v Weston Feature Film Co* [1916] 1 Ch 261. In that case Elinor Glyn complained that the defendants had made a film based on a book written by her. Younger J took a very unfavourable view of both the plain-tiff's book and the defendants' film, regarding them both as indecently offensive. On that ground, amongst others, he refused the plaintiff any relief. . . .

I entirely accept the principle stated in that case, the principle being that a court of equity will not enforce copyright, and presumably also will not enforce a duty of confidence, relating to matters which have a grossly immoral tendency. But at the present day the difficulty is to identify what sexual conduct is to be treated as grossly immoral. In 1915 there was a code of sexual morals accepted by the overwhelm-ing majority of society. A judge could therefore stigmatize certain sexual conduct as offending that moral code. But at the present day no such general code exists. There is no common view that sexual conduct of any kind between consenting adults is grossly immoral. I suspect the works of Elinor Glyn if published today would be widely regarded as, at the highest, very soft pornography.

The sexual conduct of the plaintiff was not so morally shocking in this case as to prevent the third defendant, a major national Sunday newspaper, from spreading the story all over its front and inside pages. The submission on behalf of these defendants that the actions of the plaintiff in this case are so grossly immoral as to produce a tendency towards immoral conduct and thereby to be without the law lies ill in their mouths, since they have themselves spread the news of such conduct nationwide for their own personal profit.

If it is right that there is now no generally accepted code of sexual morality applying to this case, it would be quite wrong in my judgment for any judge to apply his own personal moral views, however strongly held, in deciding the legal rights of the parties. The court's function is to apply the law, not per-sonal prejudice. Only in a case where there is a generally accepted moral code can the court refuse to enforce rights in such a way as to offend that generally accepted code.

As to the submission that there is no confidentiality in tittle-tattle and gossip, Mr. Wilson relied on a passage in the *Coco* case [1969] RPC 41, 48, where Megarry J said:

'. . . I doubt whether equity would intervene unless the circumstances are of sufficient gravity; equity ought not to be invoked merely to protect trivial tittle-tattle, however confidential.'

Since the *Coco* case was exclusively concerned with information which was of industrial value, those remarks were plainly obiter dicta. Moreover, I have the greatest doubt whether wholesale revelation of the sexual conduct of an individual can properly be described as 'trivial' tittle-tattle. Again, although it is true that the passage I have quoted occurs in that part of the judgment which deals with the nature of information which can be protected, it is to be noted that the judge appeared to be considering when equity would give a remedy, not dealing with the fundamental nature of the legal right. If, as I think he was, Megarry J was saying that the discretion to grant an injunction or to award damages would not be exercised in a case which was merely trivial, I agree. But the exercise of such a discretion can only be decided in the light of all the circumstances. Those cannot be known until there has been a trial.

Next, I consider the submission that because in all cases of sexual conduct both parties are aware of the facts, information relating to those facts cannot in law be confidential. In my judgment this submission is wholly misconceived. It is based on the premise that as between unmarried sexual partners there is no duty of confidentiality. Therefore, both parties are free to discuss the matter with the whole world. I will assume that submission to be correct, but without expressing any view on its correctness in law. Even on that assumption, the fact that the other partner to a sexual relationship *may* disclose what has happened does not mean that he or she had done so. To most people the details of their sexual lives are high on their list of those matters which they regard as confidential. The mere fact that two people know a secret does not mean that it is not confidential. If in fact information is secret, then in my judgment it is capable of being kept secret by the imposition of a duty of confidence on any person to whom it is communic-ated. Information only ceases to be capable of protection as confidential when it is in fact known to a substantial number of people.

That this is the law is shown by . . . the Court of Appeal in *A-G v Guardian Newspapers Ltd (No 2)* [1990] 1 AC 109, [1988] 2 WLR 805 . . . Sir John Donaldson M.R. said, at p. 868:

'As a general proposition, that which has no character of confidentiality because it has already been communicated to the world, i.e., made generally available to the relevant public, cannot thereafter be subjected to a right of confidentiality . . . However, this will not necessarily be the case if the information has previously only been disclosed to a limited part of that public. It is a question of degree.'. . .

In principle, therefore, I can see no reason why information relating to that most private sector of everybody's life, namely sexual conduct, cannot be the subject matter of a legally enforceable duty of confidentiality. Mr. Wilson submits that there is no case in which confidentiality of such information has been enforced. This is true. But it is equally true that no one has previously suggested that just because information related to the sexual conduct of an individual it was in someway different to any other information. In a number of cases where the point could have been argued it was not: see, for example, *Woodward v Hutchins* [below, p. 561]. In *Khashoggi v Smith* [above, p. 553, n. 1], the point was apparently argued. Sir David Cairns said that:

'He was by no means satisfied that the duty of confidentiality was inappropriate to protect matters involving the plaintiff's sexual misconduct.'

Therefore, I can see nothing either in principle or authority to support the view that information relating to sexual conduct cannot be the subject matter of a duty of confidence.

I turn to the second attack made by Mr. Wilson, namely that the circumstances in which the plaintiff is alleged to have communicated the information to Mrs. Avery are not such as to raise a duty of confidence: . . .

Mr. Wilson submits that in the absence of either a legally enforceable contract or a pre-existing relationship—such as that of employer and employee, doctor and patient, or priest and penitent—it is not possible to impose a legal duty of confidence on the recipient of the information merely by saying that the information is given in confidence. In my judgment that is wrong in law. The basis of equitable intervention to protect confidentiality is that it is unconscionable for a person who has received information on the basis that it is confidential subsequently to reveal that information. Although the relationship between the parties is often important in cases where it is said there is an implied as opposed to express obligation of confidence, the relationship between the parties is not the determining factor. It is the acceptance of the information on the basis that it will be kept secret that affects the conscience of the recipient of the information. I quote again from the judgment of Bingham LJ in the *Spycatcher* case, where he said, at p. 904:

'The cases show that the duty of confidence does not depend on any contract, express or implied, between the parties. If it did, it would follow on ordinary principles that strangers to the contract would not be bound. But the duty "depends on the broad principle of equity that he who has received information in confidence shall not take unfair advantage of it:" *Seager v Copydex Ltd* [1967] 1 WLR 923, 931, *per* Lord Denning M.R. "The jurisdiction is based not so much on property or on contract as on the duty to be of good faith": *Fraser v Evans* [1969] 1 QB 349, 361, per Lord Denning M.R.'

If, as is here alleged, the information was communicated and accepted expressly in confidence, the conscience of Mrs. Avery is just as much affected as in any other case. In my judgment the express statement that the information is confidential is the clearest possible example of the imposition of a duty of confidence. . . .

Therefore, on the specific grounds argued, in my judgment it has not been demonstrated that there is no legal basis for the plaintiff's claim. I therefore decline to strike out the statement of claim.

However, in reply, Mr. Wilson tried to expand the ambit of his attack into more general fields of public policy. To my mind this case undoubtedly does raise fundamental difficulties as to the relationship between on the one hand the privacy which every individual is entitled to expect, and on the other hand freedom of information. To many, the aggressive intrusion of sectors of the press into the private lives of individuals is unpalatable. On the other hand, the ability of the press to obtain and publish for the public benefit information of genuine public interest, as opposed to general public titillation, may be impaired if information obtained in confidence is too widely protected by the law. Moreover, is the press to be liable in damages for printing what is true? I express no view as to where or how the borderline should be drawn in such a case. . . .

Appeal dismissed with costs.

NOTES

1. *Stephens v Avery* confirms the decision in *Argyll v Argyll* that information concerning a person's sexual life may be protected by the law of breach of confidence. In this connection, it is interesting that the court limits the scope and effect of Sir Robert Megarry's exclusion of 'tittle-tattle', so that it would not prevent a remedy in breach of confidence for the 'wholesale revelation of the sexual conduct of an individual', as on the facts of the case.

2. Whereas the decision in *Argyll v Argyll* was predicated upon the fact that the information was disclosed during marriage, an institution which the law seeks to protect, *Stephens v Avery* concerns no such institution. Nor does it involve any fiduciary relationship (doctor-patient, bank manager-client, etc.) recognised by the law. As in Lord Keith's speech in *A-G v Guardian Newspapers Ltd (No 2)*, above, p. 477, the court in *Stephens v Avery* supposes instead that it is the policy of the law to uphold the moral quality of an undertaking not to disclose information given in confidence, whatever the existing relationship between the persons concerned. For criticism of this wider approach, which clearly strengthens the law of breach of confidence as a means of controlling the press, see W. Wilson, (1990) 53 MLR 43. Would it have mattered in *Stephens v Avery* if the obligation of confidence had been an implied rather than an express one?

Fraser v Evans [1969] 1 QB 349, [1969] 1 All ER 8, [1968] 3 WLR 1172, Court of Appeal

The plaintiff, a public relations consultant, was employed by the Greek Government to make a report for them. A copy of the report was obtained surreptitiously from the Greek Government and came into the hands of a *Sunday Times* reporter. The plaintiff sought an interim injunction to prevent its publication on grounds of libel, breach of copyright and breach of confidence. The *Sunday Times* admitted that the article was defamatory but said that they proposed to plead justification and fair comment. Crichton J issued an injunction restraining only the publication of extracts or information obtained from the report. The *Sunday Times* appealed against the injunction. The following extract concerns only the breach of confidence claim. The arguments based on libel and breach of copyright were also rejected.

Lord Denning MR: . . . Mr Fraser says that the report was a confidential document and that the publication of it should be restrained on the principles enunciated in the cases from *Prince Albert v Strange* to *Duchess of Argyll v Duke of Argyll*. Those cases show that the court will in a proper case restrain the publication of confidential information. The jurisdiction is based not so much on property or on contract as on the duty to be of good faith. No person is permitted to divulge to the world information which he has received in confidence, unless he has just cause or excuse for doing so. Even if he comes by it innocently, nevertheless once he gets to know that it was originally given in confidence, he can be restrained from breaking that confidence. But the party complaining must be the person who is entitled to the confidence and to have it respected. He must be a person to whom the duty of good faith is owed. It is at this point that I think Mr Fraser's claim breaks down. There is no doubt that Mr Fraser himself was under an obligation of confidence to the Greek Government. The contract says so in terms. But there is nothing in the contract which expressly puts the Greek Government under any obligation of confidence. Nor, so far as I can see, is there any implied obligation. . . . The Greek Government alone have any standing to complain if anyone obtains the information surreptitiously or proposes to publish it. . . .
Davies and **Widgery LJJ** delivered concurring judgments.
Appeal allowed. Injunction discharged.

NOTES

1. Does Lord Denning's 'good faith' basis for the doctrine suggest that the breach of confidence need not be for profit for liability to arise?

2. Suppose that a newspaper buys a story reasonably, but incorrectly, believing that it has been obtained without a breach of confidence on the part of the writer? Can the newspaper be liable for breach of confidence?[1]

3. Would a doctor who revealed to the parents of a 15 year old patient that she was on the pill be in breach of confidence in law? See *Gillick v West Norfolk and Wisbech Area Health Authority* [1986] AC 112, HL. For a complaint that confidential information about foreigners using the NHS is given by the Department of Health and Social Security to the Home Office, see *The Times*, 6 December 1979.

4. Does *Fraser v Evans* support the view that there would be no liability in breach of confidence in the following case discussed by the Law Commission (Working Paper No 58, para. 75):

'. . . suppose that a newspaper commissioned a journalist to write a candid assessment of a man's life on the understanding that it would be kept confidential until after the man's death and that the journalist furnished an article to the newspaper exposing details of the man's life which were true but likely to cause him distress, or even pecuniary loss; if the article was in fact published by the newspaper before the man's death in breach of their duty of confidence to the journalist, should the man also have a right of action against the newspaper based on their breach of confidence? It is arguable that in this situation the wrong to the man is far greater than that to the journalist and that he should be entitled to recover damages accordingly. . . . The truth seems to us to be that the man has a complaint not because his confidence has been abused but because his privacy has been infringed and that to admit an action by him for breach of confidence would amount to using the law of confidence merely as a peg on which to hang a right of privacy in his favour.'

Lion Laboratories Ltd v Evans [1985] QB 526, [1984] 2 All ER 417, [1984] 3 WLR 539, Court of Appeal

The plaintiff company manufactured the Lion Intoximeter 3000, which was in use by the police with Home Office approval for measuring the level of alcohol in the blood. A number of convictions had been obtained for drinking and driving offences based upon Intoximeter evidence. Two former employees of the plaintiffs gave to the *Daily Express* copies of company documents which they had by virtue of their employment. These revealed that there were doubts, known to the plaintiffs and the Home Office, as to the accuracy of the Intoximeter. On 8 March 1984, the plaintiffs issued a writ against the two employees and *Daily Express* representatives claiming an injunction and damages in respect of breach of confidence and/or breach of copyright. On the same day, they were granted an injunction ex parte in the terms of the writ. The following day the *Daily Express* published an article headed 'Exposed: the Great "Breath Test" Scandal' based on the documents. Adjoining the article were blank spaces attributed to the injunction. In these interlocutory proceedings, the defendants appealed against the ex parte injunction.

Stephenson LJ: The problem . . . is how best to resolve before trial a conflict of two competing public interests. The first public interest is the preservation of the right of organisations, as of individuals, to keep secret confidential information. The courts will restrain breaches of confidence, and breaches of copyright, unless there is just cause or excuse for breaking confidence or infringing copyright. The just cause or excuse with which the case is concerned is the public interest in admittedly confidential information. There is confidential information which the public may have a right to receive and others, in particular the press, now extended to the media, may have a right and even a duty to publish, even if the information has been unlawfully obtained in flagrant breach of confidence and irrespective of the motive of the informer. The duty of confidence, the public interest in maintaining it, is a restriction on the freedom of

1 On the position of innocent third parties, see Jones (1970) 86 LQR 463, 477–81; Meagher, Gummow and Lehane, *Equity Doctrines and Remedies* (3rd edn, 1992), pp. 880–881; Law Commission Report No 110, p. 25. Was the defendant in *Prince Albert v Strange*, above, or the editor of *The People* in the *Argyll* case, above, an innocent third party?

the press which is recognised by our law, as well as by art 10(2) of the European Convention [on Human Rights] . . . the duty to publish, the countervailing interest of the public in being kept informed of matters which are of real public concern, is an inroad on the privacy of confidential matters. . . .

There are four further considerations. First, 'There is a wide difference between what is interesting to the public and what it is in the public interest to make known': per Lord Wilberforce in *British Steel Corpn v Granada Television Ltd* [1981] 1 All ER 417 at 455, [1981] AC 1096 at 1168. The public are interested in many private matters which are no real concern of theirs and which the public have no pressing need to know. Second, the media have a private interest of their own in publishing what appeals to the public and may increase their circulation or the numbers of their viewers or listeners; and (I quote from the judgment of Sir John Donaldson MR in *Francome v Mirror Group Newspapers Ltd* [1984] 2 All ER 408 at 413) '. . . they are peculiarly vulnerable to the error of confusing the public interest with their own interest'. Third, there are cases in which the public interest is best served by an informer giving the confidential information not to the press but to the police or some other responsible body, as was suggested by Lord Denning MR in the *Initial Services* case and by Sir John Donaldson MR in the *Francome* case. Fourth, it was said by Page Wood V-C in *Gartside v Outram* (1856) 26 LJ Ch 113 at 114, 'there is no confidence as to the disclosure of iniquity'; and though counsel concedes on the plaintiffs' behalf that, as Salmon LJ said in *Initial Services v Putterill* [1967] 3 All ER 145 at 151, [1968] 1 QB 396 at 410, 'what was iniquity in 1856 may be too narrow, or too wide, in 1967', and in 1984 extends to serious misdeeds or grave misconduct, he submits that misconduct of that kind is necessary to destroy the duty of confidence or excuse the breach of it, and nothing of that sort is alleged against the plaintiffs in the evidence now before the court.

Counsel for the third and fourth defendants and counsel for the first and second defendants have not been able to find any case where a defendant has been able to rely on public interest in defence of a claim for breach of confidence and the plaintiff has not also been guilty of such misconduct. And there are passages in the speeches of Lord Wilberforce and Lord Fraser in *British Steel Corpn v Granada Television Ltd* in which they appear to be satisfied with describing the 'public interest rule' as the 'iniquity rule'. But I nowhere find any authority for the proposition, except perhaps in the judgment of Ungoed-Thomas J in *Beloff v Pressdram Ltd* [1973] 1 All ER 241 at 260, that some modern form of iniquity on the part of the plaintiffs is the only thing which can be disclosed in the public interest; and I agree with the judge in rejecting the 'no iniquity, no public interest' rule and in respectfully adopting what Lord Denning MR said in *Fraser v Evans* [1969] 1 All ER 8 at 11, [1969] 1 QB 349 at 362 that some things are required to be disclosed in the public interest, in which case no confidence can be prayed in aid to keep them secret, and '[iniquity] is merely an instance of a just cause and excuse for breaking confidence'.

To be allowed to publish confidential information, the defendants must do more than raise a plea of public interest: they must show 'a legitimate ground for supposing it is in the public interest for it to be disclosed'. Then, as Lord Denning MR said in *Woodward v Hutchins* [1977] 2 All ER 751 at 755, [1977] 1 WLR 760 at 764, 'the courts should not restrain it by interlocutory injunction, but should leave the complainant to his remedy in damages', after (I will assume, though I am not sure that Lord Denning MR would have agreed) considering and weighing in the balance all relevant matters, such as whether damages would be an adequate remedy to compensate the plaintiffs if they succeeded at the trial.

We cannot of course at this stage decide whether the balance will come down on the side of confidentiality or of public interest. But, to see if there is a serious defence of public interest which may succeed at the trial, we have to look at the evidence and, if we decide that there is such a defence, to perform a balancing exercise, as indicated for instance in the judgment of Lord Denning MR in *Woodward v Hutchins* and in the speech of Lord Fraser in *British Steel Corpn v Granada Television Ltd* [1981] 1 All ER 417 at 480, [1981] AC 1096 at 1202.

. . . The issue raised by the defendants is a serious question concerning a matter which affects the life, and even the liberty, of an unascertainable number of Her Majesty's subjects, and though there is no proof that any of them has been wrongly convicted on the evidence of the plaintiffs' Intoximeter, and we certainly cannot decide that any has, we must not restrain the defendants from putting before the public this further information how the Lion Intoximeter 3000 has worked, and how the plaintiffs regard and discharge their responsibility for it, although the information is confidential and was unlawfully taken in breach of confidence.

O'Connor and **Griffiths LJJ** delivered concurring judgments.
Appeal allowed. Injunction discharged.

NOTES

1. The ruling that the 'public interest' defence is not limited to cases within the 'iniquity' rule is in line with several judgments by Lord Denning (including that in

Fraser v Evans) and with the recommendation of the Law Commission (Report No 110, p. 138). There are, however, obiter dicta, by a majority of the House of Lords in *British Steel Corpn v Granada Television Ltd* [1981] AC 1096 to the contrary. For example, Lord Wilberforce stated (p. 1169):

There is an important exception to the limitations which may exist upon the right of the media to reveal information otherwise restricted. That is based on what is commonly known as the 'iniquity rule'. It extends in fact beyond 'iniquity' to misconduct generally: see *Initial Services Ltd v Putterill* [1968] 1 QB 396. It is recognised that, in cases where misconduct exists, publication may legitimately be made even if disclosure involves a breach of confidence such as would normally justify a prohibition against disclosure. It must be emphasised that we are not in this field in the present case [which concerned revelations by a 'mole' of mismanagement and government intervention in the affairs of BSC]; giving the widest extension to the expression 'iniquity' nothing within it is alleged in the present case.

2. The *Lion* case is the first in which a public interest defence was upheld in a breach of confidence case when there was no evidence of 'iniquity' on the facts. In *Hubbard v Vosper* [1972] 2 QB 84, CA, the first defendant had written a book in which he revealed damaging facts about scientology based upon his former membership. The disclosures were held to be justified in the public interest as arguably revealing 'medical quackery of a dangerous kind'. In *Woodward v Hutchins* [1977] 1 WLR 760, CA, the plaintiff 'pop' singers (Tom Jones, Englebert Humperdinck and Gilbert O'Sullivan) were refused an injunction to prevent the publication by their former public relations officer of embarrassing details of their personal lives in the *Daily Mirror* on grounds of public interest and public domain. Lord Denning MR stated (pp. 763–4):

There is no doubt whatever that this pop group sought publicity. They wanted to have themselves presented to the public in a favourable light so that audiences would come to hear them and support them. Mr Hutchins was engaged so as to produce, or help to produce, this favourable image, not only of their public lives but of their private lives also. If a group of this kind seek publicity which is to their advantage, it seems to me that they cannot complain if a servant or employee of theirs afterwards discloses the truth about them. If the image which they fostered was not a true image, it is in the public interest that it should be corrected. In these cases of confidential information it is a question of balancing the public interest in maintaining the confidence against the public interest in knowing the truth. . . .
There is a further point. The injunction . . . speaks of 'confidential information'. But what is confidential? As Bridge LJ pointed out in the course of the argument, Mr Hutchins, as a press agent, might attend a dance which many others attended. Any incident which took place at the dance would be known to all present. The information would be in the public domain. There could be no objection to the incidents being made known generally. It would not be confidential information. So in this case the incident on this jumbo jet was in the public domain. It was known to all the passengers on the flight. Likewise with several other incidents in the series.

On the public interest defence, see Y. Cripps, (1984) 4 OJLS 184.
3. In *X v Y* [1988] 2 All ER 648, QBD, the plaintiffs, a health authority, sought an injunction preventing the defendants, a reporter and newspaper publisher, from, inter alia, publishing the identity of two doctors who had AIDS who were continuing with their general practice or, as the defendants claimed in argument was now their sole intention, from revealing that two *unnamed* doctors with AIDS were continuing to practise. The information had been obtained from confidential hospital AIDS patients' records which had been leaked to the reporter by health authority employees. Granting the injunction, Rose J rejected a 'public interest' defence:

I keep in the forefront of my mind the very important public interest in freedom of the press. And I accept that there is some public interest in knowing that which the defendants seek to publish (in whichever version). But in my judgment those public interests are substantially outweighed when measured against the public interests in relation to loyalty and confidentiality both generally and with particular reference to AIDS patients' hospital records. There has been no misconduct by the plaintiffs. The records of hospital patients, particularly those suffering from this appalling condition should, in my judgment, be as confidential as the courts can properly keep them in order that the plaintiffs may 'be free from suspicion that they are harbouring disloyal employees'. The plaintiffs have 'suffered a grievous wrong in which the defendants became involved . . . with active participation'. The deprivation of the public of the information sought to be published will be of minimal significance if the injunction is granted; for, without it, all the evidence before me shows that a wide-ranging public debate about AIDS generally and about its effect on doctors is taking place among doctors of widely differing views, within and without the BMA, in medical journals and in many newspapers. . . .

4. In *Francome v Mirror Group Newspapers Ltd* [1984] 2 All ER 408, CA, the *Daily Mirror* was offered by unnamed persons tapes of telephone conversations conducted on the home telephone of the champion National Hunt jockey. The tapes, which allegedly revealed breaches of the rules of racing, were obtained by means of a 'bug'.

Pending the hearing of their claim against the Mirror Group for exemplary damages for breach of confidence and for trespass, the plaintiffs, who were the champion jockey and his wife, sought an interlocutory injunction restraining the publication by the defendants of articles based upon the tapes. In granting the injunction, Sir John Donaldson MR stated (pp. 411–414):

The defendants . . . say that the plaintiffs have no right of action against them. So far as trespass is concerned, they were not parties to it. This may well be right. They go on to say that there is no cause of action against them or the eavesdroppers for breach of an obligation of confidentiality. The authority for this rather surprising proposition is said to be *Malone v Metropolitan Police Comr (No 2)* [see above, p. 554]. Suffice it to say that Sir Robert Megarry V-C expressly stated that he was deciding nothing on the position when tapping was effected for purposes other than the prevention, detection and discovery of crime and criminals or by persons other than the police. . . . This is thus a live issue.

The defendants then go on to submit that, whatever their obligations towards the plaintiffs on grounds of confidentiality, they can rely on the classic, but ill-defined, exception of what is quaintly called 'iniquity'. The basis of this exception is that, whilst there is a public interest in maintaining confidentiality, there is a countervailing public interest in exposing conduct which involves a breach of the law or which is 'anti-social'. I use the term 'anti-social', without defining it, to describe activities which, whilst not in breach of the law, are seriously contrary to the public interest. In the defendants' submission the tapes revealed breaches by Mr Francome of the rules of racing and, bearing in mind the large sums of money which are staked on the results of the races, this conduct they say is 'anti-social' within the meaning of the iniquity rule and may also involve criminal offences. Let me say at once it is not for me to say whether the tapes bear this interpretation and I express no view on that point. That will also be an issue. . . .

5. On damages for breach of confidence (which will be the only satisfactory remedy where publication has already occurred), Sir Robert Megarry V-C stated in *Malone v Metropolitan Police Comr* (p. 360):

This is an equitable right which is still in course of development, and is usually protected by the grant of an injunction to prevent disclosure of the confidence. Under Lord Cairns' Act 1858 damages may be granted in substitution for an injunction; yet if there is no case for the grant of an injunction, as when the disclosure has already been made, the unsatisfactory result seems to be that no damages can be awarded under this head: see *Proctor v Bayley* (1889) 42 Ch D 390. In such a case, where there is no breach of contract or other orthodox foundation for damages at common law, it seems doubtful whether there is any right to damages, as distinct from an account of profits. It may be, however, that a new tort is emerging (see *Goff and Jones, The Law of Restitution* (2nd edn, 1978), pp. 518, 519, and Gareth Jones (1970) 86 LQR 463 at 491), though this has been doubted: see *Street, The Law of Torts* (6th edn, 1976), p. 377.

Damages were awarded in *Seager v Copydex* (a trade secrets case) [1967] 2 All ER 415, CA. They were to be 'assessed on the basis of reasonable compensation for the use of confidential information' (Lord Denning MR). In *Seager v Copydex (No 2)*

[1969] 2 All ER 718, CA, Winn LJ stated that the damages were to be recovered 'on a tortious basis' and Lord Denning MR drew an analogy with conversion. Relying upon this case, North (1972) 12 JoSPTL 149 argues that breach of confidence, which developed as an equitable principle, is now a tort. Presumably, if damages may be awarded for commercial loss (as in *Seager v Copydex*) they may be awarded for material loss in a privacy context (e.g. for dismissal when confidential information is passed on to an employer): see Law Commission Report No 110, p. 67. There is, however, despite the analogies that exist (see *Williams v Settle*, above, p. 549, and s. 57(4), Race Relations Act 1976, below, p. 675), 'no authority to support an award of damages for mental stress': ibid, p. 68. The Law Commission recommends that mental suffering be a head of damages for breach of confidence, ibid, p. 152.

6. With regard to interlocutory injunctions (i.e. those granted pending the hearing of a case on the merits), the Calcutt Committee commented critically on their effect on third parties (Report, p. 34):

These injunctions are to all intents and purposes binding on a third party as soon as that party is notified of its terms. In *A-G v Newspaper Publishing plc* [1988] Ch 333 (the Spycatcher case) the Court of Appeal held that newspapers, which were not party to an injunction, could be guilty of contempt at common law if they published the information covered by the injunction, provided the relevant *mens rea* (criminal state of mind) was present. The purpose of the original injunction was to protect the position pending trial because the claim of confidentiality could only be tested at that stage. However, if someone else published the information in the meantime, the proceedings would become pointless and the Court's purpose in granting the temporary injunction would be defeated.

... We are persuaded that, in general terms, it is unjust for a newspaper to be restricted by the terms of an injunction without having an opportunity to argue against it. While the reasoning of the Court of Appeal in the Spycatcher case has been widely misunderstood, we nevertheless consider that the practical consequences for third parties, whose freedom of speech is undoubtedly restricted, should be urgently addressed, possibly by the Supreme Court Procedure Committee.

(g) OTHER REMEDIES IN LAW

It has been suggested (see Dworkin, (1967) 2 U Tas LR 418, 444 and Neill (1962) 25 MLR 393, 402) that the tort of *intentional infliction of physical harm* (other than by trespass) established in *Wilkinson v Downton* [1897] 2 QB 57, QBD, could be developed to provide a remedy.[1] In that case, as a practical joke the defendant told the plaintiff that the plaintiff's husband had broken his legs in an accident. The plaintiff suffered nervous shock causing 'serious and permanent physical consequences'. Wright J awarded her damages on the following basis:

The defendant has wilfully done an act calculated to cause physical harm to the plaintiff—that is to say, to infringe her legal right to personal safety, and has in fact thereby caused physical harm to her. That proposition without more appears to me to state a good cause of action, there being no justification alleged for the act. This wilful injuria is in law malicious, although no malicious purpose to cause the harm which was caused nor any motive of spite is imputed to the defendant.'

The decision was approved and relied on by the Court of Appeal in *Janvier v Sweeney* [1919] 2 KB 316, CA. In that case, the defendants, private detectives, sought to persuade the plaintiff to hand over letters to which she had access by telling her falsely that she was wanted by Scotland Yard for corresponding with a German spy. The plaintiff recovered damages for physical illness resulting from shock. Cf. the Press Council case (11th Report 1964, p. 36) in which the press

---

1 On the use of *Wilkinson v Downton* in *Khorasandjian v Bush* (telephone harassment), see above, p. 533.

contacted a young girl and correctly informed her in the absence of her mother that her estranged father whom she had not seen since she was a baby had been granted a right of access to her by a court order. The girl 'suffered a serious emotional upset which required medical attention'.

Might there be liability in tort for *negligent misstatement* if a reporter failed to check his facts and published an inaccurate statement about someone's personal life (e.g. that he takes heroin or has a mistress) that causes him to lose his job? Is there a duty of care? In a Press Council case (14th Report 1967, p. 53), the *Sunday Times* mistakenly reported that a person had committed suicide when the coroner's verdict was otherwise. What if his widow suffered physical injury resulting from shock?

Breach of contract may provide a remedy in some cases. See, e.g., *Pollard v Photographic Co*, above, p. 552. On express or implied terms in contracts of employment, see above, p. 551.

In *criminal law*, eavesdroppers and 'peeping toms' may be bound over to be of good behaviour.[1] A compulsive 'nosey parker' who had been seen peeping through many a window and who had been trapped with her hand in someone's letter box was bound over to keep the peace. She had earlier had buckets of water and snowballs thrown at her by neighbours. *The Guardian* 6 November 1979. Eavesdropping is not a criminal offence: Criminal Law Act 1967, s. 13(1)(a). The Official Secrets Acts 1911–89, above, pp. 444–470, protect confidential information about private individuals in official hands.[2] In *DPP v Withers* [1975] AC 842, HL, the defendants were private detectives. They were convicted on two counts of conspiracy to effect a public mischief by (on the first count) obtaining confidential information from banks and building societies about private accounts by making telephone calls pretending to be officials from other banks, etc., and (on the second count) by obtaining confidential information from the Criminal Records Office, vehicle registration authorities and the Ministry of Defence. The information in relation to the second count was obtained either by deceit or by persuading a public official to act contrary to his duty. The convictions were quashed by the House of Lords on the ground that conspiracy to effect a public mischief was not a crime.[3] A majority of the House of Lords in *DPP v Withers* thought the defendants might have been guilty on the second count of a conspiracy to defraud. Two members—Lord Reid and Viscount Dilhorne—would appear to have taken the same view in respect of the first count. Lord Kilbrandon, however, was of the opinion that there could be no conspiracy to defraud bank and building society officials, because they are not public officers. The Criminal Law Act 1977 retains conspiracy to defraud as an offence, but does not resolve the question whether private detectives (and others) may commit it only if they deceive public officials or defy public officials for this purpose. One situation which criminal law does not cover is that in which a person 'steals' information (by, for example, photographing a document). In *Oxford v Moss* (1978) 68 Cr App Rep 183, DC, a university student dishonestly obtained a copy of the proof of an examination paper and read and returned it. It was held that he could not be guilty of theft because information was not 'property' that could be stolen. See A. M. Tettenborn, (1979) 129 NLJ 967. On the Younger Committee's recommendation for a new tort of disclosure or other use of information unlawfully acquired, see above, p. 555.

---

1 See *R v Wyres* (1956) 2 *Russell on Crime* (12th edn, (1964)) 1397 (spying on woman undressing).
2 For other statutory provisions, see the Younger Committee Report, Appendix I.
3 The decision is confirmed by the provisions on conspiracy (ss. 1, 5) in the Criminal Law Act 1977.

4 Invasion of privacy by the media

In addition to such remedies at law as may exist, the following regulatory bodies have powers to receive and pronounce upon (in a legally non-binding way) invasions of privacy by the press and in broadcasting.

(a) PRESS COMPLAINTS COMMISSION

Code of Practice

The Press Complaints Commission is charged with enforcing the following Code of Practice which was framed by the newspaper and periodical industry and ratified by the Press Complaints Commission in April 1994, as amended in February 1995.

All members of the Press have a duty to maintain the highest professional and ethical standards. In doing so, they should have regard to the provisions of this Code of Practice and to safeguarding the public's right to know.

Editors are responsible for the actions of journalists employed by their publications. They should also satisfy themselves as far as possible that material accepted from non-staff members was obtained in accordance with this Code.

While recognising that this involves a substantial element of self-restraint by editors and journalists, it is designed to be acceptable in the context of a system of self-regulation. The Code applies in the spirit as well as in the letter.

It is the responsibility of editors to co-operate as swiftly as possible in PCC enquiries.

Any publication which is criticised by the PCC under one of the following clauses is duty bound to print the adjudication which follows in full and with due prominence.

1. *Accuracy*
    (i) Newspapers and periodicals should take care not to publish inaccurate, misleading or distorted material.
    (ii) Whenever it is recognised that a significant inaccuracy, misleading statement or distorted report has been published, it should be corrected promptly and with due prominence.
    (iii) An apology should be published whenever appropriate.
    (iv) A newspaper or periodical should always report fairly and accurately the outcome of an action for defamation to which it has been a party.

2. *Opportunity to reply*

A fair opportunity for reply to inaccuracies should be given to individuals or organisations when reasonably called for.

3. *Comment, conjecture and fact*

Newspapers, while free to be partisan, should distinguish clearly between comment, conjecture and fact.

4. *Privacy*

Intrusions and enquiries into an individual's private life without his or her consent, including the use of long-lens photography to take pictures of people on private property without their consent, are not generally acceptable and publication can only be justified when in the public interest.
NOTE—Private property is defined as (i) any private residence, together with its garden and outbuildings, but excluding any adjacent fields or parkland and the surrounding parts of the property within the unaided view of passers-by, (ii) hotel bedrooms (but not other areas in a hotel) and (iii) those parts of a hospital or nursing home where patients are treated or accommodated.

5. *Listening devices*

Unless justified by public interest, journalists should not obtain or publish material obtained by using clandestine listening devices or by intercepting private telephone conversations.

6. *Hospitals*

  (i) Journalists or photographers making enquiries at hospitals or similar institutions should identify themselves to a responsible executive and obtain permission before entering non-public areas.

 (ii) The restrictions on intruding into privacy are particularly relevant to enquiries about individuals in hospitals or similar institutions.

7. *Misrepresentation*

  (i) Journalists should not generally obtain or seek to obtain information or pictures through misrepresentation or subterfuge.

 (ii) Unless in the public interest, documents or photographs should be removed only with the express consent of the owner.

(iii) Subterfuge can be justified only in the public interest and only when material cannot be obtained by any other means.

8. *Harassment*

  (i) Journalists should neither obtain nor seek to obtain information or pictures through intimidation or harassment.

 (ii) Unless their enquiries are in the public interest, journalists should not photograph individuals on private property (as defined in the note to Clause 4) without their consent; should not persist in telephoning or questioning individuals after having been asked to desist; should not remain on their property after having been asked to leave and should not follow them.

(iii) It is the responsibility of editors to ensure that these requirements are carried out.

9. *Payment for articles*

Payment or offers of payment for stories, pictures or information should not be made directly or through agents to witnesses or potential witnesses in current criminal proceedings or to people engaged in crime or to their associates—which includes family, friends, neighbours and colleagues—except where the material concerned ought to be published in the public interest and the payment is necessary for this to be done.

10. *Intrusion into grief or shock*

In cases involving personal grief or shock, enquiries should be carried out and approaches made with sympathy and discretion.

11. **Innocent relatives and friends**

Unless it is contrary to the public's right to know, the press should generally avoid identifying relatives or friends of persons convicted or accused of crime.

12. *Interviewing or photographing children*

  (i) Journalists should not normally interview or photograph children under the age of 16 on subjects involving the personal welfare of the child in the absence of or without the consent of a parent or other adult who is responsible for the children.

 (ii) Children should not be approached or photographed while at school without the permission of the school authorities.

13. *Children in sex cases*

1 The press should not, even where the law does not prohibit it, identify children under the age of 16 who are involved in cases concerning sexual offences, whether as victims or as witnesses or defendants.

2 In any press report of a case involving a sexual offence against a child—

     (i) The adult should be identified.

    (ii) The term 'incest' where applicable should not be used.

   (iii) The offence should be described as 'serious offences against young children' or similar appropriate wording.

   (iv) The child should not be identified.

    (v) Care should be taken that nothing in the report implies the relationship between the accused and the child.

14. *Victims of crime*

The Press should not identify victims of sexual assault or publish material likely to contribute to such identification unless, by law, they are free to do so.

15. *Discrimination*

 (i) The press should avoid prejudicial or pejorative reference to a person's race, colour, religion, sex or sexual orientation or to any physical or mental illness or handicap.
 (ii) It should avoid publishing details of a person's race, colour, religion, sex or sexual orientation unless these are directly relevant to the story.

16. *Financial journalism*

 (i) Even where the law does not prohibit it, journalists should not use for their own profit financial information they receive in advance of its general publication, nor should they pass such information to others.
 (ii) They should not write about shares or securities in whose performance they know that they or their close families have a significant financial interest without disclosing the interest to the editor or financial editor.
 (iii) They should not buy or sell, either directly or though nominees or agents, shares or securities about which they have written recently or about which they intend to write in the near future.

17. *Confidential sources*

Journalists have a moral obligation to protect confidential sources of information.

18. *The public interest*

Clauses 4, 5, 7, 8 and 9 create exceptions which may be covered by invoking the public interest. For the purpose of this code that is most easily defined as:

 (i) Detecting or exposing crime or a serious misdemeanour.
 (ii) Protecting public health and safety.
 (iii) Preventing the public from being misled by some statement or action of an individual or organisation.

In any cases raising issues beyond these three definitions the Press Complaints Commission will require a full explanation by the editor of the publication involved, seeking to demonstrate how the public interest was served.

NOTES

1. Established in 1991 following the Calcutt Committee Report, the Press Complaints Commission replaced the Press Council, which had existed since 1953. The Council had an independent chairman and an otherwise equal number of press and lay members. It was the subject of much criticism because of its limited powers and impact in curbing press intrusion into individual privacy.
2. Like its predecessor, the Press Complaints Commission is a non-statutory body established by the newspapers and periodicals industry with the object, inter alia, of hearing complaints about the conduct of the press. It has an independent chairman (Lord Wakeham) and eight non-press members and seven editors. The membership reflects an intention 'to involve every section of the newspaper industry as well as people in public life who are in a position to make impartial judgments on what might constitute unacceptable journalistic practices': *The Times*, 28 December 1990, p. 3. Any person may complain to the Commission of an invasion of privacy, whether personally affected or not. The Commission does not conduct oral hearings. It has no formal conciliation procedure, although it does informally advise the parties as to a solution where appropriate. The Commission has not adopted the

'hotline' procedure recommended by the Calcutt Committee, whereby complainants would have access to editors via the Commission prior to the publication of material in the press. The Commission decided that this would involve unacceptable censorship. Nor has the Commission formally adopted the 'fast track' procedure for the correction of significant factual errors recommended by the Calcutt Committee. It does not, however, require a complainant to waive any legal right of action, as the Press Council was criticised for doing. Instead, the Commission may call upon a complainant to wait until his case has been heard before resorting to law. The Commission has the same limited sanctions as the Press Council. It may censure a newspaper or journalist, but it has no power to fine or award compensation. Newspapers are expected to publish an adverse adjudication, although they are under no legal obligation to do so. In fact, newspapers normally cooperate; there were only 11 cases of newspapers failing to publish adjudications in the long history of the Press Council.

3. The Code of Practice was prepared by a committee of editors acting for the newspapers and periodicals industry. As far as the protection of privacy is concerned, it replaces the more detailed Press Council Declaration of Principle on Privacy (23rd Press Council Report 1976, p. 150). The Code is revised periodically. The present version of the Code was adopted in 1994.

4. The number of complaints of invasion of privacy dealt with by the Press Council was not high. The same is true of the Press Complaints Commission. In its first year of operation, only 80 of the 1,000 or so complaints found to present a prima facie case concerned privacy. Even so, as the Younger Committee Report, p. 44, stated in respect of the Press Council, although the percentage of complaints which the Council received that were on privacy are 'a tiny proportion of the whole', they are sufficient in number and diversity to indicate the hazards that press coverage present for the protection of privacy—as the examples in the chapter taken from the Council's and the Commission's practice show.

5. In his Foreword to the Press Council's 22nd Report 1975, Lord Shawcross (Chairman) was critical of gossip columns and referred approvingly to Sir Harold Wilson's suggestion 'that the test of what is permissible might be that the Press would accord to public men and women the degree of privacy they would give to their own proprietors or to their own or other editors'. Cf. the following comment by Street, *Freedom, the Individual and the Law* (5th edn, 1982) p. 262:

'What is more sinister is that the privacy of certain persons only is invaded: we are told nothing of the private lives of newspaper proprietors . . . But let Mrs Gilliatt expose the methods of the leading gossip columnists in an article in *Queen*, and she will be hounded by squads of reporters from the *Daily Telegraph* and other dailies who will report her minute-by-minute movements in the company of playwright John Osborne.'

In his Foreword in the following year, Lord Shawcross quoted the Royal Commission on the Press's opinion 'that the way in which a few national newspapers treat some private lives is one of the worst aspects of the performance of the press': *Final Report of the Commission*, 1977, p. 100. Later, the Chairman (P. Neill QC) singled out harassment by the media as a problem (27th/28th Press Council Reports, 1980/81, Foreword):

The cases which cause the most anxiety are those where the target of persistent inquiries is a person in a vulnerable position who has no organisation to protect him or her. Repeated badgering is particularly abhorrent where the victim is innocent of fault and has become an object of notoriety through some chance circumstance. But there may be cause for concern also in cases where the victim holds a public position.

6. In his *Review of Press Self-Regulation*, 1993, p. 24, Sir David Calcutt emphasised that the Commission was significantly different from the new body that had been proposed in the Calcutt Committee Report: it was appointed by a body that represented the press industry; the Code it operated had been adopted by the industry and had, inter alia, too wide a public interest defence; the Commission was not operating a hot-line; it was unwilling to initiate inquiries; generally, it was over-emphasising press freedom to the detriment of fairness to the individual.

(b) BROADCASTING COMPLAINTS COMMISSION

The Broadcasting Complaints Commission, which consists of at least three members, at present five, is a body independent of the broadcasting industry, provided for by the Broadcasting Act 1990: see further on the Commission, above, p. 345. It is competent to 'consider and adjudicate upon complaints' inter alia 'of . . . unwarranted infringement of privacy in, or in connection with the obtaining of materials included in', BBC or independent licensed television or sound broadcasts (s. 143(1), 1990 Act). The Commission receives only a small number of invasion of privacy complaints annually (ten adjudicated on in 1993). If it finds that there has been an unwarranted invasion of privacy, the Commission may give directions requiring the broadcasting body or licence holder to publish in, for example, the *Radio Times*, or broadcast a summary of the complaint and the Commission's findings (s. 156, 1990 Act). Although the number of invasion of privacy cases is small, some are upheld annually. See, for example, the *'Big Breakfast'* case, above, p. 537. For full details, see *Adjudications of the Broadcasting Complaints Commission 1994*, a Commission publication.

In *R v Broadcasting Complaints Commission, ex p. Granada Television Ltd* (1993), Times, 31 May, QBD, it was held that the Commission had not acted unreasonably under the *Wednesbury* principle in taking the view that there was an unwarranted infringement of privacy even though the material that was broadcast was in the public domain. In that case, parents of deceased children had complained to the Commission of a television programme called 'The Allergy Business' that had shown clips of their children without forewarning them, causing them great distress. Dismissing an application for judicial review of a decision made under s. 143, 1990 Act, Popplewell J held that it was not unreasonable for the Commission to decide that the recall in the film of what was in the public domain could intrude upon the parents' privacy.

5 Surveillance by technical devices

Interception of Communications Act 1985

1.—(1) Subject to the following provisions of this section, a person who intentionally intercepts a communication in the course of its transmission by post or by means of a public telecommunication system shall be guilty of an offence and liable—

    (*a*) on summary conviction, to a fine not exceeding the statutory maximum;

    (*b*) on conviction on indictment, to imprisonment for a term not exceeding two years or to a fine or to both.

(2) A person shall not be guilty of an offence under this section if—

    (*a*) the communication is intercepted in obedience to a warrant issued by the Secretary of State under section 2 below; or

    (*b*) that person has reasonable grounds for believing that the person to whom, or the person by whom, the communication is sent has consented to the interception.

(3) A person shall not be guilty of an offence under this section if—

(a) the communication is intercepted for purposes connected with the provision of postal or public telecommunication services or with the enforcement of any enactment relating to the user of those services; or

(b) the communication is being transmitted by wireless telegraphy and is intercepted, with the authority of the Secretary of State, for purposes connected with the issue of licences under the Wireless Telegraphy Act 1949 or the prevention or detection of interference with wireless telegraphy.

(4) No proceedings in respect of an offence under this section shall be instituted—

(a) in England and Wales, except by or with the consent of the Director of Public Prosecutions;

(b) In Northern Ireland, except by or with the consent of the Director of Public Prosecutions for Northern Ireland.

2.—(1) Subject to the provisions of this section and section 3 below, the Secretary of State may issue a warrant requiring the person to whom it is addressed to intercept, in the course of their transmission by post or by means of a public telecommunication system, such communications as are described in the warrant; and such a warrant may also require the person to whom it is addressed to disclose the intercepted material to such persons and in such manner as are described in the warrant.

(2) The Secretary of State shall not issue a warrant under this section unless he considers that the warrant is necessary—

(a) in the interests of national security;

(b) for the purpose of preventing or detecting serious crime; or

(c) for the purpose of safeguarding the economic well-being of the United Kingdom.

(3) The matters to be taken into account in considering whether a warrant is necessary as mentioned in subsection (2) above shall include whether the information which it is considered necessary to acquire could reasonably be acquired by other means.

(4) A warrant shall not be considered necessary as mentioned in subsection (2)(c) above unless the information which it is considered necessary to acquire is information relating to the acts or intentions of persons outside the British Islands. . . .

3.—(1) Subject to subsection (2) below, the interception required by a warrant shall be the interception of—

(a) such communications as are sent to or from one or more addresses specified in the warrant, being an address or addresses likely to be used for the transmission of communications to or from—

(i) one particular person specified or described in the warrant; or

(ii) one particular set of premises so specified or described; and

(b) such other communications (if any) as it is necessary to intercept in order to intercept communications falling within paragraph (a) above.

(2) Subsection (1) above shall not apply to a warrant if—

(a) the interception required by the warrant is the interception, in the course of their transmission by means of a public telecommunication system, of—

(i) such external communications as are described in the warrant; and

(ii) such other communications (if any) as it is necessary to intercept in order to intercept such external communications as are so described; and

(b) at the time when the warrant is issued, the Secretary of State issues a certificate certifying the descriptions of intercepted material the examination of which he considers necessary as mentioned in section 2(2) above.

(3) A certificate such as is mentioned in subsection (2) above shall not specify an address in the British Islands for the purpose of including communications sent to or from that address in the certified material unless—

(a) the Secretary of State considers that the examination of communications sent to or from that address is necessary for the purpose of preventing or detecting acts of terrorism; and

(b) communications sent to or from that address are included in the certified material only in so far as they are sent within such a period, not exceeding three months, as is specified in the certificate.

(4) A certificate such as is mentioned in subsection (2) above shall not be issued except under the hand of the Secretary of State.

(5) References in the following provisions of this Act to a certificate are references to a certificate such as is mentioned in subsection (2) above.

4.—(1) A warrant shall not be issued except—

(a) under the hand of the Secretary of State; or

(b) in an urgent case where the Secretary of State has expressly authorised its issue and a statement of that fact is endorsed thereon, under the hand of an official of his department of or above the rank of Assistant Under Secretary of State.

(2) A warrant shall, unless renewed under subsection (3) below, cease to have effect at the end of the relevant period.

(3) The Secretary of State may, at any time before the end of the relevant period, renew a warrant if he considers that the warrant continues to be necessary as mentioned in section 2(2) above.

(4) If, at any time before the end of the relevant period, the Secretary of State considers that a warrant is no longer necessary as mentioned in section 2(2) above, he shall cancel the warrant.

(5) A warrant shall not be renewed except by an instrument under the hand of the Secretary of State.

(6) In this section 'the relevant period'—

    (a) in relation to a warrant which has not been renewed, means—

        (i) if the warrant was issued under subsection (1)(a) above, the period of two months beginning with the day on which it was issued; and

        (ii) if the warrant was issued under subsection (1)(b) above, the period ending with the second working day following that day;

    (b) in relation to a warrant which was last renewed within the period mentioned in paragraph (a)(ii) above, means the period of two months beginning with the day on which it was so renewed; and

    (c) in relation to a warrant which was last renewed at any other time, means—

        (i) if the instrument by which it was so renewed is endorsed with a statement that the renewal is considered necessary as mentioned in section 2(2)(a) or (c) above, the period of six months beginning with the day on which it was so renewed; and

        (ii) if that instrument is not so endorsed, the period of one month beginning with that day.

5.—(1) The Secretary of State may at any time—

    (a) modify a warrant by the insertion of any address which he considers likely to be used as mentioned in section 3(1)(a) above; or

    (b) modify a certificate so as to include in the certified material any material the examination of which he considers necessary as mentioned in section 2(2) above.

(2) If at any time the Secretary of State considers that any address specified in a warrant is no longer likely to be used as mentioned in section 3(1)(a) above, he shall modify the warrant by the deletion of that address.

(3) If at any time the Secretary of State considers that the material certified by a certificate includes any material the examination of which is no longer necessary as mentioned in section 2(2) above, he shall modify the certificate so as to exclude that material from the certified material.

(4) A warrant or certificate shall not be modified under subsection (1) above except by an instrument under the hand of the Secretary of State or, in an urgent case—

    (a) under the hand of a person holding office under the Crown who is expressly authorised by the warrant or certificate to modify it on the Secretary of State's behalf; or

    (b) where the Secretary of State has expressly authorised the modification and a statement of that fact is endorsed on the instrument, under the hand of such an officer as is mentioned in section 4(1)(b) above.

(5) An instrument made under subsection (4)(a) or (b) above shall cease to have effect at the end of the fifth working day following the day on which it was issued.

6.—(1) Where the Secretary of State issues a warrant he shall, unless such arrangements have already been made, make such arrangements as he considers necessary for the purpose of securing—

    (a) that the requirements of subsections (2) and (3) below are satisfied in relation to the intercepted material; and

    (b) where a certificate is issued in relation to the warrant, that so much of the intercepted material as is not certified by the certificate is not read, looked at or listened to by any person.

(2) The requirements of this subsection are satisfied in relation to any intercepted material if each of the following, namely—

    (a) the extent to which the material is disclosed;

    (b) the number of persons to whom any of the material is disclosed;

    (c) the extent to which the material is copied; and

    (d) the number of copies made of any of the material,

is limited to the minimum that is necessary as mentioned in section 2(2) above.

(3) The requirements of this subsection are satisfied in relation to any intercepted material if each copy made of any of that material is destroyed as soon as its retention is no longer necessary as mentioned in section 2(2) above.

7.—(1) There shall be a tribunal (in this Act referred to as 'the Tribunal') in relation to which the provisions of Schedule 1 to this Act shall apply.

(2) Any person who believes that communications sent to or by him have been intercepted in the course of their transmission by post or by means of a public telecommunication system may apply to the Tribunal for an investigation under this section.

(3) On such an application (other than one appearing to the Tribunal to be frivolous or vexatious), the Tribunal shall investigate—

    (a) whether there is or has been a relevant warrant or a relevant certificate; and

    (b) where there is or has been such a warrant or certificate, whether there has been any contravention of sections 2 to 5 above in relation to that warrant or certificate.

(4) If, on an investigation, the Tribunal, applying the principles applicable by a court on an application for judicial review, conclude that there has been a contravention of sections 2 to 5 above in relation to a relevant warrant or a relevant certificate, they shall—

    (a) give notice to the applicant stating that conclusion;

    (b) make a report of their findings to the Prime Minister; and

    (c) if they think fit, make an order under subsection (5) below.

(5) An order under this subsection may do one or more of the following, namely—

    (a) quash the relevant warrant or the relevant certificate;

    (b) direct the destruction of copies of the intercepted material or, as the case may be, so much of it as is certified by the relevant certificate;

    (c) direct the Secretary of State to pay to the applicant such sum by way of compensation as may be specified in the order.

(6) A notice given or report made under subsection (4) above shall state the effect of any order under subsection (5) above made in the case in question.

(7) If, on an investigation, the Tribunal come to any conclusion other than that mentioned in subsection (4) above, they shall give notice to the applicant stating that there has been no contravention of sections 2 to 5 above in relation to a relevant warrant or a relevant certificate.

(8) The decisions of the Tribunal (including any decisions as to their jurisdiction) shall not be subject to appeal or liable to be questioned in any court.

(9) For the purposes of this section—

    (a) a warrant is a relevant warrant in relation to an applicant if—

        (i) the applicant is specified or described in the warrant; or

        (ii) an address used for the transmission of communications to or from a set of premises in the British Islands where the applicant resides or works is so specified;

    (b) a certificate is a relevant certificate in relation to an applicant if and to the extent that an address used as mentioned in paragraph (a)(ii) above is specified in the certificate for the purpose of including communications sent to or from that address in the certified material.

9.—(1) In any proceedings before any court or tribunal no evidence shall be adduced and no question in cross-examination shall be asked which (in either case) tends to suggest—

    (a) that an offence under section 1 above has been or is to be committed by any of the persons mentioned in subsection (2) below; or

    (b) that a warrant has been or is to be issued to any of those persons. . . .

NOTES

1. The Interception of Communications Act marks a fundamental change in the legal basis for the control of the interception of communications by telephone tapping and the interception of letters under the United Kingdom constitution – a change that was thrust upon the government of the day, not volunteered. Prior to 1985, the interception of communications was regulated not by detailed statutory provisions such as those in the 1985 Act but by administrative practice given only oblique parliamentary authority by s. 80, Post Office Act 1969. The 1985 Act was introduced in order partly[1] to comply with the judgment of the European Court of Human Rights in the *Malone* case, below, p. 804, in which the previous arrange-

---

1 It was introduced also because of the need to make provision for telephone tapping by British Telecom, a private sector company, in place of the Post Office. On the Act, see I. J. Lloyd, (1986) 49 MLR 86.

ments for the interception of communications had been found to be in breach of the European Convention on Human Rights.

2. The 1985 Act, s. 1, creates a criminal offence of unlawful interception of communications 'by post or by means of a public telecommunications system'. It does not, however, apply to cordless telephones: *R v Effick* [1994] 3 WLR 583, CA. The offence may be committed by persons in the public or private sectors, including, in the latter case, newspaper reporters or private detectives. The offence does not apply to the interception of communications by the use of electronic bugs and other listening apparatus. There are unpublished guidelines issued in a Home Office circular with regard to the use of such devices and of means of visual surveillance that are almost identical to rules in the 1985 Act by the police.

3. The 1985 Act leaves the power to issue a warrant with the competent Secretary of State. The 1981 proposal of the Royal Commission on Criminal Procedure, Cmnd. 8092, para. 3.57, that the power be exercised by a magistrates' court was not adopted. Although there is no requirement of prior judicial authorisation *in criminal cases* (which exists, for example, in the United States: see *Berger v NY* 388 US 41 (1967)), it has been held at Strasbourg that the Act complies with the European Convention on Human Rights: *Christie v United Kingdom* (1994) 78A DRE Com HR 119.

4. The three grounds upon which a warrant may be issued (see s. 2(2)) are basically those that existed under the earlier administrative arrangements. A 'serious crime' is defined in s. 10(3) as follows:

(3) For the purpose of this Act conduct which constitutes or, if it took place in the United Kingdom, would constitute one or more offences shall be regarded as a serious crime if, and only if—

 (a) it involves the use of violence, results in substantial financial gain or is conduct by a large number of persons in pursuit of a common purpose; or

 (b) the offence or one of the offences is an offence for which a person who has attained the age of twenty-one and has no previous convictions could reasonably be expected to be sentenced to imprisonment for a term of three years or more.

As to the meaning of 'economic well-being', a government spokesman stated during the passage of the bill (Lord President of the Council 464 HL Deb June 1985 col 879):

'It is concerned with the interception that is necessary for the effective protection of the country's economic interests at the international level. It is an important part of our foreign policy to protect the country from adverse developments overseas which may not necessarily affect our national security so directly as to justify interception on that ground but which may have damaging consequences for our economic well-being. . . . If I refer in a general way to a threat to the supply from abroad of a commodity [eg oil] on which our economy is particularly dependent, I hope that your Lordships will accept that I have gone . . . as far as I can by way of offering an example.'

With regard to 'national security', the 1985 Act needs to be viewed in conjunction with the Security Service Act 1989, above, p. 501. Whereas the 1985 Act concerns the interception of communications for national security purposes, the 1989 Act applies to surveillance by the security services for reasons of national security by other means.

In 1966, the Prime Minister (Mr Wilson) announced that he had given instructions after taking office that MPs' telephones were to be immune from tapping (736 HC Deb 17 November 1966 col. 639). Later Prime Ministers have confirmed this (see, e.g., Mr Heath: 803 HC Deb 16 July 1970 col 1723).

5. The application procedure for a warrant is described as follows in the Commissioner's Report for 1986 (Cm 108, pp. 2–3):

5.   Warrants are obtained on the application of the Police, HM Customs and Excise and the Security and Intelligence Agencies. They are of two kinds, postal warrants for the opening of mail, and telecommunications warrants for the interception of all forms of telecommunication, including telephone, telegraph, telex and data transmission. Postal warrants are addressed to the Post Office. Telecommunication warrants are in general addressed to the British Telecommunications plc ('B.T.'). I discuss other [security] cases in a confidential appendix.

6.   The application for a warrant under Section 3(1) of the Act contains a description of the case, the name of the person, or target, whose communications it is desired to intercept, the telephone number and address of the person and the grounds on which the application is said to be justified. The ground put forward must be one of the three grounds set out in Section 2(2) of the Act. . . .

7.   Applications in the field of national security are dealt with by the Home Office, the Foreign Office, the Scottish Home and Health Department and the Northern Ireland Office. Applications in the field of serious crime are dealt with by the Home Office, Scottish Home and Health Department and the Northern Ireland Office. Applications in the field of the economic interests of the UK are dealt with by the Foreign Office.

10.   When an application arrives at the Home Office (I take the Home Office as typical) it is processed by the Warrants Unit. It is scrutinised on arrival at Principal level, to ensure that the application is in order, and that the grounds put forward come within Section 2(2) of the Act. If there is any doubt, the application is referred back. If the application is approved at Principal level, it is referred to the Permanent Under Secretary, or in his absence the Deputy Under Secretary in charge of the Police Department. It is only after it has been approved by him, that it is put before the Home Secretary for his personal approval. The Home Secretary then considers the application, together with any background papers, and the comments of his advisors. If he approves the application, he signs the warrant personally. If the telephone is one to which the public have access, the Home Secretary requires a particularly strong case to be made out before authorising interception.

11.   In urgent cases, where the Home Secretary is not available to sign a warrant, but can be reached on the telephone, he may authorise the issue of a warrant under the hand of an official in his Department of the rank of Assistant Under Secretary, or above. But a separate authority is required from the Secretary of State for each warrant so signed. He cannot delegate a general authority. Where authority is granted in a particular case, the warrant lapses, unless renewed under the hand of the Secretary of State by the end of the second working day following the date of issue. Since the Act came into force, there have been only five occasions on which a warrant has been signed by someone other than the Secretary of State. . . .

13.   The warrant is initially effective for a period of up to two months from issue. If it is not renewed, it lapses. The procedure on renewal is the same as on initial application, except that the application for renewal will state whether or not the interception has produced intelligence of value since the warrant was originally issued or last renewed. If the warrant is renewed, then, in cases where the justification for the warrant is national security or economic well-being, the warrant is renewed for up to six months. In the case of serious crime it is renewed for one month. The reason for the difference is that in the case of serious crime, the intelligence, if it is going to be obtained at all, is usually obtained more quickly.

6. In 1993, 1,120 warrants (1,005 for telephone tapping, 115 for the interception of letters) were issued by the Home Secretary and the Secretary of State for Scotland; 409 warrants were in force at the end of the year: Report of the Commissioner for 1993, Cm 2522, Annex. These figures continue an upwards trend in numbers of warrants in recent years, mostly in connection with customs offences. Most warrants concerned 'serious crime', especially drug offences.

7. The Act provides for independent supervision of the operation of the system of warrants by means of a Commissioner appointed by the Prime Minister, who must have held 'a higher judicial office' (s. 8(1)). The present Commissioner is Sir Thomas Bingham MR.

The Commissioner's functions are set out in s. 8(1) of the 1985 Act as follows:

(*a*) to keep under review the carrying out by the Secretary of State of the functions conferred on him by sections 2 to 5 above and the adequacy of any arrangements made for the purposes of section 6 above; and

(*b*) to give to the Tribunal all such assistance as the Tribunal may require for the purpose of enabling them to carry out their functions under this Act.

The Commissioner has stated that he applies 'the principles of judicial review' when exercising his function under s. 8(1)(a): Report of the Commissioner for 1989, Cm. 1063, p. 1.

The Commissioner must report to the Prime Minister annually on the working of the system, the report being presented to Parliament and published as a command paper. If 'it appears to the Prime Minister . . . that the publication of any matter in an annual report would be prejudicial to national security, to the prevention or detection of serious crime or to the economic wellbeing of the United Kingdom', the Prime Minister may exclude it from the copy of the report presented to Parliament (s. 8(9)).

In his annual reports, the Commissioner has found a small number of unlawful interceptions. These have resulted from clerical errors in transcribing the telephone number to be tapped or from the tapping of a telephone after it has been transferred to another subscriber. The Commissioner has not found any case of a warrant being issued when this was not justified on the grounds listed in the Act.

8. In addition to the criminal offence of unlawful interception of communications (s. 1), the 1985 Act provides a remedy for individuals through the Interception of Communications Tribunal. The Tribunal's composition and function are indicated in s. 7, above. If it finds, applying judicial review principles, that the warrant procedures have not been complied with (s. 7(3)), it must inform the applicant and report to the Prime Minister (s. 7(4)). It may also make an order quashing the warrant, requiring the destruction of the intercepted material, or awarding compensation (s. 7(5)). The remedy before the Tribunal is final; it is not subject to appeal or judicial review in the courts (s. 7(8)).

9. In 1981, Sir Robert Megarry VC granted an injunction to prevent the publication in the press of the contents of tapes obtained by telephone tapping which purported to be of telephone conversations between the Prince of Wales in Australia and his fiancée, now the Princess of Wales, in the UK: *The Times*, 7 and 8 May 1981.

10. As noted earlier, the 1985 Act does not apply to technical devices such as 'bugs'. Their use by the police probably does not comply with the 'in accordance with law' requirement in the European Convention: see the *Malone* case, below, p. 804. The Younger Committee (Report, p. 154) listed the technical surveillance devices it had come across. In addition to telephoto lenses, scanners to read the contents of envelopes, and tape recorders, they included the following listening devices:

Device	Capability and other characteristics
(g) microphone using wired link, the wired link either being specially laid or using existing pair of wires or single insulated wire; can also be applied like a stethoscope to listen to sounds on the other side of a wall:	range and sensitivity in effect unlimited depending on size of the microphone; certainly able to be superior to the human ear; a microphone about the size of a match head can pick up a whisper at 20 feet.

Device	Capability and other characteristics
(h) microphone using radio link, i.e. a microphone coupled to a radio transmitter; this is the proverbial 'bug', intruded in many ways, e.g. in a cocktail olive, a cuff link, tiepin, telephone, dart shot into a wall:	sensitivity of the microphone as (g) above; size, including battery, of a lump of sugar; practical transmission range about a quarter of a mile.
(i) tap on a telephone line—this can be a metallic contact, but this is not necessary, as an induction device which picks up the pulses in the line is equally effective; these draw an almost undetectable amount of electricity from the telephone wire and give no betraying noises:	reception just as good as the telephone user's; can be applied at any point on the line, indoors or out.
(j) 'infinity transmitter', a device inserted into a telephone handset, which, when activated by dialling the number and giving an ultrasonic note on the last digit, prevents the telephone ringing and transmits over the dialler's telephone line all the sounds in the room where the telephone is situated, whether the handset is on or off the telephone:	can be installed in three minutes; reception just as good as the telephone used properly; but works only on telephones with direct Post Office lines; that is, not through a switchboard.
(k) induction device to pick up telephone conversations from the stray magnetic field of the telephone itself:	must be within about 4 feet of the telephone.
(l) directional (or 'parabolic' or 'telescopic') microphone concentrating a beam of sound from a distance onto a sensitive microphone and so hearing across intervening noises:	range about 25 yards; rather bulky and so difficult to conceal, and background noise can interfere.
(m) invisible light beams for monitoring vibrations, usually spoken of in the context of the laser; the vibrations can be sensed on any object near the speaker, including a window pane if it is coated with an invisible metallic film:	there is a lack of agreement about the capability of these; it does not appear that they yet exist in any marketable form.

For other descriptions of technical surveillance devices, see the Justice Report, Appendix D, and M. Jones (ed), *Privacy* (1974) pp. 26–40. A bugging device found hidden in a cigarette packet behind a painting of Queen Victoria's Jubilee in Burnley Town Hall just before a meeting of the town's ruling Labour group was said by the police to have a transmitting range of about 70 yards and of being capable of being received by any VHF radio. It could have been made for a few pounds and with only a basic knowledge of electronics. It was uncovered after the Labour group had become suspicious about recent 'leaks': *The Times*, 25 May 1978.

11. In *R v Maqsud Ali* [1966] 1 QB 688, CCA, the appellants had been convicted of murder. The evidence against them included tape recordings of what they had said to each other while unaware that the room in which they were was 'bugged'. The Court of Criminal Appeal rejected an argument that the tape recordings should not have been admitted in evidence. Marshall J stated at p. 701:

'Both appellants had come voluntarily to the Town Hall, they were not in custody and no charge was brought against them until June 13 and 15, 1964, respectively. They were left in the room together. They had not, of course, been warned of the presence of the microphone. The police were inquiring into a particularly savage murder and it was a matter of great public concern that those responsible should be traced. There is no question here of being in custody and subject to any Judges' Rules. The criminal does not act according to Queensberry Rules. The method of the informer and of the eavesdropper is commonly used in the detection of crime. The only difference here was that a mechanical device was the eavesdropper. If, in such circumstances and at such a point in the investigations, the appellants by in cautious talk provided evidence against themselves, then in the view of this court it would not be unfair to use it against them. The method of taking the recording cannot affect admissibility as a matter of law although it must remain very much a matter for the discretion of the judge.'

See also *R v Khan (Sultan)* (1994), above, p. 152, where an electronic device was placed by the police, following Home Office guidelines, on the outside of a house that K was visiting. In both of these cases, no arrest or charge had occurred. For a case where the conversation of two arrested persons in a police cell was taped without their knowledge, see *R v Bailey and Smith* (1993), above, p. 164. And see *Hopes and Lavery v HM Advocate* 1960 JC 104, 1960 SLT 264, High Court of Justiciary, in which a person being blackmailed was fitted with a 'bug' by the police. Tape recordings of conversations with the blackmailer obtained by means of the 'bug' were held to be admissible. Would the appellants in any of these cases have had a civil remedy?

12. Evidence that is obtained by telephone-tapping under the Act must be destroyed once it is no longer needed for a statutory purpose. A distinction is to be drawn in this connection between 'preventing' or 'detecting' crime and the prosecution of offenders; evidence is not to be retained for the purpose of prosecution: *R v Preston* [1994] 2 AC 130, [1993] 4 All ER 638, HL. In the same case, an argument that evidence obtained by telephone-tapping under the Act should not be made available to the prosecution; although it was not admissible in court because of s. 9, it might be in the interests of justice for information to be revealed, via the prosecution, to the defence.

13. The Younger Committee considered that the use, or abuse, of technical surveillance devices (by which it understood 'electronic and optical extensions of the human senses' (Report, p. 153)) was an area in which the law needed strengthening. It recommended a new criminal offence of surreptitious surveillance by means of a technical device with the following constituents (Report, p. 173):

'a. a technical device;
b. surreptitious use of the device;
c. a person who is, or his possessions which are, the object of surveillance;
d. a set of circumstances in which, were it not for the use of the device, that person would be justified in believing that he had protected himself or his possessions from surveillance whether by overhearing or observation;
e. an intention by the user to render those circumstances ineffective as protection against overhearing or observation; and
f. absence of consent by the victim.'

This recommendation has not been implemented, 'mainly because of the difficulty in defining the act which it is intended to prohibit' (Calcutt Committee Report, p. 19). The Committee also recommended a tort of unlawful surveillance by technical devices. This would have the same elements as the offence but the act would not need to be surreptitious. It too remains a recommendation only.

CHAPTER 9

Freedom of religion

1 Introduction[1]

One element of freedom of religion is freedom from discrimination between religions. The Church of England's status as the established church means some preference in law for it over other denominations, although establishment carries disadvantages too. Religious toleration has reached the point where almost all the disabilities formerly suffered by dissenters have been removed and atheism is within the policy of the law. In addition to the aid to religion that the establishment of a particular church represents, the state provides support to religion generally or to particular denominations in other ways as well. The provision made for religion in schools, for exemption from taxation and by the law of blasphemy are good examples. *Private* discrimination on religious grounds is mostly uncontrolled. There is no statute like the Race Relations Act 1976 prohibiting it in Great Britain,[2] although the concept of indirect racial discrimination in that Act may provide a remedy in some cases. This has been the case for muslims and sikhs especially.[3]

Freedom of religion also includes freedom of worship and expression and freedom to conduct one's life in accordance with one's religious beliefs. Freedom of worship is now virtually complete. Freedom of expression on religious matters is limited only by the remnants of the law of blasphemy. The Christian morality underlying English law means that most Christians have no difficulty in practising their religion in their daily lives. Members of some minority Christian and non-Christian denominations lack the same facility, as the sections in this chapter on criminal law, employment, religious holy days and immigration show.[4] Immigration from the new Commonwealth since the 1950s has provided further evidence of the link between Christianity and the law. The same development of a more multi-racial (and hence multi-religious[5]) society has increased the importance of freedom of religion.

1 On the legal aspects of freedom of religion see, A. Bradney, *Religions, Rights and Laws*, 1993; J. Montgomery, in B. Hepple and E. M. Szyszczak, op. cit. at Chap. 11, n. 1, below; S. Poulter, id., Chap. 10; and St. J. Robilliard, *Religion and the Law* (1984). On freedom of religion in Northern Ireland, which is too large and complex a subject to be considered here, see B. Dickson, ed., *Civil Liberties in Northern Ireland* (2nd edn, 1993) Chap. 11.
2 Private discrimination in employment is illegal in Northern Ireland: Fair Employment (NI) Acts 1976 and 1989.
3 See, e.g., the *Muhammed Azam* case, below, p. 608, and the *Mandla* case, below, p. 638. As to rasta-farians, see the *Dawkins* case, below, p. 645.
4 On the problems that face ethnic minorities, see S. Poulter, *English Law and Ethnic Minority Customs*, 1986.
5 In terms of community members, there are approximately 39 (7.23) million Christians; 1.2 (0.99) million Muslims; 0.5 (0.39) million Sikhs; 0.3 (0.14) million Hindus; and 0.3 (0.11) million Jews in the UK: *UK Christian Handbook*, 1992–93 edition. The figures in brackets are of active members: *Social Trends* 22, 1992. See the table in *Runnymede Bulletin* 253, p. 6 (1992).

2 What is a religion?

Re South Place Ethical Society: Barralet v A-G [1980] 3 All ER 918, [1980] 1 WLR 1565, QBD

The South Place Ethical Society sought a declaration that its objects were charitable, as being for the advancement of religion or otherwise. The objects of the society were 'the study and dissemination of ethical principles and the cultivation of a rational religious sentiment'. Counsel for the society described it as 'a wholly learned society with a deep and thoughtful philosophy'; it was 'agnostic about the existence of any god'. The society had abandoned prayer in 1869. In the society's objects, the word 'religious' was 'used in a sense which eschews all supernatural belief'. The society's beliefs were an aspect of humanism and in the Platonic tradition. The society held Sunday meetings open to the public at which lectures were given. There were also ancillary social activities. The following extract concerns the question whether the society could be regarded as charitable on religious grounds.

Dillon J: . . . The Society says that religion does not have to be theist or dependent on a god; any sincere belief in ethical qualities is religious, because such qualities as truth, love and beauty are sacred, and the advancement of any such belief is the advancement of religion.

One decision [cited to the court] is the decision of the Supreme Court of the United States in *United States v Seeger* (1965) 380 US 163. That was concerned with the exemption of a conscientious objector from conscription on the grounds of religion. . . . The judgment of the court (delivered by Clark J) gives as the ratio (at 176) that in the opinion of the court—

'A sincere and meaningful belief, which occupies in the life of its possessor a place parallel to that filled by the God of those admittedly qualifying for exemption on the grounds of religion comes within the statutory definition.' . . .

In a free country . . . it is natural that the court should desire not to discriminate between beliefs deeply and sincerely held, whether they are beliefs in a god or in the excellence of man or in ethical principles or in Platonism or some other scheme of philosophy. But I do not see that that warrants extending the meaning of the word 'religion' so as to embrace all other beliefs and philosophies. Religion, as I see it, is concerned with man's relations with God, and ethics are concerned with man's relations with man. The two are not the same, and are not made the same by sincere inquiry into the question, what is God. If reason leads people not to accept Christianity or any known religion, but they do believe in the excellence of qualities such as truth, beauty and love, or believe in the Platonic concept of the ideal, their beliefs may be to them the equivalent of a religion, but viewed objectively they are not religion. The ground of the opinion of the Supreme Court in *Seeger's* case, that any belief occupying in the life of its possessor a place parallel to that occupied by belief in God in the minds of theists is religion, prompts the comment that parallels, by definition, never meet.

In *Bowman v Secular Society Ltd* [below, p. 585], Lord Parker, in commenting on one of the objects of the society in that case, namely to promote the principle that human conduct should be based upon natural knowledge and not on supernatural belief, and that human welfare in this world is the proper end of all thought and action, said of that object:

'It is not a religious trust, for it relegates religion to a region in which it is to have no influence on human conduct.'

That comment seems to me to be equally applicable to the objects of the society in the present case, and it is not to be answered in my judgment by attempting to extend the meaning of religion. Lord Parker has used the word 'in its natural and accustomed sense'.

Again, in *United Grand Lodge of Ancient, Free and Accepted Masons of England v Holborn Borough Council* [1957] 3 All ER 281 at 285, [1957] 1 WLR 1080 at 1090 Donovan J, delivering the judgment of the Divisional Court, after commenting that freemasonry held out certain standards of truth and justice by which masons were urged to regulate their conduct, and commenting that, in particular, masons were urged to be reverent, honest, compassionate, loyal, temperate, benevolent and chaste, said:

'Admirable though these objects are, it seems to us impossible to say that they add up to the advancement of religion.'

Therefore I take the view that the objects of this society are not for the advancement of religion.

There is a further point. It seems to me that two of the essential attributes of religion are faith and worship; faith in god and worship of that god. This is supported by the definitions of religion given in the

Oxford English Dictionary, although I appreciate that there are other definitions in other dictionaries and books. The Oxford Dictionary gives as one of the definitions of religion:

'a particular system of faith and worship . . . recognition on the part of man of some higher, unseen power as having control of his destiny and as being entitled to obedience, reverence and worship.'

In *R v Registrar General, ex p Segerdal* [1970] 3 All ER 886 at 892, [1970] 2 QB 697 at 709, which was concerned with the so-called Church of Scientology, Buckley LJ in his judgment said this:

'Worship I take to be something which must have some, at least, of the following characteristics: submission to the object worshipped, veneration of that object, praise, thanksgiving, prayer or intercession.'

He went on to say that, looking at the wedding ceremony of the scientologists, he could find nothing in the form of ceremony which would not be appropriate in a purely civil, non-religious ceremony such as is conducted in a registry office, and that it contained none of the elements which he had suggested were necessary elements of worship. . . .

The society really accepts that worship by that definition, which in my view is the correct definition in considering whether a body is charitable for the advancement of religion, is not practised by the society because, indeed, it is not possible to worship in that way a mere ethical or philosophical ideal. . . .

One of the matters that has been pressed in argument and which weighed with Douglas J in *Seeger's* case is the position of Buddhism, which is accepted by everyone as being a religion. It is said that religion cannot be necessarily theist or dependent on belief in a god, a supernatural or supreme being, because Buddhism does not have any such belief. I do not think it is necessary to explore that further in this judgment because I do not know enough about Buddhism. It may be that the answer in respect of Buddhism is to treat it as an exception, as Lord Denning MR did in his judgment in *R v Registrar General* . . . Alternatively, it may be that Buddhism is not an exception, because I have been supplied with an affidavit by his Honour Judge Christmas Humphreys QC, an eminent English Buddhist, where he says that he does not accept the suggestion that 'Buddhism denies a supreme being'. I would not wish to suggest in any way that Buddhism is not a religion.

The society therefore fails in my judgment to make out its case to be charitable on the ground that its objects are for the advancement of religion. . . .

[Dillon J then held that the society was charitable as being for purposes beneficial to the community and as being for the advancement of education.]

Declarations accordingly.

NOTES

1. This case defines 'religion' in the context of the law of charities. In *R v Registrar General, ex p Segerdal* [1970] 2 QB 697, the Court of Appeal had adopted a similar approach when deciding whether the chapel of the Church of Scientology at East Grinstead was a 'place of meeting for religious worship' within the Places of Worship Registration Act 1855. That Act applies to places of worship of all denominations except the Church of England. Registration is not compulsory, but carries with it important advantages. By registration, the church 'will have taken one step towards getting a licence to celebrate marriages there; they will be outside the jurisdiction of the Charity Commissioners; and the building itself may become exempt from paying rates' (Lord Denning, p. 704). Refusing the applicants mandamus to require the Registrar General to register the chapel, Lord Denning stated:

'. . . the combined phrase, "place of meeting for religious worship" . . . connotes to my mind a place of which the principal use is as a place where people come together as a congregation or assembly to do reverence to God. It need not be the God which the Christians worship. It may be another God, or any unknown God, but it must be a reverence to deity. There may be exceptions. For instance, Buddhist temples are properly described as places of meeting for religious worship. . . .

Turning to the creed of the Church of Scientology, I must say that it seems to me to be more a *philosophy* of the existence of man or of life, rather than a *religion*. Religious worship means reverence or veneration of God or a Supreme Being. I do not find any such reverence or veneration in the creed of this church, or, indeed, in the affidavit of Mr. Segerdal. There is considerable stress on the spirit of man. The adherents of this philosophy believe that man's spirit is everlasting and moves from one human frame to another; but still, so far as I can see, it is the spirit of man and not of God. When I look through the ceremonies and the affidavits, I am left with the feeling that there is nothing in it of reverence for God or deity, but simply instruction in a philosophy.'

Winn and Buckley LJJ delivered concurring judgments. In *Church of the New Faith v Comr for Pay-roll Tax* (1983) 57 ALJR 785 (Aust HC) it was held that scientology *was* a religion so as to attract tax exemption. The definition of religion adopted by Mason ACJ and Brennan J (two members of a five man court) was (p. 789):

'. . . for the purposes of the law, the criteria of religion are twofold: first, belief in a supernatural Being, Thing or Principle; and second, the acceptance of canons of conduct in order to give effect to that belief, though canons of conduct which offend against the ordinary laws are outside the area of any immunity, privilege or right conferred on the grounds of religion.'

Insofar as belief in a principle could suffice, this definition was wider than that in *Re South Place Ethical Society*.[1]

2. The charitable status of the South Place Ethical Society was important for tax purposes. A charity, whether for the advancement of religion or for other charitable purposes, is largely exempt from tax.[2]

3. The charitable status of the Exclusive Brethren has been the subject of scrutiny. An investigation conducted on behalf of the Charity Commissioners by Mr H. Francis QC into the Brethren concluded that a faction of the Brethren which followed the teachings of James Taylor Jnr could not be regarded as charitable because it applied the 'separation from evil' doctrine in such a way that 'the advancement of such a religion, far from being beneficial to the community, is inimical to the true interests of the community' (1976 Charity Commissioners Report, 1976–77 HC 389, p. 35). In *A-G v BBC* [1981] AC 303 at 340–1, HL Lord Salmon gave this picture of the sect:

On September 26, 1976, the BBC broadcast on television what purported to be the habits, teaching and attitudes of a religious sect called the Exclusive Brethren which adhered to the principles laid down by an American called James Taylor Jnr. The broadcast was extremely hostile to the sect; it made it plain that the sect taught that anyone who is not one of its members is necessarily evil, and accordingly decreed that the sect's members must dissociate themselves from any such persons whosoever they may be—husband, wife, father, mother, brother or sister. They must not even talk to them nor eat with them. According to the broadcast, this doctrine was applied so strictly that it caused the deepest distress amongst many and led in Andover to two deaths which the coroner described as murder and suicide.

In that case, the House of Lords rejected an application for an injunction to prevent the re-broadcast of the BBC programme pending the hearing of a case before a local valuation court concerning a claim to exemption from rates because such a court was not protected by the law of contempt. See above, p. 391. Following the Francis Report (but before the *BBC* case), in *Holmes v A-G* (1981) *The Times*, 12 February, QBD, Walton J granted a declaration requested by the Brethren to the effect that they were entitled to be registered as a charity. The Brethren were clearly a religion and the presumption that their purposes were therefore charitable was not rebutted by the evidence presented to the court on the question whether the furtherance of their activities was contrary to public policy.

4. The charitable status of the Unification Church, or 'Moonies' (after their founder, Sun Myung Moon), has also been questioned.[3] In a libel action brought by the

1 See on the *New Faith* case, Sadurski, (1989) 63A LJ 834. Scientology is not registered as a charity under English law. See also on scientology, *Hubbard v Vosper*, above, p. 561; *Church of Scientology of California v Kaufman* [1973] RPC 635, 658 ('pernicious nonsense'); and the immigration section below, p. 610.
2 See G. Moffat, *Trusts Law: Text and Materials* (2nd edn, 1994), pp. 637–638.
3 See on the Moonies, A. Swetland, *Escape from the Moonies* (1982) and E. Barker, *The Making of a Moonie* (1984). On the Children of God Sect, which is registered as a charity, see the immigration section, below, p. 610. See also H. Picarda, (1981) 131 NLJ 436, 1064.

spiritual leader of the Moonies in the UK against the *Daily Mail*, which had printed an article claiming that the sect broke up families and brainwashed converts, the jury found for the defendant and added a rider to their verdict calling for the charitable status of the Moonies to be investigated on the ground that they were a political organisation (*The Times*, 1 April 1981). The Charity Commissioners considered the matter but decided that the sect should continue to be registered. In a debate in Parliament on the Moonies, a Home Office Minister (Dr S. Summerskill), responding to allegations that the Moonies tended to separate vulnerable teenagers from their families and to obtain funds by fraud, stated (926 HC Deb 23 February 1977 cols 1597–8):

> If the Government as a Government took action against organisations which they regarded as wrong-headed or even worse, we should be living in a rather different kind of society. The cost of such freedom is that some people will spend their money foolishly, be led astray by charlatans and even misunderstand the motives and feelings of their families and true friends. But when we decide that people should be treated as adults from the age of 18, this meant that they had the right to make their own choice on the way they wished to lead their lives and to make their own mistakes.

5. On new religions generally, see E. Barker, *New Religious Movements* (1989).
6. Whereas the courts do consider what qualifies as a religion for various purposes, they tend not to consider whether a particular person is a follower, etc, of a recognised religion or what the tenets of the religion are, preferring to leave this to the person or the religion concerned.[1]

3 Church and the state

(a) THE ESTABLISHED CHURCH

The Canons of the Church of England (Canons Ecclesiastical promulgated by the Convocations of Canterbury and York in 1964 and 1969)

CANON A1

The Church of England, established according to the laws of this realm under the Queen's Majesty, BELONGS to the true and Apostolic Church of Christ; . . .

CANON A7

We acknowledge that the Queen's most excellent Majesty, acting according to the laws of the realm, is the highest power under God in this kingdom, and has supreme authority over all persons in all causes, as well ecclesiastical as civil.

NOTES[2]

1. Although the Church of England had become the established church in England long before the 16th century, it is with the Reformation statutes of that time, which

1 See J. Montgomery, in B. Hepple and E. M. Szyszczak, *Discrimination: The Limits of the Law* (1992) Chap. 11. See, e.g., the *Mandla* case, below, p. 638, where the House of Lords accepted 'what the Sikhs themselves say' as to the requirements of the Sikh religion.
2 On establishment, see R. Davies, (1976) 7 Cambrian LR 11; C. Garbett, *Church and State in England* (1950); E. G. Moore, *An Introduction to English Canon Law* (1967) Chap. II; and D. Grant, in R. Blackburn, ed., *Constitutional Studies* (1992) Chap. 11. See also *Church and State* (1970), a Report of the Archbishops' Commission (Chadwick Commission) and the resulting House of Lords debate on establishment: 314 HL Deb 20 Jan 1971 cols 485–501, 506–562. For the case for disestablishment, see T. Benn, in D. Reeves, ed., *The Church and the State* (1984). Mr. Benn unsuccessfully introduced a bill for disestablishment in 1988.

severed the link with Rome and stated the doctrine of royal supremacy, that one associates the idea of establishment in its present form.[1] None of these statutes, which are now mostly repealed, expressly 'establishes' the Church of England. The above extract from the Canons of the Church of England recognises the fact of establishment as clearly as any other legislative source. Canon law is a part of the ecclesiastical law of the Church of England; it is binding upon the clergy of the Church, not the laity. The Church in Wales was disestablished by the Welsh Church Act 1914. On the special status of the Church of Scotland, see F. Lyall, 1976 JR 58, 65.

2. The Sovereign is the head of the Church of England: Canon A7, Canons of the Church of England, above. The Act of Supremacy 1558, s. 9, now repealed, referred to the Sovereign as 'the Supreme Governor of the Realm in all spiritual and ecclesiastical causes as well as temporal'. The Act of Settlement 1700, s. 3, provides that

'whosoever shall hereafter come to the possession of this crown shall join in communion with the Church of England as by law established.'

The same Act (s. 2) also provides that

'all and every person and persons who shall or may take or inherit the said crown by virtue of the limitation of this present Act and is are or shall be reconciled to or shall hold communion with the see or church of Rome or shall profess the popish religion or shall marry a papist'

are disqualified from being the Sovereign. In 1978, Prince Michael of Kent renounced his claim to the throne upon marrying a Roman Catholic. In 1980, the amendment of s. 2 was discussed when Prince Charles was considering marriage. It was understood that any such amendment would by convention require the approval of all Commonwealth countries accepting the monarch as such. The government indicated that it had no plans for amendment (989 HC Deb 29 July 1980 written answers col 607).

3. The Church of England's position as the established church gives it certain privileges in law. The Archbishops of Canterbury and York, the Bishops of London, Durham and Winchester and 21 other diocesan bishops by seniority in office are members of the House of Lords (*Erskine May* (21st edn, 1989, p. 9). The 1968 government White Paper on House of Lords reform (Cmnd. 3799, paras. 63–7) accepted that the presence of the 'lords spiritual' could be defended by reference to the control that Parliament has over Church of England affairs and suggested that they should remain 'at least for the present', although their number should be reduced to 16 in the proposed smaller chamber. The 'lords spiritual' are free to debate and vote on any matter before the House, not only on matters of direct concern to the Church. The ecclesiastical law of the Church of England is a part of the law of the land (*Mackonochie v Lord Penzance* (1881) 6 App Cas 424 at 446, HL) and is enforced by the state. The Sovereign is crowned by the Archbishop of Canterbury.

4. The price that the Church pays for these and other privileges is a certain degree of state involvement in its affairs. The state has control over law-making by the 'parliament' of the Church of England, the General Synod (formerly the National Assembly). *Canons* (which cannot be contrary to the prerogative or statutory or other law of the realm (Submission of the Clergy Act 1533, s. 3)) passed by the General Synod require the royal assent to be law (Synodical Government Measure

---

1 See, in particular, the Ecclesiastical Appeals Act 1531; the Submission of the Clergy Act 1533; the Appointment of Bishops Act 1533; the Ecclesiastical Licences Act 1533; and 26 Hen 8 c 2 (Supremacy of the Crown) (1534).

1969, s. 1). *Measures* (which have the force of statute and hence may change any law) passed by it have to be approved by the two Houses of Parliament as well as obtain the royal assent (Church of England (Assembly) Powers Act 1919). It is rare for Parliament not to approve a proposed measure.[1] Archbishops and bishops are appointed by the Crown (see 1 Co Inst 134 and the Appointment of Bishops Act 1533, s. 3) on the advice (by convention) of the Prime Minister. As of 1977, the newly established Church of England Crown Appointments Commission puts forward two candidates (in order of preference if it thinks fit) for the Prime Minister's consideration. The understanding is that he will recommend one of these candidates, normally the 'first choice' candidate if there is one. In 1981, the second choice candidate for the office of Bishop of London was, somewhat controversially, put forward by the Prime Minister. The new arrangement applies only to Archbishops and diocesan bishops; in the case of suffragan bishops, the appointment is made on the basis of a recommendation from the diocesan bishop. The Crown is also the patron of a larger number of benefices, or livings. Appointments to these are made after consultation with the Church. 'No person having been ordained to the office of priest or deacon' in the Church of England or minister of the Church of Scotland may be an MP: House of Commons (Clergy Disqualification) Act 1801. The prohibition extends beyond the Church of England to all episcopally ordained clergymen: *Re MacManaway* [1951] AC 161, HL (Church of Ireland priest). Roman Catholic priests are also excluded: Roman Catholic Relief Act 1829, s. 9. Ministers of non-conformist churches (e.g. Dr Ian Paisley) may be MPs. The Chadwick Commission (Report, p. 58) recommended that the prohibition be lifted. The 1801 Act was explained in *Re MacManaway* in terms of the spiritual, and hence non-political, nature of the priest's office. The historical evidence indicates that the intention was to prevent priests representing their patrons and because of one particular demagogic priest at the time.

(b) TOLERATION OF OTHER DENOMINATIONS

Lord Chancellor (Tenure of Office and Discharge of Ecclesiastical Functions) Act 1974

1. For the avoidance of doubt it is hereby declared that the office of Lord Chancellor is and shall be tenable by an adherent of the Roman Catholic faith.
2. In the event of the office of Lord Chancellor being held by an adherent of the Roman Catholic faith it shall be lawful for Her Majesty in Council to make provision for the exercise of any or all the visitational or the ecclesiastical functions normally performed by the Lord Chancellor, and any patronage to livings normally in the gift of the Lord Chancellor, to be performed by the Prime Minister or any other Minister of the Crown.

NOTES

1. At the time of the Reformation settlement, a consequence of the establishment of one denomination was inevitably the proscription of others. Since then the church has lost most of its temporal power and attitudes have mellowed to the point where

---

1 In 1927 and 1928, Parliament rejected proposed measures for the revision of the Prayer Book passed by the National Assembly. In 1975, the Incumbents (Vacation of Benefices) Measure was rejected, although later passed as revised. In 1990, the House of Commons approved the Clergy (Ordination) Measure, which allows a remarried man whose former spouse is still alive to be ordained as a Church of England priest, 167 HC Deb 20 February 1990 col 882, after having earlier rejected it: 157 HC Deb 17 July 1989 col 174.

it is not illegal to profess or practise any religion and nearly all of the other disabilities to which non-conformists were subject (e.g. exclusion from Parliament) have been removed.[1] The Prime Minister may be of any religion or none. So may the Lord Chancellor, as the Lord Chancellor, etc., Act 1974 makes clear. The Act was expressed in terms only of Roman Catholics because there was felt to be no doubt that adherents of other religions were eligible. And at least one Lord Chancellor had been 'a devoutly practising atheist' (352 HL Deb 11 June 1974 col 417 written answers). But the Sovereign must, as noted above, be a member of the Church of England and his or her consort may not be a Roman Catholic. Other minor disabilities (mostly affecting Roman Catholics) are listed in Moore, *An Introduction to English Canon Law* (1967) pp. 161–2.

2. Another result of religious toleration is the Oaths Act 1978 which provides (s. 5):

'**5.**—(1) Any person who objects to being sworn shall be permitted to make his solemn affirmation instead of taking an oath.

(2) Subsection (1) above shall apply in relation to a person to whom it is not reasonably practicable without inconvenience or delay to administer an oath in the manner appropriate to his religious belief as it applies in relation to a person objecting to be sworn.'

Bowman v Secular Society [1917] AC 406, House of Lords

The appellants challenged the validity of a testamentary gift to the respondent company on the ground that the latter's objects were illegal so that the gift was for an illegal purpose. Its objects were 'to promote . . . the principle that human conduct should be based upon natural knowledge, and not upon super-natural belief, and that human welfare in this world is the proper end of all thought and action'.

Lord Sumner: My Lords, the question is whether an anti-Christian society is incapable of claiming a legacy, duly bequeathed to it, merely because it is anti-Christian. . . . is the maxim that Christianity is part of the law of England true, and, if so, in what sense? If Christianity is of the substance of our law, and if a Court of law must, nevertheless, adjudge possession of its property to a company whose every action seeks to subvert Christianity and bring that law to naught, then by such judgment it stultifies the law. . . .

My Lords, with all respect for the great names of the lawyers who have used it, the phrase 'Christianity is part of the law of England' is really not law; it is rhetoric . . . One asks what part of our law may Christianity be, and what part of Christianity may it be that is part of our law? Best CJ once said in *Bird v Holbrook* (1828) 4 Bing 628 at 641 (a case of injury by setting a spring-gun): 'There is no act which Christianity forbids, that the law will not reach: if it were otherwise, Christianity would not be, as it has always been held to be, part of the law of England'; but this was rhetoric too. Spring-guns, indeed, were got rid of, not by Christianity, but by Act of Parliament. 'Thou shalt not steal' is part of our law. 'Thou shalt not commit adultery' is part of our law, but another part. 'Thou shalt love thy neighbour as thyself' is not part of our law at all. Christianity has tolerated chattel slavery; not so the present law of England. Ours is, and always has been, a Christian State. The English family is built on Christian ideas, and if the national religion is not Christian there is none. English law may well be called a Christian law, but we apply many of its rules and most of its principles, with equal justice and equally good government, in heathen communities, and its sanctions, even in Courts of conscience, are material and not spiritual. . . . In the present day reasonable men do not apprehend the dissolution or the downfall of society because religion is publicly assailed by methods not scandalous. . . . Accordingly I am of opinion that acts merely done in furtherance of paragraph 3(A) and other paragraphs of the respondents' memorandum are not now contrary to the law, and that the appeal should be dismissed.

Lords Dunedin, Parker of Waddington, and **Buckmaster** delivered concurring speeches. **Lord Finlay LC** delivered a dissenting speech.

Appeal dismissed.

---

1 See, mainly, the Toleration Act 1688 (protestant non-conformists); the Roman Catholic Relief Acts 1791 and 1829; and Religious Disabilities Act 1846 (Jews).

1. *Bowman v Secular Society* was one of two cases decided in the space of three years in which the House of Lords adjusted the policy of the common law to reflect the change in the relationship between church and state that has occurred since the Reformation. The other was *Bourne v Keane* [1919] AC 815, HL, in which it was held (overruling *West v Shuttleworth* (1835) 2 My & K 684) that a trust for the saying of Roman Catholic masses for the dead was valid. In these cases, the old idea that the 'Church must help the State to maintain its authority, and the State must help the Church to punish nonconformists and infidels' (W. Holdsworth, (1920) 36 LQR 339) gave way to one emphasising freedom of conscience instead. Nonetheless, although, in Lord Sumner's famous dictum, it may only be 'rhetoric' to say that 'Christianity is part of the law of the land', most of English law remains firmly based on Christian moral values. Consequently, members of the main Christian denominations are unlikely to find themselves out of step with the law as they practise their religion in their daily lives. As the cases later in this chapter show, the same may not be true of members of some of the minority Christian sects (see e.g. *R v Senior*, below, p. 600) or of non-Christian denominations, whether the latter are denominations that have long been well represented in the community (see e.g. *Ostreicher v Secretary of State for the Environment*, below, p. 607) or denominations that are now more common because of recent patterns of immigration (see e.g. *Ahmad v Inner London Education Authority*, below, p. 603).

2. In *Cowan v Milbourn* (1867) LR 2 Exch 230, an owner of a room refused to honour a letting when he discovered that it was to be used by the Liverpool Secular Society (not to be confused with the Liverpool Football Club, which is a religious society) for a lecture questioning Christian doctrine. The Court of Exchequer Chamber held the refusal to be justified as the intended use was for an unlawful purpose, Christianity being a part of the law of the land. The case was overruled in *Bowman v Secular Society*.

(c) ASSISTANCE TO RELIGION

(i) Education

Education Reform Act 1988

6. Collective worship
(1) Subject to section 9 of this Act, all pupils in attendance at a maintained school[1] shall on each school day take part in an act of collective worship.
(2) The arrangements for the collective worship in a school required by this section may, in respect of each school day, provide for a single act of worship for all pupils or for separate acts of worship for pupils in different age groups or in different school groups. . . .

7. Special provisions as to collective worship in county schools
(1) Subject to the following provisions of this section, in the case of a county school the collective worship required in the school by section 6 of this Act shall be wholly or mainly of a broadly Christian character.
(2) For the purposes of subsection (1) above, collective worship is of a broadly Christian character if it reflects the broad traditions of Christian belief without being distinctive of any particular Christian denomination.

1 *Ed.* A 'maintained school' is any county or voluntary school: Education Reform Act 1988, s. 25(1).

(3) Every act of collective worship required by section 6 of this Act in the case of a county school need not comply with subsection (1) above provided that, taking any school term as a whole, most such acts which take place in the school do comply with that subsection.

(4) Subject to subsections (1) and (3) above—

   (a) the extent to which (if at all) any acts of collective worship required by section 6 of this Act which do not comply with subsection (1) above take place in a county school;

   (b) the extent to which any act of collective worship in a county school which complies with subsection (1) above reflects the broad traditions of Christian belief; and

   (c) the ways in which those traditions are reflected in any such act of collective worship;

shall be such as may be appropriate having regard to any relevant considerations relating to the pupils concerned which fall to be taken into account in accordance with subsection (5) below.

(5) Those considerations are—

   (a) any circumstances relating to the family backgrounds of the pupils concerned which are relevant for determining the character of the collective worship which is appropriate in their case; and

   (b) their ages and aptitudes.

(6) Where under section 12 of this Act a standing advisory council on religious education determine that it is not appropriate for subsection (1) above to apply in the case of any county school, or in the case of any class or description of pupils at such a school, then, so long as that determination has effect—

   (a) that subsection shall not apply in relation to that school or (as the case may be) in relation to those pupils; and

   (b) the collective worship required by section 6 of this Act in the case of that school or those pupils shall not be distinctive of any particular Christian or other religious denomination (but this shall not be taken as preventing that worship from being distinctive of any particular faith).

9. Exceptions, special arrangements and supplementary and consequential provisions

(1) It shall not be required, as a condition of any pupil attending any maintained school, that he shall attend or abstain from attending any Sunday school or any place of religious worship.

(2) For the purposes of subsections (3) to (10) below 'maintained school' does not include a maintained special school.

(3) If the parent of any pupil in attendance at any maintained school requests that he may be wholly or partly excused—

   (a) from attendance at religious worship in the school;

   (b) from receiving religious education given in the school in accordance with the school's basic curriculum; or

   (c) both from such attendance and from receiving such education;

the pupil shall be so excused until the request is withdrawn.

(4) Where in accordance with subsection (3) above any pupil has been wholly or partly excused from attendance at religious worship or from receiving religious education in any school, and the responsible authority are satisfied—

   (a) that the parent of the pupil desires him to receive religious education of a kind which is not provided in the school during the periods of time during which he is so excused;

   (b) that the pupil cannot with reasonable convenience be sent to another maintained school where religious education of the kind desired by the parent is provided; and

   (c) that arrangements have been made for him to receive religious education of that kind during school hours elsewhere;

the pupil may be withdrawn from the school during such periods of time as are reasonably necessary for the purpose of enabling him to receive religious education in accordance with the arrangements. . . .

Education Act 1944

26. (1) In the case of a county school the provision for religious education for pupils at the school which is required by section 2(1)(a) of the Education Reform Act 1988 to be included in the school's basic curriculum shall be provision for religious education in accordance with an agreed syllabus adopted for the school or for those pupils.

(2) No such syllabus shall provide education to be given to pupils at such a school by means of any catechism or formulary which is distinctive of any particular religious denomination; but this provision is not to be taken as prohibiting provision in such a syllabus for the study of such catechisms or formularies.

(3) Subsection (4) below applies where a county secondary school is so situated that arrangements cannot conveniently be made for the withdrawal of pupils from the school in accordance with section 9 of that Act to receive religious education elsewhere.

(4) If in any such case the local education authority are satisfied—

(*a*) that the parents of pupils in attendance at the school desire them to receive religious education in the school in accordance with the tenets of a particular religious denomination; and

(*b*) that satisfactory arrangements have been made for the provision of such education to those pupils in the school, and for securing that the cost of providing such education to those pupils in the school will not fall upon the authority;

the authority shall, unless they are satisfied that owing to any special circumstances it would be unreasonable to do so, provide facilities for the carrying out of those arrangements.

[Sections 27 and 28 make special provisions for religious education in voluntary controlled (s. 27) and aided or special agreement (s. 28) schools.]

NOTES[1]

1. The statutory provisions on religion distinguish between county and voluntary schools. *County* schools are state schools established and maintained by local education authorities (Education Act 1944, s. 9(1)). *Voluntary* schools are schools that have been established privately but that have been voluntarily brought within the state system and as a result are, to varying degrees, financially maintained by local education authorities and subject to their control (ibid, s. 9(2)). There are three categories of voluntary schools: controlled, aided and special agreement schools, to which different rules apply. Most of the 4,000 or so voluntary schools are denominational and, with the exception of a small number of Jewish and Methodist schools, all of these are Roman Catholic or Church of England. Although Muslim schools have applied for voluntary aided status, the Secretary of State for Education, whose decision it is (Education Act 1980, s. 13), has not approved any such application as yet. In 1993, an application from the private Islamia Primary School in Brent was refused because there were extensive surplus places in state funded schools in Brent.[2] Although this is in itself a reasonable ground for refusal, it can work unfairly against Muslim schools which are largely in catchment areas with surplus places.[3]

2. *Religious education.* Religious education is a compulsory part of the 'basic curriculum' in all maintained (i.e. county and voluntary) schools, including sixth form colleges (Education Reform Act 1988, s. 2(1)(a) and (8)). It is not, however, a part of the 'national curriculum' so that there are no national attainment requirements or tests. Instead religious education must be in accordance with a locally 'agreed syllabus' (s. 26, Education Act 1944), except that provision is made for religious education in voluntary schools to be denominational in accordance with the trust deed if the parents request this (controlled schools: s. 27) or the governors so decide (aided and special agreement schools: s. 28). The 'agreed syllabus' is drawn up by a conference convened by the local education authority consisting of representatives of four groups:

---

1 On s. 26, as substituted by the Education Reform Act 1988, see E. Cox and J. M. Cairns, *Reforming Religious Education* (1989) and S. Poulter (1990) 2 *Education and the Law* 1. See also Department of Education Circular 1/1994, Religious Education and Collective Worship. The arrangements described below for religion in schools are extended to grant-maintained schools by the Education Act 1993, s. 138ff. As of 1993, collective worship and religious education in voluntary and grant-maintained schools (as well as county schools, as previously) is subject to inspection by Her Majesty's Chief Inspector of Schools: s. 13, Education (Schools) Act 1992, as amended by s. 259, Education Act 1993.

2 Department of Education News 255/93. The decision was taken after mandamus had been issued against the Secretary of State requiring him to reconsider the application because he had not informed the applicants of new information to the effect that spare places were available: *R v Secretary of State for Education, ex p Yusar Islam* (1992) Times 22 May. In the Brent school decision, the possibility of establishing a grant-maintained school was pointed out.

3 Cf. Cumper, in Harris and Joseph, op. cit. at p. 20, n. 1, p. 389, who suggests that the failure to accept any applications from Muslim schools raises a question of compliance with Article 26, ICCPR, which guarantees equality before the law. On an earlier unsuccessful Bradford application, see Cumper, (1990) Forum 60.

(i) such Christian and other religious denominations as, in the opinion of the authority, appropriately reflect the principal religious traditions in the area; (ii) such teachers' associations, as, in the opinion of the authority, ought to be represented, having regard to the circumstances of the area; (iii) the Church of England; and (iv) the authority (Education Act 1944, s. 29 and Sch. 5, as amended by the 1988 Act). 'Agreed syllabuses' adopted under the original 1944 Act (by a similarly constituted conference) were required not to be 'distinctive of any particular religious denomination'. As of 1989, any new syllabus must instead 'reflect the fact that the religious traditions in Great Britain are in the main Christian whilst taking account of the teaching and practices of the other principal religions represented in Great Britain'.[1] As amended, the 1944 Act, s. 26, refers to religious 'education', not 'instruction', in order to emphasise that the intention is to inform children about religion as a part of their social education rather than to indoctrinate them in the tenets of a particular religion. In recent years, the main problem in practice has not been the nature of the religious education provided but ensuring that schools comply with their legal obligation to provide religious education at all. An HMI report indicates that in at least 20% of primary schools inspected 'the teaching of RE was negligible' and that the 'vast majority of secondary schools did not provide enough time to teach the agreed syllabus'.[2] As to what is taught, the Christian emphasis in the new statutory criterion results from a concern felt by some members of the House of Lords that religious education in schools had ceased to reflect the country's essentially Christian character. The HMI report referred to indicates that religious education often does not comply with the agreed syllabus or the new criterion in the 1988 Act. Inspection revealed that there was very limited teaching of the world's non-Christian religions and that much 'RE teaching is confined to a rather dull exposition of basic Christian beliefs, with little attempt to examine Christianity as a major world faith' (p. 40).

3. *Collective worship.* In all maintained schools, there must be a daily act of worship (Education Reform Act 1988, s. 6). It need not, as previously under the Education Act 1944, be at the beginning of the school day or a single act of worship for all pupils. In voluntary schools, the act of worship may be denominational. In county schools, it must 'be wholly or mainly of a broadly Christian character' (1988 Act, s. 7(1)). It will be such if it 'reflects the broad traditions of Christian belief without being distinctive of any particular Christian denomination' (s. 7(2)). Not every act of worship must comply with this requirement; 'taking any school term as a whole, most such acts' must do so (s. 7(3)). Further allowance for the non-Christian character of a particular county school is made by the 'family background' provision in the 1988 Act, s. 7(5). Moreover, a county school may apply for exemption from the 'broadly Christian' requirement to the local Standing Advisory Council on Religious Education (SACRE) (a body composed of the same four representative groups as the religious education 'approved syllabus' conference: see previous note) (1988 Act, s. 12). Such exemption, which will normally be applied for by schools with a large non-Christian population, will allow the school to hold its own non-'broadly Christian' acts of worship for all or some of its pupils. Such acts of worship may be 'distinctive of any particular faith' (e.g. the Muslim faith), but not 'distinctive of any particular Christian or other religious denomination (s. 7(6)(b)) (e.g.

---

1 Education (Reform) Act 1988, s. 8(3). Provision is now made by the Education Act 1993, s. 256 requiring the reconsideration of pre-1988 Act agreed syllabuses in accordance with the new criteria. Before the 1993 Act, few had been revised.

2 *Religious Education and Collective Worship 1992–3*: Report of Her Majesty's Inspector of Schools, pp. 4–5.

Catholic or Sunni Muslim). Not unreasonably, HMI has 'assumed that "worship" required that there should be recognition of some supreme being and that "mainly Christian" meant that in the majority of occasions the material should be recognisably of a Christian character'. Compliance with the requirement is far from perfect. HMI has reported that 40% of the secondary schools inspected 'were identified as not complying with the legal requirements regarding collective worship and in the remainder there were difficulties and tensions'.[1] Commenting on the provisions for collective worship, Poulter (1990) 2 Education and the Law 1, 9 states:

. . . there would seem to be extremely persuasive arguments in favour of removing worship from school life altogether. . . . Collective *worship* is not primarily or essentially educational and is almost certainly an activity which is best organized by the faith concerned within the child's local community and subject to the continuing direction and supervision of parents.

4. *The right of withdrawal.* The parent of a child at a maintained school has the right to withdraw a child from its acts of collective worship or its religious education classes (Education Reform Act 1988, s. 9(3)). HMI report that 'very few parents exercised their right to withdraw children from RE'.[2] Parents may also withdraw their children from school 'on any day exclusively set apart for religious observance by the religious body to which his parents belong'.[3] The Department of Education and Science will not allow parents to withdraw their children in maintained schools from classes in secular subjects on grounds of religion or conscience.[4] This position was taken in connection with a request by Plymouth Brethren parents that they be allowed to withdraw their children from classes involving the use of computers or television.

5. In *Watson v Hertfordshire County Council* (1977), summarized in (1977) 150 Education 170, a teacher who was the head of religious studies in a comprehensive school in Hertfordshire was dismissed when he refused to give an undertaking to teach the story of the creation in Genesis as 'myths and legends' which did not conflict with evolutionary theories, as the 'agreed syllabus' required. He lost his claim for unfair dismissal before an industrial tribunal.

6. Mixed sex schools have presented problems for Muslim parents. In 1972, a Muslim parent in Blackburn was convicted of failing to cause his daughter to receive efficient full-time education when he kept her away from a co-educational secondary school because he 'believed that, having regard to the tone of present-day society, she would lose her virtue and become unmarriageable'.[5] The parent was fined £5. Similarly, when Peterborough amalgamated two single sex schools in 1973 in the course of local government reorganisation, the parents of Muslim children who were allocated to a co-educational secondary school appealed unsuccessfully to the Minister on the ground their religion forbade mixed schooling.[6] In the same year, a Muslim family in Bradford returned to Pakistan to avoid mixed schooling: *The Times*, 15 December 1973.

1 Op. cit. at p. 589, n. 2, above, p. 30. The position in primary schools was more satisfactory.
2 Ibid., p. 20. Most children withdrawn are Jehovah's Witnesses: *Religious Education, Assistant Masters Association Survey*, 1975.
3 S. 39(2), 1944 Act. E.g. Ascension Day (for members of the Church of England or Roman Catholics) or the Day of Atonement (for Jews). And see *Marshall v Graham* [1907] 2 KB 112, DC.
4 In its view, the European Convention on Human Rights, Article 2, First Protocol, does not require this: 158 HC Deb, 23 October 1989, written answers, col 321.
5 G. R. Barrell, *Teachers and the Law* (5th edn, 1978) p. 27, referring to a report in the *Daily Mail*, 3 November 1972.
6 The 'Islamic doctrine of purdah (seclusion) prescribes the separation of the sexes from puberty onwards': Cumper, loc. cit. at p. 588, n. 3, above, p. 389. See also G. Sarwar, *British Muslims and Schools* (rev. edn., 1994) p. 24.

7. A child's religion and his religious education are matters for the parents to decide until he reaches the age of discretion. The mother has an equal voice and responsibility with the father in the matter (Children Act 1989, s. 2). In the case of an illegitimate child, the parental responsibility for the matter is one just for the mother, unless there is agreement to the contrary or the father makes a successful court application (Children Act 1989, ss. 2, 4). If a dispute concerning the religious upbringing of a child should reach the courts, it must be decided in accordance with the welfare of the child (Children Act 1989, s. 1). On the granting of custody of children to parents belonging to minority sects such as the Jehovah's Witnesses, see F. Bates, (1981) 131 NLJ 1139.

8. *Parental choice of schools.* The duty in the Education Act 1980, s. 6(2), as amended to comply with parental choice in the allocation of school places does not prevent an oversubscribed voluntary aided school from operating an admissions policy that gives preference to children of a particular religion. In *Choudhury v Governors of Bishop Challoner Roman Catholic Comprehensive School* [1992] 3 All ER 277, HL, two girls, a Hindu and a Muslim, were not admitted to a single sex Catholic school because they did not meet the admissions criteria, which gave preference to Catholics and other Christians in that order. It was held that the admissions policy was lawful under s. 6(3)(a) by which parental preference need not be respected if it would 'prejudice the provision of efficient education'. This permitted a limit to be set on pupil numbers and it was reasonable when applying such a limit to take account of the religious character of the school. On the limited value of s. 76, 1944 Act (children 'to be educated in accordance with the wishes of their parents') as a means of ensuring compliance with the religious wishes of the parents, see *Watt v Kesteven County Council* [1955] 1 QB 408, CA, and *Cumings v Birkenhead Corpn* [1972] Ch 12, CA.

9. The Education Act provisions on religion in schools are in striking contrast with the law in the United States where the saying of prayers (*Engel v Vitale* 370 US 431 (1962)) and the reading of verses from the Bible (*Abingdon School District v Schempp* 374 US 203 (1963)) at the beginning of the school day in state (but not private) schools is an 'establishment of religion' contrary to the First Amendment. Religious instruction classes in state schools during school hours, whether given by state-employed teachers or by teachers provided by religious denominations and allowed a 'right of entry', are likewise unconstitutional (*McCollum v Board of Education* 333 US 203 (1948)).

(ii) Blasphemy and Blasphemous Libel

R v Chief Metropolitan Stipendiary Magistrate, ex parte Choudhury [1991] 1 All ER 306, [1990] 3 WLR 986, Queen's Bench Divisional Court

This case concerned the novel 'The Satanic Verses' written by Salman Rushdie and published by Viking Penguin, the first and second respondents. The Chief Magistrate refused the applicant a summons against the respondents alleging the common law offences of blasphemous libel and seditious libel. The applicant sought, by way of judicial review, an order of certiorari to quash the Chief Magistrate's decision and an order of mandamus directing him to issue the summons.

Watkins LJ (for the Divisional Court): 'The Satanic Verses' is a book, said to be a novel, published by Viking Penguin in 1988. In that year the book won the Whitbread Prize for Literature. It has been translated into 15 different languages.

The book has achieved considerable notoriety. It has been banned, so we were told by Mr Azhar, counsel for the applicant, in all Muslim countries, in South Africa, China and India. He said that there had been demonstrations abroad against the book in which people had died, notably in Bombay which is Mr Rushdie's place of birth, in Lahore and in Kashmir; that Muslims have demonstrated against the book in the United Kingdom—there are two million of that faith here—and that Muslims, otherwise of good character, have been arrested and convicted of offences against public order arising out of those demonstrations, in particular where the demonstrations by Muslims against the book have encountered groups demonstrating in favour of the book.

There can be little doubt that the contents of the book have deeply offended many law abiding Muslims who are United Kingdom citizens. . . .

The particulars [of the complaint against the book] can be summarised under six headings. First, God is described as 'The Destroyer of Man'. Secondly, the book vilifies the prophet Abraham, who is, as 'Ibrahim', a prophet revered by Muslims, by recounting the story of Abraham, Hagar and Ishmael, their son, and commenting adversely on Abraham's behaviour towards Hagar and Ishmael. Thirdly, the book refers to Muhammad as Mahound, which is a word having the meaning of a devil; that elsewhere in the book Muhammad is called 'a conjurer', a 'magician', and 'a false prophet'. Fourthly, the book grossly vilifies and profoundly insults the wives of Muhammad by calling some whores after their names. Muslims hold the prophet's wives in the highest esteem as mothers of the faithful. Fifthly, the book vilifies the close companions of Muhammad (calling them 'some sort of bums from Persia' and 'clowns') whereas the Koran recounts that they were men of high moral character and righteousness. Sixthly, the book vilifies and ridicules the teachings of Islam as containing too many rules and as seeking to control every aspect of day to day life. Moreover, insult is added to injury by the liberal use of an offensive four letter word.

Mr. Robertson [for the first respondent] pointed out that those passages form part of Gibreel's dreams and are, for the most part, words spoken by characters in the book who appear in Gibreel's dreams, some of whom have not been converted to Islam at the moment they make the utterances to which objection is taken.

That appears to be so but, in our opinion, a statement will not necessarily be prevented from being a blasphemous libel simply because the statement is put into the mouth of a character, even a disreputable character, in a novel.

. . . it appears . . . that this is the first case in which a would-be prosecutor has claimed that the offence of blasphemy is applicable to religions other than Christianity. . . .

Before the Restoration in 1660 the offence of blasphemy was dealt with in the ecclesiastical courts; it was akin to heresy, though punished less severely. The common law offence traces its origins from *Taylor's Case*[1] (1676) 1 Vent 293. . . .

For the next hundred years or so following *Taylor's Case*, the basis of prosecutions was that the defendant had aspersed the Christian religion. . . .

The most explicit statement of the law is to be found in Alderson B's direction to the jury in *Gathercole's Case*[2] (1838) 2 Lewin 237, 254, where he said:

'A person may, without being liable to prosecution for it, attack Judaism, or Mahomedanism, or even any sect of the Christian Religion (save the established religion of the country); and the only reason why the latter is in a different situation from the others is, because it is the form established by law, and is therefore a part of the constitution of the country. In like manner, and for the same reason, any general attack on Christianity is the subject of criminal prosecution, because Christianity is the established religion of the country.' . . .

By the middle of the 19th century the essential elements of the offence were beginning to change. This was no doubt as a result of the revolution in thought brought about by Darwin and others. It was no longer blasphemous to make a sober reasoned attack on the Christian religion; it had to be a scurrilous vilification of that religion. . . .

This change in the law was firmly established by 1883 . . . in *R v Ramsey and Foote*[3] (1883) 15 Cox CC 231. . . .

---

1 *Ed.* The accused, who was mentally disturbed, was convicted of blasphemy for 'uttering diverse blasphemous expressions, horrible to hear, (viz) that Jesus Christ was a bastard, a whoremaster, religion was a cheat'.

2 *Ed.* The accused was convicted of blasphemous libel for referring to certain Roman Catholic nunneries as 'houses of prostitution' and 'popish stews', inquiring 'how many popish priests enter the nunneries . . . each week . . . and how many infants are born in them . . . and whether the innocents are murdered'.

3 *Ed.* The accused published the *Freethinker*, a paper that promoted the views of some members of the secularist movement at the end of the 19th century. Walter states that 'the most objectionable material it published was a series of "Comic Bible Sketches" . . . which were crudely anti-religious and anti-semitic cartoons of appropriate biblical events – very effective, but also very offensive': Walter, *Blasphemy Ancient and Modern* (1990), p. 51. One such cartoon is printed on the back cover of Walter's book. In the reported case, the jury disagreed and the charge was dropped.

It is . . . clear from the speeches in *Bowman v Secular Society Ltd* [above, p. 585] that the House of Lords were dealing with the offence only in relation to the Christian religion. Lord Sumner after referring to Alderson B's dictum in *Gathercole's Case*, said, at pp. 459–460:

'it only shows that the gist of the offence of blasphemy is a supposed tendency in fact to shake the fabric of society generally. Its tendency to provoke an immediate breach of the peace is not the essential, but only an occasional, feature. After all, to insult a Jew's religion is not less likely to provoke a fight than to insult an Episcopalian's . . .'

Bowman v Secular Society Ltd was a civil action. Since that time there have been only two prosecutions for blasphemy. The first was *R v Gott*[1] (1922) 16 Cr App Rep 87. Avory J's direction to the jury included the following passage, at p. 89:

'What you have to ask yourselves in this case is whether these words which are published, these matters which are published in these two pamphlets are, in your opinion, indecent and offensive attacks on Christianity or the Scriptures or sacred persons or objects, calculated to outrage the feelings of the general body of the community and so lead possibly . . . to a breach of the peace.' . . .

The second was *R v Lemon* [1979] AC 617, the 'Gay News' case, the blasphemy in which related to a poem about Christ on the Cross. Mr. Azhar has referred us to a ruling by the trial judge, Judge King-Hamilton, in that case on a motion to quash the indictment on the ground that blasphemy was no longer an offence. In the course of that he said:

'In my judgment, therefore, the offence of blasphemous libel today occurs when there is published anything concerning God, Christ or the Christian religion in terms so scurrilous, abusive or offensive as to outrage the feelings of any member of or sympathiser with the Christian religion and would tend to lead to a breach of the peace. I would be prepared to extend the definition to cover similar attacks on some other religion, as we have now become a multi-religion state, but it is not necessary for me to go so far for the purpose of the present case.'

[This] . . . sentence, as the judge recognised, was obiter and was unnecessary for the decision in the case. Nevertheless, we must say that if it was intended to be a statement of the existing law it was, in our view, plainly wrong. . . . But this dictum, which was not repeated in the judge's summing up, received no support from the Court of Appeal [1979] 1 QB 10, nor the House of Lords [1979] AC 617. The only issue that arose on appeal related to the mens rea of the offence. As to that Lord Diplock said in his speech in the House of Lords, at p. 632:

'The only question in this appeal is whether in 1976 the mental element or mens rea in the common law offence of blasphemy is satisfied by proof only of an intention to publish material which in the opinion of the jury is likely to shock and arouse resentment among believing Christians or whether the prosecution must go further and prove that the accused in publishing the material in fact intended to produce that effect upon believers, or (what comes to the same thing in criminal law), although aware of the likelihood that such effect might be produced, did not care whether it was or not, so long as the publication achieved some other purpose that constituted his motive for publishing it.'

It was held, affirming the Court of Appeal, that an intention to publish the material was sufficient. Although counsel suggested to the House, at p. 620H, that the offence might no longer be restricted to Christianity, there is nothing in any of the speeches to support this. On the contrary the definitions of the offence in their Lordships' speeches refer only to the Christian religion . . . Lord Scarman[2] made it plain that, in his view, it extends only to the Christian religion and that any change in the law was a matter for Parliament. . . .

'My Lords, I do not subscribe to the view that the common law offence of blasphemous libel serves no useful purpose in the modern law. On the contrary, I think that there is a case for legislation extending it to protect the religious beliefs and feelings of non-Christians. The offence belongs to a group of criminal offences designed to safeguard the internal tranquillity of the kingdom. In an increasingly plural society such as that of modern Britain it is necessary not only to respect the differing religious beliefs, feelings and practices of all but also to protect them from scurrility, vilification, ridicule and contempt.

. . . My criticism of the common law offence of blasphemy is not that it exists but that it is not sufficiently comprehensive. It is shackled by the chains of history.

---

1 *Ed.* The accused had been found in a public place selling papers entitled 'The Rib Tickler' and 'The Liberator' containing pamphlets that described Jesus as entering Jerusalem 'like a circus clown on the back of two donkeys'. Upholding the accused's conviction for blasphemous libel and sentence to nine months' hard labour, Trevethin LCJ noted that the pamphlets contained other passages that were 'equally offensive to anyone in sympathy with the Christian religion'.

2 *Ed.* Lord Scarman has since changed his mind, now favouring abolition of the offence because of uncertainty about the meaning of religion and a preference for freedom of speech; the matter should be dealt via public order law: see S. J. D. Green, *Encounter*, June 1990, pp. 12, 15.

'While in my judgment it is not open to your Lordships' House, even under [the 1966 House of Lords Practice Statement] . . . to extend the law beyond the limits recognised by the House in *Bowman v Secular Society Ltd*, or to make by judicial decision the comprehensive reform of the law which I believe to be beneficial, this appeal does offer your Lordships the opportunity of stating the existing law in a form conducive to the social conditions of the late 20th century rather than to those of the 17th, the 18th, or even the 19th century. This is, my Lords, no mere opportunity: it is a duty.' . . .

In 1914 Sir John Simon, the Attorney-General, was asked to advise the Home Office on the current state of the law. In the course of his opinion he said:

'It seems certainly to be the fact that no offence is committed if the religious beliefs which are attacked are not those of the Church of England; this seems a gross anomaly.'

With that comment we entirely agree; but the anomaly arises from what Lord Scarman called 'the chains of history', the origins of the law in the ecclesiastical courts, and the fact that the Anglican religion is the established law of the country. Perhaps more important, and certainly more recent, are the views of the Law Commission set out in their Working Paper No. 79, Offences against Religion and Public Worship. They report, at p. 82, para. 6.9:

'Another shortcoming—or at any rate an anomaly—in the present law of blasphemy is the narrow scope of its protection. As we have seen, it is clear that that protection does not extend beyond the Christian religion, but it is less clear whether in the law of England and Wales it also protects the tenets of Christian denominations other than the established Church. Having regard to the authorities, it seems probable that at most other denominations are protected only to the extent that their fundamental beliefs are those which are held in common with the established Church.' . . .

We have no doubt that as the law now stands it does not extend to religions other than Christianity.

Can it in the light of the present conditions of society be extended by the courts to cover other religions? In our judgment where the law is clear it is not the proper function of this court to extend it; particularly is this so in criminal cases where offences cannot be retrospectively created. It is in that circumstance the function of Parliament alone to change the law. This was the view of Lord Scarman in the passage already quoted. . . .

. . . If the law is uncertain in interpreting and declaring the law the judges will do so in accordance with justice and to avoid anomaly or discrimination against certain classes of citizens; but taking that course is not open to us, even though we may think justice demands it, for the law is not, we think, uncertain. . . .

We think it right to say that, were it open to us to extend the law to cover religions other than Christianity, we should refrain from doing so. Considerations of public policy are extremely difficult and complex. It would be virtually impossible by judicial decision to set sufficiently clear limits to the offence, and other problems involved are formidable. These are considered at length in the Report of the Law Commission No. 145. We need only mention a few briefly.

Among other matters consideration would have to be given to the kinds of religions to be protected and to how religion is to be defined, see for an illustration of this problem *Church of the New Faith v Comr for Pay-Roll Tax* (1983) 57 ALJ 785 in which it was held that Scientology was a religion. Although an English jury may be expected, or certainly were in the last century, to understand the tenets of Christianity, this would not be so with other religions. There would be a need for expert evidence, no doubt for both prosecution and defence. If different sects of the same religion had differing views and the published material scandalised one sect and not another, how would the matter be decided? Since the only mental element in the offence is the intention to publish the words complained of, there would be a serious risk that the words might, unknown to the author, scandalise and outrage some sect or religion.

In any event, in the light of the majority opinion of the Law Commission in favour of abolition of the offence, it would, in our judgment, be wholly wrong to extend the law, even if, which we do not, we had the power to do so.

The resourceful Mr. Azhar [referred the Court to Articles 9, 10 and 14 ECHR]. . . . He maintained that the magistrate failed to consider and, therefore, take account of, the fact that we are a signatory to that Convention which, among many other things, guarantees freedom of religion to all citizens in equal terms. That being so, it is to be assumed, he said, that there must be a provision in our law to enforce such a freedom. If the law of blasphemy is designed to protect Christianity alone, it means, he went on, that other religions have been left unprotected ever since the Convention was signed in 1950. . . .

Mr. Lester [for the second respondent] responded impressively to Mr. Azhar's attempt to show that the absence of a domestic law of blasphemy relating to Islam would or might be in breach of the Convention.

He accepted that the obligations imposed on the United Kingdom by the Convention are relevant sources of public policy where the common law is uncertain. But, he maintained, the common law of blasphemy is, without doubt, certain. Accordingly, it is not necessary to pay any regard to the Convention. Nevertheless, he thought it necessary, and we agree, in the context of this case, to attempt to satisfy us that the United Kingdom is not in any event in breach of the Convention. Indeed, he went further and asserted that if this application were to succeed and result in successful prosecutions, the rights of Mr. Rushdie and of Viking Penguin, as protected by articles 7 and 10 of the Convention, would be violated. . . .

What the applicant seeks to do, Mr. Lester said, is to interfere with a well founded right to freedom of expression, a kind of interference never at any time foreshadowed by the common law of this country. Moreover, it would be an interference such as would contravene article 7 by creating ex post facto a criminal offence: see *Gay News Ltd v United Kingdom* (1982) 5 EHRR 123. Nothing in Mr. Azhar's argument could possibly bring either Mr. Rushdie or 'Gay News' within one of the exceptions in article 10(2). The test of necessity, if that could be said to be relevant, requires, he contended, the existence of a pressing social need for an interference with free speech for one of those purposes: see *Sunday Times v United Kingdom* (1979) 2 EHRR 245. Nothing in the book calls for additional protection of public order, or the freedom of everyone, Muslims included, to worship just as they please.

. . . freedom of religion [in Article 9, ECHR] is not absolute. It must tolerate certain restrictions including that, Mr. Lester submitted, of it not including the right to bring criminal proceedings for blasphemy where it cannot be shown that a domestic law has been offended against. There might be, Mr. Lester said, a breach of article 9 if criticism or agitation against a church or religious group reached such a level that the church or its members were prevented from manifesting their beliefs in the way set out in article 9. Nothing remotely like that had been demonstrated by the applicant.

If no law of blasphemy protects Muslims, Mr. Azhar maintained that they would be plainly discriminated against in that they would be denied the enjoyment of the rights and freedoms under the Convention. Mr. Lester dealt at length with that contention. Article 14, he said, read alongside article 9 clearly indicated that there was no such discrimination: see *Church of X v United Kingdom* (1968) 29 Collection of Decisions of the European Commission of Human Rights 70, and *Gay News Ltd v United Kingdom* 5 EHRR 123, 131, where the Commission decided that it is inadmissible to complain of discrimination in breach of article 14, read with article 9, on the ground that the law of blasphemy protects only the Christian but no other religion.

Mr. Lester [also submitted] that even if there is discrimination in the exercise of freedom of religion, it has an objective and reasonable justification and therefore involves no breach of article 14. The offence of blasphemous libel is an offence of strict liability. It is no defence that the defendant did not intend to blaspheme. As it stands, the offence is capable of resulting in unreasonable interferences with freedom of expression in breach of article 10. If the offence is extended to cover attacks upon religious doctrines, tenets, commandments, or practices of religions other than Christianity, the existence of such an extended law of blasphemy would encourage intolerance, divisiveness and unreasonable interference and interferences with freedom of expression. Fundamentalist Christians, Jews or Muslims could then seek to invoke the offence of blasphemy against each other's religion, doctrines, tenets, commandments, or practices; for example, for denying the divinity of Jesus Christ; or for denying that the Messiah has yet to come; or for denying the divine inspiration of the Prophet Mohammed, and so on. An extended law of blasphemy which applied to all religions could be used as a weapon between Protestants and Roman Catholics in Northern Ireland, or by fringe religions, such as the Church of Scientology. The fact that the offence was committed only in cases of scurrilous attacks would mitigate, but not eliminate, the resulting intolerance, divisiveness, and unreasonable interference with freedom of expression. To the extent that it has been submitted by the applicant that there is no relevant difference in Christianity, Judaism and Islam, it is clear that there are fundamental differences which would be capable of setting one religion against another under an extended law of blasphemy.

We agree that extending the law of blasphemy would pose insuperable problems and would be likely to do more harm than good. We cannot think that the makers of the Convention could have had in mind such an extension of the law in this country in giving expression to the right of freedom of religion as it has in the various articles we have referred to.

Mr. Lester has persuaded us convincingly that the Convention does not demand within any of those articles the creation of a law of blasphemy for the protection of Islam so that as signatory to the Convention the United Kingdom be in conformity with it. Thus, Mr. Azhar's attempt to invoke the assistance of the Convention is, in our judgment, unavailing.

[The Court then rejected the applicant's claim based upon seditious libel on the ground that the book did not disclose any intent to incite persons to violence against the state.]

Application dismissed

NOTES[1]

1. After lying dormant for half a century,[2] the offence of blasphemous libel has been the object of a reported case twice in recent years. The first case was in *Whitehouse v Lemon* [1979] AC 617, HL, from the speeches in which extracts are quoted in *Ex p Choudhury*. *R v Lemon* concerned the poem 'The Love that Dares to Speak its Name', by James Kirkup, an established poet and a Fellow of the Royal Society of Literature. The poem 'purports to describe in explicit detail acts of sodomy and fellatio with the body of Christ immediately after his death and to ascribe to Him during his lifetime promiscuous homosexual practices with the Apostles and with other men' (per Lord Diplock). Mrs Mary Whitehouse brought a private prosecution for blasphemous libel against the editor and publisher (Gay News plc) of *Gay News*, which had published the poem together with an illustration of the fantasy it contained.[3] Both defendants were convicted. The editor was given a suspended sentence of nine months' imprisonment that was quashed by the Court of Appeal. Fines of £1,000 and £500 on the editor and Gay News plc respectively and an order for prosecution costs were upheld. The House of Lords' ruling, when dismissing the appeal, that there was no need to prove a specific intent to shock believing Christians was by three to two, Lords Diplock and Edmund-Davies dissenting. It had been strongly argued by the defence that neither the author of the poem nor the defendants had intended to offend Christians; their intention was instead to put a homosexual point of view.

2. An application in the *Choudhury* case under Articles 9 and 14, ECHR was declared inadmissible as manifestly ill-founded because Article 9 could not be read as including a positive obligation upon states to protect religious sensibilities.[4] *Ex p Choudhury* raises a question that has become increasingly relevant as the United Kingdom has become a more multi-religious society. Is it defensible that in *R v Lemon* the publisher of a poem that offended Christians could be guilty of blasphemy when in *Ex p Choudhury* the publishers of a novel that contained passages that were at least equally offensive to Muslims could not? The Law Commission addressed this question in their 1985 Report, below, footnote 1, when recommending the abolition of the offences of blasphemy and blasphemous libel (the written form of blasphemy). The Report reads (footnote omitted):

2.4 [Law Commission] Working Paper 79 examined the rationales for retaining in the criminal law an offence penalising insults directed against religion. It distinguished four arguments—(i) the protection of religion and religious beliefs, (ii) the protection of society, (iii) the protection of individual feelings, and (iv) the protection of public order. Of these, the working paper concluded that (iii) was the most persuasive. Even so, it found that the arguments were quite evenly balanced and, in particular, that, while the

1 On blasphemy and blasphemous libel, see L. Blom-Cooper and G. Drewry, *Law and Morality* (1976), pp. 294–60; R. Buxton, [1978] Crim LR 673; P. Jones, (1980) 10 BJ Pol S 129; C. Kenny, (1922) CLJ 127; C. L. Ten, (1978) 5 BJ Law and Soc 89; Walter, *Blasphemy Ancient and Modern* (1990); R. Webster, *A Brief History of Blasphemy* (1990); *Law, Blasphemy and the Multi-Faith Society* (1990), Report of a CRE-Inter Faith Network Seminar, CRE Discussion Paper 1. See also *Criminal Law: Offences against Religion and Public Worship*, Law Commission Report No. 145 (1985). This was preceded by Law Commission Working Paper No. 79 (1981) (same title). On the Working Paper, see J. R. Spencer [1981] Crim LR 810; G. Robertson, [1981] PL 295; and St. J. Robilliard, (1981) 44 MLR 556. On the *Choudhury* case, see M. Tregilas-Davey, (1991) 54 MLR 294
2 Blasphemy was described as 'a dead letter' by Lord Denning in *Freedom under the Law* (1949), p. 46. Criminal proceedings were contemplated or attempted in certain cases in the early 1970s before the *Lemon* case; see the Law Commission Working Paper, footnote 1, above p. 18.
3 For a full account of the prosecution, see M. Tracy and D. Morrison, *Whitehouse* (1979), pp. 3–17.
4 *Choudhury v UK* No 17349/1990, 12 HRLJ 172 (1991). There may be a breach of the equality before the law guarantee in Article 26, ICCPR: see P. Cumper, D. Feldman, in D. Harris and S. Joseph, eds., *The International Covenant on Civil and Political Rights and the United Kingdom* (1995), Chaps. 11 and 12.

presence of a pressing social need might justify the imposition of penalties for incitement to racial hatred, there was no corresponding need in the context of religion which might justify an offence of blasphemy. 2.5 Accordingly, the working paper examined the form which a new offence might take in order to assess whether there were insuperable difficulties in specifying with precision its possible constituent elements, for 'where the case for a law is finely balanced, the inability to state clearly what the law requires can be allowed to weigh against it.' The paper came to the conclusion that, while an offence of wounding or outraging the feelings of adherents of any religious group could be envisaged, it seemed impossible to construct a sufficiently precise definition of what was meant by 'religion' in this context, and that other elements would also have an unacceptable degree of imprecision; this shortcoming, in the view expressed by the working paper, fatally flawed this possible offence. . . .

Two of the five members of the Commission (Gibson J, Chairman, and Mr B. Davenport) dissented. In their Note of Dissent, they stated:

We agree with the substance of the main criticisms of the existing common law offence of blasphemy and with the recommendation that it should be abolished. We attach particular importance to the defect in the existing offence that it affords protection to one religion only. Our view, however, is that in abolishing the common law offence of blasphemy the preferable course would be to enact a new offence which would be free of the defects of the present law. . . .

We agree that if there is no argument which may properly be regarded as sufficiently powerful to justify the derogation from freedom of expression which any offence of blasphemy must occasion, then no such offence should have a place in the criminal law. In our view, however, that argument is to be found in what we think should be seen as the duty on all citizens, in our society of different races and of people of different faiths and of no faith, not purposely to insult or outrage the religious feelings of others.

In the view of the two dissenting Law Commissioners, the drafting of a new, satisfactory offence, although difficult, could be achieved.

In 1994, a House of Lords amendment to a bill that would have abolished the offence of blasphemy was withdrawn in the face of Government opposition.[1] Do the difficulties of drafting a new offence extending to all religions support the Law Commission's conclusions that none should be enacted? Does the high value placed upon freedom of speech in western societies do likewise? Or should it be recognised that a person may value his or her religion so highly that verbal attacks may cause such offence to reasonable believers that the law should make blasphemous words a criminal offence and do so without regard to their tendency to cause a breach of the peace?[2] Would you agree with J. C. Smith's comments, [1979] Crim LR 311, 313, on Lord Scarman's speech in *R v Lemon*?

'Should the law protect all religions, however weird and potentially harmful to the community, from vilification, ridicule and contempt? It is submitted that vilification, ridicule and contempt may be decidedly in the public interest. Should it not be possible to attack in the strongest terms religious beliefs that adulterers should be stoned to death and that thieves should have the offending hand lopped off, however offensive that may be to the holders of the beliefs?'

Do these comments apply to the offence caused by *The Satanic Verses*?

An Archbishop of Canterbury's Working Group, chaired by the Bishop of London, agreed with the dissenting members of the Law Commission that the offence should be extended to other religions, although it is understood that, since the Salman Rushdie Affair, at least some members of the Working Group have changed their mind. The Government position is that, in the absence of any consensus, no change in the law is appropriate.

1 See the debate on Lord Lester's amendment and the Government response by Earl Ferrers, who noted a lack of consensus and foresaw practical difficulties: 555 HL Deb 16 June 1994, cols 1891–1909.
2 See A. Weale, in *Free Speech* (1990), Report of a CRE-Policy Studies Institute, CRE Discussion Paper 2, p. 49. Cf. the problem with incitement to racial hatred: below, p. 664. Arguing for an extension of the law of blasphemy to eliminate discrimination against muslims, see A. Bradney, 143 NLJ 434 (1993). See also the *Otto-Preminger* case, below, p. 839.

3. In its 1985 Report, the Law Commission identified other weaknesses in the present law of blasphemy, in addition to its application only to Christianity:[1]

2.18 The defects in the common law analysed in the working paper may be summarised as follows—

(i) The law is to an unacceptable degree uncertain. As we put it—

'Once the judge has directed the jury as to the ingredients of the offence, it is for the jury to say whether the matter is "scurrilous" or "abusive" or "insulting" in relation to the Christian religion and thereby has a tendency to induce a breach of the peace . . . It is hardly an exaggeration to say that whether or not a publication is a blasphemous libel can only be judged *ex post facto* . . . Delimitation of a criminal offence by reference to jury application of one or more of several adjectives (all of which necessitate subjective interpretation and none of which is absolute) is hardly satisfactory . . . While matter which is merely abusive is ignored in the law of defamatory libel, it becomes of the essence in blasphemous libel, provided that the jury finds it sufficiently scurrilous to amount to the offence.'

(ii) In so far as the law requires only an intention to publish the offending words and not an intention to blaspheme, the offence is to an undesirable extent one of strict liability. Furthermore, the absence of a mental element of an intent to blaspheme runs contrary to the general principle developed during the past century that a mental element is normally required as to all the elements of the prohibited conduct both in common law and statutory crimes, save in special cases of regulatory offences. The practical consequence of the exclusion of any requirement as to the intent of the defendant to blaspheme is that he cannot give admissible evidence as to what he claims to be his beliefs and purpose. It is thus quite possible for the offence to be committed by someone with profound religious beliefs and with entirely sincere motives, provided that the language in which he expresses himself is sufficiently shocking and insulting to be held blasphemous by a jury. . . .

We see no reason now to differ from the views expressed in the working paper.

Other aspects of the present law that the Commission criticised or noted were that there is no defence of 'public good' comparable to that under the Obscene Publications Act 1959, s. 4 (Working Paper, para. 3.8); that publication to just one other person may constitute an offence (ibid, para. 3.5); that there 'is no authority on the question whether statements made on television or in other broadcasts' are prohibited, although 'in principle' there 'seems to be no reason why statements or visual images' on television or radio should not be subject to the law (ibid); and that a prosecution may be brought by any member of the public without the consent of, for example, the DPP (as in *R v Lemon*) (ibid, para. 3.9). As to whether a tendency to a breach of the peace is a necessary element in the offence, the Law Commission stated (para. 6.2)

. . . if this element survives, it means in this context no more than that the publication must be such as 'to provoke or arouse angry feelings, something which is a possibility, not a probability'.[2] If blasphemy is to be regarded as an offence 'designed to safeguard the internal tranquility of the kingdom', which according to the most recent authority is still its primary function,[3] the exiguous or non-existent burden laid upon the prosecution to prove some possibility of disturbance to public order compares unfavourably with the position in other areas of the law. [For example, there are] the limits imposed by section 5 of the Public Order Act 1936, where a subjective intent to cause a breach of the peace or an objective likelihood of a breach of the peace is required.[4] If the requirements of section 5 were held to be satisfied by a requirement that the behaviour complained of might possibly, not probably, arouse angry feelings, we believe that its unacceptable character would be readily apparent and that it would be regarded as a gross infringement of freedom of expression.

1 As to whether the law protects only the established church or Christianity generally, the Law Commission stated in its Working Paper, para. 3.2, that it 'seems that the Christian religion in general is protected, together with the doctrines and rituals of the Church of England but not those of other religions or other Christian bodies'.
2 *R v Lemon*, per Judge King-Hamilton QC, transcript of summing-up, para 11a; . . .
3 See *Whitehouse v Lemon* [1979] AC 617 at pp. 658 and 662 per Lord Scarman.
4 *Ed.* see now s. 4, Public Order Act 1986, above, p. 191.

(iii) Other forms of assistance

Apart from the assistance given in schools, the law aids religion in many other ways. The Sunday Observance Act 1780, as amended, prohibits public entertainments and amusements on Sundays for which an admission charge (as opposed to a charge for a programme or car parking) is made. Its rigours have been reduced somewhat by the Sunday Entertainments Act 1932 (museums, picture galleries, zoological gardens, etc, may open) and, more recently, the Sunday Theatre Act 1972 and the Cinemas Act 1985, s. 9, as amended, which permit the opening of theatres and cinemas subject to certain limitations. In 1976, seven people were convicted under the Sunday Observance Act 1780. The Home Office consolidated circular to the police on crime states that it is assumed that the police will take the view that prosecutions under the Act can best be brought by private persons rather than the police: 952 HC Debs written answers 21 June 1978 col 204.

The Sunday Trading Act 1994 withdrew the assistance to religion that had been provided by the general prohibition on Sunday trading in the Shops Act 1950. Under the 1994 Act, large shops (defined in terms of floor area) are permitted to open for six hours on Sundays; small shops may open all day. Large shops occupied by persons of the Jewish religion are not subject to the six hours limit if they close on the Jewish Sabbath. Shopworkers may, for reasons of conscience or otherwise, decide not to work on Sundays and must not be disadvantaged for doing so.

The law allows religions to have single sex ministries: s. 19, Sex Discrimination Act 1975 excludes employment or the granting of authorisations or qualifications 'limited to one sex so as to comply with the doctrines of the religion or avoid offending the religious susceptibilities of a significant number of its followers' from the prohibition of sexual discrimination in the Act.

Account is taken of the increased diversity of religions in the United Kingdom by the Matrimonial Causes Act 1973, s. 47, by which Parliament changed the policy of the law so that matrimonial relief is now available to a party to a polygamous marriage celebrated abroad. This is, however, discrimination between religions in law in respect of the recognition of marriages celebrated in accordance with religious traditions in the United Kingdom.[1]

A Roman Catholic priest is probably not privileged in the law of evidence in respect of what is said to him in the confessional: Cross, *Evidence* (7th edn, 1990), p. 447. In the Irish case of *Schlegel v Corcoran and Gross* [1942] IR 19, H Ct Ireland, it was held that consent to the assignment of a lease was not 'unreasonably withheld' by a Roman Catholic widow who refused her consent to the assignment to a Jewish dentist of a tenancy of rooms used for a dental practice in the house which she owned and in which she lived. There is no comparable English case interpreting the same 'consent not to be reasonably withheld' provision in Landlord and Tenant Act 1927, s. 19(2). Cf. the Race Relations Act 1976, s. 24, below, p. 659. A person who is unable to vote at a parliamentary or local election 'by reason of religious observance' may vote by post (Representation of the People Act 1983, s. 19(1)(c)).

Some allowance for religious beliefs is made in the case of jury service. Although a 'serious conscientious objection arising out of a religious belief, on its own, would

---

1 See S. Poulter, loc. cit. at p. 578, n. 1, above, pp. 176–8. E.g. polygamous marriages celebrated in the UK are not recognised and no concession is made to the Muslim religion as to the place or formalities of the marriage. Likewise a Muslim divorce by talaq that occurs in the UK is not valid. On the claim to a separate Islamic system of personal law in the UK, see id., in Mallat C. and Connor, J, eds., *Islamic Family Law* (1990) p. 140.

be unlikely to amount to a "good reason" for being excused jury service', it may do so 'if the applicant's religious beliefs, for example, would be likely to prevent her from performing her duty in a proper way': *R v Crown Court at Guildford, ex p Siderfin* [1989] 3 All ER 7, 12, CA, per Watkins LJ (Plymouth Brethren member would not have been able to have talked the case over with her fellow jurors).

Arrangements exist to hear appeals by members of the regular Armed Forces whose claim for discharge on grounds of conscientious objection has been rejected by the Service authorities. Such appeals go to the Advisory Committee on Conscientious Objectors, an independent, non-statutory body established in 1970 (see 807 HC Deb 2 December 1970 col 423) whose members are appointed by the Lord Chancellor. The Committee, which hears argument in public, has advised acceptance of 8 out of 33 appeals. Its advice is normally followed. For a successful appeal by an army captain who objected to the British military presence in Northern Ireland, see *The Guardian*, 16 May 1979.

Although neither the BBC nor commercial broadcasting are legally obliged to broadcast religious programmes, there is a strong tradition that they should.

Places of worship are protected by the criminal law from 'riotous, violent or indecent behaviour'.[1] It is also an offence to use force to prevent a Minister from celebrating divine service (Offences against the Person Act 1861, s. 36).

On freedom of religion in prisons, see St. J. Robilliard, *Religion and the Law* (1984), pp. 132–7.

4 Religion and the criminal law

R v Senior [1899] 1 QB 283, Court for Crown Cases Reserved

The defendant was a member of a Christian religious sect called the 'Peculiar People'. Following its beliefs, he refused to allow his child, aged nine months, to be treated by a doctor. The child died and the defendant was convicted of manslaughter for having caused the death by an unlawful act—'wilful neglect' of a child in his custody contrary to the Prevention of Cruelty to Children Act 1894, s. 1. The defendant was the father of 12 children, of whom 7 had died. More than one would appear to have died because of the defendant's religious beliefs. The following extract concerns solely the question whether these beliefs could provide a defence to the charge.

Lord Russell of Killowen CJ: . . . Mr Sutton contended that because the prisoner was proved to be an affectionate parent, and was willing to do all things for the benefit of his child, except the one thing which was necessary in the present case, he ought not to be found guilty of the offence of manslaughter, on the ground that he abstained from providing medical aid for his child in consequence of his peculiar views in the matter; but we cannot shut our eyes to the danger which might arise if we were to accede to that argument, for where is the line to be drawn? In the present case the prisoner is shown to have had an objection to the use of medicine; but other cases might arise, such, for instance, as the case of a child with a broken thigh, where a surgical operation was necessary, which had to be performed with the aid of an anæsthetic; could the father refuse to allow the anæsthetic to be administered? Or take the case of a child that was in danger of suffocation, so that the operation of tracheotomy was necessary in order to save its life, and anæsthetic was required to be administered.

Conviction affirmed.

---

1 Ecclesiastical Courts Jurisdiction Act 1860, s. 2, interpreted recently in *Abrahams v Cavey*, [1968] 1 QB 479 and *R v Farrant* [1973] Crim LR 240.

NOTES

1. The 1894 Act offence is now found in s. 1, Children and Young Persons Act 1933. The father would not now be guilty of manslaughter by unlawful act, because his unlawful act was an omission: *R v Lowe* [1973] QB 702, CA. A genuine lack of understanding that the child requires medical care (which was not present on the facts in *R v Senior*) is a good defence to the 1933 Act offence: *R v Sheppard* [1981] AC 394, HL. A rastafarian couple, Beverley and Dwight Harris, whose religious belief caused them to refuse their diabetic daughter insulin were convicted of manslaughter by gross negligence. They believed insulin was produced from pigs and hence unclean: *Runnymede Bulletin* 271, p. 7 (1994).

2. Before the Suicide Act 1961 (which abolished the offence), a person who refused medical treatment for himself for religious or other reasons with the result that he died was guilty of suicide. A person who aids, abets, counsels or procures another to commit suicide is still guilty of the offence of complicity in suicide (Suicide Act 1961, s. 2). As a matter of criminal or civil law, a person may refuse medical treatment for religious or other reasons, provided that the refusal is not the result of the undue influence by another: *Re T* [1992] 4 All ER 649, CA (undue influence by Jehovah's Witness mother). The courts will, however, authorise medical treatment to a person despite that person's religious beliefs to save the life of another: *Re S* [1992] 4 All ER 671, Fam D ('Born-again' Christian's refusal to have caesarian birth overriden).

3. In *R v John* [1974] 1 WLR 624, CA, the Court of Appeal held that a motorist's religious beliefs cannot constitute a 'reasonable excuse' for his failure to provide a specimen of blood contrary to the Road Traffic Act 1972, s. 9(3). The appellant was a Mesmerist and believed that he was possessed of certain faith healing powers derived from the presence in his blood of certain divinely given gifts. The court followed *R v Lennard* [1973] 1 WLR 483, 487, CA in which it was held that 'no excuse can be adjudged a reasonable one unless the person from whom the specimen is required is physically or mentally unable to provide it or the provision of the specimen would entail a substantial risk to his health'. Similarly, in *Blake v DPP* 19 January 1993 QBDC, it was held that a genuinely held belief was not a 'lawful excuse' under the Criminal Damage Act 1971. So, a vicar who wrote words from the bible on a concrete pillar in protest at the use of force in the Iraq war was guilty of the offence of criminal damage.

4. In 1976, a Muslim Ugandan Asian was fined £20 by Burnham Magistrates for stopping illegally on the hard shoulder of the M4. He had been found there beside his car at sunset praying as his religion required (*Daily Telegraph*, 7 September 1976).

5. Religious belief is a statutory defence for Sikh motor-cyclists and Sikhs on construction sites. It is a principle of his religion that a Sikh wear a turban in public. The wearing of a crash helmet with or without a turban is a breach of this principle. After a series of cases (see e.g. *R v Aylesbury Crown Court, ex p Chahal* [1976] RTR 489, DC) in which Sikhs were convicted (one more than 30 times) of riding motor-cycles with turbans and without crash-helmets, the Motor-Cycle Crash-Helmets (Religious Exemption) Act 1976 provided an exemption for 'any follower of the Sikh religion while he is wearing a turban' (s. 1). The Employment Act 1989, s. 11 exempts a Sikh from any legal requirement to wear a safety helmet while on a construction site when he is wearing a turban.

Under the Criminal Justice Act 1988, s. 139(5), a person charged with the offence of having a knife in a public place has the defence that he has it for 'religious reasons', which might be the case of a Sikh carrying a kirpan.

6. The Abortion Act 1967, s. 4, provides:

'**4.**—(1) Subject to subsection (2) of this section, no person shall be under any duty, whether by contract or by statutory or other legal requirement, to participate in any treatment authorised by this Act to which he has a conscientious objection:

Provided that in any legal proceedings the burden of proof of conscientious objection shall rest on the person claiming to rely on it.

(2) Nothing in subsection (1) of this section shall affect any duty to participate in treatment which is necessary to save the life or to prevent grave permanent injury to the physical or mental health of a pregnant woman. . . .'

Section 4(1) offers a defence against criminal liability for a doctor, nurse, etc, who is unable to carry out an abortion for reasons of conscience. Cf. the Human Fertilisation and Embryology Act 1990, s. 38, which has a similarly worded conscience clause. A doctor's secretary who types a letter referring a patient to a consultant with a view to an abortion does not 'participate' in treatment for abortion for the purposes of s. 4: *Janaway v Salford Health Authority* [1989] AC 537, HL. In that case a receptionist and secretary was dismissed by the Authority for refusing to type such a letter on the ground that as a Roman Catholic she believed abortion to be morally wrong. She applied for judicial review of the Authority's decision on the ground that by virtue of the Abortion Act 1967, s. 4, her contract of employment did not require her to type correspondence concerning abortions, but was unsuccessful. The House of Commons Social Services Committee recommended that the s. 4 conscience clause be extended to some ancillary staff: 10th Report HC 123 (1989–90). It also recommended that the burden of proving a conscientious objection should not be on the person claiming it.

Cf. the limitation in s. 4(2) with the summing up by Macnaghten J in *R v Bourne* [1939] 1 KB 687:

'. . . there are people who, from what are said to be religious reasons, object to the operation being performed under any circumstances. That is not the law either. On the contrary, a person who holds such an opinion ought not to be an obstetrical surgeon, for if a case arose where the life of the woman could be saved by performing the operation and the doctor refused to perform it because of his religious opinions and the woman died, he would be in grave peril of being brought before this Court on a charge of manslaughter by negligence. He would have no better defence than a person who, again for some religious reason, refused to call in a doctor to attend his sick child, where a doctor could have been called in and the life of the child could have been saved.'

7. *R v Blaue* [1975] 1 WLR 1411, CA, concerned the religious beliefs of the victim. The question was whether a Jehovah's Witness who had been stabbed by the defendant and who refused a blood transfusion that would have saved her life had broken the chain of causation by her action so that the defendant was not guilty of manslaughter. The Court of Appeal held that she had not:

'It has long been the policy of the law that those who use violence on other people must take their victims as they find them. This in our judgment means the whole man, not just the physical man. It does not lie in the mouth of the assailant to say that his victim's religious beliefs which inhibited him from accepting certain kinds of treatment were unreasonable. The question for decision is what caused her death. The answer is the stab wound.'

8. See also the Slaughterhouses Act 1974, s. 36(3), and the Slaughter of Poultry Act 1967, s. 1(2), as amended, which exempt from the provisions of those Acts the slaughtering of animals and birds by the methods used by Jews and Muslims in the preparation of their food provided that unnecessary suffering is not inflicted.

9. 'The true Rastafarian is deeply religious . . . He believes it is as legitimate to smoke cannabis as to drink alcohol and less likely to lead to unruly behaviour; but . . . the true Rastafarian accepts the law of the land.' *Scarman Report on the*

Brixton Disorders 10–12 April 1981, Cmnd 8427, p. 44. Should the law make an exception for him?

10. Following the custom of the Yoruba tribe, Mrs Adesanya had small incisions cut into the cheeks of her two sons at puberty. This occurred at a family ceremony in England at which hymns were sung and there was 'just rejoicing in the name of the Lord'. Mrs Adesanya was convicted of assault, but given an absolute discharge: (1974) 124 NLJ 708.

11. In 1986, the Severn Trent River Authority informed Indian families who had approached the Authority for permission to scatter funeral ashes in a river that they could be prosecuted under Part II of the Control of Pollution Act 1974 for polluting controlled waters. Ashes could be scattered at selected tidal points on the Trent and the Severn with Ministry of Agriculture dispensation: *The Times*, 23rd September 1986, p. 9.

5 Religion and employment

Ahmad v Inner London Education Authority [1978] QB 36, [1977] 3 WLR 396, [1978] 1 All ER 574, Court of Appeal

The appellant, a devout Muslim, was employed as a full-time schoolteacher by the ILEA. From 1968 to 1974, he taught at a school that was too far away from a mosque for it to be necessary for him in accordance with his religion to attend one on Fridays for prayer. Upon being transferred by the ILEA to a school only 20 minutes away from a mosque, he went there for prayers on Fridays as his religion required. This meant that he missed 45 minutes of teaching time, during which his teaching had to be done by someone else. The school's work was to that extent disrupted and his colleagues objected. The ILEA informed the appellant that if he continued to go to the mosque, he would have to give up his full-time post for a part-time one at a lower salary. The appellant thereupon resigned and applied to an industrial tribunal for compensation and for reinstatement on the ground that the ILEA's conduct had forced him to resign and amounted to unfair dismissal contrary to the Trade Union and Labour Relations Act 1974. The tribunal held against him on the ground that the employer had not acted unreasonably so that the dismissal was not unfair. The Employment Appeal Tribunal rejected his appeal. The appellant appealed further to the Court of Appeal. He relied upon section 30 of the Education Act 1944, which reads:

'Subject as hereinafter provided, no person shall be disqualified by reason of his religious opinions, or of his attending or omitting to attend religious worship, from being a teacher in a county school or in any voluntary school, or from being otherwise employed for the purposes of such a school; and no teacher in any such school shall be required to give religious instruction or receive any less emolument or be deprived of, or disqualified for, any promotion or other advantage by reason of the fact that he does or does not give religious instruction or by reason of his religious opinions or of his attending or omitting to attend religious worship: Provided that, save in so far as they require that a teacher shall not receive any less emolument or be deprived of, or disqualified for, any promotion or other advantage by reason of the fact that he gives religious instruction or by reason of his religious opinions or of his attending religious worship, the provisions of this section shall not apply with respect to a teacher in an aided school or with respect to a reserved teacher in any controlled school or special agreement school.'

Lord Denning MR: . . . On the appeal, Mr Ahmad relied much on section 30 of the Education Act 1944. . . . If the words were read literally without qualification, they would entitle Mr Ahmad to take time off every Friday afternoon for his prayers without loss of pay. I cannot think this was ever intended. The school time-table was well known to Mr Ahmad when he applied for the teaching post. It was for the usual teaching hours from Monday to Friday, inclusive. If he wished to have every Friday afternoon off for his prayers, *either* he ought not to have applied for this post: *or* he ought to have made it clear at the outset and entered into a 4½-day engagement only. . . .

I think that section 30 can be applied to the situation perfectly well by reading it as subject to the qualification 'if the school time-table so permits.' . . . It has been so interpreted by the great majority of Muslim teachers in our schools. They do not take time off for their prayers. . . . The industrial tribunal said: '. . . none of the other education authorities has ever received such a request from Muslim staff and the problem would seem to be unique to the applicant, Mr Ahmad.' . . .

During the argument Scarman LJ drew attention to article 9 of the European Convention on Human Rights. . . .

The convention is not part of our English law, but . . . we will always have regard to it. We will do our best to see that our decisions are in conformity with it. But it is drawn in such vague terms that it can be used for all sorts of unreasonable claims and provoke all sorts of litigation. As so often happens with high-sounding principles, they have to be brought down to earth. They have to be applied in a work-a-day world. I venture to suggest that it would do the Muslim community no good—or any other minority group no good—if they were to be given preferential treatment over the great majority of people. If it should happen that, in the name of religious freedom, they were given special privileges or advantages, it would provoke discontent, and even resentment among those with whom they work. As, indeed, it has done in this very case. And so the cause of racial integration would suffer. So, whilst upholding religious freedom to the full, I would suggest that it should be applied with caution, especially having regard to the setting in which it is sought. Applied to our educational system, I think that Mr Ahmad's right to 'manifest his religion in practice and observance' must be subject to the rights of the education authorities under the contract and to the interests of the children whom he is paid to teach. I see nothing in the European Convention to give Mr Ahmad any right to manifest his religion on Friday afternoons in derogation of his contract of employment: and certainly not on full pay. . . .

I would dismiss the appeal.

Scarman LJ: The true construction of s. 30 is at the heart of this case . . . The reasons for its 30 years of immunity from judicial interpretation are not hard to see. First, and foremost, local education authorities, like the ILEA in this case, have treated it as no more than of negative intent—forbidding discrimination on the ground of religion in the selection and employment of teachers, but not obliging them to ensure that religious minorities are represented amongst their teachers. The ILEA, we have been told, have sought to comply with the section by not asking questions, the theory being that, if you do not know a man's religion, you cannot discriminate against him on that ground. Secondly, there were until recently no substantial religious groupings in our country which fell outside the broad categories of Christian and Jew. So long as there was no discrimination between them, no problem was likely to arise. The five-day school week, of course, takes care of the Sabbath and of Sunday as days of special religious observance. But with the advent of new religious groups in our society section 30 assumes a new importance. . . .

When the section was enacted, the negative approach to its interpretation was, no doubt, sufficient. But society has changed since 1944; so also has the legal background. Religions, such as Islam and Buddhism, have substantial followings among our people. Room has to be found for teachers and pupils of the new religions in the educational system, if discrimination is to be avoided. This calls not for a policy of the blind eye but for one of understanding. The system must be made sufficiently flexible to accommodate their beliefs and their observances: otherwise, they will suffer discrimination—a consequence contrary to the spirit of section 30, whatever the letter of that law. The change in legal background is no less momentous. Since 1944 the United Kingdom has accepted international obligations designed to protect human rights and freedoms, and has enacted a series of statutes designed for the same purpose in certain critical areas of our society. These major statutes include the Trade Union and Labour Relations Act 1974, the Employment Protection Act 1975, the Sex Discrimination Act 1975, and the race relations legislation.

They were enacted after the United Kingdom had ratified the European Convention on Human Rights . . . and in the light of our obligations under the Charter of the United Nations. Today, therefore, we have to construe and apply section 30 not against the background of the law and society of 1944 but in a multi-racial society which has accepted international obligations and enacted statutes designed to eliminate discrimination on grounds of race, religion, colour or sex. Further, it is no longer possible to argue that because the international treaty obligations of the United Kingdom do not become law unless enacted by Parliament our courts pay no regard to our international obligations. They pay very serious regard to them: in particular, they will interpret statutory language and apply common law principles wherever possible, so as to reach a conclusion consistent with our international obligations. . . .

With these general considerations in mind, I conclude that the present case, properly considered, begins but does not end with the law of contract. It ends with a very difficult problem—the application to the particular circumstances of this appellant of the new law associated with the protection of the individual's human rights and fundamental freedoms. . . .

The ILEA submits that because of its context, coming as it does as a final saving for the position of teachers at the end of a set of sections dealing with religious education in schools, the section is to be read as limited to attending or omitting to attend worship in school. . . .

Although I see the force of the submission, I reject it; because fundamentally a narrow construction of the section is in conflict with the developments in our society to which I have already referred—developments which are protected by statutes to which I have also referred. A narrow construction of the section would mean that a Muslim, who took his religious duty seriously, could never accept employment as a full-time teacher, but must be content with the lesser emoluments of part-time service. In modern British society, with its elaborate statutory protection of the individual from discrimination arising from race, colour, religion or sex, and against the background of the European Convention, this is unacceptable, inconsistent with the policy of modern statute law, and almost certainly a breach of our international obligations. Unless, therefore, the language of section 30 forces one to adopt the narrow construction, I would think it wrong to do so. But it does not: the section, linguistically speaking, can be construed broadly or narrowly. No doubt, Parliament in 1944 never addressed its mind to the problem of this case. But, if the section lends itself, as successful human rights or constitutional legislation must lend itself, to judicial interpretation in accordance with the spirit of the age, there is nothing in this point, save for the comment that Parliament by refusing to be too specific was wiser than some of us have subsequently realised. The choice of construction, while it must be exercised judicially, is ours: for the reasons which I have attempted to formulate, the decision must be in favour of the broad construction.

Construed broadly and as part of the teacher's contract for full-time service, the section means that the teacher is not to receive less emoluments by reason only that during school hours he attends religious worship. It is immaterial whether he does so in the school or elsewhere; but the right to go to church, chapel, temple or mosque whether it be inside or outside the school, which the section confers on the teacher, has to be read into his full-time contract. In the context of such a contract the right is to be exercised in such a way as not to conflict with the duty of full-time service. . . .

Nor do I think there is any substance in the point that a broad construction of section 30 imposes an unfair burden upon the teacher's colleagues. . . . If, however, my view of section 30 is correct, all that is necessary is that the authority should make its administrative arrangements on the basis of that view. It may mean employing a few more teachers either part-time or full-time, but, when the cost is compared with the heavy expenditure already committed to the cause of non-discrimination in our society, expense would not in this context appear to be a sound reason for requiring a narrow meaning to be given to the words of the statute. The question, therefore, as to whether Mr Ahmad broke his contract ultimately depends upon an examination of the particular circumstances of his case. . . . I therefore would allow the appeal . . .

Orr LJ delivered a judgment concurring with **Lord Denning MR**.
Appeal dismissed.

NOTES

1. The appellant also lost his claim under the ECHR: *Ahmad v United Kingdom* (1982) 4 EHRR 126. The European Commission dismissed the case at the admissibility stage: in relying upon the applicant's contract of employment, the ILEA had not arbitrarily disregarded the applicant's freedom of religion as protected by Article 9, ECHR.

2. In *Esson v United Transport Executive* [1975] IRLR 48, Int. Trib., a bus conductor refused to work on Saturdays after he had become a Seventh Day Adventist. His dismissal was held not to be unfair because he was in breach of contract and because his failure to take his share of Saturday work placed an unreasonable burden upon his fellow employees. Cf. *Storey v Allied Breweries* (1976) 84 IRLIB 9, Int. Trib., in which it was held that it was not unfair to dismiss a chambermaid who refused to do new Sunday rota work in order to take the elderly to church on Sunday mornings, since her refusal imposed a burden on other chambermaids and she could attend Sunday evening services.

3. British government contracts (unlike Federal government contracts in the United States) do not require that the firm awarded the contract not follow an employment policy that discriminates on religious grounds. See C. Turpin, *Government Contracts* (1972) pp. 257–8.

4. In *Yassin v Northwest Homecare Ltd* CRE Rep 1993, p. 21, Ind Trib, the applicant, a Muslim, was dropped from a sales representative training course after requesting an hour off to attend Friday prayers at the Mosque. The Tribunal awarded him £3,000 compensation for injury to feelings and loss of potential earnings for discrimination contrary to the Race Relations Act 1976. The Tribunal stated:

'The requirement not to attend the Mosque . . . seems to us to be wholly unreasonable. In a working day of 12 or 13 hours there had to be breaks of refreshment and rest. The working day was not strictly defined. One hour a week to visit the Mosque (and the hour included travelling time) could easily be accommodated, even when a high commitment to the job was required.'

Can this case be distinguished from the Ahmad case? For other employment cases concerning muslims and sikhs that have been considered as indirect racial discrimination under the Race Relations Act, see below, pp. 632–3.

6 Religious holy days

Case 130/75, Prais v EC Council [1976] ECR 1589, [1976] 2 CMLR 708, European Court of Justice

The plaintiff, a British national, applied for a job in the European Communities as a translator. By a letter of 23 April 1975 she was told that the written examination would be on 16 May 1975. By a letter of 25 April 1975, the plaintiff informed the Council that she was unable to attend on 16 May because she was Jewish and that day was a Jewish holy day. The application form had no place for an applicant's religion and the plaintiff had not otherwise informed the Council of her religion. By a letter of 5 May, the Council replied that the plaintiff could not be given an alternative date for the examination for security and administrative reasons. In her application to the European Court of Justice, the plaintiff sought the annulment of the decisions taken against her and damages.

JUDGMENT OF THE COURT

The plaintiff claims that Article 27 of the Staff Regulations ['Officials shall be selected without reference to race, creed or sex'] is to be interpreted in such a manner that the defendant should so arrange the dates of tests for competitions to enter its service as to enable every candidate to take part in these tests, whatever his religious circumstances. Alternatively the right of freedom of religion guaranteed by the European Convention [Article 9, below, p. 742] so requires. . . .
The defendant does not . . . seek to suggest that the right of freedom of religion as embodied in the European Convention does not form part of the fundamental rights recognized in Community law, but says that neither the Staff Regulations nor the European Convention are to be understood as according to the plaintiff the rights she claims.
The defendant submits that such an obligation would force it to set up an elaborate administrative machinery. Article 27 does not limit its application to any particular creeds by enumerating them, and it would be necessary to ascertain the details of all religions practised in any Member State in order to avoid fixing for a test a date or time which might offend against the tenets of any such religion and make it impossible for a candidate of that religious persuasion to take part in the test. . . .
When the competition [for posts] is on the basis of tests, the principle of equality necessitates that the tests shall be on the same conditions for all candidates, and in the case of written tests the practical difficulties of comparison require that the written tests for all candidates should be the same.
It is therefore of great importance that the date of the written tests should be the same for all candidates.
The interests of participants not to have a date fixed for the test which is unsuitable must be balanced against this necessity.
If a candidate informs the appointing authority that religious reasons make certain dates impossible for him the appointing authority should take this into account in fixing the date for written tests, and endeavour to avoid such dates.

On the other hand if the candidate does not inform the appointing authority in good time of his difficulties, the appointing authority would be justified in refusing to afford an alternative date, particularly if there are other candidates who have been convoked for the test.

If it is desirable that an appointing authority informs itself in a general way of dates which might be unsuitable for religious reasons, and seeks to avoid fixing such dates for tests, nevertheless, for the reasons indicated above, neither the Staff Regulations nor the fundamental rights already referred to can be considered as imposing on the appointing authority a duty to avoid a conflict with a religious requirement of which the authority has not been informed.

In so far as the defendant, if informed of the difficulty in good time, would have been obliged to take reasonable steps to avoid fixing for a test a date which would make it impossible for a person of a particular religious persuasion to undergo the test, it can be said that the defendant in the present case was not informed of the unsuitability of certain days until the date for the test had been fixed, and the defendant was in its discretion entitled to refuse to fix a different date when the other candidates had already been convoked.

Application dismissed.

NOTE

In his opinion in the case, the Advocate General (Mr J-P Warner) summarised British practice in regard to examinations:

'It seems to be the invariable practice of professional and academic bodies in the United Kingdom to make, when requested, alternative arrangements for observant Jewish candidates whose examinations fall on Jewish holy days. . . . The letter from the Civil Service Commission shows that its practice is quite different. Under the heading of "Criteria observed when setting examination dates" it states:

"Known factors which could affect particular groups of candidates would be taken into account as far as is possible when constructing the programme. For example, the Board of Directors of British Jews have for many years provided the Commission with a list of dates on which Jewish Holy days are given . . . [However]

(i) The Commission expects all candidates to make arrangements to attend the examination on the date(s) set.

(ii) An examination is not deferred, or the date altered, to suit the needs of individual candidates.

(iii) Special separate sittings are not arranged for individuals who cannot attend on the examination dates.'

Ostreicher v Secretary of State for the Environment [1978] 3 All ER 82, [1978] 1 WLR 810, Court of Appeal

The applicant, a devout Jewess, lodged an objection through her surveyor, Mr L, to a compulsory purchase order made by the second respondent, a local authority, which applied to houses which she owned. By a letter of 5 February 1976, Mr L was informed that the inquiry would be held on 21 April 1976. This was one of 11 annual Jewish festival days on which the applicant was forbidden to work or to employ anyone to work for her. On 1 April 1976, Mr L wrote to the first respondent stating that the applicant was unable to attend the hearing for religious reasons. He did not mention the question of representation. In the letter, Mr L indicated the reasons for the applicant's objection to the order and asked for a special hearing at which they could be put orally in respect of one of the houses.

On 7 April, the first respondent rejected this request and suggested that the applicant could be represented at the inquiry. The inquiry was held on the scheduled day and the order confirmed. By notice of motion, the applicant applied under the Housing Act 1957, Schedule 4, para. 2, for the order to be quashed for non-compliance with the rules of natural justice in not giving her an opportunity of being heard by the inspector who held the inquiry. The applicant appealed to the Court of Appeal against an order dismissing her application.

Lord Denning MR: It is one of the elementary principles of natural justice, no matter whether it is in a judicial proceeding or an administrative inquiry, that everything should be done fairly: and that any party or objector should be given a fair opportunity of being heard. . . . Sometimes a refusal of an adjournment is unfair, but quite often it is fair. It depends on the circumstances of each particular case. . . . There is a distinction between an administrative inquiry and judicial proceedings before a court. An administrative inquiry has to be arranged long beforehand. There are many objectors to consider as well as the proponents of the plan. It is a serious matter to put all the arrangements aside on the application of one objector out of many. The proper way to deal with it, if called on to do so, is to continue with the inquiry and hear all the representatives present; and then, if one objector is unavoidably absent, to hear his objections on a later day when he can be there. There is ample power in the rules for the inspector to allow adjournments as and when reasonably required.

. . . it seems to me that the men at the department acted perfectly reasonably in what they did. First, they acted reasonably in arranging the date of 21st April, the Wednesday after Easter Monday. . . . I cannot think that even in Hackney [with its high Jewish population] it would be wrong for the Secretary of State to give that date as a suitable date for the inquiry. Indeed, no objection was ever taken to it by anyone until two or three months later when this letter of 1st April 1976 was written on behalf of Mr and Mrs Ostreicher. In that letter the surveyors do not say that they could not attend themselves or that anyone else could not attend on behalf of Mr and Mrs Ostreicher to look after their interests. Moreover that letter only refers to one house, no 16. . . . The Secretary of State's representative wrote back quite reasonably. He said: 'Should your clients deem it necessary they are open of course to arrange to be represented at the inquiry in their absence.' . . . There was no reply to that letter. If Mr and Mrs Ostreicher or their representative thought that there ought to be a postponement or an adjournment, so far as their houses were concerned, they could have written back and said so. . . .

Second, the inspector acted reasonably in going on with the inquiry as he did. No representative turned up on behalf of Mr and Mrs Ostreicher. It seems to me that the inspector could well have understood from what had happened that they were content to leave the position as it was on the papers. . . . I see no want of natural justice whatever in what the inspector did either at the inquiry and later on in making his report.

. . . I would dismiss the appeal accordingly.

Shaw LJ concurred. **Waller LJ** delivered a concurring judgment.

Appeal dismissed.

NOTES

1. At first instance, Sir Douglas Frank QC, sitting as a deputy High Court judge, had rejected an argument based upon the freedom of religion guarantee in Article 9, ECHR on the ground that it was 'of little assistance because it does not apply and moreover it is in vague terms' [1978] 1 All ER 591. He also referred to the dictum in *Prais v EC Council*, above, that the administration must be given notice in good time of an objection to a proposed date.

2. In *Mohammed Azam v Walker Ltd* (1993) Ind Trib, CRE 1993 Annual Report, p. 20, Muslim employees of ten years' standing who had always been allowed to take off Eid, a religious holiday, as a part of their annual holiday or as unpaid leave were no longer allowed to do so following a change in the firm's holiday arrangements that affected all workers. This was held to be indirect discrimination contrary to the Race Relations Act 1976.

7 Religion and the law of trusts and succession

Re Lysaght [1966] Ch 191, [1965] 3 WLR 391, [1965] 2 All ER 888, Buckley J

By her will, the testatrix established a trust for scholarships tenable at the Royal College of Surgeons. To qualify, a student had to be 'of the male sex and a British born subject and not of the Jewish or Roman Catholic faith'. Buckley J rejected the

College's submission that the religious discrimination clause was void for uncertainty. He then considered in the following extract a submission by another beneficiary under the will that the trust as a whole was contrary to public policy.

Buckley J: . . . I accept that racial and religious discrimination is nowadays widely regarded as deplorable in many respects and I am aware that there is a Bill dealing with racial relations at present under consideration by Parliament, but I think that it is going much too far to say that the endowment of a charity, the beneficiaries of which are to be drawn from a particular faith or are to exclude adherents to a particular faith, is contrary to public policy. The testatrix's desire to exclude persons of the Jewish faith or of the Roman Catholic faith from those eligible for the studentship in the present case appears to me to be unamiable, and I would accept Mr Clauson's suggestion that it is undesirable, but it is not, I think, contrary to public policy. . . .

[Buckley J then, after holding that it was an essential part of the testatrix's intention that the College should be a trustee and noting that the College felt itself unable to be such if it discriminated on religious grounds, ordered by way of scheme that the trust should be administered by the College with the offending words omitted.]

Declaration accordingly.

Blathwayt v Baron Cawley [1976] AC 397, [1975] 3 WLR 684, [1975] 3 All ER 625, House of Lords

One question in this case was whether a forfeiture clause in a trust established by the will by which a beneficiary forfeited his interest if he 'be or become a Roman Catholic' was invalid for reasons of public policy. The following extract concerns this question only.

Lord Wilberforce: . . . Finally, as to public policy . . . it was said that the law of England was now set against discrimination on a number of grounds including religious grounds, and appeal was made to the Race Relations Act 1968 which does not refer to religion and to the European Convention on Human Rights of 1950 which refers to freedom of religion and to enjoyment of that freedom and other freedoms without discrimination on the ground of religion. My Lords, I do not doubt that conceptions of public policy should move with the times and that widely accepted treaties and statutes may point the direction in which such conceptions, as applied by the courts, ought to move. It may well be that conditions such as this are, or at least are becoming inconsistent with standards now widely accepted. But acceptance of this does not persuade me that we are justified, particularly in relation to a will which came into effect as long ago as 1936 and which has twice been the subject of judicial consideration, in introducing for the first time a rule of law which would go far beyond the mere avoidance of discrimination on religious grounds. To do so would bring about a substantial reduction of another freedom, firmly rooted in our law, namely that of testamentary disposition. Discrimination is not the same thing as choice; it operates over a larger and less personal area, and neither by express provision nor by implication has private selection yet become a matter of public policy.

Lord Cross of Chelsea: . . . Turning to the question of public policy, it is true that it is widely thought nowadays that it is wrong for government to treat some of its citizens less favourably than others because of differences in their religious beliefs; but it does not follow from that that it is against public policy for an adherent of one religion to distinguish in disposing of his property between adherents of his faith and those of another. So to hold would amount to saying that though it is in order for a man to have a mild preference for one religion as opposed to another it is disreputable for him to be convinced of the importance of holding true religious beliefs and the fact that his religious beliefs are the true ones. **Lord Simon, Lord Edmund-Davies** and **Lord Fraser** delivered speeches to the same effect.

NOTES

1. On *Re Lysaght*, see (1965) 29 Conv 407; (1966) 82 LQR 10.
2. Contrast the refusal of the courts in these cases to find private religious discrimination contrary to public policy with the Race Relations Act 1976 which prohibits

private racial discrimination on grounds of colour in charitable trusts. See below, p. 664.

3. Trusts for the advancement of religion are valid whatever the religion benefited.[1] They are also charitable. See *Re South Place Ethical Society*, above p. 579. This is probably true of all religions, although the cases are as yet limited to Christianity and the Jewish religion. To be charitable a trust must be for the public benefit: *Re Hetherington* [1990] Ch 1, Ch D (a trust for the saying of masses which would in practice be said in public a valid charitable trust). A trust for a Roman Catholic order of strictly cloistered and contemplative nuns is therefore not charitable: *Gilmour v Coats* [1949] AC 426, HL. See *Tudor on Charities* (7th edn, 1984) pp. 43–82. As to the charitable status of the Exclusive Brethren and the Unification Church, see above, p. 581.

4. In *Re Remnant's Settlement Trusts, Hooper v Wenhaston* [1970] Ch 560, Ch D, clauses in a will by which grandchildren would forfeit their interests under it if they became Roman Catholics were deleted under the Variation of Trusts Act 1958. The clauses were regarded as undesirable in the particular circumstances of the family and their deletion was to the advantage of all possible beneficiaries. In *Re Tepper's Will Trusts* [1987] Ch 358, Ch D grandchildren received gifts under a will 'provided that they shall remain within the Jewish faith and shall not marry outside the Jewish faith'. Responding to an argument that the proviso contained a condition subsequent that was void for uncertainty, Scott J adjourned the summons to allow evidence to be adduced as to the religion practised by the testator which might make it possible to conclude with sufficient certainty what the expression 'the Jewish faith' meant. This approach was used to avoid *Clayton v Ramsden*, below, p. 664, where a majority of the House of Lords considered that the phrase 'of the Jewish faith' was uncertain so that a similar condition subsequent was void for uncertainty. In neither case would it appear to have been argued that the limitation was contrary to public policy as being restrictive of freedom of religion.

8 Religion and immigration

Home Office Policy on Religion and Immigration 424 HC Deb 5 July 1946 cols 2580–2

Mr Ede (Home Secretary)
I am not prepared to apply religious or political tests to people who desire to come into this country unless it can be established that they desire to come here to carry on subversive propaganda as defined by the Acts concerned with seditious practices. . . .

I desire that the ancient record of this country as a place of free speech, where the flow of ideas from all parts of the world is welcome, may be maintained; and while I will not guarantee that some of the people I admit may not be charlatans, may not . . . even be false prophets on occasion, I desire to impose no censorship other than that which the law entitles me to impose against subversive propaganda on any person who desires to come to this country to meet people of his own persuasion. I am confident of this, that as far as this particular movement is concerned, there are some people in this country who gain spiritual sustenance from it. . . . Therefore I desire to live and let live in this particular matter.

NOTES

1. The 'particular movement' to which the Home Secretary referred was Moral Re-Armament, or the Oxford Group Movement, founded by Dr Buchman, an

---

1 See *Bowman v Secular Society*, above, p. 585, and *Bourne v Keane*, above, p. 586.

American evangelist. The statement was made following criticism in Parliament of Mr Ede's decision to admit into the UK a number of aliens who were members of the Movement and who intended to further its cause here. The persons admitted had committed no crime under UK law. The criticism was based mainly on the fact that certain leading members of the Group had been Nazi sympathisers.

2. It would seem that the 1946 statement still represents Home Office policy. In 1976, the Home Office was not prepared to exclude American members of the Children of God when police inquiries had produced no evidence of criminal activities in the UK (apart from minor street collection, etc, offences). Allegations that young people over 18 had been estranged from their families did not raise any issue of criminal law: Home Office Minister (Dr S. Summerskill) 905 HC Deb 11 February 1976 cols 584–8. The Home Secretary's discretionary power to exclude aliens and other non-'patrials' from the UK is based upon Immigration Act 1971, s. 3 and is exercised in accordance with Immigration Rules made by him under that section. The Rules provide for the admission of ministers of religion, missionaries and members of religious orders coming to work as such, including those engaged in teaching, see below, p. 700. On scientology, see below. On the special position under the Treaty of Rome of EU citizens who wish to enter the UK for employment, see *Van Duyn v Home Office*, below, n. 3. In 1976, when rumour had it that a Danish film maker, Jens Thorsen, was planning to enter the UK to make a film portraying the sexual life of Christ, the Under Secretary of State for the Home Department pointed out that were Thorsen, a Common Market national, actually to seek entry into the UK the question would arise whether he could be excluded under the Treaty of Rome on grounds of 'public policy' (918 HC Deb 26 October 1976 cols 239–248).

3. In 1968, the Minister of Health (Mr Robinson) announced (769 HC Deb, 25 July 1968, written answers, col 189) that the government had decided that scientology was 'socially harmful' (although not illegal) and that foreign nationals seeking entry to work or study at scientology establishments in the UK would be refused admission. The Minister described scientology as 'a pseudo-philosophical cult'; he did not refer to it as a religion. It was described by Sir John Foster in his government-sponsored *Enquiry into the Practice and Effects of Scientology*, 1971–72 HC 52, Chap. 9, as a form of psychological medicine or therapy. Sir John Foster criticised the 1968 ban on the ground that 'the mere fact that someone is a Scientologist is . . . no reason for excluding him . . . when there is nothing in law to prevent his fellows who are citizens in this country from practising Scientology here.'

In *Schmidt v Secretary of State for Home Affairs* [1969] 2 Ch 149, CA, the Court of Appeal held that the plaintiffs, who had been refused an extension of their permits to enter the United Kingdom to study at the Hubbard College of Scientology at East Grinstead in accordance with the new policy, had no cause of action in English law; the Home Secretary had acted properly within his power to exclude aliens under the Aliens Order 1953. In Case 41/74: *Van Duyn v Home Office* [1975] Ch 358, ECJ, a Dutch secretary was refused entry into the United Kingdom to work at the same College. The European Court of Justice ruled that the refusal was not contrary to Article 48 of the Treaty of Rome (by which nationals of European Communities countries have, subject to certain limitations, freedom of movement for employment purposes within the Communities); it could be justified as being 'on the grounds of public policy' (Article 48(3)). An application to Strasbourg by the Church of Scientology under Article 9, ECHR also failed because it does not protect companies (such as the Church): *Church of X v UK* 12 YBECHR 306 (1969).

In 1980, the Home Secretary (Mr Whitelaw) lifted the general ban on Scientologists, 988 HC Deb 16 July 1980 written answers col 578, so that scientology students are admitted.

CHAPTER 10

Freedom from racial discrimination

1 Introduction[1]

The Race Relations Act 1976 (the 1976 Act) is the third Act of Parliament on racial discrimination. It repeals the Race Relations Act 1968 and what remained of the Race Relations Act 1965. In much of its form and its content, the new Act follows the pattern of the Sex Discrimination Act 1975. It was understood that the two might later be merged, but there are no current plans for this.

The common law had only incidentally and exceptionally offered protection against racial discrimination before Parliament acted. See, e.g., *Constantine v Imperial Hotels Ltd*, below, p. 650, and *Scala Ballroom Ltd v Ratcliffe*.[2] In the words of Lord Simon in *Applin v Race Relations Board* [1975] AC 259, 286, HL:

> The common law before the making of the first Race Relations Act (1965) was that people could discriminate against others on the ground of colour, etc., to their hearts' content. This unbridled capacity to discriminate was the mischief and defect for which common law did not provide. The remedy Parliament resolved and appointed was to make certain acts of discrimination unlawful. The reason for the remedy must have been that discrimination was thought to be socially divisive (indeed, section 6 of the Act of 1965 [incitement to racial hatred] suggests, potentially subversive of public order) and derogatory to human dignity.

The arrival of immigrants from the West Indies and later India and Pakistan to take jobs in the 1950s and 1960s resulted in friction and discrimination. Racial incidents such as the Notting Hill riots in 1958 and the example of the Civil Rights Act 1964 in the US led Parliament, after much hesitation, to enact the Race Relations Act 1965. This made it illegal to discriminate in certain places of public resort (e.g. pubs

---

1 On the law of racial discrimination generally, see G. Bindman, in R. Blackburn, ed., *Constitutional Studies* (1992) Chap. 7; C. Bourne and J. Whitmore, *Race and Sex Discrimination Law* (2nd edn, 1993); Sir N. Browne-Wilkinson, (1988) 41 CLP 237; A. Lester and G. Bindman, *Race and Law* (1972); J. Gregory, *Sex, Race and the Law* (1987); B. Hepple and E. M. Szyszczak, eds., *Discrimination and the Limits of the Law* (1992); L. Lustgarten, *Legal Control of Racial Discrimination* (1980) (mostly concerning employment); I. A. MacDonald, *Race Relations—The New Law* (1977); M. Malone, *A Practical Guide to Discrimination Law* (1980); C. McCrudden, in C. McCrudden and G. Chambers, eds., *Individual Rights and the Law in Britain* (1994) Chap. 13; D. J. Walker and M. J. Redman, *Racial Discrimination* (1977). See also N. Glazer and K. Young, ed., *Ethnic Pluralism and Public Policy* (1983). On the interpretation of race relations legislation, see J. K. Bentil [1973] PL 157 and Rawlings, [1985] Cambrian LR 98. On the limitations of law as a means of tackling racial inequality, see L. Lustgarten, (1986) 49 MLR 68. For a critical review of the working of the 1976 Act, see C. McCrudden, D. J. Smith, C. Brown, *Racial Justice at Work*, 1991. The CRE has published a *Second Review of the Race Relations Act 1976* (1992), which makes recommendations for changes to the Act. For recommendations made in 1985 following a similar review, see *Review of the Race Relations Act 1976: Proposals for Change*, CRE, 1985. On immigration, see below, Chap. 11.
2 [1958] 3 All ER 220, CA (officials of Musicians' Union did not commit the tort of conspiracy by refusing to allow members to play in a ballroom with a colour bar to protect livelihood of its coloured members).

and dance halls) and in the disposal of tenancies, and created an offence of incitement to racial hatred. Conciliation procedures operated by the Race Relations Board (RRB) and local conciliation committees were the key to enforcement of the Act, with recourse to the courts by the Attorney General available as a last resort. These modest provisions soon proved insufficient and were replaced or supplemented by those of the Race Relations Act 1968. This was enacted in the light of evidence (see the PEP Report, *Racial Discrimination in Britain* (1967)) that much discrimination existed in areas not covered by the law and that the 1965 Act enforcement procedures needed strengthening. The violent riots in Watts in Los Angeles and elsewhere in the US in the mid-1960s also cast their shadow. The 1968 Act, which was influenced by the favourable assessment in the Street Report (H. Street, G. Howe and G. Bindman, *Report on Anti-Discrimination Legislation*, (1967)) of the effectiveness of US race legislation, extended the prohibition of discrimination to include goods, facilities and services generally, employment, housing and advertisements and modified the system of enforcement mainly by allowing the RRB to take cases to court instead of the Attorney General if conciliation failed. The Act also established a Community Relations Commission (CRC) to promote good race relations. The 1968 Act, in its turn, soon came to be seen as inadequate. The government White Paper (*Racial Discrimination*, Cmnd. 6234) introducing the present 1976 Act contains the following passages justifying legislation on racial discrimination generally and suggesting the new direction it should take:

'4. . . . The Government's proposals are based on a clear recognition of the proposition that the overwhelming majority of the coloured population[1] is here to stay, that a substantial and increasing proportion of that population belongs to this country, and that the time has come for a determined effort by Government, by industry and unions, and by ordinary men and women, to ensure fair and equal treatment for all our people, regardless of their race, colour, or national origins. Racial discrimination, and the remediable disadvantages experienced by sections of the community because of their colour or ethnic origins are not only morally unacceptable, not only individual injustices for which there must be remedies, but also a form of economic and social waste which we as a society cannot afford. . . .

23. Legislation is the essential pre-condition for an effective policy to combat the problems experienced by the coloured minority groups and to promote equality of opportunity and treatment. It is a necessary pre-condition for dealing with explicit discriminatory actions or accumulated disadvantages. Where unfair discrimination is involved, the necessity of a legal remedy is now generally accepted. To fail to provide a remedy against an injustice strikes at the rule of law. To abandon a whole group of people in society without legal redress against unfair discrimination is to leave them with no option but to find their own redress. It is no longer necessary to recite the immense damage, material as well as moral, which ensues when a minority loses faith in the capacity of social institutions to be impartial and fair. . . .

25. Legislation is capable of dealing not only with discriminatory acts but with patterns of discrimination, particularly with patterns which, because of the effects of past discrimination, may not any longer involve explicit acts of discrimination. Legislation, however, is not, and can never be, a sufficient condition for effective progress towards equality of opportunity. A wide range of administrative and voluntary measures are needed to give practical effect to the objectives of the law. But the legislative framework must be right. It must be comprehensive in its scope, and its enforcement provisions must not only be capable of providing redress for the victim of individual injustice but also of detecting and eliminating unfair discriminatory practices. . . .

31. It is not possible to provide a quantifiable measure of the practical impact of the 1968 Act. Generally, the law has had an important declaratory effect and has given support to those who do not wish to discriminate but who would otherwise feel compelled to do so by social pressure. It has also made crude, overt forms of racial discrimination much less common. Discriminatory advertisements and notices have virtually disappeared both from the press and from public advertisement boards. Discriminatory conditions have largely disappeared from the rules governing insurance and other financial matters, and they are

1 *Ed.* The 1991 census indicated that the 'ethnic' population of Great Britain was 3,015,000 ('white' population 51,874,000). This was divided as follows: 27.9% Indian; 15.8% Pakistani; 5.4% Bangladeshi; 5.2% Chinese; 6.6% 'other Asian'; 16.6% Caribbean; 7% African; 5.9% 'other black'; 9.6% 'other': *Whitaker's Almanac* (1994), p. 119.

being removed from tenancy agreements. It is less common for an employer to refuse to accept any coloured workers and there has been some movement of coloured workers into more desirable jobs. . . . 33. And yet, at the end of the decade, both statutory bodies have forcefully drawn attention to the inability of the legislation to deal with widespread patterns of discrimination, especially in employment and housing, a lack of confidence among minority groups in the effectiveness of the law, and a lack of credibility in the efficacy of the work of the Race Relations Board and the Community Relations Commission themselves. The continuing unequal status of Britain's racial minorities and the extent of the disadvantage from which they suffer provide ample evidence of the inadequacy of existing policies.'

Evidence of the 'continuing unequal status' and 'disadvantage' in employment and other areas had been produced in a series of PEP Reports.[1] A strike by Asian workers in the Mansfield Hosiery Mills in 1972, which revealed that skilled jobs were being reserved exclusively for whites (RRB Report 1972, p. 10), was also important.

The areas covered by the 1976 Act are essentially those covered in 1968 although there are a number of particular changes, including the extension of the law to cover contract workers (section 7), partnerships (section 10) and clubs (section 25).[2] The principle that the law should not apply to 'personal and intimate relationships' is retained (Cmnd. 6234 p. 15).[3] The definition of discrimination is widened to include discrimination on the ground of nationality (section 3) and, in accordance with the new strategy of attacking 'patterns of discrimination' (such as that in the Mansfield Hosiery Mills case) as well as particular 'discriminatory acts', 'indirect discrimination' (section 1(1)(b)) and 'discriminatory practices' (section 28) are prohibited too.[4]

The Crown is liable under the Act. Section 75(1) reads:

(1) This Act applies—
   (a) to an act done by or for purposes of a Minister of the Crown or government department; or
   (b) to an act done on behalf of the Crown by a statutory body, or a person holding a statutory office, as it applies to an act done by a private person.

This provision has been interpreted in the *Amin* case, below, p. 653, as excluding important areas of conduct in the public sector, such as policing and immigration control, in which many allegations of racial discrimination are made. Discrimination in the criminal justice system is also not subject to the 1976 Act. However, the Criminal Justice Act 1991, s. 95(1), reads:

'The Secretary of State shall in each year publish such information as he considers expedient for the purpose of—
   . . .
   (b) facilitating the performance by . . . persons [engaged in the administration of criminal justice] of their duty to avoid discriminating against any persons on the ground of race or sex or any other improper ground.'

1 D. Smith, *Racial Disadvantage in Employment* (1974); N. McIntosh and D. Smith, *The Extent of Racial Discrimination* (1974); D. Smith and A. Whalley, *Racial Minorities and Public Housing* (1975), and D. Smith, *The Facts of Racial Disadvantage* (1976). See since the 1976 Act, *Racial Disadvantage*, 5th Report of the Home Affairs Committee, 1980–81 HC 424–I; the *Scarman Report on the Brixton Disorders 10–12 April 1981*, Cmnd. 8427; and *Racial Discrimination: 17 Years After the Act*, a study by the Policy Studies Institute for the CRE (1985).
2 The 1976 Act originally did not make illegal discrimination by or in respect to barristers. A 1990 amendment makes unlawful discrimination on racial grounds in relation to the offering of a pupillage or tenancy or the giving of instructions to a barrister: Race Relations Act 1976, s. 26A. In 1993, racial discrimination was made a specific professional disciplinary offence for solicitors: CRE 1993 Annual Report, p. 9.
3 E.g. the Act does not apply to employment in a private household (s. 4(3)) or to accommodation in small premises (s. 22).
4 For the view that the control on indirect discrimination introduced by the 1976 Act has not proved very effective, see below, p. 680.

The 'duty' referred to does not arise from other legislation. Whether it was intended to establish such a legal duty incidentally in the course of imposing a different and more general information-giving duty upon the Secretary of State is debatable. The CRE has recommended that 'the vague non-discrimination duty applicable to the whole of the criminal justice system should be made more explicit', and should be 'backed by code-making powers together with proper ways of airing grievances.'[1]

Local authorities are subject to the particular provisions of the Act and also have a general statutory duty under s. 71, which reads:

> Without prejudice to their obligation to comply with any other provision of this Act, it shall be the duty of every local authority to make appropriate arrangements with a view to securing that their various functions are carried out with due regard to the need—
> (a) to eliminate unlawful racial discrimination; and
> (b) to promote equality of opportunity, and good relations, between persons of different racial groups.

The scope of s. 71 was considered in *Wheeler v Leicester City Council*.[2] Leicester Rugby Football Club had had its licence to use a council administered recreation ground terminated after it had failed to comply with requirements imposed by the council. These requirements followed the decision of three of the club's players to take part in a rugby tour of South Africa. The club was willing to comply with the council's demand that it should condemn apartheid. It did not, however, comply with the council's requirement that it put pressure on the players not to take part in the tour. It regarded itself as having no such jurisdiction over its players. The club sought certiorari to quash the council's decision revoking its licence. The council argued that it had, in exercising its discretionary powers as regards the licensing of the ground, properly taken into account and been guided by its duty under s. 71 of the 1976 Act to discharge its functions in such manner as would tend to promote good relations between persons of different racial groups. The Court of Appeal, by a majority, accepted this reasoning, holding that on the facts and in view of the ethnic mix in the city of Leicester it was not possible to categorise the decision of the council as improper or unreasonable in the *Wednesbury* sense (*Associated Provincial Picture Houses Ltd v Wednesbury Corpn* [1948] 1 KB 223). Browne-Wilkinson LJ dissented in strong terms. He stressed the fact that the actions of the players were in no way unlawful, and also noted the importance to be placed upon the liberty of freedom of speech and of conscience. The council's requirements of the club, in his opinion, went beyond its powers of administration of the ground for the general public benefit, and improperly sought to discriminate against a licensee on the grounds of that person's (lawful) views and beliefs. These matters were, he held, irrelevant considerations to the proper exercise of the licensing power. Browne-Wilkinson LJ did not regard s. 71 as sufficient to authorise what the council had done. To so hold, as the majority had done, was to permit the council to impose a 'penalty' on the club for behaviour which was not unlawful within the terms of the principal provisions of the 1976 Act. Section 71 should not, given its rather general terms, be interpreted as giving to local authorities such a power of punishment. The club appealed successfully to the House of Lords. Lord Roskill acknowledged that s. 71 required the council in exercising its powers to have regard to the interests of race relations. But this did not make any course of action decided upon immune from judicial review. His Lordship regarded the action of the council as unreasonable and procedurally unfair, given its inflexible attitude as regards strict compliance

---

1 *Second Review of the Race Relations Act 1976* (1992) p. 31.
2 [1985] AC 1054 HL. See on the *Wheeler* case, T. R. S. Allan, (1986) 49 MLR 121 and A. Hutchinson and M. Jones, (1988) 15 J. Law Soc. 263.

with all of the requirements it had imposed. Lord Templeman's opinion was founded on the improper purpose of the council in seeking to punish the club which had, it was stressed, committed no wrong. Lords Bridge, Brightman and Griffiths concurred with both speeches. Note also *R v Lewisham London Borough Council, ex p Shell UK Ltd* [1988] 1 All ER 938: given the multi-racial character of the borough, the council was entitled, in view of s. 71, to adopt a policy of not trading with a company that had links with South Africa. However, to adopt such a policy, as the council had done, in order to bring pressure to bear on the company to sever links with South Africa was to abuse power in the same way as in the *Wheeler* case.[1]

There is immunity from liability under the Act for acts done under statutory authority or a prerogative Order in Council. As a result, contrary to the normal rule, the Act gives way to earlier as well as later legislation. The CRE has recommended that this 'is wrong in principle for a statute which sets out a basic civil right': *Second Review of the Race Relations Act 1976* (1992) p. 35. Section 41 reads:

41.—(1) Nothing in Parts II to IV shall render unlawful any act of discrimination done—
  (*a*) in pursuance of any enactment or Order in Council; or
  (*b*) in pursuance of any instrument made under any enactment by a Minister of the Crown; or
  (*c*) in order to comply with any condition or requirement imposed by a Minister of the Crown (whether before or after the passing of this Act) by virtue of any enactment.
References in this subsection to an enactment, Order in Council or instrument include an enactment, Order in Council or instrument passed or made after the passing of this Act.
(2) Nothing in Parts II to IV shall render unlawful any act whereby a person discriminates against another on the basis of that other's nationality or place of ordinary residence or the length of time for which he has been present or resident in or outside the United Kingdom or an area within the United Kingdom, if that act is done—
  (*a*) in pursuance of any arrangements made (whether before or after the passing of this Act) by or with the approval of, or for the time being approved by, a Minister of the Crown; or
  (*b*) in order to comply with any condition imposed (whether before or after the passing of this Act) by a Minister of the Crown.

Section 41 was restrictively interpreted by the House of Lords in *Hampson v Department of Education and Science*.[2] In that case, the Education (Teachers) Regulations 1982, a statutory instrument made by the Secretary of State in the exercise of a power under the Education Act 1980, provided that a person could not be employed as a teacher unless he was qualified. The Regulations provided further that a person would be so qualified if he had successfully completed an 'approved' course, viz. one approved by the Secretary of State, in his discretion, as being 'comparable to a course within sub-paragraph (a)' of the Regulations. Lord Lowry, for the House, decided that s. 41 did not provide a defence, explaining his approach to the interpretation of s. 41 as follows:

Balcombe LJ framed the question clearly when, having summarised the respondent's point on s. 41, he said . . .

'This argument, which succeeded below, is controvertible if the words "in pursuance of any instrument" are apt in their context to include, not only acts done in necessary performance of an express obligation contained in the instrument (the narrow construction) but also acts done in exercise of a power or discretion conferred by the instrument (the wide construction). Both constructions are possible.' . . .

---

1 See also on s. 71, the *Secondary School Allocations in Reading* case, below, p. 648. The CRE has recommended that s. 71 be extended beyond local authorities to *all* public bodies.
2 [1991] 1 AC 171. The House of Lords reversed the Court of Appeal. For the facts of the case further, see below, p. 631.

. . . s. 41 . . . introduces over a wide field, namely the subject matter covered by Pts II to IV of the 1976 Act, as exceptions to the Act's general purpose of outlawing discrimination, five cases in which an act of discrimination shall not be unlawful and in each such case the relevant enactment, Order in Council, instrument, condition, requirement or arrangement may be either pre- or post-Act. In view of the wide sweep of these provisions, the exceptions ought therefore, I suggest, to be narrowly rather than widely construed where the language is susceptible of more than one meaning. The next point which strikes me is that the words 'in pursuance of' occur in sub-ss. (1)(*a*) and (*b*) and in sub-s. (2)(*a*). I take note, too, of the words 'in order to comply with' in sub-ss. (1)(*c*) and (2)(*b*) and the words 'by virtue of' also in sub-s. (1)(*c*). Even allowing for the variation of expression which may be attributed to the dictates of grammar or style, it seems to me that the phrase 'in pursuance of', while not limited to describing an act which is done *in order* to comply with an enactment etc, is more limited in its meaning than 'by virtue of', a phrase with which it could in a different context be synonymous. . . . The inference to be drawn is that, if the discriminatory act is specified in an enactment, order or instrument, but not otherwise, it is done 'in pursuance of' that enactment, order or instrument and protected by s. 41.

It is, however, the consideration of the wider context that demonstrates the need to adopt the narrow construction of the words 'in pursuance of', since the wide construction is seen to be irreconcilable with the purpose and meaning of the 1976 Act. . . . The most important weapons contained in Pts II and III of the Act would be irretrievably blunted and, indeed, would not make sense. . . .

My Lords, the alleged act of discrimination . . . was to decide the appellant's application by reference to a test of acceptability of her teacher training course (in statutory language, 'a requirement') which indirectly discriminated against her within the meaning of s. 1(1)(*b*)(i) and (iii) of the 1976 Act. That requirement was no doubt applied 'in pursuance of' the 1982 regulations according to the wide construction, as defined by Balcombe LJ, but it was not so applied according to the narrow construction, under which the requirement must be found in the regulations as, for example, is true of the courses described in para. 2(*a*)(i) of Sch. 5. On the other hand, the approval of a course as 'comparable to a course within sub-paragraph (*a*)' involved the application of a requirement (whether established or ad hoc) which was based on administrative practice and discretion and was not a requirement laid down by the regulations. Therefore the requirement of a course consisting of three consecutive years' training, assuming that it was discriminatory and also not justifiable under s. 1(1)(*b*)(ii), was not protected by s. 41(1)(*b*).

There is a sound argument, based on public policy, for drawing the line in this way. I refer to the need and the opportunity for parliamentary scrutiny. Balcombe LJ put the matter aptly ([1990] 2 All ER 25 at 32, [1989] ICR 179 at 188): . . .

If an enactment, Order in Council or statutory instrument imposes requirements compliance with which may lead to racial discrimination, those requirements can be debated in Parliament and their justification considered there. Similarly, if a minister of the Crown imposes a condition or requirement compliance with which could lead to racial discrimination (see s. 41(1)(*c*) of the 1976 Act) he can be made answerable in Parliament for his action. If what is done is not *necessary* to comply with a statutory requirement, then there can be no valid reason why it should not have to be justified before an industrial tribunal.'. . .

What I would venture to describe as the fallacy of [the Court of Appeal's] approach can be recognised when one reflects that almost every discretionary decision, such as that which is involved in the appointment, promotion and dismissal of individuals in, say, local government, the police, the national health service and the public sector or the teaching profession, is taken against a statutory background which imposes a duty on someone, just as the 1982 regulations imposed a duty on the Secretary of State. It seems to me that to apply the reasoning of the majority here to the decisions I have mentioned would give them the protection of s. 41 and thereby achieve results which no member of the Court of Appeal would be likely to have thought acceptable.

Acts 'done for the purpose of safeguarding national security' are also exempt: s. 42, 1976 Act.

As in the 1968 Act, discrimination is treated as a statutory tort. Apart from the offences of incitement to racial hatred (now in the Public Order Act 1986, below, p. 664) and certain minor offences (e.g. that in the 1976 Act, s. 29(5) below, p. 662), the remedies provided by the law remain civil, not criminal. In other respects the enforcement machinery in the 1976 Act differs markedly from that which predated it. The emphasis in the earlier legislation had been on enforcement by conciliation by the RRB following complaints by individuals of particular 'discriminatory acts'. Three major changes have been made. Firstly, conciliation has been largely abandoned; nearly all complaints may be taken straight to court instead. Secondly, the decision to take a case to court is in most cases in the hands of the individual complainant; the CRE is there simply to offer him assistance if he wants it. The CRE may take legal proceedings in a few 'reserved' cases. Thirdly, in keeping again with the realisation that underlying 'patterns of discrimination' need to be tackled as well as (and perhaps more than) individual cases of 'discriminatory acts', the CRE is given wide-ranging authority to conduct formal investigations on its own initiative. Armed with a new power to subpoena evidence in 'named person investigations', the CRE may investigate 'discriminatory acts' or 'patterns of discrimination' and may issue non-discrimination notices that are binding in law. Unfortunately, the power to conduct formal investigations has been seriously undermined by judicial interpretation.[1]

If a UK Bill of Rights incorporating the ECHR were enacted, the 1976 Act would continue to apply in parallel with the guarantee of freedom from 'degrading treatment' in Article 3, ECHR (which prohibits racial discrimination in immigration at least: *East African Asians* cases, below, p. 772) and the guarantees in Article 14, ECHR of freedom from racial discrimination in the protection of the rights in the Convention.

The remainder of this chapter deals with most aspects of the 1976 Act, but does not consider in detail the provisions of Part II of the Act on employment and related matters. Although discrimination in employment is of prime importance, it is best seen as an area of employment law and is fully treated in books on that subject.[2]

Contract compliance. It may be noted, however, in connection with employment that, although not required by the 1976 Act, since 1969 central government contracts contain a term by which contractors must comply with the non-discrimination provisions of the 1976 Act in respect of their workforce.[3] Local authorities have commonly followed a similar practice, although their freedom to do so has been considerably restricted by the Local Government Act 1988, ss. 17–18, which, subject to certain exceptions reflecting s. 71 of the 1976 Act, require them not to take 'non-commercial matters', which include the terms and conditions of employment of a contractor's workforce, into account in their contracts.

Neither the courts nor the police when investigating crime are subject to the 1976 Act.[4] Allegations of racial discrimination in the administration of justice are widespread, but the matter is a complicated one, there being various factors that may contribute to statistics indicating that there are disproportionate numbers of black persons who are stopped and searched, arrested and convicted of criminal offences. The Royal Commission on Criminal Justice[5] stated that there was 'no comprehensive information which would establish the extent to which members of the ethnic minority communities suffer discrimination within the criminal justice system'. It recommended further research and, referring to s. 95 of the Criminal Justice Act 1991, recommended a 'system of ethnic monitoring to establish how minorities are treated and thus to identify the measures which are needed to ensure as far as

---

1 See the *Prestige* and *Amari* cases, below, pp. 671 and 672. For the view that formal investigations have failed to play the key role that was envisaged for them, see below, p. 674.
2 See e.g. I. T. Smith and J. Wood, *Industrial Law* (5th edn, 1993), Chap. 5.
3 *Second Review of the Race Relations Act 1976* (1992) p. 41. However, Whitehall does not monitor compliance: ibid.
4 See s. 41, above, p. 617 (courts) and s. 20, below, p. 652 (police).
5 Cm 2263 (1993), pp. 7–8. A system of ethnic monitoring has been introduced: see CRE Report 1993, p. 29. For a study of arrests and disposal of suspects that showed no clear pattern of racial discrimination when the treatment of blacks and whites from the same geographic areas was compared, see T. Jefferson and M. Walker, [1992] Crim LR 83. Training programmes are being introduced by the Lord Chancellor to educate judges to avoid racial discrimination: see *Runnymede Bulletin* No. 271, p. 8 (1994). On allegations of racial discrimination by the police, see the 1993 Annual Report of Police Complaints Authority, pp. 41–2. Racial discrimination against policemen by their colleagues or superior officers is subject to the 1976 Act and a number of successful tribunal cases have been brought: see, e.g., *Singh v Nottinghamshire Constabulary*, CRE Report 1993, p. 31.

possible that the rules, procedures and practices of the criminal justice system are applied, and seen to be applied, in the same way to all'.

2 The meaning of discrimination

Race Relations Act 1976

1. Racial discrimination

(1) A person discriminates against another in any circumstances relevant for the purposes of any provision of this Act if—

(a) on racial grounds he treats that other less favourably than he treats or would treat other persons; or

(b) he applies to that other a requirement or condition which he applies or would apply equally to persons not of the same racial group as that other but—

(i) which is such that the proportion of persons of the same racial group as that other who can comply with it is considerably smaller than the proportion of persons not of that racial group who can comply with it; and

(ii) which he cannot show to be justifiable irrespective of the colour, race, nationality or ethnic or national origins of the person to whom it is applied; and

(iii) which is to the detriment of that other because he cannot comply with it.

(2) It is hereby declared that, for the purposes of this Act, segregating a person from other persons on racial grounds is treating him less favourably than they are treated.

2. Discrimination by way of victimisation

(1) A person ('the discriminator') discriminates against another person ('the person victimised') in any circumstances relevant for the purposes of any provision of this Act if he treats the person victimised less favourably than in those circumstances he treats or would treat other persons, and does so by reason that the person victimised has—

(a) brought proceedings against the discriminator or any other person under this Act; or

(b) given evidence or information in connection with proceedings brought by any person against the discriminator or any other person under this Act; or

(c) otherwise done anything under or by reference to this Act in relation to the discriminator or any other person; or

(d) alleged that the discriminator or any other person has committed an act which (whether or not the allegation so states) would amount to a contravention of this Act,

or by reason that the discriminator knows that the person victimised intends to do any of those things, or suspects that the person victimised has done, or intends to do, any of them.

(2) Subsection (1) does not apply to treatment of a person by reason of any allegation made by him if the allegation was false and not made in good faith.

NOTES

1. Discrimination in any of the three forms prohibited by ss. 1–2 (direct and indirect discrimination and victimisation) is only illegal if it occurs in one of the areas of conduct or activity covered by Part II (employment and related matters), Part III (education; goods, facilities or services; housing; clubs), or Part IV (advertisements) of the 1976 Act. Racial questions that raise issues of discrimination may arise in other areas of the law. For example, it has been held that a jury must be chosen at random in order best to ensure a fair trial; a court has no residual discretion to interfere with the random selection of jury members to achieve a multiracial jury: *R v Ford* [1989] QB 868, CA (trial judge correct to reject request by black accused for black jury members). In adoption proceeding the best interests of the child may require that the adoptive parents not be the child's foster parents where they are not of the same race as the child.[1]

1 *Re P (A Minor)* [1990] FCR 260, CA. The 1976 Act does not apply to the fostering of children: s. 23(2), below, p. 656. The Children Act 1989, s. 22(5)(c), requires local authorities to give due consideration to a child's 'religious persuasion, racial origin and cultural and linguistic background' when taking decisions concerning children being looked after by them.

Racial harassment may be less favourable treatment so as to amount to direct discrimination contrary to s. 1(1)(2). In the sex discrimination case of *Porcelli v Strathclyde Regional Council* [1986] ICR 564, Ct Sess, a female employee had been subjected to a campaign of sexually suggestive remarks and physical advances. Arguing that the industrial tribunal's decision rejecting the applicant's claim should be upheld, the employer submitted that the campaign was meted out to her not because she was a woman but because she was disliked as a colleague; a disliked male colleague would have been equally badly treated, although the harassment would have taken a different form. Rejecting this submission, the Court of Session found that the case involved less favourable treatment of the applicant 'on the ground of her sex' (1975 Act, s. 1(1)(a)). Lord Emslie stated:

'The industrial tribunal reached their decision by finding that Coles' and Reid's treatment of an equally disliked male colleague would have been just as unpleasant. Where they went wrong, however, was in failing to notice that a material part of the campaign against the applicant consisted of sexual harassment, a particularly degrading and unacceptable form of treatment which it must be taken to have been the intention of Parliament to restrain. From their reasons it is to be understood that they were satisfied that this form of treatment – sexual harassment in any form – would not have figured in a campaign by Coles and Reid directed against a man. In this situation the treatment of the applicant fell to be seen as very different in a material respect from that which would have been inflicted on a male colleague, regardless of equality of overall unpleasantness, and that being so it appears to me that upon a proper application of section 1(1)(a) the industrial tribunal ought to have asked themselves whether in that respect the applicant had been treated by Coles (on the ground of her sex) "less favourably" than he would have treated a man with whom her position fell to be compared. Had they asked themselves that question it is impossible to believe that they would not have answered it in the affirmative.'

This reasoning applies equally to racial harassment. For there to be illegal racial discrimination, however, it is necessary to show that discrimination in the sense of s. 1(1)(a) of the 1976 Act has occurred in the context of some other provision of the Act. In *De Souza v Automobile Association*,[1] a coloured employee overheard the manager tell a clerk to give some typing to the 'wog', viz herself. The Court of Appeal was prepared to hold that the applicant had been treated less favourably for the purposes of s. 1(1)(a) provided that 'he intended her to overhear the conversation in which it was used, or knew or ought reasonably to have anticipated that the person he was talking to would pass the insult on or that the employee would become aware of it in some other way'. The question was then whether the discrimination was to the applicant's 'detriment' as an employee contrary to s. 4 of the Act. Holding that it was not, May LJ stated for a unanimous court:

'. . . the detriment or disadvantage to the employee . . . [must be] in connection with . . . his employment context . . . I think that this necessarily follows upon a proper construction of section 4, and in particular section 4(2)(c) of the Act. Racially to insult a coloured employee is not enough by itself, even if that insult caused him or her distress; before the employee can be said to have been subjected to some "other detriment" the court or tribunal must find that by reason of the act or acts complained of a reasonable worker would or might take the view that he had thereby been disadvantaged in the circumstances in which he had thereafter to work.'

As well as being unlawful to discriminate, it is illegal to instruct someone to discriminate (s. 30, below, p. 634) or to 'induce or attempt to induce' a breach of Parts II or III of the Act (s. 31). In the latter case, 'inducement' does not necessarily involve an element of benefit or threat; any attempt to persuade is sufficient: *Commission for Racial Equality v Imperial Society of Teachers of Dancing* [1983] ICR 473, EAT. A person who 'knowingly aids another person to do an act made unlawful by this Act shall be treated for the purposes of this Act as himself doing an unlawful act

---

1 [1986] ICR 514, CA. See H. Carty, (1986) 49 MLR 653.

of the like description' (s. 33). For example, in the *Cottrell and Rothon* case, F. Invest. Rep. 1980, an estate agent was found by the CRE to have accepted discriminating instructions from vendors and landlords. Employers and principals are liable vicariously for the acts of their employees and agents (s. 32).

2. *Section 1(1)(a): direct discrimination.* A single act of discrimination is illegal. Following attempts to extend criminal law ideas of motive and intention to the concept of direct discrimination, it is now established that a 'but for' test applies when deciding whether a person has been treated less favourably on racial grounds: '. . . it is common ground that this does not depend on intention or motive but simply on whether "but for" their race, persons would have been more favourably treated'.[1] The leading authority is the sex discrimination case of *James v Eastleigh Borough Council*.[2] There, a husband and wife, both aged 61, went to a public swimming bath where persons of retirement age were admitted free of charge. Because of the different retirement ages for men and women (65 and 60) in UK law, the wife qualified for free entry; the husband did not. In the Court of Appeal ([1990] 1 QB 61) it was held that this situation was not direct discrimination contrary to the Sex Discrimination Act 1975 because the intention was not to discriminate 'on the ground of sex'. The crucial question was not the result of applying a retirement age rule but the reason for doing so. In this case, the reason for the retirement age rule was not to discriminate against men but, Sir Nicolas Browne-Wilkinson stated (p. 918), to benefit 'those whose resources would be likely to have been reduced by retirement'. The House of Lords, by the narrow majority of three to two (Lords Griffiths and Lowry dissenting), took a different approach and held that there had been direct discrimination. The majority applied a 'but for' test. Lord Goff stated:

'. . . as I see it, cases of direct discrimination under s. 1(1)(a) can be considered by asking the simple question: would the complainant have received the same treatment from the defendant but for his or her sex? This simple test possesses the double virtue that, on the one hand, it embraces both the case where the treatment derives from the application of a gender-based criterion, and the case where it derives from the selection of the complainant because of his or her sex; and on the other hand it avoids, in most cases at least, complicated questions relating to concepts such as intention, motive, reason or purpose, and the danger of confusion arising from the misuse of those elusive terms. I have to stress, however, that the "but for" test is not appropriate for cases of indirect discrimination under s. 1(1)(b), because there may be indirect discrimination against persons of one sex under that subsection, although a (proportionately smaller) group of persons of the opposite sex is adversely affected in the same way.'

The two dissenting judges rejected the majority's adoption of an objective test, arguing that the wording 'on racial grounds' suggested a subjective test. In terms of causation, there is authority for the view that when applying the 'but for' test, it does not have to be established that the victim's race was the sole reason for his less favourable treatment: it is sufficient that racial grounds are 'an important factor' or 'a substantial reason for what has happened'.[3]

Section 1(2) makes it clear that segregation (e.g. in public houses) is illegal. In *Furniture, Timber and Allied Trades Union v Modgill; Pel Ltd v Modgill* [1980] IRLR

---

1 Per Rose LJ in *R v LB Tower Hamlets London Borough Council, ex p Mohib Ali* 25 HLR 218, 225 (1993).
2 [1990] 2 AC 751, HL. Cf. *Equal Opportunities Commission v Birmingham City Council* [1989] AC 115, HL, in which the House of Lords had also used a 'but for' test (higher pass mark for girls for grammar school entry because fewer places for them was direct discrimination). The decision for the victim in *R v Commission for Racial Equality, ex p Westminster City Council* [1984] ICR 770, QBD, which is reasoned in terms of motive and intention, can be justified using the 'but for' test. There a Council official, who was not racially motivated, had failed to appoint a black candidate as a refuse collector because of trade union opposition.
3 *Owen and Briggs v James* [1982] ICR 618, 622, 626, CA. Although this case pre-dates the adoption of the 'but for' test, it is likely to apply in cases where there is more than one reason for the defendant's action.

142, EAT, only Asians were employed in a factory paintshop. White employees had worked there, but as vacancies had arisen they had been filled by Asians who had been alerted to their existence by Asians already employed in the paintshop. For two years, all vacancies had been filled 'by word of mouth' in this way, without the employer having to advertise for candidates or otherwise take the initiative. An allegation of segregation contrary to the Act made by some of the Asian paintshop workers was rejected (p. 166):

'. . . had there been evidence of a policy to segregate, and of the fact of segregation arising as a result of the company's acts, that might well have constituted a breach of the legislation; but it does not seem to us that there was evidence to support that position. We do not consider that the failure of the company to intervene and to insist on white or non-Asian workers going into the shop, contrary to the wishes of the men to introduce their friends, itself constituted the act of segregating persons on racial grounds within the meaning of s. 1(2) of the Act.'

For a comment on the case, see J. M.T., (1981) 97 LQR 10. In *Qadus v Henry Robinson (Ironfounders) Ltd* (1980) CRE Report 1980 p. 84, it was held by an industrial tribunal that the defendant had infringed s. 1(1)(a) by having separate toilets for Asian and white employees.

Words of discouragement may amount to less favourable treatment.[1] Less favourable treatment of V because of the colour, etc., of someone other than V (e.g. V's companion) is discrimination against V contrary to s. 1(1)(a): see *Showboat Entertainment Centre v Owens*, below, p. 634.

3. *Section 1(1)(b): indirect discrimination; generally.*[2] The 1976 Act made indirect racial discrimination illegal for the first time. The government White Paper (Cmnd. 6234, pp. 8, 13) explained the reason for this and gave examples:

'One important weakness in the existing legislation is the narrowness of the definition of unlawful discrimination upon which it is based. . . . [I]t is insufficient for the law to deal only with overt discrimination. It should also prohibit practices which are fair in a formal sense but discriminatory in their operation and effect. . . .

The new Bill . . . will, for example, cover the situation where an employer requires applicants to pass an educational test before obtaining employment if (a) the test operates to disqualify coloured applicants at a substantially higher rate than white applicants and (b) it cannot be shown to be significantly related to job performance. The employer will be required to stop using such a test. . . . The provision will similarly apply to requirements concerning the clothing worn by employees (e.g. preventing the wearing of turbans or saris) or their minimum height, where such requirements cannot be shown to be justifiable.'

The concept was consciously imported from US law. In *Griggs v Duke Power Co* 401 US 424 (1971), the US Supreme Court used it in the employment context to rule against a requirement for certain jobs in a power station that the occupant have graduated from high school or have passed an intelligence test. The Court stated (p. 431):

'Congress has now provided that tests or criteria for employment or promotion may not provide equality of opportunity merely in the sense of the fabled offer of milk to the stork and the fox. . . . The Act proscribes not only overt discrimination but also practices that are fair in form, but discriminatory in operation. The touchstone is business necessity. If an employment practice which operates to exclude Negroes cannot be shown to be related to job performance, the practice is prohibited.'

Indirect discrimination was introduced into English law in the Sex Discrimination Act 1975 which contains in s. 1(1)(b) the same provision mutatis mutandis as the

---

1 *Simon v Brimham Associates* [1987] ICR 596, 600, CA, per Balcombe LJ. See also *Tower Hamlets London Borough Council v Rabib* [1989] ICR 693, EAT. The cases concerned remarks that Jews or persons who could not work on Saturdays might have difficulty in being employed.
2 See G. Bindman, (1979) 129 NLJ 408: L. Lustgarten, [1978] PL 178: and D. Pannick, (1982) 132 NLJ 885, 903.

Race Relations Act 1976, s. 1(1)(b). The caselaw that has developed under the Sex Discrimination Act is helpful in interpreting the Race Relations Act.

4. *Indirect discrimination: 'requirement or condition'.* A 'requirement or condition' need not be formally contained in any rules. It is sufficient that it is 'the normal practice': *Steel v Union of Post Office Workers* [1978] ICR 181, EAT (practice by which postal rounds allocated by seniority was indirect sex discrimination). In the *Broomfield Ltd* case, F. Invest. Rep., 1980, the CRE concluded that an employer's practice of giving first consideration to applicants recommended by existing employees was, although not formally set down, a 'requirement or condition' in practice (and one that was indirectly discriminatory on the facts).[1] A 'requirement or condition' must be 'something which has to be complied with'; it is not sufficient that it is just a relevant factor. In *Perera v Civil Service Commission (No 2)* [1983] ICR 428, CA, a candidate for the post of legal assistant in the Civil Service *had* to be a barrister or solicitor, so that this was a 'requirement or condition'. Other allegedly discriminatory factors such as command of English and experience in the UK were taken into account, but were not by themselves crucial, so that they were not: '. . . a brilliant man whose personal qualities made him suitable as a legal assistant might well have been sent forward . . . in spite of being, perhaps, below standard on his knowledge of English . . .' (per Stephenson LJ). The *Perera* case has been criticised as being too strict, placing ethnic minority applicants at a serious disadvantage. In *Meer v London Borough of Tower Hamlets* [1988] IRLR 399, 403, CA, although following it as a binding precedent, Balcombe LJ stated that there were 'strong arguments' for saying that the *Perera* case 'may not be consistent with the object of the Act'. See Sylvester, 23 Law Teacher 202 (1989).

The CRE has recommended a new definition of indirect discrimination 'making unlawful any practice, policy or situation as well as any requirement or condition which is continued, allowed or introduced and which has an adverse impact on a particular racial group and which cannot be demonstrated to be necessary': *Second Review of the Race Relations Act 1976* (1992) p. 28. This would (i) make it sufficient to show a 'practice, policy or situation' rather than a 'requirement or condition'; (ii) abandon the *Pereira* 'absolute bar' rule; and (iii) limit the justification defence to cases of 'necessity'.

5. *Indirect discrimination: 'proportionality' requirement and justification defence.* See the *Orphanos* and *Hampson* cases, below, pp. 628 and 631, respectively.

6. *Indirect discrimination: 'detriment'.* 'Detriment' in s. 1(1)(b)(iii) does not require financial or other material loss. It simply means being put 'under a disadvantage', provided it is not de minimis.[2]

7. *Indirect discrimination: damages.* In many cases, a person may not appreciate that a 'requirement or condition' that he has imposed is indirectly discriminatory. Although he is nonetheless liable under the Act, allowance is made by the rule that damages may not be awarded if there is 'no intention of treating the claimant unfavourably on racial grounds' (s. 57(3)). A declaration or other civil remedy is available in such cases. See, e.g. the *Orphanos* case, below, p. 628.

---

1 Whether the CRE's conclusion on this point in the *Bloomfield* case is correct has yet to be decided in court. Word of mouth recruitment within the exsiting workforce is against the Race Relations Code of Practice in Employment, para. 1.10, where the workforce is predominantly white or black and the labour market is multi-racial. G. Bindman, LS Gaz No. 8, 1991, p. 24, argues that word-of-mouth recruitment of judges is indirect discrimination.
2 *BL Cars Ltd v Brown* [1983] ICR 143 at 147, EAT, following *Ministry of Defence v Jeremiah* [1980] ICR 13 at 26, CA (a sex discrimination case). See also *De Souza v Automobile Association*, above, p. 621. G. Bindman, in Hepple and Szyszczak, op. cit. at p. 613, n. 1, above, p. 52 questions whether Lord Denning's de minimis exception in *Jeremiah* ever applies to discrimination in the light of *Gill v El Vino* [1983] 1 All ER 398, CA.

8. *Discriminatory practices.* The prohibition of indirect discrimination in s. 1(1)(b) is supplemented by that in s. 28. This provides:

'(1) In this section "discriminatory practice" means the application of a requirement or condition which results in an act of discrimination which is unlawful by virtue of any provision of Part II or III taken with section 1(1)(*b*), or which would be likely to result in such an act of discrimination if the persons to whom it is applied included persons of any particular racial group as regards which there has been no occasion for applying it.
(2) A person acts in contravention of this section if and so long as—
  (*a*) he applies a discriminatory practice; or
  (*b*) he operates practices or other arrangements which in any circumstances would call for the application by him of a discriminatory practice.'

The purpose of s. 28 is indicated in the government White Paper (Cmnd. 6234, p. 13):

'It will also be unlawful to apply a requirement or condition which results or would be likely to result in an act of discrimination as defined above, irrespective of whether the requirement or condition is actually applied to a particular victim. . . . This will, for example, cover the situation where an employer operates recruiting arrangements which result in there being no coloured applicants for job vacancies and thus no act of discrimination against any individual victim.'

Section 28 is enforceable only by a non-discrimination notice issued by the CRE after a formal investigation, see below, p. 669; it is not enforceable by court proceedings. Thus in the *Barlavington Manor Children's Home* case, F. Invest. Rep. 1979, a private children's home which had made it known that it was not prepared to accept black children from local authorities so that no such children had been sent to it was found to have operated a discriminatory practice contrary to s. 28 and a non-discrimination notice was issued.

9. *Section 2: victimisation.* The fear of victimisation and the absence of any protection from it was identified by the RRB as one of the reasons why minority groups had been reluctant to complain under the 1968 Act (RRB Report 1973, p. 14). Section 2 covers victimisation by a third person as well as the person against whom proceedings have been brought, etc. It also protects persons who are not themselves victims of direct or indirect discrimination. In *Kirby v Manpower Services Commission* [1980] ICR 420, EAT, however, an employee at a Job Centre was transferred to other less desirable work after he had reported to a Community Relations Council incidents of alleged discrimination at the Centre. It was held that he had not been 'victimised' contrary to s. 2 because an employee who improperly disclosed confidential information of any sort would have been similarly treated, whether the context was racial or not. The plaintiff therefore had not been 'treated less favourably for doing something under or by reference to' the 1976 Act. B. Hepple and P. O'Higgins, *Employment Law* (4th edn, 1981), p. 189, criticise this decision on the grounds that 'the employees with which comparison should have been made were not those who (hypothetically) committed a similar act but those who did not do so' and that 'once the causal link between the treatment received and the act of informing . . . was established, the EAT was in error in allowing the treatment to be justified on any ground (e.g. breach of confidence) except those allowed by the statute'. Could the plaintiff in the *Kirby* case have succeeded under s. 1(1)(a)? See *Showboat Entertainment Centre Ltd v Owens*, below, p. 634.

Subsequently, in *Aziz v Trinity Street Taxis* [1989] QB 463, the Court of Appeal disapproved *Kirby* as regards the persons with whom the comparison should be made. In that case, the appellant taxi driver, who was of Asian origin, was a member of an organisation of taxi operators who considered the fee that he was charged by the organisation to operate another taxi to be unfair and racially discriminatory. He made a complaint under the Act to an industrial tribunal, disclosing during the course of the proceedings that he had made secret tape recordings of conversations with other members of the organisation who were sympathetic to his case but not prepared to speak out in public. On learning of the existence of the tapes, the organisation expelled the appellant, who thereupon claimed victimisation contrary to s. 2. The Court of Appeal held that in such a case the proper test was whether the applicant had been less favourably treated than persons who had not made such recordings. Clearly he had. His claim under s. 2 failed, however, because he had to show that his less favourable treatment was because he had done something 'under or by reference to' the 1976 Act in relation to the organisation (s. 2(1)(d)).[1] The Court accepted the evidence of the organisation that its motive in expelling the appellant was to act against a person who had breached the trust of the other members; it was not to act against someone for seeking to bring the Act's provisions into operation. In cases like *Kirby* and *Aziz* attention must therefore centre on the reasons underlying the alleged act of victimisation.

10. *Positive action.* Sometimes called 'affirmative action', 'positive discrimination' or 'reverse discrimination', positive action means discrimination in favour of a racial group whose members have previously suffered from extensive racial discrimination. An employment training programme or a quota of reserved places in higher education are examples. Although writers have made constructive attempts to distinguish between the above terms, unfortunately usage varies.[2] There is no one or more recognised term or terms in English law; instead there is a spectrum of positive action that may be taken, with all kinds of such action involving 'less favourable' treatment or another on a prohibited ground being illegal, unless permitted by a particular provision of the Act. The government White Paper (Cmnd. 6234, p.14) was against positive action and the definition of 'discrimination' in s. 1 makes it generally illegal. Thus in *Riyat v London Borough of Brent* (1983), cited in *IDS Employment Law Handbook 28* (1984), p. 57, a tribunal held that an employer had infringed the 1976 Act by discriminating in favour of black applicants for employment. Likewise, in *Lambeth London Borough Council v Commission for Racial Equality* [1990] IRLR 231, 234, CA, Balcombe LJ indicated that the policy of the Act was not such as generally to authorise positive action:

It is undoubtedly the case that certain sections of the Act encourage positive action to meet the special needs of particular racial groups in certain defined fields, by providing that acts of discrimination that would otherwise be unlawful shall not be so if done for those purposes. [ss. 35–38, below] . . . It is also correct that s. 71 imposes on local authorities the duty to promote equality of opportunity between persons of different racial groups, although this is expressly stated to be 'without prejudice to their obligation to comply with any other provision of this Act'.

Nevertheless . . . I am wholly unpersuaded that one of the two main purposes of the Act is to promote positive action to benefit racial groups. . . .

However, I should make it clear that . . . I express no view of the case for or against positive action in favour of ethnic minorities in order to counter the effects of past discrimination; I confine my attention to the present meaning of the 1976 Act.

As Balcombe LJ states, the 1976 Act, ss. 35–38, allows for some exceptions. Thus it is not unlawful to afford 'persons of a particular racial group access to facilities or services to meet the special needs of persons of that group in regard to their education,

---

1 The CRE has recommended that this limitation be repealed: *Second Review of the Race Relations Act 1976* (1992) p. 29.
2 Contrast, e.g., B. Parekh and G. Pitt, in Hepple and Szyszczak, op. cit. at p. 613, n. 1, above, Chaps. 15 and 16. See also on positive action, G. Bindman, (1980) *New Community* 248.

training or welfare, or any ancillary benefit' (s. 35) and special training schemes (public or private) to boost the number of members of a racial group in an occupation in which their number is disproportionately low are lawful (ss. 37–38). Sections 37–38 also permit employers to encourage applications from members of particular racial groups where these are under-represented in their workforce. Special provision 'for the benefit of persons not ordinarily resident in Great Britain in affording them access to facilities for education or training' is also permitted (s. 36). As to s. 35, English language instruction is an obvious case. Bindman states (loc cit above, p. 626, n. 2) that a 'number of "special access courses" have been introduced with the encouragement of the Department of Education and Science in colleges of further education and polytechnics' and that while 'a number of these courses are foundation courses which are not related to specific kinds of work, others are designed to direct members of ethnic minorities into specific occupations such as teaching'. As to ss. 37 and 38, training may be provided by public bodies such as the Manpower Services Commission or by private employers. Preference by way of *training* only may be given; the clear intention is that there should be no positive action in the *selection* or *promotion* of employees.[1]

Parekh[2] suggests, however, that practice is ahead of the law in that places on some public bodies are reserved for members of ethnic minority groups (and women) and that similar employment quotas are common:

'For years the Home Office has ensured that one of the ten governors of the BBC is black. There is no reason to believe that the black appointee is among the top ten "most distinguished" men and women in the country or is "uniquely equipped" to look after black interests. . . . The same is true of the appointments of blacks and women to the Independent Broadcasting Authority, the Equal Opportunities Commission, the Commission for Racial Equality, and to countless other government bodies. Local authorities are guided by similar considerations when they appoint school governors. And all political parties, albeit in different ways and with different degrees of enthusiasm, appoint blacks and women to important committees or select them as their local and parliamentary candidates.

Several private and public organizations too . . . set informal quotas (or what are euphemistically called targets) and go out of their way to recruit black and female staff, sometimes to important positions and in preference to equally or more qualified whites and males. Although their motives are mixed, they include a sense of social responsibility, the need to integrate blacks and other disadvantaged groups into mainstream society, the desire to encourage and tap talent, and the concern to counter the still pervasive preferential treatment of the traditional racist and sexist kind.'

Positive action was considered by Lord Scarman in his *Report on the Brixton Disorders 10–12 April 1981* (Cmnd. 8427) in the following paragraph, which attracted a good deal of public attention:

6.32. This leads me to the question how far it is right to go in order to meet ethnic minority needs. It is clear from the evidence of ethnic minority deprivation I have received that, if the balance of racial

---

1 See, however, the facts of the *Cardiff Women's Aid* case, below, p. 663, where a job was advertised as just for a 'black or Asian woman'. This would seem to cross the line between legal encouragement under s. 38 and an act of discrimination contrary to s. 1. It could only be lawful if the job came within s. 5(2), which permits selection for employment on racial grounds where this is 'a genuine occupational qualification for a job'. See, e.g., *Tottenham Green Under Fives Centre v Marshall (No. 2)* [1991] ICR 320, EAT. An example of a scheme within the Act was one involving the reservation for ethnic minorities of nearly half of the places on a BBC regional radio news training scheme: *Runnymede Bulletin* No. 179, p. 3 (1994). Following a formal investigation that revealed considerable under-representation of ethnic minorities in management, supervisory and clerical grades in the hotel industry, the CRE recommended that ss. 37 and 38 be used by hotel groups to improve the situation: *Working in Hotels*, F. Invest. Rep. 1991.

2 In Hepple and Szyszczak, op. cit. at p. 613, n. 1, above, p. 279. London Underground has set equality targets (15%) for the employment of ethnic minority senior managers following a CRE formal investigation (*Lines of Progress*, 1990) that concluded that the selection procedures involved indirect discrimination: *Race and Immigration, Runnymede Trust Bulletin*, No. 241, p. 5 (1991).

disadvantage is to be redressed, as it must be, positive action is required. . . . Given the special problems of the ethnic minorities, exposed in evidence, justice requires that special programmes should be adopted in areas of acute deprivation. In this respect, the ethnic minorities can be compared with any other group with special needs, such as the elderly, or one-parent families. I recognise the existence of a legitimate and understandable fear on the part of both public and private institutions that programmes which recognise and cater for the special needs of minority groups will stimulate a backlash from the majority. . . . Nevertheless, it must not be allowed to prevent necessary action. Certainly special programmes for ethnic minority groups should only be instituted where the need for them is clearly made out. But need must be the criterion, and no other. The principle has already been recognised by Parliament (ss. 35, 37, 38 of the Race Relations Act 1976), and must be made effective.

Orphanos v Queen Mary College [1985] AC 761, [1985] 2 All ER 233, [1985] 2 WLR 703, House of Lords

The plaintiff, a Cypriot national, was required to pay an 'overseas student' university tuition fee of £3,600. Had he been 'ordinarily resident' in the EEC for the preceding three years (which then meant residence for purposes other than purely educational purposes), he would have had to have paid only the home/EEC student fee of £480. He claimed, inter alia, that this 'requirement' amounted to indirect discrimination contrary to ss. 1(1)(b) and 17, Race Relations Act 1976.

In the following extract from his speech, Lord Fraser considered whether the ordinary residence requirement fell within the three conditions set by s. 1(1)(b).

Lord Fraser: That requirement will only be discriminatory within the meaning of paragraph (*b*) [of s. 1(1), 1976 Act] if it falls within all three sub-paragraphs (i), (ii), (iii). Clearly it does fall within sub-paragraph (iii) because Mr. Orphanos, not having been 'ordinarily resident' in the area of the EEC for three years before 1 September 1982, cannot now comply with that requirement. Sub-paragraph (i) is more doubtful, but the college has conceded that it also applies.

. . . Strictly speaking the House could proceed simply on the basis of the admission [i.e. concession] without considering whether it had been made correctly, but as this is a test case, and as the point does not seem to be covered by any authority, I think it is right to attempt to clarify a somewhat obscure provision. The draftsman of the notice of admission evidently had in mind section 3(2) of the Act of 1976 . . . which provides in effect that a racial group may comprise two or more distinct racial groups.

The admission seems to be made on the footing that Mr. Orphanos belongs to three racial groups (Cypriot, non-British, and non-EEC) and that it makes no difference which of these groups is chosen for the comparison required by section 1(1)(*b*)(i). I agree that Mr. Orphanos belongs to each of these groups, and that each is a 'racial group' as defined by section 3(1) as extended by section 3(2). But I do not agree that it makes no difference which of these groups is used for the comparison under section 1(1)(*b*)(i). The comparison must be between the case of a person of the same racial group as Mr. Orphanos and the case of a person not of that racial group, but it must be such that 'the relevant circumstances in the one case are the same, or not materially different, in the other': see section 3(4). The 'relevant circumstances' in the present case are, in my view, that Mr. Orphanos wished to be admitted as a pupil at the college, so the comparison must be between persons of the same racial group as him who wish to be admitted to the college, and persons not of that racial group who so wish. Consider first the two largest groups—namely persons of non-British and non-EEC nationality (omitting the reference to national origins brevitatis causa.) I have no doubt that the proportion of persons of non-British and non-EEC nationality who wish to attend the college and who can comply with the requirement of having ordinarily resided in the EEC area for three years immediately before 1 September 1982 is substantially smaller than the proportion of persons not of that group (i.e., persons who *were* British or EEC nationals) who wish to attend the college and who can comply with it. That seems obvious and causes no difficulty. But consider now the group consisting of persons of Cypriot (or Greek Cypriot) nationality and compare it with the group consisting of persons not of Cypriot (or Greek Cypriot) nationality, i.e., consisting of all persons (except Cypriots) of every nationality from Chinese to Peruvian inclusive. If the comparison is between persons of those groups who wish to be admitted to the college as pupils I do not see how any sensible comparison can be made because it would be impracticable to ascertain the numbers of persons so wishing. On the other hand if it is limited to persons who actually apply to the college for admission it would omit all those who may have been deterred from applying because they knew that they would not comply with the residence qualification. A comparison limited to applicants would, in my view, be entirely unsatisfactory.

I am accordingly of opinion that the concession should not have been made with regard to persons of Cypriot nationality. But the omission of that part of the concession would make no difference to the result because in terms of section 3(1), references to a person's racial group refer to *any* racial group into which he falls. As Mr. Orphanos falls into two racial groups, both of which are caught by section 1(1)(*b*)(i), that is enough to make that paragraph apply to his case.

On the assumption that the residence qualification is therefore caught by section 1(1)(*b*)(i), it is necessary to consider under 1(1)(*b*)(ii) whether the requirement is 'justifiable irrespective of the colour, race, nationality or ethnic or national origins of the [student] to whom it is applied.' Nationality is the only one of these grounds which is in question in this appeal. 'Justifiable' means, in my opinion, 'capable of being justified.' 'Irrespective of' in that subsection means 'without regard to,' as I said in *Mandla (Sewa Singh) v Dowell Lee* [below, p. 638], and I see no reason to alter that opinion. No doubt the main reason for introducing the residence requirement was, as Mr. Scrivener said, to curtail public expenditure on education in the interest of economy. That reason itself did not involve discrimination on racial grounds.

. . . But the economy was to be effected at the expense of foreign students. That may have been a perfectly reasonable and justifiable policy for the British Government to adopt but in my opinion the college, on whom the onus lies under section 1(1)(*b*)(ii), has not been able to justify the requirement without having regard to the nationality of the applicants at whose expense the policy was carried into effect. The typical example of a requirement which was caught by section 1(1)(*b*)(i) but which was nevertheless justifiable irrespective of racial grounds was *Panesar v Nestlé Co Ltd* [1980] ICR 144 where it was held that a rule forbidding the wearing of beards in the respondent's chocolate factory was justifiable on hygienic grounds notwithstanding that the proportion of Sikhs who could conscientiously comply with it was considerably smaller than the proportion of non-Sikhs who could comply with it. The justification there was purely a matter of public health and nothing whatever to do with racial grounds. But in the present case the discrimination is in accordance with a policy directed against persons who are not ordinarily resident in the EEC area, and ordinary residence is in my view so closely related to their nationality that the discrimination cannot be justified irrespective of nationality.

For these reasons I agree . . . that the college did discriminate on racial grounds against Mr. Orphanos.

NOTES

1. Although deciding that indirect racial discrimination had occurred,[1] Lord Fraser dismissed the plaintiff's appeal against the decisions of the county court and the Court of Appeal rejecting his claim to restitution of the difference between the overseas and home student fee because the discrimination was not intentional: see s. 57(3), 1976 Act, below, p. 675. Lord Fraser's speech was concurred in by the other four members of the House of Lords. The following notes concern the 'considerably smaller' requirement in s. 1(1)(b)(i). See on this aspect of the case, I. Leigh, (1986) 49 MLR 235. The justification defence is considered below in the notes following the *Hampson* case, below, p. 631.

2. When considering the proportion of members of V's 'racial group' who can comply with a 'requirement or condition', the comparison must, in terms appropriate to an employment context, be with the 'pool of qualified persons', not the population at large: *Price v Civil Service Commission* [1978] ICR 27 at 32, EAT (sex discrimination). In *Perera v Civil Service Commission (No 2)*, above, p. 624, Stephenson LJ stated that this was made clear by s. 3(4) of the 1976 act, below, p. 635, and continued:

'. . . you do not compare all the population of, in this case, Sri Lanka with all the population of England or any other racial group; you compare the persons in those two groups similarly qualified, and if you do that it is quite plain that in this case there was no evidence to prove that a substantially smaller proportion of persons from Sri Lanka who had got over the hurdle of Bar examinations or solicitor's final examinations than the proportion of barristers or solicitors from other racial groups could comply with anything that might be called a requirement or condition which would satisfy these examiners, as it were, of their suitability for the post of legal assistant.'

---

1 Note that higher overseas student fees are now authorised by the Education (Fees and Awards) Act 1983 and delegated legislation thereunder so that s. 41, 1976 Act, see above, p. 617, excludes liability under the Act.

If an Englishman complained of the refusal of a publican in Wales to serve anyone who did not speak Welsh, what comparison would be made? Between Welsh and non-Welsh persons who could comply? Or between Welsh and English persons? In addition to the *Orphanos* case, see the *Bohon Mitchell* case, below, p. 633.

3. In the *Mandla* case, below, p. 638, it was established that 'can comply' means 'can in practice' or 'can consistently with the customs and cultural conditions of the racial group'; it does not mean 'can physically'.

4. The phrase 'considerably smaller' has been given a 'common sense' meaning: *Clarke v Eley (IMI) Kynoch Ltd* [1982] IRLR 131, 137, Ind Trib (sex discrimination). There is no required method of proof. Judicial notice has been taken of well known facts about the population: *Perera v Civil Service Commission (No 2)*, above, p. 624. Because of the cost, elaborate statistical evidence is not required, at least not in all cases: ibid. In cases in which statistics have been relied upon, no particular threshold percentage has been identified. In *Meeks v National Union of Agricultural and Allied Workers* [1976] IRLR 198, Ind Trib, a female part-time typist complained that a lower hourly rate of pay for part-time, as opposed to full-time, typing was indirect discrimination under the Sex Discrimination Act. Although rejecting her claim on another ground, the industrial tribunal accepted her contention that the 'considerably smaller' criterion had been fulfilled. It did so on the basis of statistical evidence showing that 97% of employed men were in full-time employment (and hence satisfied the requirement for the higher rate of pay) but that only 68% of female employees were in such employment. Statistical evidence was also used in *Hussein v Saints Complete House Furnishers,* below, p. 633. It has been held that a 'requirement or condition' that *no* member of a racial group can comply with cannot be indirect discrimination because the Act imagines 'a smaller proportion who can comply, not zero': *Wong v GLC* (1980) EAT, cited in *IDS Employment Law Handbook 28* (1984), p. 11. Slynn J stated, obiter, that it was 'obvious that someone who is brown cannot comply at all with the condition [imposed in the case] that the candidate has to be white' so that it was 'quite impossible to look for a smaller proportion of people who are able to satisfy the condition'. This dictum has, however, been doubted. In *Greencroft Social Club and Institute v Mullen* [1985] ICR 796, 802, EAT, a sex discrimination case, Waite J stated:

It will be sufficient to say of this citation that we are satisfied that the appeal tribunal did not intend in that case to lay down any general principle to the effect that nil can never for discrimination purposes be a proportion of the whole. If there was any such intention, we would feel justified in declining to follow it, because now that the matter has been raised before us for direct consideration powerful arguments come to our mind to the contrary. It would, in our view, run counter to the whole spirit and purpose of the sex discrimination legislation if a requirement or condition which otherwise fell within the definition in section 1(1)(b) because a negligible proportion of women as against men could comply with it was held to lie outside the legislation if the proportion was so negligible as to amount to no women at all.

In most such cases, however, a claim of direct discrimination will be available. The dictum in the *Wong* case might be crucial, however, in claims of 'discriminatory practices' in the sense of s. 28, 1976 Act, above, p. 625. As noted above, s. 28 forbids discriminatory practices that amount to indirect discrimination. It is designed to meet the situation where, because of a known requirement, no applicants have applied for a job, house, etc. In the absence of individual victims, the—CRE instigated—procedure is applicable. The procedure does not apply where the discrimination which would have been practised is direct, not indirect, discrimination. In such cases there may be no victims so that a direct discrimination claim cannot be brought. See the *Percy Ingle Bakeries Ltd* case, F. Invest. Rep. 1983; *IDS Employment Law Handbook* 28 (1984) p. 54, in which a non-discrimination notice requiring a company not to contravene s. 28 by refusing to employ Pakistanis or black persons to serve in their bakery shops was quashed by an industrial tribunal. On the authority of *Wong v GLC*, it was considered that such discrimination would have been direct, not indirect, Only one shop employee out of 140 was black, although there was a high ethnic minority population in the area. A manageress reported no job applications from black persons in three years.

Hampson v Department of Education [1989] ICR 179, [1990] 2 All ER 25, Court of Appeal

The appellant, of Hong Kong Chinese origin, had qualified as a teacher in Hong Kong, having taken a two year teacher training course there. In 1978, after teaching for eight years, she took a further one year teacher training course in Hong Kong and then became a teaching inspector. In 1984, the appellant came to the United Kingdom, where her application for qualified teacher status was rejected, inter alia, on the ground that her initial training did not meet a Department of Education requirement of a three year teacher training course. In this connection, the 1978 course that the appellant had taken was not regarded as an integral part of her initial training. The appellant claimed that the Department of Education requirement amounted to indirect discrimination contrary to ss. 1(1)(*b*) and 12, 1976 Act (for s. 12, see below, p. 633). In argument before the Court of Appeal, it was accepted that the three year rule was a 'requirement' for the purposes of s. 1(1)(*b*) and that it had, in terms of s. 1(1)(*b*)(i), a disproportionate effect upon persons of the appellant's racial origin. The following extract concerns the justification defence under s. 1(1)(*b*)(ii).

Balcombe LJ: In *Ojutiku v Manpower Services Commission* [1982] ICR 661 this court was concerned with the meaning of 'justifiable' where it appears in section 1(1)(*b*)(ii) of the Act of 1976 and of course that decision is binding on us in so far as it decides that meaning. . . . However, I regret that I do not find, in two of the judgments in *Ojutiku*, any clear decision as to that meaning. . . . With all due respect to Eveleigh and Kerr LJJ, I derive little help from these judgments. 'Justifiable' and 'justify' are words which connote a value judgment, as is evident from the dictionary definition cited by Eveleigh LJ—'to produce adequate grounds for,' but neither Lord Justice indicates what test should be applied. Kerr LJ says it applies a lower standard than 'necessary,' but does not indicate how much lower. It was, however, accepted by Mr. Carlisle, and rightly so, that whatever test is to be applied it is an objective one: it is not sufficient for the employer to establish that he considered his reasons adequate. However I do derive considerable assistance from the judgment of Stephenson LJ. At p. 674, he referred to
  'the . . . judgment of the appeal tribunal given by Phillips J. in *Steel v Union of Post Office Workers* [1978] ICR 181, 187–188 . . . What Phillips J. there said is valuable as rejecting justification by convenience and requiring the party applying the discriminatory condition to prove it to be justifiable in all the circumstances on balancing its discriminatory effect against the discriminator's need for it. But that need is what is reasonably needed by the party who applies the condition; . . .'
In my judgment 'justifiable' requires an objective balance between the discriminatory effect of the condition and the reasonable needs of the party who applies the condition. This construction is supported by the recent decision of the House of Lords in *Rainey v Greater Glasgow Health Board* [1987] ICR 129, a case under the Equal Pay Act 1970, and turning on the provisions of section 1(3) of that Act . . .
  The House of Lords held, applying the decision of the European Court in *Bilka-Kaufhaus GmbH v Weber von Hartz* (Case 170/84) [1987] ICR 110, that to justify a material difference under section 1(3) of the Equal Pay Act 1970, the employer had to show a real need on the part of the undertaking, objectively justified, although that need was not confined to economic grounds; it might, for instance, include administrative efficiency in a concern not engaged in commerce or business. Clearly it may, as in the present case, be possible to justify by reference to grounds other than economic or administrative efficiency. . . .
  Mr. Sedley constructed an elaborate argument designed to show that *Ojutiku* had been overruled by *Rainey*. . . . However I do not find it necessary to consider this argument further here. For my part I can find no significant difference between the test adopted by Stephenson LJ in *Ojutiku* and that adopted by the House of Lords in *Rainey*. Since neither Eveleigh LJ nor Kerr LJ in *Ojutiku* indicated what they considered the test to be—although Kerr LJ said what it was not—I am content to adopt Stephenson LJ's test as I have expressed it above, which I consider to be consistent with *Rainey*. It is obviously desirable that the tests of justifiability applied in all these closely related fields should be consistent with each other.

NOTES

1. Nourse and Parker LJJ concurred in the judgment of Balcombe LJ on the interpretation of the justification defence. The case went on appeal to the House of Lords on a separate question whether the Department of Education had a defence under s. 41, 1976 Act on the basis that its refusal to recognise the appellant's course was an act done under lawful authority. The House of Lords reversed the Court of Appeal's decision, Balcombe LJ dissenting, that the Department of Education was immune by virtue of s. 41 (see further on this point, above, p. 617) and remitted the case to an industrial tribunal for a rehearing. The House of Lords did not consider the Court of Appeal's interpretation of the justification defence.

2. The 'justification' defence in s. 1(1)(b) has been the subject of disagreement. In *Steel v Union of Post Office Workers* [1978] ICR 181, EAT (a sex discrimination case), Phillips J stated:

'. . . it is right to distinguish between a requirement or condition which is necessary and one which is merely convenient and for this purpose it is relevant to consider whether the employer can find some other and non-discriminatory method of achieving his object'.

This is consistent with the 'business necessity' test adopted in the American employment case (*Griggs v Duke Power Co*, above, p. 623) from which the concept of indirect discrimination derives, but is probably not what Parliament intended.[1]

Since *Steel*, a less demanding test has evolved. The approach that first prevailed was that indicated by Eveleigh LJ in *Ojutiku v Manpower Services Commission*:[2]

'For myself, it would be enough simply to ask myself: is it justifiable? But if I have to give some explanation of my understanding of that word, I would turn to a dictionary definition which says "adduce adequate grounds for"; and it seems to me that if a person produces reasons for doing something, which would be acceptable to right-thinking people as sound and tolerable reasons for so doing, then he has justified his conduct.'

In the course of applying the *Ojutiku* approach in *Clarke v Eley (IMI) Kynoch Ltd* [1983] ICR 165, 174–5, EAT, Browne-Wilkinson J was critical of the discretion that a 'right-thinking people' test left to industrial tribunals on such emotive matters as racial or sex discrimination. In the *Hampson* case the Court of Appeal has itself responded to this criticism. Eveleigh LJ's 'acceptable to right-thinking people' formula in *Ojutiku* has now been replaced by the *Hampson* 'balancing' test.[3] The new test places a greater onus of proof upon the defendant than its predecessor. Even so, the test is not as strict as the unavoidable necessity test suggested earlier in *Steel*.

3. The following are examples of 'requirements or conditions' that have been held, by courts or tribunals not always applying the same test, to be justified: a rule prohibiting beards in a chocolate factory, for reasons of public hygiene (the *Panesar* case, above); a requirement that a person have managerial experience to be sponsored for a management course, because persons without such experience were unlikely to gain employment subsequently (the *Ojutiku* case, above); and a requirement that a Sikh factory employee wear a hard-hat in place of his turban.[4] It was also justifiable under

1   In the drafting of the provision parallel to s. 1(1)(b) in the Sex Discrimination Act 1975, amendments to replace 'justifiable' by 'necessary' were rejected as being too strict: HC, Standing Committee B, 24 April 1975, cols 64–79 and 362 HL Deb 14 July 1975 cols 1013–20. On the justification defence, see L. Lustgarten, (1983) 133 NLJ 1057 and (1984) 134 NLJ 9.
2   [1982] ICR 661, 667–8, CA. Cf. Kerr LJ in the same case.
3   In *Webb v EMO Air Cargo* [1993] 1 WLR 49, the House of Lords approved the *Hampson* test as replacing that of Eveleigh LJ in *Ojutiku*. On the *Hampson* case, see E. Ellis, [1990] PL 461 and B. W. Napier, [1989] CLJ 187.
4   *Dhanjal v British Steel General Steels* (1993) Ind Trib, cited in G. Welhengama, 144 NLJ 671 (1994). The statutory exception for construction workers on religious grounds, see above, p. 601, did not apply.

the *Hampson* balancing test for a Church of England school to advertise for a committed communicant Christian as headmaster: *Board of Governors of St Matthias Church of England School v Crizzle* [1993] ICR 401, EAT.

Cases in which a justification defence has been rejected include the *Mandla* case, below, p. 638; *Hussein v Saints Complete House Furnishers* [1979] IRLR 337, Ind Trib, and *Bohon-Mitchell v Common Professional Examination Board* [1978] IRLR 525, Ind Trib. In the *Hussein* case, an employer decided not to employ youths from the 'City Centre' of Liverpool because 'lads who live within walking distance of our shop have a lot of friends out of work who stand in front of the shop, distracting their mates and putting customers off.' When the requirement was imposed, approximately 50% of the people in the City Centre were black whilst outside that zone the percentage of black residents was no more than 2%. It was held that the requirement could not be justified under the 1976 Act. In the *Bohon-Mitchell* case, the claimant was an American national and a graduate of an American university. She was married to a UK citizen and had been resident in the UK for five years overall. It was held that a requirement that she should, as a non-law graduate of a university other than a British or an Irish one, have to take a 21 month course to qualify for the Bar when non-law graduates of British or Irish universities need only take a course lasting 12 months, was indirect discrimination contrary to ss. 1(1)(b) and 12 of the Act. (Section 12 prohibits discrimination by authorities or bodies 'which can confer an authorisation or qualification which is needed for, or facilitates, engagement in a particular profession or trade'.) The tribunal considered that the proportion of graduates not of British or Irish nationality who could qualify for the shorter course was 'considerably smaller' than those who were of such nationality and, applying *Steel*, that the Council's aim of ensuring that barristers be familiar with the English way of life could be attained in a way that was less detrimental to overseas graduates (by assessing their familiarity on a case by case basis) and was therefore not 'justifiable'. The defence was also unsuccessful in the *Orphanos* case, above, p. 628. The House of Lords there rejected the College's attempt to justify charging overseas students a higher tuition fee on economic grounds. Economic considerations could not justify the choice of a policy that was racially discriminatory. See also *Malik v British Home Stores*[1] in which a shop uniform that did not permit trousers was held to be unjustified. The tribunal 'accepted the evidence of an expert witness that the wearing of skirts without trousers by mature Muslim girls was forbidden and that some 14% of Blackburn's population was of Indian or Pakistani origin, mainly of the Muslim faith'.

Racial Justice at Work, op. cit. at p. 613, n. 1, above, p. 271, concludes that the extension of the law to control indirect discrimination has not proved as effective as had been expected:

'A central finding [of the present study] is that the attempt to extend the law to cover something wider than direct discrimination has not worked; and this has been one factor limiting the success of the strategic approach to combating institutional discrimination. The vast majority of cases heard by industrial tribunals were concerned only with direct discrimination, hence the tribunals were articulating concepts only in that area. . . . In its role of assisting individual complainants, the CRE also concentrated on direct discrimination. . . . In its strategic role . . . it has since 1983 concentrated on direct discrimination in formal investigations of specified organisations; though the recommendations to employers following such investigations typically went wider, the investigations themselves were almost exclusively concerned with direct discrimination, so it was over direct discrimination that the main battles were fought. . . .'

1 (1980) CRE Report 1980, p. 78. In *Kingston and Richmond Area Health Authority v Kaur* [1981] ICR 631, EAT, it was held that a requirement, based upon statutory authority, that if nurses wore a uniform it must not include trousers, was justified. The requirement has since been abolished: S.I. 1981 No. 1533.

Showboat Entertainment Centre v Owens [1984] 1 WLR 384, Employment Appeal Tribunal

The appellant, who was white, was dismissed from his post as the manager of an amusement centre for failure to obey an order to exclude black youths. He was awarded £1,350 compensation for discrimination against him contrary to s. 1(1)(a) and 4(2)(c) (employment provision) of the 1976 Act. The employer appealed.

Browne-Wilkinson J (for the Tribunal). In essence, the question raised by this appeal is whether, for the purposes of the Act of 1976, A can unlawfully discriminate against B on the ground of C's race. . . .

The racially discriminatory instructions given by the employers to the applicant were unlawful by virtue of s. 30.[1] But under s. 63 only the Commission for Racial Equality has the right to bring proceedings based on such illegality. The applicant can only bring a complaint if he brings himself within s. 54(1)(a) by showing that there has been unlawful discrimination 'against' him. Therefore the question is whether the racially discriminatory instruction not to admit blacks (which constituted discrimination 'against' the blacks excluded) can also be regarded as discrimination 'against' the applicant.

In _Zarczynska v Levy_ [1979] 1 WLR 125, the circumstances were broadly the same as in the present case: an employee [a barmaid in a pub] who had not got the necessary qualifying period to complain of unfair dismissal was dismissed because of her refusal to obey an instruction not to serve black customers. This appeal tribunal held that she had been unlawfully discriminated against contrary to s. 4(2)(c) of the Act of 1976. . . .

In our judgment, the words of section 1(1)(a) are capable of two possible meanings, the one reflecting the broad approach of Mr Hytner and the other the narrower approach of Mr Harvey. It is plain that the person 'against' whom there has been discrimination is the person who is being treated less favourably by the discriminator, i.e. the words 'that other' in paragraph (a) refer back to 'another' in the phrase 'a person discriminates against another' at the beginning of the subsection. Therefore the only question is whether the applicant was treated less favourably 'on racial grounds.' Certainly the main thrust of the legislation is to give protection to those discriminated against on the grounds of their own racial characteristics. But the words 'on racial grounds' are perfectly capable in their ordinary sense of covering any reason for an action based on race, whether it be the race of the person affected by the action or of others.

. . . The fact that the giving of racialist instructions is dealt with separately in section 30 in a part of the Act headed 'Other unlawful acts' is in our judgment explicable without requiring the words 'on racial grounds' to be given a narrow meaning. . . . [A]part from s. 30, the mere giving of the instruction unaccompanied by an action pursuant to such an instruction which falls within Parts II or III would not be rendered unlawful by Parts II or III of the Act. Therefore s. 30 by making unlawful the giving of the instruction itself is creating another unlawful act, namely, the mere giving of the instruction. Moreover there is nothing manifestly absurd in giving the Commission for Racial Equality the right to take proceedings to stop the giving of such instructions . . . at the same time as giving a right to individual redress to someone who has actually suffered as a result of such instruction.

At this stage we should note a point . . . which has caused us some hesitation. . . . It seems to us clear that in relation to indirect discrimination under sub-s. (1)(b) the discrimination must relate to the race of the person against whom it is exercised. Thus, the requirement or condition is applied to 'that other'; it is the racial group of 'that other' whose ability to comply with the requirement has to be considered; it is detriment to 'that other' which has to be shown. . . . it might be argued that the same must also be true in relation to direct discrimination under s. 1(1)(a). However . . . Mr Hytner provided the answer. He said that if, for example, an employee refused to carry out an indirectly discriminatory recruitment policy on the ground that it was racially discriminatory and was dismissed for such refusal, his dismissal would be 'on racial grounds' within s. 1(1)(a) not withstanding that his refusal was a refusal to be a party to indirect discrimination within s. 1(1)(b).

. . . We find it impossible to believe that Parliament intended that a person dismissed for refusing to obey an unlawful discriminatory instruction should be without a remedy. It places an employee in an impossible position if he has to choose between being party to an illegality and losing his job. It seems to us that Parliament must have intended such an employee to be protected so far as possible from the consequences of doing his lawful duty by refusing to obey such an instruction. . . .

---

1 Section 30 reads:
It is unlawful for a person—
   (a) who has authority over another person; or
   (b) in accordance with whose wishes that other person is accustomed to act,
to instruct him to do any act which is unlawful by virtue of Part II or III, or procure or attempt to procure the doing by him of any such act.

We, like the appeal tribunal in the *Levy* case, gain considerable support from certain remarks made in the Court of Appeal in *Race Relations Board v Applin* [1973] QB 815.[1] That case was concerned with incitement by Mr Applin to stop foster parents taking in coloured children placed with them by the local authority. . . .

The Court of Appeal held that such conduct [by the foster parents] would have amounted to discrimination against the children themselves. But Lord Denning MR said that they would also have discriminated against the local authority. Counsel had put to the Court of Appeal the example of two white women who were refused entrance to a public house if accompanied by coloured men. After quoting section 1 of the Act of 1968, Lord Denning MR said, at p. 828:

'That definition of discrimination is wide enough to cover the case of the two women. They are treated less favourably than other women on the ground of colour. Similarly in this case [the foster parents] would discriminate against the local authorities on the ground of colour if they said: "We will take white children only." '

Stephenson LJ [agreed] . . .

We therefore agree with the decision in *Zarczynska v Levy* . . . (although for rather different reasons) and hold that on the facts as found by the industrial tribunal . . . the applicant had been unlawfully discriminated against.

Appeal dismissed.

NOTES

1. In *Zarczynska v Levy*, the CRE took proceedings in the county court against the publican for a declaration that his instruction had been contrary to s. 30. Kilner Brown J stated:

'Can it not be said in the instant case that in dismissing the one barmaid because she wanted to serve some coloured men, and not dismissing a barmaid who was prepared to apply the embargo, the employer treated the one less favourably than the other on racial grounds? We recognise that s. 1(1) of the Act of 1976 has to be read in conjunction with the other provisions to which reference has been made and that a broad approach to s. 1(1) may be prevented or delimited by the effect of other provisions. If we could say, however, that such other provisions are explanatory of or provide remedies for instances of breach of the general principle, then the general principle would not be restricted. This might involve reading into section 1 the purposive intent of Parliament to make it a section which overrides subsequent sections which might otherwise be deemed to limit the provisions of that section. If this is not done the strict interpretation of the relevant sections taken as a whole may well create an absurd—or unjust situation which Parliament would not have intended if they had contemplated its possibility.

. . . We are of opinion here that if Parliament had had pre-knowledge of this unfortunate complainant's predicament they would have made clear that the great civilised principle upon which the Act was based was one which overrode all apparent limitations expressed in other sections which had the effect of denying justice to someone who was victimised.'

Earlier, Kilner Brown J had referred to s. 2(1)(d). Would it have been possible to have decided either the *Levy* or the *Owens* case in favour of the claimant under s. 2?

2. In *Wilson v TB Steelwork Co Ltd* (1978), cited in *IDS Employment Law Handbook 28* (1984), p. 7, a white woman was held by an industrial tribunal to have been discriminated against contrary to the 1976 Act when she was refused employment because she was married to a West Indian.

Race Relations Act 1976

3. Meaning of 'racial grounds', 'racial group' etc.

(1) In this Act, unless the context otherwise requires—

'racial grounds' means any of the following grounds, namely colour, race, nationality or ethnic or national origins;

'racial group' means a group of persons defined by reference to colour, race, nationality or ethnic or national origins, and references to a person's racial group refer to any racial group into which he falls.

---

1 *Ed.* See further on this case, p. 656, below.

(2) The fact that a racial group comprises two or more distinct racial groups does not prevent it from constituting a particular racial group for the purposes of this Act.

(3) In this Act—

    (a) references to discrimination refer to any discrimination falling within section 1 or 2; and

    (b) references to racial discrimination refer to any discrimination falling within section 1, and related expressions shall be construed accordingly.

(4) A comparison of the case of a person of a particular racial group with that of a person not of that group under section 1(1) must be such that the relevant circumstances in the one case are the same, or not materially different, in the other.

NOTES[1]

1. The term 'national origins' as it appeared in the 1968 Act was examined by the House of Lords in *Ealing London Borough Council v Race Relations Board* [1972] AC 342, HL. In that case the appellants had refused to put a person of Polish nationality – a Mr Zesko – on their council housing waiting list because he was not, as their rules required, a British subject. The House of Lords held that discrimination based upon nationality was not discrimination on the ground of 'national origins' and, since discrimination on the ground of 'nationality' was not prohibited, the 1968 Act had not been infringed. Lord Simon said (pp. 362–3):

'The Acts of 1965 and 1968 do not provide a complete code against discrimination or socially divisive propaganda. The Acts do not deal at all with discrimination on the grounds of religion or political tenet. It is no offence under the Acts to stir up class hatred. It is, therefore, unquestionably with a limited sort of socially disruptive conduct that the Acts are concerned, and it is, on any reading, within a limited sphere that Parliament put its ameliorative measures into action.

. . . Moreover, "racial" is not a term of art, either legal or, I surmise, scientific. I apprehend that anthropologists would dispute how far the word "race" is biologically at all relevant to the species amusingly called homo sapiens. . . .

The ["colour, race or ethnic or national origins"] is rubbery and elusive language—understandably when the draftsman is dealing with so unprecise a concept as "race" in its popular sense and endeavouring to leave no loophole for evasion.

. . . "Origin", in its ordinary sense, signifies a source, someone or something from which someone or something else has descended. "Nation" and "national", in their popular in contrast to their legal sense, are also vague terms. They do not necessarily imply statehood. For example, there were many submerged nations in the former Hapsburg Empire. Scotland is not a nation in the eye of international law, but Scotsmen constitute a nation by reason of those most powerful elements in the creation of national spirit—tradition, folk memory, a sentiment of community. . . .

. . . To discriminate against Englishmen, Scots or Welsh[2] as such, would, in my opinion, be to discriminate against them on the ground of their national origins. To have discriminated against Mr Zesko on the ground of his Polish descent would have been to have discriminated against him on the ground of his national origins.

There is another situation which the phrase is apt to cover, namely, where a person of foreign nationality by birth has acquired British nationality or where a person of British nationality by birth is descended from someone of foreign nationality. There are those who are apt to say "The leopard cannot change his spots; once an Erehwonian always an Erehwonian." To discriminate against a British subject on the grounds of his foreign nationality by birth or alien lineage would be to discriminate against him on the ground of his national origins. To have discriminated against Mr Zesko on the ground of Russian nationality by birth (if such was his case, which is not clear) would have been to have discriminated against him on the ground of his national origins. . . .'

Lord Cross said (pp. 365–6);

1 On 'racial grounds', see L. Lustgarten, (1979) 28 ICLQ 221. On the *Ealing* case, see J. Hucker (1975) 24 ICLQ 284.

2 Ed. Cf. *Gwynedd County Council v Jones* [1986] ICR 833, EAT (Welsh a 'nation and an ethnic group'; industrial tribunal erred, however, in distinguishing between two racial sub-groups of Welsh and English-speaking Welsh persons).

'There is no definition of "national origins" in the Act and one must interpret the phrase as best one can. To me it suggests a connection subsisting at the time of birth between an individual and one or more groups of people who can be described as a "nation"—whether or not they also constitute a sovereign state. The connection will normally arise because the parents or one of the parents of the individual in question are or is identified by descent with the nation in question, but it may also sometimes arise because the parents have made their home among the people in question. Suppose, for example, that a man of purely French descent marries a woman of purely German descent and that the couple have made their home in England for many years before the birth of the child in question. It could, I think, fairly be said that the child had three "national origins": French through his father, German through his mother and English not because he happened to have been born here but because his parents had made their home here. Of course, in most cases a man has only a single "national origin" which coincides with his nationality at birth in the legal sense and again in most cases his nationality remains unchanged through-out his life. But "national origins" and "nationality" in the legal sense are two quite different conceptions and they may well not coincide or continue to coincide. . . . It is not difficult to see why the legislature in enacting the Race Relations Act 1965 used this new phrase "national origins" and not the word "nationality" which had a well-established meaning in law. It was because "nationality" in the strict sense was quite irrelevant to the problem with which they were faced. Most of the people against whom dis-crimination was being practised or hatred stirred up were in fact British subjects. The reason why the words "ethnic or national origins" were added to the words "racial grounds" which alone appear in the long title was, I imagine, to prevent argument over the exact meaning of the word "race". For example, a publican who had no objection to West Indians might refuse to serve Pakistanis. He would hardly be said to be discriminating against them on grounds of colour and it might well be argued that Pakistanis do not constitute a single "race". On the other hand, it could hardly be argued that they did not all have the same "national origin".'

What emerges from these speeches is that the terms used in s. 3 are to be understood in their popular rather than their scientific meaning (insofar as there is an agreed scientific meaning for them: see A. Dickey, 1974 JR 282), and to be read as cover-ing, under one head or another, members of all of those minority groups that might popularly be regarded as having a racial character. This approach is in tune with the statement made by the Home Secretary (Sir Frank Soskice) when the 1965 Bill was before Parliament (716 HC Deb 16 July 1965 cols 970–1):

'It is an objective which is of prime importance in the Bill that no grouping of citizens of whom one could, in ordinary English parlance, predicate that they have, or are thought to have, or are merely repre-sented to have, some common feature or characteristics or origins that, broadly speaking, one relates to the stem from which they proceed . . . should be excluded.
   The word "colour" is one which ordinarily would be understood. . . .
   The word "race" is perhaps a little more ambiguous. The words "ethnic or national origin" are delib-erately introduced into the Clause to make certain that no one is left out of the description "colour or race". We want to be certain that, because of some accident of language, some ambiguity of outline attaching to the words "colour or race", we do not fail to cover anybody who could possibly have fallen outside the ambit of these two words.'

2. Discrimination on the ground of 'nationality' was added by the 1976 Act in the light of the *Ealing* case. The 1976 Act s. 78(1) provides that 'unless the context otherwise requires' ' "nationality" includes "citizenship" '. See further on both con-cepts in the context of United Kingdom law, below, p. 684. Discrimination against aliens by legislation or with legislative authority in areas covered by the Act (e.g. higher tuition fees for overseas students) is protected by the 1976 Act, s. 41, see above, pp. 617, 628); other laws (e.g. those preventing an alien from owning a British ship or voting) are not within the Act because of their subject-matter.

3. Discrimination on religious or political grounds is not covered by the Act: see Lord Simon in the *Ealing* case, above and Lords Fraser and Templeman in the *Mandla* case, below. Lord Templeman supposed that Parliament 'considered that the amount of discrimination on religious grounds does not constitute a severe burden on members of religious groups.' An attempt to include discrimination on religious grounds in the 1976 Act was unsuccessful, the government arguing that a separate tailor-made bill would be necessary to deal with all of the issues peculiar to religion that would arise and that the Act's prohibition of indirect racial discrimination would (like that of direct discrimination) deal with a lot of cases of religious discrimination. See HC, Standing Committee A, 29 April 1976 and 4 May 1976, cols 84–118. Although some cases may be caught in this way (e.g. a 'No Hindus' rule would be indirect racial discrimination against Indians and the requirement in the *Malik* case, above, p. 632, was similarly discriminatory for Muslims), there are many cases that would escape. A 'No Catholics' rule would not be illegal if applied to an English Catholic. Whether a case is to be seen as religious or racial discrimination will in some cases turn upon the view of the court as to whether a person is being discriminated against by reference to his religion or his ethnic status: *Tower Hamlets London Borough Council v Rabin* [1989] ICR 693, EAT (Jewish faith or being a Jew).

Mandla v Dowell Lee [1983] 2 AC 548, [1983] 1 All ER 1062, [1983] 2 WLR 620, House of Lords

A Sikh solicitor resident in Birmingham applied for his son's admission to a private school. The application was refused because, as an orthodox Sikh, the son would have had to have worn a turban, contrary to school rules. The father complained to the CRE which supported county court proceedings, inter alia, for a declaration that the refusal was indirect discrimination contrary to ss. 1(1)(b) and 17(a) of the 1976 Act. The county court rejected the claim. The Court of Appeal, [1983] QB 1, dismissed an appeal on the ground that Sikhs were not a 'racial group' in the sense of s. 3(1), 1976 Act. The House of Lords unanimously allowed the appeal. The interval between the Court of Appeal and House of Lords hearings was marked by demonstrations indicating the strength of feeling in the Sikh community.

Lord Fraser. . . . the first question is whether the Sikhs are a racial group . . .

It is not suggested that Sikhs are a group defined by reference to colour, race, nationality or *national* origins. In none of these respects are they distinguishable from many other groups, especially those living, like most Sikhs, in the Punjab. The argument turns entirely upon whether they are a group defined by *'ethnic* origins.'. . .

The *Oxford English Dictionary* (1897 ed) gives two meanings of 'ethnic'. The first is 'Pertaining to nations not Christian or Jewish; gentile, heathen, pagan.' That clearly cannot be its meaning in the Act of 1976, because it is inconceivable that Parliament would have legislated against racial discrimination intending that the protection should not apply either to Christians or (above all) to Jews. . . . The second meaning . . . was 'Pertaining to race; peculiar to a race or nation; ethnological.' A slightly shorter form of that meaning (omitting 'peculiar to a race or nation') was given by the *Concise Oxford Dictionary* in 1934 and was expressly accepted by Lord Denning MR as the correct meaning for the present purpose. Oliver and Kerr LJJ also accepted that meaning as being substantially correct, and Oliver LJ . . . said that the word 'ethnic' in its popular meaning involved 'essentially a racial concept—the concept of something with which the members of the group are born; some fixed or inherited characteristic.' . . .

My Lords, I recognise that 'ethnic' conveys a flavour of race but it cannot, in my opinion, have been used in the Act of 1976 in a strictly racial or biological sense. For one thing, it would be absurd to suppose that Parliament can have intended that membership of a particular racial group should depend upon scientific proof that a person possessed the relevant distinctive biological characteristics (assuming that such characteristics exist). The practical difficulties of such proof would be prohibitive, and it is clear that Parliament must have used the word in some more popular sense. For another thing, the briefest glance at the evidence in this case is enough to show that, within the human race, there are very few, if any, distinctions which are scientifically recognised as racial. . . .

I turn therefore, to the third and wider meaning which is given in the *Supplement to the Oxford English Dictionary* (1972). It is as follows: 'pertaining to or having common racial, cultural, religious, or linguistic characteristics, esp. designating a racial or other group within a larger system; . . .' . . . The 1972 meaning is, in my opinion, too loose and vague to be accepted as it stands. It is capable of being read as implying that any one of the adjectives, 'racial, cultural, religious, *or* linguistic' would be enough to constitute an ethnic group. That cannot be the sense in which 'ethnic' is used in the Act of 1976, as that Act is not concerned at all with discrimination on religious grounds. . . . But in seeking for the true meaning of 'ethnic' in the statute, we are not tied to the precise definition in any dictionary. The value of the 1972 definition is, in my view, that it shows that ethnic has come to be commonly used in a sense appreciably wider than the strictly racial or biological. That appears to me to be consistent with the ordinary experience of those who read newspapers at the present day. In my opinion, the word 'ethnic' still retains a racial flavour but it is used nowadays in an extended sense to include other characteristics which may be commonly thought of as being associated with common racial origin.

For a group to constitute an ethnic group in the sense of the Act of 1976, it must, in my opinion, regard itself, and be regarded by others, as a distinct community by virtue of certain characteristics. Some of these characteristics are essential; others are not essential but one or more of them will commonly be found and will help to distinguish the group from the surrounding community. The conditions which appear to me to be essential are these: (1) a long shared history, of which the group is conscious as distinguishing it from other groups, and the memory of which it keeps alive; (2) a cultural tradition of its own, including family and social customs and manners, often but not necessarily associated with religious observance. In addition to those two essential characteristics the following characteristics are, in my opinion, relevant; (3) either a common geographical origin, or descent from a small number of common ancestors; (4) a common language, not necessarily peculiar to the group; (5) a common literature peculiar to the group; (6) a common religion different from that of neighbouring groups or from the general community surrounding it; (7) being a minority or being an oppressed or a dominant group within a larger community, for example a conquered people (say, the inhabitants of England shortly after the Norman conquest) and their conquerors might both be ethnic groups.

A group defined by reference to enough of these characteristics would be capable of including converts, for example, persons who marry into the group, and of excluding apostates. Provided a person who joins the group feels himself or herself to be a member of it, and is accepted by other members, then he is, for the purposes of the Act, a member. That appears to be consistent with the words at the end of s. 3(1): 'references to a person's racial group refer to any racial group into which he falls.' In my opinion, it is possible for a person to fall into a particular racial group either by birth or by adherence, and it makes no difference, so far as the Act of 1976 is concerned, by which route he finds his way into the group. This view does not involve creating any inconsistency between direct discrimination under paragraph (*a*) and indirect discrimination under paragraph (*b*). A person may treat another relatively unfavourably 'on racial grounds' because he regards that other as being of a particular race, or belonging to a particular racial group, even if his belief is, from a scientific point of view, completely erroneous.

Finally . . . I think it is proper to mention that the word 'ethnic' is . . . derived from the Greek word 'ethnos', the basic meaning of which appears to have been simply 'a group' not limited by reference to racial or any other distinguishing characteristics . . . I do not suggest that the meaning of the English word in a modern statute ought to be governed by the meaning of the Greek word from which it is derived, but the fact that the meaning of the latter was wide avoids one possible limitation on the meaning of the English word.

. . . The conclusion at which I have arrived by construction of the Act itself is greatly strengthened by consideration of the decision of the Court of Appeal in New Zealand . . . in *King-Ansell v Police* [1979] 2 NZLR 531. . . . If it had been before the Court of Appeal it might well have affected their decision. In that case the appellant had been convicted by a magistrate of an offence under the New Zealand Race Relations Act 1971, the offence consisting of publishing a pamphlet with intent to incite ill-will against Jews, 'on the ground of their ethnic origins.' . . . The decision of the Court of Appeal was that Jews in New Zealand did form a group with common ethnic origins within the meaning of the Act.

. . . Richardson J. said . . . :

'a group is identifiable in terms of its ethnic origins if it is a segment of the population distinguished from others by a sufficient combination of shared customs, beliefs, traditions and characteristics derived from a common or presumed common past, even if not drawn from what in biological terms is a common racial stock. It is that combination which gives them an historically determined social identity in their own eyes and in the eyes of those outside the group. They have a distinct social identity based not simply on group cohesion and solidarity but also on their belief as to their historical antecedents.'

–My Lords, that last passage sums up in a way upon which I could not hope to improve the views which I have been endeavouring to express . . .

. . . [Sikhs] were originally a religious community founded about the end of the 15th century in the Punjab by Guru Nanak . . . but the community is no longer purely religious in character. Their present position is summarised sufficiently for present purposes in the opinion of the learned judge in the county court in the following passage:

'The evidence in my judgment shows that Sikhs are a distinctive and self-conscious community. They have a history going back to the 15th century. They have a written language which a small proportion of Sikhs can read but which can be read by a much higher proportion of Sikhs than of Hindus. They were at one time politically supreme in the Punjab.'

The result is, in my opinion, that Sikhs are a group defined by a reference to ethnic origins for the purpose of the Act of 1976, although they are not biologically distinguishable from the other people living in the Punjab. . . . It is, therefore, necessary to consider whether the respondent has indirectly discriminated against the appellants in the sense of section 1(1)(*b*) of the Act. . . .

It is obvious that Sikhs, like anyone else, 'can' refrain from wearing a turban, if 'can' is construed literally. But if the broad cultural/historic meaning of ethnic is the appropriate meaning of the word in the Act of 1976, then a literal reading of the word 'can' would deprive Sikhs and members of other groups defined by reference to their ethnic origins of much of the protection which Parliament evidently intended the Act to afford to them. They 'can' comply with almost any requirement or condition if they are willing to give up their distinctive customs and cultural rules. On the other hand, if ethnic means inherited or unalterable, as the Court of Appeal thought it did, then 'can' ought logically to be read literally. The word 'can' is used with many shades of meaning. In the context of section 1(1)(*b*)(i) of the Act of 1976 it must, in my opinion, have been intended by Parliament to be read not as meaning 'can physically,' so as to indicate a theoretical possibility, but as meaning 'can in practice' or 'can consistently with the customs and cultural conditions of the racial group.' The latter meaning was attributed to the word by the Employment Appeal Tribunal in *Price v Civil Service Commission* [1978] ICR 27, on a construction of the parallel provision in the Sex Discrimination Act 1975. I agree with their construction of the word in that context. Accordingly I am of opinion that the 'No turban' rule was not one with which the second appellant could, in the relevant sense, comply.

The word 'justifiable' occurs in section 1(1)(*b*)(ii). It raises a problem which is, in my opinion, more difficult than the problem of the word 'can'. . . . Regarded purely from the point of view of the respondent, it was no doubt perfectly justifiable. He explained that he had no intention of discriminating against Sikhs. In 1978 the school had about 300 pupils (about 75 per cent boys and 25 per cent girls) of whom over 200 were English, five were Sikhs, 34 Hindus, 16 Persians, six negroes, seven Chinese and 15 from European countries. The reasons for having a school uniform were largely reasons of practical convenience—to minimise external differences between races and social classes, to discourage the 'competitive fashions' which he said tend to exist in a teenage community, and to present a Christian image of the school to outsiders, including prospective parents. The respondent explained the difficulty for a headmaster of explaining to a non-Sikh pupil why the rules about wearing correct school uniform were enforced against him if they were relaxed in favour of a Sikh. In my view these reasons could not, either individually or collectively, provide a sufficient justification for the respondent to apply a condition that is prima facie discriminatory under the Act.

An attempted justification of the 'No turban' rule, which requires more serious consideration, was that the respondent sought to run a Christian school, accepting pupils of all religions and races, and that he objected to the turban on the ground that it was an outward manifestation of a non-Christian faith. Indeed he regarded it as amounting to a challenge to that faith. I have much sympathy with the respondent on this part of the case and I would have been glad to find that the rule was justifiable within the meaning of the statute, if I could have done so. But in my opinion that is impossible. The onus under paragraph (ii) is on the respondent to show that the condition which he seeks to apply is not indeed a necessary condition, but that it is in all circumstances justifiable 'irrespective of the colour, race, nationality or ethnic or national origins of the person to whom it is applied'; that is to say that it is justifiable without regard to the ethnic origins of that person. But in this case the principal justification on which the respondent relies is that the turban is objectionable just because it is a manifestation of the second appellant's ethnic origins. That is not, in my view, a justification which is admissible under paragraph (ii). The kind of justification that might fall within that provision would be one based on public health, as in *Panesar v Nestlé Co Ltd (Note)* [1980] ICR 144, where the Court of Appeal held that a rule forbidding the wearing of beards in the respondent's chocolate factory was justifiable within the meaning of section 1(1)(*b*)(ii) on hygienic grounds, notwithstanding that the proportion of Sikhs who could [sc. conscientiously] comply with it was considerably smaller than the proportion of non-Sikhs who could comply with it. Again, it might be possible for the school to show that a rule insisting upon a fixed diet, which included some dish (for example, pork) which some racial groups could not conscientiously eat was justifiable if the school proved that the cost of providing special meals for the particular group would be prohibitive. Questions of that sort would be questions of fact for the tribunal of fact, and if there was evidence on which it could find the condition to be justifiable its finding would not be liable to be disturbed on appeal.

But in the present case I am of opinion that the respondents have not been able to show that the 'No turban' rule was justifiable.

Before parting with the case I must refer to some observations by the Court of Appeal . . . which suggest that the conduct of the Commission for Racial Equality in this case has been in some way unreasonable or oppressive. Lord Denning MR . . . merely expressed regret that the Commission had taken up the case. But Oliver LJ . . . used stronger language and suggested that the machinery of the Act had been operated against the respondent as 'an engine of oppression,' Kerr LJ . . . referred to notes of an interview between the respondent and an official of the Commission which he said read in part 'more like an inquisition than an interview' and which he regarded as harassment of the respondent.

My Lords, I must say I regard these strictures on the Commission and its officials as entirely unjustified. The Commission has a difficult task, and no doubt its inquiries will be resented by some and are liable to be regarded as objectionable and inquisitive. But the respondent in this case, who conducted his appeal with restraint and skill, made no complaint of his treatment at the hands of the Commission. . . . Opinions may legitimately differ as to the usefulness of the Commission's activities, but its functions have been laid down by Parliament and, in my view, the actions of the Commission . . . were perfectly proper and in accordance with its statutory duty.

I would allow this appeal. . . .

Lord Templeman: I agree with the Court of Appeal that in this context ethnic origins have a good deal in common with the concept of race just as national origins have a good deal in common with the concept of nationality. But the statutory definition of a racial group envisages that a group defined by reference to ethnic origins may be different from a group defined by reference to race, just as a group defined by reference to national origins may be different from a group defined by reference to nationality. In my opinion, for the purposes of the Race Relations Act a group of persons defined by reference to ethnic origins must possess some of the characteristics of a race, namely group descent, a group of geographical origin and a group history. The evidence shows that the Sikhs satisfy these tests. They are more than a religious sect, they are almost a race and almost a nation. As a race, the Sikhs share a common colour, and a common physique based on common ancestors from that part of the Punjab which is centred on Amritsar. they fail to qualify as a separate race because in racial origin prior to the inception of Sikhism they cannot be distinguished from other inhabitants of the Punjab. As a nation the Sikhs defeated the Moghuls, and established a kingdom in the Punjab which they lost as a result of the first and second Sikh wars; they fail to qualify as a separate nation or as a separate nationality because their kingdom never achieved a sufficient degree of recognition or permanence. The Sikhs qualify as a group defined by ethnic origins because they constitute a separate and distinct community derived from the racial characteristics I have mentioned. They also justify the conditions enumerated by my noble and learned friend, Lord Fraser of Tullybelton. The Sikh community has accepted converts who do not comply with those conditions. Some persons who have the same ethnic origins as the Sikhs have ceased to be members of the Sikh community. But the Sikhs remain a group of persons forming a community recognisable by ethnic origins within the meaning of the Act.

I agree that the appeal should be allowed.

Lords Edmund Davies, Roskill and **Brandon** concurred in both of the above speeches.

Appeal allowed.

NOTES[1]

1. This case makes it clear that Sikhs are protected by the 1976 Act, as a 'group of persons defined by reference to . . . ethnic origins'. This would appear to have been the intention of Parliament.[2] For further discussion of the cultural distinctiveness of the Sikh people, see the Court of Appeal judgment in the case, [1983] QB 1. Sikhs must comply with 'five Ks': they must leave their hair uncut (hence the turban to keep it in order); secure it with a comb; wear a long undergarment and a steel bracelet; and carry a symbolic dagger.

2. Is the meaning of 'ethnic origins' adopted by Lords Fraser and Templeman the same? Does Lord Templeman mention the second of Lord Fraser's two 'essential' characteristics (a 'cultural tradition')? Are all of the three necessary characteristics listed by Lord Templeman ('group descent', 'group of geographical origin', 'group history') regarded as essential by Lord Fraser? Does Lord Templeman refer to the

---

1 For comments on the case, see Beynon and Love, (1984) 100 LQR 120; Jefferson, (1983) 5 Liverpool LR 75; McKenna, (1983) 46 MLR 759; Robilliard, [1983] PL 348; Saunders, (1983) 7 Trent LJ 23.

2 See the reference to Sikhs by the government spokesman (Lord Harris), 373 HL Deb 27 September 1976 col 73.

other relevant characteristics referred to by Lord Fraser? Note that (1) Lord Templeman does say that Sikhs do 'justify the conditions enumerated by' Lord Fraser and (2) that the other three judges concurred in both speeches.[1] In 1965, the Home Secretary (Sir Frank Soskice), when asked what the word 'ethnic' added in the phrase 'colour, race or ethnic or national origins', replied (711 HC Deb 3 May 1965 col 932):

'We have chosen that connotation [quaere "combination"] of words to try to ensure that we include every possible minority group in the country . . . We hope, by the use of the word "ethnic", to cover everybody who is neither of a particular national origin nor of a particular racial origin but [quaere "or"] who would be distinguishable by colour'.

In 1976, the government spokesman (Lord Harris) explained that the wording 'ethnic or national origins' was intended to 'cover the examples which do not fit comfortably into "colour" or "race" ' and that this formula 'gets away from the idea of physical characteristics which inform the words "colour" and "race" and introduces the idea of groups defined by reference to cultural characteristics, geographic location, social organisation and so on'.[2]

3. *Mandla* also confirms that Jews are a 'racial group' within the 1976 Act. The definitions of 'ethnic origins' in both speeches include Jews. See too the specific references to Jews by Lord Fraser and in the Court of Appeal. In *Seide v Gillette Industries Ltd* [1980] IRLR 427, 430, EAT, alleged employment discrimination against a Jew was said to be within the Act if 'what happened . . . was not because Mr Seide was of the Jewish faith but [as was held] because he was a member of the Jewish race or of Jewish ethnic origin'. The absence of discrimination on religious grounds from the Act had raised the question whether Jews are protected by it: see Jewish Employment Group, [1983] PL 4. In the debate on the 1965 Act, the Home Secretary had no doubt:[3]

'It is certainly the intention of the Government that people of Jewish faith should be covered. The words have to be construed in law according to the ordinary canons of construction, as an ordinary person would read ordinary English language. I would have thought a person of Jewish faith, if not regarded as caught by the word "racial" would undoubtedly be caught by the word "ethnic", but if not caught by the word "ethnic" would certainly be caught by the scope of the word "national", as certainly having a national origin.'

Hepple (*Race, Jobs and the Law* (2nd edn, 1970), p. 37) suggests the following approach in cases where it is unclear whether a person is being less favourably treated because of his race or his religion:

'. . . [T]he problem is not really one of definition but of proof . . . it is erroneous to lay down, in the abstract, whether discrimination against Jews or Sikhs is on racial grounds rather than for religious reasons. In each case, . . . the actual relationship of the parties must be examined to determine whether the discriminator believed his victim to be a member of some distinct race and for that reason discriminated against him.'

Cf. the approach of the RRB in the following case (RRB Report 1970–1, p. 7):

---

1 In the *Dawkins* case, below, p. 645, the Court of Appeal stated that the two speeches in the *Mandla* case (1) were not to be read as the closely drafted text of a statute and (2) had the same meaning. In fact, Lord Fraser's speech was the one cited in *Dawkins*.
2 373 HL Deb 27 September 1976 col 74. There is a hotel in Glencoe which has a notice saying 'Positively no Campbells' (373 HL Deb 27 September 1976 col 75 (Lord Hailsham)). Is this contrary to the 1976 Act?
3 711 HC Deb 3 May 1965 cols 932–3. Some members were sceptical, believing that 'the Jewish identity is essentially a religious one' (Mr N. St. John–Stevas, Standing Committee B, col 70, 27 May 1965.

'Two complaints dealt with in the field of private education concerned allegations that children had been refused admission to certain schools because of their Jewish ethnic origin. The Act does not deal with discrimination on religious grounds; and it was maintained by the schools complained against that to admit more than a certain proportion of children of the Jewish faith would affect the Christian character of their schools, and that the schools therefore operated Jewish quotas which varied from 25 to 50 per cent. Enquiries showed that one of the schools was established by its charter as an Anglican foundation. The Christian character of the other school was not so apparent, but enquiries showed that the parents of the children concerned had answered "Jewish" to questions on the school's application form which asked for their religious denomination. In both of these cases the Board concluded that the discrimination was religious and not ethnic.'

What if D were to discriminate against V in the belief that V was a French national and for that reason when V was in fact a British citizen? Would that be direct discrimination? Can one rely on the understanding and motive of the discriminator in respect of *indirect* discrimination? Or is it necessary to decide to what 'racial group' V actually belongs?

4. In the *Ealing* case, above, p. 636, the House of Lords understood the phrase 'national origins' to refer to a connection *at birth*. Cf. Oliver and Kerr LJJ in the Court of Appeal in *Mandla v Dowell Lee*. Neither speech in the House of Lords imposes such a limitation when interpreting 'ethnic origins'. Sikhs were held to be a 'racial group' even though, as was acknowledged, the Sikh (like the Jewish) community accepts converts and excludes apostates.

5. On the meaning of 'can comply' and the 'justification' defence, see above, pp. 630, 631.

6. There were echoes of the *Mandla* case on its facts in a 1990 incident concerning two Muslim sisters who were refused permission to wear a hijab, or headscarf, to Altrincham Grammar School in accordance with their religious beliefs because this was contrary to school uniform rules. Following an approach from the CRE and much publicity, the school allowed the sisters to wear hijabs in the school colours: CRE Report 1990, p. 44.

Commission for Racial Equality v Dutton [1989] QB 783, [1989] 2 WLR 17, [1989] 1 All ER 306, Court of Appeal

The defendant was the licensee of the 'Cat and Mutton', Hackney. Having previously had trouble with persons who lived in illegally parked caravans, he put up a 'No Travellers' notice in his pub window. A local resident informed the CRE, who, acting under s. 63, 1976 Act, brought proceedings seeking a declaration that the notice was an unlawful advertisement contrary to s. 29. The claim having been rejected in the county court (gipsies not a racial group), the CRE appealed to the Court of Appeal.

Nicholls LJ: One of the difficulties in the present case, in my view, is that the word 'gipsy' has itself more than one meaning. The classic dictionary meaning can be found as the primary meaning given in the *Oxford English Dictionary* (1933):
  'A member of a wandering race (by themselves called *Romany*), of Hindu origin, which first appeared in England about the beginning of the 16th c. and was then believed to have come from Egypt.'.
Alongside this meaning, the word 'gipsy' also has a more colloquial, looser meaning. This is expressed in the *Longman Dictionary of Contemporary English* (1984), where two meanings are attributed to 'gipsy'. The first meaning is along the lines I have already quoted. The second is: 'a person who habitually wanders or who has the habits of someone who does not stay for long in one place': in short, a nomad.
I can anticipate here by noting that if the word 'gipsy' is used in this second, colloquial sense it is not definitive of a racial group within the 1976 Act. To discriminate against such a group would not be on racial grounds, namely on the ground of ethnic origins. As the judge observed, there are many people who travel around the country in caravans, vans, converted buses, trailers, lorries and motor vehicles, leading a peripatetic or nomadic way of life. They include didicois, mumpers, peace people, new age

travellers, hippies, tinkers, hawkers, self-styled 'anarchists', and others, as well as Romany gipsies. They may all be loosely referred to as 'gipsies', but as a group they do not have the characteristics requisite of a racial group within the Act. . . .

Like most English words, the meaning of the word 'traveller' depends on the context in which it is being used. It has one meaning when seen on a railway station . . . In my view, in the windows of the Cat and Mutton 'No travellers' will be understood by those to whom it is directed, namely potential customers, as meaning persons who are currently leading a nomadic way of life, living in tents or caravans or other vehicles. Thus the notices embrace gipsies who are living in that way. But the class of persons excluded from the Cat and Mutton is not confined to gipsies. The prohibited class includes all those of a nomadic way of life mentioned above. . . .

For this reason I cannot accept that Mr Dutton's notices indicate, or might reasonably be understood as indicating, an intention by him to do an act of discrimination within s. 1(1)(a). Excluded from the Cat and Mutton are all 'travellers', whether or not they are gipsies. All 'travellers', all nomads, are treated equally, whatever their race. They are not being discriminated against on racial grounds. . . .

That suffices to dispose of the claim based on s. 1(1)(a) of the 1976 Act, but . . . I must now turn to consider s. 1(1)(b), . . .

On this the first question which arises is whether gipsies are a racial group. . . .

The definition of 'racial group' in s. 3(1) includes a group of persons defined by reference to 'ethnic . . . origins'. This definition was considered by the House of Lords in *Mandla v Dowell Lee* [above, p. 638].

. . . with all respect to the judge, I am unable to agree with his conclusion on what have been called the *Mandla* conditions when applied, not to the larger amorphous group of 'travellers' or 'gipsies' (colloquially so-called), but to 'gipsies' in the primary, narrower sense of that word. On the evidence it is clear that such gipsies are a minority, with a long shared history and a common geographical origin. They are a people who originated in northern India. They migrated thence to Europe through Persia in medieval times. They have certain, albeit limited, customs of their own regarding cooking and the manner of washing. They have a distinctive traditional style of dressing, with heavy jewellery worn by the women, although this dress is not worn all the time. They also furnish their caravans in a distinctive manner. They have a language or dialect, known as 'pogadi chib', spoken by English gipsies (Romany chals) and Welsh gipsies (Kale) which consists of up to one-fifth of Romany words in place of English words. They do not have a common religion, nor a peculiar, common literature of their own, but they have a repertoire of folk-tales and music passed on from one generation to the next. No doubt, after all the centuries which have passed since the first gipsies left the Punjab, gipsies are no longer derived from what, in biological terms, is a common racial stock, but that of itself does not prevent them from being a racial group as widely defined in the 1976 Act.

I come now to the part of the case which has caused me most difficulty. Gipsies prefer to be called 'travellers' as they think that term is less derogatory. This might suggest a wish to lose their separate distinctive identity so far as the general public is concerned. Half or more of them now live in houses, like most other people. Have gipsies now lost their separate, group identity so that they are no longer a community recognisable by ethnic groups within the meaning of the Act? The judge held that they had. This is a finding of fact.

Nevertheless, with respect to the judge, I do not think that there was before him any evidence justifying his conclusion that gipsies has been absorbed into a larger group, if by that he meant that substantially all gipsies have been so absorbed. . . . In my view the evidence was sufficient to establish that, despite their long presence in England, gipsies have not merged wholly in the population, as have the Saxons and the Danes, and altogether lost their separate identity. They or many of them, have retained a separateness, a self-awareness, of still being gipsies. . . .

Having concluded that gipsies are a racial group, each of sub-paras (i) to (iii) in s. 1(1)(b) of the 1976 Act must be satisfied before the conduct complained of amounts to discrimination within the meaning of the Act. . . .

Clearly the proportion of gipsies who will satisfy the 'no travellers' condition is considerably smaller than the proportion of non-gipsies. Of the estimated gipsy population in the United Kingdom of some 80,000, between one-half and two-thirds now live in houses. But this still means that a far higher proportion of gipsies are leading a nomadic way of life than the rest of the population in general or, more narrowly, than the rest of the population who might wish to resort to the Cat and Mutton.

Counsel for Mr Dutton submitted that the word 'can' in the expression 'can comply' in sub-para (i) means 'can comply without giving up the distinctive customs and cultural rules of gipsies'. He submitted that gipsies can cease to be nomadic, and become house-dwellers, and comply with the 'no travellers' condition, without giving up their customs and cultures and that, therefore, sub-para (i) is not satisfied in this case. I do not accept this. Lord Fraser's words in *Mandla*'s case . . . were used in the context of a 'no turban' condition being applied in relation to a Sikh. Lord Fraser was rejecting the submission that 'can' meant 'can physically'. But that does not assist the solution of the present case. Indeed, gipsies can and do cease to be nomadic, but that will be of little use to a particular nomadic gipsy when he chances on the Cat and Mutton and wishes to go in for a drink. At that stage he is, in practice, unable to comply. In the present case the problem is a different one: at what moment of time does ability to comply fall to be judged? Is it when the condition is invoked (in this case, when the gipsy is outside the public house wishing to enter) or is it at some earlier date (which would give the gipsy sufficient opportunity to acquire housing accommodation for himself before turning up at the Cat and Mutton)?

A similar question was considered by the Employment Appeal Tribunal in *Clarke v Eley (IMI) Kynoch Ltd* [1983] ICR 165 with regard to s. 1(1) of the Sex Discrimination Act 1975, the wording of which does not differ materially from s. 1(1)(*b*) of the 1976 Act. Browne-Wilkinson J delivered the judgment of the tribunal to the effect that the relevant point of time at which the ability or inability to comply has to be shown is the date at which the requirement or condition has to be fulfilled. I find his reasoning compelling, and I agree with his conclusion (see [1983] ICR 165 at 171–172).

In my view, therefore, sub-para (i) is satisfied in the present case.

Sub-paragraph (iii) requires the applied condition to be to the relevant person's detriment because he cannot comply with it. Rightly, it was not disputed that sub-para (iii) is satisfied in the present case, by the hypothetical nomad gipsy being excluded from the Cat and Mutton (I say hypothetical, because there was no evidence that there were any gipsies among the travellers on the nearby sites). . . .

In these circumstances for my part I would remit the action to the county court for the judge to determine whether s. 1(1)(*b*)(ii) is satisfied in the present case and, if it is, for him to make such order as he considers appropriate. I would allow this appeal accordingly.

NOTES

1. The decision in the *Dutton* case that gipsies are a racial group follows clearly from the reasoning in the *Mandla* case. It has also been the view of the CRE. Acting on this basis, in the *Brymbo* Case, F. Invest. Rep. 1981, the CRE had issued non-discrimination notices after local residents had urged that a gipsy family not be re-housed in council housing.

2. The obligation imposed upon local authorities by the Caravan Sites Act 1968, s. 6(2), 'to provide adequate accommodation for gypsies' was repealed by the Criminal Justice and Public Order Act 1994, s. 80. For the purposes of the 1968 Act, 'gypsies' include not only gypsies in the *Dutton* racial group sense, but all 'persons of nomadic habit of life', provided that there is some connection between a person's nomadic way of life and the means by which he earns his living.[1] It has been argued that the removal of the duty to provide accommodation for gypsies and the new law of criminal trespass may amount to a breach of Article 8, ECHR, from which may be inferred a right to engage in a nomadic lifestyle.[2]

3. In *Crown Suppliers (PSA) v Dawkins*,[3] it was held that rastafarians are not an ethnic group in the sense of the *Mandla* case, so that failure to employ the applicant as a van driver because, as a rastafarian, he refused to cut his dreadlocks was not discrimination contrary to the 1976 Act. Neill LJ stated:

'It is clear that Rastafarians have certain identifiable characteristics. They have a strong cultural tradition which includes a distinctive form of music known as reggae music. They adopt a distinctive form of hairstyle by wearing dreadlocks. They have other shared characteristics of which both the industrial tribunal and the appeal tribunal were satisfied. But the crucial question is whether they have established some

---

1 1968 Act, s. 6, as interpreted in *R v South Hams District Council, ex p Gibb* [1994] 4 All ER 1012, CA. The duty is replaced by a power on the part of local authorities to provide a place of accommodation in their discretion.

2 Response to Consultation Paper on the Reform of the Caravan Sites Act 1968, memorandum prepared by and available from Justice.

3 [1993] ICR 517, 528. Neill LJ's judgment was concurred in by a unanimous court. On the *Dawkins* case, see N. Parpworth, 143 NLJ 610 (1993). On rastafarians, see M. Banton, (1989) 16 New Community 153. See generally on state education and the 1976 Act, L. Lustgarten and V. Giles, (1981) 4 Urban Law and Policy 55.

separate identity by reference to their ethnic origins. In speaking about Rastafarians in this context I am referring to the core group, because I am satisfied that a core group can exist even though not all the adherents of the group could, if considered separately, satisfy any of the relevant tests.

It is at this stage that one has to take account of both the racial flavour of the word "ethnic" and Lord Fraser's requirement of a long shared history. Lord Meston submitted that if one compared Rastafarians with the rest of the Jamaican community in England, or indeed with the rest of the Afro-Caribbean community in this country, there was nothing to set them aside as a separate *ethnic* group. They are a separate group but not a separate group defined by reference to their ethnic origins. I see no answer to this submission.

Mr. Whitmore quite rightly stressed that this case is concerned with identity. The question is: have the Rastafarians a separate *ethnic* identity? Do they stand apart by reason of *their* history from other Jamaicans?

In my judgment it is not enough for Rastafarians now to look back to a past when their ancestors, in common with other peoples in the Caribbean, were taken there from Africa. They were not a separate group then. The *shared* history of Rastafarians goes back only 60 years or so. One can understand and admire the deep affection which Rastafarians feel for Africa and their longing for it as their real home. But, as Mr. Riza recognises, the court is concerned with the language of the statute.'

3 Education

Race Relations Act 1976

17. Discrimination by bodies in charge of educational establishments
It is unlawful, in relation to an educational establishment falling within column 1 of the following table [omitted], for a person indicated in relation to the establishment in column 2 (the 'responsible body') to discriminate against a person—
  (a) in the terms on which it offers to admit him to the establishment as a pupil; or
  (b) by refusing or deliberately omitting to accept an application for his admission to the establishment as a pupil; or
  (c) where he is a pupil of the establishment—
      (i) in the way it affords him access to any benefits, facilities or services, or by refusing or deliberately omitting to afford him access to them; or
      (ii) by excluding him from the establishment or subjecting him to any other detriment.

18. Other discrimination by local education authorities
(1) It is unlawful for a local education authority, in carrying out such of its functions under the Education Acts 1944 to [1980] as do not fall under section 17, to do any act which constitutes racial discrimination. . . .

19. General duty in public sector of education
(1) Without prejudice to its obligation to comply with any other provision of this Act, a body to which this subsection applies shall be under a general duty to secure that facilities for education provided by it, and any ancillary benefits or services, are provided without racial discrimination.

NOTES

1. Section 17 applies, by virtue of the Table attached to it, to all state and independent primary and secondary schools in England and Wales, including private schools for handicapped children and private community homes (education). It also applies to most institutions of higher education. Universities, polytechnics, colleges of education, colleges of further education and designated institutions (such as the College of Nursing and the Co-operative College) are within the section. Other non-designated institutions are controlled by s. 20, below, p. 649, not s. 17.
2. Although the 1968 Act did not contain any provision comparable to s. 17 dealing just with discrimination in education, a number of cases arose under the equivalent provision to the 1976 Act, s. 20, below, in respect of educational facilities. A case in which a private preparatory school was found by the RRB to have

unlawfully refused to admit a child of Iranian origin (Case 6, RRB Report 1974, p. 36) would now come within s. 17(1)(b). For the 'Jewish quota' case, see above, p. 643. The RRB also examined under the 1968 Act the London Borough of Ealing's dispersal policy for immigrant children. By this policy, Asian children were not admitted to local schools in Southall but 'bussed' to 'white' schools elsewhere within the Borough's jurisdiction. White children were not 'bussed'. After obtaining the opinion of an expert assessor, the RRB reported on the policy as follows (RRB Report 1975–76, p. 6):

'30. In his report Professor Kogan explained that dispersal was introduced in Ealing in the mid-1960s. In 1976 nearly 3,000 Asian children of primary school age were sent by coach every day to other parts of the Borough. In the great majority of cases the dispersal was on educational grounds, but there was evidence which suggested that a number of these children were dispersed away from their neighbourhood schools even though their knowledge of the English language was perfectly adequate. The local authority argued that any such Asian children were dispersed because of cultural needs. The Board formed the opinion that such children were being treated less favourably than other children for no other reason than their ethnic origins. Attempts at conciliation failed and the Board determined to bring proceedings.'

After legal proceedings had been instituted against the Borough (see *Race Relations Board v London Borough of Ealing (No 2)* [1978] 1 WLR 112, CA), an out of court settlement was reached (CRE Report 1978, p. 101):

'The central feature of the settlement was that in future no child would be "bussed" except on the basis of educational need, and a special assessment procedure was introduced to enable the language needs of children entering the education system for the first time to be individually defined. Moreover, no additional children would be "bussed" after September 1979 and it was expected that new school building in the Southall area would enable "bussing" to be completely phased out by 1981.'

See also the dispersal case reported in RRB Report 1974, p. 6. What would have to be proved to establish that 'bussing' in these dispersal cases was direct or indirect discrimination? Note the dictum in *Cumings v Birkenhead Corpn* [1972] Ch 12, CA, that the allocation of children to particular schools on the basis of the colour of their skin would be unlawful as an 'abuse of power' (quite apart from race relations legislation). In the US, the Supreme Court has, controversially, required the 'bussing' of children (white children to black neighbourhood schools and vice-versa) to overcome the effects of segregation previously imposed by law in state schools (*Swann v Charlotte-Mecklenburg* 402 US 1 (1971)). Other courts have permitted state educational authorities to operate two-way 'bussing' systems in their discretion to overcome de facto segregation resulting from natural population trends (see, e.g., *Addabbo v Donovan* 209 NE 2d 112 (1965), NY Ct App). No such 'bussing' has been required or undertaken in the UK.

Another issue has been the testing and classification of school children as educationally subnormal and their placement in special schools. Following a complaint concerning Haringey, 'the Board noted that West Indian children in the borough concerned, and in a number of other local education authority areas, were over-represented in the group considered to be educationally sub-normal. The evidence suggested that this situation had come about because the intelligence tests in general use do not effectively distinguish the educationally sub-normal from those whose performance is at a similar level as a result of educational or cultural deprivation' (RRB Report 1970–71, p. 7). The RRB did not consider that there had been any unlawful discrimination contrary to the 1968 Act. Might there be *indirect* discrimination under the 1976 Act?

In the *Teaching of English as a Second Language* case F. Invest. Rep. 1986, Calderdale, in West Yorkshire, had required all children whose language at home was not English to undergo language scrutiny, with the likely consequence of being placed in separate language units instead of the usual school classes. Such units might be located at places requiring pupils to be bussed to school; their curriculum was also more restricted than the normal curriculum. The CRE concluded that these arrangements could not be justified on educational grounds and amounted to indirect discrimination.

In another complaint to the RRB it was alleged (but not proven) that a headmaster had discriminated in the protection of school children from assault by other children (Case 5, RRB Report 1972, p. 35). Would this be unlawful discrimination under any part of s. 17?

3. Unlike s. 17, ss. 18 and 19 apply only to 'racial discrimination', which (see s. 3(3) above, p. 636) excludes victimisation contrary to s. 2. The allocation of local authority grants for higher education is subject to s. 18. A three year residence condition for eligibility for such grants was considered by the RRB to work harshly against some immigrant pupils seeking further education but was not thought to be contrary to the 1968 Act (RRB Report 1969–70, p. 9). It is lawful under s. 41, 1976 Act, above, p. 617.

4. In the *Secondary School Allocations in Reading* case, F. Invest. Rep. 1983, the CRE investigated allegations of discrimination in new school zoning arrangements adopted by Berkshire LEA. Although it did not find the arrangements to be discriminatory, the CRE did conclude that 'the Authority had carried out no analysis of what the consequence of their scheme would be for ethnic minority pupils. . . . To that extent the Authority had taken insufficient account of their duties under [ss. 19 and 71 of the] Race Relations Act' (Report, p. vi). In 1982, the CRE considered a complaint that a group of parents of children at the Greenfield Primary School, Hyde, had attempted to induce the local authority to limit the number of children of Asian origin attending the school. It concluded that s. 31 of the 1976 Act had been infringed. The parents accepted this finding and undertook not to contravene the Act again (CRE Report 1982, p. 12).

The 1976 Act imposes no duty of positive action upon a local education authority to ensure that there are Asian children in a school's catchment area: *R v Bradford Metropolitan Borough Council, ex p Sikander Ali* (1993) Times, 21 October.

An admissions procedure by which parents were required to give at least four reasons for the admission of their children to particular schools was indirect discrimination against Asian parents because of their difficulties with English and their relative lack of knowledge and experience of the British education system: *Secondary Schools Admissions*, F. Invest. Rep. 1992.

5. For a case arising under s. 17 concerning tuition fees for overseas students, see the *Orphanos* case, above, p. 628.

6. On the special rules for the enforcement of ss. 17–19, see below, p. 677.

7. The duty of a local education authority under the Education Act 1980, s. 6, to comply with a parent's request to transfer a child to another school is not limited by s. 18 of the Race Relations Act. In *R v Cleveland County Council, ex p Commission for Racial Equality* (1993) 91 LGR 139, CA, an education authority complied with a mother's request to transfer her five year old daughter, who was of mixed English and African descent, from a primary school that had nearly all Asian pupils to one that was predominantly white. The request was made for fear that the daughter would learn a Pakistani language at the expense of her English. It was held that the education authority had not committed an act of discrimination contrary to s. 18; its duty to transfer the child was not limited by s. 18 (since the duty fell under s. 17) and, in any event, the transfer was not, as argued, an act of segregation contrary to

s. 2 of the Race Relations Act so that the authority had not committed any act of racial discrimination. The CRE had reached the contrary conclusion in a formal investigation report: *Racial Segregation in Education* (1989).

4 Goods, facilities and services

Race Relations Act 1976

20. Discrimination in provision of goods, facilities or services
(1) It is unlawful for any person concerned with the provision (for payment or not) of goods, facilities or services to the public or a section of the public to discriminate against a person who seeks to obtain or use those goods, facilities or services—
    (*a*) by refusing or deliberately omitting to provide him with any of them; or
    (*b*) by refusing or deliberately omitting to provide him with goods, facilities or services of the like quality, in the like manner and on the like terms as are normal in the first-mentioned person's case in relation to other members of the public or (where the person so seeking belongs to a section of the public) to other members of that section.
(2) The following are examples of the facilities and services mentioned in subsection (1)—
    (*a*) access to and use of any place which members of the public are permitted to enter;
    (*b*) accommodation in a hotel, boarding house or other similar establishment;
    (*c*) facilities by way of banking or insurance or for grants, loans, credit or finance;
    (*d*) facilities for education;
    (*e*) facilities for entertainment, recreation or refreshment;
    (*f*) facilities for transport or travel;
    (*g*) the services of any profession or trade, or any local or other public authority.

NOTES

1. *Goods, facilities or services*. These terms are not defined in the Act. A. Lester and G. Bindman, *Race and Law* (1972) p. 260, suggest:

'They must be given their ordinary and natural meaning. "Goods" are any movable property, including merchandise or wares. "Facilities" include any opportunity for obtaining some benefit or for doing something. "Services" refer to any conduct tending to the welfare or advantage of other people, especially conduct which supplies their needs. Each of these expressions is deliberately vague and general; taken together, they cover a very wide range of human activity.'

Manufacturers, wholesalers and retailers are all subject to s. 20. Thus a wholesaler who refused to supply a retailer (retailers being a 'section of the public') with goods on racial grounds would be in breach of the Act. In *Dockers' Labour Club and Institute Ltd v Race Relations Board* [1976] AC 285 at 297, HL, Lord Diplock stated that 'normally' (now 'normal' in the 1976 Act) indicated that the Act was not intended to deal with persons who supplied goods, etc., 'on an isolated occasion'; it concerned only persons who did so 'regularly'.
2. Section 20(2) gives certain examples of 'facilities and services'. Places 'which members of the public are permitted to enter' include shops, banks, public houses, restaurants, public parks, dance halls, and theatres. This first example overlaps with the subsequent ones in that many of the places that come within it (e.g. public houses) provide a 'facility' (e.g. refreshment) listed in another. The place may be publicly or privately owned. There need be no legal right of entry; a licence to enter is sufficient. The test is whether the public or a section of it (e.g. persons over 18) are customarily or on a particular occasion (e.g. garden open to the public one day in the year) 'permitted to enter'.[1] Would the organisers of the meeting in *Thomas v*

1 See further A. Lester and G. Bindman, *Race and Law*, (1972) pp. 261–2, and M. Supperstone, *Brownlie's Law of Public Order and National Security* (2nd edn, 1981), pp. 33–34.

Sawkins, above, p. 259, have been entitled to exclude a black member of the public from the meeting because of his colour? A District Registrar provides 'facilities or services' when carrying out 'his duties' in the course of applications for marriage licences.[1] Prison work is a 'facility' for prisoners, who constitute a 'section of the public', for the purposes of s. 20: *Alexander v Home Office*, below, p. 678.

3. 'Hotel' in the phrase 'hotel, boarding house or other similar establishment' can be taken to have the meaning that it has in the Hotel Proprietors Act 1956, s. 1(3):

'An establishment held out by the proprietor as offering food, drink and if so required sleeping accommodation, without special contract, to any traveller presenting himself who appears able and willing to pay a reasonable sum for the services and facilities provided and who is in a fit state to be received.'

This definition is also that of an inn at common law. An innkeeper is obliged at common law to receive allcomers without discrimination. Thus in the famous case of *Constantine v Imperial Hotels Ltd* [1944] 1 KB 693, KBD, judgment was awarded against an innkeeper for refusing to accommodate a well known black West Indian cricketer (and later a member of the Race Relations Board) during the Second World War for fear of upsetting members of the US armed forces. The case would now fall within the 1976 Act, s. 20 and the plaintiff would have to bring proceedings under the Act and not at common law (see the 1976 Act, s. 53, below, p. 674). The wording 'boarding house or other similar establishment' includes bed and breakfast establishments and other establishments insofar as they offer *short-term* (see 'similar') residential accommodation for travellers. A holiday camp might qualify; it might also be said to offer facilities for 'recreation'. The longer term 'facilities' offered by private or residential hotels, 'bed-sits', and university halls probably fall within s. 21, below, and not s. 20. (But note that a *long-term* private children's home was treated by the CRE as being within s. 20 in the *Barlavington Manor Children's Home* case, F. Invest. Rep. 1979.) But the examples listed in s. 20(2) are not exhaustive[2] and it could be that as far as accommodation is concerned there is some overlap between ss. 20 and 21, below. In that case, the generality of the wording of s. 20 ('facilities for . . .') might in a few cases make it more useful than the more precise wording of s. 21. In the *Hackney* case, below, p. 658, an enforcement notice was issued in respect of both ss. 20 and 21. In the *Racial Discrimination in Liverpool City Council Housing Department* case, F. Invest. Rep. 1989, in which the CRE found that the Housing Department had consistently allocated poorer quality council housing to ethnic minority applicants, the enforcement notice was in respect of s. 20 only. The 'small premises' exception in s. 22, below, applies to both s. 20 and s. 21.

4. The prohibition of discrimination in respect of the making of 'loans' includes the granting of mortgages. In the *Race and Mortgage Lending* case F. Invest. Rep. 1985, the CRE found that certain rules applied in the allocation of mortgages by building societies in Rochdale (e.g. no mortgages for houses without front gardens, which were mostly city centre houses where ethnic minorities tended to live) was indirect discrimination contrary to s. 20.

5. Although s. 20 refers to 'facilities for education' without qualification, the 1976 Act, s. 23(1), provides that s. 20 does not apply to discrimination in education rendered unlawful by ss. 17–18, above. As a result, s. 20 has only a modest role. It applies to establishments not covered by s. 17, such as driving schools, foreign language schools, crammers, and to piano lessons (whether in the pupil's home or that of the teacher).

---

1 *Tejani v Superintendent Registrar for the District of Peterborough* [1986] IRLR 502, CA. See J. Gardner, (1987) 50 MLR 345.
2 See Lord Simon in *Applin v Race Relations Board* [1975] AC 259, 291, HL.

6. For a case of discrimination by a restaurant ('facilities for refreshment'), see the *Genture Restaurants Ltd* case, F. Invest. Rep. 1978 (restrictions on black persons and Chinese: illegal discrimination).

7. 'Facilities for transport and travel' include sleeping cabins for passengers on board ship. The 1968 Act, s. 7(6), permitted the segregation of persons of different 'racial groups' in such cabins as a result of pressure from British shipping companies to protect them from international competition. As with innkeepers, the obligation of the common carrier at common law to accept allcomers is placed upon a statutory basis and any proceedings against him for racial discrimination must be brought under the 1976 Act, s. 53 below, p. 674.

8. 'Trade' in the phrase 'the services of any profession or trade or any local or other public authority' includes 'any business' (1976 Act, s. 78(1)). Estate agents and accommodation bureaux come within this wording (they *may* be subject to s. 21 too, see below). A PEP Report in 1974 (McIntosh and Smith, *The Extent of Racial Discrimination* (1974)) showed that discrimination by estate agents against Asian and West Indian house buyers had dropped a lot in the five years since the law was extended to cover housing in 1968. There had been discrimination in 64% of cases in tests conducted in 1967. In tests in 1973 there was discrimination in one form or another in 17% of cases. According to one manager of an accommodation agency, '95 per cent of landlords using the agency gave racially discriminating instructions' (RRB Report 1974, p. 12). The CRE has issued non-discrimination notices in several cases against estate agents.[1] Estate agents are also controlled in respect of racial discrimination by the Estate Agents Act 1979.[2] An estate agent is defined as 'a person who, by way of profession or trade, provides services for the purpose of finding premises for persons seeking to acquire them or assisting in the disposal of premises' (1976 Act, s. 78(1)). An estate agent (or accommodation bureau) may rely upon the 'small premises' exception (1976 Act, s. 22, below) even if the property does not fall within it if he has taken 'all reasonable steps in the circumstances to ensure that the accommodation with which he is concerned and in respect of which racial stipulations are sought to be imposed falls within' it: *Race Relations Board v Furnished Rooms Bureau*, Westminster C Ct 1972 RRB Report p. 38. Normally, 'the agent could be expected in relation to each property to ascertain and record the specific facts relevant to section 7 [1968 Act, see now the 1976 Act s. 22] and would, where any doubt existed, carry out further investigation to satisfy himself that the criteria in the section were met': ibid.

The 1976 Act is supplemented by the Consumer Credit Act 1974, s. 25(2)(c), which provides that in determining whether an applicant for a licence to carry on a consumer credit or consumer hire business is a 'fit person', account must be taken of evidence that he has practised discrimination on grounds of sex, colour, race or ethnic or national origins in or in connection with the carrying on of any business.

9. The wording 'local or other public authority' covers discrimination in the provision of public housing (as does s. 21) and other 'services'. See, e.g., the *Hackney Council Housing* case, below, p. 658. In *Hillingdon London Borough Council v Commission for Racial Equality* [1982] AC 779, HL, the Council was obliged by statute to house homeless persons within its area, which included Heathrow airport,

---

1 See, e.g. *Racial Discrimination in an Oldham Estate Agency*, F. Invest. Rep. 1990 and *Allen's Accommodation Bureau* case, F. Invest. Rep. 1980.
2 The Director General of Fair Trading may stop a person from doing estate agency work if he is satisfied that the person has been discriminating: 1979 Act, s. 1(3)(b). The Director may also revoke a licence to grant mortgages of an estate agent who has practised discrimination: Consumer Credit Act 1974, s. 25(2).

at ratepayers' expense. In protest, a Councillor drove a Kenyan Asian family, then recently arrived, to Whitehall and left them on the steps of the Foreign Office. A white Rhodesian family that arrived in the same period was housed without difficulty. It was accepted in argument that s. 20 had been infringed. In *Commission for Racial Equality v Riley* (1982) CRE Report 1982, p. 18, Manchester C Ct, it was held that the granting of planning permission was a 'service' or 'facility' (injunction restraining National Front officer from bringing pressure to bear (contrary to s.31) on the planning authority to refuse planning applications from black persons). Following the *Amin* case, below, p. 653, doubts were expressed as to the correctness of this decision. These doubts have been resolved by s. 19A, 1976 Act, added by the Housing and Planning Act 1986, by which 'it is unlawful for a planning authority to discriminate against a person in carrying out their planning functions'. The police were intended by Parliament to be covered only in the few areas where they offer 'services' (e.g. crime prevention advice); discrimination in the course of their operational duties was understood to be subject not to s. 20 of the 1976 Act, but to the police complaints procedure under other legislation (see above, p. 47): cf. 374 HL Deb 29 September 1976 col 525. The work of other public servants such as immigration officers, public health inspectors and Inland Revenue officials likewise was understood not to constitute a 'service'; cf. ibid.

In *Savjani v IRC* [1981] QB 458, CA, however, the IRC had a policy by which a taxpayer born in the Indian subcontinent who was claiming tax relief for the first time for a child born in the UK had to provide a full birth certificate, which gave details of the parents and cost £2.50. In the case of other taxpayers, a short birth certificate, which gave no such details and cost nothing, was sufficient. The policy had been introduced because fraudulent claims to relief had been made by persons originating from the Indian subcontinent based upon false documents. The Court of Appeal held unanimously that, in its operation of the tax relief system, the Inland Revenue was providing a 'service' in the sense of s. 20(2)(g), which was infringed on the facts of the case. Templeman LJ stated:

'. . . the board and the inspector are performing duties. . . . The duty is to collect the right amount of revenue; but, in my judgment, there is a service to the taxpayer provided by the board and the inspector by the provision, dissemination and implementation of regulations which will enable the taxpayer to know that he is entitled to a deduction or a repayment which will entitle him to know how he is to satisfy the inspector or the board if he is so entitled, and which will enable him to obtain the actual deduction or repayment which Parliament said he is to have. For present purposes, in my judgment, the inspector and the board provide the inestimable services of enabling a taxpayer to obtain that relief which Parliament intended he should be able to obtain as a matter of right subject only to proof.

Now if the inspector or the board make it more difficult for a taxpayer—who is entitled to relief if he does satisfy all the conditions—to obtain that relief than they do for other taxpayers, they are discriminating in the provision of the service to the public and the service to him of enabling tax relief to be obtained.'

It was pointed out by the Court of Appeal that it would have been possible for the Minister concerned to have sanctioned the illegal policy in accordance with s. 41(2)(a), see above, p. 617.

The Court of Appeal distinguished *R v Immigration Appeal Tribunal, ex p Kassam* [1980] 2 All ER 330, [1980] 1 WLR 1037, CA, in which it was held that the Home Secretary was not providing a 'facility' in the sense of s. 29 of the Sex Discrimination Act 1975 (the equivalent provision to s. 20) when exercising powers under the Immigration Act 1971 in respect of entry to the UK. In that case, Stephenson LJ stated:

'The kind of facilities with which the sections of the Acts of 1975 and 1976 are concerned is of the same order as goods and services, and though it may not always be easy to say whether a particular person (or body of persons) is a person concerned with the provision of any of those three things to the public or a section of the public and although a Minister of the Crown or a government department might be such a person (for instance, in former days the Postmaster General . . .), I am clearly of the opinion that the Secretary of State in acting under the Immigration Act and Rules is not such a person, and he cannot be held to have discriminated against the appellant by refusing to give him leave to remain here while his wife was a student, or by refusing to interpret or alter the immigration rule . . . which is relevant to this appeal. He is operating in a field outside the fields in which Parliament has forbidden sex discrimination.'

Both the *Kassam* and *Savjani* cases were approved by the House of Lords in *Re Amin* [1983] 2 AC 818. In that case, an Asian woman who was a UK citizen was refused a special entry voucher for admission to the UK because she was not a head of household. Her claim that this was sex discrimination contrary to the 1975 Act was rejected by the House of Lords by the narrow majority of 3 to 2. Lord Fraser, giving the only speech for the majority, stated (p. 835):

My Lords, I accept that the examples in s. 29(2) are not exhaustive, but they are, in my opinion, useful pointers to aid in the construction of subsection (1). S. 29 as a whole seems to me to apply to the direct provision of facilities or services, and not to the mere grant of permission to use facilities. That is in accordance with the words of subsection (1), and it is reinforced by some of the examples in subsection (2). Example (*a*) is 'access to *and use of* any place' and the words that I have emphasised indicate that the paragraph contemplates actual provision of facilities which the person will use. Example (*d*) refers, in my view, to the actual provision of schools and other facilities for education, but not to the mere grant of an entry certificate or a special voucher to enable a student to enter the United Kingdom in order to study here. Example (*g*) seems to me to be contemplating things such as medical services, or library facilities, which can be directly provided by local or other public authorities. So in *Savjani*, Templeman LJ took the view that the Inland Revenue performed two separate functions—first a duty of collecting revenue and secondly a service of providing taxpayers with information. . . . In the present case the entry clearance officer in Bombay was in my opinion not providing a service for would-be immigrants; rather he was performing his duty of controlling them.

Counsel for the appellant sought to draw support for his contention from section 85(1) of the Act of 1975 [cf. s. 75(1), 1976 Act, above, p. 615: identical wording] . . . . That section puts an act done on behalf of the Crown on a par with an act done by a private person, and it does not in terms restrict the comparison to an act *of the same kind* done by a private person. But in my opinion it applies only to acts done on behalf of the Crown which are of a kind similar to acts that might be done by a private person. It does not mean that the Act is to apply to any act of any kind done on behalf of the Crown by a person holding statutory office. There must be acts . . . done in the course of formulating or carrying out government policy, which are quite different in kind from any act that would ever be done by a private person, and to which the Act does not apply. I would respectfully agree with the observations on the corresponding provision of the Race Relations Act 1976 made by Woolf J in *Home Office v Commission for Racial Equality* [1982] QB 385 at 395B–C. Part V of the Act of 1975 makes exceptions for certain acts including acts done for the purpose of national security (s. 52 [cf. s. 42, 1976 Act]) and for acts which are 'necessary' in order to comply with certain statutory requirements: s. 51 [cf. s. 41, 1976 Act]. These exceptions will no doubt be effective to protect acts which are of a kind that would otherwise be unlawful under the Act. But they do not in my view obviate the necessity for construing s. 29 as applying only to acts which are at least similar to acts that could be done by private persons.

In *Home Office v Commission for Racial Equality*, Woolf J had stated:

In relation to [s. 75] sub-s. (1) it was contended on behalf of the Home Office that that only applies to acts which could be done by a private person. . . . Thus, in the course of argument, Mr Scott contended that if an immigration officer treated coloured immigrants in a wholly different manner from the way in which he treated white immigrants, this would not be an act to which section 75 referred, because it was not an act capable of being done by an individual.

I cannot accept this restricted interpretation of section 75. It is true that only an immigration officer and not a private person can purport to exercise immigration control. However, the type of act to which I have just made reference is one which a private person in a different capacity is quite able to perform, for example a doorkeeper at a nightclub, and so it seems to me that that would be an act falling within section 75. After all it is only a government department who can engage immigration officers. A private individual cannot do that. But the Home Office concedes that such an engagement would be an act within section 75.

. . . It appears to me that an act, for the purposes of section 75, which is defined in section 78 as including a deliberate omission, means some act which, while not necessarily the same, is one similar to the kind of act which can amount to unlawful discrimination under the Act of 1976.

What if an income tax official were to discriminate when investigating a person's income? Would this be contrary to s. 20? Is the *Riley* case, above, consistent with the interpretation of ss. 20 and 75 of the 1976 Act in the *Amin* case?

The CRE has recommended that the *Amin* decision be reversed by Parliament, so that s. 20 should apply to 'all areas of governmental and regulatory activity, whether central or local, such as acts in the course of immigration control, the prison and police services, and planning control'.[1] The particular areas of the public sector listed above are ones in which there have been allegations and some proven instances of racial discrimination. As the CRE states, the lack of a remedy in most of the public sector is serious given the importance of many of the decisions taken for individuals and the fact that, in contrast with the case of discrimination by a private person, there is usually no opportunity to go elsewhere.

10. In *Applin v Race Relations Board* [1975] AC 259, HL, Lord Wilberforce, after studying the examples given in it, drew the following conclusion from s. 2(2) of the 1968 Act (now the 1976 Act s. 20(2)):

'What it suggests, in combination with section 2(1), is that the area in which discrimination is forbidden is that in which a person is concerned to provide something which in its nature is generally offered to and needed by the public at large, or a section of it, which is offered impersonally to all who choose to go through the doors or approach the counter: things which, in their nature, would be provided to anyone, and the refusal of which to persons of different colour etc., could only be ascribed to discrimination on grounds of colour etc. Conversely, they do not extend to matters, the provision of which is a private matter, as to which the motives of the refusing provider may reasonably have nothing to do with colour etc., at all.'

11. An early problem in cases referred to the RRB was discrimination in motor and life insurance. A number of complaints revealed that it was common for insurance companies to refuse car hire insurance if the applicant was born abroad. The Board took the view that this was illegal discrimination ('national origins') (RRB Report 1968–69, p. 14) and negotiated an agreement with the Lloyd's Motor Underwriters' Association by which members of the Association would replace their 'born abroad' test by one of three years' residence together with appropriate driving experience. (RRB Report 1969-70, p. 50). A 'born abroad' restriction was imposed in *Kelsall v National Motor and Accident Insurance Union* (1980) CRE Report 1980, p. 84, Westminster C Ct (named driver restriction in car insurance for German born car owner resident in UK 16 years; liability under s. 20 admitted). On the question of residence, the CRE takes the view that, with the introduction of indirect discrimination in 1976, a general three years' residence requirement, which remains common practice, may be illegal: *Zone Insurance Co Ltd* case, F. Invest. Rep. 1982, p. 13. In respect of life insurance, the RRB took up a case in which a form used by a life assurance society asked the proposer to state whether he was 'Caucasian, Negroid or Asian'. The company agreed to abandon this question and to ask instead about the proposer's length of residence in the United Kingdom. The Board took the view that 'dubious anthropological concepts such as caucasian, or negroid, can have no actuarial relevance to life or sickness assurance' (RRB Report 1971–72, p. 9) and that discrimination based upon them was illegal (RRB Report 1970–71, p. 9).

1 *Second Review of the Race Relations Act 1976* (1992) p. 30. Planning control is subject to the 1976 Act to a small extent: see s. 19A. As to the control of discrimination in the criminal justice system, see above, p. 619.

Discrimination in pubs may take various forms.[1] In 1973, the RRB reported 'an increase in the number of complaints in which it was alleged that licensees told Asian customers they would only be served if they and their friends talked to each other in English'. The Board stated that 'to refuse any group merely for speaking a language other than English is unreasonable; where the real ground for the refusal is racial, it is also unlawful' (RRB Report 1973, p. 4). Summarising the effect of the 1968 Act, the RRB stated (RRB Report 1975–76, pp. 5–6):

'We are of the view that the Act has worked well in relation to public houses and that whereas before 1968 members of minorities were never sure whether they would be served, they can now enter the vast majority of public houses reasonably confident that they will be treated in the same way as others. Since 1968 brewers and the National Union of Licensed Victuallers have done a great deal to ensure that licensees are made familiar with the Act and we believe that their work has played an important part in reducing discrimination.'

Complaints about discrimination in dance halls (like some complaints about pubs) have raised the question whether it is lawful for the owner to exclude all persons belonging to a particular 'racial group' because one or more members of that group have caused 'trouble' in the past. In *Race Relations Board v Mecca Ltd (Hammersmith Palais)*, Westminster C Ct 1974 RRB Report, p. 39, at the time that the complainant, a West Indian, was refused admission to the Palais 'a temporary ban had been imposed on West Indians and the Company claimed that the ban was imposed following a disturbance involving some coloured youths'. Judge Ruttle gave judgment for the Board. Repeating what he had said in *Race Relations Board v Morris*,[2] he stated:

'... I think he [the licensee] has to consider them as individuals and not jump to the conclusion because a man happens to come from a particular country that he will be in the gang. He has to bring his judgment to bear upon the individuals as such as distinct from being of a particular colour, race or ethnic origin'.

There have not been many complaints of discrimination in shops. In *Race Relations Board v Beckton*, Leeds C Ct 1975–1976 RRB Report, p. 52, a declaration was made against a shopkeeper who 'lost his temper and went beyond the bounds of proper behaviour when he shouted at Mrs Robinson and ordered her out of his shop' because 'colour was a matter which played a very large part in the defendant's conduct'. In another case, RRB Report 1970–71, p. 44, a complaint was made against a hairdresser who charged more for cutting 'Asiatic' and 'Negroid' hair. The local conciliation committee appointed an assessor who 'gave it as his opinion that there was no technical difference between the cutting of European and the cutting of Asian hair. Negroid hair required a different technique, but this could be learnt and, once learnt, could be carried out as quickly as cutting European hair'. The committee took the view that unlawful discrimination had occurred. 'The respondent gave an assurance against future unlawful discrimination and removed the words "Asiatic" and "Negroid" from his price list.'

In *Commission for Racial Equality v Marr, Cleanersweep Ltd*, CRE Report 1977, p. 120, the Newcastle County Court issued a declaration against a chimney sweep who refused to sweep a Pakistani chimney ('we don't deal with you people'). See also *Race Relations Board v Botley, Motor Vehicle Repairs*, Westminster C Ct ibid, p. 118, (declaration against garage for refusal to re-spray car: 'You're coloured and that's enough for me').

1 E.g. overcharging (*Antwerp Arms Public House* case, F. Invest. Rep. 1979), discrimination in the time allowed for drinking (*Race Relations Board v Royal Oak Public House, London E15*, Westminster C Ct, 1977 CRE Report, p. 118), or refusal to serve (*Race Relations Board v White Hart Public House, Kent* Westminster C Ct, 1973 RRB Report p. 42).

2 Reported in 1973 RRB Report, p. 42, as *Race Relations Board v White Hart Public House, Kent*. See also the *Rank Leisure Ltd* case, F. Invest. Rep. 1983, and *Hussain v Canklow Community Centre* (1980) CRE Report 1980, p. 85, Leeds C Ct (refusal to let hall for Pakistani wedding illegal).

Are Irish jokes prohibited by s. 20, or any other part of the 1976 Act?

12. The meaning of a 'section of the public' in s. 2, 1968 Act (now s. 20, 1976 Act) was considered by the House of Lords in several cases. In *Charter v Race Relations Board* [1973] AC 868, the complainant was an Indian living in East Ham. He applied for membership of the East Ham South Conservative Club. As a Conservative male of 18 or more, he was eligible for admission. The Club committee rejected his application on the casting vote of the Chairman. The vote was taken after the Chairman had said, in reply to a question from a committee member, that he regarded the applicant's colour as relevant to the decision. It was held that the members of a club were not a 'section of the public' so that s. 2 did not apply. The ruling was extended to associate club members in the *Dockers' Labour Club* case, above, p. 649. Although clubs therefore can be taken not now to be within s. 20, 1976 Act, they have been brought within the law by s. 25, 1976 Act, below, p. 660, which in effect reverses *Charter*. The above is true only of what might be called genuine clubs. A club that does not have a 'genuine system of personal selection of members' (Lord Reid's phrase) falls on the public side of the division between public and private groups that the House of Lords sought to draw. It is thus 'a section of the public' and subject to s. 20, not s. 25. The RAC (*associate* membership: contrast *full* membership) and the London (and other) Co-operative Societies are examples. They do not under their constitutions apply a 'genuine system of personal selection': they take all motorists or all comers. A club which provides for 'personal selection' in its rules but in which 'in practice the rules are disregarded' (Lord Reid) is similarly not a genuine club. An example of the latter kind is to be found in the facts of *Panama (Piccadilly) Ltd v Newberry* [1962] 1 WLR 610, DC. The proprietor of the Panama Club appealed against convictions for keeping premises for public dancing, etc., without a licence on the ground that only members and guests were allowed to enter the club. The appeal was rejected because any member of the public was in fact admitted at the door upon payment of a 25s. annual membership fee. Although there was provision for the nomination and seconding of applicants, the procedure was not followed. To Lord Parker CJ's mind, it was 'open to any member of the public to go in, pay 25s. and see the show'. The case was referred to by two members of the House of Lords in *Charter* as that of a club that would be 'a section of the public' for the purposes of s. 2. Although the distinction between genuine and other clubs drawn in *Charter* would appear to survive the 1976 Act in law, it is no longer important in view of s. 25 (unless the more general wording of s. 20 offers a fuller remedy).

13. In *Applin v Race Relations Board* [1975] AC 259, Mr and Mrs W had for many years fostered children in care of local authorities. They normally had four or five children in their home, each staying for about three weeks. About 60 per cent of the children were coloured. The appellant, a member of the National Front, learnt of this and brought pressure to bear upon Mr and Mrs W to stop fostering coloured children. The RRB sought a declaration that the appellant's conduct was incitement to commit an act of unlawful discrimination, contrary to the 1968 Act, s. 12 (now the 1976 Act, s. 31). The House of Lords ruled in favour of the Board on the ground that the fostering of children in care was the provision of facilities or services to a 'section of the public' (children in care) so that the refusal to take in children because of their colour would be unlawful discrimination. The decision in the case was reversed by the 1976 Act, s. 23(2) which creates an exception to s. 20:

'Section 20(1) does not apply to anything done by a person as a participant in arrangements under which he (for reward or not) takes into his home, and treats as if they were members of his family, children, elderly persons, or persons requiring a special degree of care and attention.'

5 Housing, etc

Race Relations Act 1976

21. Discrimination in disposal or management of premises

(1) It is unlawful for a person, in relation to premises in Great Britain of which he has power to dispose, to discriminate against another—

    (a) in the terms on which he offers him those premises; or

    (b) by refusing his application for those premises; or

    (c) in his treatment of him in relation to any list of persons in need of premises of that description.

(2) It is unlawful for a person, in relation to premises managed by him, to discriminate against a person occupying the premises—

    (a) in the way he affords him access to any benefits or facilities, or by refusing or deliberately omitting to afford him access to them; or

    (b) by evicting him, or subjecting him to any other detriment.

(3) Subsection (1) does not apply to a person who owns an estate or interest in the premises and wholly occupies them unless he uses the services of an estate agent for the purposes of the disposal of the premises, or publishes or causes to be published an advertisement in connection with the disposal.

NOTES

1. *'Premises'*. These 'include land of any description' (the 1976 Act s. 78(1)). The use (residential, business, recreational, etc.) to which the land is put does not matter, although racial discrimination is mostly a problem of housing. In *Race Relations Board v Geo Haigh & Co Ltd* (1969) Times, 11 September, Leeds C Ct, it was held that a builder who refused to sell a house under construction on a housing estate to the complainant because of his colour had acted contrary to the 1968 Act, s. 5(a), which prohibited discrimination in the disposal of 'housing accommodation, business premises or other land'. The partly-built house was 'housing accommodation' although not ready for occupation. The case would have the same outcome on this point under the different wording of s. 21. After the case, the builder stated that he would 'reluctantly' change his policy and sell to coloured applicants: *The Guardian*, 11 September 1969, quoted in A. Lester and G. Bindman, *Race and Law* (1972), p. 235.

2. *Power of disposal*. A 'power of disposal' includes the power to grant a right to occupy the premises (the 1976 Act, s. 78(1)). Generally, the 'disposal' of premises would appear to include the sale of a fee simple, the assignment or granting of a lease or tenancy, and the granting of a licence to occupy premises. Public housing authorities have the 'power to dispose' of housing within their control. An estate agent or accommodation bureau will be subject to s. 21 (as well as s. 20) if, as is sometimes the case, he or it is given a 'power to dispose'.

3. Would a covenant by which land may not be sold to persons 'not of the caucasian race' be unlawful under s. 21? Or at common law on grounds of public policy?[1]

4. Section 21(1) does not apply to disposals of property that come within s. 21(3). This was an exception that would have been available to the defendant in *Race Relations Board v Relf*, below, p. 663, had he, when selling his house, refrained from advertising it as well as from using an estate agent. Since a 'for sale' or 'vacancies' notice on the premises is an advertisement, the exception is a very narrow one. The 'small premises' exception in s. 22, below, also applies to s. 21(1).

---

1 See S. Cretney (1968) 118 NLJ 1094; J. F. Garner, (1972) 35 MLR 478; and J. D. A. Brooke-Taylor, (1978) 42 Conv(ns) 24. And see the public policy cases in Chap. 9, section 7, above, p. 608. See also *Shelley v Kraemer* 334 US 1 (1948).

5. *Management of premises.* A case of discrimination in the management of premises under the 1968 Act that would now come within the 1976 Act, s. 1(2) was reported by the RRB as follows (RRB Report 1970–71, p. 11):

'During the year the Board formed the opinion that a local authority had acted unlawfully by treating a Cypriot tenant less favourably than other tenants. The complainant received a letter from the local housing manager concerning his children's behaviour which stated that because of his limited residence in the country he was fortunate to have local authority accommodation, and indicated that his tenancy might be terminated if a further complaint were received. No such warning was sent to an English tenant whose children had also been the subject of adverse reports by the same caretaker. The Council apologised to the tenant and gave an assurance against further acts of unlawful discrimination.'

Other examples suggested by I. A. Macdonald, *Race Relations – The New Law* (1977), p. 90, are 'separate toilet or bathroom facilities for coloured tenants in a boarding house or the situation where the landlord sends a rent collector to white families but makes the coloured families call in at the rent office'.

6. Examples of discrimination in the terms on which premises are offered (s. 21(1)(a)) that occurred under the 1968 Act are the refusal on racial grounds to allow a house purchaser mortgage facilities available to other purchasers (RRB Report 1969–70, p. 13) and insistence upon a coloured house purchaser buying both houses in a two house development (for fear that the other house would otherwise be difficult to sell) when such a requirement would not have been placed upon a white purchaser (Case 7, RRB Report 1974, p. 36). Charging a higher purchase price would be another obvious example. Refusal to renew a lease (*Race Relations Board v Wharton*, 1977 CRE Report, p. 119), to rent a flat (RRB Report 1974, p. 11), or to sell a house (Case 8, RRB Report 1975–76, p. 46) come within s. 21(1)(b).[1] For an investigation into the practices of a housing association, see *Racial Discrimination in Hostel Accommodation*, F. Invest. Rep. 1992. Section 21(1)(c) applies to waiting lists kept, for example, by a caravan site owner or a local authority.

7. *Discrimination in the allocation of public housing.* Local authority waiting list rules were the subject of several investigations by the RRB. Wolverhampton Corporation's 'housing waiting list rule which, broadly speaking, treated people on the waiting list who were born outside the country less favourably than others by applying to them a longer qualifying waiting period' was declared by the RRB to be unlawful and later abandoned by the Corporation (RRB Report 1970–71, p. 11). The rule was replaced by one which applied a residence (as opposed to a place of birth) test, a longer qualifying waiting period being applied to persons who had lived in the United Kingdom for less than 10 years. This rule was dropped after the RRB began an investigation of it (RRB Report 1970–71, p. 10). It was reported in 1975 (Smith and Whalley, *Racial Minorities and Public Housing* (1975) p. 36) that a number of local authorities in the London area required an applicant for council housing to have lived within its area for five years. Might such a rule be indirect discrimination (the 1976 Act, s. 1(1)(b))? What of a rule by which residence in a borough is effective for waiting list purposes only from the date that the applicant is joined by his family.[2] In the *Hackney Council Housing* case,[2] a non-discrimination notice was issued

---

1 RRB Report 1969–70, p. 12 and RRB Report 1970–71, p. 11. On nationality restrictions, see the *Ealing* case, below, p. 636. A rule whereby priority for public housing on a new estate was given to the largely white residents of an existing estate was indirect discrimination: *Out of Order*, F. Invest. Rep. 1990.

2 F. Invest. Rep. 1984. See Bryan, [1984] PL 194. For a finding of illegal segregation in public housing, see *Housing Allocation in Oldham*, 1993. See also the *Homelessness and Discrimination in the London Borough of Tower Hamlets* case, F. Invest. Rep. 1988, in which an enforcement notice was issued in respect of ss. 20(1)(b) and 21(1)(c) on the ground of discrimination against Bangladeshi families in need of emergency rehousing.

against the Council for breaches of ss. 20(1)(b) and 21(1)(c). The CRE concluded that Council officials had discriminated between black and white persons when allocating accommodation (newer housing, houses and maisonettes as opposed to flats, ground floor flats as opposed to high rise flats predominantly for whites). Hackney was selected not because of any complaints against it. It was chosen 'as an inner-city area with a large ethnic minority population' that could be considered as a 'suitable and representative borough on which to concentrate a comprehensive investigation of the causes of the discrimination and disadvantage in public sector housing that research had shown ethnic minorities had suffered' (Report, p. 5). The findings of the CRE, which were accepted by the Council, were for the first time in any formal investigation based solely upon statistical evidence:

Until now, findings of discrimination have generally been centred on individual acts of discrimination. The practical difficulty of relying on this approach is that the scope for comparison, to determine whether there has been less favourable treatment on racial grounds, is necessarily narrow. When one finds less favourable treatment there will often be factors present which might appear to explain away the differences on non-racial grounds. However, when large numbers of cases are examined statistically, and less favourable treatment of a racial group is established, and one then examines all possible non-racial explanations statistically, it becomes possible to say with statistical certainty whether they can in fact explain the difference. In practice, non-racial explanations start falling away when subject to this kind of scrutiny. This is the reason why the Commission is insistent that ethnic record keeping and monitoring are essential to securing equality of opportunity, not only in the housing field, but elsewhere. And it is for this reason also that this investigation represents a significant milestone on the long road toward eliminating racial discrimination.

8. *Discrimination in the private sector.* A formal investigation of racial discrimination in the private sector revealed that discrimination was practised by about 20% of the accommodation agencies investigated: *Sorry Its Gone*, F. Invest. Rep. 1990. There was less discrimination by private landlords and very little by guesthouses and private hotels.
9. Section 24 makes it illegal (subject to a 'small premises' exception) for a landlord to discriminate in refusing to agree to the assignment of a tenancy. See also the Landlord and Tenant Act 1927, s. 19, and *Schegel v Corcoran*, above, p. 599.

Race Relations Act 1976

22. Exceptions from ss. 20(1) and 21: small dwellings
(1) Sections 20(1) and 21 do not apply to the provision by a person of accommodation in any premises, or the disposal of premises by him, if—
  (a) that person or a near relative of his ('the relevant occupier') resides, and intends to continue to reside, on the premises; and
  (b) there is on the premises, in addition to the accommodation occupied by the relevant occupier, accommodation (not being storage accommodation or means of access) shared by the relevant occupier with other persons residing on the premises who are not members of his household; and
  (c) the premises are small premises.
(2) Premises shall be treated for the purposes of this section as small premises if—
  (a) in the case of premises comprising residential accommodation for one or more households (under separate letting or similar agreements) in addition to the accommodation occupied by the relevant occupier, there is not normally residential accommodation for more than two such households and only the relevant occupier and any member of his household reside in the accommodation occupied by him;
  (b) in the case of premises not falling within paragraph (a), there is not normally residential accommodation on the premises for more than six persons in addition to the relevant occupier and any members of his household.

NOTE

The exception in s. 22 applies to s. 21(2) as well as s. 21(1), the management of premises being covered by the wording 'the provision by a person of accommodation in any premises'. A person is a near relative of another 'if that person is the wife or husband, a parent or child, a grandparent or grandchild, or a brother or sister of the other (whether of full blood or half blood or by affinity), and "child" includes an illegitimate child and the wife or husband of an illegitimate child' (1976 Act, s. 78(1)(5)). 'Accommodation . . . shared' (s. 22(1)(b)) includes a bathroom, kitchen, or toilet; it does not include a stairway. 'Hotels, boarding houses and other similar establishments' that would otherwise be subject to the 1976 Act, s. 20 are exempt from it if they can be brought within the 'small premises' exception in s. 22.

6 Clubs

Race Relations Act 1976

25. Discrimination: associations not within s.11

(1) This section applies to any association of persons (however described, whether corporate or unincorporate, and whether or not its activities are carried on for profit) if—

    (a) it has twenty-five or more members; and

    (b) admission to membership is regulated by its constitution and is so conducted that the members do not constitute a section of the public within the meaning of section 20(1); and

    (c) it is not an organisation to which section 11 applies [trade unions, etc].

(2) It is unlawful for an association to which this section applies, in the case of a person who is not a member of the association, to discriminate against him—

    (a) in the terms on which it is prepared to admit him to membership; or

    (b) by refusing or deliberately omitting to accept his application for membership.

(3) It is unlawful for an association to which this section applies, in the case of a person who is a member or associate of the association, to discriminate against him—

    (a) in the way it affords him access to any benefits, facilities or services, or by refusing or deliberately omitting to afford him access to them; or

    (b) in the case of a member, by depriving him of membership, or varying the terms on which he is a member; or

    (c) in the case of an associate, by depriving him of his rights as an associate, or varying those rights; or

    (d) in either case, by subjecting him to any other detriment.

(4) For the purposes of this section—

    (a) a person is a member of an association if he belongs to it by virtue of his admission to any sort of membership provided for by its constitution (and is not merely a person with certain rights under its constitution by virtue of his membership of some other association), and references to membership of an association shall be construed accordingly;

    (b) a person is an associate of an association to which this section applies if, not being a member of it, he has under its constitution some or all of the rights enjoyed by members (or would have apart from any provision in its constitution authorising the refusal of those rights in particular cases).

26. Exception from s. 25 for certain associations

(1) An association to which section 25 applies is within this subsection if the main object of the association is to enable the benefits of membership (whatever they may be) to be enjoyed by persons of a particular racial group defined otherwise than by reference to colour; and in determining whether that is the main object of an association regard shall be had to the essential character of the association and to all relevant circumstances including, in particular, the extent to which the affairs of the association are so conducted that the persons primarily enjoying the benefits of membership are of the racial group in question.

(2) In the case of an association within subsection (1), nothing in section 25 shall render unlawful any act not involving discrimination on the ground of colour.

NOTES

1. As noted earlier, p. 656, in the *Charter* case, it was held that genuine clubs were not subject to the 1968 Act's prohibition of discrimination in the provision of goods, facilities and services. In enacting the 1976 Act, Parliament decided that such clubs should be controlled in this respect. It decided to achieve this result not by amending the section on goods, facilities and services (now the 1976 Act, s. 20), but by adding a new section—s. 25—specifically dealing with clubs. The government White Paper explained its reason for wanting to bring clubs within the Act as follows (Cmnd. 6234, p. 18):

'72 . . . Some 4,000 working men's clubs, with a total membership of about $3\frac{1}{2}$ million people, are affiliated to the Club and Institute Union and are not covered by the 1968 Act. In some towns they have replaced public houses as the main providers of facilities for entertainment, recreation and refreshment. In addition, thousands of golf, squash, tennis and other sporting clubs registered as members' clubs are, almost certainly, also outside the 1968 Act, except in so far as they may offer only limited playing facilities to the public generally. Many clubs do not discriminate on racial grounds but at present they may lawfully do so. The Government considers that it is right that all clubs should be allowed to apply a test of personal acceptability to candidates for membership, but it considers that it is against the public interest that they should be entitled to do this on racial grounds. The Government believes that the relationship between members of clubs is no more personal and intimate than is the relationship between people in many situations which are rightly covered by the 1968 Act; for example, the members of a small firm or trade union branch, children at school, or tenants in multi-occupied housing accommodation. In principle it is justifiable to apply the legislation in all these situations because of the inherently unjust and degrading nature of racial discrimination and its potentially grave social consequences. In practice the objectives of the legislation will be seriously undermined if its protection does not extend beyond the workplace and the market-place to enable workers and other members of the public to obtain entertainment, recreation and refreshment together on the basis of equality, irrespective of colour or race.

The Bill will therefore make it unlawful for a club or other voluntary body to discriminate as regards the admission of members or the treatment accorded to members. Subject to this the Bill will not, of course, affect the right of such a body to withhold membership or facilities from someone who does not qualify for them in accordance with its rules. Small voluntary bodies will be exempted from this provision so as to avoid interference with the kind of regular social gathering which is genuinely private and domestic in character. In addition, there will be an expectation to enable bona fide social, welfare, political or sporting organisations whose main object is to confer benefits on a particular ethnic or national group to continue to do so.'

A club that is not a genuine club in the sense of the *Charter* case, so that its members are a 'section of the public', is subject to s. 20 and not s. 25.

2. Section 25(3) reverses the *Dockers' Labour Club* case, above, p. 656, so that discrimination by a club against an associate member is prohibited by the 1976 Act. The RRB reported in 1974 that there were about one million members of working men's clubs who held associate member cards valid in other clubs that are members of the Working Men's Club and Institute Union (RRB Report 1974, p. 4). The CRE takes the view that discrimination against a member's guest is discrimination against the member contrary to s. 25.

3. The exemption for small clubs (s. 25(1)) was set at 25 members because that is the minimum number of members that a club must have to qualify for registration under the Licensing Acts. It was suggested in debate in Parliament that there will be few clubs with a list, as opposed to an active, membership of less than 25 (374 HL Deb 29 September 1976 col 538).

4. Section 26 safeguards such clubs as the Caledonian Club, the London Welsh Rugby Club and the Indian Workers Association.[1] It would not allow a person who was otherwise qualified for membership of such a club to be excluded because of his colour. It would, however, allow him to be excluded on 'racial grounds' other than colour.

5. The CRE has issued non-discrimination notices in several cases of discriminations in respect of club membership. In *Handsworth Horticultural Institute Ltd v CRE*

---

1 See Standing Committee A, Race Relations Bill, 9th Sitting HC Deb col 400, 25 May 1976.

(1992),[1] a social club had a rule (rule 7) whereby an applicant for membership had to be sponsored by two members and approved by a selection committee. Although 60% of the local population was non-white, no non-white person had every applied for membership. Following a formal investigation, the CRE found that rule 7 constituted a discriminatory practice involving indirect discrimination in breach of ss. 28 and 1(1)(b). The club's appeal against the resulting non-discrimination notice was rejected by the Birmingham County Court:

'It seems to us that given the circumstances in which the Club finds itself . . ., surrounded by a population of half black and half white, the evidence is clear, that, whether intended or not, experience has shown that not a single black person has ever been proposed for membership of the Club of 1500 members, and that leads us to the view that while the rule remains in being it has an adverse impact, and it is not likely that one will be proposed. It is true that black people can comply, ie become members, but in practice one will not be asked. Further we are of the view that the failure of the Club committee ever formally to discuss the matter between themselves, and their failure ever to raise the situation with the members once the Commission had drawn attention to it, exhibited clear disingenuousness.

. . . We accept that no other system is quite as satisfactory as that set out in Rule 7. However, looking at the matter objectively, we have asked ourselves whether what we accept are marginal disadvantages of a reference system, as an alternative method of applying for membership, sufficiently outweigh the desirability of maintaining good order as effected by the present sponsorship system. We have come to the conclusion that they do not, and accordingly we hold that the Club cannot show that the rule which provides for the sole means of entry by proposer and seconder can in all the circumstances of the case be justified.'

7 Advertisements

Race Relations Act 1976

29. Discriminatory advertisements

(1) It is unlawful to publish or to cause to be published an advertisement which indicates, or might reasonably be understood as indicating, an intention by a person to do an act of discrimination, whether the doing of that act by him would be lawful or, by virtue of Part II or III, unlawful.

(2) Subsection (1) does not apply to an advertisement—

(a) if the intended act would be lawful by virtue of any of sections 5, 6, 7(3) and (4), 10(3), 26, 34(2)(b), 35 to 39 and 41; or

(b) if the advertisement relates to the services of an employment agency (within the meaning of section 14(1)) and the intended act only concerns employment which the employer could by virtue of section 5, 6 or 7(3) or (4) lawfully refuse to offer to persons against whom the advertisement indicates an intention to discriminate.

(3) Subsection (1) does not apply to an advertisement which indicates that persons of any class defined otherwise than by reference to colour, race or ethnic or national origins are required for employment outside Great Britain.

(4) The publisher of an advertisement made unlawful by subsection (1) shall not be subject to any liability under that subsection in respect of the publication of the advertisement if he proves—

(a) that the advertisement was published in reliance on a statement made to him by the person who caused it to be published to the effect that, by reason of the operation of subsection (2) or (3), the publication would not be unlawful; and

(b) that it was reasonable for him to rely on the statement.

(5) A person who knowingly or recklessly makes a statement such as is mentioned in subsection (4)(a) which in a material respect is false or misleading commits an offence, and shall be liable on summary conviction to a fine not exceeding £400.

---

1 Birmingham County Court judgment in *Ruled Out*, F. Invest. Rep. 1992, Appendix C. See also the *Woodhouse Recreation Club, Leeds*, F. Invest. Rep. 1980. A Sikh was awarded £150 damages by the Birmingham County Court for exclusion from a golf club on racial grounds: *The Guardian* 25 February 1984.

NOTES

1. The number of discriminatory advertisements would appear to have dropped considerably since 1968 when they were first prohibited. In 1973, the RRB reported that 'advertisements and notices indicating an intention to discriminate . . . have virtually disappeared both from the press and from public advertisement boards.[1] Nonetheless, in 1983 the CRE disposed of complaints about 23 advertisements. Seven were found to be unlawful and the complaint was settled informally in all cases (CRE Report 1982, p. 12). In 1982, there were several complaints about notices refusing service to Argentinians during the Falklands War. The CRE considered these illegal, but took no action (CRE Report 1982, p. 25).

2. 'Advertisement' is defined very widely. Section 78(1) of the 1976 Act reads:

' "advertisement" includes every form of advertisement or notice, whether to the public or not, and whether in a newspaper or other publication, by television or radio, by display of notices, signs, labels, showcards or goods, by distribution of samples, circulars, catalogues, price lists or other material, by exhibition of pictures, models or films, or in any other way, and references to the publishing of advertisements shall be construed accordingly;'

The display of a 'notice' was the reason for the well publicised case of *Race Relations Board v Relf*,[2] in which a notice in a house window: 'For sale to an English Family' was held contrary to the 1968 Act by the county court.

3. The 'Scottish porridge' case also illustrates the wide field of application of s. 29. It was reported by the RRB as follows (RRB Report 1969–70, p. 6):

'Here a Scottish doctor living in Eastbourne sought a "daily" able to cook plain Scottish food. But he advertised for a "Scottish daily". There can be few who would regard such a restriction as anything but innocuous, but a member of the public insisted that the Board should investigate a complaint. The regional conciliation committee understandably formed the opinion that the advertisement contravened section 6 of the Act [now the 1976 Act s. 29]. Having called the doctor's attention to section 6 of the Act, the committee proposed to do no more.'

Would the doctor have infringed the Act if he had advertised for a 'daily' who could cook plain Scottish food?

4. Partly because of cases like the 'Scottish porridge' case, enforcement of s. 29 is placed solely in the hands of the CRE, which may issue a non-discrimination notice after a formal investigation (s. 58) or bring legal proceedings for a declaration or an injunction (ss. 63, 64). Damages may not be awarded. Placing an advertisement for a post 'designated for a black or Asian woman under the terms of s. 38' of the 1976 Act was not an act of discrimination contrary to s. 4 of the 1976 Act (employment discrimination); instead it fell within s. 29 as indicating an 'intention' to do such an act, so that only the CRE could enforce it: *Cardiff Women's Aid v Hartup*.[3] The Tribunal did not consider the question whether the case fell within s. 38. If an advertisement is published by someone (e.g. a newspaper) other than the advertiser, the publisher is liable under s. 29 as well as the advertiser. The publisher has a defence of 'reliance' in such cases (s. 29(4)).

1 RRB Report 1973, p. 13. Comparing advertisements in one London newspaper in July 1968 and July 1969, the Board noted that it had 18 discriminatory advertisements ('no coloured', 'Europeans wanted', 'coloured only', 'Jew preferred') in 1968 and none a year later (RRB Report 1969–70, p. 53). A similar survey of newsagents' noticeboards in 1970 revealed one discriminatory accommodation advertisement out of 36: ibid.

2 RRB Report 1975, p. 56. The 'no travellers' notice in the *Dutton* case, above, p. 643, was an advertisement.

3 [1994] IRLR 390, EAT. The Tribunal did not follow *Brindley v Tayside Health Board* [1976] IRLR 364, Ind Trib, a sex discrimination case in which it had been held that an advertisement was an 'act' of discrimination.

5. Section 29 has been criticised for making it illegal, subject to s. 29(2), to advertise something that may in itself be perfectly lawful, as in the case of a letting of accommodation exempted from the Act by the 'small premises' exception (s. 22). The justification for this in the government White Paper (Cmnd. 6234, p. 19) was that 'the public display of racial prejudices and preferences is inherently offensive and likely to encourage the spread of discriminatory attitudes and practices'.

8 Charities

Race Relations Act 1976

34. Charities

(1) A provision which is contained in a charitable instrument (whenever that instrument took or takes effect) and which provides for conferring benefits on persons of a class defined by reference to colour shall have effect for all purposes as if it provided for conferring the like benefits—

    (a) on persons of the class which results if the restriction by reference to colour is disregarded; or

    (b) where the original class is defined by reference to colour only, on persons generally; but nothing in this subsection shall be taken to alter the effect of any provision as regards any time before the coming into operation of this subsection.

(2) Nothing in Parts II to IV shall—

    (a) be construed as affecting a provision to which this subsection applies or;

    (b) render unlawful an act which is done in order to give effect to such a provision.

(3) Subsection (2) applies to any provision which is contained in a charitable instrument (whenever that instrument took or takes effect) and which provides for conferring benefits on persons of a class defined otherwise than by reference to colour (including a class resulting from the operation of subsection (2)). . . .

NOTE

Quite a number of charitable trusts apply in areas covered by the Act, particularly education and housing. Section 34 only concerns those that discriminate on grounds of colour. Others that do so on grounds of race, etc. (see s. 3) are not affected, although they may be void at common law for reasons of uncertainty or public policy. As to uncertainty, see, for example, *Clayton v Ramsden* [1943] AC 320, HL, in which a condition subsequent in a will by which a beneficiary was to forfeit a legacy upon marrying a person 'not of Jewish parents and not of Jewish faith' was held void for uncertainty. As to public policy, see *Re Lysaght*, above, p. 608.

9 Incitement to racial hatred

Public Order Act 1986

17. Meaning of 'racial hatred'

In this Part 'racial hatred' means hatred against a group of persons in Great Britain defined by reference to colour, race, nationality (including citizenship) or ethnic or national origins.

18. Use of words or behaviour or display of written material

(1) A person who uses threatening, abusive or insulting words or behaviour, or displays any written material which is threatening, abusive or insulting, is guilty of an offence if—

    (a) he intends thereby to stir up racial hatred, or

    (b) having regard to all the circumstances racial hatred is likely to be stirred up thereby.

(2) An offence under this section may be committed in a public or a private place, except that no offence is committed where the words or behaviour are used, or the written material is displayed, by a person inside a dwelling and are not heard or seen except by other persons in that or another dwelling.

(3) A constable may arrest without warrant anyone he reasonably suspects is committing an offence under this section.

(4) In proceedings for an offence under this section it is a defence for the accused to prove that he was inside a dwelling and had no reason to believe that the words or behaviour used, or the written material displayed, would be heard or seen by a person outside that or any other dwelling.

(5) A person who is not shown to have intended to stir up racial hatred is not guilty of an offence under this section if he did not intend his words or behaviour, or the written material, to be, and was not aware that it might be, threatening, abusive or insulting.

(6) This section does not apply to words or behaviour used, or written material displayed, solely for the purpose of being [included in a programme service].

19. Publishing or distributing written material

(1) A person who publishes or distributes written material which is threatening, abusive or insulting is guilty of an offence if—

   (a) he intends thereby to stir up racial hatred, or

   (b) having regard to all the circumstances racial hatred is likely to be stirred up thereby.

(2) In proceedings for an offence under this section it is a defence for an accused who is not shown to have intended to stir up racial hatred to prove that he was not aware of the content of the material and did not suspect, and had no reason to suspect, that it was threatening, abusive or insulting.

(3) References in this Part to the publication or distribution of written material are to its publication or distribution to the public or a section of the public.

23. Possession of racially inflammatory material

(1) A person who has in his possession written material which is threatening, abusive or insulting, or a recording of visual images or sounds which are threatening, abusive or insulting, with a view to—

   (a) in the case of written material, its being displayed, published, distributed, [or included in a cable programme service], whether by himself or another, or

   (b) in the case of a recording, its being distributed, shown, played, [or included in a programme service], whether by himself or another,

is guilty of an offence if he intends racial hatred to be stirred up thereby or, having regard to all the circumstances, racial hatred is likely to be stirred up thereby.

(2) For this purpose regard shall be had to such display, publication, distribution, showing, playing, [or inclusion in a programme service] as he has, or it may reasonably be inferred that he has, in view.

(3) In proceedings for an offence under this section it is a defence for an accused who is not shown to have intended to stir up racial hatred to prove that he was not aware of the content of the written material or recording and did not suspect, and had no reason to suspect, that it was threatening, abusive or insulting.

NOTES[1]

1. The sections in the Public Order Act 1986, as amended by the Broadcasting Act 1990, on incitement to racial hatred replace s. 5A, Public Order Act 1936. As the government White Paper leading to the 1986 Act (Cmnd. 9510, p. 39) makes clear, the general purpose remains the protection of public order, not the prevention of the expression of offensive views:

A variety of amendments to the section were suggested, many of which would alter the basis of the offence, so that the criminal law would be used against the production of material or the expression of views which are offensive in a multi-racial society. The Government believes that the reasonable exercise of freedom of expression should be protected, however unpleasant the views expressed, and has concluded that section 5A should continue to be based on considerations of public order.

1 On the earlier law and incitement to racial hatred generally, see G. Bindman, (1982) 132 NLJ 299; id., in S. Coliver, ed., *Striking a Balance: Hate Speech, Freedom of Expression and Non-discrimination* (1992) Chap. 28; R. Cotterrell, [1982] PL 278; A. Dickey, [1968] Crim LR 489; Gordon, *Incitement to Racial Hatred* (1982), Runnymede Trust publication; Khan, (1978) 122 Sol Jo 256; P. Leopold, [1977] PL 389; D. G. T. Williams, [1966] Crim LR 320; *Review of the Public Order Act 1936 and Related Legislation* (Cmnd. 7891), pp. 29–31. On ths 1986 Act, see W. J. Wolffe, [1987] PL 85.

2. The Public Order Act 1936, s. 5A replaced the offence in the Race Relations Act 1965, s. 6. Referring to incitement to racial hatred and to the similar offence in section 5 of the Theatres Act 1968 (now replaced by s. 20, Public Order Act 1986, above, p. 366), the government White Paper explained its reason for moving the former offence from the Race Relations Act to the Public Order Act as follows (Cmnd. 6234, p. 30):

'125. These offences are entirely separate from the anti-discrimination provisions of the race relations legislation. They deal with the stirring up of racial hatred rather than with acts of racial discrimination; they are criminal rather than civil; and they are enforced in the criminal courts rather than by the Race Relations Board in the civil courts. In several respects they are similar to the offence under section 5 of the Public Order Act 1936 of using threatening, abusive or insulting words, in any public place or at any public meeting, with intent to provoke a breach of the peace or whereby a breach of the peace is likely to be occasioned. They are concerned to prevent the stirring up of racial hatred which may beget violence and public disorder.'

3. As defined in the 1965 Act, s. 6, the offence of incitement to racial hatred required an 'intent to stir up hatred' against a racial group. As redefined in s. 5A of the Public Order Act 1936, it no longer required this subjective intent. It was necessary only to prove that hatred was likely to be stirred up by the defendant's act; no mention was made of intent. The government White Paper justified this widening of the offence as follows (Cmnd. 6234, p. 30):

'126. Relatively few prosecutions have been brought under section 6 of the 1965 Act . . . However, during the past decade, probably largely as a result of section 6, there has been a decided change in the style of racialist propaganda. It tends to be less blatantly bigoted, to disclaim any intention of stirring up racial hatred, and to purport to make a contribution to public education and debate. Whilst this shift away from crudely racialist propaganda and abuse is welcome, it is not an unmixed benefit. The more apparently rational and moderate is the message, the greater is its probable impact on public opinion. But it is not justifiable in a democratic society to interfere with freedom of expression except where it is necessary to do so for the prevention of disorder or for the protection of other basic freedoms. The present law penalises crude verbal attacks if and only if it is established that they have been made with the deliberate intention of causing groups to be hated because of their racial origins. In the Government's view this is too narrow an approach. . . . It therefore proposes to ensure that it will no longer be necessary to prove a subjective intention to stir up racial hatred.
127. The present law does not, however, penalise the dissemination of ideas based on an assumption of racial superiority or inferiority or facts (whether true or false) which may encourage racial prejudice or discrimination. It is arguable that false and evil publications of this kind may well be more effectively defeated by public education and debate than by prosecution and that in practice the criminal law would be ineffective to deal with such material. Due regard must also of course be paid to allowing the free expression of opinion. The Government is not therefore at this stage putting forward proposals to extend the criminal law to deal with the dissemination of racialist propaganda in the absence of a likelihood that group hatred will be stirred up by it. It recognises, however, that strong views are held on this important question and will carefully consider any further representations that may be made to it.'

4. Under s. 18(1)(b) and s. 19(1)(b), 1986 Act it remains the case that an intention to stir up racial hatred is not required where racial hatred is in fact likely to be stirred up. However, the 1986 Act amends the law as it existed previously so that, by virtue of s. 18(1)(a) and s. 19(1)(a), a person may be guilty of an offence where he intends to stir up racial hatred even though the stirring up of such hatred is not a likely effect of his conduct. The White Paper leading to the 1986 Act (Cmnd. 9510 p. 39) explained the reason for this further extension of the offence:

6.6 One area in which difficulties have been experienced with section 5A is where circulation of the material is to selected groups of people, such as clergymen or Members of Parliament who might be thought unlikely to be incited to racial hatred. At present, the more level-headed the recipients of racially inflammatory material, the more difficult it is to show that racial hatred is likely to be stirred up, even when the material itself is so threatening, insulting or abusive that this was clearly the intention of the distributor. The public order consideration is relevant here since the material may well find its way to other, less equable, audiences, although not directly distributed to them, and its effect may be to stir up racial hatred. The Government proposes that section 5A should be re-cast to penalise conduct which is either *likely* to stir up racial hatred or which is intended to do so. The offence will then be in similar terms to the main section 5 offence of conduct which is *likely* or *intended* to cause a breach of the peace.

5. Amendments to the offence introduced by the 1986 Act are that there are now two separate offences of *using* threatening, etc., words or behaviour and of *publishing* threatening, etc., written material (ss. 18 and 19) and a new offence of possessing racially inflammatory material has been introduced (s. 23). Other changes are (i) that the s. 18 offence may be committed in a 'public or a private place' (other than a dwelling); previously it could only be committed 'in any public place or at any public meeting' and (ii) that the exception in respect of publication or distribution of written material to members of an organisation to which the publisher or distributor belongs is not retained in s. 19. This omission is justified in the White Paper (p. 39) as follows:

This provision was intended to protect freedom of expression within a group holding particular views, but it is possible that even those who already hold racialist views may be incited or incited further to racial hatred, and the mischief at which section 5A is aimed could occur. The Government sees no justification for allowing material to be circulated privately when it would be open to prosecution if circulated more generally and may have the same effect in both cases; accordingly it proposes to remove the exemption for material circulated to members of an association.

6. Prosecutions may only be brought 'by or with the consent of' the Attorney-General. In practice, all complaints are referred for investigation to the local police, who may, if they find a complaint to have substance, refer it back to the Attorney-General, through the Crown Prosecution Service. Although there are quite a number of complaints, there are usually only two or so prosecutions a year. Under the 1986 Act, the Attorney-General had by the end of 1993 given his consent for prosecution in 13 cases and there had been seven convictions: CRE Report 1993, p. 24. One reason for the small number of prosecutions is that racist literature has not been so intemperate since the 1986 Act as previously. Cases under the Act have concerned incitement to hatred against black persons or, increasingly, Jews. In 1990, following the choice of John Taylor as a Conservative parliamentary candidate for Cheltenham, a Major Galbraith, a party member, was charged with incitement for calling Mr Taylor a 'bloody nigger', although the defendant died before the trial. In 1994, Lady Birdwood, aged 80, was convicted of the offence for distributing anti-semitic literature (the holocaust was a 'holohoax'; Jack the Ripper was Jewish, etc). She was given a three months suspended sentence.

7. The common law offence of sedition and ss. 4–5 Public Order Act 1986, above, pp. 213–214, also control conduct tending to cause racial hatred. Sections 18 and 19 have effectively replaced sedition, although the latter may still be of use if it extends to conduct causing hatred against religious groups within society. In *R v Caunt* (1947), see (1948) 64 LQR 203, the jury was directed that an article aimed at Jews could be seditious.

8. There is considerable evidence of large and increased numbers of racially motivated attacks upon members of ethnic minorities or persons who support them and of many incidents of racial abuse and sustained harassment.[1] In 1994, proposals for a specific criminal offence of racially-motivated violence were rejected by the

1 See the records of such attacks and incidents collected in the issues of the *Runnymede Bulletin*. In 1993, 3,500 racial attacks or other incidents were reported to the Metropolitan Police, including a 300% increase in the Isle of Dogs since the election of a British National Party local government candidate: *Runnymede Bulletin* No. 274, p. 7 (1994). On the resulting problem and the need for tailor-made legislation, see G. Bindman, 91 *Guardian Gazette*, No. 4, p. 23 (1994).

Government.[1] As to racial abuse and harassment, the offence of incitement to racial hatred deals with only a small part of the problem. A 1994 private members' bill[2] that would have strengthened the existing incitement to racial hatred law and introduced an offence of group defamation – by which it would have been an offence to publish offensive written material intended to vilify a racial group – failed for lack of government support. The government preferred to treat of the matter generally, adding an offence of intentionally causing harassment, alarm or distress in s. 4A of the Public Order Act 1986: see above, p. 213. On racial harassment at work as discrimination under the 1976 Act, see above, p. 621.

9. The problem of racial abuse at football matches is dealt with by the Football (Offences) Act 1991, s. 3, as follows:

'**3.**—(1) It is an offence to take part at a designated football match in chanting of an indecent or racialist nature.

(2) For this purpose—
   (a) "chanting" means the repeated uttering of any words or sounds in concert with one or more others; and
   (b) "of a racialist nature" means consisting of or including matter which is threatening, abusive or insulting to a person by reason of his colour, race, nationality (including citizenship) or ethnic or national origins.'

There are regularly convictions for the offence, which is punishable by fine.

10 The Commission for Racial Equality

Race Relations Act 1976

43. Establishment and duties of Commission
(1) There shall be a body of Commissioners named the Commission for Racial Equality consisting of at least eight but not more than fifteen individuals each appointed by the Secretary of State on a full-time or part-time basis, which shall have the following duties—
   (a) to work towards the elimination of discrimination;
   (b) to promote equality of opportunity, and good relations, between persons of different racial groups generally; and
   (c) to keep under review the working of this Act and, when they are so required by the Secretary of State or otherwise think it necessary, draw up and submit to the Secretary of State proposals for amending it.

NOTES[3]

1. The CRE has its full complement of 15 members. The Chair is Mr Herman Ouseley. Extra commissioners may be appointed *ad hoc* for the purposes of a particular investigation (s. 49(2)). The CRE is a body corporate (1976 Act, Sch. 1). It is

---

1 House of Commons Home Affairs Committee, *Racial Attacks and Harassment*, 27 HC 71–I (1993–4), recommendation 27. So did the Association of Chief Police Officers: *Runnymede Bulletin* 273, p. 3. Cf. the CRE recommendation: *Second Review of the Race Relations Act 1976*, p. 74. The Government argued that violence was already a criminal offence; that special treatment of ethnic minorities might be resented by others; and that racial motivation would be difficult to prove.
2 The Racial Hatred and Violence bill, introduced by Mr Hartley Booth. The CRE has recommended that racial harassment should become a specific ground for eviction under housing legislation and that consideration be given to creating a tort of racial harassment. A family lost their council house for breach of a tenancy agreement because they had engaged in racial harassment: *Race and Immigration, Runnymede Trust Bulletin*, No. 243, p. 12 (1993).
3 On the CRE, see G. Bindman, (1976) 3 Br Jo of Law and Soc 110; I. Leigh, (1982) 132 NLJ 24; L. Lustgarten, [1982] PL 229; *A Review of the Race Relations Act 1976*, Runnymede Trust, (1979).

wholly independent of the government. It is 'not an emanation of the Crown, and shall not act or be treated as the servant or agent of the Crown' (ibid).

2. The CRE replaces and merges the enforcement and promotional functions of the RRB and the CRC. In carrying out the very wide duties listed in s. 43, it is authorised (i) to 'give financial and other assistance to any organisation appearing to the Commission to be concerned with the promotion of equality of opportunity, and good relations, between persons of different racial groups' (s. 44(1)); (ii) to 'undertake or assist (financially or otherwise) the undertaking by other persons of any research and any educational activities, which appear to the Commission necessary or expedient for the purposes of s. 43(1)' (s. 45(1)); (iii) to issue codes of practice aimed at the elimination of discrimination in employment and/or 'the promotion of equality of opportunity in that field between persons of different racial groups' and in respect of housing[1] (s. 47(1)); (iv) to give assistance to an individual bringing a claim under the Act (s. 66, and see below, p. 675), and (v) to conduct formal investigations, as to which see below. The CRE's work is summarised in its annual reports.

3. The *First Report of the Home Affairs Committee*, 1981–82 HC 46–I contained many criticisms of the CRE's work. One general criticism was of the CRE's tending to see itself as a spokesman for ethnic minorities and to prefer this role to its 'true one of a quasi-judicial Statutory Commission': ibid., p. xiv. On the strongly critical comments on the CRE's conduct by the Court of Appeal in *Mandla v Dowell Lee*—comments rejected by the House of Lords in that case,—see above, p. 641.

11 Formal investigations

Race Relations Act 1976

48. Power to conduct formal investigations

(1) Without prejudice to their general power to do anything requisite for the performance of their duties under section 43(1), the Commission may if they think fit, and shall if required by the Secretary of State, conduct a formal investigation for any purpose connected with the carrying out of those duties. . . .

49.—(1) The Commission shall not embark on a formal investigation unless the requirements of this section have been complied with.

(2) Terms of reference for the investigation shall be drawn up by the Commission or, if the Commission were required by the Secretary of State to conduct the investigation, by the Secretary of State after consulting the Commission.

(3) It shall be the duty of the Commission to give general notice of the holding of the investigation unless the terms of reference confine it to activities of persons named in them, but in such a case the Commission shall in the prescribed manner give those persons notice of the holding of the investigation.

(4) Where the terms of reference of the investigation confine it to activities of persons named in them and the Commission in the course of it propose to investigate any act made unlawful by this Act which they believe that a person so named may have done, the Commission shall—

    (*a*) inform that person of their belief and of their proposal to investigate the act in question; and

    (*b*) offer him an opportunity of making oral or written representations with regard to it (or both oral and written representations if he thinks fit);

and a person so named who avails himself of an opportunity under this subsection of making oral representations may be represented—

---

1 Section 47 was amended to extend to housing by the Housing Act 1988, s. 137 (rented housing), and the Local Government and Housing Act 1989, s. 180 (other housing). There are Statutory Codes on Employment (1984), S.I. 1983 No. 1083; Rented Housing (1991), S.I. 1991 No. 227; and Non-Rented (Owner Occupied) Housing 1992, S.I. 1992 No. 619. Statutory codes do not have the force of law, but may be taken into account by courts: 1976 Act, s. 47(10). There are also non-statutory CRE Codes on Education and Primary Health Care. On s. 47 codes, see C. McCrudden (1988), 51 MLR 409.

(i) by counsel or a solicitor; or

(ii) by some other person of his choice, not being a person to whom the Commission object on the ground that he is unsuitable.

(5) The Commission or, if the Commission were required by the Secretary of State to conduct the investigation, the Secretary of State after consulting the Commission may from time to time revise the terms of reference; and subsections (1), (3) and (4) shall apply to the revised investigation and terms of reference as they applied to the original.

50.—(1) For the purposes of a formal investigation the Commission, by a notice in the prescribed form served on him in the prescribed manner—

(a) may require any person to furnish such written information as may be described in the notice, and may specify the time at which, and the manner and form in which, the information is to be furnished;

(b) may require any person to attend at such time and place as is specified in the notice and give oral information about, and produce all documents in his possession or control relating to, any matter specified in the notice.

(2) Except as provided by section 60 [investigations as to compliance with non-discrimination notices], a notice shall be served under subsection (1) only where—

(a) service of the notice was authorised by an order made by the Secretary of State; or

(b) the terms of reference of the investigation state that the Commission believe that a person named in them may have done or may be doing acts of all or any of the following descriptions—

(i) unlawful discriminatory acts;

(ii) contraventions of section 28; and

(iii) contraventions of sections 29, 30 or 31,

and confine the investigation to those acts.

NOTES

1. The CRE's power to conduct formal investigations is a key part of the 1976 Act.[1] Formal investigations may be initiated by the Secretary of State (none so far) or by the CRE (s. 48(1)). They may be conducted for any purpose connected with the execution of the CRE's duties under s. 41(1). In *Home Office v Commission for Racial Equality* [1982] QB 385, QBD, Woolf J held that the CRE was entitled to conduct a formal investigation into racial discrimination in the immigration service. Such an investigation could not be seen as coming within s. 43(1)(a) because 'discrimination' there referred to discrimination within the 1976 Act and the court was bound by the ruling in the *Kassam* case, above, p. 652, that discrimination in immigration practice was outside the Act. It did, however, come within s. 43(1)(b) as being aimed at 'promoting "good relations . . . between persons of different racial groups" '. Woolf J pointed out that the CRE's powers to conduct the investigation would be limited in that it would only be able to require the Home Office to produce evidence if the Secretary of State authorised it to do so (s. 50(2)(a)). In fact, the Home Office co-operated fully. See *Immigration Control and Procedures: Report of a Formal Investigation*, F. Invest. Rep. 1985. One incident which led the CRE to undertake the investigation was the disclosure that Asian women had been required by immigration officials to undergo virginity tests before entry into the UK (*The Guardian* 20 July 1979.)

2. The procedure to be followed in the conduct of formal investigations is indicated in ss. 49–50 of the Act. The meaning of these sections, which have proved difficult to interpret, has been considered in two House of Lords cases: the *Hillingdon* and

---

1 On formal investigations, see Appleby and Ellis, [1984] PL 236; ibid, (1984) 100 LQR 349; M. Coussey, in Hepple and Szyszczak, op. cit. at p. 613, n. 1, Chap. 3; C. McCrudden, in R. Baldwin and C. McCrudden, eds, *Regulation and Public Law* (1987) p. 227; *Racial Justice at Work*, op. cit. at p. 613, n. 1, above, Chaps. 3 and 4; Pardoe, (1982) 132 NLJ 670.

Prestige cases,[1] with the one speech in each case being delivered by Lord Diplock. The cases established, inter alia, that the CRE is subject to judicial review in the exercise of its statutory powers in respect of formal investigations.

3. The Act provides for named person and general investigations. A *named person investigation* may only occur if the CRE has a 'belief' that the person named has acted illegally: s. 49(4). In the *Hillingdon* case, it was said (p. 791):

. . . to embark upon the full investigation it is enough that there should be material before the Commission sufficient to raise in the minds of reasonable men, possessed of the experience of covert racial discrimination that has been acquired by the Commission, a suspicion that there may have been acts by the person named of racial discrimination of the kind which it is proposed to investigate.

In the *Prestige* case, Lord Diplock added (p. 342):

. . . it should be a condition precedent to the exercise by the CRE of its power to conduct named-persons investigations that the CRE should in fact have already formed a suspicion that the persons named may have committed some unlawful act of discrimination and had at any rate *some* grounds for so suspecting, albeit that the grounds upon which any such suspicion was based might, at that stage, be no more than tenuous because they had not yet been tested.

In the *Prestige* case, a non-discrimination notice was quashed because the CRE had had no 'belief' at all that the company had acted illegally when it decided to conduct an investigation into 'the employment of persons of different racial groups by the Prestige Group Ltd.' The House of Lords rejected the CRE's view that there could be a second, non-accusatorial kind of named person investigation within the Act, to which s. 49(4) did not apply, of the sort represented by the facts of that case.

The decision in the *Prestige* case was a considerable blow to the CRE which had a number of similar investigations pending. They were all investigations into a particular sector of activity which seemed to merit inquiry (e.g. because of the small number of black persons employed in an industry or allocated public housing) and in which the CRE had chosen to investigate a particular company or body as a test case. In each case, the named company or body was chosen not because it was believed to have been discriminating but because it would, for one reason or another, make a good subject for study. One such case was the *Hackney Council Housing* case, above, p. 658. This case was completed and a non-discrimination notice issued. Although the decision to conduct it could almost certainly have been quashed under the *Prestige* case, the Council decided not to challenge the notice and agreed to comply with it. As a result of the *Prestige* case, in which the House of Lords showed its concern for a named person who would appear to many to have been accused, such test cases can only be conducted as general investigations, in respect of which the CRE has no automatic right to subpoena evidence and from which a non-discrimination notice cannot result. If, in the course of a general investigation, a belief emerges that discrimination has occurred, a separate named person investigation may be initiated, after the framing of new named person terms of reference. The CRE has called for the repeal of s. 49(4), with the result that the *Prestige* case would be reversed and the CRE would be free to conduct formal investigations for any purpose connected with the carrying out of its duties: *Second Review of the Race Relations Act* (1992) p. 43.

In a named person investigation proceedings begin with a preliminary inquiry (s. 49(4)), the purpose of which was described in the *Hillingdon* case as being to 'give the persons named in the terms of reference an opportunity of making written or

---

1 *R v Commission for Racial Equality, ex p London Borough of Hillingdon* [1982] AC 779 (see above, p. 651 for the facts) and *Re Prestige Group plc, Commission for Racial Equality v Prestige Group plc* [1984] 1 WLR 335. On the *Prestige* case, see M. Munroe, (1985) 14 Anglo-American LR 187.

oral representations or both . . . that the proposed full investigation should not be proceeded with at all, or that its terms of reference should be made narrower . . . or as to the manner in which the full investigation should be conducted'. In other words, Lord Diplock stated, 'audi alteram partem, the first rule of natural justice, is expressly required to be observed . . .'. The named person is entitled to be legally represented at an oral hearing, although he has no right to cross-examine witnesses against him (see *R v CRE, ex p Cottrell and Rothon*, below, which presumably applies at the preliminary inquiry stage as well as later). The oral hearing in the *Hillingdon* case took over three days. In the *Prestige* case, the CRE had infringed s. 49(4) because it had not conducted a preliminary inquiry.

If the CRE decides to proceed with a named person investigation after the s. 49(4) inquiry, a full investigation occurs. CRE staff question individuals and collect documentary evidence, backed by the power to subpoena persons to give evidence or to produce documents (s. 50(2)(b)). Lord Denning MR described these powers as 'immense' and, in somewhat exaggerated fashion, has stated: 'You might think that we were back in the days of the Inquisition': *Science Research Council v Nassé; Leyland Cars Ltd v Vyas* [1979] QB 144 at 172, CA. The Act contains no provision giving the named person a right to a hearing at the full investigation stage. The reason for this can be traced to the drafting history of s. 49(4). This was intended by its author (Lord Hailsham) to apply at the full investigation stage; it was included in s. 49 and phrased in terms of a preliminary inquiry by mistake, as Lord Denning MR acknowledged in the *Hillingdon* case, [1982] QB 276, 285, CA. It is by virtue of this drafting error that the preliminary inquiry stage and many of the difficulties in the working of the formal investigation procedure exist. In the *Hillingdon* case, in the Court of Appeal, Griffiths LJ stated (ibid., p. 297) 'if the Act is to be construed as giving a right of audience and legal representation before the formal investigation even commences, it must be implicit that there is a similar right during the course of the formal investigation itself'. In practice, although the named person will be allowed to make written and oral representations, there is no formal oral hearing in the sense that this can occur at the preliminary inquiry stage until the 'minded' stage is reached (below).

The CRE may issue a non-discrimination notice (other than in education cases within s. 58(6)) following a named person investigation (s. 58). Before a notice is issued, the CRE must, if 'minded' to make one, offer the person who will be subject to it the chance to make representations (s. 58(5)). In *R v Commission for Racial Equality, ex p Cottrell and Rothon* [1980] 1 WLR 1580, QBD, it was held that there was no right at this stage to cross-examine witnesses relied upon by the CRE. The rules of natural justice applied to formal investigations but in the view of Lord Lane LCJ in that case they meant only 'that the proceedings must be conducted in a way which is fair . . . in all the circumstances' and that in an investigatory process of a largely administrative kind which did not lead to the imposition of criminal sanctions, the right to cross-examine was not required. (*Quaere* whether this approach is consistent with Lord Diplock's emphasis on natural justice later in the *Hillingdon* case). A non-discrimination notice is subject to judicial review which may occur before an appeal is made in the case: *R v Commission for Racial Equality, ex p Westminster City Council* [1985] ICR 827, CA. There is a right of appeal against a notice to an industrial tribunal or a county court (s. 59). This allows the person concerned to challenge the CRE's findings of fact as well as raise points of law: *Commission for Racial Equality v Amari Plastics Ltd* [1982] QB 1194, CA. Commenting on the court's 'finding of fact' jurisdiction, Griffiths LJ stated (pp. 1204–5):

'There is no doubt that before a non-discrimination notice is served, the Commission have carried out a searching inquisitorial inquiry to satisfy themselves of the truth of the facts upon which the notice is based and have given at least two and probably three opportunities to the person to put his case, either orally or in writing, either by himself or through solicitors, counsel or any person of his choice. This is necessarily an expensive and a time-consuming process. In the present case it has already been going on over four years, and I can understand the frustration that the commissioners must feel if the Act requires that their findings of fact are liable to be reopened and reversed on appeal.

. . . If it were not for the plain wording of section 59(2), I should be most sympathetic to the commission's argument. If Parliament empowers a body to carry out a formal investigation and hedges the procedure with safeguards to ensure that the person investigated shall have every opportunity to state his case and then requires that body to publish its findings, one might be forgiven for thinking that Parliament intended that that would be the end of the matter. But it is to my mind clear from the language of this statute that such is not the case.'

Lord Denning also appreciated the CRE's difficulty (p. 1203):

'The machinery [of formal investigations] is so elaborate and cumbersome that it is in danger of grinding to a halt. I am very sorry for the Commission, but they have been caught up in a spider's web spun by Parliament, from which there is little hope of their escaping.'

He noted, however, that under the *Cottrell and Rothon* case, above, the company would have had no opportunity to cross-examine witnesses before the CRE and that the hearing before the court or tribunal would be the one occasion on which it would be able to put its case to a body other than the CRE.

The CRE must keep a register of non-discrimination notices and make it available for public inspection (s. 61). It is kept in the CRE's library in London. A non-discrimination notice will require the person named not to commit further discriminatory acts. If, during the following five years, it appears likely to the CRE that discrimination persists, it may apply for an injunction to enforce the notice (s. 62(1)). At the end of 1993, there were eight non-discrimination notices in force. One had been issued in 1993.

A named person investigation is completed by the adoption of a report, to which any non-discrimination notice may be appended. A formal investigation report must be published by the Secretary of State if the investigation was one required by him (s. 51(3)). Otherwise the CRE has the choice of publishing the report or simply making it available for inspection (s. 51(4)). The reports made so far have been published. The CRE may make recommendations in its report, including recommendations for a change in the law (s. 51(1)).

4. In the case of a *general investigation*, once the terms of reference have been adopted, the CRE begins its full investigation, interviewing individuals and collecting evidence. In general investigations, the power of subpoena is only available if the Secretary of State agrees (s. 50(2)(a)). The question of a right to a hearing for any interested party is not dealt with by statute and has not as yet been considered judicially. In the case of some general investigations, although no person is named in the terms of reference (they must not be: the *Hillingdon* and *Prestige* cases), the nature of the investigation (e.g. specific to the immigration service) or the way in which the investigation develops (so as to focus upon a particular person) suggests that a right to representation should exist, even though the reasoning in the *Hillingdon* and *Prestige* cases indicates that the CRE may not issue a non-discrimination notice following a general investigation. The outcome of a general investigation is a report which is otherwise subject to the same rules as a report resulting from a named person investigation. A draft of the report is submitted to any interested party for comment.

5. By the end of 1993, the CRE had completed 59 formal investigations. Fourteen investigations were pending. Most formal investigations have been in employment or housing, particularly the former. Whereas in the early years the great majority of investigations were 'named person' investigations, following the *Prestige* case the number of general investigations has increased. The response to the *Prestige* case has been for most general investigations to be narrower in scope, following the success of the *Beaumont Leys* case.[1] Coussey, loc. cit. at p. 670, n. **1**, above, p. 45, has described the post-Prestige strategy for general investigations as follows:

'The investigation must be narrowly-defined, either by industry or organised structure or by function or geographical location. It must include in its scope employers regarded as a model or leader by others, and it must focus on an issue or practice about which the industry itself has a concern, to maximise self-interest and the potential for negotiating change.'

As of 1989, a further shift in strategy has occurred, with increased emphasis on the use of formal investigations as a basis for the private negotiation of change rather than public, accusatory enforcement: see Coussey, ibid., who states that this strategy has had 'mixed success'.

Overall, formal investigations have not played the key enforcement role that was envisaged for them under the 1976 Act. This has been partly because of the *Prestige* case and delays and upsets that have resulted from legal challenges through judicial review or appeals against non-discrimination notices. It is also partly to do with a lack of resources and different views within the CRE as to the relative importance of its enforcement and promotional roles. As is concluded in *Racial Justice at Work*, op. cit. at p. 613, n. **1**, above, p. 275, the result is that, contrary to Parliament's intentions, the individual complaint is a more effective means of enforcement than the formal investigation:

'Formal investigations are not playing the central role now that might have been expected. On the other hand, the use of the CRE's power to assist individual complainants has expanded over the period since it was established in 1977, in spite of the legislators' intention to reduce the dominance of the law enforcement agency and give individuals direct access to the tribunals and courts. This may be to do with the failure of alternative legal strategies. As one senior officer said: "Complaints were regarded as the scout cars of the CRE powers, whereas formal investigations were supposed to be the tanks. What has happened is that the scout cars have become the more effective." '

12 Enforcement in the courts

Race Relations Act 1976

53. Restriction of proceedings for breach of Act
(1) Except as provided by this Act no proceedings, whether civil or criminal, shall lie against any person in respect of an act by reason that the act is unlawful by virtue of a provision of this Act.
(2) Subsection (1) does not preclude the making of an order of certiorari, mandamus or prohibition.

[Sections 54–6 provide for remedies in employment and similar (partnerships, trade unions, etc) cases arising under Part II (ss. 4–16) of the Act. A person alleging discrimination against him may take his case directly to an industrial tribunal (s. 54(1)). If conciliation through ACAS (s. 55) proves unsuccessful, the tribunal will hear the case and may make an order declaring that discrimination has occurred, award compensation, or recommend action to rectify the wrong done (s. 56).]

57. Claims under Part III
(1) A claim by any person ('the claimant') that another person ('the respondent')—
  (a) has committed an act of discrimination against the claimant which is unlawful by virtue of Part III [ss. 17–27]; or
  (b) is by virtue of section 32 [vicarious liability of employers and principals] or 33 [aiding unlawful acts] to be treated as having committed such an act of discrimination against the claimant,

---

1 F. Invest. Rep. 1985. The general investigation there was into the numbers of black employees in shops, including leading stores, at a new Leicester shopping precinct.

may be made the subject of civil proceedings in like manner as any other claim in tort or (in Scotland) in reparation for breach of statutory duty.

(2) Proceedings under subsection (1)—

(*a*) shall, in England and Wales, be brought only in a designated county court; and

(*b*) shall, in Scotland, be brought only in sheriff court;

but all such remedies shall be obtainable in such proceedings as, apart from this subsection and section 53(1), would be obtainable in the High Court or the Court of Session, as the case may be.

(3) As respects an unlawful act of discrimination falling within section 1(1)(*b*), no award of damages shall be made if the respondent proves that the requirement or condition in question was not applied with the intention of treating the claimant unfavourably on racial grounds.

(4) For the avoidance of doubt it is hereby declared that damages in respect of an unlawful act of discrimination may include compensation for injury to feelings whether or not they include compensation under any other head. . . .

NOTES

1. Section 53 excludes the few common law remedies that might be available, e.g. a claim in tort against an innkeeper (see above, p. 650). The prerogative orders remain available where they apply and may be cheaper and quicker to use in some cases.

2. The Act provides for the first time[1] for direct and immediate access to court for an aggrieved individual to challenge acts of discrimination contrary to the Race Relations Act. Under the 1968 Act, his only remedy was to complain to the RRB which attempted conciliation and took the case to court if conciliation failed. This approach was criticised as 'paternalistic' and an individual may now take a case claiming a breach (either directly or by virtue of ss. 32 or 33) of Part II (employment and related matters) to an industrial tribunal and of Part III (education, goods, facilities, services, housing, and clubs) to a county court. The CRE has recommended a radical change in these arrangements.[2] It has proposed that a single 'discrimination division within the industrial tribunal system should be established to hear both employment and non-employment race and sex discrimination cases'.

3. The limitation period is very short. Cases must be brought within three months of the alleged act of discrimination before any industrial tribunal (s. 68(1)) and within six months before a county court, except for public sector education cases under ss. 17–18 (eight months) and cases where assistance is sought from the CRE (eight or nine months) (s. 68(2)–(4)).[3] The claimant does not have to inform the CRE that he is bringing proceedings, although he will obviously do so if (as in practice he normally does) he seeks the assistance which the CRE can give him (s. 66). In 1993, the CRE received 1,630 applications for assistance, over two thirds of which concerned employment. In the same year, the CRE offered representation in 250 county court or industrial tribunal cases. In such cases, the claimant retains control over his case in the sense that he is always free to terminate proceedings.

Legal aid is available in county court cases. Guidance to local legal aid committees has suggested that legal aid should be given in accordance with the importance of

---

1 Except for unfair dismissal cases under (now) the Employment Protection (Consolidation) Act 1978, as amended.

2 *Second Review of the Race Relations Act 1976* (1992) p. 48. Cf. the similar proposal made by the Home Office sponsored Policy Studies Institute study: *Racial Justice at Work* (1992) pp. 227–8. The CRE has been concerned at the very small number of non-employment cases going to county courts, with their inappropriately formal procedures, and the problems in race cases before industrial tribunals (see below).

3 The time limit may be waived if this would be 'just and equitable' (s. 68(6)). It does not prevent a claim being brought in the case of a continuing act of discrimination: see *Barclays Bank plc v Kapur* [1991] 1 All ER 646, HL. See also *Sougrin v Haringey Health Authority* [1991] IRLR 447.

the case to the individual and not the likely amount of damages (which may not be great). Legal aid is not available in the much more numerous industrial tribunal cases—which makes CRE assistance particularly important.[1] The 'green form' legal advice scheme applies, however, and trade union representation may be available. In *Freeman v Salford Health Authority*,[2] an industrial tribunal argued in favour of extending legal aid to employment cases as follows:

'So much of an applicant's case depends upon in-depth cross-examination of the respondent's witnesses. Such a cross-examination can in most cases only be conducted by a skilled advocate. Fortunately in this case the applicant's representation was financed by the Commission for Racial Equality. Unfortunately their resources only permit them to represent in selected cases. There must clearly be a case for the availability of legal aid, with proper safeguards, in discrimination cases.'

The absence of legal aid in employment cases is one reason for the low success level of racial discrimination claims. Other reasons that apply to employment and other cases include the fact that '[r]acial discrimination is not normally practised openly. . . . It may take a whole variety of subtle forms that are not easy to uncover'[3]. There are also problems as to the burden of proof. Under the Act, this is the normal civil law burden of proof upon the balance of probabilities. It falls upon the claimant, although in a case of indirect discrimination the burden of proving that a requirement or condition is 'justifiable' is upon the defendant (see above, p. 620).

Although recognising the particular problem of proving racial discrimination, the courts have declined to adopt an approach whereby the burden of proof would shift to the defendant once less favourable treatment consistent with discrimination is proved; instead, it is for the court to draw its own conclusion as to whether there has been unlawful racial discrimination on the basis of the findings of fact, taking into account any failure of the defendant to prove a convincing explanation. The position was explained in *King v GB China Centre*:[4]

'(1) It is for the applicant who complains of racial discrimination to make out his or her case. Thus if the applicant does not prove the case on the balance of probabilities he or she will fail. (2) It is important to bear in mind that it is unusual to find direct evidence of racial discrimination. Few employers will be prepared to admit such discrimination even to themselves. In some cases the discrimination will not be ill-intentioned but merely based on an assumption that "he or she would not have fitted in." (3) The outcome of the case will therefore usually depend on what inferences it is proper to draw from the primary facts found by the tribunal. These inferences can include, in appropriate cases, any inferences that it is just and equitable to draw in accordance with section 65(2)(b) of the Act of 1976 from an evasive or equivocal reply to a questionnaire. (4) Though there will be some cases where, for example, the non-selection of the applicant for a post or for promotion is clearly not on racial grounds, a finding of discrimination and a finding of a difference in race will often point to the possibility of racial discrimination. In such circumstances the tribunal will look to the employer for an explanation. If no explanation is then put forward or if the tribunal considers the explanation to be inadequate or unsatisfactory it will be legitimate for the tribunal to infer that the discrimination was on racial grounds. This is not a matter of law but, as May LJ put it in *North West Thames Regional Health Authority v Noone* [1988] ICR 813, 822, "almost common sense." (5) It is unnecessary and unhelpful to introduce the concept of a shifting evidential burden of proof. At the conclusion of all the evidence the tribunal should make findings as to the primary facts and draw such inferences as they consider proper from those facts. They should then reach a conclusion on the balance of probabilities, bearing in mind both the difficulties which face a person who complains of unlawful discrimination and the fact that it is for the complainant to prove his or her case.'

1 Legal aid is available on appeal to the Employment Appeal Tribunal.
2 Quoted in *Second Review of the Race Relations Act 1976*, p. 52. The CRE has recommended that legal aid be available in industrial tribunal cases. The Home Office sponsored Policy Studies Institute study reached the same conclusion: *Racial Discrimination at Work* (1991) p. 277.
3 Per Lord Diplock in *Hillingdon London Borough Council v Commission for Racial Equality* [1982] AC 779, HL.
4 [1992] ICR 526 at 528, CA, per Neill LJ for a unanimous court. The position may be contrasted with that in unfair dismissal cases where the burden of proof is always upon the employer to show that the dismissal is fair: Employment Protection (Consolidation) Act 1978, s. 57(1).

Commenting on the low success level in racial discrimination claims, the CRE has stated:[1]

'The Commission has long expressed concern at the low number of ethnic minority chairs and members in industrial tribunals. During the year the President of Tribunals and the Department of Employment agreed that more ethnic minority chairs and members were needed. . . . The approach some tribunals took towards applicants alleging racial discrimination, and the quality of some tribunal decisions, also gave us cause for concern. . . . In recent years, cases taken to the Employment Appeals Tribunal have met with little success. Whether this was because the cases were weak, or the issues of law misunderstood, was a matter much debated. . . . There was a worrying number of cases where the industrial tribunal found discrimination but this was then overturned at the EAT—in some cases because the tribunal had issued a defective written decision. This reinforces the need to improve training for tribunal members.'

4. There are special arrangements for the enforcement of the education provisions in ss. 17–19. Sections 17 and 18 cases arising in the public sector (i.e. mainly cases concerning LEAs, but excluding universities and independent schools) must be taken first to the Minister for Education (s. 57(5)). They may be referred to a county court if no satisfactory solution has been reached within two months. The general duty in s. 19 is not enforceable under the Act through the courts or by a non-discrimination notice (although a formal investigation is possible: see the *Reading* case, above, p. 648). It is enforceable instead by the Secretary of State for Education acting under his Education Act 1944 powers (1944 Act, s. 19(4)).

5. By s.75(8), 1976 Act, a member of the armed forces has no remedy before an industrial tribunal or in the courts. Instead any complaint of racial discrimination contrary to the Act must be considered through internal armed forces procedures. When considering a racial discrimination complaint from a serving soldier, the Army Board of the Defence Council must allow the complainant to see all of the evidence seen by the Board and allow him a proper opportunity to respond, which will require the Board to consider in its discretion giving the complainant an oral hearing: *R v Army Board of Defence Council, ex p Anderson* [1991] 3 All ER 375, DC (Army Board decision quashed on judicial review for failure to consider oral hearing and to allow discovery). In 1993, a soldier was awarded £8,500 compensation from the Ministry of Defence for racial bullying and constant racial abuse and physical violence by the Army Board: CRE Report 1993, p. 9. The Ministry has issued a Code of Practice for the Armed Forces that deals with racial discrimination: ibid., p. 22.

6. *Evidence.* The question of discovery of documents has been dealt with encouragingly by the courts. In *Science Research Council v Nassé; BL Cars Ltd v Vyas*[2] it was held that discovery must be ordered, notwithstanding confidentiality, where this was 'necessary for disposing fairly of the proceedings' (Lord Wilberforce, at p. 1065). In an important ruling it has also been held that the discovery of statistical material as to the ethnic composition of an employer's workforce may be ordered in a case of direct (as well as indirect) discrimination as probative evidence of a policy of racial discrimination that may have been applied to the plaintiff: *West Midlands Passenger Transport Executive v Singh* [1988] ICR 614, CA. In that case, a coloured bus inspector who had failed in his application for promotion, successfully sought an order requiring his employer to disclose a schedule indicating the number of white and non-white persons who had applied for and been appointed to the post of traffic supervisor for which he had applied. See Gardner, (1989) 105 LQR 183. A separate question concerns the s. 65 questionnaire procedure. A defendant is not obliged to

---

1 CRE 1993 Annual Report, p. 9. Only 15% of racial discrimination claims heard by industrial tribunals succeeded in 1990–1: *Second Review of the Race Relations Act 1976*, p. 22.
2 [1980] AC 1028, HL. See also *Metropolitan Police Comr v Locker* [1993] ICR 440, EAT.

complete the questionnaire properly, although if he does not the court or tribunal may draw any inference 'that it considers just and equitable'. The CRE has recommended that the court or tribunal should be under a duty to draw the appropriate inference.[1]

7. The remedies available to an individual in a county court are those available in any tort claim (s. 57(1)). Damages, which are unlimited, may include damages for injured feelings (s. 57(4)). As noted above, p. 624, no damages may be awarded for indirect discrimination if there is no wrongful intention.[2] In employment cases, a declaration or compensation corresponding to damages that could have been ordered in the case by a county court may be awarded by an industrial tribunal (s. 56(1)). There is now no statutory limit to the amount of damages that may be awarded by an industrial tribunal in a claim under the 1976 Act.[3] A tribunal may recommend that the victim be offered employment or reinstated. The recommendation is not legally binding, but the tribunal may award further compensation if it is not carried out. Unlike a county court, a tribunal has no power to issue an injunction against a defendant to prevent acts of discrimination.

The measure of damages in racial discrimination cases was discussed in *Alexander v Home Office* [1988] 1 WLR 968, CA. In that case, the plaintiff, who was black, was a convicted prisoner who successfully complained of direct racial discrimination contrary to s. 20, 1976 Act by being refused employment in the prison kitchens because of his colour. Relevant to his treatment were initial assessments of him by the prison authorities, of which the appellant only became aware during the legal proceedings, which contained racial stereotyping remarks, in particular that he displayed 'the usual traits associated with people of his ethnic background being arrogant, suspicious of staff, anti-authority, devious and possessing a very large chip on his shoulder.' The Court of Appeal allowed an appeal against the quantum of damages, increasing the damages from £50 to £500. On the measure of damages, May LJ stated (pp. 975–6):

As with any other awards of damages, the objective of an award for unlawful racial discrimination is restitution. Where the discrimination has caused actual pecuniary loss, such as the refusal of a job, then the damages referable to this can be readily calculated. For the injury to feelings, however, for the humiliation, for the insult, it is impossible to say what is restitution and the answer must depend on the experience and good sense of the judge and his assessors. Awards should not be minimal, because this would tend to trivialise or diminish respect for the public policy to which the Act gives effect. On the other hand, just because it is impossible to assess the monetary value of injured feelings, awards should be restrained. To award sums which are generally felt to be excessive does almost as much harm to the policy and the results which it seeks to achieve as do nominal awards. Further, injury to feelings, which is likely to be of a relatively short duration, is less serious than physical injury to the body or the mind which may persist for months, in many cases for life.

Nevertheless damages for this relatively new tort of unlawful racial discrimination are at large, that is to say that they are not limited to the pecuniary loss that can be specifically proved. Further, even where exemplary or punitive damages are not sought, nevertheless compensatory damages may and in some instances should include an element of aggravated damages where, for example, the defendant may have behaved in a high-handed, malicious, insulting or oppressive manner in committing the act of discrimination: see per Lord Devlin in *Rookes v Barnard*. . . .

Although damages for racial discrimination will in many cases be analogous to those for defamation, they are not necessarily the same. In the latter the principal injury to be compensated is that to the

---

1 *Second Review of the Race Relations Act 1976* (1992) p. 55. For criticism of the s. 65 procedure, see L. Lustgarten, *Legal Controls of Racial Discrimination* (1980), p. 205.
2 The CRE has recommended that compensation should now be available for indirect discrimination even in cases of unintentional discrimination on the basis that the victim suffers injury in all cases and that people generally should by now be aware of the likely effect for racial groups of any requirement or condition that they impose: *Second Review of the Race Relations Act 1976*, 1992, p. 60.
3 Race Relations (Remedies) Act 1994. Interest may be included in a compensation award: S.I. 1994 No. 1748.

plaintiff's reputation: I doubt whether this will play a large part in the former. On the other hand, if the plaintiff knows of the racial discrimination and that he has thereby been held up to 'hatred, ridicule or contempt,' then the injury to his feelings will be an important element in the damages. That the injury to feelings for which compensation is sought must have resulted from knowledge of the discrimination is clear from the decision of this court in *Skyrail Oceanic Ltd v Coleman* [1981] ICR 864: see per Lawton LJ, at p. 871. (This was a case concerned with sex discrimination and not racial discrimination, but in my opinion the principle must be the same.)

Whereas May LJ countenanced the possibility of exemplary damages in racial discrimination cases, it has since been established that such damages are not available for torts, such as the statutory tort of racial discrimination, that have been established since 1964.[1] Aggravated damages remain available so that when assessing compensatory damages the court 'can take into account the motives and conduct of the defendant where they aggravate the injury done to the plaintiff'.[2] Since the *Alexander* case, the level of damages in racial discrimination cases has increased. Although a very high award of £5,000 was reduced to £3,000 in *Noone v North West Thames Regional Health Authority* [1988] IRLR 195, the Court of Appeal in that case, which included May LJ, reaffirmed the general statement of principle in the *Alexander* case. £500 is the minimum that should be awarded for injury to feelings: *Sharifi v Strathclyde Regional Council* [1992] IRLR 259, EAT.

8. Enforcement through the CRE by formal investigation and non-discrimination notices has been dealt with in the previous section. Although it lacks the power the RRB had to refer cases in any area covered by the Act arising out of individual complaints to the courts, the CRE retains an important enforcement role in the courts, particularly in giving assistance to claimants bringing their own cases. The CRE also has the exclusive right to bring legal proceedings before a county court or industrial tribunal to enforce ss. 29 (advertisements), 30 (instructions to discriminate), and 31 (inducement to do so). In each of these cases the tribunal or court may only make a declaration or issue an injunction; no damages or compensation may be awarded (s. 63). On the power to seek injunctions when persistent discrimination continues following non-discrimination notices, see above, p. 673.

9. Assessing the value of the individual complaint system under the 1976 Act, *Racial Justice at Work*, pp. 156–7, concludes:

'The number of complaints of racial discrimination made to the tribunals has increased substantially over the period since the 1976 Act came into force, and the number of complaints upheld (though not the proportion) has also increased. The system seems to have attracted complaints from a broad cross-section of the population belonging to non-white ethnic minorities. The system has proved far more popular with ethnic minorities than the comparable system has with women.

. . . Complaints of . . . race discrimination have tended to be against organisations in the public sector, which are trying to introduce equal opportunity policies, and in this sector the success rate of complainants has been low; too few complaints have been made against private sector organisations, although the success rate in this sector has been higher. It may be that organisations that pursue equal opportunity policies tend to raise the level of consciousness of racial discrimination, thereby stimulating complaints, while those which allow discriminatory policies to continue are relatively untouched.

. . . The CRE is much better equipped than any other organisation to provide advice and representation to complainants, and it is the major source of free representation. At the same time, it has a limited budget to spend on this aspect of its work. The result is that a twin-track system has developed. Applicants who are granted assistance by the CRE have a substantially better chance of success than others, for at least three reasons: first, the CRE tries to select the stronger cases; second, it is likely to provide more effective advice and representation than any other body; third, and perhaps most important, it provides moral support to the applicant throughout the earlier stages, thus greatly reducing the chance

1 *Deane v Ealing Borough Council* [1993] ICR 329, applying *AB v South West Water Services Ltd* [1993] 2 WLR 507, CA.
2 Per Lord Devlin in *Rookes v Barnard* [1964] AC 1027, 1221, HL.

that he or she will withdraw. Because the minority of applicants who are granted CRE assistance have a substantial advantage, the determining factor becomes the CRE's decision about whether or not to assist. This means that the CRE retains a dominant and quasi-judicial function. Another consequence is that there has been no development of campaigning organisations which sponsor individual complaints, although the CRE is currently making efforts to develop a complainant aid organisation.

The industrial tribunal process is simpler and quicker than most processes of civil action through the courts. Three-quarters of cases took up to six months from start to finish. Yet the objective of creating an informal system which would be worth entering for the prospect of modest rewards has not really been achieved. . . .

The prospects of success for racial discrimination cases in the industrial tribunal system are much lower than for other types of cases, such as unfair dismissal. . . . For the cases included in the PSI database, which mostly fall within the 12 months ending 31 March 1988, 18 per cent ended in a judgment or settlement in which the applicant was paid £500 or more. (It is possible that the level of financial awards has tended since to increase, following the *Alexander* and *Noone* cases.) It seems clear from these results that a rational person would not embark on the process of making a complaint of racial discrimination to a tribunal simply for the prospect of securing monetary compensation. . . . To achieve a further substantial increase in the number of complaints it will probably be necessary to increase the prospects of success and the size of the remedies.[1]

Evidence presented in later chapters suggests that honour and self-respect are at stake more than monetary compensation.

13 The impact of the 1976 Act on racial discrimination

B. Hepple, 'Have Twenty-Five Years of the Race Relations Acts in Britain been a Failure?' in Hepple and Szyszczak, op. cit. at p. 613, n. 1, pp. 19–20 (footnotes omitted)

Judged in terms of the aims expressed in the White Paper on *Racial Discrimination*[2] – to reduce discrimination and by so doing to help break the 'familiar cycle of cumulative disadvantage' – the ineffectiveness of the Race Relations Act 1976 is irrefutable. The Policy Studies Institute's (PSI) third survey (1982–85) showed a continued gap in the unemployment rates, job levels, earnings, household income and quality of housing between black and white people.[3] This has been confirmed by successive Labour Force Surveys.[4] Seventeen years after the Act of 1968, the PSI found that 'even at a conservative estimate' there were still 'tens of thousands of acts of racial discrimination in job recruitment every year'.[5] The most recent report by Colin Brown[6] shows that differential unemployment rates between whites and ethnic minorities cannot be explained by differences in levels of qualifications. They reflect instead employer discrimination against ethnic minorities and the concentration of workers from minority groups in jobs that are most vulnerable to redundancy. While there has been some narrowing of the gap between white and ethnic minority unemployment rates in recent years, this mainly reflects the tendency for unemployment among minorities to rise faster than white unemployment during economic downturns and to fall faster during periods of growth. Brown points out that ethnic minorities might benefit from changes in labour supply conditions in the next few years but one cannot expect lasting improvement without a serious assault on racial discrimination.

Even the severest critics of the Acts would concede that they have broken down some barriers for individuals in their quest for jobs, housing and services and that they have driven underground those overt expressions of discrimination which were current twenty years ago. Yet most of the reformers expected more than this from the legislation. They usually acknowledge the obvious difficulties in ascribing to an Act of Parliament specific responsibility for any degree of social change, especially where the long-term aim of the Act is to alter entrenched attitudes and behaviour. But they tend to focus their critique, and strategies for future changes, on the perceived weaknesses of the legislation and its enforcement. If only the Act had 'more teeth', imposing cost-deterrent sanctions on discriminators, there would be more significant impacts upon discrimination and disadvantage, according to this line of argument.

1 *Ed.* The limit on industrial tribunal compensation has since been lifted: see above, p. 678.
2 *Ed.* Above, p. 614.
3 Brown, C. *Black and White Britain: The Third PSI Survey* (London, Policy Studies Institute, 1984).
4 'Ethnic Origin and the Labour Market' (1991) *Employment Gazette* 59–72; compare 'Ethnic Origin and Economic Status' (1987) *Employment Gazette* 18–29.
5 Policy Studies Institute *Racial Discrimination: Seventeen Years after the Act* (London, Policy Studies Institute, 1985) p. 31.
6 Brown, C. *Racial Discrimination in the British Labour Market* (London, Employment Institute Economic Report, Vol. 5, No. 4, June 1990).

This approach shows little familiarity with the insights provided by sociologists into law as an instrument of social change. If these scholars teach us anything, it is that law is more likely to be effective in facilitating action which people want to take than in creating new rights to protect weaker parties.[1] The lack of social change following the Race Relations Acts is not unique. It is characteristic of most legislation which seeks to protect those who lack economic and social power, through the mechanism of individual rights enforced by private litigation.

NOTE

The 'serious assault' to which Hepple refers would require Government action. For the view that the Government's policy on racial discrimination in recent years has been one of 'benign neglect', see McCrudden, loc. cit. at p. 613, n. **1**, above, p. 439. McCrudden, p. 453, also quotes and agrees with the following critical assessment by J. Solomos, 67 Pub. Admin. 79, 90 (1989): 'The translation of policies into practice has been hampered by a weak legal framework, organisational marginality and a lack of political legitimacy'. Government action could be required by European Union legislation comparable to that which has led to remarkable advances in the UK law on sex discrimination: see Lord Lester and S. L. Joseph, in Harris and Joseph, op. cit. at p. 739, n. 2, below. For the view that the legal basis for such a development of European Union law exists, see C. Docksey, [1991] ILJ 258. See also *Second Review of the Race Relations Act 1976* (1992) p. 68.

---

1 This distinction is made and developed in the context of the Race Relations Acts by L. Lustgarten, 'Racial Discrimination and the Limits of Law' (1986) 49 *Modern Law Review* 68 at p. 71.

CHAPTER 11

Freedom of movement: immigration and deportation

1 Introduction

A variety of civil liberties issues arise out of the law and practice of immigration control, and it is these which provide the principal focus of this chapter. Given the particularly complex nature of much of the subject-matter with which we shall deal it seems appropriate to highlight at the outset some of the main questions which will recur.

We may begin by noting that a number of purposes may be served by a system of immigration control. In an underpopulated country with an inadequate labour force the principal concern might simply be the individual, personal, acceptability of intending entrants, together with powers to remove those admitted who subsequently may prove unacceptable. More commonly though, in circumstances where existing population levels are placing some strains on housing and the various social services, and levels of unemployment are a matter of concern, immigration controls will seek to exert also a numerical control on entry. In limiting numbers of entrants it is likely that certain categories of applicant will be favoured as compared with others. For example, those with special skills, those with significant assets who may bring wealth into the country, those with apparent ability to support themselves and their families, those from countries with particular historical links with the country exercising control, those who are seeking entry to join other family members previously admitted for settlement, and those seeking entry as refugees seeking political asylum. Much is likely also to turn on the purpose, and duration, for which permission to enter is sought. Is the visit to be relatively short-term (e.g. holiday, education, short-term employment, medical treatment), or is entry being sought with a view to permanent settlement?

As we shall see, the exercise of immigration control in the UK in the period from the end of the Second World War has shifted from the former to the latter approach. Immediately following the war, immigration, particularly from the Caribbean, was very much encouraged as a means of tackling labour shortages in certain sectors. By the late 1950s concern began to be expressed at this 'open' immigration policy in respect of the Commonwealth, and from 1962 onwards legislation, and administrative rules, have imposed increasingly strict and increasingly complex controls restricting entry. Perhaps inevitably, the criteria adopted in limiting entry have engendered considerable and continuing controversy. Charges have been laid, for example, of over-zealous protection of the labour market, of undue favouritism towards the wealthy, of failure to honour 'obligations' stemming from our Imperial past (in stark contrast to the freedom of movement of EC, and more recently EEA, Nationals, as required by EU law), of policies based on 'ancestral connection' which advantage those from the 'white' as compared with the 'coloured' Commonwealth, of policies which are said to fail to recognise the importance of family unity and have resulted in the separation between continents of close-knit extended families, and of over-cautious attitudes in relation to refugee and asylum cases.

We should also note the debate which has surrounded the question of the impact of the law and practice of immigration control on the establishment of good domestic race relations. Starkly opposing views have been expressed on this matter. To some, the imposition of close control over the number of non-temporary entrants to the UK is essential to progress in community relations. Put crudely, it is said to be essential for the promotion of good race relations to reassure the majority white population that the influx of persons of other races is subject to effective powers of control. Integration and racial harmony, on this view, depend on the elimination of fears of mass entry and consequent associated problems in relation to housing, employment, social services and so on. Others regard this issue very differently, arguing that a strict policy of immigration control may be a hindrance to racial harmony. Unless the greatest care is taken in the formulation of the favoured immigration categories, and in relation also to the day to day administration of controls, the immigration system itself may, it is argued, become regarded as a symbol of a lack of true commitment towards racial equality, tolerance, and integration. On this controversial issue the consistent approach of British governments has been to acknowledge some force in each of the contentions, by following what they have commonly proclaimed to be 'firm but fair' immigration control. Note in this context the terms of rule 2 of the Immigration Rules 1994:

'Immigration Officers, Entry Clearance Officers and all staff of the Home Office Immigration and Nationality Department will carry out their duties without regard to the race, colour or religion of persons seeking to enter or remain in the United Kingdom.'

Lastly by way of introduction, we should draw attention to the importance in this area, as elsewhere, of good administrative practice and of fair procedures. The administration of immigration control should reflect the often very great significance of the decisions taken to the lives of those concerned. To decide to deport or to remove a person from the UK, to refuse a person permission to join a spouse or other family member, or to refuse a plea for asylum, is to take a decision which is likely to be of very considerable importance to the lives of the applicant and others. The procedures and processes for taking such decisions should reflect this fact, and mechanisms should exist for appeal against decisions, or for some other review of decisions. In the UK a fairly sophisticated and extensive tribunal appeal system has been established. However, as we shall see, it does not operate in relation to all immigration decisions taken; moreover, in certain situations an appellant may not be able to exercise the right of appeal whilst remaining within the UK.

These various matters should be borne in mind in assessing the materials and explanatory notes which follow. The leading works on immigration law are I. MacDonald and N. Blake, *Immigration Law and Practice* (3rd edn, 1991); M. Supperstone and D. O'Dempsey, *Immigration Law* (3rd edn, 1994); J. M. Evans, *Immigration Law* (2nd edn, 1983); L. Grant and I. Martin, *Immigration Law and Practice* (1982 and Supplements); V. Bevan, *The Development of British Immigration Law* (1986); A. Dummett and A. Nicol, *Subjects, Citizens, Aliens and Others – Nationality and Immigration Law* (1990); C. Vincenzi and D. Marrington, *Immigration Law: The Rules Explained* (1992). Note also, the discussion in C. Harlow and R. Rawlings, *Law and Administration* (1984) Chaps. 16 and 17; and the reports of the Commission for Racial Equality, *Immigration Control and Procedures: Report of a Formal Investigation*

(1985), and the Select Committee on Home Affairs: *Immigration from the Indian Subcontinent* (1981–82, HC 90–1).

2 Emergence of immigration controls

The exercise of strict control over immigration into the UK is of fairly modern origin. Until as recently as 1962 all *British subjects* (i.e. all citizens of independent Commonwealth countries, and including 'citizens of the UK and Colonies' (CUKCs)) had complete freedom to enter and remain in the UK. Prior to 1962 immigration control extended only to *aliens* (i.e. persons not British subjects, though not including citizens of the Republic of Ireland or British Protected Persons). However, even in respect of aliens, non-temporary statutory controls had only existed since the Aliens Act 1905, an Act passed in response to anti-Jewish sentiment triggered by Jewish immigration from Eastern Europe in the latter part of the nineteenth century; this rather modest measure, giving powers to deny entry to 'undesirable aliens' arriving on immigrant ships, being soon superseded, at the commencement of the First World War, by the more comprehensive Aliens Restriction Acts of 1914 and 1919 and the Orders in Council made thereunder (e.g. the Aliens Order 1953).

The freedom of all British subjects to enter and remain in the UK survived the 'fracturing', during the 1940s, of the single, uniform, 'Empire', citizenship of 'British subjecthood' into the newly emergent local-based citizenship units within the Commonwealth (i.e. the new citizenships of Canada, Australia, UK and Colonies, etc.). Thereafter, the status of British subject became a derivative status shared by all those possessing any such local-based citizenship (hence the expressions 'British subject' and 'Commonwealth citizen' were synonymous). The status of British subject/Commonwealth citizen continued, until 1962, to afford full entry and settlement rights in respect of the UK.

This simple equation of freedom from immigration control with the British citizenship possessed by millions around the world, was uncontroversial and unproblematic all the while there were labour shortages which needed to be met (e.g. health service and public transport), and so long as relatively few sought to take advantage of their entry rights. However, as net immigration rose during the late 1950s (from 42,700 in 1955 to 136,000 in 1961 – nearly half a million entrants in the seven years up to 1962, many subsequently to be joined by spouses and families), incidents expressing ill-feeling towards the new entrants occurred (e.g. the Notting Hill 'race' riots of 1959). Such feelings and events soon led to the passage of the Commonwealth Immigrants Act of 1962, extending immigration control for the first time beyond aliens, and restricting the entry rights of certain defined categories of British subjects. The scheme of the Act was to extend control to all British subjects except:

(1) those born in the UK; and
(2) those who were CUKCs and held 'UK passports' (as defined in the Act); and
(3) those included in the passports of persons exempt from immigration control under (1) or (2) above.

The expression 'UK passport' did not extend to the passports of those CUKCs who had that citizenship by virtue of their links with a colony rather than with the UK itself, and who accordingly possessed passports issued by the UK government on behalf of the colonial government. The term did, however, extend to passports obtained by CUKCs from High Commissions in *independent* Commonwealth countries. In this way the Act not only subjected Commonwealth citizens who were not

CUKCs to immigration control, it also extended immigration control to those CUKCs who were regarded as 'belonging' to one of the colonies rather than to the UK itself. Those now subject to control were subject to an employment voucher scheme, the terms of which were significantly tightened in 1965. The effect of the 1962 Act was intended to be to render subject to control the numbers of would-be entrants except for those possessing personal or ancestral connections with the UK itself.

The 1962 Act proved, in fact, to be of only limited effect in securing such governmental control over numbers entering the UK. In particular its provisions did not extend control to large sections of the Asian community in Kenya and Uganda who, largely as a result of 'Africanisation' policies operated in those countries (i.e. progressively excluding non-citizens from trading or taking employment), entered the UK in increasing numbers in the mid-1960s. On Kenya's independence in 1963, Asian residents had had the option of acquiring the new Kenyan citizenship or of retaining their citizenship of the UK and Colonies. Many opted for the latter, and acquired passports issued through the British High Commission in independent Kenya on behalf of the UK Government. They therefore qualified as 'UK passport' holders within the terms of the 1962 Act. Many 'Ugandan' Asians were in a similar position.

To subject entry of these Asian citizens of the UK and Colonies to governmental regulation, the Commonwealth Immigrants Act 1968 was hurriedly passed. This Act extended controls to cover holders of UK passports issued outside the UK, unless the would-be entrant could show requisite defined personal or ancestral (parental or grandparental) links with the UK itself: a test immediately criticised as being 'neutral' in form but which neatly divided the world of Commonwealth citizens into 'predominantly blacks' and 'predominantly whites'. It should be noted also that whereas the 1962 Act had restricted the residence rights of some CUKCs to the colony to which they 'belonged', the 1968 Act had considerably more drastic effects. It withdrew UK entry and settlement rights from persons who, not being citizens of the countries from which they sought entry, accordingly found themselves in a precarious position. Some were, in fact, permitted entry under the 'Special Voucher' quota scheme (see below, p. 699); others sought entry unsuccessfully without such vouchers only then to find themselves also refused entry on being returned to E. Africa, thus giving rise to the problem of the 'shuttlecock' Asians. This strict control had, however, to be relaxed in the face of the mass expulsion of Asian CUKCs and British Protected Persons from Uganda in 1972; the UK ultimately accepting some 28,000 such refugees for settlement (see *R v Secretary of State for the Home Department, ex p Thakrar* [1974] QB 684). On the background to the 1962 and 1968 Acts, see P. Foot, *Immigration and Race in British Politics* (1965), D. Steel, *No Entry* (1969), V. Bevan, *The Development of British Immigration Law* (1986), A. Dummett and A. Nicol, *Subjects, Citizens, Aliens and others* (1990). For the East African Asians cases before the European Commission on Human Rights, see below, Chap. 12, p. 772. Note that the UK has not ratified the Fourth Protocol to the ECHR: 'no one shall be deprived of the right to enter the territory of the State of which he is a national' (see below, p. 743).

The Aliens Restriction Acts and the Commonwealth Immigrants Acts were in due course replaced by the Immigration Act 1971, which, as amended, is the current governing legislation. The 1971 Act, unlike the 1962 and 1968 Acts, was not primarily designed to extend further the ambit of immigration control. Indeed, it *removed* from control Commonwealth citizens with certain parental connections with the UK. Moreover, the Immigration Rules, governing the exercise of immigration control, have recognised the very generous 'rights' to enter and to remain of EC (and, now, EEA) nationals under European Community law: see below, p. 705, n. **1**. The Rules, since 1973, have also eased entry of Commonwealth citizens with grandparental connections with the UK. Nevertheless, the passage of the 1971 Act did mark some tightening of control. For example, its provisions relating to deportation weakened the position of those Commonwealth citizens who had entered and remained by permission rather than as of right, denying them the 'privileged' position such citizens hitherto had possessed. In general, the Act went far towards the general equation of the rights of aliens and the rights of those Commonwealth citizens who were subject to control. Furthermore, the Immigration Rules made under the Act, regulating the entry, and the control after entry, of those subject to control, were generally more restrictive than before (except, importantly, in relation to EC nationals and Commonwealth citizens with grandparental connections).

The 1971 Act introduced the concept of 'patriality', signifying persons with the 'right of abode' in the UK (i.e. having the right to enter and remain, free from immigration control and free from the power of deportation). The complexity of the definition of those who were 'patrials' (see the original s. 2 of the 1971 Act, below p. 689) revealed very clearly the inadequacy of the then existing citizenship categories for immigration purposes. The right of abode could not be defined directly in terms of citizenship; nor did possession of any particular citizenship of itself ensure the right of abode.

The British Nationality Act 1981 has sought to return immigration control directly to distinctions of citizenship, by revision of those citizenship categories. 'British citizens', as there defined, are immune from controls. All others are subject to control, including those former CUKCs who fall now within the new categories of 'British Dependent Territories Citizens' (BDTCs: most significantly, residents of Hong Kong – the term 'dependent territory' superseding the term 'colony') and 'British Overseas Citizens' (BOCs – a residual category comprising those CUKCs who under the Act did not qualify as British citizens or BDTCs: mostly CUKCs resident in independent Commonwealth countries without citizenship of those countries). The return of immigration control to distinctions directly based on citizenship categories is, however, only a superficial simplification because the concept of British citizen is itself defined to include all those who had the right of abode when the 1981 Act came into force. This definition, protecting 'acquired rights', means that for many years it will be necessary to refer back to the complex original definitions of the 1971 Act.

This policy of exclusion of numbers of citizens abroad from entry to the UK itself has, however, continued to give rise to problems. Following the conclusion of the Falklands war it was decided to enhance the immigration rights of certain of the islanders. Under the British Nationality (Falklands Islands) Act 1983 those born in the Falklands to parents who were settled there have become British citizens rather than merely BDTCs. The problem of Hong Kong remains. The Hong Kong Act 1985 provides that after 1 July 1997 those who are BDTCs shall become what will be called 'British Nationals (Overseas)' – a new category carrying with it no UK residence rights. Fear that 'key' figures in Hong Kong's political and economic life might leave Hong Kong (e.g. for Canada) prior to 1997 has, however, caused the British government to grant British citizenship (*with* entry rights) to such persons. The aim has been to try to engender in them the confidence to remain in Hong

Kong, in the knowledge that a 'bolt-hole' to the UK exists. Critics have commented on this preferential treatment afforded to this small minority of Hong Kong BDTCs. See, further, the British Nationality (Hong Kong) Act 1990 and S.I. 1990 No. 2292.

In considering the scope of immigration control it is important to emphasise the following fundamental distinctions: firstly, between those categories of persons who are subject to immigration control and those not so subject (i.e. the question of the 'right of abode'); and secondly, in respect of those who *are* subject to control, between those categories of persons who may expect to be permitted to enter and remain, and those with no such expectations. The first distinction – who has the right of abode? – is determined, as we shall see, by more or less precise *statutory* provisions. The latter distinction – how will control powers be exercised? – is dependent, in large part at least, on the Immigration Rules: rules of guidance issued, under statutory authority and subject to some degree of parliamentary supervision, by the Home Secretary, indicating the manner of exercise of discretionary powers by immigration officers, entry clearance officers and by the Home Secretary himself. This distinction between 'entitlement' and 'discretionary entry' does not, however, very satisfactorily depict the 'rights' of EU and EEA nationals. See Article 7, Treaty of European Union and the Immigration (European Economic Area) Order 1994 (S.I. 1994 No. 1895); and below, pp. 704–707.

The materials which follow cover the following matters: the ambit of immigration control (i.e. who has, or has not, the right of abode?); the administration of immigration control; the substance of the Immigration Rules indicating how immigration control powers will normally be exercised; powers of deportation (who is subject to deportation? and on what grounds?); powers to remove summarily persons who are 'illegal entrants'; and finally, appeals against immigration and deportation decisions. The reader should at the outset be alerted to the complexities of the subject matter. This chapter aims to provide an outline only of the scope and administration of controls.

References in this chapter to the '1971 Act' and the '1981 Act' are to the Immigration Act 1971 and the British Nationality Act 1981. References to the 'Immigration Rules 1994' are to the 'Statement of Changes in Immigration Rules' which came into effect on 1 October 1994 (1993–4 HC 395). Note also the following abbreviations: SSHD – Secretary of State for the Home Department; ECO – Entry Clearance Officer; IAT – Immigration Appeal Tribunal; CIO – Chief Immigration Officer.

3 The ambit of immigration control: the right of abode

Immigration Act 1971

1.—(1) All those who are in this Act expressed to have the right of abode in the United Kingdom shall be free to live in, and to come and go into and from, the United Kingdom without let or hindrance except such as may be required under and in accordance with this Act to enable their right to be established or as may be otherwise lawfully imposed on any person.

(2) Those not having the right may live, work and settle in the United Kingdom by permission and subject to such regulation and control of their entry into, stay in and departure from the United Kingdom as is imposed by this Act; and indefinite leave to enter or remain in the United Kingdom shall by virtue of this provision, be treated as having been given under this Act to those in the United Kingdom at its coming into force, if they are then settled there (and not exempt under this Act from the provisions relating to leave to enter or remain).

NOTES

1. The Immigration (European Economic Area) Order 1994 (S.I. 1994 No. 1895) came into force on 20 July 1994. Its purpose is to implement within the UK the terms of the Agreement on the European Economic Area (Oporto 1992, Brussels 1993). One aspect of the Agreement has been to extend the 'traditional' EC freedom of movement provisions to nationals of Austria, Finland, Iceland, Norway and Sweden.

Prior to the 1994 Order the rights of EC nationals were provided for under the, administrative, Immigration Rules rather than by primary, or even secondary, legislation. (For the status of the Rules, see below, p. 693, n. **1.**) Nevertheless, it was clear that in so far as such EC rights had direct effect under EC law, no EC national could legally be prejudiced by any failure to have properly transposed EC obligations into the terms of the Rules.

The position has since July 1994 been altered by the bringing into force of s. 7 of the Immigration Act 1988: a person does not require leave to enter or remain in the UK in any case where he is entitled to do so by virtue of an enforceable Community right. Such persons should, therefore, be considered alongside those who enter 'as of right', rather than as formerly as a category of persons seeking administrative permission.

On arrival EEA nationals must produce a valid EEA passport or national identity card. At most points of entry EEA nationals are processed separately from those requiring leave to enter.

See further, below, pp. 704–707.

2. The 1971 Act came into force on 1 January 1973. The purpose of the latter part of s. 1(2) was to preserve 'acquired rights' of persons so settled at that date. See, however, *R v SSHD, ex p Mughal* [1974] QB 313. The word 'settled' means 'being ordinarily resident . . . without being subject under the immigration laws to any restriction on the period for which he may remain' (1971 Act s. 33(1), (2), (2A)); and by virtue of s. 33(2) 'a person is not to be treated for the purposes of any provision of this Act as ordinarily resident in the United Kingdom or any of the Islands at any time when he is there in breach of the immigration laws'. The meaning of 'ordinarily resident', an expression used in a variety of statutory contexts, was fully considered in the House of Lords in *Shah v Barnet London Borough Council* [1983] 2 AC 309; eligibility for mandatory educational awards. A person should be regarded as 'ordinarily resident' in the UK if he habitually and normally resided in the UK from choice and for a settled purpose (e.g. education) at or during the time in question even if his real or permanent home remained elsewhere, and even if his future intention might be to leave the UK. 'Settled in the United Kingdom' is similarly defined for the purposes of the Immigration Rules 1994: see Rule 6.

3. A person who has the right of abode is not, in law, 'hindered' in the exercise of that right, within the terms of s. 1(1) above, by the fact that that person's spouse may, if a person not having the right of abode, require entry clearance to enter; and that obtaining such entry clearance may take some time. See *R v Secretary of State for the Home Department, ex p Rofathullah* [1989] QB 219, [1988] 3 All ER 1, CA.

Immigration Act 1971

2.—(1) A person is under this Act to have the right of abode in the United Kingdom if—

(a) he is a British citizen; or

(b) he is a Commonwealth citizen who—

(i) immediately before the commencement of the British Nationality Act 1981 was a Commonwealth citizen having the right of abode in the United Kingdom by virtue of section 2(1)(*d*) or section 2(2) of this Act as then in force; and

(ii) has not ceased to be a Commonwealth citizen in the meanwhile.

(2) In relation to Commonwealth citizens who have the right of abode in the United Kingdom by virtue of subsection (1)(*b*) above, this Act, except this section and section 5(2), shall apply as if they were British citizens; and in this Act (except as aforesaid) 'British citizen' shall be construed accordingly.

NOTES

1. The provisions set out above were substituted for the original s. 2 by the British Nationality Act 1981, s. 39(2). The original section is set out below. The commencement date of the 1981 Act was 1 January 1983.

2. The term 'British citizen' is defined by the British Nationality Act 1981 Part 1. Section 11 of that Act defines those who became British citizens 'at commencement' (i.e. on 1 January 1983). It provides that:

'a person who immediately before commencement (a) was a citizen of the United Kingdom and Colonies; and (b) had the right of abode in the United Kingdom under the Immigration Act 1971 as then in force, shall at commencement become a British citizen'.

In other words, no citizen of the UK and Colonies who immediately before commencement had the right of abode under the 1971 Act was prejudicially affected by the 1981 Act. Nor, by virtue of s. 2(1)(b) of the amended 1971 Act, was any Commonwealth citizen who had at that time the right of abode under the 1971 Act. Sections 2(1)(d) and 2(2) of the original 1971 Act were the only provisions of that Act under which a Commonwealth citizen could have the right of abode. The result is that the 1981 Act prejudiced no such acquired rights to enter and remain in the UK free from immigration control.

Who, then, had such right of abode under the 1971 Act as in force immediately prior to commencement of the 1981 Act? The original s. 2 of the 1971 Act provided:

2.—(1) A person is under this Act to have the right of abode in the United Kingdom if—

(*a*) he is a citizen of the United Kingdom and Colonies who has that citizenship by his birth, adoption, naturalisation or (except as mentioned below) registration in the United Kingdom or in any part of the Islands; or

(*b*) he is a citizen of the United Kingdom and Colonies born to or legally adopted by a parent who had that citizenship at the time of the birth or adoption, and the parent either—

(i) then had that citizenship by his birth, adoption, naturalisation or (except as mentioned below) registration in the United Kingdom or in any of the Islands; or

(ii) had been born to or legally adopted by a parent who at the time of that birth or adoption so had it; or

(*c*) he is a citizen of the United Kingdom and Colonies who has at any time been settled in the United Kingdom and Islands and had at that time (and while such a citizen) been ordinarily resident there for the last five years or more; or

(*d*) he is a Commonwealth citizen born to or legally adopted by a parent who at the time of the birth or adoption had citizenship of the United Kingdom and Colonies by his birth in the United Kingdom or in any of the Islands.

(2) A woman is under this Act also to have the right of abode in the United Kingdom if she is a Commonwealth citizen and either—

(*a*) is the wife of any such citizen of the United Kingdom and Colonies as is mentioned in subsection (1)(*a*), (*b*) or (*c*) above or any such Commonwealth citizen as is mentioned in subsection (1)(*d*); or

(*b*) has at any time been the wife—

(i) of a person then being such a citizen of the United Kingdom and Colonies or Commonwealth citizen; or

(ii) of a British subject who but for his death would on the date of commencement of the British Nationality Act 1948 have been such a citizen of the United Kingdom and Colonies as is mentioned in subsection (1)(*a*) or (*b*);

but in subsection (1)(*a*) and (*b*) above references to registration as a citizen of the United Kingdom and Colonies shall not, in the case of a woman, include registration after the passing of this Act under or by virtue of s. 6(2) (wives) of the British Nationality Act 1948 unless she is so registered by virtue of her marriage to a citizen of the United Kingdom and Colonies before the passing of this Act.

3. Note that those with the right of abode under s. 2(1)(b) of the amended 1971 Act constitute a 'wasting' category. Only those with 'acquired rights' at commencement of the 1981 Act can so qualify. In time this category will reduce in size and eventually disappear. It is the category of 'British citizens' which is the ongoing category, embracing not only those with acquired rights at commencement (1983) but also those who have acquired that citizenship since commencement.

4. Prior to 1988 it was possible for the several wives of polygamous marriages, recognised as valid under English law, to qualify for rights of abode. The Immigration Act 1988 now restricts this possibility. The Act does not prevent any polygamous wife from exercising a right of abode which she may possess in her own right (e.g. by virtue of being herself a British citizen). However, in the case of women who claim right of abode in their capacity of 'wife' under s. 2(2) of the 1971 Act (before amendment) it is now provided that the first polygamous wife to exercise such right, by entry or by obtaining a certificate of entitlement (see below, p. 692) shall, by so doing, exclude the rights of others.

Wives not falling within s. 2(2) do not as wives have rights of abode. Their entry is regulated, instead, by the Immigration Rules. These Rules were amended, with the coming into force of the 1988 Act, to provide similar restrictions on the entry of any but one of the wives of a polygamous marriage. See Rules 281–289.

5. Acquisition of British citizenship *after commencement* (i.e. since 1983) is by the standard mechanisms of birth, adoption, descent, registration and naturalisation. The rules governing such acquisition of citizenship are complex – see ss. 1–11 of the 1981 Act. For our purposes the following comments must suffice:

(i) *Birth in the United Kingdom.* Prior to 1983 the mere fact of birth in the UK or a colony was sufficient for the acquisition of citizenship of the United Kingdom and Colonies. For British citizenship since 1983, a closer link than simply the fact of birth in the UK is necessary. Section 1(1) provides that it is also necessary that the child's father or mother be, at that time, either a British citizen or 'settled' in the UK. The meaning of settled here is similar to that referred to above at p. 688 – see 1981 Act, s. 50(2)–(5) (i.e. ordinarily resident, not in breach of immigration laws, and not with only limited leave to remain: thus, e.g. the child of an illegal entrant will not acquire citizenship by birth). In the case of an illegitimate child it is the status or circumstances (i.e. settled or not) of the mother which is crucial – see s. 50(9)(b). Notwithstanding recommendation by the Law Commission (Law Com No. 118 para. 11.20) the opportunity was not taken in the Family Law Reform Act 1987 to equate the positions of legitimate and illegitimate children in this respect.

Although the mere fact of birth in the UK may no longer in itself be sufficient for the acquisition of British citizenship, it is provided by subsections (3) and (4) that such a person shall be entitled to be registered as a British citizen if (a) while he is under 18 his father or mother becomes a British citizen or becomes settled in the UK; or (b) if as regards each of the first ten years of his life, the number of days on which he is absent from the UK does not exceed 90. Note also the Home Secretary's discretion to register even where the 90-day period has been exceeded in any or all of those first ten years: s. 1(7).

By imposing a requirement of 'birth plus parent ordinarily resident (i.e. settled) at the time of birth' in cases where neither parent is at that time a British citizen, some uncertainty has been introduced as to what a child's citizenship may be. The concept of 'ordinary residence' is notoriously imprecise; much will depend on the residence intentions of the parents at the time of the birth. Where the child becomes entitled to be registered under subsection (3) or (4), such registration, in due course, will remove uncertainty.

(ii) *Adoption in the United Kingdom.* A minor becomes a British citizen on being adopted by a British citizen; or in the case of a joint adoption, where either adoptive parent is a British citizen. A measure of sexual equality has here been achieved. Prior to the 1981 Act it was only, in joint adoptions, where the father was a citizen that that citizenship was acquired by the adopted child.

(iii) *Descent.* Section 2 of the 1981 Act provides that a person born outside the UK after commencement shall be a British citizen if at the time of the birth either parent was a British citizen (otherwise than by descent). A measure of sexual equality has again been achieved. Prior to 1983, citizenship by descent could only be acquired through a citizen father. In the case of *illegitimate* children born abroad it is the citizenship of the mother that is critical. Somewhat controversially the opportunity was not taken with the enactment of the Family Law Reform Act 1987 (which removes most of the legal disadvantages which had attached to the status of illegitimacy) to alter the nationality position so that nationality rights can be derived from the illegitimate child's father.

(iv) *Registration.* We have already noted the rights to be registered of certain persons born since 1983 in the UK who did not thereby acquire citizenship at birth. Other cases of entitlement to registration include:

(1) Registration of persons born outside the UK to a parent who is a citizen by descent, who has or had a parent who was, or if not dead would have been, a British citizen (otherwise than by descent) at the time of birth. Registration must be sought within 12 months of the birth and, except in the case of otherwise stateless children, a specified period of parental residence in the UK prior to the birth is necessary (1981 Act, s. 3(2) and (3)).

(2) Registration of persons under 18 born outside the UK to a parent who is a citizen by descent where the minor seeking citizenship and the parents have resided in the UK for a specified period immediately prior to the application, and the parents consent to the registration (1981 Act, s. 3(5) and (6)).

(3) Registration of
  (a) *BDTCs* (i.e. former citizens of the UK and Colonies who did not under the 1981 Act become British citizens but became citizens of any of the territories listed in Schedule 6 to that Act; and persons who have subsequently acquired such citizenship under Part II of the 1981 Act),
  (b) *BOCs* (i.e. former citizens of the UK and Colonies who did not at commencement of the 1981 Act thereby become British citizens or BDTCs),
  (c) *British subjects under the 1981 Act* (a smallish category; not to be confused with British subjects at common law – a category formerly coterminous with that of Commonwealth citizen – but no longer a recognised citizenship status: s. 37(4), 1981 Act) and
  (d) *British Protected Persons* (again, a smallish category of persons with close connections with protectorates, protected states or trust territories). Such persons are entitled to be registered as British citizens if they have resided without breach of the immigration laws in the UK for the five years prior to the

application, and for the twelve months prior to the application have been free from restriction on the period during which they may remain in the UK (i.e. persons who have been accepted for settlement) (1981 Act, s. 4(2)).
(4) Registration of BDTCs who are nationals of the UK under the European Community treaties – i.e. Gibraltarians (1981 Act, s. 5).
(5) Persons with certain connections with the Falklands Islands (British Nationality (Falkland Islands) Act 1983).

In addition to such *rights* as these to be registered as British citizens there exists power in the Home Secretary to register certain persons as citizens at his *discretion*. See e.g. 1981 Act, s. 3(1) – power to register any minor; ss. 1(7), 3(4), and (5), 7(6) and (8) – power to register persons notwithstanding failure by them to satisfy certain requirements which if fulfilled would have placed the Home Secretary under a duty to register them.

(v) *Naturalisation.* Whereas certain categories of persons have an entitlement to citizenship by registration, citizenship by naturalisation is in all cases entirely at the discretion of the Home Secretary. Section 6 of the 1981 Act provides that he 'may, if he thinks fit' grant a certificate of naturalisation to any person of full age and capacity whom he is satisfied fulfils the requirements of Schedule 1. This Schedule lays down requirements as to past residence in the UK, good character, knowledge of language, and intention to remain. These requirements are slightly relaxed (e.g. in relation to knowledge of language, duration of residence) where the applicant is married to a British citizen – compare Schedule 1 paras. 1 and 2, with paras. 3 and 4.

Prior to the 1981 Act, wives of citizens of the UK and Colonies were by virtue of their marriage entitled as of right to obtain such citizenship by registration; husbands of citizens of the UK and Colonies had no such right but could apply for naturalisation. The 1981 Act secured sexual equality by 'downward equalisation' – i.e. by removing the registration rights of wives, rather than by granting such rights to husbands. In each case the grant of citizenship is now discretionary and dependent, inter alia, on residence in the UK for the stipulated period.

6. Section 3(9), 1971 Act, as amended, imposes on persons claiming the right of abode certain restrictions as to how that right is to be proven. The position, broadly, is that persons claiming the right of abode who are not British citizens (i.e. seeking to qualify under the 1971 Act, s. 2(1)(b), above p. 689) must prove that right of abode by means of a certificate of entitlement. By contrast, persons who are British citizens may enter simply upon production of a passport showing them to be such. Cf. *R v IAT, ex p Minta* [1992] Imm AR 380 (British Visitor's passport insufficient: does not describe holder as a British Citizen). The aim in each case is to avoid difficult decisions as to 'right of abode' arising at ports of entry.

A problem which confronted would-be entrants who considered themselves to have the right of abode but required certificates of entitlement (formerly, of 'patriality') was that it might take many months, even years, before they could obtain such certificates in their countries of origin. Such applications were handled alongside applications, for entry clearance documents, from persons who were subject to immigration control. Procedures were altered, however, following the decision of the Court of Appeal in *R v Secretary of State for the Home Department, ex p Phansopkar* [1976] QB 606. The applicants, who claimed to have the right of abode, travelled from India to the UK and sought entry notwithstanding not having obtained certificates prior to departure. The Court of Appeal issued mandamus ordering the Secretary of State to consider the applications for certificates which they had made on their arrival in the UK. The Secretary of State, it was held, had no power to insist that proof of right of abode take place prior to departure for the UK, since this would unreasonably restrict their rights of entry under the 1971 Act. (Cf. *R v Secretary of State for the Home Department, ex p Akhtar* [1975] 3 All ER 1087, DC.)

Following the decision in *Phansopkar* administrative changes were made so that such certificate applications are now dealt with abroad separately from entry clearance applications, thereby reducing waiting time. Moreover, it may be noted that since 1985 entry clearance applications have been dealt with in several 'queues' in order to deal more expeditiously with certain categories of applicant – e.g. dependants over 70, special compassionate cases, children. Nevertheless, delays remain a problem.

4 The administration of immigration control

(a) IMMIGRATION RULES

Immigration Act 1971

3.—(2) The Secretary of State shall from time to time (and as soon as may be) lay before Parliament statements of the rules, or of any changes in the rules, laid down by him as to the practice to be followed in the administration of this Act for regulating the entry into and stay in the United Kingdom of persons required by this Act to have leave to enter, including any rules as to the period for which leave is to be given and the conditions to be attached in different circumstances; . . .

NOTES

1. Some uncertainty has existed as to the juridical status of the Immigration Rules. It appears that they are not rules of law in the sense of being delegated legislation (see *R v Secretary of State for the Home Department, ex p Hosenball* [1977] 1 WLR 766; *Pearson v Immigration Appeal Tribunal* [1978] Imm AR 212). Cf. *R v Chief Immigration Officer, Heathrow Airport, ex p Salamat Bibi* [1976] 1 WLR 979. However, by virtue of s. 19 of the 1971 Act (see below, p. 736), in situations where a right of appeal lies to an adjudicator or to the Immigration Appeal Tribunal (or both), the appeal will succeed if the appellant can show that the decision taken 'was not in accordance with the law or with any immigration rules applicable to the case'. (For other grounds of appeal, see below pp. 736 and 737.) To this extent at least the Rules have, in effect, the force of law. Moreover, any decision of an adjudicator or the IAT is challengeable in the High Court by judicial review if it is not in accordance with the Immigration Rules (most commonly for error of law on the face of the record – the error of law being the failure to reach a correct decision in accordance with the duties under section 19). In other words, the Rules may be considered to be 'law' in the context of cases that can be taken through the immigration appeal system. It has also been held that it is an erro. of 'law', for the purpose of challenge by way of judicial review, for an immigration officer to take a decision or to act on the basis of an incorrect interpretation of the Immigration Rules – see *R v Chief Immigration Officer, Gatwick Airport, ex p Kharrazi* [1980] 3 All ER 373, [1980] 1 WLR 1396, CA. Note, however, the general principle that in deciding whether or not to grant leave to apply for judicial review the High Court will take account of the availability to the applicant of 'alternative remedies', such as a right of appeal. In *R v Secretary of State for the Home Department, ex p Swati* [1986] 1 All ER 717, CA this principle was applied so as to refuse leave to seek judicial review to an applicant who had, but had preferred not to exercise, a right of appeal against the decision in question; albeit a right which was not exercisable without first having left the UK (for this common feature of immigration appeal rights see further below p. 729). The applicant was therefore held to possess an alternative remedy. Although there might be advantages apparent to the applicant to be able to proceed by way of judicial review whilst still within the UK, for the court to permit this would, thought the Court of Appeal, have been to have undermined the statutory scheme of appeal. See also *R v Secretary of State for the Home Department, ex p Chong* [1990] Imm AR 397, QBD; *Suarez v Secretary of State for the Home Department* [1991] Imm AR 54; *Soon Ok Ryoo v Secretary of State for the Home Department* [1992] Imm AR 59; *Doorga v Secretary of State for the Home Department* [1990] Imm AR 98. The Court of Appeal, in *Swati*, did however acknowledge that there might be exceptional circumstances in which the exercise of a right of appeal from abroad would be more than usually less advantageous than to proceed by way of judicial review. In such a case judicial review would be available. Such a case, it felt, was *Kharrazi*. The applicant would there have had to return to Iran before exercising his right of appeal. At the time it was evident that Iran was not permitting children of the applicant's age to leave the country. The appeal would therefore, even if successful, have been nugatory. It had therefore been appropriate in that case to have allowed the challenge by way of judicial review to proceed. Cf. *Grazales v Secretary of State for the Home Department* [1990] Imm AR 505; *R v Secretary of State for the Home Department, ex p Pulgarin* [1992] Imm AR 96; *R v Secretary of State for the Home Department, ex p Salamat* [1993] Imm AR 239.

2. Note that the Home Secretary may depart from the Rules in order to *favour* an individual. See F. Webber, *Legal Action* February 1994, p. 18; C. Vincenzi, [1992] Pub. Law 300. Accordingly, the Home Office was regularly lobbied by, and on behalf of, individuals (e.g. by MPs, friends, relatives) to exercise this discretion. The power has, however, not frequently been exercised; and the decision whether or not to depart from the Rules is not itself a discretionary decision upon which an appeal may be brought before the appellate authorities (s. 19(2), 1971 Act, below p. 736; and see *Wirdestedt v Secretary of State for the Home Department* [1982] Imm AR 186). The progressive 'tightening' of controls in the Rules led to an increase in petitions to the Home Office. See the discussion in C. Harlow and R. Rawlings, *Law and Administration* (1984) pp. 553–558. This has itself led to a change to the former Home Office policy of automatically 'staying' action in respect of an individual when an MP intervenes – see 140 HC Deb col 516, 10 November, 1988; 143 HC Deb col 576, 14 December, 1988.

3. In administering the Immigration Rules the immigration officers act in accordance with unpublished instructions issued from the Home Office. These must not be inconsistent with the Rules (1971 Act, Sch. 2, para. 1(3)). On occasions the content of such instructions may become known – see e.g. *Legal Action* October 1984, p. 119 (interpretation of what is now Rule 290, below p. 708) – and so provide valuable information as to how the Rules will be interpreted and applied by officers. Should not such instructions be made more generally available for the benefit of would-be entrants and their advisers?

(b) LEAVE TO ENTER – CONDITIONS – TIME LIMITS

Immigration Act 1971

3.—(1) Except as otherwise provided by or under this Act, where a person is not [a British citizen][1]
 (a) he shall not enter the United Kingdom unless given leave to do so in accordance with this Act;
 (b) he may be given leave to enter the United Kingdom (or, when already there, leave to remain in the United Kingdom) either for a limited or for an indefinite period;

1 Words in brackets substituted by the British Nationality Act 1981, s. 39(6), Sch. 4, para. 2.

(c) if he is given a limited leave to enter or remain in the United Kingdom, it may be given subject to conditions restricting his employment or occupation in the United Kingdom, or requiring him to register with the police, or both.

(3) In the case of a limited leave to enter or remain in the United Kingdom,—

(a) a person's leave may be varied, whether by restricting, enlarging or removing the limit on its duration, or by adding, varying or revoking conditions, but if the limit on its duration is removed, any conditions attached to the leave shall cease to apply;

(b) . . . .

NOTES

1. Sections 24–27 of the 1971 Act, as amended, create a number of criminal offences in relation to immigration control. By virtue of s. 24(1) it is an offence for a person who does not have the right of abode, inter alia:

(1) knowingly to enter the UK in breach of a deportation order or without leave; or

(2) knowingly to remain in the UK beyond the time limit on his leave to enter, or knowingly to fail to observe a condition on his leave to enter; or

(3) without reasonable excuse to fail to comply with any requirement imposed on him under Sch. 2 of the 1971 Act to report to a medical officer of health and to submit to tests or examinations as required by such an officer (see Sch. 2, para. 7).

Section 24(2) confers on police and immigration officers a power to arrest without warrant any person who has or who is reasonably suspected to have committed (or attempted to commit) any offence under s. 24 (except the offence in category (3) above).

Section 25 creates offences (i) of being knowingly concerned in assisting entry into the UK of an illegal entrant and (ii) of knowingly harbouring an illegal entrant, or a person who has committed an offence under s. 24 of knowingly exceeding a time limit or breaching an entry condition. Sub-s. (3) confers on police and immigration officers powers to arrest without warrant persons reasonably suspected of having committed such offences. Sub-s. (5) provides for the extra-territorial application of the offence of assisting entry so as to cover things done outside the UK so long as done by British citizens, BDTCs, BOCs, British Protected Persons or British subjects (as defined by the 1981 Act). Sub-ss. (6)–(8) contain provisions authorising in certain circumstances the forfeiture by the court, following conviction on indictment for assisting illegal entry, of any ship, aircraft or vehicle used or intended to be used in connection with that offence.

Section 26 creates a number of summary offences in connection with the administration of immigration control. These include failing or refusing to submit to examination by an immigration officer or medical inspector under Sch. 2; failing or refusing to furnish or produce any document in his possession or control which he is required under Sch. 2 to produce – note also the power in Sch. 2, para. 3 to search persons being examined and their luggage for this purpose; making statements or representations during the examination which are known to be false or not believed to be true (the examination may be in pursuit of inquiries *away* from the port of entry, and *after* the permission for entry – see *Singh v Hammond* [1987] 1 All ER 829); altering immigration documents or possessing documents with knowledge (or constructive knowledge) of their falsification, with intent to use them; and obstructing an immigration officer or other person acting lawfully in the execution of the (1971) Act. For limits to the scope of this last offence, see *R v Clarke* [1985] AC 1037, [1985] 2 All ER 777, HL.

2. Rule 10, 1994 Immigration Rules, provides:

'The power to refuse leave to enter the United Kingdom is not to be exercised by an Immigration Officer acting on his own. The authority of a Chief Immigration Officer or of an Immigration Inspector must always be obtained.'

Cf. *Oladehindi v Secretary of State for the Home Department* [1991] AC 254: delegability of functions of Secretary of State for the Home Department.

(c) ENTRY CLEARANCES

Immigration Rules 1994

Entry clearance

24. A visa national and any other person who is seeking entry for a purpose for which prior entry clearance is required under these Rules must produce to the Immigration Officer a valid passport or other identity document endorsed with a United Kingdom entry clearance issued to him for the purpose for which he seeks entry. Such a person will be refused leave to enter if he has no such current entry clearance. Any other person who wishes to ascertain in advance whether he is eligible for admission to the United Kingdom may apply for the issue of an entry clearance.

25. Entry clearance takes the form of a visa (for visa nationals) or an entry certificate (for non-visa nationals). These documents are to be taken as evidence of the holder's eligibility for entry into the United Kingdom . . .

28. An applicant for an entry clearance must be outside the United Kingdom and Islands at the time of the application. . . .

General grounds for refusal of entry

320. In addition to the grounds for refusal of entry clearance or leave to enter set out in Parts 2–8 of these Rules,[1] and subject to paragraph 321 below, the following grounds for the refusal of entry clearance or leave to enter apply:

Grounds on which entry clearance or leave to enter the United Kingdom is to be refused

(1) the fact that entry is being sought for a purpose not covered by these Rules;
(2) the fact that the person seeking entry to the United Kingdom is currently the subject of a deportation order;
(3) failure by the person seeking entry to the United Kingdom to produce to the Immigration Officer a valid national passport or other document satisfactorily establishing his identity and nationality;
(4) . . . .
(5) failure, in the case of a visa national, to produce to the Immigration Officer a passport or other identity document endorsed with a valid and current United Kingdom entry clearance issued for the purpose for which entry is sought;
(6) where the Secretary of State has personally directed that the exclusion of a person from the United Kingdom is conducive to the public good;
(7) save in relation to a person settled in the United Kingdom or where the Immigration Officer is satisfied that there are strong compassionate reasons justifying admission, confirmation from the Medical Inspector that, for medical reasons, it is undesirable to admit a person seeking leave to enter the United Kingdom.

Grounds on which entry clearance or leave to enter the United Kingdom should normally be refused

(8) failure by a person arriving in the United Kingdom to furnish the Immigration Officer with such information as may be required for the purpose of deciding whether he requires leave to enter and, if so, whether and on what terms leave should be given;
(9) . . . .

---

1 *Ed*. Rules 40–319: the *substantive* Rules as regards admission to, and rights to remain in, the UK.

(10) production by the person seeking leave to enter the United Kingdom of a national passport or travel document issued by a territorial entity or authority which is not recognised by Her Majesty's Government as a state or is not dealt with as a government by them, or which does not accept valid United Kingdom passports for the purpose of its own immigration control; or a passport or travel document which does not comply with international passport practice;

(11) failure to observe the time limit or conditions attached to any grant of leave to enter or remain in the United Kingdom;

(12) the obtaining of a previous leave to enter or remain by deception;

(13) failure, except by a person eligible for admission to the United Kingdom for settlement or a spouse eligible for admission under paragraph 282, to satisfy the Immigration Officer that he will be admitted to another country after a stay in the United Kingdom;

(14) refusal by a sponsor of a person seeking leave to enter the United Kingdom to give, if requested to do so, an undertaking in writing to be responsible for that person's maintenance and accommodation for the period of any leave granted;

(15) whether or not to the holder's knowledge, the making of false representations or the failure to disclose any material fact for the purpose of obtaining a work permit;

(16) . . . .

(17) save in relation to a person settled in the United Kingdom, refusal to undergo a medical examination when requested to do so by the Immigration Officer;

(18) save where the Immigration Officer is satisfied that admission would be justified for strong compassionate reasons, conviction in any country including the United Kingdom of an offence which, if committed in the United Kingdom, is punishable with imprisonment for a term of 12 months or any greater punishment or, if committed outside the United Kingdom, would be so punishable if the conduct constituting the offence had occurred in the United Kingdom;

(19) where, from information available to the Immigration Officer, it seems right to refuse leave to enter on the ground that exclusion from the United Kingdom is conducive to the public good; if, for example, in the light of the character, conduct or associations of the person seeking leave to enter it is undesirable to give him leave to enter.

Refusal of leave to enter in relation to a person in possession of an entry clearance

321. A person seeking leave to enter the United Kingdom who holds an entry clearance which was duly issued to him and is still current may be refused leave to enter only where the Immigration Officer is satisfied that:

(i) whether or not to the holder's knowledge, false representations were employed or material facts were not disclosed, either in writing or orally, for the purpose of obtaining the entry clearance; or

(ii) a change of circumstances since it was issued has removed the basis of the holder's claim to admission . . .; or

(iii) refusal is justified on grounds of restricted returnability; on medical grounds; on grounds of criminal record; because the person seeking leave to enter is the subject of a deportation order or because exclusion would be conducive to the public good.

Appendix

Visa requirements for the United Kingdom

1. Subject to paragraph 2 below the following persons need a visa for the United Kingdom:

(a) Nationals or citizens of the following countries or territorial entities:

Afghanistan	Gabon	Philippines
Albania	Georgia	Romania
Algeria	Ghana	Russia
Angola	Guinea	Rwanda
Armenia	Guinea-Bissau	Sao Tome e Principe
Azerbaijan	Haiti	Saudi Arabia
Bangladesh	India	Senegal
Belarus	Indonesia	Somalia
Benin	Iran	Sri Lanka
Bhutan	Iraq	Sudan
Bosnia-Herzegovina	Jordan	Syria
Bulgaria	Kazakhstan	Taiwan
Burkina	Kirgizstan	Tajikistan
Burma	Korea (North)	Thailand

Burundi	Laos	Togo
Cambodia	Lebanon	Tunisia
Cameroon	Liberia	Turkey
Cape Verde	Libya	Turkmenistan
Central African Republic	Macedonia	Uganda
Chad	Madagascar	Ukraine
China	Mali	Uzbekistan
Comoros	Mauritania	Vietnam
Congo	Moldova	Yemen
Cuba	Mongolia	Zaire
Djibouti	Morocco	The territories formerly
Egypt	Mozambique	comprising the Socialist
Equatorial Guinea	Nepal	Federal Republic of
Eritrea	Nigeria	Yugoslavia excluding
Ethiopia	Oman	Croatia and Slovenia.
	Pakistan	

(*b*) Persons who hold passports or travel documents issued by the former Soviet Union or by the former Socialist Federal Republic of Yugoslavia.

(*c*) Stateless persons.

(*d*) Persons who hold non-national documents.

2. . . . .

NOTES

1. The imposition of visa requirements (as distinct from other forms of entry clearance) on Commonwealth citizens from Bangladesh, India, Ghana, Nigeria, Pakistan and Sri Lanka is of quite recent origin, and has been controversial. It has been criticised on the grounds of the additional inconvenience caused to would-be entrants, and also because of the adverse effect on community relations within the UK of the singling out of the 'new' (black) Commonwealth for such additional controls.

2. The Rules set out above show the critical importance to a would-be entrant of possession of the appropriate entry documents. A person subject to immigration control who has the appropriate entry clearance documents will normally experience no difficulties at the port of entry. (See Rule 321, above, p. 697.) A person subject to control who arrives without entry clearance documents may be in a very different position. In several contexts the possession of appropriate entry clearance documents is mandatory. Note also the possibility of obtaining entry clearance prior to embarkation for the UK even in non-obligatory cases: Rule 24 above.

5 Immigration Rules: substantive provisions

The substantive provisions of the 1994 Rules deal successively with the following main categories:

(1) visitors;

(2) students; their spouses and children;

(3) au pairs;

(4) working holiday-makers, persons coming for training or for work experience: their spouses and children;

(5) persons seeking to enter and remain for employment purposes, plus their spouses and children;

(6) persons seeking to enter and remain as businessmen, self-employed persons, investors, writers, composers or artists: plus their spouses and children;

(7) holders of special vouchers and their dependants (see above, p. 685);
(8) EEA Nationals and their families;
(9) retired persons of independent means, their spouses and children;
(10) persons who apply as family members (spouses, fiancé(e)s, children, parents, grandparents and other dependent relatives) of persons admitted for settlement;
(11) persons seeking asylum.

Note that the materials which follow set out the Rules in relation to certain of these categories only.

(a) PERSONS SEEKING LEAVE TO ENTER OR REMAIN IN THE UNITED KINGDOM FOR EMPLOYMENT

Immigration Rules 1994

Work permit employment

128. The requirements to be met by a person coming to the United Kingdom to seek or take employment . . . are that he:
   (i) holds a valid Department of Employment work permit; and
   (ii) is not of an age which puts him outside the limits for employment; and
   (iii) is capable of undertaking the employment specified in the work permit; and
   (iv) does not intend to take employment except as specified in his work permit; and
   (v) is able to maintain and accommodate himself and any dependants adequately without recourse to public funds; and
   (vi) in the case of a person in possession of a work permit which is valid for a period of 12 months or less, intends to leave the United Kingdom at the end of his approved employment.

Leave to enter for work permit employment

129. A person seeking leave to enter the United Kingdom for the purpose of work permit employment may be admitted for a period not exceeding 4 years (normally as specified in his work permit), subject to a condition restricting him to employment approved by the Department of Employment, provided the Immigration Officer is satisfied that each of the requirements of paragraph 128 is met.

Refusal of leave to enter for employment

130. Leave to enter for the purpose of employment is to be refused if the Immigration Officer is not satisfied that each of the requirements of paragraph 128 is met. . . .

Requirements for an extension of stay for work permit employment

131. The requirements for an extension of stay to seek or take employment . . . are that the applicant:
   (i) entered the United Kingdom with a valid work permit under paragraph 129; and
   (ii) has written approval from the Department of Employment for the continuation of his employment; and
   (iii) meets the requirements of paragraph 128 (ii)–(v).

Extension of stay for work permit employment

132. An extension of stay for work permit employment may be granted for a period not exceeding the period of approved employment recommended by the Department of Employment provided the Secretary of State is satisfied that each of the requirements of paragraph 131 is met. An extension of stay is to be subject to a condition restricting the applicant to employment approved by the Department of Employment.

Refusal of extension of stay for employment

133. An extension of stay for employment is to be refused if the Secretary of State is not satisfied that each of the requirements of paragraph 131 is met. . . .

Indefinite leave to remain for a work permit holder

134. Indefinite leave to remain may be granted, on application, to a person admitted as a work permit holder provided:
   (i)   he has spent a continuous period of 4 years in the United Kingdom in this capacity; and
  (ii)   he has met the requirements of paragraph 131 throughout the 4 year period; and
 (iii)   he is still required for the employment in question, as certified by his employer.

Refusal of indefinite leave to remain for a work permit holder

135. Indefinite leave to remain in the United Kingdom for a work permit holder is to be refused if the Secretary of State is not satisfied that each of the requirements of paragraph 134 is met.

NOTES

1. Work permits are issued by the Department of Education and Employment. There is no right of appeal against the refusal of a permit: *Pearson v Immigration Appeal Tribunal* [1978] Imm AR 212; although, in an appropriate case, the discretionary decision may be challenged by way of judicial review: *R v Department of Employment, ex p Barry Allan* [1991] Imm AR 336. Conditions for the award of work permits are not laid down in the Act or in the Rules: they are governed by internal departmental rules of policy. The basic principle is that permits are only available to persons who satisfy conditions as regards their age, their possession of professional qualifications or possession of a high degree of skill or experience. They are issued for a particular job with a particular employer when there appears to be no suitable worker within the UK or EU country. A very small quota of permits exists, however, for the benefit of unskilled and semi-skilled workers from dependent territories, provided again that no resident labour is available.

2. These provisions on work permit employment are followed (Rules 136–193) by provisions relating to the non-work permit entry of certain categories of persons, including: representatives of foreign newspapers, newsagencies and broadcasting organisations; representatives of overseas firms which have no branch, subsidiary or other representative in the UK; private servants in diplomatic households; overseas government employees; ministers of religion, missionaries, and members of religious orders; persons with United Kingdom ancestry. Rules 194–199 deal with the admission of spouses and children of persons admitted under Rules 128–193.

(b) PERSONS WITH UNITED KINGDOM ANCESTRY

Immigration Rules 1994

Requirements for leave to enter on the grounds of United Kingdom ancestry

186. The requirements to be met by a person seeking leave to enter the United Kingdom on the grounds of his United Kingdom ancestry are that he:
   (i)   is a Commonwealth citizen; and
  (ii)   is aged 17 or over; and
 (iii)   is able to provide proof that one of his grandparents was born in the United Kingdom and Islands; and
 (iv)   is able to work and intends to take or seek employment in the United Kingdom; and
  (v)   will be able to maintain and accommodate himself and any dependants adequately without recourse to public funds; and
 (vi)   holds a valid United Kingdom entry clearance for entry in this capacity.

Leave to enter the United Kingdom on the grounds of United Kingdom ancestry

187. A person seeking leave to enter the United Kingdom on the grounds of his United Kingdom ancestry may be given leave to enter for a period not exceeding 4 years provided he is able to produce to the Immigration Officer, on arrival, a valid United Kingdom entry clearance for entry in this capacity.

Refusal of leave to enter on the grounds of United Kingdom ancestry

188. Leave to enter the United Kingdom on the grounds of United Kingdom ancestry is to be refused if a valid United Kingdom entry clearance for entry in this capacity is not produced to the Immigration Officer on arrival.

Requirements for an extension of stay on the grounds of United Kingdom ancestry

189. The requirements to be met by a person seeking an extension of stay on the grounds of United Kingdom ancestry are that he is able to meet each of the requirements of paragraph 186 (i)–(v).

Extension of stay on the grounds of United Kingdom ancestry

190. An extension of stay on the grounds of United Kingdom ancestry may be granted for a period not exceeding 4 years provided the Secretary of State is satisfied that each of the requirements of paragraph 186 (i)–(v) is met.

Refusal of extension of stay on the grounds of United Kingdom ancestry

191. An extension of stay on the grounds of United Kingdom ancestry is to be refused if the Secretary of State is not satisfied that each of the requirements of paragraph 186 (i)–(v) is met.

Indefinite leave to remain on the grounds of United Kingdom ancestry

192. Indefinite leave to remain may be granted, on application, to a Commonwealth citizen with a United Kingdom born grandparent provided:
   (i)   he meets the requirements of paragraph 186 (i)–(v); and
   (ii) he has spent a continuous period of 4 years in the United Kingdom in this capacity.

Refusal of indefinite leave to remain on the grounds of United Kingdom ancestry

193. Indefinite leave to remain in the United Kingdom on the grounds of a United Kingdom born grandparent is to be refused if the Secretary of State is not satisfied that each of the requirements of paragraph 192 is met.

NOTE

Those entering under Rules 186 and 187, mostly white Commonwealth citizens from the 'old' Commonwealth, may arrive without any particular job to go to: an intention to seek employment will suffice. Note that the 'working holiday' rule (Rule 95) is not dependent on any ancestral connection. However, in practice it may be that those from the 'new' Commonwealth may have more difficulty persuading officials of their intentions later to settle down in their own countries than will those from Australia, New Zealand or Canada. See e.g. *Gunatilake v Entry Clearance Officer, Colombo* [1975] Imm AR 23.

(c) PERSONS SEEKING TO ENTER OR REMAIN IN THE UNITED KINGDOM AS A BUSINESSMAN, INVESTOR, ETC.

Immigration Rules 1994

Requirements for leave to enter the United Kingdom as a person intending to establish himself in business

200. For the purpose of paragraphs 201–210 a business means an enterprise as:

- a sole trader; or
- a partnership; or
- a company registered in the United Kingdom.

201. The requirements to be met by a person seeking leave to enter the United Kingdom to establish himself in business are:
   (i) that he satisfies the requirements of either paragraph 202 or paragraph 203; and
   (ii) that he has not less than £200,000 of his own money under his control and disposable in the United Kingdom which is held in his own name and not by a trust or other investment vehicle and which he will be investing in the business in the United Kingdom; and
   (iii) that until his business provides him with an income he will have sufficient additional funds to maintain and accommodate himself and any dependants without recourse to employment (other than his work for the business) or to public funds; and
   (iv) that he will be actively involved full-time in trading or providing services on his own account or in partnership, or in the promotion and management of the company as a director; and
   (v) that his level of financial investment will be proportional to his interest in the business; and
   (vi) that he will have either a controlling or equal interest in the business and that any partnership or directorship does not amount to disguised employment; and
   (vii) that he will be able to bear his share of liabilities; and
   (viii) that there is a genuine need for his investment and services in the United Kingdom; and
   (ix) that his share of the profits of the business will be sufficient to maintain and accommodate himself and any dependants without recourse to employment (other than his work for the business) or to public funds; and
   (x) that he does not intend to supplement his business activities by taking or seeking employment in the United Kingdom other than his work for the business; and
   (xi) that he holds a valid United Kingdom entry clearance for entry in this capacity.

202. Where a person intends to take over or join as a partner or director an existing business in the United Kingdom he will need, in addition to meeting the requirements at paragraph 201, to produce:
   (i) a written statement of the terms on which he is to take over or join the business; and
   (ii) audited accounts for the business for previous years; and
   (iii) evidence that his services and investment will result in a net increase in the employment provided by the business to persons settled here to the extent of creating at least 2 new full-time jobs.

203. Where a person intends to establish a new business in the United Kingdom he will need, in addition to meeting the requirements at paragraph 201 above, to produce evidence:
   (i) that he will be bringing into the country sufficient funds of his own to establish a business; and
   (ii) that the business will create full-time paid employment for at least 2 persons already settled in the United Kingdom.

Leave to enter the United Kingdom as a person seeking to establish himself in business

204. A person seeking leave to enter the United Kingdom to establish himself in business may be admitted for a period not exceeding 12 months with a condition restricting his freedom to take employment provided he is able to produce to the Immigration Officer, on arrival, a valid United Kingdom entry clearance for entry in this capacity.

Refusal of leave to enter the United Kingdom as a person seeking to establish himself in business

205. Leave to enter the United Kingdom as a person seeking to establish himself in business is to be refused if a valid United Kingdom entry clearance for entry in this capacity is not produced to the Immigration Officer on arrival.

Requirements for an extension of stay in order to remain in business

206. The requirements for an extension of stay in order to remain in business in the United Kingdom are that the applicant can show:
   (i) that he entered the United Kingdom with a valid United Kingdom entry clearance as a businessman; and
   (ii) audited accounts which show the precise financial position of the business and which confirm that he has invested not less than £200,000 of his own money directly into the business in the United Kingdom; and

(iii) that he is actively involved on a full-time basis in trading or providing services on his own account or in partnership or in the promotion and management of the company as a director; and

(iv) that his level of financial investment is proportional to his interest in the business; and

(v) that he has either a controlling or equal interest in the business and that any partnership or directorship does not amount to disguised employment; and

(vi) that he is able to bear his share of any liability the business may incur; and

(vii) that there is a genuine need for his investment and services in the United Kingdom; and

(viii) (a) that where he has established a new business, new full-time paid employment has been created in the business for at least 2 persons settled in the United Kingdom; or

(b) that where he has taken over or joined an existing business, his services and investment have resulted in a net increase in the employment provided by the business to persons settled here to the extent of creating at least 2 new full-time jobs; and

(ix) that his share of the profits of the business is sufficient to maintain and accommodate him and any dependants without recourse to employment (other than his work for the business) or to public funds; and

(x) that he does not and will not have to supplement his business activities by taking or seeking employment in the United Kingdom other than his work for the business.

Extension of stay in order to remain in business

207. An extension of stay in order to remain in business with a condition restricting his freedom to take employment may be granted for a period not exceeding 3 years provided the Secretary of State is satisfied that each of the requirements of paragraph 206 is met.

Refusal of extension of stay in order to remain in business

208. An extension of stay in order to remain in business is to be refused if the Secretary of State is not satisfied that each of the requirements of paragraph 206 is met.

Indefinite leave to remain for a person established in business

209. Indefinite leave to remain may be granted, on application, to a person established in business provided he:

(i) has spent a continuous period of 4 years in the United Kingdom in this capacity and is still engaged in the business in question; and

(ii) has met the requirements of paragraph 206 throughout the 4 year period; and

(iii) submits audited accounts for the first 3 years of trading and management accounts for the 4th year.

Refusal of indefinite leave to remain for a person established in business

210. Indefinite leave to remain in the United Kingdom for a person established in business is to be refused if the Secretary of State is not satisfied that each of the requirements of paragraph 209 is met.

Requirements for leave to enter the United Kingdom as an investor

224. The requirements to be met by a person seeking leave to enter the United Kingdom as an investor are that he:

(i) has money of his own under his control and disposable in the United Kingdom amounting to no less than £1 million; and

(ii) intends to invest not less than £750,000 of his capital in the United Kingdom by way of United Kingdom Government bonds, share capital or loan capital in active and trading United Kingdom registered companies (other than those principally engaged in property investment and excluding investment by the applicant by way of deposits with a bank, building society or other enterprise whose normal course of business includes the acceptance of deposits); and

(iii) intends to make the United Kingdom his main home; and

(iv) is able to maintain and accommodate himself and any dependants without taking employment (other than self-employment or business) or recourse to public funds; and

(v) holds a valid United Kingdom entry clearance for entry in this capacity.

Leave to enter as an investor

225. A person seeking leave to enter the United Kingdom as an investor may be admitted for a period not exceeding 12 months with a restriction on his right to take employment, provided he is able to produce to the Immigration Officer, on arrival, a valid United Kingdom entry clearance for entry in this capacity.

Refusal of leave to enter as an investor

226. Leave to enter as an investor is to be refused if a valid United Kingdom entry clearance for entry in this capacity is not produced to the Immigration Officer on arrival.

Requirements for an extension of stay as an investor

227. The requirements for an extension of stay as an investor are that the applicant:
  (i) entered the United Kingdom with a valid United Kingdom entry clearance as an investor; and
  (ii) has no less than £1 million of his own money under his control in the United Kingdom; and
  (iii) has invested not less than £750,000 of his capital in the United Kingdom on the terms set out in paragraph 224 (ii) above and intends to maintain that investment on the terms set out in paragraph 224 (ii); and
  (iv) has made the United Kingdom his main home; and
  (v) is able to maintain and accommodate himself and any dependants without taking employment (other than his self-employment or business) or recourse to public funds.

Extension of stay as an investor

228. An extension of stay as an investor, with a restriction on the taking of employment, may be granted for a maximum period of 3 years, provided the Secretary of State is satisfied that each of the requirements of paragraph 227 is met.

Refusal of extension of stay as an investor

229. An extension of stay as an investor is to be refused if the Secretary of State is not satisfied that each of the requirements of paragraph 227 is met.

Indefinite leave to remain for an investor

230. Indefinite leave to remain may be granted, on application, to a person admitted as an investor provided he:
  (i) has spent a continuous period of 4 years in the United Kingdom in this capacity; and
  (ii) has met the requirements of paragraph 227 throughout the 4 year period including the requirement as to the investment of £750,000 and continues to do so.

Refusal of indefinite leave to remain for an investor

231. Indefinite leave to remain in the United Kingdom for an investor is to be refused if the Secretary of State is not satisfied that each of the requirements of paragraph 230 is met.

(d) EEA NATIONALS AND THEIR FAMILIES

Immigration Rules 1994

Settlement

255. An EEA national (other than a student) and the family member of such a person, who has been issued with a residence permit or residence document valid for 5 years, and who has remained in the United Kingdom in accordance with the provisions of the 1994 EEA Order for 4 years and continues to do so may, on application, have his residence permit or residence document (as the case may be) endorsed to show permission to remain in the United Kingdom indefinitely.

256. A self-employed EEA national who has a right to reside in the United Kingdom by virtue of having ceased such activity in the United Kingdom within the meaning of the 1994 EEA Order, and the family member of such a person, will be permitted to remain in the United Kingdom indefinitely.

257. In addition, the following persons will be permitted to remain in the United Kingdom indefinitely:
  (i) an EEA national who has been continuously resident in the United Kingdom for at least 3 years, has been in employment in the United Kingdom or any other Member State of the EEA for the preceding 12 months, and has reached the age of entitlement to a state retirement pension;
  (ii) an EEA national who has ceased to be employed owing to a permanent incapacity for work arising out of an accident at work or an occupational disease entitling him to a state disability pension;

(iii) an EEA national who has been continuously resident in the United Kingdom for at least 2 years, and who has ceased to be employed owing to a permanent incapacity for work;
(iv) a member of the family of an EEA national as (defined in the 1994 EEA Order) to whom (i), (ii) or (iii) above applies;
(v) a member of the family of an EEA national (as defined in the 1994 EEA Order) who dies during his working life after having resided continuously in the United Kingdom for at least 2 years, or whose death results from an accident at work or an occupational disease.

The EEA family permit

258. An 'EEA family permit' means an entry clearance issued, free of charge, to a family member (as defined in the 1994 EEA Order) who is not an EEA national and who is a visa national or a person who wishes to install himself in the United Kingdom with an EEA national who is a qualified person in the terms of the 1994 EEA Order.

Requirements for the issue of an EEA family permit

259. The requirements for the issue of an EEA family permit are that:
 (i) the applicant is the family member (as defined in the 1994 EEA Order) of an EEA national who is a qualified person in the terms of the 1994 EEA Order; and
 (ii) the applicant is coming to the United Kingdom for a purpose provided for in the 1994 EEA Order; and
 (iii) the applicant is not a person who falls to be excluded on grounds of public policy, public security or public health.

Issue of an EEA family permit

260. An application for an EEA family permit shall be granted provided the Entry Clearance Officer is satisfied that each of the requirements of paragraph 259 is met.

Refusal of an application for an EEA family permit

261. An application for an EEA family permit is to be refused if the Entry Clearance Officer is not satisfied that each of the requirements of paragraph 259 is met.

NOTES

1. EU law provides for freedom of movement for economic purposes between the various Union states. The rights are afforded to EU nationals. They do not, however, extend beyond movement for economic purposes – i.e. freedom of movement does not extend to those wishing to enter and remain to exercise civil or political rights. See e.g. *Levin v Secretary of State for Justice* [1982] ECR 1035; and *Re a Belgian Prostitute* [1976] 2 CMLR 527 – prostitution not a protected economic activity.

The economic purposes for which free movement of EEC nationals must be ensured were stated in the Treaty of Rome 1957 to consist of:
(1) free movement to work (and to seek work – *R v Secretary of State for the Home Department, ex p Muhammad Ayub* [1982] Imm AR 20); *Hoth v Secretary of State for the Home Department* [1985] Imm AR 20; *Bouanimba v Secretary of State for the Home Department* [1986] Imm AR 343 IAT (Arts. 48–51);
(2) freedom to establish or join a business (Arts. 52–58);
(3) free movement to provide services (Arts. 59–66).
These Articles provide a basic framework which has been supplemented by EC regulations and directives. Also, there have been enacted within the EC complex provisions for the mutual recognition of professional and other qualifications. Note also, rights to remain, in certain circumstances even on ceasing to be economically active because of involuntary unemployment, illness or simply age.

Article 8a(1) of the Treaty of European Union provides that 'Every citizen of the Union shall have the right to move freely within the territory of the Member States, subject to the limitations laid down in the Treaty and by the measures adopted to give it effect.'

This right of free movement extends also to those covered by the terms of Part III of the European Economic Area Agreement (i.e. originally, nationals of Austria, Finland, Iceland, Norway, and Sweden: although all except the Norwegians now have right by virtue of full EU membership). For transposition into UK law, see the European Economic Area Act 1993 and the EEA Order 1994.

For the direct effect of rights of EU citizens, and of nationals of the European Economic Area, see above, p. 686.

2. EU law permits a member state to refuse a Community national permission to enter and remain on certain defined grounds of personal unacceptability (i.e. public policy (*ordre public*), public security, public health). See Arts. 48(3), 56(1) and 66. The provisions of the Treaty of Rome have in this connection been supplemented by Council Directives 64/221, 72/194 and 75/35. Thus, in the case of refusal of entry on medical grounds, the wide discretion to refuse to admit many, though not all, categories of non-EC nationals is confined in respect of EC nationals to refusal on the basis of belief that the would-be entrant is suffering from one of a defined list of diseases – Art. 4 and Annex: Directive 64/221. The list also restricts the scope of discretion to refuse to grant a residence permit, or to deport on 'public health' grounds.

Directive 64/221 also contains important limits to the powers of member states to derogate from the basic freedoms of movement on grounds of public policy and public security. The powers may only be exercised on grounds of personal unacceptability – see Art. 3(1) and *Van Duyn v Home Office (No 2)* [1974] ECR 1337. Thus, exclusion or deportation *solely* on grounds of past membership of an undesirable organisation is not permissible; the undesirability of the specific individual in question must be demonstrable. However, membership which connotes identification of the individual with the aims and objectives of an objectionable organisation, together with involvement in its activities, may suffice. The directive also provides that the mere fact of commission of a criminal offence does not, without more, justify exclusion or deportation. Where offences are not serious, or where further commission of crime is not expected, the 'public policy' condition will not be satisfied and the EC national's rights to enter and stay will remain intact. See *Bonsignore v Oberstadtdirektor of the City of Cologne* [1975] ECR 297 – (negligent causing of death of brother in firearm accident; no likelihood of repetition). In *R v Bouchereau* [1977] ECR 1999 it seemed, however, to be accepted that in the case of certain kinds of offence, the defendant's assumed propensity to reoffend, and the seriousness of the offence if (when) recommitted, may suffice. Note also, *R v Secretary of State for the Home Department, ex p Marchon* [1993] 1 CMLR 207, [1993] 2 CMLR 132. See also *Puttick v Secretary of State for the Home Department* [1984] Imm AR 118. *R v Immigration Appeal Tribunal, ex p Tamdjid-Nezhad* [1986] Imm AR 396. (Contrast the non-EEC deportation position – *R v Immigration Appeal Tribunal, ex p Florent* [1985] Imm AR 141, CA.) Note also, that in relation to *court recommended* deportations, in cases where the Home Secretary's decision is reached after the custodial sentence has been served, it may be necessary to allow EC nationals to make representations as to any changed circumstances since the court recommendation. Directive 64/221 requires that action be taken on the basis of facts as they currently exist – see *R v Secretary of State for the Home Department, ex p Santillo* [1980] ECR 1585 – though note the liberal application of the rule in this case; *R v Secretary of State for the Home Department, ex p Allegret* [1989] Imm AR 211, QBD. In *R v Secretary of State for the Home Department, ex p Dannenberg* [1984] 2 All ER 481 it was held in the Court of Appeal that Directive 64/221 requires the magistrates or the

Crown Court judge to send a short statement of reasons for recommending deportation to the defendant and to the Home Secretary. See also *R v Escauriaza* (1987) 87 Cr App Rep 344, CA.

Note, however, that provided the *ordre public* or public security condition is satisfied it does not matter that the conduct in question does not amount to a criminal offence – see Case 115–116/81, *Adoui and Cornvaille v Belgian State* [1982] ECR 1665: deportation of immoral waitress.

(e) FAMILY MEMBERS

(i) Spouses

Immigration Rules 1994

Requirements for leave to enter the United Kingdom with a view to settlement as the spouse of a person present and settled in the United Kingdom or being admitted on the same occasion for settlement

281. The requirements to be met by a person seeking leave to enter the United Kingdom with a view to settlement as the spouse of a person present and settled in the United Kingdom or who is on the same occasion being admitted for settlement are that:
    (i) the applicant is married to a person present and settled in the United Kingdom or who is on the same occasion being admitted for settlement; and
    (ii) the marriage was not entered into primarily to obtain admission to the United Kingdom; and
    (iii) the parties to the marriage have met; and
    (iv) each of the parties intends to live permanently with the other as his or her spouse and the marriage is subsisting; and
    (v) there will be adequate accommodation for the parties and any dependants without recourse to public funds in accommodation which they own or occupy exclusively; and
    (vi) the parties will be able to maintain themselves and any dependants adequately without recourse to public funds; and
    (vii) the applicant holds a valid United Kingdom entry clearance for entry in this capacity.

Leave to enter as the spouse of a person present and settled in the United Kingdom or being admitted for settlement on the same occasion

282. A person seeking leave to enter the United Kingdom as the spouse of a person present and settled in the United Kingdom or who is on the same occasion being admitted for settlement may be admitted for an initial period not exceeding 12 months provided a valid United Kingdom entry clearance for entry in this capacity is produced to the Immigration Officer on arrival.

Refusal of leave to enter as the spouse of a person present and settled in the United Kingdom or being admitted on the same occasion for settlement

283. Leave to enter the United Kingdom as the spouse of a person present and settled in the United Kingdom or who is on the same occasion being admitted for settlement is to be refused if a valid United Kingdom entry clearance for entry in this capacity is not produced to the Immigration Officer on arrival.

Requirements for an extension of stay as the spouse of a person present and settled in the United Kingdom

284. The requirements for an extension of stay as the spouse of a person present and settled in the United Kingdom are that:
    (i) the applicant has limited leave to remain in the United Kingdom; and
    (ii) is married to a person present and settled in the United Kingdom; and
    (iii) the marriage was not entered into primarily to obtain settlement here; and
    (iv) the parties to the marriage have met; and
    (v) the applicant has not remained in breach of the immigration laws; and
    (vi) the marriage has not taken place after a decision has been made to deport the applicant or he has been recommended for deportation or been given notice under Section 6(2) of the Immigration Act 1971; and

(vii) each of the parties intends to live permanently with the other as his or her spouse and the marriage is subsisting; and

(viii) there will be adequate accommodation for the parties and any dependants without recourse to public funds in accommodation which they own or occupy exclusively; and

(ix) the parties will be able to maintain themselves and any dependants adequately without recourse to public funds.

Extension of stay as the spouse of a person present and settled in the United Kingdom

285. An extension of stay as the spouse of a person present and settled in the United Kingdom may be granted for a period of 12 months in the first instance, provided the Secretary of State is satisfied that each of the requirements of paragraph 284 is met.

Refusal of extension of stay as the spouse of a person present and settled in the United Kingdom

286. An extension of stay as the spouse of a person present and settled in the United Kingdom is to be refused if the Secretary of State is not satisfied that each of the requirements of paragraph 284 is met.

Requirements for indefinite leave to remain for the spouse of a person present and settled in the United Kingdom

287. The requirements for indefinite leave to remain for the spouse of a person present and settled in the United Kingdom are that:

(i) the applicant was admitted to the United Kingdom or given an extension of stay for a period of 12 months and has completed a period of 12 months as the spouse of a person present and settled here; and

(ii) the applicant is still the spouse of the person he or she was admitted or granted an extension of stay to join and the marriage is subsisting; and

(iii) each of the parties intends to live permanently with the other as his or her spouse.

Indefinite leave to remain for the spouse of a person present and settled in the United Kingdom

288. Indefinite leave to remain for the spouse of a person present and settled in the United Kingdom may be granted provided the Secretary of State is satisfied that each of the requirements of paragraph 287 is met.

Refusal of indefinite leave to remain for the spouse of a person present and settled in the United Kingdom

289. Indefinite leave to remain for the spouse of a person present and settled in the United Kingdom is to be refused if the Secretary of State is not satisfied that each of the requirements of paragraph 287 is met.

(ii) Fiancé(e)s

Immigration Rules 1994

Requirements for leave to enter the United Kingdom as a fiancé(e) (ie with a view to marriage and permanent settlement in the United Kingdom)

290. The requirements to be met by a person seeking leave to enter the United Kingdom as a fiancé(e) are that:

(i) the applicant is seeking leave to enter the United Kingdom for marriage to a person present and settled in the United Kingdom or who is on the same occasion being admitted for settlement; and

(ii) it is not the primary purpose of the intended marriage to obtain admission to the United Kingdom; and

(iii) the parties to the proposed marriage have met; and

(iv) each of the parties intends to live permanently with the other as his or her spouse after the marriage; and

(v) adequate maintenance and accommodation without recourse to public funds will be available for the applicant until the date of the marriage; and

(vi) there will, after the marriage, be adequate accommodation for the parties and any dependants without recourse to public funds in accommodation which they own or occupy exclusively; and

(vii) the parties will be able after the marriage to maintain themselves and any dependants adequately without recourse to public funds; and

(viii) the applicant holds a valid United Kingdom entry clearance for entry in this capacity.

Leave to enter as a fiancé(e)

291. A person seeking leave to enter the United Kingdom as a fiancé(e) may be admitted, with a prohibition on employment, for a period not exceeding 6 months to enable the marriage to take place provided a valid United Kingdom entry clearance for entry in this capacity is produced to the Immigration Officer on arrival.

Refusal of leave to enter as a fiancé(e)

292. Leave to enter the United Kingdom as a fiancé(e) is to be refused if a valid United Kingdom entry clearance for entry in this capacity is not produced to the Immigration Officer on arrival.

Requirements for an extension of stay as a fiancé(e)

293. The requirements for an extension of stay as a fiancé(e) are that:
 (i) the applicant was admitted to the United Kingdom with a valid United Kingdom entry clearance as a fiancé(e); and
 (ii) good cause is shown why the marriage did not take place within the initial period of leave granted under paragraph 291; and
 (iii) there is satisfactory evidence that the marriage will take place at an early date; and
 (iv) the requirements of paragraph 290 (ii)–(vii) are met.

Extension of stay as a fiancé(e)

294. An extension of stay as a fiancé(e) may be granted for an appropriate period with a prohibition on employment to enable the marriage to take place provided the Secretary of State is satisfied that each of the requirements of paragraph 293 is met.

Refusal of extension of stay as a fiancé(e)

295. An extension of stay is to be refused if the Secretary of State is not satisfied that each of the requirements of paragraph 293 is met.

NOTE

The Rules relating to entry for marriage, and the entry of spouses of persons already in the UK, have been controversial. These Rules have been amended on numerous occasions – e.g. in 1974, 1977, 1980, 1982, 1983 and 1985.

Between 1977 and 1985 the Rules contained provisions which were quite different in substance as regards (i) the admission of men as fiancés or husbands of women in the UK, and (ii) the admission of women as fiancées or wives of men in the UK. The Rules were considerably stricter as regards admission of men than they were in relation to admission of women. To put it another way, women had to satisfy more stringent conditions to be joined by their men, than did men to be joined by their fiancées or wives.

The discrimination between the sexes contained in these rules was successfully challenged in the European Court of Human Rights in *Abdulaziz, Cabales and Balkandali v United Kingdom* (1985) 7 EHRR 471; the court rejecting the UK argument that the discrimination was justified as a reasonable measure to protect the local workforce, men being more prone to take employment than women. See further, below p. 849. Following this decision the Rules were revised in 1985 in order to secure equality. This was achieved, however, not by elevating the rights of women to be joined by their partners, but by restricting the rights of men. Since 1985 the rules governing entry of fiancés and husbands have been abolished and the former rules about fiancées and wives made applicable to both sexes. For unsuccessful challenge by way of judicial review, see *Rajput v Immigration Appeal Tribunal* [1989] Imm AR 350.

A consequence of this is that the much-criticised 'genuine marriage–primary purpose' rule (Rules 281 and 290) now applies to all such admissions, and not just to the admission of men. Note on whom lies the burden of proof on this matter. The applicant must satisfy the officer that the marriage, or intended marriage, satisfies the requirement of the Rules that the primary purpose of the marriage is not settlement in the UK and that the parties intend to live permanently together as man and wife. See further, *Entry Clearance Officer, Islamabad v Mohamed Hussain* [1991] Imm AR 476; *R v Immigration Appeal Tribunal, ex p Kumar* [1986] Imm AR 446; *Bhatia v Immigration Appeal Tribunal* [1985] Imm AR 50; *R v Immigration Appeal Tribunal, ex p Hoque* [1988] Imm AR 216; *R v Immigration Appeal Tribunal, ex p Kaur* [1991] Imm AR 107 – see per McCullough J, at 110, '. . . it is fatally easy but wrong to treat an admission on the part of a man that he seeks to obtain admission to the United Kingdom as evidence that that was the primary purpose of the marriage. Equally, it is easy but wrong to treat the fact that a man has lied about the strength of his desire to obtain admission . . . as evidence that this was the primary purpose of the marriage.' Cf. *R v Immigration Appeal Tribunal, ex p Gondalia* [1991] Imm AR 519. In a comprehensive discussion in *ex p Hoque*, Slade LJ also explained, however, that the mere fact that parties do intend to live permanently together as man and wife does not, of itself, mean that the primary purpose was not to obtain admission. Note also, *Islam Choudhry v Immigration Appeal Tribunal* [1990] Imm AR 211. Note also, the statement in *Hoque* that 'arranged marriages' do not *ipso facto* fall foul of this Rule.

(iii) Children

Immigration Rules 1994

Requirements for indefinite leave to enter the United Kingdom as the child of a parent, parents or a relative present and settled or being admitted for settlement in the United Kingdom

297. The requirements to be met by a person seeking indefinite leave to enter the United Kingdom as the child of a parent, parents or a relative present and settled or being admitted for settlement in the United Kingdom are that he:
  (i) is seeking leave to enter to accompany or join a parent, parents or a relative in one of the following circumstances:
    (a) both parents are present and settled in the United Kingdom; or
    (b) both parents are being admitted on the same occasion for settlement; or
    (c) one parent is present and settled in the United Kingdom and the other is being admitted on the same occasion for settlement; or
    (d) one parent is present and settled in the United Kingdom or being admitted on the same occasion for settlement and the other parent is dead; or
    (e) one parent is present and settled in the United Kingdom or being admitted on the same occasion for settlement and has had sole responsibility for the child's upbringing; or
    (f) one parent or a relative is present and settled in the United Kingdom or being admitted on the same occasion for settlement and there are serious and compelling family or other considerations which make exclusion of the child undesirable and suitable arrangements have been made for the child's care; and
  (ii) is under the age of 18; and
  (iii) is not leading an independent life, is unmarried, and has not formed an independent family unit; and
  (iv) can, and will, be maintained and accommodated adequately without recourse to public funds in accommodation which the parent, parents or relative own or occupy exclusively; and
  (v) holds a valid United Kingdom entry clearance for entry in this capacity.

Requirements for indefinite leave to remain in the United Kingdom as the child of a parent, parents or a relative present and settled or being admitted for settlement in the United Kingdom

298. The requirements to be met by a person seeking indefinite leave to remain in the United Kingdom as the child of a parent, parents or a relative present and settled in the United Kingdom are that he:
  (i) is seeking to remain with a parent, parents or a relative in one of the following circumstances:
      (a) both parents are present and settled in the United Kingdom; or
      (b) one parent is present and settled in the United Kingdom and the other parent is dead; or
      (c) one parent is present and settled in the United Kingdom and has had sole responsibility for the child's upbringing; or
      (d) one parent or a relative is present and settled in the United Kingdom and there are serious and compelling family or other considerations which make exclusion of the child undesirable and suitable arrangements have been made for the child's care; and
  (ii) has limited leave to enter or remain in the United Kingdom, and
      (a) is under the age of 18; or
      (b) was given leave to enter or remain with a view to settlement under paragraph 302; and
  (iii) is not leading an independent life, is unmarried, and has not formed an independent family unit; and
  (iv) can, and will, be maintained and accommodated adequately without recourse to public funds in accommodation which the parent, parents or relative own or occupy exclusively.

Indefinite leave to enter or remain in the United Kingdom as the child of a parent, parents or a relative present and settled or being admitted for settlement in the United Kingdom

299. Indefinite leave to enter the United Kingdom as the child of a parent, parents or a relative present and settled or being admitted for settlement in the United Kingdom may be granted provided a valid United Kingdom entry clearance for entry in this capacity is produced to the Immigration Officer on arrival. Indefinite leave to remain in the United Kingdom as the child of a parent, parents or a relative present and settled in the United Kingdom may be granted provided the Secretary of State is satisfied that each of the requirements of paragraph 298 is met.

Refusal of indefinite leave to enter or remain in the United Kingdom as the child of a parent, parents or a relative present and settled or being admitted for settlement in the United Kingdom

300. Indefinite leave to enter the United Kingdom as the child of a parent, parents or a relative present and settled or being admitted for settlement in the United Kingdom is to be refused if a valid United Kingdom entry clearance for entry in this capacity is not produced to the Immigration Officer on arrival. Indefinite leave to remain in the United Kingdom as the child of a parent, parents or a relative present and settled in the United Kingdom is to be refused if the Secretary of State is not satisfied that each of the requirements of paragraph 298 is met.

Requirements for limited leave to enter or remain in the United Kingdom with a view to settlement as the child of a parent or parents given limited leave to enter or remain in the United Kingdom with a view to settlement

301. The requirements to be met by a person seeking limited leave to enter or remain in the United Kingdom with a view to settlement as the child of a parent or parents given limited leave to enter or remain in the United Kingdom with a view to settlement are that he:
  (i) is seeking leave to enter to accompany or join or remain with a parent or parents in one of the following circumstances:
      (a) one parent is present and settled in the United Kingdom or being admitted on the same occasion for settlement and the other parent is being or has been given limited leave to enter or remain in the United Kingdom with a view to settlement; or
      (b) one parent is being or has been given limited leave to enter or remain in the United Kingdom with a view to settlement and has had sole responsibility for the child's upbringing; or
      (c) one parent is being or has been given limited leave to enter or remain in the United Kingdom with a view to settlement and there are serious and compelling family or other considerations which make exclusion of the child undesirable and suitable arrangements have been made for the child's care; and
  (ii) is under the age of 18; and
  (iii) is not leading an independent life, is unmarried, and has not formed an independent family unit; and

(iv) can, and will, be maintained and accommodated adequately without recourse to public funds in accommodation which the parent or parents own or occupy exclusively; and

(v) (where an application is made for limited leave to remain with a view to settlement) has limited leave to enter or remain in the United Kingdom; and

(vi) if seeking leave to enter, holds a valid United Kingdom entry clearance for entry in this capacity or, if seeking leave to remain, was admitted with a valid United Kingdom entry clearance for entry in this capacity.

Limited leave to enter or remain in the United Kingdom with a view to settlement as the child of a parent or parents given limited leave to enter or remain in the United Kingdom with a view to settlement

302. A person seeking limited leave to enter the United Kingdom with a view to settlement as the child of a parent or parents given limited leave to enter or remain in the United Kingdom with a view to settlement may be admitted for a period not exceeding 12 months provided he is able, on arrival, to produce to the Immigration Officer a valid United Kingdom entry clearance for entry in this capacity. A person seeking limited leave to remain in the United Kingdom with a view to settlement as the child of a parent or parents given limited leave to enter or remain in the United Kingdom with a view to settlement may be given limited leave to remain for a period not exceeding 12 months provided the Secretary of State is satisfied that each of the requirements of paragraph 301(i)–(v) is met.

Refusal of limited leave to enter or remain in the United Kingdom with a view to settlement as the child of a parent or parents given limited leave to enter or remain in the United Kingdom with a view to settlement

303. Limited leave to enter the United Kingdom with a view to settlement as the child of a parent or parents given limited leave to enter or remain in the United Kingdom with a view to settlement is to be refused if a valid United Kingdom entry clearance for entry in this capacity is not produced to the Immigration Officer on arrival. Limited leave to remain in the United Kingdom with a view to settlement as the child of a parent or parents given limited leave to enter or remain in the United Kingdom with a view to settlement is to be refused if the Secretary of State is not satisfied that each of the requirements of paragraph 301(i)–(v) is met.

(iv) Parents, grandparents and other dependent relatives of persons present and settled in the United Kingdom

Immigration Rules 1994

Requirements for indefinite leave to enter or remain in the United Kingdom as the parent, grandparent or other dependent relative of a person present and settled in the United Kingdom

317. The requirements to be met by a person seeking indefinite leave to enter or remain in the United Kingdom as a parent, grandparent or other dependent relative of a person present and settled in the United Kingdom are that the person:

(i) is related to a person present and settled in the United Kingdom in one of the following ways:

(a) mother or grandmother who is a widow aged 65 years or over; or

(b) father or grandfather who is a widower aged 65 years or over; or

(c) parent or grandparents travelling together of whom at least one is aged 65 or over; or

(d) a parent or grandparent aged 65 or over who has remarried but cannot look to the spouse or children of the second marriage for financial support; and where the person settled in the United Kingdom is able and willing to maintain the parent or grandparent and any spouse or child of the second marriage who would be admissible as a dependant; or

(e) a parent or grandparent under the age of 65 if living alone outside the United Kingdom in the most exceptional compassionate circumstances and mainly dependent financially on relatives settled in the United Kingdom; or

(f) the son, daughter, sister, brother, uncle or aunt over the age of 18 if living alone outside the United Kingdom in the most exceptional compassionate circumstances and mainly dependent financially on relatives settled in the United Kingdom; and

(ii) is joining or accompanying a person who is present and settled in the United Kingdom or who is on the same occasion being admitted for settlement; and

(iii) is financially wholly or mainly dependent on the relative present and settled in the United Kingdom; and

(iv) can, and will, be maintained and accommodated adequately, together with any dependants, without recourse to public funds in accommodation which the sponsor owns or occupies exclusively; and

(v) has no other close relatives in his own country to whom he could turn for financial support; and

(vi) if seeking leave to enter, holds a valid United Kingdom entry clearance for entry in this capacity.

Indefinite leave to enter or remain as the parent, grandparent or other dependent relative of a person present and settled in the United Kingdom

318. Indefinite leave to enter the United Kingdom as the parent, grandparent or other dependent relative of a person present and settled in the United Kingdom may be granted provided a valid United Kingdom entry clearance for entry in this capacity is produced to the Immigration Officer on arrival. Indefinite leave to remain in the United Kingdom as the parent, grandparent or other dependent relative of a person present and settled in the United Kingdom may be granted provided the Secretary of State is satisfied that each of the requirements of paragraph 317 (i)–(v) is met.

Refusal of indefinite leave to enter or remain in the United Kingdom as the parent, grandparent or other dependent relative of a person present and settled in the United Kingdom

319. Indefinite leave to enter the United Kingdom as the parent, grandparent or other dependent relative of a person settled in the United Kingdom is to be refused if a valid United Kingdom entry clearance for entry in this capacity is not produced to the Immigration Officer on arrival. Indefinite leave to remain in the United Kingdom as the parent, grandparent or other dependent relative of a person present and settled in the United Kingdom is to be refused if the Secretary of State is not satisfied that each of the requirements of paragraph 317 (i)–(v) is met.

NOTES

1. Such applicants must be 'necessarily' dependent on sons or daughters settled in the UK. Thus, self-induced dependency (e.g. by giving up employment or giving away assets) does not qualify – see *Entry Clearance Officer, Port Louis v Grenade* [1978] Imm AR 143; *Mohammed Zaman v Entry Clearance Officer, Lahore* [1973] Imm AR 71. Contrast, *Chavda v Entry Clearance Officer, Bombay* [1978] Imm AR 40; *Entry Clearance Officer, New Delhi v Malhan* [1978] Imm AR 209.

2. Note that the 1994 Rules refer to being 'financially wholly or mainly dependent'. Earlier Rules omitted the first of these words. In *R v Immigration Appeal Tribunal, ex p Singh* [1987] 3 All ER 690, Dillon LJ discussed decisions interpreting the earlier Rules and concluded that matters in respect of which such entrants must be at least mainly dependent upon children in the UK, and in respect of which they must have no close relatives in their own country to whom they could instead turn, include a wider range of things than just a home and financial support. Limiting the scope of an earlier decision, *R v Immigration Appeal Tribunal, ex p Bastiampillai* [1983] 2 All ER 844, he said that in addition to those things there were also needs arising out of loneliness and isolation. 'One obvious instance is the need for some close relative to turn to in the event of chronic illness. Another, . . . is the need for a close relative to turn to, and who will be willing and able to cope, in the event of accident or sudden emergency to the elderly parent; it is difficult to imagine anything more worrying to a loving child settled here than the fear of an accident to a parent thousands of miles away with no one to cope. . . . [T]he rule is one of broad humanity. . .'. Note also, *R v Immigration Appeal Tribunal, ex p Kara* [1989] Imm AR 120, QBD; *R v Immigration Appeal Tribunal, ex p Jan* [1989] Imm AR 162, QBD; *R v Immigration Appeal Tribunal, ex p Khatun* [1989] Imm AR 482 QBD. The 1994 Rules appear to restore the *Bastiampillai* principle.

3. On the 'most exceptional compassionate circumstances' extension, see e.g.

Mukhopadyoy v Entry Clearance Officer, Calcutta [1975] Imm AR 42; *Entry Clearance Officer, Nairobi v Seth* [1979–80] Imm AR 63; *Gheithy v Entry Clearance Officer, Dar-Es-Salaam* [1981] Imm AR 113; *R v Immigration Appeal Tribunal, ex p Joseph* [1988] Imm AR 329, QBD.

(f) ASYLUM

Immigration Rules 1994

Definition of asylum applicant

327. Under these Rules an asylum applicant is a person who claims that it would be contrary to the United Kingdom's obligations under the United Nations Convention and Protocol relating to the Status of Refugees for him to be removed from or required to leave the United Kingdom. All such cases are referred to in these Rules as asylum applications.

Applications for asylum

328. All asylum applications will be determined by the Secretary of State in accordance with the United Kingdom's obligations under the United Nations Convention and Protocol relating to the Status of Refugees.[1] Every asylum application made by a person at a port or airport in the United Kingdom will be referred by the Immigration Officer for determination by the Secretary of State in accordance with these Rules.

329. Until an asylum application has been determined by the Secretary of State, no action will be taken to require the departure of the asylum applicant or his dependants from the United Kingdom.

331. If a person seeking leave to enter is refused asylum, the Immigration Officer will then resume his examination to determine whether or not to grant him leave to enter under any other provision of these Rules.

332. If a person who has been refused leave to enter applies for asylum and that application is refused, leave to enter will again be refused unless the applicant qualifies for admission under any other provisions of these Rules.

333. A person who is refused leave to enter following the refusal of an asylum application will be provided with a notice informing him of the decision and of the reasons for refusal. The notice of refusal will also explain any rights of appeal available to the applicant and will inform him of the means by which he may exercise those rights. The applicant will not be removed from the United Kingdom so long as any appeal which he may bring is pending.

Grant of asylum

334. An asylum applicant will be granted asylum in the United Kingdom if the Secretary of State is satisfied that:
  (i)   he is in the United Kingdom or has arrived at a port of entry in the United Kingdom; and
  (ii) he is a refugee, as defined by the Convention and Protocol; and
  (iii) refusing his application would result in his being required to go (whether immediately or after the time limited by an existing leave to enter or remain) in breach of the Convention and Protocol, to a country in which his life or freedom would be threatened on account of his race, religion, nationality, political opinion or membership of a particular social group.

Refusal of asylum

336. An application which does not meet the criteria set out in paragraph 334 will be refused.

337. The Secretary of State may decide not to consider the substance of a person's claim to refugee status if he is satisfied that the person's removal to a third country does not raise any issue as to the United Kingdom's obligations under the Convention and Protocol. More details are given in paragraphs 345 and 347.

1 *Ed.* Cmnd. 9171 and Cmnd. 3906.

Consideration of cases

340. A failure, without reasonable explanation, to make a prompt and full disclosure of material factors, either orally or in writing, or otherwise to assist the Secretary of State to the full in establishing the facts of the case may lead to refusal of an asylum application. This includes failure to comply with a notice issued by the Secretary of State requiring the applicant to report to a designated place to be fingerprinted, or failure to complete an asylum questionnaire, or failure to comply with a request to attend an interview concerning the application.

341. In determining an asylum application the Secretary of State will have regard to matters which may damage an asylum applicant's credibility if no reasonable explanation is given. Among such matters are:
   (i) that the applicant has failed to apply forthwith upon arrival in the United Kingdom, unless the application is founded on events which have taken place since his arrival in the United Kingdom;
   (ii) that the applicant has made false representations, either orally or in writing;
   (iii) that the applicant has destroyed, damaged or disposed of any passport, other document or ticket relevant to his claim;
   (iv) that the applicant has undertaken any activities in the United Kingdom before or after lodging his application which are inconsistent with his previous beliefs and behaviour and calculated to create or substantially enhance his claim to refugee status;
   (v) that the applicant has lodged concurrent applications for asylum in the United Kingdom or in another country.
If the Secretary of State concludes for these or any other reasons that an asylum applicant's account is not credible, the application will be refused.

342. The actions of anyone acting as an agent of the asylum applicant may also be taken into account in regard to the matters set out in paragraphs 340 and 341.

343. If there is a part of the country from which the applicant claims to be a refugee in which he would not have a well-founded fear of persecution, and to which it would be reasonable to expect him to go, the application may be refused.

344. Cases will normally be considered on an individual basis but if an applicant is part of a group whose claims are clearly not related to the criteria for refugee status in the Convention and Protocol he may be refused without examination of his individual claim. However, the Secretary of State will have regard to any evidence produced by an individual to show that his claim should be distinguished from those of the rest of the group.

Third country cases

345. If the Secretary of State is satisfied that there is a safe country to which an asylum applicant can be sent, his application will normally be refused without substantive consideration of his claim to refugee status. A safe country is one in which the life or freedom of the asylum applicant would not be threatened (within the meaning of Article 33 of the Convention) and the government of which would not send the applicant elsewhere in a manner contrary to the principles of the Convention and Protocol. The Secretary of State shall not remove an asylum applicant without substantive consideration of his claim unless:
   (i) the asylum applicant has not arrived in the United Kingdom directly from the country in which he claims to fear persecution and has had an opportunity at the border or within the territory of a third country to make contact with that country's authorities in order to seek their protection; or
   (ii) there is other clear evidence of his admissibility to a third country.
Provided that he is satisfied that a case meets these criteria, the Secretary of State is under no obligation to consult the authorities of the third country before the removal of an asylum applicant.

Previously rejected applications

346. Where an asylum applicant has previously been refused asylum in the United Kingdom and can demonstrate no relevant and substantial change in his circumstances since that date, his application will be refused.

347. When an asylum applicant has come to the United Kingdom from another country which is a party to the United Nations Convention relating to the Status of Refugees or its Protocol and which has considered and rejected an application for asylum from him, his application for asylum in the United Kingdom may be refused without substantive consideration of his claim to refugee status. He may be removed to that country, or another country meeting the criteria of paragraph 345, and invited to raise any new circumstances with the authorities of the country which originally considered his application.

Rights of appeal

348. Special provisions governing appeals in asylum cases are set out in the Asylum and Immigration Appeals Act 1993 and the Asylum Appeals (Procedure) Rules 1993. Where asylum is refused the applicant will be provided with a notice informing him of the decision and of the reasons for refusal. At the same time that asylum is refused the applicant may be notified of removal directions or served with a notice of intention to deport, as appropriate. The notice of refusal of asylum will also explain any rights of appeal available to the applicant and will inform him of the means by which he may exercise those rights.

Dependants

349. A husband or wife or minor children accompanying a principal applicant may be included in an application for asylum. If the principal applicant is granted asylum any such dependants will be granted leave to enter or remain of the same duration. . . .

Unaccompanied children

350. Unaccompanied children may also apply for asylum and, in view of their potential vulnerability, particular priority and care is to be given to the handling of their cases.

351. A person of any age may qualify for refugee status under the Convention and the criteria in paragraph 334 apply to all cases. However, account should be taken of the applicant's maturity and in assessing the claim of a child more weight should be given to objective indications of risk than to the child's state of mind and understanding of his situation. An asylum application made on behalf of a child should not be refused solely because the child is too young to understand his situation or to have formed a well-founded fear of persecution. Close attention should be given to the welfare of the child at all times.

352. A child will not be interviewed about the substance of his claim to refugee status if it is possible to obtain by written enquiries or from other sources sufficient information properly to determine the claim. . . .

NOTES

1. The Immigration Rules relating to 'refugees' are based upon international treaty obligations – the Geneva Convention of 1951, as amended by a 1967 Protocol. Note that s. 2 of the Asylum and Immigration Appeals Act 1993 provides that 'nothing in the immigration rules . . . shall lay down any practice which would be contrary to' the Convention or Protocol. Neither the Treaty nor the Protocol have been enacted directly into the law of the UK. Neither the Treaty/Protocol nor the Rules apply to 'economic' refugees (e.g. those fleeing from famine or other disaster), as distinct from those fleeing from the various kinds of persecution described in the Rules above. Whether those who leave a country during the turmoil of a civil war do so because of persecution or for other reasons can present difficult questions.

The Convention and Protocol do not impose any direct duties on ratifying states to grant asylum to refugees. Instead, as is suggested in the Rules above, they proceed on the basis of imposing restrictions on the return or removal ('refoulement') of refugees to territories where their life or freedom is threatened with such persecution. Where, however, no safe haven can be found for a refugee, the effect of the 'no return' obligation will be to impose a duty to afford asylum. Exceptions to the obligation not to so remove or return refugees exist where the refugee is reasonably regarded as a danger to the security of the country he is in, or where he constitutes a danger to the community in that country (evidenced by the fact of having been convicted of a particularly serious crime).

There was established, also in 1951, within the framework of the General Assembly of the United Nations, an Office of High Commissioner for Refugees. An advisory Executive Committee to this Office has, over the years, provided valuable guidance as to the meaning and operation of, the Treaty and Protocol. See its *Handbook on Procedures and Criteria for Determining Refugee Status* (1988). Such guidance may be considered by the Secretary of State in his decision–making under the Immigration Rules – it is not, however binding upon him. See *Miller v Immigration Appeal Tribunal* [1988] Imm AR 358, CA; *Bugdaycay v Secretary of State for the Home Department* [1987] AC 514, HL; *R v Immigration Appeal Tribunal, ex p Yassine* [1990] Imm AR 354, QBD.

2. Article 1A(2) of the Convention defines refugee in terms of a person who has a *well-founded fear of being persecuted* for reasons of race, religion and so on. Fear of persecution must be actual and must be 'well-founded'. The onus of proof lies on the applicant. The House of Lords held, in *R v Secretary of State for the Home Department, ex p Sivakumaran* [1988] AC 958, [1988] 1 All ER 193, that in reaching his decision on this issue the Secretary of State is entitled to take into account all facts and information of which he is aware. This may go beyond what is known to the applicants themselves. On the basis of this information the Secretary of State is required to ask himself whether there has been demonstrated a 'real likelihood' of persecution. In other words, the onus on the applicants is less than to have to prove that persecution is, on a 'balance of probabilities' more likely than not to occur. Indeed, approval was given by Lord Keith to the expressions 'reasonable chance', 'substantial grounds for thinking' and '–serious possibility', as describing the extent of likelihood that the objective evidence must suggest – expressions taken from Lord Diplock's judgment in *Fernandez v Government of Singapore* [1971] 2 All ER 691 at 697. On the facts the House of Lords upheld the decision of the Secretary of State to refuse the asylum applications of the six applicant Tamils from Sri Lanka. In due course the applicants appealed from abroad (see 1971 Act s. 13(3), below p. 729) against the Secretary of State for the Home Department's decision, and their appeal was upheld by the adjudicator, who, on the evidence before him, found a sufficient risk of persecution based upon race, religion and political opinion. See N. Blake, (1989) Immigration and Nationality Law and Practice Vol. 4 No. 1 p. 7; D. Burgess (1991) 141 NLJ 50; *R v Immigration Appeal Tribunal, ex p Secretary of State for the Home Department* [1990] 3 All ER 652, CA.

3. 'Persecution' has been held to be a strong term – 'to pursue with malignancy', 'to oppress for holding a heretical opinion or belief' – see per Nolan J in *R v Immigration Appeal Tribunal, ex p Jonah* [1985] Imm AR 7. Mere discriminatory treatment may not therefore suffice. See *Ahmad v Secretary of State for the Home Department* [1990] Imm AR 61 – distinction drawn between prevention of the practice of a religious faith, and prevention of the proselytisation of that faith. Nor may 'harassment' be sufficient to amount to persecution – see *R v Secretary of State for the Home Department, ex p Yurekli* [1990] Imm AR 334, QBD; but contrast, *Asante v Secretary of State for the Home Department* [1991] Imm AR 78. The position of an applicant who only need fear persecution if he 'speaks his mind', but who claims he feels obliged so to do, was considered, inconclusively, in *Mendis v Immigration Appeal Tribunal* [1989] Imm AR 6, CA.

4. The meaning of 'social group' was considered in *R v Secretary of State for the Home Department, ex p Binbasi* [1989] Imm AR 595. Kennedy J regarded the concept as involving persons with common characteristics which they cannot change, or should not be expected to change because they are fundamental to their individual consciences. The court assumed that homosexuals can be so regarded. See also, *Secretary of State for the Home Department v Otchere* [1988] Imm AR 21, Immigration Appeal Tribunal.

5. A person may only seek asylum after having left his country of persecution. In other words, claims to asylum are made on arrival, not prior to departure. In this connection the Immigration (Carriers' Liability) Act 1987 may present asylum seekers with difficulties. This Act provides that carriers of travellers to the UK shall be liable, on demand, to make a payment of £2,000 (S.I. 1991/1497) to the Secretary of State for the Home Department in respect of each passenger on their ship or aircraft who arrives to enter the UK without, inter alia, a visa where such is required. Asylum-seekers will commonly come from visa countries: the very reason for imposing the visa requirement appears, in some cases, to have been to hinder asylum claimants. Such persons, by definition not being persons who will have obtained visas for entry on one of the other entry grounds, may find it difficult to persuade carriers to carry them to the UK. See Schiemann J in *R v Secretary of State for the Home Department, ex p Yassine* [1990] Imm AR 354. To seek to assuage fears of carriers on this matter the Immigration Service announced, in 1987, certain conditions which, if satisfied, would result in the financial penalty not being demanded. The conditions have, however, been criticised as over-strict and unlikely to reassure carriers. See *MacDonald* pp. 303–304. The guidance has more recently been updated, and contains advice to carriers as to the performance of their 'immigration filtering' functions.

The Asylum and Immigration Appeals Act 1993 has sought to respond to a strategy adopted by some asylum-seekers: that of booking a ticket to a third country involving a transit stop in the UK. Such a passenger would be permitted to travel by the airline, yet could seek asylum in the UK. The 1993 Act amends the 1987 Act and instigates a system of visas for transit passengers travelling from certain countries designated by order (see S.I. 1993 No. 1678).

6 Deportation

Immigration Act 1971

3.—(5) A person who is not [a British citizen][1] shall be liable to deportation from the United Kingdom—
  (a) if, having only a limited leave to enter or remain, he does not observe a condition attached to the leave or remains beyond the time limited by the leave; or
  (b) if the Secretary of State deems his deportation to be conducive to the public good; or
  (c) if another person to whose family he belongs is or has been ordered to be deported.
(6) Without prejudice to the operation of subsection (5) above, a person who is not [a British citizen][1] shall also be liable to deportation from the United Kingdom if, after he has attained the age of seventeen, he is convicted of an offence for which he is punishable with imprisonment and on his conviction is recommended for deportation by a court empowered by this Act to do so.

5.—(1) Where a person is under s. 3(5) or (6) above liable to deportation, then subject to the following provisions of this Act the Secretary of State may make a deportation order against him, that is to say an order requiring him to leave and prohibiting him from entering the United Kingdom; and a deportation order against a person shall invalidate any leave to enter or remain in the United Kingdom given him before the order is made or while it is in force.
(2) A deportation order against a person may at any time be revoked by a further order of the Secretary of State, and shall cease to have effect if he becomes [a British citizen].[1]
(3) A deportation order shall not be made against a person as belonging to a family of another person if more than eight weeks have elapsed since the other person left the United Kingdom after the making of the deportation order against him; and a deportation order made against a person on that ground shall cease to have effect if he ceases to belong to the family of the other person, or if the deportation order made against the other person ceases to have effect.
(4) For purposes of deportation the following shall be those who are regarded as belonging to another person's family—
  (a) where that other person is a man, his wife and his or her children under the age of eighteen; and
  (b) where that other person is a woman, her children under the age of eighteen;

1 Words in brackets substituted by the British Nationality Act 1981, s. 39(6), Sch. 4, para. 2.

and for purposes of this subsection an adopted child, whether legally adopted or not, may be treated as the child of the adopter and, if legally adopted, shall be regarded as the child only of the adopter; an illegitimate child (subject to the foregoing rule as to adoptions) shall be regarded as the child of the mother; and 'wife' includes each of two or more wives.

(6) Where a person is liable to deportation under s. 3(5) or (6) above but, without a deportation order being made against him, leaves the United Kingdom to live permanently abroad, the Secretary of State may make payments of such amounts as he may determine to meet the person's expenses in so leaving the United Kingdom, including travelling expenses for members of his family or household.

Immigration Rules 1994

Deportation

364. In considering whether deportation is the right course on the merits, the public interest will be balanced against any compassionate circumstances of the case. While each case will be considered in the light of the particular circumstances, the aim is an exercise of the power of deportation which is consistent and fair as between one person and another, although one case will rarely be identical with another in all material respects. Deportation will normally be the proper course where a person has failed to comply with or has contravened a condition or has remained without authority. Before a decision to deport is reached the Secretary of State will take into account all relevant factors known to him including:
  (i) age;
  (ii) length of residence in the United Kingdom;
  (iii) strength of connections with the United Kingdom;
  (iv) personal history, including character, conduct and employment record;
  (v) domestic circumstances;
  (vi) previous criminal record and the nature of any offence of which the person has been convicted;
  (vii) compassionate circumstances;
  (viii) any representations received on the person's behalf.

Deportation of family members

365. . . . The Secretary of State will not normally decide to deport the wife of a deportee where:
  (i) she has qualified for settlement in her own right; or
  (ii) she has been living apart from the deportee.

366. The Secretary of State will not normally decide to deport the child of a deportee where:
  (i) he and his mother are living apart from the deportee; or
  (ii) he has spent some years in the United Kingdom and is nearing the age of 18; or
  (iii) he has left home and established himself on an independent basis; or
  (iv) he married before deportation came into prospect.

367. In considering whether to require a wife or child to leave with the deportee the Secretary of State will take account of the factors listed in paragraph 364 as well as the following:
  (i) the ability of the wife to maintain herself and any children in the United Kingdom, or to be maintained by relatives or friends without charge to public funds, not merely for a short period but for the foreseeable future; and
  (ii) in the case of a child of school age, the effect of removal on his education; and
  (iii) the practicability of any plans for a child's care and maintenance in this country if one or both of his parents were deported; and
  (iv) any representations made by or on behalf of the wife or child.

Arrangements for removal

385. A person against whom a deportation order has been made will normally be removed from the United Kingdom. The power is to be exercised so as to secure the person's return to the country of which he is a national, or which has most recently provided him with a travel document, unless he can show that another country will receive him. In considering any departure from the normal arrangements, regard will be had to the public interest generally, and to any additional expense that may fall on public funds.

386. The person will not be removed as the subject of a deportation order while an appeal may be brought against the removal directions or such an appeal is pending.

Supervised departure

387. A person liable to deportation may, in certain circumstances, leave the United Kingdom by means of supervised departure without having a deportation order made against him.

Returned deportees

388. Where a person returns to this country when a deportation order is in force against him, he may be deported under the original order. The Secretary of State will consider every such case in the light of all the relevant circumstances before deciding whether to enforce the order.

Returned family members

389. Persons deported in the circumstances set out in paragraph 365–368 above (deportation of family members) may be able to seek re-admission to the United Kingdom under the Immigration Rules where:
   (i)   a child reaches 18 (when he ceases to be subject to the deportation order); or
   (ii) in the case of a wife, the marriage comes to an end.

Revocation of deportation order

390. An application for revocation of a deportation order will be considered in the light of all the circumstances including the following:
   (i)   the grounds on which the order was made;
   (ii)   any representations made in support of revocation;
   (iii) the interests of the community, including the maintenance of an effective immigration control;
   (iv)   the interests of the applicant, including any compassionate circumstances.

391. In the case of an applicant with a serious criminal record continued exclusion for a long term of years will normally be the proper course. In other cases revocation of the order will not normally be authorised unless the situation has been materially altered, either by a change of circumstances since the order was made, or by fresh information coming to light which was not before the court which made the recommendation or the appellate authorities or the Secretary of State. The passage of time since the person was deported may also in itself amount to such a change of circumstances as to warrant revocation of the order. However, save in the most exceptional circumstances, the Secretary of State will not revoke the order unless the person has been absent from the United Kingdom for a period of at least 3 years since it was made.

392. Revocation of a deportation order does not entitle the person concerned to re-enter the United Kingdom; it renders him eligible to apply for admission under the Immigration Rules. Application for revocation of the order may be made to the Entry Clearance Officer or direct to the Home Office.

NOTES

1. Note the obligation under Rule 364 to take into account all relevant circumstances. Such would, in any case, be a requirement imposed by the principles of administrative law relating to the exercise of discretionary powers. In *Singh v Immigration Appeal Tribunal* [1986] 2 All ER 721, HL, the House held that the immigration adjudicatory authorities ought to have taken into account, as a relevant factor or circumstance, the effect which deportation of the applicant 'overstayer' would have on the Sikh community in the UK. The applicant was a valued member of that community by virtue of his religious, charitable and cultural activities. The effect of a person's deportation on the interests of third parties was a relevant consideration in the exercise of this discretionary power.

2. In *R v Nazari* [1980] 3 All ER 880, the Court of Appeal stated that no court should 'make an order recommending deportation without full inquiry into all the circumstances. It should not be done, as has sometimes happened in the past, . . . as if by an afterthought at the end of observations about any sentence of imprisonment'. Lawton LJ, giving the judgment of the court, explained:

'We now indicate some guidelines which courts should keep in mind when considering whether to make an order recommending deportation. But we stress that these are guidelines, not rigid rules. . . .

First, the court must consider, as was said by Sachs LJ in *R v Caird* (1970) 54 Cr App Rep 499 at 510, whether the accused's continued presence in the United Kingdom is to its detriment. This country has no use for criminals of other nationalities, particularly if they have committed serious crimes or have long criminal records. That is self-evident. The more serious the crime and the longer the record the more obvious it is that there should be an order recommending deportation. On the other hand, a minor offence would not merit an order recommending deportation. In the Greater London area, for example, shoplifting is an offence which is frequently committed by visitors to this country. Normally an arrest for shoplifting followed by conviction, even if there were more than one offence being dealt with, would not merit a recommendation for deportation. But a series of shoplifting offences on different occasions may justify a recommendation for deportation. Even a first offence for shoplifting might merit a recommendation if the offender were a member of a gang carrying out a planned raid on a departmental store.

Second, the courts are not concerned with the political systems which operate in other countries. They may be harsh; they may be soft; they may be oppressive; they may be the quintessence of democracy. The court has no knowledge of those matters over and above that which is common knowledge, and that may be wrong. In our judgment it would be undesirable for this court or any other court to express views about regimes which exist outside the United Kingdom of Great Britain and Northern Ireland. It is for the Home Secretary to decide in each case whether an offender's return to his country of origin would have consequences which would make his compulsory return unduly harsh. The Home Secretary has opportunities of informing himself about what is happening in other countries which the courts do not have. The sort of argument which was put in Nazari's case is one which we did not find attractive. It may well be that the regime in Iran at the present time is likely to be unfavourable from his point of view. Whether and how long it will continue to be so we do not know. Whether it will be so by the end of this man's sentence of imprisonment must be a matter of speculation. When the time comes for him to be released from prison the Home Secretary, we are sure, will bear in mind the very matters which we have been urged to consider, namely whether it would be unduly harsh to send him back to his country of origin.

The next matter to which we invite attention by way of guidelines is the effect that an order recommending deportation will have on others who are not before the court and who are innocent persons. This court and all other courts would have no wish to break up families or impose hardship on innocent people. The case of Fernandez illustrates this very clearly indeed. Mrs Fernandez is an admirable person, a good wife and mother, and a credit to herself and someone whom most of us would want to have in this country. As we have already indicated, if her husband is deported she will have a heartrending choice to make; whether she should go with her husband or leave him and look after the interests of the children. That is the kind of situation which should be considered very carefully before a recommendation for deportation is made.

We have considered the case of Fernandez in the light of those considerations and have come to the conclusion that the recommendation for deportation should be quashed. . . .

That concludes all the cases except to say a word in relation to deportation in the case of Dissanayake. He wants to go back to Sri Lanka, but says that he does not want to go back under an order of deportation. . . . It is often said in this class of case that there is no need to recommend deportation, because the accused is willing to go back of his own free will when he has served his sentence of imprisonment. We are not impressed with that argument. Assertions of intention made in this court are often forgotten on leaving the court and even more frequently forgotten once the prison gates have opened and the appellant is at large once again.

In our judgment there were very good grounds in the case of Dissanayake for making a recommendation. He had committed a serious offence, and he committed it, according to the case put forward on his behalf, when he was in a state of diminished responsibility by reason of what in his case must be inherent causes. Where there is evidence of mental instability connected with or resulting in the commission of a serious criminal offence it seems to us, again as a matter of guidelines, that that in itself is a good reason why a recommendation for deportation should be made. Whether it is carried out is entirely a matter for the Home Secretary. . . .'

The Court of Appeal also indicated that a recommendation normally *should* be made in cases of persons convicted of immigration offences e.g. overstayers.

Note also, *R v Serry* (1980) 2 Cr App Rep (S) 336 – single offence of shoplifting insufficiently serious; *R v Tshuma* (1981) 3 Cr App Rep (S) 97 – repetition of serious offence unlikely, so no recommendation; *R v Singh and Saini* (1979) 1 Cr App Rep (S) 90 and *R v Thoseby and Krawczyk* (1979) 1 Cr App Rep (S) 280 – no recommendation notwithstanding conviction of immigration offences owing to exceptional circumstances.

For general criticism of the procedure of court recommended deportation, see G. Zellick, [1973] Crim LR 612.

3. The 'conducive to public good' ground for deportation (and exclusion, see above p. 718) seems most commonly to be used in respect of persons who have been convicted of offences but where the court itself made no recommendation for deportation, and in respect of persons whose criminal activity abroad makes them undesirable. See J. M. Evans, *Immigration Law* (2nd edn, 1983) p. 272; *Butt v Secretary of State for the Home Department* [1979–80] Imm AR 82; *Patel v Secretary of State for the Home Department* [1986] Imm AR 457; *R v Immigration Appeal Tribunal, ex p Florent* [1985] Imm AR 141; *Martinez-Tobon v Immigration Appeal Tribunal* [1988] Imm AR 319, CA. This use has aroused little criticism. In addition the powers have been used in a few instances, and controversially, to deport or exclude persons not because their activities appear to be criminal, but because of their undesirability in a broader 'political' sense. Note, e.g. the deportation of the former militant student leader, Rudi Deutschke, back to West Germany in 1969, thereby terminating his studies at Cambridge (see B. Hepple (1971) 45 MLR 501); the blanket exclusion of Scientologists for a number of years prior to 1980 (see above p. 611); the exclusion of members of the Ku Klux Klan; and of persons associated with the then illegal regime in Southern Rhodesia. The deportation of journalists, Agee and Hosenball, on national security grounds may fall on the borderline between exercise of the power against 'political unacceptables' and the use of the power against those suspected of criminal activity – note the prosecution of two British journalists and a soldier on charges under the Official Secrets Acts in respect of similar activities, involving revelation of the existence and functions of the then officially unacknowledged Government Communications Headquarters at Cheltenham (see further above pp. 459, 462).

In *R v Brixton Prison Governor, ex p Soblen* [1963] 2 QB 243, S challenged a deportation order on the grounds that the Secretary of State had acted for an improper purpose – i.e. that the deportation was being ordered so as to comply with an alleged request from the United States for S's return, formal extradition proceedings not being possible because of the nature of S's offences (espionage). The Court of Appeal upheld the deportation order. The fact that deportation would achieve the same result as the 'barred' extradition proceedings was not, of itself, sufficient to invalidate the order; nor was the mere fact of the request for S's return. The Secretary of State could act for a plurality of purposes. Was it necessary, though, for the removal of S from the UK to have been the dominant purpose? Although this had been stated to be the proper test in other contexts (see e.g. *Westminster Corpn v London and North Western Rly Co* [1905] AC 426), the court suggested a more limited scope of review, stating that so long as the Minister was genuine in his opinion that the public good required the removal of S from the UK (i.e. that the order was not a 'sham') it did not matter if the Minister's main motive for acting might have been to comply with the request from the USA. Note, however, the decision in Rhodesia in *Minister of Information, Immigration and Tourism v Mackeson* [1980] 1 SA 747, where a challenge to a deportation order succeeded on it being shown that the 'true purpose' or 'main reason' for the order was to comply with a request for M's return to the UK to face charges of fraud. Subsequently, in the English Court of Appeal, Lord Lane CJ explained the Rhodesian decision in terms more in line with the *Soblen* approach – i.e. that the 'object of the exercise was *simply* to achieve extradition by the back door' – *R v Bow Street Magistrates, ex p Mackeson* (1982) 75 Cr App Rep 24 (italics added). See further, on the approach generally adopted by the courts to the issue of 'plurality of purposes': *R v Inner London Education Authority, ex p Westminster City Council* [1986] 1 All ER 19; *R v Broadcasting Complaints Commission, ex p Owen* [1985] QB 1153; and *R v Lewisham London Borough Council, ex p Shell UK Ltd* [1988] 1 All ER 938. These decisions suggest a 'motivating purpose' test – that a decision will not be interfered with so long as the reviewing court is satisfied that the same decision would have been reached even in the absence of consideration of the 'bad' purpose.

4. In *Patel v Immigration Appeal Tribunal* [1988] 2 All ER 378 HL, it was held that deception practised either in order originally to obtain entry to the UK, or thereafter to seek leave to remain, could constitute grounds upon which the SSHD could regard a person's continued presence as not conducive to the public good. See also *R v Immigration Appeal Tribunal, ex p Sheikh*, (1994) Times, 17 March: original entry by bribery.

5. Note the use of the 'conducive to public good' power of deportation in *R v Immigration Appeal Tribunal, ex p (Mahmud) Khan* [1983] QB 790. The applicant, a citizen of Pakistan, had been served with a deportation order on the grounds that his marriage to a person with a number of convictions for prostitution was a marriage of convenience entered into to obtain settlement in the UK with no intention of living together as man and wife. The applicant successfully challenged the IAT's dismissal of his appeal against deportation, on the ground that the tribunal's reasons for its decision failed to show it had properly considered whether the marriage was truly one of convenience – it seemed not to have considered whether the couple intended to live together as man and wife. Though the matter was not in issue, no doubt was expressed as to the legitimacy of such use of the 'conducive to public good' power. See also *R v Immigration Appeal Tribunal, ex p Ghazi Zubalir Ali Khan* [1983] Imm AR 32 (failure properly to consider whether marriage was 'of convenience' – also, 'public good' relates to likely future behaviour; mere fact of *past* wrongdoing not sufficient); *Malik v Secretary of State for the Home Department* [1981] Imm AR 134; *R v Immigration Appeal Tribunal, ex p Ullah* (1983) Times, 14 January.

6. For the applicability of Article 8 of the European Convention on Human Rights, see *Berrehab v Netherlands* (1988) 11 EHRR 322; *Beldjoudi v France* (1992) Times, 10 April; *Supperstone* pp. 270–271.

7 Removal of illegal entrants

R v Secretary of State for the Home Department, ex p Khera; ibid, ex p Khawaja [1984] AC 74, [1983] 1 All ER 765, [1983] 2 WLR 321, [1982] Imm AR 139 House of Lords

The House of Lords heard together two appeals brought by appellants who had unsuccessfully sought judicial review of the Home Secretary's determinations that each of them was an illegal entrant who should be detained and removed under the powers contained in s. 4(2) of, and Schedule 2 paras. 9 and 16(2) to, the 1971 Act.

Khawaja, a Pakistani citizen, had in December 1979 while living in Belgium gone through a bigamous form of marriage with a Mrs Butt, a woman settled in England. He arrived in the UK in March 1980, told an immigration officer that he had come for a temporary visit and made no mention of his 'marriage'. He was granted leave to enter for one month. He promptly 'remarried' Mrs Butt, whose previous marriage had by now been dissolved. He applied to the Home Office successively for leave to remain for a further temporary period (again not mentioning his marriage) and then for indefinite leave to remain on the grounds of his marriage. The Home Secretary ordered his removal on the basis that there were reasonable grounds to conclude that he was an illegal entrant, his entry having been achieved by deception, i.e. that had he disclosed his 'marriage' to Mrs Butt this would have destroyed the credibility of his statement that he intended only to visit temporarily.

The Home Office's claim to power to remove the other appellant, Khera, was, by the time of the hearing in the House of Lords, based solely on there being reasonable grounds for belief that in securing admission he had positively lied about his marital status.

Lord Bridge of Harwich: . . . Before turning to the facts of the two cases under appeal, I propose to consider [certain] clearly defined questions of law.

Who is an illegal entrant?

Section 33(1) of the 1971 Act provides:

'. . . "entrant" means a person entering or seeking to enter the United Kingdom and "illegal entrant" means a person unlawfully entering or seeking to enter in breach of a deportation order or of the immigration laws, and includes also a person who has so entered . . . "immigration laws" means this Act and any law for purposes similar to this Act which is for the time being or has (before or after the passing of this Act) been in force in any part of the United Kingdom and Islands . . .'

Before examining these definitions it is necessary to consider their significance in the scheme of the Act. . . . Once a non-patrial has entered and is resident in the United Kingdom he may be liable to expulsion by one or other of two distinct procedures, viz (i) by deportation under s. 5 and Sch. 3, (ii) by summary removal under s. 4 and Sch. 2. . . .

The grounds for deportation of a non-patrial, so far as relevant are: (i) that 'having only a limited leave to enter or remain, he does not observe a condition attached to the leave or remains beyond the time limited by the leave' (see s. 3(5)(*a*)); (ii) that 'the Secretary of State deems his deportation to be conducive to the public good' (see s. 3(5)(*b*)); (iii) that he has been recommended for deportation by a court on conviction of an offence punishable with imprisonment (see s. 3(6)).

The procedure for deportation ensures that, before the deportation order is made, i.e. while the person proposed to be deported is still in the United Kingdom, certain rights of appeal are exercisable. These are in case (i) appeal to an adjudicator and a limited right of further appeal from the adjudicator to the Immigration Appeal Tribunal, in case (ii) a limited right of appeal direct to the Immigration Appeal Tribunal (see s. 15). There is no appeal to the statutory appellate authorities in case (iii).

The only ground for summary removal by directions given pursuant to para. 8 or 10 of Sch. 2 of a resident non-patrial is that he is an illegal entrant, which, in this context, must mean that he comes within the relevant words of the definition as 'a person who has entered the United Kingdom in breach of a deportation order or of the immigration laws'. A deportation order invalidates any leave to enter granted before or after the order was made and remains in force until it is revoked or the person to whom the order applies becomes patrial (see s. 5). Hence, entry in breach of a deportation order presents no problem. The relevant problem of illegal entry is that of entry 'in breach of the immigration laws', which in turn, more shortly, means 'entry in breach of the Act'. A right of appeal against directions for removal lies to the adjudicator with a limited further right of appeal to the Immigration Appeal Tribunal but these rights are not exercisable while the appellant is still in the United Kingdom, i.e. in effect until the directions for removal have been implemented (see s. 16).

There is a clear and unbroken line of authority that where permission to enter has been obtained by the fraud of the entrant he is an illegal entrant and can be removed by the summary procedure. The principle was first stated in the unreported decision of the Divisional Court in *R v Risley Remand Centre (Governor) ex p Maqbool Hussain* on 4 May 1976, when it does not seem to have been contested . . . The principle was applied by the Court of Appeal in *R v Secretary of State for the Home Dept, ex p Hussain* [1978] 1 WLR 700 and *R v Secretary of State for the Home Dept, ex p Choudhary* [1978] 1 WLR 1177, which have been followed in numerous subsequent cases. The whole line of authority received the imprimatur of this House in the speech of Lord Wilberforce in *Zamir v Secretary of State for the Home Department* [1980] AC 930 at 947 (concurred in by all the other noble Lords). . . .

Counsel for the appellant Khera challenges this principle. He submits that the only resident non-patrial who can be removed summarily as an illegal entrant is one who, having entered clandestinely, has never passed through immigration control and has thus succeeded in entering without the grant of any leave whatever.

If it is desired to expel one who has obtained leave to enter by fraud, this, says counsel for the appellant Khera, can be achieved in one of two ways, viz (i) by securing a conviction coupled with a recommendation for deportation under s. 26(1)(*c*) by which a person is guilty of an offence punishable with a fine or imprisonment if 'he makes or causes to be made to an immigration officer or other person lawfully acting in the execution of this Act a return, statement or representation which he knows to be false or does not believe to be true' or (ii) by deportation under s. 3(5)(*b*) on the ground that the Secretary of State deems his deportation to be conducive to the public good. Both these procedures, counsel points out, incorporate suitable safeguards for the person alleged to have entered by fraud. In the one case he has his full rights, including appellate rights, as a defendant in criminal proceedings. In the other he has his rights of appeal to the appellate authorities under the 1971 Act. These are contrasted with the right of appeal given by s. 16, which, being exercisable only after the appellant has left the country, is virtually valueless. We were indeed told by counsel for the Secretary of State in the course of argument that only one s. 16 appeal has ever succeeded.

I see great force in the contention that the illegal entrant proposed to be removed by the summary procedure requires the protection of some effective judicial process before the removal. But I shall return to this when considering the second main question raised by these appeals, to which, in my view, it is primarily relevant. I do not find it persuasive in considering who is an illegal entrant. On the contrary, if the only procedures available to secure the expulsion of a non-patrial who has obtained leave to enter by fraud are those suggested by counsel for the appellant Khera, it seems to me that there is a startling lacuna in the Act. A conviction under s. 26(1)(*c*) would not necessarily lead to a recommendation for deportation; moreover, being a summary offence, it must normally be prosecuted within six months of commission, though, exceptionally, this time limit may be extended to a maximum of three years (see s. 28). Those who have obtained leave to enter by fraud are frequently not exposed until after three years from their arrival. On the other hand, the power given to the Secretary of State to deem deportation to be conducive to the public good seems to me to be intended for cases where the continued presence of the deportee would be objectionable on some positive and specific ground. The examples given in s. 15(3), 'that his deportation is conducive to the public good as being in the interests of national security or of the relations between the United Kingdom and any other country or for other reasons of a political nature', although clearly not exhaustive, nevertheless illustrate the kind of objection contemplated. I cannot suppose that this power was ever intended to be invoked as a means of deporting a perfectly respectable established resident on the grounds arising from the circumstances of his original entry. On the other hand, no one has suggested in argument that a non-patrial who has obtained leave to enter by fraud should not be liable to expulsion when the fraud is exposed, nor doubted that one would expect the Act to provide for such a case. That provision, I conclude, has to be found, if anywhere in the statutory machinery for the removal of an illegal entrant.[1]

Despite the wealth of authority on the subject, there is nowhere to be found in the relevant judgments (perhaps because none was thought necessary) a definitive exposition of the reasons why a person who has obtained leave to enter by fraud is an illegal entrant.

My Lords, . . . the question whether a person who has obtained leave to enter by fraud 'has entered in breach of the Act' is purely one of construction. If the fraud was a contravention of s. 26(1)(*c*) of the Act, the provisions of which I have already quoted, and if that fraud was the effective means of obtaining leave to enter, in other words, if but for the fraud, leave to enter would not have been granted, then the contravention of the Act and the obtaining of leave to enter were the two inseparable elements of the single process of entry and it must inevitably follow that the entry itself was 'in breach of the Act'.

It remains to consider some of the implications of the principle stated in the foregoing paragraph. First, it is clear that a *mere* non-disclosure to the immigration officer by the person seeking permission to enter of a fact known to him cannot, by itself, amount to a contravention of s. 26(1)(*c*). In so far as the passage in the speech of Lord Wilberforce in *Zamir* [1980] AC 930 at 950 may be understood as imposing on an applicant for leave to enter a duty of candour approximating to uberrima fides the breach of which would have the same effect as fraud, it cannot, I think, be accepted. If intended in that sense, it was obiter, was not supported in the present case by counsel for the Secretary of State and, as I understand, does not now find favour with my noble and learned friend Lord Wilberforce himself. On the other hand, as Lord Wilberforce said in *Zamir*: 'It is clear on general principles of law that deception may arise from conduct, or from conduct accompanied by silence as to a material fact.' The relevant words of s. 26(1)(*c*), 'a statement or representation which he knows to be false or does not believe to be true', embodying as they do the classic definition of a fraudulent deception, are amply wide enough to allow for the operation of this salutary principle.

Finally, I would wish to leave for consideration on a future occasion the difficult questions that may arise when leave to enter has been obtained by the fraud of a third party, but the person entering had no knowledge of the fraud. I am not convinced that *Khan v Secretary of State for the Home Dept* [1977] 1 WLR 1466, where it was held that the innocent wife who obtained leave to enter on a false passport procured for her by her husband was an illegal entrant, was rightly decided. In such cases the proper

---

1 *Ed*. Note that Lord Bridge has subsequently held s. 3(5)(b) not to be of such limited effect—see *Patel v IAT*, above, p. 723.

conclusion may depend on a variety of circumstances and I think it safer to express no present view but to leave such cases to be decided as they arise.[1]

The court's power to review a decision to detain and remove an illegal entrant

The 1971 Act provides by s. 4(2):

'The provisions of Schedule 2 to this Act shall have effect with respect to . . . (c) the exercise by immigration officers of their powers in relation to entry into the United Kingdom, and the removal from the United Kingdom of persons refused leave to enter or entering or remaining unlawfully . . .'

The vital provisions [of Schedule 2] for present purposes are the following:

'9. Where an illegal entrant is not given leave to enter or remain in the United Kingdom, an immigration officer may give any such directions in respect of him as in a case within paragraph 8 above are authorised by para. 8(1) . . .

16 . . . (2) A person in respect of whom directions may be given under any of paragraphs 8 to 14 above may be detained under the authority of an immigration officer pending the giving of directions and pending his removal in pursuance of any directions given . . .'

Here again the authorities from *R v Secretary of State for the Home Dept, ex p Hussain* to *Zamir* have consistently affirmed the principle that the decision of an immigration officer to detain and remove a person as an illegal entrant under these provisions can only be attacked successfully on the ground that there was no evidence on which the immigration officer could reasonably conclude that he was an illegal entrant.

It will be seen at once that this principle gives to an executive officer, subject no doubt, in reaching his conclusions of fact to a duty to act fairly a draconian power of arrest and expulsion based on his own decision of fact which, if there was any evidence to support it, cannot be examined by any judicial process until after it has been acted on and then in circumstances where the person removed, being unable to attend the hearing of his appeal, has no realistic prospect of prosecuting it with success. It will be further observed that to justify the principle important words have to be read into para. 9 of Sch. 2 by implication. That paragraph, on the face of the language used, authorises the removal of a person who is an illegal entrant. The courts have applied it as if it authorised the removal of a person whom an immigration officer on reasonable grounds believes to be an illegal entrant. The all-important question is whether such an implication can be justified.

My Lords, we should, I submit, regard with extreme jealousy any claim by the executive to imprison a citizen without trial and allow it only if it is clearly justified by the statutory language relied on. The fact that, in the case we are considering, detention is preliminary and incidental to expulsion from the country in my view strengthens rather than weakens the case for a robust exercise of the judicial function in safeguarding the citizen's rights.

So far as I know, no case before the decisions under the Act which we are presently considering has held imprisonment without trial by executive order to be justified by anything less than the plainest statutory language, with the sole exception of the majority decision of your Lordships' House in *Liversidge v Anderson* [1942] AC 206. No one needs to be reminded of the now celebrated dissenting speech of Lord Atkin in that case, or of his withering condemnation of the process of writing into the statutory language there under consideration the words which were necessary to sustain the decision of the majority. Lord Atkin's dissent now has the approval of your Lordships' House in *IRC v Rossminster Ltd* [1980] AC 952.

A person who has entered the United Kingdom without leave and who is detained under Sch. 2, para. 16(2) pending removal as an illegal entrant on the ground that he obtained leave to enter by fraud is entitled to challenge the action taken and proposed to be taken against him both by application for habeas corpus and by application for judicial review. On the view I take, para. 9 of Sch. 2 must be construed as meaning no more and no less than it says. There is no room for any implication qualifying the words 'illegal entrant'. From this it would follow that, while, prima facie, the order for detention under para. 16(2) would be a sufficient return to the writ of habeas corpus, proof by the applicant that he had been granted leave to enter would shift the onus back to the immigration officer to prove that the leave had been obtained in contravention of s. 26(1)(c) of the Act, in other words by fraud.

The question about which I have felt most difficulty concerns the standard of proof required to discharge that onus. I was at first inclined to regard the judgment of Lord Parker CJ in *Ahson's* case as sufficient authority for the proposition that proof is required beyond reasonable doubt. But I have been

---

1   *Ed.* Cf. the words of Woolf LJ in *R v Secretary of State for the Home Department, ex p Miah* [1990] 2 All ER 523 at 530, CA, speaking of the *Khan* case: 'I can see considerable force in the logic of the judgment of Megaw LJ in that case'. Note also *R v Secretary of State for the Home Department, ex p Khan* [1990] 2 All ER 531, CA; *R v Secretary of State for the Home Department, ex p Salim* [1990] Imm AR 316, QBD; *R v Immigration Officer, ex p Chan* [1992] 1 WLR 541 and *Hamid v Secretary of State for the Home Department* [1993] Imm AR 216.

persuaded by the reasoning on this point in the speech of my noble and learned friend Lord Scarman and by the authorities which he cites that that proposition cannot be sustained. These have led me to the conclusion that the civil standard of proof by a preponderance of probability will suffice, always provided that, in view of the gravity of the charge of fraud which has to be made out and of the consequences which will follow if it is, the court should not be satisfied with anything less than probability of a high degree. I would add that the inherent difficulties of discovering and proving the true facts in many immigration cases can afford no valid ground for lowering or relaxing the standard of proof required. If unlimited leave to enter was granted perhaps years before and the essential facts relied on to establish the fraud alleged can only be proved by documentary and affidavit evidence of past events which occurred in some remote part of the Indian subcontinent, the courts should be less, rather than more, ready to accept anything short of convincing proof. On the other hand it must be accepted that proof to the appropriate standard can, and in the vast majority of cases will, be provided, in accordance with the established practice of the Divisional Court, by affidavit evidence alone. I understand all your Lordships to be agreed that nothing said in the present case should be construed as a charter to alleged illegal entrants who challenge their detention and proposed removal to demand the attendance of deponents to affidavits for cross-examination. Whether to permit cross-examination will remain a matter for the court in its discretion to decide. It may be that the express discretion conferred on the court to permit cross-examination by the new procedure for judicial review under RSC Ord 53 has been too sparingly exercised when deponents could readily attend court. But, however that may be, the discretion to allow cross-examination should only be exercised when justice so demands. The cases will be rare when it will be essential, in the interests of justice, to require the attendance for cross-examination of a deponent from overseas. If the alleged illegal entrant applying for habeas corpus, certiorari or both files an affidavit putting in issue the primary facts alleged against him he will himself be readily available for cross-examination, which should enable the court in the great majority of cases to decide whether or not he is a witness of truth. If he is believed, he will succeed in his application. If he is disbelieved, there will be nothing to stop the court relying on affidavit evidence, provided it is inherently credible and convincing, to prove the fraud alleged against him, even though it has not been tested by cross-examination.

The instant appeals

In the case of Khera it is sufficient to say that the evidence fails to prove that the appellant's leave to enter was obtained by any kind of fraud or deception. The appellant Khawaja, on arrival at Manchester Airport on 17 March 1980, told the immigration officer that he was visiting the United Kingdom for one week to see a cousin, that he would then return to Brussels, and he showed the officer a return ticket dated 23 March 1980. He was given leave to enter for one month. The surrounding circumstances, fully disclosed in the evidence, lead to the irresistible inference that what he told the officer was a deliberate lie. The appellant had travelled from Brussels to Manchester with a lady who had the right to reside in the United Kingdom with whom he had already gone through a bigamous ceremony of marriage. They entered through different desks at immigration control to conceal the connection between them. The lady's previous marriage was dissolved on 3 April. The appellant married her on 10 April. Having applied on 11 April for an extension of his temporary leave to remain, without disclosing the marriage, he made a further application on 29 April for indefinite leave to remain as the husband of the lady entitled to reside here. It was perfectly clear that the appellant's intention from the outset was to settle in the United Kingdom with his wife. He may or may not have believed, erroneously, that the marriage would entitle him to leave to settle here, but that is immaterial. His blatant lie to the immigration officer as to his intention was a contravention of s. 26(1)(*c*) of the 1971 Act. If he had disclosed his true intention, he would not have been granted leave to enter. In this case the evidence clearly proves that the appellant was an illegal entrant. My Lords, I would allow the appeal of Khera and dismiss the appeal of Khawaja.

Lords Fraser of Tullybelton, Wilberforce, Scarman and **Templeman** delivered concurring speeches.

NOTES

1. In *Zamir* the House of Lords had held that the entrants owed a positive duty to disclose information known to be material to the immigration officer's decision. Breach of the duty rendered such persons 'illegal entrants'. It is doubtful whether the principle extended to entrants who failed to disclose material information but who did not appreciate that the information was material to the entry decision. See Lord Wilberforce's speech – [1980] AC 930 at 940. The Home Office appears to have taken a stricter view of the decision, regarding as excused only those whose failure to realise the material nature of their non-disclosure was reasonable. See J. M. Evans, *Immigration Law* (2nd edn, 1983, p. 323, note 37). Since *Khawaja* the position would appear to be as follows:

(1) There is a duty not to make positive statements known to be false or not believed to be true. It seems to be necessary to show that the false statement was a material factor in securing entry (though note that there seems to be no such limit to the scope of the criminal offence under s. 26). See *R v Secretary of State for the Home Department, ex p Jayakody* [1982] 1 WLR 405; *R v Secretary of State for the Home Department, ex p Pembe Unal* [1983] Imm AR 182. If such a material misstatement is made it matters not that the entrant might have been successful in obtaining entry had he told only the truth and applied for entry under some different ground – e.g. asylum. See *R v Secretary of State for the Home Department, ex p Bugdaycay* [1986] 1 All ER 458 at 464–5, CA; *R v Secretary of State for the Home Department, ex p Saichon Chomsuk* [1991] Imm AR 29, 32 QBD. The fact that an entrant did not realise that his lie was material to his securing entry may also not prevent him being an illegal entrant. In *Khawaja* itself the appellant, their Lordships considered, may not have realised that he would not have been admitted entry had he not lied about his intent only to visit temporarily – see the final words of Lord Bridge's speech. See also *R v Secretary of State for the Home Department, ex p Adesina* [1988] Imm AR 288, QBD.

(2) An obligation of disclosure exists where a positive representation though not untrue in itself will mislead the immigration (or entry clearance) officer unless further information is provided. For example, where a change of status or circumstances has taken place since the date of a document which has been presented. Again, the matter in issue must be material to the entry decision and, in this situation, it seems that it must be shown that the entrant appreciated the materiality of the matter.

(3) In other situations, where non-disclosure does not render misleading that which has been disclosed, there is no duty of disclosure. The onus is on the immigration and entry clearance officers to seek out by their questions positive statements about the matters which are material to their decisions. For failure to correct a statement made by somebody else, see *R v Secretary of State for the Home Department, ex p Dordas* [1992] Imm AR 99.

These principles were clearly stated in the speech of Lord Scarman [1984] AC 74 at 107:

'It is certainly an entrant's duty to answer truthfully the questions put to him and to provide such information as is required of him (see Sch. 2, para. 4). But the Act goes no further. He may, or may not, know what facts are material. The immigration officer does, or ought to, know the matters relevant to the decision he has to make. Immigration control is, no doubt, an important safeguard for our society. Parliament has entrusted the control to immigration officers and the Secretary of State (see s. 4). To allow officers to rely on an entrant honouring a duty of positive candour, by which is meant a duty to volunteer relevant information, would seem perhaps a disingenuous approach to the administration of control: some might think it conducive to slack rather than to "sensitive" administration (see *Zamir* [1980] AC 930 at 950). The 1971 Act does impose a duty not to deceive the immigration officer. It makes no express provision for any higher or more comprehensive duty; nor is it possible, in my view, to imply any such duty. Accordingly, I reject the view that there is a duty of positive candour imposed by the immigration laws and that mere non-disclosure by an entrant of material facts in the absence of fraud is a breach of the immigration laws.'

(4) There may be positive statements *implicit* in other actions. Thus, the presentation of a passport and entry clearance to enter as a 'visitor' may constitute a false representation as to the absence of intention to remain beyond such short period. See *Patel v Secretary of State for the Home Department* [1986] Imm AR 515, CA;

and note *R v Secretary of State for the Home Department, ex p Olasebikan* [1986] Imm AR 337, QBD; *R v Immigration Appeal Tribunal, ex p Kasim* [1986] Imm AR 428, QBD; *Adesina v Secretary of State for the Home Department* [1988] Imm AR 442; *R v Secretary of State for the Home Department, ex p Chomsuk* [1991] Imm AR 29; *Mokuolo v Secretary of State for the Home Department* [1989] Imm AR 51. Contrast *R v Secretary of State for the Home Department, ex p Ku* [1995] 2 WLR 589.

2. In *Ali v Secretary of State for the Home Department* [1984] 1 All ER 1009, the applicant appealed against the dismissal by Webster J, at first instance, of his application for judicial review to quash the Home Secretary's decision that he was an illegal entrant. The issue was as to the true identity of the applicant. If he was Momin, son of Cherig Ali, he was lawfully present in the UK. If he was Fozlu, son of Roquib Ali, he was an illegal entrant. After his arrival in the UK the Home Office received anonymous information that the applicant was Fozlu, as the authorities had originally believed prior to an adjudicator's decision to the contrary. Investigations ensued both in the UK and also in India, at Cherig Ali's former village. The investigation produced evidence which gave rise to 'serious doubts' as to whether the applicant was Momin. In the Court of Appeal it was held that, since the decision in *Khawaja*, the onus of proof that the person to be removed was an illegal entrant rested on the Secretary of State, and that the burden of proof was 'that appropriate to an allegation of a serious character and . . . involving the liberty of the subject'. Moreover, in this case there had earlier been an adjudicator's decision that the applicant was Momin. The proper approach for the reviewing court (following *R v Secretary of State for the Home Department, ex p Miah* [1983] Imm AR 91) was to accept that decision of the adjudicator as correct unless the Home Office could prove to a standard appropriate to such an allegation that fraud had been practised on the adjudicator. 'That decision may not render the issue of his status res judicata, but it comes very close to it' (per Sir John Donaldson MR at p. 1015). The 'serious doubts' raised by the evidence were 'quite insufficient' to warrant a finding of fraud on the part of the applicant. In determining the various questions the reviewing court should have regard to all evidence presently available: it should not confine itself to the evidence available to the Secretary of State for the Home Department at the time of his decision: *R v Secretary of State for the Home Department, ex p Mahoney* [1992] Imm AR 275 and *R v Secretary of State for the Home Department, ex p Muse* [1992] Imm AR 282.

8 Appeals

(a) APPEALS AGAINST REFUSALS OF ENTRY, REFUSALS OF CERTIFICATES OF ENTITLEMENT, REFUSALS OF ENTRY CLEARANCES

Immigration Act 1971

13.—(1) Subject to the provisions of this Part of this Act, a person who is refused leave to enter the United Kingdom under this Act may appeal to an adjudicator against the decision that he requires leave or against the refusal.

(2) Subject to the provisions of this Part of this Act, a person who, on an application duly made, is refused a [certificate of entitlement]¹ or an entry clearance may appeal to an adjudicator against the refusal.

(3) [A person shall not be entitled to appeal, on the ground that he has a right of abode in the United Kingdom, against a decision that he requires leave to enter the United Kingdom, unless he holds such a passport or certificate as is mentioned in section 3(a) above]² and a person shall not be entitled to appeal

1 Words in brackets substituted by the British Nationality Act 1981, s. 39(6), Sch. 4, para. 3(1).
2 Words in brackets substituted by the Immigration Act 1988, s. 3(2).

against a refusal of leave to enter so long as he is in the United Kingdom, unless he was refused leave at a port of entry and at a time when he held a current entry clearance or was a person named in a current work permit.

(3A) A person who seeks to enter the United Kingdom—

   (*a*) as a visitor, or

   (*b*) in order to follow a course of study of not more than six months duration for which he has been accepted, or

   (*c*) with the intention of studying but without having been accepted for any course of study, or

   (*d*) as a dependent of a person within paragraph (a), (b) or (c) above,

shall not be entitled to appeal against refusal of an entry clearance and shall not be entitled to appeal against a refusal of leave to enter unless he held a current entry clearance at the time of refusal.

(3AA) The Secretary of State shall appoint a person, not being an officer of his, to monitor, in such cases as the Secretary of State shall determine, refusals of entry clearance in cases where there is, by virtue of subsection (3A) above, no right of appeal; and the person so appointed shall make an annual report on the discharge of his functions to the Secretary of State who shall lay a copy of it before each House of Parliament.

(3B) A person shall not be entitled to appeal against a refusal of an entry clearance if the refusal is on the ground that—

   (*a*) he or any person whose dependent he is does not hold a relevant document which is required by the immigration rules; or

   (*b*) he or any person whose dependent he is does not satisfy a requirement of the immigration rules as to age or nationality or citizenship; or

   (*c*) he or any person whose dependent he is seeks entry for a period exceeding that permitted by the immigration rules;

and a person shall not be entitled to appeal against a refusal of leave to enter if the refusal is on any of those grounds.

(3C) For the purposes of subsection (3B)(a) above, the following are 'relevant documents'—

   (*a*) entry clearances

   (*b*) passports and other identity documents

   (*c*) work permits.

(4) An appeal against a refusal of leave to enter shall be dismissed by the adjudicator if he is satisfied that the appellant was at the time of the refusal an illegal entrant, and an appeal against a refusal of entry clearance shall be dismissed by the adjudicator if he is satisfied that a deportation order was at the time of the refusal in force in respect of the appellant.

(5) A person shall not be entitled to appeal against a refusal of leave to enter, or against a refusal of an entry clearance, if the Secretary of State certifies that directions have been given by the Secretary of State (and not by a person acting under his authority) for the appellant not to be given entry to the United Kingdom on the ground that his exclusion is conducive to the public good, or if the leave to enter or entry clearance was refused in obedience to any such directions.

NOTE

Subsections (3A), (3AA) and (3B) were added by ss. 10 and 11 of the Asylum and Immigration Appeals Act 1993. Subsection (3A) abolishes rights of appeal of visitors, short-term students and persons wishing to enter to study but who have not yet obtained places on any course. The explanation given for withdrawal of such rights was the backlog of immigration appeals and the need to target resources on the more important appeals: ones which have a more fundamental impact on the individuals concerned. Note that there may remain the opportunity to challenge a decision by way of judicial review, albeit on the more limited grounds which may found such an application.

Subsection (3B) also removes previously established rights of appeal. Controversially the removal is based upon the grounds given for refusal of an entry clearance. The justification given for the withdrawal of appeal rights is that such persons are bound under the rules to be refused entry clearance (i.e. cases where refusal is, under the rules, mandatory). However, such persons are only 'bound' to be refused an entry clearance if the understandings of fact held by entry clearance officers are correct. It is disputes as to such issues of fact (e.g. as regards an applicant's age) that formed a valuable basis for the previous rights of appeal.

(b) APPEALS AGAINST VARIATIONS OF LEAVE, AND AGAINST REFUSALS TO VARY LEAVE

Immigration Act 1971

14.—(1) Subject to the provisions of this Part of this Act, a person who has a limited leave under this Act to enter or remain in the United Kingdom may appeal to an adjudicator against any variation of the leave (whether as regards duration or conditions), or against any refusal to vary it; and a variation shall not take effect so long as an appeal is pending under this subsection against the variation, nor shall any appellant be required to leave the United Kingdom by reason of the expiration of his leave so long as his appeal is pending under this subsection against a refusal to enlarge or remove the limit on the duration of the leave.

(3) A person shall not be entitled to appeal under subsection (1) above against any variation of his leave which reduces its duration, or against any refusal to enlarge or remove the limit of its duration, if the Secretary of State certifies that the appellant's departure from the United Kingdom would be conducive to the public good, as being in the interests of national security or of the relations between the United Kingdom and any other country or for any other reasons of a political nature, or the decision questioned by the appeal was taken on that ground by the Secretary of State (and not by a person acting under his authority). . . .

(5) Where a deportation order is made against a person any pending appeal by that person under subsection (1) shall lapse.[1]

NOTE

In an appeal under section 14 of the 1971 Act an appellant is not restricted to challenging the Secretary of State's decision not to vary leave to enter on the grounds of misconstruction or misapplication of the *post*-entry Immigration Rules. The appellant may appeal on the ground that 'his entry permit was subject to conditions which could not be justified under the terms of the pre-entry Rules and . . . that the Secretary of State has refused to put the matter right' (per Sir John Donaldson MR in *R v Immigration Appeal Tribunal, ex p Coomasaru* [1983] 1 WLR 14).

(c) ASYLUM APPEALS

Asylum and Immigration Appeals Act 1993

8.—(1) A person who is refused leave to enter the United Kingdom under the 1971 Act may appeal against the refusal to a special adjudicator on the ground that his removal in consequence of the refusal would be contrary to the United Kingdom's obligations under the Convention.

(2) A person who has limited leave under the 1971 Act to enter or remain in the United Kingdom may appeal to a special adjudicator against any variation of, or refusal to vary, the leave on the ground that it would be contrary to the United Kingdom's obligations under the Convention for him to be required to leave the United Kingdom after the time limited by the leave.

(3) Where the Secretary of State—

(a) has decided to make a deportation order against a person by virtue of section 3(5) of the 1971 Act, or

(b) has refused to revoke a deportation order made against a person by virtue of section 3(5) or (6) of that Act,

the person may appeal to a special adjudicator against the decision or refusal on the ground that his removal in pursuance of the order would be contrary to the United Kingdom's obligations under the

1 Added by Immigration Act 1988, Sch.

Convention; but a person may not bring an appeal under both paragraphs (*a*) and paragraph (*b*) above.
(4) Where directions are given as mentioned in section 16(1)(*a*) or (*b*) of the 1971 Act for a person's removal from the United Kingdom, the person may appeal to a special adjudicator against the directions on the ground that his removal in pursuance of the directions would be contrary to the United Kingdom's obligations under the Convention.

NOTE

This section provides for the first time a right of appeal, prior to removal, for asylum seekers refused entry at their port of arrival. It also permits an appeal on grounds of asylum against the exercise by the Secretary of State of his powers of deportation following recommendation by a criminal court (as to which lacuna, see *R v Immigration Appeal Tribunal, ex p Murugunandarajah* [1986] Imm AR 382. For procedure see the Asylum Appeals (Procedure) Rules 1993 (S.I. 1993 No. 1661).

(d) APPEALS AGAINST DEPORTATION DECISIONS

Immigration Act 1971

15.—(1) Subject to the provisions of this Part of this Act, a person may appeal to an adjudicator against—
   (*a*) a decision of the Secretary of State to make a deportation order against him by virtue of section 3(5) above; or
   (*b*) a refusal by the Secretary of State to revoke a deportation order made against him.
(3) A person shall not be entitled to appeal against a decision to make a deportation order against him if the ground of the decision was that his deportation is conducive to the public good as being in the interests of national security or of the relations between the United Kingdom and any other country or for other reasons of a political nature.
(4) A person shall not be entitled to appeal under this section against a refusal to revoke a deportation order, if the Secretary of State certifies that the appellant's exclusion from the United Kingdom is conducive to the public good or if revocation was refused on that ground by the Secretary of State (and not by a person acting under his authority).
(5) A person shall not be entitled to appeal under this section against a refusal to revoke a deportation order so long as he is in the United Kingdom, whether because he has not complied with the requirement to leave or because he has contravened the prohibition on entering.
(6) On an appeal against a decision to make a deportation order against a person as belonging to the family of another person, or an appeal against a refusal to revoke a deportation order so made, the appellant shall not be allowed, for the purpose of showing that he does not or did not belong to another person's family, to dispute any statement made with a view to obtaining leave for the appellant to enter or remain in the United Kingdom (including any statement made to obtain an entry clearance) unless the appellant shows that the statement was not so made by him or by any person acting with his authority and that, when he took the benefit of the leave, he did not know that any such statement had been made to obtain it or, if he did know, was under the age of eighteen.
(7) An appeal under this section shall be to the Appeal Tribunal in the first instance, instead of to an adjudicator, if
   (*a*) it is an appeal against a decision to make a deportation order and the ground of the decision was that the deportation of the appellant is conducive to the public good; or
   (*b*) it is an appeal against a decision to make a deportation order against a person as belonging to the family of another person, or an appeal against a refusal to revoke a deportation order so made; or
   (*c*) there is pending a related appeal to which paragraph (*b*) above applies.
(8) Where an appeal to an adjudicator is pending under this section, and before the adjudicator has begun to hear it a related appeal is brought, the appeal to the adjudicator shall be dealt with instead by the Appeal Tribunal and be treated as an appeal duly made to the Tribunal in the first instance.
(9) In relation to an appeal under this section in respect of a deportation order against any person (whether an appeal against a decision to make or against a refusal to revoke the order), any other appeal under this section is a 'related appeal' if it is an appeal in respect of a deportation order against another person as belonging to the family of the first-mentioned person.

Immigration Rules 1994

DEPORTATION

Right of appeal against destination

369. In all cases of deportation the person in respect of whom the order has been or is to be made has a right of appeal against the removal directions on the ground that he ought to be removed (if at all) to a country or territory specified by him, other than the one named in the direction (Section 17 of the 1971 Act).

Restricted right of appeal against deportation in cases of breach of limited leave

370. By virtue of Section 5(1) of the Immigration Act 1988, a person who was last given leave to enter the United Kingdom less than 7 years before the date of the decision to make a deportation order against him:
(i) by virtue of Section 3(5)(a) of the Immigration Act 1971 (breach of limited leave); or
(ii) by virtue of Section 3(5)(c) of that Act (as belonging to the family of a person who is or has been ordered to be deported by virtue of Section 3(5)(a))
shall not be entitled to appeal under Section 15 of the 1971 Act against that decision except on the ground that on the facts of his case there is in law no power to make the deportation order for the reasons stated in the notice of the decision.

A deportation order made on the recommendation of a court

373. There is no appeal within the immigration appeal system against the making of a deportation order on the recommendation of a court; but there is a right of appeal to a higher court against the recommendation itself. An order may not be made while it is still open to the person to appeal against the relevant conviction, sentence or recommendation, or while an appeal is pending.

Where deportation is deemed to be conducive to the public good

374. There is no right of appeal except as to the country of destination (see paragraph 369) where a deportation order is made on the ground that the Secretary of State deems the person's deportation to be conducive to the public good as being in the interests of national security or of the relations between the United Kingdom and any other country or for other reasons of a political nature. Such cases are subject to a non-statutory advisory procedure and the person proposed to be deported on that ground will be informed, so far as possible, of the nature of the allegations against him and will be given the opportunity to appear before the advisers, and to make representations to them, before they tender advice to the Secretary of State.

375. Where it is proposed to deport a person because it is deemed that his expulsion will be conducive to the public good on *other* than security or political grounds there is a right of appeal, under Section 15 of the 1971 Act, direct to the Immigration Appeal Tribunal.

Persons who have claimed asylum

379. In addition to the rights of appeal mentioned above, except where the ground of the decision to make a deportation order is that it is conducive to the public good and is certified by the Secretary of State as being in the interests of national security, a person who has claimed asylum may also appeal under Section 8 of the Asylum and Immigration Appeals Act 1993 against:
(i) a decision to make a deportation order against him by virtue of Section 3(5) of the 1971 Act; or
(ii) a refusal to revoke a deportation order made against him by virtue of Section 3(5) or (6) of the 1971 Act; or
(iii) directions for his removal from the United Kingdom given under Section 16(1)(a) or (b) of the 1971 Act. In such circumstances the appeal will be before a special adjudicator who will also consider any appeal under Part II of the 1971 Act.

380. A deportation order will not be made against any person if his removal in pursuance of the order would be contrary to the United Kingdom's obligations under the Convention and Protocol relating to the Status of Refugees.

Procedure

381. When a decision to make a deportation order has been taken (otherwise than on the recommendation of a court) a notice will be given to the person concerned informing him of the decision and of his

right of appeal, or facility to make representations in the case of the security and political cases subject to the advisory procedure.

382. Following the issue of such a notice the Secretary of State may make a detention order, or any order restricting a person as to residence, employment or occupation and requiring him to report to the police, pending the making of a deportation order.

383. Where a person is detained pending an appeal, he may apply to an adjudicator for release on bail.

384. If a notice of appeal is given within the period allowed, a summary of the facts of the case on the basis of which the decision was taken will be sent to the appellate authorities, who will notify the appellant of the arrangements for the appeal to be heard.

Rights of appeal in relation to a decision not to revoke a deportation order

393. Where an application for revocation is refused there is a right of appeal, in the first instance to an adjudicator, unless the order was made against a person as belonging to the family of another person in which case it lies to the Tribunal.

394. No appeal lies while the person is in the United Kingdom or where the Secretary of State personally decides that continued exclusion from the United Kingdom is conducive to the public good.

395. Where an appeal does lie the right of appeal will be notified at the same time as the decision to refuse to revoke the order.

NOTE

Note that except as provided in ss. 13–17 no rights of appeal exist against decisions taken in the context of immigration and deportation. Thus, there is no right of appeal against decisions in respect of work permits; nor the refusal to issue a Special Voucher to a BOC – see *Amin v Entry Clearance Officer, Bombay* [1983] 2 AC 818.

The provisions above also demonstrate the denial in specific situations of any right of appeal in respect of decisions from which normally a right of appeal does lie; for example, against deportation decisions where the ground for deportation is that of having been convicted of a criminal offence, the court having recommended such deportation. Appeal rights here are restricted to the right of appeal against sentence imposed by the criminal court – the recommendation being part of the sentence. Such appeal will take place at the time of conviction. No further right of appeal exists at the time of exercise of the power to deport. This may be some time later, perhaps following completion of a penalty of imprisonment. Note, however, that the Home Office has accepted that where such a convicted person indicates a wish to argue against deportation on 'asylum' grounds, it should proceed under s. 3(5)(b) instead – thereby giving that person opportunity to appeal.

Equally, where a decision to deport (or to refuse leave to remain) is stated to have been taken for reasons of 'public good' and specifically on grounds of 'national security', 'diplomatic relations' or for 'reasons of a political nature' the ordinary right of appeal is excluded. Similarly, a person refused entry on grounds of public good (without anything more specific as to reason) has no right of appeal. See above ss. 15(5), 14(3), and 15(3), (4).

In the case of deportation decisions from which no statutory appeal lies, there exists instead, following government concessions during the passage of the 1971 Act through Parliament, an 'ex gratia' hearing before the Three Advisers. For these, see above p. 492. The ex gratia procedure was described by the then Home Secretary in the following words:

'. . . proceedings start with a personal decision by the Home Secretary. . . . The person concerned . . . will be given . . . such particulars of allegations as will not entail disclosure of sources of evidence. He will be notified that he can make representations to the three advisers. . . . The advisers will . . . allow him to appear before them, if he wishes. . . . As well as speaking for himself he may arrange for a third party to testify on his behalf. Neither the sources of evidence nor evidence that might lead to disclosure of sources can be revealed to the person concerned, but the advisers will ensure that the person is able to make his points effectively and . . . will give him the best opportunity to make the points he wishes to bring to their notice. . . . Since the evidence against a person necessarily has to be received in his absence, the advisers in assessing the case will bear in mind that it has not been tested by cross-exanmination and that the person has not had the opportunity to rebut it. . . . On receiving the advice of the advisers the Secretary of State will reconsider his original decision, but the advice given to him will not be revealed' (819 HC Deb Written Answer 15 June 1971 col 376).

A challenge to this procedure was brought by a journalist, Mark Hosenball, following such a hearing into the Home Secretary's intention to deport him on grounds of national security – *R v Secretary of State for the Home Department, ex p Hosenball* [1977] 3 All ER 452, CA. He argued that the deportation procedures had not complied with the principles of natural justice, in that he had not been given adequate particulars of the allegations against him. However, the Court of Appeal acknowledged that ordinarily the principles of natural justice require that persons should know what charges they face before being condemned, and should know what evidence there is against them so that they may seek to refute it. However, said the court, there are circumstances where national security is involved when 'our cherished freedoms have to take second place' and 'even natural justice itself may suffer a set-back' (per Lord Denning MR); and when 'the rights of the individual must be subordinated to the protection of the realm' (per Geoffrey Lane LJ). In such circumstances the balance between the interests of national security and the freedom of the individual, said Lord Denning, is for the Home Secretary to determine and not for the courts of law. See also, *NSH v Secretary of State for the Home Department* [1988] Imm AR 389, CA.

At the outset of hostilities in the Gulf War of 1991 the Home Office detained, pending deportation on the ground of threat to national security, some 160 Iraqis and Palestinians. The list, selected from the very much larger number of such citizens within the UK, had been drawn up by the police Special Branch and by MI5. Immediately, concern was expressed at the accuracy of the information upon which the list had been compiled. It included a respected author on Arab affairs whose writings and actions had displayed a sympathetic approach towards Israel; a businessman employing some 600 employees; a person who had lived in the UK for 21 years and who had been granted permanent residence only shortly before. Many had British wives and children. A habeas corpus challenge on the ground that the SSHD had failed sufficiently to state his reasons for his decision failed in *R v Secretary of State for the Home Department, ex p Cheblak* [1991] 2 All ER 319, CA. In due course the three advisers, sitting in Pentonville Prison, heard a considerable number of cases, the Home Secretary in late February 1991 taking the precautionary step of appointing two 'reserve' advisers. Following receipt of the advice of the advisers on the first dozen cases the Secretary of State for the Home Department ordered the release of five detainees. It is, of course, not known what advice the Secretary of State for the Home Department received from the advisers; in particular it is not known whether the Secretary of State for the Home Department followed their advice in all the cases. Note also, *R v Secretary of State for the Home Department, ex p Chahel* [1995] 1 WLR 526.

Critics of these procedures have drawn comparisons with procedures adopted in other contexts where it is necessary to protect sources of information (e.g. criminal prosecutions in espionage and terrorist cases). Such proceedings commonly will take place in camera and witnesses' identities may be withheld; but the accused will know with some particularity the charges that he faces, he is entitled to legal representation, his lawyer may cross-examine witnesses to test the evidence given, he will know what decision the court comes to, and that decision will not simply be a recommendation to a politician as to what action to take.

(e) APPEALS FROM THE IMMIGRATION APPEAL TRIBUNAL

Asylum and Immigration Appeals Act 1993

Appeals from Immigration Appeal Tribunal

9.—(1) Where the Immigration Appeal Tribunal has made a final determination of an appeal brought under Part II of the 1971 Act any party to the appeal may bring a further appeal to the appropriate appeal court on any question of law material to that determination.
(2) An appeal under this section may be brought only with the leave of the Immigration Appeal Tribunal or, if such leave is refused, with the leave of the appropriate appeal court.
(3) In this section 'the appropriate appeal court' means—
  (a) if the appeal is from the determination of an adjudicator or special adjudicator and that determination was made in Scotland, the Court of Session; and
  (b) in any other case, the Court of Appeal.

NOTE

This section provides a belated link-up between the immigration tribunal machinery and the courts of law: a linkage which is commonplace in other contexts of tribunal adjudication. It is hoped that the appeal rights may remove some burdens from the judicial review procedure. See further, the Immigration Appeals (Procedure) Rules 1993 (S.I. 1993 No. 1662).

(f) GROUNDS OF APPEAL

Immigration Act 1971

19.—(1) Subject to sections 13(4) and 16(4) above, and to any restriction on the grounds of appeal, an adjudicator on an appeal to him under this Part of this Act—
  (a) shall allow the appeal if he considers
    (i) that the decision or action against which the appeal is brought was not in accordance with the law or with any immigration rules applicable to the case; or
    (ii) where the decision or action involved the exercise of discretion by the Secretary of State or an officer, that the discretion should have been exercised differently; and
  (b) in any other case, shall dismiss the appeal.
(2) For the purposes of subsection (1)(a) above, the adjudicator may review any determination of a question of fact on which the decision or action was based; and for the purposes of subsection (1)(a)(ii) no decision or action which is in accordance with the immigration rules shall be treated as having involved the exercise of a discretion by the Secretary of State by reason only of the fact that he has been requested by or on behalf of the appellant to depart, or to authorise an officer to depart, from the rules and has refused to do so.
(3) Where an appeal is allowed, the adjudicator shall give such directions for giving effect to the determination as the adjudicator thinks requisite, and may also make recommendations with respect to any other action which the adjudicator considers should be taken in this case under this Act; and, . . . it shall be the duty of the Secretary of State and any officer to whom directions are given under this subsection to comply with them.

(4) Where in accordance with section 15 above a person appeals to the Appeal Tribunal in the first instance, this section shall apply with the substitution of references to the Tribunal for references to an adjudicator.

20.—(1) Subject to any requirement of rules of procedure as to leave to appeal, any party to an appeal to an adjudicator may, if dissatisfied with his determination thereon, appeal to the Appeal Tribunal, and the Tribunal may affirm the determination or make any other determination which could have been made by the adjudicator.

NOTES

1. In a number of cases certain limits to the functions of the adjudicators and the IAT have been stressed. Thus it has been held that on appeal against the decision of an entry clearance officer the function of the adjudicator and the IAT is to review the correctness of the officer's decision on the facts as they existed at the time of his decision. No evidence of changes of facts or circumstances may therefore be adduced in the appeal proceedings – see *R v Immigration Appeal Tribunal, ex p Kotecha* [1983] 2 All ER 289; and also *R v Immigration Appeal Tribunal, ex p Weerasuriya* [1983] 1 All ER 195; *R v Immigration Appeal Tribunal, ex p Bastiampillai* [1983] 2 All ER 844; *Patel v Secretary of State for the Home Department* [1983] Imm AR 187 (appeals from decisions of the Secretary of State). Contrast, the power to consider new ('fresh') evidence to show that the decision was taken on the basis of incorrect or incomplete findings of fact as they existed at the time of the decision. See *R v Immigration Appeal Tribunal, ex p Hassanin* [1987] 1 All ER 74, CA. Nevertheless, in the interests of finality in litigation the appellate body may be reluctant to admit such evidence except where the failure to adduce the evidence at the earlier stages was not due to any lack of reasonable diligence – see *Ali v Secretary of State for the Home Department* [1984] 1 All ER 1009.

2. A decision (or action taken) may be 'not in accordance with the law or an Immigration Rule applicable to the case' either because of misconstruction or misapplication of the law or Rule, or because of erroneous findings of fact. In the latter case the adjudicator or the Immigration Appeal Tribunal can hold that the decision was not, on the facts which should have been found, in accordance with the law or an Immigration Rule. Under s. 19(1)(a)(ii), appeals against the exercise of discretionary powers are appeals 'on the merits' – i.e. the adjudicator and the Immigration Appeal Tribunal should consider the matter de novo and reach their own decisions as to how the discretionary power ought to have been exercised. See *R v Peterkin, ex p Soni* [1972] Imm AR 253; *R v Immigration Appeal Tribunal, ex p Zaman* [1982] Imm AR 61; *R v Immigration Appeal Tribunal, ex p Husbadek* [1982] Imm AR 8; *R v Immigration Appeal Tribunal, ex p Hubbard* [1985] Imm AR 110.

Section 19 draws an apparently clear distinction between challenge for error of law or fact in relation to a decision reached on the basis of the law or the Rules, and challenging the exercise of discretion where neither the law nor the Rules dictate a particular decision but confer discretion. In fact the distinction is not a very clear one. Some Rules do state 'X shall be allowed (or not allowed) . . .' in particular (more or less clearly defined) circumstances – others state that X 'may' or 'may normally' be allowed. Some Rules confer discretions 'at large' – others indicate factors to be taken into account. Accordingly, the borderline between reaching a wrong decision on the basis of an Immigration Rule, and reaching a decision in the exercise of discretion which is different from the one the adjudicator or the IAT would have reached, is not clear-cut.

CHAPTER 12

The European Convention on Human Rights

1 Introduction

As well as being relevant to the interpretation of statutes and the development of the common law by British courts, see above, pp. 11–12, the ECHR also provides a remedy of its own at Strasbourg for 'victims' of a breach of the ECHR by the UK.[1] If a Bill of Rights were to be enacted in the UK, this international law remedy would continue in parallel with the remedy that would exist in the British courts. A large number of cases have been taken to Strasbourg against the UK.[2] The purpose of this chapter is to consider the substantive guarantee offered by the ECHR and to give some indication of the remedy provided.

The ECHR was drafted under the auspices of the Council of Europe, an international organisation now composed of 34 European states which was formed in 1949 as the result of the first post-war attempt at unifying Europe. The impetus for the ECHR came from the need to define more closely the obligations of members of the Council concerning 'human rights',[3] and, more generally, from the wish to provide a bulwark against communism and to prevent a recurrence of conditions which Europe had then recently witnessed. It was believed that the ECHR would serve as an alarm that would bring violations of human rights to the attention of the international community in time for it to take action to suppress them. In practice, this function of the ECHR, which imagines large-scale violations of human rights, has largely remained dormant.[4] The ECHR has instead been used primarily to raise questions of isolated weaknesses in legal systems that basically conform to its requirements and which are representative of the 'common heritage of political traditions, ideals, freedom and the rule of law' to which the Preamble to the

---

1 See on the ECHR generally, see R. Beddard, *Human Rights and Europe* (3rd edn 1993); J. E. S. Fawcett, *The Application of the European Convention on Human Rights* (2nd edn 1987); D. J. Harris, M. O'Boyle and C. Warbrick, *The Law of the European Convention on Human Rights* (1995); A. H. Robertson and J. Merrills, *Human Rights in Europe* (3rd edn 1993); P. Van Dijk and F. Van Hoof, *Theory and Practice of the European Convention on Human Rights* (2nd edn 1990).

2 For a survey of UK cases at Strasbourg, see A. Bradley, in W. Finnie, ed., *Edinburgh Essays in Public Law* (1991), p. 185.

3 See Arts. 1 and 3, Council of Europe Statute 1949, UKTS 51 (1949), Cmnd 7778: 87 UNTS 103.

4 It did apply in the *Greek* case, (1969) 12 YBECHR (The Greek case): CM resolution DH (70) 1. In 1967, the 'Regime of the Colonels', which had taken power by revolution, suspended the Greek Constitution and detained its opponents. State applications were brought against it by Denmark, the Netherlands, Norway and Sweden. The Committee of Ministers confirmed the opinion of the Commission that the Regime had tortured persons contrary to Article 3 and that breaches of nine other Articles of the Convention had occurred. Greece withdrew from the Council and denounced the Convention in 1970. Following the overthrow of the Colonels, Greece returned to the fold in 1974.

ECHR refers. Most commonly such questions have concerned the administration of justice, although the impact of the ECHR has by now been felt by states in many other areas. Important features of the approach of the European Court of Human Rights to its task are its emphasis upon the 'dynamic' character of the ECHR and its adoption of a teleological, or purpose-based, method of interpretation. As to the former, see the *Tyrer* case, below, p. 767. As to the latter, see the *Golder* case, below, p. 792.

The ECHR entered into force on 3 September 1953. There are 30 parties. They are Austria, Belgium, Bulgaria, Cyprus, Czech Republic, Denmark, Finland, France, Germany, Greece, Hungary, Iceland, Ireland, Italy, Liechtenstein, Luxembourg, Malta, the Netherlands, Norway, Poland, Portugal, Romania, San Marino, Slovakia, Slovenia, Spain, Sweden, Switzerland, Turkey and the UK. The Convention is open only to Council of Europe members. Andorra, Estonia, Latvia and Lithuania are the four members that are not yet parties. Ratification of the ECHR is a political condition of Council of Europe membership. An important recent development has been the ratification of the ECHR by new Council of Europe states in Central and Eastern Europe that were formerly parts of the USSR or under its influence.

The ECHR is concerned with civil and political rights. Economic and social rights are protected by another regional Council of Europe treaty – the 1961 European Social Charter,[1] which is enforced through the assessment of national reports by a Committee of Independent Experts in Strasbourg, but which does not have a system of petitions.

At a universal level, the UK is a party to the 1966 International Covenant on Civil and Political Rights[2] and the 1966 International Covenant on Economic, Social and Cultural Rights[3] and to other United Nations human rights treaties specific to particular rights.[4] The Civil and Political Rights Covenant is accompanied by a 1966 Optional Protocol[5] allowing a right of individual petition to an independent Human Rights Committee that meets in Geneva and New York. The UK is not one of the 77 states that have accepted the Protocol. As a result, the Civil and Political Rights Covenant, which protects, in some respects more extensively, the same range of rights as the ECHR, is, like the Economic, Social and Cultural Rights Covenant, enforceable vis à vis the UK only through the assessment of national reports.

The Strasbourg system of applications is a valuable adjunct to the possibilities provided under UK law for the protection of civil liberties, particularly in the absence of a Bill of Rights. The numbers of applications to Strasbourg would clearly decrease if, in the exhaustion of local remedies, one had first to go to a British court which would, under the private members' bills unsuccessfully put to Parliament, see above, p. 20, apply the ECHR.

---

1 UKTS 38 (1965), Cmnd 2643; 529 UNTS 89. In force 1965. There are 20 parties including the UK. See D. J. Harris, *The European Social Charter* (1984).
2 UKTS 6 (1977), Cmnd 6702; 999 UNTS 171. See D. McGoldrick, *The Human Rights Committee: its Role in the Development of the International Covenant on Civil and Political Rights* (1991) and M. Nowak, *UN Covenant on Civil and Political Rights: CCPR Commentary* (1993). On UK compliance with the ICCPR, see D.J. Harris and S.L. Joseph, eds, *The International Covenant on Civil and Political Rights and the UK* (1995).
3 UKTS 6 (1977), Cmnd 6702; 999 UNTS 3.
4 For a list of these to which the United Kingdom is a party, see above, p. 4, n. 6.
5 UKTS 6 (1977), Cmnd 6702; 999 UNTS 302. Optional rights of individual petition are also provided under the Racial Discrimination and Torture Conventions; the UK has yet to accept them.

European Convention on Human Rights 1950 Cmd. 8969

ARTICLE 1

The High Contracting Parties shall secure to everyone within their jurisdiction[1] the rights and freedoms in Section 1 of this Convention [Articles 2 to 18].

ARTICLE 2

1. Everyone's right to life shall be protected by law. No one shall be deprived of his life intentionally save in the execution of a sentence of a court following his conviction of a crime for which this penalty is provided by law.
2. Deprivation of life shall not be regarded as inflicted in contravention of this Article when it results from the use of force which is no more than absolutely necessary:
    (*a*) in defence of any person from unlawful violence;
    (*b*) in order to effect a lawful arrest or to prevent the escape of a person lawfully detained;
    (*c*) in action lawfully taken for the purpose of quelling a riot or insurrection.

ARTICLE 3

No one shall be subjected to torture or to inhuman or degrading treatment or punishment.

ARTICLE 4

1. No one shall be held in slavery or servitude.
2. No one shall be required to perform forced or compulsory labour.
3. For the purpose of this Article the term 'forced or compulsory labour' shall not include:
    (*a*) any work required to be done in the ordinary course of detention imposed according to the provisions of Article 5 of this Convention or during conditional release from such detention;
    (*b*) any service of a military character or, in case of conscientious objectors in countries where they are recognised, service exacted instead of compulsory military service;
    (*c*) any service exacted in case of an emergency or calamity threatening the life or well-being of the community;
    (*d*) any work or service which forms part of normal civic obligations.

ARTICLE 5

1. Everyone has the right to liberty and security of person. No one shall be deprived of his liberty save in the following cases and in accordance with a procedure prescribed by law:
    (*a*) the lawful detention of a person after conviction by a competent court;
    (*b*) the lawful arrest or detention of a person for non-compliance with the lawful order of a court or in order to secure the fulfilment of any obligation prescribed by law;
    (*c*) the lawful arrest or detention of a person effected for the purpose of bringing him before the competent legal authority on reasonable suspicion of having committed an offence or when it is reasonably considered necessary to prevent his committing an offence or fleeing after having done so;

6 *Ed.* The term 'jurisdiction' in Art. 1 was interpreted in *Loizidou v Turkey* E Ct HRR A 310 para 62 (1995), in which it was held that Turkey was responsible under the ECHR for the acts of its troops in the northern part of Cyprus following their invasion of that territory. The Court stated:

'. . . the Court recalls that . . . the concept of "jurisdiction" under this provision is not restricted to the national territory of the High Contracting Parties. According to its established case-law, for example, the Court has held that the extradition or expulsion by a Contracting State may give rise to an issue under Article 3, and hence engage the responsibility of that State under the Convention (see, the *Soering v UK* judgment [below, p. 758] . . .). In addition, the responsibility of Contracting Parties can be involved because of acts of their authorities, whether performed within or outside national boundaries, which produce effects outside their own territory (see the *Drozd and Janousek v France and Spain* judgment of 26 June 1992, Series A No. 240, p. 29, para 91).

Bearing in mind the object and purpose of the Convention, the responsibility of a Contracting Party may also arise when as a consequence of military action – whether lawful or unlawful – it exercises effective control of an area outside its national territory. The obligation to secure, in such an area, the rights and freedoms set out in the Convention, derives from the fact of such control whether it be exercised directly, through its armed forces, or through a subordinate local administration.'

A party may make a declaration extending the application of the ECHR to 'territories for whose international relations it is responsible': Art. 63(1). The UK has made such a declaration for the Isle of Man and the Channel Islands and for most of its overseas territories, including Gibraltar, but not Hong Kong.

(*d*) the detention of a minor by lawful order for the purpose of educational supervision or his lawful detention for the purpose of bringing him before the competent legal authority;

(*e*) the lawful detention of persons for the prevention of the spreading of infectious diseases, of persons of unsound mind, alcoholics or drug addicts or vagrants;

(*f*) the lawful arrest or detention of a person to prevent his effecting an unauthorised entry into the country or of a person against whom action is being taken with a view to deportation or extradition.

2. Everyone who is arrested shall be informed promptly, in a language which he understands, of the reasons for his arrest and of any charge against him.

3. Everyone arrested or detained in accordance with the provisions of paragraph 1(*c*) of this Article shall be brought promptly before a judge or other officer authorised by law to exercise judicial power and shall be entitled to trial within a reasonable time or to release pending trial. Release may be conditioned by guarantees to appear for trial.

4. Everyone who is deprived of his liberty by arrest or detention shall be entitled to take proceedings by which the lawfulness of his detention shall be decided speedily by a court and his release ordered if the detention is not lawful.

5. Everyone who has been the victim of arrest or detention in contravention of the provisions of this Article shall have an enforceable right to compensation.

ARTICLE 6

1. In the determination of his civil rights and obligations or of any criminal charge against him, everyone is entitled to a fair and public hearing within a reasonable time by an independent and impartial tribunal established by law. Judgment shall be pronounced publicly but the press and public may be excluded from all or part of the trial in the interest of morals, public order or national security in a democratic society, where the interests of juveniles or the protection of the private life of the parties so require, or to the extent strictly necessary in the opinion of the court in special circumstances where publicity would prejudice the interests of justice.

2. Everyone charged with a criminal offence shall be presumed innocent until proved guilty according to law.

3. Everyone charged with a criminal offence has the following minimum rights:

(*a*) to be informed promptly, in a language which he understands and in detail, of the nature and cause of the accusation against him;

(*b*) to have adequate time and facilities for the preparation of his defence;

(*c*) to defend himself in person or through legal assistance of his own choosing or, if he has not sufficient means to pay for legal assistance, to be given it free when the interests of justice so require;

(*d*) to examine or have examined witnesses against him and to obtain the attendance and examination of witnesses on his behalf under the same conditions as witnesses against him;

(*e*) to have the free assistance of an interpreter if he cannot understand or speak the language used in court.

ARTICLE 7

1. No one shall be held guilty of any criminal offence on account of any act or omission which did not constitute a criminal offence under national or international law at the time when it was committed. Nor shall a heavier penalty be imposed than the one that was applicable at the time the criminal offence was committed.

2. This Article shall not prejudice the trial and punishment of any person for any act or omission which, at the time when it was committed, was criminal according to the general principles of law recognised by civilised nations.

ARTICLE 8

1. Everyone has the right to respect for his private and family life, his home and his correspondence.

2. There shall be no interference by a public authority with the exercise of this right except such as is in accordance with the law and is necessary in a democratic society in the interests of national security, public safety or the economic well-being of the country, for the prevention of disorder or crime, for the protection of health or morals, or for the protection of the rights and freedoms of others.

ARTICLE 9

1. Everyone has the right to freedom of thought, conscience and religion; this right includes freedom to change his religion or beliefs and freedom, either alone or in community with others and in public or private, to manifest his religion or belief, in worship, teaching, practice and observance.
2. Freedom to manifest one's religion or beliefs shall be subject only to such limitations as are prescribed by law and are necessary in a democratic society in the interests of public safety, for the protection of public order, health or morals, or for the protection of the rights and freedoms of others.

ARTICLE 10

1. Everyone has the right to freedom of expression. This right shall include freedom to hold opinions and to receive and impart information and ideas without interference by public authority and regardless of frontiers. This Article shall not prevent States from requiring the licensing of broadcasting, television or cinema enterprises.
2. The exercise of these freedoms, since it carries with it duties and responsibilities, may be subject to such formalities, conditions, restrictions or penalties as are prescribed by law and are necessary in a democratic society, in the interests of national security, territorial integrity or public safety, for the prevention of disorder or crime, for the protection of health or morals, for the protection of the reputation or rights of others, for preventing the disclosure of information received in confidence, or for maintaining the authority and impartiality of the judiciary.

ARTICLE 11

1. Everyone has the right to freedom of peaceful assembly and to freedom of association with others, including the right to form and to join trade unions for the protection of his interests.
2. No restrictions shall be placed on the exercise of these rights other than such as are prescribed by law and are necessary in a democratic society in the interests of national security or public safety, for the prevention of disorder or crime, for the protection of health or morals or for the protection of the rights and freedoms of others. This Article shall not prevent the imposition of lawful restrictions on the exercise of these rights by members of the armed forces, of the police or of the administration of the State.

ARTICLE 12

Men and women of marriageable age have the right to marry and to found a family, according to the national laws governing the exercise of this right.

ARTICLE 13

Everyone whose rights and freedoms as set forth in this Convention are violated shall have an effective remedy before a national authority notwithstanding that the violation has been committed by persons acting in an official capacity.

ARTICLE 14

The enjoyment of the rights and freedoms set forth in this Convention shall be secured without discrimination on any ground such as sex, race, colour, language, religion, political or other opinion, national or social origin, association with a national minority, property, birth or other status.

ARTICLE 15

1. In time of war or other public emergency threatening the life of the nation any High Contracting Party may take measures derogating from its obligations under this Convention to the extent strictly required by the exigencies of the situation, provided that such measures are not inconsistent with its other obligations under international law.
2. No derogation from Article 2, except in respect of deaths resulting from lawful acts of war, or from Articles 3, 4 (paragraph 1) and 7 shall be made under this provision.
3. Any High Contracting Party availing itself of this right of derogation shall keep the Secretary-General of the Council of Europe fully informed of the measures which it has taken and the reasons therefor. It shall also inform the Secretary-General of the Council of Europe when such measures have ceased to operate and the provisions of the Convention are again fully executed.

ARTICLE 16

Nothing in Articles 10, 11 and 14 shall be regarded as preventing the High Contracting Parties from imposing restrictions on the political activity of aliens.

ARTICLE 17[1]

Nothing in this Convention may be interpreted as implying for any State, group or person any right to engage in any activity or perform any act aimed at the destruction of any of the rights and freedoms set forth herein or at their limitation to a greater extent than is provided for in the Convention.

ARTICLE 18

The restrictions permitted under this Convention to the said rights and freedoms shall not be applied for any purpose other than those for which they have been prescribed.

First Protocol to the Convention 1952 Cmd 9221[2]

ARTICLE 1

Every natural or legal person is entitled to the peaceful enjoyment of his possessions. No one shall be deprived of his possessions except in the public interest and subject to the conditions provided for by law and by the general principles of international law.

The preceding provisions shall not, however, in any way impair the right of a State to enforce such laws as it deems necessary to control the use of property in accordance with the general interest or to secure the payment of taxes or other contributions or penalties.

ARTICLE 2[3]

No person shall be denied the right to education. In the exercise of any functions which it assumes in relation to education and to teaching, the State shall respect the right of parents to ensure such education and teaching in conformity with their own religious and philosophical convictions.

ARTICLE 3

The High Contracting Parties undertake to hold free elections at reasonable intervals by secret ballot, under conditions which will ensure the free expression of the opinion of the people in the choice of the legislature.

Fourth Protocol to the Convention 1963[4] Cmnd 2309

ARTICLE 1

No-one shall be deprived of his liberty merely on the ground of inability to fulfil a contractual obligation.

1 *Ed.* Acting under Art. 17, the European Commission of Human Rights declared inadmissible an application from the West German Communist Party alleging that government action banning it was contrary to Arts. 9, 10 and 11 of the Convention: *A.250/57*, (1955–57) 1 YBECHR 222.
2 *Ed.* All of the parties to the Convention except Liechtenstein and Switzerland are parties to the Protocol, which entered into force on 18 May 1954.
3 *Ed.* The UK has made the following reservation to Article 2:
   '. . . in view of certain provisions of the Education Acts in force in the United Kingdom, the principle affirmed in the second sentence of Article 2 is accepted by the United Kingdom only so far as it is compatible with the provision of efficient instruction and training, and the avoidance of unreasonable public expenditure.'
   In *Kjeldsen, Busk Madsen and Pedersen v Denmark* (the *Danish Sex Education Case*), E Ct HRR A 23 (1976), 1 EHRR 711, the Court held the system of compulsory sex education in Danish schools was not contrary to Art. 2, First Protocol. The judgment confirms that Art. 2 applies to education in state, as well as private, schools. In the *Campbell* and *Cosans* cases below, p. 772, the Court held, by six votes to one, that the applicant's right to respect for their 'philosophical convictions' in the state's education of their children had been infringed by the system of corporal punishment in Scottish schools. The Court considered that 'conviction' meant more than opinions or ideas, which were protected by Art. 10. A conviction was more akin to a 'belief' (cf. Art. 9), and denoted 'views that attain a certain level of cogency, seriousness, cohesion and importance'. 'Philosophical convictions' were 'such convictions as are worthy of respect in a "democratic society" . . . and are not incompatible with human dignity'. Judge Sir Vincent Evans dissented. In his opinion, for which he found support in the *travaux préparatoires*, Art. 2 was concerned with the ideological indoctrination of children in class and not with the organisation or administration of schools. He pointed out that parents also held 'convictions' about mixed sex schools, mixed ability classes, and independent schools. He also considered that the case came within the British reservation to Art. 2.
4 *Ed.* The Fourth Protocol entered into force on 2 May 1968. There are 22 contracting parties. The UK is not a party.

ARTICLE 2

1. Everyone lawfully within the territory of a State shall, within that territory, have the right to liberty of movement and freedom to choose his residence.
2. Everyone shall be free to leave any country, including his own.
3. No restrictions shall be placed on the exercise of these rights other than such as are in accordance with law and are necessary in a democratic society in the interests of national security or public safety, for the maintenance of *ordre public*, for the prevention of crime, for the protection of health or morals, or for the protection of the rights and freedoms of others.
4. The rights set forth in paragraph 1 may also be subject, in particular areas, to restrictions imposed in accordance with law and justified by the public interest in a democratic society.

ARTICLE 3

1. No-one shall be expelled, by means either of an individual or of a collective measure, from the territory of the State of which he is a national.
2. No-one shall be deprived of the right to enter the territory of the State of which he is a national.

ARTICLE 4

Collective expulsion of aliens is prohibited.

Sixth Protocol to the Convention 1983[1] (1983) 5 EHRR 167

ARTICLE 1

The death penalty shall be abolished. No one shall be condemned to such penalty or executed.

ARTICLE 2

A state may make provision in its law for the death penalty in respect of acts committed in time of war or imminent threat of war. . . .

Seventh Protocol to the Convention 1984 (1984)[2] 7 EHRR 1

ARTICLE 1

1. An alien lawfully resident in the territory of a State shall not be expelled therefrom except in pursuance of a decision reached in accordance with law and shall be allowed:
    (*a*) to submit reasons against his expulsion,
    (*b*) to have his case reviewed, and
    (*c*) to be represented for these purposes before the competent authority or a person or persons designated by that authority.
2. An alien may be expelled before the exercise of his rights under paragraph 1(*a*), (*b*) and (*c*) of this Article, when such expulsion is necessary in the interests of public order or is grounded on reasons of national security.

ARTICLE 2

1. Everyone convicted of a criminal offence by a tribunal shall have the right to have his conviction or sentence reviewed by a higher tribunal. The exercise of this right, including the grounds on which it may be exercised, shall be governed by law.
2. This right may be subject to exceptions in regard to offences of a minor character, as prescribed by law, or in cases in which the person concerned was tried in the first instance by the highest tribunal or was convicted following an appeal against acquittal.

ARTICLE 3

When a person has by a final decision been convicted of a criminal offence and when subsequently his conviction has been reversed, or he has been pardoned, on the ground that a new or newly discovered fact

---

1 *Ed.* The Sixth Protocol entered into force on 1 March 1985. There are 23 contracting parties. The UK is not a party.
2 *Ed.* The Seventh Protocol entered into force on 1 November 1988. There are 17 contracting parties. The UK is not a party.

shows conclusively that there has been a miscarriage of justice, the person who has suffered punishment as a result of such conviction shall be compensated according to the law or the practice of the State concerned, unless it is proved that the non-disclosure of the unknown fact is wholly or partly attributable to him.

ARTICLE 4

1. No one shall be liable to be tried or punished again in criminal proceedings under the jurisdiction of the same State for an offence for which he has already been finally acquitted or convicted in accordance with the law and penal procedure of that State.
2. The provisions of the preceding paragraph shall not prevent the re-opening of the case in accordance with the law and penal procedure of the State concerned, if there is evidence of new or newly discovered facts, or if there has been a fundamental defect in the previous proceedings, which could affect the outcome of the case.
3. No derogation from this Article shall be made under Article 15 of the Convention.

ARTICLE 5

Spouses shall enjoy equality of rights and responsibilities of a private law character between them, and in their relations with their children, as to marriage, during marriage and in the event of its dissolution. This Article shall not prevent States from taking such measures as are necessary in the interests of the children.

NOTES

1. The ECHR is enforced by means of *state* and *individual* applications (Articles 24, 25), which go in the first place to the European Commission of Human Rights at Strasbourg (Article 19). The Commission, which is part-time, consists of a number of members equal to the number of parties to the Convention, with, in practice, one national from each contracting party (Article 20). The members are independent experts, and usually lawyers.
2. Applications[1] by *states* under Article 24 have been few in number. To take one example, in 1971, Ireland brought an application against the UK which resulted in the judgment in *Ireland v United Kingdom*.[2] Although, for political reasons, *state* applications will always be less numerous than *individual* applications, they are potentially more useful in two respects: (1) they may concern a violation of rights defined in the Convention even though there has, at the same time, been no 'victim' of it and (2) they may concern *any* provision of the Convention whether one guaranteeing a right or not (although this has not been important in practice). They are also not subject to the admissibility requirements in Article 27.
3. An individual may not bring an application against a party unless it has made a declaration under Article 25 accepting the right of individuals to petition against it. All of the parties to the ECHR have such declarations in force. Some have no time limit; the remainder are valid for two to five years. The UK's declaration was first made on 14 January 1966. It applies only to violations occurring as of that date. It was renewed most recently for five years from 14 January 1991. The 1991 declaration extends to Guernsey and Jersey and most remaining British overseas territories, including Gibraltar and the Falklands. It does not extend to Hong Kong.[3]
4. Only 'victims' may bring claims under Article 25, but this term has been interpreted widely. See for example, the *Dudgeon* case, below, p. 812, and the *Malone* case, below, p. 804. Aliens and nationals may bring claims against a party. Legal aid may be granted in appropriate cases.

1 The term 'application' has come to be used in connection with both Art. 24 and Art. 25 instead of 'petition'.
2 Below, p. 749.
3 The right of petition was extended to the Isle of Man in 1993, after a 12-year lapse following the *Tyrer* case, below, p. 767.

5. By the end of 1994, the Commission had registered over 25,000 individual applications. Of these, 2,027, i.e. less than 10% of those in respect of which decisions as to admissibility had been taken, had been admitted for consideration on the merits. The number of annual applications has risen sharply in recent years.

6. Both state and individual applications are first considered by the Commission at the admissibility stage, when they are examined to see whether, in accordance with Article 26, *local remedies* have been exhausted and whether they have been brought '- within a period of six months from the date on which the final decision was taken'. The Commission has developed a substantial jurisprudence applying the local remedies requirement.[1] Only 'effective' remedies need to be exhausted. The Commission takes the view, for example, that there is no need to resort to the House of Lords or even the Court of Appeal if 'settled legal opinion' indicates that an appeal would be pointless.[2] There is no need to resort to a court at all if a legal aid certificate is refused for lack of a prima facie case. Administrative remedies such as a petition to the Home Secretary by a prisoner (*Golder v United Kingdom* (1971) 14 YBECHR 416) must be exhausted. A petition for clemency in the exercise of the royal prerogative is not required (*A. 458/59* (1960) 3 YBECHR 222). Local remedies need not be exhausted in the case of a state application where the allegation is that a law is contrary to the ECHR *in abstracto* or that an administrative practice (as opposed to an isolated breach) has been developed by a state's officials that is in breach of the ECHR. It was because such practices existed that the victims concerned did not have to exhaust the remedies available in the Northern Irish courts before the Irish government could bring its state application in *Ireland v United Kingdom* below, p. 749. In *Donnelly v United Kingdom* (1973) 16 YBECHR 212, the Commission held (again in the Northern Ireland context) that an *individual* applicant need not exhaust local remedies where the breach of the ECHR of which he claims to be a victim results from an administrative practice and the existence of the practice has rendered local remedies ineffective. The *6 months rule* is tempered somewhat by the rule in *Ringeisen v Austria* E Ct HRR A 13 (1968), 1 EHRR 455, by which an application may be lodged before the final stage in the exhaustion of local remedies is over, although it must be completed before the decision as to admissibility is taken. The Commission has also developed the idea of a 'continuing violation', which overcomes the six months rule in some cases: see the *De Becker* case (1958–9) 2 YBECHR 214 (deprivation of freedom of speech for life).

7. Individual applications have also to comply with Article 27. An application will be rejected as 'incompatible with . . . the Convention', inter alia, if it does not raise a question of the violation of the Convention as a matter of law, i.e. if the facts do not bring the case within the scope of a right as defined in the Convention (e.g. where the application concerns the right to food, which is not protected at all, or the right to jury trial, which is not included in the Article 6 guarantee of the right to a fair trial). It will be rejected as 'manifestly ill-founded' if a right as defined in the Convention is in issue but the facts show no evidence of a breach of it (i.e. no prima facie case). An individual application may also be rejected under Article 27 if it is anonymous, an abuse of the right of petition, or 'is substantially the same as a matter which has already been examined by the Commission or has already been submitted to another procedure of international investigation or settlement (e.g. the International Covenant on Civil and Political Rights) and if it contains no relevant

---

1 See A. A. Cançado Trindade, *The Application of the Rule of Exhaustion of Local Remedies in International Law* (1983) (mostly on the ECHR).
2 *McFeeley v United Kingdom* (1980) 20 DR E Com HR 44, 71–6.

new information'. The decision by the Commission to reject an application is final. This being so, and the final word as to the interpretation of the Convention resting with the European Court of Human Rights,[1] not the Commission, there is a strong case for arguing that the Commission should be reluctant to reject an application on a ground that involves its interpretation of the meaning of the Convention.

8. If a state or individual application is admitted for consideration on the merits, a fact-finding inquiry is conducted by the Commission on the basis of written pleadings by the parties (who include at this stage any individual applicant) (Article 28). This may, exceptionally, involve an on-the-spot visit by members of the Commission for which the government concerned must provide the necessary facilities. The Commission visited Greece in the *Greek* case, above, p. 738, n. 1. It left abruptly when it was not accorded all the facilities it sought. The Commission has visited Broadmoor to examine conditions there: *B v United Kingdom*, below, p. 765. There may be an oral hearing on the merits if, exceptionally, none has occurred at the admissibility stage. Having established the facts, the Commission acts as a conciliator, placing itself 'at the disposal of the parties concerned with a view to securing a friendly settlement of the matter on the basis of respect for human rights as defined' in the Convention (Article 28). Friendly settlements had been obtained in over 200 cases by the end of 1994.

9. If no friendly settlement is reached, the Commission drafts a report in which it states its findings of fact and expresses an opinion, which is not legally binding, on the existence of a breach of the Convention (Article 31). The report is sent to the Committee of Ministers of the Council of Europe (ibid.). This consists of the Foreign Ministers (in practice their deputies) of all of the Council of Europe members. It may be referred to the European Court of Human Rights within three months of being so sent. The Court is composed of a number of judges, who are part-time, equal to the number of members of the Council of Europe. No state may have more than one national on the Court. A case may be referred to the Court only if the defendant state has made a declaration under Article 46 accepting the Court's compulsory jurisdiction or if it agrees to the Court's jurisdiction ad hoc in a particular case. All of the parties to the ECHR have made declarations under Article 46 that are in force. Some are without any time limit, the others are for periods of two to five years. All declarations with time limits have been renewed so far. The current UK declaration is for five years from 14 January, 1991. If the defendant state has accepted the Court's jurisdiction, a case may be referred to the Court by the Commission, a defendant state, a state bringing an application, or a contracting party whose national is an alleged victim. In practice, most cases that reach the Court are referred to it by the Commission. In respect of cases where the defendant state is a party to the Ninth Protocol to the ECHR,[2] 'the person, non-governmental organisation or group of individuals having lodged the complaint with the Commission' may also refer a case to the Court (Article 48, ECHR as amended by Article 5, Ninth Protocol) otherwise an individual applicant may not refer his case to the Court. The workload of the Court has increased remarkably in the last few years. Whereas the number of cases referred to it annually was in single figures until 1981, it now stands at over 50 each year. Breaches of the Convention have been found in a majority of the cases decided by the Court on the merits.

---

1 *Vagrancy* cases, E Ct HRR A 12 (1971), 1 EHRR 373. The Court may rule on a question of admissibility in a case that reaches it, although it seldom does so. In *Van Oosterwijck v Belgium*, E Ct HRR A 40 (1980), 3 EHRR 557, the Court held, contrary to the decision of the Commission, that local remedies had not been exhausted.

2 ETS 140. In force 1994; 17 parties. The UK is not a party.

10. The question of the applicant's standing in proceedings brought before the Court was raised in *Lawless v Ireland* E Ct HRR A 1 (1960), 1 EHRR 1. There, after confirming that the individual applicant could not initiate proceedings before it, the Court stated that 'it is in the interests of the proper administration of justice that the Court should have knowledge of and, if need be, take into consideration, the Applicant's point of view' since the proceedings were 'upon issues which concern' him. These views, the Court said, would become known to the Court through the Commission's report. In addition, the Commission, which does have standing before the Court, 'as defender of the public interest, is entitled of its own accord, even if it does not share them, to make known the Applicant's views to the Court as a means of throwing light on the points at issue'. The Court could also hear the Applicant as a witness. As of 1983, an applicant is allowed to plead his own case before the Court, either through a lawyer or, with the Court's permission, in person (Rule 30, Revised Rules of Court). He is still, however, not a party to the proceedings.

11. The Court's judgment, which is binding (Article 53), is declaratory. If the Court finds that a breach of the ECHR has occurred, this brings into operation the defendant state's obligation in international law to make reparation. However, the Court may award 'just satisfaction' to the 'injured party'. Article 50 provides:

If the Court finds that a decision or a measure taken by a legal authority or any other authority of a High Contracting Party is completely or partially in conflict with the obligations arising from the present Convention, and if the internal law of the said Party allows only partial reparation to be made for the consequences of this decision or measure, the decision of the Court shall, if necessary, afford just satisfaction to the injured party.

Under Rule 47 *bis* of its Rules, the Court may rule upon the question of 'satisfaction' when the issue of liability is being determined if the question is 'ready for decision'. Otherwise, separate proceedings are conducted before the Court (with the Commission participating) after the defendant state has had an opportunity to make reparation in accordance with the Court's judgment. In the exercise of its essentially secondary power under Article 50, the Court has made monetary awards in a number of cases, including the *Sunday Times* case, below, p. 823, (£22,000) and the *Young, James and Webster* case, below, p. 844 (£130,000 for the three applicants altogether). The award in the *Sunday Times* case was wholly in respect of the costs of taking the case to Strasbourg. In the *Young, James and Webster* case, the award was for costs, pecuniary loss (loss of earnings, etc.) and 'moral damage' (i.e. injury to feelings, etc.). So far, 'satisfaction' has always taken the form of monetary compensation. The execution of the Court's judgments is the responsibility of the Committee of Ministers (Article 54). As yet, all judgments have been complied with to the Committee's satisfaction, i.e. the required 'satisfaction' has been paid or any offending law or practice has been changed.

12. If a case is not referred to the Court for a final decision, it is decided by the Committee of Ministers by a two-thirds majority vote of the members of the Committee (Article 32).[1] This alternative procedure was provided for because states were not prepared to accept a Convention in which every case might finally be decided by a court. There is no judicial hearing of the evidence by the Committee of Ministers. It has the Commission's report on the case before it and hears the comments of the defendant state, which is allowed to vote. The Committee's decision is not reasoned. The existence of alternative bodies competent to take a final decision in a case is not in the interests of the development of a consistent jurisprudence interpret-

---

1   The Tenth Protocol to the ECHR, ETS 146, reduces the requirement to a simple majority. 20 ratifications. Not yet in force.

ing the Convention. The unsatisfactory nature of an arrangement whereby a case may be determined by the Committee of Ministers was illustrated in the *Huber* case, (1971) 14 YBECHR 572. There, the Committee rejected (CM Resolution DH (75)2) an eight to two majority opinion by the Commission that Austria had detained the applicant contrary to Article 5(3). This was done after a discussion of the case in which, in accordance with the usual procedure, the Austrian representative explained his state's defence and in the absence of any hearing of the Commission or applicant. For the Committee to reject in these circumstances the considered and independent judgment of a clear majority of the Commission, arrived at after a full hearing of the facts and legal arguments of the parties, is scarcely what one would hope for in the administration of a human rights guarantee that protects the right to a fair trial.

13. *Reform of ECHR procedures.*[1] For some time there has been concern that the system for enforcement of the ECHR was in need of reform. The main reason has been the need to expedite proceedings, with cases typically taking five years before a final decision by the Court. These delays have developed as individuals have become more aware that there is a chance of success at Strasbourg and as more states have become ECHR parties, including now an increasing number of states from Central and Eastern Europe. The remedy decided upon is a merger of the Commission and the Court into one full-time institution called the European Court of Human Rights which will deal with questions of admissibility and the merits. Chambers of the Court will be reduced from nine to seven members, which will allow more than one chamber to sit at the same time. The occasion has been used to make other important improvements. In particular, the right of individual petition will be compulsory and all cases will be decided by the Court (not the Committee of Ministers). The new procedures are provided for by the Eleventh Protocol to the ECHR. This was adopted in 1994 and will enter into force one year after it has been ratified by all of the contracting parties (8 ratifications so far). The signs are that this will be before the end of the century.

2 Article 3: Freedom from torture or inhuman or degrading treatment or punishment

Ireland v United Kingdom, E Ct HRR A 25 (1978), 2 EHRR 25, Eur Court HR

In 1971, Ireland lodged an application against the UK arising out of events in Northern Ireland. The claims in the application that were admitted for consideration on the merits concerned the introduction and operation of the policy of internment and detention that applied in Northern Ireland between 1971 and 1975. Following an increase in IRA activities it was decided in 1971 to intern without trial persons suspected of serious terrorist activities but against whom there was not sufficient evidence to bring court proceedings. Powers to detain persons for questioning over a 48 hour period or longer were also brought into operation. Implementation of this policy, which was originally based upon regulations made under the Civil Authorities (Special Powers) Act (NI) 1922, began with 'Operation Demetrius' on 9 August 1971. Some 350 persons were arrested, of whom 104 were released within 48 hours. Of those detained further, 12 were sent to unidentified centres for

---

1 On the reforms, see A. Drzemczecwski and J. Meyer-Ladewig, 15 HRLJ 81 (1994); D. J. Harris, M. O'Boyle and C. Warbrick, *The Law of the European Convention on Human Rights* (1995), Chap 26, and A. R. Mowbray, [1994] PL 54. For the text of the Eleventh Protocol and the Explanatory Report, see 17 EHRR 501 and (1994) 1–3 IHHR 206.

'interrogation in depth'. This involved use of the 'five techniques' described in the Court's judgment. Many more suspects were interned or detained for questioning in the following months. Of these, two more (making a total of 14) were subjected to the 'five techniques'. The claims admitted for consideration on their merits were mainly to the effect that the policy of internment and detention infringed Articles 5 and 6 and that persons interned or detained had been subjected to ill-treatment that constituted an 'administrative practice' in violation of Article 3. The ill-treatment, it was alleged, had occurred at the unidentified interrogation centres where the 'five techniques' were used and at other named interrogation centres including Palace Barracks, where, it was alleged, more familiar forms of assault occurred. In support of its allegations, the Irish Government presented evidence relating to the treatment of 228 persons. The procedure agreed upon by the Commission and parties to handle this mass of evidence was for the Commission to concentrate on 16 'illustrative cases' selected by Ireland. The Commission heard oral as well as written evidence in these cases and received medical reports. The Commission had regard to another 'forty-one cases' in respect of which it heard written (but not oral) evidence and received medical reports. It also took account of the remaining cases, but did not examine them in detail.

In its report, the Commission, inter alia, unanimously expressed the opinion that the combined use of the 'five techniques' constituted a practice of inhuman treatment and of torture contrary to Article 3; that there had been at Palace Barracks a practice of inhuman treatment contrary to Article 3; and that other instances of inhuman and, in some cases, degrading, treatment had occurred in other places of detention.

Following the Commission's report, Ireland referred the case to the Court. The following extracts from the Court's judgment concern the Article 3 claims. Claims under Articles 5, 6 and 14 failed because of the UK's notice of derogation under Article 15: see below, p. 851.

JUDGMENT OF THE COURT

As to the facts . . .

III Allegations of ill-treatment . . .

B. The unidentified interrogation centre or centres

96. Twelve persons arrested on 9 August 1971 and two persons arrested in October 1971 were singled out and taken to one or more unidentified centres. There, between 11 to 17 August and 11 to 18 October respectively, they were submitted to a form of 'interrogation in depth' which involved the combined application of five particular techniques.

These methods, sometimes termed 'disorientation' or 'sensory deprivation' techniques, were not used in any cases other than the fourteen so indicated above. It emerges from the Commission's establishment of the facts that the techniques consisted of:

(a) *wall-standing*: forcing the detainees to remain for periods of some hours in a 'stress position', described by those who underwent it as being 'spreadeagled against the wall, with their fingers put high above the head against the wall, the legs spread apart and the feet back, causing them to stand on their toes with the weight of the body mainly on the fingers';

(b) *hooding*: putting a black or navy coloured bag over the detainees' heads and, at least initially, keeping it there all the time except during interrogation;

(c) *subjection to noise*: pending their interrogations, holding the detainees in a room where there was a continuous loud and hissing noise;

(d) *deprivation of sleep*: pending their interrogations, depriving the detainees of sleep;

(e) *deprivation of food and drink*: subjecting the detainees to a reduced diet during their stay at the centre and pending interrogations. . . .

97. From the start, it has been conceded by the respondent Government that the use of the five techniques was authorised at 'high level'. . . .

98. The two operations of interrogation in depth by means of the five techniques led to the obtaining of a considerable quantity of intelligence information, including the identification of 700 members of both IRA factions and the discovery of individual responsibility for about 85 previously unexplained criminal incidents.

99. Reports alleging physical brutality and ill-treatment by the security forces were made public within a few days of Operation Demetrius. . . . A committee of enquiry under the chairmanship of Sir Edmund Compton was appointed by the United Kingdom Government on 31 August 1971 to investigate such allegations. Among the 40 cases this Committee examined were 11 cases of persons subjected to the five techniques in August 1971; its findings were that interrogation in depth by means of the techniques constituted physical ill-treatment but not physical brutality as it understood that term. The Committee's report [Cmnd. 4823], adopted on 3 November 1971, was made public, as was a supplemental report of 14 November by Sir Edmund Compton in relation to 3 further cases occurring in September and October, one of which involved the techniques.

100. The Compton reports came under considerable criticism in the United Kingdom. On 16 November 1971, the British Home Secretary announced that a further Committee had been set up under the chairmanship of Lord Parker of Waddington to consider 'whether, and if so in what respects, the procedures currently authorised for interrogation of persons suspected of terrorism and for their custody while subject to interrogation require amendment'.

The Parker report . . . contained a majority and a minority opinion. The majority report concluded that the application of the techniques, subject to recommended safeguards against excessive use, need not be ruled out on moral grounds. On the other hand, the minority report by Lord Gardiner disagreed that such interrogation procedures were morally justifiable, even in emergency terrorist conditions. Both the majority and the minority considered the methods to be illegal under domestic law, although the majority confined their view to English law and to 'some if not all the techniques'.

101. The Parker report [Cmnd. 4901] was published on 2 March 1972. . . . directives expressly prohibiting the use of the techniques, whether singly or in combination, were then issued to the security forces by the Government. . . .

102. At the hearing before the Court on 8 February 1977, the United Kingdom Attorney-General made the following declaration:

'The Government of the United Kingdom have considered the question of the use of the "five techniques" with very great care and with particular regard to Article 3 of the Convention. They now give this unqualified undertaking, that the "five techniques" will not in any circumstances be introduced as an aid to interrogation.'

103. The Irish Government referred to the Commission 8 cases of persons submitted to the five techniques during interrogation at the unidentified centre or centres between 11 and 17 August 1971. The Commission examined as illustrative the cases of T 6 and T 13, which were among the 11 cases investigated by the Compton Committee.

104. T 6 and T 13 were arrested on 9 August 1971 during Operation Demetrius. Two days later they were transferred from Magilligan Regional Holding Centre to an unidentified interrogation centre where they were medically examined on arrival. Thereafter, with intermittent periods of respite, they were subjected to the five techniques during four or possibly five days; neither the Compton or Parker Committees nor the Commission were able to establish the exact length of the periods of respite.

The Commission was satisfied that T 6 and T 13 were kept at the wall for different periods totalling between twenty to thirty hours, but it did not consider it proved that the enforced stress position had lasted all the time they were at the wall. It stated in addition that the required posture caused physical pain and exhaustion. The Commission noted that, later on during his stay at the interrogation centre, T 13 was allowed to take his hood off when he was alone in the room, provided that he turned his face to the wall. It was not found possible by the Commission to establish for what periods T 6 and T 13 had been without sleep, or to what extent they were deprived of nourishment and whether or not they were offered food but refused to take it.

The Commission found no physical injury to have resulted from the application of the five techniques as such, but loss of weight by the two case-witnesses and acute psychiatric symptoms developed by them during interrogation were recorded in the medical and other evidence. The Commission, on the material before it, was unable to establish the exact degree of any psychiatric after-effects produced on T6 and T 13, but on the general level it was satisfied that some psychiatric after-effects in certain of the fourteen persons subjected to the techniques could not be excluded. . . .

105. . . . T 6 . . . alleged that he was also assaulted in various ways at, or during transport to and from, the centre. On 17 August 1971 he was medically examined on leaving the centre and also on his subsequent arrival at Crumlin Road Prison where he was then detained until 3 May 1972. The medical reports of

these examinations and photographs taken on the same day revealed on T 6's body bruising and contusions that had not been present on 11 August. While not accepting all T 6's allegations, the Commission was 'satisfied beyond a reasonable doubt that certain of these injuries . . . [were] the result of assaults committed on him by the security forces at the centre'. As a general inference from the facts established in T 6's case, the Commission also found it 'probable that physical violence was sometimes used in the forcible application of the five techniques'.

107. T 13 and T 6 instituted civil proceedings in 1971 to recover damages for wrongful imprisonment and assault; their claims were settled in 1973 and 1975 respectively for £15,000 and £14,000. The twelve other individuals against whom the five techniques were used have all received in settlement of their civil claims compensation ranging from £10,000 to £25,000.

C. Palace Barracks

110. . . . Despite the absolute denials given in evidence by witnesses from the security forces at Palace Barracks, the Commission held the following facts, amongst others, to be established beyond reasonable doubt:

> 'The four men [T 2, T 8, T 12 and T 15] . . . were severely beaten by members of the security forces. . . . The beating was not occasional but it was applied in a sort of scheme in order to make them speak. . . .'

Each man instituted civil proceedings for damages and rejected the offer of £750 made in settlement of his claim. . . .

111. . . . The medical evidence disclosed injuries described as 'substantial' in T 9's case and 'massive' in T 14's case. The Commission concluded that 'the proved injuries must have been caused while the two men were at Palace Barracks'. Fourteen members of the security forces at the centre gave evidence completely denying any knowledge of the injuries or their causes, but these denials were not believed by the Commission. While viewing certain of the two men's assertions as exaggerated, invented or improbable, the Commission made the following finding:

> 'T 9 and T 14 . . . were subjected to physical violence, especially kicking and beating, during or between a series of "interviews" conducted by Special Branch.'

Civil proceedings seeking damages were instituted by T 14 and T 9; their claims were settled for £2,250 and £1,975 respectively. They also, it seems, complained to the police, but no evidence was produced to the Commission of a police enquiry into their complaints. . . .

118. The Commission considered on a number of grounds that the police officers in command at Palace Barracks at the relevant time could not have been ignorant of the acts of ill-treatment.

Knowledge on the part of the higher authorities of allegations regarding this centre was inferred by the Commission from various facts. Nevertheless, no evidence of police investigations into these allegations was produced to the Commission and, apart from Sir Edmund Compton's 'supplemental' report into three Palace Barracks cases . . ., no general enquiry took place. Furthermore, no disciplinary or criminal proceedings seem to have been instituted against any of the police officers who either committed or failed to react against the acts established. No special instructions relating to the proper treatment of persons in custody were issued to the RUC until April 1972. . . . Through their inaction, the authorities in Northern Ireland were held by the Commission to have shown indifference towards the treatment of prisoners at Palace Barracks in the autumn of 1971.

[The court then reviewed evidence of ill-treatment at Girdwood Park and Ballykinler Regional Holding Centres, and at various army posts, police stations, a prison, at home or during transport.]

G. Measures concerning the treatment of persons arrested or held by the security forces . . .

Compensation

142. Procedures to obtain compensation were available before the domestic courts to all persons who considered themselves to have been ill-treated by the security forces. There is no suggestion that domestic courts were or are anything other than independent, fair and impartial. . . . Like any plaintiff in a civil action, a plaintiff alleging ill-treatment by the security forces was entitled to obtain disclosure of relevant documents, for example medical reports, in the possession of the defendant authorities.

143. Between 9 August 1971 and 31 January 1975, compensation totalling £302,043 had been paid in settlement of 473 civil claims for wrongful arrest, false imprisonment, assault and battery, leaving 1,193 actions still outstanding. At the time of the Commission's report, compensation ranging from about £200

to £25,000, had been paid in settlement of 45 of the 228 cases submitted by the applicant Government. In the only case of alleged physical ill-treatment which seems to have been fought, namely the case of *Moore v Shillington* (18 February (1972), Armagh County Court), the judge disbelieved the evidence of the security forces.

As to the law . . .

II. On Article 3 . . .

A. Preliminary questions . . .

158. . . . the Irish Government indicated . . . that they were asking the Court to hold that there had been in Northern Ireland, from 1971 to 1974, a practice or practices in breach of Article 3 and to specify, if need be, where they had occurred. . . .

159. A practice incompatible with the Convention consists of an accumulation of identical or analogous breaches which are sufficiently numerous and inter-connected to amount not merely to isolated incidents or exceptions but to a pattern or system; a practice does not of itself constitute a violation separate from such breaches.

It is inconceivable that the higher authorities of a State should be, or at least should be entitled to be, unaware of the existence of such a practice. Furthermore, under the Convention those authorities are strictly liable for the conduct of their subordinates; they are under a duty to impose their will on sub-ordinates and cannot shelter behind their inability to ensure that it is respected.

The concept of practice is of particular importance for the operation of the rule of exhaustion of domestic remedies. This rule, as embodied in Article 26 of the Convention, applies to State applications (Article 24), in the same way as it does to 'individual' applications (Article 25), when the applicant State does no more than denounce a violation or violations allegedly suffered by 'individuals' whose place, as it were, is taken by the State. On the other hand and in principle, the rule does not apply where the applicant State complains of a practice as such, with the aim of preventing its continuation or recurrence, but does not ask the Commission or the Court to give a decision on each of the cases put forward as proof or illustra-tions of that practice. The Court agrees with the opinion which the Commission, following its earlier case-law, expressed on the subject in its decision of 1 October 1972 on the admissibility of the Irish Government's original application. Moreover, the Court notes that that decision is not contested by the respondent Government. . . .

160. In order to satisfy itself as to the existence or not in Northern Ireland of practices contrary to Article 3, the Court will not rely on the concept that the burden of proof is borne by one or other of the two Governments concerned. In the cases referred to it, the Court examines all the material before it, whether originating from the Commission, the Parties or other sources, and, if necessary, obtains material *proprio motu.* . . .

161. . . . To assess this evidence, the Court adopts the standard of proof 'beyond reasonable doubt' but adds that such proof may follow from the coexistence of sufficiently strong, clear and concordant infer-ences or of similar unrebutted presumptions of fact. In this context, the conduct of the Parties when evidence is being obtained has to be taken into account. . . .

C. Questions concerning the merits

162. As was emphasised by the Commission, ill-treatment must attain a minimum level of severity if it is to fall within the scope of Article 3. The assessment of this minimum is, in the nature of things, relative; it depends on all the circumstances of the case, such as the duration of the treatment, its physical or mental effects and, in some cases, the sex, age and state of health of the victim, etc. . . .

1. The unidentified interrogation centre or centres

(A) *The 'five techniques'*

165. The facts concerning the five techniques are summarised at paragraphs 96–104 and 106–107 above. In the Commission's estimation, those facts constituted a practice not only of inhuman and degrading treatment but also of torture. The applicant Government ask for confirmation of this opinion which is not contested before the Court by the respondent Government.

166. The police used the five techniques on fourteen persons in 1971. . . . Although never authorised in writing in any official document, the five techniques were taught orally by the English Intelligence Centre to members of the RUC at a seminar held in April 1971. There was accordingly a practice.

167. The five techniques were applied in combination, with premeditation and for hours at a stretch; they caused, if not actual bodily injury, at least intense physical and mental suffering to the persons sub-jected thereto and also led to acute psychiatric disturbances during interrogation. They accordingly fell

into the category of inhuman treatment within the meaning of Article 3. The techniques were also degrading since they were such as to arouse in their victims feelings of fear, anguish and inferiority capable of humiliating and debasing them and possibly breaking their physical or moral resistance. . . .

In order to determine whether the five techniques should also be qualified as torture, the Court must have regard to the distinction, embodied in Article 3, between this notion and that of inhuman or degrading treatment.

In the Court's view, this distinction derives principally from a difference in the intensity of the suffering inflicted.

The Court considers in fact that, whilst there exists, on the one hand violence which is to be condemned both on moral grounds and also in most cases under the domestic law of the Contracting States but which does not fall within Article 3 of the Convention, it appears on the other hand that it was the intention that the Convention, with its distinction between 'torture' and 'inhuman or degrading treatment', should by the first of these terms attach a special stigma to deliberate inhuman treatment causing very serious and cruel suffering.

Moreover, this seems to be the thinking lying behind Article 1 *in fine* of Resolution 3452 (XXX) adopted by the General Assembly of the United Nations on 9 December 1975, which declares: 'Torture constitutes an *aggravated* and deliberate form of cruel, inhuman or degrading treatment or punishment.'

Although the five techniques, as applied in combination, undoubtedly amounted to inhuman and degrading treatment, although their object was the extraction of confessions, the naming of others and/or information and although they were used systematically, they did not occasion suffering of the particular intensity and cruelty implied by the word torture as so understood. . . .

168. The Court concludes that recourse to the five techniques amounted to a practice of inhuman and degrading treatment, which practice was in breach of Article 3. . . .

(B) *Ill-treatment alleged to have accompanied the use of the five techniques* . . .

170. As far as T 6 is concerned, the Court shares the Commission's opinion that the security forces subjected T6 to assaults severe enough to constitute inhuman treatment. This opinion, which is not contested by the respondent Government, is borne out by the evidence before the Court. . . .

[As this was the only case where ill-treatment in addition to the use of the five techniques was established, the Court was unable to hold that there was a 'practice' of ill-treatment.]

2. Palace Barracks

174. In so far as the Commission has found that a practice of inhuman treatment was followed in the autumn of 1971 [at Palace Barracks], for example in the cases of T 2, T 8, T 12, T 15 . . . the facts summarised above . . . bear out its opinion. The evidence before the Court reveals that, at the time in question, quite a large number of those held in custody at Palace Barracks were subjected to violence by members of the RUC. This violence, which was repeated violence occurring in the same place and taking similar forms, did not amount merely to isolated incidents; it definitely constituted a practice. It also led to intense suffering and to physical injury which on occasion was substantial; it thus fell into the category of inhuman treatment.

According to the applicant Government, the violence in question should also be classified, in some cases, as torture.

. . . Admittedly, the acts complained of often occurred during interrogation and, to this extent, were aimed at extracting confessions, the naming of others and/or information, but the severity of the suffering that they were capable of causing did not attain the particular level inherent in the notion of torture as understood by the Court. . . .

FOR THESE REASONS, THE COURT

On Article 3 . . .

3. *holds* by sixteen votes to one that the use of the five techniques in August and October 1971 constituted a practice of inhuman and degrading treatment, which practice was in breach of Article 3;
4. *holds* by thirteen votes to four that the said use of the five techniques did not constitute a practice of torture within the meaning of Article 3;
5. *holds* by sixteen votes to one that no other practice of ill-treatment is established for the unidentified interrogation centres;
6. *holds* unanimously that there existed at Palace Barracks in the autumn of 1971 a practice of inhuman treatment, which practice was in breach of Article 3;

7. *holds* by fourteen votes to three that the last-mentioned practice was not one of torture within the meaning of Article 3;
8. *holds* unanimously that it is not established that the practice in question continued beyond the autumn of 1971;
9. *holds* by fifteen votes to two that no practice in breach of Article 3 is established as regards other places. . . .

On Article 50

18. *holds* unanimously that it is not necessary to apply Article 50 in the present case.

NOTES

1. *Ireland v UK* is the leading case on the meaning of 'torture' and 'inhuman treatment'. In that case, the Court held – in contrast, remarkably, to the opinion of a unanimous Commission – that torture had not occurred because the intensity of suffering inflicted had not been sufficient. The only case in which torture has been held to have occurred contrary to Article 3 as a matter of final decision is the *Greek* case, see above, p. 738, n. 4, in which the Commission's finding to that effect was confirmed by the Committee of Ministers. In that case, the Commission concluded that political detainees had been subjected by the Athens security police to 'torture and ill-treatment' contrary to Article 3, this most often taking the form of *falanga* or severe beatings of all parts of the body with a view to extracting confessions and information as to the political activities of subversive individuals. It is implicit in *Ireland v UK* that mental anguish alone may constitute torture; suffering caused by bodily injury is not essential. More explicitly, in the *Greek* case, (1969) 12 YBECHR (The Greek case) 1, 461, the Commission referred to 'non-physical torture', which it described as 'the infliction of mental suffering by creating a state of anguish and stress by means other than bodily assault'. Evidence which the Commission considered under this heading, without concluding that any amounted to torture on the facts, involved mock executions and threats of death, humiliating acts and threats of reprisal against a detainee's family.
2. In addition to the definition of 'torture' in the 1975 UN Declaration to which the Court refers, see also the definition in the later 1984 UN Torture Convention, Article 1:

'For the purposes of this Convention, the term "torture" means any act by which severe pain or suffering, whether physical or mental, is intentionally inflicted on a person for such purposes as obtaining from him or a third person information or a confession, punishing him for an act he or a third person has committed or is suspected of having committed, or intimidating or coercing him or a third person, or for any reason based on discrimination of any kind, when such pain or suffering is inflicted by or at the instigation of or with the consent or acquiescence of a public official or other person acting in an official capacity. It does not include pain or suffering arising only from, inherent in or incidental to lawful sanctions.'

3. The distinction between 'torture' and other forms of ill treatment in breach of Article 3 may be relevant to the level of compensation awarded under Article 50 or to a state's reputation. With regard to the latter, the UK's concession before the Court in *Ireland v UK* that the use of the 'five techniques' was 'torture', not just 'inhuman or degrading treatment', proved not to be a good tactic.
4. Looking at Article 3 more generally, it is noticeable that it contains an absolute guarantee of the rights it protects. It does so in two senses. Firstly, it cannot be derogated from even in time of war or other public emergency: see Article 15. It is

this, as well as the historical background to the ECHR, that has led to the argument that it should not be trivialised, ie understood to prohibit other than the most serious forms of ill-treatment. Secondly, Article 3, unlike almost all other ECHR guarantees, is expressed in unqualified terms. As a result, 'torture', for example, is not permitted for even the highest reasons of public interest.

Tomasi v France, E Ct HRR A 241-A (1992), 15 EHRR 1, Eur Court HR

The applicant was arrested for a murder related to Corsican terrorist activities. He claimed that he had been assaulted to the point of ill-treatment in breach of Article 3 while in custody at a police station. In its report, the Commission expressed the opinion, by 12 votes to 3, that there had been a breach of Article 3.

JUDGMENT OF THE COURT

1. The causal connection between the treatment complained of and the injuries noted

110. . . . the Court bases its view on several considerations.

In the first place, no one has claimed that the marks noted on the applicant's body could have dated from a period prior to his being taken into custody or could have originated in an act carried out by the applicant against himself or again as a result of an escape attempt.

In addition, at his first appearance before the investigating judge, he drew attention to the marks which he bore on his chest and his ear; the judge took note of this and immediately designated an expert . . .

Furthermore, four different doctors – one of whom was an official of the prison authorities – examined the accused in the days following the end of his police custody. Their certificates contain precise and concurring medical observations and indicate dates for the occurrence of the injuries which correspond to the period spent in custody on police premises. . . .

2. The gravity of the treatment complained of

112. Relying on the *Ireland v the United Kingdom* judgment of 18 January 1978 (Series A no. 25), the applicant maintained that the blows which he had received constituted inhuman and degrading treatment. They had not only caused him intense physical and mental suffering; they had also aroused in him feelings of fear, anguish and inferiority capable of humiliating him and breaking his physical or moral resistance.

He argued that special vigilance was required of the Court in this respect in view of the particular features of the French system of police custody, notably the absence of a lawyer and a lack of any contact with the outside world.

113. The Commission stressed the vulnerability of a person held in police custody and expressed its surprise at the times chosen to interrogate the applicant. Although the injuries observed might appear to be relatively slight, they nevertheless constituted outward signs of the use of physical force on an individual deprived of his liberty and therefore in a state of inferiority. The treatment had therefore been both inhuman and degrading.

114. According to the Government, on the other hand, the 'minimum level of severity' required by the Court's case-law . . . had not been attained. It was necessary to take into account not only that the injuries were slight, but also the other facts of the case: Mr Tomasi's youth and good state of health, the moderate length of the interrogations (fourteen hours, three of which were during the night), 'particular circumstances' obtaining in Corsica at the time and the fact that he had been suspected of participating in a terrorist attack which had resulted in the death of one man and grave injuries to another. In the Government's view, the Commission's interpretation of Article 3 in this case was based on a misunderstanding of the aim of that provision.

115. The Court cannot accept this argument. It does not consider that it has to examine the system of police custody in France and the rules pertaining thereto, or, in this case, the length and the timing of the applicant's interrogations. It finds it sufficient to observe that the medical certificates and reports, drawn up in total independence by medical practitioners, attest to the large number of blows inflicted on Mr Tomasi and their intensity; these are two elements which are sufficiently serious to render such treatment inhuman and degrading. The requirements of the investigation and the undeniable difficulties inherent in the fight against crime, particularly with regard to terrorism, cannot result in limits being placed on the protection to be afforded in respect of the physical integrity of individuals. . . .

FOR THESE REASONS, THE COURT UNANIMOUSLY [9–0] . . .

2. *Holds* that there has been a violation of . . . Article 3. . . .

NOTES

1. In the *Tomasi* case,[1] the Court placed the burden of proof upon the state in respect of what happened in police custody. The case was distinguished in the case of an 'on the street' incident in *Klaas v Germany*, E Ct HRR A 269 (1993), 18 EHRR 305. There a woman driver suffered injuries in the course of being arrested by the police outside her block of flats in order to be taken to a police station for a blood test for alcohol. Whereas the applicant argued that the injuries had been caused by excessive police force, the defendant state claimed that the applicant had injured herself while resisting a lawful arrest. Faced with this conflict of evidence, a German court had rejected a civil claim for compensation against the police because the applicant, who had the burden of proof, had not satisfied it that the injuries had been caused by the use of excessive force. Accepting the findings of fact by the national court, the European Court held against the applicant, by six votes to three. It stated:

'29. The Court recalls . . . that it is not normally within the province of the European Court to substitute its own assessment of the facts for that of the domestic courts and, as a general rule, it is for these courts to assess the evidence before them. . . .

30. The admitted injuries sustained by the first applicant were consistent with either her or the police officers' version of events. The national courts, however, found against her. In reaching the conclusion that she could have injured herself while resisting arrest and that the arresting officers had not used excessive force, the Regional Court, in particular, had the benefit of seeing the various witnesses give their evidence and of evaluating their credibility. No material has been adduced in the course of the Strasbourg proceedings which could call into question the findings of the national courts and add weight to the applicant's allegations either before the Commission or the Court.

The Court would distinguish the present case from that of *Tomasi v France* . . . where certain inferences could be made from the fact that Mr Tomasi had sustained unexplained injuries during forty-eight hours spent in police custody.

No cogent elements have been provided which could lead the Court to depart from the findings of fact of the national courts.

31. Accordingly no violation of Article 3 can be found to have occurred.'

Judge Walsh dissented, adopting a different approach to the burden of proof. He stated:

'. . . the applicant had apparently driven her motor car . . . through a red traffic light. . . . Because the police detected a smell of alcohol on her breath she was requested to take a breathalyser test. . . . As that test would involve her going to the police station she was formally arrested by one of the police officers who physically restrained her. There is no doubt that, as from that moment, she was in the custody of the police. All the subsequent injuries sustained by the applicant accordingly took place during that period of custody. I cannot therefore accept as a valid distinction the fact that in the case of *Tomasi v France* . . . the applicant had been in custody for many hours. Whether one is in the custody of the police for but a few minutes or for a few days makes no difference to the principle involved. When the police take a person into custody they have automatically assumed the duty and obligation to save such person from harm whether from members of the police or from any other party. Once a person's liberty has been restrained by the police, she or he is in police custody, whether or not formal words of arrest have been pronounced. Once it has been established that physical injury has been sustained by such person while in police custody, the burden falls upon the police or their State to show that such injuries were not caused or brought about by the actions of the police or their want of care.

2. In the *Tomasi* case, the Court did not question that the level of suffering caused by the physical assaults was sufficient to bring Article 3 into play. In that case, the

---

1 On the *Tomasi* case, see Tompkins, (1993) 52 CLJ 9.

medical evidence established that the applicant had abrasions and bruises on the face, abrasions on the chest and an injury to an ear. It is also noticeable that in the *Klaas* case the suffering caused to the applicant was not said by the Court to have fallen below the threshold of Article 3, although the claim failed on another point. In that case, the applicant sustained a serious and probably long-term injury to her left shoulder and bruises on her right arm. Physical assault was also found to have reached the level of 'inhuman treatment' in *Ireland v UK*, above, and in *Cyprus v Turkey* (1984) 4 EHRR 482, 537 (rapes by Turkish soldiers).

Soering v United Kingdom, E Ct HRR A 161 (1989), 11 EHRR 439, Eur Ct HR

The applicant, an FRG national, and his girl-friend, a Canadian national, were wanted for the brutal murder by stabbing, when they were aged 18 and 20 respectively, of the girl-friend's parents in Virginia in 1985. The couple having been arrested in the UK, the US applied for their extradition under the 1846 extradition treaty between the two states. The girl-friend was extradited and, after pleading guilty as an accessory to the murders, was sentenced to 90 years' imprisonment (45 years on each count). The extradition proceedings against the applicant were delayed while he completed a prison sentence in the UK for cheque fraud. While he was in prison, the FRG also sought the applicant's extradition for the Virginia murders under its extradition treaty with the UK. However, the UK government gave the US application priority because it was made earlier and the German application did not show a prima facie case. While the UK–US extradition treaty does not prohibit extradition for capital offences, it does provide that where the offence for which extradition is requested is a capital offence and the death penalty is not provided for in a similar case under the law of the requested state, the requested state may refuse extradition 'unless the requesting Party gives assurances satisfactory to the requested Party that the death penalty will not be carried out' (Article IV). In applying Article IV, the UK had followed a practice of requesting and accepting as sufficient an assurance from the prosecuting authorities in the jurisdiction concerned that a representation would be made by them to the judge at the time of sentencing that the UK government wished that the death penalty neither be imposed nor carried out. As yet, there has not been a case in which such an assurance has been put to the test. In the applicant's case, such an assurance was obtained. However, during the course of proceedings in the case before the European Court of Human Rights, the prosecuting authorities in Virginia made it clear to the UK government that, although the requested representation would be made to the judge, the death penalty would nonetheless be demanded.

In July 1988, following his committal for extradition by the Chief Metropolitan Magistrate, the applicant made an application to Strasbourg claiming that his extradition to the US would be 'inhuman treatment' by the UK in breach of Article 3, ECHR, particularly because of the 'death row phenomenon' to which he would be subjected if he were convicted and sentenced to death, which was a likely outcome of the trial. The applicant also alleged breaches of Article 6(3)(c), because of the absence of legal aid in Virginia, and Article 13, because he lacked effective remedies under UK law in respect of his Article 3 claim. In August 1988, the Secretary of State issued a warrant ordering the applicant's extradition. Acting under Rule 36 of its Rules of Procedure, the Commission requested that the extradition not take place pending its consideration of the applicant's case. The UK government complied with this request. The Commission concluded, by 6 votes to 5, that Article 3 had not been infringed; unanimously, that Article 6(3)(c) had not been infringed; and, by 7 votes to 4, that there had been a violation of Article 13. The case was referred to the Court by the UK government. The plenary Court held unanimously that there had been no breach of Articles 6(3)(c) or 13. The following extracts concern the claim under Article 3.

JUDGMENT OF THE COURT

A. Applicability of Article 3 in cases of extradition . . .

85. As results from Article 5 § 1 (f), which permits 'the lawful . . . detention of a person against whom action is being taken with a view to . . . extradition', no right not to be extradited is as such protected by the Convention. Nevertheless, in so far as a measure of extradition has consequences adversely affecting the enjoyment of a Convention right, it may, assuming that the consequences are not too remote, attract the obligations of a Contracting State under the relevant Convention guarantee. . . . What is at issue in the present case is whether Article 3 can be applicable when the adverse consequences of extradition are, or may be, suffered outside the jurisdiction of the extradition State as a result of treatment or punishment administered in the receiving State.
86. Article 1 of the Convention . . . sets a limit, notably territorial, on the reach of the Convention. In particular, the engagement undertaken by a Contracting State is confined to 'securing' ('*reconnaître*' in the French text) the listed rights and freedoms to persons within its own 'jurisdiction'. Further, the Convention does not govern the actions of States not Parties to it, nor does it purport to be a means of requiring the Contracting States to impose Convention standards on other States. Article 1 cannot be read as justifying a general principle to the effect that, notwithstanding its extradition obligations, a Contracting State may not surrender an individual unless satisfied that the conditions awaiting him in the country of destination are in full accord with each other of the safeguards of the Convention. Indeed, as the United Kingdom Government stressed, the beneficial purpose of extradition in preventing fugitive offenders from evading justice cannot be ignored in determining the scope of application of the Convention and of Article 3 in particular.
   In the instant case it is common ground that the United Kingdom has no power over the practices and arrangements of the Virginia authorities which are the subject of the applicant's complaints. It is also true that in other international instruments cited by the United Kingdom Government – for example the 1951 United Nations Convention relating to the Status of Refugees (Article 33), the 1957 European Convention on Extradition (Article 11) and the 1984 United Nations Convention against Torture and Other Cruel, Inhuman and Degrading Treatment or Punishment (Article 3) – the problems of removing a person to another jurisdiction where unwanted consequences may follow are addressed expressly and specifically.
   These considerations cannot, however, absolve the Contracting Parties from responsibility under Article 3 for all and any foreseeable consequences of extradition suffered outside their jurisdiction.
87. In interpreting the Convention regard must be had to its special character as a treaty for the collective enforcement of human rights and fundamental freedoms (see the *Ireland v the United Kingdom* judgment of 18 January 1978, Series A no. 25, p. 90, § 239). Thus, the object and purpose of the Convention as an instrument for the protection of individual human beings require that its provisions be interpreted and applied so as to make its safeguards practical and effective (see, *inter alia*, the *Artico* judgment of 13 May 1980, Series A no. 37, p. 16 § 33). In addition, any interpretation of the rights and freedoms guaranteed has to be consistent with 'the general spirit of the Convention, an instrument designed to maintain and promote the ideals and values of a democratic society' (see the *Kjeldsen, Busk Madsen and Pedersen* judgment of 7 December 1976, Series A no. 23, p. 27, § 53).
88. Article 3 makes no provision for exceptions and no derogation from it is permissible under Article 15 in time of war or other national emergency. This absolute prohibition of torture and of inhuman or degrading treatment or punishment under the terms of the Convention shows that Article 3 enshrines one of the fundamental values of the democratic societies making up the Council of Europe. It is also to be found in similar terms in other international instruments such as the 1966 International Covenant on Civil and Political Rights and the 1969 American Convention on Human Rights and is generally recognised as an internationally accepted standard.
   The question remains whether the extradition of a fugitive to another State where he would be subjected or be likely to be subjected to torture or to inhuman or degrading treatment or punishment would itself engage the responsibility of a Contracting State under Article 3. That the abhorrence of torture has

such implications is recognised in Article 3 of the United Nations Convention Against Torture and Other Cruel, Inhuman or Degrading Treatment or Punishment, which provides that 'no State Party shall . . . extradite a person where there are substantial grounds for believing that he would be in danger of being subjected to torture'. The fact that a specialised treaty should spell out in detail a specific obligation attaching to the prohibition of torture does not mean that an essentially similar obligation is not already inherent in the general terms of Article 3 of the European Convention. It would hardly be compatible with the underlying values of the Convention, that 'common heritage of political traditions, ideals, free-doms and the rule of law' to which the Preamble refers, were a Contracting State knowingly to surrender a fugitive to another State where there were substantial grounds for believing that he would be in danger of being subjected to torture, however heinous the crime allegedly committed. Extradition in such cir-cumstances, while not explicitly referred to in the brief and general wording of Article 3, would plainly be contrary to the spirit and intendment of the Article, and in the Court's view this inherent obligation not to extradite also extends to cases in which the fugitive would be faced in the receiving State by a real risk of exposure to inhuman or degrading treatment or punishment proscribed by that Article.

89. What amounts to 'inhuman or degrading treatment or punishment' depends on all the circumstances of the case (see paragraph 100 below). Furthermore, inherent in the whole of the Convention is a search for a fair balance between the demands of the general interest of the community and the requirements of the protection of the individual's fundamental rights. As movement about the world becomes easier and crime takes on a larger international dimension, it is increasingly in the interest of all nations that sus-pected offenders who flee abroad should be brought to justice. Conversely, the establishment of safe havens for fugitives would not only result in danger for the State obliged to harbour the protected person but also tend to undermine the foundations of extradition. These considerations must also be included among the factors to be taken into account in the interpretation and application of the notions of inhuman and degrading treatment or punishment in extradition cases.

90. It is not normally for the Convention institutions to pronounce on the existence or otherwise of potential violations of the Convention. However, where an applicant claims that a decision to extradite him would, if implemented, be contrary to Article 3 by reason of its foreseeable consequences in the requesting country, a departure from this principle is necessary, in view of the serious and irreparable nature of the alleged suffering risked, in order to ensure the effectiveness of the safeguard provided by that Article (see paragraph 87 above).

91. In sum, the decision by a Contracting State to extradite a fugitive may give rise to an issue under Article 3, and hence engage the responsibility of that State under the Convention, where substantial grounds have been shown for believing that the person concerned, if extradited, faces a real risk of being subjected to torture or to inhuman or degrading treatment or punishment in the requesting country. The establishment of such responsibility inevitably involves an assessment of conditions in the requesting country against the standards of Article 3 of the Convention. Nonetheless, there is no question of adjudi-cating on or establishing the responsibility of the receiving country, whether under general international law, under the Convention or otherwise. In so far as any liability under the Convention is or may be incurred, it is liability incurred by the extraditing Contracting State by reason of its having taken action which has as a direct consequence the exposure of an individual to proscribed ill-treatment.

B. Application of Article 3 in the particular circumstances of the present case . . .

1. Whether the applicant runs a real risk of a death sentence and hence of exposure to the 'death row phenomenon'

95. Under Virginia law, before a death sentence can be returned the prosecution must prove beyond reasonable doubt the existence of at least one of the two statutory aggravating circumstances, namely future dangerousness or vileness. . . . In this connection, the horrible and brutal circumstances of the kill-ings would presumably tell against the applicant, regard being had to the case-law on the grounds for establishing the 'vileness' of the crime. . . .

Admittedly, taken on their own the mitigating factors do reduce the likelihood of the death sentence being imposed. No less than four of the five facts in mitigation expressly mentioned in the Code of Virginia could arguably apply to Mr Soering's case. These are a defendant's lack of any previous criminal history, the fact that the offence was committed while a defendant was under extreme mental or emotional disturbance, the fact that at the time of commission of the offence the capacity of a defendant to appreciate the criminality of his conduct or to conform his conduct to the requirements of the law was significantly diminished, and a defendant's age. . . .

96. These various elements arguing for or against the imposition of a death sentence have to be viewed in the light of the attitude of the prosecuting authorities.

97. The Commonwealth's Attorney for Bedford County, Mr Updike, who is responsible for conducting the prosecution against the applicant, has certified that 'should Jens Soering be convicted of the offence of capital murder as charged . . . a representation will be made in the name of the United Kingdom to the

judge at the time of sentencing that it is the wish of the United Kingdom that the death penalty should not be imposed or carried out' . . .

98. . . . notwithstanding the diplomatic context of the extradition relations between the United Kingdom and the United States, objectively it cannot be said that the undertaking to inform the judge at the sentencing stage of the wishes of the United Kingdom eliminates the risk of the death penalty being imposed. In the independent exercise of his discretion the Commonwealth's Attorney has himself decided to seek and to persist in seeking the death penalty because the evidence, in his determination, supports such action. If the national authority with responsibility for prosecuting the offence takes such a firm stance, it is hardly open to the Court to hold that there are no substantial grounds for believing that the applicant faces a real risk of being sentenced to death and hence experiencing the 'death row phenomenon'.

99. The Court's conclusion is therefore that the likelihood of the feared exposure of the applicant to the 'death row phenomenon' has been shown to be such as to bring Article 3 into play.

2. Whether in the circumstances the risk of exposure to the 'death row phenomenon' would make extradition a breach of Article 3

(A) GENERAL CONSIDERATIONS

100. As is established in the Court's case-law, ill-treatment, including punishment, must attain a minimum level of severity if it is to fall within the scope of Article 3. The assessment of this minimum is, in the nature of things, relative; it depends on all the circumstances of the case, such as the nature and context of the treatment or punishment, the manner and method of its execution, its duration, its physical or mental effects and, in some instances, the sex, age and state of health of the victim (see the above-mentioned *Ireland v the United Kingdom* judgment. Series A no. 25, p. 65, § 162; and the *Tyrer* judgment of 25 April 1978, Series A no. 26, pp. 14–15, §§ 29 and 30).

Treatment has been held by the Court to be both 'inhuman' because it was premeditated, was applied for hours at a stretch and 'caused, if not actual bodily injury, at least intense physical and mental suffering', and also 'degrading' because it was 'such as to arouse in [its] victims feelings of fear, anguish and inferiority capable of humiliating and debasing them and possibly breaking their physical or moral resistence' (see the above-mentioned *Ireland v the United Kingdom* judgment p. 66, § 167). In order for a punishment or treatment associated with it to be 'inhuman' or 'degrading', the suffering or humiliation involved must in any event go beyond that inevitable element of suffering or humiliation connected with a given form of legitimate punishment (see the *Tyrer* judgment, loc. cit.). In this connection, account is to be taken not only of the physical pain experienced but also, where there is a considerable delay before execution of the punishment, of the sentenced person's mental anguish of anticipating the violence he is to have inflicted on him.

101. Capital punishment is permitted under certain conditions by Article 2 § 1 of the Convention. . .

102. . . . 'the Convention is a living instrument which . . . must be interpreted in the light of present-day conditions'; and, in assessing whether a given treatment or punishment is to be regarded as inhuman or degrading for the purposes of Article 3, 'the Court cannot but be influenced by the developments and commonly accepted standards in the penal policy of the member States of the Council of Europe in this field' (see the above-mentioned *Tyrer* judgment, Series A no. 26, pp. 15–16, § 31). *De facto* the death penalty no longer exists in time of peace in the Contracting States to the Convention. In the few Contracting States which retain the death penalty in law for some peacetime offences, death sentences, if ever imposed, are nowadays not carried out. This 'virtual consensus in Western European legal systems that the death penalty is, under current circumstances, no longer consistent with regional standards of justice', to use the words of Amnesty International, is reflected in Protocol No. 6 to the Convention, which provides for the abolition of the death penalty in time of peace. Protocol No. 6 was opened for signature in April 1983, which in the practice of the Council of Europe indicates the absence of objection on the part of any of the Member States of the Organisation; it came into force in March 1985 and to date has been ratified by thirteen Contracting States to the Convention, not however, including the United Kingdom.

Whether these marked changes have the effect of bringing the death penalty *per se* within the prohibition of ill-treatment under Article 3 must be determined on the principles governing the interpretation of the Convention.

103. The Convention is to be read as a whole and Article 3 should therefore be construed in harmony with the provisions of Article 2 (see, *mutatis mutandis*, the *Klass and Others* judgment of 6 September 1978, Series A no. 28, p. 31, § 68). On this basis Article 3 evidently cannot have been intended by the drafters of the Convention to include a general prohibition of the death penalty since that would nullify the clear wording of Article 2 § 1.

Subsequent practice in national penal policy, in the form of a generalised abolition of capital punishment, could be taken as establishing the agreement of the Contracting States to abrogate the exception provided for under Article 2 § 1 and hence to remove a textual limit on the scope for evolutive interpretation of Article 3. However, Protocol No. 6, as a subsequent written agreement, shows that the intention of the Contracting Parties as recently as 1983 was to adopt the normal method of amendment of the text in order to introduce a new obligation to abolish capital punishment in time of peace and, what is more, to do so by an optional instrument allowing each State to choose the moment when to undertake such an engagement. In these conditions, notwithstanding the special character of the Convention (see paragraph 87 above), Article 3 cannot be interpreted as generally prohibiting the death penalty.

104. That does not mean however that circumstances relating to a death sentence can never give rise to an issue under Article 3. The manner in which it is imposed or executed, the personal circumstances of the condemned person and a disproportionality to the gravity of the crime committed, as well as the conditions of detention awaiting execution, are examples of factors capable of bringing the treatment or punishment received by the condemned person within the proscription under Article 3. Present-day attitudes in the Contracting States to capital punishment are relevant for the assessment whether the acceptable threshold of suffering or degradation has been exceeded.

(B) THE PARTICULAR CIRCUMSTANCES . . .

106. The period that a condemned prisoner can expect to spend on death row in Virginia before being executed is on average six to eight years. . . . This length of time awaiting death is . . . in a sense largely of the prisoner's own making in that he takes advantage of all avenues of appeal which are offered to him by Virginia law. The automatic appeal to the Supreme Court of Virginia normally takes no more than six months. . . . The remaining time is accounted for by collateral attacks mounted by the prisoner himself in habeas corpus proceedings before both the State and Federal courts and in applications to the Supreme Court of the United States for *certiorari* review, the prisoner at each stage being able to seek a stay of execution. . . . The remedies available under Virginia law serve the purpose of ensuring that the ultimate sanction of death is not unlawfully or arbitrarily imposed.

Nevertheless, just as some lapse of time between sentence and execution is inevitable if appeal safeguards are to be provided to the condemned person, so it is equally part of human nature that the person will cling to life by exploiting those safeguards to the full. However well-intentioned and even potentially beneficial is the provision of the complex of post-sentence procedures in Virginia, the consequence is that the condemned prisoner has to endure for many years the conditions on death row and the anguish and mounting tension of living in the ever-present shadow of death. . . .

107. As to conditions in Mecklenburg Correction Center, where the applicant could expect to be held if sentenced to death, the Court bases itself on the facts which were uncontested by the United Kingdom Government, without finding it necessary to determine the reliability of the additional evidence adduced by the applicant, notably as to the risk of homosexual abuse and physical attack undergone by prisoners on death row. . . .

The stringency of the custodial regime in Mecklenburg, as well as the services (medical, legal and social) and the controls (legislative, judicial and administrative) provided for inmates, are described in some detail above. . . . In this connection, the United Kingdom Government drew attention to the necessary requirement of extra security for the safe custody of prisoners condemned to death for murder. Whilst it might thus well be justifiable in principle, the severity of a special regime such as that operated on death row in Mecklenburg is compounded by the fact of inmates being subject to it for a protracted period lasting on average six to eight years. . .

108. At the time of the killings, the applicant was only 18 years old and there is some psychiatric evidence, which was not contested as such, that he 'was suffering from [such] an abnormality of mind . . . as substantially impaired his mental responsibility for his acts'. . . .

Unlike Article 2 of the Convention, Article 6 of the 1966 International Covenant on Civil and Political Rights and Article 4 of the 1969 American Convention on Human Rights expressly prohibit the death penalty from being imposed on persons aged less than 18 at the time of commission of the offence. Whether or not such a prohibition be inherent in the brief and general language of Article 2 of the European Convention, its explicit enunciation in other, later international instruments, the former of which has been ratified by a large number of States Parties to the European Convention, at the very least indicates that as a general principle the youth of the person concerned is a circumstance which is liable, with others, to put in question the compatibility with Article 3 of measures connected with a death sentence. . . .

It is in line with the Court's case-law . . . to treat disturbed mental health as having the same effect for the application of Article 3.

109. Virginia law, as the United Kingdom Government and the Commission emphasised, certainly does not ignore these two factors. . . . Under the Virginia Code account has to be taken of mental disturbance in a defendant, either as an absolute bar to conviction if it is judged to be sufficient to amount to insanity or, like age, as a fact in mitigation at the sentencing stage. . . . Additionally, indigent capital murder defendants are entitled to the appointment of a qualified mental health expert to assist in the preparation of their submissions at the separate sentencing proceedings. . . . These provisions in the Virginia Code undoubtedly serve, as the American courts have stated, to prevent the arbitrary or capricious imposition of the death penalty and narrowly to channel the sentencer's discretion. . . . They do not however remove the relevance of age and mental condition in relation to the acceptability, under Article 3, of the 'death row phenomenon' for a given individual once condemned to death.

Although it is not for this Court to prejudge issues of criminal responsibility and appropriate sentence, the applicant's youth at the time of the offence and his then mental state, on the psychiatric evidence as it stands, are therefore to be taken into consideration as contributory factors tending, in his case, to bring the treatment on death row within the terms of Article 3. . . .

110. For the United Kingdom Government and the majority of the Commission, the possibility of extra-diting or deporting the applicant to face trial in the Federal Republic of Germany . . . where the death penalty has been abolished under the Constitution . . . is not material for the present purposes. Any other approach, the United Kingdom Government submitted, would lead to a 'dual standard' affording the protection of the Convention to extraditable persons fortunate enough to have such an alternative des-tination available but refusing it to others not so fortunate.

This argument is not without weight. Furthermore, the Court cannot overlook either the horrible nature of the murders with which Mr Soering is charged or the legitimate and beneficial role of extradi-tion arrangements in combating crime. The purpose for which his removal to the United States was sought, in accordance with the Extradition Treaty between the United Kingdom and the United States, is undoubtedly a legitimate one. However, sending Mr Soering to be tried in his own country would remove the danger of a fugitive criminal going unpunished as well as the risk of intense and protracted suffering on death row. It is therefore a circumstance of relevance for the overall assessment under Article 3 in that it goes to the search for the requisite fair balance of interests and to the proportionality of the contested extradition decision in the particular case. . . .

(C) CONCLUSION

111. For any prisoner condemned to death, some element of delay between imposition and execution of the sentence and the experience of severe stress in conditions necessary for strict incarceration are inevitable. The democratic character of the Virginia legal system in general and the positive features of Virginia trial, sentencing and appeal procedures in particular are beyond doubt. The Court agrees with the Commission that the machinery of justice to which the applicant would be subjected in the United States is in itself neither arbitrary nor unreasonable, but, rather, respects the rule of law and affords not inconsiderable procedural safeguards to the defendant in a capital trial. Facilities are available on death row for the assistance of inmates, notably through provision of psychological and psychiatric services. . . .

However, in the Court's view, having regard to the very long period of time spent on death row in such extreme conditions, with the ever present and mounting anguish of awaiting execution of the death penalty, and to the personal circumstances of the applicant, especially his age and mental state at the time of the offence, the applicant's extradition to the United States would expose him to a real risk of treat-ment going beyond the threshold set by Article 3. A further consideration of relevance is that in the particular instance the legitimate purpose of extradition could be achieved by another means which would not involve suffering of such exceptional intensity or duration.

Accordingly, the Secretary of State's decision to extradite the applicant to the United States would, if implemented, give rise to a breach of Article 3.

This finding in no way puts in question the good faith of the United Kingdom Government, who have from the outset of the present proceedings demonstrated their desire to abide by their Convention obligations, firstly by staying the applicant's surrender to the United States authorities in accord with the interim measures indicated by the Convention institutions and secondly by themselves referring the case to the Court for a judicial ruling. . . .

FOR THESE REASONS, THE COURT UNANIMOUSLY

1. *Holds* that, in the event of the Secretary of State's decision to extradite the applicant to the United States of America being implemented, there would be a violation of Article 3. . . .

NOTES

1. Following indications by the Commission and the Court, acting under their Rules of Procedure, that it was desirable in the interests of the parties and the conduct of the case that the applicant not be extradited while the Strasbourg proceedings were pending, the UK agreed not to execute the extradition warrant until the case was over. After the Court's judgment, Mr Soering was extradited to the United States by the UK following an assurance that he would be prosecuted on murder charges that did not involve a possible death sentence.

2. Would you agree with the Court that, in a human–rights context, it was appropriate to assess the treatment to which a person would be subjected to by a sovereign state that was not a party to the ECHR? How special were the circumstances of the case? Would the Court have reached the same decision just on the basis of conditions on death row?[1]

3. In *Cruz Varas v Sweden* E Ct HRR A 201 (1991), 14 EHRR 1, the European Court of Human Rights held that its decision in the *Soering* case in the context of extradition applied equally to cases of expulsion or deportation. On the facts of that case, however, it decided that there was no real risk that the applicant would be subjected to inhuman or degrading treatment in Chile when the decision was taken by the Swedish authorities to deport him there.

4. There must be a 'real risk', not just a 'mere possibility', of proscribed ill-treatment. In *Vilvarajah v United Kingdom*, E Ct HRR A 215 (1991), 14 EHRR 248, the return to Sri Lanka of five Sri Lankan Tamils who had been refused asylum in the UK and who claimed to be at risk of ill-treatment at the hands of state security forces in the conflict between the Sri Lankan government and the Tamil Liberation movement was held not to be a breach of Article 3. Whereas there had earlier been substantial government violence against all members of the Tamil community, the danger had now been reduced to the point where Tamils were returning voluntarily to Sri Lanka. As a result, it was necessary for an applicant to show that if he remained he was at risk in his particular circumstances, and this the applicants had not done.

5. As well as the kinds of ill-treatment in the *Soering* case and *Ireland v United Kingdom*, 'inhuman treatment' may also result from the conditions in which a person is detained. The conditions in which many political detainees were kept in the *Greek* case, were held to be 'inhuman treatment' by reference to overcrowding and to inadequate heating, toilets, medical facilities, sleeping arrangements, food, recreation and provision for contact with the outside world. In *Cyprus v Turkey*, (1984) 4 EHRR 482, 541, the withholding of food and water and medical treatment from detainees was 'inhuman treatment'. In *Guzzardi v Italy*, E Ct HRR A 39 (1980), 3 EHRR 333, the preventive detention of a Mafia suspect in dilapidated, insanitary buildings in a restricted part of an isolated island was not. In *A v United Kingdom* (1980) 20 DR E Comm HR 5, a Broadmoor offender patient complained of a breach of Article 3 because of the conditions (cell conditions, clothing, lack of exercise and of association with others) of his detention when placed in seclusion for five weeks on suspicion of having started a fire. A friendly settlement was reached by which the UK agreed to pay £500 compensation, without admitting liability. The

---

1 On the *Soering* case, see J. Quigley and S. A. Shank, (1989–90) 30 Virg JIL 241; M. O'Boyle, in O'Reilly, ed., *Human Rights and Constitutional Law* (1992), p. 93; C. Van Den Wyngaert, (1990) 39 ICLQ 757; and C. Warbrick, (1990) 11 MJIL 1073.

UK also indicated that the intensive care unit within which the applicant had been detained had since been renovated and that an additional secure hospital was being built. In *B v United Kingdom*, (1984) 6 EHRR 204, the Committee of Ministers, agreeing with the Commission's Report, held that the conditions in which B had been kept in Broadmoor were not in breach of Article 3, although 'there was no doubt that there was deplorable overcrowding in the dormitory accommodation'. A friendly settlement was reached in *Simon-Herold v Austria*, (1971) 14 YBECHR 352, Rep E Com HR, 19 December 1972, in which a remand prisoner was transferred for physical examination to a hospital where he was kept for over a week in a closed ward with violent, mentally ill patients, several of whom died in his presence. By the terms of the settlement, Austria accepted that the transfer to such a ward of a prisoner who was not suspected of mental illness might be 'inhuman treatment', and indicated steps it had taken to prevent such transfers in future.

Solitary confinement, or segregation, of prisoners is not in itself a breach of Article 3; it is permissible for reasons of security or discipline or to protect the segregated prisoner from other prisoners or vice versa. It may also be justified in the interests of the administration of justice, e.g. to prevent collusion between prisoners in respect of pending proceedings. In each case, 'regard must be had to the surrounding circumstances, including the particular conditions, the stringency of the measure, its duration, the objective pursued and its effects on the person concerned': *Ensslin, Baader and Raspe v Federal Republic of Germany*, (1979) 14 DR E Com HR 64 at 109. The arrangements for the segregation of troublesome prisoners typically found in the law of states parties to the ECHR are consistent with Article 3. For example, the restrictions imposed in the United Kingdom on prisoners segregated under Rule 43, Prison Rules, are not 'inhuman treatment': for an extreme case, see *A.9907/82*, (1984) 6 EHRR 576. It is recognised, however, that 'complete sensory isolation coupled with complete social isolation can no doubt destroy the personality': *Ensslin, Baader and Raspe* case, loc. cit. above. At that point, Article 3 is infringed, however strong the justification for segregation may be. The case which has come the closest to the limits set by Article 3 is *Kröcher and Möller v Switzerland*, (1984) 34 DR E Com HR 25, 6 EHRR 345. In that case, two West Germans were detained on remand in Switzerland on charges of attempted murder following terrorist activities. They were subjected to a severe regime of sensory and social deprivation to prevent their suicide or escape. The applicants were detained in separate, non-adjacent cells, with no other prisoners on the same floor or in the cells immediately above or below theirs. Their cell windows were frosted over and lights burnt continuously in their cells. They were placed under constant television surveillance and allowed 20 minutes' exercise outside their cell during weekdays only. Newspapers, radio and television were prohibited and the applicants' watches and diaries were removed. They were not allowed contact with each other, with other prisoners or with lawyers, although any request for a visit from close relatives would not have been refused. These conditions prevailed for a month; some of them were relaxed during the remaining five months of detention on remand. The Commission accepted that the West German terrorist climate of late 1977 justified severe security measures. Referring to the arrangements for television surveillance (constant cell lighting, later replaced by an infra-red device), the Commission expressed 'serious concern with the need for such measures, their usefulness and their compatibility with Article 3'. Nonetheless, by a majority of 8 to 5, it was of the opinion that because of (i) the gradual relaxation of the conditions of sensory and social isolation and the medical evidence of their effect, and (ii) the refusal of the applicants to take advantage of certain opportunities for outside contact, the applicants had not been 'subject to a form of physical or moral suffering designed to punish them, destroy the personality or break their resistance' in breach of Article 3. In a joint dissenting opinion, four members of the Commission took the view that the Commission should have focused more upon the conditions in the first month and that these amounted to 'inhuman treatment', however great the security need. The Committee of Ministers confirmed the Commission's report.

In *Delazarus v United Kingdom*,[1] a prisoner in solitary confinement complained, inter alia, of the general conditions of detention at Wandsworth Prison. Relying upon reports of the European Prevention of Torture Committee and the Chief Inspector of Prisons in England and Wales, the Commission referred in particular to overcrowding, the confinement of prisoners to their cells for 23 hours a day and the use of chamberpots in cells. The Commission declared the claim inadmissible, however, because, the applicant, being in solitary confinement, could not complain of overcrowding and was less affected by the need to use chamberpots.

A person in detention must be given the medical treatment (including psychiatric care) necessitated by his condition; if such treatment cannot be made available, he must be released at least temporarily to allow it to be obtained elsewhere (e.g. in a specialist clinic). Failure to adopt either course may amount to inhuman treatment contrary to Article 3 where the result of that failure is to cause serious injury to health. Article 3 was infringed in *Hurtado v Switzerland*[2] when a person who had been forcibly arrested was not given an X-ray, which revealed a fractured rib, until six days after he had requested it.

In *Herczegfalvy v Austria*, E Ct HRR A 244 (1992), 15 EHRR 437, food and drugs had been forcibly administered to a violent, mentally ill patient detained in a mental hospital on hunger strike who was deemed unable to take decisions for himself. In finding that there was no breach of Article 3, the Court stated:

'82. The Court considers that the position of inferiority and powerlessness which is typical of patients confined in psychiatric hospitals calls for increased vigilance in reviewing whether the Convention has been complied with. While it is for the medical authorities to decide, on the basis of the recognised rules of medical science, on the therapeutic methods to be used, if necessary by force, to preserve the physical and mental health of patients who are entirely incapable of deciding for themselves and for whom they are therefore responsible, such patients nevertheless remain under the protection of Article 3, the requirements of which permit of no derogation.

The established principles of medicine are admittedly in principle decisive in such cases; as a general rule, a measure which is a therapeutic necessity cannot be regarded as inhuman or degrading. The Court must nevertheless satisfy itself that the medical necessity has been convincingly shown to exist.

83. In this case it is above all the length of time during which the handcuffs and security bed were used which appears worrying. However, the evidence before the Court is not sufficient to disprove the Government's argument that, according to the psychiatric principles generally accepted at the time, medical necessity justified the treatment in issue.'

6. Experimental medical treatment may be 'inhuman treatment', if not 'torture', in the absence of consent: *A.9610/81*, (1984) 6 EHRR 110. Compulsory sterilisation was understood to be contrary to the ECHR during its drafting. Ordinary medical treatment without consent, particularly psychiatric treatment and the use of drugs, may raise issues under Article 3, although they are more likely to do so under Article 8 (the right to a personality) instead.

---

1 A 17525/90 (1993), unreported.
2 E Ct HRR A 280-A, (1994) Com Rep F Sett before the Court. See also *Bonnechaux v Switzerland*, (1981) 18 DR E Com HR 100, 3 EHRR 259 and *Chartier v Italy*, (1982) 33 DR E Com HR 41, 6 EHRR 387, both Committee of Ministers decisions.

Tyrer v United Kingdom, E Ct HRR A 26 (1978), 2 EHRR 1, Eur Ct HR

The applicant was a UK citizen resident in the Isle of Man. In 1972, when aged 15, he was sentenced by a juvenile court to three strokes of the birch for an assault occasioning actual bodily harm contrary to Manx law. A sentence of corporal punishment could be imposed on males for certain offences under Manx law. It ceased to be a permissible sentence in England, Wales and Scotland in 1968. The ECHR extends to the Isle of Man as a result of a declaration made by the UK government under Article 63, which permits the extension of the ECHR to any territory 'for whose international relations' a party is responsible, subject to any 'local requirements'. The applicant complained that the birching he was given was contrary to Article 3. Although the applicant sought to withdraw his application after it had been admitted for consideration on the merits, the Commission refused to permit this because it raised issues of a general character affecting the operation of the Convention. In its report on the case, the Commission expressed the opinion, by fourteen votes to one, that the punishment was 'degrading' contrary to Article 3 and referred the case to the Court. The Court ruled that the suffering undergone by the applicant was not such as to amount to 'torture' and that his punishment was not 'inhuman'. It then considered whether it was 'degrading'.

JUDGMENT OF THE COURT

30. The Court notes first of all that a person may be humiliated by the mere fact of being criminally convicted. However, what is relevant for the purposes of Article 3 is that he should be humiliated not simply by his conviction but by the execution of the punishment which is imposed on him. In fact, in most if not all cases this may be one of the effects of judicial punishment, involving as it does unwilling subjection to the demands of the penal system.

However, as the Court pointed out in the case of *Ireland v United Kingdom* [above, p. 749], the prohibition contained in Article 3 of the Convention is absolute: no provision is made for exceptions and, under Article 15(2), there can be no derogation from Article 3. It would be absurd to hold that judicial punishment generally, by reason of its usual and perhaps almost inevitable element of humiliation, is 'degrading' within the meaning of Article 3. Some further criterion must be read into the text. Indeed, Article 3, by expressly prohibiting 'inhuman' and 'degrading' punishment, implies that there is a distinction between such punishment and punishment in general.

In the Court's view, in order for a punishment to be 'degrading' and in breach of Article 3, the humiliation or debasement involved must attain a particular level and must in any event be other than that usual element of humiliation referred to in the preceding sub-paragraph. The assessment is, in the nature of things, relative; it depends on all the circumstances of the case and, in particular on the nature and context of the punishment itself and the manner and method of its execution.

31. The Attorney-General for the Isle of Man argued that the judicial corporal punishment at issue in this case was not in breach of the Convention since it did not outrage public opinion in the Island. However, even assuming that local public opinion can have an incidence on the interpretation of the concept of 'degrading punishment' appearing in Article 3, the Court does not regard it as established that judicial corporal punishment is not considered degrading by those members of the Manx population who favour its retention: it might well be that one of the reasons why they view the penalty as an effective deterrent is precisely the element of degradation which it involves. As regards their belief that judicial corporal punishment deters criminals, it must be pointed out that a punishment does not lose its degrading character just because it is believed to be, or actually is, an effective deterrent or aid to crime control. Above all, as the Court must emphasise, it is never permissible to have recourse to punishments which are contrary to Article 3, whatever their deterrent effect may be.

The Court must also recall that the Convention is a living instrument which, as the Commission rightly stressed, must be interpreted in the light of present-day conditions. In the case now before it the Court cannot but be influenced by the developments and commonly accepted standards in the penal policy of the Member States of the Council of Europe in this field. Indeed, the Attorney General for the Isle of Man mentioned that, for many years, the provisions of Manx legislation concerning judicial corporal punishment had been under review.

32. As regards the manner and method of execution of the birching inflicted on Mr Tyrer, the Attorney-General for the Isle of Man drew particular attention to the fact that the punishment was carried out in private and without publication of the name of the offender.

Publicity may be a relevant factor in assessing whether a punishment is 'degrading' within the meaning of Article 3, but the Court does not consider that absence of publicity will necessarily prevent a given punishment from falling into that category: it may well suffice that the victim is humiliated in his own eyes, even if not in the eyes of others.

The Court notes that the relevant Isle of Man legislation, as well as giving the offender a right of appeal against sentence, provides for certain safeguards. Thus, there is a prior medical examination; the number of strokes and dimensions of the birch are regulated in detail; a doctor is present and may order the punishment to be stopped; in the case of a child or young person, the parent may attend if he so desires; the birching is carried out by a police constable in the presence of a more senior colleague.

33. Nevertheless, the Court must consider whether the other circumstances of the applicant's punishment were such as to make it 'degrading' within the meaning of Article 3.

The very nature of judicial corporal punishment is that it involves one human being inflicting physical violence on another human being. Furthermore, it is institutionalised violence, that is in the present case violence permitted by the law, ordered by the judicial authorities of the State and carried out by the police authorities of the State. Thus, although the applicant did not suffer any severe or long-lasting physical effects, his punishment—whereby he was treated as an object in the power of the authorities—constituted an assault on precisely that which it is one of the main purposes of Article 3 to protect, namely a person's dignity and physical integrity. Neither can it be excluded that the punishment may have had adverse psychological effects.

The institutionalised character of this violence is further compounded by the whole aura of official procedure attending the punishment and by the fact that those inflicting it were total strangers to the offender.

Admittedly, the relevant legislation provides that in any event birching shall not take place later than six months after the passing of the sentence. However, this does not alter the fact that there had been an interval of several weeks since the applicant's conviction by the juvenile court and a considerable delay in the police station where the punishment was carried out. Accordingly, in addition to the physical pain he experienced, Mr Tyrer was subjected to the mental anguish of anticipating the violence he was to have inflicted on him.

34. In the present case, the Court does not consider it relevant that the sentence of judicial corporal punishment was imposed on the applicant for an offence of violence. Neither does it consider it relevant that, for Mr Tyrer, birching was an alternative to a period of detention: the fact that one penalty may be preferable to, or have less adverse effects or be less serious than, another penalty does not of itself mean that the first penalty is not 'degrading' within the meaning of Article 3.

35. Accordingly, viewing these circumstances as a whole, the Court finds that the applicant was subjected to a punishment in which the element of humiliation attained the level inherent in the notion of 'degrading punishment' as explained at paragraph 30 above. The indignity of having the punishment administered over the bare posterior aggravated to some extent the degrading character of the applicant's punishment but it was not the only or determining factor.

NOTES

1. The Court held, by six votes to one, that Article 3 had been infringed. Sir Gerald Fitzmaurice was the dissenting judge. Responding to the Court's arguments, he could not see the relevance of the fact that the violence involved was 'institutionalised', since this was a characteristic of any punishment for crime. Nor could he agree that the 'whole aura' of official procedure attending any punishment and the infliction of the birching by strangers 'further compounded' the institutionalised character of the violence. Any institutionalised activity was bound to have the aura described and some offenders might feel *less* degraded because the punishment was administered by someone they did not know. As to the psychological effect of a birching (which was purely a matter of conjecture) and the delay in carrying out the punishment, these were considerations that might concern the humanity of the punishment, but not its degrading character. In Judge Sir Gerald Fitzmaurice's view, the gravamen of the Court's complaint was that judicial corporal punishment was degrading per se and that the circumstances of its imposition and application were irrelevant. This was an opinion with which Sir Gerald could not agree. Examining

the facts of the case, he considered it to be decisive that the applicant was a juvenile. Whereas corporal punishment had come to be regarded as an undesirable form of punishment, it had 'not been generally regarded as degrading when applied to juveniles and young offenders . . .' In Judge Sir Gerald Fitzmaurice's opinion, the corporal punishment of juveniles was not degrading for the purposes of Article 3 in the absence of 'seriously aggravating circumstances' which were not present in this case. *Did* the Court decide the case on the basis that *judicial* corporal punishment is 'degrading' per se? In what circumstances would its imposition not be in breach of the ECHR? Was the UK's problem that judicial corporal punishment is no longer 'commonly accepted' in European penal policy (see para. 31, judgment). Note in this connection the Court's emphasis upon the 'dynamic', or evolving, nature of the obligations in the ECHR. The ECHR, Article 2, permits the death penalty, which is the ultimate in 'institutionalised violence'. Article 5, ECHR, also allows, as the Court indicated, incarceration, which, however good the conditions in prison, must be at least as 'degrading' as birching. It follows that the ECHR draws a distinction between acceptable and unacceptable kinds, as well as degrees, of degradation. One guideline as to the kind of conduct proscribed by Article 3 is that, unlike most of the ECHR guarantees, Article 3 cannot be derogated from even in time of war: see Article 15, below, p. 851. Did the Court take this into account in the *Tyrer* case?

2. No sentence of birching was carried out after the *Tyrer* case before the eventual abolition of judicial corporal punishment in 1993 by statute by the Tynwald, the Isle of Man Parliament.[1]

Costello-Roberts v United Kingdom, E Ct HRR A 247-C (1993), 19 EHRR 112, Eur Court HR

The applicant was a seven year old pupil at a private boarding school. As a disciplinary punishment, he was given three 'whacks' with a gym shoe over his trousers by the headmaster with no one else present. The applicant alleged breaches of Articles 3, 8 and 13. In its report, the Commission expressed the opinion, by nine votes to four, that there had been a breach of Article 8, but not of Article 3 and, by eleven votes to two, that there had been a breach of Article 13. The Court held unanimously that there had been no breach of Articles 8 or 13. The following extract concerns the claim under Article 3.

JUDGMENT OF THE COURT

I. RESPONSIBILITY OF THE RESPONDENT STATE . . .

25. . . . Whilst conceding that the State exercised a limited degree of control and supervision over independent schools, such as the applicant's, the Government denied that they were directly responsible for every aspect of the way in which they were run; in particular, they assumed no function in matters of discipline.

Accordingly, it must first be considered whether the facts complained of by the applicant are such as may engage the responsibility of the United Kingdom under the Convention.

26. The Court has consistently held that the responsibility of a State is engaged if a violation of one of the rights and freedoms defined in the Convention is the result of non-observance by that State of its obligation under Article 1 to secure those rights and freedoms in its domestic law to everyone within its jurisdiction (see, *mutatis mutandis*, the *Young, James and Webster v the United Kingdom* judgment of 13 August 1981, Series A no. 44, p. 20, § 49). Indeed, it was accepted by the Government for the purposes of the present proceedings that such an obligation existed as regards securing the rights guaranteed by

---

1 In *Teare v Callaghan* (1982) 4 EHRR 232, a birching sentence was quashed by the Isle of Man High Court on the ground that the Isle of Man should comply with its treaty obligations as far as possible and that on the facts there were alternative sentences available not involving a breach of the ECHR. See S. Ghandhi, (1983) 46 MLR 513 and G.T.Z. 1982 PL 5.

Articles 3 and 8 to pupils in independent schools. Notwithstanding this, they argued that the responsibility of the United Kingdom was not in fact engaged because the English legal system had adequately secured the rights guaranteed by Articles 3 and 8 of the Convention by prohibiting the use of any corporal punishment which was not moderate or reasonable.

27. The Court notes first that . . . the State has an obligation to secure to children their right to education under Article 2 of Protocol No. 1. It recalls that the provisions of the Convention and its Protocols must be read as a whole. . . . Functions relating to the internal administration of a school, such as discipline, cannot be said to be merely ancillary to the educational process (see, *mutatis mutandis*, the *Campbell and Cosans v the United Kingdom* judgment of 25 February 1982, Series A no. 48, p. 14, § 33). That a school's disciplinary system falls within the ambit of the right to education has also been recognised, more recently, in Article 28 of the United Nations Convention on the Rights of the Child of 20 November 1989 which entered into force on 2 September 1990 and was ratified by the United Kingdom on 16 December 1991. This Article, in the context of the right of the child to education, provides as follows:

'2. States Parties shall take all appropriate measures to ensure that school discipline is administered in a manner consistent with the child's human dignity and in conformity with the present Convention.'

Secondly, in the United Kingdom, independent schools co-exist with a system of public education. The fundamental right of everyone to education is a right guaranteed equally to pupils in State and independent schools, no distinction being made between the two (see, *mutatis mutandis*, the above-mentioned *Kjeldsen, Busk Madsen and Pedersen* judgment, Series A no. 23, p. 24, § 50).

Thirdly, the Court agrees with the applicant that the State cannot absolve itself from responsibility by delegating its obligations to private bodies or individuals (see, *mutatis mutandis*, the *Van der Mussele v Belgium* judgment of 23 November 1983, Series A no. 70, pp. 14–15, §§ 28–30).[1]

28. Accordingly, in the present case, which relates to the particular domain of school discipline, the treatment complained of, although it was the act of a headmaster of an independent school, is none the less such as may engage the responsibility of the United Kingdom under the Convention if it proves to be incompatible with Article 3 or Article 8 or both.

II. ALLEGED VIOLATION OF ARTICLE 3

29. Jeremy Costello-Roberts claimed that the corporal punishment inflicted on him constituted 'degrading punishment'. . . .

He maintained that although the actual physical force to which he had been subjected had been moderate, there had, nevertheless, been an assault on his dignity and physical integrity. . . . The degrading character had, he claimed, been aggravated by his age at the time (seven years), the fact that he had been at the school for only about five weeks, the humiliating site of the punishment, the impersonal and automatic way in which it had been administered as a result of 'totting up' demerit marks for minor offences, and the three-day wait between the 'sentence' and its implementation. . . .

30. In its *Tyrer v the United Kingdom* judgment . . . the Court has already held that corporal punishment may constitute an assault on a person's dignity and physical integrity as protected under Article 3. However, as was pointed out in paragraph 30 of that judgment, in order for punishment to be 'degrading' and in breach of Article 3, the humiliation or debasement involved must attain a particular level of severity and must in any event be other than that usual element of humiliation inherent in any punishment. . . .

The assessment of this minimum level of severity depends on all the circumstances of the case. Factors such as the nature and context of the punishment, the manner and method of its execution, its duration, its physical and mental effects and, in some instances, the sex, age and state of health of the victim must all be taken into account (see the *Ireland v the United Kingdom* judgment. . . .)

31. The circumstances of the applicant's punishment may be distinguished from those of Mr Tyrer's which was found to be degrading within the meaning of Article 3. Mr Costello-Roberts was a young boy punished in accordance with the disciplinary rules in force within the school in which he was a boarder. This amounted to being slippered three times on his buttocks through his shorts with a rubber-soled gym shoe by the headmaster in private. . . . Mr Tyrer, on the other hand, was a young man sentenced in the local juvenile court to three strokes of the birch on the bare posterior. His punishment was administered some three weeks later in a police station where he was held by two policemen whilst a third administered the punishment, pieces of the birch breaking at the first stroke.

---

1 *Ed.* In this case, concerning 'forced labour' contrary to Article 4, ECHR, the Court had rejected the defendant state's argument that it was not responsible for the conduct of a private professional body, the *ordre des avocats*, concerning legal aid when the defendant state relied upon the arrangements for legal aid made by the *ordre* so as to comply with the right to legal aid in Article 6(3)(c).

32. Beyond the consequences to be expected from measures taken on a purely disciplinary plane, the applicant had adduced no evidence of any severe or long-lasting effects as a result of the treatment complained of. A punishment which does not occasion such effects may fall within the ambit of Article 3 . . . provided that in the particular circumstances of the case it may be said to have reached the minimum threshold of severity required. While the Court has certain misgivings about the automatic nature of the punishment and the three-day wait before its imposition, it considers that minimum level of severity not to have been attained in this case.

Accordingly, no violation of Article 3 has been established.

FOR THESE REASONS, THE COURT

1. *Holds* by five votes to four that there has been no violation of Article 3. . . .

Joint partly dissenting opinion of Judges Ryssdal, Thór Vilhjálmsson, Matscher and Wildhaber

We agree with the majority that the United Kingdom may indeed incur responsibility under the Convention on account of the administration of corporal punishment in independent schools. Primary education is compulsory in the United Kingdom as elsewhere. In such fields, the State must exercise some measure of control over private schools so as to safeguard the essence of the Convention guarantees. A State can neither shift prison administration to the private sector and thereby make corporal punishment in prisons lawful, nor can it permit the setting up of a system of private schools which are run irrespective of Convention guarantees. On the other hand, it is granted that the Convention is not applicable as such in all respects to relations between private persons. It therefore becomes a matter of balancing whether and to what extent private schools must respect Convention guarantees, in particular Articles 3 and 8. . . .

However, in the present case, the ritualised character of the corporal punishment is striking. After a three-day gap, the headmaster of the school 'whacked' a lonely and insecure 7-year-old boy. A spanking on the spur of the moment might have been permissible, but in our view, the official and formalised nature of the punishment meted out, without adequate consent of the mother,[1] was degrading to the applicant and violated Article 3.

At the relevant time the laws relating to corporal punishment applied to all pupils in both State and independent schools in the United Kingdom. However, reflecting developments throughout Europe, such punishment was made unlawful for pupils in State and certain independent schools. Given that such punishment was being progressively outlawed elsewhere, it must have appeared all the more degrading to those remaining pupils in independent schools whose disciplinary regimes persisted in punishing their pupils in this way.

NOTES

1. In contrast with the *Costello-Roberts* case, in which neither the Court nor the Commission considered that Article 3 had been infringed, in two other cases – *Warwick v United Kingdom*[2] and *Y v United Kingdom*[3] – the Commission was of the opinion that there had been a breach of Article 3. In the *Warwick* case, a 16 year old girl at a state school who had been caught smoking a cigarette was given one stroke of the cane on the hand, causing bruising, by the headmaster in his office in the presence of the deputy headmaster and another similarly delinquent girl immediately after being reported. The Committee of Ministers could not decide whether Article 3 had been infringed, being unable to obtain a two thirds majority either way.[4] In

---

1 *Ed.* The school prospectus stated that a high standard of discipline was maintained, but did not mention corporal punishment. Nor did the mother enquire.
2 60 DR 5 (1986) Com Rep; CM Resolution DH (89) 5. There have been several other UK cases. See e.g. *X v UK* No. 7907/77, 24 YB 402 (1981), in which the UK made an ex gratia payment of £1,200 compensation and £1,000 costs where a 14 year old girl at a state school had been caned.
3 E Ct HRR A 247-C (1992) Com Rep, 17 EHRR 238.
4 It is likely that the voting was influenced in favour of the defendant state by the changes in the law referred to below, in note 2, of which the Committee was informed. The Committee did, however, recommend that the UK pay the applicants' costs.

Y v United Kingdom, a 15 year old schoolboy at a private school was given four strokes of the cane on his bottom through his trousers, resulting in heavy bruising. The caning was administered by the headmaster in private as soon as the pupil was sent to him for defacing another boy's file. A county court claim in assault had been unsuccessful on the basis that the parents had agreed by contract to caning as a disciplinary punishment and the force used was reasonable. The *Y v United Kingdom* case was not decided by the court, having been struck off its list following a friendly settlement. The UK government agreed to pay £8,000 compensation and £9,000 in costs. In the one other case on school corporal punishment that has reached the Court, it was held in *Campbell and Cosans v United Kingdom*[1] that the *threat* of corporal punishment (resulting from its availability in a state school) did not cause sufficient suffering or degradation to be 'inhuman' or 'degrading' *treatment*. As yet there has been no ruling as to corporal punishment administered by parents or child-minders.[2] Bearing in mind that the problem would appear to be uniquely British, it should be noted that UK disciplinary corporal punishment cases will become less frequent following legislative changes. Corporal punishment of all pupils in state schools and of publicly funded (but not other) pupils in independent schools in Great Britain has been abolished.[3] In addition, independent boarding schools in England and Wales with less than 50 boarders are required under the Children Act 1989, s. 60, to register as children's homes and, as such, are prohibited from using corporal punishment.

2. The *Tyrer* and *Costello-Roberts* cases concern degrading punishment. There have also been cases of degrading treatment. In the *East African Asians* cases, (1977) 78A DR E Com HR 5, CM Resolution DH (77)2, 3 EHRR 76 (extracts), the applicants were 31 UK citizens or British protected persons who had been resident in Kenya or Uganda and who had fled because of anti-Asian government policies. They were refused entry into the UK following the enactment of the Commonwealth Immigrants Act 1968, which the Commission concluded was racially motivated. In 1973, the Commission found that the exclusion of the 25 applicants who were UK citizens, and who therefore had had a right to entry before the 1968 Act, was 'degrading' treatment contrary to Article 3. The Commission stated (p. 86):

'The Commission recalls in this connection that, as generally recognised, a special importance should be attached to discrimination based on race; [publicly] to single out a group of persons for differential treatment on the basis of race might, in certain circumstances, constitute a special form of affront to human dignity; and that differential treatment of a group of persons on the basis of race might therefore be capable of constituting degrading treatment when differential treatment on some other ground would raise no such question.

The Commission considers that the racial discrimination, to which the applicants have been publicly subjected by the application of the above immigration legislation, constitutes an interference with their human dignity which, in the special circumstances described above [i.e. the reasonable expectation of those Asians who retained their UK citizenship following independence that they would retain a right of entry to the UK], amounted to "degrading treatment" in the sense of Article 3 of the Convention.'

After much delay, and after all 31 applicants in the case had been admitted to the UK, the Committee of Ministers decided in 1977 that 'no further action' was called for: CM Resolution DH (77) 2. The Committee did not rule on the question whether Article 3 had been infringed. Note that the UK is not bound by Article 3(2), Fourth Protocol, ECHR.

---

1 E Ct HRR A 48 (1982), 4 EHRR 293. There was a breach of Article 2, First Protocol in this case: see above, p. 743, n. 3.
2 As to punishment by child-minders in English law, see *Sutton London Borough Council v Davis* (1994) Times, 17 March.
3 Education (No. 2) Act 1986, s. 47 and the Education (Scotland) Act 1980, s. 48A.

3. Confirming its opinion in the East African Asian cases, in *Abdulaziz, Cabales and Balkandali v United Kingdom*[1] (which concerned UK Immigration Rules which discriminated against women) the Commission stated that although a state has a sovereign power to admit persons to its territory, by virtue of Article 3, 'the state's discretion in immigration matters is not of an unfettered character, for a State may not implement policies of a purely racist nature, such as a policy prohibiting the entry of any person of a particular skin colour'.

4. A number of allegations of degrading treatment have concerned persons in detention. In *Hurtado v Switzerland*,[2] the applicant had defecated in his trousers because of the shock caused by a stun grenade used in his arrest. The Commission concluded that there had been degrading treatment when he was not able to change his clothing until the next day and after he had been transported between buildings and questioned.

3 Article 5: Freedom of the person

Fox, Campbell and Hartley v United Kingdom, E Ct HRR A 182 (1990), 13 EHRR 157, Eur Court HR

The applicants were arrested in Northern Ireland by a police constable exercising his statutory power under s. 11, Northern Ireland (Emergency Provisions) Act 1978 'to arrest without warrant any person whom he suspects of being a terrorist'. This power had been interpreted in *McKee v Chief Constable for Northern Ireland* [1984] 1 WLR 1358, HL as incorporating a subjective test, so that an arrest was permissible if the policeman had an 'honestly held suspicion'. On their arrest, the applicants were told only that they were being arrested under s. 11 on suspicion of being terrorists; they were given no facts in support of the suspicion. The applicants claimed, inter alia, that Articles 5(1)(c) and 5(2) had been infringed. In its report, the Commission expressed the opinion, by seven votes to five, that both provisions had been infringed in respect of all three applicants.

JUDGMENT OF THE COURT

32. The 'reasonableness' of the suspicion on which an arrest must be based forms an essential part of the safeguard against arbitrary arrest and detention which is laid down in Article 5 § 1(c). The Court agrees with the Commission and the Government that having a 'reasonable suspicion' presupposes the existence of facts or information which would satisfy an objective observer that the person concerned may have committed the offence. What may be regarded as 'reasonable' will however depend upon all the circumstances.

In this respect, terrorist crime falls into a special category. Because of the attendant risk of loss of life and human suffering, the police are obliged to act with utmost urgency in following up all information, including information from secret sources. Further, the police may frequently have to arrest a suspected terrorist on the basis of information which is reliable but which cannot, without putting in jeopardy the source of the information, be revealed to the suspect or produced in court to support a charge.

As the Government pointed out, in view of the difficulties inherent in the investigation and prosecution of terrorist-type offences in Northern Ireland, the 'reasonableness' of the suspicion justifying such

---

1 Eur Com HR Rep para 113, reprinted in E Ct HRR A 94 (1985). The Commission found no breach of Article 3. For the facts of the case and the Court's ruling under Articles 8 and 14, see below, p. 849. The Court dismissed the claim under Article 3 summarily: 'The Court observes that the difference of treatment complained of did not denote any contempt or lack of respect for the personality of the applicants and that it was not designed to, and did not, humiliate or debase but was intended solely to achieve the aims referred to (protect the labour market, etc) ...'. If an intention to degrade is required, some cases of indirect racial discrimination could not be in breach of Article 3.

2 E Ct HRR A 280-A (1994) Com Rep. F Sett before the Court.

arrests cannot always be judged according to the same standards as are applied in dealing with conventional crime. Nevertheless, the exigencies of dealing with terrorist crime cannot justify stretching the notion of 'reasonableness' to the point where the essence of the safeguard secured by Article 5 § 1(c) is impaired. . . .

34. Certainly Article 5 § 1(c) of the Convention should not be applied in such a manner as to put disproportionate difficulties in the way of the police authorities of the Contracting States in taking effective measures to counter organised terrorism (see, *mutatis mutandis*, the *Klaas and Others* judgment of 6 September 1978, Series A no. 28, pp. 27 and 30–31, §§ 58 and 68). It follows that the Contracting States cannot be asked to establish the reasonableness of the suspicion grounding the arrest of a suspected terrorist by disclosing the confidential sources of supporting information or even facts which would be susceptible to indicating such sources or their identity.

Nevertheless the Court must be enabled to ascertain whether the essence of the safeguard afforded by Article 5 § 1(c) has been secured. Consequently the respondent Government have to furnish at least some facts or information capable of satisfying the Court that the arrested person was reasonably suspected of having committed the alleged offence. This is all the more necessary where, as in the present case, the domestic law does not require reasonable suspicion, but sets a lower threshold by merely requiring honest suspicion.

35. The Court accepts that the arrest and detention of each of the present applicants was based on a *bona fide* suspicion that he or she was a terrorist, and that each of them, including Mr Hartley, was questioned during his or her detention about specific terrorist acts of which he or she was suspected.

The fact that Mr Fox and Ms Campbell both have previous convictions for acts of terrorism connected with the IRA . . ., although it could reinforce a suspicion linking them to the commission of terrorist-type offences, cannot form the sole basis of a suspicion justifying their arrest in 1986, some seven years later.

The fact that all the applicants, during their detention, were questioned about specific terrorist acts, does no more than confirm that the arresting officers had a genuine suspicion that they had been involved in those acts, but cannot satisfy an objective observer that the applicants may have committed these acts.

The aforementioned elements on their own are insufficient to support the conclusion that there was 'reasonable suspicion'. The Government have not provided any further material on which the suspicion against the applicants was based. Their explanations therefore do not meet the minimum standard set by Article 5 § 1(c) for judging the reasonableness of a suspicion for the arrest of an individual. . . .

40. Paragraph 2 of Article 5 contains the elementary safeguard that any person arrested should know why he is being deprived of his liberty. This provision is an integral part of the scheme of protection afforded by Article 5: by virtue of paragraph 2 any person arrested must be told, in simple, non-technical language that he can understand, the essential legal and factual grounds for his arrest, so as to be able, if he sees fit, to apply to a court to challenge its lawfulness in accordance with paragraph 4. . . . Whilst this information must be conveyed 'promptly' (in French: '*dans le plus court delai*'), it need not be related in its entirety by the arresting officer at the very moment of the arrest. Whether the content and promptness of the information conveyed were sufficient is to be assessed in each case according to its special features.

41. On being taken into custody, Mr Fox, Ms Campbell and Mr Hartley were simply told by the arresting officer that they were being arrested under section 11(1) of the 1978 Act on suspicion of being terrorists. . . . This bare indication of the legal basis for the arrest, taken on its own, is insufficient for the purposes of Article 5 § 2, as the Government conceded.

However, following their arrest all of the applicants were interrogated by the police about their suspected involvement in specific criminal acts and their suspected membership of proscribed organisations. . . . There is no ground to suppose that these interrogations were not such as to enable the applicants to understand why they had been arrested. The reasons why they were suspected of being terrorists were thereby brought to their attention during their interrogation.

42. Mr Fox and Ms Campbell were arrested at 3.40 p.m. on 5 February 1986 at Woodbourne RUC station and then separately questioned the same day between 8.15 p.m. and 10.00 p.m. at Castlereagh Police Office. . . . Mr Hartley, for his part, was arrested at his home at 7.55 a.m. on 18 August 1986 and taken to Antrim Police Station where he was questioned between 11.05 a.m. and 12.15 p.m. . . . In the context of the present case these intervals of a few hours cannot be regarded as falling outside the constraints of time imposed by the notion of promptness in Article 5 § 2. . . .

FOR THESE REASONS, THE COURT

1. *Holds* by four votes to three that there has been a breach of Article 5 § 1;
2. *Holds* unanimously that there has been no breach of Article 5 § 2; . . .

Joint dissenting opinion of Judges Sir Vincent Evans, Bernhardt and Palm

We are unable to agree with the finding of the majority of the Court that there has been a violation of Article 5 § 1(c) in this case. . . .

The majority accept – and on this we agree – that the arrest and detention of each of the applicants was based on a *bona fide* suspicion that he or she was a terrorist and that each of them was questioned during his or her detention about specific terrorist acts of which he or she was suspected. But, in the opinion of the majority the latter fact does no more than confirm that the arresting officers had a genuine suspicion and a genuine suspicion was not the equivalent of a reasonable suspicion.

In our view the 'genuine suspicion' on the part of the arresting officers that the applicants were involved in the specific terrorist acts about which they were questioned must have had some basis in information received by them, albeit from sources which the Government maintain that they are unable to disclose for security reasons. In the situation in Northern Ireland the police must have a responsibility to follow up such information of involvement in terrorist activities and, if circumstances so warrant, to arrest and detain the suspect for further investigation.

In cases such as these it is not possible to draw a sharp distinction between genuine suspicion and reasonable suspicion. Having regard to all the circumstances and to the facts and information between the Court, including in the case of Mr Fox and Ms Campbell the fact that they had previously been involved in and convicted of terrorist activities, we are satisfied that there were reasonable grounds for suspicion justifying the arrest and detention of the applicants in accordance with Article 5 § 1(c). . . .

NOTES

1. On the abolition of the arrest power in s. 11, 1978 Act, see above, p. 290. The *Fox, Campbell and Hartley* case was followed on Articles 5(1)(c) and 5(2) in *Murray v United Kingdom*, E Ct HRR A 300-A (1994), 19 EHRR 193.

2. Should it be sufficient, as the Court allows, that a person may infer the information to which he is entitled under Article 5(2) from what might be said during questioning? Might the Court have been unduly influenced by the terrorist context of the case when stating what it appears to intend as an interpretation of Article 5(2) of general application?

Brogan v United Kingdom, E Ct HRR A 145 (1988), 11 EHRR 117, Eur Ct HR

The four applicants were arrested by the police in Northern Ireland under s. 12, Prevention of Terrorism (Temporary Provisions) Act 1984 as persons suspected on reasonable grounds of being 'concerned in the commission, preparation or instigation of acts of terrorism' connected with the affairs of Northern Ireland. They were then questioned in respect of specific criminal offences resulting from terrorist activities and of membership of proscribed organisations. All four applicants were later released without being charged with any offence, having been detained for periods ranging from four days and six hours to six days and sixteen and a half hours. Under the 1984 Act, it was lawful to detain a person for an initial period of 48 hours and, on the authorisation of the Secretary of State for Northern Ireland, for up to five more days, making a total of seven days' detention, without bringing him before a magistrate. In this case, the applicants alleged breaches of Article 5(1)(c), 5(3), 5(4), and 5(5), ECHR. On the Article 5(1)(c) claim, see note 3, below. As to Article 5(4), the Court held, unanimously, that habeas corpus provided the remedy required by Article 5(4). The following extract from the Court's judgment concerns Article 5(3), (5). The Commission had expressed the opinion in its report that Article 5(3) had been infringed in respect of the two applicants who had been detained for over five days, but not in respect of the two who had been detained for four to five days. The Commission had also expressed the opinion that Article 5(5) had been infringed in respect of the first two applicants.

JUDGMENT OF THE COURT

57.   The Commission, in its report, cited its established case-law to the effect that a period of four days in cases concerning ordinary criminal offences and of five days in exceptional cases could be considered compatible with the requirement of promptness in Article 5 § 3 (see respectively the admissibility decisions in *application no. 2894/66, X v Netherlands*, Yearbook of the Convention, Vol. 9, p. 568 [1966], and in *application No. 4960/71, X v Belgium*, Collection of Decisions, Vol. 42, pp. 54–55 [1973]). In the Commission's opinion, given the context in which the applicants were arrested and the special problems associated with the investigation of terrorist offences, a somewhat longer period of detention than in normal cases was justified. The Commission concluded that the periods of four days and six hours (Mr McFadden) and four days and eleven hours (Mr Tracey) did satisfy the requirement of promptness, whereas the periods of five days and eleven hours (Mr Brogan) and six days and sixteen and a half hours (Mr Coyle) did not.

58.   The fact that a detained person is not charged or brought before a court does not in itself amount to a violation of the first part of Article 5 § 3. No violation of Article 5 § 3 can arise if the arrested person is released 'promptly' before any judicial control of his detention would have been feasible (see the *de Jong, Baljet and van den Brink* judgment of 22 May 1984, Series A no. 77, p. 25, § 52). If the arrested person is not released promptly, he is entitled to a prompt appearance before a judge or judicial officer.

The assessment of 'promptness' has to be made in the light of the object and purpose of Article 5. . . . The Court has regard to the importance of this Article in the Convention system: it enshrines a fundamental human right, namely the protection of the individual against arbitrary interferences by the State with his right to liberty (see the *Bozano* judgment of 18 December 1986, Series A no. 111, p. 23, § 54). Judicial control of interferences by the executive with the individual's right to liberty is an essential feature of the guarantee embodied in Article 5 § 3, which is intended to minimise the risk of arbitrariness. . . .

59.   The obligation expressed in English by the word 'promptly' and in French by the word '*aussitôt*' is clearly distinguishable from the less strict requirement in the second part of paragraph 3 ('reasonable time'/'*délai raisonnable*') and even from that in paragraph 4 of Article 5 ('speedily'/'*à bref délai*'). The term 'promptly' also occurs in the English text of paragraph 2, where the French text uses the words '*dans le plus court délai*'. As indicated in the *Ireland v the United Kingdom* judgment (18 January 1978, Series A no. 25, p. 76, § 199), 'promptly' in paragraph 3 may be understood as having a broader significance than '*aussitôt*', which literally means immediately. Thus confronted with versions of a law-making treaty which are equally authentic but not exactly the same, the Court must interpret them in a way that reconciles them as far as possible and is most appropriate in order to realise the aim and achieve the object of the treaty (see, *inter alia*, the *Sunday Times* judgment of 26 April 1979, Series A no. 30, p. 30, § 48, and Article 33 § 4 of the Vienna Convention of 23 May 1969 on the Law of Treaties).

The use in the French text of the word '*aussitôt*', with its constraining connotation of immediacy, confirms that the degree of flexibility attaching to the notion of 'promptness' is limited, even if the attendant circumstances can never be ignored for the purposes of the assessment under paragraph 3. Whereas promptness is to be assessed in each case according to its special features (see the above-mentioned *de Jong, Baljet and van den Brink* judgment, Series A no. 77, p. 25, § 52), the significance to be attached to those features can never be taken to the point of impairing the very essence of the right guaranteed by Article 5 § 3, that is to the point of effectively negativing the State's obligation to ensure a prompt release or a prompt appearance before a judicial authority.

60.   The instant case is exclusively concerned with the arrest and detention, by virtue of powers granted under special legislation, of persons suspected of involvement in terrorism in Northern Ireland. . . . There is no call to determine in the present judgment whether in an ordinary criminal case any given period, such as four days, in police or administrative custody would as a general rule be capable of being compatible with the first part of Article 5 § 3.

None of the applicants was in fact brought before a judge or judicial officer during his time in custody. The issue to be decided is therefore whether, having regard to the special features relied on by the Government, each applicant's release can be considered as 'prompt' for the purposes of Article 5 § 3.

61.   The investigation of terrorist offences undoubtedly presents the authorities with special problems. . . . The Court takes full judicial notice of the factors adverted to by the Government in this connection. It is also true that in Northern Ireland the referral of police requests for extended detention to the Secretary of State and the individual scrutiny of each police request by a Minister do provide a form of executive control. . . . In addition, the need for the continuation of the special powers has been constantly monitored by Parliament and their operation regularly reviewed by independent personalities. . . . The Court accepts that, subject to the existence of adequate safeguards, the context of terrorism in Northern Ireland has the effect of prolonging the period during which the authorities may, without violating Article 5 § 3, keep a person suspected of serious terrorist offences in custody before bringing him before a judge or other judicial officer.

The difficulties, alluded to by the Government, of judicial control over decisions to arrest and detain suspected terrorists may affect the manner of implementation of Article 5 § 3, for example in calling for appropriate procedural precautions in view of the nature of the suspected offences. However, they cannot justify, under Article 5 § 3, dispensing altogether with 'prompt' judicial control.

62.   As indicated above (paragraph 59), the scope for flexibility in interpreting and applying the notion of 'promptness' is very limited. In the Court's view, even the shortest of the four periods of detention, namely the four days and six hours spent in police custody by Mr McFadden . . ., falls outside the strict constraints as to time permitted by the first part of Article 5 § 3. To attach such importance to the special features of this case as to justify so lengthy a period of detention without appearance before a judge or other judicial officer would be an unacceptably wide interpretation of the plain meaning of the word 'promptly'. An interpretation to this effect would import into Article 5 § 3 a serious weakening of a procedural guarantee to the detriment of the individual and would entail consequences impairing the very essence of the right protected by this provision. The Court thus has to conclude that none of the applicants was either brought 'promptly' before a judicial authority or released 'promptly' following his arrest. The undoubted fact that the arrest and detention of the applicants were inspired by the legitimate aim of protecting the community as a whole from terrorism is not on its own sufficient to ensure compliance with the specific requirements of Article 5 § 3.

There has thus been a breach of Article 5 § 3 in respect of all four applicants. . . .

67.   . . . In the instant case, the applicants were arrested and detained lawfully under domestic law but in breach of paragraph 3 of Article 5. This violation could not give rise, either before or after the findings made by the European Court in the present judgment, to an enforceable claim for compensation by the victims before the domestic courts; this was not disputed by the Government.

Accordingly, there has also been a breach of paragraph 5 in this case in respect of all four applicants. . . .

FOR THESE REASONS, THE COURT. . . .

2. *Holds* by twelve votes to seven that there has been a violation of Article 5 § 3 in respect of all four applicants; . . .

4. *Holds* by thirteen votes to six that there has been a violation of Article 5 § 5 in respect of all four applicants; . . .

NOTES

1. The UK's response to the decision in the *Brogan* case was to derogate under Article 15, ECHR from its obligations under, inter alia, Article 5(3), ECHR in respect of the public emergency which it judged to exist in Northern Ireland. The UK had on several occasions previously derogated under Article 15 in respect of Northern Ireland: see above, p. 750, and below, p. 851. No such derogation was in operation at the time of the *Brogan* case. The United Kingdom decided upon this response to the *Brogan* case after failing to find a way of bringing its law into line with the judgment that was consistent with its traditions and that also allowed it to counteract sufficiently the threat posed by terrorism in Northern Ireland. In *Brannigan and McBride v United Kingdom*, E Ct HR A 258-B (1993), 17 EHRR 539, the Court held that the UK derogation notice was valid, so that the detention of terrorist suspects under the same power as in the *Brogan* case and for similar periods was not in breach of Article 5(3). For the legislation that has replaced, in similar terms, the Prevention of Terrorism (Temporary Provisions) Act 1984, see above, p. 301.

2. The right to 'liberty' in Article 5, which the Court interpreted in the *Brogan* case, concerns individual liberty in the classic sense, that is to say the physical liberty of the person; it is not to do with freedom of movement, as to which see Art. 2 of the Fourth Protocol, above, p. 744: *Engel v Netherlands*, E Ct HR A 22 (1976), 1 EHRR 647. The distinction between the two is not always easy to make. Confinement of a soldier to an unlocked room in barracks during off duty hours was not within Article 5; detention in a locked cell therein during off and on duty hours was: *Engel* case, above. The restriction of a suspected Mafia member to a part of a small island where he was subject to constant surveillance was controlled by Article 5; his later transfer and restriction to a mainland village and subjection only to a daily reporting obligation was not: *Guzzardi v Italy*, E Ct HRR A 39 (1980), 3 EHRR 333.

3. In the *Brogan* case, the Court held, by 16 votes to 3, that although no charges were eventually brought, there was no breach of Article 5(1)(c), inter alia, because the purpose of the arrest had been one justified by Article 5(1)(c), viz to bring the arrested persons before a competent legal authority with a view to prosecution for a criminal offence. Article 5(1)(c) does not authorise preventive detention: *Lawless v Ireland*, E Ct HRR A 1 (1961), 1 EHRR 15.

4. In the *Brogan* case, the Court left the question whether in an ordinary, non-terrorist criminal case four days in police custody would be compatible with Article 5(3). The Commission has taken the view that four days is 'in principle' permissible.[1] It is to be hoped that the Court would not find such a length of time acceptable.[2] In the *Brogan* case, the Court was stricter in a terrorist context than the Commission, finding in favour of all four applicants.

Wemhoff v Federal Republic of Germany, E Ct HRR A 7 (1968), 1 EHRR 55, Eur Ct HR

The applicant, a West German national, was arrested on 9 November 1961, on suspicion of complicity in offences of breach of trust. The investigation of the case by the West Berlin Prosecutor's Office was completed on 24 February 1964. An indictment was filed on 23 April 1964, and on 17 July 1964, the applicant was committed for trial. The trial began in the Regional Court of Berlin on 9 November 1964, and the applicant was convicted on 7 April 1965, of a 'particularly serious case of prolonged abetment to breach of trust' for which he was sentenced to six-and-a-half-years' penal servitude. The period of time spent in detention pending trial was counted as a part of this sentence. The applicant's appeal against conviction was rejected on 17 December 1965. The applicant had remained in detention since he was first arrested. The case was very complicated. It involved 12 other accused and required the examination of a mass of bank accounts and transactions. The Commission admitted the application for consideration on its merits in respect of alleged violations by West Germany of Articles 5(3) and 6(1). In its report, the Commission expressed the opinion, by seven votes to three, that Article 5(3) had been violated because the applicant had not been brought to trial "within a reasonable time" and, unanimously, that there had been no violation of Article 6(1). The Commission referred the case to the Court. The following extracts concern Article 5(3). The Court held unanimously that Article 6 had not been infringed.

JUDGMENT OF THE COURT

4. . . . As the word 'reasonable' applies to the time within which a person is entitled to trial, a purely grammatical interpretation would leave the judicial authorities with a choice between two obligations, that of conducting the proceedings until judgment within a reasonable time or that of releasing the accused pending trial, if necessary against certain guarantees.
5. The Court is quite certain that such an interpretation would not conform to the intention of the High Contracting Parties. It is inconceivable that they should have intended to permit their judicial authorities, at the price of release of the accused, to protract proceedings beyond a reasonable time. This would, moreover, be flatly contrary to the provision in Article 6(1) cited above. . . .

1 *Egue v France* (1988) 57 DR E Commn HR 47, 70.
2 For the position in English law, see above, p. 127.

Article 5, which begins with an affirmation of the right of everyone to liberty and security of person, goes on to specify the situations and conditions in which derogations from this principle may be made. . . . It is thus mainly in the light of the fact of the detention of the person being prosecuted that national courts, possibly followed by the European Court, must determine whether the time that has elapsed, for whatever reason, before judgment is passed on the accused has at some stage exceeded a reasonable limit, that is to say imposed a greater sacrifice than could, in the circumstances of the case, reasonably be expected of a person presumed to be innocent.

In other words it is the provisional detention of accused persons which must not, according to Article 5(3), be prolonged beyond a reasonable time. . . .

6. Another question relating to the interpretation of Article 5(3) . . . is that of the period of detention covered by the requirement of a 'reasonable time. . . .'

The representative of the German Government expounded the reasons which led him to maintain the interpretation, accepted in the Commission's Report, that it is the time of appearance before the trial court that marks the end of the period with which Article 5(3) is concerned.

7. The Court cannot accept this restrictive interpretation. It is true that the English text of the Convention allows such an interpretation. . . .

But while the English text permits two interpretations the French version, which is of equal authority, allows only one. According to it the obligation to release an accused person within a reasonable time continues until that person has been '*jugée*,' that is until the day of the judgment that terminates the trial. Moreover, he must be released '*pendant la procédure*,' a very broad expression which indubitably covers both the trial and the investigation.

8. Thus confronted with two versions of a treaty which are equally authentic but not exactly the same the Court must, following established international law precedents, interpret them in a way that will reconcile them as far as possible. Given that it is a law-making treaty, it is also necessary to seek the interpretation that is most appropriate in order to realise the aim and achieve the object of the treaty, not that which would restrict to the greatest possible degree the obligations undertaken by the Parties. It is impossible to see why the protection against unduly long detention on remand which Article 5 seeks to ensure for persons suspected of offences should not continue up to delivery of judgment rather than cease at the moment the trial opens.

9. It remains to ascertain whether the end of the period of detention with which Article 5(3) is concerned is the day on which a conviction becomes final or simply that on which the charge is determined, even if only by a court of first instance.

The Court finds for the latter interpretation.

One consideration has appeared to it as decisive, namely that a person convicted at first instance, whether or not he has been detained up to this moment, is in the position provided for by Article 5(1)(a) which authorises deprivation of liberty '*after conviction.*' This last phrase cannot be interpreted as being restricted to the case of a final conviction, for this would exclude the arrest at the hearing of convicted persons who appeared for trial while still at liberty, whatever remedies are still open to them. Now, such a practice is frequently followed in many Contracting States and it cannot be believed that they intended to renounce it. It cannot be overlooked moreover that the guilt of a person who is detained during the appeal or review proceedings, has been established in the course of a trial conducted in accordance with requirements of Article 6. . . . A person who has cause to complain of the continuation of his detention after conviction because of delay in determining his appeal, cannot avail himself of Article 5(3) but could possibly allege a disregard of the 'reasonable time' provided for by Article 6(1). . . .

10. The reasonableness of an accused person's continued detention must be assessed in each case according to its special features. The factors which may be taken into consideration are extremely diverse. Hence the possibility of wide differences in opinion in the assessment of the reasonableness of a given detention. . . .

13. The arrest warrant taken out in Wemhoff's name on 9 November 1961 was based on the fear that if he were left at liberty, he would abscond and destroy the evidence against him, in particular by communicating with persons who might be involved. . . . Both of these reasons continued to be invoked until 5 August 1963 in the decisions of the courts rejecting Wemhoff's many applications for release pending trial.

On that date, however, although the investigation had yet to be concluded, the Court of Appeal accepted that there was some doubt as to whether any danger of suppression of evidence still existed, but it considered that the other reason was still operative . . ., and the same reasoning was repeated in later decisions dismissing the Applicant's appeals.

14. With regard to the existence of a danger of suppression of evidence, the Court regards this anxiety of the German courts to be justified in view of the character of the offences of which Wemhoff was suspected and the extreme complexity of the case.

As to the danger of flight, the Court is of opinion that, while the severity of the sentence which the accused may expect in the event of conviction may legitimately be regarded as a factor encouraging him to abscond – though the effect of such fear diminishes as detention continues and, consequently, the balance of the sentence which the accused may expect to have to serve is reduced, nevertheless the possibility of a severe sentence is not sufficient in this respect. The German courts have moreover been careful to support their affirmations that a danger of flight existed by referring at an early stage in the proceedings to certain circumstances relating to the material position and the conduct of the accused. . . .

15. The Court wishes, however, to emphasise that the concluding words of Article 5(3) of the Convention show that, when the only remaining reason for continued detention is the fear that the accused will abscond and thereby subsequently avoid appearing for trial, his release pending trial must be ordered if it is possible to obtain from him guarantees that will ensure such appearance.

It is beyond doubt that, in a financial case such as that in which Wemhoff was involved, an essential factor in such guarantees should have been the deposit by him of bail or the provision of security for a large amount. The positions successively taken up by him on this matter (statement of the facts, paras. 5 and 14)[1] are not such as to suggest that he would have been prepared to furnish such guarantees.

16. In these circumstances the Court could not conclude that there had been any breach of the obligations imposed by Article 5(3) unless the length of Wemhoff's provisional detention between 9 November 1961 and 7 April 1965 had been due either (a) to the slowness of the investigation, which was only completed at the end of February 1964, or (b) to the lapse of time which occurred either between the closing of the investigation and the preferment of the indictment (April 1964) or between then and the opening of the trial (9 November 1964) or finally (c) to the length of the trial (which lasted until 7 April 1965). It cannot be doubted that, even when an accused person is reasonably detained during these periods for reasons of the public interest, there may be a violation of Article 5(3) if, for whatever cause, the proceedings continue for a considerable length of time.

17. On this point the Court shares the opinion of the Commission that no criticism can be made of the conduct of the case by the judicial authorities. The exceptional length of the investigation and of the trial are justified by the exceptional complexity of the case and by further unavoidable reasons for delay. . . .

FOR THESE REASONS, THE COURT

Holds, by six votes to one, that there has been no breach of Article 5(3) of the Convention; . . .

Individual dissenting opinion of Judge Zekia

The legal system of a country, governing the provisions of the criminal law and procedure relating to pre-trial proceedings—such as preliminary enquiries, investigation and arraignment—as well as the presentation of a case to the court and the power of the court itself in reopening investigations, has a lot to do with the time taken in the conclusion of a trial. . . .

In [a common law system] . . . it is the police and the prosecution who conduct the enquiries and collect the evidence. They present the case to a court either for trial or—in indictable offences—for preliminary enquiries for the purpose of committal before the Assizes. Under [a civil law] . . . system the investigation is carried out by a judge and the trial of the accused is started after judicial investigations are closed and after the decision is taken for remitting the case before trial. . . .

While in the former system sufficient evidence to build up a prima facie case against the suspected person is normally expected to be available before he is charged and is taken into custody, in the latter case, i.e. continental system, it appears that the availability of such evidence at an early stage is not essential. Information to the satisfaction of the judicial officials seems to be sufficient for the arrest and detention of a suspect.

As a consequence of these basic divergences inherent in the two systems, suspected persons are, as a rule, kept in detention considerably longer on the continent than in the case of those in England or other countries where the system of common law prevails.

. . . My intention is neither to touch on the merits or demerits of either system. My digression from the track is to emphasise the fact that—if in England, a Member of the Council of Europe—the concept of 'reasonable time' regarding the period of detention of an unconvicted person awaiting his trial does not allow us to stretch the time beyond six months even in an exceptionally difficult and complicated case, could we say that in the continent in a similar case, the period of detention might be six times longer and yet it could be considered as reasonable and therefore compatible with the Convention?

. . . it may fairly be inferred that the Governments signatories of the Convention, intended amongst other things, to set a common standard of right to liberty, the scope of which could not differ so vastly from one country to another. . . .

1 *Ed.* In August 1962, the applicant offered to deposit 200,000 DM but withdrew the offer two days later, apparently before the court had considered it. After his conviction, an offer of 100,000 DM was accepted by the court, but then replaced by a much lower one which the court could not accept.

If a man, presumably innocent, is kept in custody for years, this is bound to ruin him. It is true in the case of Wemhoff that the trial ended with a conviction, but it might have ended with an acquittal as well
...

I believe that in all systems of law there exist always ways and means of avoiding unreasonably long delayed trials. ...

NOTES

1. In deciding that the 'reasonable time' guarantee in Article 5(3) provided a basis for reviewing the *grounds* upon which a person detained pending trial under Article 5(1)(c) continues to be detained after his initial arrest as well as providing a means of control over the *length* of the procedure against a person detained pending trial, the Court clearly filled what would otherwise have been a significant gap in the Convention and made sense of an obscure text.

2. In *Stögmuller v FRG*, E Ct HRR A 9, 1 EHRR 155, the Court expressed the general test that should be applied in deciding whether the danger of the accused disappearing is too great to permit his release as follows:

'There must be a whole set of circumstances . . . which give reason to suppose that the consequences and hazards of flight will seem to him [the accused] to be a lesser evil than continued imprisonment.'

Apart from the dangers of flight and of the suppression of evidence, the Court also, in *Matznetter v Austria*, E Ct HR A 10 (1969), 1 EHRR 198, by four votes to three, accepted prevention of crime as a permissible ground for detention 'in the special circumstances of the case'. These would seem to have been that there was good reason to believe that the accused, if released, would have committed an offence or offences of the same and serious kind as those with which he was already charged, although there was no particular offence which could be identified at the time that the question of release arose as one which it was reasonably believed he would commit. Note that in English law magistrates have been judicially urged to refuse bail in such circumstances. See, eg *R v Phillips* (1947) 32 Cr App R 47.

In *Letellier v France*, E Ct HRR A 207 (1992), 14 EHRR 83, the Court has added as a fourth ground the threat to public order that might be caused by an accused's release. It stated: 'The Court accepts that, by reason of their particular gravity and public reaction to them, certain offences may give rise to a social disturbance capable of justifying pre-trial detention, at least for a time.'

X v United Kingdom, E Ct HRR A 46 (1981), 4 EHRR 188, Eur Ct HR

Following his conviction for a wounding with intent to cause grievous bodily harm by Sheffield Assizes in 1968, X, the applicant, was ordered by the court to be detained in Broadmoor as a restricted offender patient under s. 85, Mental Health Act 1959. In 1971, the Home Secretary, acting under s. 66, 1959 Act, ordered X's conditional discharge on the ground that X's condition had improved. After some three years of normal life, X was recalled to Broadmoor by the Home Secretary, acting under s. 66, 1959 Act, in the light of evidence that his condition had deteriorated. X at once applied, unsuccessfully, to the High Court for habeas corpus. After six months' detention following his recall, X was entitled by s. 66, 1959 Act to apply to the Mental Health Tribunal for release, which he did without success. Had the Tribunal recommended in his favour, the Home Secretary would have retained a discretion whether or not to accept the recommendation. The applicant claimed a breach, inter alia, of Article 5(4), ECHR.

JUDGMENT OF THE COURT

50.   As their main submission, the Government contended that the requirements of Article 5 § 4 were met by the proceedings before the Sheffield Assizes in 1968. In this connection, they relied on a passage from the *De Wilde, Ooms and Versyp* judgment of 18 June 1971 [*Vagrancy* cases] . . .:

'At first sight, the wording of Article 5 § 4 might make one think that it guarantees the right of the detainee always to have supervised by a court the lawfulness of a previous decision which has deprived him of his liberty. . . . Where [this] decision . . . is one taken by an administrative body, there is no doubt that Article 5 § 4 obliges the Contracting States to make available to the person detained a right of recourse to a court; but there is nothing to indicate that the same applies when the decision is made by a court at the close of judicial proceedings. In the latter case the supervision required by Article 5 § 4 is incorporated in the decision; this is so, for example, where a sentence of imprisonment is pronounced after "conviction by a competent court" (Article 5 § 1(a) of the Convention).'

51.   In point of fact, this passage speaks only of 'the decision depriving a person of his liberty'; it does not purport to deal with an ensuing period of detention in which new issues affecting the lawfulness of the detention might subsequently arise. . . .

52.   Furthermore, as the Government themselves pointed out, the content of the obligation imposed on the Contracting States by Article 5 § 4 will not necessarily be the same in all circumstances and as regards every category of deprivation of liberty (see, *mutatis mutandis*, the above-mentioned *De Wilde, Ooms and Versyp* judgment, pp. 41–42, § 78).

X's detention fell within the ambit of sub-paragraph (e) of Article 5 § 1 at least as much as within that of sub-paragraph (a) . . . The 'detention of persons of unsound mind' constitutes a special category with its own specific problems (see the above-mentioned *Winterwerp* judgment, pp. 23–24, §§ 57 and 60). In particular, 'the reasons initially warranting confinement of this kind may cease to exist'. This leads, so the *Winterwerp* judgment noted, to a consequence of some importance (p. 23, § 55):

'. . . it would be contrary to the object and purpose of Article 5 . . . to interpret paragraph 4 . . . as making this category of confinement immune from subsequent review of lawfulness merely provided that the initial decision issued from a court. The very nature of the deprivation of liberty under consideration would appear to require a review of lawfulness to be available at reasonable intervals.'

By virtue of Article 5 § 4, a person of unsound mind compulsorily confined in a psychiatric institution for an indefinite or lengthy period is thus in principle entitled, at any rate where there is no automatic periodic review of a judicial character, to take proceedings at reasonable intervals before a court to put in issue the 'lawfulness' – within the meaning of the Convention (see paragraph 57 below) – of his detention, whether that detention was ordered by a civil or criminal court or by some other authority.

53.   It is not within the province of the Court to inquire into what would be the best or most appropriate system of judicial review in this sphere, for the Contracting States are free to choose different methods of performing their obligations. Thus, in Article 5 § 4 the word 'court' is not necessarily to be understood as signifying a court of law of the classic kind, integrated within the standard judicial machinery of the country. This term, as employed in several Articles of the Convention including Article 5 § 4, serves to denote 'bodies which exhibit not only common fundamental features, of which the most important is independence of the executive and of the parties to the case . . ., but also the guarantees' – 'appropriate to the kind of deprivation of liberty in question' – 'of [a] judicial procedure', the forms of which may vary from one domain to another (see the above-mentioned *De Wilde, Ooms and Versyp* judgment, pp. 41–42, §§ 76 and 78). . . .

55.   The Government maintained, in the alternative, that the 'lawfulness' of the said detention had in fact been 'decided speedily by a court', namely by the Divisional Court of the Queen's Bench Division when hearing X's application for a writ of habeas corpus. . . .

57.   Although X had access to a court which ruled that his detention was 'lawful' in terms of English law, this cannot of itself be decisive as to whether there was a sufficient review of 'lawfulness' for the purposes of Article 5 § 4.

58.   Notwithstanding the limited nature of the review possible in relation to decisions taken under section 66 § 3 of the 1959 Act, the remedy of habeas corpus can on occasions constitute an effective check against arbitrariness in this sphere. It may be regarded as adequate, for the purposes of Article 5 § 4, for emergency measures for the detention of persons on the ground of unsoundness of mind. Such measures, provided they are of short duration . . . are capable of being 'lawful' under Article 5 § 1(e) even though not attended by the usual guarantees such as thorough medical examination. . . . The authority empowered to order emergency detention of this kind must, in the nature of things, enjoy a wide discretion, and this inevitably means that the role of the courts will be reduced.

On the other hand, in the Court's opinion, a judicial review as limited as that available in the habeas corpus procedure in the present case is not sufficient for a continuing confinement such as the one undergone by X. Article 5 § 4, the Government are quite correct to affirm, does not embody a right to judicial control of such scope as to empower the court, on all aspects of the case, to substitute its own discretion for that of the decision-making authority. The review should, however, be wide enough to bear on those conditions which, according to the Convention, are essential for the 'lawful' detention of a person on the ground of unsoundness of mind, especially as the reasons capable of initially justifying such a detention may cease to exist. . . . This means that in the instant case, Article 5 § 4 required an appropriate procedure allowing a court to examine whether the patient's disorder still persisted and whether the Home Secretary was entitled to think that a continuation of the compulsory confinement was necessary in the interests of public safety. . . .

59.   The habeas corpus proceedings brought by X in 1974 did not therefore secure him the enjoyment of the right guaranteed by Article 5 § 4; this would also have been the case had he made any fresh application at a later date. . . .

61.   The Government drew the Court's attention to four ways by which the continued need for detention may come to be reviewed by the Home Office, namely a recommendation from the responsible medical officer that the patient be discharged, the intervention of a Member of Parliament with the Home Secretary, a direct request by the patient to the Home Secretary asking for release or for his case to be referred to a Mental Health Review Tribunal.

The first three do not, however, bring into play any independent review procedure, whether judicial or administrative.

The fourth calls for closer examination since, in relation to the confinement of restricted patients, the 1959 Act provides the opportunity for a periodic review on a comprehensive factual basis by Mental Health Review Tribunals. There is nothing to preclude a specialised body of this kind being considered as a 'court' within the meaning of Article 5 § 4, provided it enjoys the necessary independence and offers sufficient procedural safeguards appropriate to the category of deprivation of liberty being dealt with. . . . Nonetheless, even supposing Mental Health Review Tribunals fulfilled these conditions, they lack the competence to decide 'the lawfulness of [the] detention' and to order release if the detention is unlawful, as they have advisory functions only . . .

Therefore, without underestimating the undoubted value of the safeguards thereby provided, the Court does not find that the other machinery adverted to by the Government serves to remedy the inadequacy, for the purposes of Article 5 § 4, of the habeas corpus proceedings.

62.   In conclusion, there has been a breach of Article 5 § 4 . . .

FOR THESE REASONS, THE COURT . . .

2.   *Holds* unanimously [7–0] that there has been a breach of Article 5 § 4. . . .

NOTES

1. *X v UK* concerned Article 5(4), the purpose of which is to ensure judicial consideration of administrative decisions by the police, mental institutions, etc., to detain someone. If the original decision is taken by a 'court' which meets the requirements of Article 5(4), that provision does not require a further judicial hearing: *Vagrancy* cases, *loc. cit.* at p. 782, above. To qualify as a 'court,' an institution must be independent of the executive and the parties and offer appropriate procedural safeguards: ibid. The latter are those necessary to do justice, bearing in mind that the issue is the deprivation of liberty. Compliance with all of the 'fair trial' safeguards in Article 6 of the Convention is not required. To comply with Article 5(4), a remedy must allow a person to challenge the grounds for his detention as well as the legality of the procedures followed. Thus, in *X v UK*, habeas corpus was not a sufficient remedy. (Note that habeas corpus was a sufficient remedy on the facts of the *Brogan* case, above, p. 775). Nor was the possibility of recourse to a Mental Health Review Tribunal because, as the Court indicated, the Tribunal could only make a recommendation to the Home Secretary who took the final decision. In its report in the case, the Commission had expressed the opinion that the Tribunal remedy was insufficient also because it was only available after six months' detention, so that the question of release was not decided 'speedily'. The Mental Health (Amendment) Act 1982 (see now the Mental Health Act 1983) brought English law into line with *X v UK*.

2. As *X v UK*, following the *Winterwerp* case, also indicates, Article 5(4) requires that in cases in which a detained person's condition or circumstances may change so that the justification for his detention may cease to exist, he must be provided with a remedy meeting the requirements of Article 5(4) on a continuing basis at reasonable intervals. This is the case where, as in *X v UK* and the *Winterwerp* case, the ground for detention is mental disorder.

A continuing remedy was also required in *Weeks v United Kingdom*, E Ct HRR A 114 (1987), 10 EHRR 293. In 1966, the applicant, aged 17, had been given a discretionary life sentence for armed robbery. In fact, he had stolen 35 pence from a pet shop after threatening the owner with a starting pistol. The life sentence was given because the alternative was a definite term of imprisonment for a number of years and the court thought that the more merciful approach was to impose a life sentence so that the applicant, who was emotionally immature, could be released on licence as soon as he was thought to have become sufficiently responsible, which might well be much sooner than a determinate sentence would allow him to be released. In fact, the applicant was not released on parole by the Home Secretary, on the recommendation of the Parole Board, until 1976. A year later, following incidents involving minor offences, the Parole Board confirmed an order by the Home Secretary for the applicant's recall. Thereafter the applicant was twice released and recalled, following the same procedures, as a result of other minor offences. The applicant claimed, inter alia, that he had not been provided with the remedy required by Article 5(4) to challenge his recall to prison or his continued detention. As to whether the requirements of Article 5(4) were met, as the *Vagrancy* cases allowed, by the fact that the original decision to detain was taken by a court, the Court stated:

58 . . . the stated purpose of social protection and rehabilitation for which the "indeterminate" sentence was passed on Mr. Weeks, taken together with the particular circumstances of the offence for which he was convicted, places the sentence in a special category . . . unlike the case of a person sentenced to life imprisonment because of the gravity of the offence committed, the grounds relied on by the sentencing judges for deciding that the length of the deprivation of Mr. Weeks' liberty should be subject to the discretion of the executive for the rest of his life are by their nature susceptible of change with the passage of time. . . . The Court inferred from this that if the decisions not to release or to re-detain were based on grounds inconsistent with the objectives of the sentencing court, Mr. Weeks' detention would no longer be "lawful" for the purposes of sub-paragraph (a) of paragraph 1 of Article 5. . . .

It follows that, by virtue of paragraph 4 of Article 5, Mr. Weeks was entitled to apply to a "court" having jurisdiction to decide "speedily" whether or not his deprivation of liberty had become "unlawful" in this sense; this entitlement should have been exercisable by him at the moment of any return to custody after being at liberty and also at reasonable intervals during the course of his imprisonment . . .

Considering then the remedies available to the applicant on his recall and thereafter before the Parole Board and by way of judicial review, the Court concluded first that the Parole Board was independent and impartial, as required. It also noted that, although the Board's recommendations for the release on licence of life sentence prisoners that result from the exercise of its powers of periodic review are not binding upon the Home Secretary, its recommendation for the release of a recalled life sentence prisoner, such as the applicant, were binding upon the Home Secretary and thus met the requirements of Article 5(4). However, the Court found a procedural deficiency in the functioning of the Board:

66. The Board deals with individual cases on consideration of the documents supplied to it by the Home Secretary and of any reports, information or interviews with the individual concerned it has itself called for (section 59(4) and (5) of the 1967 Act – see paragraph 28 above). The prisoner is entitled to make representations with respect to his recall, not only in writing to the Board but also orally to a member of the Local Review Committee (sections 59(5)–(6) and 62(3) of the 1967 Act – see paragraphs 26 and 29 above). The individual is free to take legal advice in preparing such representations. Furthermore, he must be sufficiently informed of the reasons for his recall in order to enable him to make sensible representations (section 62(3) of the 1967 Act and the judgments in the *Gunnell* and *Wilson* cases – ibid.).

Whilst these safeguards are not negligible, there remains a certain procedural weakness in the case of a recalled prisoner. Thus, the Court of Appeal established in the *Gunnell* case that the duty on the Board to act fairly, as required under English law by the principles of natural justice, does not entail an entitlement to full disclosure of the adverse material which the Board has in its possession (see paragraphs 30 and 31 above). The procedure followed does not therefore allow proper participation of the individual adversely affected by the contested decision, this being one of the principal guarantees of a judicial procedure for the purposes of the Convention, and cannot therefore be regarded as judicial in character. . . .

Since the Parole Board did not for this procedural reason by itself provide the remedy required by Article 5(4), the Court examined the remedy available by way of judicial review of the decision to recall the applicant. Noting the limited grounds upon which judicial review may be granted (i.e. *ultra vires* grounds such as illegality, irrationality), the Court held, by 13 votes to 4, that there had been a breach of Article 5(4):

69 . . . the scope of the control afforded [by judicial review] is thus not wide enough to bear on the conditions essential for the "lawfulness", in the sense of Article 5 § 4 of the Convention, of Mr. Weeks' detention, that is to say, whether it was consistent with and therefore justified by the objectives of the indeterminate sentence imposed on him. . . . In the Court's view, having regard to the nature of the control it allows, the remedy of judicial review can neither itself provide the proceedings required by Article 5 § 4 nor serve to remedy the inadequacy, for the purposes of that provision, of the procedure before the Parole Board.

3. The Court followed its approach in the *Weeks* case in three more normal cases of discretionary life sentences in *Thynne, Wilson and Gunnell v United Kingdom*, E Ct HRR A 190, 13 EHRR 135 (1991). There the applicants had been convicted of very grave offences for which they would have been sentenced to long terms of imprisonment had definite terms been imposed. Instead, since the applicants were regarded as unstable and likely to commit other such offences if released, they were, in accordance with an established sentencing policy, given discretionary life sentences, which contained a number of years calculated as punishment for the offence committed and thereafter were justified in terms of the public interest in keeping dangerous criminals secure. In all three cases, the applicants had moved from the punishment to the security phase of their life sentences and could be released on licence by the Home Secretary on the recommendation of the Parole Board if they were no longer thought a danger to society. The Court considered that, at this stage, the applicants were entitled under Article 5(4) to a continuing remedy at reasonable intervals to challenge the legality of their detention. Without going into details, the Court stated that it saw 'no reason to depart from its finding in the *Weeks* judgment . . . that neither the Parole Board nor judicial review proceedings . . . satisfy the requirements of Article 5(4)' and, accordingly, held against the UK by 18 votes to 1.

In contrast with a discretionary life sentence case, there is no requirement of a continuing remedy in the case of a mandatory life sentence, even though the latter will also contain a notional tariff period and the possibility of release on licence thereafter: *Wynne v United Kingdom*, E Ct HRR A 294 (1994), 19 EHRR 333. This is because a mandatory life sentence is 'imposed automatically as the punishment for the offence of murder irrespective of considerations pertaining to the dangerousness of the offender'.

4   Article 6: The right to a fair trial

Ringeisen v Austria, E Ct HRR A 13 (1968), 1 EHRR 455, Eur Ct HR

In 1962, the applicant, an Austrian national, made a contract with a Mr and Mrs Roth for the purchase from them of land in the Austrian province of Upper Austria. In accordance with an Upper Austrian statute, the transaction needed the approval of an administrative tribunal because the land was agricultural. The tribunal refused to approve the transaction on the statutory ground that the land was going to be used by the applicant for speculative building. As a result, the transaction was, in accordance with the statute, null and void. The applicant appealed, as the statute allowed, to a higher tribunal which rejected the applicant's appeal. In its judgment, the Court rejected the applicant's complaints that the proceedings in his case in Austria had not been consistent with Article 6. The following extract from the judgment is on the preliminary question whether Article 6 applied to the applicant's case in the first place. Were his 'civil rights and obligations' being determined?

JUDGMENT OF THE COURT

For Article 6, paragraph (1), to be applicable to a case (*contestation*) it is *not* necessary that both parties to the proceedings should be private persons, which is the view of the majority of the Commission and of the Government. The wording of Article 6, paragraph (1), is far wider; the French expression '*contestations sur (des) droits et obligations de caractère civil*' covers all proceedings the result of which is decisive for private rights and obligations. The English text, 'determination of . . . civil rights and obligations,' confirms this interpretation.

The character of the legislation which governs how the matter is to be determined (civil, commercial, administrative law, etc.) and that of the authority which is invested with jurisdiction in the matter (ordinary court, administrative body, etc.) are therefore of little consequence.

In the present case, when Ringeisen purchased property from the Roth couple, he had a right to have the contract for sale which they had made with him approved if he fulfilled, as he claimed to do, the conditions laid down in the Act. Although it was applying rules of administrative law, the Regional Commission's decision was to be decisive for the relations in civil law ('*de caractère civil*') between Ringeisen and the Roth couple.[1]

NOTES

1. This extract concerns the field of application of Article 6, viz. the kind of cases to which the right to a fair trial in Article 6 applies. It is clear from this passage that the term 'civil rights' in Article 6(1) refers to the distinction between private and public law found in civil law systems, but until recently, absent from English law,[2] and that Article 6, accordingly, applies only to the determination of private law rights and obligations and not to the determination of public law ones. On the meaning of 'civil rights and obligations', see further below, p. 789.
2. As to when a person's private law rights are being determined, the *Ringeisen* case indicates that this is not only in private litigation, as when two private parties to a contract take their case to court. It is also when a decision is taken by the state (e.g. by refusing to approve a private law transaction, as in the *Ringeisen* case, or by terminating a licence to practice medicine, as in the *Konig* case, below) where the outcome is 'decisive' for a person's private law rights. In *Le Compte v Belgium*, E Ct

---

1   The Court's ruling on this point was unanimous (7–0).
2   The distinction is now relevant to applications for judicial review: see *O'Reilly v Mackman* [1983] 2 AC 237, HL.

HRR A 43 (1981), 4 EHRR 1, the Court confirmed its approach in the *Ringeisen* case on this last point, but added (Series A, Vol. 43, p. 21):

'As regards the question whether the dispute related to the abovementioned right, the Court considers that a tenuous connection or remote consequences do not suffice for Article 6, § 1 . . .; civil rights and obligations must be the object – or one of the objects – of the '*contestation*' (dispute); the result of the proceedings must be directly decisive for such a right.'

So, for example, in one case the Commission held that deportation proceedings against an individual were not subject to Article 6 just because a decision to deport would be decisive for his rights under a private law contract of employment; the latter 'were not in any sense in themselves the subject of the proceedings,' which was the individual's right to remain in the United Kingdom: *X v United Kingdom*, (1977) 9 DR E Comm HR 224. What if the proceedings in the case had been an appeal against the refusal to issue a work permit when the permit was a condition of the applicant's contract of employment? In the *Le Compte* case, the applicants were Belgian doctors who had been suspended from medical practice by a disciplinary tribunal for breaches of rules of professional conduct. The Court held that Article 6 had been infringed because the proceedings had not been conducted in public. Article 6 applied because the right to practise medicine in Belgium was a private law right. Although the disciplinary proceedings were a matter of public law, the outcome in this case was 'directly decisive' for a private law right. Contrast the position, for example, if the doctors had been fined, not suspended.

In one sense, an extension of the scope of Article 6 beyond private litigation is welcome. It is mostly in respect of the functioning of administrative tribunals and authorities that the need for a fair trial guarantee is most evident in Europe. On the other hand, it is arguable that the better approach would be to draft a new text in a protocol tailored to the specific needs of administrative law rather than to apply a text which does not easily fit accepted procedures for decision-making by administrative authorities and tribunals.

The *Ringeisen* case concerned administrative tribunals. A more difficult question is the application of Article 6 to decision making by administrative authorities. Article 6 does not require that the initial decision be taken by means of a procedure that complies with it. Instead there must be the possibility of challenging an administrative decision in a court that does so. The question then is whether there must be a right of appeal on the merits to such a court, or whether judicial review is sufficient. In *W v United Kingdom*, E Ct HRR A 121 (1988), 10 EHRR 29, the Court held that the possibility of judicial review by a tribunal complying with Article 6 of a decision by a local authority concerning parental access to children in case was not sufficient to meet the requirements of Article 6:

'82. . . . on an application for judicial review, the courts will not review the merits of the decision but will confine themselves to ensuring, in brief, that the authority did not act illegally, unreasonably or unfairly. . . . Where a care order or a parental rights resolution is in force, the scope of the review effected in the context of wardship proceedings will normally be similarly confined. . . .

In a case of the present kind, however, there will in the Court's opinion be no possibility of a "determination" in accordance with the requirements of Article 6 § 1 of the parent's right in regard to access . . . unless he or she can have the local authority's decision reviewed by a tribunal having jurisdiction to examine the merits of the matter. And it does not appear from the material supplied by the Government or otherwise available to the Court that the powers of the English courts were of sufficient scope to satisfy fully this requirement during the currency of the parental rights resolution.

83. There was accordingly a violation of Article 6 § 1.'

However, in cases in which the law leaves a discretion to the executive and there are policy considerations involved, judicial review may be sufficient. This appeared to be accepted by the Court in *Zumtobel v Austria*, E Ct HRR A 268-A (1993), 17 EHRR 116. The case concerned the opportunities available to the applicant to question a decision to expropriate his land. In holding against him, the Court stated:

'31. As regards the review effected by the Administrative Court, its scope must be assessed in the light of the fact that expropriation . . . is not a matter exclusively within the discretion of the administrative authorities, because Article 44 § 1 of the Regional Highways Law makes the lawfulness of such a measure subject to a condition: the impossibility "of constructing or retaining a section of highway which is more suitable from the point of view of traffic requirements, environmental protection and the financial implications". . . . It was for the Administrative Court to satisfy itself that this provision had been complied with. . . .

32. In addition, it should be stressed that the submissions relied upon before the Administrative Court concerned solely the proceedings before the Government Office. The Administrative Court in fact considered these submissions on their merits, point by point, without ever having to decline jurisdiction in replying to them or in ascertaining various facts. The European Court should confine itself as far as possible to examining the question raised by the case before it. Accordingly, it should only decide whether, in the circumstances of the case, the scope of the competence of the Administrative Court satisfied the requirements of Article 6 § 1.

Regard being had to the respect which must be accorded to decisions taken by the administrative authorities *on grounds of expediency* and to the nature of the complaints made by the Zumtobel partnership, the review by the Administrative Court accordingly, in this instance, fulfilled the requirements of Article 6 § 1.'

As this extract also indicates, Article 6 is complied with if the applicant is allowed to argue the points he wishes to raise before a body that complies with Article 6; if he only wishes to raise an ultra vires point, it does not matter that the remedy does not provide a right of appeal on the merits, whether a question of policy ('expediency') is involved in the making of the decision or not.

The *Zumtobel* case was followed by the Commission on the 'policy' point in *IKSCON v UK*, (1994) 76A DR E Comm HR 90, 110–1. There the only remedy in the courts available to the applicants to challenge the Secretary of State's decision upholding a local authority enforcement notice for using land in breach of the planning laws was judicial review on a point of law. The Commission decided that this was not a breach of Article 6:

'The Commission recalls that appeals against the decisions of administrative bodies, which themselves do not comply with Article 6, will only be consistent with Article 6 para. 1 of the Convention if they are conducted before "judicial bodies that have full jurisdiction" (Eur Court HR, *Albert and Le Compte* judgment of 10 February 1983, Series A no. 58, p. 16, para. 29). It is true that section 289 of the Town and Country Planning Act 1990 provides that appeals to the High Court against enforcement notices may only be made "on a point of law".

The local authority did not, however, have a complete discretion in taking enforcement proceedings. In particular, it could only take proceedings in circumstances within the limits defined by section 174 of the Town and Country Planning Act 1990 (which sets out the grounds of appeal to the Secretary of State), and in accordance with its own structure plans and the policy guidance laid down in various documents by the Secretary of State. ISKCON were then able to have a determination from the High Court of whether the legal aspects (that is, "points of law",) of these requirements had been met.

The Commission recalls that the High Court dealt with each of ISKCON's grounds of appeal on its merits, point by point, without ever having to decline jurisdiction. Moreover, it was open to ISKCON to contend in the High Court that findings of fact by the Inspector and/or the Secretary of State were unsupported by evidence, as they could have argued that the administrative authorities failed to take into account an actual fact or did take into account an immaterial fact. Finally, the High Court could have interfered with the administrative authorities' decisions if those decisions had been irrational having regard to the facts established by the authorities.

It is not the role of Article 6 of the Convention to give access to a level of jurisdiction which can substitute its opinion for that of the administrative authorities on questions of expediency and where the courts do not refuse to examine any of the points raised: Article 6 gives a right to a court that has "full jurisdiction" (cf. Eur Court HR, *Zumtobel* judgment of 21 September 1993, Series A no. 268-A, para. 32).

In these circumstances, the Commission finds that the review by the High Court fulfilled the requirements of Article 6 para. 1 of the Convention.'

3. The Court's adoption of a private law meaning of 'civil rights and obligations' raises the question of the boundary between private and public law. The precise point at which the boundary should be drawn is a difficult question, with different parties to the Convention marking it differently in certain marginal cases. A doctrine of *renvoi* would therefore mean that Article 6 applied differentially according to the classification adopted by each defendant state. In fact, the Court, as with the parallel concept of a 'criminal charge', has held that the concept of 'civil rights and obligations' has an autonomous, Convention meaning: *Konig v Federal Republic of Germany*, E Ct HRR A 27 (1978), 2 EHRR 170. This meaning, it has become clear, is very different from that found in national law. One consequence of the Court's use of an autonomous concept is that in a particular case a right that falls within the public law of the state concerned may be classified as a private law right at Strasbourg.[1] The local law is not totally irrelevant, however; it necessarily provides the framework within which the Convention concept applies. Thus, in the *Konig* case, it was relevant to the Court's characterisation of the rights involved as civil rights for Convention purposes that the medical profession did not provide a public service in West German law. Similarly, in a case coming from the UK the Court would look to the legal position of a doctor under the National Health Service.

Although adopting a Convention meaning of 'civil rights and obligations', both the Court and the Commission have refrained from formulating any abstract test by which private and public law rights and obligations may be distinguished. They have instead preferred an inductive approach, ruling on particular cases as they have arisen. Applying this approach, the Commission and the Court have invariably found that the rights and obligations of private persons in their relations *inter se* in such areas as the law of contract, employment law and the law of property are 'civil rights and obligations'. In addition, the Court has identified certain 'rights and obligations' (mostly rights) of a very general kind that an individual may be said to have that may be interfered with by the state. Article 6 then applies to any dispute resulting from the state's intervention. Thus a number of cases held to be subject to Article 6 have concerned the regulation by the state of the right to practise a profession. In the *Konig* case the case was held to fall within Article 6 because the right to practise a liberal profession, such as medicine, was in principle a private law right no different in kind from the right to engage in any other occupation. In the *Konig* case, the Court also established that the right of an individual to engage in a commercial or business activity (in that case the running of a private medical clinic) is a private law, or 'civil' right and that, accordingly, Article 6 applies to any dispute arising out of its regulation by the state. Similarly, in *Benthem v Netherlands*, E Ct HRR A 97 (1985), 8 EHRR 1, the right to sell liquid petroleum gas at a garage, for the exercise of which the applicant required a licence from the state, was a 'civil right', being an aspect of the general right of an individual to engage in commercial activities. There have also been cases in which the state's regulation of an individual's property rights, and hence 'civil rights', have been held to be subject to Article 6: see, for example, the *Zumtobel* case, above, p. 788 (expropriation). The rights to engage in a commercial activity and to property share a common pecuniary character. Consistently with such a link, the Court's jurisprudence also recognises as a civil right the right to compensation for pecuniary loss resulting from illegal state acts. In *X v France*, E Ct HRR A 234-C (1991), 14 EHRR 483, the Court held that a claim for damages for contracting AIDS from a blood transfusion because of

1 This happened, for example, in *Feldbrugge v Netherlands* and *Deumeland v FRG*, below, p. 791.

government negligence fell within Article 6. Although the case concerned the exercise of a general regulatory power by a Minister and hence was clearly a matter of public law in France, its outcome was 'decisive for private rights and obligations', namely those concerning pecuniary compensation for physical injury. A right of a non-pecuniary character to which Article 6 applies is the right to respect for family life. Thus state action that is directly decisive for this right, such as a decision concerning parental access to children, has been held to be subject to Article 6: *W v United Kingdom*, E Ct HRR A 121 (1988), 10 EHRR 29.

Schuler-Zgraggen v Switzerland, E Ct HRR A 263 (1993), 16 EHRR 405, Eur Ct HR

The applicant was awarded a state invalidity pension when she was no longer able to work because of tuberculosis. However, the pension was cancelled when she gave birth to a child since her health was sufficient to allow her to look after her child at home. An Appeals Board and the Federal Insurance Court rejected her appeal, the sole basis for the latter's reasoning being that many married women give up their jobs when their first child is born. By eight votes to one, the European Court rejected the applicant's claim that Article 6(1) had been infringed because she had not been granted an oral hearing and had been denied access to her medical file. However, by the same majority, the Court did find a breach of Article 14 taken together with Article 6(1) because of the sexual discriminatory reasoning of the Federal Insurance Court.

Before reaching the merits, the European Court decided unanimously that the case concerned the applicant's 'civil rights' so that Article 6 applied. The following extract from the judgment concerns this point only. Relevant to it were the following facts. The applicant was entitled to the pension under the Swiss Invalidity Insurance Act, which was a part of Swiss social security law and characterised as being a matter of public law. It was financed by the state and by obligatory and salary-related insurance contributions deducted from the applicant's salary. The applicant had an enforceable, legal right to the pension provided she satisfied the statutory requirements.

JUDGMENT OF THE COURT

46. The Court is here once again confronted with the issue of the applicability of Article 6 § 1 to social-security disputes. The question arose earlier in the cases of *Feldbrugge v the Netherlands* and *Deumeland v Germany*, in which it gave judgment on 29 May 1986 (Series A nos. 99 and 100). At that time the Court noted that there was great diversity in the legislation and practice of the member States of the Council of Europe as regards the nature of the entitlement to insurance benefits under social-security schemes. Nevertheless, the development in the law that was initiated by those judgments and the principle of equality of treatment warrant taking the view that today the general rule is that Article 6 § 1 does apply in the field of social insurance, including even welfare assistance (see the *Salesi v Italy* judgment of 26 February 1993, Series A no. 257-E, pp. 59–60, § 19).

As in the two cases decided in 1986, State intervention is not sufficient to establish that Article 6 § 1 is inapplicable; other considerations argue in favour of the applicability of Article 6 § 1 in the instant case. The most important of these lies in the fact that despite the public-law features pointed out by the Government, the applicant was not only affected in her relations with the administrative authorities as such but also suffered an interference with her means of subsistence; she was claiming an individual, economic right flowing from specific rules laid down in a federal statute (see paragraph 35 above).

In sum, the Court sees no convincing reason to distinguish between Mrs Schuler-Zgraggen's right to an invalidity pension and the rights to social insurance benefits asserted by Mrs Feldbrugge and Mr Deumeland.

Article 6 § 1 therefore applies in the instant case.

NOTES

1. One particularly difficult question of classification for the purposes of Article 6 has been the classification of social security and social assistance rights.[1] In *Feldbrugge v Netherlands* E Ct HRR A 99 paras 32–40 (1986), 8 EHRR 425, the Court held, by ten votes to seven, that the right to a state employed person's sickness allowance, which was classified as a matter of public law in the Netherlands, was a private law right to which Article 6 applied. The Court found that it had mixed public and private law characteristics, but found 'the latter to be predominant'. As to the former, the allowance was a part of an obligatory state health insurance scheme, involving a state commitment to social protection. As to the latter:

'37. To begin with, Mrs. Feldbrugge was not affected in her relations with the public authorities as such, acting in the exercise of discretionary powers, but in her personal capacity as a private individual. She suffered an interference with her means of subsistence and was claiming a right flowing from specific rules laid down by the legislation in force.

For the individual asserting it, such a right is often of crucial importance; this is especially so in the case of health insurance benefits when the employee who is unable to work by reason of illness enjoys no other source of income. In short, the right in question was a personal, economic and individual right, a factor that brought it close to the civil sphere. . . .

38. Secondly, the position of Mrs. Feldbrugge was closely linked with the fact of her being a member of the working population, having been a salaried employee. The applicant was admittedly unemployed at the relevant time, but the availability of the health benefits was determined by reference to the terms of her former contract of employment and the legislation applicable to that contract.

The legal basis of the work that she had performed was a contract of employment governed by private law. Whilst it is true that the insurance provisions derived directly from statute and not from an express clause in the contract, these provisions were in a way grafted onto the contract. They thus formed one of the constituents of the relationship between employer and employee.

In addition, the sickness allowance claimed by Mrs. Feldbrugge was a substitute for the salary payable under the contract, the civil character of this salary being beyond doubt. This allowance shared the same nature as the contract and hence was also invested with a civil character for the purposes of the Convention. . . .

39. Finally, the Dutch health insurance is similar in several respects to insurance under the ordinary law. . . .

See also *Deumeland v Federal Republic of Germany*, E Ct HRR A 100 (1986) in which using similar reasoning, the Court held, by nine votes to eight, that a West German industrial injuries benefit was a 'private law right. The *Feldbrugge* and *Deumeland* cases were followed in *Schouten and Meldrum v Netherlands*[2] which concerned an employer's obligation – found to be a 'civil obligation' within Article 6 – to pay social security contributions for his employees. In *Salesi v Italy*,[3] the Court held that a right to social assistance for persons in need was a 'civil right'. The key consideration in this case was that the benefit was a matter of legal right, not a matter of discretion for the state.

2. *Criminal charge.* Like 'civil rights and obligations', the concept of a 'criminal' charge has an autonomous Convention meaning – although in a special, 'oneway' sense. In *Engel v Netherlands*, E Ct HRR A 22 (1976), 1 EHRR 647, in which certain military disciplinary offences were held to be 'criminal' for the purposes of Article 6, the Court stated that if a state classified an offence as 'criminal,' it would be such for the purposes of Article 6. If it classified it as 'disciplinary,' it might nonetheless be 'criminal' for the purposes of Article 6. When deciding whether an offence was 'criminal' in this latter situation, three factors were relevant: (1) the

---

1 The distinction between social security and assistance is itself difficult to draw. One distinction is between rights which involve benefits that are available equally to all persons who qualify (social security) and those that result in benefits that are allocated differentially according to individual need (social assistance).

2 E Ct HRR A 304 (1994). See also *Lombardo v Italy*, E Ct HRR A 249-B (1992) (policeman's pension).

3 E Ct HRR A 249-B (1992)

classification of the offence in the local law (disciplinary or disciplinary *and* criminal): (2) the nature of the offence, so that one (e.g. absence without leave) to do primarily with the operation of the armed forces would be disciplinary rather than 'criminal'; and (3) the nature of the punishment, so that an offence which might result in deprivation of a person's liberty to any significant extent would in principle be 'criminal'. In *Campbell and Fell v United Kingdom*, E Ct HRR A 80 (1984), 7 EHRR 165, the Court held that Article 6 applied to prison disciplinary proceedings where a prisoner risked a substantial loss of remission (570 days).

As well as disciplinary offences, other kinds of offences not classified as criminal in the national legal system concerned have been characterised as 'criminal' for the purposes of Article 6 because of their nature or possible penalty.[1] A person is subject to a 'charge' when he is 'substantially affected' by the steps taken against him.[2] This will normally be when he is arrested or he is served with a summons.

Golder v UK, E Ct HRR A 18 (1975), 1 EHRR 524, Eur Ct HR

The applicant was serving a prison sentence at Parkhurst Prison in 1969 when a serious disturbance occurred in which L, a prison officer, was assaulted. L made a statement which identified the applicant as one of the assailants. L later made a second statement in which he indicated that he might have been mistaken in his identification and another prison officer gave evidence that the applicant had taken no part in the disturbance. Thereupon, disciplinary charges which it had been proposed to bring against the applicant were dropped and the entry in his prison record about the matter was marked 'charges not proceeded with'. The applicant understood that L's first statement was still on his record and believed that this was why he had been refused parole. For this reason, he sought permission from the Home Secretary in 1970 to communicate with a solicitor with a view to bringing a libel action against L. Permission was refused under Rule 34(8), Prison Rules, as then drafted. The applicant then applied to Strasbourg in the same year. The case reached the European Court of Human Rights in 1975 when the Court considered whether the refusal to allow the applicant to communicate with a solicitor was a violation of Article 6 or 8, ECHR. The applicant had in the meantime been released on parole in 1972. He did not pursue his libel action.

JUDGMENT OF THE COURT

1. On the alleged violation of Article 6(1)

26. . . . Clearly, no one knows whether Golder would have persisted in carrying out his intention to sue Laird if he had been permitted to consult a solicitor. Furthermore, the information supplied to the Court by the Government gives reason to think that a court in England would not dismiss an action brought by a convicted prisoner on the sole ground that he had managed to cause the writ to be issued – through an attorney for instance – without obtaining leave from the Home Secretary under Rules 33 § 2 and 34 § 8 of the Prison Rules 1964, which in any event did not happen in the present case.

The fact nonetheless remains that Golder had made it most clear that he intended 'taking civil action for libel': it was for this purpose that he wished to contact a solicitor, which was a normal preliminary step in itself and in Golder's case probably essential on account of his imprisonment. By forbidding Golder to make such contact, the Home Secretary actually impeded the launching of the contemplated action. Without formally denying Golder his right to institute proceedings before a court, the Home

---

1 See *Öztürk v Federal Republic of Germany*, E Ct HRR A 73 (1984), 6 EHRR 409 (regulatory road traffic offence); *Weber v Switzerland*, E Ct HRR A 177 (1990), 12 EHRR 508 (offence akin to contempt of court); and *Demicoli v Malta*, E Ct HRR A 210 (1991), 14 EHRR 47 (breach of parliamentary privilege).
2 *Deweer v Belgium*, E Ct HRR A 35 (1980), 2 EHRR 439.

Secretary did in fact prevent him from commencing an action at that time, 1970. Hindrance in fact can contravene the Convention just like a legal impediment.

It is true that – as the Government have emphasised – on obtaining his release Golder would have been in a position to have recourse to the courts at will, but in March and April 1970 this was still rather remote and hindering the effective exercise of a right may amount to a breach of that right, even if the hindrance is of a temporary character. . . .

28. . . . Article 6 § 1 does not state a right of access to the courts or tribunals in express terms. It enunciates rights which are distinct but stem from the same basic idea and which, taken together, make up a single right not specifically defined in the narrower sense of the term. It is the duty of the Court to ascertain, by means of interpretation, whether access to the courts constitutes one factor or aspect of this right. . . .

[After examining the text of the Convention, its object and purpose and also general principles of law, the Court continued:]

36. Taking all the preceding considerations together, it follows that the right of access constitutes an element which is inherent in the right stated by Article 6 § 1. This is not an extensive interpretation forcing new obligations on the Contracting States: it is based on the very terms of the first sentence of Article 6 § 1 read in its context and having regard to the object and purpose of the Convention, a lawmaking treaty (see the *Wemhoff* judgment of 27 June 1968, Series A no. 7, p. 23, § 8), and to general principles of law. . . .

38. The Court considers . . . that the right of access to the courts is not absolute. As this is a right which the Convention sets forth (see Articles 13, 14, 17 and 25) without, in the narrower sense of the term, defining, there is room, apart from the bounds delimiting the very content of any right, for limitations permitted by implication. . . .

39. The Government and the Commission have cited examples of regulations, and especially of limitations, which are to be found in the national law of states in matters of access to the courts, for instance regulations relating to minors and persons of unsound mind. Although it is of less frequent occurrence and of a very different kind, the restriction complained of by Golder constitutes a further example of such a limitation.

It is not the function of the Court to elaborate a general theory of the limitations admissible in the case of convicted prisoners, nor even to rule *in abstracto* on the compatibility of Rules 33 §2, 34 § 8 and 37 § 2 of the Prison Rules 1964 with the Convention. Seised of a case which has its origin in a petition presented by an individual, the Court is called upon to pronounce itself only on the point whether or not the application of those Rules in the present case violated the Convention to the prejudice of Golder. . . .

40. . . . In petitioning the Home Secretary for leave to consult a solicitor with a view to suing Laird for libel, Golder was seeking to exculpate himself of the charge made against him by that prison officer on 25 October 1969 and which had entailed for him unpleasant consequences, some of which [mainly the entry still in his record and the refusal of parole] still subsisted by 20 March 1970. . . . Furthermore, the contemplated legal proceedings would have concerned an incident which was connected with prison life and had occurred while the applicant was imprisoned. Finally, those proceedings would have been directed against a member of the prison staff who had made the charge in the course of his duties and who was subject to the Home Secretary's authority.

In these circumstances, Golder could justifiably wish to consult a solicitor with a view to instituting legal proceedings. It was not for the Home Secretary himself to appraise the prospects of the action contemplated; it was for an independent and impartial court to rule on any claim that might be brought. In declining to accord the leave which had been requested, the Home Secretary failed to respect, in the person of Golder, the right to go before a court as guaranteed by Article 6 § 1.

II. On the alleged violation of Article 8 . . .

43. The Home Secretary's refusal of the petition of 20 March 1970 had the direct and immediate effect of preventing Golder from contacting a solicitor by any means whatever, including that which in the ordinary way he would have used to begin with, correspondence. While there was certainly neither stopping nor censorship of any message, such as a letter, which Golder would have written to a solicitor – or vice-versa – and which would have been a piece of correspondence within the meaning of paragraph 1 of Article 8, it would be wrong to conclude therefrom, as do the Government, that this text is inapplicable. Impeding someone from even initiating correspondence constitutes the most far-reaching form of 'interference' (paragraph 2 of Article 8) with the exercise of the 'right to respect for correspondence'; it is inconceivable that that should fall outside the scope of Article 8 while mere supervision indisputably falls within it. In any event, if Golder had attempted to write to a solicitor notwithstanding the Home Secretary's decision or without requesting the required permission, that correspondence would have been stopped and he could have invoked Article 8; one would arrive at a paradoxical and hardly equitable

result, if it were considered that in complying with the requirements of the Prison Rules 1964 he lost the benefit of the protection of Article 8. . . .

44. In the submission of the Government, the right to respect for correspondence is subject, apart from interference covered by paragraph 2 of Article 8, to implied limitations resulting, *inter alia*, from the terms of Article 5 § 1(a): a sentence of imprisonment passed after conviction by a competent court inevitably entails consequences affecting the operation of other Articles of the Convention, including Article 8.

. . . that submission conflicts with the explicit text of Article 8. The restrictive formulation used at paragraph 2 ('There shall be no interference . . . except such as . . .') leaves no room for the concept of implied limitations. In this regard, the legal status of the right to respect for correspondence, which is defined by Article 8 with some precision, provides a clear contrast to that of the right to a court (paragraph 38 above).

45. The Government have submitted in the alternative that the interference complained of satisfied the explicit conditions laid down in paragraph 2 of Article 8.

It is beyond doubt that the interference was 'in accordance with the law', that is Rules 33 § 2 and 34 § 8 of the Prison Rules 1964.

The Court accepts, moreover, that the 'necessity' for interference with the exercise of the right of a convicted prisoner to respect for his correspondence must be appreciated having regard to the ordinary and reasonable requirements of imprisonment. The 'prevention of disorder or crime', for example, may justify wider measures of interference in the case of such a prisoner than in that of a person at liberty. To this extent, but to this extent only, lawful deprivation of liberty within the meaning of Article 5 does not fail to impinge on the application of Article 8. . . .

In order to show why the interference complained of by Golder was 'necessary', the Government advanced the prevention of disorder or crime and, up to a certain point, the interests of public safety and the protection of the rights and freedoms of others. Even having regard to the power of appreciation left to the Contracting States, the Court cannot discern how these considerations, as they are understood 'in a democratic society', could oblige the Home Secretary to prevent Golder from corresponding with a solicitor with a view to suing Laird for libel. The Court again lays stress on the fact that Golder was seeking to exculpate himself of a charge made against him by that prison officer acting in the course of his duties and relating to an incident in prison. In these circumstances, Golder could justifiably wish to write to a solicitor. It was not for the Home Secretary himself to appraise – no more than it is for the Court today – the prospects of the action contemplated; it was for a solicitor to advise the applicant on his rights and then for a court to rule on any action that might be brought.

The Home Secretary's decision proves to be all the less 'necessary in a democratic society' in that the applicant's correspondence with a solicitor would have been a preparatory step to the institution of civil legal proceedings and, therefore, to the exercise of a right embodied in another Article of the Convention, that is, Article 6.

The Court thus reaches the conclusion that there has been a violation of Article 8 . . .

FOR THESE REASONS, THE COURT

1. *Holds* by nine votes to three [Judges Verdross, Zekia and Sir Gerald Fitzmaurice dissented] that there has been a breach of Article 6 § 1,
2. *Holds* unanimously that there has been a breach of Article 8; . . .

NOTES

1. On the Article 8 aspects of the *Golder* case, see below, p. 807. In the *Golder* case, the Court read into Article 6 the right of access to a court. The judgment is of more general importance in that it sets out the 'object and purpose' – or teleological – approach to the interpretation of the Convention that it has followed ever since.[1]

2. The three dissenting judges considered that Article 6 did not guarantee a right of access to the courts. Judge Sir Gerald Fitzmaurice, the judge of British nationality, was the only dissenting judge to take the view that, supposing that there were a right of access protected by Article 6, it had not been infringed in the applicant's case:

1 On the *Golder* case, see (1975) 38 MLR 683, (1974–5) 47 BYIL 391; and G. Triggs, (1976) 50 Aust LJ 229. A breach of the right of access to the courts under the Prison Rules as they existed prior to the *Golder* case was also found to have occurred in the *Hilton* case (CM Res DH (79) 3, (1981) 3 EHRR 104) and the *Silver* case, E Ct HRR A61 (1983).

'if, *de facto*, the act of refusing to allow Golder to consult a solicitor had had the effect of permanently and finally cutting him off from all chances of recourse to the courts for the purpose of the proceedings he wanted to bring. But this was not the case: he would still have been in time to act even if he had served his full term, which he did not do, being soon released on parole.'

3. In order to comply with the Article 6 ruling in the *Golder* case, the Home Secretary added Rule 37A(4) to the Prison Rules. This abolished the need to obtain permission before writing to a solicitor to discuss or institute civil proceedings.

4. The right of access to a court was relied upon successfully in *Airey v Ireland*, E Ct HRR A 32 (1979), 2 EHRR 305. In that case, the applicant was an indigent Irish wife whose marriage had broken down and whose husband was violent. Under Irish law, divorce is illegal but the courts may grant an order for judicial separation. Applying the *Golder* case, the Court held, by five votes to two, that Ireland had infringed Article 6 by not providing legal aid to the applicant in such proceedings. In the Court's opinion, the right of access meant a right of *effective* access. The Court emphasised that it did not follow from its ruling that legal aid should be provided in all civil proceedings for indigent persons. The particular circumstances that meant that it was required in the present case were as follows:

'It seems certain to the Court that the applicant would be at a disadvantage if her husband were represented by a lawyer and she were not. Quite apart from this eventuality, it is not realistic . . . to suppose that, in litigation of this nature, the applicant could effectively conduct her own case, despite the assistance which . . . the judge affords to parties acting in person.

. . . litigation of this kind, in addition to involving complicated points of law, necessitates proof of adultery, unnatural practices or, as in the present case, cruelty; to establish the facts, expert evidence may have [to be] tendered and witnesses may have to be found, called and examined. What is more, marital disputes often entail an emotional involvement that is scarcely compatible with the degree of objectivity required by advocacy in court.'

The Court found corroboration for its view in the fact that in 'each of the 255 judicial separation proceedings initiated in Ireland in the period from January 1972 to December 1978, without exception, the petitioner was represented by a lawyer'. The Court was not persuaded by the argument that by its judgment it was imposing an economic burden on states and that in doing so it might be said to be going against the grain of a guarantee of civil and political (as opposed to economic and social) rights by requiring states to take positive action to improve the lot of their inhabitants rather than just to refrain from interference with their rights:

'Whilst the Convention sets forth what are essentially civil and political rights, many of them have implications of a social and economic nature. The Court therefore considers, like the Commission, that the mere fact that an interpretation of the Convention may extend into the sphere of social and economic rights should not be a decisive factor against such an interpretation; there is no water-tight division separating that sphere from the field covered by the Convention.'

Ireland ratified the Convention subject to a reservation in respect of the legal aid obligation in *criminal* cases expressly included in Article 6(3)(c). Clearly it did not anticipate any comparable obligation in *civil* cases. This is a situation in which states are increasingly likely to find themselves as the Court develops the meaning of the Convention.

The right of access is infringed if the applicant's waiver of his right to a trial in a criminal case against him is made under constraint: *De Weer v Belgium*, E Ct HRR A 35 (1980), 2 EHRR 439. (Breach of Article 6(1) when a Belgian butcher accused under a price control law was constrained to pay a small out of court fine to avoid shop closure pending trial, with serious financial loss.)

As the Court indicated in the *Golder* case, the right of access to a court is not an absolute one; it may be subject to limitations that do not impair the very essence of the right and that are proportionate to the attainment of a legitimate purpose for which they are imposed. It was on this basis that the applicant failed in his claim in *Ashingdane v United Kingdom*, E Ct HRR A 93 (1985), 7 EHRR 528. There the Secretary of State had given his consent to the transfer of the applicant, a restricted offender patient detained at Broadmoor, to an ordinary mental hospital, the applicant's condition having improved. When the trade union at the mental hospital opposed the transfer, the Secretary of State, acting under the Mental Health Act 1959, decided that the transfer should not occur. The applicant's attempt to challenge the legality of the Secretary of State's decision in the High Court failed because of s. 141, 1959 Act. This provided no person should be liable in civil proceedings for acts under the Act unless they were done in bad faith or negligently. It also provided that civil proceedings could not be commenced unless leave was given by the High Court, which had to be satisfied that there were substantial grounds for believing that there had been bad faith or negligence. When the applicant was refused leave to commence proceedings, he applied to Strasbourg. The Court held, by six votes to one, that the right of access to a court had not been infringed. Given that the 1959 Act left the Secretary of State considerable discretion in the performance of his statutory duty – which the applicant sought to enforce – to provide reasonable hospital accommodation, the applicant's right of access to a court in this case was one of very limited potential and the essence of it was not taken away by limiting the possibility of a claim to cases of bad faith and negligence. The purpose of limitation – to prevent the harassment of persons acting under the Act by mental patients bringing claims without merit – was legitimate and the restriction in s. 141 was proportionate to its attainment. Section 141, 1959 Act has since been replaced by a narrower limitation in s. 139(4), Mental Health Act 1983.

The right of access to a court does not require a state to provide a substantive right for an individual in any particular area of law; it requires access only if he has an arguable case to present to a court under the existing national law. For example, in *Powell and Rayner v United Kingdom*, below, p. 855, the applicants, who wanted to bring an action in nuisance in respect of aircraft noise, argued that s. 76(1), Civil Aviation Act 1982, which excluded liability in nuisance arising out of aircraft flight, infringed their right of access to a court. The Court held that the effect of s. 76 was that the applicants had no substantive right in nuisance in English law and accordingly no case to argue in court. As a result, there was no breach of the right of access to a court and the applicants had no claim under Article 6.

However, a limit to this approach was set in *Fayed v United Kingdom*, E Ct HRR A 294-B (1994), 18 EHRR 393. There the applicants wanted to bring a claim in defamation arising out of a Government inspector's report under the Companies Act 1985 which found that they had been dishonest. Whereas the law of defamation extended to cover the facts of their claim, it would, as was generally agreed, have been successfully met by a defence of absolute or qualified privilege. After referring with approval to its approach in the *Powell and Rayner* and other cases, the Court drew a distinction between substantive and procedural limitations:

'Whether a person has an actionable domestic claim may depend not only on the substantive content, properly speaking, of the relevant civil right as defined under national law but also on the existence of procedural bars preventing or limiting the possibilities of bringing potential claims to court. In the latter kind of case Article 6(1) may have a degree of applicability. Certainly the Convention enforcement bodies may not create by way of interpretation of Article 6(1) a substantive civil right which has no legal basis in the state concerned. However, it would not be consistent with the rule of law in a democratic society or with the basic principle underlying Article 6(1)—namely that civil claims must be capable of being submitted to a judge for adjudication—if, for example, a state could, without restraint or control by the Convention enforcement bodies, remove from the jurisdiction of the courts a whole range of civil claims or confer immunities from civil liability on large groups or categories of persons. . . .'

Thus, in the 'no legal basis' kind of case, the reasoning in the *Powell and Rayner* case continues to apply. In the 'removal from jurisdiction' or 'immunities' kind of case, however, the rule of law dictates some kind of Convention 'restraint or control' through the medium of the right of access. However, in the *Fayed* case, the Court concluded that the privilege defence to a defamation claim could be justified as having a legitimate aim and being proportionate.

Zimmerman and Steiner v Switzerland, E Ct HRR A 66 (1984), 6 EHRR 17, Eur Ct HR

In 1974, the applicants claimed compensation for the damage caused by noise and air pollution from an airport near their places of residence. In April 1977, they were served with the Commission's decision rejecting their claims. In the same month they lodged an administrative law appeal with the Swiss Federal Court. The appeal was dismissed in October 1980. The applicants alleged a breach of the trial within a 'reasonable time' guarantee in Article 6(1) in respect of the time taken by the Federal Court to decide their cases. In its report, the Commission expressed the unanimous opinion that there had been a breach of Article 6(1).

JUDGMENT OF THE COURT

23. . . . The period to be taken into consideration thus runs from 18 April 1977, when Mr. Zimmermann and Mr. Steiner lodged their appeal, to 15 October 1980, when the Federal Court gave judgment (see paragraphs 9 and 11 above), that is nearly three and a half years. For a case dealt with at a single jurisdictional level, such a lapse of time is considerable and calls for close scrutiny under Article 6 § 1.

24. The reasonableness of the length of proceedings coming within the scope of Article 6 § 1 must be assessed in each case according to the particular circumstances (see the *Buchholz* judgment of 6 May 1981, Series A no. 42, p. 15, § 49). The Court has to have regard, *inter alia*, to the complexity of the factual or legal issues raised by the case, to the conduct of the applicants and the competent authorities and to what was at stake for the former; in addition, only delays attributable to the State may justify a finding of a failure to comply with the 'reasonable time' requirement. . . .

1. Complexity of the case

25. . . . there was nothing particularly complicated about the case . . . no investigation into the facts was required and the legal issues arising do not appear to have been of exceptional difficulty.

2. Conduct of the applicants

26. The delays complained of cannot be attributed to Mr. Zimmermann and Mr. Steiner. Under Swiss law—as the Government admitted—they had no means of expediting matters. . . .

3. Conduct of the Swiss authorities

27. It was common ground between Government, Commission and applicants that the principal cause of the length of the proceedings was the manner in which the Federal Court carried out its task. After seeking the views of the Federal Assessment Commission on 27 April 1977, it received in May that body's observations and then those of the Canton of Zürich administrative authorities; subsequently, it did no more than reply to the above-mentioned letters from the applicants. . . . Swiss law . . . empowered the Federal Court to take a decision on the basis of the documents before it; it did not do so until about three and a half years later.

The Government cited the above-mentioned *Buchholz* judgment of 6 May 1981 . . . for there the Court had not found a violation of Article 6 § 1 although almost five years had elapsed before the final domestic decision was rendered. However, in that case the proceedings complained of had passed through three jurisdictional levels and had been characterised throughout by the taking of numerous measures, either to ascertain the facts or for other purposes. In the present case, on the other hand, the Court is faced with a single and lengthy period of total inactivity, which could have been justified only by exceptional circumstances.

28. The Government, supporting their argument with statistical evidence, relied in the main on the Federal Court's excessive workload. . . . In their view, the backlog of pending business meant that cases had to be sorted according to their urgency and importance . . ., neither of which criteria militated in favour of a more rapid examination of the appeal by Mr. Zimmermann and Mr. Steiner. In addition, it was maintained that the Swiss Parliament had taken such steps as were necessary to remedy the situation. . . .

29. The Court would point out in the first place that the Convention places a duty on the Contracting States to organise their legal systems so as to allow the courts to comply with the requirements of Article 6 § 1, including that of trial within a 'reasonable time'. Nonetheless, a temporary backlog of business does not involve liability on the part of the Contracting States provided that they take, with the requisite promptness, remedial action to deal with an exceptional situation of this kind (see the above-mentioned *Buchholz* judgment, Series A no. 42, p. 16, § 51, and the *Foti and others* judgment of 10 December 1982, Series A no. 56, p. 21, § 61).

Methods which may fall to be considered, as a provisional expedient, admittedly include choosing to deal with cases in a particular order, based not just on the date when they were brought but on their degree of urgency and importance and, in particular, on what is at stake for the persons concerned. However, if a state of affairs of this kind is prolonged and becomes a matter of structural organisation, such methods are no longer sufficient and the State will not be able to postpone further the adoption of effective measures.

30. The statistics supplied by the Government show that since 1969 there has been a progressive increase in the volume of litigation before the Federal Court, above all in the area of administrative law.

Initially, the Swiss authorities may have thought that it was a matter of a temporary excess of work, but as early as 1973 the situation—which, moreover, finds an equivalent in many other Contracting States—was seen by the Federal Court to be one that depended on questions of structural organisation. . . .

31. However, although the steps taken during the period ending on 15 October 1980, the date of the Federal Court's judgment, reflected a genuine willingness to tackle the problem, they did not give sufficient weight to the structural aspect and therefore only produced results that were not very satisfactory. The Federal Court did recommend in 1973 certain urgent measures, but it asked for them to be deferred pending a full-scale revision of the Constitution of the Courts Act. . . . It renewed its request therefor in December 1977, when the position became more critical; they were adopted by the Federal Assembly in 1978, entered into force on 1 February 1979 and consisted, *inter alia*, of an increase in the number of judges from 28 to 30 and in the number of registrars and secretaries from 24 to 28. In addition, the Federal Court effected a general revision of its Rules of Procedure. . . . Nevertheless, these measures could not be regarded as sufficient, even at that time; in fact, the backlog of cases grew progressively worse, the reason being that the volume of litigation continued to increase. The more drastic measures voted on 20 March 1981—that is, after the appeal by Mr. Zimmermann and Mr. Steiner had been dismissed—will probably prove to be more effective . . .; however, the Court does not have to make any assessment thereof.

32. The proceedings in question lasted for nearly three and a half years, and during most of that period the applicants' case remained stationary. Having regard to all the circumstances of the case, the Court finds this lapse of time excessive; the difficulties undeniably encountered by the Federal Court could by then no longer be considered to be temporary, nor could they deprive the applicants of their right to a hearing within a 'reasonable time'. . . .

There has therefore been a violation of Article 6 § 1. The Court does not have to specify to which national authority this violation is attributable: the sole issue is the international responsibility of the State. . . .

FOR THESE REASONS, THE COURT UNANIMOUSLY [7–0]

1. *Holds* that there has been a violation of Article 6 § 1 of the Convention; . . .

NOTES

1. Some cases in which breaches of the Article 6 'reasonable time' guarantee have been found involved inefficiency on the part of the officials or judges in a particular case in the context of a basically satisfactory system of justice: see, for example, *Kemmache v France*, E Ct HRR A 218 (1991) (failure to separate cases). The *Zimmerman and Steiner* case differed in that it involved delays that followed from an overloading of the Swiss Federal Court of which the state had long been aware. The

European Court did not shrink from insisting that in such a situation the state must appoint more judges or revise its court procedures to overcome the general problem. More delicate still is the question whether a state can be expected to undertake fundamental reforms of its court system to expedite proceedings.

This issue arose in *Neumeister v Austria*, E Ct HRR A 8 (1969), 1 EHRR 91, in which much of the delay had occurred at the preliminary investigation stage. Under some civil law systems of criminal justice, including that in Austria, a person is likely to spend a considerable length of time waiting for a 'charge' against him in the sense of Article 6 to be fully examined by an investigating judge. Some of that examination is a repetition of work already done by the police in its investigation. If such a system, which has merits in other respects, were altered to eliminate this overlap of time, the period during which an accused had a charge hanging over him would generally be reduced. In *Neumeister v Austria*, the Court confirmed that preliminary investigation systems of the kind described are not in themselves contrary to Article 6; the requirement is only that they be administered efficiently. The Court stated:

'It should moreover be pointed out that a concern for speed cannot dispense those judges who in the system of criminal procedure in force on the continent of Europe are responsible for the investigation or the conduct of the trial from taking every measure likely to throw light on the truth or falsehood of the charges. . . .'

The same question arose again in *Konig v Federal Republic of Germany*, E Ct HRR A 27 (1978), 2 EHRR 170, in the different context of the complicated system of administrative courts in West Germany. Faced with one set of proceedings in the case that lasted nearly 11 years and were still pending, the Court first noted that it was not its function to comment on the structure of the courts concerned which, it conceded, was aimed at providing a full set of remedies for the individual's grievances. It added, however, that if efforts to this end 'result in a procedural maze, it is for the State alone to draw the conclusions and, if need be, to simplify the system with a view to complying with Article 6(1) of the Convention'. The implication is that if a case takes what is on the face of it an unreasonably long time, a state will not escape liability by proving that it has been dealt with efficiently within the limits of an unduly elaborate court structure.

2. As the Court indicated in the *Zimmerman and Steiner* case (para. 23, judgment), it takes into account what is 'at stake' for the applicant when deciding whether a case has been determined within a reasonable time. For example, in *H v United Kingdom*, E Ct HRR A 120 (1987), 10 EHRR 95, the Court held that the period of two years and seven months taken to decide on the applicant's access to her child in public care was in breach of Article 6, 'above all' because of what was at stake for the applicant.

3. The only other case in which the UK has been in breach of the 'reasonable time' guarantee was *Darnell v United Kingdom* (claim for unfair NHS dismissal took nearly nine years).[1]

Funke v France, E Ct HRR A 256-A (1993), 16 EHRR 297, Eur Ct HR

Three French customs officers, accompanied by a senior police officer, searched the applicant's house in connection with alleged offences involving financial dealings with foreign countries. Having discovered and seized foreign bank statements and cheque books, they asked the applicant to produce all of his foreign bank account statements for the past three years and other documents relating to property abroad. When the applicant refused to do this, he was convicted and fined under the

1 E Ct HRR A 272 (1993), 18 EHRR 205. The many cases of breaches of the 'reasonable time' guarantee established by the Court mostly have concerned civil law states, especially Italy.

criminal provisions of French customs law, which are treated as a part of French criminal law. No criminal proceedings were ever brought against the applicant for illegal financial dealings with foreign countries. The applicant claimed breaches of Articles 6 and 8. In its report, the Commission expressed the opinion that there had been no breach of either Article.

JUDGMENT OF THE COURT

41. In the applicant's submission, his conviction for refusing to disclose the documents asked for by the customs ... had infringed his right to a fair trial as secured in Article 6 § 1. He claimed that the authorities had violated the right not to give evidence against oneself, a general principle enshrined both in the legal orders of the Contracting States and in the European Convention and the International Covenant on Civil and Political Rights, as although they had not lodged a complaint alleging an offence against the regulations governing financial dealings with foreign countries, they had brought criminal proceedings calculated to compel Mr Funke to co-operate in a prosecution mounted against him. Such a method of proceeding was, he said, all the more unacceptable as nothing prevented the French authorities from seeking international assistance and themselves obtaining the necessary evidence from the foreign States.

42. The Government ... [noted that in] the instant case the customs had not required Mr Funke to confess to an offence or to provide evidence of one himself; they had merely asked him to give particulars of evidence found by their officers and which he had admitted, namely the bank statements and chequebooks discovered during the house search. As to the courts, they had assessed, after adversarial proceedings, whether the customs' application was justified in law and in fact.

43. The Commission reached the same conclusion, mainly on the basis of the special features of investigation procedures in business and financial matters. It considered that neither the obligation to produce bank statements nor the imposition of pecuniary penalties offended the principle of a fair trial; the former was a reflection of the State's confidence in all its citizens in that no use was made of stricter supervisory measures, while responsibility for the detriment caused by the latter lay entirely with the person affected where he refused to co-operate with the authorities.

44. The Court notes that the customs secured Mr Funke's conviction in order to obtain certain documents which they believed must exist, although they were not certain of the fact. Being unable or unwilling to procure them by some other means, they attempted to compel the applicant himself to provide the evidence of offences he had allegedly committed. The special features of customs law ... cannot justify such an infringement of the right of anyone 'charged with a criminal offence', within the autonomous meaning of this expression in Article 6, to remain silent and not to contribute to incriminating himself. ...

47. In the applicant's submission, the house search and seizures made in the instant case were in breach of Article 8. ...

48. ... The Court considers that all the rights secured in Article 8 § 1 are in issue, except for the right to respect for family life. It must accordingly be determined whether the interferences in question satisfied the conditions in paragraph 2. ...

53. In Mr Funke's submission, the interferences could not be regarded as 'necessary in a democratic society'. Their scope was unlimited and they went well beyond what was required in the public interest, since they were not subject to judicial supervision; furthermore, they had not only taken place in the absence of any flagrant offence (*flavrant délit*), circumstantial evidence or presumption but had also been carried out in an improper manner.

54. The Government, whose contentions the Commission accepted in substance, argued that house searches and seizures were the only means available to the authorities for investigating offences against the legislation governing financial dealings with foreign countries and thus preventing the flight of capital and tax evasion. In such fields there was a *corpus delicti* only very rarely if at all; the 'physical manifestation' of the offence therefore lay mainly in documents which a guilty party could easily conceal or destroy. Such persons, however, had the benefit of substantial safeguards, strengthened by very rigorous judicial supervision: decision-making by the head of the customs district concerned, the rank of the officers authorised to establish offences, the presence of a senior police officer (*officier de police judiciaire*), the timing of searches, the preservation of lawyers' and doctors' professional secrecy, the possibility of invoking the liability of the public authorities, etc. In short, even before the reform of 1986–89, the French system had ensured that there was a proper balance between the requirements of law enforcement and the protection of the rights of the individual.

55. The Court has consistently held that the Contracting States have a certain margin of appreciation in assessing the need for an interference, but it goes hand in hand with European supervision. The exceptions provided for in paragraph 2 of Article 8 are to be interpreted narrowly (see the *Klass and Others v*

Germany judgment of 6 September 1978, Series A no. 28, p. 21, § 42), and the need for them in a given case must be convincingly established.

56. Undoubtedly, in the field under consideration – the prevention of capital outflows and tax evasion – States encounter serious difficulties owing to the scale and complexity of banking systems and financial channels and to the immense scope for international investment, made all the easier by the relative porousness of national borders. The Court therefore recognises that they may consider it necessary to have recourse to measures such as house searches and seizures in order to obtain physical evidence of exchange-control offences and, where appropriate, to prosecute those responsible. Nevertheless, the relevant legislation and practice must afford adequate and effective safeguards against abuse (see, among other authorities and *mutatis mutandis*, the *Klass and Others* judgment previously cited, Series A no. 28, p. 23, § 50).

57. This was not so in the instant case. At the material time – and the Court does not have to express an opinion on the legislative reforms of 1986 and 1989, which were designed to afford better protection for individuals ... the customs authorities had very wide powers; in particular, they had exclusive competence to assess the expediency, number, length and scale of inspections. Above all, in the absence of any requirement of a judicial warrant the restrictions and conditions provided for in law, which were emphasised by the Government (see paragraph 54 above), appear too lax and full of loopholes for the interferences with the applicant's rights to have been strictly proportionate to the legitimate aim pursued.

58. To these general considerations may be added a particular observation, namely that the customs authorities never lodged a complaint against Mr Funke alleging an offence against the regulations governing financial dealings with foreign countries. . . .

FOR THESE REASONS, THE COURT . . .

2. *Holds* by eight votes to one that, for want of a fair trial, there has been a violation of Article 6 § 1. . . .

4. *Holds* by eight votes to one that there has been a breach of Article 8. . . .

NOTES

1. On the Article 8 search warrant aspect of this case, see below, p. 811. As to Article 6, the Court interpreted the general 'fair hearing' guarantee in Article 6(1) as including freedom from self-incrimination. The Court's ruling was applied by the Commission in *Saunders v United Kingdom* (1994), unreported. There, on pain of criminal sanction, including imprisonment, the applicant was required by law to answer questions put to him by Department of Trade and Industry inspectors in the course of their investigation into a company takeover. The information that he gave was later introduced as 'a not insignificant part of the evidence against him at his trial', at which the applicant was convicted and sentenced to imprisonment for offences involving commercial fraud. In its report, the Commission expressed the opinion that there had been a breach of the applicant's freedom from self-incrimination. The case is pending before the Court. Would the limitations upon the accused's freedom from self-incrimination recently introduced into English law in the Criminal Justice and Public Order Act 1994, see above, pp. 145 –146, be in breach of Article 6(1)?

2. The 'fair hearing' requirement has also been used to read into Article 6(1) other particular guarantees in civil or criminal cases, most clearly the right to 'equality of arms', i.e. the right of the parties to a case to equal procedural rights. In *Borgers v Belgium*,[1] the applicant appealed against his conviction to the Court of Cassation. He complained that he was not allowed to address the Court after and in reply to the *avocat general*, who argued against his appeal, and that the *avocat general* had participated, without a vote, in the private deliberations of the Court on the case. The European Court held, by 18 votes to 4, that the right to 'equality of arms' had been infringed. It accepted that the *avocat general* did not act as the prosecuting authority

---

1 E Ct HRR A 214-A (1991), 15 EHRR 92. The decision reverses *Delcourt v Belgium*, E Ct HRR A 11 (1970), 1 EHRR 355, which had been heavily criticised.

before the Court of Cassation and that his function instead was the independent one of advising and assisting the Court of Cassation in ensuring that its case law was consistent and in drafting its judgment. Nevertheless, once the *avocat general* spoke against the applicant's appeal, the latter should have been allowed to respond to the arguments of someone who was now his opponent. As to the *avocat general's* participation in the Court's deliberations, even if it was limited to questions of drafting, his presence could reasonably be thought, contrary to the idea of objective justice, to have provided a further opportunity for him to argue against the appeal when the applicant could not respond.

3. The 'fair hearing' requirement was applied in conjunction with Article 6(3)(d) in *Edwards v United Kingdom*, E Ct HRR A 247-B (1992), 15 EHRR 417. There the police had failed to disclose evidence to the defence. The Court held, by seven votes to two, that whereas this might have been in breach of Article 6(1) and (3)(d), the deficiency had been made good by consideration of the evidence by the Court of Appeal so that there was no breach of these provisions. The Court stated:

'35. The applicant's conviction was based mainly on police evidence, which he contested, that he had confessed to the offences. It subsequently came to light that certain facts . . . had not been disclosed by the police to the defence which would have enabled it to attack the credibility and veracity of police testimony.

36. The Court considers that it is a requirement of fairness under paragraph 1 of Article 6, indeed one which is recognised under English law, that the prosecution authorities disclose to the defence all material evidence for or against the accused and that the failure to do so in the present case gave rise to a defect in the trial proceedings.

However, when this was discovered, the Secretary of State, following an independent police investigation, referred the case to the Court of Appeal which examined the transcript of the trial including the applicant's alleged confession and considered in detail the impact of the new information on the conviction. . . .

37. In the proceedings before the Court of Appeal the applicant was represented by senior and junior counsel who had every opportunity to seek to persuade the court that the conviction should not stand in view of the evidence of non-disclosure. Admittedly the police officers who had given evidence at the trial were not heard by the Court of Appeal. It was, none the less, open to counsel for the applicant to make an application to the Court – which they chose not to do – that the police officers be called as witnesses. . . .

39. Having regard to the above, the Court concludes that the defects of the original trial were remedied by the subsequent procedure before the Court of Appeal. . . .

NOTES ON OTHER GUARANTEES IN ARTICLE 6, ECHR

1. There are a number of other specific guarantees in Article 6 in addition to the trial 'within a reasonable time' and 'fair hearing' guarantees considered in the cases above. The following are notes on some of those that have given rise to litigation.

2. *Independent and impartial tribunal.* In *Campbell and Fell v United Kingdom*, E Ct HRR A 80 (1984), 7 EHRR 165, the Court indicated the considerations it takes into account when assessing independence:

'In determining whether a body can be considered to be "independent"—notably of the executive and of the parties to the case—the Court has had regard to the manner of appointment of its members and the duration of their term of office, the existence of guarantees against outside pressures and the question whether the body presents an appearance of independence.'

In *Piersack v Belgium*, E Ct HRR A 53 (1982), 5 EHRR 169, the Court held that the requirement of 'impartiality' includes an objective as well as a subjective element; in common law terms, justice must not only be done, but be seen to be done. In that case, the President of the Assize Court that convicted the applicant of murder had, before his appointment as a judge, been the head of a section of the Public Prosecutor's Department when it had investigated the case against the applicant. According to the applicant, the judge had taken part in the investigation; according to the government, his involvement in the case had been administrative only. Without finding it necessary to determine the extent of the judge's involvement, the Court unanimously held that there had been a breach of the requirement of 'impartiality' in Article 6(1):

30. Whilst impartiality normally denotes absence of prejudice or bias, its existence or otherwise can, notably under Article 6 § 1 of the Convention, be tested in various ways. A distinction can be drawn in this context between a subjective approach, that is endeavouring to ascertain the personal conviction of a given judge in a given case, and an objective approach, that is determining whether he offered guarantees sufficient to exclude any legitimate doubt in this respect.

(a) As regards the first approach, the Court notes that the applicant is pleased to pay tribute to Mr. Van de Walle's personal impartiality; . . .

However, it is not possible to confine oneself to a purely subjective test. In this area, even appearances may be of a certain importance . . . As the Belgian Court of Cassation observed in its judgment of 21 February 1979 . . ., any judge in respect of whom there is a legitimate reason to fear a lack of impartiality must withdraw. What is at stake is the confidence which the courts must inspire in the public in a democratic society.

(b) It would be going too far to the opposite extreme to maintain that former judicial officers in the public prosecutor's department were unable to sit on the bench in every case that had been examined initially by that department, even though they had never had to deal with the case themselves. So radical a solution . . . would erect a virtually impenetrable barrier between that department and the bench. It would lead to an upheaval in the judicial system of several Contracting States where transfers from one of those offices to the other are a frequent occurrence. Above all, the mere fact that a judge was once a member of the public prosecutor's department is not a reason for fearing that he lacks impartiality . . .

(d) . . . In order that the courts may inspire in the public the confidence which is indispensable, account must also be taken of questions of internal organisation. If an individual, after holding in the public prosecutor's department an office whose nature is such that he may have to deal with a given matter in the course of his duties, subsequently sits in the same case as a judge, the public are entitled to fear that he does not offer sufficient guarantees of impartiality.

31. This was what occurred in the present case. . . .

The same approach was applied in *Belilos v Switzerland*, E Ct HRR A 132 (1988), 10 EHRR 466, without reference to the *Piersack* case. In the *Belilos* case, the applicant had been convicted of the criminal offence of participation in an unauthorised demonstration by the Police Board, its only member being a lawyer from police headquarters appointed by the local authority. Although the lawyer sat in his personal capacity and was not subject to orders in the exercise of his judicial function, the Court held that this situation infringed the requirement of an 'independent and impartial tribunal' taken as a whole:

The ordinary citizen will tend to see him as a member of the police force subordinate to his superiors and loyal to his colleagues. A situation of this kind may undermine the confidence which must be inspired by the courts in a democratic society.

In short, the applicant could legitimately have doubts as to the independence and organisational impartiality of the Police Board, which accordingly did not satisfy the requirements of Article 6(1) in this respect.

3. *The right to legal represenation: Article 6(3)(c)*. In *Poitrimol v France*, E Ct HRR A 277-A (1993), 18 EHRR 130, the Court stated: 'Although not absolute, the right of everyone charged with a criminal offence to be effectively defended by a lawyer, assigned officially if need be, is one of the fundamental features of a fair trial'. The right is not dependent upon the attendance of the accused. In *Campbell and Fell v United Kingdom*, E Ct HRR A 80 (1984), 7 EHRR 165, the first applicant was not allowed legal representation at a prison disciplinary hearing before a Board of Visitors. The Court found a breach of Article 6(3)(b) and (c):

'99. As regards sub-paragraph (c) of Article 6 para. 3, it is true that Mr Campbell elected not to attend the Board's hearing, but the Convention requires that a "person charged with a criminal offence who does not wish to defend himself in person must be able to have recourse to legal assistance of his own choosing". . . .

Moreover, a lawyer could scarcely "assist" his client—in terms of sub-paragraph (c)—unless there had been some previous consultation between them. This latter consideration leads the Court to the conclusion that the "facilities" contemplated by sub-paragraph (b) were not afforded.'

Legal aid must be provided if 'the interests of justice so require'. If a convicted person is allowed a right of appeal, he cannot be refused legal aid because his chances of success are slight. In *Bonner v United Kingdom*, E Ct HRR A 300-B (1994), 19 EHRR 246, the applicant was denied legal aid on the statutory ground that he did not have 'substantial grounds for making the appeal'. Holding that there had been a breach of Article 6(3)(c), the Court focused upon the fact that the applicant had been allowed an appeal; that he required legal assistance to argue effectively the point that he wanted to make; and that a great deal (an eight year sentence) was at stake for him. In another Scottish case, *Granger v United Kingdom*, E Ct HRR A 174 (1990), 12 EHRR 469, it was held that there was a breach of Article 6(3)(c) because the decision to refuse the applicant legal aid was not reviewed in terms of 'the interests of justice' when it became clear that the case was more complicated than had been supposed. The 'interests of justice' limitation does not require actual prejudice to the applicant; it is sufficient that 'it appears plausible that in the particular circumstances' legal representation would have helped: *Artico v Italy*, E Ct HRR A 37 (1980), 3 EHRR 1.

The right to effective legal assistance in Article 6(3)(c) includes a right of private access to a lawyer, both at the pre-trial stage and later. In *S v Switzerland*,[1] Article 6(3)(c) was infringed when the accused, who was in detention on remand, was not allowed to consult with his lawyer out of the hearing of a prison officer. As the Court stated, 'if a lawyer were unable to confer with his client and receive confidential instructions from him without such surveillance, his assistance would lose much of its usefulness, whereas the Convention is intended to guarantee rights that are practical and effective'. On the question whether an accused's lawyer may attend interrogation sessions, see *Imbrioscia v Switzerland* A275 (1993).

5 Article 8: The right to privacy, family life, etc

Malone v United Kingdom, E Ct HRR A 82 (1984), 7 EHRR 14, Eur Ct HR

Having lost in the High Court in *Malone v Metropolitan Police Comr*, see above, p. 554, the applicant took his case to Strasbourg. He alleged violations of Article 8 resulting from the tapping of his telephone and interference with his correspondence. He also claimed that details of calls he had made which the Post Office had obtained by 'metering' for its own record purposes had been passed on to the police contrary to Article 8. The Commission expressed the opinion, by 11 to 0, with one abstention, that the applicant's rights under Article 8 had been infringed 'by reason of the admitted interception of his telephone conversations and the law and practice governing the interception of postal and telephone communications on behalf of the police'.

JUDGMENT OF THE COURT

63 . . . the present case 'is directly concerned only with the question of interceptions effected by or on behalf of the police' – and not other government services such as H.M. Customs and Excise and the

---

1 E Ct HRR A 220 (1991), 8 EHRR 121. Cf. *Can v Switzerland* A 96 (1985) Com Rep, F Sett before Court.

Security Service – 'within the general context of a criminal investigation, together with the legal and administrative framework relevant to such interceptions'. . . .

66. The Court held in [the] *Silver* [case, E Ct HRR A61 (1983)] . . . that, at least as far as interferences with prisoners' correspondence were concerned, the expression 'in accordance with the law/*prévue par la loi*' in paragraph 2 of Article 8 should be interpreted in the light of the same general principles as were stated in the *Sunday Times* [case, below, p. 823] . . . to apply to the comparable expression 'prescribed by law/ *prévues par la loi*' in paragraph 2 of Article 10. . . .

[The Court restated the *Sunday Times* principles and continued:]

67 . . . The Court would reiterate its opinion that the phrase 'in accordance with the law' does not merely refer back to domestic law but also relates to the quality of the law, requiring it to be compatible with the rule of law, which is expressly mentioned in the preamble to the Convention (see, *mutatis mutandis*, the . . . *Silver* [case] . . ., and the *Golder* [case, above, p. 792]. . . . The phrase thus implies – and this follows from the object and purpose of Article 8 – that there must be a measure of legal protection in domestic law against arbitrary interferences by public authorities with the rights safeguarded by paragraph 1. . . . Especially where a power of the executive is exercised in secret, the risks of arbitrariness are evident (see the . . . *Klass* [case]). . . . Undoubtedly, as the Government rightly suggested, the requirements of the Convention, notably in regard to foreseeability, cannot be exactly the same as in the special context of interception of communications for the purposes of police investigations as they are where the object of the relevant law is to place restrictions on the conduct of individuals. In particular, the requirement of foreseeability cannot mean that an individual should be enabled to foresee when the authorities are likely to intercept his communications so that he can adapt his conduct accordingly. Nevertheless, the law must be sufficiently clear in its terms to give citizens an adequate indication as to the circumstances in which and the conditions on which public authorities are empowered to resort to this secret and potentially dangerous interference with the right to respect for private life and correspondence.

68. There was also some debate in the pleadings as to the extent to which, in order for the Convention to be complied with, the 'law' itself, as opposed to accompanying administrative practice, should define the circumstances in which and the conditions on which a public authority may interfere with the exercise of the protected rights. . . . in the case of *Silver* . . . the Court held that 'a law which confers a discretion must indicate the scope of that discretion', although the detailed procedures and conditions to be observed do not necessarily have to be incorporated in rules of substantive law. . . . The degree of precision required of the 'law' in this connection will depend upon the particular subject-matter (see the . . . *Sunday Times* . . . [case]). Since the implementation in practice of measures of secret surveillance of communications is not open to scrutiny by the individuals concerned or the public at large, it would be contrary to the rule of law for the legal discretion granted to the executive to be expressed in terms of an unfettered power. Consequently, the law must indicate the scope of any such discretion conferred on the competent authorities and the manner of its exercise with sufficient clarity, having regard to the legitimate aim of the measure in question, to give the individual adequate protection against arbitrary interference. . . .

69. Whilst the exact legal basis of the executive's power in this respect was the subject of some dispute, it was common ground that the settled practice of intercepting communications on behalf of the police in pursuance of a warrant issued by the Secretary of State for the purposes of detecting and preventing crime, and hence the admitted interception of one of the applicant's telephone conversations, were lawful under the law of England and Wales. The legality of this power to intercept was established in relation to telephone communications in the judgment of Sir Robert Megarry dismissing the applicant's civil action . . . and, as shown by the independent findings of the Birkett report . . ., is generally recognised for postal communications.

70. The issue to be determined is therefore whether, under domestic law, the essential elements of the power to intercept communications were laid down with reasonable precision in accessible legal rules that sufficiently indicated the scope and manner of exercise of the discretion conferred on the relevant authorities. . . .

[The Court then reviewed English law on the interception of communications and continued:]

79. The foregoing considerations disclose that, at the very least, in its present state the law in England and Wales governing interception of communications for police purposes is somewhat obscure and open to differing interpretations. The Court would be usurping the function of the national courts if it were to attempt to make an authoritative statement on such issues of domestic law. . . . The Court is, however, required under the Convention to determine whether, for the purposes of paragraph 2 of Article 8, the

relevant law lays down with reasonable clarity the essential elements of the authorities' powers in this domain.

Detailed procedures concerning interception of communications on behalf of the police in England and Wales do exist. . . . What is more, published statistics show the efficacy of those procedures in keeping the number of warrants granted relatively low, especially when compared with the rising number of indictable crimes committed and telephones installed. . . . The public have been made aware of the applicable arrangements and principles through publication of the Birkett report and the White Paper and through statements by responsible Ministers in Parliament. . . .

Nonetheless, on the evidence before the Court, it cannot be said with any reasonable certainty what elements of the powers to intercept are incorporated in legal rules and what elements remain within the discretion of the executive. In view of the attendant obscurity and uncertainty as to the state of the law in this essential respect, the Court cannot but reach a similar conclusion to that of the Commission. In the opinion of the Court, the law of England and Wales does not indicate with reasonable clarity the scope and manner of exercise of the relevant discretion conferred on the public authorities. To that extent, the minimum degree of legal protection to which citizens are entitled under the rule of law in a democratic society is lacking. . . .

82. . . . In view of its foregoing conclusion that the interferences found were not 'in accordance with the law', the Court considers that it does not have to examine further the content of the other guarantees required by paragraph 2 of Article 8 and whether the system complained of furnished those guarantees in the particular circumstances.

83. The process known as 'metering' involves the use of a device . . . which registers the numbers dialled on a particular telephone and the time and duration of each call. . . .

84. As the Government rightly suggested, a meter check printer registers information that a supplier of a telephone service may in principle legitimately obtain, notably in order to ensure that the subscriber is correctly charged or to investigate complaints or possible abuses of the service. By its very nature, metering is therefore to be distinguished from interception of communications, which is undesirable and illegitimate in a democratic society unless justified. The Court does not accept, however, that the use of data obtained from metering, whatever the circumstances and purposes, cannot give rise to an issue under Article 8. The records of metering contain information, in particular the numbers dialled, which is an integral element in the communications made by telephone. Consequently, release of the information to the police without the consent of the subscriber also amounts, in the opinion of the Court, to an interference with a right guaranteed by Article 8. . . .

87. Section 80 of the Post Office Act 1969 has never been applied so as to 'require' the Post Office, pursuant to a warrant of the Secretary of State, to make available to the police in connection with the investigation of crime information obtained from metering. On the other hand, no rule of domestic law makes it unlawful for the Post Office voluntarily to comply with a request from the police to make and supply records of metering. . . . The practice described above, including the limitative conditions as to when the information may be provided, has been made public in answer to parliamentary questions. . . . However, on the evidence adduced before the Court, apart from the simple absence of prohibition, there would appear to be no legal rules concerning the scope and manner of exercise of the discretion enjoyed by the public authorities. Consequently, although lawful in terms of domestic law, the interference resulting from the existence of the practice in question was not 'in accordance with the law', within the meaning of paragraph 2 of Article 8. . . .

88. This conclusion removes the need for the Court to determine whether the interference found was 'necessary in a democratic society' for one of the aims enumerated in paragraph 2 of Article 8. . . .

FOR THESE REASONS, THE COURT

1. *Holds* unanimously[1] that there has been a breach of Article 8 of the Convention; . . .

NOTES[2]

1. The Court had no difficulty in treating telephone tapping as an interference with 'correspondence' (see para. 63). On interference with prisoner's correspondence, see

1 *Ed.* The case was heard by the full Court.
2 On the *Malone* case, see J. Michael, (1984) 134 NLJ 646, 669, 698. For other cases in which arrangements for telephone tapping were in breach of the 'in accordance with the law' requirement, see *Huvig v France*, E Ct HRR A 176-B (1990), 12 EHRR 528 and *Kruslin v France*, E Ct HRR A 176-A (1990), 12 EHRR 528.

the *Golder* case, above, *Silver v United Kingdom*, E Ct HRR A 61 (1983), 5 EHRR 347 and *Campbell v United Kingdom*, E Ct HRR A 233 (1992), EHRR. The UK law and practice concerning the censorship of prisoners' correspondence has been radically changed as a result of the adverse judgments in these and other cases: see S. Livingstone and T. Owen, *Prison Law* (1993), pp. 143–157.

2. When the *Malone* case was decided, telephone tapping in the UK was regulated by administrative practice, the up-to-date details of which were not readily accessible to the public. There was no express statutory authorisation or regime. Nor was there a common law basis. The position was essentially that telephone tapping was lawful because there was no law (it involved no trespass, no breach of confidence, etc) prohibiting it: *Malone v Metropolitan Police Comr* [1979] Ch 344, Ch D. As a matter of practice, the Home Secretary authorised telephone tapping in accordance with internal, government guidelines, the details of which only became known to the public from time to time through reports such as the Birkett Report, Cmnd. 283, in 1957 in response to telephone tapping incidents giving cause for concern.

3. The legality of the interception of postal communications and telephone tapping under the Convention had earlier been considered by the Court in *Klass v Federal Republic of Germany*.[1] There the Court held that the West German law permitting the interception of postal and telephonic communications in national security cases was consistent with Article 8; although an 'interference by a public authority' with the 'right to respect for' a person's 'private and family life . . . and his correspondence', it was justified as being necessary 'in the interests of national security' and/or for 'the prevention of disorder or crime'. The Court accepted that some power of interception was permissible to prevent espionage and terrorism and, bearing in mind the 'margin of appreciation' doctrine, concluded that the controls built into the West German system to prevent abuse were sufficient. Under that system, permission to intercept communications is given by a government minister applying certain criteria as to 'reasonable suspicion', etc. An independent Commission, chaired by a person qualified for judicial office, reviews and may reverse the Minister's decisions. A Board composed of government and opposition members of parliament keeps a more general watch on the system. A person whose communications are intercepted must be told that this has happened afterwards if national security allows. He may challenge the legality of current or past interceptions in the courts (so far as he is aware of their occurrence). Although the Court stated that it was 'in principle desirable to entrust supervisory control to a judge', the above safeguards were sufficient, at least in a national security context. An interesting aspect of the *Klass* case was that the Court regarded the applicants as 'victims' able to bring a claim under Article 25 even though their telephones had not been tapped. Whereas an applicant under Article 25 normally cannot challenge the validity of a law *in abstracto* (as a state can under Article 24) but has to show that the law 'has been applied to his detriment', the position is different in a case in which 'owing to the secrecy of the measures objected to, he cannot point to any concrete measure specifically affecting him'. In such a case the need to make the application procedure effective dictates that the 'individual may, *under certain conditions*, claim to be the victim of a violation occasioned by the mere existence of secret measures or of legislation permitting secret measures. . .'. Moreover, the Court stated, the mere prospect that a telephone may be tapped is such as to inhibit conversation and thereby directly interfere with respect for privacy. In the *Malone* case, the Court

---

1 E Ct HRR A 28 (1978), 2 EHRR 214. See P. J. Duffy and P. T. Muchlinski, (1980) 130 NLJ 949.

similarly did not find it necessary to establish that interception or metering of the applicant's postal or telephonic communications had actually occurred. (Only one instance of telephone tapping and no metering had been admitted by the defendant Government.) The Court observed that, as a suspected receiver of stolen goods, the applicant was a member of a class of persons whose privacy was likely to be invaded in these ways. It is not clear from the Court's judgment whether it was necessary for the applicant to have been a member of such a class (as opposed to any person making a telephone call, etc.) where a system of secret surveillance was in operation to have been a 'victim' and for Article 8 to apply.

4. In the *Malone* case, the Court was prepared to accept that the interception of communications could be justified under the Convention as being necessary to prevent crime (para. 81) as well as (see the *Klass* case) for reasons of national security. Because of its ruling on the 'in accordance with the law' point, the Court did not find it necessary to specify what procedural safeguards were required in criminal cases. They must be at least as stringent as those spelt out in the *Klass* case for national security cases.

5. In order to comply with the *Malone* case, the UK enacted the Interception of Communications Act 1985: see above, p. 569. In *Christie v United Kingdom* (1994) 78-A DR E Com HR 119, the Commission held that the Act met the 'in accordance with the law' requirement in Article 8(2). It also held that, 'having regard to the wide margin of appreciation . . . in this area', the procedural safeguards provided by the Act (Commissioner, Tribunal, etc) were sufficient for a case such as that before it where the applicant was a trade unionist with links with communist Eastern Europe whose telephone was being tapped on 'national security' and 'economic well-being' grounds. The complaint under Article 8 was declared inadmissible.

6. In *Hewitt and Harman v United Kingdom*, (1992) 67 DR E Comm HR 88, 14 EHRR 657, CM Resolution DH (90) 36, the Commission expressed the opinion that 'secret surveillance activities for the purpose of gathering and storing on file information concerning a person's private life' was an interference with that person's private life requiring justification under Article 8(2). In that case, the applicants were a legal officer and the General Secretary respectively of the National Council for Civil Liberties, which, a former MI5 officer had stated, was classified as a communist controlled subversive organisation. Because of their links with it, files were compiled on them by the Security Service in which were recorded political and some personal information about them. Although it would appear that they were never the direct subjects of telephone or mail intercepts, references to them or information about them on intercepts of other persons would be kept on their files, as would information obtained from other sources. The Security Service's authority for such activities was the 1952 Directive issued by the Home Secretary to the Director-General of the Security Service. The Directive stated that 'the Security Service's task is the defence of the Realm as a whole, from external and internal dangers arising from attempts at espionage and sabotage, or from actions of persons and organisations whether directed from within or without the country, which may be judged to be subversive to the State'. It was not claimed by the UK government that the Directive had the force of law. In addition, in the view of the Commission, the Directive did not 'provide a framework which indicates with the requisite degree of certainty the scope and manner of the exercise of discretion by the authorities'. As a result, the surveillance of the applicants was in breach of Article 8 as not being 'in accordance with the law'. Following the case, the UK enacted the Security Service Act 1989, which places the work of the Security Service on a statutory footing: see above, p. 501. In *Esbester v United Kingdom* (1993) and *Harman v United Kingdom* (1994), referred to in *Christie v UK*, see previous note, otherwise unreported, the Commission held that the 1989 Act complied with the 'in accordance with the law' and, at least in a national security context, the procedural requirements of Article 8(2).

7. In *Leander v Sweden*, E Ct HRR A 116 (1987), 9 EHRR 443, to which the Court refers, it had held, by seven votes to none, that the storing of information about an individual on a secret police register for national security purposes and its release to other government agencies for civil service employment security vetting purposes was not a breach of the right to respect for private life in Article 8. This was so provided that adequate and effective procedural safeguards were provided to ensure that there was no abuse of power in the storage and release of information. In the *Leander* case, the applicant was refused employment as a technician at a naval museum. The reason was that the job involved occasional access to an adjoining top security naval base. Because of this, the Navy had checked with the National Police Board Security Department which gave the Navy information from its register of potentially subversive persons which led the Navy to believe that the applicant was a security risk. The nature of the information was never revealed to the applicant so that he had never had an opportunity to challenge it. However, the applicant did acknowledge that he had at one time been a member of the communist party and had been active in trade union politics during his military service. The Court held that the storage and release of information about the applicant on the facts of the case were justified in terms of the 'national security' exception in Article 8(2). This was so given that (i) there were remedies by way of recourse to the ombudsman and the Chancellor of Justice, who were each persons independent of the government who could consider complaints concerning the work of the National Police Board, and (ii) decisions to release information in the register for security purposes were taken by a National Police Board panel that included three present or former Members of Parliament, including an opposition member, and three other lay persons.

8. The above cases concern the collection of information about an individual. Neither Article 8 nor Article 10 provide a general right of access to information that is collected by the state about an individual. Such a right was found in Article 8, exceptionally, on the special facts of *Gaskin v United Kingdom*, E Ct HRR A 160 (1990), 12 EHRR 36. There the applicant had been a child in public care from babyhood until his 18th birthday, living with a long sequence of foster parents. He was refused access to those documents (the large majority) on his local authority file in respect of which the authors refused consent to their disclosure. The Court recognised that the file was important to the applicant as a record of his childhood and development, and thereby related to his private life. While accepting that there was a legitimate interest in confidentiality and that a system of consent was appropriate, the Court held the UK to be in breach of Article 8 because such 'a system is only in conformity with the principle of proportionality if it provides that an independent authority finally decides whether access has to be granted in cases in where a contributor fails to answer or withholds consent'. See now the Access to Personal Files Act 1987 and regulations made thereunder.

Niemietz v Germany, E Ct HRR A 251-B (1992), 16 EHRR 97, Eur Ct HR

A letter was sent to the judge in criminal proceedings being brought against an individual who refused to co-operate in the collection of the Church tax. The letter was critical of the judge and put pressure upon him to acquit. It was signed 'Klaus Wegner' and written 'on behalf of the Anti-Clerical Working Group' of the Freiburg *Bunte Liste*, a local political party. Criminal proceedings were instituted against Klaus Wegner for the offence of 'insulting behaviour'. In order to identify Klaus Wegner, which was possibly a fictitious name, the police obtained a search warrant to search, inter alia, the applicant's office. The applicant was a lawyer who had been the chairman of the *Bunte Liste* and a committed supporter of the Anti-Clerical Working Group. His law office had been used until recently as an address to which the Post Office forwarded Freiburg *Bunte Liste* correspondence addressed to a box number.

The search warrant authorised the entry of the applicant's office for the search and seizure of 'documents which reveal the identity of Klaus Wegner (sic)'. The search was conducted by representatives of the Public Prosecutor's Office and the police in the presence of two office assistants and, later, the applicant and his colleague. Four filing cabinets with data concerning clients and six client files were examined. No documents were seized and the criminal proceedings were later discontinued. The applicant stated in the proceedings at Strasbourg that he had destroyed documents revealing the identity of Klaus Wegner.

The applicant claimed breaches of Articles 8, 13 and Article 1, First Protocol. In its report, the Commission expressed the opinion unanimously that the applicant's rights to respect for private life and home in Article 8 had been infringed. It did not consider the other claims. The first question considered by the Court below was whether the search of an office could be said to affect a person's 'private life' or 'home'.

JUDGMENT OF THE COURT

29. The Court does not consider it possible or necessary to attempt an exhaustive definition of the notion of 'private life'. However, it would be too restrictive to limit the notion to an 'inner circle' in which the individual may live his own personal life as he chooses and to exclude therefrom entirely the outside world not encompassed within that circle. Respect for private life must also comprise to a certain degree the right to establish and develop relationships with other human beings.

There appears, furthermore, to be no reason of principle why this understanding of the notion of 'private life' should be taken to exclude activities of a professional or business nature since it is, after all, in the course of their working lives that the majority of people have a significant, if not the greatest, opportunity of developing relationships with the outside world. This view is supported by the fact that, as was rightly pointed out by the Commission, it is not always possible to distinguish clearly which of an individual's activities form part of his professional or business life and which do not. Thus, especially in the case of a person execising a liberal profession, his work in that context may form part and parcel of his life to such a degree that it becomes impossible to know in what capacity he is acting at a given moment of time.

To deny the protection of Article 8 on the ground that the measure complained of related only to professional activities – as the Government suggested should be done in the present case – could moreover lead to an inequality of treatment, in that such protection would remain available to a person whose professional and non-professional activities were so intermingled that there was no means of distinguishing between them. In fact, the Court has not heretofore drawn such distinctions: it concluded that there had been an interference with private life even where telephone tapping covered both business and private calls (see the *Huvig v France* judgment of 24 April 1990, Series A no. 176-B, p. 41, § 8, and p. 52, § 25); and, where a search was directed solely against business activities, it did not rely on that fact as a ground for excluding the applicability of Article 8 under the head of 'private life' (see the *Chappell v the United Kingdom* judgment of 30 March 1989, Series A no. 152-A, pp. 12–13, § 26, and pp. 21–22, § 51.)

30. As regards the word 'home', appearing in the English text of Article 8, the Court observes that in certain Contracting States, notably Germany . . ., it has been accepted as extending to business premises. Such an interpretation is, moreover, fully consonant with the French text, since the word '*domicile*' has a broader connotation than the word 'home' and may extend, for example, to a professional person's office.

In this context also, it may not always be possible to draw precise distinctions, since activities which are related to a profession or business may well be conducted from a person's private residence and activities which are not so related may well be carried on in an office or commercial premises. A narrow interpretation of the words 'home' and '*domicile*' could therefore give rise to the same risk of inequality of treatment as a narrow interpretation of the notion of 'private life'. . . .

31. More generally, to interpret the words 'private life' and 'home' as including certain professional or business activities or premises would be consonant with the essential object and purpose of Article 8, namely to protect the individual against arbitrary interference by the public authorities (see, for example, the *Marckx v Belgium* judgment of 13 June 1979, Series A no. 31, p. 15, § 31). Such an interpretation would not unduly hamper the Contracting States, for they would retain their entitlement to 'interfere' to the extent permitted by paragraph 2 of Article 8; that entitlement might well be more far-reaching where professional or business activities or premises were involved than would otherwise be the case.

32. To the above-mentioned general considerations, which militate against the view that Article 8 is not applicable, must be added a further factor pertaining to the particular circumstances of the case. The warrant issued by the Munich District Court ordered a search for, and seizure of, 'documents' – without qualification or limitation – revealing the identity of Klaus Wegner. . . . Furthermore, those conducting the search examined four cabinets with data concerning clients as well as six individual files . . .; their operations must perforce have covered 'correspondence' and materials that can properly be regarded as such for the purposes of Article 8. In this connection, it is sufficient to note that that provision does not use, as it does for the word 'life', any adjective to qualify the word 'correspondence'. And, indeed, the Court has already held that, in the context of correspondence in the form of telephone calls, no such qualification is to be made (see the above-mentioned *Huvig* judgment, Series A no. 176-B, p. 41, § 8, and p. 52, § 25). Again, in a number of cases relating to correspondence with a lawyer (see, for example, the *Schönenberger and Durmaz v Switzerland* judgment of 20 June 1988, Series A no. 137, and the *Campbell v the United Kingdom* judgment of 25 March 1992, Series A no. 233), the Court did not even advert to the possibility that Article 8 might be inapplicable on the ground that the correspondence was of a professional nature.

33. Taken together, the foregoing reasons lead the Court to find that the search of the applicant's office constituted an interference with his rights under Article 8. . . .

37. As to whether the interference was 'necessary in a democratic society', the Court inclines to the view that the reasons given therefor by the Munich District Court . . . can be regarded as relevant in terms of the legitimate aims pursued. It does not, however, consider it essential to pursue this point since it has formed the opinion that, as was contended by the applicant and as was found by the Commission, the measure complained of was not proportionate to those aims.

It is true that the offence in connection with which the search was effected, involving as it did not only an insult to but also an attempt to bring pressure on a judge, cannot be classified as no more than minor. On the other hand, the warrant was drawn in broad terms, in that it ordered a search for and seizure of 'documents', without any limitation, revealing the identity of the author of the offensive letter; this point is of special significance where, as in Germany, the search of a lawyer's office is not accompanied by any special procedural safeguards, such as the presence of an independent observer. More importantly, having regard to the materials that were in fact inspected, the search impinged on professional secrecy to an extent that appears disproportionate in the circumstances; it has, in this connection, to be recalled that, where a lawyer is involved, an encroachment on professional secrecy may have repercussions on the proper administration of justice and hence on the rights guaranteed by Article 6 of the Convention. In addition, the attendant publicity must have been capable of affecting adversely the applicant's professional reputation, in the eyes both of his existing clients and of the public at large. . . .

FOR THESE REASONS, THE COURT UNANIMOUSLY [9–0]

1. *Holds* that there has been a violation of Article 8 of the Convention; . . .

NOTES

1. On the need for adequate procedural guarantees, including judicial authorisation, for search warrants, see the *Funke* case, above, p. 801.

2. The enforcement of an Anton Piller order was held not to be in breach of Article 8 in *Chappell v United Kingdom*, E Ct HRR A 152 (1990), 12 EHRR 1. An Anton Piller order is one by which the High Court may, without hearing the defendant, authorise the plaintiff in civil proceedings to search the defendant's premises to seize property that is the subject of court proceedings to prevent its disappearance. There is no need for police officers to be present. In the *Chappell* case, the applicant, a video tape dealer, was being sued in breach of copyright by the plaintiffs who obtained an order against him to search for pirate videos. The order was executed in the defendant's offices and home (he lived upstairs) by five private persons acting for the plaintiffs, including their solicitor. At the same time, as pre-arranged, eleven policemen executed a search warrant for obscene videos. The Court held by seven votes to none, that although there had been an interference with the applicant's private life and home in the sense of Article 8(1), the grant and terms of the Anton Piller order issued in the case, and its manner of execution, could be justified, in terms of Article 8(2), as being necessary for 'the protection of the rights of others'.

3. Interference with a person's 'home' of a quite different kind occurred in *Gillow v United Kingdom*, E Ct HRR A 109 (1986), 11 EHRR 335. There the applicant husband and wife, who had let their home in Guernsey for a number of years while the husband was employed abroad, were refused a residence licence when he retired. This was because there were other people who could live in the house who would be more valuable to the island's economy in a situation of housing shortage. The Court held unanimously that this restriction was in breach of Article 8. Although it had the legitimate aim of furthering the 'economic well being' of the island, it was disproportionate.

Dudgeon v United Kingdom, E Ct HRR A 45 (1981), 4 EHRR 149, Eur Ct HR

The applicant, a 35-year-old UK citizen resident in Northern Ireland, was a homosexual. In 1976, the police seized evidence concerning his homosexual activities from his flat while searching it lawfully for drugs. He was taken to a police station and questioned about his sexual life. Later it was decided not to prosecute and his papers were returned. The applicant complained that the existence of the law in Northern Ireland making buggery (Offences against the Person Act 1861) and 'gross indecency' (Criminal Law Amendment Act 1885) between consenting males a criminal offence was a breach of his right to privacy under Article 8.

JUDGMENT OF THE COURT

41. . . . the maintenance in force of the impugned legislation constitutes a continuing interference with the applicant's right to respect for his private life (which includes his sexual life) within the meaning of Article 8 § 1 . . . [E]ither he respects the law and refrains from engaging—even in private with consenting male partners—in prohibited sexual acts to which he is disposed by reason of his homosexual tendencies, or he commits such acts and thereby becomes liable to criminal prosecution.

It cannot be said that the law in question is a dead letter in this sphere. It was, and still is, applied so as to prosecute persons with regard to private consensual homosexual acts involving males under 21 years of age . . . Although no proceedings seem to have been brought in recent years with regard to such acts involving only males over 21 years of age, apart from mental patients, there is no stated policy on the part of the authorities not to enforce the law in this respect. . . . Furthermore . . . there always remains the possibility of a private prosecution. . . .

Moreover the police investigation in . . . 1976 showed that the threat hanging over him was real. . . .

49. There can be no denial that some degree of regulation of male homosexual conduct, as indeed of other forms of sexual conduct, by means of the criminal law can be justified as 'necessary in a democratic society'. . . . In practice there is legislation on the matter in all the member States of the Council of Europe, but what distinguishes the law in Northern Ireland from that existing in the great majority of the member States is that it prohibits generally gross indecency between males and buggery whatever the circumstances. . . .

[The Court then considered the meaning of 'necessary,' etc., following its approach in the *Sunday Times* and *Handyside* cases, below, pp. 823, 826.]

As was illustrated by the *Sunday Times* judgment, the scope of the margin of appreciation is not identical in respect of each of the aims justifying restrictions on a right. . . . It is an indisputable fact, as the Court stated in the *Handyside* judgment, that 'the view taken . . . of the requirements of morals varies from time to time and from place to place, especially in our era,' and that 'by reason of their direct and continuous contact with the vital forces of their countries, State authorities are in principle in a better position than the international judge to give an opinion on the exact content of those requirements' (p. 22, § 48).

However, . . . [t]he present case concerns a most intimate aspect of private life. Accordingly, there must exist particularly serious reasons before interferences on the part of the public authorities can be legitimate for the purposes of paragraph 2 of Article 8.

53. . . . According to the Court's case-law, a restriction on a Convention right cannot be regarded as 'necessary in a democratic society'—two hallmarks of which are tolerance and broadmindedness—unless, amongst other things, it is proportionate to the legitimate aim pursued . . .

57. . . . the moral climate in Northern Ireland in sexual matters . . . is one of the matters which the national authorities may legitimately take into account in exercising their discretion. There is, the Court accepts, a strong body of opposition stemming from a genuine and sincere conviction shared by a large number of responsible members of the Northern Irish community that a change in the law would be seriously damaging to the moral fabric of society . . .

Whether this point of view be right or wrong, and although it may be out of line with current attitudes in other communities, its existence among an important sector of Northern Irish society is certainly relevant for the purposes of Article 8 § 2.

58. . . . Nevertheless, this cannot of itself be decisive as to the necessity for the interference with the applicant's private life resulting from the measures being challenged . . .

60. The Convention right affected by the impugned legislation protects an essentially private manifestation of the human personality . . .

As compared with the era when that legislation was enacted, there is now a better understanding, and in consequence an increased tolerance, of homosexual behaviour to the extent that in the great majority of the member States of the Council of Europe it is no longer considered to be necessary or appropriate to treat homosexual practices of the kind now in question as in themselves a matter to which the sanctions of the criminal law should be applied; the Court cannot overlook the marked changes which have occurred in this regard in the domestic law of the member States . . . In Northern Ireland itself, the authorities have refrained in recent years from enforcing the law in respect of private homosexual acts between consenting males over the age of 21 years capable of valid consent. . . . No evidence has been adduced to show that this has been injurious to moral standards in Northern Ireland or that there has been any public demand for stricter enforcement of the law.

It cannot be maintained in these circumstances that there is a 'pressing social need' to make such acts criminal offences, there being no sufficient justification provided by the risk of harm to vulnerable sections of society requiring protection or by the effects on the public. On the issue of proportionality, the Court considers that such justifications as there are for retaining the law in force unamended are outweighed by the detrimental effects which the very existence of the legislative provisions in question can have on the life of a person of homosexual orientation like the applicant. Although members of the public who regard homosexuality as immoral may be shocked, offended or disturbed by the commission by others of private homosexual acts, this cannot on its own warrant the application of penal sanctions when it is consenting adults alone who are involved.

61. . . . 'Decriminalisation' does not imply approval, and a fear that some sectors of the population might draw misguided conclusions in this respect from reform of the legislation does not afford a good ground for maintaining it in force with all its unjustifiable features. . . .

62. In the opinion of the Commission, the interference complained of by the applicant *can*, in so far as he is prevented from having sexual relations with young males under 21 years of age, be justified as necessary for the protection of the rights of others . . .

The Court has already acknowledged the legitimate necessity in a democratic society for some degree of control over homosexual conduct notably in order to provide safeguards against the exploitation and corruption of those who are specially vulnerable by reason, for example, of their youth. . . . However, it falls in the first instance to the national authorities to decide on the appropriate safeguards of this kind required for the defence of morals in their society and, in particular, to fix the age under which young people should have the protection of the criminal law. . . .

FOR THESE REASONS THE COURT

. . . *holds* by 15 votes to four that there is a breach of Article 8. . . .

NOTES

1. Northern Irish law has been changed in response to the judgment: Homosexual Offences (Northern Ireland) Order 1982. Only two of the dissenting judges – Judge Zekia (Cypriot) and Walsh (Irish) – dissented on the ground that no breach of Article 8 had occurred. Both are nationals of states that had laws similar to those in question in the case. The other two judges dissented on the ground that the applicant was not a 'victim.'

2. The case, which is a good example of the Court's 'dynamic' approach to the interpretation of the Convention (see the *Tyrer* case, above, p. 767), is of importance in recognising that the right to a personality is a part of the right to privacy in Article 8.

3. In *A.9237/81*, (1984) 6 EHRR 354, the Commission declared inadmissible an application by a UK soldier who had been discharged from the army following convictions for homosexual offences contrary to s. 66, Army Act 1955. The Commission distinguished the *Dudgeon* case on the grounds that s. 66 could be justified under Article 8(2) as being 'for the prevention of disorder' in the armed forces and that the charges had concerned relations with a soldier under 21 ('protection of morals').

4. The *Dudgeon* case was applied in *Norris v Ireland*,[1] in which the Court held, by eight votes to six, that an identical Irish statute was in breach of the right to privacy in Article 8. The case differed on its facts from the *Dudgeon* case in that the applicant had not been threatened. Although there had been no prosecution of consenting adults since at least 1974, the Court found that there was no policy of non-prosecution. The possibility of criminal sanctions reinforced prejudice against homosexuals, which caused feelings of anxiety and guilt which had an effect on their privacy. The six dissenting judges took the view that in the absence of a threat of prosecution, the applicant was not a 'victim' in the sense of Article 25, ECHR.

5. In *Bruggeman and Scheuten v Federal Republic of Germany*, Report of the Commission, 12 July 1977, (1978) 10 DR E Com HR 100, the Commission was of the opinion that the right to respect for privacy (in the sense of the right to a personality) did not guarantee a pregnant woman the right to an abortion in her discretion. The Commission held that the 1976 West German abortion law, which only permits abortions to protect the life or physical or mental health of the mother or on eugenic grounds, was consistent with Article 8. The case was not referred to the Court. The Committee of Ministers confirmed the Commission's opinion: CM Resolution DH (78) 1.

X and Y v Netherlands, E Ct HRR A 91 (1986), 8 EHRR 235, Eur Ct HR

Y, a mentally handicapped, 16-year-old girl, was forced by the son-in-law of the governor of the private home for mentally handicapped children in which Y was resident, to have sexual intercourse with him, causing traumatic mental consequences for Y. There proved to be no criminal law offence in Dutch law for which the son-in-law could be prosecuted. There was insufficient force to constitute rape. There was an offence (Article 248 *ter*, Criminal Code) of abuse of a dominant position, causing a minor to commit an indecent act, but the authorities did not prosecute the son-on-law for this because a complaint could only be laid by the victim, which Y was unable to do because of mental incompetence. X, Y's father, who had complained to the police, was not competent to lay a complaint

---

1 E Ct HRR A 142 (1988), 13 EHRR 186. See also *Modinos v Cyprus*, E Ct HRR A 259 (1993), 16 EHRR 485.

upon which the police could act. Another offence (Article 239, Criminal Code) applied only to indecent exposure. There were civil remedies available, including a claim equivalent to a claim in tort for damages and an injunction to prohibit a reoccurence. X and Y claimed a breach of the right to privacy.

JUDGMENT OF THE COURT

22. There was no dispute as to the applicability of Article 8: the facts underlying the application to the Commission concern a matter of 'private life', a concept which covers the physical and moral integrity of the person, including his or her sexual life.

23. The Court recalls that although the object of Article 8 is essentially that of protecting the individual against arbitrary interference by the public authorities, it does not merely compel the State to abstain from such interference: in addition to this primarily negative undertaking, there may be positive obligations inherent in an effective respect for private or family life (see the *Airey* judgment [see above, p. 795] . . .). These obligations may involve the adoption of measures designed to secure respect for private life even in the sphere of the relations of individuals between themselves. . . .

24. . . . The Court . . . observes that the choice of the means calculated to secure compliance with Article 8 in the sphere of the relations of individuals between themselves is in principle a matter that falls within the Contracting States' margin of appreciation. In this connection, there are different ways of ensuring 'respect for private life', and the nature of the State's obligation will depend on the particular aspect of private life that is at issue. Recourse to the criminal law is not necessarily the only answer. . . .

[The Court then examined the civil law remedies available in Dutch law and continued:]

27. The Court finds the protection afforded by the civil law in the case of wrongdoing of the kind inflicted on Miss Y is insufficient. This is a case where fundamental values and essential aspects of private life are at stake. Effective deterrence is indispensable in this area and it can be achieved only by criminal-law provisions; indeed, it is by such provisions that the matter is normally regulated.

Moreover . . . this is in fact an area in which the Netherlands has generally opted for a system of protection based on the criminal law. The only gap, so far as the Commission and the Court have been made aware, is as regards persons in the situation of Miss Y; in such cases, this system meets a procedural obstacle which the Netherlands legislature had apparently not foreseen. . . .

29. Two provisions of the Criminal Code are relevant to the present case, namely Article 248 ter and Article 239 § 2.

Article 248 ter requires a complaint by the actual victim before criminal proceedings can be instituted against someone who has contravened this provision. . . . The Arnhem Court of Appeal held that, in the case of an individual like Miss Y, the legal representative could not act on the victim's behalf for this purpose. The Court of Appeal did not feel able to fill this gap in the law by means of a broad interpretation to the detriment of Mr. B. It is in no way the task of the European Court of Human Rights to take the place of the competent national courts in the interpretation of domestic law (see, *mutatis mutandis*, the *Handyside* judgment of 7 December 1976, Series A no. 24, p. 23, § 50); it regards it as established that in the case in question criminal proceedings could not be instituted on the basis of Article 248 ter.

As for Article 239 § 2 . . . this is apparently designed to penalise indecent exposure and not indecent assault, and was not clearly applicable to the present case. . . .

30. Thus, neither Article 248 ter nor Article 239 § 2 of the Criminal Code provided Miss Y with practical and effective protection. It must therefore be concluded, taking account of the nature of the wrongdoing in question, that she was the victim of a violation of Article 8 of the Convention. . . .

FOR THESE REASONS, THE COURT UNANIMOUSLY [7–0]

1. *Holds* that there has been a violation of Article 8 as regards Miss Y. . . .

NOTE

The case is not one of the state interfering through its law or its officials with the privacy of an individual, but of the state failing to protect interference with an individual's privacy by another private individual. Cf. the *Young, James and Webster* cases, below, p. 844, and, for a different approach, *Costello-Roberts v UK*, above, p. 769. The obligation to take steps to prevent infringements of individuals' ECHR rights by other private individuals could be extended to require a state to provide adequate controls of the invasion of privacy by the press, which is a live issue in the UK, see above, Chap. 8. However, in *Winer v United Kingdom*, (1986) 48 DR E Comm HR 154, 156–7, the Commission rejected on its facts a claim based upon such an obligation. In that case, a book was published with a chapter entitled 'The smearing of Stan Winer'. The chapter included, inter alia, an intimate account of the applicant's relations with his wife. Insofar as the allegations were untrue, the applicant brought proceedings in defamation and obtained compensation from the publisher in an out of court settlement. Insofar as the statements were true, he claimed that their publication was an unjustified invasion of his privacy for which, in breach of Article 8, English law did not provide a remedy. Declaring the application inadmissible, the Commission stated:

'The Commission would next note that there is no question in the present case of any involvement by the respondent Government in the publication of "Inside BOSS". The applicant is therefore complaining about a lack of restriction on a third party, and is alleging that this omission involves the respondent Government's responsibility. In this regard the applicant is, in effect, calling for a positive obligation to be imposed on States to interfere with other individuals' right to freedom of expression, a right guaranteed by Article 10 of the Convention. However, the Commission considers that Article 10 must be taken into account when establishing the positive obligations which may be imposed by Article 8 of the Convention.

The question remains, however, to what extent the High Contracting Party must impose positive obligations on persons within its jurisdiction in order to ensure compliance with Article 8 of the Convention. In this respect, the Commission recalls the previous case-law of the Convention organs that, although positive obligations may be required by Article 8 of the Convention, the way in which a High Contracting Party may meet such obligations is largely within its discretion (c.f., for example, Eur Court HR *Abdulaziz, Cabales and Balkandali* judgment of 28 May 1985, Series A no. 94, para. 67 and further references contained there). The Commission notes the public debate in the United Kingdom on reforms to the law of privacy with the conclusions of the Law Commission that the existing law of breach of confidence should be replaced by a statutory tort, contrasted with the conclusions of the Younger Report on privacy, which expressed general satisfaction with the various existing remedies for breaches of privacy [see above, p. 551].

In the present case the Commission does not consider that the absence of an actionable right to privacy under English law shows a lack of respect for the applicant's private life and his home. Whilst it is true that this state of the law gives greater protection to other individuals' freedom of expression, the applicant's right to privacy was not wholly unprotected, as was shown by his defamation action and settlement, and his own liberty to publish. The Commission, therefore, concludes that the case does not disclose a failure to respect the applicant's rights under Article 8 of the Convention.'

Rees v United Kingdom, E Ct HRR A 106 (1986), 9 EHRR 56, Eur Ct HR

The applicant, who was born a woman, was diagnosed a trans-sexual and had a sex change operation in 1974 at the age of 32. He found that under UK law he could not have his birth certificate altered to record his new sex. This was an embarrassment because a birth certificate was required for certain purposes, including an application for a passport, entry to university, applying for employment in the civil service and obtaining some kinds of insurance. He also could not marry, as marriage was limited to persons who were biologically male and female. The applicant complained of breaches of Articles 8 and 12.

JUDGMENT OF THE COURT

35. The Court has already held on a number of occasions that, although the essential object of Article 8 is to protect the individual against arbitrary interference by the public authorities, there may in addition be

positive obligations inherent in an effective respect for private life, albeit subject to the State's margin of appreciation (see, as the most recent authority, the *Abdulaziz, Cabales and Balkandali* judgment [see below, p. 849] . . .).

In the present case it is the existence and scope of such 'positive' obligations which have to be determined. The mere refusal to alter the register of birth or to issue birth certificates whose contents and nature differ from those of the birth register cannot be considered as interferences. . . .

37. As the Court pointed out in its above-mentioned *Abdulaziz, Cabales and Balkandali* judgment the notion of "respect" is not clear-cut, especially as far as those positive obligations are concerned: having regard to the diversity of the practices followed and the situations obtaining in the Contracting States, the notion's requirements will vary considerably from case to case.

These observations are particularly relevant here. Several States have, through legislation or by means of legal interpretation or by administrative practice, given trans-sexuals the option of changing their personal status to fit their newly-gained identity. They have, however, made this option subject to conditions of varying strictness and retained a number of express reservations (for example, as to previously incurred obligations). In other States, such an option does not – or does not yet – exist. It would therefore be true to say that there is at present little common ground between the Contracting States in this area and that, generally speaking, the law appears to be in a transitional stage. Accordingly, this is an area in which the Contracting Parties enjoy a wide margin of appreciation.

In determining whether or not a positive obligation exists, regard must be had to the fair balance that has to be struck between the general interest of the community and the interests of the individual, the search for which balance is inherent in the whole of the Convention (see, *mutatis mutandis*, amongst others, the *James and Others* judgment [E Ct HRR A 98 (1986)] . . . and the *Sporrong and Lönnroth* judgment [E Ct HRR A 52 (1982)]). . . . In striking this balance the aims mentioned in the second paragraph of Article 8 may be of a certain relevance, although this provision refers in terms only to "interferences" with the right protected by the first paragraph – in other words is concerned with the negative obligations flowing therefrom (see, *mutatis mutandis*, the *Marckx* judgment, [below, p. 819]. . . .

39. In the United Kingdom no uniform, general decision has been adopted either by the legislature or by the courts as to the civil status of post-operative trans-sexuals. Moreover, there is no integrated system of civil status registration, but only separate registers for births, marriages, deaths and adoption. These record the relevant events in the manner they occurred without, except in special circumstances . . . mentioning changes (of name, address, etc.) which in other States are registered.

40. However, trans-sexuals, like anyone else in the United Kingdom, are free to change their first names and surnames at will. . . . Similarly, they can be issued with official documents bearing their chosen first names and surnames and indicating, if their sex is mentioned at all, their preferred sex by the relevant prefix (Mr., Mrs., Ms. or Miss). . . . This freedom gives them a considerable advantage in comparison with States where all official documents have to conform with the records held by the registry office.

Conversely, the drawback – emphasised by the applicant – is that, as the country's legal system makes no provision for legally valid civil-status certificates, such persons have on occasion to establish their identity by means of a birth certificate which is either an authenticated copy of or an extract from the birth register. The nature of this register, which furthermore is public, is that the certificates mention the biological sex which the individuals had at the time of their birth. . . . The production of such a birth certificate is not a strict legal requirement, but may on occasion be required in practice for some purposes. . . .

It is also clear that the United Kingdom does not recognise the applicant as a man for all social purposes. Thus, it would appear that, at the present stage of the development of United Kingdom law, he would be regarded as a woman, *inter alia* as far as marriage, pension rights and certain employments are concerned. . . . The existence of the unamended birth certificate might also prevent him from entering into certain types of private agreements as a man. . . .

42. To require the United Kingdom to follow the example of other Contracting States is from one perspective tantamount to asking that it should adopt a system in principle the same as theirs for determining and recording civil status.

Albeit with delay and some misgivings on the part of the authorities, the United Kingdom has endeavoured to meet the applicant's demands to the fullest extent that its system allowed. The alleged lack of respect therefore seems to come down to a refusal to establish a type of documentation showing, and constituting proof of, current civil status. The introduction of such a system has not hitherto been considered necessary in the United Kingdom. It would have important administrative consequences and would impose new duties on the rest of the population. The governing authorities in the United Kingdom are fully entitled, in the exercise of their margin of appreciation, to take account of the requirements of the situation pertaining there in determining what measures to adopt. While the requirement of striking a fair balance, as developed in paragraph 37 above, may possibly, in the interests of persons in the applicant's situation, call for incidental adjustments to the existing system, it cannot give rise to any direct obligation on the United Kingdom to alter the very basis thereof.

. . . Interpreted somewhat more narrowly, the applicant's complaint might be seen as a request to have such an incidental adjustment in the form of an annotation to the present birth register.

Whilst conceding that additions can be made to the entries in the birth register in order to record, for example, subsequent adoption or legitimation . . . the Government disputed that the proposed annotation was comparable to additions of this kind. They submitted that, in the absence of any error or omission at the time of birth, the making of an alteration to the register as to the sex of the individual would constitute a falsification of the facts contained therein and would be misleading to other persons with a legitimate interest in being informed of the true situation. They contended that the demands of the public interest weighed strongly against any such alteration.

The Court notes that the additions at present permitted as regards adoption and legitimation also concern events occurring after birth and that, in this respect, they are not different from the annotation sought by the applicant. However, they record facts of legal significance and are designed to ensure that the register fulfils its purpose of providing an authoritative record for the establishment of family ties in connection with succession, legitimate descent and the distribution of property. The annotation now being requested would, on the other hand, establish only that the person concerned henceforth belonged to the other sex. Furthermore, the change so recorded could not mean the acquisition of all the biological characteristics of the other sex. In any event, the annotation could not, without more, constitute an effective safeguard for ensuring the integrity of the applicant's private life, as it would reveal his change of sexual identity.

43. The applicant has accordingly also asked that the change, and the corresponding annotation, be kept secret from third parties.

However, such secrecy could not be achieved without first modifying fundamentally the present system for keeping the register of births, so as to prohibit public access to entries made before the annotation. Secrecy could also have considerable unintended results and could prejudice the purpose and function of the birth register by complicating factual issues arising in, *inter alia*, the fields of family and succession law. Furthermore, no account would be taken of the position of third parties, including public authorities (e.g. the armed services) or private bodies (e.g. life insurance companies) in that they would be deprived of information which they had a legitimate interest to receive.

44. In order to overcome these difficulties there would have to be detailed legislation as to the effects of the change in various contexts and as to the circumstances in which secrecy should yield to the public interest. Having regard to the wide margin of appreciation to be afforded the State in this area and to the relevance of protecting the interests of others in striking the requisite balance, the positive obligations arising from Article 8 cannot be held to extend that far.

45. This conclusion is not affected by the fact, on which both the Commission and the applicant put a certain emphasis, that the United Kingdom cooperated in the applicant's medical treatment.

If such arguments were adopted too widely, the result might be that Government departments would become over-cautious in the exercise of their functions and the helpfulness necessary in their relations with the public could be impaired. In the instant case, the fact that the medical services did not delay the giving of medical and surgical treatment until all legal aspects of persons in the applicant's situation had been fully investigated and resolved, obviously benefited him and contributed to his freedom of choice.

46. Accordingly, there is no breach of Article 8 in the circumstances of the present case.

47. That being so, it must for the time being be left to the respondent State to determine to what extent it can meet the remaining demands of trans-sexuals. However, the Court is conscious of the seriousness of the problems affecting these persons and the distress they suffer. The Convention has always to be interpreted and applied in the light of current circumstances (see, *mutatis mutandis*, amongst others, the *Dudgeon* judgment [above, p. 812]). The need for appropriate legal measures should therefore be kept under review having regard particularly to scientific and societal developments. . . .

FOR THESE REASONS, THE COURT

1. *Holds* by twelve votes to three that there is no violation of Article 3. . . .

NOTES

1. The Court also held unanimously that the applicant's right to marry under Article 12 had not been infringed because marriage was a relationship between persons of biologically different sexes.

2. The Court was called upon to consider again the question of the legal status of trans-sexuals in the UK in relation to Article 8 in *Cossey v United Kingdom*.[1] Finding that the facts in this case (of a trans-sexual who became a woman) could not be distinguished from those in the *Rees* case, the Court considered whether it should reverse its judgment in that case. Deciding, by ten votes to eight, that it should not do so, the Court stated:

'35. It is true that, as [the applicant] . . . submitted, the Court is not bound by its previous judgments; indeed, this is borne out by Rule 51 § 1 of the Rules of Court. However, it usually follows and applies its own precedents, such a course being in the interests of legal certainty and the orderly development of the Convention case-law. Nevertheless, this would not prevent the Court from departing from an earlier decision if it was persuaded that there were cogent reasons for doing so. Such a departure might, for example, be warranted in order to ensure that the interpretation of the Convention reflects societal changes and remains in line with present-day conditions. . .

40. In the *Rees* judgment, the Court . . . pointed out that the need for appropriate legal measures concerning transsexuals should be kept under review having regard particularly to scientific and societal developments. . . .

The Court has been informed of no significant scientific developments that have occurred in the meantime; in particular, it remains the case – as was not contested by the applicant – that gender reassignment surgery does not result in the acquisition of all the biological characteristics of the other sex.

There have been certain developments since 1986 in the law of some of the member States of the Council of Europe. However, the reports accompanying the resolution adopted by the European Parliament on 12 September 1989 (OJ No C 256, 9. 10. 1989, p. 33) and Recommendation 1117 (1989) adopted by the Parliamentary Assembly of the Council of Europe on 29 September 1989 – both of which seek to encourage the harmonisation of laws and practices in this field – reveal, as the Government pointed out, the same diversity of practice as obtained at the time of the *Rees* judgment. Accordingly this is still, having regard to the existence of little common ground between the Contracting States, an area in which they enjoy a wide margin of appreciation (see the *Rees* judgment, p. 15 § 37). In particular, it cannot at present be said that a departure from the Court's earlier decision is warranted in order to ensure that the interpretation of Article 8 on the point at issue remains in line with present-day conditions. . . .'

The eight dissenting judges considered that societal attitudes had changed sufficiently in Europe to require a reversal of the *Rees* judgment.

3. It is apparent from the *Rees* and *Cossey* cases that the Court's approach to moral, as well as other, questions that arise before it is considerably influenced by the pattern of law and practice in European states as a whole. A state whose law or practice is out of step with that of other European states generally is at risk of an adverse finding: see, e.g. the *Tyrer* case, above, p. 767, concerning corporal punishment.[2] Where attitudes and values are changing, but only to the point where the law and practice of European states are as yet various and do not point uniformly in a new direction, the Court is less likely to find a breach. This seems to be the position in respect of the legal status of trans-sexuals.

Marckx v Belgium, E Ct HRR A 31 (1979), 2 EHRR 330, Eur Ct HR

The applicant, an unmarried Belgian national, claimed on behalf of her infant daughter and herself. She complained of the law in Belgium on the maternal affiliation of an illegitimate child, its family relationships and its patrimonial rights. Under Belgian law, an illegitimate child was only regarded as the child of his mother if the latter in her discretion formally recognised her maternity. If she did so, the affiliation was retroactive to the date of birth. In the case of a legitimate child, there was no such need or delay: affiliation was proved simply by the legally obligatory entry of the married mother's name on the birth certificate. As regards family relationships,

1 E Ct HRR A 184 (1990), 13 EHRR 622. See also *B v France*, E Ct HRR A 232-C (1992), EHRR (breach of Article 8).
2 Note, however, the *Johnston* case, below, p. 822, which concerned the sensitive question of divorce in Ireland.

an illegitimate child remained, even after recognition, in principle a stranger to the parents' families. Thus, for example, in the absence of the child's mother, it was the guardian rather than the grandparents who had the power to consent to marriage. The reverse was true of legitimate children. Similarly, the patrimonial rights of an illegitimate child were in certain ways less than those of a legitimate child, both in respect of inheritance and of *inter vivos* gifts.

The Commission expressed the opinion in its report *inter alia* that Article 8 had been infringed both taken by itself and in conjunction with Article 14 and referred the case to the Court.

JUDGMENT OF THE COURT

31. . . . By guaranteeing the right to respect for family life, Article 8 presupposes the existence of a family. The Court concurs entirely with the Commission's established case-law on a crucial point, namely that Article 8 makes no distinction between the 'legitimate' and the 'illegitimate' family. Such a distinction would not be consonant with the word 'everyone,' and this is confirmed by Article 14 with its prohibition, in the enjoyment of the rights and freedoms enshrined in the Convention, of discrimination grounded on 'birth'. In addition, the Court notes that the Committee of Ministers of the Council of Europe regards the single woman and her child as one form of family no less than others (Resolution (70) 15 of 15 May 1970 . . .).

Article 8 thus applies to the 'family life'[1] of the 'illegitimate' family as it does to that of the 'legitimate' family. Besides, it is not disputed that Paula Marckx assumed responsibility for her daughter Alexandra from the moment of her birth and has continuously cared for her, with the result that a real family life existed and still exists between them. . .

By proclaiming in paragraph 1 the right to respect for family life, Article 8 signifies firstly that the State cannot interfere with the exercise of that right otherwise than in accordance with the strict conditions set out in paragraph 2. . . . the object of the Article is 'essentially' that of protecting the individual against arbitrary interference by the public authorities. . . . Nevertheless it does not merely compel the State to abstain from such interference: in addition to this primarily negative undertaking, there may be positive obligations inherent in an effective 'respect' for family life.

This means amongst other things, that when the State determines in its domestic legal system the régime applicable to certain family ties such as those between an unmarried mother and her child, it must act in a manner calculated to allow those concerned to lead a normal family life. As envisaged by Article 8, respect for family life implies in particular, in the Court's view, the existence in domestic law of legal safeguards that render possible as from the moment of birth the child's integration in his family. In this connection, the State has a choice of various means, but a law that fails to satisfy this requirement violates paragraph 1 of Article 8 without there being any call to examine it under paragraph 2. . . .

Dissenting opinion of Judge Sir Gerald Fitzmaurice

It is abundantly clear (at least it is to me)—and the nature of the whole background against which the idea of the European Convention on Human Rights was conceived bears out this view—that the main, if not indeed the sole object and intended sphere of application of Article 8, was that of what I will call the 'domiciliary protection' of the individual. He and his family were no longer to be subjected to the four o'clock in the morning rat-a-tat on the door; to domestic intrusions, searches and questionings; to examinations, delayings and confiscation of correspondence; to the planting of listening devices (buggings); to restrictions on the use of radio and television; to telephone tapping and disconnection; to measures of coercion such as cutting off the electricity or water supply; to such abominations as children being required to report upon the activities of their parents, and even sometimes the same for one spouse against another—in short the whole gamut of fascist and communist inquisitorial practices such as had scarcely been known, at least in Western Europe, since the eras of religious intolerance and oppression, until (ideology replacing religion) they became prevalent again in many countries between the two world wars and subsequently. Such, and not the internal, domestic regulation of family relationships, was the object of Article 8, and it was for the avoidance of these horrors, tyrannies and vexations that 'private and family life . . . home and . . . correspondence' were to be respected, and the individual endowed with a right to enjoy that respect—not for the regulation of the civil status of babies.

1 *Ed.* Elsewhere in its judgment (para. 45), the Court indicated that it understood 'family life' as including 'at least the ties between near relatives, for instance those between grandparents and grandchildren, since such relatives may play a considerable part in family life'.

NOTES

1. Having established that Article 8 applied, the Court examined the complaints in turn. As far as the *affiliation* rules in Belgian law were concerned, the Court held that they infringed Article 8 taken by itself with respect to both the mother (by 10 votes to 5) and the daughter (by 12 votes to 3). Similarly, the Court held that Article 8 had been infringed when read with Article 14 with respect both to the mother (by 11 votes to 4) and the daughter (by 13 votes to 2). In doing so, the Court stated that while 'support and encouragement of the traditional family is in itself legitimate or even praiseworthy', it could not be given at the expense of the 'illegitimate' family, which was equally protected by Article 8. The Convention 'must be interpreted in the light of present-day conditions' and the Court could not 'but be struck by the fact that the domestic law of the great majority of the member states of the Council of Europe has evolved and is continuing to evolve, in company with the relevant international instruments, towards full jurisdictional recognition of the maxim *mater semper certa est*'.

On the question of *family relationships*, the Court held, by 12 votes to 3, that there had been a breach of Article 8 with respect to both applicants because the daughter was not in Belgian law regarded as a member of her mother's family. The Court held by 13 votes to 2, that the same facts amounted to a breach of Article 8 as read with Article 14. Although 'the tranquillity of "legitimate" families may sometimes be disturbed if an "illegitimate" child is included, in the eyes of the law, in his mother's family on the same footing as a child born in wedlock', this was not sufficient to justify depriving such a child of 'fundamental rights'. Applying Article 8 to the *patrimonial rights* of the applicants, the Court held that there had been no breach of that Article taken by itself in respect of either the mother (by 9 votes to 6) or the daughter (unanimously). Article 8 did not mean that a state has to ensure that all children were entitled to a share in their parents' or other relatives' estates on intestacy or to a share in any gifts made by will or *inter vivos*. Similarly, from the mother's standpoint. Article 8 did not prevent a state from imposing any limitation on her right to give property to her children. But when Article 8 was read in conjunction with Article 14, the position was different. The Court held, by 13 votes to 2, that these provisions taken together were infringed in respect both of the mother and of the daughter. Whereas the State was free to control or limit the rights of entitlement to property within the family subject to the obligation indicated above, there was no justifiable reason for distinguishing between 'legitimate' and 'illegitimate' families when doing so. The Court also held by 10 votes to 5, that there had been a breach of Article 1, First Protocol, when read with Article 14 as far as the mother was concerned.

2. The *Marckx* case is of importance beyond its immediate context of illegitimacy because of the almost unanimous ruling of the plenary Court that Article 8 has a positive private law aspect as well as a negative public law one. The obligation to ensure *effective* respect for family life requires that a state take steps to provide that its law is such that individuals may enjoy a proper family life. The *Marckx* case was at once relied upon by a Chamber of the Court as the basis for a finding of a breach of Article 8 in the *Airey* case, above, p. 795. There the Court stated:

'In Ireland . . . husband and wife are . . . entitled. . . to petition for a decree of judicial separation; this amounts to recognition of the fact that the protection of their private or family life may sometimes necessitate their being relieved from the duty to live together.

Effective respect for private or family life obliges Ireland to make this means of protection effectively accessible, when appropriate, to anyone who may wish to have recourse thereto. However, it was not effectively accessible to the applicant . . . She has therefore been the victim of a violation of Art. 8.'

3. In *Johnston v Ireland*, E Ct HRR A 112 (1987), 9 EHRR 203, the first applicant's marriage had broken down and he had been living with the second applicant as man and wife for 15 years. The third applicant was a child of the relationship. Although the Court accepted that the applicants could be regarded as a family for the purposes of Article 8, it held, by 16 votes to one, that 'the absence of provision for divorce under Irish law and the resultant inability of the first and second applicants to marry each other do not give rise to a violation of Article 8 or Article 12'. With regard to Article 8, the Court stated;

'57. It is true that, on this question, Article 8, with its reference to the somewhat vague notion of "respect" for family life, might appear to lend itself more readily to an evolutive interpretation than does Article 12. Nevertheless, the Convention must be read as a whole and the Court does not consider that a right to divorce, which it has found to be excluded from Article 12 . . . can, with consistency, be derived from Article 8, a provision of more general purpose and scope. The Court is not oblivious to the plight of the first and second applicants. However, it is of the opinion that, although the protection of private or family life may sometimes necessitate means whereby spouses can be relieved from the duty to live together (see the above-mentioned *Airey* judgment, Series A, no. 32 p. 17, § 33), the engagements undertaken by Ireland under Article 8 cannot be regarded as extending to an obligation on its part to introduce measures permitting the divorce and the re–marriage which the applicants seek.'

4. In *Berrehab v Netherlands*,[1] the Court held, by six votes to one, that 'family life' may include the relationship between a divorced parent and a child of the marriage. In that case, the applicant, a Moroccan, married a Dutch woman. A child was born after their divorce in 1979, some 18 months after their marriage. The applicant saw the daughter after the divorce regularly, four times a week. Following the divorce, the Dutch authorities refused to renew the applicant's residence permit and, after unsuccessful appeals against this decision, the applicant was arrested in 1983 with a view to deportation. The Court held, by six votes to one, that the measures taken to deport the applicant, which would greatly affect his access to his child, were in breach of his right to respect for family life. Although accepting that the action was taken in pursuance of an immigration policy bearing upon employment that had a legitimate aim (the 'economic well-being of the country'), the Court considered that it was applied disproportionately on the facts of the case. The Court stated:

'29. . . . As to the aim pursued, it must be emphasised that the instant case did not concern an alien seeking admission to the Netherlands for the first time but a person who had already lawfully lived there for several years, who had a home and a job there, and against whom the Government did not claim to have any complaint. Furthermore, Mr. Berrehab already had real family ties there – he had married a Dutch woman, and a child had been born of the marriage.

As to the extent of the interference, it is to be noted that there had been very close ties between Mr. Berrehab and his daughter for several years (see paragraphs 9 and 21 above) and that the refusal of an independent residence permit and the ensuing expulsion threatened to break those ties. That effect of the interferences in issue was the more serious as Rebecca needed to remain in contact with her father, seeing especially that she was very young.

Having regard to these particular circumstances, the Court considers that a proper balance was not achieved between the interests involved and that there was therefore a disproportion between the means employed and the legitimate aim pursued. That being so, the Court cannot consider the disputed measures as being necessary in a democratic society. It thus concludes that there was a violation of Article 8.'

5. In *W v United Kingdom*, E Ct HRR A 121 (1987), it was held, by 17 votes to none, that the right to respect for family life in Article 8 requires parental participation in procedures by which certain decisions concerning their children are taken by

---

1 E Ct HRR A 138 (1988), 11 EHRR 322. See also *Beldjouti v France*, E Ct HRR A 234–A (1992), 14 EHRR 801 and *Moustaquim v Belgium*, E Ct HRR A 193 (1991), 13 EHRR 802. In these cases, it was held that the deportation of non-national immigrants with strong family connections (wife, parents and siblings) in the defendant state because of their criminal records would be a breach of Article 8. In the *Beldjouti* case, Judge Martens referred to the concept of the 'integrated alien' who could not be deported.

public authorities. In that case, the parents of a child in care were not informed or consulted prior to a decision to place the child with long-term foster parents and were not consulted before their access to the child was terminated. Ruling that this situation infringed Article 8, the Court stated:

'62. . . . It is true that Article 8 contains no explicit procedural requirements, but this is not conclusive of the matter. The local authority's decision-making process clearly cannot be devoid of influence on the substance of the decision, notably by ensuring that it is based on the relevant considerations and is not one-sided and, hence, neither is nor appears to be arbitrary. Accordingly, the Court is entitled to have regard to that process to determine whether it has been conducted in a manner that, in all the circumstances, is fair and affords due respect to the interests protected by Article 8. . . .

64. . . . In the Court's view, what . . . has to be determined is whether, having regard to the particular circumstances of the case and notably the serious nature of the decisions to be taken, the parents have been involved in the decision-making process, seen as a whole, to a degree sufficient to provide them with the requisite protection of their interests. If they have not, there will have been a failure to respect their family life and the interference resulting from the decision will not be capable of being regarded as "necessary" within the meaning of Article 8.'

6. In *Keegan v Ireland*, E Ct HRR A 290 (1994), 18 EHRR 342, the applicant and his girlfriend lived together for a year, having had a relationship for a year before that. They decided to have a baby and planned to marry. Shortly after the girlfriend became pregnant, the couple separated. The girlfriend gave birth to a daughter which, as Irish law permitted, she placed for adoption without the applicant's knowledge or consent. The Court held unanimously (i) that the de facto relationship between the applicant and his girlfriend and, later, between the applicant and his daughter was a 'family' one for the purposes of Article 8, and (ii) that Ireland had not complied with the applicant's right to respect for family life by permitting the adoption of his daughter without his involvement.

6 Article 10: The right to freedom of expression

Sunday Times v United Kingdom, E Ct HRR A 30 (1979), 2 EHRR 245, Eur Ct HR

Following *A-G v Times Newspapers Ltd*, above, p. 405, the present application was brought by the publisher, editor, and a group of journalists of *The Sunday Times*. The Commission expressed the opinion, by 8 votes to 5, that the injunction granted by the House of Lords against *The Sunday Times* was a breach of Article 10. The case was referred to the Court by the Commission. The Court held that Article 10 had been infringed because the restriction, although 'prescribed by law' and imposed for a legitimate purpose, was not 'necessary in a democratic society' for the maintenance of the 'authority . . . of the judiciary.' The full Court reached this conclusion by 11 votes to 9.

JUDGMENT OF THE COURT

49. In the Court's opinion, the following are two of the requirements that flow from the expression 'prescribed by law'. Firstly, the law must be adequately accessible: the citizen must be able to have an indication that is adequate in the circumstances of the legal rules applicable to a given case. Secondly, a norm cannot be regarded as a 'law' unless it is formulated with sufficient precision to enable the citizen to regulate his conduct: he must be able—if need be with appropriate advice—to foresee, to a degree that is reasonable in the circumstances, the consequences which a given action may entail. Those consequences need not be foreseeable with absolute certainty: experience shows this to be unattainable. Again, whilst certainty is highly desirable, it may bring in its train excessive rigidity and the law must be able to keep pace with changing circumstances. Accordingly, many laws are inevitably couched in terms which, to a greater or lesser extent, are vague and whose interpretation and application are questions of practice.

[The Court, having confirmed that the term 'law' in the above phrase included unwritten law such as the common law, concluded that although the English law of contempt was not as clear as it might be, the applicants 'were able to foresee to a degree that was reasonable in the circumstances, a risk that publication of the draft article' might be contempt. The Court also held that the injunction could be justified as having an aim permitted by Article 10(2), viz. 'the maintenance of the authority . . . of the judiciary'. More difficult was the question whether it was 'necessary,' etc., to achieve that aim:]

59. . . . The Court has noted[1] that, whilst the adjective 'necessary,' within the meaning of Article 10 § 2, is not synonymous with 'indispensable' neither has it the flexibility of such expressions as 'admissible', 'ordinary', 'useful', 'reasonable' or 'desirable' and that it implies the existence of a 'pressing social need. . . .'

In the second place, the Court has underlined that the initial responsibility for securing the rights and freedoms enshrined in the Convention lies with the individual Contracting States. Accordingly, 'Article 10 § 2 leaves to the Contracting States a margin of appreciation. This margin is given both to the domestic legislator . . . and to the bodies, judicial amongst others, that are called upon to interpret and apply the laws in force. . . .'

'Nevertheless, Article 10 § 2 does not give the Contracting States an unlimited power of appreciation:' 'The Court . . . is empowered to give the final ruling on whether a "restriction" . . . is reconcilable with freedom of expression as protected by Article 10. . . .'

The Court has deduced from a combination of these principles that 'it is in no way [its] task to take the place of the competent national courts but rather to review under Article 10 the decisions they delivered in the exercise of their power of appreciation. . . .'

This does not mean that the Court's supervision is limited to ascertaining whether a respondent State exercised its discretion reasonably, carefully and in good faith. Even a Contracting State so acting remains subject to the Court's control as regards the compatibility of its conduct with the engagements it has undertaken under the Convention. . . .

Again, the scope of the domestic power of appreciation is not identical as regards each of the aims listed in Article 10 § 2. The *Handyside* case concerned the 'protection of morals.' The view taken by the Contracting States of the 'requirements of morals', observed the Court, 'varies from time to time and from place to place, especially in our era'. Precisely the same cannot be said of the far more objective notion of the 'authority' of the judiciary. The domestic law and practice of the Contracting States reveal a fairly substantial measure of common ground in this area. This is reflected in a number of provisions of the Convention, including Article 6, which have no equivalent as far as 'morals' are concerned. Accordingly, here a more extensive European supervision corresponds to a less discretionary power of appreciation. . . .

60. Both the minority of the Commission and the Government attach importance to the fact that the institution of contempt of court is peculiar to common-law countries and suggest that the concluding words of Article 10 § 2 were designed to cover this institution which has no equivalent in many other member States of the Council of Europe.

However, even if this were so, the Court considers that the reason for the insertion of those words would have been to ensure that the general aims of the law of contempt of court should be considered legitimate aims under Article 10 § 2 but not to make that law the standard by which to assess whether a given measure was 'necessary.' . . .

62. It must now be decided whether the 'interference' complained of corresponded to a 'pressing social need', whether it was 'proportionate to the legitimate aim pursued . . .'

63. . . . The speeches in the House of Lords emphasised above all the concern that the processes of the law may be brought into disrespect and the functions of the courts usurped either if the public is led to form an opinion on the subject-matter of litigation before adjudication by the courts or if the parties to litigation have to undergo 'trial by newspaper'. Such concern is in itself 'relevant' to the maintenance of the 'authority of the judiciary.' . . .

Nevertheless, the proposed *Sunday Times* article was couched in moderate terms and did not present just one side of the evidence or claim that there was only one possible result at which a court could arrive . . . Accordingly, even to the extent that the article might have led some readers to form an opinion on the negligence issue, this would not have had adverse consequences for the 'authority of the judiciary', especially since, as noted above, there had been a nationwide campaign in the meantime.

65. . . . Whilst . . . [the courts] are the forum for the settlement of disputes, this does not mean that there can be no prior discussion of disputes elsewhere, be it in specialised journals, in the general press or

1 *Ed.* In the *Handyside* case, below, p. 826. The quotations and paraphrases in the remainder of the Court's judgment are from that case.

amongst the public at large. . . . Not only do the media have the task of imparting such information and ideas: the public also has a right to receive them. . . . The Court observes . . . that, following a balancing of the conflicting interests involved, an absolute rule was formulated by certain of the Law Lords to the effect that it was not permissible to prejudge issues in pending cases. . . . Whilst emphasising that it is not its function to pronounce itself on an interpretation of English law adopted in the House of Lords . . . the Court points out that it has to take a different approach. The Court is faced not with a choice between two conflicting principles but with a principle of freedom of expression [in Article 10] that is subject to a number of exceptions which must be narrowly interpreted . . . the Court has to be satisfied that the interference was necessary having regard to the facts and circumstances prevailing in the specific case before it . . . the families of numerous victims of the tragedy, who were unaware of the legal difficulties involved, had a vital interest in knowing all the underlying facts and the various possible solutions. They could be deprived of this information, which was crucially important for them, only if it appeared absolutely certain that its diffusion would have presented a threat to the 'authority of the judiciary'.

66. The thalidomide disaster was a matter of undisputed public concern . . . fundamental issues concerning protection against and compensation for injuries resulting from scientific developments were raised and many facets of the existing law on these subjects were called in question.

. . . the facts of the case did not cease to be a matter of public interest merely because they formed the background to pending litigation. By bringing to light certain facts, the article might have served as a brake on speculative and unenlightened discussion.

67. Having regard to all the circumstances of the case . . . the Court concludes that the interference complained of did not correspond to a social need sufficiently pressing to outweigh the public interest in freedom of expression within the meaning of the Convention. The Court therefore finds the reasons for the restraint imposed on the applicants not to be sufficient under Article 10 § 2. That restraint proves not to be proportionate to the legitimate aim pursued; it was not necessary in a democratic society for maintaining the authority of the judiciary.

NOTES[1]

1. In their joint dissenting opinion, the nine dissenting judges, who included Judge Sir Gerald Fitzmaurice, disagreed with the majority essentially on the question whether the injunction was 'necessary' and on the latitude to be given to the defendant state under the 'margin of appreciation' doctrine. They pointed out that the 'authority and impartiality of the judiciary' exception allowed by Article 10(2) was inserted on the proposal of the United Kingdom when the Convention was drafted to take account of the common law of contempt which is 'peculiar to the legal traditions of the common-law countries . . . and . . . is unknown in the law of most of the member states.' In the opinion of the dissenting judges, the conclusion of the majority that the 'authority . . . of the judiciary' was a far more objective notion than that of 'the protection of morals' (so that less discretion should be allowed to the defendant state) was erroneous. It was 'by no means divorced from national circumstances and cannot be determined in a uniform way.' Evidence for this was to be found in the different ways in which states went about protecting that authority. A state such as the United Kingdom that relied upon the law of contempt to protect it should be given sufficient latitude to apply it as national circumstances warranted or required.

2. The *Sunday Times* case was the first in which the Court was called upon to consider whether a judgment applying a rule of common law complied with the Convention. Crucial to the Court's decision was its understanding of the difference between the approach that it could adopt under Article 10 and that open to the House of Lords at common law. Whereas it had to give priority to freedom of

---

1 For casenotes, see P. J. Duffy, (1980) 5 H Rts Rev 17; F. A. Mann, (1979) 95 LQR 348; W-W. M. Wong, (1984) 17 N.Y. Univ. J.I.L. & Pol. 35. On Article 10, see D. Korff, (1988) 9 J. Media L. & P. 143.

expression, the House of Lords could give equal weight to two competing freedoms. Even so, it is difficult to avoid the conclusion that had the House of Lords been applying Article 10 (and it is interesting to note that the Convention was not referred to by any of their Lordships) it would have found the injunction to have been 'necessary' in the sense in which the Court interpreted that term. It would seem, moreover, that when applying the 'margin of appreciation' doctrine in this context, the Court reduced it almost to vanishing point. It appears to have made its own assessment of the situation *de novo* and simply to have disagreed with that of the House of Lords. This raises the question of the relationship between the Strasbourg authorities and local courts. (Cf. the *Handyside* case, below, in which a court judgment applying statutory law was in issue.) As the Court indicated in the *Sunday Times* case, (para. 59), it is not a court of appeal from national courts. It seems likely that the Court found confidence to disagree with the House of Lords from the lack of unanimity among English judges on the proper scope of the law of criminal contempt and its application in this case. Certainly it was affected by the fact, to which it refers, that the Phillimore Committee had suggested that the 'prejudgment' principle should be reconsidered (Cmnd 5794, para. 111) and that the British government White Paper (Cmnd 7145, para. 43) had not called in question this suggestion. The Contempt of Court Act 1981 was enacted partly to bring United Kingdom law into line with the Convention.

3. In *Handyside v United Kingdom*, E Ct HRR A 24 (1976), 1 EHRR 737, to which the Court refers in the *Sunday Times* case, the applicant was the publisher of *The Little Red Schoolbook*. The book, which was aimed at children, had chapters on education, learning, teachers, pupils and 'the system'. The chapter on pupils had subsections giving advise on sexual matters. The applicant was convicted under the Obscene Publications Acts of having in his possession obscene articles for gain. The European Court of Human Rights held, by 13 votes to 1, that the conviction was not a breach of the freedom of speech guarantee in Article 10, ECHR. It could be justified as being for 'the protection of morals' (Article 10(2)).

The *Handyside* case is of special importance as the one in which the Court fixed its interpretation of the 'necessary in a democratic society' formula that is found in paragraphs (2) of Articles 8, 9, 10 and 11: the Court applies a proportionality test and, when doing so, allows a certain margin of appreciation or discretion, the extent of which varies from one context to another,[1] to the defendant state in its assessment of what the public interest requires. The Court stated:

'48. The Court points out that the machinery of protection established by the Convention is subsidiary to the national systems safeguarding human rights (judgment of 23 July 1968 on the merits of the "Belgian Linguistic" case, Series A no. 6, p. 35, § 10 *in fine*). The Convention leaves to each Contracting State, in the first place, the task of securing the rights and freedoms it enshrines. The institutions created by it make their own contribution to this task but they become involved only through contentious proceedings and once all domestic remedies have been exhausted (Article 26).

These observations apply, notably, to Article 10 § 2. In particular, it is not possible to find in the domestic law of the various Contracting States a uniform European conception of morals. The view taken by their respective laws of the requirements of morals varies from time to time and from place to place, especially in our era which is characterised by a rapid and far-reaching evolution of opinions on the subject. By reason of their direct and continuous contact with the vital forces of their countries, State authorities are in principle in a better position than the international judge to give an opinion on the exact content of these requirements as well as on the "necessity" of a "restriction" or "penalty" intended

---

1   Generally a wider margin of appreciation in the context of 'public morals' and 'national security' than, for example, 'the administration of justice'. Note that the principles of proportionality and of a margin of appreciation are also used extensively by the Court in connection with other ECHR articles in addition to Articles 8–11.

to meet them. The Court notes at this juncture that, whilst the adjective "necessary", within the meaning of Article 10 § 2, is not synonymous with "indispensable" (c.f., in Articles 2 § 2 and 6 § 1, the words "absolutely necessary" and "strictly necessary" and, in Article 15 § 1, the phrase "to the extent strictly required by the exigencies of the situation"), neither has it the flexibility of such expressions as "admissible", "ordinary" (c.f. Article 4 § 3), "useful" (c.f. the French text of the first paragraph of Article 1 of Protocol No. 1), "reasonable" (c.f. Articles 5 § 3 and 6 § 1) or "desirable". Nevertheless, it is for the national authorities to make the initial assessment of the reality of the pressing social need implied by the notion of "necessity" in this context.

Consequently, Article 10 § 2 leaves to the Contracting States a margin of appreciation. This margin is given both to the domestic legislator ("prescribed by law") and to the bodies, judicial amongst others, that are called upon to interpret and apply the laws in force. . . .

49. Nevertheless, Article 10 § 2 does not give the Contracting States an unlimited power of appreciation. The Court, which, with the Commission, is responsible for ensuring the observance of thos States' engagements (Article 19), is empowered to give the final ruling on whether a "restriction" or "penalty" is reconcilable with freedom of expression as protected by Article 10. The domestic margin of appreciation thus goes hand in hand with a European supervision. Such supervision concerns both the aim of the measure challenged and its "necessity"; it covers not only the basic legislation but also the decision applying it, even one given by an independent court. . . .'

Lingens v Austria, E Ct HRR A 103 (1986), 8 EHRR 407, Eur Ct HR

The applicant published two articles in an Austrian magazine in which he criticised Mr Bruno Kreisky, an Austrian politician. The articles were written shortly after an Austrian General Election in which the party of which Mr Kreisky, the retiring Chancellor (Prime Minister), was the leader had won. At a time when Mr Kreisky was forming a new government and in this connection had consulted Mr Peter, the leader of another party, Mr Kreisky defended Mr Peter in a television interview from criticism of his Nazi past by Mr Wiesenthal of the Jewish Documentation Centre. The applicant's first article accused Mr Kreisky of protecting Mr Peter and other former SS members for political reasons and described Mr Kreisky's attack in the television interview on Mr Peter's accuser as displaying 'the basest opportunism.' In the second article, the applicant criticised Mr Kreisky's accommodating attitude towards former Nazis who had taken part in politics and described his attitude as 'immoral' and 'undignified'. Following private prosecutions by Mr Kreisky, the applicant was convicted of the criminal offence of defamation for using the words 'the basest opportunism', 'immoral' and 'undignified' about Mr Kreisky. The applicant claimed a breach of Article 10.

JUDGMENT OF THE COURT

35. It was not disputed that there was 'interference by public authority' with the exercise of the freedom of expression. This resulted from the applicant's conviction for defamation. . . .

Such interference contravenes the Convention if it does not satisfy the requirements of paragraph 2 of Article 10. It therefore falls to be determined whether the interference . . . had an aim or aims that is or are legitimate under Article 10 § 2 and was 'necessary in a democratic society' for the aforesaid aim or aims. . . .

36. . . . the Court agrees with the Commission and the Government that the conviction in question was . . . designed to protect 'the reputation or rights of others' and there is no reason to suppose that it had any other purpose (see Article 18 of the Convention). The conviction . . . accordingly . . . had a legitimate aim under Article 10 § 2 of the Convention. . . .

39. The adjective 'necessary', within the meaning of Article 10 § 2, implies the existence of a 'pressing social need'. . . . The Contracting States have a certain margin of appreciation in assessing whether such a need exists . . . but it goes hand in hand with a European supervision, embracing both the legislation and the decisions applying it, even those given by an independent court (see the *Sunday Times* judgment [above, p. 823]). The Court is therefore empowered to give the final ruling on whether a 'restriction' or 'penalty' is reconcilable with freedom of expression as protected by Article 10 (ibid.).

40. In exercising its supervisory jurisdiction, the Court . . . must determine whether the interference at issue was 'proportionate to the legitimate aim pursued'. . . .

41. In this connection, the Court has to recall that freedom of expression, as secured in paragraph 1 of Article 10, constitutes one of the essential foundations of a democratic society and one of the basic conditions for its progress and for each individual's self-fulfilment. Subject to paragraph 2, it is applicable not only to 'information' or 'ideas' that are favourably received or regarded as inoffensive or as a matter of indifference, but also to those that offend, shock or disturb. Such are the demands of that pluralism, tolerance and broadmindedness without which there is no 'democratic society' (see the *Handyside* judgment above, p. 826).

These principles are of particular importance as far as the press is concerned. Whilst the press must not overstep the bounds set, *inter alia*, for the 'protection of the reputation of others', it is nevertheless incumbent on it to impart information and ideas on political issues just as on those in other areas of public interest. Not only does the press have the task of imparting such information and ideas: the public also has a right to receive them (see, *mutatis mutandis*, the above-mentioned *Sunday Times* judgment . . .). In this connection, the Court cannot accept the opinion, expressed in the judgment of the Vienna Court of Appeal, to the effect that the task of the press was to impart information, the interpretation of which had to be left primarily to the reader. . . .

42. Freedom of the press furthermore affords the public one of the best means of discovering and forming an opinion of the ideas and attitudes of political leaders. More generally, freedom of political debate is at the very core of the concept of a democratic society which prevails throughout the Convention.

The limits of acceptable criticism are accordingly wider as regards a politician as such than as regards a private individual. Unlike the latter, the former inevitably and knowingly lays himself open to close scrutiny of his every word and deed by both journalists and the public at large, and he must consequently display a greater degree of tolerance. No doubt Article 10 § 2 enables the reputation of others – that is to say, of all individuals – to be protected, and this protection extends to politicians too, even when they are not acting in their private capacity; but in such cases the requirements of such protection have to be weighed in relation to the interests of open discussion of political issues.

43. The applicant was convicted because he had used certain expressions ('basest opportunism', 'immoral' and 'undignified') apropos of Mr. Kreisky, who was Federal Chancellor at the time, in two articles published in the Viennese magazine *Profil* on 14 and 21 October 1975. . . . The articles dealt with political issues of public interest in Austria which had given rise to many heated discussions concerning the attitude of Austrians in general – and the Chancellor in particular – to National Socialism and to the participation of former Nazis in the governance of the country. The content and tone of the articles were on the whole fairly balanced but the use of the aforementioned expressions in particular appeared likely to harm Mr. Kreisky's reputation.

However, since the case concerned Mr. Kreisky in his capacity as a politician, regard must be had to the background against which these articles were written. They had appeared shortly after the general election of October 1975. Many Austrians had thought beforehand that Mr. Kreisky's party would lose its absolute majority and, in order to be able to govern, would have to form a coalition with Mr. Peter's party. When, after the elections, Mr. Wiesenthal made a number of revelations about Mr. Peter's Nazi past, the Chancellor defended Mr. Peter and attacked his detractor, whose activities he described as 'mafia methods'; hence Mr. Lingens' sharp reaction. . . .

The impugned expressions are therefore to be seen against the background of a post-election political controversy . . . in this struggle each used the weapons at his disposal; and these were in no way unusual in the hard-fought tussles of politics.

In assessing, from the point of view of the Convention, the penalty imposed on the applicant and the reasons for which the domestic courts imposed it, these circumstances must not be overlooked.

44. On final appeal the Vienna Court of Appeal sentenced Mr. Lingens to a fine; it also ordered confiscation of the relevant issues of *Profil* and publication of the judgment. . . .

As the Government pointed out, the disputed articles had at the time already been widely disseminated, so that although the penalty imposed on the author did not strictly speaking prevent him from expressing himself, it nonetheless amounted to a kind of censure, which would be likely to discourage him from making criticisms of that kind again in future; the Delegate of the Commission rightly pointed this out. In the context of political debate such a sentence would be likely to deter journalists from contributing to public discussion of issues affecting the life of the community. By the same token, a sanction such as this is liable to hamper the press in performing its task as purveyor of information and public watchdog. . . .

45. The Austrian courts applied themselves first to determining whether the passages held against Mr. Lingens were objectively defamatory; they ruled that some of the expressions used were indeed defamatory – 'the basest opportunism', 'immoral' and 'undignified'. . . .

The defendant had submitted that the observations in question were value-judgments made by him in the exercise of his freedom of expression. . . . The Court, like the Commission, shares this view. The applicant's criticisms were in fact directed against the attitude adopted by Mr. Kreisky, who was Federal

Chancellor at the time. What was at issue was not his right to disseminate information but his freedom of opinion and his right to impart ideas; the restrictions authorised in paragraph 2 of Article 10 nevertheless remained applicable.

46. The relevant courts then sought to determine whether the defendant had established the truth of his statements; this was in pursuance of Article 111 § 3 of the Criminal Code. . . . They held in substance that there were different ways of assessing Mr. Kreisky's behaviour and that it could not logically be proved that one interpretation was right to the exclusion of all others; they consequently found the applicant guilty of defamation. . . .

In the Court's view, a careful distinction needs to be made between facts and value-judgments. The existence of facts can be demonstrated, whereas the truth of value-judgments is not susceptible of proof. The Court notes in this connection that the facts on which Mr. Lingens founded his value-judgment were undisputed, as was also his good faith. . . .

Under paragraph 3 of Article 111 of the Criminal Code, read in conjunction with paragraph 2, journalists in a case such as this cannot escape conviction for the matters specified in paragraph 1 unless they can prove the truth of their statements. . . .

As regards value-judgments this requirement is impossible of fulfilment and it infringes freedom of opinion itself, which is a fundamental part of the right secured by Article 10 of the Convention. . . .

47. From the various foregoing considerations it appears that the interference with Mr. Lingens' exercise of the freedom of expression was not 'necessary in a democratic society . . . for the protection of the reputation . . . of others'; it was disproportionate to the legitimate aim pursued. There was accordingly a breach of Article 10 of the Convention. . . .

FOR THESE REASONS, THE COURT UNANIMOUSLY

1. *Holds* that there has been a breach of Article 10 of the Convention; . . .

NOTE

The *Lingens* case is important because of the emphasis placed by the plenary Court upon the value of freedom of expression and also because of the distinction it draws between public and private figures, with the former being properly subject to closer scrutiny by way of comment in the public interest than the latter. There are echoes here of *New York Times v Sullivan* (1964) 376 US 254 in the American law of defamation: see D. Elder, (1986) 35 ICLQ 891. As to a comparable distinction between public and private individuals in the law of privacy, see above, p. 538. Austria's difficulty in this case was that its law did not draw a distinction between assertions of fact and expression of opinion by way of comment. A defendant had to prove the truth of the latter as well as the former; it was not sufficient just to show that a comment was made without malice. What the Court in effect requires is that a state provide a defence of fair comment on matters of public concern in its law of defamation in order to comply with Article 10.

The Observer and the Guardian v United Kingdom, E Ct HRR A 216 (1991), 14 EHRR 153, Eur Ct HR

The applicants were the proprietors and publishers, editors and certain reporters of the above two newspapers. In June 1986, the two newspapers published articles which (i) gave details of alleged improper and criminal activities by the British Security Service derived from the manuscript of *Spycatcher*, a planned book written by a retired member of MI5, Peter Wright, and (ii) reported on Australian court proceedings in which the Attorney-General sought to prevent the publication of *Spycatcher* in Australia. The allegations were in part that the Security Service had routinely burgled and bugged foreign diplomats and had plotted against Harold Wilson while he was Prime Minister. In the next week, the Attorney-General

obtained interlocutory injunctions in the English High Court preventing the publication in the two newspapers of further articles containing more information
obtained by Peter Wright in the course of his employment as a civil servant. The
injunctions were upheld by the Court of Appeal and, in later proceedings, confirmed by the House of Lords. They were granted to safeguard the
Attorney-General's position in connection with a High Court application by him
for a permanent injunction to prevent the newspapers publishing material from
the *Spycatcher* manuscript on grounds of breach of confidence. On 30 July 1987,
the injunctions were maintained by the House of Lords despite the publication of
the book two weeks earlier in the US and the resulting circulation of copies in the
UK.

At Strasbourg, the applicants claimed that the interlocutory injunctions were in
breach of Articles 10, 13 and 14. In its report, the Commission expressed the
opinion that there had been a breach of Article 10 both before 30 July 1987, by six
votes to five, and afterwards, unanimously. The Commission and the Court unanimously rejected the claims under Articles 13 and 14. The following extracts concern
Article 10.

JUDGMENT OF THE COURT

B. Did the interference have aims that are legitimate under Article 10 § 2? . . .

56. The Court is satisfied that the injunctions had the direct or primary aim of 'maintaining the authority
of the judiciary', which phrase includes the protection of the rights of litigants. . . .
It is also incontrovertible that a further purpose of the restrictions complained of was the protection of
national security. They were imposed, as has just been seen, with a view to ensuring a fair trial of the
Attorney General's claim for permanent injunctions against O.G. and the evidential basis for that claim
was the two affidavits sworn by Sir Robert Armstrong, in which he deposed to the potential damage
which publication of the *Spycatcher* material would cause to the Security Service. . . . Not only was that
evidence relied on by Mr. Justice Millett when granting the injunctions initially . . ., but considerations of
national security featured prominently in all the judgments delivered by the English courts in this case. . . .
The Court would only comment – and it will revert to this point in paragraph 69 below – that the precise
nature of the national security considerations involved varied over the course of time.
57. The interference complained of thus had aims that were legitimate under paragraph 2 of Article 10.

C. Was the interference 'necessary in a democratic society'?

1. General principles

59. The Court's judgments relating to Article 10 . . . enounce the following major principles.
(a) Freedom of expression constitutes one of the essential foundations of a democratic society; subject to
paragraph 2 of Article 10, it is applicable not only to 'information' or 'ideas' that are favourably received
or regarded as inoffensive or as a matter of indifference, but also to those that offend, shock or disturb.
Freedom of expression, as enshrined in Article 10, is subject to a number of exceptions which, however,
must be narrowly interpreted and the necessity for any restrictions must be convincingly established.
(b) These principles are of particular importance as far as the press is concerned. Whilst it must not
overstep the bounds set, *inter alia*, in the 'interests of national security' or for 'maintaining the authority of
the judiciary', it is nevertheless incumbent on it to impart information and ideas on matters of public
interest. Not only does the press have the task of imparting such information and ideas: the public also
have a right to receive them. Were it otherwise, the press would be unable to play its vital role of 'public
watchdog'.
(c) The adjective 'necessary', within the meaning of Article 10 § 2, implies the existence of a 'pressing
social need'. The Contracting States have a certain margin of appreciation in assessing whether such a
need exists, but it goes hand in hand with a European supervision, embracing both the law and the decisions applying it, even those given by independent courts. The Court is therefore empowered to give the
final ruling on whether a 'restriction' is reconcilable with freedom of expression as protected by Article
10.
(d) The Court's task, in exercising its supervisory jurisdiction, is not to take the place of the competent

national authorities but rather to review under Article 10 the decisions they delivered pursuant to their power of appreciation. This does not mean that the supervision is limited to ascertaining whether the respondent State exercised its discretion reasonably, carefully and in good faith; what the Court has to do is to look at the interference complained of in the light of the case as a whole and determine whether it was 'proportionate to the legitimate aim pursued' and whether the reasons adduced by the national authorities to justify it are 'relevant and sufficient'.

60. For the avoidance of doubt, and having in mind the written comments that were submitted in this case by 'Article 19' . . ., the Court would only add to the foregoing that Article 10 of the Convention does not in terms prohibit the imposition of prior restraints on publication, as such. This is evidenced not only by the words 'conditions', 'restrictions', 'preventing' and 'prevention' which appear in that provision, but also by the Court's *Sunday Times* judgment of 26 April 1979 and its *markt intern Verlag GmbH* and *Klaus Beermann* judgment of 20 November 1989 (Series A no. 165). On the other hand, the dangers inherent in prior restraints are such that they call for the most careful scrutiny on the part of the Court. This is especially so as far as the press is concerned, for news is a perishable commodity and to delay its publication, even for a short period, may well deprive it of all its value and interest.

2. The period from 11 July 1986 to 30 July 1987 . . .

62. Mr. Justice Millett's decision to grant injunctions – which, in the subsequent stages of the interlocutory proceedings, was accepted as correct not only by the Court of Appeal but also by all the members of the Appellate Committee of the House of Lords . . . – was based on the following line of reasoning. The Attorney General was seeking a permanent ban on the publication of material the disclosure of which would, according to the credible evidence presented on his behalf, be detrimental to the Security Service; to refuse interlocutory injunctions would mean that O.G. would be free to publish that material immediately and before the substantive trial; this would effectively deprive the Attorney General, if successful on the merits, of his right to be granted a permanent injunction, thereby irrevocably destroying the substance of his actions and, with it, the claim to protect national security.

In the Court's view, these reasons were 'relevant' in terms of the aims both of protecting national security and of maintaining the authority of the judiciary. The question remains whether they were 'sufficient'.

63. . . . In forming its . . . opinion, the Court has borne in mind its observations concerning the nature and contents of *Spycatcher* . . . and the interests of national security involved; it has also had regard to the potential prejudice to the Attorney General's breach of confidence actions, this being a point that has to be seen in the context of the central position occupied by Article 6 of the Convention and its guarantee of the right to a fair trial (see the above-mentioned *Sunday Times* judgment, Series A no. 30, p. 34, § 55). Particularly in the light of these factors, the Court takes the view that, having regard to their margin of appreciation, the English courts were entitled to consider the grant of injunctive relief to be necessary and that their reasons for so concluding were 'sufficient' for the purposes of paragraph 2 of Article 10.

64. It has nevertheless to be examined whether the actual restraints imposed were 'proportionate' to the legitimate aims pursued.

In this connection, it is to be noted that the injunctions did not erect a blanket prohibition. Whilst they forbade the publication of information derived from or attributed to Mr. Wright in his capacity as a member of the Security Service, they did not prevent O.G. from pursuing their campaign for an independent inquiry into the operation of that service. . . . Moreover, they contained provisos excluding certain material from their scope, notably that which had been previously published in the works of Mr. Chapman Pincher and in the Granada Television programmes. . . . Again, it was open to O.G. at any time to seek – as they in fact did . . . – variation or discharge of the orders.

It is true that although the injunctions were intended to be no more than temporary measures, they in fact remained in force – as far as the period now under consideration is concerned – for slightly more than a year. And this is a long time where the perishable commodity of news is concerned (see paragraph 60 above). As against this, it may be pointed out that the Court of Appeal . . . certified the case as fit for a speedy trial – which O.G. apparently did not seek – and that the news in question, relating as it did to events that had occurred several years previously, could not really be classified as urgent. Furthermore, the Attorney General's actions raised difficult issues of both fact and law: time was accordingly required for the preparation of the trial, especially since, as Lord Brandon of Oakbrook pointed out (see paragraph 36(a) (v) above), they were issues on which evidence had to be adduced and subjected to cross-examination.

65. Having regard to the foregoing, the Court concludes that, as regards the period from 11 July 1986 to 30 July 1987, the national authorities were entitled to think that the interference complained of was 'necessary in a democratic society'.

3. The period from 30 July 1987 to 13 October 1988

66. On 14 July 1987 *Spycatcher* was published in the United States of America.... This changed the situation that had obtained since 11 July 1986. In the first place, the contents of the book ceased to be a matter of speculation and their confidentiality was destroyed. Furthermore, Mr. Wright's memoirs were obtainable from abroad by residents of the United Kingdom, the Government having made no attempt to impose a ban on importation. . . .

68. The fact that the further publication of *Spycatcher* material could have been prejudicial to the trial of the Attorney General's claims for permanent injunctions was certainly, in terms of the aim of maintaining the authority of the judiciary, a 'relevant' reason for continuing the restraints in question. The Court finds, however, that in the circumstances it does not constitute a 'sufficient' reason for the purposes of Article 10.

It is true that the House of Lords had regard to the requirements of the Convention, even though it is not incorporated into domestic law.... It is also true that there is some difference between the casual importation of copies of *Spycatcher* into the United Kingdom and mass publication of its contents in the press. On the other hand, even if the Attorney General had succeeded in obtaining permanent injunctions at the substantive level, they would have borne on material the confidentiality of which had been destroyed in any event – and irrespective of whether any further disclosures were made by O.G. – as a result of the publication in the United States. Seen in terms of the protection of the Attorney General's rights as a litigant, the interest in maintaining the confidentiality of that material had, for the purposes of the Convention, ceased to exist by 30 July 1987. . . .

69. As regards the interests of national security relied on, the Court observes that in this respect the Attorney General's case underwent, to adopt the words of Mr. Justice Scott, 'a curious metamorphosis' (*Attorney General v Guardian Newspapers Ltd (No. 2)* [1990] 1 Appeal Cases 140F). As emerges from Sir Robert Armstrong's evidence . . ., injunctions were sought at the outset, *inter alia*, to preserve the secret character of information that ought to be kept secret. By 30 July 1987, however, the information had lost that character and, as was observed by Lord Brandon of Oakbrook . . ., the major part of the potential damage adverted to by Sir Robert Armstrong had already been done. By then, the purpose of the injunctions had thus become confined to the promotion of the efficiency and reputation of the Security Service, notably by: preserving confidence in that Service on the part of third parties; making it clear that the unauthorised publication of memoirs by its former members would not be countenanced; and deterring others who might be tempted to follow in Mr. Wright's footsteps.

The Court does not regard these objectives as sufficient to justify the continuation of the interference complained of. It is, in the first place, open to question whether the actions against O.G. could have served to advance the attainment of these objectives any further than had already been achieved by the steps taken against Mr. Wright himself. Again, bearing in mind the availability of an action for an account of profits . . ., the Court shares the doubts of Lord Oliver of Aylmerton . . . as to whether it was legitimate, for the purpose of punishing Mr. Wright and providing an example to others, to use the injunctive remedy against persons, such as O.G., who had not been concerned with the publication of *Spycatcher*. Above all, continuation of the restrictions after July 1987 prevented newspapers from exercising their right and duty to purvey information, already available, on a matter of legitimate public concern.

70. Having regard to the foregoing, the Court concludes that the interference complained of was no longer 'necessary in a democratic society' after 30 July 1987. . . .

FOR THESE REASONS, THE COURT

1. *Holds* by fourteen votes to ten that there was no violation of Article 10 of the Convention during the period from 11 July 1986 to 30 July 1987;
2. *Holds* unanimously that there was a violation of Article 10 during the period from 30 July 1987 to 13 October 1988; . . .

NOTES

1. On the *Spycatcher* litigation in the English courts, see above, p. 474. At Strasbourg, in addition to the *Observer* and *Guardian* cases, see the companion case of *Sunday Times v United Kingdom (No 2)*, E Ct HRR A 217 (1991), 14 EHRR 29.

2. In the *Observer* and *Guardian* cases there were several dissenting opinions by judges who considered that the Court should have found a breach of Article 10 in respect of the period before 30 July 1987. Judge Pettiti, joined by Judge Pinheiro Farinha stated:

'One gets the impression that the extreme severity of Millett J.'s injunction and of the course adopted by the Attorney General was less a question of the duty of confidentiality than the fear of disclosure of certain irregularities carried out by the security service in the pursuit of political rather than intelligence aims.

In this respect there was a violation of the right to receive information, which is the second component of Article 10. To deprive the public of information on the functioning of State organs is to violate a fundamental democratic right. . . .

If the state believes that a publication puts at risk state secrets or national security, there are other procedural means at its disposal. If the state contests a failure to comply with the duty of discretion on the part of a retired civil servant, appropriate procedures are available. In the present case the state did not prosecute Mr. Wright. . . .

An interim injunction, not subsequently lifted after a short period, is in effect a disguised means of instituting censure or restraint on the freedom of the press.'

3. In *Harman v United Kingdom*, (1986) 46 DR E Comm HR 57, the applicant, solicitor and NCCL legal adviser, had allowed a journalist to inspect Home Office documents disclosed to her client by order of court. Her conviction for contempt of court was upheld by the House of Lords because an implied obligation of confidence continued even though the documents had been read out in open court. After the application was admitted under Articles 10 and 14, a friendly settlement was reached by which the UK agreed to pay the applicant £36,000 expenses and undertook to change the law, which it did by amending the Supreme Court's Rules of Court.

Open Door Counselling and Dublin Well Woman v Ireland, E Ct HRR A 246 (1992), 15 EHRR 244, Eur Ct HR

The applicants were two limited companies with the above names, trained counsellors for them and Mrs X and Mrs G, two women of child-bearing age. An injunction was issued by the Irish High Court against the two companies in a relator action at the suit of the Attorney-General. As upheld by the Supreme Court, the injunction stated that they and their servants or agents were 'perpetually restrained from assisting pregnant women within the jurisdiction to travel abroad to obtain abortions by referral to a clinic, by the making for them of travel arrangements, or by informing them of the identity and location of and the method of communication with a specified clinic or clinics or otherwise'. The applicants claimed that the injunction was in breach of their rights under Article 10. Mrs X and Mrs G claimed a breach of Article 8 (right to respect for private life) and of Articles 8 and 10 in conjunction with Article 14. In its report, the Commission expressed the opinion that there had been a breach of Article 10 in respect both of the two companies and their counsellors, by eight votes to five, and of Mrs X and Mrs G, by seven votes to six. The remaining claims were either unanimously rejected (the claim under Articles 8 and 14) or not considered. The Court only considered the claims under Article 10. It first rejected an objection by the defendant state that only the two companies could bring a claim. The Court held both the counsellors and Mrs X and G were 'directly affected' by the injunction so that they could claim under Article 25 to be 'victims' of a breach of Article 10.

JUDGMENT OF THE COURT

C. Did the restriction have aims that were legitimate under Article 10 § 2? . . .

63. . . . it is evident that the protection afforded under Irish law to the right to life of the unborn is based on profound moral values concerning the nature of life which were reflected in the stance of the majority of the Irish people against abortion as expressed in the 1983 referendum. . . . The restriction thus pursued the legitimate aim of the protection of morals of which the protection in Ireland of the right to life of the unborn is one aspect. It is not necessary in the light of this conclusion to decide whether the term 'others' under Article 10 § 2 extends to the unborn.

D. Was the restriction necessary in a democratic society? . . .

1. Article 2 . . .

66. The Court observes at the outset that in the present case it is not called upon to examine whether a right to abortion is guaranteed under the Convention or whether the foetus is encompassed by the right to life as contained in Article 2. The applicants have not claimed that the Convention contains a right to abortion, as such, their complaint being limited to that part of the injunction which restricts their freedom to impart and receive information concerning abortions abroad. . . .

Thus the only issue to be addressed is whether the restrictions on the freedom to impart and receive information contained in the relevant part of the injunction are necessary in a democratic society for the legitimate aim of the protection of morals as explained above. . . . It follows from this approach that the Government's argument based on Article 2 of the Convention does not fall to be examined in the present case.

2. Proportionality . . .

68. The Court . . . acknowledges that the national authorities enjoy a wide margin of appreciation in matters of morals, particularly in an area such as the present which touches on matters of belief concerning the nature of human life. As the Court has observed before, it is not possible to find in the legal and social orders of the Contracting States a uniform European conception of morals, and the State authorities are, in principle, in a better position than the international judge to give an opinion on the exact content of the requirements of morals as well as on the 'necessity' of a 'restriction' or 'penalty' intended to meet them (see, *inter alia*, the *Handyside v the United Kingdom* judgment . . .).

However, this power of appreciation is not unlimited. It is for the Court, in this field also, to supervise whether a restriction is compatible with the Convention. . . .

70. Accordingly, the Court must examine the question of 'necessity' in the light of the principles developed in its case-law (see, *inter alia*, the *Observer and Guardian v the United Kingdom* judgment . . .). It must determine whether there existed a pressing social need for the measures in question and, in particular, whether the restriction complained of was 'proportionate to the legitimate aim pursued' (ibid.). . . .

72. While the relevant restriction, as observed by the Government, is limited to the provision of information, it is recalled that it is not a criminal offence under Irish law for a pregnant woman to travel abroad in order to have an abortion. Furthermore, the injunction limited the freedom to receive and impart information with respect to services which are lawful in other Convention countries and may be crucial to a woman's health and well-being. Limitations on information concerning activities which, notwithstanding their moral implications, have been and continue to be tolerated by national authorities, call for careful scrutiny by the Convention institutions as to their conformity with the tenets of a democratic society.

73. The Court is first struck by the absolute nature of the Supreme Court injunction which imposed a 'perpetual' restraint on the provision of information to pregnant women concerning abortion facilities abroad, regardless of age or state of health or their reasons for seeking counselling on the termination of pregnancy. The sweeping nature of this restriction has since been highlighted by the case of *The Attorney General v X and Others* and by the concession made by the Government at the oral hearing that the injunction no longer applied to women who, in the circumstances as defined in the Supreme Court's judgment in that case, were now free to have an abortion in Ireland or abroad. . . .

74. On that ground alone the restriction appears over broad and disproportionate. Moreover, this assessment is confirmed by other factors.

75. In the first place, it is to be noted that the corporate applicants were engaged in the counselling of pregnant women in the course of which counsellors neither advocated nor encouraged abortion, but confined themselves to an explanation of the available options. . . . The decision as to whether or not to act on the information so provided was that of the woman concerned. There can be little doubt that following such counselling there were women who decided against a termination of pregnancy. Accordingly, the link between the provision of information and the destruction of unborn life is not as definite as contended. Such counselling had in fact been tolerated by the State authorities even after the passing of the Eighth Amendment in 1983 until the Supreme Court's judgment in the present case. Furthermore, the information that was provided by the relevant applicants concerning abortion facilities abroad was not made available to the public at large.

76. It has not been seriously contested by the Government that information concerning abortion facilities abroad can be obtained from other sources in Ireland such as magazines and telephone directories . . . or by persons with contacts in Great Britain. Accordingly, information that the injunction sought to restrict was already available elsewhere although in a manner which was not supervised by qualified personnel and thus less protective of women's health. Furthermore, the injunction appears to have been largely

ineffective in protecting the right to life of the unborn since it did not prevent large numbers of Irish women from continuing to obtain abortions in Great Britain. . . .

77. In addition, the available evidence, which has not been disputed by the Government, suggests that the injunction has created a risk to the health of those women who are now seeking abortions at a later stage in their pregnancy, due to lack of proper counselling, and who are not availing themselves of customary medical supervision after the abortion has taken place. . . . Moreover, the injunction may have had more adverse effects on women who were not sufficiently resourceful or had not the necessary level of education to have access to alternative souces of information. . . . These are certainly legitimate factors to take into consideration in assessing the proportionality of the restriction. . . .

FOR THESE REASONS, THE COURT

3. *Holds* by fifteen votes to eight that there has been a violation of Article 10; . . .

Jersild v Denmark, E Ct HRR A 298 (1994), 19 EHRR 1, Eur Ct HR

A serious Danish television programme dealing with social and political issues broadcast in one of its weekly programmes an interview in which the applicant, a journalist, interviewed three members of the Greenjackets, a group of young people with extreme racist views. No complaints were made to the competent complaints authority or to the television station. However, a leading churchman complained to the Minister of Justice and the three Greenjacket members were convicted of the criminal offence of 'publicly or with the intention of disseminating it to a wide circle of people' making a statement 'threatening, insulting or degrading a group of persons on account of their race, colour, national or ethnic origin'. Statements in the interview that provided the basis for the conviction included the following: 'Just take a picture of a gorilla . . . and then look at a nigger . . .'; 'A nigger is not a human being, it's an animal, that goes for all the other foreign workers as well, Turks, Yugoslavs . . .'; and 'what we don't like is when they walk around in those Zimbabwe-clothes and then speak this hula-hula language in the street'. The applicant was convicted of aiding and abetting the three Greenjacket members. When the Supreme Court rejected his appeal, the following reasons were given. The applicant had taken the initiative in contacting the Greenjacket members and caused them to make racial assertions that he knew they had previously made and would be likely to repeat; he had edited the interview, lasting several hours, down to a few minutes containing the strongest racial assertions; and he had caused the statements to be brought to the attention of a 'wide circle' of viewers. For these reasons, the applicant was guilty of aiding and abetting. He could have been acquitted if on balance there were reasons 'clearly outweighing the wrongfulness' of his actions. In deciding that there were not, the Supreme Court noted that the statements consisted of 'inarticulate, defamatory remarks and insults spoken by members of an insignificant group whose opinions could hardly be of interest to many people'. Extremist views could be reported in the media but 'such reports must be carried out in a more balanced and comprehensive manner than was the case in the television programme in question'.

The applicant claimed that his conviction was a breach of Article 10. In its report, the Commission expressed the opinion, by twelve votes to four, that there had been such a breach.

JUDGMENT OF THE COURT

. . . it is uncontested that the interference pursued a legitimate aim, namely the 'protection of the reputation or rights of others'.

The only point in dispute is whether the measures were 'necessary in a democratic society'. . . .

30. The Court would emphasise at the outset that it is particularly conscious of the vital importance of combating racial discrimination in all its forms and manifestations. It may be true, as has been suggested by the applicant, that as a result of recent events the awareness of the dangers of racial discrimination is sharper today than it was a decade ago, at the material time. Nevertheless, the issue was already then of general importance, as is illustrated for instance by the fact that the UN Convention dates from 1965. Consequently, the object and purpose pursued by the UN Convention are of great weight in determining whether the applicant's conviction, which – as the Government have stressed – was based on a provision enacted in order to ensure Denmark's compliance with the UN Convention, was 'necessary' within the meaning of Article 10 § 2.

In the second place, Denmark's obligations under Article 10 must be interpreted, to the extent possible, so as to be reconcilable with its obligations under the UN Convention. In this respect it is not for the Court to interpret the 'due regard' clause in Article 4 of the UN Convention, which is open to various constructions. The Court is however of the opinion that its interpretation of Article 10 of the European Convention in the present case is compatible with Denmark's obligations under the UN Convention.

31. A significant feature of the present case is that the applicant did not make the objectionable statements himself but assisted in their dissemination in his capacity of television journalist responsible for a news programme of *Danmarks Radio*. . . . In assessing whether his conviction and sentence were 'necessary', the Court will therefore have regard to the principles established in its case-law relating to the role of the press (as summarised in for instance the *Observer and Guardian v the United Kingdom* judgment of 26 November 1991, Series A no. 216, pp. 29–30, § 59).

The Court reiterates that freedom of expression constitutes one of the essential foundations of a democratic society and that the safeguards to be afforded to the press are of particular importance (ibid.). Whilst the press must not overstep the bounds set, *inter alia*, in the interest of 'the protection of the reputation and rights of others', it is nevertheless incumbent on it to impart information and ideas of public interest. Not only does the press have the task of imparting such information and ideas: the public also has a right to receive them. Were it otherwise, the press would be unable to play its vital role of 'pubic watchdog' (ibid.). Although formulated primarily with regard to the print media, these principles doubtless apply also to the audio-visual media.

In considering the 'duties and responsibilities' of a journalist, the potential impact of the medium concerned is an important factor and it is commonly acknowledged that the audio-visual media have often a much more immediate and powerful effect than the print media. . . . The audio-visual media have means of conveying through images meanings which the print media are not able to impart.

At the same time, the methods of objective and balanced reporting may vary considerably, depending among other things on the media in question. It is not for this Court, nor for the national courts for that matter, to substitute their own views for those of the press as to what technique of reporting should be adopted by journalists. In this context the Court recalls that Article 10 protects not only the substance of the ideas and information expressed, but also the form in which they are conveyed (see the *Oberschlick v Austria* judgment of 23 May 1991, Series A no. 204, p. 25, § 57).

The Court will look at the interference complained of in the light of the case as a whole and determine whether the reasons adduced by the national authorities to justify it are relevant and sufficient and whether the means employed were proportionate to the legitimate aim pursued (see the above-mentioned *Observer and Guardian* judgment, pp. 29–30, § 59). In doing so the Court has to satisfy itself that the national authorities did apply standards which were in conformity with the principles embodied in Article 10 and, moreover, that they based themselves on an acceptable assessment of the relevant facts. . . .

The Court's assessment will have regard to the manner in which the Greenjackets feature was prepared, its contents, the context in which it was broadcast and the purpose of the programme. Bearing in mind the obligations on States under the UN Convention and other international instruments to take effective measures to eliminate all forms of racial discrimination and to prevent and combat racist doctrines and practices . . ., an important factor in the Court's evaluation will be whether the item in question, when considered as a whole, appeared from an objective point of view to have had as its purpose the propagation of racist views and ideas.

32. The national courts laid considerable emphasis on the fact that the applicant had himself taken the initiative of preparing the Greenjackets feature and that he not only knew in advance that racist statements were likely to be made during the interview but also had encouraged such statements. He had edited the programme in such a way as to include the offensive assertions. Without his involvement, the remarks would not have been disseminated to a wide circle of people and would thus not have been punishable. . . .

The Court is satisfied that these were relevant reasons for the purposes of paragraph 2 of Article 10.

33. On the other hand, as to the contents of the Greenjackets item, it should be noted that the TV presenter's introduction started by a reference to recent public discussion and press comments on racism in

Denmark, thus inviting the viewer to see the programme in that context. He went on to announce that the object of the programme was to address aspects of the problem, by identifying certain racist individuals and by portraying their mentality and social background. There is no reason to doubt that the ensuing interviews fulfilled that aim. Taken as a whole, the feature could not objectively have appeared to have as its purpose the propagation of racist views and ideas. On the contrary, it clearly sought – by means of an interview – to expose, analyse and explain this particular group of youths, limited and frustrated by their social situation, with criminal records and violent attitudes, thus dealing with specific aspects of a matter that already then was of great public concern.

The Supreme Court held that the news or information value of the feature were not such as to justify the dissemination of the offensive remarks. . . . However, in view of the principles stated in paragraph 31 above, the Court sees no cause to question the *Sunday News Magazine* staff members' own appreciation of the news or information value of the impugned item, which formed the basis for their decisions to produce and broadcast it.

34. Furthermore, it must be borne in mind that the item was broadcast as a part of a serious Danish news programme and was intended for a well-informed audience. . . .

The Court is not convinced by the argument, also stressed by the national courts . . . that the Greenjackets item was presented without any attempt to counterbalance the extremist views expressed. Both the TV presenter's introduction and the applicant's conduct during the interviews clearly dissociated him from the persons interviewed, for example by describing them as members of 'a group of extremist youths' who supported the Ku Klux Klan and by referring to the criminal records of some of them. The applicant also rebutted some of the racist statements for instance by recalling that there were black people who had important jobs. It should finally not be forgotten that, taken as a whole, the filmed portrait surely conveyed the meaning that the racist statemens were part of a generally anti-social attitude of the Greenjackets.

Admittedly, the item did not explicitly recall the immorality, dangers and unlawfulness of the promotion of racial hatred and of ideas of superiority of one race. However, in view of the above-mentioned counter-balancing elements and the natural limitations on spelling out such elements in a short item within a longer programme as well as the journalist's discretion as to the form of expression used, the Court does not consider the absence of such precautionary reminders to be relevant.

35. News reporting based on interviews, whether edited or not, constitutes one of the most important means whereby the press is able to play its vital role of 'public watchdog' (see, for instance, the above-mentioned *Observer and Guardian* judgment, pp. 29–30, § 59). The punishment of a journalist for assisting in the dissemination of statements made by another person in an interview would seriously hamper the contribution of the press to discussion of matters of public interest and should not be envisaged unless there are particularly strong reasons for doing so. In this regard the Court does not accept the Government's argument that the limited nature of the fine is relevant; what matters is that the journalist was convicted.

There can be no doubt that the remarks in respect of which the Greenjackets were convicted . . . were more than insulting to members of the targeted groups and did not enjoy the protection of Article 10 (see, for instance, the Commission's admissibility decisions in *Glimmerveen and Hagenbeek v the Netherlands*, applications nos. 8348/78 and 8406/78, DR 18, p. 187; and *Künen v Germany*, application no. 9235/81, DR 29, p. 194). However, even having regard to the manner in which the applicant prepared the Greenjackets item (see paragraph 32 above), it has not been shown that, considered as a whole, the feature was such as to justify also his conviction of, and punishment for, a criminal offence under the Penal Code.

36. It is moreover undisputed that the purpose of the applicant in compiling the broadcast in question was not racist. Although he relied on this in the domestic proceedings, it does not appear from the reasoning in the relevant judgments that they took such a factor into account. . . .

37. Having regard to the foregoing, the reasons adduced in support of the applicant's conviction and sentence were not sufficient to establish convincingly that the interference thereby occasioned with the enjoyment of his right to freedom of expression was 'necessary in a democratic society'; in particular the means employed were disproportionate to the aim of protecting 'the reputation or rights of others'. Accordingly the measures gave rise to a breach of Article 10 of the Convention.

FOR THESE REASONS, THE COURT

1. *Holds* by twelve votes to seven that there has been a violation of Article 10 of the Convention; . . .

Joint dissenting opinion of Judges Ryssdal, Bernhardt, Spielmann and Loizou

1. This is the first time that the Court has been concerned with a case of dissemination of racist remarks which deny to a large group of persons the quality of 'human beings'. In earlier decisions the Court has –

in our view, rightly – underlined the great importance of the freedom of the press and the media in general for a democratic society, but it has never had to consider a situation in which 'the reputation or rights of others' (Article 10 § 2) were endangered to such an extent as here.

2. We agree with the majority (paragraph 35 of the judgment) that the Greenjackets themselves 'did not enjoy the protection of Article 10'. The same must be true of journalists who disseminate such remarks with supporting comments or with their approval. This can clearly not be said of the applicant. Therefore it is admittedly difficult to strike the right balance between the freedom of the press and the protection of others. But the majority attributes much more weight to the freedom of the journalist than to the protection of those who have to suffer from racist hatred.

3. Neither the written text of the interview (paragraph 11 of the judgment) nor the video film we have seen makes it clear that the remarks of the Greenjackets are intolerable in a society based on respect for human rights. The applicant has cut the entire interview down to a few minutes, probably with the consequence or even the intention of retaining the most crude remarks. That being so, it was absolutely necessary to add at least a clear statement of disapproval. The majority of the Court sees such disapproval in the context of the interview, but this is an interpretation of cryptic remarks. Nobody can exclude that certain parts of the public found in the television spot support for their racist prejudices.

And what must be the feelings of those whose human dignity has been attacked, or even denied, by the Greenjackets? Can they get the impression that seen in context the television broadcast contributes to their protection? A journalist's good intentions are not enough in such a situation, especially in a case in which he has himself provoked the racist statements.

4. The International Convention on the Elimination of All Forms of Racial Discrimination probably does not require the punishment of journalists responsible for a television spot of this kind. On the other hand, it supports the opinion that the media too can be obliged to take a clear stand in the area of racial discrimination and hatred.

5. The threat of racial discrimination and persecution is certainly serious in our society, and the Court has rightly emphasised the vital importance of combating racial discrimination in all its forms and manifestations (paragraph 30 of the judgment). The Danish courts fully recognised that protection of persons whose human dignity is attacked has to be balanced against the right to freedom of expression. They carefully considered the responsibility of the applicant, and the reasons for their conclusions were relevant. The protection of racial minorities cannot have less weight than the right to impart information, and in the concrete circumstances of the present case it is in our opinion not for this Court to substitute its own balancing of the conflicting interests for that of the Danish Supreme Court. We are convinced that the Danish courts acted inside the margin of appreciation which must be left to the Contracting States in this sensitive area. Accordingly, the findings of the Danish courts cannot be considered as giving rise to a violation of Article 10 of the Convention.

NOTES

1. Article 4 of the International Convention on the Elimination of All Forms of Racial Discrimination,[1] to which the Court refers, requires that parties:

'With due regard to the principles embodied in the Universal Declaration of Human Rights and the rights expressly set forth in Article 5 of this Convention [which both include freedom of expression], inter alia, (a) shall declare an offence punishable by law all dissemination of ideas based on racial superiority or hatred, incitement to racial discrimination, as well as all acts of violence or incitement to such acts against any race or group of persons of another colour or ethnic origin. . . .'

2. Does the Court strike the right balance between freedom of expression and freedom from racial discrimination? The judgment is a typically European (and North American) one. The experience of the Committee that operates the 1965 Racial Discrimination Convention is that states from the developing world place less emphasis upon freedom of speech, both generally and when balanced against the reinforcement of prejudice by race hate speech.

1 60 UNTS 195, UKTS 77 (1969), Cmnd. 4108. On Article 4, see K. J. Partsch in S. Coliver, ed., *Striking a Balance: Hate Speech, Freedom of Expression and Non-discrimination* (1992), Chap. 3.

Otto-Preminger Institute v Austria, E Ct HRR A 295-A (1994), 19 EHRR 34, Eur Ct HR

The applicant Institute, which operated an art cinema in Innsbruck, had scheduled six showings of a film, *Das Liebeskinzil*. The showings, for which a fee was charged, were to be at 10 p.m. at night, except for one 4 p.m. matinee. Persons under the age of 17 would be excluded. An announcement in an information bulletin distributed to Institute members and displayed in various windows in Innsbruck and outside the cinema described the play upon which the film was based as a 'satirical tragedy'. The announcement stated that the play started 'from the assumption that syphilis was God's punishment for man's fornication and sinfulness at the time of the Reformation' and that in the film 'trivial imagery and absurdities of the Christian creed are targeted in a caricatural mode and the relationship between religious beliefs and worldly mechanisms of oppression is investigated'. The European Court's judgment states that the film

'portrays the God of the Jewish religion, the Christian religion and the Islamic religion as an apparently senile old man. . . . Other scenes show the Virgin Mary permitting an obscene story to be read to her and the manifestation of a degree of erotic tension between the Virgin Mary and the devil. The adult Jesus Christ is portrayed as a low grade mental defective and in one scene is shown lasciously attempting to fondle and kiss her breasts, which she is shown as permitting.'

At the request of the Roman Catholic Church, the Public Prosecutor brought criminal proceedings against Mr Zingl, the Institute manager, for the offence of 'disparaging religious doctrines', an offence which required behaviour 'likely to arouse justified indignation'. The Austrian courts had held that indignation would be 'justified' only if the behaviour in question was such as to offend the religious feelings of an average person with normal sensitivity (European Court judgment, para. 13). While the proceedings were pending, a court order for the seizure and forfeiture of the film made on the basis that it involved the commission of the above criminal offence was upheld by the Innsbruck Court of Appeal. The proceedings against Mr Zingl were discontinued. The applicant claimed a breach of Article 10. In its report, the Commission expressed the opinion that there was a breach of Article 10 by the seizure (by nine votes to five) and forfeiture (by 13 votes to one) of the film.

JUDGMENT OF THE COURT

C. Whether the interferences had a 'legitimate aim'

46. The Government maintained that the seizure and forfeiture of the film were aimed at 'the protection of the rights of others', particularly the right to respect for one's religious feelings, and at 'the prevention of disorder'.

47. As the Court pointed out in its judgment in the case of *Kokkinakis v Greece* of 25 May 1993 (Series A no. 260, p. 17, § 31), freedom of thought, conscience and religion, which is safeguarded under Article 9 of the Convention, is one of the foundations of a 'democratic society' within the meaning of the Convention. It is, in its religious dimension, one of the most vital elements that go to make up the identity of believers and their conception of life.

Those who choose to exercise the freedom to manifest their religion, irrespective of whether they do so as members of a religious majority or a minority, cannot reasonably expect to be exempt from all criticism. They must tolerate and accept the denial by others of their religious beliefs and even the propagation by others of doctrines hostile to their faith. However, the manner in which religious beliefs and doctrines are opposed or denied is a matter which may engage the responsibility of the State, notably its responsibility to ensure the peaceful enjoyment of the right guaranteed under Article 9 to the holders of those beliefs and doctrines. Indeed, in extreme cases the effect of particular methods of opposing or denying religious beliefs can be such as to inhibit those who hold such beliefs from exercising their freedom to hold and express them.

In the *Kokkinakis* judgment the Court held, in the context of Article 9, that a State may legitimately consider it necessary to take measures aimed at repressing certain forms of conduct, including the imparting of information and ideas, judged incompatible with the respect for the freedom of thought, conscience and religion of others (ibid., p. 21, § 48). The respect for the religious feelings of believers as guaranteed in Article 9 can legitimately be thought to have been violated by provocative portrayals of objects of religious veneration; and such portrayals can be regarded as malicious violation of the spirit of tolerance, which must also be a feature of democratic society. The Convention is to be read as a whole and therefore the interpretation and application of Article 10 in the present case must be in harmony with the logic of the Convention (see, *mutatis mutandis*, the *Klass and Others v Germany* judgment of 6 September 1978, Series A no. 28, p. 31, § 68).

48. The measures complained of were based on section 188 of the Austrian Penal Code, which is intended to suppress behaviour directed against objects of religious veneration that is likely to cause 'justified indignation'. It follows that their purpose was to protect the right of citizens not to be insulted in their religious feelings by the public expression of views of other persons. Considering also the terms in which the decisions of the Austrian courts were phrased, the Court accepts that the impugned measures pursued a legitimate aim under Article 10 § 2, namely 'the protection of the rights of others'.

D. Whether the seizure and the forfeiture were 'necessary in a democratic society'

1. General principles

49. As the Court has consistently held, freedom of expression constitutes one of the essential foundations of a democratic society, one of the basic conditions for its progress and for the development of everone. Subject to paragraph 2 of Article 10, it is applicable not only to 'information' or 'ideas' that are favourably received or regarded as inoffensive or as a matter of indifference, but also to those that shock, offend or disturb the State or any sector of the population. Such are the demands of that pluralism, tolerance and broadmindedness without which there is no 'democratic society' (see, particularly, the *Handyside v the United Kingdom* judgment of 7 December 1976, Series A no. 24, p. 23, § 49).

However, as is borne out by the wording itself of Article 10 § 2, whoever exercises the rights and freedoms enshrined in the first paragraph of that Article undertakes 'duties and responsibilities'. Amongst them – in the context of religious opinions and beliefs – may legitimately be included an obligation to avoid as far as possible expressions that are gratuitously offensive to others and thus an infringement of their rights, and which therefore do not contribute to any form of public debate capable of furthering progress in human affairs.

This being so, as a matter of principle it may be considered necessary in certain democratic societies to sanction or even prevent improper attacks on objects of religious veneration, provided always that any 'formality', 'condition', 'restriction' or 'penalty' imposed be proportionate to the legitimate aim pursued (see the *Handyside* judgment referred to above, ibid.).

50. As in the case of 'morals' it is not possible to discern throughout Europe a uniform conception of the significance of religion in society (c.f. the *Müller and Others v Switzerland* judgment of 24 May 1988, Series A no. 133, p. 20, § 30, and p. 22, § 35); even within a single country such conceptions may vary. For that reason it is not possible to arrive at a comprehensive definition of what constitutes a permissible interference with the exercise of the right to freedom of expression where such expression is directed against the religious feelings of others. A certain margin of appreciation is therefore to be left to the national authorities in assessing the existence and extent of the necessity of such interference.

The authorities' margin of appreciation, however, is not unlimited. It goes hand in hand with Convention supervision, the scope of which will vary according to the circumstances. In cases such as the present one, where there has been an interference with the exercise of the freedoms guaranteed in paragraph 1 of Article 10, the supervision must be strict because of the importance of the freedoms in question. The necessity for any restriction must be convincingly established (see, as the most recent authority, the *Informationsverein Lentia and Others v Austria* judgment of 24 November 1993, Series A no. 276, p. 15, 35).

2. Application of the above principles . . .

54. The Court notes first of all that although access to the cinema to see the film itself was subject to payment of an admission fee and an age–limit, the film was widely advertised. There was sufficient public knowledge of the subject-matter and basic contents of the film to give a clear indication of its nature; for these reasons, the proposed screening of the film must be considered to have been an expression sufficiently 'public' to cause offence.

55. The issue before the Court involves weighing up the conflicting interests of the exercise of two fundamental freedoms guaranteed under the Convention, namely the right of the applicant association to impart to the public controversial views and, by implication, the right of interested persons to take cognisance of such views, on the one hand, and the right of other persons to proper respect for their freedom

of thought, conscience and religion, on the other hand. In so doing, regard must be had to the margin of appreciation left to the national authorities, whose duty it is in a democratic society also to consider, within the limits of their jurisdiction, the interests of society as a whole.

56. The Austrian courts, ordering the seizure and subsequently the forfeiture of the film, held it to be an abusive attack on the Roman Catholic religion according to the conception of the Tyrolean public. Their judgments show that they had due regard to the freedom of artistic expression, which is guaranteed under Article 10 of the Convention (see the *Müller and Others* judgment referred to above, p. 22, § 33) and for which Article 17a of the Austrian Basic Law provides specific protection. They did not consider that its merit as a work of art or as a contribution to public debate in Austrian society outweighed those features which made it essentially offensive to the general public within their jurisdiction. The trial courts, after viewing the film, noted the provocative portrayal of God the Father, the Virgin Mary and Jesus Christ (see paragraph 16 above). The content of the film (see paragraph 22 above) cannot be said to be incapable of grounding the conclusions arrived at by the Austrian courts.

The Court cannot disregard the fact that the Roman Catholic religion is the religion of the over-whelming majority of Tyroleans.[1] In seizing the film, the Austrian authorities acted to ensure religious peace in that region and to prevent that some people should feel the objects of attacks on their religious beliefs in an unwarranted and offensive manner. It is in the first place for the national authorities, who are better placed than the international judge, to assess the need for such a measure in the light of the situation obtaining locally at a given time. In all the circumstances of the present case, the Court does not consider that the Austrian authorities can be regarded as having overstepped their margin of appreciation in this respect.

(b) *The forfeiture*

57. The foregoing reasoning also applies to the forfeiture, which determined the ultimate legality of the seizure and under Austrian law was the normal sequel thereto.

Article 10 cannot be interpreted as prohibiting the forfeiture in the public interest of items whose use has lawfully been adjudged illicit (see the *Handyside* judgment referred to above, p. 30, § 63). Although the forfeiture made it permanently impossible to show the film anywhere in Austria, the Court considers that the means employed were not disproportionate to the legitimate aim pursued and that therefore the national authorities did not exceed their margin of appreciation in this respect. . . .

FOR THESE REASONS, THE COURT . . .

3. *Holds*, by six votes to three, that there has been no violation of Article 10 of the Convention as regards either the seizure or the forfeiture of the film.

Joint dissenting opinion of Judges Palm, Pekkanen and Makarczyk

1. We regret that we are unable to agree with the majority that there has been no violation of Article 10.

2. The Court is here faced with the necessity of balancing two apparently conflicting Convention rights against each other. In the instant case, of course, the rights to be weighed up against each other are the right to freedom of religion (Article 9), relied on by the Government, and the right to freedom of expression (Article 10), relied on by the applicant association. Since the case concerns restrictions on the latter right, our discussion will centre on whether these were 'necessary in a democratic society' and therefore permitted by the second paragraph of Article 10.

3. As the majority correctly stated, echoing the famous passage in the *Handyside v the United Kingdom* judgment, (7 December 1976, Series A no. 24), freedom of expression is a fundamental feature of a 'democratic society'; it is applicable not only to 'information' or 'ideas' that are favourably received or regarded as inoffensive or as a matter of indifference, but *particularly* to those that shock, offend or disturb the State or any sector of the population. There is no point in guaranteeing this freedom only as long as it is used in accordance with accepted opinion.

It follows that the terms of Article 10 § 2, within which an interference with the right to freedom of expression may exceptionally be permitted, must be narrowly interpreted; the State's margin of appreciation in this field cannot be a wide one.

In particular, it should not be open to the authorities of the State to decide whether a particular statement is capable of 'contributing to any form of public debate capable of furthering progress in human affairs'; such a decision cannot but be tainted by the authorities' idea of 'progress'.

4. The necessity of a particular interference for achieving a legitimate aim must be convincingly established (see, as the most recent authority, the *Informationsverein Lentia and Others v Austria* judgment of 24

---

1 *Ed.* The Court had earlier noted that it was 78% of Austrians and 87% of Tyroleans.

November 1993, Series A no. 276, p. 15, § 35). This is all the more true in cases such as the present, where the interference as regards the seizure takes the form of prior restraint (see, *mutatis mutandis*, the *Observer and Guardian v the United Kingdom* judgment of 26 November 1991, Series A no. 216, p. 30, § 60). There is a danger that if applied to protect the perceived interests of a powerful group in society, such prior restraint could be detrimental to that tolerance on which pluralist democracy depends.

5. The Court has rightly held that those who create, perform, distribute or exhibit works of art contribute to exchange of ideas and opinions and to the personal fulfilment of individuals, which is essential for a democratic society, and that therefore the State is under an obligation not to encroach unduly on their freedom of expression (see the *Müller and Others v Switzerland* judgment of 24 May 1988, Series A no. 133, p. 22, § 33). We also accept that, whether or not any material can be generally considered a work of art, those who make it available to the public are not for that reason exempt from their attendant 'duties and responsibilities'; the scope and nature of these depend on the situation and on the means used (see the *Müller and Others* judgment referred to above, p. 22, § 34).

6. The Convention does not, in terms, guarantee a right to protection of religious feelings. More particularly, such a right cannot be derived from the right to freedom of religion, which in effect includes a right to express views critical of the religious opinions of others.

Nevertheless, it must be accepted that it may be 'legitimate' for the purpose of Article 10 to protect the religious feelings of certain members of society against criticism and abuse to some extent; tolerance works both ways and the democratic character of a society will be affected if violent and abusive attacks on the reputation of a religious group are allowed. Consequently, it must also be accepted that it may be 'necessary in a democratic society' to set limits to the public expression of such criticism or abuse. To this extent, but no further, we can agree with the majority.

7. The duty and the responsibility of a person seeking to avail himself of his freedom of expression should be to limit, as far as he can reasonably be expected to, the offence that his statement may cause to others. Only if he fails to take necessary action, or if such action is shown to be insufficient, may the State step in.

Even if the need for repressive action is demonstrated, the measures concerned must be 'proportionate to the legitimate aim pursued'; according to the case-law of the Court, which we endorse, this will generally not be the case if another, less restrictive solution was available (see, as the most recent authority, the *Informationsverein Lentia and Others* judgment referred to above, p. 16, § 39).

The need for repressive action amounting to complete prevention of the exercise of freedom of expression can only be accepted if the behaviour concerned reaches so high a level of abuse, and comes so close to a denial of the freedom of religion of others, as to forfeit for itself the right to be tolerated by society.

8. As regards the need for any State action at all in this case, we would stress the distinctions between the present case and that of *Müller and Others*, in which no violation of Article 10 was found. Mr Müller's paintings were accessible without restriction to the public at large, so that they could be – and in fact were – viewed by persons for whom they were unsuitable.

9. Unlike the paintings by Mr Müller, the film was to have been shown to a paying audience in an 'art cinema' which catered for a relatively small public with a taste for experimental films. It is therefore unlikely that the audience would have included persons not specifically interested in the film.

This audience, moreover, had sufficient opportunity of being warned beforehand about the nature of the film. Unlike the majority, we consider that the announcement put out by the applicant association was intended to provide information about the critical way in which the film dealt with the Roman Catholic religion; in fact, it did so sufficiently clearly to enable the religiously sensitive to make an informed decision to stay away.

It thus appears that there was little likelihood in the instant case of anyone being confronted with objectionable material unwittingly.

We therefore conclude that the applicant association acted responsibly in such a way as to limit, as far as it could reasonably have been expected to, the possible harmful effects of showing the film.

10. Finally, as was stated by the applicant association and not denied by the Government, it was illegal under Tyrolean law for the film to be seen by persons under seventeen years of age and the announcement put out by the applicant association carried a notice to that effect.

Under these circumstances, the danger of the film being seen by persons for whom it was not suitable by reason of their age can be discounted.

The Austrian authorities thus had available to them, and actually made use of, a possibility less restrictive than seizure of the film to prevent any unwarranted offense.

11. We do not deny that the showing of the film might have offended the religious feelings of certain segments of the population in Tyrol. However, taking into account the measures actually taken by the applicant association in order to protect those who might be offended and the protection offered by Austrian legislation to those under seventeen og age, we are, on balance, of the opinion that the seizure and forfeiture of the film in question were not proportionate to the legitimate aim pursued.

NOTES

1. Did the Court find the seizure and forfeiture justified by reference to the 'rights of others', considerations of 'public order' or both? Would the Court have reached the same decision if the seizure and forfeiture had been of a film offensive to a *minority* religion? Does the judgment *require* a state to take steps to protect the religious feelings of others? In *Choudhury v United Kingdom*[1] (the Salman Rushdie case), the Commission held that the fact blasphemy protected only the feelings of Christians was not a breach of Article 9. In *X and Y v United Kingdom*[2] (the *Gay News* case), the Commission held that the applicant's conviction for blasphemy was not a breach of Article 10. Are these decisions consistent with the *Otto-Preminger* case?

2. The *Otto-Preminger* case is one of a number of cases concerning artisitic expression. The first was the *Handyside* case: see above, p. 826. In *Müller v Switzerland*, E Ct HRR A 133 (1991), 13 EHRR 212, the first applicant, an established artist whose paintings had been exhibited on many occasions, had, with the other applicants, the organisers of an exhibition, been convicted under a Swiss obscenity law for publishing obscene articles, viz three paintings by the applicant that had been displayed at a public exhibition of contemporary art. The trial court commented on the paintings as follows:

'The overall impression is of persons giving free rein to licentiousness and even perversion. The subjects – sodomy, fellatio, bestiality, the erect penis – are obviously morally offensive to the vast majority of the population.'

Holding, by six votes to one, that the conviction was not in breach of Article 10, the Court, referring to its earlier obscenity judgment in the *Handyside* case, above, p. 826, stated:

'35. The applicants' conviction on the basis of Article 204 of the Swiss Criminal Code was intended to protect morals. Today, as at the time of the *Handyside* judgment . . . it is not possible to find in the legal and social orders of the Contracting States a uniform European conception of morals. The view taken of the requirements of morals varies from time to time and from place to place, especially in our era, characterised as it is by a far-reaching evolution of opinions on the subject. By reason of their direct and continuous contact with the vital forces of their countries, state authorities are in principle in a better position than the international judge to give an opinion on the exact content of these requirements as well as on the "necessity" of a "restriction" or "penalty" intended to meet them.

36. In the instant case, it must be emphasised that – as the Swiss courts found both at the cantonal level at first instance and on appeal and at the federal level – the paintings in question depict in a crude manner sexual relations, particularly between men and animals. . . . They were painted on the spot – in accordance with the aims of the exhibition, which was meant to be spontaneous – and the general public had free access to them, as the organisers had not imposed any admission charge or any age-limit. Indeed, the paintings were displayed in an exhibition which was unrestrictedly open to – and sought to attract – the public at large.

The Court recognises, as did the Swiss courts, that conceptions of sexual morality have changed in recent years. Nevertheless, having inspected the original paintings, the Court does not find unreasonable the view taken by the Swiss courts that those paintings, with their emphasis on sexuality in some of its crudest forms, were "liable grossly to offend the sense of sexual propriety of persons of ordinary sensitivity". . . . In the circumstances, having regard to the margin of appreciation left to them under Article 10 § 2, the Swiss courts were entitled to consider it "necessary" for the protection of morals to impose a fine on the applicants for publishing obscene material.

The applicants claimed that the exhibition of the pictures had not given rise to any public outcry and indeed that the press on the whole was on their side. It may also be true that Josef Felix Müller has been able to exhibit works in a similar vein in other parts of Switzerland and abroad, both before and after the "Fri-Art 81" exhibition. . . . It does not, however, follow that the applicants' conviction in Fribourg did not, in all the circumstances of the case, respond to a genuine social need, as was affirmed in substance by all three of the Swiss courts which dealt with the case.'

1 12 HRLJ 172 (1991). On the *Chowdhury* case in the English courts, see above, p. 591.
2 28 DR 77 (1982). On the *Gay News* case in the English courts, see above, p. 596.

3. Article 10 applies to commercial, as well as political and artistic speech, although less protection is given to commercial speech than to these other kinds of speech. In *Markt Intern and Beermann v Federal Republic of Germany*,[1] the applicants, the publishers and editors of an information bulletin for chemists and beauty product retailers, published an article voicing the complaint of a consumer about the practices of a cosmetics mail order firm and asking for information about similar experiences at the hands of the firm. A court order was obtained by the firm against the publishers under a 1909 FRG unfair competition law restraining them from repeating the statements they had previously published. The Court held, by nine votes to nine, with the casting vote of the President, that the court order had not infringed Article 10. On the scope of Article 10, the Court stated:

'26. The Court recalls that the writer of the article in question reported the dissatisfaction of a consumer who had been unable to obtain the promised reimbursement for a product purchased from a mail-order firm, the Club; it asked for information from its readers as to the commercial practices of that firm. It is clear that the article in question was addressed to a limited circle of tradespeople and did not directly concern the public as a whole; however, it conveyed information of a commercial nature. Such information cannot be excluded from the scope of Article 10(1) which does not apply solely to certain types of information or ideas or forms of expression.'

4. Article 10 'applies not only to the contents of information but also to the means of transmission or reception since any imposed on the means necessarily interferes with the right to receive and impart information': *Autronic AG v Switzerland*.[2] In that case the Swiss authorities rejected an application from the applicant Swiss company for permission to receive for private use uncoded broadcasts via telecommunication satellites from another state (in that case the USSR) without that other state's consent. The Court held, by 16 votes to 2, that although the resulting interference with the applicant company's right to receive information had legitimate aims (the 'prevention of disorder' in telecommunications and the need to avoid the disclosure of confidential information), the Swiss government's approach was disproportionate to the attainment of these objectives. Confidential information would not be at risk and the 1989 European Convention on Transfrontier Television did not require consent.

7 Article 11: The right to freedom of association

Young James and Webster v UK, E Ct HRR A 44 (1982), 4 EHRR 38, Eur Ct HR

In 1975, British Rail entered into a closed shop agreement with three rail trade unions, by which membership of one of them was a condition of employment. The three applicants, who were British Rail employees before the agreement was negotiated, refused to become members and were dismissed. All three objected to membership on the ground that no one should be compelled to join a trade union; Y and W objected also to the political activities of trade unions; Y objected further to the political affiliations of the specified trade unions. The Commission was of the opinion, by 14 votes to 3, that Article 11 had been infringed and referred the case to the Court.

---

1 E Ct HRR A 164 (1989), 12 EHRR 1. For other commercial cases, see *Bathold v Federal Republic of Germany*, E Ct HRR A 90 (1985), 7 EHRR 383 and *Jacobouski v Germany*, E Ct HRR A 291 (1994), 19 EHRR 64. Article 10 applies to advertising: *Casado Coca v Spain*, E Ct HRR A 185 (1994) and *Colman v United Kingdom*, E Ct HRR A 258-D (1993), 18 EHRR 119.
2 E Ct HRR A 178 (1990), 12 EHRR 485. For other regulation cases, see *Groppera Radio AG v Switzerland*, E Ct HRR A 173 (1990), 12 EHRR 485 (technical licensing) and *Informationsverein Lentia v Austria*, E Ct HRR A 276 (1993), 17 EHRR 93 (state broadcasting monopoly a breach).

JUDGMENT OF THE COURT

49. Under Article 1 of the Convention, each Contracting State 'shall secure to everyone within [its] juris-diction the rights and freedoms defined in . . . [the] Convention'; hence, if a violation of one of those rights and freedoms is the result of non-observance of the obligation in the enactment of domestic legisla-tion, the responsibility of the State for that violation is engaged. Although the proximate cause of the events giving rise to this case was the 1975 agreement between British Rail and the railway unions, it was the domestic law in force at the relevant time[1] that made lawful the treatment of which the applicants complained. The responsibility of the respondent State for any resultant breach of the Convention is thus engaged on this basis. Accordingly, there is no call to examine whether, as the applicants argued, the State might also be responsible on the ground that it should be regarded as employer or that British Rail was under its control. . . .

51. A substantial part of the pleadings before the Court was devoted to the question whether Article 11 guarantees not only freedom of association, including the right to form and to join trade unions, in the positive sense, but also, by implication, a 'negative right' not to be compelled to join an association or a union. . . .

52. The Court does not consider it necessary to answer this question on this occasion.

The Court recalls, however, that the right to form and to join trade unions is a special aspect of free-dom of association . . . it adds that the notion of freedom implies some measure of freedom of choice as to its exercise.

Assuming for the sake of argument that, for the reasons given in . . . the *travaux préparatoires*,[2] a general rule such as that in Article 20 § 2 of the Universal Declaration of Human Rights was deliberately omitted from, and so cannot be regarded as itself enshrined in, the Convention, it does not follow that the negative aspect of a person's freedom of association falls completely outside the ambit of Article 11 and that each and every compulsion to join a particular trade union is compatible with the intention of that provision. . . .

53. The Court emphasises . . . that . . . in the present case, it is not called upon to review the closed shop system as such in relation to the Convention or to express an opinion on every consequence or form of compulsion which it may engender; it will limit its examination to the effects of that system on the applicants. . . .

55. The situation facing the applicants clearly runs counter to the concept of freedom of association in its negative sense.

Assuming that Article 11 does not guarantee the negative aspect of that freedom on the same footing as the positive aspect, compulsion to join a particular trade union may not always be contrary to the Convention.

However, a threat of dismissal involving loss of livelihood is a most serious form of compulsion and, in the present instance, it was directed against persons engaged by British Rail before the introduction of any obligation to join a particular trade union.

In the Court's opinion, such a form of compulsion, in the circumstances of the case, strikes at the very substance of the freedom guaranteed by Article 11. For this reason alone, there has been an interference with that freedom as regards each of the three applicants.

56. Another facet of this case concerns the restriction of the applicants' choice as regards the trade unions which they could join of their own volition. An individual does not enjoy the right to freedom of asso-ciation if in reality the freedom of action or choice which remains available to him is either non-existent or so reduced as to be of no practical value.

. . . the applicants . . . would . . . have been dismissed if they had not become members of one of the specified unions.

57. Moreover . . . [t]he protection of personal opinion afforded by Articles 9 and 10 . . . is also one of the purposes of freedom of association as guaranteed by Article 11. Accordingly, it strikes at the very sub-stance of this Article to exert pressure, of the kind applied to the applicants, in order to compel someone to join an association contrary to his convictions.

1 *Ed.* i.e. the Trade Unions and Labour Relations Act 1974. This repealed the Industrial Relations Act 1971, which had prohibited most closed shops and protected the right not to join a union. Under the 1974 Act dismissal for refusal to join a union required by a closed shop agreement was lawful (not 'unfair dismissal') except where the refusal was 'on grounds of religious belief to being a member of any union whatsoever or on any reasonable grounds to being a member of a particular union' (First Schedule, Part II, 1974 Act).

2 *Ed.* These stated that '[o]n account of the difficulties raised by the "closed shop system" in certain countries, the Conference [of Senior Government Officials drafting the Convention] . . . considered that it was undesirable to introduce into the Convention a rule under which "no one may be com-pelled to belong to an association" which features in [Article 20(2), Universal Declaration of Human Rights]' 4 *Travaux Préparatoires*, p. 262.

In this further respect, the treatment complained of—in any event as regards Mr Young and Mr Webster—constituted an interference with their Article 11 rights.

[The Court next considered and rejected the argument that the restrictions could be justified under Article 11(2) as being 'necessary', etc.]

FOR THESE REASONS, THE COURT . . .

Holds by 18 votes to three that there has been a breach of Article 11 of the Convention.

NOTES[1]

1. Would the Court have ruled in favour of the applicants if (i) they had been free to join a trade union of their choice or (ii) they had become British Rail employees after the closed shop agreement had entered into force?

2. UK law has changed again since the case so that an employee cannot be 'fairly' (and hence lawfully) dismissed for refusing to comply with a 'pre-' or (as in the *Young* case) 'post' entry closed shop agreement.

3. The Court's judgment (para. 49) touches upon the question whether the Convention makes a state responsible for conduct by private individuals that interferes with rights protected by it.[2] How far does the Court go? Is it saying that a state would be liable if its law were such, for example, as to permit (i) a private detective to tap telephones contrary to Article 8 or (ii) the press to comment on pending criminal proceedings contrary to the fair trial guarantee in Article 6? (In the latter case, a balance would have to be struck between the right to a fair trial and freedom of speech (Article 10): see the *Sunday Times* case, above, p. 823.) How important was it in the present case that the UK Parliament had legislated since the Convention so as to legalise private action contrary to Article 11 which had previously been unlawful under UK law?

4. Note that the Court was faced with a very clear statement of the intention of the draftsmen in the *travaux préparatoires*. While not contradicting it expressly, would it be correct to say that the Court largely subverts that expressed intention?

5. In *Reid v United Kingdom*, (1984) 6 EHRR 387, the UK agreed to pay £30,129 by way of friendly settlement to an employee who had lost his job with British Aluminium because of a 'closed shop' agreement in circumstances comparable with those in the *Young, James and Webster* cases.

6. The Court has interpreted Article 11 in a number of other cases. In *National Union of Belgian Police v Belgium*, E Ct HRR A 19 (1975), 1 EHRR 578, the Court held that the words 'for the protection of his interests' indicated that, as far as trade unions are concerned, Article 11 has a *functional* as well as an *organisational* side. Individuals, that is, are not only entitled to 'form and join' trade unions, but have the right to expect that these be allowed such rights as are necessary to protect their members' interests effectively. These rights include the "right to be heard" by the employer, although this does not necessarily mean a right to be consulted by him; an employer may, as in the *Belgian Police* case, limit the number of trade unions with which it consults. In *Swedish Engine Drivers' Union v Sweden*, E Ct HRR A 20

---

1 On the *Young* case, see C. M. Shea, (1982) 15 Cornell I.L.J. 489 and F. Von Prondzynski, (1982) 41 CLJ 256. In *Sigurjonsson v Iceland*, E Ct HRR A 264 (1993), 16 EHRR 462, the Court held, by eight votes to one, that a pre-entry requirement by which a taxi driver was obliged by law to be a member of a taxi drivers' association was in breach of Article 11.
2 See also *X and Y v Netherland*, above, p. 814.

(1975), 1 EHRR 617, the Court ruled that the right to conclude a collective agreement with an employer was also not in itself a necessary condition of effective trade union action; an employer may, as on the facts of that case, limit the number of trade unions with which it concludes such agreements. In *Schmidt and Dahlström v Sweden*, E Ct HRR A 21 (1976), 1 EHRR 637, the Court held that Article 11 also did not require that benefits from a collective agreement negotiated by a trade union be made retroactive, so that the failure to make them retroactive for members of unions that had taken strike action was not a violation of any right to strike that Article 11 might contain. The Court has yet to rule on the question whether the right to strike or a more general right to take industrial action is necessary to effective trade union functioning and hence protected by Article 11. However, reading between the lines, the *Schmidt and Dahlström* case does not suggest that the Court would hold that Article 11 does guarantee a right to strike. Moreover, the Court's jurisprudence on Article 11 generally does not lead to the conclusion that there is much in Article 11 from the standpoint of organised labour. On the Court's jurisprudence generally, see M. Forde, (1983) 31 AJCL 301.

7. In the *Council of Civil Service Unions v United Kingdom*, (1987) 20 DR E Com HR 228, 10 EHRR 269, the Commission declared inadmissible an application claiming that the withdrawal of the right of the 7,000 civil servants employed by the Government Communications Headquarters (GCHQ) to join a trade union was a breach of Article 11. GCHQ's function is to ensure the security of the UK's military and official communications and to provide signals intelligence by monitoring telecommunications. The right of GCHQ employees to join a trade union was withdrawn in 1984 on the ground that industrial action, such as had occurred in the recent past, posed a threat to national security. Without concluding that all civil servants could be so classified, the Commission was of the opinion that, given their functional relationship to the armed forces and the police (who were also mentioned in Article 11(2)), the civil servants working at GCHQ were 'members . . . of the administration of the state' within Article 11(2). Accordingly, restrictions could be imposed upon their exercise of the right to freedom of association in Article 11 and these could include the complete suppression of the right to be a trade union member. The requirement that the restrictions be 'lawful' included a requirement of proportionality, but this was met in the present case given the wide margin of appreciation that applied in cases of national security and the UK's concern about the disruptive effect of industrial action. The ILO Committee on Freedom of Association (which has no power to make a decision legally binding upon the UK) had earlier found that the same facts amounted to a breach of the differently worded 1947 ILO Freedom of Association Convention (Convention 87).

8 Article 14: Freedom from discrimination

Belgian Linguistic cases (Merits), E Ct HRR A 6 (1968), 1 EHRR 252, Eur Ct HR

For the purpose of determining the language of instruction in its state and state-supported schools, Belgium is divided territorially by law into unilingual and bilingual areas. In the former, which consist of Dutch, French and German speaking areas, the predominant language of the region is the language of instruction. In the latter, including six communes surrounding Brussels, special arrangements exist. In this case, the Court held, by eight votes to seven, that this system 'does not comply with the requirements of Article 14 read in conjunction with the first sentence of Article 2 of the First Protocol, in so far as it prevents certain children, solely on the basis of the residence of their parents, from having access to the French-language schools existing in the six communes on the periphery of Brussels invested with a special status, of which Kraainem is one. . . .' On the other five questions put to the Court concerning the arrangements in other areas, no violation of the ECHR was found. In the following extract from its judgment, the Court examines the meaning of Article 14.

JUDGMENT OF THE COURT

While it is true that this guarantee has no independent existence in the sense that under the terms of Article 14 it relates solely to 'rights and freedoms set forth in the Convention,' a measure which in itself is in conformity with the requirements of the Article enshrining the right or freedom in question may however infringe this Article when read in conjunction with Article 14 for the reason that it is of a discretionary nature.

Thus, persons subject to the jurisdiction of a Contracting State cannot draw from Article 2 of the [First] Protocol the right to obtain from the public authorities the creation of a particular kind of educational establishment; nevertheless, a State which had set up such an establishment could not, in laying down entrance requirements, take discriminatory measures within the meaning of Article 14.

To recall a further example . . . Article 6 of the Convention does not compel States to institute a system of appeal courts. . . . However it would violate that Article, read in conjunction with Article 14, were it to debar certain persons from these remedies without a legitimate reason while making them available to others in respect of the same type of actions.

In such cases there would be a violation of a guaranteed right or freedom as it is proclaimed by the relevant Article read in conjunction with Article 14. It is as though the latter formed an integral part of each of the Articles laying down rights and freedoms. No distinctions should be made in this respect according to the nature of these rights and freedoms and of their correlative obligations, and for instance as to whether the respect due to the right concerned implies positive action or mere abstention. . . .

In spite of the very general wording of the French version ('*sans distinction aucune*'), Article 14 does not forbid every difference in treatment in the exercise of the rights and freedoms recognised. This version must be read in the light of the more restrictive text of the English version ('without discrimination'). In addition, and in particular, one would reach absurd results were one to give Article 14 an interpretation as wide as that which the French version seems to imply. One would, in effect, be led to judge as contrary to the Convention every one of the many legal or administrative provisions which do not secure to everyone complete equality of treatment in the enjoyment of the rights and freedoms recognised. . . .

. . . the Court, following the principles which may be extracted from the legal practice of a large number of democratic States, holds that the principle of equality of treatment is violated if the distinction has no objective and reasonable justification. The existence of such a justification must be assessed in relation to the aim and effects of the measure under consideration, regard being had to the principles which normally prevail in democratic societies. A difference of treatment in the exercise of a right laid down in the Convention must not only pursue a legitimate aim: Article 14 is likewise violated when it is clearly established that there is no reasonable relationship of proportionality between the means employed and the aim sought to be realised.

In attempting to find out in a given case, whether or not there has been an arbitrary distinction, the Court cannot disregard those legal and factual features which characterise the life of the society in the State which, as a Contracting Party, has to answer for the measure in dispute. In so doing it cannot assume the role of the competent national authorities, for it would thereby lose sight of the subsidiary nature of the international machinery of collective enforcement established by the Convention. The national authorities remain free to choose the measures which they consider appropriate in those matters which are governed by the Convention. Review by the Court concerns only the conformity of these measures with the requirements of the Convention.

In the present case the Court notes that Article 14, even when read in conjunction with Article 2 of the Protocol, does not have the effect of guaranteeing to a child or to his parent the right to obtain instruction in a language of his choice. The object of these two Articles, read in conjunction, is more limited: it is to ensure that the right to education shall be secured by each Contracting Party to everyone within its jurisdiction without discrimination on the ground, for instance, of language. This is the natural and ordinary meaning of Article 14 read in conjunction with Article 2. Furthermore, to interpret the two provisions as conferring on everyone within the jurisdiction of a State a right to obtain education in the language of his own choice would lead to absurd results, for it would be open to anyone to claim any language of instruction in any of the territories of the Contracting Parties.

NOTES

1. The Court has taken the view that it is not necessary for the obligations which the Convention contains in respect of a right which it protects to be infringed for there to be a breach of the Article protecting that right *when read in conjunction with Article 14*. It is sufficient that the discrimination occurs within the area of the right protected. See, e.g. the Court's example concerning the right of appeal and Article 6.

2. Not all inequalities of treatment will be discrimination contrary to Article 14. As the Court states in the sixth paragraph above, an inequality will be consistent with Article 14 if there is an 'objective and reasonable justification' for it. There must, that is, be a 'legitimate aim' (objective) and what is done must be in realisation of it and must be proportionate in the circumstances (reasonable). The Court held that there was a 'legitimate aim' behind the language discrimination in the *Belgian Linguistics* case, viz. the efficient instruction of children in schools. Similarly, in the *National Union of Belgian Police* case, above, p. 846, the limitation of the right of consultation to the main and most representative trade unions had the 'legitimate aim' of ensuring effective negotiations. The 'proportionality' requirement was not met in the one situation in the *Belgian Linguistics* case in which a breach of Article 14 was found, because it would have been possible to have devised another language instruction scheme for the region concerned that placed a lesser burden upon minority language children.

3. 'Other status' in Article 14 has been held, for example, to include the status of illegitimacy (*Marckx* case, above, p. 819) or of being a category-based trade union (*National Union of Belgian Police* case).

4. Discrimination on sexual grounds is particularly suspect; it will only be held to be consistent with Article 14 if there are 'very weighty reasons' for it: *Abdulaziz, Cabales and Balkandali v United Kingdom*.[1] The same is true of discrimination based upon the ground that a person is born out of wedlock.[2] In the *Abdulaziz* case, the three applicants were women (two British citizens, one stateless) who were entitled under British nationality and immigration law to live in the UK. They were married to husbands who lacked British citizenship and who had no right to enter and settle in the UK. The UK immigration authorities, acting under the 1980 Immigration Rules, refused the husbands entry, arguing that in each case the couple could settle in the husband's home country. Had the position been reversed, with the three wives seeking to join their husbands lawfully resident in the UK, it would have been much easier for the wives to have gained admission. The Court held, by 14 votes to none, that the exclusion of the husbands in these circumstances was a breach of Article 8 read with Article 14, involving discrimination on grounds of sex in the respect afforded to family life. The Court accepted that the stricter policy in respect of the admission of men had a legitimate aim, viz the protection of the labour market. However,

---

1 E Ct HRR A 94 (1985), 7 EHRR 471. See G. Cvetic, (1987) 36 ICLQ 647 and H. Storey, (1990) 39 ICLQ 328. For other cases of sexual discrimination, see *Rasmussen v Denmark*, E Ct HRR A 87 (1984), 7 EHRR 371 and *Schmidt v Germany*, E Ct HRR A 291-B (1994), 18 EHRR 513.
2 *Inze v Austria*, E Ct HRR A 94 (1985), 7 EHRR 471.

the measure adopted was not reasonable, particularly since sexual discrimination was involved. The Court stated:

'78. The Court accepts that the 1980 Rules had the aim of protecting the domestic labour market. . . .

Whilst the aforesaid aim was without doubt legitimate, this does not in itself establish the legitimacy of the difference made in the 1980 Rules as to the possibility for male and female immigrants settled in the United Kingdom to obtain permission for, on the one hand, their non-national wives or fiancées and, on the other hand, their non-national husbands or fiancés to enter or remain in the country.

Although the Contracting States enjoy a certain "margin of appreciation" in assessing whether and to what extent differences in otherwise similar situations justify a different treatment, the scope of the margin will vary according to the circumstances, the subject-matter and its background (see the above-mentioned *Rasmussen* judgment, Series A no. 87, p. 15, § 40).

As to the present matter, it can be said that the advancement of the equality of the sexes is today a major goal in the member States of the Council of Europe. This means that very weighty reasons would have to be advanced before a difference of treatment on the ground of sex could be regarded as compatible with the Convention.

79. In the Court's opinion, the Government's arguments . . . are not convincing.

It may be correct that on average there is a greater percentage of men of working age than of women of working age who are "economically active" . . . and that comparable figures hold good for immigrants. . . .

Nevertheless, this does not show that similar differences in fact exist – or would but for the effect of the 1980 Rules have existed – as regards the respective impact on the United Kingdom labour market of immigrant wives and of immigrant husbands. In this connection, other factors must also be taken into account. Being "economically active" does not always mean that one is seeking to be employed by someone else. Moreover, although a greater number of men than of women may be inclined to seek employment, immigrant husbands were already by far outnumbered, before the introduction of the 1980 Rules, by immigrant wives . . . many of whom were also "economically active". Whilst a considerable proportion of those wives, in so far as they were "economically active", were engaged in part-time work, the impact on the domestic labour market of women immigrants as compared with men ought not to be underestimated.

In any event, the Court is not convinced that the difference that may nevertheless exist between the respective impact of men and of women on the domestic labour market is sufficiently important to justify the difference of treatment, complained of by the applicants, as to the possibility for a person settled in the United Kingdom to be joined by, as the case may be, his wife or her husband. . . .

82. There remains a more general argument advanced by the Government, namely that the United Kingdom was not in violation of Article 14 by reason of the fact that it acted more generously in some respects – that is, as regards the admission of non-national wives and fiancées of men settled in the country – than the Convention required.

The Court cannot accept this argument. It would point out that Article 14 is concerned with the avoidance of discrimination in the enjoyment of the Convention rights in so far as the requirements of the Convention as to those rights can be complied with in different ways. The notion of discrimination within the meaning of Article 14 includes in general cases where a person or group is treated, without proper justification, less favourably than another, even though the more favourable treatment is not called for by the Convention.'

The Court considered, but unanimously rejected, a claim that there had also been racial discrimination contrary to Article 8 read with Article 14. Surprisingly it did so without identifying racial discrimination as particularly suspect.[1] The Court stated:

'The 1980 Rules, which were applicable in general to all "non-patrials" wanting to enter and settle in the United Kingdom, did not contain regulations differentiating between persons or groups on the ground of their race or ethnic origin. The rules included in paragraph 2 a specific instruction to immigration officers to carry out their duties without regard to the race, colour or religion of the intending entrant . . ., and they were applicable across the board to intending immigrants from all parts of the world, irrespective of their race or origin.

As the Court has already accepted, the main and essential purpose of the 1980 Rules was to curtail "primary immigration" in order to protect the labour market at a time of high unemployment. This means that their reinforcement of the restrictions on immigration was grounded not on objections regarding the origin of the non-nationals wanting to enter the country but on the need to stem the flow of immigrants at the relevant time.

1 Note, however, the Commission's approach to racial discrimination in the *East African Asians* cases, above, p. 772.

That the mass immigration against which the rules were directed consisted mainly of would-be immigrants from the New Commonwealth and Pakistan, and that as a result they affected at the material time fewer white people than others, is not a sufficient reason to consider them as racist in character: it is an effect which derives not from the content of the 1980 Rules but from the fact that, among those wishing to immigrate, some ethnic groups outnumbered others.'

Note that since Article 14 only applies in conjunction with other articles of the ECHR, it provides only an imperfect remedy in respect of most kinds of racial discrimination. In particular, it does not apply to racial discrimination in respect of employment, housing or the provision of goods, facilities or services.

Does Article 14 prohibit 'indirect discrimination', as to which see above, p. 622? Does it require a state to make private discrimination illegal in areas of conduct covered by the ECHR?

9 Article 15: Derogation in time of emergency

Lawless v Ireland (Merits), E Ct HRR A 3 (1961), 1 EHRR 15, Eur Ct HR

The applicant, an Irish national, was arrested and detained without trial for five months in 1957 at a time when the activities of the Irish Republican Army were causing much violence. The European Court held that Ireland's action in the applicant's case violated Article 5(1)(c). The question then arose, however, whether Article 15 applied.

JUDGMENT OF THE COURT

28. Whereas, in the general context of Article 15 of the Convention, the natural and customary meaning of the words 'other public emergency threatening the life of the nation' is sufficiently clear; whereas they refer to an exceptional situation of crisis or emergency which affects the whole population and constitutes a threat to the organised life of the community of which the State is composed: . . . whereas the existence at the time of a 'public emergency threatening the life of the nation', was reasonably deduced by the Irish Government from a combination of several factors, namely: in the first place, the existence in the territory of the Republic of Ireland of a secret army engaged in unconstitutional activities and using violence to attain its purposes; secondly, the fact that this army was also operating outside the territory of the State, thus seriously jeopardising the relations of the Republic of Ireland with its neighbour; thirdly the steady and alarming increase in terrorist activities from the autumn of 1956 and throughout the first half of 1957.

29. Whereas, despite the gravity of the situation, the Government had succeeded, by using means available under ordinary legislation, in keeping public institutions functioning more or less normally, but whereas the homicidal ambush on the night of 3 to 4 July 1957 in the territory of Northern Ireland near the border had brought to light, just before 12 July—a date, which, for historical reasons[1] is particularly critical for the preservation of public peace and order—the imminent danger to the nation caused by the continuance of unlawful activities in Northern Ireland by the IRA and various associated groups, operating from the territory of the Republic of Ireland;

30. Whereas, in conclusion, the Irish Government were justified in declaring that there was a public emergency in the Republic of Ireland threatening the life of the nation and were hence entitled, applying the provisions of Article 15, paragraph 1, of the Convention for the purposes for which those provisions were made, to take measures derogating from their obligations under the Convention; . . .

36. Whereas, however, considering, in the judgment of the Court, that in 1957 the application of the ordinary law had proved unable to check the growing danger which threatened the Republic of Ireland; whereas the ordinary criminal courts, or even the special criminal courts or military courts, could not suffice to restore peace and order; whereas, in particular, the amassing of the necessary evidence to convict persons involved in activities of the IRA and its splinter groups was meeting with great difficulties caused by the military, secret and terrorist character of those groups and the fear they created among the population; whereas the fact that these groups operated mainly in Northern Ireland, their activities in the

---

1 *Ed.* It is the day on which the anniversary of the Battle of the Boyne 1690, in which the protestant William of Orange defeated the catholic James II, is celebrated.

Republic of Ireland being virtually limited to the preparation of armed raids across the border, was an additional impediment to the gathering of sufficient evidence; whereas the sealing of the border would have had extremely serious repercussions on the population as a whole, beyond the extent required by the exigencies of the emergency; . . .

37. Whereas, moreover, the Offences against the State (Amendment) Act of 1940, was subject to a number of safeguards designed to prevent abuses in the operation of the system of administrative detention; whereas the application of the Act was thus subject to constant supervision by Parliament, which not only received precise details of its enforcement at regular intervals but could also at any time, by a Resolution, annul the Government's Proclamation which had brought the Act into force; whereas the Offences against the State (Amendment) Act 1940 provided for the establishment of a 'Detention Commission' made up of three members, which the Government did in fact set up, the members being an officer of the Defence Forces and two judges; whereas any person detained under this Act could refer his case to that Commission whose opinion, if favourable to the release of the person concerned, was binding upon the Government; whereas, moreover, the ordinary courts could themselves compel the Detention Commission to carry out its functions; . . .

Whereas, therefore, it follows from the foregoing that the detention without trial provided for by the 1940 Act, subject to the above-mentioned safeguards, appears to be a measure strictly required by the exigencies of the situation within the meaning of Article 15 of the Convention;

38. Whereas, in the particular case of G. R. Lawless, there is nothing to show that the powers of detention conferred upon the Irish Government by the Offences against the State (Amendment) Act 1940, were employed against him, either within the meaning of Article 18 of the Convention, for a purpose other than that for which they were granted, or within the meaning of Article 15 of the Convention, by virtue of a measure going beyond what was strictly required by the situation at that time; . . .

47. Whereas the Court is called upon in the first instance, to examine whether, in pursuance of paragraph 3 of Article 15 of the Convention, the Secretary-General of the Council of Europe was duly informed both of the measures taken and of the reasons therefor; whereas the Court notes that a copy of the Offences against the State (Amendment) Act 1940, and a copy of the Proclamation of 5 July, published on 8 July 1957, bringing into force Part II of the aforesaid Act were attached to the letter of 20 July; that it was explained in the letter of 20 July that the measures had been taken in order 'to prevent the commission of offences against public peace and order and to prevent the maintaining of military or armed forces other than those authorised by the Constitution'; that the Irish Government thereby gave the Secretary-General sufficient information of the measures taken and the reasons therefor; that, in the second place, the Irish Government brought this information to the Secretary-General's attention only twelve days after the entry into force of the measures derogating from their obligations under the Convention; and that the notification was therefore made without delay; whereas in conclusion, the Convention does not contain any special provision to the effect that the Contracting State concerned must promulgate in its territory the notice of derogation addressed to the Secretary-General of the Council of Europe.

Whereas the Court accordingly finds that, in the present case, the Irish Government fulfilled their obligations as Party to the Convention under Article 15, paragraph 3, of the Convention;

THE COURT

Unanimously [7–0] . . . [decided that Ireland was not in breach of the Convention by virtue of its valid derogation under Article 15.]

NOTES[1]

1. Derogations from Article 4, Seventh Protocol are also prohibited. Derogations under Article 15 have been made from time to time by Greece, Ireland, Turkey and the UK (in respect of overseas territories and Northern Ireland). In *Brannigan and McBride v UK*, above, p. 777, the Court accepted as valid the current UK derogation concerning Article 5(3). Might it reach a different conclusion now following the cease-fire? In the *Greek Case* (1969) 12 YB (The Greek Case) 1, the Commission expressed the opinion that the state of emergency claimed by Greece did not exist.

1 On Article 15, see B. Mangan, (1988) 10 HRQ 372; D. Shraga, (1986) 16 Israel YHR 217; C. Schreuer, (1982) 9 Yale Studies World Public Order 113.

This is the one case in which the Strasbourg authorities have not accepted as valid a derogation made under Article 15.

2. A derogation in respect of Northern Ireland was accepted in *Ireland v UK*, above, p. 750. In that case, the Court made it clear that it allowed states a wide margin of appreciation when applying Article 15:

'It falls in the first place to each Contracting State, with its responsibility for "the life of [the] nation", to determine whether that life is threatened by a "public emergency" and, if so, how far it is necessary to go in attempting to overcome the emergency. By reason of their direct and continuous contact with the pressing needs of the moment, the national authorities are in principle in a better position than the international judge to decide both on the presence of such an emergency and on the nature and scope of derogations necessary to avert it. In this matter Article 15(1) leaves the authorities a wide margin of appreciation.'

3. Might the requirement that a state's derogation not be 'inconsistent with its other obligations under international law' include obligations under Article 4, International Covenant on Civil and Political Rights, which is the Covenant derogation provision equivalent to Article 15? This was argued, but not decided, in the *Brannigan and McBride* case. The question is relevant in that Article 4 is more rigorous than Article 15. It requires an 'official proclamation' of the emergency (which was held to have occurred in the *Brannigran and McBride* case) and makes more rights non-derogable.

4. What would be the effect of failure to comply with Article 15(3)? Would the derogation be invalid? Or would there just be a breach of the particular treaty obligation in Article 15(3), of which a state could complain under Article 24?

10 Article 13: The right to an effective remedy in national law

Silver v United Kingdom, E Ct HRR A 61 (1983), 5 EHRR 347, Eur Ct HR

In this case, the Court held that the censorship of the applicants' correspondence by the prison authorities was in breach of Article 8. The following extract concerns the applicants' claim that they had not been provided with the effective remedy in national law that Article 13 required.

JUDGMENT OF THE COURT

113. The principles that emerge from the Court's jurisprudence on the interpretation of Article 13 include the following:

(a) where an individual has an arguable claim to be the victim of a violation of the rights set forth in the Convention, he should have a remedy before a national authority in order both to have his claim decided and, if appropriate, to obtain redress. . . .

(b) the authority referred to in Article 13 may not necessarily be a judicial authority but, if it is not, its powers and the guarantees which it affords are relevant in determining whether the remedy before it is effective. . . .

(c) although no single remedy may itself entirely satisfy the requirements of Article 13, the aggregate of remedies provided for under domestic law may do so . . .

(d) neither Article 13 nor the Convention in general lays down for the Contracting States any given manner for ensuring within their internal law the effective implementation of any of the provisions of the Convention – for example, by incorporating the Convention into domestic law . . .

It follows from the last-mentioned principle that the application of Article 13 in a given case will depend upon the manner in which the Contracting State concerned has chosen to discharge its obligation under Article 1 directly to secure to anyone within its jurisdiction the rights and freedoms set out in section 1 (see the above-mentioned *Ireland v The United Kingdom* judgment, Series A, no. 25, p. 91, § 239).

114. In the present case, it was not suggested that any remedies were available to the applicants other than the four channels of complaint examined by the Commission, namely an application to the Board of Visitors, an application to the Parliamentary Commissioner for Administration, a petition to the Home Secretary and the institution of proceedings before the English courts.

115. As regards the first two channels, the Court, like the Commission, considers that they do not constitute an 'effective remedy' for the present purposes.

The Board of Visitors cannot enforce its conclusions . . . nor can it entertain applications from individuals like Mrs. Colne who are not in prison.

As regards the Parliamentary Commissioner, it suffices to note that he has himself no power to render a binding decision granting redress.

116. As for the Home Secretary, if there were a complaint to him as to the validity of an Order or Instruction under which a measure of control over correspondence had been carried out, he could not be considered to have a sufficiently independent standpoint to satisfy the requirements of Article 13 . . .: as the author of the directives in question, he would in reality by judge in his own cause. The position, however, would be otherwise if the complainant alleged that a measure of control resulted from a misapplication of one of those directives. The Court is satisfied that in such cases a petition to the Home Secretary would in general be effective to secure compliance with the directive, if the complaint was well-founded. The Court notes, however, that even in these cases, at least prior to 1 December 1981, the conditions for the submission of such petitions imposed limitations on the availability of this remedy in some circumstances . . .

117. The English courts, for their part, are endowed with a certain supervisory jurisdiction over the exercise of the powers conferred on the Home Secretary and the prison authorities by the Prison Act and the Rules. . . . However, their jurisdiction is limited to determining whether or not those powers have been exercised arbitrarily, in bad faith, for an improper motive or in an *ultra vires* manner.

In this connection, the applicants stressed that the Convention, not being incorporated into domestic law, could not be directly invoked before the English courts; however, they acknowledged that it was relevant for the interpretation of ambiguous legislation, according to the presumption of the latter's conformity with the treaty obligations of the United Kingdom.

118. The applicants made no allegation that the interferences with their correspondence were contrary to English law. . . . Like the Commission, the Court has found that the majority of the measures complained of in the present proceedings were incompatible with the Convention. . . . In most of the cases, the Government did not contest the Commission's findings. Neither did they maintain that the English courts could have found the measures to have been taken arbitrarily, in bad faith, for an improper motive or in an *ultra vires* manner.

In the Court's view, to the extent that the applicable norms, whether contained in the Rules or in the relevant Orders or Instructions, were incompatible with the Convention there could be no effective remedy as required by Article 13 and consequently there has been a violation of that Article.

To the extent, however, that the said norms were compatible with Article 8, the aggregate of the remedies available satisfied the requirements of Article 13, at least in those cases in which it was possible for a petition to be submitted to the Home Secretary . . .: a petition to the Home Secretary was available to secure compliance with the directives issued by him and, as regards compliance with the Rules, the English courts had the supervisory jurisdiction described in paragraph 117 above.

119. To sum up, in those instances where the norms in question were incompatible with the Convention and where the Court has found a violation of Article 8 to have occurred there was no effective remedy and Article 13 has therefore also been violated. In the remaining cases, there is no reason to assume that the applicants' complaints could not have been duly examined by the Home Secretary and/or the English courts and Article 13 has therefore not been violated; this, however, is subject to the exception of Mr. Silver's letter no. 7, in respect of which the remedy of petition to the Home Secretary was not available. . . .

FOR THESE REASONS, THE COURT UNANIMOUSLY [7–0] . . .

5. *Holds* that there has been a violation of Article 13 to the extent specified in paragraph 119 of the judgment.

NOTES

1. As stated in the *Silver* case, a remedy is required by Article 13 where there is an 'arguable case' that there has been a breach of the ECHR. In *Powell and Rayner v*

United Kingdom, E Ct HRR A 172 (1990), 12 EHRR 355, the applicants, who were owners of properties close to Heathrow affected by excessive aircraft noise, claimed a breach of Article 13 in that there were no effective remedies in English law in respect of breaches, which they also claimed, of Articles 6(1) and 8. The European Commission had held the Articles 6 and 8 claims to be inadmissible as 'manifestly ill-founded'. It had, however, admitted the claim based upon Article 13, drawing a distinction between 'manifestly ill-founded' and 'arguable'. The Court commented on this distinction as follows:

'32. The majority of the Commission, however, drew a distinction between the notions of "manifestly ill-founded" and lack of "arguability". It was "implicit in the Commission's established case-law that the term 'manifestly ill-founded' extends further than the literal meaning of the word 'manifest' would suggest at first reading" (see paragraph 59 of the report). Thus, some serious claims might give rise to a prima facie issue but, after "full examination" at the admissibility stage, ultimately be rejected as manifestly ill-founded notwithstanding their arguable character. . . .

33. As the Court stated in the *Boyle and Rice* judgment, "on the ordinary meaning of the words, it is difficult to conceive how a claim that is 'manifestly ill-founded' can nevertheless be 'arguable', and vice versa" ([Eur Court HR, Series A, Vol. 131], p. 24, § 54). Furthermore, Article 13 and Article 27 § 2 are concerned, within their respective spheres, with the availability of remedies for the enforcement of the same Convention rights and freedoms. The coherence of this dual system of enforcement is at risk of being undermined if Article 13 is interpreted as requiring national law to make available an "effective remedy" for a grievance classified under Article 27 § 2 as being so weak as not to warrant examination on its merits at international level. Whatever threshold the Commission has set in its case-law for declaring claims "manifestly ill-founded" under Article 27 § 2, in principle it should set the same threshold in regard to the parallel notion of "arguability" under Article 13.

This does not mean, however, that in the present case the Court is bound to hold Article 13 inapplicable solely as a result of the Commission's decisions . . . declaring the applicants' substantive claims under Articles 6 § 1 and 8 to be manifestly ill-founded. Whilst those decisions as such are unreviewable, the Court is competent to take cognisance of all questions of fact and law arising in the context of the Article 13 complaints duly referred to it, including the "arguability" or not of each of the substantive claims. . . . In order to determine the latter question, the particular facts and the nature of the legal issues raised must be examined, notably in the light of the Commission's admissibility decisions and the reasoning contained therein. In that connection, as the case of *Boyle and Rice* and the case of *Plattform "Ärzte für das Leben"* show, a claim is not necessarily rendered arguable because before rejecting it as inadmissible, the Commission has devoted careful consideration to it and to its underlying facts (loc. cit., pp. 27–29, §§ 68–76, and pp. 30–31, §§ 79–83; and the *Plattform "Ärzte für das Leben"* judgment of 21 June 1988, Series A no. 139, pp. 11–13, §§ 28–39).'

The Court then considered the Article 13 claims in respect of Articles 6 and 8 and found no 'arguable' case in respect of either of them, so that there was no breach of Article 13. For criticism of the Court's approach, see F. Hampson, (1990) 39 ICLQ 891.

2. In *Soering v United Kingdom*,[1] the Court held that the remedy of judicial review met the requirements of Article 13 for an applicant who wished to challenge his extradition on the ground that he would be subjected to ill-treatment contrary to Article 3, ECHR if extradited. The Court stated:

'121. In judicial review proceedings the court may rule the exercise of executive discretion unlawful on the ground that it is tainted with illegality, irrationality or procedural impropriety. In an extradition case the test of "irrationality", on the basis of the so-called "*Wednesbury* principles", would be that no reasonable Secretary of State could have made an order for surrender in the circumstances. According to the United Kingdom Government, a court would have jurisdiction to quash a challenged decision to send a fugitive to a country where it was established that there was a serious risk of inhuman or degrading treatment, on the ground that in all the circumstances of the case the decision was one that no reasonable Secretary of State could take. Although the Convention is not considered to be part of United Kingdom law, the Court is satisfied that the English courts can review the "reasonableness" of an extradition decision in the light of the kind of factors relied on by Mr. Soering before the Convention institutions in the context of Article 3.'

---

1 E Ct HRR A 161 (1989); 11 EHRR 439. Followed in *Vilvarajah v United Kingdom*, E Ct HRR A 215 (1991) 14 EHRR 248 (judicial review sufficient remedy for person seeking asylum and alleging ill-treatment contrary to Article 3).

As to whether proportionality may become a ground for judicial review in UK law, see the *Brind* case, above, p. 11. A high percentage of Strasbourg cases under Article 13 come from the UK. Might the UK comply more easily with Article 13 if the ECHR were incorporated into its law so that a person could rely upon it directly in the UK courts?

Index

857